OAT® REVIEW NOTES

Special thanks to the staff of Kaplan Test Prep who worked on this book.

This publication is designed to provide accurate information in regard to the subject matter covered as of its publication date, with the understanding that knowledge and best practice constantly evolve. The publisher is not engaged in rendering medical, legal, accounting, or other professional service. If medical or legal advice or other expert assistance is required, the services of a competent professional should be sought. This publication is not intended for use in clinical practice or the delivery of medical care. To the fullest extent of the law, neither the Publisher nor the Editors assume any liability for any injury and/or damage to persons or property arising out of or related to any use of the material contained in this book.

© 2016 by Kaplan, Inc.

Published by Kaplan Publishing, a division of Kaplan, Inc.
750 Third Avenue
New York, NY 10017

10 9 8 7 6 5 4 3 2 1

ISBN: 978-1-5062-2399-5

TABLE OF CONTENTS

SECTION I: OAT STRATEGIES

SECTION II: BIOLOGY

SECTION III: GENERAL CHEMISTRY

SECTION IV: ORGANIC CHEMISTRY

SECTION V: READING COMPREHENSION

SECTION VI: QUANTITATIVE REASONING

SECTION VII: PHYSICS

STUDY SHEETS

Late-Breaking Developments

kaptest.com/publishing

The material in this book is up to date at the time of publication. However, the test makers may release more information on test changes after this book is published. Be sure to read carefully the materials you receive when you register for the test. If there are any important late-breaking developments—or any changes or corrections to the Kaplan test preparation materials in this book—we will post that information online at **kaptest.com/publishing**.

Feedback and Comments

Email us: **booksupport@kaplan.com**

We would appreciate your comments and suggestions about this book. Please provide any feedback you have for the improvements of this book to **booksupport@kaplan.com**. Your feedback is extremely helpful as we continue to develop high-quality resources to meet your needs.

NOTE TO INTERNATIONAL STUDENTS

If you are an international student hoping to attend an optometry school in the United States, Kaplan can help you explore your options. Here are some things to think about.

- If English is not your first language, most optometry schools will require you to take the TOEFL (Test of English as a Foreign Language) or provide some other evidence that you are proficient in English.
- Plan to take the OAT. All U.S. optometry schools require it.
- Begin the process of applying to optometry schools at least 12 months before the fall of the year you plan to start your studies. Some programs start as early as July.
- You will need to obtain an I-20 Certificate of Eligibility from the school you plan to attend if you intend to apply for an F-1 Student Visa to study in the United States.
- If you've already completed an optometry degree outside the United States, get information from U.S. schools—some may have special programs for international graduates of optometry.

HOW TO USE THIS BOOK

- Familiarize yourself with Kaplan's "Introduction to the OAT" and "Studying Effectively" recommendations.

- Create a plan to study the Survey of Natural Sciences (Biology, General Chemistry, and Organic Chemistry), Reading Comprehension, Physics, and Quantitative Reasoning sections, using the end-of-chapter practice questions to assess your progress.

- Begin the reading for each section with the introduction which outlines the goals, content, and key study strategies for that section.

- Complete your assigned readings for each session in advance. You can find these assignments in your online study plan at **kaplanOAT.com.** Use the recommendations to help prioritize what you will need to do to improve your score.

- After each session, spend extra time reviewing and practicing with the most difficult content areas, but don't re-read every word of every chapter without a good reason.

Section I

OAT STRATEGIES

SECTION GOALS

Throughout the OAT, you will be asked to respond to questions that require application of a strategic approach and critical thinking. The first portion of this book is designed to introduce you to the OAT, as well as the major Kaplan strategies for raising your score. This section is designed to help you achieve the following goals:

- Identify common themes within OAT test sections
- Recall the key content areas and timing guidelines for each section of the OAT
- Recognize opportunities for a strategic approach within test sections and questions
- Study and review the materials within this book using clear, effective rules that will assist with recall
- Troubleshoot problematic test questions with previously learned strategic techniques
- Apply the Kaplan strategies systematically across the sections of the OAT

CONTENT OVERVIEW

Test Day Format	Chapter 1: Introduction to the OAT
Strategy	Chapter 2: Studying Effectively Chapter 3: Test Strategies

KEY STUDY STRATEGIES

These chapters are designed to serve as both an introduction to the OAT and the Kaplan approach, and a resource that can be referred back to with frequency. This is the first section you should read through within this book. Special focus should be given to the unique strategies detailed within Chapter 3. As you study, refer back to this section of the book for a refresher on OAT structure and best study habits. Make sure to apply the strategies detailed within this portion of the book across every relevant section of the OAT. In early practice, it may help to either flip back to this material, or to your notes on this material, every time you work practice problems. In later practice, ensure you are using the Kaplan strategies on each practice problem. By Test Day, the materials within these chapters should be completely internalized. The OAT is a critical thinking test, and high scores are accomplished through a combination of content knowledge and effective strategy.

CHAPTER ONE

Introduction to the OAT

The Optometry Admissions Test (OAT) is a component of a complete application for admission to most optometry schools in the United States and Canada. The American Dental Association (ADA) Department of Testing Services administers the OAT at Prometric Test Centers on behalf of the Association of Schools of Colleges of Optometry (ASCO) as part of the application process for optometry school. Scores earned by examinees are an important part of the optometry school admissions process because they provide a common factor for schools to use in comparing applications for admission. Your Kaplan program is designed to launch you along the path to your career in optometry by helping you achieve the best score possible on the OAT.

The OAT is likely different from any other test you have encountered in your academic career. It is unlike the knowledge-based exams common in high schools and colleges that emphasize memorizing information; optometry schools can assess your academic prowess by looking at your transcript instead. The OAT is not even like other standardized tests that focus on proving your general skills. Optometry schools use OAT scores to assess whether you possess the foundation upon which to build a successful optometry career. Though you certainly need to know the content to do well, the focus is on thought processes. The OAT emphasizes reasoning, critical thinking, reading comprehension, data analysis, and problem-solving skills.

The OAT's power comes from its use as an indicator of your abilities: Good scores can open up many opportunities for you. Your power comes from preparation and mindset. The key to OAT success is knowing what you are up against. That's where this book helps. You'll learn the philosophy behind the test, review the sections one by one, attempt sample questions, master Kaplan's proven methods, and understand what the test makers really want. You'll get a handle on the process; find a confident, new perspective; and achieve your highest possible scores.

The OAT should be viewed as an opportunity to show optometry schools who you are and what you can do, just like any other part of your application. Take control of your OAT experience.

THE COMPUTER-BASED TEST

The OAT is conducted by the Association of Schools and Colleges of Optometry (ASCO) and administered by the American Dental Association (ADA). The OAT is administered year-round at test centers operated by Prometric. The official OAT website is found at **ada.org/oat** and is where you begin the process of registering for the OAT. You will also find the OAT Guide and a PDF of Frequently Asked Questions as well as many other resources for OAT test takers.

All 20 optometry schools in the United States, as well as the Interamerican University of Puerto Rico and the University of Waterloo in Canada, require applicants to have taken the OAT. You may submit an electronic application at **ada.org** using a credit card. To request a paper application, call 1-800-232-2159.

After your application and fee are processed, you will receive instructions to contact Prometric (**prometric.com**) to arrange a date, time, and location for your test. Plan to register several weeks in advance of when you want to take the test so you can arrange the best time and location. Any corrections to your application must be completed at least two weeks prior to your test date, and rescheduling your test incurs a rescheduling fee that varies according to the advance notice you provide.

The OAT is administered exclusively on the computer and can be taken almost any day of the year. To check in for your testing session, you will need your admission ticket (emailed to you as confirmation of your registration) and two forms of valid, nonexpired identification with signature, one of which must be government-issued and contain a photograph of you, such as a driver's license, passport, state ID, or military ID. The first and last names on your admission ticket must match your personal IDs exactly; however, IDs with only middle initial or with no middle name included will be accepted. At the testing center, additional security procedures such as photos or digital fingerprints may be taken to confirm and record your identity.

During the test, time is kept via a countdown timer in the corner of the screen. You will not be allowed to wear a watch and may not have access to a clock. One 15-minute rest break is scheduled for the middle of the test. You may take additional breaks with the permission of the proctor, but the test timer will continue running, and you will lose that time. Even if you are not at the computer, the test will continue to run itself, and successive sections will start automatically if time for the previous section has elapsed.

An on-screen periodic table is provided for only the Survey of Natural Sciences section, and an on-screen calculator is provided for only the Quantitative Reasoning section. The testing center provides a noteboard and marker to use for taking notes and writing out calculations. If you need to replace your noteboard or marker, you may ask the proctor for a new set any time during the test (although if this is during a section, your time will continue to elapse). You will not be allowed to bring your own calculator, writing utensils, or paper.

CONTENT

The OAT is, among other things, an endurance test. It consists of four sections and 230 multiple-choice questions. Add in the administrative details at both ends of the testing experience plus the break halfway through the test, and you can count on being in the test room for almost five hours. It can be a grueling experience, to say the least. If you do not approach the OAT with sufficient confidence and stamina, you may quickly lose your composure. That's why taking control of the test is so important.

The OAT consists of four timed sections: the Survey of Natural Sciences (with Biology, General Chemistry, and Organic Chemistry), Reading Comprehension, Physics, and Quantitative Reasoning. In this book, we'll take an in-depth look at each OAT section with content review, sample questions, and specific, test-smart hints.

Survey of the Natural Sciences

Time: 90 minutes (54 seconds per question)

Format: 100 multiple-choice questions, subdivided into Biology, General Chemistry, and Organic Chemistry

What it tests: Knowledge of university-level sciences

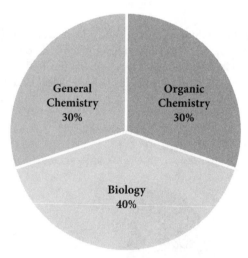

The distribution of Survey of Natural Sciences questions

Figure 1.1

Biology (40 questions): Structure and Function of Systems (Anatomy and Physiology) (22.5%); Developmental Biology (10%); Diversity of Life (7.5%); Cell and Molecular Biology (32.5%); Genetics (17.5%); Evolution, Ecology, and Behavior (10%)

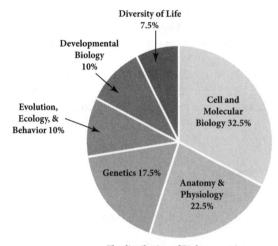

The distribution of Biology questions

Figure 1.2

General Chemistry (30 questions): Stoichiometry and General Concepts (10%), Gases (7%), Liquids and Solids (10%), Solutions (10%), Acids and Bases (10%), Chemical Equilibria (7%), Thermodynamics and Thermochemistry (7%), Chemical Kinetics (7%), Oxidation-Reduction Reactions (7%), Atomic and Molecular Structure (10%), Periodic Properties (7%), Nuclear Reactions (3%), and Laboratory Techniques (7%)

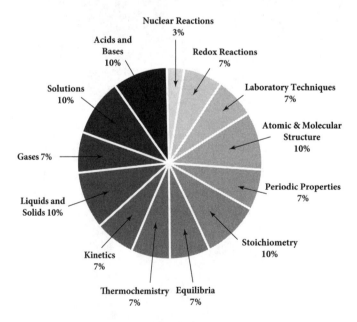

The distribution of General Chemistry questions

Figure 1.3

Organic Chemistry (30 questions): Reaction Mechanisms (17%), Chemical and Physical Properties of Molecules (17%), Stereochemistry (10%), Nomenclature (7%), Reactions (30%), Acid-Base Chemistry (10%), and Aromatics and Bonding (10%)

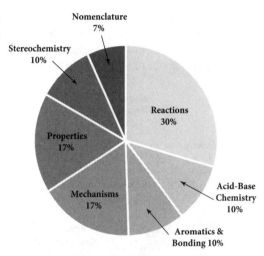

The distribution of Organic Chemistry questions

Figure 1.4

Reading Comprehension

Time: 60 minutes (20 minutes per passage)

Format: 50 multiple-choice questions; three passages with 16–17 questions following each

What it tests: ability to comprehend, analyze, and interpret reading passages on scientific topics

Physics

Time: 50 minutes (75 seconds per question)

Format: 40 multiple-choice questions

What it tests: Units and Vectors, Linear Kinematics, Rotational Motion, and Force Statics and Dynamics (40%); Electrostatics, D.C. Circuits, and Magnetism (15%); Energy and Momentum (10%); Simple Harmonic Motion and Waves (10%); Optics (10%); Thermal Chemistry and Thermodynamics (7.5%), Fluid Statics (5%), and Modern Physics (2.5%)

The approximate distribution of Physics questions

Figure 1.5

STRAIGIES

Quantitative Reasoning

Time: 45 minutes (67.5 seconds per question)

Format: 40 multiple-choice questions

What it tests: Algebra (22.5%), Numerical Calculations (15%), Conversions (7.5%), Probability and Statistics (10%), Geometry (10%), Trigonometry (10%), and Applied Mathematics (Word) Problems (25%).

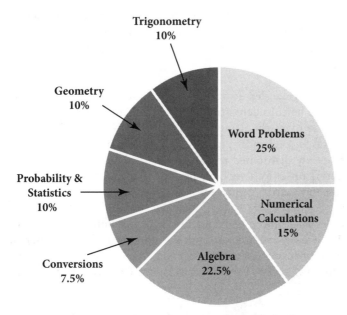

The distribution of Quantitative Reasoning questions

Figure 1.6

SCORING

The OAT is scored on a 200 to 400 scale. For each section of the test, the actual number of multiple-choice questions you answer correctly per section is your **raw score**. All multiple-choice questions are worth the same amount—one raw point—and there's no penalty for incorrect answers. That means you should always fill in an answer for every question whether you have time to fully invest in that question or not. Never let time run out on any section without filling in an answer for every question.

Your raw scores will not appear on your score report. Instead, they are converted to yield your **scaled scores**, the ones that fall somewhere in that 200–400 range. These scaled scores are reported to schools as your OAT scores.

In addition to scaled scores for individual sections, schools are also provided a **composite score**, which is a scaled score that factors in your performance on all the sections. Your composite score is not merely an average of the scores from all the sections but rather an evaluation of your performance on the entire test.

Your score report will tell you—and your potential optometry schools—not only your scaled scores but also the **percentile** ranking that corresponds with your scaled score in each section. A percentile ranking reflects how many test takers out of 100 scored at or below your level. For example, a percentile of 80 means that 80 percent of test takers did as well as or worse than you did, and only 20 percent did better.

What's a Good Score?

What defines a good score can vary significantly based on personal situation. Much depends on the strength of the rest of your application (e.g., if your transcript is first-rate, then the pressure to do well on the OAT isn't as intense) and on where you want to go to school (e.g., different schools have different score expectations).

For each administration, the average scaled scores are approximately 300 for each section; this equates to the 50th percentile. To be considered competitive, you'll likely want to score above the 50th percentile. Especially competitive schools may want scores above the 70th percentile range. It's important to check the scores for each individual school. One commonality is that most schools will consider scores that are evenly distributed across sections to be more favorable than a very high performance on one section offset by a very low performance on another section of the test. Performing consistently across the board is preferred.

Because all of your section scores factor into your cumulative score, maximizing your performance on every question is important. Just a few questions one way or the other can make a big difference in your scaled score. Make an extra effort to score well on a test section if you did poorly in a corresponding class; the best revenge for getting a C in chemistry class is acing the Chemistry section of the OAT!

WHAT THE OAT REALLY TESTS

It's important to grasp not only the nuts and bolts of the OAT (so you know what to do on Test Day) but also the underlying principles of the test (so you know why you're doing what you're doing). The straightforward facts tested by the OAT are covered throughout this book, but now it's time to examine the heart and soul of the exam to see what it's really about.

The Myth

Most people preparing for the OAT fall prey to the myth that the OAT is a straightforward science test. They think something like this:

> *The OAT covers the two years of science I had to take in school: biology, chemistry, and basic organic chemistry, plus math and physics. The important stuff is the science, though. After all, we're going to be optometrists.*

Here's a little-known secret: the OAT is not just a science test; it's also a critical thinking test. This means the test is designed to let you demonstrate your thought processes as well as your thought content. The implications are vast. Once you shift your test-taking paradigm to match the test makers', you'll find a new level of confidence and control over the test. You'll begin to work with the nature of the exam rather than against it. You'll be more efficient and insightful as you prepare for the test, and you'll be more relaxed on Test Day. In fact, you'll be able to see the test for what it actually is rather than for what students fear it to be. We want your Test Day to feel familiar, not awkward!

The Zen of OAT

Optometry schools do not need to rely on the OAT to evaluate what content you already know; admission committees can measure your subject-area proficiency using your undergraduate coursework and grades. Schools are interested instead in the potential of your mind. In recent years, many optometry schools have shifted pedagogic focus away from an information-heavy curriculum to a concept-based curriculum. Currently, more emphasis is placed on problem solving, holistic thinking, and cross-disciplinary study. This trend affects you right now because it's reflected in the OAT. Every good tool matches its task. In this case, the tool is the OAT, which is used to measure you and other candidates, and the task is to quantify how likely it is you will succeed in optometry school. In fact, research shows the OAT is correlated with success in optometry school, and, together with undergraduate GPA, is an excellent tool for schools to determine which applicants are likely to be the top—and the bottom—students.

Therefore, your intellectual potential—how skillfully you annex new territory into your mental boundaries, how quickly you build connections between ideas, and how confidently and creatively you solve problems—is far more important to admission committees than your ability to recite the pK_a for every acid known to humankind. Schools assume they can expand your knowledge base. They choose applicants carefully because expansive knowledge is not enough to succeed in optometry school or in the profession. There's something more, and it's this something more that the test is trying to measure. Every section on the OAT tests essentially the same higher-order thinking skills: analytical reasoning, abstract thinking, and problem solving. Most test takers get trapped into thinking they are being tested strictly about their knowledge of science and math. Thus, they approach each section with a new outlook on what's expected. This constant mental shifting of gears can be exhausting and counterproductive. Instead of perceiving the OAT as parsed into radically different sections, maintain your focus on the underlying nature of the test; each section presents a variation on the same theme. The OAT is not just about what you know; it's also about how you think.

What About the Science?

With this perspective, you may be left asking questions: *What about the science? What about the content? Don't I need to know the basics?* The answer to each is a resounding *Yes!* You must be fluent in the different languages of the test. You cannot do well on the OAT if you don't know the basics of biology, general chemistry, organic chemistry, physics, and mathematics. The best approach to learning that content is to take one year each of biology, general physics, chemistry, and organic chemistry and then review the content in this book thoroughly before taking the OAT. Knowing these basics is just the beginning of doing well on the OAT, though. That's a shock to most test takers. They presume that once they relearn their undergraduate science they are ready to do battle against the OAT. Wrong! Test takers with only this minimum of knowledge merely have directions to the battlefield and lack what they need to actually beat the test: an understanding of the test makers' battle plans. You won't merely be drilled on facts and formulas on the OAT; you will need to demonstrate the ability to reason based on ideas and concepts. The science questions are painted with a broad brush to test your general understanding.

THE OAT MINDSET

In addition to being a thinking test, the OAT is a standardized test. As such, it has its own consistent patterns and idiosyncrasies, which can actually work in your favor. This is the key to why test preparation works: You have the opportunity to familiarize yourself with those consistent peculiarities and adopt the proper test-taking mindset.

The OAT mindset is something to bring to every question, passage, and section you encounter. Being in the OAT mindset means reshaping the test-taking experience so you are in control. Answer questions *when* you want to; feel free to skip tough but feasible passages and questions, coming back to them only after you've racked up points on easy ones. Answer questions *how* you want to; use Kaplan shortcuts and methods to get points quickly and confidently, even if those methods aren't exactly what the test makers had in mind when they wrote the test.

Some overriding principles of the OAT mindset that will be covered in-depth in the chapters to come are as follows:

- Read actively and critically.
- Translate prose into your own words.
- Save the toughest questions and passages for last.
- Know the test and its components inside and out.
- Do OAT-style problems in each topic area after you've reviewed it.
- Allow your confidence to build on itself.
- Complete full-length practice tests to break down the mystique of the real experience.
- Know that you are going to make mistakes and learn from those mistakes to get the most out of your practice.
- Stick with the new methods you'll be learning. Some might take more practice than others, but when mastered, all will pay off on Test Day by saving you valuable time and earning you more points.
- Look at the OAT as a challenge and the first step in your new career rather than as an arbitrary obstacle.

The OAT mindset boils down to being proactive and taking control of the testing experience so you can get as many points possible as quickly and as easily as you can. Keep this in mind as you read and work through the material in this book and as you face the challenge on Test Day.

The Four Basic Principles of Good Test Mentality

Knowing the test content arms you with the tools you need to do well on the OAT, but you must wield those tools with the right frame of mind and in the right spirit. Good test mentality involves taking a certain stance toward the entire test. Here's what's involved:

1. Test awareness

To do your best on the OAT, always keep in mind that the test is like no other test you've taken before, both in terms of content and in terms of the scoring system. If you took a test in high school or college and got a number of the questions wrong, you generally wouldn't receive a perfect grade. However, on the OAT, you can get a handful of questions wrong and still earn a fantastic—if not perfect—score. The test is geared so that only the very best test takers are able to finish every section, but even these people rarely get every question right.

What does this mean for you? Just as you shouldn't let one bad question ruin an entire section, you shouldn't let what you consider to be a subpar performance on one section ruin your performance on the entire test. Often when you think you did not do well you are mistaken. If you allow a feeling of failure to rattle you, it can have a cumulative negative effect, setting in motion a downward spiral that does serious damage to your score. Losing a few points won't ruin your cumulative score, but losing your cool will. If you feel you did poorly on a section, don't sweat it: Chances are it was just a difficult section, and that factor will already be figured into the scoring curve. The point is to remain calm and collected. Do your best on each section, and, once a section is over, forget about it and move on.

2. Stamina

Improving your test-taking stamina can be just as beneficial as learning more content. Overall, the OAT is a fairly grueling experience, and some test takers simply run out of mental endurance on the last section, which happens to be one of the toughest in terms of timing and mental capacity required: Quantitative Reasoning. To avoid running out of steam, prepare by taking full-length practice tests in the weeks before your exam so that, on Test Day, completing all four sections will seem like a breeze. (Well, maybe not a breeze, but at least not a hurricane.) Taking online practice tests also ensures you are comfortable with the computer-based format and allows you to review the explanations and assess your performance. Although the scores you earn on your Kaplan practice tests will be quite realistic, the scores are far less important than the practice itself.

3. Confidence

Confidence feeds on itself; unfortunately, so does the opposite of confidence: self-doubt. Confidence in your ability leads to quick, sure answers and a sense of well-being that translates into more points. If you lack confidence, you may end up reading the sentences and answer choices two, three, or four times until you confuse yourself. This leads to timing difficulties, which only perpetuate the downward spiral, causing anxiety and a rush to finish each section.

However, if you subscribe to the right OAT mindset, you'll gear all of your practice toward the major goal of taking control of the test. When you've achieved that goal, you'll be ready to face the test with supreme confidence—armed with the principles, techniques, strategies, and approaches set forth in this book—and that's the one sure way to score your best on Test Day.

4. The right attitude

Those students who approach the OAT as an obstacle, rail against the necessity of taking it, or make light of its importance rarely fare as well as those who see the OAT as an opportunity to show off the reading and reasoning skills that optometry schools are looking for. Don't waste time making value judgments about the OAT. It's not going away, so you have to deal with it. Those who look forward to doing battle with the OAT—or, at least, who enjoy the opportunity to distinguish themselves from the rest of the applicants—tend to score better than do those who resent or dread it.

It may sound a little dubious, but attitude adjustment is a proven test-taking technique. Just as a successful athlete prepares mentally and uses positive visualization before a big game, so too should you. Here are a few steps you can take to make sure you develop the right OAT attitude:

- Look at the OAT as a challenge but don't obsess over it; you certainly don't want to psych yourself out of the game.
- Remember that, yes, the OAT is important, but this one test will not single-handedly determine the outcome of your life (contrary to what some students think).
- Have fun with the test. Learning how to match your wits against the test makers' can be a very satisfying experience, and the reading and thinking skills you'll acquire will benefit you in optometry school as well as in your future optometry career.
- Remember that you're more prepared than most people. You're training with Kaplan. You will have the tools you need and know how to use them.
- Get in shape; you wouldn't run a marathon without working on your stamina well in advance of the race, and the same goes for taking the OAT.

CHAPTER TWO

Studying Effectively

The first year of optometry school is a frenzied experience for most students. To meet the requirements of a rigorous work schedule, students either learn to prioritize and budget their time or else fall hopelessly behind. It's no surprise, then, that the OAT, the test specifically designed to predict success in the first year of optometry school, is a high-speed, time-intensive test. The OAT demands excellent time-management skills as well as grace under pressure, both during the test as well as while preparing for it. Having a solid plan of attack and sticking with it are key to giving you the confidence and structure you need to succeed.

CREATING A STUDY PLAN

The best time to create a study plan is at the beginning of your OAT preparation. If you don't already use a calendar, you will want to start. You can purchase a planner from an office store, print out a free calendar from the Internet, use a built-in calendar or app for one of your smart devices, or keep track using an interactive online calendar. Pick the option that is most practical for you and that you are most likely to see and use consistently.

Once you have a calendar, write in all your professional obligations: class sessions, work shifts, meetings, etc. Then add in personal obligations: appointments, lunch dates, family time, etc. As part of your personal obligations, schedule in specific time for family and friends, working out, or other hobbies. Making an appointment in your calendar for family dinner or going to see a movie may seem strange at first, but planning social activities in advance helps your loved ones cope with your busy schedule (soon to become even busier once you start optometry school!) and helps you balance your personal and professional obligations. When life gets busy, social appointments are often the first to be sacrificed, but this can lead to strained relationships and both physical and mental exhaustion. Having a happy balance allows you to be more focused and productive when it comes time to study, so stay well-rounded and don't neglect anything important to you.

Once you have established your calendar's framework, add in study blocks around your obligations, keeping your study schedule as consistent as possible across days and across weeks. Studying at the same time of day as your official test is ideal for promoting the best recall, but if that's not possible, then fit in study blocks whenever you can.

Next, add in your full-length practice tests. Take one test earlier in your preparation, but save any remaining tests until you've reviewed all the content and are beginning to feel confident about the OAT. Staggering your tests in this way allows you to form a baseline for comparison and to determine which areas to focus on right away, while also providing realistic feedback as to how you will perform on Test Day. For each test scheduled, set aside five hours to take the test and then another five hours the next day to thoroughly review the test (discussed more later in this chapter).

When planning your calendar, aim to finish your full-length practice tests and the majority of your studying by one week before Test Day, which will allow you to spend that final week completing a final, brief review of what you already know.

Study Blocks

To make studying as efficient as possible, block out short, frequent periods of study time throughout the week. From a learning perspective, studying one hour per day for six days per week is much more valuable than studying for six hours all at once one day per week. Spacing out your preparation allows your brain time to consolidate its new memories, and seeing the material repeatedly over a longer period of time makes recalling the information on Test Day easier and faster. Specifically, Kaplan recommends studying for no longer than three hours in one sitting. In fact, three hours is an ideal length of time to study: It's long enough to build up your stamina for the five-hour Test Day but not so long that you become overwhelmed with too much information.

Within those three-hour blocks, also plan to take 10-minute breaks every hour. Use these breaks to get up from your seat, do some quick stretches, get a snack and a drink, and clear your mind. Although 10 minutes of break for every 50 minutes of studying may sound like a lot, these breaks will allow you to deal with distractions and rest your brain so that, during the 50-minute study blocks, you can remain completely focused. Taking breaks more often than this, however, can be detrimental; research shows that becoming fully engaged in a mentally-taxing activity generally takes 10 minutes, so if you stop to check your email or social media, talk with your roommates, or grab yet another snack every ten minutes while studying, you will never be completely engaged and will not be using your time effectively.

If you would like to study for more than three hours in one day, space out your studying with a significant break in the middle. For example, you may study for three hours in the morning, take a two-hour break to have lunch with your friends, then study for another two hours in the afternoon.

If you are unable to study for a full three hours in one sitting, shorter amounts of time can work as well, but you'll get the most benefit from your studying if you immerse yourself in the material uninterrupted for at least one hour. For brief practice when you only have a few minutes, use the Study Sheets located at the back of this book. These sheets contain the most important information to memorize before Test Day, so take them with you wherever you go or put them somewhere you'll see them frequently. These can be a great way to fit in extra studying when you wouldn't be doing anything productive otherwise, such as when waiting for the bus to arrive or for a class or meeting to start or even while brushing your teeth (you can hang them up on your bathroom mirror!). Even five or ten minutes per day quickly adds up to hours of additional studying over the course of a few weeks.

The total amount of time you spend studying each week will depend on your schedule and your test date, but it is recommended that you spend 200–250 hours before taking the official OAT. One way you could break this down is to study for three hours per day, five days per week, for three months. But this is just one way. You might study six days per week (though avoid studying every day!) or for more than three hours per day. You might study over a longer period of time if you don't have as much time to study each week. Or you might find that you need more or fewer hours based on your personal performance and goal scores.

One way you could use this book is to complete at least one chapter per day. Note that the length of each chapter varies considerably, so only use this as a rough guideline, remembering each week to spend additional time practicing, memorizing vocabulary, and reviewing material previously covered. Furthermore, for best studying, don't just review all of the chapters in order; instead, start thinking about all of the sections of the test right away and reinforce long-term learning by staggering the material.

No matter what your plan is, ensure you complete enough practice to feel completely comfortable with the OAT and its content. A good sign you're ready for Test Day is when you begin to earn your goal score consistently in practice.

Time Off

Taking some time off can be just as important as studying. Just as you should take breaks during study blocks, take breaks during the week as well. Kaplan recommends taking at least one full day off per week, ideally from all of your professional obligations but at minimum from studying for the OAT. Taking this time allows you to recharge mentally, and any fun or relaxing activities you plan for those days give you something to look forward to during the rest of the week.

HOW TO STUDY

The OAT covers a large amount of material, so studying for Test Day can initially seem daunting. To put studying more into your control, break the content down into specific goals for each day and each week instead of attempting to approach the test as a whole. A goal of "I want to increase my cumulative score by thirty points" is too big, abstract, and difficult to measure on the small scale. More reasonable goals are "I will read one chapter each day this week" or "I will be able to recite all the digestive enzymes by Friday." Goals like these are much less overwhelming and help break studying into manageable pieces. As you achieve these smaller goals, you may be surprised to see how quickly you begin achieving your bigger goals, too.

Once you've established your next short-term goals, you will want to achieve them as efficiently and effectively as possible, which means making the most of your study time. Always take notes when reading and practicing. Don't just passively read this book. Instead, read actively: Use the free margin spaces to jot down important ideas, draw diagrams, and make charts as you read. Active participation increases your retention and makes rereading your notes at a later date a great way to refresh your memory.

As you go through your Kaplan program, much of the information may be familiar to you. After all, you have probably seen most of the content before. However, be very careful: Familiarity with a subject does not necessarily translate to knowledge or mastery of that subject. Do not assume that if you recognize a concept you actually know it and can apply it quickly at an appropriate level. Frequently stop and ask yourself questions while you read (e.g., *What is the main point? How does this fit into the overall scheme of things? Could I thoroughly explain this to someone else?*). By making connections and focusing on the grander scheme, not only will you ensure you know the essential content, but you will also prepare yourself for the level of critical thinking required by the OAT.

If you are limited by only having a minimal amount of time to prepare before Test Day, focus on your biggest areas of opportunity first. You likely won't have time to take detailed notes for every page of this book; instead, use your results from practice questions and tests to determine which areas are your biggest opportunities and seek those out. Skim over content matter for which you are already demonstrating proficiency, pausing to read more thoroughly when something looks unfamiliar or particularly difficult. If you are already feeling confident with the topic of a specific chapter, consider starting with the Review Problems at the end of the chapter. If you can get all of those questions correct within a reasonable amount of time, you may be able to quickly skim through that chapter, but if the questions prove to be more difficult, then you may need to spend time reading the chapter or certain subsections of that chapter more thoroughly, taking notes.

Leave time to review your practice questions and your notes from previous chapters, too. You lead a busy life in addition to preparing for the OAT, and fitting in so much study time can often feel difficult. You may be tempted to push ahead and cover new material as quickly as possible, but failing to schedule ample time for review will actually throw away your greatest opportunity to improve your performance. The brain rarely remembers anything it sees or does only once. When you build a connection in the brain and then don't follow up on it, that knowledge may still be in your memory somewhere but not in the accessible way you need it to be on Test Day. When you carefully review notes you've taken or problems you've solved (and the explanations for them), the process of retrieving that information reopens and reinforces the connections you've built in your brain. This builds long-term retention and repeatable skill sets—exactly what you need to beat the OAT!

While reviewing, take notes about the specific reasons why you missed questions you got wrong or had to guess on, perhaps by using a spreadsheet like the one below in Table 2.1. Keep adding to the same Why I Missed It Sheet (WIMIS) as you complete more practice, and periodically review your WIMIS to identify any patterns you see, such as consistently missing questions in certain content areas or falling for the same test-maker traps.

Section	Q #	Topic or type	Wrong answer chosen	Why I missed it
Chemistry	42	Nuclear Chem.	Opposite	Confused electron absorption and emission
Chemistry	47	K_{eq}	Miscalculation	Need to memorize Kaplan steps
Reading Comp.	2	Detail	Opposite	Didn't read "not" in answer choice; slow down!
Reading Comp.	4	Inference	Out of Scope	Forgot to make a prediction

Table 2.1

As you move through your OAT program, adjust your study plan based on your available study time and the results of your practice questions. Your strengths and weaknesses are likely to change over the course of this program. Keep addressing the areas that are most important to your score, shifting your focus as those areas change.

Where to Study

One often-overlooked aspect of studying is the environment where the learning actually occurs. Although studying at home is many students' first choice, several problems can arise in this environment, chief of which are distractions. At home, many people have easy access to family, roommates, books, television, movies, food, the Internet, chores yet to be completed—the list goes on. Studying can be a mentally draining process, so as time passes these distractions become ever more tempting as escape routes. As discussed earlier, the moment you lose focus due to one of these distractions, you also lose the time it takes to return to the level of concentration you just had (not to mention any time clearly spent not studying!).

Although you may have considerable willpower, there's no reason to make staying focused harder than it needs to be. Instead of studying at home, head to a library, quiet coffee shop, or similar location whenever possible. This will eliminate many of the usual distractions and also promote efficient studying; instead of studying off and on at home over the course of an entire day, you can stay at the library for three hours of effective studying and enjoy the rest of the day off from the OAT.

If you must study at home, consider ways to prevent distractions. Give copies of your schedule to family and friends and ask them not to interrupt your study blocks. Complete all the essential tasks you can before studying so they do not become distractions. If the Internet is a distraction for you, consider temporarily disabling your social media accounts or downloading an extension for your Internet browser that blocks certain websites while you are studying. Rather than fighting distractions with willpower alone, remove as many distractions as possible in advance to avoid the problem entirely.

An additional advantage of studying at libraries, however, is that their environments tend to be akin to those of the Prometric testing centers. Similar to a library, your testing center will be quiet but not completely silent. Not everyone at the test center will be taking the OAT, and not everyone will start at exactly the same time. While you are in the middle of a multiple choice section, other test takers may be entering the testing room to start their tests, taking breaks, typing essays, or talking with their proctors. Practicing in this type of environment (as opposed to in complete silence or while listening to music at home) means you will be less distracted in the actual testing center on Test Day.

Finally, no matter where you study, make your practice as much like Test Day as possible. Just as required during the official test, don't have snacks or chew gum during your intense, 50-minute study blocks. Turn off your music, television, and phone. Practice on the computer to simulate the computer-based test environment. When completing practice questions, do your work on scratch paper or noteboard sheets rather than writing directly on any printed materials since you won't have that option on Test Day. Study at the same time of day as your official test, especially on the same day of the week, to get in the habit of thinking about the test at those times. Because memory is tied to all of your senses, the more test-like you can make your studying environment, the easier it will be on Test Day to recall the information you're putting in so much work to learn.

In the end, you want to personalize your studying to be as effective as possible for you individually, follow a strict calendar that contains your study blocks and breaks, and make the most of those study blocks by focusing on your opportunity areas while simulating the testing environment. In this way, you'll learn more and at a faster rate than you could otherwise. Sticking with your efficient plan leads to effectively learning the material you need to ace the OAT—this way, you can do well the first time and not need to study for the test again. Being committed now will definitely pay off in the end.

CHAPTER THREE

Test Strategies

Even someone with perfect knowledge of all the science and math on the OAT is unlikely to achieve a perfect score without adequate test strategies. Understanding the test question formats and having a clear plan for how to tackle each question while finishing every section on time can be just as important as content knowledge. In fact, using Kaplan's strategies allows you to use the test structure in your favor and determine correct answers even without knowledge of all the content. Specific strategies for each test section will be covered in the corresponding sections of this book, but this chapter will serve as an introduction to several overarching principles to apply throughout the OAT.

KAPLAN QUESTION STRATEGY

The OAT has only one question type: multiple choice. You won't find any fill-in-the-blank, matching, short response, or true/false problems on the test. Instead, every question will provide you with the option to select one of five (or rarely four) answer choices. Every time. This means two important things. First, you won't need to prepare your knowledge in such a way that you can recite formulas, facts, or statistics from rote memory. Instead, all you'll need to do is recognize and apply those ideas using the choices provided. This means your focus when studying and answering questions should be on recognizing relationships and patterns more than on memorizing lists. Second, the fact that every question is multiple choice means you can identify patterns among the questions and answer choices to help you choose the correct answer even when you're not completely confident regarding the content. Upcoming chapters in this book outline specific strategies for how to use question types and answer choices to your advantage in different subject areas of the test.

All the specific strategies for each section start with one key process: Stop-Think-Predict-Match. Although you will make slight modifications to this strategy depending on which question type you are tackling, the core ideas remain the same: Carefully analyze each question and determine what the correct answer will look like *before* reading the corresponding answer choices. This will allow you to use the question format to your advantage. You will quickly bypass wrong answer choices without needing to analyze them fully or falling for the test makers' trap choices, and you will also leave yourself open to using alternative strategies, such as the process of elimination, when necessary. Each step of Stop-Think-Predict-Match is outlined in more detail below.

Stop

Your very first step when attempting any question is to Stop: Don't fully read the question or answer choices but instead **triage**, analyzing the question's subject matter, length, and difficulty to determine if you should tackle it immediately, later, or not at all. For most questions, you will also use this opportunity to characterize the answer choices (e.g., as vocabulary terms, sentences, equations, numbers with units, graphs, etc.).

As discussed later in this chapter, the Stop step allows you to make the most of the limited amount of time you have available. Determining each question's general characteristics before tackling it also allows you to get in the right mindset for that question. If you know you will need to calculate a specific value, you may list the variables you see on your noteboard as you read the question stem; if you know the answer will instead be a graph, you may sketch a quick plot of the variables instead of listing them.

Think

Once you've characterized the question stem and answer choices and decided to tackle a problem, the next step is to actually read the question stem—but still don't read the answer choices yet. While reading the question, don't just read passively; instead, paraphrase as you read so you can determine what the question is really asking. You won't be able to answer the question correctly if you misunderstand what the question is asking you to do, so don't minimize the importance of this step. This step ensures that you do not rush through the question, potentially leading to additional work that is not needed. Establish what the correct answer will look like as specifically as possible (e.g., velocity on the *x*-axis in meters per second) while being careful to note any negative words, such as *not*, *except*, or *false*.

Predict

Once you have a clear idea of what the question is asking and have all the information you need to answer it, your next step is to formulate a framework of what the correct answer will look like. At this point, you still should not have read the answer choices, so you are essentially treating the problem as a fill-in-the-blank question. A great prediction will answer the question as thoroughly as possible; however, if you're not certain what to expect from wordy answer choices or don't have strong content knowledge for the subject being tested, a simpler prediction could be nearly as useful and is always better than no prediction at all.

Although the Stop-Think-Predict-Match strategy may sound like a radical change to the way you approach a multiple-choice test, chances are it's not entirely different from what you normally do. The major difference is likely the order: Most test takers who are not Kaplan students read the answer choices first and then determine what the correct answer will be. However, the advantages of predicting before reviewing the answer choices are many. First, making a prediction saves you time. Instead of analyzing all four answer choices, you can quickly skip the wrong choices that don't match your prediction without needing to disprove them specifically. Second, having a clear idea of what the correct answer will look like helps you avoid wrong answer choices that might otherwise be tempting. For example, although choice A of a hypothetical Reading Comprehension question might have sounded reasonable had you read it first, after making a prediction you instead realize it doesn't answer the question and in fact wasn't mentioned in the passage at all. In this way, you avoid the trap of "that sounds good" and home in on the correct answer right away instead. Finally, you will feel much more confident with your answer if you predict it and then find it among the choices. As discussed in Chapter 1, confidence builds upon itself, so this aspect of the Predict step is great for Test Day.

Match

After preparing a prediction, your last step is to select the answer choice that truly meets the requirements of your prediction. When matching, your goal is not to judge each answer choice based on its own merits but rather to identify if a choice corresponds with the framework you predicted. To that end, answer choices will fall into one of three categories:

- *The choice matches your prediction:* In this case, read the entire choice thoroughly to ensure all components of the choice are correct, paraphrasing as needed. If the choice looks completely correct, select it and move on to the next question.

- *The choice is clearly the opposite of your prediction or otherwise incorrect:* If at any point you realize a choice is definitely incorrect, stop reading that choice and mark it as eliminated on your noteboard (see noteboard strategies later in this chapter). If one component of a choice is incorrect, the entire choice must be incorrect, so there's no need to read the entire option.

- *The choice does not match your prediction:* When an answer choice is not obviously wrong but also doesn't align with what you were anticipating, skip that choice. Don't spend time at this point attempting to definitively prove the choice is incorrect; one of the other answer choices is likely to match your prediction instead, meaning you won't ever need to determine why this option is incorrect.

  Note that just because a choice doesn't match your prediction doesn't mean you should eliminate it right away. In some cases, you may find that no answer choice matches your original prediction. When this happens, you will need to return to the Think and Predict steps, incorporating more information to modify your prediction by making it more general or more specific as needed. Using this modified prediction, you can then complete the Match step again on the choices you did not already eliminate.

As you first start using the Stop-Think-Predict-Match strategy, you may find yourself moving through questions more slowly, especially when you need to modify your predictions, but don't give up! With practice, you will begin to perform these steps automatically and find both your speed and accuracy increased. Because mastery of all the OAT strategies does require practice, use them consistently throughout your practice tests and questions so you can use them effectively by Test Day.

TEST TIMING

For complete Test Day success, you must answer as many questions correctly as possible in the time allotted. Knowing the content and question strategies is important, but not enough; you also must hone your time-management skills so you have the opportunity to use those strategies on as many questions as possible. It's one thing to answer a Reading Comprehension question correctly; it's quite another to answer all of the questions in the section in the limited time allotted. The same applies for the other sections; it's a completely different experience to move from handling an individual passage or problem at leisure to handling a full section under timed conditions. Time is a factor that affects every test taker, and the good news is that you can easily improve your scores by adhering to the following basic principles.

The Four Basic Principles of Test Timing

On some tests, if a question seems particularly difficult, you can spend significantly more time on it because you are given more points for correctly answering hard questions. This is not true on the OAT. Every OAT question, no matter how difficult, is worth a single point. There's no partial credit. Because there are so many questions to do in so little time, you can seriously hurt your score by spending five minutes earning one point for a hard question and then not having time to get several quick points from easier questions later in the section.

Given this combination—limited time and all questions equal in weight—you must manage the test sections to ensure you earn as many points possible as quickly and easily as you can.

1. Feel free to skip around

One of the most valuable strategies to help you finish sections in time is recognizing and dealing with the questions and passages that are easier and more familiar to you first. That means temporarily skipping those that promise to be more difficult and time-consuming. You can always come back to these at the end, and, if you run out of time, you're much better off having spent time on the questions that will definitely earn you points rather than those you might have gotten incorrect anyway. Because there's no guessing penalty, always fill in an answer to every question on the test whether you have time to fully attempt it or not.

This strategy is difficult for most test takers; we're conditioned to do things in order, but it just doesn't pay off on the OAT. Don't let your ego sabotage your score by wasting time on questions you can't do. Sometimes it isn't easy to give up on a tough, time-consuming question, but often it's better simply to move on. The computer won't be impressed if you get the toughest question right. If you dig in your heels on a tough question, refusing to move on until you've cracked it, you're letting your ego get in the way of your test score. A test section is too short to waste on lost causes. There's no point of honor at stake here, but there are OAT points at stake.

Give skipping around a try when you practice. Remember, if you do the test in the exact order given, you're letting the test makers control you. Be mindful of the clock, and don't get bogged down with the tough questions. On the computer-based test, you can skip around within a section but not among sections.

2. Seek out questions you can answer correctly

Being able to identify which questions will be most difficult for you personally is essential to making decisions about which ones to skip. Unlike items on some other standardized tests, questions and passages on the OAT are not presented in order of difficulty. There's no rule that says you have to work through the questions within a section in any particular order; in fact, the test makers scatter the easy and difficult questions throughout the section, in effect rewarding those who actually get to the end. Don't lose sight of what you're being tested for along with your reading and thinking skills: efficiency and cleverness. If general chemistry questions are your area of expertise, head straight for them when you first begin the Survey of Natural Sciences section and save the organic chemistry and biology questions until the end of that section.

Ideally, you'll be able to determine if a question is easier or more difficult and time-consuming within the first five seconds. If you only realize a question is difficult after spending two minutes working on it, you've already lost time there and forfeited much of the advantage of skipping around.

When evaluating the difficulty of a question, consider factors such as length of question stem and answer choices, type of question, type of answer choices provided (e.g., numbers, expressions, terms, or sentences), vocabulary used, content area being tested, etc. Also consider how long a question will take you; even if you know exactly how to perform a calculation, if it involves multiple steps and will take you several minutes, you may want to skip that question initially. If you do decide you can't do a question or realize you won't get to it, guess! Fill in an answer—any answer—for every question. There's no penalty if you're wrong, but you score a point if you're right. Note that no answer choice is more frequently correct on the OAT than any other, so avoid looking for big-picture patterns and instead make educated guesses based on logic and elimination.

3. Use the process of elimination judiciously

There are two ways to get all the answers right on the OAT: You either know all the right answers, or you know all the wrong answers. Because there are four times as many wrong answers, you should be able to eliminate some, if not all, of them. Therefore, if you don't know the right answer, eliminate as many wrong answers as you can. By doing so, you either get to the correct response or increase your chances of guessing the correct response. You start out with a 20 percent chance of picking the right answer, and with each eliminated answer your odds go up. Eliminate one choice, and you have a 25 percent chance of picking the right answer; eliminate two choices, and you have a 33 percent chance; and so on. Remember to look for wrong-answer traps when eliminating. Some answers are designed to seduce you by distorting the correct answer and therefore can be quickly eliminated. For more information about common wrong answer pathologies, see Chapter 53, Question Types.

However, note that using the process of elimination can be slow. If you attempt to use the process of elimination on every question, you undoubtedly will run out of time before getting to all the questions. Evaluating five choices is much more time-consuming than directly homing in on the correct answer and picking it without worrying about why all the wrong choices are incorrect. The process of elimination can be a powerful tool, but save it as a backup for when tackling the question directly with Stop-Think-Predict-Match has not yielded the correct answer.

4. Keep track of time

While working on a section, maintain a general sense of your timing without constantly looking at the clock. For most multiple choice sections, you must average from 55 to 65 seconds per question in order to finish in time. These are averages, though; you will be able to answer some basic questions in 15 seconds, whereas other questions, such as those that involve lengthy calculations, may take over 60 seconds. Especially because of such discrepancies, constantly looking at the countdown timer after every question can be unnecessarily stressful and potentially misleading; you may have just tackled a particularly difficult question for which taking more time was perfectly acceptable, so trying to stick too closely to the average for every question can be counterproductive. Nevertheless, to ensure you finish each section, you still shouldn't spend a wildly disproportionate amount of time on any one question or group of questions.

A good strategy, therefore, is to look at the clock every 5 or 10 minutes with a specific goal, such as "I should have more minutes than questions remaining in the Quantitative Reasoning section" (meaning there will be at least one minute for every remaining question). Having specific guidelines in mind helps avoid spending time calculating how much time is left out of the total, which can use up valuable testing time.

When planning out your time, leave at least 30 seconds at the end of each section to review any questions you intended to come back to later and make quick educated guesses for questions you left blank (if any). The last thing you want to happen is for time to elapse for a particular section before you've gotten to half the questions. Therefore, it's essential that you pace yourself, keeping in mind the general guidelines for how long to spend on any individual question or passage. With practice, you will develop an innate sense of how long you have to complete each question so you know when you're exceeding the limit and should start to move faster.

Section-Specific Pacing

Let's now look at the section-specific timing requirements and some tips for meeting them. As described previously, keep in mind that the times per question or passage are only averages; some questions are bound to take less time, whereas others will take more. Try to stay balanced. Every question is of equal worth, so don't get hung up on any one. Think about it: If a question is so hard that it takes you a long time to answer it, chances are you may get it wrong anyway. In that case, you'd have nothing to show for your extra time but a lower score.

Reading Comprehension

Allow yourself approximately 20 minutes per passage set, which includes reading a passage and answering the associated questions. On average, give yourself 7–8 minutes to read a passage and 10–12 minutes to answer the corresponding questions. Some longer passages may take more time to read, but limit yourself to eight minutes as a maximum so you have time to answer the questions, which are what actually contribute to your overall score.

Do the easiest passages first. This may mean avoiding topics that are extremely unfamiliar or passages that seem to include a lot of challenging vocabulary. For passage-based questions, choose an answer based only on the information given. Be careful not to overthink the question by inserting too much of your own logic. Passages might generate their own data. Your answer choices must be consistent with the information in the passage, even if that means an answer choice is inconsistent with the science of ideal, theoretical situations.

The Survey of Natural Sciences

You have about 55 seconds for each Biology, General Chemistry, or Organic Chemistry question in the Survey of Natural Sciences. However, Biology and Organic Chemistry questions typically take less time than complex General Chemistry calculations, so it's important to keep track of your overall progress. A good goal is to spend 30 seconds per Biology question, up to 75 seconds per General Chemistry question, and then 60 seconds per Organic Chemistry question. Completing the mostly fact-based Biology questions quickly will allow you to have plenty of time for the more time-consuming chemistry questions and set yourself up for success in the section as a whole.

Physics and Quantitative Reasoning

Physics averages 75 seconds per question, but different question types use less or more time depending on the level of calculation required. You have about 67 seconds for each Quantitative Reasoning question, but again, some will take more time and others less.

NOTEBOARD STRATEGIES

Other resources to maximize on Test Day are your two noteboards and markers. Using the noteboards when you need them, but not so much that you waste your limited time, is important. One efficient strategy is to make an elimination table, like the one at the top of Figure 3.1. Rather than rewriting the letters A, B, C, D, and E for each question, write them only once and use a table to keep track of which choices you have eliminated. This has the added benefit of clearly retaining which choices you have eliminated for any given question, which is helpful for those questions you plan to return to later. As discussed previously, don't use elimination for every question since it can be time-consuming even with this shortcut.

Figure 3.1

Write clearly on your noteboard. Conserve space by keeping all your work for a given problem in the same area. Number each question and box off its notes when you are finished so you can come back to it later, if needed, and so you do not confuse your work for one question with the work for another. When you finish a section, ask your proctor for a new noteboard (and a new marker if you sense yours is beginning to run out of ink).

KAPLAN'S TOP TEN OAT STRATEGIES

1. **Relax!**

   Just by reading the first few chapters of this book you are already ahead of your competition. By the time Test Day arrives, you will have mastered the Kaplan strategies and OAT content needed to conquer the exam. Have fun with the process; you're almost in optometry school already!

2. **Know what the OAT tests.**

   Never forget the purpose of the OAT: to test your powers of analytical reasoning. You need to know the content because each section has its own particular language, but the underlying OAT intention is consistent throughout the test.

3. **Develop the OAT mindset.**

   The OAT is designed to let you show off everything you've learned so far. Don't let your spirit fall, or your attitude will slow you down. Don't let yourself worry about a question or section once you've finished it; instead, change your mindset and tackle the next item as if you're just starting the day.

4. **Build your stamina.**

   Prepare your mind for Test Day by completing practice tests and studying for three-hour blocks while remembering to take breaks every hour and one day off per week.

5. **Master the art of predicting.**

   Kaplan's Stop-Think-Predict-Match strategy allows you to break up each question into manageable steps. Carefully determine what a question is really asking, then anticipate answers before you read the answer choices. This helps protect you from persuasive, tricky, and time-consuming incorrect choices.

6. **Skip around within each section by seeking out questions you can answer correctly.**

   Attack each section confidently. You're in charge. Since every question is worth one point each, work your best areas first to maximize your opportunity for OAT points. Don't be a passive victim of the test structure, and don't let any one question drag you down!

7. **Use the process of elimination judiciously.**

   Most wrong answer choices are logical twists on the correct choice. Quickly move past any obvious traps to more easily match your prediction, but only use the full process of elimination when you cannot find a match.

8. **Keep track of time.**

   Pace yourself to avoid spending too much time on any individual question. Don't let the clock add stress to Test Day; it's just another tool designed to help you.

9. **Make the most of your noteboard.**

   Keep track of all the notes you need on your noteboard by being neat and methodical. You aren't given many resources to use on Test Day, so take full advantage of those provided.

10. **Have the right attitude.**

    Your attitude toward the test really does affect your performance. You don't necessarily have to think nice thoughts about the OAT, but work to develop confidence and a positive mental stance toward the test. You can do this!

Section II

BIOLOGY

SECTION GOALS

Biology is a topic area integral to mastery of the Survey of Natural Sciences portion of the OAT. The biology strategies, content, and practice presented within this section are designed to help you to accomplish the following goals:

- Recall key biology content terms and ideas
- Identify when and how Test Day questions are using biological concepts
- Distinguish key differences in similar answer choices using knowledge of biological concepts
- Connect new information given in a question to previously existing knowledge of biology
- Predict answers to OAT Biology questions accurately and quickly, using the Kaplan methods

CONTENT OVERVIEW

Cell and Molecular Biology (32.5%)	Chapter 5: Cellular Biology Chapter 6: DNA and RNA* Chapter 7: Metabolism
Genetics (17.5%)	Chapter 6: DNA and RNA* Chapter 8: Genetics
Structure and Function of Systems (22.5%)	Chapter 10: Integumentary and Immunological Systems Chapter 11: Nervous System Chapter 12: Muscular and Skeletal Systems Chapter 13: Circulatory and Respiratory Systems Chapter 14: Digestive System Chapter 15: Urinary System Chapter 16: Endocrine System Chapter 17: Reproductive System
Developmental Biology (10%)	Chapter 18: Developmental Biology
Evolution, Ecology, and Behavior (10%)	Chapter 9: Evolution Chapter 19: Animal Behavior Chapter 20: Ecology
Diversity of Life (7.5%)	Chapter 21: Taxonomy

*Note: An understanding of DNA and RNA is necessary for both Cellular and Molecular Biology and Genetics.

KEY STUDY STRATEGIES

The biology review in this book begins with a chapter on strategy that should be read thoroughly before any other chapters within the section. Once Chapter 4 has been read and internalized, this section can be used in a number of versatile ways. Most of the chapters can be perused in any order, but it is recommended that you prioritize the chapters of greatest need to your individual prep. Boldface vocabulary terms are likely to show up on Test Day. Make sure that you know not only the definitions of these bold terms, but also how they relate to other key terms within biology. Recognition of relevant terms, or "buzzwords," is one of the basic skills required for success on the OAT. Consider using Kaplan flashcards to review these terms, or build your own flashcard set. Use the table above, in combination with practice, to determine which chapters to prioritize in prep. After reviewing a chapter, use the associated quiz to test your knowledge of that content, and review the quiz to find any missing knowledge gaps.

CHAPTER FOUR

Biology Strategies

The biology knowledge you need for the OAT encompasses a wide variety of topics in the categories of cell and molecular biology, diversity of life, vertebrate anatomy and physiology, developmental biology, genetics and evolution, and ecology and behavior. Mastering biology on the OAT means not only memorizing biology vocabulary and facts but also learning to integrate your knowledge, make connections, and otherwise approach the multiple-choice questions in the Biology subtest and the entire Survey of Natural Sciences section in the best way possible.

THE SURVEY OF NATURAL SCIENCES

Biology content appears in the Survey of Natural Sciences section, which contains the Biology, General Chemistry, and Organic Chemistry subtests. The Survey of Natural Sciences has a total of 100 questions that must be completed in 90 minutes. Questions 1–40 are always related to biology, questions 41–70 are always related to general chemistry, and questions 71–100 are always related to organic chemistry. The content in each subtest does overlap in some areas (such as chemical bonding, which is tested in both General Chemistry and Organic Chemistry), but the questions always remain in three discrete groups, and you will receive separate scores for each subtest in addition to your cumulative Survey of Natural Sciences score. Therefore, when you first begin studying for the Survey of Natural Sciences, it's generally best to treat the section as three separate tests and master each content area separately, except for those topics that obviously overlap.

Survey of Natural Sciences Pacing

On Test Day you will be able to freely navigate among all 100 questions in the Survey of Natural Sciences section. Time is shared for all three subtests, giving you an average of 54 seconds per problem. Because the Survey of Natural Sciences is one long section, some test takers find themselves overwhelmed by the need to keep track of time, since there are so many questions yet less than one minute per question. Therefore, you should not only study each subtest separately but also consider each separately when managing the entire section.

Among the three subtests, you should complete Biology in the least amount of time since its questions are mostly fact based and require few calculations. Spend 30 seconds or less on each question to finish the Biology subtest within 20 minutes.

General Chemistry, which involves many more calculations and therefore more use of your scratch work, will take the most time. You should average 75 seconds for each General Chemistry question, which means the entire subtest will take you a total of 37.5 minutes.

Finally, Organic Chemistry will be somewhere in the middle, with some questions that involve drawing out reactions or complex figures taking longer and other questions that require just naming or identifying molecules taking less time. With 60 seconds per question, you will be able to complete this section in 30 minutes.

The Kaplan timing guidelines for the Survey of Natural Sciences are summarized below:

> Biology: 20 minutes (30 seconds per question)
>
> General Chemistry: 37.5 minutes (75 seconds per question)
>
> Organic Chemistry: 30 minutes (60 seconds per question)
>
> Review Marked Questions: 2.5 minutes
>
> Total: 90 minutes

Following these guidelines will allow you to break down the Survey of Natural Sciences into more reasonable pieces and give you a more realistic sense of how you're progressing through the section than if you were to use the overall average of 54 seconds per question. If you stick to the Kaplan guidelines closely, you'll also have 2.5 minutes left at the end of the section to review any questions that you marked to return to later because they involved lengthy calculations or otherwise would take too long to answer during your first pass through the section. By adhering to this Kaplan pacing strategy, using the Test Timing tips from Chapter 1 and the Test Strategies from Chapter 3, and continually practicing, you undoubtedly will find the timing of the Survey of Natural Sciences much more reasonable than you previously thought.

BIOLOGY QUESTION STRATEGY

Kaplan's Stop-Think-Predict-Match strategy is useful for all sections of the test and is especially helpful for the Survey of Natural Sciences section due to the limited time given per question. Before spending a significant amount of time on any one question, *Stop* to consider what content area is being tested and whether you want to attempt that question right away or mark it for later. Each question within a section is worth the same number of points, so answer the easiest and fastest questions first to ensure you've earned as many points as possible before attempting the most difficult and time-consuming problems. Once you've committed to a question, *Think* about what is being asked by carefully reading and paraphrasing the question stem. Next, recall any pertinent outside information and apply that to the question to *Predict* the answer. Only when you have a strong prediction in mind should you read the answer choices, and even then, your goal should be to find a *Match* to your prediction rather than to analyze each answer choice on its own merits. Not reading the answer choices in advance is especially important for the Biology subtest because it contains many questions with lengthy trap answer choices that initially seem correct. For a more thorough review of Stop-Think-Predict-Match, see Chapter 3, Test Strategies.

STUDYING BIOLOGY CONTENT

The OAT assesses test takers' memories of discrete biological facts with particular focus on the molecular basis of life. However, the OAT also assesses test takers' proficiency with integrative questions that focus on biological systems as wholes, including the complex interactions within them. This means that the test rewards both breadth of knowledge and the ability to make connections. Learn both approaches; you'll still need to memorize a wide range of biology facts, but you'll also need to understand how those pieces work together.

To help you learn this wide range of material, it's important to use a wide range of methods while studying. The following chapters contain the biology content you need for Test Day, but you may still see questions on your official test about content that doesn't look familiar at first. That won't be a problem, though, because you'll be able to figure out the answers to those types of questions using critical thinking: bringing different ideas together to determine the correct answers and eliminate impossible choices. You may see a question about a particular enzyme you didn't study, but you can still use information in the question about where it is produced and your knowledge of other molecules with similar names to find the correct answer. For example, if a question asks you about carboxypeptidase formed in the pancreas but you can't remember its function, you can take what you do know to infer that coming from the pancreas means it acts in the small intestine. Since *peptid* refers to peptide bonds, carboxypeptidase must help digest proteins.

To ensure the facts you need come readily to mind, supplement your reading by memorizing flashcards as well as the science study sheets, which contain some of the most important content for Test Day, located at the end of this book. Once you have the basics down, use practice questions to evaluate your knowledge in a test-like setting, remembering to spend plenty of time reviewing the explanations for every question. Although it's unlikely you'll see the exact same questions on Test Day, carefully evaluating exactly why you answered correctly or incorrectly will allow you to apply the concepts to any similar questions you see in the future.

Finally, no matter how you're studying, don't neglect to keep a broad focus on the interactions within and among biological systems. It's important to know that aldosterone is produced by the adrenal cortex and increases salt reabsorption in the nephrons, but it's even more valuable to realize that damage to the adrenal glands (in the exocrine system) can cause low blood pressure (in the circulatory system). By making these connections, not only will you be prepared to answer challenging integrative questions on Test Day, but you'll also ensure you have a solid knowledge of the basics as well. Even if you come from a strong biology background, many of the other test takers do as well, and you might not be very familiar with every topic tested, so it's important to have very thorough knowledge to earn a higher score than your competition.

CHAPTER FIVE

Cellular Biology

The cell is the fundamental unit of all living things. Every function in biology involves a process that occurs within cells or at the interface between cells. Therefore, to understand biology, you need to appreciate the structure and function of different parts of the cell.

CELL THEORY AND STRUCTURE

Cell Theory

The cell was not discovered or studied in detail until the development of the microscope in the 17th century. Since then, much more has been learned, and a unifying theory known as the Cell Theory has been proposed.

The Cell Theory may be summarized as follows:
- All living things are composed of cells.
- The cell is the basic functional unit of life.
- The chemical reactions of life take place inside the cell.
- Cells arise only from pre-existing cells.
- Cells carry genetic information in the form of **DNA**. This genetic material is passed from parent cell to daughter cell.

Cell Structure

The components of the cell are specialized in their structure and function. These components, or **organelles,** include the nucleus, ribosomes, endoplasmic reticulum, Golgi apparatus, vesicles, vacuoles, lysosomes, mitochondria, chloroplasts, and centrioles.

Figure 5.1

There are millions of species of "living things" that can be divided into six kingdoms: **Bacteria, Archaea, Protista, Fungi, Plantae,** and **Animalia.** Within these six kingdoms are two major types of cells: **prokaryotic** and **eukaryotic**. The word prokaryote means "before nucleus," and prokaryotic cells lack membrane-bound nuclei and in fact any membrane-bound organelles. That means the main internal components of prokaryotic cells are ribosomes and genetic material. Note that scientists formerly divided life into only five kingdoms but recently separated the kingdom of Monera (Prokaryota) into Bacteria and Archaea due to differing evolutionary origins.

Cell membrane

The cell membrane (plasma membrane) encloses the cell and exhibits selective permeability; it regulates the passage of materials into and out of the cell. According to the generally accepted **fluid mosaic model**, the cell membrane consists of a phospholipid bilayer with proteins embedded throughout. The lipids and many of the proteins can move freely within the membrane.

The phospholipid bilayer has a specific structure that forms spontaneously. Phospholipid molecules are arranged such that the long, nonpolar, hydrophobic, "fatty" chains of carbon and hydrogen face each other, with the phosphorus-containing, polar, hydrophilic heads facing outward. The hydrophilic heads face the watery regions inside and outside the cell, while the hydrophobic tails face each other in a water-free region.

As a result of its lipid bilayer structure, a plasma membrane is readily permeable to both small, nonpolar, hydrophobic molecules, such as oxygen, and small polar molecules, such as water. Small charged particles are usually able to cross the membrane through protein channels. However, charged ions and larger charged molecules cross the membrane with the assistance of **carrier proteins**.

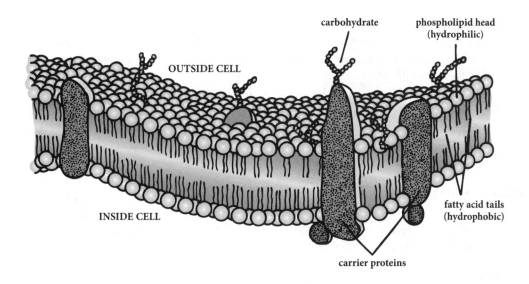

Figure 5.2

Nucleus

The nucleus controls the activities of the cell, including cell division. It is surrounded by a nuclear membrane. The nucleus contains DNA, which is complexed with structural proteins called **histones** to form **chromosomes**. DNA winds around histones to make it more compact, and these histones are also involved in regulation of gene transcription. The **nucleolus** is a dense structure in the nucleus where **ribosomal RNA** (rRNA) synthesis occurs (ribosomal RNA is necessary for protein synthesis at the ribosome).

Ribosome

Ribosomes are the sites of protein production and are synthesized by the nucleolus. Free ribosomes are found in the cytoplasm, whereas bound ribosomes line the outer membrane of the endoplasmic reticulum.

Endoplasmic reticulum

The endoplasmic reticulum (ER) is a network of membrane-enclosed spaces involved in the transport of materials throughout the cell, particularly those materials destined to be secreted by the cell. There are two kinds of endoplasmic reticuli, rough ER and smooth ER. **Smooth ER** does not contain ribosomes and so is not involved with protein synthesis but instead is involved with metabolism and the production of lipids. **Rough ER** contains ribosomes (which gives it a "rough" appearance under microscopy) and plays an important role in the production of proteins.

Golgi apparatus

The Golgi apparatus receives vesicles and their contents from the smooth ER and then modifies them (via processes such as glycosylation), repackages them into vesicles, and distributes them to the cell surface for exocytosis.

Mitochondria

Mitochondria are the sites of aerobic respiration within the cell and hence the suppliers of energy, especially in the form of adenosine triphosphate (ATP). Each mitochondrion is composed of an outer and inner phospholipid bilayer.

Cytoplasm

Most of the cell's metabolic activity occurs in the cytoplasm, which includes the **cytosol** (the cellular fluid contained within the cell membrane) and all the organelles of the cell. Transport within the cytoplasm occurs by **cyclosis** (streaming movement within the cell).

Vacuoles/Vesicles

Vacuoles and vesicles are membrane-bound sacs involved in the transport and storage of materials that are ingested, secreted, processed, or digested by the cell. Vacuoles are larger than vesicles and are more likely to be found in plant than in animal cells.

Centrioles

Centrioles are composed of microtubules and are involved in spindle organization during cell division. They are not bound by a membrane. Animal cells usually have a pair of centrioles oriented at right angles to each other that lie in a region called the centrosome. The centrosome organizes microtubules and helps regulate the progression of the cell cycle. Plant cells do not contain centrioles.

Lysosomes

Lysosomes are membrane-bound vesicles that contain **hydrolytic enzymes** involved in intracellular digestion. Lysosomes break down material ingested by the cell. An injured or dying cell may self-destruct by rupturing the lysosome membrane and releasing its hydrolytic enzymes; this process is called **autolysis**.

Cytoskeleton

The cytoskeleton supports the cell, maintains its shape, and aids in cell motility. It is composed of microtubules, microfilaments, and intermediate filaments.

Microtubules are hollow rods made up of polymerized **tubulin** that radiate throughout the cell and provide it with support. Microtubules provide a framework for organelle movement within the cell. Centrioles, which direct the separation of chromosomes during cell division, are composed of microtubules. **Cilia** and **flagella** are specialized arrangements of microtubules that extend from certain cells and are involved in cell motility and cytoplasmic movement.

Microfilaments are solid rods of **actin,** which are important in cell movement as well as support. Muscle contraction, for example, is based on the interaction of actin with myosin. Microfilaments move materials across the plasma membrane, for instance, in the contraction phase of cell division and in amoeboid movement.

CELLULAR TRANSPORT

Substances can move into and out of cells in various ways. Some methods occur passively, without energy, whereas others are active and require energy expenditure (via hydrolysis of ATP).

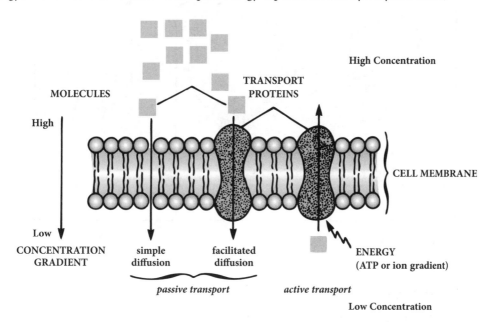

Figure 5.3

Simple Diffusion

Simple diffusion is the net movement of dissolved particles down their concentration gradients—from a region of higher concentration to a region of lower concentration. This is a passive process that requires no external source of energy.

Osmosis

Osmosis is the simple diffusion of water from a region of lower solute concentration to a region of higher solute concentration. When the cytoplasm of a cell has a lower solute concentration than the extracellular medium, the medium is said to be **hypertonic** to the cell, and water will flow out of the cell into the surrounding medium. This process, also called **plasmolysis**, will cause the cell to shrivel.

If the extracellular environment is less concentrated than the cytoplasm of the cell, the extracellular medium is said to be **hypotonic** and water will flow into the cell, causing it to swell and **lyse** (burst). For example, red blood cells will burst if placed in distilled water. Freshwater protozoa have contractile vacuoles to pump out excess water and prevent bursting.

If the extracellular environment has the same concentration of solutes as the cell cytoplasm, the cell is said to be **isotonic** to the environment, and water will move back and forth in equal amounts across the cell membrane.

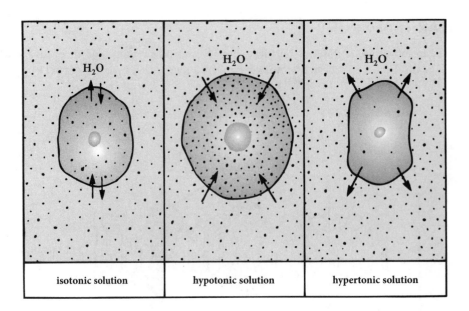

| isotonic solution | hypotonic solution | hypertonic solution |

Figure 5.4

Facilitated Diffusion

Facilitated diffusion (passive transport) is the net movement of dissolved particles down their concentration gradient through special channels or carrier proteins in the cell membrane. This process, like simple diffusion, does not require energy.

Active Transport

Active transport is the net movement of dissolved particles against their concentration gradients with the help of transport proteins. Unlike diffusion, active transport requires energy. These carrier molecules or transport proteins aid in the regulation of the cell's internal content of ions and large molecules. The passage of specific ions and molecules is facilitated by these carrier molecules, which include the following:

- **Symporters**: move two or more ions or molecules in the same direction across the membrane
- **Antiporters**: exchange one or more ions (or molecules) for another ion or molecule across the membrane
- **Pumps**: energy-dependent carriers (require ATP); e.g., sodium-potassium pump

Endocytosis

Endocytosis is a process in which the cell membrane invaginates, forming a vesicle that contains extracellular medium (see Figure 5.5). This allows the cell to bring large volumes of extracellular material inside the cell. **Pinocytosis** is the ingestion of fluids or small particles, and **phagocytosis** is the engulfing of large particles. Particles may bind to receptors on the cell membrane before being engulfed.

Exocytosis

In exocytosis, a vesicle within the cell fuses with the cell membrane and releases a large volume of contents to the outside. Fusion of the vesicle with the cell membrane can play an important role in cell growth and intercellular signaling (see Figure 5.5). For example, neurotransmitters, which act as signals to neighboring cells, are often released from neurons in this manner. Note that in both endocytosis and exocytosis, material never actually passes through the cell membrane.

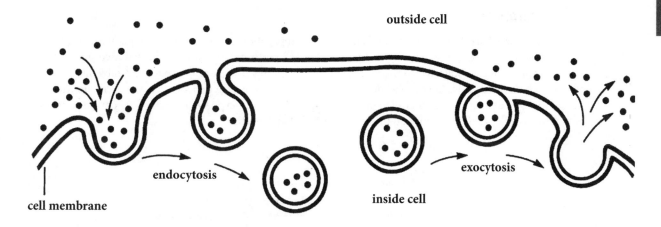

Figure 5.5

Intracellular Circulation

Materials move about within a cell in a number of ways. Some examples include the following:

- **Brownian movement**: Kinetic energy spreads small suspended particles throughout the cytoplasm of the cell.
- **Cyclosis or streaming**: The circular motion of cytoplasm around the cell transports molecules.
- **Endoplasmic reticulum**: The ER forms a network of channels throughout the cytoplasm and provides a direct continuous passageway from the plasma membrane to the nuclear membrane.

Extracellular Circulation

A number of systems deal with the movement of materials on a larger scale through the body of an organism. Examples include:

- **Diffusion**: If cells are in direct or close contact with the external environment, diffusion can serve as a sufficient means of transport for food and oxygen from the environment to the cells. In larger, more complex animals, diffusion is important for the transport of materials between cells and the interstitial fluid that bathes the cells.
- **Circulatory system**: Complex animals, whose cells are too far from the external environment to transport materials by diffusion, require a circulatory system. It generally includes vessels to transport fluid and a pump to drive the circulation. See Chapter 13, Circulatory and Respiratory Systems, for more information.

CELL DIVISION

Cell division is the process by which a cell doubles its organelles and cytoplasm, replicates its DNA, and then divides in two. For **unicellular organisms**, cell division is a means of reproduction, whereas for **multicellular organisms**, it is a method of growth, development, and replacement of worn-out cells. Cell division can follow two different courses, mitosis or meiosis, but each is preceded by interphase. The entire series of events leading to cellular replication constitutes the cell cycle.

Interphase

Interphase is a period of growth and chromosome replication. A cell normally spends at least 90 percent of its life in interphase. During this period, the cell performs its normal cellular functions, and each chromosome is replicated so that during division a complete copy of the genome can be distributed to both daughter cells. After replication, the chromosomes consist of two identical **sister chromatids** held together at a central region called the **centromere**. During interphase the individual chromosomes are not visible; the DNA is instead uncoiled and called **chromatin**.

Figure 5.6

Interphase consists of the following three parts:

1. **G1**: This phase initiates interphase. It is described as the active growth phase and can vary in length. The cell increases in size and synthesizes proteins. The length of the G1 phase determines the length of the entire cell cycle.
2. **S**: This is the period of DNA synthesis.
3. **G2**: The cell prepares to divide in G2. It grows and synthesizes proteins.

The last phase of the cell cycle is the M phase. During M phase mitosis or meiosis occurs, generally resulting in either two identical or four non-identical daughter cells.

Mitosis

Mitosis is the division and distribution of the cell's DNA to its two daughter cells such that each cell receives a complete copy of the original genome. This type of cell division takes place in somatic cells (as opposed to gametes). Nuclear division (**karyokinesis**) is followed by cell division (**cytokinesis**).

Animal Cytokinesis

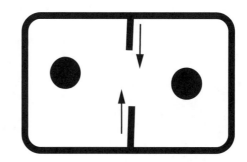

Plant Formation of Cell Plate

Figure 5.7

Prophase

During prophase, the chromosomes condense and the centriole pairs (in animals) separate and move toward the opposite poles of the cell. The spindle apparatus forms between them and the nuclear membrane dissolves, allowing the spindle fibers to interact with the chromosomes.

Metaphase

The centriole pairs are now at opposite poles of the cell. The fibers of the spindle apparatus attach to each chromatid at its corresponding **kinetochore**, a protein location on the centromere. The spindle fibers align the chromosomes at the center of the cell (equator), forming the **metaphase plate**.

Anaphase

The centromeres split so that each chromatid has its own distinct centromere, thus allowing sister chromatids to separate. The sister chromatids are pulled toward the opposite poles of the cell by the shortening of the spindle fibers. Spindle fibers are composed of microtubules.

Telophase

The spindle apparatus disappears. A nuclear membrane forms around each set of newly formed chromosomes. Thus, each nucleus contains the same number of chromosomes (the **diploid** number, $2N$) as the original or parent nucleus. The chromosomes uncoil, resuming their interphase form.

Cytokinesis

Near the end of telophase the cytoplasm divides into two daughter cells, each with a complete nucleus and its own set of organelles. In animal cells, a **cleavage furrow** forms, and the cell membrane indents along the equator of the cell, eventually pinching through the cell and separating the two nuclei. In plant cells a cell plate forms between the two nuclei, effectively splitting the plant cell in half and allowing the cell to divide.

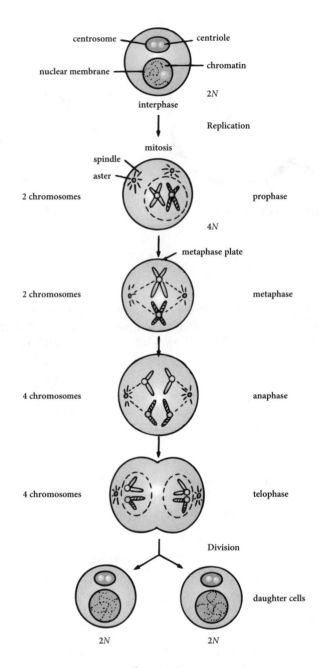

Figure 5.8

Meiosis

Sexual reproduction differs from asexual reproduction in that there are two parents involved. Sexual reproduction occurs via the fusion of two gametes—specialized sex cells produced by each parent. **Meiosis** is the process by which these sex cells are produced. Meiosis is similar to mitosis in that a cell duplicates its chromosomes before undergoing the process. However, whereas mitosis preserves the diploid number of the cell, meiosis produces **haploid** ($1N$) cells, halving the number of chromosomes. Meiosis involves two divisions of **primary sex cells**, resulting in four haploid cells called **gametes**.

Interphase

As in mitosis, the parent cell's chromosomes are replicated during interphase, resulting in the $2N$ number of sister chromatids.

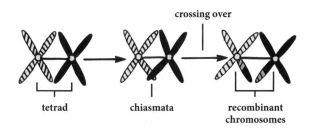

Figure 5.9

First meiotic division

The first division produces two intermediate daughter cells with N chromosomes and sister chromatids.

Prophase I: The chromatin condenses into chromosomes, the spindle apparatus forms, and the nucleoli and nuclear membrane disappear. Homologous chromosomes (chromosomes that code for the same traits, one inherited from each parent) come together and intertwine in a process called **synapsis**. Since at this stage each chromosome consists of two sister chromatids, each synaptic pair of homologous chromosomes contains four chromatids and is therefore often called a **tetrad**. Sometimes chromatids of homologous chromosomes break at corresponding points and exchange equivalent pieces of DNA; this process is called **crossing over**. The points of contact between these homologous chromosomes where crossing over can occur are called chiasmata. Note that crossing over occurs between homologous chromosomes and not between sister chromatids of the same chromosomes (the latter are identical, so **crossing over** would not produce any genetic variation). The chromatids involved are left with an altered but complete set of genes. Recombination among chromosomes results in increased genetic diversity within a species. Note that the two pairs of sister chromatids are no longer identical after recombination has occurred.

Figure 5.10

Metaphase I: Homologous pairs (tetrads) align at the equatorial plane and each pair attaches to a separate spindle fiber at the kinetochore.

Anaphase I: The homologous pairs separate and are pulled to opposite poles of the cell. This process is called **disjunction** and it accounts for a fundamental Mendelian law. During disjunction, each chromosome of paternal origin separates (or disjoins) from its homologue of maternal origin, and either chromosome can end up in either daughter cell. Thus, the distribution of homologous chromosomes to the two intermediate daughter cells is random with respect to parental origin. Each daughter cell will have a unique pool of genes from a random mixture of maternal and paternal origin.

Nondisjunction occurs when cells do not separate appropriately during meiosis. This results in the daughter cells having an incorrect number of chromosomes and is discussed in greater detail in Chapter 8.

Telophase I: A nuclear membrane forms around each new nucleus. At this point, each chromosome still consists of sister chromatids joined at the centromere.

Second meiotic division

This second division is very similar to mitosis, except that meiosis II is not preceded by chromosomal replication. The chromosomes align at the equator, separate and move to opposite poles, and are surrounded by a re-formed nuclear membrane. The new cells have the haploid number of chromosomes. Note that, in women, only one of these daughter cells becomes a functional gamete; the other two or three cells are destroyed by the body.

REVIEW PROBLEMS

1. All of the following are components of the Cell Theory EXCEPT the idea that
   A. all living things are composed of cells.
   B. all living things contain mitochondria.
   C. cooperation among cells allows for complex functioning in living things.
   D. all cells arise from preexisting cells.
   E. cells carry genetic information in the form of DNA.

2. A eukaryotic cell contains organelles specialized for various activities. Name the organelles involved and the role they play in the following activities.
   A. Ingestion
   B. Digestion
   C. Transport of proteins

3. Which of the following activities occurs in the Golgi apparatus?
   A. Synthesis of proteins
   B. Breakdown of lipids and carbohydrates
   C. Catalysis of various oxidative reactions
   D. Modification and packaging of proteins
   E. Aerobic respiration

4. Draw the fluid mosaic model of the cell membrane. How does this model account for the passage of materials across the membrane?

5. Prokaryotes and eukaryotes differ in a number of ways. Compare them in terms of the following characteristics.
   A. Organization of genetic material
   B. Site of cellular respiration
   C. Presence of membrane-bound organelles

6. A researcher treats a solution containing animal cells with ouabain, a substance that interferes with the Na^+/K^+ pump embedded in the cell membrane and causes the cell to lyse. Which of the following statements best explains ouabain's mechanism of action?
   A. Treatment with ouabain results in high levels of extracellular Ca_2^+.
   B. Treatment with ouabain results in high levels of extracellular K^+ and Na^+.
   C. Treatment with ouabain increases intracellular concentrations of Na^+.
   D. Treatment with ouabain decreases intracellular concentrations of Na^+.
   E. Treatment with ouabain results in high levels of extracellular Na^+ only.

7. Prokaryotic cells and eukaryotic animal cells both have
    A. DNA.
    B. ribosomes.
    C. cell walls.
    D. chloroplasts.
    E. A and B

8. What is the significance of the lysosomal membrane?

9. What roles do microtubules and microfilaments play in cell division?

10. If the haploid number of an organism is 13, what is its diploid number?

11. Fill in the blanks with the name of the appropriate stage of mitosis.
    A. During _____, the chromosomes separate and move to opposite poles of the cell.
    B. The nuclear membrane begins to dissolve during _____.
    C. The centromeres of the replicated chromosomes have completely split by _____.
    D. During _____, nucleoli disappear.
    E. Chromosomes condense, shorten, and coil during _____.
    F. Centromeres line up at the equatorial plate during _____.
    G. During _____, a cleavage furrow is formed.

12. How do metaphase and anaphase of mitosis differ from metaphase I and anaphase I of meiosis?

BIO

SOLUTIONS TO REVIEW PROBLEMS

1. **B** Discussed in cell theory section of this chapter.

2. **A** Cellular ingestion is a function of the cell membrane and vesicles. The cell membrane invaginates around a food particle and pinches off, enclosing the material in a vesicle that can travel freely in the cytoplasm. This is known as endocytosis.

   B The organelles involved in digestion are lysosomes, vesicles, and mitochondria. A lysosome is a membrane-bound sac containing hydrolytic enzymes. It fuses with a vesicle, allowing its enzymes to chemically degrade the ingested material. The products of lysosomal digestion are released into the cytoplasm, where they can be used by the cell. Glucose is metabolized in mitochondria via aerobic respiration.

   C The endoplasmic reticulum forms a long, interconnecting series of passageways through which proteins are transported. Rough ER secretes proteins into cytoplasmic vesicles that are transported to the Golgi apparatus. Microtubules are involved in the transport of proteins in some specialized cells, such as neurons.

3. **D** Discussed in cell structure section of this chapter.

4. According to the fluid mosaic model in Figure 5.2, the individual molecules of the lipid bilayer are in constant motion within the plane of the membrane. This fluidity allows ions and small molecules to diffuse directly across the cell membrane. However, large molecules cannot cross the membrane without the aid of special carrier protein molecules, which are embedded within the phospholipid bilayer. Some substances cannot cross the membrane at all. This selective permeability allows the cell membrane to tightly control the passage of materials into and out of the cell.

5. **A** In prokaryotes, the genetic material is composed of a single circular molecule of DNA localized in a region of the cell called the nucleoid. Eukaryotes have highly coiled linear strands of DNA organized into chromosomes within a membrane-bound nucleus.

   B In prokaryotes, cellular respiration occurs directly at the cell membrane, whereas in eukaryotes, cellular respiration occurs across the mitochondrial membrane and within the mitochondrion itself.

   C Prokaryotes do not contain any membrane-bound organelles, whereas eukaryotes contain a number of membrane-bound organelles, such as the nucleus, lysosomes, vesicles, ER, and mitochondria.

6. **C** This question requires an understanding of osmosis and the action of the Na^+/K^+ pump, also known as Na^+/K^+ adenosine triphosphatase (ATPase). When a cell is placed in a hypertonic solution (a solution having a higher solute concentration than the cell), fluid will diffuse out of the cell into the solution, resulting in cell shrinkage. When a cell is placed in a hypotonic solution (a solution having a lower solute concentration than the cell), fluid will diffuse from the solution into the cell, causing the cell to expand and possibly lyse. Na^+/K^+ ATPase moves three sodium ions out for every two potassium ions it lets into the cell. Therefore, inhibition of Na^+/K^+ ATPase by ouabain will cause a net increase in the Na^+ concentration inside the cell, and water will diffuse down its concentration gradient and into the cell, causing the cell to swell and then lyse.

7. **E**   Discussed in cell structure section of this chapter.

8.   The lysosomal membrane serves an important function. It protects the cell from the hydrolytic actions of the enzymes it contains. If the membrane were to burst, these enzymes would digest cellular components and ultimately kill the cell.

9.   Microtubules and microfilaments play important roles in cell division. Microtubules form the mitotic spindle, which is responsible for separating sister chromatids. During prophase, a radial array of microtubules forms around the centrioles. The microtubules "push" the centrioles to opposite poles of the cell, forming the bipolar spindle apparatus. When the chromosomes align at the metaphase plate, these spindle fibers attach to the centromeres. During anaphase, the fibers shorten and pull on the centromeres, separating the sister chromatids and moving them toward opposite poles of the cell.

   After anaphase, microfilaments (actin filaments) and myosin filaments under the cell membrane contract, leading to the indentation of the membrane at the metaphase plate and the subsequent division of the parent cell into two daughter cells.

10.   Haploid gametes are produced by meiosis, a process in which the chromosome number of the parent cell is reduced by one half. Thus, if the haploid number (N) of a particular organism is 13, then the diploid number ($2N$) must be 26.

11. **A** anaphase
     B prophase
     C anaphase
     D prophase
     E prophase
     F metaphase
     G telophase

12.   In metaphase of mitosis, replicated chromosomes line up in single file; during anaphase, sister chromatids separate and move to opposite poles of the cell. In metaphase I of meiosis, homologous pairs of replicated chromosomes line up; during anaphase I, the homologous chromosomes separate, but sister chromatids remain attached to each other.

CHAPTER SIX

DNA and RNA

Genes are composed of **DNA** (deoxyribonucleic acid), which contains information coded in the sequence of its base pairs. This information can be transcribed into **RNA** (ribonucleic acid), which is then translated into a sequence of amino acids called a **protein**. Therefore, the DNA sequence is essentially a blueprint for protein synthesis. These proteins regulate all life functions. DNA is also able to **self-replicate**, an essential step in cell division and therefore for cell (and organism) reproduction.

DEOXYRIBONUCLEIC ACID

Deoxyribonucleic acid (DNA) is the basis for heredity. Its ability to self-replicate makes sure that the coded DNA sequence will be passed on to future generations. This concept, along with the sequences of events described above, is the **central dogma** of molecular genetics. DNA is **mutable** and can be altered under certain conditions. These changes alter the proteins produced and therefore the organism's characteristics. Changes in DNA are usually stable and are passed down from generation to generation. This provides the basis for evolution.

Figure 6.1

DNA Structure

The basic unit of DNA is the **nucleotide**. A nucleotide is composed of deoxyribose (a sugar) bonded to both a phosphate group and a nitrogenous base. There are two types of bases: **purines** and **pyrimidines**. Purines in DNA include **adenine** (A) and **guanine** (G); pyrimidines are **cytosine** (C) and **thymine** (T). Purines are larger in structure than pyrimidines because they possess a two-ring nitrogenous base, whereas pyrimidines have a one-ring nitrogenous base. The phosphate and sugar form a chain with the bases arranged as side groups off the chain.

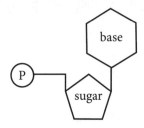

Figure 6.2

The directionality of DNA is designated by a 3′ (read as "three prime") and a 5′ (read as "five prime") end. This naming convention is based on which carbon of the sugar molecule of the DNA strand is the terminus of the helix. If the 5′ carbon is at the end of the DNA strand, then that end is referred to as the 5′ end. Similarly, if the 3′ carbon is at the end of the DNA strand, then that end is referred to as the 3′ end.

DNA is most commonly found in humans as double-stranded helices of complementary strands with the sugar-phosphate chains on the outside of the helix and the nitrogenous bases on the inside. These strands are held together by hydrogen bonds between the bases oriented toward the center. Purines pair with pyrimidines in the following pattern: T forms two hydrogen bonds with A, and G forms three hydrogen bonds with C. This pairing holds the two strands of the double helix together and links the polynucleotide chains. When arranged this way, one DNA strand has its 5′ end pointing up, and the other strand has its 3′ end pointing up, resulting in an **antiparallel** arrangement. This structure was discovered by James Watson and Francis Crick with the help of Rosalind Franklin and others and is therefore known as the **Watson-Crick DNA model**.

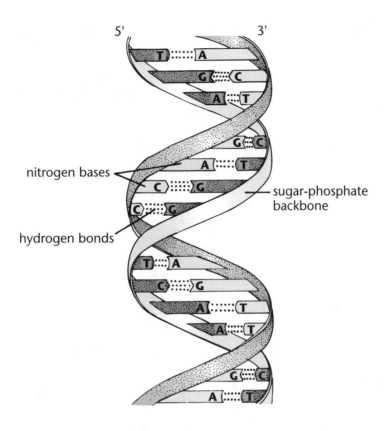

5'   3'

nitrogen bases

hydrogen bonds

sugar-phosphate backbone

Figure 6.3

DNA Function

DNA replication

In order to replicate, the double-stranded DNA helix must unwind and separate into two single strands. This involves uncoiling the strands by **topoisomerase** and breaking the hydrogen bonds between the nitrogenous bases of each nucleotide by **DNA helicase**. The opening in the DNA molecule created by DNA helicase is known as the **replication fork**.

With their hydrogen bonds broken, each single strand can act as a template for complementary base-pairing. This allows for the synthesis of two new daughter strands. Each new daughter helix contains an intact strand from the parent helix and a newly synthesized strand; this type of replication is called **semiconservative**. The daughter strands of DNA formed from the parent strands are identical to the parent strands.

Creation of these daughter strands is a result of the action of **DNA polymerase**. DNA polymerase reads the parent DNA strand and creates a complementary, antiparallel daughter strand. DNA polymerase always reads the parent strand in the $3' \rightarrow 5'$ direction, creating a new daughter strand in the $5' \rightarrow 3'$ direction. One daughter strand is the **leading strand**, and the other is the **lagging strand**. The leading strand is continually synthesized by DNA polymerase, which attaches nucleotides to the exposed 3' end of the parent strand and follows the replication fork to the 5' end. However, the other daughter strand, the lagging strand, is synthesized discontinuously because the 5′ end of the parent strand is the one exposed. Therefore, DNA polymerase, which can only read in the 3′ → 5′ direction, must continually reattach to the 3′ ends of the parent strand since these ends are continually exposed as new section of helices unwinds. The short fragments that result from this discontinuous synthesis are known as **Okazaki fragments**; as the lagging daughter strand is being formed, DNA ligase joins these fragments together.

Figure 6.4

The genetic code

DNA is made up of four different nucleosides: **adenine** (A), **thymine** (T), **cytosine** (C), and **guanine** (G). In RNA, the nucleosides are identical except for thymine, which is replaced with **uracil** (U). DNA is transcribed into mRNA and arranged into **triplets** (sets of three). These triplets (also known as **codons**) are then translated from mRNA into amino acids. There are 20 amino acids that can be formed from all possible combinations of the four nucleosides. A sequence of three consecutive bases codes for a particular amino acid; e.g., the codon GGC specifies glycine, and the codon GUG specifies valine. The genetic code is universal for almost all organisms.

Given that 64 different codons are possible based on the triplet code and four possible nucleotides, and only 20 amino acids need to be coded, the code must contain synonyms. This means that most amino acids have more than one codon coding for them. This is referred to as the degeneracy or **redundancy** of the genetic code.

Second Base

First Base (5′)		U	C	A	G		Third Base (3′)
	U	UUU⎫ UUC⎭ Phe UUA⎫ UUG⎭ Leu	UCU⎫ UCC ⎬ Ser UCA ⎪ UCG⎭	UAU⎫ UAC⎭ Tyr UAA⎫ UAG⎭ *Stop*	UGU⎫ Cys UGC⎭ UGA⎬ *Stop* UGG⎬ Trp	U C A G	
	C	CUU⎫ CUC ⎬ Leu CUA ⎪ CUG⎭	CCU⎫ CCC ⎬ Pro CCA ⎪ CCG⎭	CAU⎫ CAC⎭ His CAA⎫ CAG⎭ Gln	CGU⎫ CGC ⎬ Arg CGA ⎪ CGG⎭	U C A G	Third Base (3′)
	A	AUU⎫ AUC ⎬ Ile AUA⎭ AUG⎬ *Start or Met*	ACU⎫ ACC ⎬ Thr ACA ⎪ ACG⎭	AAU⎫ AAC⎭ Asn AAA⎫ AAG⎭ Lys	AGU⎫ Ser AGC⎭ AGA⎫ Arg AGG⎭	U C A G	
	G	GUU⎫ GUC ⎬ Val GUA ⎪ GUG⎭	GCU⎫ GCC ⎬ Ala GCA ⎪ GCG⎭	GAU⎫ GAC⎭ Asp GAA⎫ GAG⎭ Glu	GGU⎫ GGC ⎬ Gly GGA ⎪ GGG⎭	U C A G	

Figure 6.5

RIBONUCLEIC ACID

RNA Structure

Ribonucleic acid (RNA) is a polynucleotide that is very structurally similar to DNA but with three major exceptions:

- Its sugar is ribose (instead of deoxyribose).
- It contains uracil instead of thymine.
- It is usually single-stranded.

RNA can be found in both the nucleus and the cytoplasm of the cell. There are several types of RNA, all of which are involved in protein synthesis. The three major types are mRNA, tRNA, and rRNA.

Messenger RNA

Messenger RNA (mRNA) carries the complement of a DNA sequence (except that thymine is substituted with **uracil**). It transports this complement from the nucleus to the ribosomes for protein synthesis. mRNA is made from ribonucleotides complementary to the template strand of DNA. This means that mRNA has the complementary code to the original DNA. For example, because the DNA code for the amino acid valine is AAC, the mRNA sequence is the complementary UUG: A pairs with U, and C pairs with G. mRNA is monocistronic, meaning that one mRNA strand codes for one polypeptide.

Transfer RNA

Transfer RNA (tRNA) is a small RNA molecule found in the cytoplasm. It assists in the translation of mRNA's nucleotide code into a sequence of amino acids. It does this by bringing the amino acids coded for in the mRNA sequence to the ribosomes during protein synthesis. tRNA recognizes both the mRNA codon and its corresponding amino acid. This dual function is reflected in its three-dimensional structure. One end contains a three-nucleotide sequence, the **anticodon**, which is complementary to one of the mRNA codons. The other end is the site of attachment of the corresponding amino acid. Each amino acid has its own aminoacyl-tRNA synthetase, which has an active site that binds to both the amino acid and its corresponding tRNA, catalzying their attachment to form an aminoacyl-tRNA complex. There is at least one type of tRNA for each amino acid (there are approximately 40 known types of tRNA).

Ribosomal RNA

Ribosomal RNA (rRNA) is a structural component of ribosomes and is the most abundant of all RNA types. The mRNA sequence passes through two subunits of the rRNA structure and is translated into amino acids at this time. rRNA is synthesized in the nucleolus.

Transcription

Transcription is the process through which information coded in the base sequence of DNA is used to direct the synthesis of a strand of mRNA, when then leaves the nucleus through nuclear pores. Each human chromosome is a long strand of DNA that is used to make approximately 1,000 different sequences of RNA; therefore, RNA molecules are much shorter than DNA molecules since only a segment of each original DNA strand is used as a template. The first step of transcription occurs when RNA polymerase binds to the DNA at a **promoter region**, a short DNA sequence found upstream from the site where transcription of a specific RNA is going to take place. In humans, this is most commonly a TATA box.

Transcription factors then help **RNA polymerase** bind to the DNA molecule and initiate transcription. In a process very similar to DNA replication, the RNA polymerase surrounds the DNA molecule after it has been opened by the actions of DNA helicase and topoisomerase. The RNA polymerase then recruits and adds complementary RNA nucleotides based on the DNA sequence. As with DNA polymerase, RNA polymerase reads DNA in the $3' \to 5'$ direction and creates a new daughter strand of RNA in the $5' \to 3'$ direction. The RNA sequence is complementary to the original DNA sequence except that A binds with uracil (U) rather than T. RNA also uses a slightly different sugar backbone than that used in DNA: ribose (with an oxygen on C–2) instead of deoxyribose (without an oxygen on C–2).

After transcription is complete, mRNA undergoes post-transcriptional processing. RNA that has not yet been processed is known as hetero-nuclear RNA (hnRNA), or pre-RNA, and contains extra nucleotides that are not necessary to create the corresponding protein. These extra sequences are called **introns**; in contrast, **exons** are the nucleotides necessary to make the protein. The introns are **spliced** out (removed) by the spliceosome, leaving only the exons behind. Additionally, a **guanine cap** and a series of adenines known as a **poly-A tail** are added to the ends of the new molecule to provide protection from enzyme degradation once the RNA leaves the nucleus.

Translation

Translation is the process through which mRNA codons are translated into a sequence of amino acids. Translation occurs in the cytoplasm and involves tRNA, ribosomes, mRNA, amino acids, enzymes, and other proteins and can be divided into four distinct stages: initiation, elongation, translocation, and termination (see Figure 6.6).

Initiation begins when the ribosome binds to the mRNA near its 5′ end. The ribosome scans the mRNA until it binds to a **start codon** (AUG). The initiator aminoacyl-tRNA complex, methionine-tRNA (with the anticodon 3′–UAC–5′), base pairs with the start codon.

In **elongation**, hydrogen bonds form between the mRNA codon in the A site of the ribosome and its complementary anticodon on the incoming aminoacyl-tRNA complex. A peptide bond is formed between the amino acid attached to the tRNA in the A site and the amino acid attached to the tRNA in the P site of the ribosome. After the peptide bond formation, a ribosome carries uncharged tRNA in the P site and peptidyl-tRNA in the A site.

The cycle is completed by **translocation**, in which the ribosome advances three nucleotides along the mRNA in the 5′ to 3′ direction. In a concurrent action, the uncharged tRNA from the P site is expelled and the peptidyl-tRNA from the A site moves into the P site. The ribosome then has an empty A site ready for the entry of the aminoacyl-tRNA corresponding to the next codon.

Polypeptide synthesis undergoes **termination** when one of three special mRNA termination codons, or **stop codons** (UAA, UAG, or UGA), arrives in the A site. These codons signal the ribosome to terminate translation; they do not code for amino acids. Frequently, numerous ribosomes simultaneously translate a single mRNA molecule, forming a structure known as a **polyribosome**.

After the release of the protein from the ribosome, the protein immediately assumes its characteristic three-dimensional native conformation. This conformation is determined by the primary sequence of amino acids. Additional secondary and tertiary structural folding occurs based on the primary sequence. Furthermore, the polypeptide chains can form intramolecular and intermolecular cross-bridges with disulfide bonds. The result is a functional protein or complex of multiple proteins.

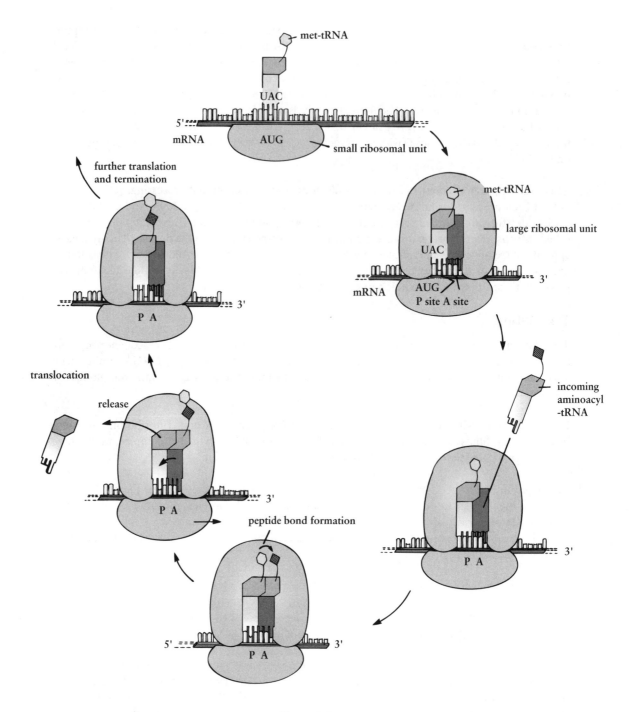

Figure 6.6

Ribosomes, where translation takes place, are composed of two subunits, one small and one large, each consisting of proteins and rRNA. These bind together only during protein synthesis. As previously discussed, ribosomes also have three binding sites for tRNA: the A, P, and E sites. The **A site** (aminoacyl-tRNA complex binding site) binds to the next incoming tRNA complex. The tRNA complex is then transferred to the **P site** (peptidyl-tRNA binding site), where the tRNA contributes its amino acid to the growing polypeptide chain. Finally, having already given up its amino acid, the tRNA is released at the **E site** (exit site).

Humans and bacteria have different types of subunits that make up their ribosomes. This is a difference that drug manufacturers capitalize on when designing antibiotics. Many antibiotics target only the ribosomal structures specific to bacteria, thereby harming bacterial cells while leaving human cells unharmed.

REVIEW PROBLEMS

1. What is the central dogma of molecular genetics?

2. What of the following is NOT true about pyrimidines and purines?
    A. Pyrimidines have a two-ring nitrogenous base.
    B. Purines have a two-ring nitrogenous base.
    C. Purines always bind to pyrimidines when a DNA helix is formed.
    D. Purines and pyrimidines make up the "rungs" of the DNA ladder.
    E. Purines and pyrimidines bind together using hydrogen bonds.

3. What is the difference between the 3′ and the 5′ ends of a DNA molecule?

4. Which model of DNA replication describes one parental strand and one new strand of DNA making up each new helix?
    A. Semiconservative
    B. Conservative
    C. Dispersive
    D. Redundancy
    E. Degeneracy

5. Describe the process of DNA replication, including the roles of topoisomerase and DNA helicase and the definitions of Okazaki fragments and the replication fork.

6. What is the redundancy of the genetic code?

7. What are the three major differences between RNA and DNA?

8. Distinguish between transcription and translation and describe the process that takes place within the ribosome during translation.

SOLUTIONS TO REVIEW PROBLEMS

1. The central dogma of molecular genetics states that genetic information goes from DNA to RNA to protein.

2. **A** Purines are larger molecules than pyrimidines and have a two-ring nitrogenous base, whereas pyrimidines only have a one-ring nitrogenous base. It is true that purines and pyrimidines bind to each other via hydrogen bonds when the DNA helix is formed and that they are on the inside of the helix ("rungs" of the DNA ladder) rather than the outside of the structure.

3. The 3′ end of DNA is where the carbon on the sugar molecule at the farthest end of the DNA molecule is the 3′ carbon within the ring structure. Similarly, the 5′ end is where the carbon on the sugar molecule at the DNA terminus is the 5′ carbon.

4. **A** Semiconservative replication produces two copies of DNA that each contain one parent strand and one new strand. In conservative replication there is one DNA copy with both parent strands and one with two new strands. In dispersive replication there are two copies of DNA that both have pairs of parent and new genetic material interspersed throughout the helix. Redundancy and degeneracy describe the multiple codons that code for the same amino acid in the genetic code.

5. DNA helicase "unzips" the DNA helix, exposing the two parent DNA strands. This opening is called the replication fork. DNA polymerase moves in a 3′ ⟶ 5′ direction along both parent DNA strands, recruiting complementary nucleotides and creating the daughter strands. The leading strand is made continuously, whereas the lagging strand is made discontinuously because DNA polymerase only moves in a 3′ ⟶ 5′ direction. This means that on the lagging strand DNA pieces are made in short sequences rather than one long strand. The short pieces of new DNA on the lagging strand are called Okazaki fragments. Topoisomerase prevents DNA from overcoiling during replication.

6. The genetic code is redundant because more than one codon (sequence of three base pairs) codes for many amino acids. Because there are four possible nucleotides for a codon consisting of a combination of three nucleotides, 64 possible combinations of nucleotides exist to make each codon. However, since only 20 amino acids are coded for, most amino acids can be coded for by more than one sequence of nucleotides. This is referred to as the redundancy of the genetic code.

7. Three major differences between RNA and DNA are that RNA (1) contains ribose instead of deoxyribose as its sugar, (2) contains uracil instead of thymine, and (3) is usually single-stranded.

8. Transcription is the process by which DNA is turned into RNA, whereas in translation RNA is turned into protein. In translation the ribosome locates a start codon near the 5′ end of the mRNA. The ribosome then reads the mRNA sequence, codon by codon, and recruits the corresponding amino acid (attached to a tRNA) encoded by the mRNA. After each codon is read, the mRNA molecule translocates within the ribosome to make room for the next codon. Once a stop codon is reached, termination occurs, and the ribosome falls off the mRNA sequence. At this point the primary structure of the protein is complete, and it assumes its three-dimensional conformation based on its primary sequence.

CHAPTER SEVEN

Metabolism

Humans use energy obtained from the digestion of food to maintain their internal environment and power the basic activities of life. The following terms are used to describe the acquisition, the conversion, and some of the uses of energy by a living organism:

- **Metabolism**: The sum of all chemical reactions that occur in the body. Metabolism can be divided into **catabolic reactions**, which break down large chemicals and release energy, and **anabolic reactions**, which build up large chemicals and require energy.

- **Ingestion**: The acquisition and consumption of food and other raw materials.

- **Digestion**: The process of converting food into a usable soluble form so it can pass through membranes in the digestive tract and enter the body.

- **Absorption**: The passage of nutrient molecules through the lining of the digestive tract into the body proper. Absorbed molecules pass through cells lining the digestive tract by diffusion or active transport.

- **Transport**: The circulation of essential compounds required to nourish the tissues and the removal of waste products from the tissues.

- **Assimilation**: The building up of new tissues from digested food materials.

- **Respiration**: The consumption of oxygen by the body. Cells use oxygen to convert glucose into ATP, a ready source of energy for cellular activities.

- **Excretion**: The removal of waste products (such as carbon dioxide, water, and urea) produced during metabolic processes like respiration and assimilation.

- **Synthesis**: The creation of complex molecules from simple ones (anabolism).

- **Regulation**: The control of physiological activities. The body's metabolism functions to maintain its internal environment in a changing external environment. The steady state of the internal environment is known as **homeostasis** and includes regulation by hormones and the nervous system. **Irritability** is the ability to respond to a stimulus and is part of regulation.

- **Growth**: An increase in size caused by cell division and synthesis of new materials.

- **Reproduction**: The generation of additional individuals of a species.

RESPIRATION

Respiration involves the conversion of the chemical energy in molecular bonds into the usable energy needed to drive the processes of living cells. All living cells need energy for growth, maintenance of homeostasis, defense mechanisms, repair, and reproduction. The cells of the human body and those of other organisms obtain this energy from aerobic respiration (respiration in the presence of oxygen). This process includes the intake of oxygen from the environment, the transport of oxygen in the blood, and the ultimate oxidation of fuel molecules in the cell. **External respiration** refers to the entrance of air into the lungs and the gas exchange between the alveoli and the blood (see Chapter 13, Circulatory and Respiratory Systems). **Internal respiration** includes the exchange of gas between the blood and the cells and the intracellular processes of respiration.

Carbohydrates and fats are the favored **fuel** molecules in living cells. As hydrogen is removed, bond energy is made available. The C-H bond is energy rich; in fact, compared with many other bonds, it is capable of releasing a relatively large amount of energy per mole. In contrast, carbon dioxide contains little usable energy. It is the stable, energy-exhausted end product of respiration.

During respiration, high-energy hydrogen atoms are removed from organic molecules. This is called **dehydrogenation** and is an oxidation reaction. The subsequent acceptance of hydrogen by a hydrogen acceptor (oxygen in the final step) is the reduction component of the redox reaction. Energy released by this reduction is used to form a high-energy phosphate bond in ATP. Although the initial oxidation step requires energy input, the net result of the redox reaction is energy production. If all of this energy was released in a single step, little could be harnessed. Instead, the reductions occur in a series of small steps called the **electron transport chain.**

GLUCOSE CATABOLISM

The degradative oxidation of glucose occurs in two stages: **glycolysis** and **cellular respiration.**

Figure 7.1

Glycolysis

The first stage of glucose catabolism is glycolysis. Glycolysis is a series of reactions that leads to the oxidative breakdown of glucose into two molecules of **pyruvate** (the ionized form of pyruvic acid), the production of ATP, and the reduction of NAD^+ into NADH. All of these reactions occur in the **cytoplasm** and are mediated by specific enzymes.

The process of glycolysis is defined as the sequence of reactions that converts glucose into pyruvate with the concomitant production of ATP. Glycolysis begins when glucose reacts with hexokinase to form glucose 6-phosphate. When this compound interacts with the enzyme phosphoglucose isomerase, the compound fructose 6-phosphate is formed. Fructose 6-phosphate interacts with the enzyme phosphofructokinase to form the compound fructose 1,6-biphosphate. The enzyme aldolase converets 1,6-biphosphate into glyceraldehyde 3-phosphate. After a number of enzymatic reactions, the compound phosphoenolpyruvate is formed. The enzyme pyruvate kinase converts phosphoenolpyruvate into pyruvate, and the glycolytic pathway is complete.

Glycolytic pathway

Step 1   Glucose

ATP
ADP

Step 2   Glucose 6-phosphate

Step 3   Fructose 6-phosphate

ATP
ADP

Step 4   Fructose 1,6-biphosphate

Step 5   Glyceraldehyde 3-phosphate ⇌ Dihydroxyacetone
           (PGAL)   phosphate

Step 6   1,3-Diphosphoglycerate

ADP
ATP

Step 7   3-Phosphoglycerate

Step 8   2-Phosphoglycerate

Step 9   Phosphoenolpyruvate

ADP
ATP

           Pyruvate

*Note: Steps 5–9 occur twice per molecule of glucose

Figure 7.2

Note that at step 4, fructose 1,6-biphosphate is split into two three-carbon molecules: **dihydroxyacetone phosphate** and **glyceraldehyde 3-phosphate (PGAL).** Dihydroxyacetone phosphate is isomerized into PGAL so that it can be used in subsequent reactions. Thus, two molecules of PGAL are formed per molecule of glucose, and all of the subsequent steps occur twice for each glucose molecule.

From one molecule of glucose (a six-carbon molecule), two molecules of pyruvate (a three-carbon molecule) are obtained. During this sequence of reactions, two ATP are used (in steps 1 and 3) and four ATP are generated (two in step 6 and two in step 9). Thus, there is a net production of two ATP per glucose molecule. This type of phosphorylation is called **substrate level phosphorylation** because ATP synthesis is directly coupled with the degradation of glucose without the participation of an intermediate molecule such as NAD^+. Anaerobic metabolism, which ends in fermentation, produces only two ATP per glucose molecule.

The net reaction for glycolysis is:

$$\text{Glucose} + 2\ \text{ADP} + 2\ \text{P}_i + 2\ \text{NAD}^+ \longrightarrow 2\ \text{Pyruvate} + 2\ \text{ATP} + 2\ \text{NADH} + 2\ \text{H}^+ + 2\ \text{H}_2\text{O}$$

At this stage much of the initial energy stored in the glucose molecule has not been released and is still present in the chemical bonds of pyruvate. Depending on the capabilities of the organism, pyruvate degradation can proceed in one of two directions. Under **anaerobic** conditions (in the absence of oxygen), pyruvate is reduced during the process of fermentation. Under aerobic conditions (in the presence of oxygen), pyruvate is further oxidized during cellular respiration in the mitochondria.

Fermentation

NAD^+ must be regenerated for glycolysis to continue in the absence of O_2. This is accomplished by reducing pyruvate into ethanol or lactic acid. Fermentation refers to all of the reactions involved in this process (i.e., glycolysis and the additional steps leading to the formation of ethanol or lactic acid). Fermentation produces only two ATP per glucose molecule.

Alcohol fermentation occurs in yeast and some bacteria. The pyruvate produced in glycolysis is converted to ethanol. In this way, NAD^+ is regenerated, and glycolysis can continue.

Lactic acid fermentation occurs in certain fungi and bacteria and in human muscle cells during strenuous activity. When the oxygen supply to muscle cells lags behind the rate of glucose catabolism, the pyruvate generated is reduced to lactic acid. As in alcohol fermentation, the NAD^+ used in step 5 of glycolysis is regenerated when pyruvate is reduced.

Cellular Respiration

Cellular respiration is the most efficient catabolic pathway used by organisms to harvest the energy stored in glucose. Whereas glycolysis yields only **2 ATP** per molecule of glucose, cellular respiration can yield **36–38 ATP**. Cellular respiration is an **aerobic** process; **oxygen** acts as the final acceptor of electrons that are passed from carrier to carrier during the final stage of glucose oxidation. The metabolic reactions of cell respiration occur in the eukaryotic mitochondrion and are catalyzed by reaction-specific enzymes.

Cellular respiration can be divided into three stages: pyruvate decarboxylation, the citric acid cycle, and the electron transport chain.

Pyruvate decarboxylation

The pyruvate formed during glycolysis is transported from the cytoplasm into the mitochondrial matrix where it is decarboxylated (i.e., it loses a CO_2), and the acetyl group that remains is transferred to coenzyme A to form acetyl-CoA. In the process, NAD^+ is reduced to NADH.

Citric acid cycle

The citric acid cycle is also known as the **Krebs cycle**. The cycle begins when the two-carbon acetyl group from acetyl-CoA combines with oxaloacetate, a four-carbon molecule, to form the six-carbon citrate. Through a series of reactions, two CO_2 are released, and oxaloacetate is regenerated for use in another turn of the cycle.

For each turn of the citric acid cycle one ATP is produced by substrate-level phosphorylation via a GTP intermediate. In addition, electrons are transferred to NAD^+ and FAD, generating NADH and $FADH_2$, respectively. These coenzymes then transport the electrons to the electron transport chain, where more ATP is produced via oxidative phosphorylation (see below). Studying the cycle, we can do some bookkeeping; keep in mind that for each molecule of glucose, two pyruvate are decarboxylated and channeled into the citric acid cycle. Therefore, two of each type of molecular product at this stage of the cycle are created for each glucose molecule.

$$2 \times 3 \text{ NADH} \quad \rightarrow \quad 6 \text{ NADH}$$
$$2 \times 1 \text{ FADH}_2 \quad \rightarrow \quad 2 \text{ FADH}_2$$
$$2 \times 1 \text{ GTP (ATP)} \quad \rightarrow \quad 2 \text{ ATP}$$

The net reaction of the citric acid cycle per glucose molecule is:

$$2 \text{ acetyl-CoA} + 6 \text{ NAD}^+ + 2 \text{ FAD} + 2 \text{ GDP} + 2 \text{ P}_i + 4 \text{ H}_2\text{O} \longrightarrow$$
$$4 \text{ CO}_2 + 6 \text{ NADH} + 2 \text{ FADH}_2 + 2 \text{ GTP} + 4 \text{ H}^+ + 2\text{CoA}$$

Electron transport chain

The electron transport chain (ETC) is a complex carrier mechanism located on the inside of the **inner mitochondrial membrane.** During oxidative phosphorylation, ATP is produced when high-energy potential electrons are transferred from NADH and $FADH_2$ to oxygen by a series of carrier molecules located in the inner mitochondrial membrane. As the electrons are transferred from carrier to carrier, free energy is released, which is then used to form ATP. Most molecules of the ETC are **cytochromes**, electron carriers that resemble hemoglobin in the structure of their active site. The functional unit contains a central iron atom that is capable of undergoing a reversible redox reaction (i.e., it can be alternatively reduced and oxidized). Sequential redox reactions continue to occur as the electrons are transferred from one carrier to the next; each carrier is reduced as it accepts an electron and is then oxidized when it passes it on to the next carrier. The last carrier of the ETC passes its electron to the final electron acceptor, O_2. In addition to the electrons, O_2 picks up a pair of hydrogen ions from the surrounding medium, forming water.

$$2 \text{ H}^+ + 2 \text{ e}^- + \tfrac{1}{2} \text{ O}_2 \longrightarrow \text{H}_2\text{O}$$

Total Energy Production

To calculate the net amount of ATP produced per molecule of glucose, we need to tally the number of ATP produced by substrate-level phosphorylation and the number of ATP produced by oxidative phosphorylation.

Substrate-level phosphorylation

Degradation of one glucose molecule yields a net of two ATP from glycolysis and one ATP for each turn of the citric acid cycle. Thus, a total of four ATP are produced by substrate-level phosphorylation.

Oxidative phosphorylation

Oxidative phosphorylation is the process that produces more than 90 percent of the ATP used by the cells in our body. The major steps involved in this process occur within the ETC or respiratory chain of the mitochondria. The steps at the end of the electron transport chain, where ATP is generated, are as follows. Along the ETC, the respiratory enzymes continually pump hydrogen ions from the matrix of the mitochondria to the intermembrane space, which creates a large concentration gradient. At the end of the ETC, hydrogen ions pass through channels in the respiratory enzymes along the concentration gradient. As the hydrogen ions pass through these enzymes, the energy released is used to convert ADP to ATP. Now, specifically looking at the process of oxidative phosphorylation, two pyruvate decarboxylations yield one NADH each for a total of two NADH. Each turn of the citric acid cycle yields three NADH and one $FADH_2$, for a total of six NADH and two $FADH_2$ per glucose molecule. Each $FADH_2$ generates two ATP, as previously discussed. Each NADH generates three ATP except for the two NADH that were reduced during glycolysis. These NADH cannot cross the inner mitochondrial membrane and must transfer their electrons to an intermediate carrier molecule, which delivers the electrons to the second carrier protein complex, Q. Therefore, because one ATP is used in this transfer, these NADH generate only two ATP per glucose. So the two NADH of glycolysis yield four ATP, the other eight NADH yield 24 ATP, and the two $FADH_2$ produce four ATP, for a total of 32 ATP produced by oxidative phosphorylation.

The total amount of ATP produced during eukaryotic glucose catabolism is therefore four via substrate-level phosphorylation plus 32 via oxidative phosphorylation, for a total of 36 ATP. (For prokaryotes, the yield is 38 ATP because the two NADH of glycolysis don't have any mitochondrial membranes to cross and therefore don't lose energy.)

Eukaryotic ATP Production per Glucose Molecule

Glycolysis

2 ATP invested (steps 1 and 3)	− 2 ATP
4 ATP generated (steps 6 and 9)	+ 4 ATP (substrate)
2 NADH × 2 ATP/NADH (step 5)	+ 4 ATP (oxidative)

Pyruvate decarboxylation

2 NADH × 3 ATP/NADH	+ 6 ATP (oxidative)

Citric acid cycle

6 NADH × 3 ATP/NADH	+ 18 ATP (oxidative)
2 $FADH_2$ × 2 ATP/$FADH_2$	+ 4 ATP (oxidative)
2 GTP × 1 ATP/GTP	+ 2 ATP (substrate)
Total	+ 36 ATP

ALTERNATE ENERGY SOURCES

When glucose supplies run low, the body uses other energy sources. These sources are used by the body in the following preferential order: other carbohydrates, fats, and proteins. These substances are first converted to either glucose or glucose intermediates, which can then be degraded in the glycolytic pathway and the citric acid cycle.

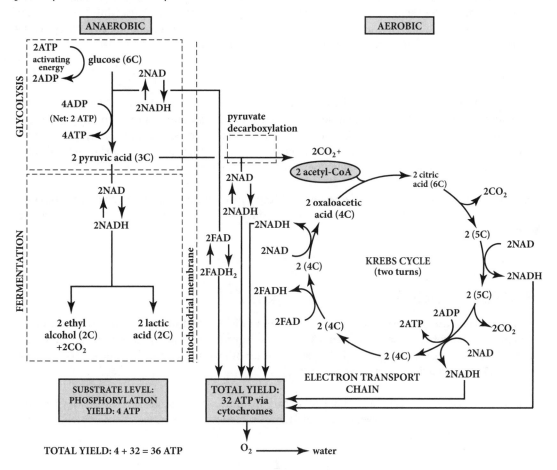

Figure 7.3

Carbohydrates

Disaccharides are hydrolyzed into monosaccharides, most of which can be converted into glucose or glycolytic intermediates. Glycogen stored in the liver can be converted, when needed, into a glycolytic intermediate.

Fats

Fat molecules are stored in adipose tissue in the form of triglycerides. When needed, they are hydrolyzed by **lipases** to **fatty acids** and **glycerol** and are carried by the blood to other tissues for oxidation. Glycerol can be converted into PGAL, a glycolytic intermediate. A fatty acid must first be "activated" in the cytoplasm; this process requires two ATP. Once activated, the fatty acid is transported into the mitochondrion and taken through a series of beta-oxidation cycles that convert it into two-carbon fragments, which are then converted into acetyl-CoA. Acetyl-CoA then enters the citric acid cycle. With each round of β-oxidation of a saturated fatty acid, one NADH and one $FADH_2$ are generated.

Of all the high-energy compounds used in cellular respiration, fats yield the greatest number of ATP per gram. This makes them extremely efficient energy storage molecules. Thus, while the amount of glycogen stored in humans is enough to meet short-term energy needs for about a day, the stored fat reserves can meet the long-term energy needs for about a month.

Proteins

The body degrades proteins only when not enough carbohydrate or fat is available. Most amino acids undergo a **transamination reaction** in which they lose an amino group to form an α-keto acid. The carbon atoms of most amino acids are converted into acetyl-CoA, pyruvate, or one of the intermediates of the citric acid cycle. These intermediates enter their respective metabolic pathways, allowing cells to produce fatty acids, glucose, or energy in the form of ATP.

Oxidative deamination removes an ammonia molecule directly from the amino acid. **Ammonia** is a toxic substance in vertebrates. Fish can excrete ammonia, whereas insects and birds convert it to uric acid, and mammals convert it to urea for excretion.

PHOTOSYNTHESIS

All green plants use **photosynthesis** to convert carbon dioxide and water into glucose and oxygen. Glucose can be stored as starch or used as an energy source. In plants, photosynthesis takes place in a specialized organelle called a chloroplast. Photosynthetic bacteria lack chloroplasts but have membranes that function in a similar manner.

Photosynthesis involves the reduction of CO_2 to carbohydrate accompanied by release of oxygen from water. The net reaction is the reverse of respiration—reduction occurs instead of oxidation. This net reaction is shown below:

$$6\ CO_2 + 12\ H_2O + \text{light energy} \longrightarrow C_6H_{12}O_6 + 6\ O_2 + 6\ H_2O$$

Photosynthesis can be divided into two distinct reactions, the **light reactions** and the dark reactions. The light reactions convert solar energy into chemical energy in the form of ATP (by photophosphorylation) and NADPH. These reactions must take place in the light. The dark reactions are coupled to the light reactions. They incorporate CO_2 into organic molecules in a process called carbon fixation. The **dark reactions** are also called reduction synthesis because carbohydrates are produced by reducing CO_2. Both reactions take place in the chloroplasts.

The Light Reactions

The light reactions, also called photolysis reactions, begin with the absorption of a photon of light by a chlorophyll molecule. When light strikes the special chlorophyll a P700 molecule in photosystem I, it excites electrons to a higher energy level. These high energy electrons can flow along two pathways giving cyclic electron flow or noncyclic electron flow.

Cyclic Electron Flow

In cyclic electron flow, the excited electrons of P700 move along a chain of electron carriers. A series of redox reactions ultimately returns the electrons to P700. The reactions are harnessed to produce ATP from ADP and P_i in a process called cyclic photophosphorylation. The coenzyme carrier ferrodoxin is one of the early electron carriers in this electron transport chain.

Noncyclic Electron Flow

This is the key pathway of the light reactions and involves reactions of both photosystems. Again, photons of light excite electrons in P700 in photosystem I. However, instead of returning to P700 along the carrier chain, the high-energy electrons are transferred to the electron acceptor $NADP^+$. $NADP^+$ is very similar to NAD^+ which functions in cellular respiration. $NADP^+$ accepts the high energy electrons and forms NADPH. P700 is left with electron "holes" and thus is a powerful oxidizing agent. When light strikes P680 in photosystem II, electrons are excited. These electrons travel down the same electron carrier chain used by cyclic electron flow until they reach P700 and fill the electron "holes." This cascade produces ATP by noncyclic photophosphorylation.

Now, P680 has electron "holes." P680 is a strong enough oxidizing agent to oxidize water and fill its holes. Water is split into two hydrogen ions and an oxygen atom and the electrons produced reduce P680. Oxygen atoms combine to form O_2. The net result of noncyclic electron flow is the production of NADPH and ATP and the photolysis (breakdown) of water.

The Dark Reactions

The dark reactions use the ATP and NADPH produced by the light reactions to reduce CO_2 to carbohydrates. Although these reactions do not directly require light, they will only occur during the day, when the light reactions are replenishing the supply of ATP and NADPH. The dark reactions are also called carbon-fixation or reduction synthesis reactions. CO_2 is the source of carbon for carbohydrate production in the **Calvin cycle**. The product of the cycle is the three carbon sugar phosphoglyceraldehyde (PGAL). In order to produce a three carbon sugar from CO_2, the cycle must take place three times. The cycle begins with the addition of CO_2 to ribulose bisphosphate, a five carbon sugar, to produce an unstable six-carbon intermediate that immediately splits to give 2 three-carbon molecules of 3-phosphoglyceric acid. This acid is phosphorylated by ATP and reduced by NADPH to give glyceraldehyde-3-phosphate (PGAL). Two molecules of PGAL can be converted to glucose which can then be oxidized to provide usable energy. The Calvin cycle is similar to the Krebs cycle in reverse: (1) carbon dioxide is fed into the cycle; in the Krebs cycle it was produced and released; (2) reducing power is utilized during the cycle (NADPH); in the Krebs cycle NADH was removed; (3) energy is used in the cycle (conversion of ATP to ADP); in the Krebs cycle, energy was produced when ATP was formed from ADP and inorganic phosphate.

Summary of the Calvin Cycle

Carbon dioxide is fixed to RBP (ribulose bisphosphate), a five carbon sugar. The resulting unstable 6 carbon molecule splits to form 2 molecules of PGA (phosphoglyceric acid). PGA is then phosphorylated and reduced (by ATP and NADPH) to form PGAL. Most of the PGAL is recycled to RBP by a complex series of reactions. In six turns of the Calvin Cycle, 12 PGAL are formed from 6 carbon dioxide and 6 RBP. The 12 PGAL recombine to form 6 RBP and 1 molecule of glucose, the net product. PGAL is generally considered the prime end-product of photosynthesis and it can be used as an immediate food nutrient, combined and rearranged to form monosaccharide sugars (e.g. glucose) which can be transported to other cells, or packaged for storage as insoluble polysaccharides such as starch.

ENZYMES

Enzymes are organic catalysts. A catalyst is any substance that affects the rate of a chemical reaction without itself being changed. Enzymes are crucial to living things because all living systems must have continuously controlled chemical activity. Enzymes regulate metabolism by speeding up certain chemical reactions. They affect the reaction rate by decreasing the activation energy.

Enzymes are proteins, and thus, thousands of different enzymes can conceivably be formed. Many enzymes are conjugated proteins (proteins that consist of amino acids attached to other groups via covalent bonds) and have a nonprotein **coenzyme**. In these cases, both components must be present for the enzyme to function.

Enzymes are very selective; they may catalyze only one reaction or one specific class of closely related reactions. The molecule upon which an enzyme acts is called the **substrate**. There is an area on each enzyme to which the substrate binds called the **active site**. The following characteristics are true for all enzymes:

- Enzymes do NOT alter the equilibrium constant.
- Enzymes are NOT consumed in the reaction. This means that they will appear in both the reactants and the products.
- Enzymes are pH- and temperature-sensitive, with optimal activity at specific pH ranges and temperatures.

Most enzyme-catalyzed reactions are reversible. The product synthesized by an enzyme can be decomposed by the same enzyme. An enzyme that synthesizes maltose from glucose can also hydrolyze maltose back to glucose. The two models that follow describe the binding of the enzyme to the substrate.

Lock and Key Theory

This theory holds that the spatial structure of an enzyme's active site is exactly complementary to the spatial structure of its substrate. The two fit together like a lock and key. In other words, receptors are large proteins that contain a recognition site (lock) that is directly linked to transduction systems. When a drug or endogenous substance (key) binds to the receptor, a sequence of events is started. Although this theory has been largely discounted, it is still frequently used as a teaching tool when explaining drug interactions with receptors and enzymes.

Induced Fit Theory

This more widely accepted theory describes the active site as having flexibility of shape. When the appropriate substrate comes in contact with the active site, the conformation of the active site changes to fit the substrate.

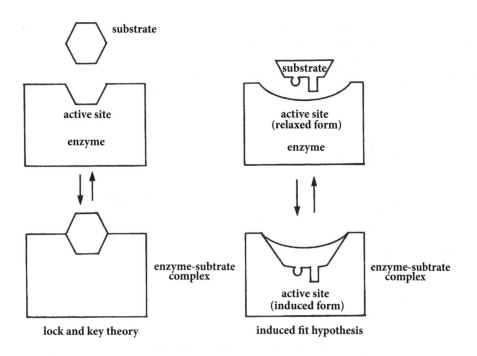

Figure 7.4

Enzyme Specificity

Enzyme action and the reaction rate depend on several environmental factors including temperature, pH, and the concentration of enzyme and substrate.

In general, as the temperature increases, the rate of enzyme action increases until an optimum temperature is reached (usually around 40°C). Beyond optimal temperature, heat alters the shape of the active site of the enzyme molecule and deactivates it, leading to a rapid drop in rate of action.

Figure 7.5

For each enzyme there is an optimal pH; above and below that, enzymatic activity declines. Maximal activity of many human enzymes occurs around pH 7.2, which is the pH of most body fluids. Exceptions include **pepsin**, which works best in the highly acidic conditions of the stomach (pH = 2), and pancreatic enzymes, which work optimally in the alkaline conditions of the small intestine (pH = 8.5). In most cases the optimal pH matches the conditions under which the enzyme operates.

The concentrations of substrate and enzyme greatly affect the reaction rate. When the concentrations of both enzyme and substrate are low, many of the active sites on the enzyme are unoccupied, and the reaction rate is low. Increasing the substrate concentration will increase the reaction rate until all of the active sites are occupied. After this point, further increase in substrate concentration will not increase the reaction rate, and the reaction is said to have reached the maximum velocity, V_{max}.

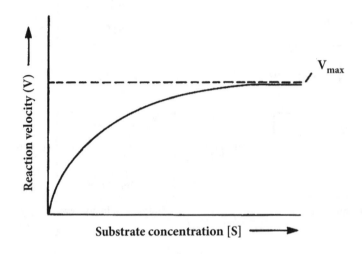

Figure 7.6

Competitive Inhibition

The active site of an enzyme is specific for a particular substrate or class of substrates. However, it is possible for molecules that are similar to the substrate to bind to the active site of the enzyme. If a similar molecule is present in a concentration comparable to the concentration of the substrate, it will compete with the substrate for binding sites on the enzyme and interfere with enzyme activity. This is known as competitive inhibition because the enzyme is inhibited by the inactive substrate, or competitor. If sufficient quantities of the substrate are introduced, however, the substrate can outcompete the competitor and will still be able to reach the V_{max}; however, this will require much higher concentrations of substrate than would be necessary without the competitor.

Noncompetitive Inhibition

A noncompetitive inhibitor is a substance that forms strong covalent bonds with an enzyme, making it unable to bind with its substrate, and consequently a noncompetitive inhibitor cannot be displaced by the addition of excess substrate. Therefore, noncompetitive inhibition is irreversible. Because this inhibition is noncompetitive, addition of excess substrate will not influence the rate of the reaction, and the reaction will never reach V_{max}. A noncompetitive inhibitor may be bound at, near, or far from the active site. When the inhibition takes place at a site other then the active site, this is called **allosteric inhibition**. (**Allosteric** means "other site" or "other structure.") The interaction of an inhibitor at an allosteric site changes the structure of the enzyme so that the active site is also changed.

Examples of enzyme activity

Every reaction in the body is regulated by enzymes. Some of the basic reaction types are listed below.

Hydrolysis reactions function to digest large molecules into smaller components. **Lactase** hydrolyzes lactose to the monosaccharides glucose and galactose. **Proteases** degrade proteins to amino acids, and **lipases** break down lipids to fatty acids and glycerol.

In multicellular organisms, digestion can begin outside of the cells in the gut. Other hydrolytic reactions occur within cells.

Synthesis reactions (including dehydrations) can be catalyzed by the same enzymes as hydrolysis reactions, but the directions of the reactions are reversed.

These reactions occur in different parts of the cell. For example, protein synthesis occurs in the ribosomes and involves dehydration reactions between amino acids.

Synthesis is required for growth, repair, regulation, protection, and production of food reserves such as fat and glycogen by the cell. The survival of an organism depends on its ability to ingest substances that it needs but cannot synthesize. Once ingested, these substances are converted into useful products.

Certain vitamin cofactors and essential amino acids cannot be synthesized by humans. If they are not available in the diet, deficiency diseases will occur.

Many enzymes require the incorporation of a nonprotein molecule to become active. These molecules, called **cofactors**, can be metal cations such as Zn^{2+} or Fe^{2+} or small organic groups called coenzymes. Most coenzymes cannot be synthesized by the body and are obtained from the diet as vitamin derivatives. Cofactors that bind to the enzyme by strong covalent bonds are called **prosthetic groups**.

BIO

REVIEW PROBLEMS

1. What is the net reaction for glycolysis? For the citric acid cycle?

2. In glucose catabolism
   A. oxygen must be the final electron acceptor.
   B. oxygen is necessary for any ATP synthesis.
   C. inorganic phosphate is produced.
   D. ATP is generated.
   E. all of the above occur.

3. Fatty acids enter the degradative pathway in the form of
   A. glycerol.
   B. glucose.
   C. acetyl-CoA.
   D. brown adipose tissue.
   E. pyruvate.

4. How do ATP, NADH, and $FADH_2$ store energy?

5. How is NAD^+ regenerated and why is this important?

6. Describe the production of ATP via oxidative phosphorylation.

7. Which of the following is LEAST likely to occur during oxygen debt?
   A. Buildup of lactic acid
   B. Buildup of pyruvate
   C. Decrease in pH
   D. Fatigue
   E. Decrease in pO_2

8. Which of the following is true of the dark reactions of photosynthesis?
   A. They occur in the mitochondria.
   B. They occur at night.
   C. They do not require light directly but are linked to the light reactions.
   D. They require light in the UV range.
   E. They produce more energy than the light reactions.

9. What are the primary differences between cyclic electron flow and noncyclic electron flow?

10. Describe the kinetic effects of increasing substrate concentration while enzyme concentration remains constant.

11. What determines enzyme specificity?

SOLUTIONS TO REVIEW PROBLEMS

1.   The net reaction for glycolysis is:

Glucose + 2ATP + 4ADP + 2P$_i$ + 2NAD$^+$ →
2 Pyruvate + 2ADP + 4ATP + 2NADH + 2H$^+$ + 2H$_2$O

The net reaction for the citric acid cycle is:

2 Acetyl-CoA + 6NAD$^+$ + 2FAD + 2GDP + 2P$_i$ + 4H$_2$O →
4CO$_2$ + 6NADH + 2FADH$_2$ + 2GTP + 4H$^+$ + 2CoA

2. **D** Although oxygen is necessary as the final electron receptor for aerobic catabolism (respiration), anaerobic catabolism (fermentation) can occur in the absence of oxygen to still consume ADP and inorganic phosphate as reactants to create ATP.

3. **C** Discussed in alternate energy sources section of this chapter.

4.   Energy is stored in ATP as high-energy bonds created by the covalent bonding of three phosphates to adenosine. The hydrolysis of ATP to ADP releases inorganic phosphate (P$_i$) and 7 kcal of energy. Hydrolysis of ADP to AMP releases an additional 7 kcal. Alternatively, ATP hydrolysis to AMP + PP$_i$ releases 7 kcal.

NADH and FADH$_2$ are reducing agents that carry chemical energy in the form of high-potential electrons, which can be transferred as hydride ions. In cellular respiration, these hydride ions are transferred to the electron transport chain, where energy release is coupled with ATP synthesis during a series of redox reactions.

5.   Step 5 of glycolysis involves the reduction of NAD$^+$ to NADH. Because NAD$^+$ is necessary for glycolysis to continue, it must be regenerated in one of two ways. In the presence of oxygen, oxidative phosphorylation and the ETC can be used to oxidize NADH to NAD$^+$. Alternatively, alcohol or lactic acid fermentation can be used to regenerate NAD$^+$ under anaerobic conditions.

6.   In the electron transport chain, the release of hydrogen ions is coupled with the transfer of electrons. H$^+$ ions accumulate in the mitochondrial matrix and are shuttled across the inner mitochondrial membrane, creating a proton gradient. To cross the inner membrane, the hydrogen ions must pass through ATP synthetases, which catalyze the phosphorylation of ADP into ATP.

7. **B** Discussed in fermentation section of this chapter.

8. **C** However, they depend on the ATP and NADPH which is generated by the light reactions, and so, occur only during the day.

9.   Cyclic electron flow involves only photosystem I and leads to the production of ATP by cyclic photophosphorylation. Noncyclic electron flow is the key pathway of photosynthesis. Electrons are excited from P680 in photosystem II to P700 in photosystem I, leading to production of ATP by noncyclic photophosphorylation. Electrons are then removed from water to fill electron "holes" in P680. Water is split and oxygen is formed. This process leads to the formation of NADPH which helps power the dark reactions.

10. When substrate concentration is low, the reaction proceeds slowly. Initial increases in substrate concentration greatly increase the reaction rate because of the binding of substrate to available active sites. Eventually, a point is reached at which all of the active sites are occupied, and the addition of more substrate will not hasten the reaction appreciably. Eventually, at very high levels of substrate, the reaction rate approaches a maximum, V_{max}.

11. Enzyme specificity is determined by the unique three-dimensional spatial structure of the active site. According to the induced fit hypothesis, an enzyme's active site is capable of undergoing a conformational change when the appropriate substrate comes into contact with it, such that the substrate is held in place to form an enzyme-substrate complex.

CHAPTER EIGHT

Genetics

Genetics is the study of how traits are inherited from one generation to the next. The basic unit of heredity is the **gene**. Genes are composed of DNA and are located on **chromosomes**. When a gene exists in more than one form, the alternative forms are called **alleles**. The genetic makeup of an individual is the individual's **genotype**; the physical manifestation of the genetic makeup is the individual's **phenotype**. Some phenotypes correspond to a single genotype, whereas other phenotypes correspond to several different genotypes. Knowledge of genetics will help clarify the concepts of evolution by the process of natural selection.

MENDELIAN GENETICS

In the 1860s Gregor Mendel developed the basic principles of genetics through his experiments with the garden pea. Mendel studied the inheritance of individual pea traits by performing **genetic crosses**. He took true-breeding individuals (which, if self-crossed, produce progeny only with the parental phenotype) with different traits, mated them, and statistically analyzed the inheritance of the traits in the progeny.

Mendel's First Law: Law of Segregation

Mendel postulated four principles of inheritance:

1. Genes exist in alternative forms (now referred to as alleles). A gene controls a specific trait in an organism.

2. An organism has two alleles for each inherited trait, one inherited from each parent.

3. The two alleles **segregate** during meiosis, resulting in gametes that carry only one allele for any given inherited trait.

4. If two alleles in an individual organism are different, only one will be fully expressed, and the other will be silent. The expressed allele is said to be **dominant**, the silent allele, **recessive**. In genetics problems dominant alleles are typically assigned capital letters, and recessive alleles are assigned lowercase letters. Organisms that contain two copies of the same allele are **homozygous** for that trait; organisms that carry two different alleles are **heterozygous**. The dominant allele is expressed in the phenotype. This is known as **Mendel's Law of Dominance**. For example, for the following genotypes Yy and YY will both be yellow:

Genes	Genotype	Phenotype
YY	Homozygous	Yellow
Yy	Heterozygous	Yellow
yy	Homozygous	Green

Monohybrid cross

The principles of Mendelian inheritance can be illustrated in a cross between two true-breeding pea plants, one with purple flowers and the other with white flowers. Because only one trait is being studied in this particular mating, it is referred to as a **monohybrid cross**. The individuals being crossed are the **parental** or **P generation**; the progeny generations are the **filial** or **F generations**, with each generation numbered sequentially (e.g., F1, F2, etc.).

The purple flower parent has the genotype PP (i.e., it has two P alleles) and is homozygous dominant. The white flower parent has the genotype pp and is homozygous recessive. When these individuals are crossed, they produce F1 plants that are 100 percent heterozygous (genotype = Pp). Because purple is dominant to white, all the F1 progeny have the purple flower phenotype.

Punnett square

One way of predicting the genotypes expected from a cross is by drawing a **Punnett square diagram**. The parental genotypes are arranged around a grid. Because the genotype of each progeny will be the sum of the alleles donated by the parental gametes, their genotypes can be determined by looking at the intersections on the grid. A Punnett square indicates all the potential progeny genotypes, and the relative frequencies of the different genotypes and phenotypes can be easily calculated.

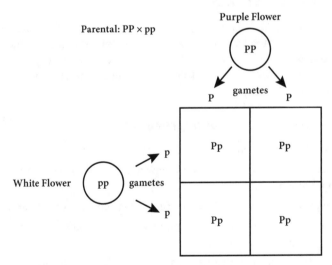

F_1 genotypes: 100% Pp (heterozygous)
F_1 phenotypes: 100% purple flowers

Figure 8.1

When the F1 generation from our monohybrid cross is self-crossed (i.e., Pp × Pp), the F2 progeny are more genotypically and phenotypically diverse than their parents. Because the F1 plants are heterozygous, they will donate a P allele to half of their descendants and a p allele to the other half. One-fourth (25 percent) of the F2 plants will have the genotype PP, 50 percent will have the genotype Pp, and 25 percent will have the genotype pp. Because the homozygous dominant and heterozygous genotypes both produce the dominant phenotype purple flowers, 75 percent of the F2 plants will have purple flowers, and 25 percent will have white flowers.

This is a standard pattern of Mendelian inheritance. Its hallmarks are the disappearance of the silent (recessive) phenotype in the F1 generation and its subsequent reappearance in 25 percent of the individuals in the F2 generation. If we were to take a closer look at the physical characteristics of the plants themselves, we would find that the 1:2:1 genotypic ratio produces a 3:1 phenotypic ratio.

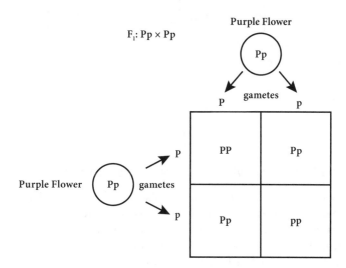

F_2 genotypes: 1:2:1; 1PP: 2Pp:1pp)
F_2 phenotypes: 3:1; 3 purple:1 white

Figure 8.2

Testcross

Mendel also developed the **testcross,** a diagnostic tool used to determine the genotype of an organism. Only with a recessive phenotype can genotype be predicted with 100 percent accuracy. If the dominant phenotype is expressed, the genotype can be either homozygous dominant or heterozygous. Thus, homozygous recessive organisms always breed true. This fact can be used to determine the unknown genotype of an organism with a dominant phenotype, such as when an organism with a dominant phenotype of unknown genotype (Ax) is crossed with a phenotypically recessive organism (genotype aa). Since the recessive parent is homozygous, it can donate only the recessive allele, a, to the progeny. If the dominant parent's genotype is AA, all of its gametes will carry an A, and all of the progeny will have genotype Aa. If the dominant parent's genotype is Aa, half of the progeny will be Aa and express the dominant phenotype, and half will be aa and express the recessive phenotype. In a testcross, the appearance of the recessive phenotype in the progeny indicates that the phenotypically dominant parent is genotypically heterozygous.

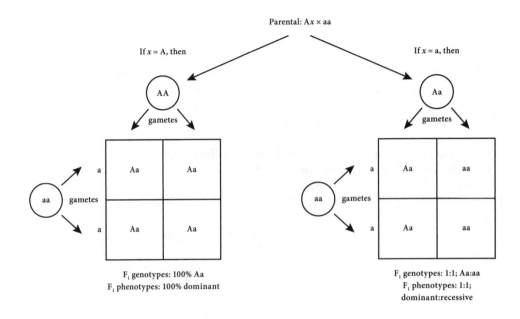

Figure 8.3

Mendel's Second Law: Law of Independent Assortment

The segregation principle provides a satisfactory explanation for the inheritance of a single allele and also can be extended to a dihybrid cross, in which the parents differ in two traits, as long as the genes are on separate chromosomes and assort independently during meiosis. Mendel postulated that the inheritance of one such trait is completely independent of any other. In this way, a plant with purple flowers is no more likely to be a dwarf than a plant with white flowers (see the example below). This is known as **Mendel's Law of Independent Assortment**.

Note that according to modern, non-Mendelian genetics, genes on the same chromosome will not follow this rule and instead will stay together unless **crossing over** occurs (see Chapter 5, Cellular Biology). Nevertheless, crossing over exchanges information between chromosomes and may break the linkage of certain patterns. For example, red hair is usually linked with freckles, but some blondes and brunettes have freckles as well. Generally, the closer the genes are on the chromosome, the more likely they are to be inherited together.

Dihybrid cross

In the following example, a purple-flowered tall pea plant is crossed with a white-flowered dwarf pea plant; both plants are doubly homozygous (tall is dominant to dwarf, T = tall allele, t = dwarf allele; purple is dominant to white, P = purple allele, p = white allele). The purple parent's genotype is TTPP, and it thus produces only TP gametes; the white parent's genotype is ttpp and produces only tp gametes. The F1 progeny will all have the genotype TtPp and will be phenotypically dominant for both traits.

When the F1 generation is self-crossed (TtPp × TtPp), it produces four different phenotypes: tall purple, tall white, dwarf purple, and dwarf white, in the ratio 9:3:3:1, respectively. This is the typical pattern for Mendelian inheritance in a dihybrid cross between heterozygotes with independently assorting traits.

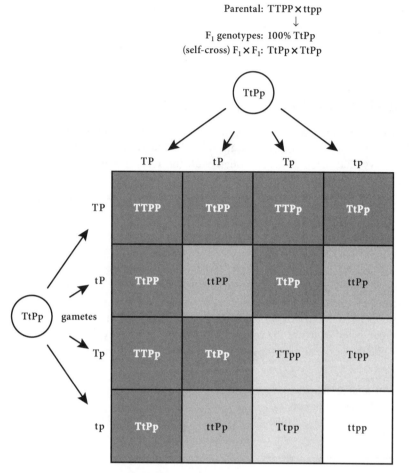

Parental: TTPP × ttpp
↓
F₁ genotypes: 100% TtPp
(self-cross) F₁ × F₁: TtPp × TtPp

F₂ phenotypes: 9:3:3:1
F₂ tall purple: 3 tall white:3 dwarf purple:1 dwarf white

Figure 8.4

Drosophila melanogaster

Modern work with the fruit fly (*Drosophila melanogaster*) helped to provide explanations for Mendelian genetic patterns. The fruit fly possesses several advantages for genetic research:

- It reproduces often (short life cycle).
- It reproduces in large numbers (large sample size).
- Its chromosomes (especially in the salivary gland) are large and easily recognizable in size and shape.
- Its chromosomes are few (4 pairs, $2N = 8$).
- Mutations occur relatively frequently.

Through genetic and mutational analyses of *D. melanogaster*, scientists have elucidated the patterns of embryological development, discovering how genes expressed early in development can affect the adult organism.

NON-MENDELIAN INHERITANCE PATTERNS

In most practical applications, inheritance patterns are often more complicated than Mendel would have hoped. One major source of complications is in the relationship between **phenotype** and **genotype**. In theory, 100 percent of individuals with the recessive phenotype have a homozygous recessive genotype, and 100 percent of individuals with the dominant phenotype have either homozygous or heterozygous genotypes. Such clean concordance between genotype and phenotype is not always the case.

Incomplete Dominance

Some progeny phenotypes are apparently **blends** of the parental phenotypes. The classic example is flower color in snapdragons: homozygous dominant red snapdragons, when crossed with homozygous recessive white snapdragons, produce 100 percent pink progeny in the F1 generation. When F1 progeny are self-crossed, they produce red, pink, and white progeny in the ratio of 1:2:1, respectively. The pink color is the result of the combined effects of the red and white genes in heterozygotes. An allele is incompletely dominant if the phenotype of the heterozygote is an intermediate of the phenotypes of the homozygotes.

R = allele for red flowers
r = allele for white flowers
Parental: RR × rr (red × white)   F$_1$: Rr × Rr (pink × pink)

	R	R
r	Rr	Rr
r	Rr	Rr

	R	r
R	RR	Rr
r	Rr	rr

F$_1$ genotype ratio: 100% Rr   F$_1$ genotype ratio: 1RR:2Rr:1rr
F$_1$ phenotype ratio: 100% pink   F$_2$ phenotype ratio: 1 red:2 pink:1 white

Figure 8.5

Codominance

Codominance occurs when **multiple** alleles exist for a given gene and more than one of them is **dominant**. Each dominant allele is fully dominant when combined with a recessive allele, but when two dominant alleles are present, the phenotype is the result of the expression of both dominant alleles simultaneously.

The classic example of codominance and multiple alleles is the inheritance of **ABO blood groups** in humans. Blood type is determined by three different alleles: I^A, I^B, and i. Only two alleles are present in any single individual, but the population contains all three alleles. I^A and I^B are both dominant to i. Individuals who are homozygous I^A or heterozygous I^Ai have blood type A; individuals who are homozygous I^B or heterozygous I^Bi have blood type B; and individuals who are homozygous ii have blood type O. However, I^A and I^B are codominant; individuals who are heterozygous I^AI^B have a distinct blood type, AB, which combines characteristics of both the A and B blood groups.

Codominance differs from incomplete dominance because in incomplete dominance the phenotype expressed is a blend of both genotypes. In codominance, however, both alleles in the genotype are expressed at the same time without a blending of phenotype.

Sex Determination

The two members of each of the chromosome pairs are identical in shape except for one pair: the sex chromosomes. Different species vary in their systems of sex determination. In sexually differentiated species most chromosomes exist as pairs of homologues called **autosomes**, but sex is determined by a pair of sex chromosomes. All humans have 22 pairs of autosomes; additionally, women have a pair of homologous X chromosomes, and men have a pair of heterologous chromosomes, an X and a Y chromosome. The sex chromosomes pair during meiosis and segregate during the first meiotic division. Since females can produce only gametes containing the X chromosome, the gender of a zygote is determined by the genetic contribution of the male gamete. If the sperm carries a Y chromosome, the zygote will be male; if it carries an X chromosome, the zygote will be female. For every mating, there is a 50 percent chance that the zygote will be male and a 50 percent chance that it will be female.

Genes located on the X or Y chromosome are called **sex-linked**. In humans, most sex-linked genes are located on the X chromosome, although some Y-linked traits have been found (e.g., hair on the outer ear).

Figure 8.6

Sex Linkage

In humans, women have two X chromosomes and men have only one. As a result, recessive genes carried on the X chromosome will produce the recessive phenotypes whenever they occur in men because no dominant allele is present to mask them. The recessive phenotype will thus be much more frequently found in men. Examples of sex-linked recessives in humans are the genes for **hemophilia** and **color-blindness**.

The pattern of inheritance for a sex-linked recessive trait is somewhat complicated. Because men pass the X chromosome only to their daughters and the gene is carried only on the X chromosome, affected men cannot pass the trait to their male offspring. Affected men will, however, pass the gene to all of their daughters. Nevertheless, unless the daughter also receives the gene from her mother, she will be a phenotypically normal carrier of the trait. Because all of the daughter's male children will receive their only X chromosome from her, half of her sons will receive the recessive sex-linked allele. Thus, sex-linked recessives generally affect only men; they cannot be passed from father to son, but they can be passed from grandfather to grandson via a daughter who is a carrier, thereby skipping a generation.

Environmental Factors

The environment can often affect the expression of a gene. Interaction between the environment and the genotype produces the phenotype. For example, *Drosophila* with a given set of genes have crooked wings at low temperatures but straight wings at higher temperatures.

Temperature also influences the hair color of the Himalayan hare. The same genes for color result in white hair on the warmer parts of the body and black hair on colder parts. If the naturally warm portions are cooled (e.g., by the application of ice), the hair will grow in black.

Cytoplasmic Inheritance

Heredity systems exist outside the nucleus. For example, DNA is found in mitochondria and other cytoplasmic bodies. These cytoplasmic genes may interact with nuclear genes and are important in determining the characteristics of their organelles. Drug resistance in many microorganisms is regulated by cytoplasmic DNA, known as plasmids, that contain one or more genes. Plasmids can be passed from one bacterial cell to another via transformation (described below).

GENETIC PROBLEMS

Although genetic replication is very accurate, chromosome number and structure can be altered by abnormal cell division during meiosis or by mutagenic agents. This can result in the appearance of abnormal characteristics of the offspring in question.

Nondisjunction

Nondisjunction is either the failure of homologous chromosomes to separate properly during meiosis I or the failure of sister chromatids to separate properly during meiosis II. The resulting **zygote** might either have three copies of that chromosome, called **trisomy** (somatic cells will have $2N + 1$ chromosomes), or a single copy of that chromosome, called **monosomy** (somatic cells will have $2N - 1$ chromosomes). A classic case of trisomy is the birth defect **Down syndrome**, which is caused by trisomy of chromosome 21. Most monosomies and trisomies are lethal, causing the embryo to spontaneously abort early in the pregnancy.

Nondisjunction of the sex chromosomes may also occur, resulting in individuals with extra or missing copies of the X or Y chromosomes.

Chromosomal Breakage

Chromosomal breakage may occur spontaneously or be induced by environmental factors, such as mutagenic agents and X-rays. The chromosome that loses a fragment is said to have a deficiency.

Mutations

Mutations are changes in the genetic information coded in the DNA of a cell. Mutations that occur in **somatic** cells can lead to tumors in the individual. Mutations that occur in the sex cells (**gametes**) will be passed down to the offspring. Most mutations occur in regions of DNA that do not code for proteins and are silent (not expressed in the phenotype). Mutations that do change the sequence of amino acids in proteins are most often recessive and deleterious.

Mutagenic agents

Mutagenic agents induce mutations. These include cosmic rays, X-rays, ultraviolet rays, and radioactivity as well as chemical compounds such as colchicine, which inhibits spindle formation, or mustard gas, which alkylates guanine in DNA. Mutagenic agents are sometimes also **carcinogenic** (cancer-causing).

Mutation types

In a gene mutation, nitrogen bases are **added**, **deleted**, or **substituted**, thus altering the amino acid sequence. Inappropriate amino acids may be inserted into polypeptide chains, and a mutated protein may be produced. Therefore, a mutation is a genetic "error" with the "wrong" base or a missing base in the DNA at any particular position.

In a **point mutation** a nucleic acid is replaced by another nucleic acid. The number of nucleic acids substituted may vary, but generally point mutations involve between one and three nucleotides. There are three possible effects on the **codon**, the sequence of three nucleotides that determines the identity of the amino acid. First, the new codon may code for the same amino acid (a **silent mutation**), and no change in the resulting protein is seen. Second, the new codon may code for a different amino acid (a **missense mutation**). This may or may not lead to a problem with the resulting protein, depending on the role of that amino acid in determining the protein structure. Finally, the new codon may be a stop codon (a **nonsense mutation**). Nonsense mutations are often lethal or severely inhibit the functioning of the protein, which can lead to many different problems depending on the role of that protein in organism function. The length of the genome does not change with any of these mutations, but the primary structure of the proteins formed from an RNA sequence with a nonsense mutation could be much shorter due to the premature stop.

In a **frameshift mutation** nucleic acids are deleted or inserted into the genome sequence. This frequently is lethal. The insertion or deletion of nucleic acids throws off the entire sequence of codons from that point on because the genome is "read" in groups of three nucleic acids. Since nucleic acids are inserted or deleted, the length of the genome changes.

Examples of genetic disorders

- **Phenylketonuria** (PKU) is a molecular disease caused by the inability to produce the proper enzyme for the metabolism of phenylalanine. A degradation product (phenylpyruvic acid) accumulates as a result. The administration of any product that contains phenylalanine, such as aspartame, to an individual with any of the hyperphenylaninemia conditions could be detrimental to his or her general health. Therefore, these individuals are unable to consume products containing aspartame. Hyperphenylaninemia may result from an impaired conversion of phenylalanine to tyrosine. The most common and clinically important impairment is phenylketonuria, which is characterized by an increased concentration of phenylalanine in blood, increased concentration of phenylalanine and its by-products (such as phenylpyruvate, phenylacetate, and phenyllactate) in urine, and mental retardation. Phenylketonuria is caused by a deficiency of phenylalanine hydrolase.
- **Sickle-cell anemia** is a disease in which red blood cells become crescent-shaped because they contain defective hemoglobin. The sickle-cell hemoglobin carries less oxygen. This disease is caused by a substitution of valine (coded by GUA or GUG) for glutamic acid (coded by GAA or GAG) because of a single base-pair substitution in the gene coding for hemoglobin. While the decreased ability to carry oxygen can have negative effects on patients, these individuals do have less severe symptoms of malaria should they become infected, indicating a possible evolutionary advantage in regions where malaria infection is common.

BACTERIAL GENETICS

Bacterial Genome

The bacterial genome consists of a single circular chromosome located in the **nucleoid** region of the cell. Many bacteria also contain smaller circular rings of DNA called **plasmids**, which contain accessory genes. **Episomes** are plasmids that are capable of integration into the bacterial genome.

Replication

Replication of the bacterial chromosome begins at a unique origin of replication and proceeds in both directions simultaneously. DNA is synthesized in the 5′ to 3′ direction.

Genetic Variance

Bacterial cells reproduce by **binary fission** and proliferate very rapidly under favorable conditions. Although binary fission is an **asexual** process, bacteria have three mechanisms for increasing the genetic variance of a population: **transformation**, **conjugation**, and **transduction**.

Transformation

Transformation is the process by which a foreign chromosome fragment (**plasmid**) is incorporated into the bacterial chromosome via recombination, creating new inheritable genetic combinations.

Conjugation

Conjugation can be described as **sexual mating** in bacteria; it is the transfer of genetic material between two bacteria that are temporarily joined. A cytoplasmic conjugation bridge is formed between the two cells, and genetic material is transferred from the donor male (+) type to the recipient female (−) type. Only bacteria containing plasmids called sex factors are capable of conjugating. The best studied sex factor is the **F factor** in *E. coli*. Bacteria possessing this plasmid are termed F$^+$ cells; those without it are called F$^-$ cells. During conjugation between an F$^+$ and an F$^-$ cell, the F$^+$ cell replicates its F factor and donates the copy to the recipient, converting it to an F$^+$ cell. Genes that code for other characteristics, such as **antibody resistance**, may be found on the plasmids and transferred into recipient cells along with these factors.

Sometimes the sex factor becomes integrated into the bacterial genome. During conjugation, the entire bacterial chromosome replicates and begins to move from the donor cell into the recipient cell. The conjugation bridge usually breaks before the entire chromosome is transferred, but the bacterial genes that enter the recipient cell can easily recombine with the genes already present to form novel genetic combinations. These bacteria are called **Hfr** cells, meaning that they have a **high frequency of recombination**.

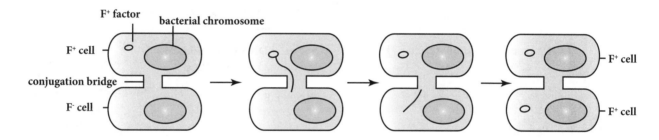

Figure 8.7

Transduction

A **bacteriophage** is a virus that infects its host bacterium by attaching to the bacterium, boring a hole through the bacterial cell wall, and injecting its viral DNA while its protein coat remains attached to the cell wall. Transduction occurs when fragments of the bacterial chromosome become packaged into the viral progeny produced during such a viral infection. These virions may infect other bacteria and introduce new genetic arrangements through recombination with the new host cell's DNA. The closer two genes are to one another on a chromosome, the more likely they will be to transduce together; this fact allows geneticists to map genes to a high degree of precision.

BIO

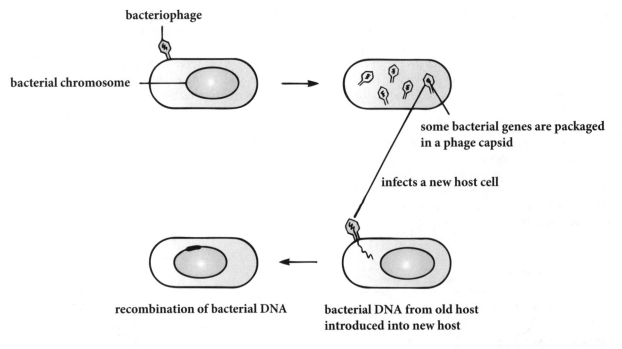

Figure 8.8

Recombination

Recombination occurs when linked genes are separated. It occurs by breakage and rearrangement of adjacent regions of DNA when organisms carrying different genes or alleles for the same traits are crossed.

Gene Regulation

The regulation of **transcription,** one of the steps of gene expression, enables prokaryotes to control their metabolism. Regulation of transcription is based on the accessibility of **RNA polymerase** to the genes being transcribed and is directed by an **operon,** which consists of **structural** genes, an **operator** region, and a **promoter** region on the DNA before the protein coding genes. Structural genes contain sequences of DNA that code for proteins. The operator is the sequence of nontranscribable DNA that is the **repressor** binding site. The promoter is the noncoding sequence of DNA that serves as the initial binding site for RNA polymerase. There is also a **regulator** gene, which codes for the synthesis of a repressor molecule that binds to the operator and blocks RNA polymerase from transcribing the structural genes.

RNA polymerase must also move past the operator to transcribe the structural genes. Regulatory systems function by preventing or permitting the RNA polymerase to pass on to the structural genes. Regulation may be via **inducible systems** or **repressible systems.** Inducible systems are those that require the presence of a substance, called an **inducer,** for transcription to occur. Repressible systems are in a constant state of transcription unless a **corepressor** is present to inhibit transcription.

Inducible systems

In an inducible system the repressor binds to the operator, forming a barrier that prevents RNA polymerase from transcribing the structural genes. For transcription to occur, an inducer must bind to the repressor, forming an **inducer-repressor complex**. This complex cannot bind to the operator, thus removing it as a barrier and permitting transcription. The proteins synthesized are thus said to be inducible. The structural genes typically code for an enzyme, and the inducer is usually the substrate, or a derivative of the substrate, upon which the enzyme normally acts. When the substrate (inducer) is present, enzymes are synthesized; when it is absent, enzyme synthesis is negligible. In this manner, enzymes are transcribed only when they are actually needed.

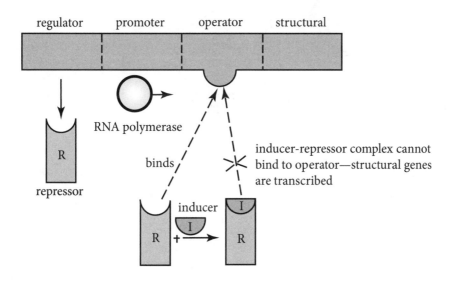

Figure 8.9

Repressible systems

In a repressible system the repressor is inactive until it combines with the corepressor. The repressor can bind to the operator and prevent transcription only when it has formed a repressor-corepressor complex. Corepressors are often the **end products** of the biosynthetic pathways they control. The proteins produced (usually enzymes) are said to be repressible because they are normally being synthesized; transcription and translation occur until the corepressor is synthesized. Operons containing mutations, such as deletions, or whose regulator genes code for defective repressors are incapable of being turned off; their enzymes, which are always being synthesized, are referred to as **constitutive**.

Figure 8.10

REVIEW PROBLEMS

1. A woman with blood genotype I^Ai and a man with blood genotype I^Bi have two children, both type AB. What is the probability that a third child will be blood type AB?

    A. 25%
    B. 33%
    C. 50%
    D. 66%
    E. 75%

2. In humans, the allele for black hair (B) is dominant to the allele to brown hair (b), and the allele for curly hair (C) is dominant to the allele for straight hair (c). When a person of unknown genotype is crossed against a straight- and brown-haired individual, the phenotypic ratio is:

    > 25% curly black hair
    >
    > 25% straight black hair
    >
    > 25% curly brown hair
    >
    > 25% straight brown hair

    What is the genotype of the unknown parent?

    A. BBCC
    B. BbCC
    C. bbCc
    D. BbCc
    E. BBCc

3. Assuming classical Mendelian inheritance, how can one differentiate between a homozygous dominant individual and one who is heterozygous for the dominant trait?

    A. By crossing the individuals in question with one another
    B. By crossing each individual with a known homozygous recessive individual and examining the offspring
    C. By crossing each individual with a known heterozygote and examining the offspring
    D. By crossing each individual with a known homozygous dominant individual and examining the offspring
    E. Both B and C

4. If a male hemophiliac (X^hY) is crossed with a female carrier of both color blindness and hemophilia (X^cX^h), what is the probability that a female child will be phenotypically normal?

    A. 0%
    B. 25%
    C. 50%
    D. 75%
    E. Same as for a male child

BIO

5. Explain the concept of Mendel's law of segregation.

6. Why are lethal dominant alleles much less common than lethal recessive alleles?

7. Many point mutations do not have any effect on the gene product. What are two possible explanations for this observation?

SOLUTIONS TO REVIEW PROBLEMS

1. **A** This is a cross between two heterozygotes for a trait that has codominant alleles. The inheritance pattern for human blood groups is not a simple dominant/recessive pattern because the A and B alleles are both phenotypically expressed when the genotype is I^AI^B.

    This is a cross between a woman heterozygous for blood type A and a man heterozygous for blood type B: $I^Ai \times I^Bi$.

F1 genotypes:	25% I^AI^B	phenotypes:	25% type AB
	25% I^Bi		25% type B
	25% I^Ai		25% type A
	25% ii		25% type O

    The birth of each child is an independent event. Hence, the fact the first two children this couple had were type AB has no influence whatsoever on the probability that a third child will be AB. So there is a 25 percent chance that any child, not just the third, will be type AB.

2. **D** In this dihybrid problem, a doubly recessive individual is crossed with an individual of unknown genotype—this is known as a testcross. The straight- and brown-haired individual has the genotype bbcc and can thus produce only bc gametes. Looking at the F1 offspring, there is a 1:1:1:1 phenotypic ratio. The fact that both the recessive and dominant traits are present in the offspring means that the unknown parental genotype must contain both recessive alleles (b and c). The unknown parental genotype must therefore be BbCc. If you want to double-check the answer, you can work out the Punnett square for the cross BbCc × bbcc: BbCc can produce four different types of gametes, BC, Bc, bC, and bc, whereas bbcc can produce only bc gametes, as previously mentioned.

    So the unknown parental genotype is BbCc, choice (D).

3. **E** To differentiate between a homozygous dominant and a heterozygous dominant for a trait that exhibits classic dominant/recessive Mendelian inheritance, one must perform a cross that results in offspring that reveal the unknown parental genotype; this is known as a testcross. If we cross the homozygous dominant with a homozygous recessive, we will get 100 percent phenotypically dominant offspring; if we cross the heterozygous dominant with the homozygous recessive, we will get 50 percent phenotypically dominant and 50 percent phenotypically recessive offspring. Thus, using a homozygous recessive as a testcrosser will allow us to distinguish between the two. We can also use a known heterozygote as the testcrosser because when this is crossed with the homozygous dominant, 100 percent phenotypically dominant offspring are produced, and when it is crossed with the heterozygote, the phenotypic ratio of the offspring is 3:1 dominant:recessive. Hence, the correct answer is (E), because both (B) and (C) are viable options. Crossing the individuals in question with one another or with a homozygous dominant individual, as in (A) and (D), will result in 100 percent phenotypically dominant offspring and hence will not be helpful.

4. **C** In this problem, we are told that the female in this cross is a carrier of two sex-linked traits: color blindness and hemophilia. We are also told that the genes for these traits are not found on the same X chromosome, as indicated by her genotype, X^cX^h. So of the female offspring, half, or 50 percent, will be phenotypically normal.

BIO

5. The chromosomal basis for Mendel's Law of Segregation is as follows: For any given trait, all individuals have two alleles located on separate but homologous chromosomes, one inherited from each parent. During meiosis, or gamete formation, these homologous chromosomes pair and line up along the equatorial plate. As meiosis proceeds, the spindle fibers attached to the homologues move them toward opposite poles of the cell. Because the alleles are on different chromosomes, they segregate and wind up in different gametes. The paired condition of the alleles is restored with the fusion of egg and sperm during fertilization.

6. Lethal dominant alleles are much less common than lethal recessive alleles because a lethal dominant allele kills both heterozygotes and homozygotes, preventing the transmission of the allele to offspring (unless the gene is late-acting). Dominant lethals usually appear in an individual as a result of spontaneous mutations and die with that individual. Thus, the frequency with which dominant lethals appear in the gene pool always remains very low. Lethal recessive alleles only kill homozygotes; however, heterozygotes are phenotypically normal and will not die as a result of their single copy of the lethal recessive. Hence, heterozygotes are able to pass on the lethal allele to offspring and thus maintain the frequency of the allele in the gene pool.

7. A point mutation causes the substitution of one base pair for another. Sometimes, as in the case of sickle-cell anemia, it may have a very profound effect on the gene product (hemoglobin) because it changes the message carried by the gene. In some cases, however, a mutated gene codes for the same product. This can be explained by the redundancy of the genetic code: most amino acids have more than one triplet coding for them. The substitution of the third cytosine in the triplet CCC (proline) by any of the remaining bases (G, A, or U) will not change the amino acid sequence because the codons CCG, CCA, and CCU code for proline as well. In eukaryotes, a point mutation may occur in an intron (noncoding region) and thus will not affect the gene product because noncoding regions are excised after transcription.

CHAPTER NINE

Evolution

The change in the genetic makeup of a population with time is termed **evolution**. Evolution is explained by the constant propagation of new variations in the genes of a species, some of which impart an adaptive advantage. All living things (past and present) are descendents from a single common ancestor. Each of these organisms arose as a direct result of some genetic alteration in the species that lived before them, and this process is called evolution. Most evolutionary changes occur slowly over a long period of time.

THEORIES OF EVOLUTION

Lamarckian Evolution

This discredited theory proposed by Jean-Baptiste Lamarck held that new organs or changes in existing ones arose because of the needs of the organism. The amount of change was thought to be based on the **use or disuse** of the organ. The theory of use and disuse was based upon a fallacious understanding of genetics. Any useful characteristic acquired in one generation was thought to be transmitted to the next. An example of an **acquired characteristic** was the long necks of giraffes. Supposedly, early giraffes permanently stretched their necks to reach for leaves on higher branches of trees. The offspring were believed to inherit the valuable trait of longer necks as a result of this excessive use.

Modern genetics has disproved theories of acquired characteristics. In reality, only changes in the DNA of the sex cells can be inherited. In contrast, changes acquired during an individual's life are changes in somatic cells. August Weismann showed that these changes are not inherited in an experiment in which he cut off the tails of mice for 20 generations (somatic change) only to find that the 21st generation was born with tails.

Darwin's Theory of Natural Selection

In Charles Darwin's theory, pressures in the environment select for the organism most **fit** to survive and reproduce. In the evolutionary sense, **fitness** is the ability to survive and reproduce. Darwin essentially concluded that a member of a particular species that is equipped with beneficial traits, allowing it to cope effectively with the immediate environment, will produce more offspring than individuals with less favorable genetic traits. The genes of parents that are

BIO

more fit are therefore passed down to more offspring and become increasingly prevalent in the gene pool. Darwin subsequently chose the words **natural selection** to describe his theory because nature selects the best set of parents for the next generation. Darwin outlined a number of basic agents leading to evolutionary change.

Overpopulation

More offspring are produced than can survive. Thus, the food, air, light, and space are insufficient to support the entire population.

Variations

Offspring naturally show differences (variations) in their characteristics compared to those of their parents. Darwin did not know the source of these differences. Hugo de Vries later suggested mutations as the cause of variations. Some mutations are beneficial, although most are harmful.

Competition

The developing population must compete for the necessities of life. Many young must die, and the number of adults in the population generally remains constant from generation to generation.

Natural selection

Some organisms in a species have variations that give them an advantage over other members of the species. In the struggle for existence, these organisms may have adaptations that are advantageous for survival. For example, a giraffe with a variation of a longer neck would be able to get more food from higher branches of a tree and therefore would be more fit. This principle is encapsulated in the phrase "survival of the fittest."

Inheritance of the variations

The individuals that survive (those with the favorable variations) live to adulthood to reproduce and thus **transmit** these favorable variations or adaptations to their offspring. These favored genes gradually dominate the gene pool.

Evolution of new species

Over many generations of natural selection, the favorable changes (adaptations) are perpetuated in the species. The accumulation of these favorable changes eventually results in such significant changes in the gene pool that we can say a new species has evolved. These physical changes in the gene pool were perpetuated or selected for by environmental conditions.

For example, the rapid evolution of DDT-resistant insects illustrates the theory of natural selection and speciation. A change in the environment such as the introduction of DDT (an insecticide) constitutes a favorable change for the DDT-resistant mutant flies. These mutants existed before the environmental change. Now, conditions select for survival of DDT-resistant mutants.

COMPONENTS OF EVOLUTION

Speciation

Speciation is the evolution of new species, which are groups of individuals that can interbreed freely with each other but not with members of other species. Gene flow is impossible between different species.

Different selective pressures act upon the gene pools of each group, causing them to evolve independently. Genetic variation, changes in the environment, migration to new environments, adaptation to new environments, natural selection, genetic drift, and isolation are all factors that can lead to speciation.

Before speciation, small, local populations called **demes** often form within a species. For example, all the beavers along a specific portion of a river form a deme. There may be many demes belonging to a specific species. Members of a deme resemble one another more closely than they resemble members of other demes. They are closely related genetically since mating between members of the same deme occurs more frequently. They are also influenced by similar environmental factors and thus are subject to the same selection processes.

If these demes become **isolated**, speciation may occur. When groups are isolated from each other, there is no gene flow among them. Any difference arising from mutations or new combinations of genes will be maintained in the isolated population. Over time, these genetic differences may become significant enough to make mating impossible. If the gene pools within a species become sufficiently different so that two individuals cannot mate and produce fertile offspring, two different species have developed and one or more new species have formed. Genetic and eventually reproductive isolation often results from the geographic isolation of a population.

Evolutionary History

Biologists seek to understand the evolutionary relationships among species alive today. This evolutionary history is termed **phylogeny**. Evolutionary history may be visualized as a branching tree on which the common ancestor is found at the trunk and the modern species are found at the tips of the branches.

Convergent evolution

Groups among the branches often develop in similar ways when exposed to similar environments. When two species from different ancestors develop similar traits, this is known as **convergent evolution**. For example, sharks and dolphins have come to resemble one another physically despite belonging to different classes of vertebrates (sharks are members of Chondrichthyes, whereas dolphins are members of Mammalia). Despite different recent ancestors, they evolved certain similar features in adapting to the conditions of aquatic life.

Parallel evolution

Parallel evolution is similar to convergent evolution but occurs when a more recent ancestor can be identified. For example, marsupial (pouched) mammals and placental mammals are both in the class Mammalia but diverged due to geographic separation. Descendants of the ancestral marsupial mammal include the pouched wolf, anteater, mouse, and mole. These species have developed parallel to the placental wolf, anteater, mouse, and mole. Despite their geographic separation, the pouched mammals and their placental counterparts faced similar environments; thus, they developed similar adaptations.

Divergent evolution

In contrast, **divergent evolution** occurs when species with a shared ancestor develop differing traits due to dissimilarities between their environments. For example, bears of the family Ursidae within the class Mammalia share many similar traits but have diverged from a common ancestor to adapt to their specific environments. Polar bears have white coats to blend in with their arctic environment, whereas black bears have developed darker fur to blend in with their wet, forest environments. Over time, additional changes accumulated between these bears, resulting in the inability to cross-breed and eventual speciation.

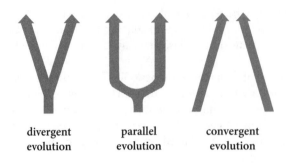

divergent   parallel   convergent
evolution   evolution   evolution

Figure 9.1

Adaptive radiation is the emergence of a number of lineages from a single ancestral species. A single species may diverge into a number of distinct species; the differences between them are those adaptive to a distinct lifestyle, or **niche**. A classic example is Darwin's finches of the Galápagos island chain. Over a comparatively short period of time, a single species of finch underwent adaptive radiation, resulting in 13 separate species of finches, some of them on the same island. Such adaptations minimized competition among the birds, enabling each emerging species to become firmly established in its own environmental niche.

Population Genetics

A **population** includes all members of a particular species inhabiting a given location. The **gene pool** of a population is the sum total of all the alleles for any given trait in the population. **Gene frequency** is the decimal fraction representing the presence of an allele for all members of a population that have this particular gene. In basic Mendelian genetics, only two alleles exist for a given trait: one dominant and one recessive. The letter p is used for the frequency of the dominant allele of a particular gene. The letter q represents the frequency of the recessive allele. Since by definition these are the only two alleles that can be present, for a given gene, $p + q = 1$.

The Hardy-Weinberg principle

Evolution can be viewed as a result of changing gene frequencies within a population. Gene frequency is the relative frequency of a particular allele. When the gene frequencies of a population are not changing, the gene pool is stable and the population is not evolving. However, this is true only in ideal situations in which the following conditions are met:

- The population is very large.
- No mutations affect the gene pool.
- Mating between individuals in the population is random.
- There is no net migration of individuals into or out of the population.
- The genes in the population are all equally successful at reproducing.

Under these idealized conditions, a certain equilibrium will exist among all of the genes in a gene pool, which is described by the **Hardy-Weinberg equation**.

For a gene with only two alleles, T and t, p = the frequency of allele T and q = the frequency of allele t. For that gene, $p + q = 1$ since the combined frequencies of the alleles must total 100 percent. Thus,

$$(p + q)^2 = (1)^2 \text{, and}$$

$$p^2 + 2pq + q^2 = 1$$

where p^2 = frequency of TT (dominant homozygotes)
$2pq$ = frequency of Tt (heterozygotes)
q^2 = frequency of tt (recessive homozygotes)

The Hardy-Weinberg equation may be used to determine gene frequencies in a large population in the absence of microevolutionary change (defined by the five conditions given previously).

For example, individuals from a nonevolving population can be randomly crossed to demonstrate that the gene frequencies remain constant from generation to generation. If you know that the gene frequency of the dominant gene for tallness, T, is 0.80, and the gene frequency of the recessive gene for shortness, t, is 0.20, then $p = 0.80$ and $q = 0.20$. In a cross between two heterozygotes, the resulting F1 genotype frequencies will be 64% TT, 16% + 16% = 32% Tt, and 4% tt:

	$p = 0.80$ (T)	$q = 0.20$ (t)
$p = 0.80$ (T)	($p^2 = 0.64$) TT = 64%	($pq = 0.16$) Tt = 16%
$q = 0.20$ (t)	($pq = 0.16$) Tt = 16%	($q^2 = 0.04$) tt = 4%

The gene frequencies of the F1 generation can be calculated as follows:

64% TT = 64% T allele + 0% t allele
32% Tt = 16% T allele + 16% t allele
4% tt = 0% T allele + 4% t allele

Gene frequencies = 80% T allele + 20% t allele

Thus, $p = 0.80$ and $q = 0.20$. These frequencies are the same as those in the parent generation, demonstrating Hardy-Weinberg equilibrium in a nonevolving population.

Microevolution

No population can be represented indefinitely by the Hardy-Weinberg equilibrium because such idealized conditions do not exist in nature. Real populations have **unstable** gene pools and **migrating** populations. The agents of microevolutionary change—natural selection, mutation, assortive mating, genetic drift, and gene flow—are all deviations from the five conditions of a Hardy-Weinberg population.

Natural selection

Genotypes with favorable variations are selected through natural selection, and the frequency of favorable genes increases within the gene pool. Genotypes with low adaptive values tend to disappear.

Mutation

Gene mutations change allele frequencies in a population, shifting gene equilibria by introducing additional alleles. These gene mutations can either be favorable or detrimental for the offspring.

Assortive mating

If mates are not randomly chosen but rather selected according to criteria such as phenotype and proximity (**sexual selection**), the relative genotype ratios will be affected and will depart from the predictions of the Hardy-Weinberg equilibrium.

Genetic drift

Genetic drift refers to changes in the composition of the gene pool due to chance. Genetic drift tends to be more pronounced in small populations or new populations, where it is sometimes called the **founder effect**.

Gene flow

Migration of individuals between populations will result in a loss or gain of genes, thus changing the composition of a population's gene pool.

EVIDENCE OF EVOLUTION

Fossil Record

Fossils are direct evidence of evolutionary change. They represent the preserved remains of an organism. Fossils are generally found in sedimentary rocks.

Types of fossils

Many types of fossils can provide information. Paleontologists can find actual remains, including teeth, bones, etc., in rock, tar pits, ice, and **amber** (the fossil resin of trees). **Petrification** is the process by which minerals replace the cells of an organism. **Imprints** are impressions left by an organism (e.g., footprints). **Molds** form hollow spaces in rocks as the organisms within decay. **Casts** are formed by minerals deposited in molds.

Significant fossil discoveries

The trilobite is a primitive arthropod (similar to lobsters and crabs), which was a dominant form of the early Paleozoic era. Dinosaurs were ancient animals related to both reptiles and birds. Various forms lived on all the ancient continents. They were a dominant form of the Mesozoic era. Eohippus, the dawn horse, was a primitive horse the size of a fox with four toes and short teeth with pointed cusps for feeding on soft leaves. Fossil evidence indicates a gradual evolution within the horse lineage to the modern horse, which has one toe (hoof) and two vestigial toes as side splints, flat teeth with ridges for grinding grain and tough prairie grass, and long legs for running. The woolly mammoth was a hairy elephant found in the Siberian ice. Saber-tooth tigers have been preserved in asphalt tar pits. Insects have been discovered preserved in amber. *Archaeopteryx* is a link between reptiles (it has teeth and scales) and birds (it also has feathers).

Comparative Anatomy

Homologous structures

Homologous structures have the same basic anatomical features and evolutionary origins. They demonstrate similar evolutionary patterns with late divergence of form due to differences in exposure to evolutionary forces. Although the origins and anatomical features of these structures are similar, their functions may not be. Examples of homologous structures include the wings of a bat, the flipper of a whale, the forelegs of horses, and the arms of humans.

Analogous structures

Analogous structures have similar functions but may have different evolutionary origins and entirely different patterns of development. The wings of a fly (membranous) and the wings of a bird (bony and covered with feathers) are analogous structures. Analogous organs demonstrate a superficial resemblance that cannot be used as a basis for classification.

Comparative Embryology

The **stages of development** of the embryo resemble the stages in an organism's evolutionary history. The human embryo passes through stages that demonstrate common ancestry with other organisms. The two-layer **gastrula** is similar to the structure of the hydra, a cnidarian. The three-layer gastrula is similar in structure to the flatworm. Gill slits in the embryo indicate a common ancestry with fish. The similarity of these stages suggests a common ancestry and development history.

The earlier the stage at which the development begins to diverge, the more dissimilar the adult organisms will be. For example, it is difficult to differentiate between the embryo of a human and that of a gorilla until relatively late in the development of each embryo.

Embryological development suggests other evidence of evolution from common ancestors. The avian embryo has teeth, suggesting shared ancestry with reptiles. The larvae of some mollusks resemble annelids. Human embryos possess a tail, like most other mammals.

Comparative Biochemistry (Physiology)

Most organisms demonstrate the same basic needs and metabolic processes. They require the same nutrients and contain similar cellular organelles and energy storage forms (ATP). For example, respiratory processes are very similar in most organisms. The similarity of the enzymes involved in these processes suggests that all organisms must contain some DNA sequences in common. The more recently organisms shared a common ancestor, the greater the similarity of their chemical constituents (enzymes, hormones, antibodies, blood) and genetic information. Thus, we can conclude that all organisms are descended from a single common ancestral form. The chemical similarity of the blood of different organisms very closely parallels the evolutionary pattern. A chimpanzee's blood shows close similarity to that of a human but is quite different from that of a rabbit or fish. Thus, the more time that has elapsed since the divergence of two species, the more different their biochemical characteristics.

Vestigial Structures

Vestigial structures have no known current function but apparently had some ancestral function. There are many examples of vestigial structures in humans, other animals, and plants:

- In humans, the appendix is small and useless. In herbivores, it assists in the digestion of cellulose.
- In humans, the tail is reduced to a few useless bones (coccyx) at the base of the spine.
- Splints on the legs of horses are the vestigial remains of the two side toes of more primitive horses.
- Python "legs" are reduced to useless bones embedded in the sides of the adult. The whale has similar hind-limb bones.

Geographic Barriers

Species multiplication is generally accompanied by **migration** to lessen **intraspecific competition**. Separation of a widely distributed population by emerging geographic barriers increases the likelihood of genetic adaptations on either side of the barrier. Each population may evolve specific adaptations to the environment in which it lives in addition to accumulating neutral (random, nonadaptive) changes. These adaptations will remain unique to the population in which they evolve—provided that interbreeding is prevented by the barrier. In time, genetic differences will reach the point where interbreeding becomes impossible between the populations and **reproductive isolation** would be maintained even if the barrier were removed. Following are two examples:

- **Marsupials:** A lineage of pouched mammals (marsupials) paralleling the development of placental mammals developed on the Australian side of a large water barrier. The geographic barrier protected the pouched mammals from competition and hybridization with modern placental mammals. This barrier resulted in the development of uniquely Australian marsupials, such as kangaroos and pouched wolves, as well as other Australian plants and animals, such as the eucalyptus tree and the duck-billed platypus.
- **Darwin's finches**: Over a comparatively short period of time, a single species of Galápagos finch underwent adaptive radiation to form 13 different species of finches. Slight variations in the beak, for example, favored ground or tree feeding. Such adaptations minimized the competition among the birds, enabling each emerging species to become firmly entrenched in its environmental niche. The evolution of these adaptations was helped by the geographic isolation of some of these species on different islands of the Galápagos island chain.

ORIGIN AND EARLY EVOLUTION OF LIFE

The Heterotroph Hypothesis

The first forms of life lacked the ability to synthesize their own nutrients; they required preformed molecules. These "organisms" were heterotrophs, which depended upon outside sources for food. The primitive seas contained simple inorganic and organic compounds such as salts, methane, ammonia, hydrogen, and water. Energy was present in the form of heat, electricity, solar radiation (including X-rays and ultraviolet light), cosmic rays, and radioactivity.

The presence of these building blocks and energy may have led to the synthesis of simple organic molecules such as sugars, amino acids, purines, and pyrimidines. These molecules dissolved in the "**primordial soup**," and after many years, the simple monomeric molecules combined to form a supply of macromolecules.

Evidence of organic synthesis

In 1953, Stanley L. Miller set out to demonstrate that the application of ultraviolet radiation, heat, or a combination of these to a mixture of methane, hydrogen, ammonia, and water could result in the formation of complex organic compounds. Miller set up an apparatus in which the four gases were continuously circulated past electrical discharges from tungsten electrodes.

After circulating the gases for one week, Miller analyzed the liquid in the apparatus and found that an amazing variety of organic compounds, including urea, hydrogen cyanide, acetic acid, and lactic acid had been synthesized.

Formation of primitive cells

Colloidal protein molecules tend to clump together to form **coacervate droplets** (a cluster of colloidal molecules surrounded by a shell of water). These droplets tend to absorb and incorporate substances from the surrounding environment. In addition, the droplets tend to possess a definite internal structure. It is highly likely that such droplets developed on the early Earth. Although these coacervate droplets were not living, they did possess some properties normally associated with living organisms.

Most of these systems were unstable; however, a few systems may have arisen that were stable enough to survive. A small percentage of the droplets possessing favorable characteristics may have eventually developed into the first primitive cells. These first primitive cells probably possessed nucleic acid polymers and became capable of reproduction.

Development of Autotrophs

The primitive heterotrophs slowly evolved complex **biochemical pathways**, enabling them to use a wider variety of nutrients. They evolved anaerobic respiratory processes to convert nutrients into energy. However, these organisms required nutrients at a faster rate than they were being synthesized. Life would have ceased to exist if autotrophic nutrition had not developed. Autotrophs are able to produce organic compounds, including energy-containing molecules, from substances in their surroundings. The pioneer autotrophs developed primitive photosynthetic pathways, capturing solar energy and using it to synthesize carbohydrates from carbon dioxide and water.

Development of Aerobic Respiration

The primitive autotrophs fixed carbon dioxide during the synthesis of carbohydrates and released molecular oxygen as a waste product. The addition of molecular oxygen to the atmosphere converted the atmosphere from a **reducing** to an **oxidizing** one. Some molecular oxygen was converted to ozone, which functions in the atmosphere to block high-energy radiation. In this way, living organisms destroyed the conditions that made their development possible. Once molecular oxygen became a major component of the Earth's atmosphere, both heterotrophs and autotrophs evolved the biochemical pathways of aerobic respiration. Now equilibrium exists between oxygen-producing and oxygen-consuming organisms.

General Categories of Living Organisms

All living organisms can be divided into four basic categories. The **autotrophic anaerobes** include chemosynthetic bacteria. The **autotrophic aerobes** include the green plants and photoplankton. The **heterotrophic anaerobes** include yeasts. The **heterotrophic aerobes** include amoebas, earthworms, and humans.

REVIEW PROBLEMS

1. Can the muscular strength that a weight lifter gains be inherited by the athlete's children?

2. Which organism has a greater evolutionary fitness: one that lives 70 years and has five fertile offspring or one that lives 40 years and has ten fertile offspring?

3. Homologous structures are
   A. similar in function but not in origin.
   B. similar in origin but not necessarily in function.
   C. completely dissimilar.
   D. found only in mammals.
   E. similar in function and origin.

4. Will chance variation have a greater effect in a large or a small population? What is this effect called?

5. As the climate got colder during the Ice Age, a particular species of mammal evolved a thicker layer of fur. This is an example of what kind of selection?

6. At what point are two populations descended from the same ancestral stock considered separate species?

7. In a nonevolving population, there are two alleles, R and r, which code for the same trait. The frequency of R is 30 percent. What are the frequencies of all the possible genotypes?

8. As the ocean became saltier, whales and fish independently evolved mechanisms to maintain the concentration of salt in their bodies. This can be explained by
   A. homologous evolution.
   B. analogous evolution.
   C. convergent evolution.
   D. parallel evolution.
   E. heterologous evolution.

9. In a particular Hardy-Weinberg population, there are only two eye colors: brown and blue. Thirty-six percent of the population has blue eyes, the recessive trait. What percentage of the population is heterozygous for brown eyes?

10. In a certain population, 64 percent of individuals are homozygous for curly hair (CC). The gene for curly hair is dominant to the gene for straight hair, c. Use the Hardy-Weinberg equation to determine what percentage of the population has curly hair.

11. Which of the following was NOT a belief of Darwin's?

    A.   Evolution of species occurs gradually and evenly over time.

    B.   There is a struggle for survival among organisms.

    C.   Genetic mutation and recombination are the driving forces of evolution.

    D.   Those individuals with fitter variants will survive and reproduce.

    E.   More offspring are produced in a population than can survive.

12. The proposed "primordial soup" was composed of organic precursor molecules formed by interactions between all of the following elements EXCEPT

    A.   oxygen.

    B.   helium.

    C.   nitrogen.

    D.   hydrogen.

    E.   carbon.

Section II: Biology

BIO

SOLUTIONS TO REVIEW PROBLEMS

1. No. The only characteristics that are inherited are those genetically coded for, not those acquired through the use or disuse of body parts. Therefore, the musculature of the weight lifter, an acquired characteristic, cannot be inherited by that athlete's children.

2. The organism that lives 40 years and has ten fertile offspring has the greater evolutionary fitness because it makes a greater genetic contribution to the next generation. It has twice as many direct descendants as the organism that lives 70 years and has five fertile offspring.

3. **B** Homologous structures are similar in origin but not necessarily similar in function. Analogous structures are similar in function but not in origin. Homologous structures are not limited to mammals; e.g., the forelimbs of crocodiles and birds are homologous structures.

4. Chance variation will have a greater effect in a small population because any one variant individual is a greater percentage of the whole population. This effect is called genetic drift.

5. This is an example of natural selection, the phenotypic norm of a particular species shifting to adapt to a selective pressure, such as an increasingly colder environment. Only those individuals with a thick layer of fur were able to survive during the Ice Age, thus that trait led to greater fitness (the production of more offspring, in this case due to living longer).

6. Two populations are considered separate species when they can no longer interbreed and produce viable, fertile offspring.

7. The frequency of R = 30%. Thus, $p = 0.30$. The frequency of recessive gene r = 100% − 30% = 70%. Thus, $q = 0.70$. Frequency of genotypes = $p^2 + 2pq + q^2 = 1$, where p^2 = RR, $2pq$ = Rr, and q^2 = rr.

p^2	=	$(0.3)^2$	=	0.09	=	9% RR
$2pq$	=	$2(0.3)(0.7)$	=	0.42	=	42% Rr
q^2	=	$(0.7)^2$	=	0.49	=	49% rr

8. **C** Whales and fish have similar body structures (streamlined body with fins and tail), although they belong to different classes of vertebrates. When organisms that differ phylogenetically develop in similar ways when exposed to similar environments, the process is known as convergent evolution.

9. The percentage of the population with blue eyes (genotype = bb) = 36% = $q^2 = 0.36$; therefore, $q = 0.6$. Because $p + q = 1$, $p = 0.4$. The frequency of heterozygous brown eyes is $2pq = 2(0.4)(0.6) = 0.48$. So 48% of the population is heterozygous for brown eyes.

10. The variable p represents the frequency of the dominant allele (C), and q represents the frequency of the recessive allele (c). The CC frequency is 64%, which means that $p^2 = 0.64$, or $p = 0.8$. Because $p + q = 1$, $q = 1 − 0.8 = 0.2$.

    The problem asks for the percentage of the population with curly hair; this includes both homozygotes and heterozygotes (CC and Cc). The genotype frequencies can be found using the equation $p^2 + 2pq + q^2$.

CC	=	p^2	= $(0.8)^2$	=	0.64	=	64% homozygous curly
Cc	=	$2pq$	= $2(0.8)(0.2)$	=	0.32	=	32% heterozygous curly
cc	=	q^2	= $(0.2)^2$	=	0.04	=	4% straight hair

Therefore, the percentage of the population with curly hair is 64% + 32% = 96%.

11. **C** Darwin believed the driving force behind evolution was the fitness of the organism for its particular environment.

12. **B** He, a noble gas, is inert and does not form molecules with other atoms.

BIO

CHAPTER TEN

Integumentary and Immunological Systems

The body's ability to resist infection is highly dependent on both the integumentary and immunological systems. The integument serves as the initial barrier to infection and prevents a large proportion of environmental microorganisms from entering the body. Should the organisms penetrate the integument, the immune system has several mechanisms to protect the body from infection and destroy the invading organisms.

THE INTEGUMENTARY SYSTEM

The **integument**, which is composed of the skin, hair, and nails, provides a physical barrier to prevent the entrance of pathogens into the body. Many microorganisms live on the surface of human skin and make up the normal skin flora, also known as the **skin microbiome**. These microorganisms often participate in mutualism (relationships that benefit both the microorganisms and the human). By occupying the surface of the skin, these microorganisms prevent other, more harmful organisms from occupying that same space; in return, the microorganisms get a stable environment with access to nutrients. However, some of the normal flora can become pathogenic if they penetrate the integument.

The **skin** itself is also a nonspecific defense mechanism that protects against pathogenic invasion. Sebaceous glands in the skin secrete oil onto the surface of the skin to keep its pH relatively acidic (a range of approximately 4–6), which decreases bacterial growth. These secretions also help keep the skin moist. **Sweat** is secreted from other glands and helps cool the skin by evaporative cooling. Sweat also contains enzymes that help destroy bacterial cell walls as well as pheromones used in chemical communication among humans.

The skin is divided into two different layers, the **dermis** and the **epidermis**, which are connected together by the **basement membrane**. The dermis contains the blood supply to the skin and most of the specialized cells, whereas the epidermis contains mainly keratinocytes, which differentiate into corneocytes: protective, waterproof cells that do not undergo further replication and are routinely sloughed off and replaced.

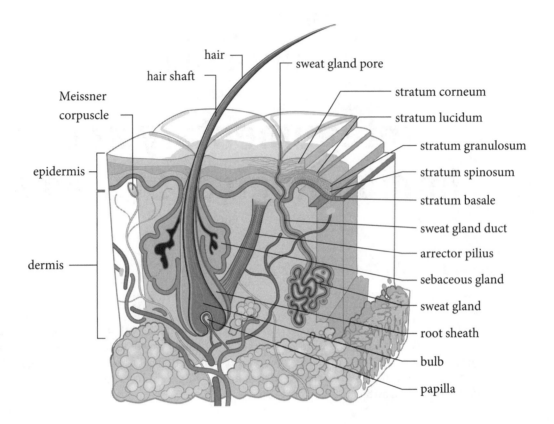

Figure 10.1

Parts of the skin are covered with **hair**, which aids the skin with the above functions. Hair serves to direct sweat and waste away from the skin, helping with evaporative cooling when the body is hot. Conversely, hair also traps heat, preventing the body from becoming too cool. Hair also serves as a sensory organ, allowing the detection of nearby motion.

Other components of the integument help prevent infection as well. **Mucous** secretions in the nose and aqueous secretions in the eyes help prevent foreign organisms from entering the body and resist infection. Similarly, **enzymes** in the mouth and throat break down many entering microorganisms and decrease their pathogenicity. Finally, **nails** protect the tips of the fingers and toes from physical injury and can be used as tools.

THE IMMUNOLOGICAL SYSTEM

In addition to the integument, the **immune system** plays a key role in the destruction of internal pathogens. The body can distinguish between self and nonself and can recognize and remember nonself qualities in other cells (**antigens**). This allows the body to recognize pathogens it has previously encountered and to mount a quicker immune response against these antigens if exposed to them again. The immune system has two major types of immunity: **humoral**, which involves antibody production, and **cell-mediated**, which involves cells that combat fungal and viral infections.

Another nonspecific defense mechanism employed by the immune system is the **inflammatory response**. When white blood cells are activated, they release chemicals, such as **histamine**, that activate the immune response. This response dilates and increases the permeability of blood vessels. These effects together increase the flow of white blood cells and other immune cells to the affected area, allowing the body to more effectively ward off infection. Inflammation is often accompanied by the rise in body temperature termed a **fever**, which in theory increases the ability to fight infection by killing temperature-dependent pathogens and speeding up healing processes. However, whether or not fever is practically beneficial is still a topic of scientific debate.

The **lymphatic system** is another important part of the immune system and is found in the extravascular space of most tissues. **Lymph** flows through the lymphatic vessels from lymph node to lymph node. The **lymph nodes** and **spleen** serve as reservoirs of white blood cells and filters for lymph, removing antigen-presenting cells and foreign matter and activating the immune system when necessary (see Chapter 13, Circulatory and Respiratory Systems).

Cell-Mediated Immunity

The immune system contains several varieties of white blood cells, or **leukocytes**, each with a specific function.

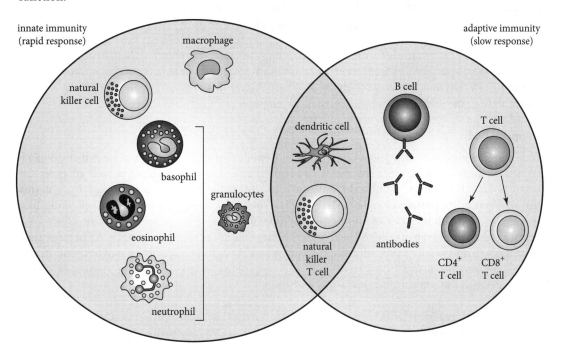

Figure 10.2

Granulocytes

Granulocytes are attracted to the site of injury, where they phagocytize antigens and antigenic material.

Neutrophils, the most common type of granulocyte, are often the first responders to sites of inflammation. These cells are attracted to cytokines and in turn attract additional white blood cells once they arrive at the site of tissue damage. Although they can help moderate various infections and environmental trauma, neutrophils are particularly adapted to attack bacteria. Neutrophil counts are often elevated during the acute stages of inflammation and are the main component of pus.

Eosinophils are much less common and are responsible for immune responses, especially allergic and asthmatic responses. Elevated eosinophil counts on a complete blood count (CBC) often indicate an allergic response or infection by a parasite, including those that live on the surface of the skin (ectoparasites), such as fleas and ticks, and those that live in intercellular spaces (endoparasites), such as the parasitic worms known as helminths.

Basophils and the related **mast cells** are similarly involved in allergic responses and parasite infections and often are responsible for the release of histamine, which stimulates blood vessel dilation as previously described.

Monocytes

Monocytes are large, long-lived immune cells that can differentiate into macrophages and dendritic cells.

The main role of **macrophages** is to phagocytize dead cells and pathogens. If a pathogen is ingested, its antigens are then presented on the surface of the macrophage to stimulate other immune cells to mount a specific immune response to the invading pathogen.

Dendritic cells are even more focused on processing antigens and presenting them to other immune cells and therefore serve as important links between the innate and adaptive immune systems. Dendritic cells are found in areas of the body where contact with the external environment is more common (e.g., the skin, intestine, and mucous membranes).

T lymphocytes

T cells are an important component in specific immunity. Through random rearrangement of gene sequences, each T cell becomes reactive to only one specific antigen. If infection with an organism that displays this antigen occurs, the antigen from the pathogen will be presented by a **major histocompatibility protein complex (MHC)** on the surface of an antigen-presenting cell, indicating that the corresponding T-cell should perform its function. The vast majority of T cells created are deactivated and undergo apoptosis because they either will not react with the MHC or because they react too well and would attack self cells. Nevertheless, although each T cell can only respond to one specific antigen and many T cells are destroyed during development, a sufficient number of T cells exists to defend the body against nearly any pathogen.

The two major types of histocompatibility proteins are MHC I and MHC II. **Cytotoxic T (T_C) cells** (also known as **CD8+ T cells** because they contain the CD8 protein) recognize and respond to antigens presented by MHC I complexes. These complexes come from cells infected with viruses or developing tumors and signal T_C cells to destroy those cells. In contrast, **T helper (T_H) cells** (also known as CD4+ T cells) recognize and respond to antigens presented by MHC II complexes. Activated T_H cells release cytokines to stimulate the immune response, causing other white blood cells to mature and attack. **Natural killer T (NKT) cells** behave similarly to both T_C and T_H cells but respond to antigens presented by other types of cells.

Once a reaction has occurred, **memory T cells** reactive to the same antigens are formed and remain in circulation for long periods of time, allowing a quicker, more targeted response if the antigen reappears. **Regulatory** or **suppressor T (T_{reg}) cells** have the opposite function, serving to tone down T cell response to self cells or following an infection.

T cells begin their development in the bone marrow, where T lymphocyte precursor cells are formed. They travel via the bloodstream to the **thymus**, where they mature. It is because these cells mature in the thymus that they are referred to as T cells. Once maturation is complete, the cells are released into the lymph to perform their immune function.

T cells are a vital component of the immune system. Patients with acquired immunodeficiency syndrome (AIDS) have very low levels of certain types of T cells and as a result are particularly subject to infection because their immune systems are so weakened by this loss.

B lymphocytes

B cells, when stimulated, create and express **antibodies** (also known as **immunoglobulins**) that have a high affinity for the antigen expressed by the stimulating T lymphocyte. Immunoglobulins have a very particular structure (outlined later in this chapter) and utilize the specificity of this structure to aid in the targeted destruction of pathogens. Like T cells, B cells can also stimulate the formation of memory cells.

B lymphocytes, like T cells, begin their development in the bone marrow. However, unlike T cells, their development is completed there; they do not travel to other parts of the body to mature.

The following table outlines the most important cells found in the immune system as well as their functions.

Cell Type	Function
Granulocytes	
Basophil	Least common of all the granulocytes (1%); fight parasites; mediate allergic response
Eosinophil	Much less common than neutrophils (5%); fight parasites; mediate allergic response
Neutrophils	Most common of the granulocytes (94%); phagocytic
Monocytes	
Macrophage	Phagocytic; secrete cytokines; present antigens
Dendritic cells	Present antigens; activate immune system
Lymphocytes	
B cells	Produce antigen-specific antibodies
T cells	Helper T (CD4$^+$) cells activate other immune cells; cytotoxic T (CD8$^+$) cells and natural killer T (NKT) cells destroy cells marked for destruction; memory T cells remain after an infection so a response can be mounted more quickly if infected again

Table 10.1

Humoral Immunity

The immune system also contains components that are not cells. Various chemicals, hormones, and enzymes supplement the action of the cells and serve equally important roles.

Antibodies

Large proteins secreted by B cells known as antibodies or **immunoglobulins** provide specific, targeted responses to a given antigen. Several types of immunoglobulins exist within the immune system, and each plays a unique role in immunity. Nevertheless, the structure of all immunoglobulins is relatively consistent and resembles a "Y," with antigen binding sites at either end of the top of the "Y." Each side of the structure consists of two chains, a light chain and a heavy chain, which are held together with disulfide bonds. The variable portion of the structure is the antigen-binding region.

Figure 10.3

The antigen-binding region of the antibody is unique to each antigen and is the reason that specificity for a particular antigen exists. The immune system can generate millions of unique antigen-binding sites, which confers the ability to mount an immune response against any number of antigens.

Antibody-mediated immunity includes both active and passive immunity. **Active immunity** occurs as a result of an immune response. This can be due to exposure to a pathogen or antigen, such as during an infection. It can also be the result of **vaccination**, where an individual is deliberately exposed to a weakened, inactivated, or killed form of the antigen. This exposure stimulates the body's immune system to mount an immune response against the antigen presented. The features of this antigen are then stored in the "nonself" memory, allowing the body to mount a similar immune response should the antigen present itself again. This type of immune response, because it requires the development of cells specific to a particular antigen, can take weeks or months to build up.

Passive immunity, in contrast, is acquired by the transfer of antibodies from one individual to another. This can occur during pregnancy, for example, when maternal antibodies cross the placenta and enter fetal circulation. Injections of gamma globulin, which is the fraction of the blood containing antibodies, can also provide passive immunity by transferring antibodies to a particular illness to a given individual. While passive immunity is effective immediately upon transfer of antibodies, once the antibodies are no longer circulating in the immune system the effect of the immunity is lost.

Types of Immunity

While immunity can be characterized by the types of immune components involved, it can also be divided into **innate** and **adaptive immunity** based on how the immunity is acquired. Each of these categories involves components from both cell-mediated and humoral immunity.

Innate immunity

Innate immunity is comprised of the body's initial, generalized defenses against pathogens. This type of immunity does not require the cells of the immune system to be previously exposed to any given antigen to be activated. However, it is not a specific response, and the body is limited in the types of immune response it can mount. Innate immunity includes:

- anatomic features (including the integument, as described above)
- physiologic response (fever, pH change, enzymes)
- phagocytic cells (monocytes, neutrophils, macrophages)
- inflammation

Adaptive immunity

Acquired or **specific** immunity consists of cells capable of recognizing self versus nonself cells—for example, cells that can differentiate invading cells from host cells—and that are specific to a particular antigen. The activity of cells that participate in an adaptive immune response is increased with each exposure. Thus, there are memory components to acquired immunity: Cells recognize antigens they have been exposed to previously, and the immune response mounted against increases in magnitude after each repeat exposure to an antigen. Cells that are involved in adaptive immunity are:

- lymphocytes (B and T cells)
- plasma cells
- antigen-presenting cells (macrophages, B cells)

Innate and acquired immunity work together to protect the host and defend against invading pathogens. Phagocytic cells can stimulate production of specific T lymphocytes to assist in pathogen killing and destruction. T lymphocytes, in turn, can release cytokines, which increase the killing activities of phagocytes. Other examples of this type of cooperation exist, and they work to increase the function and efficacy of the immune system.

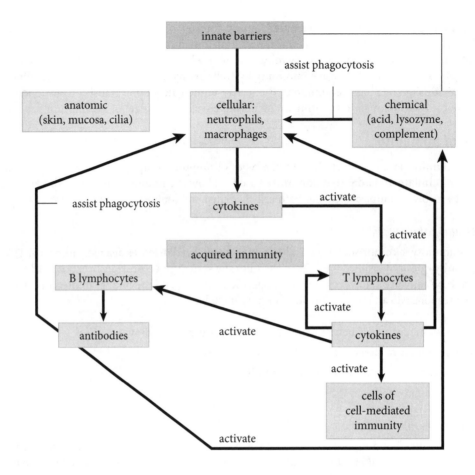

Figure 10.4

Transplant rejection

Transplanted tissues or organs are detected as nonself by the recipient's immune system. This is because the antigens on the donated organ are those of the donor, not of the recipient. As a result, the recipient's immune system attacks the transplanted organ. This attack can lead to rejection of the organ, which can ultimately result in destruction of the organ or death of the patient. As a result, immunosuppressing drugs are used to lower the immune response to transplants and decrease the likelihood of rejection. These work by lowering the body's immune response to antigens; while this decreases the likelihood of rejecting the organ, it also lowers the recipient's overall immune response. The recipient is then referred to as **immunocompromised** because his immune system is not functioning at its full capacity.

REVIEW PROBLEMS

1. What is the role of histamine in the immune response?
    - A. To induce a fever
    - B. To reduce inflammation
    - C. To dilate the blood vessels
    - D. To recruit immunoglobulin
    - E. To increase inflammation

2. Describe the roles of the three types of granulocytes (basophils, eosinophils, and neutrophils) and the two types of monocytes (macrophages and dendritic cells).

3. What type of cell responds to activated MHC II complexes?
    - A. Cytotoxic T cell
    - B. Helper T cell
    - C. Natural killer cell
    - D. Plasma cell
    - E. B cell

4. Which cells produce a memory-driven response to pathogens?
    - A. Neutrophils
    - B. Macrophages
    - C. Cytokines
    - D. B lymphocytes
    - E. Basophils

5. Compare and contrast the maturation process of T lymphocytes and B lymphocytes.

6. Differentiate between active and passive immunity and give examples of each.

7. Where is the antigen-binding region found on the immunoglobulin structure?
    - A. Heavy chain
    - B. Light chain
    - C. N-terminus
    - D. Cytoplasmic tail
    - E. Complement-binding region

SOLUTIONS TO REVIEW PROBLEMS

1. **C** Histamine triggers the inflammatory response and dilates blood vessels, thereby increasing blood flow to an injured area, which increases the number of immune cells that can reach the damaged tissue. In contrast, cytokines trigger the fever response and activate B lymphocytes, which in turn produce immunoglobulin.

2. Neutrophils are the first responders to inflammation and phagocytize pathogens. Eosinophils and basophils are involved in inflammation and the allergic response, and both are involved in combating parasites. Among other actions, basophils specifically stimulate histamine release. Macrophages phagocytize pathogens and dead or damaged cells. Dendritic cells present antigens to allow for a targeted immune response.

3. **B** The major histocompatibility complex (MHC) presents proteins to immune cells. MHC II in particular is found on antigen-presenting cells and B cells and presents to helper T lymphocytes, and these cells then activate other T cells and B cells. Cytotoxic T cells recognize and attack foreign antigens, natural killer cells similarly destroy tumor cells and cells infected with viruses, and plasma cells release large quantities of antibodies, but none of these types of cells interact with MHC.

4. **D** Macrophages are part of the general immune response and do not exert a targeted effect or retain memory of antigens. Cytokines activate B cells but do not themselves possess a memory for antigens. Neutrophils are phagocytic and also do not have a memory for specific antigens. Basophils stimulate histamine due to stimulation of an allergic reaction.

5. Both T lymphocytes and B lymphocytes begin development in the bone marrow. Immature T cells are released into the bloodstream and travel to the thymus. It is in the thymus that T cells complete the maturation process and develop their permanent characteristics. B cells, however, complete their maturation in the bone marrow. When B cells are released from the bone they are mature and ready to undertake their anti-pathogenic activities.

6. Active immunity is due to exposure to an antigen, for example during infection or vaccination. Passive immunity requires the transfer of antibodies from one individual to another, for example from a pregnant woman to her fetus.

7. **C** The heavy chain, light chain, complement-binding region, and cytoplasmic tail are all components of antibody structure, but none of them plays a role in binding antigens. It is only the N-terminus that binds to antigens and thus determines the specificity of the antibody.

CHAPTER ELEVEN

Nervous System

The **nervous system** is responsible for controlling most body functions, enabling organisms to receive and respond to **stimuli** from their external and internal environments. Signals from the nervous system travel quickly, reaching in excess of 100 meters per second in some cases, which results in transmission of information much more rapidly than through the endocrine system (see Chapter 16).

The nervous system is composed of both **neurons** (specialized nervous tissue) and **neuroglia** (cells that support and protect the neurons). These cells work together to form the major organs of the nervous system, which include the brain and spinal cord as well as complex sensory organs, such as the eye and ear. In turn, these organs can be grouped into two divisions: the **central nervous system (CNS)** and the **peripheral nervous system (PNS)**.

NEURON

Structure

Neurons are the functional units of the nervous system and are used to convert stimuli into **electrochemical signals** and conduct these signals through the body. Each neuron is generally an elongated cell consisting of **dendrites**, a **cell body**, and an **axon**. **Dendrites** are cytoplasmic extensions that receive information and transmit it toward the cell body. The cell body (**soma**) contains the nucleus and controls the metabolic activity of the neuron. The **axon** is a long cellular process that transmits impulses, or **action potentials**, away from the cell body. Most mammalian axons are sheathed by an insulating substance known as **myelin**, which prevents leakage of signal from the axons and allows for faster conduction of impulses. The gaps between segments of myelin, the **nodes of Ranvier**, are where the action potential actually propagates; this occurs through a process known as saltatory ("hopping") conduction. Myelin itself is produced by glial cells known as **oligodendrocytes** in the central nervous system and by **Schwann cells** in the peripheral nervous system. The axons end in swellings known as **synaptic terminals** (also called boutons or knobs). **Neurotransmitters** are released from these terminals into the **synapse** (or synaptic cleft), which is the gap between the axon terminals of one cell and the dendrites of the next cell. Axons may be very long, such as the axon of a neuron traveling from the spinal cord to the tip of the foot.

BIO

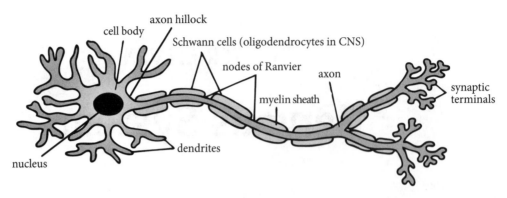

Figure 11.1

The four major types of cells in the CNS and two major types in the PNS are summarized in the following table:

Cells in the CNS and PNS	
Cell Type	**Cell Function**
CNS	
Astrocytes	Maintain the integrity of the blood–brain barrier, regulate nutrient and dissolved gas concentrations, and absorb and recycle neurotransmitters
Oligodendrocytes	Myelinate CNS axons as well as provide structural framework for the CNS
Microglia	Remove cellular debris and pathogens
Ependymal cells	Line the brain ventricles and aid in the production, circulation, and monitoring of cerebral spinal fluid
PNS	
Satellite cells	Surround the neuron cell bodies in the ganglia
Schwann cells	Enclose the axons in the PNS and aid in the myelination of some peripheral axons

Table 11.1

Function

Neurons are specialized to receive signals from sensory receptors or from other neurons in the body. These signals create action potentials, which travel the length of the axon to invade the nerve terminal, thereby causing the release of neurotransmitter into the synapse.

Resting potential

Even at rest, a neuron is **polarized** due to unequal distribution of ions between the inside and outside of the cell. The potential difference at rest between the extracellular space and the intracellular space is called the **resting potential**. A typical resting membrane potential is –70 millivolts (mV), which means the inside of the neuron is more negative than the outside. This difference is caused by selective ionic permeability of the neuronal cell membrane and is maintained by the active transport of ions by the **Na$^+$/K$^+$ pump** (also called the Na$^+$/K$^+$ ATPase), which pumps 3 Na$^+$ out of the cell for every 2 K$^+$ it transports into the cell. This uneven exchange results in one more positive charge leaving the cell than entering it, creating a negative internal environment. Furthermore, the cell membrane is more permeable to K$^+$ than to Na$^+$, allowing some of the K$^+$ that was pumped into the cell to move back out through facilitated diffusion, making the internal environment even more negative.

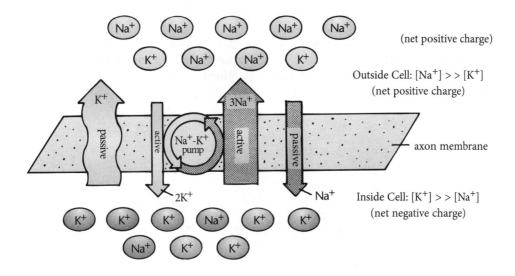

Figure 11.2

Action potential

The nerve cell body receives both excitatory and inhibitory impulses from other cells. If the cell body becomes sufficiently excited and **depolarized** (i.e., the inside of the cell becomes less negative and more positive) to reach the **threshold potential**, then **voltage-gated ion channels** located in the nerve cell membrane open in response. An action potential begins when voltage-gated Na$^+$ channels open in response to depolarization, allowing Na$^+$ to rush down its electrochemical gradient into the cell and causing further, rapid depolarization of that segment of the axon. The Na$^+$ also causes the next portion of the axon toward the terminal to become depolarized, causing voltage-gated Na$^+$ channels to open there as well, continuing the process and moving the action potential toward the terminal. Once the action potential reaches the synaptic terminal, a final voltage-gated channel specific for calcium is opened. This allows Ca^{2+} to rush in and trigger the exocytosis of **synaptic vesicles** containing neurotransmitters.

After the signal has been propagated through a segment of the axon, the high voltage there causes voltage-gated K^+ channels to open, allowing K^+ to rush down its electrochemical gradient and out of the cell. Meanwhile, the voltage-gated Na^+ channels also close, and the Na^+/K^+ pump begins to pump Na^+ out of the cell again. Together, these processes return the cell to a negative potential in a process known as **repolarization**. In fact, the neuron's voltage shoots past the resting potential and becomes even more negative inside than normal due to the K^+ still being free to leave the cell; this is called **hyperpolarization**. This results in the **refractory period**, a period of time after an action potential during which new action potentials are very difficult or impossible to initiate immediately. The refractory period allows the neuron time to regenerate neurotransmitter and also helps ensure the action potential only moves in the forward direction, toward the terminal.

The action potential itself can be described as an all-or-none response. This means that if and only if the threshold membrane potential is reached, an action potential with a consistent size and duration is produced; the neuron fires maximally or not at all. Stimulus intensity is therefore coded by the **frequency** of action potentials and not their magnitude.

Figure 11.3

Impulse propagation

Although axons can theoretically propagate action potentials bidirectionally, information transfer will occur only in one direction: from dendrite to synaptic terminal. This is because synapses operate only in one direction and because refractory periods make the backward travel of action potentials impossible.

Nevertheless, different axons do propagate action potentials at **different speeds**. The greater the **diameter** of the axon and the more heavily it is **myelinated**, the faster the impulses travel. Myelin increases the conduction velocity by insulating segments of the axon such that the membrane is permeable to ions only in the nodes of Ranvier. In this way, the action potential "hops" from node to node.

Figure 11.4

Synapse

The synapse is the gap between the axon terminal of one neuron (called the **presynaptic neuron** because it is before the synapse) and the dendrites of another neuron (the **postsynaptic neuron**). Neurons may also communicate with postsynaptic cells other than neurons, such as cells in muscles or glands; these are called **effector cells**.

The nerve terminal contains thousands of membrane-bound vesicles full of chemical messengers known as **neurotransmitters**. When the action potential arrives at the nerve terminal and depolarizes it, the synaptic vesicles fuse with the presynaptic membrane and release neurotransmitter into the synapse. The neurotransmitter diffuses across the synapse and acts on receptor proteins embedded

BIO

in the postsynaptic membrane. The released neurotransmitter will lead to depolarization of the postsynaptic cell and consequent firing of an action potential.

Neurotransmitter is removed from the synapse in a variety of ways: it may be taken back up into the nerve terminal (via a protein known as an uptake carrier) where it may be reused or degraded; it may be degraded by enzymes located in the synapse (e.g., acetylcholinesterase inactivates the neurotransmitter acetylcholine); or it may simply diffuse out of the synapse.

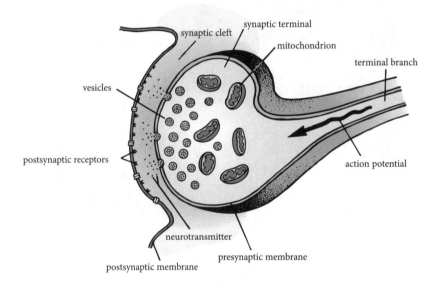

Figure 11.5

Effects of drugs

- **Curare** blocks postsynaptic nicotinic acetylcholine receptors, such as those on muscles, so acetylcholine is unable to interact with them. This leads to muscle relaxation and paralysis by blocking the ability to constrict muscles.
- **Botulinum toxin** prevents the release of acetylcholine from the presynaptic membrane and also results in paralysis.
- **Anticholinesterases** are used as nerve gases and in the insecticide parathion. As the name implies, these substances inhibit the activity of the acetylcholinesterase enzyme responsible for degrading acetylcholine released into the synapse. As a result, acetylcholine is not degraded and continues to affect the postsynaptic membrane. Therefore, no coordinated muscular contractions can take place.

Neuron Types

Although their general characteristics remain the same, neurons can become specialized to perform specific tasks. Neurons that carry **sensory** information about the external or internal environment to the brain or spinal cord are called **afferent neurons**. Neurons that carry **motor** commands from the brain or spinal cord to various parts of the body (e.g., muscles or glands) are called **efferent neurons**. Some neurons (**interneurons**) participate only in local circuits, linking sensory and motor neurons in the brain and spinal cord; their cell bodies and their nerve terminals are in the same location.

Nerves are essentially bundles of axons covered with connective tissue. A network of nerve fibers is called a **plexus**. Neuronal cell bodies often cluster together: such clusters are called **ganglia** in the periphery; in the central nervous system, they are called **nuclei**.

ORGANIZATION OF THE NERVOUS SYSTEM

The human nervous system can be viewed as having several different divisions, each with unique properties and functions:

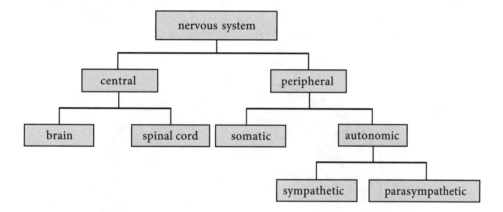

Figure 11.6

Central Nervous System

The central nervous system (CNS) consists of the brain and spinal cord.

Brain

The brain is a mass of neurons that resides in the skull. Its functions include interpreting sensory information, forming motor plans, and cognitive function (thinking). The brain consists of an outer portion of cell bodies called the **gray matter** and an inner portion of myelinated axons called the **white matter**. The brain also can be divided into the forebrain, midbrain, and hindbrain.

Forebrain (Prosencephalon)

- The **forebrain** consists of the **telencephalon** and the **diencephalon**. A major component of the telencephalon is the **cerebral cortex**, which is the highly convoluted gray matter that can be seen on the surface of the brain. The cortex processes and integrates sensory input and motor responses and is important for memory and creative thought. The **olfactory bulb** is the center for reception and integration of olfactory (smell-related) input.

- The diencephalon contains the thalamus and hypothalamus. The **thalamus** is a relay and integration center for the spinal cord and cerebral cortex. The **hypothalamus** controls visceral functions such as hunger, thirst, sex drive, water balance, blood pressure, and temperature regulation. It also plays an important role in the control of the endocrine system.

Midbrain (Mesencephalon)

- The **midbrain** is a relay center for visual and auditory impulses. It also plays an important role in motor control.

Hindbrain (Rhombencephalon)

- The **hindbrain** is the posterior part of the brain and consists of the cerebellum, the pons, and the medulla. The **cerebellum** helps to modulate motor impulses initiated by the cerebral cortex and is important in the maintenance of balance, hand-eye coordination, and the timing of rapid movements. One function of the **pons** is to act as a relay center to allow the cortex to communicate with the cerebellum. The **medulla** (also called the medulla oblongata) controls many vital functions such as breathing, heart rate, and gastrointestinal activity. Together, the midbrain, pons, and medulla constitute the **brainstem**.

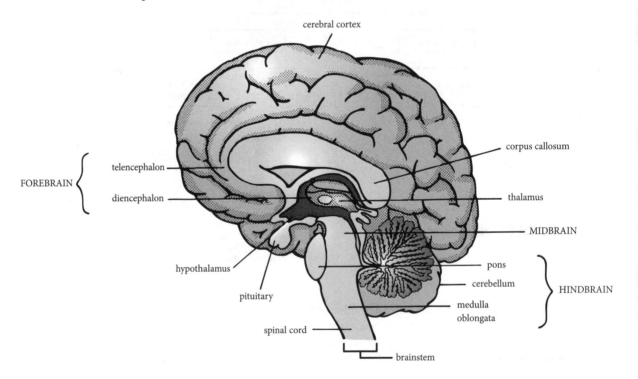

Figure 11.7

Spinal cord

The spinal cord is an elongated extension of the brain that acts as the conduit for sensory information to the brain and motor information from the brain. The spinal cord can also integrate simple motor responses (e.g., **reflexes**) by itself. A cross-section of the spinal cord reveals an outer white matter area containing motor and sensory axons and an inner gray matter area containing nerve cell bodies. Sensory information enters the spinal cord through the **dorsal horn**; the cell bodies of these sensory neurons are located in the dorsal root ganglia. All motor information exits the spinal cord through the **ventral horn**. For simple reflexes like the knee-jerk reflex, sensory fibers (entering through the dorsal root ganglion) synapse directly on ventral horn motor fibers. Other reflexes include interneurons between the sensory and motor fibers that allow for some processing in the spinal cord.

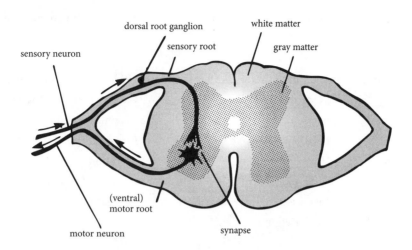

Figure 11.8

Peripheral Nervous System

The peripheral nervous system (PNS) consists of nerves and ganglia. The sensory nerves that enter the CNS and the motor nerves that leave the CNS are part of the peripheral nervous system. The PNS has two primary divisions: the **somatic** and the **autonomic** nervous systems, each of which has both motor and sensory components.

Somatic nervous system

The somatic nervous system (SNS) innervates skeletal muscles and is responsible for voluntary movement as well as reflex arcs (pathways that control motor reflexes).

Autonomic nervous system

The autonomic nervous system (ANS) is sometimes also called the **involuntary nervous system** because it regulates the body's internal environment without the aid of conscious control. The autonomic innervation of the body includes both sensory and motor fibers. The ANS innervates cardiac and smooth muscle. Smooth muscle is located in areas such as blood vessels, the digestive tract, the bladder, and bronchi (see Chapter 13), so the ANS is important in blood pressure control, gastrointestinal motility, excretion, respiration, and reproduction. The ANS is comprised of two subdivisions, the **sympathetic** and the **parasympathetic** nervous systems, which generally act in opposition to one another.

- **Sympathetic nervous system:** The sympathetic division is responsible for the "**flight or fight**" responses that ready the body for action in an emergency situation. It increases blood pressure and heart rate, increases blood flow to skeletal muscles, and decreases gut motility. It also dilates the bronchioles to increase gas exchange. The sympathetic nervous system uses **norepinephrine** as its primary neurotransmitter.

- **Parasympathetic nervous system:** The parasympathetic division acts to conserve energy and restore the body to resting activity levels after exertion ("**rest and digest**"). It acts to lower heart rate and increase gut motility. One very important parasympathetic nerve that innervates many of the thoracic and abdominal viscera is called the **vagus nerve**. It uses **acetylcholine** as its primary neurotransmitter.

Below is a summary table that lists the major functions of the parasympathetic and sympathetic nervous systems.

Comparison of Sympathetic and Parasympathetic Autonomic Functions		
Organ	**Sympathetic Effect**	**Parasympathetic Effect**
Lens	n/a	Accommodation
Iris	Dilates pupil	Constricts pupil
Salivary glands	Vasoconstriction	Secretion
Sweat glands	Secretion (specific)	Secretion (generalized)
Heart (force and rate)	Increases	Decreases
Peripheral blood vessels	Constriction	Dilation
Visceral blood vessels	Constriction	Dilation
Lungs	Bronchodilation	Bronchoconstriction
Gastrointestinal tract	Decreases peristalsis and secretion	Increases peristalsis and secretion
Rectum and anus	Inhibits smooth muscle in rectum and constricts sphincter	Increases smooth muscle tone and relaxes sphincter
Adrenal medulla	secretion	n/a
Bladder	Relaxation of the detrusor muscle and constriction of internal sphincter	Contraction of the detrusor muscle and inhibition of internal sphincter
Genitalia	Ejaculation	Penile erection / engorgement of clitoris and labia

Table 11.2

SPECIAL SENSES

The human body has a number of organs that are specialized receptors adapted to detect stimuli.

The Eye

The eye detects light energy (photons) and transmits information about intensity, color, and shape to the brain. The eyeball is covered by a thick, opaque layer known as the **sclera**, which is also known as the white of the eye. Beneath the sclera is the **choroid** layer, which helps to supply the retina with blood. The choroid is a dark, pigmented area that reduces reflection in the eye. The innermost layer of the eye is the **retina**, which contains the **photoreceptors** that sense light.

The transparent **cornea** at the front of the eye bends and focuses light rays. The rays then travel through an opening called the **pupil**, whose diameter is controlled by the pigmented, muscular **iris**. The iris responds to the intensity of light in the surroundings (light makes the pupil constrict). The light continues through the lens, which is suspended behind the pupil. The **lens**, the shape and focal length of which is controlled by the **ciliary muscles**, focuses the image onto the retina.

In the retina are **photoreceptors** that transduce light into action potentials. The two main types of photoreceptors are cones and rods. **Cones** respond to high-intensity illumination and are sensitive to color, whereas **rods** detect low-intensity illumination and are important in night vision. Cones and rods contain various pigments that absorb specific wavelengths of light. Cones contain three different pigments that absorb red, green, and blue wavelengths; the rod pigment, **rhodopsin**, only absorbs a single wavelength. The photoreceptor cells synapse onto **bipolar cells**, which in turn synapse onto **ganglion cells**. Axons of the ganglion cells bundle to form the optic nerve, which conducts visual information to the brain. The point at which the optic nerve exits the eye is called the **blind spot** because photoreceptors are not present there. The **fovea**, a small area of the retina above the blind spot, is densely packed with cones and is important for high-acuity vision.

The eye also contains a jelly-like material called **vitreous humor** that helps maintain its shape and optical properties. **Aqueous humor** is a more watery substance that fills the space between the lens and the cornea.

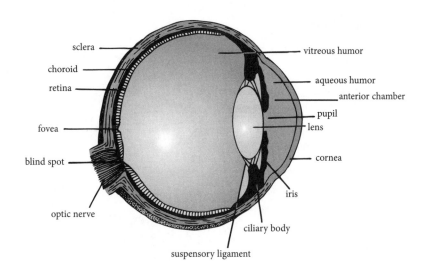

Figure 11.9

Disorders of the eye

- **Myopia (nearsightedness)** occurs when the image is focused in front of the retina.
- **Hyperopia (farsightedness)** occurs when the image is focused behind the retina.
- **Astigmatism** is caused by an irregularly shaped cornea.
- **Cataracts** develop when the lens becomes opaque; light cannot enter the eye, and blindness results.
- **Glaucoma** is an increase of pressure in the eye because of blocking of the outflow of the aqueous humor, which results in optic nerve damage.

THE EAR

The ear transduces sound energy (**pressure waves**) into impulses perceived by the brain as sound. Sound waves pass through three regions as they enter the ear. First, they enter the **outer ear**, which consists of the **auricle** (external ear) and the **auditory canal**. At the end of the auditory canal is the **tympanic membrane** (eardrum) of the middle ear, which vibrates at the same frequency as the incoming sound. Next, the three bones, or **ossicles** (malleus, incus, and stapes or hammer, anvil, and stirrup), of the middle ear amplify the stimulus and transmit it through the oval window, which leads to the fluid-filled inner ear. The inner ear consists of the **cochlea** and the **vestibular apparatus**, which is involved in maintaining equilibrium. Vibration of the ossicles exerts pressure on the fluid in the cochlea, stimulating **hair cells** in the **basilar membrane** to transduce the pressure into action potentials, which travel via the **auditory (cochlear) nerve** to the brain for processing.

Figure 11.10

REVIEW PROBLEMS

1. Which of the following statements best characterizes an axon?

   A. It is a long, slender process that fires every time neurotransmitters bind to the postsynaptic membrane.

   B. It transmits nonelectrical impulses.

   C. It transmits information from the cell body to the axon terminals.

   D. It releases neurotransmitter at the synaptic cleft.

   E. None of the above

2. Resting membrane potential is NOT dependent on

   A. the differential distribution of ions across the axon membrane.

   B. active transport.

   C. selective permeability.

   D. passive diffusion.

   E. pinocytosis.

3. All of the following are associated with the myelin sheath EXCEPT

   A. faster conduction of nervous impulses.

   B. nodes of Ranvier forming gaps along the axon.

   C. increased energy output for nervous impulse conduction.

   D. saltatory conduction of action potentials.

   E. insulation of axon segments.

4. The all-or-none law states that

   A. all hyperpolarizing stimuli will be carried to the axon terminal without a decrease in size.

   B. the size of the action potential is proportional to the size of the stimulus that produced it.

   C. increasing the intensity of the depolarization increases the size of the impulse.

   D. once an action potential is triggered, an impulse of a given magnitude and speed is produced.

   E. the greater the depolarization, the greater the impulse.

5. Discuss two major differences between the somatic and the autonomic divisions of the peripheral nervous system.

6. By increasing the intensity of the stimulus, the action potential will

   A. increase in amplitude.

   B. increase in frequency.

   C. increase in speed.

   D. increase in wavelength.

   E. increase in period.

BIO

7. Which of the following pairings is correct?

   A. Sensory nerves–Afferent
   B. Motor nerves–Afferent
   C. Sensory nerves–Efferent
   D. Sensory nerves–Ventral
   E. Motor nerves–Ventral

8. When a sensory receptor receives a threshold stimulus, it will do all of the following EXCEPT

   A. become depolarized.
   B. transduce the stimulus to an action potential.
   C. inhibit the spread of the action potential to sensory neurons.
   D. cause the sensory neuron to send action potentials to the central nervous system.
   E. have a more positive charge.

9. Which of the following structures is most important for focusing light on the retina?

   A. Cornea
   B. Aqueous humor
   C. Vitreous humor
   D. Sclera
   E. Lens

10. When the potential across the axon membrane is more negative than the normal resting potential, the neuron is said to be in a state of

   A. depolarization.
   B. hyperpolarization.
   C. repolarization.
   D. refraction.
   E. hypopolarization

11. Chemical X is found to denature all enzymes in the synaptic cleft. What are the effects on acetylcholine if chemical X is added to the cleft?

   A. Acetylcholine is not released from the presynaptic membrane.
   B. Acetylcholine does not bind to the postsynaptic membrane.
   C. Acetylcholine is not inactivated in the synaptic cleft.
   D. Acetylcholine is degraded before it acts on the postsynaptic membrane.
   E. Acetylcholine cannot be taken up into the axon terminal.

12. Which of the following statements concerning the somatic division of the peripheral nervous system is INCORRECT?

   A. Its pathways innervate skeletal muscles.
   B. Its pathways are usually voluntary.
   C. Some of its pathways are referred to as reflex arcs.
   D. It includes the vagus nerve.
   E. It controls motor reflexes.

13. In the ear, what structure transduces pressure waves to action potentials?

    A. Tympanic membrane

    B. Hair cells

    C. Oval window

    D. Semicircular canals

    E. Hammer, anvil, and stirrup

SOLUTIONS TO REVIEW PROBLEMS

1. **C** Axons carry information from the cell body of the neuron to the axon terminal by way of action potentials. From there, the impulse is transmitted to another neuron or to an effector. However, the axon does not fire unless the impulse is strong enough to depolarize the axon membrane to the threshold membrane potential.

2. **E** Resting membrane potential is a result of an unequal distribution of ions between the inside and the outside of the cell, and of all the other facets of cell structure listed. It is NOT dependent on pinocytosis, als known as "cellular drinking," which is a form of endocytosis by which the cell engulfs a portion of the extracellular fluid; this process requires much more ATP and would not be energetically efficient.

3. **C** Discussed in impulse propagation section of this chapter.

4. **D** Discussed in action potential section of this chapter.

5.   First, the somatic nervous system regulates voluntary actions (except in the cases of monosynaptic and polysynaptic reflexes), whereas the autonomic nervous system regulates involuntary actions. Second, the somatic nervous system innervates skeletal muscle, whereas the autonomic nervous system innervates cardiac and smooth muscle.

6. **B** Discussed in action potential section of this chapter.

7. **A** Discussed in vertebrate nervous system section of this chapter.

8. **C** Discussed in vertebrate nervous system section of this chapter.

9. **E** Discussed in special senses section of this chapter.

10. **B** When the neuron goes past the resting potential and becomes even more negative inside than normal, this is termed hyperpolarization.

11. **C** Acetylcholine is inactivated in the synaptic cleft by the enzyme acetycholinesterase after it has acted upon the postsynaptic membrane. If chemical X denatures acetylcholinesterase, acetylcholinesterase will not be able to inactivate acetylcholine and prevent the continuous depolarization of the effector membrane.

12. **D** Discussed in peripheral nervous system section of this chapter.

13. **B** Discussed in special senses section of this chapter.

CHAPTER TWELVE

Muscular and Skeletal Systems

The musculoskeletal system forms the basic internal framework of the vertebrate body. Muscles and bones work in close coordination to produce voluntary movement. In addition, bone and muscle perform a number of other independent functions. Physical support and locomotion are the functions of animal skeletal systems, while the muscular system generates force.

SKELETAL SYSTEM

An endoskeleton serves as the framework within all vertebrate organisms. Muscles are attached to the bones, permitting movement. The endoskeleton also provides protection by surrounding delicate internal organs with bone. The rib cage protects the thoracic organs (heart and lungs), whereas the skull and vertebral column protect the brain and spinal cord. The two major components of the skeleton are cartilage and bone.

Structure of the Skeleton

Cartilage

Cartilage is a type of connective tissue that is softer and more flexible than bone. Cartilage is retained in adults in places where firmness and flexibility are needed. For example, in humans, the external ear, nose, walls of the larynx and trachea, and skeletal joints contain cartilage. **Chrondrocytes** are cells responsible for synthesizing cartilage.

Bone

Bone is a specialized type of mineralized connective tissue that has the ability to withstand physical stress. Ideally adapted for body support, bone tissue is hard and strong while at the same time somewhat elastic and lightweight. There are two basic types of bone: compact bone and spongy bone.

1. **Compact bone** is dense bone that does not appear to have any cavities when observed with the naked eye. The bony matrix is deposited in structural units called **osteons** (Haversian systems). Each osteon consists of a central microscopic channel called a **Haversian canal**, surrounded by a number of concentric circles of bony matrix (calcium phosphate) called **lamellae**.

2. **Spongy bone** is much less dense and consists of an interconnecting lattice of bony **spicules** (trabeculae); the cavities between the spicules are filled with yellow or red bone marrow. **Yellow marrow** is inactive and infiltrated by adipose tissue; **red marrow** is involved in blood cell formation.

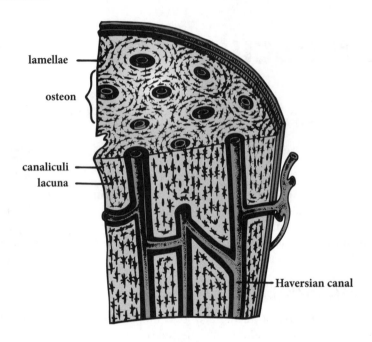

Figure 12.1

Osteocytes

Two types of cells found in bone tissue are osteoblasts and osteoclasts. **Osteoblasts** synthesize and secrete the organic constituents of the bone matrix; once they have become surrounded by their matrix they mature into osteocytes. **Osteoclasts** are large, multinucleated cells involved in bone reabsorption, wherein bone is broken down and minerals are released into the blood.

Bone formation

Bone formation occurs by either endochondral ossification or by intramembranous ossification. In **endochondral ossification**, existing cartilage is replaced by bone. Long bones arise primarily through endochondral ossification. In **intramembranous ossification**, mesenchymal (embryonic or undifferentiated) connective tissue is transformed into and replaced by bone.

Organization of the Skeleton

The axial skeleton is the basic framework of the body, consisting of the skull, vertebral column, and rib cage. It is the point of attachment of the appendicular skeleton, which includes the bones of the appendages (limbs) and the pectoral and pelvic girdles.

Bones are held together in a number of ways. Sutures or immovable joints hold the bones of the skull together. Bones that move relative to one another are held together by movable joints and are additionally supported and strengthened by ligaments. Ligaments serve as bone-to-bone connectors. Tendons attach skeletal muscle to bones and bend the skeleton at the movable joints.

The point of attachment of a muscle to a stationary bone (proximal end in limb muscles) is called the **origin**. The point of attachment of a muscle to the bone that moves (distal end in limb muscles) is called the **insertion**. **Extension** indicates a straightening of a joint, whereas **flexion** refers to a bending of a joint.

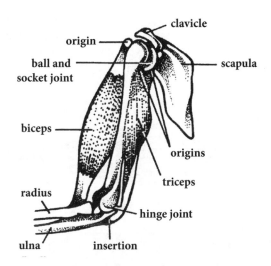

Figure 12.2

MUSCULAR SYSTEM

Muscle tissue consists of bundles of specialized contractile fibers held together by connective tissue. There are three morphologically and functionally distinct types of muscle in mammals: skeletal muscle, smooth muscle, and cardiac muscle.

Nervous control of the muscular system involves the axons of the pyramidal cells of the motor cortex, which descend from the brain to synapse on lower motor neurons in the brain stem and spinal cord. Because there are no intervening synapses, the **pyramidal system** is able to provide rapid commands to the skeletal muscles and various other organs. Several other centers can issue somatic motor commands as a result of processing performed at the unconscious, involuntary level. These centers and their associated tracts comprise the **extrapyramidal system**. The red nucleus, located in the mesencephalon, is the component of the extrapyramidal system primarily in control of skeletal muscle tone.

BIO

Skeletal Muscle

Skeletal muscle is responsible for voluntary movements and is innervated by the somatic nervous system. Each fiber is a multinucleated cell created by the fusion of several mononucleated embryonic cells. Embedded in the fibers are filaments called **myofibrils**, which are further divided into contractile units called **sarcomeres**. The myofibrils are enveloped by a modified endoplasmic reticulum that stores calcium ions and is called the **sarcoplasmic reticulum**. The cytoplasm of a muscle fiber is called sarcoplasm, and the cell membrane is called the sarcolemma. The **sarcolemma** is capable of propagating an action potential and is connected to a system of transverse tubules (T system) oriented perpendicularly to the myofibrils. The **T system** provides channels for ion flow throughout the muscle fibers and can also propagate an action potential. Because of the high-energy requirements of contraction, mitochondria are very abundant in muscle cells and are distributed along the myofibrils. Skeletal muscle has striations of light and dark bands and is therefore also referred to as **striated muscle**.

Figure 12.3

BIO

Sarcomeres

The sarcomere is composed of thin and thick filaments. The thin filaments are chains of actin molecules. The thick filaments are composed of organized bundles of myosin molecules.

Electron microscopy reveals that the sarcomere is organized as follows: **Z lines** define the boundaries of a single sarcomere and anchor the thin filaments. The **M line** runs down the center of the sarcomere. The **I band** is the region containing thin filaments only. The **H zone** is the region containing thick filaments only. The **A band** spans the entire length of the thick filaments and any overlapping portions of the thin filaments. When the muscles contract, the Z lines move toward each other. Note that during contraction, the A band is not reduced in size, whereas the H zone and I band are.

Figure 12.4

Contraction

Muscle contraction is stimulated by a message from the somatic nervous system sent via a motor neuron. The link between the nerve terminal (synaptic bouton) and the sarcolemma of the muscle fiber is called the **neuromuscular junction**. The space between the two is known as the synapse, or synaptic cleft. Depolarization of the motor neuron results in the release of neurotransmitters (e.g., acetylcholine) from the nerve terminal. The neurotransmitter diffuses across the synaptic cleft and binds to special receptor sites on the sarcolemma. If enough of these receptors are stimulated, the permeability of the sarcolemma is altered and an action potential is generated.

Once an action potential is generated, it is conducted along the sarcolemma and the T system and into the interior of the muscle fiber. This causes the sarcoplasmic reticulum to release calcium ions into the sarcoplasm. Calcium ions initiate the contraction of the sarcomere by binding to troponin C on the actin filaments. Allosteric changes occur in the proteins that allow myosin heads to bind to these sites on the actin. Use of energy allows a power stroke to occur, pulling the Z bands closer together. Actin and myosin slide past each other, and the sarcomere contracts.

An interesting point is that several hours after death, all of the muscles in the body go into a state of **rigor mortis**. In this condition, the muscles contract and become rigid, even without action potentials. The rigidity is caused by an absence of adenosine triphosphate (ATP), which is required for the myosin heads to be released from the actin filaments. The muscles typically remain rigid for 12 to 24 hours after death until the muscle proteins degrade.

There are five major types of muscle contractions: isotonic, dynamic, concentric, eccentric, and isometric. An **isotonic** contraction occurs when a muscle shortens against a fixed load while the tension on that muscle remains constant. A **dynamic** contraction includes both concentric and eccentric types of contractions. In general, a dynamic contraction results in a change in length of the muscle with a corresponding change in tension on that muscle. A **concentric** contraction is a type of dynamic contraction where the muscle fibers shorten and the tension on the muscle increases. An **eccentric** contraction is a type of dynamic contraction where the muscle fiber lengthens and the tension on the muscle increases. An **isometric** contraction occurs when both ends of the muscle are fixed and no change in length occurs during the contraction, but the tension increases.

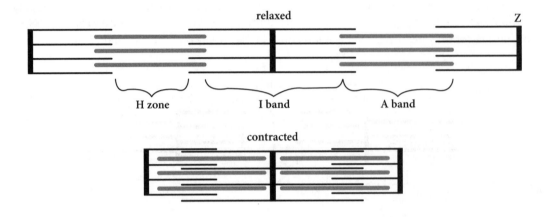

Figure 12.5

Stimulus and muscle response

Individual muscle fibers generally exhibit an all-or-none response; only a stimulus above a minimal value, called the threshold value, can elicit a contraction. The strength of the contraction of a single muscle fiber cannot be increased, regardless of the strength of the stimulus. However, the strength of contraction of the entire muscle can be increased by recruiting more muscle fibers. The different types of muscle responses are summarized as follows:

- A **simple twitch** is the response of a single muscle fiber to a brief stimulus at or above the threshold stimulus and consists of a latent period, a contraction period, and a relaxation period. The latent period is the time between stimulation and the onset of contraction. During this time lag, the action potential spreads along the sarcolemma, and Ca^{2+} ions are released. After the contraction period, there is a brief relaxation period during which the muscle is unresponsive to a stimulus; this period is known as the **absolute refractory period**.

- When the fibers of a muscle are exposed to very frequent stimuli, the muscle cannot fully relax. The contractions begin to combine, becoming stronger and more prolonged. This is known as **temporal summation**. The contractions become continuous when the stimuli are so frequent that the muscle cannot relax. This type of contraction is known as **tetanus** and is stronger than a simple twitch of a single fiber. If tetanus is maintained, the muscle will fatigue, and the contraction will weaken.

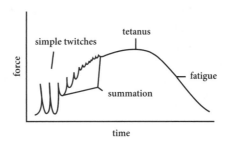

Figure 12.6

- **Tonus** is a state of partial contraction. Muscles are never completely relaxed and maintain a partially contracted state at all times.

During periods of strenuous activity, skeletal muscles convert glucose to pyruvic acid through the process of glycolysis. This process enables skeletal muscles to continue contracting even in the absence of oxygen. Lactic acid is generated when pyruvic acid reacts with the enzyme lactate dehydrogenase. This process allows the pyruvate to enter the citric acid (or Krebs) cycle.

The purpose of the **Cori cycle** during periods of strenuous activity is to convert lactic acid in the liver to glucose for discharge into the bloodstream. Once the glucose is in the blood, the muscles are then able to use the glucose as an immediate source of energy or to rebuild their glycogen reserves. Conversion of glucose into pyruvate in the muscle cells is necessary for the creation of ATP during periods of strenuous exercise and does not involve the Cori cycle. During periods of intense exercise, the production of lactic acid is increased and glycogen is broken down into glucose; however, it is not by means of the Cori cycle.

Smooth Muscle

Smooth muscle is responsible for involuntary actions and is innervated by the autonomic nervous system. Smooth muscle is found in the digestive tract, bladder, uterus, and blood vessel walls, among other places. Smooth muscle cells possess one centrally located nucleus and lack the striations of skeletal muscle.

Cardiac Muscle

The muscle tissue of the heart is composed of cardiac muscle fibers. These fibers possess characteristics of both skeletal and smooth muscle fibers. As in skeletal muscle, actin and myosin filaments are arranged in sarcomeres, giving cardiac muscle a striated appearance. However, cardiac muscle cells generally have only one or two centrally located nuclei.

BIO

Comparison of Different Muscle Types		
Smooth Muscle	**Cardiac Muscle**	**Skeletal Muscle**
• Nonstriated • One nucleus per cell • Involuntary/autonomic nervous system • Smooth, continuous contractions	• Striated • One to two nuclei per cell • Involuntary/autonomic nervous system • Strong, forceful contractions	• Striated • Multinucleated cells • Voluntary/somatic nervous system • Strong, forceful contractions

Table 12.1

Energy Reserves

ATP is the primary source of energy for muscle contraction. Very little ATP is actually stored in the muscles, so other forms of energy must be stored and rapidly converted to ATP.

Creatine phosphate

In vertebrates, energy can be temporarily stored in a high-energy compound called creatine phosphate.

Myoglobin

Myoglobin is a hemoglobin-like protein found in muscle tissue. Myoglobin has a high oxygen affinity and maintains the oxygen supply in muscles by tightly binding to oxygen.

REVIEW PROBLEMS

Questions 1, 2, and 3 are based on the following diagram:

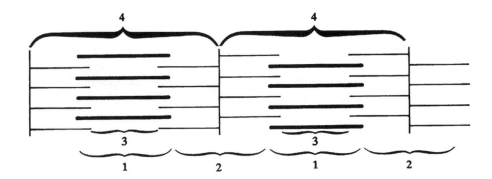

1. During muscle contraction, which of the following regions decrease(s) in length?

   A. 1 only

   B. 2 only

   C. 4 only

   D. 2, 3, and 4

   E. 2 and 3

2. Region 1 refers to

   A. the thick filaments only.

   B. the thin filaments only.

   C. the A band.

   D. the I band.

   E. the Z band.

3. Which of the following region(s) represents exactly one sarcomere?

   A. 1

   B. 2

   C. 3

   D. 4

   E. 1 and 2 together

4. Which of the following cells is correctly coupled with its definition?

   A. Osteoblasts—bone cells involved in the secretion of bone matrix

   B. Osteoclasts—immature bone cells

   C. Osteocytes—multinucleated cells actively involved in bone reabsorption

   D. Chondrocytes—undifferentiated bone marrow cells

   E. Chondrocytes—multinucleated cells actively involved in bone reabsorption

5. Describe the microscopic structure of compact bone. Include the following terms in your discussion: bone matrix, osteon, Haversian canal, lamellae, and osteocyte.

BIO

6. When a muscle fiber is subjected to very frequent stimuli

   A. an oxygen debt is incurred.
   B. a muscle tonus is generated.
   C. the threshold value is reached.
   D a simple twitch is repeatedly generated.
   E. tetanus occurs.

7. When a muscle is attached to two bones, usually only one of the bones moves. The part of the muscle attached to the stationary bone is referred to as

   A. proximal.
   B. distal.
   C. origin.
   D. insertion.
   E. ventral.

8. Two processes are involved in bone formation. How do they differ from one another?

Questions 9–11 refer to the following types of muscle:

   I. Cardiac muscle
   II. Skeletal muscle
   III. Smooth muscle

9. Which type of muscle is always multinucleated?

   A. I only
   B. II only
   C. III only
   D. Both I and II
   E. Both II and III

10. Which type of muscle has strong, forceful contractions?

   A. I only
   B. II only
   C. III only
   D. Both I and III
   E. Both I and II

11. Which type of muscle lacks sarcomeric striations?

   A. I only
   B. II only
   C. III only
   D. Both II and III
   E. None of the above

SOLUTIONS TO REVIEW PROBLEMS

1. **D** Discussed in the sarcomere section in this chapter.

2. **C** Discussed in the sarcomere section in this chapter.

3. **D** Discussed in the sarcomere section in this chapter.

4. **A** Discussed in structure of vertebrate skeleton section in this chapter.

5. Discussed in structure of vertebrate skeleton section in this chapter.

6. **E** Discussed in summation section of stimulus and muscle response in this chapter.

7. **C** Discussed in muscle/bone interactions section in this chapter.

8. The processes involved in bone formation are endochondral ossification and intramembranous ossification. In endochrondral ossification, cartilage is replaced with bone. In intramembranous ossification, mesenchyme, or undifferentiated cells, are transformed into bone cells.

9. **B** Discussed in skeletal muscle section in this chapter.

10. **E** Discussed in smooth muscle and cardiac muscle sections in this chapter.

11. **C** Discussed in smooth muscle section in this chapter.

CHAPTER THIRTEEN

Circulatory and Respiratory Systems

The human cardiovascular system is composed of a muscular, four-chambered heart, a network of blood vessels, and the blood itself. Blood is pumped into the **aorta**, which branches into a series of **arteries**. The arteries branch into **arterioles** and then into microscopic **capillaries**. Exchange of gases, nutrients, and cellular waste products occurs via diffusion across capillary walls. The capillaries then converge into **venules** and eventually into **veins**, which carry deoxygenated blood back toward the heart. From the heart, deoxygenated blood is pumped to the **lungs**, where CO_2 is exchanged for O_2, and this oxygenated blood returns to the heart to be pumped throughout the body once more.

Figure 13.1

THE HEART

The heart is the driving force of the circulatory system. The right and left halves can be viewed as two separate pumps: the right side of the heart pumps **deoxygenated** blood into **pulmonary** circulation (toward the lungs), whereas the left side pumps **oxygenated** blood into **systemic** circulation (throughout the body). The two upper chambers are called **atria**, and the two lower chambers are called **ventricles**. The atria are thin-walled, whereas the ventricles are extremely muscular. The left ventricle is more muscular than the right ventricle because it is responsible for generating the force that propels the systemic circulation and because it pumps against a higher resistance. As a result, in patients with increased systemic resistance, the left ventricle can become hypertrophied (enlarged), which over time can lead to congestive heart failure and other cardiovascular diseases.

Blood returning from the body first flows through the right atrium, then through the tricuspid valve into the right ventricle, and finally through the pulmonary semilunar valve into the pulmonary arteries to continue to the lungs. Blood returning from the lungs flows through the pulmonary veins into the left atrium, then through the mitral valve into the left ventricle, and finally out through the aortic semilunar valve into the systemic circulation.

Figure 13.2

BIO

Valves

The **atrioventricular valves**, located between the atria and ventricles on both sides of the heart, prevent backflow of blood into the atria. The valve on the right side of the heart has three cusps and is called the **tricuspid valve**. The valve on the left side of the heart has two cusps and is called the **mitral valve**. The **semilunar valves** have three cusps and are located between the left ventricle and the aorta (the aortic valve) and between the right ventricle and the pulmonary artery (the pulmonic valve). The "lub-dub" sound of a heartbeat is made by the successive closing of the atrioventricular and semilunar valves.

Contraction

The heart's pumping cycle is divided into two alternating phases, **systole** and **diastole,** which together make up the **heartbeat.** Systole is the period during which the ventricles contract, forcing blood out of the heart into the pulmonary and systemic circulation. Diastole is the period of cardiac muscle relaxation during which blood drains into all four chambers. This is reflected in physiologic measurements such as blood pressure. Systolic blood pressure measures the pressure in a patient's blood vessels when the ventricles are contracting, and diastolic blood pressure measures the pressure during cardiac relaxation. **Cardiac output** is defined as the total volume of blood the left ventricle pumps out per minute. Cardiac output = **heart rate** (number of beats per minute) × **stroke volume** (volume of blood pumped out of the left ventricle per contraction).

Control of heart rate

Cardiac muscle contracts rhythmically without stimulation from the nervous system, producing impulses that spread through its internal conducting system. An ordinary cardiac contraction originates in, and is regulated by, the **sinoatrial (SA) node** (the **pacemaker**), a small mass of specialized tissue located in the wall of the right atrium. The SA node spreads impulses through both atria, stimulating them to contract simultaneously. The impulse arrives at the **atrioventricular (AV) node**, which slowly conducts impulses to the rest of the heart, allowing enough time for atrial contraction and for the ventricles to fill with blood. The impulse is then carried by the **bundle of His (AV bundle)**, which branches into the right and left bundle branches, and finally through the **Purkinje fibers** in the walls of both ventricles, stimulating a strong contraction. This contraction forces blood out of the heart into circulation.

BIO

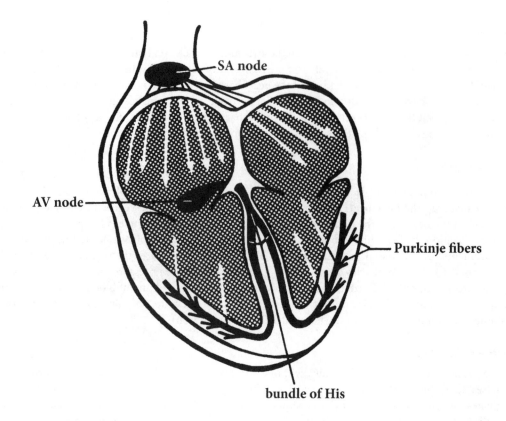

Figure 13.3

The **autonomic nervous system** modifies the rate of heart contraction. The parasympathetic nervous system innervates the heart via the **vagus nerve** and causes a decrease in heart rate. The sympathetic nervous system innervates the heart via the cervical and upper thoracic ganglia and causes an increase in heart rate. The adrenal medulla exerts hormonal control via epinephrine (adrenaline) secretion, which causes an increase in heart rate.

BLOOD VESSELS

The three types of blood vessels are arteries, veins, and capillaries. **Arteries** are thick-walled, muscular, elastic vessels that transport oxygenated blood away from the heart—except for the **pulmonary arteries**, which transport deoxygenated blood from the heart to the lungs. **Veins** are relatively thin-walled, inelastic vessels that conduct deoxygenated blood toward the heart—except for the **pulmonary veins**, which carry oxygenated blood from the lungs to the heart. Much of the blood flow in veins depends on their compression by skeletal muscles during movement rather than on the pumping of the heart. Venous circulation is often at odds with gravity; thus, larger veins, especially those in the legs, have valves that prevent backflow. Capillaries have very thin walls composed of a single layer of endothelial cells across which respiratory gases, nutrients, enzymes, hormones, and wastes can readily diffuse. **Capillaries** have the smallest diameter of all three types of vessels; red blood cells must often travel through them single file.

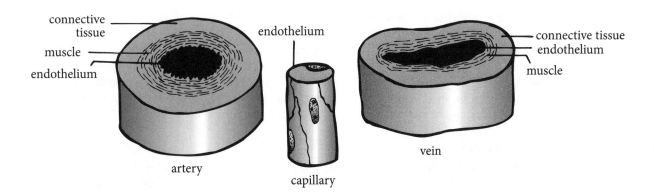

Figure 13.4

Lymph Vessels

The lymphatic system is a secondary circulatory system distinct from the cardiovascular circulation. Its vessels transport excess **interstitial fluid**, called **lymph**, to the cardiovascular system, thereby keeping **fluid** levels in the body constant. The smallest lymphatic vessels (**lacteals**) collect fats, in the form of chylomicrons, from the villi in the small intestine and deliver them into the bloodstream, bypassing the liver. **Lymph** nodes are swellings along lymph vessels containing phagocytic cells (**lymphocytes**) that filter the lymph, removing and destroying foreign particles and pathogens (see Chapter 10, Integumentary and Immunological Systems).

BLOOD

On average, the human body contains four to six liters of blood. Blood has both liquid components (55 percent) and cellular components (45 percent). **Plasma** is liquid portion of the blood. It is an aqueous mixture of nutrients, salts, respiratory gases, wastes, hormones, and blood proteins (e.g., immunoglobulins, albumin, and fibrinogen). The cellular components of blood are erythrocytes, leukocytes, and platelets.

Leukocytes

Leukocytes (known as **white blood cells,** or WBCs) are larger than erythrocytes and serve protective functions. White blood cells are discussed further in the context of immunity in Chapter 10.

Platelets

Platelets are cell **fragments** that lack nuclei and are involved in clot formation. Many drugs inhibit platelet formation or adhesion to decrease clot development.

Erythrocytes

Erythrocytes (known as **red blood cells,** or RBCs) are the oxygen-carrying components of blood. An erythrocyte contains approximately 250 million molecules of hemoglobin, each of which can bind up to four molecules of oxygen. When hemoglobin binds oxygen it is called **oxyhemoglobin**. This is the primary form of oxygen transport in the blood. Erythrocytes have a distinct biconcave, disk-like shape that gives them both increased surface area for gas exchange and greater flexibility for movement through tiny capillaries. **Erythrocytes** are formed from stem cells in the **bone marrow**; their formation is stimulated by erythropoietin, a hormone made in the kidneys. In the bone marrow, erythrocytes lose their nuclei, mitochondria, and membranous organelles. Once mature, erythrocytes circulate in the blood for about 120 days, after which they are phagocytized by special cells in the spleen and liver. Finding immature erythrocytes circulating in the bloodstream—that is, before they have lost their organelles—can be an indicator of a number of disease states, such as hemolytic anemia, which is caused by the rapid destruction of red blood cells due to an infection or disorder.

ABO blood types

Erythrocytes have characteristic cell-surface proteins (**antigens**). Antigens are macromolecules that are foreign to the host organism and trigger an immune response. The two major groups of red blood cell antigens are the **ABO group** and the **Rh factor**.

Characteristics of Human Blood Types				
Blood Type	**Antigen**	**Antibody**	**Can Donate To**	**Can Receive From**
A	A	anti-B	A and AB	A and O
B	B	anti-A	B and AB	B and O
AB	A and B	none	AB only	all (universal acceptor)
O	none	anti-A and anti-B	all (universal donor)	O only

Table 13.1

It is extremely important during blood transfusions that **donor** and **recipient** blood types be appropriately matched. The aim is to avoid transfusion of red blood cells that will be clumped ("rejected") by antibodies (proteins in the immune system that bind specifically to antigens) present in the recipient's plasma. For example, a person with blood type A has antigens for type A blood and antibodies for type B blood. This means that, if transfused with any blood containing type B antigens (type B or type AB blood), they will mount an immune response, and their anti-B antibodies will clump and "reject" the transfusion. Therefore, to avoid rejection of the transfusion, the recipient must have a natural blood type with the same antigens as the blood type being transfused. For example, if a patient with type O blood is given blood of any type except type O, they will reject the transfusion because they do not have type A or type B antigens and as a result have anti-A and anti-B antibodies.

Type AB blood is termed the "**universal recipient**," as it has neither anti-A nor anti-B antibodies and therefore will not reject transfusions of any blood type. **Type O** blood is considered to be the "**universal donor**"; it will not elicit a response from the recipient's immune system because it does not possess any surface antigens.

Rh factor

The Rh factor is another antigen that may be present on the surface of red blood cells. Individuals may be Rh+, possessing the Rh antigen, or Rh−, lacking the Rh antigen. Consideration of the Rh factor is particularly important during **pregnancy**. An Rh− woman can be sensitized by an **Rh+ fetus** if fetal red blood cells (which will have the Rh factor) enter maternal circulation during birth. If this woman subsequently carries another Rh+ fetus, the anti-Rh antibodies she produced when sensitized by the first birth may cross the placenta and destroy fetal red blood cells. This results in a type of severe anemia in the fetus known as **erythroblastosis fetalis**. Erythroblastosis is not caused by ABO blood-type mismatches between mother and fetus because anti-A and anti-B antibodies cannot cross the placenta. Rhogam is a drug comprised of a mixture of antibodies given to mothers who are Rh– to prevent their immune systems from attacking the fetal red blood cells.

Rh factor is also an issue with blood transfusions. If patients who do not possess the Rh antigen (that is, who are Rh–) are given blood that is Rh+, their bodies can mount an immune response and reject the transfusion.

FUNCTIONS OF THE CIRCULATORY SYSTEM

Blood transports nutrients and O_2 to tissue and wastes and CO_2 from tissue. Platelets in the blood are involved in injury repair, and leukocytes in the blood are the main component of the immune system (see Chapter 10).

Transport of Gases

Erythrocytes transport O_2 throughout the circulatory system. The hemoglobin molecules in erythrocytes bind to O_2. Hemoglobin contains iron and each hemoglobin molecule is capable of binding to four molecules of O_2. Hemoglobin also binds to CO_2, in which case it is referred to as carbaminohemoglobin.

Transport of Nutrients and Waste

Amino acids and **simple sugars** are absorbed into the bloodstream at the intestinal capillaries. Throughout the body, metabolic **waste products** (e.g., water, urea, and carbon dioxide) diffuse into capillaries from surrounding cells; these wastes are then delivered to the appropriate excretory organs.

Clotting

When platelets come into contact with the exposed collagen of a damaged vessel, they release a chemical that causes neighboring platelets to adhere to one another, forming a **platelet plug**. Subsequently, both the platelets and the damaged tissue release the clotting factor thromboplastin. **Thromboplastin**, with the aid of its cofactors calcium and vitamin K, converts the inactive plasma protein **prothrombin** to its active form, **thrombin**. Thrombin then converts **fibrinogen** (another plasma protein) into fibrin. Threads of **fibrin** coat the damaged area and trap blood cells to form a clot. Clots prevent extensive blood loss while the damaged vessel heals itself. The fluid left after blood clotting is called **serum**. This complex series of reactions is called the **clotting cascade.**

Warfarin, a commonly used anticoagulant, works by inhibiting the recycling of vitamin K. Without this essential cofactor, the clotting cycle is inhibited and patients are less likely to be able to form clots. Other types of anticoagulant medications work at other points along the clotting cascade.

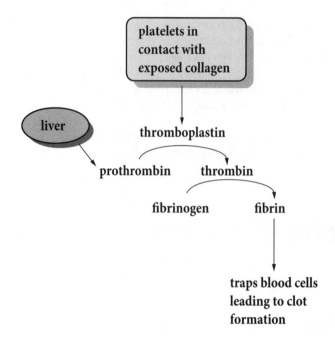

Figure 13.5

THE RESPIRATORY SYSTEM

In the human respiratory system, air enters the **lungs** after traveling through a series of respiratory **airways**. The air passages consist of the nose, pharynx (throat), larynx, trachea, bronchi, bronchioles, and alveoli. Gas exchange between the lungs and the circulatory system occurs across the very thin walls of the **alveoli,** which are air-filled sacs at the terminals of the airway branches. Three hundred million alveoli provide approximately 100 m^2 of moist respiratory surface for gas exchange. After gas exchange, air travels back through the respiratory pathway and is exhaled.

The respiratory system also provides a very large area for gas exchange, continually moving oxygenated air over this area and protecting the respiratory surface from infection, dehydration, and temperature changes. It moves air over the vocal cords for the production of sound and assists in the regulation of body pH by regulating the rate of carbon dioxide removal from the blood.

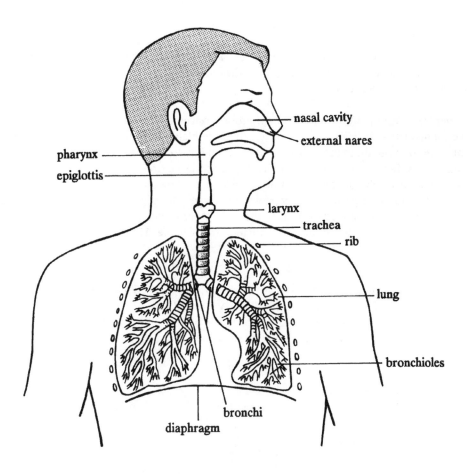

Figure 13.6

Ventilation

Ventilation of the lungs (breathing) is the process by which air is inhaled and exhaled. The purpose of ventilation is to take in oxygen from the atmosphere and eliminate carbon dioxide from the body.

During **inhalation,** the diaphragm contracts and flattens, and the external intercostal muscles contract, pushing the rib cage and chest wall up and out. The phrenic nerve innervates the diaphragm and causes it to contract and flatten. These actions cause the thoracic cavity to increase in volume. This volume increase reduces the pressure, causing the lungs to expand and fill with air.

Exhalation is generally a passive process. The lungs and chest wall are highly elastic and tend to recoil to their original positions after inhalation. The diaphragm and external intercostal muscles relax and the chest wall pushes inward. The consequent decrease in thoracic cavity volume causes the pressure to increase. This forces air out of the alveoli, causing the lungs to deflate.

Surfactant is a protein complex secreted by cells in the lungs. Surfactant keeps the lungs from collapsing by decreasing surface tension in the alveoli. Babies born prematurely do not always produce surfactant and must be given artificial surfactants until they can produce their own.

Control of ventilation

Ventilation is regulated by neurons (referred to as **respiratory centers**) located in the **medulla oblongata.** When the partial pressure of CO_2 in the blood rises, the medulla oblongata stimulates an increase in the rate of ventilation.

The primary goal of respiration is to maintain proper concentrations of oxygen, carbon dioxide, and hydrogen ions in tissues. Hence, respiratory activity is highly responsive to changes in the blood levels of these compounds. Excessive carbon dioxide and hydrogen ion levels are the primary stimuli for respiration. When carbon dioxide and hydrogen ion levels are increased, the respiratory center stimulates both the inspiratory and expiratory muscles of the lungs. Oxygen blood levels do not have a significant effect on the respiratory center. However, oxygen blood levels are monitored by peripheral **chemoreceptors**, which indirectly stimulate the respiratory center. Changes in acid-base chemistry due to kidney function can also influence ventilation (see Chapter 15, Urinary System).

Gas Exchange

A dense network of minute blood vessels called **pulmonary capillaries** surrounds the alveoli. Gas exchange occurs by diffusion across these capillary walls and those of the alveoli; gases move from regions of higher partial pressure to regions of lower partial pressure. Oxygen diffuses from the alveolar air into the blood, while carbon dioxide diffuses from the blood into the lungs.

Figure 13.7

Lung Capacities

The volume of air in the lungs changes throughout respiration. **Total lung capacity** represents the maximum volume of air the lungs can hold. The volume of air moved during a normal resting breath is known as the tidal volume, which is significantly less than the total lung capacity. The volume of air that could be additionally inhaled into the lungs at the end of a normal, resting inhalation is called the inspiratory reserve volume. The volume of air left in the lungs at the end of a normal, resting exhalation is called the expiratory reserve volume. The vital capacity is the volume of air moved during a maximum inhalation followed by a maximum exhalation. Even after maximum exhalation, there is always some air left in the lungs. This is known as the residual volume.

Figure 13.8

REVIEW PROBLEMS

1. Erythrocytes are anaerobic. Why is this advantageous for the organism?

2. The lymphatic system
    A. transports hormones throughout the body.
    B. transports absorbed chylomicrons to the circulatory system.
    C. filters the blood.
    D. contains vessels that are nearly identical to arteries.
    E. contains more erythrocytes than leukocytes.

3. Draw the reactions of the clotting process. Include all of the proteins and cofactors involved.

4. What role do the surface proteins on erythrocytes play in blood transfusions?

5. All of the following facilitate gas exchange in the lungs EXCEPT
    A. thin alveolar surfaces.
    B. moist alveolar surfaces.
    C. differences in the partial pressures of O_2 and CO_2.
    D. active transport.
    E. large surface areas.

6. What muscles play a role in ventilation? Compare the muscular motions involved in inhalation with those involved in exhalation.

7. Which is the correct sequence of the passages that air travels through during inhalation?
    A. Pharynx → Trachea → Bronchioles → Bronchi → Alveoli
    B. Pharynx → Trachea → Lungs → Bronchi → Alveoli
    C. Pharynx → Larynx → Bronchi → Trachea → Alveoli
    D. Pharynx → Larynx → Trachea → Bronchi → Alveoli
    E. Pharynx → Trachea → Larynx → Bronchi → Alveoli

8. Which of the following is generally an active process?
    A. Inhalation
    B. Exhalation
    C. Gas exchange
    D. Diffusion
    E. Osmosis

SOLUTIONS TO REVIEW PROBLEMS

1. If erythrocytes were aerobic, they would use some of the O_2 that they carry for their own energy requirements, thus decreasing the amount of O_2 transported to the rest of the body. Because they are anaerobic, they do not have any O_2 requirements of their own and can deliver all the O_2 they carry to other cells.

2. **B** The main function of the lymphatic system is to collect excess interstitial fluid and return it to the circulatory system, maintaining the balance of body fluids. However, this is not one of the answer choices. A second function of the lymphatic system is to absorb chylomicrons from the small intestine and deliver them to cardiovascular circulation; this is choice (B). The remaining answer choices describe the circulatory system but not the lymphatic system.

3. See Figure 13.5.

4. In a blood transfusion, the donor blood must be carefully matched with the blood of the recipient. If the erythrocytes in the donor blood have a different class of surface proteins (antigens) than the recipient's erythrocytes, the recipient's immune system might "attack" the surface protein of the donor, thus rejecting the donor blood. For example, if the donor blood is type A and the recipient blood is type B, the recipient's anti-A antibodies would attack the donor's erythrocytes, because type A blood has type A antigens.

5. **D** Discussed in gas exchange section of this chapter.

6. The muscles involved in ventilation are the diaphragm, which separates the thoracic cavity from the abdominal cavity, and the intercostal muscles of the rib cage. During inhalation the diaphragm contracts and flattens while the external intercostals contract, pushing the rib cage up and out. These actions cause an overall increase in the volume of the thoracic cavity. During exhalation both the diaphragm and the external intercostals relax, causing a decrease in the volume of the thoracic cavity. In forced expiration the internal intercostals contract, pulling the rib cage down.

7. **D** Discussed in vertebrate respiratory system section of this chapter.

8. **A** Exhalation is generally a passive process involving elastic recoil of the lungs and relaxation of both the diaphragm and the external intercostal muscles. (However, during vigorous exercise, active muscular contraction assists in expiration.) Gas exchange, diffusion, and osmosis are also passive processes and involve molecules moving down their partial pressure gradients. Inhalation is an active process requiring contraction of the diaphragm and the external intercostals.

CHAPTER FOURTEEN

Digestive System

Humans are **heterotrophic** and thus unable to synthesize all of their own nutrients. Instead, food provides the raw material for energy, repair, and growth of tissues. This food must first be **ingested** (eaten), after which **digestion** (breakdown) occurs. **Digestion** consists of the degradation of large molecules into smaller molecules that can be **absorbed** into the bloodstream and used directly by cells. **Intracellular** digestion occurs within the cell, usually in membrane-bound vesicles. **Extracellular** digestion refers to a digestive process that occurs outside of the cell, within a lumen or tract.

DIGESTIVE TRACT

The human digestive tract begins with the **oral cavity** and continues with the **pharynx, esophagus, stomach, small intestine, large intestine,** and **anus.** Accessory organs, such as the salivary glands, pancreas, liver, and gallbladder, also play essential roles in digestion.

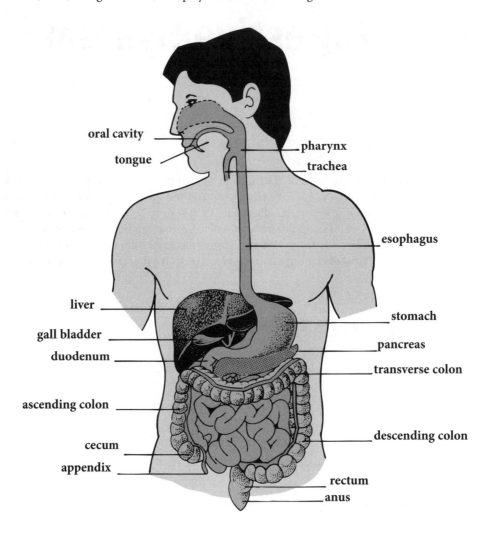

Figure 14.1

Oral Cavity

The oral cavity (the mouth) is where **mechanical** and **chemical** digestion of food begins. Mechanical digestion is the breakdown of large food particles into smaller particles through physical actions, such as the biting and chewing action of teeth (**mastication**) or the churning motion of the stomach. Chemical digestion refers to the enzymatic breakdown of macromolecules into smaller molecules and begins in the mouth when the salivary glands secrete **saliva**. Saliva **lubricates** food to facilitate swallowing and provides a solvent for food particles. Saliva is secreted in response to the presence of food in the oral cavity. Saliva contains the enzyme **salivary amylase** (**ptyalin**), which hydrolyzes starch to maltose (a disaccharide). Food that has been moistened and chewed enough to be swallowed is called a **bolus**.

Esophagus

The esophagus is the muscular tube leading from the mouth to the stomach. Food is moved down the esophagus by rhythmic waves of involuntary muscular contractions called **peristalsis**. The esophagus is closed off from the stomach by contraction of a muscular structure called the **lower esophageal (cardiac) sphincter**.

The body of the esophagus lies within the thoracic cavity, which is negatively pressured relative to the environment on inhalation. The abdominal cavity has a relative positive pressure. Therefore, without normal defense mechanisms, the pressure gradients favor a continual reflux of gastric (stomach) materials into the esophagus, resulting in a pathological condition known as gastroesophageal reflux disease (GERD). Physiologic changes associated with the gastroesophageal reflux are as follows:

- Reflux can occur after spontaneous transient lower esophageal sphincter relaxations not associated with swallowing.
- Patients with GERD usually have a decreased lower esophageal sphincter pressure (5–10 mmHg above gastric baseline pressure), leading to an increased passage of stomach contents into the esophagus.
- Resting pressures of the lower esophageal sphincter normally range from 15–35 mmHg above gastric baseline pressure.

Stomach

The stomach, a large, muscular organ located in the upper abdomen, stores and partially digests food. The walls of the stomach are lined by the gastric mucosa, a mucous membrane that contains the gastric glands. Mucous cells in gastric pits along the membrane secrete **mucus** to protect the stomach lining from the harshly acidic juices (pH = 2) present in the stomach. Chief cells found within the gastric glands synthesize pepsinogen, which is converted to **pepsin** upon contact with stomach acid and breaks down proteins. Parietal cells, also present within gastric glands, synthesize and release hydrochloric acid (HCl), which alters the pH of the stomach and kills bacteria, and intrinsic factor, which is necessary for the absorption of vitamin B_{12}. The churning of the stomach (mechanical digestion), combined with this enzymatic activity (chemical digestion), produces an acidic, semifluid mixture of partially digested food known as **chyme**. The chyme passes into the first segment of the small intestine, the **duodenum**, through the pyloric sphincter.

Small Intestine

Chemical digestion is completed in the small intestine. The small intestine is divided into three sections: the **duodenum**, the **jejunum**, and the **ileum**. The small intestine is highly adapted to **absorption**. To maximize the surface area available for digestion and absorption, the intestine is extremely long (greater than six meters in length) and highly coiled. In addition, numerous finger-like projections called **villi** extend out of the intestinal wall. Villi contain capillaries and lacteals (vessels of the lymphatic system). Amino acids and monosaccharides pass through the villi walls into the capillary system. Blood from the digestive tract enters the portal system of the liver, where it is detoxified and stripped of some of its nutrients. Large fatty acids and glycerol pass into the lacteals and are then reconverted into triglycerides (fatty acid + glycerol) in the liver. Note that some nutrients, such as glucose and amino acids, are actively absorbed (i.e., requiring energy), whereas others are passively absorbed.

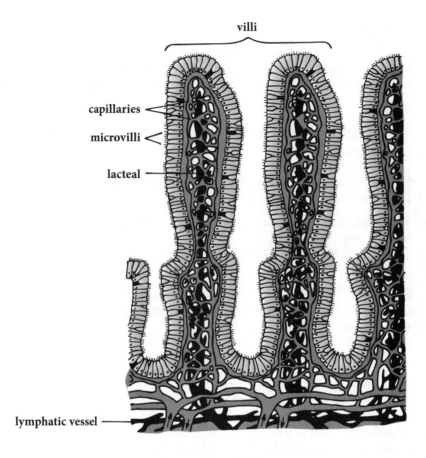

Figure 14.2

Most digestion in the small intestine occurs in the duodenum, where the secretions of the intestinal glands, pancreas, liver, and gallbladder mix together with the acidic chyme entering from the stomach. The intestinal mucosa secretes **lipases** (for fat digestion), **aminopeptidases** (for polypeptide digestion), and **disaccharidases** (for maltose, lactose, and sucrose digestion). For example, the disaccharidase **lactase** breaks down lactose (milk sugar). This enzyme is present in most infants, but many adults lack the enzyme and are **lactose-intolerant**. In these people, lactose in the small intestine cannot be digested and is instead metabolized by bacteria, producing large quantities of gas and resulting in intestinal discomfort.

Digestion Hormones

The activity of the digestive system is regulated by several hormones, which allow for optimum flow of materials through the digestive tract and help regulate the hunger and satiation mechanisms. These hormones include:

- **Gastrin**: produced in the G cells of the duodenum, gastrin primarily functions to stimulate histamine and pepsinogen secretion as well as increase gastric blood flow. Gastrin also stimulates the parietal cells to produce HCl, which denatures proteins and activates digestive enzymes.

- **Intrinsic factor**: a secretion of the parietal cells that facilitates the absorption of vitamin B_{12} across the intestinal lining.

- **Cholecystokinin (CCK)**: produced and stored in the I cells of the duodenal and jejunal mucosa. It is involved in stimulation of pancreatic enzyme and somatostatin secretion as well as gallbladder contraction. CCK also acts as a hunger suppressant.
- **Secretin**: synthesized and stored in the S cells of the upper intestine. It stimulates the secretion of bicarbonate-containing substances from the pancreas and inhibits gastric emptying and gastric acid production.

Liver

The liver produces **bile** that is stored in the **gallbladder** before being released into the small intestine. Bile contains no enzymes; it **emulsifies** fats, breaking down large globules into small droplets. Emulsification of fat exposes a greater surface area of the fat to the action of pancreatic lipase. In the absence of bile, fats cannot be digested. The liver's functions also include storage of glycogen, conversion of ammonia to urea, protein synthesis, detoxification, and cholesterol metabolism.

Pancreas

The pancreas produces enzymes such as **amylase** for carbohydrate digestion, **trypsin** for protein digestion, and **lipase** for fat digestion. When the pancreas releases chymotrypsin and enterokinase, enterokinase cleaves trypsinogen to trypsin. Trypsin then cleaves and activates the other zymogens (enzyme precursors). The pancreas secretes a bicarbonate-rich juice that neutralizes the acidic chyme arriving from the stomach in the duodenum. The pancreatic enzymes operate optimally at this higher pH.

Large Intestine

The large intestine is approximately 1.5 m long and absorbs salts and any water not already absorbed by the small intestine. The **rectum** provides for transient storage of feces before elimination through the anus.

REVIEW PROBLEMS

1. Define extracellular digestion. How is the stomach specialized for extracellular digestion?

2. Where are proteins digested?
   A. Mouth and stomach
   B. Stomach and large intestine
   C. Small intestine and large intestine
   D. Mouth and small intestine
   E. Stomach and small intestine

3. All of the following processes occur in the mouth EXCEPT
   A. mechanical digestion.
   B. moistening of food.
   C. bolus formation.
   D. chemical digestion of proteins.
   E. saliva secretion.

4. The graphs below show the relative activities of pepsin and chymotrypsin in solutions of varying pH. Which graph refers to which enzyme?

5. Outline the digestion of a piece of bread.

6. Why is pancreatic juice alkaline, and what would happen if its alkaline components were removed?

7. Starch is hydrolyzed into maltose by
   A. aminopeptidase.
   B. maltase.
   C. pancreatic amylase.
   D. sucrase.
   E. cholecystokinin.

8. The intestinal capillaries transport nutrients from the intestines to the
   A. large intestine.
   B. liver.
   C. kidney.
   D. heart.
   E. lungs.

SOLUTIONS TO REVIEW PROBLEMS

1. Digestion refers to a mechanical or chemical process whereby macromolecules are converted into smaller molecules that are more readily absorbed and used by cells. Extracellular digestion describes a process in which molecules are broken down outside of the cell. The stomach is a cavity perfectly adapted for extracellular digestion. Macromolecules are digested in an environment confined by the lower esophageal and pyloric sphincters. The cells lining the stomach walls are specialized for HCl and pepsinogen secretion by their ability to withstand acidic conditions. Muscular contractions aid in digestion by churning and crushing food. Little absorption occurs in the stomach; chyme is propelled into the small intestine, where further digestion and absorption occur.

2. **E** Protein digestion begins in the stomach with pepsin and continues in the small intestine.

3. **D** Chewing, the mechanical digestion of food, occurs in the mouth, as does moistening of food by saliva and bolus formation. In addition, salivary amylase begins digestion of complex carbohydrates.

4. Graph A refers to pepsin, whereas graph B refers to chymotrypsin. Pepsin is a gastric enzyme; it works best under the highly acidic conditions of the stomach. Chymotrypsin is an enzyme of the small intestine and thus operates optimally in alkaline environments.

5. In the mouth, teeth chew the bread into smaller particles, and salivary amylase digests some of the starch (the major component of bread) into maltose. The bread enters the stomach, where there is mechanical digestion of the bread into semiliquid chyme but no chemical digestion of starch. Chyme then enters the small intestine. In the small intestine, pancreatic amylase hydrolyzes starch into maltose while maltase, sucrase, and lactase hydrolyze various disaccharides into their respective monosaccharides. Most of the monosaccharides (e.g., glucose, fructose, and galactose) are absorbed into the circulatory system through the intestinal wall.

6. Pancreatic juice is an alkaline (basic) fluid that helps neutralize the acidity of the chyme entering the small intestine from the stomach. This is necessary because the small intestine enzymes work optimally at a neutral or alkaline pH. Also, the walls (mucosa) of the small intestine are not specialized for protection against acidic conditions. Therefore, without alkaline pancreatic juice, the intestinal enzymes would not function, and the intestinal walls would be damaged.

7. **C** Amylase, whether it is produced in the mouth or the pancreas, digests starch into maltose, a disaccharide.

8. **B** Intestinal capillaries transport amino acids and monosaccharides to the liver, where initial processing of many nutrients begins.

CHAPTER FIFTEEN

Urinary System

Excretion refers to the removal of **metabolic wastes** produced in the body. Most of the body's activities produce metabolic wastes, including mineral salts, that must be removed. **Aerobic respiration** leads to the production of **carbon dioxide** and water. **Deamination** of amino acids in the liver leads to the production of **nitrogenous wastes,** such as urea and ammonia. Excretion is distinguished from **elimination**, the removal of indigestible material, such as dietary fiber.

The principal organs of excretion in humans are the lungs, liver, skin, and kidneys. In the **lungs**, carbon dioxide and water vapor diffuse from the blood and are continually exhaled. Sweat glands in the **skin** excrete water and dissolved salts (and a small quantity of urea). Perspiration serves to regulate body temperature since the evaporation of sweat removes heat from the body. The **liver** processes nitrogenous wastes, hemoglobin, and other chemicals for excretion. Urea is produced by the deamination of amino acids in the liver and diffuses into the blood for ultimate excretion in the **kidneys**. Bile salts are excreted as bile and pass out with the feces. The kidneys function to maintain the osmolarity of the blood, excrete numerous waste products and toxic chemicals, and conserve glucose, salt, and water.

KIDNEYS

The kidneys regulate the concentration of salt and water in the blood through the formation and excretion of urine. The kidneys are bean-shaped and are located behind the stomach and liver. Each kidney is composed of approximately one million units called **nephrons**.

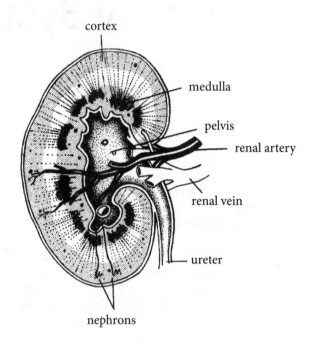

Figure 15.1

Structure

The kidney is divided into three regions: the outer **cortex**, the inner **medulla**, and the renal **pelvis**. A **nephron** consists of a bulb called **Bowman's capsule**, which embraces a special capillary bed called a **glomerulus**. Bowman's capsule leads to a long, coiled tubule divided into functionally distinct units: the **proximal convoluted tubule**, the **loop of Henle**, the **distal convoluted tubule**, and the **collecting duct**. The nephron is positioned such that the loop of Henle and collecting duct run through the medulla, while the convoluted tubules and Bowman's capsule are in the cortex. Concentrated urine in the collecting tubules flows into the pelvis of the kidney, a funnel-like region that opens into the **ureter**. The ureters from the kidneys empty into the **urinary bladder**, where urine collects until expelled via the **urethra**. Most of the nephron is surrounded by a complex **peritubular capillary** network that facilitates reabsorption of amino acids, glucose, salts, and water.

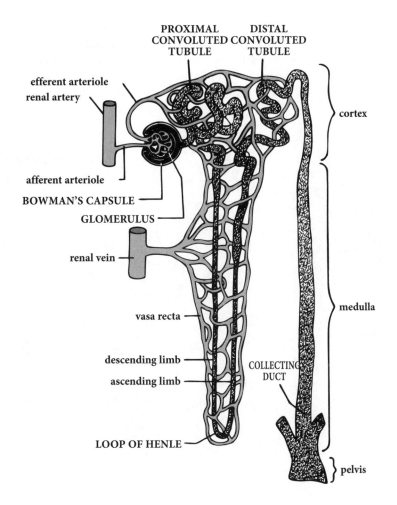

Figure 15.2

Urine Formation

Filtration, secretion, and reabsorption are the three processes that lead to urine formation.

- **Filtration**: Blood pressure forces 20 percent of the blood plasma entering the glomerulus through its capillary walls and into the surrounding Bowman's capsule. The fluid and small solutes entering the nephron are called the **filtrate**. The filtrate is isotonic with blood plasma. Particles too large to filter through the glomerulus, such as blood cells and albumin, remain in the circulatory system. Filtration is a passive process driven by the hydrostatic pressure of the blood. Having high blood pressure results in an increased hydrostatic pressure, which exerts extra pressure on the kidney tissues and can lead to kidney damage over time.

- **Secretion**: The nephron secretes waste substances such as acids, ions, and other metabolites from the interstitial fluid into the filtrate by both **passive** and **active** transport.

- **Reabsorption**: Essential substances (**glucose**, **salts**, and **amino acids**) and water are reabsorbed from the filtrate and returned to the blood. Reabsorption occurs primarily in the proximal convoluted tubule and is an active process. Movement of these molecules is accompanied by the passive movement of water because water passively follows solute. This results in the formation of **concentrated urine**, which is hypertonic to the blood.

Figure 15.3

Nephron Function

Through the **selective permeability** of its walls and the maintenance of an **osmolarity gradient**, the nephron is able to regulate the balance of salt and water in the body.

A primary function of the nephron is to clean the blood plasma of unwanted substances as the filtrate passes through the kidney. Because blood plasma contains both wanted and unwanted substances, the nephron will selectively reabsorb wanted substances back into the plasma, while the remaining substances are excreted in the urine. The primary site of nutrient reabsorption in the nephron is the proximal convoluted tubule. The loop of Henle and collecting duct play major roles in the regulation of water, sodium, and potassium concentrations in the nephron. The distal convoluted tubule is a major site for secretion of substances into the filtrate.

Each part of the loop of Henle plays a distinct role in regulating water absorption and electrolyte concentrations. The descending loop of Henle is very permeable to water but not to ions or urea. The thin ascending limb of the loop of Henle, however, is impermeable to water but is permeable to ions, allowing for passive diffusion of ions. In the thick ascending limb of the loop of Henle, sodium, potassium, and chloride are actively reabsorbed from the urine.

The production of concentrated urine is made possible by the establishment of an osmolarity gradient between the tubules and the interstitial fluid that surrounds them. By exiting and then re-entering at different segments of the nephron, solutes, such as Na^+ and Cl^-, create this osmolarity gradient, with tissue osmolarity increasing from the **cortex** to the **inner medulla**. The gradient depends upon a **counter-current-multiplier system,** a system in which energy is used to create a concentration gradient.

The counter-current multiplier system causes the interstitial space in the medulla of the kidney to be **hyperosmolar** with respect to the dilute filtrate flowing through the renal tubule. As the filtrate travels down the collecting ducts on its way to the pelvis and ureter, water flows from the ducts to the interstitial fluid through **osmosis**. This water returns to the systemic circulation via capillaries present in the medulla. The reabsorption of water in this zone of the kidney, which permits the concentration of urine, depends on the permeability of the collecting ducts to water. Regulation of the permeability of the collecting ducts to water is accomplished by **antidiuretic hormone (ADH),** also known as **vasopressin.** ADH increases the permeability of the collecting duct to water, allowing more water to be absorbed and more concentrated urine to be formed. In some disease states, people have excess secretion of ADH, which causes them to retain too much fluid.

Aldosterone is a steroid hormone that causes increased transport of sodium and potassium ions along the distal convoluted tubule and collecting duct, resulting in decreased excretion of sodium ions and increased excretion of potassium ions in the urine. Since water flows to the area of higher solute concentration through osmosis, this also causes additional water reabsorption. Furthermore, aldosterone does not affect renal blood flow.

ADH has the same net effect of increased water reabsorption as aldosterone. However, as discussed previously, ADH directly affects water absorption by the distal convoluted tubule and collecting ducts, opening additional **aquaporins** (water channels) in these structures to allow water to be reasborbed more readily. Both ADH and aldosterone cause a decrease in urine output and a corresponding increase in blood pressure, allowing the human body to compensate for periods of dehydration or other causes of low blood pressure.

Diuretics are drugs that target different parts of the kidneys to cause an increase in urine production. For example, loop diuretics inhibit sodium reabsorption in the ascending loop of the nephron, whereas thiazide diuretics inhibit the sodium-chloride transporter in the distal convoluted tubule. Both have the net effect of increasing the amount of water present in the urine and therefore increase urine excretion.

Maintenance of pH

Body fluid **pH** remains relatively constant at 7.4; this consistency is attained by the removal of carbon dioxide by the lungs and hydrogen ions by the kidneys. pH is assessed via the following laboratory tests:

- arterial pH
- arterial partial pressure of carbon dioxide (P_{CO_2})
- plasma bicarbonate (HCO_3^-)

There are two types of acid-base disorders:

1. **Respiratory**: affects the blood acidity by causing changes in the P_{CO_2}
2. **Metabolic**: affects the blood acidity by causing changes in the HCO_3^-

Below is a summary of acid-base disorders and compensatory mechanisms by the human body:

	Condition	Defect	Blood pH	Compensation
Respiratory	Acidosis	Increased P_{CO_2}	Decreased	Increased HCO_3^-
	Alkalosis	Decreased P_{CO_2}	Increased	Decreased HCO_3^-
Metabolic	Acidosis	Decreased HCO_3^-	Decreased	Decreased P_{CO_2}
	Alkalosis	Increased HCO_3^-	Increased	Increased P_{CO_2}

Table 15.1

Compensation mechanisms that affect P_{CO_2} are performed by the respiratory system and can effect change quite quickly. However, compensation mechanisms that affect HCO_3^- are performed by the kidneys, and therefore the compensatory effect can take longer to manifest. These changes in acid-base chemistry within the body, as well as the cause of the change (respiratory or metabolic), dictate how a patient will be treated medically. For example, a change in pH due to a change in respiratory rate or function may be the result of airway obstruction or chronic obstructive pulmonary disease (COPD), whereas metabolic acidosis may be due to kidney dysfunction or volume loss, so these disorders must be treated accordingly.

REVIEW PROBLEMS

1. Which of the following would most likely filter through the glomerulus into Bowman's capsule?

    A.   Erythrocytes

    B.   Monosaccharides

    C.   Leukocytes

    D.   Platelets

    E.   Monocytes

2. Draw a nephron and label all of its segments.

3. Which region of the kidney has the lowest solute concentration?

    A.   Nephron

    B.   Cortex

    C.   Medulla

    D.   Pelvis

    E.   Glomerulus

4. In the nephron, amino acids enter the peritubular capillaries via

    A.   filtration.

    B.   secretion.

    C.   reabsorption.

    D.   osmoregulation.

    E.   passive diffusion.

5. Glucose reabsorption in the nephron occurs in the

    A.   loop of Henle.

    B.   distal tubule.

    C.   proximal tubule.

    D.   collecting duct.

    E.   Bowman's capsule.

6. Urine is

    A.   hypotonic to the blood.

    B.   hypertonic to the blood.

    C.   hypertonic to the filtrate.

    D.   hypotonic to the vasa recta.

    E.   isotonic to the blood.

SOLUTIONS TO REVIEW PROBLEMS

1. **B** Monosaccharides would most likely filter through the glomerulus. Cells, cell fragments, and proteins remain on the circulatory side.

2. See Figure 15.2.

3. **B** Discussed in nephron function section in this chapter.

4. **C** Discussed in osmoregulation section in this chapter.

5. **C** Discussed in function of nephron section in this chapter.

6. **B** Discussed in function of nephron section in this chapter.

CHAPTER SIXTEEN

Endocrine System

The endocrine system acts as a means of internal communication, coordinating the activities of the organ systems. **Endocrine glands** synthesize and secrete chemical substances called **hormones** directly into the circulatory system. In contrast, **exocrine glands**, such as the gallbladder, secrete substances transported by ducts.

ENDOCRINE GLANDS

Glands or organs that synthesize or secrete hormones include the pituitary, hypothalamus, thyroid, parathyroids, adrenals, pancreas, testes, ovaries, pineal gland, kidneys, gastrointestinal glands, heart, and thymus. Some hormones regulate a single type of cell or organ, whereas others have more widespread effects. The specificity of hormonal action is determined by the presence of specific receptors on or in the target cells.

Figure 16.1

Adrenal Glands

The adrenal glands are located on top of the kidneys and consist of the adrenal cortex and the adrenal medulla.

Adrenal cortex

In response to stress, adrenocorticotropic hormone (ACTH), which is produced by the anterior pituitary, stimulates the adrenal cortex to produce more than two dozen different steroid hormones, collectively known as **adrenocortical steroids**, or simply **corticosteroids**. In the bloodstream, these corticosteroids are bound to transport proteins called **transcortins**. Corticosteroids exert their action by determining which genes are transcribed in the nuclei of their target cells and at what rate. The subsequent changes in the nature and concentration of the proteins produced in the target cells will affect metabolism and other cellular functions. The three major classes of corticosteroids are described below:

- **Glucocorticoids:** Glucocorticoids, such as **cortisol** and **cortisone**, are involved in glucose regulation and protein metabolism. Glucocorticoids raise blood glucose levels by promoting protein breakdown and **gluconeogenesis** and decreasing protein synthesis. Glucocorticoids increase plasma glucose levels and are antagonistic to the effects of insulin. Glucocorticoids release amino acids from skeletal muscle as well as lipids from adipose tissue. They also promote the peripheral use of lipids and have anti-inflammatory effects.

- **Mineralocorticoids:** Mineralocorticoids, particularly **aldosterone**, regulate plasma levels of sodium and potassium and, consequently, the total extracellular fluid volume. Aldosterone causes active reabsorption of sodium and passive reabsorption of water in the **nephron** of the kidney. This results in an increase in both blood volume and blood pressure. Excess production of aldosterone results in excess retention of water with resulting hypertension (high blood pressure). The mineralocorticoids are stimulated by angiotensin II and inhibited by ANP (atrial natriuretic peptide). See Chapter 15, Urinary System, for more information on the action of aldosterone.

- **Cortical sex hormones:** In both men and women, the adrenal cortex secretes small quantities of **androgens** (male sex hormones) like androstenedione and dehydroepiandrosterone. In men, most of the androgens are produced by the **testes**, so the physiologic effect of the adrenal androgens is quite small. In women, however, overproduction of the adrenal androgens may have masculinizing effects, such as excessive facial hair.

Adrenal medulla

The adrenal medulla produces **epinephrine** (adrenaline) and **norepinephrine** (noradrenaline), both of which belong to a class of amino acid–derived compounds called **catecholamines**.

Epinephrine increases the conversion of glycogen to glucose in liver and muscle tissue, causing an increase in blood glucose levels and an increase in the basal metabolic rate. Both epinephrine and norepinephrine increase the rate and strength of the heartbeat and dilate and constrict blood vessels in such a way as to increase the blood supply to the skeletal muscles, heart, and brain, while decreasing the blood supply to the kidneys, skin, and digestive tract. Both epinephrine and norepinephrine will also promote the release of lipids by adipose tissue. These effects are known as the "fight or flight response" and are elicited by sympathetic nervous stimulation in response to stress.

Epinephrine will inhibit other functions, such as digestion, that are not immediately important for survival. Both of these hormones are also **neurotransmitters**, proteins used by neurons to transmit signals.

Pituitary Gland

The pituitary (**hypophysis**) is a small, trilobed gland at the base of the brain. The two main lobes, anterior and posterior, are functionally distinct. (In humans, the third lobe, the intermediate lobe, is rudimentary.) Specifically, the pituitary gland hangs below the hypothalamus and is connected to it by a slender cord known as the **infundibulum**.

Anterior pituitary

The anterior pituitary synthesizes both direct hormones, which directly act on their target organs, and tropic hormones, which stimulate other endocrine glands to release hormones. The hormonal secretions of the anterior pituitary are regulated by hypothalamic hormones called releasing/inhibiting hormones or factors.

The **tropic hormones** of the anterior pituitary include:

- **Follicle-stimulating hormone (FSH):** In women, FSH causes maturation of ovarian follicles, which in turn secrete estrogen; in men, FSH stimulates maturation of the seminiferous tubules and sperm production.

- **Luteinizing hormone (LH):** In women, LH stimulates ovulation and maintenance of the **corpus luteum**. LH is also responsible for regulating progesterone secretion in women. In men, LH stimulates the interstitial cells of the testes to synthesize testosterone.

- **Adrenocorticotropic hormone (ACTH):** ACTH stimulates the adrenal cortex to synthesize and secrete glucocorticoids and is regulated by corticotropin-releasing factor (CRF).

- **Thyroid-stimulating hormone (TSH):** TSH stimulates the thyroid gland to synthesize and release thyroid hormones, including thyroxine.

The **direct hormones** of the anterior pituitary include:

- **Prolactin:** Prolactin stimulates milk production in female mammary glands.

- **Endorphins**: These are neurotransmitters that have pain-relieving properties.

- **Growth hormone (GH, somatotropin):** GH promotes bone and muscle growth. GH also promotes protein synthesis and lipid mobilization and catabolism. In children, a GH deficiency can lead to stunted growth (**dwarfism**), while overproduction of GH results in **gigantism**. Overproduction of GH in adults causes **acromegaly**, a disorder characterized by a disproportionate overgrowth of bone, especially in the skull, jaw, feet, and hands.

- **Melanocyte-stimulating hormone (MSH):** MSH is secreted by the intermediate lobe of the pituitary. In mammals, the function of MSH is unclear, but in frogs, MSH causes darkening of the skin via the induced dispersion of molecules of pigment in melanophore cells.

Posterior pituitary

The posterior pituitary (**neurohypophysis**) does not synthesize hormones; it stores and releases the peptide hormones **oxytocin** and **antidiuretic hormone**, which are produced by the neurosecretory cells of the hypothalamus. Hormone secretion is stimulated by action potentials descending from the hypothalamus.

- **Oxytocin:** Oxytocin, which is secreted during childbirth, increases the strength and frequency of uterine muscle contractions. Oxytocin secretion is also induced by suckling; oxytocin stimulates milk secretion in the mammary glands.

- **Antidiuretic hormone (ADH; vasopressin):** ADH increases the permeability of the nephron's **collecting duct** to water, thereby promoting water reabsorption and increasing blood volume, which subsequently increases blood pressure. ADH is secreted when plasma osmolarity increases, as sensed by osmoreceptors in the hypothalamus, or when blood volume decreases, as sensed by baroreceptors in the circulatory system.

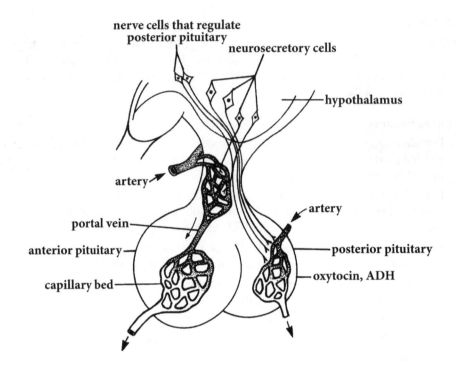

Figure 16.2

Hypothalamus

The hypothalamus is part of the forebrain and is located directly above the pituitary gland. The hypothalamus receives neural transmissions from other parts of the brain and from peripheral nerves that trigger specific responses from its **neurosecretory cells**. The neurosecretory cells regulate pituitary gland secretions via negative feedback mechanisms and through the actions of inhibiting and releasing hormones.

Interactions with the anterior pituitary

Hypothalamic-releasing hormones stimulate or inhibit the secretions of the anterior pituitary. For example, GnRH stimulates the anterior pituitary to secrete FSH and LH. Releasing hormones are secreted into the hypothalamic-hypophyseal portal system. In this circulatory pathway, blood from the capillary bed in the hypothalamus flows through a portal vein into the anterior pituitary, where it diverges into a second capillary network. In this way, releasing hormones can immediately reach the anterior pituitary.

A complicated feedback system regulates the secretions of the endocrine system. For example, when the plasma levels of adrenal cortical hormones drop, hypothalamic cells (via a negative feedback mechanism) release corticotropin-releasing factor (CRF) into the portal system, which signals the pituitary cells to release ACTH. ACTH then acts on the adrenal cortex to increase glucocorticoid levels. When the plasma concentration of corticosteroids exceeds the normal plasma level, the steroids themselves exert an inhibitory effect on the hypothalamus.

Interactions with the posterior pituitary

Neurosecretory cells in the hypothalamus synthesize both oxytocin and ADH and transport them via their axons into the posterior pituitary for storage and secretion.

Thyroid

Thyroid hormones affect the function of nearly every organ system in the body. In children, thyroid hormones are essential for growth and neurological development; in adults, thyroid hormones increase the rate of metabolism throughout the body and are essential for maintenance of metabolic stability.

Thyroid hormones (thyroxine and triiodothyronine)

The thyroid hormones, **thyroxine (T4)** and **triiodothyronine (T3)**, are formed from the glycoprotein **thyroglobulin**, which is synthesized in thyroid cells. Because of the specific tertiary structure of this glycoprotein, iodinated tyrosine residues present in thyroglobulin are able to bind together to form active thyroid hormones. The thyroid hormones possess the following characteristics:

- T3 is five times more potent than T4.
- T4 and T3 are transported via plasma proteins. Approximately 99.5% of these hormones are bound to proteins, but only an unbound hormone is able to enter a cell and elicit a cellular response.
- All of the T4 in the body is formed and secreted by the thyroid gland; however, only 20% of T3 is produced by the thyroid gland.
- The majority of T3 is produced by the conversion of T4 to T3 by the enzyme 5′-monodeiodase, found primarily in the peripheral tissues.

In **hypothyroidism**, thyroid hormones are undersecreted or not secreted at all. Common symptoms of hypothyroidism include a slowed heart rate and respiratory rate, fatigue, cold intolerance, and weight gain. Hypothyroidism in newborn infants, called **cretinism**, is characterized by mental retardation and short stature. In **hyperthyroidism**, the thyroid is overstimulated, resulting in the oversecretion of thyroid hormones. Symptoms often include increased metabolic rate, feelings of excessive warmth, profuse sweating, palpitations, weight loss, and protruding eyes. In both disorders the thyroid often enlarges, forming a bulge in the neck called a goiter.

Hypothyroidism is often treated with supplementation of thyroid hormones via synthetic or animal-derived products. Hyperthyroidism can be treated by antithyroid medications that suppress the thyroid's release of excess hormone or ablation of the thyroid with radiation. After ablation, the thyroid no longer produces thyroid hormone, and the patient must take thyroid supplementation for the rest of his or her life.

BIO

Calcitonin

Calcitonin decreases plasma Ca^{2+} concentration by inhibiting the release of Ca^{2+} from bone. Calcitonin secretion is regulated by plasma Ca^{2+} levels. Calcitonin is antagonistic to parathyroid hormone.

Pancreas

The pancreas is both an **exocrine** organ and an **endocrine** organ. The exocrine function is performed by the cells that secrete digestive enzymes into the small intestine via a series of ducts. The endocrine function is performed by small glandular structures called the **islets of Langerhans**, which are composed of alpha and beta cells. Alpha cells produce and secrete glucagon; beta cells produce and secrete insulin. The endocrine hormones secreted by the pancreas include the following:

- **Glucagon:** Glucagon stimulates protein and fat degradation, the conversion of glycogen to glucose, and gluconeogenesis, all of which serve to increase blood glucose levels. Glucagon's actions are largely antagonistic to those of insulin.

- **Insulin**: Insulin is a protein hormone secreted in response to a high blood glucose concentration. It stimulates the uptake of glucose by muscle and adipose cells and the storage of glucose as glycogen in muscle and liver cells, thus lowering blood glucose levels. It also stimulates the synthesis of fats from glucose and the uptake of amino acids. Insulin's actions are antagonistic to those of **glucagon** and the **glucocorticoids**. Underproduction of insulin, or insensitivity to insulin, leads to **diabetes mellitus**, which is characterized by hyperglycemia (high blood glucose levels). Diabetes is the most common endocrine disorder and, if not treated, can lead to long-term complications involving the eyes, nerves, kidneys, and blood vessels. Table 16.1 identifies the distinguishing characteristics of Type I and Type II diabetes.

Distinguishing Characteristics	Type I	Type II
% diabetics	10	90
Age of onset	Usually <30 years	Usually >30 years
Pathogenesis	Presence of islet cell antibodies Autoimmune Decreased insulin secretion	Resistance to insulin Increased hepatic glucose production
Plasma insulin	Usually none	Low, normal, or high Etiology dependent
Family history	Usually none	Strong
Obesity	Uncommon	Common

Table 16.1

Parathyroid Glands

The parathyroid glands are four small, pea-shaped structures embedded in the posterior surface of the thyroid. These glands synthesize and secrete **parathyroid hormone (PTH)**, which regulates plasma Ca^{2+} concentration. PTH raises the Ca^{2+} concentration in the blood by stimulating Ca^{2+} release from the bone and decreasing Ca^{2+} excretion in the kidneys. Calcium in bone is bonded to phosphate, and breakdown of the bone releases phosphate as well as calcium. Parathyroid hormone compensates for this by stimulating excretion of phosphate by the kidneys.

Kidneys

When blood volume falls, the kidneys produce **renin**—an enzyme that converts the plasma protein angiotensinogen to angiotensin I. Angiotensin I is converted to angiotensin II, which stimulates the adrenal cortex to secrete **aldosterone**. Aldosterone helps restore blood volume by increasing sodium reabsorption by the kidneys, leading to an increase in fluid retention. This removes the initial stimulus for renin production. The kidneys also produce **erythropoietin (EPO)**. EPO is a glycoprotein that stimulates red blood cell production; it is normally produced in the kidneys. This hormone causes the following:

- stimulation of the stem cells to differentiate into rubriblasts (least mature erythrocytes)
- increased rate of mitosis
- increased release of reticulocytes from the bone marrow
- increased hemoglobin (HgB) formation, which results in the critical HgB concentration necessary for RBC maturity to be reached at a more rapid rate

Gastrointestinal Hormones

Ingested food stimulates the stomach to release the hormone gastrin. **Gastrin** is carried to the gastric glands and stimulates the glands to secrete HCl in response to food in the stomach. Secretion of pancreatic juice, the exocrine product of the pancreas, is also under hormonal control. The hormone **secretin** is released by the small intestine when acidic chyme enters from the stomach. Secretin stimulates the secretion of an alkaline bicarbonate solution from the pancreas that neutralizes the acidity of the chyme. The hormone **cholecystokinin** is released by the small intestine in response to the presence of fats and causes the contraction of the gallbladder and release of bile into the small intestine. **Bile,** which is not a hormone, is involved in the emulsification and digestion of fats.

Pineal Gland

The pineal gland is a tiny structure at the base of the brain that secretes the hormone **melatonin**. The role of melatonin in humans is unclear, but it is believed to play a role in the regulation of **circadian rhythms**—physiological cycles lasting approximately 24 hours. Melatonin secretion is regulated by light and dark cycles in the environment. In primitive vertebrates, melatonin lightens the skin by concentrating pigment granules in melanophores (melatonin is an antagonist to MSH).

MECHANISM OF HORMONE ACTION

Hormones are classified on the basis of their chemical structure into two major groups: peptide hormones and steroid hormones. There are two ways in which hormones affect the activities of their target cells: via extracellular receptors or intracellular receptors.

Peptides

Peptide hormones range from simple short peptides (amino acid chains), such as ADH, to complex polypeptides, such as insulin. Peptide hormones act as **first messengers.** When they bind to **specific receptors** on the surface of their target cells, they trigger a series of enzymatic reactions within each cell, the first of which may be the conversion of ATP to cyclic adenosine monophosphate (cyclic AMP); this reaction is catalyzed by the membrane-bound enzyme adenylate cyclase. **Cyclic AMP** acts as a **second messenger**, relaying messages from the extracellular peptide hormone to cytoplasmic

BIO

enzymes and initiating a series of reactions in the cell. This is an example of a **cascade effect**; with each step, the hormone's effects are amplified. Cyclic AMP activity is inactivated by the cytoplasmic enzyme phosphodiesterase.

Steroids

Steroid hormones, such as estrogen and aldosterone, belong to a class of lipid-derived molecules with a characteristic ring structure. They are produced by the testes, ovaries, placenta, and adrenal cortex. Because they are lipid soluble, steroid hormones cross the phospholipid bilayer and enter their target cells directly in order to bind to specific receptor proteins in the cytoplasm. This receptor-hormone complex enters the nucleus and directly activates the expression of specific genes by binding to receptors on the chromatin. This induces a change in mRNA transcription and protein synthesis.

REVIEW PROBLEMS

1. Name the different parts of the adrenal gland and the hormones secreted from each.

2. Discuss the relationship between the hypothalamus and the pituitary gland.

3. Increased activity of the parathyroid gland leads to
   A. a decrease in blood glucose levels.
   B. an increase in metabolic rate.
   C. a decrease in body temperature.
   D. an increase in blood Ca^{2+} concentrations.
   E. a decrease in blood phosphate concentrations.

4. Which of the following statements concerning growth hormone is NOT true?
   A. Overproduction of growth hormone in children results in gigantism.
   B. Overproduction of growth hormone in adults results in acromegaly.
   C. A deficiency of growth hormone results in dwarfism.
   D. Growth hormone is secreted by the hypothalamus.
   E. Growth hormone promotes protein synthesis.

5. Describe the regulation of plasma Ca^{2+} concentration. Include all of the hormones and organs involved.

6. Thyroid hormone deficiency may result in
   A. acromegaly.
   B. cretinism.
   C. gigantism.
   D. hyperthyroidism.
   E. ablation.

7. Match the following hormones with their respective functions.
   A. Growth hormone   1. Promotes growth of muscle
   B. ACTH   2. Stimulates the release of glucose into the blood
   C. Oxytocin   3. Prepares the uterus for implantation of a fertilized egg
   D. Progesterone   4. Stimulates the secretion of glucocorticoids
   E. Aldosterone   5. Increases the rate of metabolism
   F. Glucagon   6. Induces water reabsorption in the kidneys
   G. Thyroxine   7. Increases uterine contractions during childbirth

8. What is negative feedback?

9. Why is the level of blood glucose so important? What hormones are involved in the regulation of blood glucose levels?

BIO

10. Destruction of all beta cells in the pancreas would cause
    A. glucagon secretion to stop and a decrease in blood glucose.
    B. glucagon secretion to stop and an increase in blood glucose.
    C. insulin secretion to stop and an increase in blood glucose.
    D. insulin secretion to stop and a decrease in blood glucose.
    E. none of the above.

11. A man trapped for three days underneath the ruins of a collapsed building was rescued and rushed to the nearest hospital. He suffered from internal bleeding and was very dehydrated. Why was a high level of aldosterone found in his blood?

12. Oxytocin and vasopressin are
    A. produced and released by the hypothalamus.
    B. produced and released by the pituitary.
    C. produced by the hypothalamus and released by the pituitary.
    D. produced by the pituitary and released by the hypothalamus.
    E. produced by both the hypothalamus and pituitary but released by neither.

SOLUTIONS TO REVIEW PROBLEMS

1. The adrenal gland is divided into the adrenal cortex and the adrenal medulla. The adrenal cortex secretes steroid hormones called mineralocorticoids (e.g., aldosterone) as well as glucocorticoids (e.g., cortisol) and sex hormones (e.g., androstenedione). The adrenal medulla secretes the catecholamines norepinephrine and epinephrine, which are amino acid derivatives.

2. The posterior pituitary stores and secretes hormones produced by the neurosecretory cells of the hypothalamus. In contrast, the anterior pituitary produces hormones that are regulated by hypothalamic releasing hormones. Hypothalamic releasing hormones stimulate the anterior pituitary to secrete a particular hormone, whereas hypothalamic inhibiting hormones inhibit anterior pituitary secretions. The releasing and inhibiting hormones are secreted into a circulatory pathway known as the hypothalamic-hypophyseal portal system, which allows for high, localized concentrations of the various stimulating and inhibitory hormones and rapid, direct transport of these hormones to the pituitary.

3. **D** Discussed in section on parathyroid glands in this chapter.

4. **D** Discussed in section on hormones of the anterior pituitary in this chapter.

5. Calcium levels in the blood are regulated by two hormones: calcitonin and parathyroid hormone (PTH). Calcitonin is secreted by the thyroid gland when plasma Ca^{2+} levels are high and decreases the plasma Ca^{2+} concentration by inhibiting bone resorption (which releases Ca^{2+} into the blood). When plasma Ca^{2+} levels are low, PTH is secreted by the parathyroid glands. PTH increases plasma Ca^{2+} concentration by increasing bone resorption, increasing Ca^{2+} reabsorption in the kidney (thus reducing the amount of Ca^{2+} excreted in the urine), and stimulating the conversion of vitamin D into its active form (1,25-dihydroxycholecalciferol), which increases intestinal absorption of Ca^{2+}.

6. **B** Discussed in section on thyroid gland in this chapter.

7. **A** 1
    B 4
    C 7
    D 3
    E 6
    F 2
    G 5

8. Negative feedback is a means of regulation whereby an end product inhibits one or more of the earlier steps that lead to its production or secretion. For example, high plasma levels of thyroxine inhibit the pituitary gland from secreting TSH, thus removing the stimulus on the thyroid to secrete more thyroxine. Negative feedback mechanisms are also used by the body to regulate enzyme production and activity.

9. Glucose is the primary source of energy used by cells during aerobic respiration, so blood glucose levels determine the amount of energy available for cellular activity. Many

hormones involved in the regulation of blood glucose levels do so by stimulating the liver either to store or release glucose. When glucose levels are low, the adrenal medulla secretes epinephrine, which stimulates the liver to convert glycogen stores into glucose and release it into the blood. Epinephrine also acts on muscles, transforming their glycogen stores into lactic acid, which is transported to the liver and converted to glucose. The pancreas secretes glucagon, which also stimulates the liver to convert glycogen to glucose. When additional glucose is needed, the adrenal cortex secretes glucocorticoids, which stimulate the liver to synthesize glucose in a process called gluconeogenesis. Insulin is antagonistic to glucagon, epinephrine, and glucocorticoids; it lowers blood glucose levels by stimulating the uptake of glucose by adipose and muscle tissue and by promoting the conversion of glucose into glycogen in liver and muscle cells.

10. **C** Discussed in section on endocrine functions of the pancreas in this chapter.

11. Internal bleeding leads to a decrease in the volume of blood in the circulatory system. When blood volume falls, the kidney produces renin, which leads to an increase in aldosterone. Aldosterone causes increased water reabsorption in the nephrons, leading to an increase in blood volume. Thus, the man's body responded to the blood loss by secreting aldosterone.

12. **C** Discussed in section on anterior pituitary in this chapter.

CHAPTER SEVENTEEN

Reproductive System

Reproduction in animals is a complex process involving the formation and fertilization of gametes and regulation of these processes by both parents. Once fertilization occurs, an embryo is formed, and that embryo matures into a fetus through rapid division and differentiation.

SEXUAL REPRODUCTION

Sexual reproduction differs from asexual reproduction in that the genetic material of two organisms combines and results in a genetically unique offspring. Sexual reproduction occurs via the fusion of two gametes, specialized sex cells produced by each parent. Sexual reproduction requires the following:

- The production of **functional sex cells** or **gametes** by adult organisms
- The union of these cells (**fertilization** or **conjugation**) to form a zygote
- The development of the zygote into another adult, completing the cycle

Gonads

The gametes are produced in specialized organs called **gonads**. The male gonads, the **testes**, produce **sperm** in the tightly coiled seminiferous tubules. The female gonads, the **ovaries**, produce **oocytes** (eggs). Some species are **hermaphrodites**, which possess both functional male and female gonads. These include the hydra and the earthworm.

Gametogenesis

The production of functional sex cells is called **gametogenesis**. In males, the process is called **spermatogenesis**, or sperm production, and occurs in the seminiferous tubules of the testes. In females, the process is called **oogenesis**, or egg production, and occurs in the ovaries. Spermatogenesis and oogenesis will be discussed in more detail in the sections on the male and female reproductive systems, respectively.

Fertilization

Fertilization is the union of the egg and sperm nuclei to form a zygote with a diploid number of chromosomes. **Internal fertilization** is practiced by terrestrial vertebrates and provides a direct route for sperm to reach the egg cell. This increases the chance for fertilization success, and females produce fewer eggs. The number of eggs produced is affected by other factors as well. If the early development of the offspring occurs outside of the mother's body, more eggs will be produced to increase the chances of offspring survival. The amount of parental care after birth is also related to the number of eggs produced. Species that care for their young produce fewer eggs.

MALE REPRODUCTIVE SYSTEM

The **testes** are located in the **scrotum** , an external pouch that maintains the testes' temperature at 2°C to 4°C lower than body temperature, a condition essential for sperm survival. Sperm pass from the testes through the **vas deferens** to the **ejaculatory duct** and then to the **urethra**. The urethra passes through the **penis** until it terminates with an external opening at the **glans** of the penis. In males, the urethra is a common passageway for both the reproductive and excretory systems.

The testes are also the sites of production of testosterone. **Testosterone** regulates secondary male sex characteristics including facial and pubic hair, and voice changes.

Figure 17.1

Spermatogenesis

Spermatogenesis, or sperm production, occurs in the seminiferous tubules. Diploid cells called **spermatogonia** differentiate into diploid cells called **primary spermatocytes**, which undergo a meiotic division to yield two haploid **secondary spermatocytes** of equal size; a second meiotic division produces four haploid **spermatids** of equal size. After meiosis the spermatids undergo a final series of changes that increase their mobility, resulting in mature sperm, or **spermatozoa**. The mature sperm is an elongated cell with a head, neck, body, and tail. The head consists almost entirely of the nucleus. The tail (flagellum) propels the sperm, while mitochondria in the neck and body provide energy for locomotion. A caplike structure called the **acrosome**, derived from the Golgi apparatus, develops over the anterior half of the head. The acrosome contains enzymes needed to penetrate the tough outer covering of the ovum. After a male has reached sexual maturity, approximately 3 million primary spermatocytes begin to undergo spermatogenesis per day.

FEMALE REPRODUCTIVE SYSTEM

The **ovaries** are found in the abdominal cavity below the digestive system. The ovaries consist of thousands of follicles; a **follicle** is a multilayered sac of cells that contains, nourishes, and protects an immature ovum. It is actually the follicle cells that produce estrogen. Approximately once a month, an immature ovum is released from the ovary into the abdominal cavity and drawn by cilia into the nearby **oviduct**, also known as a **fallopian tube.** Each fallopian tube opens into the upper end of a muscular chamber called the **uterus**, the site of fetal development. The lower, narrow end of the uterus is called the **cervix**. The cervix connects with the vaginal canal, which is the site of sperm deposition during intercourse and is also the passageway through which a baby is expelled during childbirth.

Figure 17.2

Oogenesis

Oogenesis, the production of female gametes, occurs in the ovarian follicles. At birth, most of the immature ova, known as **primary oocytes,** that a female will produce during her lifetime have already formed. Primary oocytes are diploid cells that form by mitosis in the ovary. After menarche (the first time a female menstruates), one primary oocyte per month completes meiosis I, yielding two daughter cells of unequal size—a **secondary oocyte** and a small cell known as a **polar body**. The secondary oocyte is expelled from the follicle during ovulation. Meiosis II does not occur until fertilization. The oocyte cell membrane is surrounded by two layers of cells; the inner **zona pellucida layer** and the outer **corona radiata layer**. Meiosis II is triggered when these layers are penetrated by a sperm cell, yielding two haploid cells—a mature ovum and another polar body. The mature ovum is a large cell containing cytoplasm, RNA, organelles, and nutrients needed by the developing embryo. When polar bodies are formed, they lack these resources and rapidly degenerate.

Female Sex Hormones

The ovaries synthesize and secrete female sex hormones, including estrogens and progesterone. The secretion of both estrogens and progesterone is regulated by **luteinizing hormone (LH)** and **follicle stimulating hormone (FSH)**, which, are regulated by gonadotropin-releasing hormone (GnRH).

Estrogens

Estrogens are steroid hormones necessary for normal female maturation. They stimulate the development of the female reproductive tract, contribute to the development of secondary sexual characteristics, and influence libido. Estrogens are also responsible for the thickening of the endometrium (the inner lining of the uterine wall). Estrogens are secreted by the ovarian follicles and the corpus luteum.

Progesterone

Progesterone is a steroid hormone secreted by the corpus luteum during the luteal phase of the menstrual cycle. Progesterone stimulates the development and maintenance of the endometrium in preparation for implantation.

The Menstrual Cycle

The hormonal secretions of the ovaries, hypothalamus, and anterior pituitary play important roles in the female reproductive cycle. From puberty through menopause, interactions between these hormones result in a monthly cyclical pattern known as the menstrual cycle. The menstrual cycle is divided into the follicular phase, ovulation, the luteal phase, and menstruation.

Follicular phase

The follicular phase begins with the cessation of the menstrual flow from the previous cycle. During this phase, FSH from the anterior pituitary promotes the development of the follicle, which grows and begins secreting estrogen.

BIO

Ovulation

Midway through the cycle, ovulation occurs—a mature ovarian follicle bursts and releases an ovum. Ovulation is caused by a surge in LH that is preceded, and in part caused by, a peak in estrogen levels.

Women ovulate approximately once every four weeks (except during pregnancy and, usually, lactation) until menopause, which typically occurs between the ages of 45 and 50. During menopause the ovaries become less sensitive to the hormones that stimulate follicle development (FSH and LH) and eventually atrophy. The remaining follicles disappear, estrogen and progesterone levels greatly decline, and ovulation stops. The profound changes in hormone levels are often accompanied by physiological and psychological changes that persist until a new balance is reached.

Luteal phase

After ovulation, LH maintains the remnant of the ruptured follicle, called the **corpus luteum**, which secretes estrogen and progesterone. **Progesterone** causes the glands of the endometrium to mature and produce secretions that prepare it for the implantation of an embryo. Progesterone and estrogen are essential for the maintenance of the endometrium.

Menstruation

If the ovum is not fertilized, the corpus luteum atrophies. The resulting drop in progesterone and estrogen levels causes the endometrium (with its superficial blood vessels) to slough off, giving rise to the menstrual flow (**menses**).

If fertilization occurs, the developing placenta produces **hCG** (human chorionic gonadotropin), maintaining the corpus luteum as well as the supply of estrogen and progesterone that maintains the uterus. Eventually the placenta will take over production of these hormones.

Fertilization

An egg can be fertilized during the 12–24 hours after ovulation. Fertilization most often occurs in the lateral, widest portion of the fallopian tube. Sperm must travel through the vaginal canal, cervix, uterus, and into the fallopian tubes to reach the ovum. Sperm remain viable and capable of fertilization for 1–2 days after intercourse.

The first barrier that the sperm must penetrate is the corona radiata. Enzymes secreted by the sperm aid in penetration of the corona radiata. The acrosome is responsible for penetrating the zona pellucida; it releases enzymes that digest this layer, thereby allowing the sperm to come into direct contact with the ovum cell membrane. Once in contact with the membrane, the sperm forms a tubelike structure called the **acrosomal process**, which extends to the cell membrane and penetrates it, fusing the sperm cell membrane with that of the ovum. The sperm nucleus now enters the ovum's cytoplasm. It is at this stage of fertilization that the ovum completes meiosis II.

The acrosomal reaction triggers a **cortical reaction** in the ovum, causing calcium ions to be released into the cytoplasm; this initiates a series of reactions that result in the formation of the **fertilization membrane**. The fertilization membrane is a hard layer that surrounds the ovum cell membrane and prevents multiple fertilizations. The release of Ca^{2+} also stimulates metabolic changes within the ovum, greatly increasing its metabolic rate. This is followed by the fusion of the sperm nucleus with the ovum nucleus to form a diploid zygote. The first mitotic division of the zygote soon follows.

BIO

pituitary hormones

ovarian hormones

ovarian phases

endometrail changes

Figure 17.3

BIO

Multiple Births

Monozygotic (identical) twins

Monozygotic twins result when a single zygote splits into two embryos. If the splitting occurs at the two-cell stage of development, the embryos will have separate chorions and separate placentas; if it occurs at the blastula stage, the embryos will have only one chorionic sac and will therefore share a placenta and possibly an amnion. Occasionally the division is incomplete, resulting in the birth of "Siamese" (conjoined) twins, which are attached at some point on the body, often sharing limbs or organs. Monozygotic twins are genetically identical because they develop from the same zygote. Monozygotic twins are therefore of the same sex, blood type, and so on.

Dizygotic (fraternal) twins

Dizygotic twins result when two ova are released in one ovarian cycle and are fertilized by two different sperm. The two embryos implant in the uterine wall individually, and each develops its own placenta, amnion, and chorion (although the placentas may fuse if the embryos implant very close to each other). Fraternal twins share no more characteristics than any other siblings because they develop from two distinct zygotes.

BIO

REVIEW PROBLEMS

1. Upon ovulation, the oocyte is released into the
   A. fallopian tube.
   B. ovary.
   C. follicle.
   D. abdominal cavity.
   E. uterus.

2. Describe three ways in which sexual reproduction promotes genetic variability. How does genetic variability benefit a species?

3. All of the following describe glands in the male reproductive system EXCEPT
   A. prostate.
   B. bulbourethral.
   C. Cowper's.
   D. seminal vesicles.
   E. suprarenal.

4. Which of the following correctly describes the order of maturation of a sperm?
   A. spermatazoa → spermatogonia → primary spermatocyte → secondary spermatocyte → spermatid
   B. spermatogonia → spermatazoa → primary spermatocyte → secondary spermatocyte → spermatid
   C. spermatogonia → primary spermatocyte → secondary spermatocyte → spermatid → spermatazoa
   D. primary spermatocyte → secondary spermatocyte → spermatid → spermatazoa → spermatogonia
   E. spermatazoa → primary spermatocyte → secondary spermatocyte → spermatogonia

5. Ovulation is directly caused by
   A. a surge in estrogen.
   B. lack of inhibition from follicle-stimulating hormone.
   C. a decrease in progesterone.
   D. a sharp increase in luteinizing hormone.
   E. inhibition from gonadotropin-releasing hormone.

SOLUTIONS TO REVIEW PROBLEMS

1. **D** This subtle point about ovulation eludes most people and remains hard to believe until the organs are examined in anatomy class. The ruptured ovarian follicle releases an oocyte into the abdominal cavity, close to the entrance of the fallopian tube. With the aid of beating cilia, the oocyte is drawn into the fallopian tube, through which it travels until it reaches the uterus. If it is fertilized (in the fallopian tube), it will implant in the uterine wall; if it is not fertilized, it will be expelled along with the uterine lining during menstruation.

2. Sexual reproduction promotes genetic variability through the independent assortment of homologous chromosomes, the crossing over between homologous chromosomes during meiosis, and the random fertilization of an egg by a sperm.

    The independent assortment of chromosomes during gametogenesis allows for tremendous genetic variability by creating numerous possible combinations of chromosomes in a given gamete. During metaphase I, homologous chromosomes pair and randomly align at the metaphase plate. The random positioning of the homologous pairs determines which chromosomes are pulled toward each pole of the cell during anaphase. Thus, each resultant daughter cell has a random assortment of chromosomes, some of maternal origin and some of paternal origin.

    In addition to independent assortment, a random exchange of genes between chromosomes can occur via recombination. This allows for greater genetic variability by creating new combinations of genes on each chromosome. Recombination occurs during prophase I of meiosis, when homologous pairs of chromosomes align themselves side by side and exchange genetic information in a process called crossing over.

    Genetic variability is further enhanced by fertilization. An egg cell containing one of the millions of possible gene combinations fuses with a sperm cell containing another of the millions of possible combinations of different genes to create a zygote with a unique assortment of maternal and paternal genes.

    Genetic variability increases the chances of some members of a species surviving potential environmental stresses and conditions and promotes evolution over many generations.

3. **E** The suprarenal glands, also known as the adrenal glands, are located on the kidneys and are not part of the reproductive system, so (E) is the correct answer. The prostate, bulbourethral (Cowper's) gland, and seminal vesicles all contribute to the formation of semen in the male reproductive system.

4. **C** In spermatogenesis, a spermatogonia matures into a primary spermatocyte, which undergoes meiosis I to form two secondary spermatocytes, which in turn undergo meiosis II to form a total of four spermatid. These spermatid then undergo spermiogenesis to become spermatazoa.

5. **D** Ovulation occurs when luteinizing hormone (LH) spikes in response to a sharp increase in follicle-stimulating hormone (FSH), which in turn was caused by rising estrogen levels from the developing follicle. LH causes the follicle to rupture, releasing its ovum, and this is ovulation. The follicle leaves behind the corpus luteum, which is what gives LH its name.

CHAPTER EIGHTEEN

Developmental Biology

Embryology is the study of the development of a unicellular zygote into a complete, multicellular organism. Over the course of nine months, a unicellular human zygote undergoes cell division, cellular differentiation, and morphogenesis in preparation for life outside the uterus.

Early Developmental Stages

Fertilization

In mammals, an egg can be fertilized within 12–24 hours after ovulation. Fertilization occurs in the lateral, widest portion of the oviduct where sperm traveling from the vagina encounter an egg. If more than one egg is fertilized, **fraternal (dizygotic) twins** may be conceived. **Identical (monozygotic) twins**, in contrast, occur when one zygote divides into two separate embryos.

Cleavage

Early embryonic development is characterized by a series of rapid mitotic divisions known as **cleavage**. These divisions lead to an increase in cell number without a corresponding growth in cell protoplasm (i.e., the total volume of cytoplasm remains constant). Thus, cleavage results in progressively smaller cells with an increasing ratio of nuclei to cytoplasm. Cleavage also increases the surface-area-to-volume ratio of each cell, thereby improving gas and nutrient exchange.

The first complete cleavage of a zygote occurs approximately 32 hours after fertilization. The second cleavage occurs after 60 hours, and the third cleavage after approximately 72 hours, at which point the eight-celled embryo reaches the uterus. As cell division continues, a solid ball of embryonic cells, known as the **morula**, is formed. **Blastulation** begins when the morula develops a fluid-filled cavity called the **blastocoel**, which by the fourth day becomes a hollow sphere of cells called the **blastula**. The blastula is the stage of the embryo that implants in the uterus. Emergency contraception works partially by inhibiting implantation of the blastula in the uterus, which is why it is most effective if taken within 72 hours of the time of potential fertilization.

In a normal pregnancy, the blastula implants in the uterus. In an ectopic pregnancy, the embryo implants outside the uterus, for example, in the fallopian tube. An embryo typically cannot be maintained for long outside of the uterus; it will usually abort spontaneously, and hemorrhaging may occur. Ectopic pregnancies can be fatal if not caught in time and managed appropriately.

Development

The final developmental processes can be divided into three different components that continue even after gestation (described below):

- **Organogenesis:** The body organs begin to form. In this process, the cells interact, differentiate, change physical shape, proliferate, and migrate.
- **Growth:** The organs increase in size, which is a continual process from infancy through childhood to adulthood.
- **Gametogenesis:** Eggs develop in women and sperm develop in men, which permits reproduction to occur.

Placental development

The growing fetus receives oxygen directly from its mother through a specialized circulatory system. This system not only supplies oxygen and nutrients to the fetus but removes carbon dioxide and metabolic wastes as well. The two components of this system are the **placenta** and the **umbilical cord**, which both develop in the first few weeks after fertilization.

The placenta and the umbilical cord are outgrowths of the four extra-embryonic membranes formed during development: the **amnion**, **chorion**, **allantois**, and **yolk sac**. The **amnion** is a thin, tough membrane containing a watery fluid called amniotic fluid. Amniotic fluid acts as a shock absorber of external pressure during gestation and localized pressure from uterine contractions during labor. Placenta formation begins with the **chorion**, a membrane that completely surrounds the amnion. The chorion assists with transfer of nutrients from the mother to the fetus. A third membrane, the **allantois**, develops as an outpocketing of the gut. The blood vessels of the allantoic wall enlarge and become the umbilical vessels, which will connect the fetus to the developing placenta. The **yolk sac**, the site of early development of blood vessels, becomes associated with the umbilical vessels.

Figure 18.2

Gestation

Human pregnancy, or gestation, is approximately nine months (266 days) long and can be subdivided into three **trimesters**. The primary developments that occur during each trimester are described below.

First trimester

During the first weeks the major organs begin to develop. The heart begins to beat at approximately 22 days, and soon afterward the eyes, gonads, limbs, and liver start to form. By five weeks the embryo is 10 mm in length; by six weeks the embryo has grown to 15 mm. The cartilaginous skeleton begins to turn into bone by the seventh week. By the end of eight weeks, most of the organs have formed, the brain is fairly developed, and the embryo is referred to as a fetus. At the end of the third month, the fetus is about 9 cm long.

Second trimester

During the second trimester the fetus does a tremendous amount of growing. It begins to move around in the amniotic fluid, its face appears human, and its toes and fingers elongate. By the end of the sixth month, the fetus is 30–36 cm long.

Third trimester

The seventh and eighth months are characterized by continued rapid growth and further brain development. During the ninth month, antibodies are transported by highly selective active transport from the mother to the fetus. The growth rate slows and the fetus becomes less active as it has less room to move about.

Birth and maturation

Childbirth is accomplished by **labor**, a series of strong uterine contractions. Labor can be divided into three distinct stages. In the first stage, the **cervix** thins and dilates, and the amniotic sac ruptures, releasing its fluids. During this time contractions are relatively mild. The second stage is characterized by rapid contractions, resulting in the birth of the baby (the umbilical cord is usually cut after this stage). During the final stage, the uterus contracts, expelling the placenta and the umbilical cord.

The embryo develops into an adult through the process of maturation, which involves cell division, growth, and differentiation. Differentiation of cells is complete when all organs reach adult form.

Congenital Disorders

In some cases, errors occur during fetal development, often because of deleterious genes or problems with the gestation environment. These **congenital disorders,** also known as birth defects, can present with a wide variety of symptoms, including death. Chemical and biological agents that cause such disorders are called **teratogens** and include some drugs, such as alcohol and tobacco, as well as some microorganisms, such as viruses and bacteria. When a mother passes on an infection directly to her developing offspring, this is called **vertical transmission** and can occur either during development or during birth. Other environmental factors that can lead to birth defects include poor nutrition, radiation, and physical trauma or restraint.

Experimental embryology

The field of **experimental embryology** aims to investigate the effects of these and other factors on development. Experimental embryologists use the techniques of molecular biology, such as visualizing antigens using immunohistochemistry, as well as those of geneticists, such as manipulating specific genes and performing research on the behavior of stem cells. By investigating embryos, scientists hope to identify risk factors for women who could become pregnant as well as treatments applicable throughout the human life cycle.

PLANT EMBROYOLOGY

Seed Formation

The zygote divides mitotically to form the mass of cells called the embryo. The embryo consists of the following parts:

- **Epicotyl:** precursor of the upper stem and leaves.
- **Cotyledons:** seed leaves; dicots have two seed leaves, while monocots have only one.
- **Hypocotyl:** the lower stem and root.
- **Endosperm:** feeds the embryo; in dicots, the cotyledon absorbs the endosperm.
- **Seed coat:** develops from the outer covering of the ovule; the embryo and its seed coat together comprise the seed.

Seed Dispersal

The fruit, in which most seeds develop, is formed from the ovary walls, the base of the flower, and other consolidated flower pistil components. The fruit may be fleshy like a tomato or dry like a nut. It serves as a means of seed dispersal. The fruit enables the seed to be carried more frequently or effectively by air, water, or animals (which in animals involves ingestion and subsequent elimination). The seed is released from the ovary and will germinate under proper conditions of temperature, moisture, and oxygen.

Plant Development

Growth in higher plants is restricted to the embryonic (undifferentiated) cells called **meristem** cells. These tissues undergo active cell reproduction. Gradually, the cells elongate and differentiate into cell types characteristic of the species.

Apical meristem

The apical meristem is found in the tips of roots and stems. Growth in length occurs only at these points.

Lateral meristem

The lateral meristem or **cambium** is located between the xylem and phloem. This tissue permits growth in diameter and can differentiate into new xylem and phloem cells. It is not an active tissue in monocots (grasses) or herbaceous dicots (alfalfa) but is predominant in woody dicots like oaks.

REVIEW PROBLEMS

1. Which of the following developmental stages has the greatest nuclear-to-cytoplasmic material ratio?
   A. Four-celled zygote
   B. Eight-celled zygote
   C. Morula
   D. Blastula
   E. Neurula

2. Name the three embryonic germ layers. Identify the embryological origin of the following structures: nails, thyroid, lens, testes, aorta, peripheral nerves, and lung epithelium.

3. Describe the structure of a blastula.

4. What is cleavage? When does the embryo first differentiate into germ layers?

5. Describe the difference between the apical and lateral meristem.

6. What is the difference between dicots and monocots?

7. Which of the following is not a stage of cell cleavage?

   A. Morula
   B. Blastocoel
   C. Blastula
   D. Mesoderm
   E. Gastrula

8. Describe the function of the four extra-embryonic membranes formed during development.

SOLUTIONS TO REVIEW PROBLEMS

1. **D** Discussed in early development section of this chapter.

2. The three embryonic germ layers are the endoderm, mesoderm, and ectoderm. The thyroid and lung epithelium are of endodermal origin. The testes and the aorta are of mesodermal origin. The nails, lens, and peripheral nerves are of ectodermal origin.

3. The name *blastula* refers to an early stage of development in which the embryo consists of a hollow ball of cells surrounding a cavity called the blastocoel.

4. Cleavage is the rapid division of cells early in the embryo's development. A determinate cleavage results in cells whose differentiation pathways are clearly defined; these cells are incapable of individually developing into complete organisms. The appearance of the three primary germ layers—the endoderm, mesoderm, and ectoderm—from such processes occurs during gastrulation.

5. The apical meristem is in the tips of roots and stems, and growth occurs at these points. The lateral meristem is between the xylem and phloem and permits growth in diameter.

6. Dicots have two seed leaves (cotyledons), whereas monocots only have one.

7. **D** The mesoderm is a primary germ layer that differentiates into the musculoskeletal system, circulatory system, and other areas throughout the body.

8. The amnion contains the amniotic fluid, which is a shock absorber for external pressure and uterine contractions. The chorion completely surrounds the amnion. The allantois contains blood vessels that become the umbilical vessels and connect the fetus to the placenta. The yolk sac is the site of early development of blood vessels.

CHAPTER NINETEEN

Animal Behavior

The preceding biology chapters focused mainly on vertebrate systems (with some information about plants as well). However, on Test Day you will see a few questions about non-vertebrate, non-plant systems: three questions on the diversity of life and taxonomic relationships as well as four questions on evolution, ecology, and behavior, which will contain a mixture of questions about human and nonhuman populations. This chapter on Animal Behavior and the following two chapters on Ecology and Taxonomy contain the information you need to successfully answer questions about non-vertebrate systems on Test Day. However, as you are studying, keep in mind that these types of questions will likely constitute only ten percent or less of the Biology questions on your exam.

This chapter on animal behavior describes the individual and social activities of various organisms, how evolution has shaped those behaviors in the long term, and how learning can influence those behaviors in the short term.

PATTERNS OF ANIMAL BEHAVIOR

Simple Reflexes

Reflexes are automatic responses to simple stimuli and are recognized as reliable behavioral responses following a given environmental stimulus. A **simple reflex** is controlled at the **spinal cord,** connecting a two-neuron pathway from the **receptor** (afferent neuron) to the **motor** (efferent neuron). The efferent nerve innervates the effector (e.g., a muscle or gland). Reflex behavior is important in the behavioral response of lower animals. It is less important in the behavior in higher forms of life, such as vertebrates. A simple reflex arc is shown in Figure 19.1.

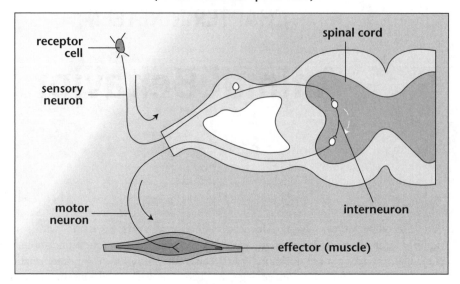

sensory neuron $\longrightarrow$ interneuron $\longrightarrow$ motor neuron
(contained in the spinal cord)

Figure 19.1

Complex Reflexes

More complex reflex patterns involve neural integration at a higher level of the **brainstem** or even the **cerebrum.** For example, the "**startle response**" alerts an animal to a significant stimulus. It can occur in response to potential danger or to hearing one's name called. The startle response involves the integration of many neurons in a system termed the **reticular activating system,** which is responsible for sleep–wake transitions and behavioral motivation.

Fixed-action Pattern

Fixed-action patterns are complex, coordinated, **innate** behavioral responses to specific patterns of stimulation in the environment. The stimulus that elicits the behavior is referred to as the **releaser.** Because fixed-action patterns are innate, they are relatively unlikely to be modified by learning. An animal has a repertoire of fixed-action patterns and only a limited ability to develop new ones. The particular stimuli that trigger a fixed-action pattern are more readily modified, provided certain cues or elements of the stimuli are maintained. An example of a fixed-action pattern is the retrieval and maintenance response of many female birds to an egg of their species.

Certain kinds of stimuli are more effective than others in triggering a fixed-action pattern. For example, an egg with the characteristics of that species will be more effective than one that only crudely resembles the natural egg. Another type of fixed-action pattern is the characteristic movements made by animals that herd or flock together, such as the swimming actions of fish and the flying actions of locusts.

Behavior Cycles

Daily cycles of behavior are called **circadian rhythms**. Animals with such behavior cycles lose their exact 24-hour periodicity if they are isolated from the natural phases of light and dark. Cyclical behavior, however, will continue with approximate day-to-day phasing. The cycle is thus initiated intrinsically but modified by external factors.

Daily cycles of eating, maintained by many animals, provide a good example of cycles with both internal and external control. The internal controls are the natural bodily rhythms of eating and satiation. External modulators include the elements of the environment that occur in familiar cyclic patterns, such as dinner bells and clocks.

Sleep and wakefulness are the most obvious examples of cyclic behavior. In fact, these behavior patterns have been associated with particular patterns of brain waves.

Environmental Rhythms

In many situations, patterns of behavior are established and maintained mainly by periodic **environmental stimuli.** (A human example of this is the response to traffic light signals.) Just as environmental stimuli influence many naturally occurring biological rhythms, biological factors influence behavior governed by periodic environmental stimuli.

LEARNING

Learned behavior involves **adaptive responses** to the environment. Learning is a complex phenomenon that occurs to some extent in all animals. In lower animals, instinctual or innate behaviors are the predominant determinants of behavior patterns, and learning plays a relatively minor role in the modification of these predetermined behaviors. In higher animals, learning plays a more significant role. The capacity for learning adaptive responses is closely correlated with the degree of **neurologic development** (i.e., the capacity of the nervous system, particularly the cerebral cortex, for flexibility and plasticity).

Habituation

Habituation is one of the simplest learning patterns involving the suppression of the normal start response to stimuli. In habituation, repeated stimulation results in decreased responsiveness to that stimulus. The normal autonomic response to that stimulus would serve no useful purpose since the stimulus becomes a part of the background environment; thus, the response to the stimulus is suppressed. If the stimulus is no longer regularly applied, the response tends to recover over time. This is referred to as **spontaneous recovery.** Recovery of the response can also occur with modification of the stimulus.

Classical Conditioning

Classical or **Pavlovian** conditioning involves the association of a normally **autonomic** or visceral response with an environmental stimulus. For this reason, the response learned through Pavlovian conditioning is sometimes called a **conditioned reflex.** In Pavlovian conditioning, the normal, innate stimulus for a reflex is replaced by one chosen by the experimenter. This is illustrated in Figure 19.2.

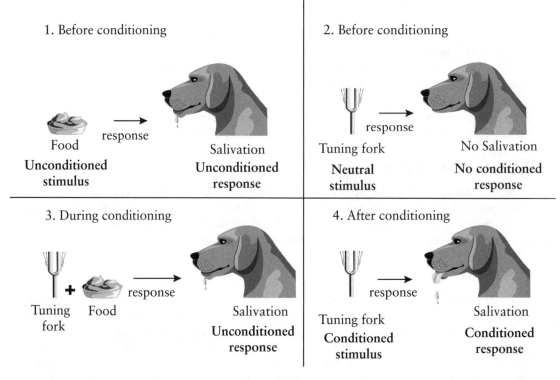

Figure 19.2

Pavlov's experiments

Ivan Pavlov, who won a Nobel Prize for his work on digestive physiology, studied the **salivation reflex** in dogs. In 1927, he discovered that if a dog was presented with an **arbitrary stimulus** (e.g., a bell) and then presented with food, it would eventually salivate on hearing the bell alone. The food elicited the unconditioned response of salivation. After repeated association of the bell with the food, the bell alone could elicit the salivation reflex. Thus, the innate or unconditioned response would occur with the selected stimulus. Pavlov's terminology, still used today, is described below:

- An established (innate) reflex consists of an **unconditioned stimulus** (e.g., food) and the response that is naturally elicited, termed the **unconditioned response** (e.g., salivation).

- A neutral stimulus is a stimulus that will not by itself elicit the response (prior to conditioning). During conditioning, the neutral stimulus (the bell) and the unconditioned stimulus (the food) are presented together. Eventually, the neutral stimulus is able to elicit the response in the absence of the unconditioned stimulus, and it is then called the conditioned stimulus. Pavlov's example of a conditioned stimulus is the sound of a bell for salivation.

- The product of the conditioning experience is termed the **conditioned reflex.** The conditioned reflex in Pavlov's experiment was salivation (the conditioned response) following a previously neutral stimulus (now the conditioned stimulus), such as the sound of a bell.

- Pavlov defined **conditioning** as the establishment of a new reflex (association of stimulus with response) by the addition of a new, previously neutral stimulus to the set of stimuli that are already capable of triggering the response.

Pseudoconditioning

Pseudoconditioning is a phenomenon that can be confused with true classical conditioning. A critical test of conditioning is the determination of whether the conditioning process is actually necessary for the production of a response by a previously "neutral" stimulus. In many cases, the "neutral" stimulus is able to elicit the response even before conditioning and, hence, is not really a neutral stimulus. Pseudoconditioning can be avoided by carefully evaluating all prospective stimuli before conditioning begins.

Operant or Instrumental Conditioning

Operant or instrumental conditioning involves conditioning responses to stimuli with the use of **reward** or **reinforcement.** When the organism exhibits a specific behavioral pattern that the experimenter would like to see repeated, the animal is rewarded. The reinforcement or reward increases the likelihood that the behavior will appear; it has been "reinforced." Although this instrumental conditioning was originally applied to conditioning responses under the voluntary control of the organism, it has been successfully applied more recently to the conditioning of visceral responses, such as changes in heartbeat.

Experiments of B. F. Skinner

B. F. Skinner first demonstrated the principles of operant conditioning and reinforcement. In the original operant conditioning experiments he used the well-known "Skinner box," which consists of a cage with a lever or key and a food dispenser. A food pellet was delivered whenever the animal pressed the lever. Thus, depression of the lever was the **operant response** under study. In later experiments, Skinner varied the type of reinforcement. Reinforcement fell into two categories: positive reinforcement and negative reinforcement.

Positive reinforcement

Positive reinforcement or reward includes providing food, light, or electrical stimulation of the animal's brain "pleasure centers." Following positive reinforcement, the animal was much more likely to repeat the desired behavioral response (e.g., to press the bar). In a sense, the animal has developed a positive connection between the action (response) and the reward (stimulus that followed). This type of conditioning is likely to be involved in normal habit formation.

Negative reinforcement

Negative reinforcement also involves stimulating the brain's pleasure centers. However, in contrast to positive reinforcement, negative reinforcement links the lack of certain behavior with a reward (e.g., a bird may learn that it will receive a food pellet if it does *not* peck on a yellow circle in its cage).

In this case, the animal has developed a negative connection between action (response) and reward (stimulus that followed). Thus, the animal has developed a *positive* connection between the lack of the action and the reward, and the animal is less likely to repeat the behavioral response.

Punishment

Punishment involves conditioning an organism so that it will stop exhibiting a given behavior pattern. Punishment may involve painfully shocking the organism each time the chosen behavior appears. After punishment, the organism is less likely to repeat the behavioral response. The animal develops a negative connection between the stimulus and the response.

Habit family hierarchy

A stimulus is usually associated with several possible responses, each response having a different probability of occurrence. These stimulus–behavioral associations are believed to be ordered in a **habit family hierarchy.** For example, a chicken may respond to a light in many ways, but if one particular response is rewarded, the rewarded response will occur with a higher probability in the future. Reward strengthens a specific behavioral response and raises its order in the hierarchy. Punishment weakens a specific behavioral response and lowers its order in the hierarchy.

Modifications of Conditioned Behavior

Extinction

Extinction is the gradual **elimination** of conditioned responses in the absence of reinforcement (i.e., the "unlearning" of the response pattern). In **instrumental** and **operant conditioning,** the response is diminished and finally eliminated in the absence of reinforcement. The response is not completely unlearned but rather is inhibited in the absence of reinforcement. It will rapidly reappear if the reinforcement is returned. In **classical conditioning,** extinction occurs when the unconditioned stimulus is removed or was never sufficiently paired with the conditioned stimulus. The conditioned stimulus must be paired with the unconditioned stimulus, at least part of the time, for the maintenance of the conditioned response. After sufficient time elapses following extinction, the conditioned response may again be elicited by the conditioned stimulus. The recovery of the conditioned response after extinction is called **spontaneous recovery.**

Generalization and discrimination

Stimulus generalization is the ability of a conditioned organism to respond to stimuli that are similar, but not identical, to the original conditioned stimulus. The less similar the stimulus is to the original conditioned stimulus, the less the response will be. For example, an organism may be conditioned to respond to a stimulus of a 1,000 Hz tone, but it may respond to stimuli somewhat higher or lower in pitch as well. **Stimulus discrimination** involves the ability of the learning organism to respond differentially to slightly different stimuli. For example, if rewards are given during only a very narrow range of sound frequencies (such as a tone of 990 to 1,010 Hz) but not to stimuli outside this range, the organism will learn not to respond to stimuli that are different in tone. A **stimulus generalization gradient** is established after the organism has been conditioned, whereby stimuli further and further away from the original conditioned stimulus elicit responses with decreasing magnitude.

LIMITS OF BEHAVIORIAL CHANGE

Imprinting

Imprinting is a process in which environmental patterns or objects presented to a developing organism during a brief **critical period** in early life become accepted permanently as an element of its behavioral environment (i.e., "stamped in" and included in an animal's behavioral response). A duckling passes through a critical period in which it learns that the first large moving object it sees is its mother. In the natural environment, the first large moving object it sees is typically its mother. However, other objects can be substituted during this period, and the duckling will follow anything that is substituted for its mother. This phenomenon was first identified by the ethologist Konrad Lorenz, who swam in a pond amongst newly hatched ducklings separated from their mother and found that they eventually followed him as if he was their mother.

Critical Period

Critical periods are specific time periods during an animal's early development when it is physiologically able to develop specific behavioral patterns. If the proper environmental pattern is not present during the critical period, the behavioral pattern will not develop properly. Some animals have a **visual critical period.** If light is not present during this period, visual effectors will not develop properly.

INTRASPECIFIC INTERACTIONS

Intraspecific interactions occur as a means of communication between members of a species.

Behavioral Displays

A display may be defined as an **innate behavior** that has evolved as a signal for **communication** between members of the same species. According to this definition, a song, call, or intentional change in an animal's physical characteristics is considered a display. Categories of displays include the following:

- **Reproductive displays** are specific behaviors found in all animals, including humans. Many animals have evolved a variety of complex actions that function as signals in preparation for mating.

- **Agonistic displays** are such things as a dog's display of appeasement when it wags its tail or the dog's antagonistic behavior when it directs its face straight and raises its body.

- Other displays include various **dancing** procedures exhibited by **honeybees,** especially the scout honeybee, to convey information concerning the quality and location of food sources. Displays utilizing auditory, visual, chemical, and tactile elements are often used as a means of communication.

Pecking Order

The relationships among members of the same species living as a contained social group frequently become stable for a period of time. When food, mates, or territory are disputed, a **dominant** member of the species will prevail over a **subordinate** one. The social hierarchy is frequently referred to as the **pecking order.** It minimizes violent intraspecific aggressions by defining stable relationships among members of the group.

Territoriality

Members of most land-dwelling species defend a limited area or **territory** from intrusion by other members of the species. These territories are typically occupied by a male or a male–female pair and are frequently used for mating, nesting, and feeding. Territoriality serves the adaptive functions of distributing members of the species, so the environmental resources are not depleted in a small region, and reducing intraspecific competition. Although there is frequently a minimum size for any species' territory, the territory size varies with the population size and density. The larger the population, the smaller the territories are likely to be.

Response to Chemicals

The **olfactory sense** is immensely important as a means of communication in many animals. Many animals secrete substances called **pheromones,** which influence the behavior of other members of the same species. Pheromones can be classified as one of two types:

- Releaser pheromones trigger a reversible behavioral change in the recipient. For example, female silkworms secrete a very powerful attracting pheromone so powerful that a male responds to one ten-millionth of a gram from a distance of two miles or more. **Sex-attractant** pheromones are secreted by many animals, including cockroaches, queen honeybees, and gypsy moths. In addition to serving as sex attractants, releaser pheromones may also be secreted as **alarm** or **toxic defensive** substances.

- Primer pheromones produce long-term behavioral and physiological alterations in receiving animals. For example, pheromones from male mice may affect the estrous cycles of females. Pheromones have also been shown to limit sexual reproduction in areas of high animal density. Primer pheromones are important in social insects such as ants, bees, and termites, where they regulate role determination and reproductive capacities.

REVIEW PROBLEMS

1. Explain the difference between a complex reflex and a fixed-action pattern.
2. How does pseudoconditioning differ from classical conditioning?
3. What is negative reinforcement?
4. Describe the critical period.
5. What is the difference between releaser pheromones and primer pheromones?

BIO

SOLUTIONS TO REVIEW PROBLEMS

1. A complex reflex involves neural integration at a high level, such as the brainstem or the cerebrum. It involves the neurons within the reticular activation system and as such has a more complex reflex arc than a simple reflex. Fixed-action patterns are coordinated behavioral responses to patterns of stimulation. They are innate, as with reflexes, and the triggers that stimulate a fixed-action pattern can be modified.

2. The determining factor is whether the conditioning process is necessary to get a response by a stimulus that previously did not evoke such a response. That is, often the stimulus being tested could elicit the response even without conditioning and therefore is not a "neutral stimulus." In pseudoconditioning, the stimulus that the animal has been conditioned to respond to can evoke the conditioned response without conditioning, therefore differentiating it from classical conditioning.

3. In contrast to positive reinforcement, where a reward is given following a desired behavior, in negative reinforcement the reward is given following a lack of a certain behavior. In both cases a reward is given, but in negative reinforcement it is rewarding a behavior the animal did not do rather than one it did do.

4. The critical period is a time in an animal's early development when it can develop specific behavior patterns. If the animal does not properly interact with the environment during this time, the behavioral pattern will not develop or will not develop properly.

5. Releaser pheromones trigger a reversible change in the recipient, whereas primer pheromones produce long-term behavioral and physiological changes in the recipient.

CHAPTER TWENTY

Ecology

Ecology is the study of the interactions between organisms and their environment. The **environment** encompasses all that is external to the organism and is necessary for its existence. An organism's environment contains two components: the physical or nonliving (**abiotic**) environment, and the living (**biotic**) environment. The abiotic environment includes climate, temperature, availability of light and water, and the local topology. The biotic environment includes all living things that directly or indirectly influence the life of the organism, including the relationships that exist between organisms.

LEVELS OF BIOLOGICAL ORGANIZATION

Organism

The organism is the individual unit of an ecological system, but the organism itself is composed of smaller units. The organism contains many organ systems, which are made up of **organs.** Organs are formed from **tissues,** tissues from **cells,** cells from many different **molecules,** molecules from **atoms,** and atoms from subatomic particles.

Population

A **species** is any group of similar organisms that are capable of producing fertile offspring. A **population** is a group of organisms of the same species living together in the same location. Examples of populations include dandelions on a lawn, flies in a barn, minnows of a certain species in a pond, and lions in a grassland. Environmental factors, such as nutrients, water, and sunlight limitations, aid in maintaining populations at relatively constant levels.

Communities

A community consists of populations of different plants and animal species interacting with each other in a given environment. The term **biotic community** is used to include only the population and not their physical environment. An **ecosystem** includes the community and the environment. Generally, a community contains populations from all six kingdoms (archea, eubacteria, protists, plants, fungi, and animals), all depending upon each other for survival. The following are examples of communities:

- A lawn contains dandelions, grasses, mushrooms, earthworms, nematodes, bacteria, etc.
- A pond contains dragonflies, algae, minnows, insect larva, etc.

- A forest contains moss, pine, bacteria, lichens, ferns, deer, chipmunks, spiders, foxes, etc.
- A sea contains fish, whales, plankton, etc.

Ecosystem

An ecosystem or ecological community encompasses the interaction between living biotic communities and the nonliving environment. In studying the ecosystem, the biologist emphasizes the effects of the biotic community on the environment and the environment on the community. The examples listed previously for communities are also examples of ecosystems.

Biosphere

The biosphere includes all portions of the planet that support life: the **atmosphere,** the **lithosphere** (rock and soil surface), and the **hydrosphere** (the oceans). It is a relatively thin zone extending a few feet beneath the Earth's surface several miles into the deepest sea, and several miles into the atmosphere.

THE ENVIRONMENT

Physical Environment

Water

Water is the major component of the internal environment of all living things. Water may be readily available, or the organism may possess adaptations for storage and conservation of water.

Temperature

Temperature must be maintained at an optimal level. Protoplasm is destroyed at temperatures below 0°C and at high temperatures. Organisms have adaptations necessary for protection against these extremes. The temperature of a geographic location depends upon its latitude and altitude. In fact, the same changes in habitat that occur as one approaches colder polar regions (changes in latitude) occur as one ascends toward the colder regions of a mountain top (changes in altitude).

Sunlight

Sunlight is the ultimate source of energy for all organisms. Green plants must compete for sunlight in forests. They have adapted to capture as much sunlight as possible by growing broad leaves, branching, growing to greater height, or producing vine growths. The **photic zone,** the top layer of water through which light can penetrate, is where all aquatic photosynthetic activity takes place. In the **aphotic zone,** only animal life and other heterotrophic life exist.

Oxygen supply

This poses no problem for **terrestrial** life since the air contains approximately 20 percent oxygen. Aquatic plants and animals utilize the small amount of oxygen dissolved in water. Pollution can significantly lower oxygen content in water and threaten aquatic life.

Substratum (soil or rock)

The substratum determines the nature of plant and animal life in the soil. Soil is affected by a number of factors:

- Soil **acidity,** or **pH,** may determine what types of plants grow in what types of soil. Some plants, such as rhododendrons and pines, are more suited for growth in acid soil. Acid rain may make soil pH too low for most plant growth.
- The **texture** of soil and its clay content determine the water-holding capacity of the soil. Willows require moist soil. Most plans grow well in **loams,** which contain high percentages of each type of soil.
- **Minerals,** including **nitrates** and **phosphates,** affect the type of vegetation that can be supported. Beach sand has been leached of all minerals and is generally unable to support plant life.
- **Humus** quantity is determined by the amount of decaying plant and animal life in the soil.

Biotic Factors in the Environment

Organisms belonging to the same or different species influence each other's development. Living things interact with other living organisms and with their physical environment.

INTERACTIONS WITHIN THE ECOSYSTEM

Complex interactions exist among the constituents of an ecosystem. These interactions involve a cyclic flow of energy and materials.

The Niche

The **niche** defines the functional role of an organism in its ecosystem. The niche is distinct from the **habitat**—the latter is the physical place where an organism lies. The characteristics of the habitat aid in defining the niche, but additional factors must also be considered. The niche describes what the organism eats, where and how it obtains its food, what climactic factors it can tolerate and which are optimal, the nature of its parasites and predators, where and how it reproduces, etc. The concept of niche embodies every aspect of an organism's existence.

It is implicit in the definition of niche that no two species can ever occupy the same niche in the same location. Organisms occupying the same niche compete for the same limited resources: food, water, light, oxygen, space, minerals, and reproductive sites. There may be many organisms in this niche, but they are all of the same species and thus have the same requirements. The niche is so specific that a species can be identified by the niche it occupies.

Species occupying similar niches utilize at least one resource in common. Therefore, they will compete for that resource. This competition can have a number of outcomes:

- One species may be competitively superior to another and drive the second to **extinction.**
- One species may be competitively superior in some regions, and the other may be superior in other regions under different environmental conditions. This would result in the elimination of one species in some places and the other in other places.
- The two species may rapidly evolve in **divergent** directions under the strong selection pressure resulting from intense competition. Thus, the two species would rapidly evolve greater differences in their niches.

BIO

Nutritional Interactions within the Ecosystem

Autotrophs

Autotrophs are organisms that manufacture their own food. Green plants utilize the energy of the sun to manufacture food. Chemosynthetic bacteria obtain energy from the oxidation of inorganic sulfur, iron, and nitrogen compounds.

Heterotrophs

Heterotrophs cannot synthesize their own food and must depend upon autotrophs or other heterotrophs in the ecosystem to obtain food and energy.

Herbivores

These animals consume only plants or plant foods. The toughness of cellulose-containing plant tissues has led to the development of structures for crushing and grinding that can extract plant fluids. Herbivores have long digestive tracts that provide greater surface area and time for digestion. However, they cannot digest much of the food they consume. **Symbiotic bacteria** capable of digesting cellulose inhabit the digestive tracts of herbivores and allow the breakdown and utilization of cellulose.

Herbivores are more adept in defense than carnivores because they are often prey. Many herbivores, such as cows and horses, have hoofs instead of toes for faster movement on the grasslands. They have incisors adapted for cutting and molars adapted for grinding their food. Insects or other invertebrates can also be herbivores.

Carnivores

Carnivores are animals that eat only other animals. In general, carnivores, such as hyenas, possess pointed teeth and fanglike canine teeth for eating flesh. They have shorter digestive tracts due to the easier digestibility of animal food.

Omnivores

Omnivores, such as humans, are animals that eat both plants and animals.

Interspecific Interactions

A community is not simply a collection of different species living within the same area. It is an integrated system of species that are dependent upon one another for survival. The major types of interspecific interactions are symbiosis, predation, saprophytism, and scavenging.

Symbiosis

Symbionts live together in an intimate, often permanent association, which may or may not be beneficial to both participants. Some symbiotic relationships are **obligatory**; that is, one or both organisms cannot survive without the other. Symbiotic relationships are classified according to the benefits the symbionts receive. The types of symbiotic relationships include commensalism, mutualism, and parasitism.

Commensalism (+/0)

One organism is benefited (+) by the association, and the other is not affected (0). The host neither discourages nor fosters the relationship. Some examples include the following:

- Remora and shark: The remora (suckerfish) attaches itself by a holdfast device on the underside of a shark. Through this association the remora obtains the food the shark discards, wide geographic dispersal, and protection from enemies. The shark is totally indifferent to the association.
- Barnacle and whale: The barnacle is a sessile crustacean that attaches to the whale and obtains wider feeding opportunities through the migrations of the whale.

Mutualism (+/+)

A symbiotic relationship from which both organisms derive some benefit (+). Some examples include the following:

- Tick bird and rhinoceros: The bird receives food in the form of ticks on the skin of the rhinoceros. The rhinoceros has its ticks removed and is warned of danger by the rapid departure of the bird.
- Fungi and algae: In a lichen, the green algae produces food for itself and the fungus by **photosynthesis**. The meshes of fungal threads support the algae and conserve rainwater. The fungus also provides carbon dioxide and nitrogenous wastes for the algae, all of which are needed for photosynthesis and protein synthesis.
- Nitrogen-fixing bacteria and legumes: Nitrogen-fixing bacteria invade the roots of legumes, and infected cells grow to form root nodules. In the nodule, the legume provides nutrients for the bacteria and the bacteria fixes nitrogen (by changing it into a soluble nitrate, a mineral essential for protein synthesis by the plant). These bacteria are a major source of usable nitrogen, which is needed by all plants and animals.
- Protozoa and termites: Termites chew and ingest wood but are unable to digest the cellulose. Protozoa in the digestive tract of the termite secrete an enzyme that digests the cellulose. Both organisms share the carbohydrates. Thus, the protozoan is guaranteed protection and a steady food supply, while the termites are able to obtain nourishment from the ingested wood.
- Intestinal bacteria and humans; Bacteria utilize some of the food material not fully digested by humans and manufacture vitamin K.

Parasitism (+/−)

A parasite benefits (+) at the expense (−) of the host. Parasitism exists when competition for food is most intense. Few autotrophs (green plants) exist as parasites (mistletoe is an exception). Parasitism instead flourishes among organisms such as bacteria, fungi, and animals. Some parasites cling to the exterior surface of the host (**ectoparasites**) using suckers or clamps. They may bore through the skin and suck out blood and nutrients. Leeches, ticks, and sea lampreys employ these techniques. Other parasites (**endoparasites**) live within the host. To gain entry, they must pass through defenses such as skin, digestive juices, antibodies, and white blood cells. Parasites possess special adaptations to overcome these defenses.

Parasitism is advantageous and efficient. The parasite lives with a minimum expenditure of energy. Parasites may even have parasites of their own. Thus, a mammal may have parasitic worms, which in turn are parasitized by bacteria, which in turn are victims of bacteriophages. It is interesting to note that successful parasites do not kill their hosts; this would lead to the death of the parasite. The more dangerous the parasite, the less the chance it will survive. Some examples are the following:

- Virus and host cell: All viruses are parasites. They contain nucleic acids surrounded by a protein and are nonfunctional outside the host. Upon entry of the viral nucleic acids into the host, the virus takes over the host cell functions and redirects them into replication of itself. The life functions of the bacterial cell slow down or cease in favor of viral replication.

BIO

- Disease bacteria and animals: Most bacteria are either chemosynthetic (energy producing) or **saprophytic** (bacteria of decay). For example, diphtheria is parasitic upon humans, anthrax is parasitic upon sheep, and tuberculosis is parasitic upon cows or humans.
- Disease fungi and animals: Most fungi are saprophytic. Ringworm is parasitic on humans.
- Worms and animals: An example is the parasitic relationship that exists between the tapeworm and humans.

Predation

Predators are free-living organisms that feed on other living organisms. This definition of predation includes both **carnivores** and **herbivores**. The effects of predators on their prey vary. The predator may severely limit the numbers or distribution of the prey, and the prey may become extinct. On the other hand, the predator may only slightly affect the prey because the predator is scarce or commonly utilizes another food source. In many cases, the predator aids in controlling the numbers of the prey but not so much as to endanger the existence of the prey population. Predator–prey relationships evolve toward a balance in which the predator is a regulatory influence on the prey but not a threat to its survival. Examples of predators include the hawk, lion, human, and Venus flytrap.

Saprophytism

Saprophytes include those protists and fungi that **decompose** (digest) dead organism matter externally and absorb the nutrients; they constitute a vital link in the cycling of material within the ecosystem. Examples of saprophytes include mold, mushrooms, bacteria of decay, and slime molds.

Scavengers

Scavengers are animals that consume dead animals. They therefore require no adaptations for hunting and killing their prey. Decomposers, such as the bacteria of decay, may be considered scavengers. Examples of scavengers include the vulture and hyena. The snapping turtle is an organism that may be considered both a scavenger and a predator.

Intraspecific Interactions

Competition is not restricted to interspecific interactions (relations between species). Individuals belonging to the same species utilize the same resources; if a particular resource is limited, then these organisms compete with one another. Members of the same species compete, but they must also **cooperate**. Intraspecific cooperation may be extensive (as with the formation of societies in animal species) or may be nearly nonexistent. Relationships between individuals within a species are influenced by both disruptive and cohesive forces. Competition is the chief disruptive force. Cohesive forces include reproduction and protection from predators and destructive weather.

Interactions between Organisms and Their Environment

Osmoregulation

Animals have developed many adaptations for maintaining their internal osmolarity and conserving water.

- Saltwater fish live in a hyperosmotic environment, which causes them to lose water and take in salt. They are constantly in danger of dehydration and must compensate by constant drinking and active secretion of salt across their gills.

- Freshwater fish live in a hypoosmotic environment, which causes intake of excess water and excessive salt loss. These fish correct this condition by seldom drinking, absorbing salt through the gills, and excreting dilute urine.

- Insects excrete solid uric acid crystals to conserve water.

- Desert animals possess adaptations for avoiding desiccation (drying up). The camel can tolerate a wide range of body temperatures and possesses fat layers in regions that are exposed to solar radiation. The horned toad has thick, scaly skin, which prevents water loss. Other desert animals burrow in the sand during the day and search for food at night, thereby avoiding the intense heat that causes water loss.

- Plants possess adaptations for conservation of water. Nondesert plants possess waxy **cuticles** on leaf surfaces and stomata on the lower leaf surfaces only. They shed leaves in winter to avoid water loss. Desert plants have extensive root systems, fleshy stems to store water, spiny leaves to limit water loss, extra thick cuticles, and few stomata.

Thermoregulation

Cellular respiration only transfers a fraction of the energy derived from the oxidation of carbohydrates into the high-energy bonds of ATP. Roughly 60 percent of the total energy is given off as heat. The vast majority of animals and plants are cold-blooded or **poikilothermic**, and most of their heat energy escapes to the environment. The body temperature of poikilotherms is very close to that of their surroundings. Since an organism's metabolism is closely tied to its body temperature, the activity of poikilothermic animals is radically affected by environmental temperature changes. As the temperature rises, these organisms become more active. As temperatures fall, they become sluggish and lethargic.

Some animals, notably mammals and birds, are warm-blooded or **homeothermic**. They have evolved physical mechanisms that allow them to make use of the heat produced as a consequence of respiration. Physical adaptations like fat, hair, and feathers retard heat loss. Homeotherms maintain constant body temperatures that are higher than the temperature of environment. They are less dependent upon environmental temperature than poikilothermic animals and are able to inhabit a comparatively wider range of environments.

RELATIONSHIPS WITHIN THE ECOSYSTEM

Energy Flow

All living things require energy to carry on their life functions. The complex pathways involved in the transfer of energy through the living components of the ecosystem (biotic community) may be mapped in the form of a **food chain** or **food web**.

Food chain

A food chain is a single chain showing the transfer of energy. For example, energy from the sun enters living systems through the **photosynthetic** production of glucose by green plants. Within the food chain, energy is transferred from the original sources in green plants through a series of organisms, with repeated stages of consumption and finally decomposition. Thus, these are producers, primary consumers, secondary consumers, and decomposers.

BIO

Producers

The **autotrophic** green plants and **chemosynthetic** bacteria are the producers. They utilize the energy of the sun and simple raw materials (carbon dioxide, water, minerals), respectively, to manufacture carbohydrates, proteins, and lipids. The radiant energy of the sun is captured and stored in the C–H bond. Producers always form the initial step in any food chain. The wheat plant is a typical producer.

Primary consumers

Primary consumers are animals that consume green plants (herbivores). Examples include the cow, grasshopper, and elephant.

Secondary consumers

Secondary consumers are animals that consume the primary consumers (carnivores). These include frogs, tigers, and dragonflies.

Tertiary consumers

These are animals that feed on secondary consumers (also called carnivores).

Decomposers

Decomposers include saprophytic organisms and organisms of decay, which include bacteria and fungi. The producers and consumers concentrate and organize materials of the environment into complex living substances. Living things give off wastes during their lifetimes and eventually die. Bacteria and fungi decompose the organic wastes and dead tissues to simpler compounds, such as nitrates and phosphates, which are returned to the environment to be used again by living organisms. These processes are demonstrated in **food webs** and **material cycles** (nitrogen, carbon, and water).

Food web

The food web is not simply a linear chain but an intricate collection of interconnected food chains. Almost every species is consumed by one or more other species, some of which are on different food chain levels. The result is a series of branches and cross-branches among all the food chains of a community to form a web. The greater the number of pathways in a community food web, the more stable the community. For example, owls eat rabbits. If rabbits died off because of disease, there would be more vegetation available to mice. Mice would provide substitute food for owls. Meanwhile, the decimated rabbit population would have a better chance of recovering while owls concentrated their predation on mice.

Food pyramids

Without a constant input of energy from the sun, an ecosystem would soon run down. As food is transferred from one level of the food chain to the next, a transfer of energy occurs. According to the second law of thermodynamics, energy transfer involves a loss of energy. In addition to the energy lost in the transfer, each level of the food chain utilizes some of the energy it obtains from food for its own metabolism (i.e., to support life functions) and loses some additional energy in the form of heat. A pyramid of energy is thus a fundamental property of all ecosystems at all levels.

BIO

Pyramid of Energy

Each member of a food chain utilizes some of the energy it obtains from its food for its own metabolism (life functions) and loses some additional energy in the form of heat. Since this means a loss of energy at each feeding level, the producer organism at the base of the pyramid contains the greatest amount of energy. Less energy is available for the primary consumer and still less for secondary and tertiary consumers. The smallest amount of available energy is thus at the top of the pyramid.

Pyramid of Mass

Since organisms at the upper levels of the food chain derive their food energy from organisms at lower levels, and since energy is lost from one level to the next, each level can support a successively smaller biomass. Three hundred pounds of foliage (producer) may support 125 pounds of insects. This may support 50 pounds of insectivorous hens, which in turn may be just the right amount to sustain 25 pounds of hawks.

Pyramid of Numbers

Consumer organisms that are highest in the food chain are usually larger and heavier than those further down. Since the lower organism has a greater total mass, there must be a greater number of lower-level organisms. (A large bass eats tiny minnows but eats many of them.) With the greatest number of organisms at the base (producer level) and the smallest number at the top (final consumer level), we have a pyramid of numbers.

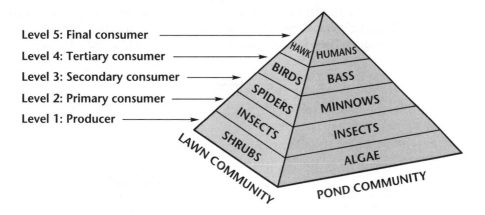

Figure 20.1

Since other factors, such as the generation time of the size of the organisms must be considered, the pyramids of numbers and biomass do not apply to all levels at all times (unlike the pyramid of energy). In general, as the pyramid is ascended, there is less energy content, less mass, and a lesser number of organisms.

Material Cycles

Material is cycled and recycled between organisms and their environments, passing from inorganic forms to organic forms and then back to the inorganic forms. Many of these cycles are accomplished largely through the action of scavengers (such as hyenas and vultures) and decomposers (saprophytes such as bacteria and fungi).

Nitrogen cycle

Nitrogen is an essential component of amino acids and nucleic acids, which are the building blocks of all living things. Since there is a finite amount of nitrogen on the Earth, it is important that it be recovered and reused.

- Elemental nitrogen is chemically inert and cannot be used by most organisms. Lightning and nitrogen-fixing bacteria in the roots of legumes change the nitrogen to usable, soluble nitrates.

- The nitrates are absorbed by plants and are used to synthesize nucleic acids and plant proteins.

- Animals eat the plants and synthesize specific animal proteins from the plant proteins.

- Nitrogen locked up in waste and dead tissues is released by the action of bacteria of decay, which convert the proteins into ammonia (NH_3).

- Two fates await the ammonia. Some is nitrified to nitrites by chemosynthetic bacteria and then to usable nitrates by nitrifying bacteria. The rest is denitrified. This means the ammonia is broken down to release free nitrogen, which returns to the beginning of the cycle. Note the four kinds of bacteria that are involved in this cycle: **decay, nitrifying, denitrifying,** and **nitrogen fixing**. The bacteria have no use for the excretory ammonia, nitrites, nitrates, and nitrogen they produce. These materials are essential, however, for the existence of other living organisms.

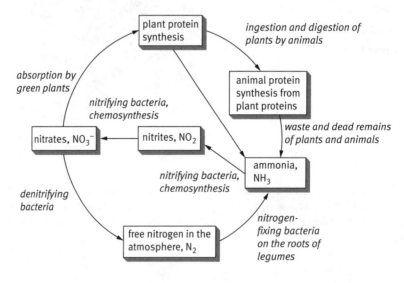

Figure 20.2

Carbon cycle

- **Gaseous CO_2** enters the living world when plants use it to produce glucose via photosynthesis. The carbon atoms from CO_2 are bonded to hydrogen and other carbon atoms. Plants use the glucose to make starch, proteins, and fats.
- Animals eat plants and use the digested nutrients to form carbohydrates, fats, and proteins characteristic of the species. A part of these organic compounds is used as fuel in respiration in both plants and animals.
- The metabolically produced CO_2 is released into the air. The rest of the organic carbon remains locked within an organism until its death (except for wastes given off), at which time decay processes by bacteria return CO_2 to the air.

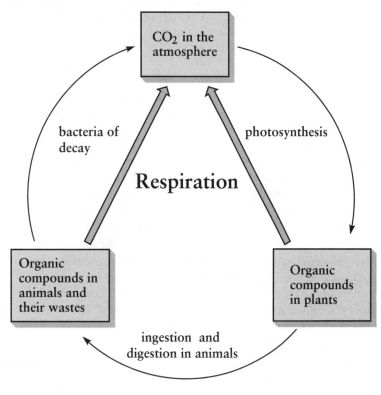

Figure 20.3

Other cycles

Other cycles recycle water, oxygen, and phosphorus. These substances are used by almost all living things and must be returned by the biotic community to the environment for reuse.

STABILITY WITHIN THE ECOSYSTEM

Conditions for Stability in an Ecosystem

An ecosystem is self-sustaining and, therefore, will be stable if three conditions are met. First, it needs a relatively stable physical environment (abiotic factors) and a relatively stable biotic community. Second, a stable ecosystem requires a constant energy source and a living system incorporating this energy into organic compounds. Lastly, the cycling of materials between the living system and its environment is critical for a stable ecosystem.

BIO

Ecological Succession

Ecological succession is the orderly process by which one biotic community replaces or succeeds another until a climax community is established. Each community stage, or **sere**, in an ecological succession is identified by a **dominant** species—the one that exerts control over the other species that are present. Thus, in a grassland community, grass is the dominant species.

Changes occur because each community that establishes itself changes the environment, making it more unfavorable for itself and more favorable for the community that is to succeed it. Successive communities are composed of populations that are able to exist under the new conditions. Finally, a stage occurs in which a population alters the environment in such a way that the original conditions giving rise to that population are recreated. Replacement stops and the climax community is created, which is the final and most stable stage of ecological succession. This climax community is permanent in the ecosystem unless the abiotic factors are drastically altered by climatic or geological upheavals. If this happens, a new series of successions is initiated.

- Example 1: Consider a barren rocky area in the northeastern United States, barren perhaps as a result of a severe forest fire. Lichen may be the first or pioneer organism to resettle this area. Recall that lichen is an association between an algae and a fungus. Acids produced by lichen attack the rocks and help to form bits of soil. Since lichens thrive only on a solid surface, conditions are now worse for the lichen but better for mosses. Airborne spores of mosses land on the soil and germinate. The result is a new sere with the moss as the dominant species in the community. As the remains of the moss build up the soil still more, annual grasses and then perennial grasses with deeper roots become the dominant species. As time goes on, we find shrubs and trees. The first trees are the sun-loving gray birch and poplar. As more and more trees compete for the sun, these trees are replaced by white pine and finally maples and beeches, which grow in deep shade—the climax community.

  The growth of maples and beeches produces the same conditions that originally favored their appearance. And so this community remains for thousands of years. In the final maple-beech community, you would find foxes, deer, chipmunks, and plant-eating insects. These are animals that would not have been found in the original barren rock terrain. However, one forest fire can kill the entire community. Ecological succession then starts all over again, commencing with lichen and bare rock.

  It is important to note again that the dominant species of the climax community depends on such physical factors as temperature, nature of the soil, rainfall, etc. Thus, the climax community in New York at higher elevations is hemlock-beech-maple, while at lower elevations, the climax plants are more often oak-hickory. In cold Maine, the climax community is dominated by pine; in the wet areas of Wisconsin, by cypress; in sandy New Jersey, by pine; on a cold windy mountain top, by scrub oak.

- Example 2: Ecological succession in a pond. A quick summary:

  Step 1: The pond contains plants such as algae and pondweed and animals such as protozoa, water insects, and small fish.

  Step 2: Shallow pools formed as the pond fills in bring reeds, cattails, and water lilies.

  Step 3: Moist land brings grass, herbs, shrubs, willow trees, frogs, and snakes.

  Step 4: Woodland brings the climax tree, perhaps pine or oak.

The Climax Community

A climax community is the stable, living (biotic) part of an ecosystem, in which populations exist in balance with each other and with the environment. The type of climax community depends upon all the abiotic factors: rainfall, soil conditions, temperature, shade, etc. A climax community persists until a major climactic or geological change disturbs the abiotic factors or a major biotic change (disease, mutation, etc.) affects the populations. Once the equilibrium is upset, new climax conditions are produced and new communities will be established in the ecosystem.

WORLD BIOMES (MAJOR COMMUNITIES)

Terrestrial Biomes

The evolutionary origin of plants and animals can be traced to the seas. To survive on land, these organisms had to develop adaptations to face an environment with: (1) a relative lack of water; (2) a relative lack of food and supporting medium; (3) varying temperature (as compared to the oceans, which have a relatively constant temperature); and (4) varying composition of the soil as compared to the definite salt composition in the oceans. The conditions in different terrestrial and climate regions selected for plants and animals possessing suitable adaptations. Each **geographic region** is inhabited by a distinct community, called a **biome**, existing in the major climate areas.

Land biomes are characterized and named according to the **climax vegetation** of the region. The climax vegetation is the vegetation that becomes dominant and stable after years of evolutionary development. Since plants are important as food producers, they determine the nature of the inhabiting animal population, and thus the climax vegetation determines the **climax animal population**. Some types of terrestrial biomes are as follows:

Desert biome

Deserts receive fewer than ten inches of rain each year; the rain is concentrated within a few heavy cloudbursts. The main growing season in the desert is restricted to those days after rainfalls. Generally, small plants and animals inhabit the desert. Most desert plants conserve water actively (cactus, sagebrush, and mesquite). Desert animals live in burrows (insects and lizards). Few birds and mammals are found in deserts except those that have developed adaptations for maintaining constant body temperatures. Examples of deserts include the Sahara in Africa and the Gobi in Asia.

Grassland biome

Grasslands are characterized by low rainfall (usually 10–30 inches per year), although this is considerably more than the desert biomes receive. Grasslands provide no shelter for **herbivorous mammals** (bison, antelope, cattle, and zebra) from carnivorous predators. Land animals that do inhabit the grasslands frequently have developed long legs, and many are hoofed. Examples of grasslands include the prairies east of the Rockies, the steppes of the Ukraine, and the pampas of Argentina.

Rainforest biome

Rainforests, sometimes known as jungles, are characterized by torrential rains. Tropical rainforests have high temperatures, whereas temperature rainforests are more moderate. They both include climax communities with dense growth of vegetation that does not shed its leaves. Vegetation, such as vines and **epiphytes** (plants growing on other plants), and animals, such as monkeys, lizards, snakes, and birds, inhabit rainforests. Trees grow closely together, and sunlight hardly reaches the forest floor. The floor is inhabited by **saprophytes,** which live off of dead organic matter. Tropical rainforests are found in Central Africa, Central America, the Amazon basin, and Southeast Asia. Temperate rainforests are much more rare but can be found in western North and South America as well as on islands off of eastern Asian and Australian coasts.

Temperate deciduous forest biome

Temperate deciduous forests have cold winters, warm summers, and moderate rainfall. Inhabitants include beech, maple, oaks, and willow trees, which shed their leaves during the cold winter months. Animals in temperate deciduous forests include deer, foxes, woodchucks, squirrels, and birds. These biomes are found in the northeastern and central-eastern United States and in Central Europe.

Temperate coniferous forest biome

These forests are cold, dry, and inhabited mainly by trees that do not lose their leaves, such as fir, pine, and spruce trees. Much of the vegetation has evolved adaptations for water conservation, such as needle-shaped leaves. These forests are found in the extreme northern part of the United States and in southern Canada and contain the largest biomass of any terrestrial biome, in large part due to massive trees, such as the redwood. Animal inhabitants include beavers, bears, sheep, squirrels, and birds.

Taiga biome

Taigas receive less rainfall than temperate forests. They have long, cold winters and, like coniferous forests, are inhabited by trees that do not lose their leaves, especially the spruce. The forest floors in the taiga are characterized by thin soil covered in moss and lichens. The chief animal inhabitants are moose and deer; however, bears, wolves, rodents, and birds are also found there. Taigas exist in the extreme northern parts of Canada and Russia.

Tundra biome

The tundra is a treeless, frozen plain found between the taiga and the northern ice sheets. The ground is covered in snow and ice for much of the year and can be described as **permafrost.** There is only a very short summer and thus growing season, during when the ground becomes wet and marshy. Lichens, mosses, polar bears, musk oxen, and arctic hares are found in the tundra.

Polar region

Polar regions surround the **polar ice caps** and are frozen areas with no vegetation and few terrestrial animals. Animals that do inhabit polar regions generally live near the oceans and include penguins and polar bears. Although ice is present, there is little precipitation (falling rain or snow), so most polar regions can also be considered deserts.

Terrestrial Biomes and Altitude

The sequence of biomes between the equator and the poles is comparable to the sequence of regions on mountains. The nature of those regions is determined by the same decisive factors—temperature and rainfall. For example, the base of a mountain would resemble the biome of a temperate deciduous area. As one ascends the mountain, one would pass a coniferous-like biome, then taiga-like, tundra-like, and polar-like biomes.

Aquatic Biomes

More than 70 percent of the Earth's surface is covered by water. Most of the Earth's plant and animal life is found in water. As much as 90 percent of the Earth's food and oxygen production (**photosynthesis**) takes place in the water. Aquatic biomes are classified according to criteria quite different from the criteria used to classify terrestrial biomes. Plants have little controlling influence on communities of aquatic biomes compared to their role in terrestrial biomes. Aquatic areas are the most stable ecosystems: the conditions affecting temperature, the amount of available oxygen and carbon dioxide, and the amount of suspended or dissolved materials are stable over very large areas with little tendency to change. Therefore, aquatic food webs and aquatic communities are balanced. There are two types of major aquatic biomes: **marine** and **freshwater**.

Marine biomes

The oceans connect to form one continuous body of water, which controls the Earth's temperature by absorbing solar heat. Water has the distinctive property of being able to absorb or utilize large amounts of heat without undergoing a great temperature change. Marine biomes contain a relatively constant amount of nutrient materials and dissolved salts.

Although ocean conditions are more uniform than those on land, distinct zones in the marine biomes exist.

- **Intertidal zone:** The region exposed at low tides that undergoes variations in temperature and periods of dryness. Populations in the intertidal zones include algae, sponges, clams, snails, sea urchins, starfish, and crabs.
- **Neritic zone:** The region on the continental shelf that contains ocean with depths up to 600 feet and extends several hundred miles from the shores. Populations in littoral zone regions include algae, crabs, crustaceans, and many different species of fish.
- **Pelagic zone:** Typical of the open seas, this can be divided into photic and aphotic zones (see Figure 20.4).
- **Photic zone:** The sunlit layer of the open sea extending to a depth of 250–600 feet. It contains **plankton**, passively drifting masses of microscopic photosynthetic and heterotrophic organisms, and **nekton**, active swimmers such as fish, sharks, or whales that feed on plankton and smaller fish. The chief autotroph is the **diatom**, an alga.
- **Aphotic zone:** The region beneath the photic zone that receives no sunlight. There is no photosynthesis in the aphotic zone, and only heterotrophs exist here. Deep-sea organisms in this zone have adaptations enabling them to survive in very cold water with high pressures and in complete darkness. The zone contains nekton and **benthos** (the crawling and sessile organisms). Some are scavengers, and some are predators. The habitat of the aphotic zone is fiercely competitive.

Figure 20.4

BIO

Freshwater biomes

Rivers, lakes, ponds, and marshes—the links between the oceans and land—contain freshwater. Rivers are the routes by which ancient marine organisms reached land and evolved terrestrial adaptations. Many forms failed to adapt to land and developed adaptations for freshwater. Others developed special adaptations suitable for both land and freshwater. As in marine biomes, factors affecting life in freshwater include temperature, transparency (suspended mud particles decrease illumination), depth of water, available carbon dioxide and oxygen, and most important, salt concentration. Freshwater biomes are different from saltwater biomes in three basic ways:

- Freshwater is **hypotonic**, creating a diffusion gradient that results in the passage of water into the cell. Freshwater organisms have homeostatic mechanisms to maintain water balance by the regular removal of excess water. These include the contractile vacuoles of protozoa and excretory systems of fish. Plant cells have rigid cell walls and thus build up cell pressure (cell **turgor**) as water flows in. This pressure counteracts the gradient pressure, stops the influx of water, and establishes water balance.

- In rivers and streams, strong, swift currents exist, and thus selection favored the survival of fish that developed strong muscles and plants with root-like **holdfasts**.

- Freshwater biomes, except very large lakes, are affected by variations in climate and water. The temperature of freshwater bodies may vary considerably; they may freeze or dry up; and mud from their floors may be stirred up by storms.

REVIEW PROBLEMS

1. Which of the following does not affect soil?

   A. Texture

   B. Nitrates

   C. Phosphates

   D. Loams

   E. Acidity

2. What is NOT true about niches?

   A. There may be many organisms of different species within the same niche.

   B. What the organism eats helps define the niche.

   C. Organisms in the same niche compete for resources.

   D. A species can be identified by the niche it occupies.

   E. Niches are different from habitats.

3. Which is an example of symbiosis?

   A. Predation

   B. Saprophytism

   C. Scavenging

   D. Commensalism

   E. Cooperation

4. Which is an example of a secondary consumer?

   A. Autotrophs

   B. Herbivores

   C. Carnivores

   D. Decomposers

   E. Bacteria

5. Which of the following is NOT true about the nitrogen cycle?

   A. Elemental nitrogen cannot be used by most organisms.

   B. Nitrates cannot be absorbed by plants.

   C. Bacteria of decay convert proteins into ammonia.

   D. Ammonia is broken down to release free nitrogen.

   E. Chemosynthetic bacteria turn ammonia intro nitrites.

6. Which is NOT a region of a marine biome?

   A. Intertidal zone

   B. Nekton zone

   C. Pelagic zone

   D. Aphotic zone

   E. Neritic zone

SOLUTIONS TO REVIEW PROBLEMS

1. **D** Loams contain high percentages of each type of soil, and most plants grow well in this type of environment. The other characteristics of soil affect the nature of plant and animal life that are able to live within the soil.

2. **A** No two species can ever occupy the same niche in the same location. All the other statements about niches are true.

3. **D** Symbionts live together in an association that may or may not be beneficial to both participants. In commensalism, one organism benefits from the association and the other is not affected. In predation, one free-living organism feeds on other living organisms. Saprophytes decompose dead organic matter to absorb the nutrients, and scavengers consume dead animals. Cooperation is an example of intraspecific interactions within members of the same species.

4. **C** Carnivores are secondary consumers because they consume primary consumers, which are herbivores. Autotrophs and bacteria are producers.

5. **B** Nitrates are in fact absorbed by plants and are used to synthesize nucleic acids and plant proteins. For a diagram of the nitrogen cycle, see Figure 20.2.

6. **B** Nekton are active swimmers such as fish and whales that feed on plankton and smaller fish. They are found in the photic zone.

CHAPTER TWENTY-ONE

Taxonomy

Billions of years of evolution have led to the great diversity of living organisms we see today. Scientists have tried to categorize relationships among the vast number of different organisms. The science of classification and the nomenclature used are known as **taxonomy**. The modern classification system seeks to group organisms on the basis of **evolutionary relationships**. In this system the bat, whale, horse, and humans are placed in the same class of animals because they have all descended from a common ancestor. Since much of early evolutionary history is not known, there is some disagreement among biologists as to the best classification system to employ, particularly with regard to groups of unicellular organisms. Taxonomy takes into account anatomical and structural characteristics; modes of excretion, movement, and digestion; genetic makeup; and biochemical capabilities. Taxonomic organization proceeds from the largest, broadest group to the smallest, most specific subgroups.

TAXONOMIC CLASSIFICATIONS

Biologists originally divided all living things into two categories: plants and animal. This division ignored a number of different organisms, and since then, several new systems have been proposed as additional knowledge is gained. The modern classification system used on the exam now separates the largest divisions of life by **domain** based on the degree of differences among them. The three domains are Archaea, Bacteria, and Eukarya. Within those domains are six **kingdoms**: Archaea, Eubacteria, Protista, Fungi, Plantae, and Animalia. Viruses fall somewhere outside of this system.

The modern scheme of taxonomy includes not only the three domains and six kingdoms but also further division. Each kingdom is divided into several major **phyla** (in the animal kingdom) or **divisions** (in other kingdoms). A phylum or division is further divided into **classes**. Each class includes multiple **orders**. Orders are subdivided into **families**, and each family is made up of many **genera** (singular *genus*). The **species** is the final major subdivision. Organisms of the same species can mate with one another to produce fertile offspring.

BIO

Each level also may have additional subdivisions, especially when many branching evolutionary paths are represented at one level. For example, humans can be classified as **Domain**: Eukarya, **Kingdom**: Animalia, **Phylum**: Chordata, **Subphylum**: Vertebrata, **Class**: Mammalia, **Order**: Primates, **Family**: Hominidae, **Tribe**: Homini, **Genus**: *Homo*, **Species**: *sapiens*.

All organisms are assigned a binomial name consisting of the genus and species name of that organism. Thus, humans are *Homo sapiens*, and the common housecat is *Felis domestica*.

The following sections outline specific information about the domains and kingdoms as well as examples of specific subdivisions within them. However, on Test Day, the entire field of taxonomy will only contribute to three Biology questions, which constitutes only 7.5 percent of the subtest. Since some (or all) of those questions may pertain to the broader ideas behind taxonomy listed above, the probability of seeing a specific species or even group is very low. Therefore, efficient use of your study time means not focusing on memorizing every phylum, class, and order but rather learning the general characteristics of the kingdoms and only quickly reviewing the more specific groupings. A good way to do this is to pick a model organism from each category that exemplifies the traits of that group. In that way, remembering one species will allow you to remember characteristics about all the members of that group. The following organisms will serve as great examples to memorize, or you can choose models of your own.

MONERA (ARCHAEA AND EUBACTERIA)

Monerans are **prokaryotes** (e.g., bacteria). They lack a nucleus or any membrane-bound organelles and are single-celled organisms that reproduce asexually. Monerans may exist as single cells or as aggregates of cells that stick together after division.

The kingdom Monera was part of the former, five-kingdom system but has since been divided into two separate kingdoms based on newly discovered differences among its members: the eubacteria and the archaea. Although both new kingdoms are composed of single-celled, prokaryotic organisms, they likely split down different evolutionary paths over three billion years ago.

Eubacteria

Bacteria are generally single-celled prokaryotes with a single double-stranded circular loop of DNA that is not enclosed by a nuclear membrane. Almost all forms have **cell walls**. They play active roles in **biogeochemical cycles**, recycling various chemicals such as carbon, nitrogen, phosphorus, and sulfur. Bacteria may be classified by their **morphological** appearances: **cocci** (round), **bacilli** (rods), and **spirilla** (spiral). Some forms are **duplexes** (diplo–), **clusters** (staph–), and **chains** (strepto–). Bacteria are ubiquitous, and many possess a wide variety of complex biochemical pathways.

Cyanobacteria

Cyanobacteria are types of bacteria that live primarily in fresh water but also exist in marine environments. They possess a cell wall and **photosynthetic pigments** but have no flagella, true nuclei, chloroplasts, or mitochondria. They can withstand extreme temperatures and are believed to be directly descended from the first organisms that developed photosynthetic capabilities. Cyanobacteria are sometimes called blue-green algae, but be careful not to confuse them with other forms of algae, which are eukaryotic and members of the Protista kingdom instead.

Archaea

Archaea were formerly thought to be types of bacteria, but recent evidence shows that they are fundamentally different and in fact compose both their own domain and kingdom. Archaea are prokaryotes, like bacteria, and often have cell walls and flagella. However, they also exhibit several unique variations on the basic prokaryote plan, such as having cell membranes composed of glycerol-ether lipids, which is different from both Bacteria and Eukarya since they use glycerol-ester lipids instead. Further differences include changes to the molecules involved in basic biochemical processes, such as metabolism and translation; some of Archaea's enzymes correspond instead with Eukarya, and some are wholly unique. This may be due to the fact that Archaea inhabit a wide variety of environments, including extreme areas with high temperatures or high acidity. Scientists still have much to learn about Archaea, so having only a basic knowledge of their existence will be sufficient for Test Day.

PROTISTA

The Protist kingdom contains primitive eukaryotic organisms with membrane-bound nuclei and organelles. These organisms are either single cells or colonies of similar cells with no differentiation of specialized tissues. Each protist cell possesses the capability to carry out all of the life processes. The Protist kingdom contains all simple eukaryotes that cannot be classified as plants or animals. For example, the protists of the genus *Euglena* demonstrate the motility of animals and the photosynthetic capabilities of plants. The kingdom is divided into many phyla, which fall primarily into the categories of **protozoa** and **algae**.

Protozoa

Protozoa are single-celled organisms that are **heterotrophic** and in some ways are similar to little animals. This category of protists includes a number of different groups. The **rhizopods**, including amoebas, move with cellular extensions called pseudopods. The **ciliophors** have cilia that are used for feeding and locomotion.

Algae

Algae are primarily **photosynthetic** organisms. Blue, green, red, and brown algae all fit in this category. However, blue-green algae are not traditional algae and do *not* fit in this kingdom because they are prokaryotic rather than eukaryotic (see the Cyanobacteria section above). Examples of algae include the tiny **phytoplankton**, which are important sources of food for many marine organisms, as well as the **kelp**, which are large seaweeds of the brown algae family that can grow to be longer than 150 feet.

Slime Molds

The **slime molds** were formerly placed in the Fungi kingdom. However, they are now considered to belong to the Protist kingdom. They are arranged in a **coenocytic** (many nuclei) mass of **protoplasm**. The slime mold undergoes a unique life cycle containing animal-like and plant-like stages. These stages include fruiting bodies and unicellular flagellated spores. Slime molds reproduce asexually by sporulation.

FUNGI

Fungi may be considered nonphotosynthetic plants (i.e., they resemble plants in that they are eukaryotic, multicellular, differentiated, and nonmotile). However, their cell walls are composed of chitin and not cellulose, which is used by plants.

Fungi are eukaryotes and primarily multicellular. All fungi are **heterotrophs**. This differentiates them from the plant kingdom. They may be **saprophytic,** decomposing dead organic material (e.g., bread mold), or parasitic, extracting nutrients from their hosts (e.g., the fungus that causes athlete's foot, *Epidermophyton floccosum*). In either case, fungi absorb food from their environment.

Fungi reproduce by asexual **sporulation** or by intricate sexual processes. Notable types are **mushrooms** (traditional macroscopic fungi), **yeast** (unicellular fungi), and **lichens** (fungi in symbiotic relationships with other, photosynthetic organisms).

PLANTAE

The plant kingdom includes multicellular organisms that exhibit differentiation of tissues and are **nonmotile photosynthetic**. Because plants are able to make their own energy rather than relying on consuming other organisms, they are known as **autotrophs**. Many plants also exhibit an alternation of generations and a distinct embryonic phase.

Plants have developed complex differentiated tissues to adapt to a terrestrial life. Photosynthetic tissue layers contain **chloroplasts** for the manufacture of carbohydrates. Supportive tissues provide mechanical support facilitating the typical upright radial construction of plants. Absorptive tissues, like specialized roots and simpler **rhizoids**, project into soil to absorb water and minerals. **Conducting** or **vascular** tissues include specialized tubes that transport water, minerals, and nutrients to all parts of the plant. Waxy **cuticles** on exposed surfaces minimize loss of water while permitting the transmittance of light. Cells are in direct contact with the external environment by means of air spaces called **stomata**, making elaborate respiratory and excretory systems unnecessary.

Bryophytes

The bryophyta, hepatophyta, and anthocerotophyta divisions (informally called **bryophytes** as a collective) are simple plants with few specialized organs and tissues. They lack the water-conducting woody material (**xylem**) that functions as support in tracheophytes and retain flagellated sperm cells that must swim to the eggs, which means they must live in moist places.

These types of plants undergo alternation of generations. The **gametophyte** is the dominant generation; it is the "main" plant and is larger and nutritionally independent. The **sporophyte** is smaller and shorter-lived, growing off the gametophyte from the **archegonium**. It resembles a heterotrophic parasite in that it obtains its organic and inorganic materials from the autotrophic gametophyte.

Mosses are classic bryophytes in which the sporophyte and gametophyte generations grow together. **Liverworts** are flat, horizontal, and leaf-like plants with differentiated dorsal and ventral surfaces.

BIO

Tracheophytes

Vascular plants (**tracheophytes**) are complex plants with a great degree of cell differentiation. They contain vascular tissues: **xylem** (water-conducting) and **phloem** (food-conducting). Tracheophytes have radial symmetry about a main vertical axis and are anchored by deep roots instead of rhizoids. Their extensive woody or nonwoody support systems allow them to grow to great heights. They have developed excellent provisions for water conservation (waxy surfaces) and gas exchange (stomata). Cellular water storage creates turgid cells.

In contrast to bryophytes, in vascular plants, the sporophyte generation is dominant. The gametophyte is short-lived and either independent (in primitive tracheophytes such as ferns) or small and parasitic (in more advanced tracheophytes such as seed plants).

Non-seed-bearing

There are two extant divisions of non-seed-bearing vascular plants: Pteriodphyta and Lycophyta. Those that remain are evidence of prior evolutionary linkage to the bryophytes.

Pterophytes, of the division Pteridophyta, include the familiar **fern**. They grow from an underground stem called the **rhizome** and contain large leaves (megaphylls) that possess many vascular bundles. Ferns grow lengthwise, not in diameter, and contain xylem with elongated **tracheid** cells that transport water and salts. They do not produce seeds, and their short-lived gametophyte generation possesses heart-shaped leaves; the fern's normal leaves are part of the sporophyte generation. Sporangium on the underside of the leaves produce monoploid spores, which germinate to form gametophytes.

Lycophytes belong to an ancient subdivision known as Lycopodiophyta. They have roots, are nonwoody, and contain microphyll leaves (e.g., **club mosses**).

Angiosperms

Angiosperms are members of the division Angiospermae, which contains the greatest number of different plant species of all the extant plant divisions. They have covered seeds and are the most abundant of all plants. Angiosperms have flowers, not cones, as their principal reproductive structures. The **anther** of the male **stamen** produces **microspores** (pollen grains), while the ovary of the female **pistil** produces **megaspores**. Successful pollination results in the germination of pollen tubes, which aid in fertilization of female eggs in the gametophyte. The embryo develops into a seed within the ovary. The ovary eventually ripens into fruit, which is how the seeds are dispersed. Xylem-conducting cells are in the form of vessels as well as tracheids, allowing for better conduction of water.

Dicotyledons (dicots) are angiosperms with net-veined leaves and vascular bundles around a ring within the central cylinder. Dicotyledons contain two **cotyledons** (seed leaves) within the seed. Many have cambium and can be woody. They have flower parts in multiples of four or five. Some examples of dicotyledons are the maple and apple trees, potatoes, carrots, goldenrods, and buttercups.

Monocotyledons (monocots) are angiosperms that contain leaves with parallel veins, scattered vascular bundles, and seeds with single cotyledons. Most monocots do not possess cambium and therefore are nonwoody (herbaceous). They contain flower parts in multiples of three. Some examples are **grasses** such as wheat, corn, rye, and rice. Other monocots include sugar cane, pineapple, irises, bananas, orchids, and palms (woody monocots).

BIO

Gymnosperms

Gymnosperms are naked-seeded plants. The gametophyte stage of gymnosperms is short-lived and microscopic. The male microspore produces pollen that can be carried by the wind; thus, the requirement of a water environment for flagellated sperm is eliminated and the gymnosperms are truly terrestrial. Sperm nuclei fertilize the egg with the aid of a pollen tube, and the embryo develops within the exposed seed.

The presence of a specialized cambium tissue allows for secondary growth of secondary xylem (wood) and secondary phloem. Gymnosperms can grow in diameter as well as in length and are woody, not herbaceous (green with soft stems) plants. Most gymnosperms are evergreens (non-deciduous).

Conifers of the division Pinophyta make up the largest grouping of gymnosperms. They include pines, spruce, and firs. Conifers have cones, spiral clusters of modified leaves. There are two different types of cones: large female cones with sporangia that produce **megaspores** and small male cones with sporangia that produce microspores.

The remaining three divisions of gymnosperms contain fewer species and are Cycadophyta (**cycads**), Gnetophyta (**gnetophytes**), and Ginkgophyta (**ginkgo**). Cycads are stout, cylindrical trees with pinnate (feather-like) leaves. Gnetophytes have widely varying properties but tend to be vine like. Ginkgophyta only has one extant species: *Ginkgo biloba*, also known as the Ginkgo tree, which grows pungent seeds and is sometimes used in herbal medicine.

ANIMALIA

The animal kingdom contains **multicellular**, generally **motile**, **heterotrophic** organisms that have **differentiated** tissues (and organs in higher forms). With the exception of some parasites like the tapeworm, animals ingest bulk foods, digest them, and then eliminate the remains. Animals usually employ some form of locomotion to acquire nutrients, but some are **sessile** (stationary) and create currents to trap food. Nevertheless, locomotion can also be important for protection, mate selection, and reproduction.

Simple multicellular animals, such as sponges, coelenterates, and flatworms, have minimal differentiation. Most of their cells are in direct contact with the outside environment. In these organisms, only a few systems (such as the digestive and reproductive systems) are required to support the life processes. In more advanced animals, specialized tissues and systems facilitate digestion, locomotion, circulation, message conduction (nervous system), and support.

Most animals also have right and left sides that are mirror images of one another, which is known as **bilateral symmetry**. However, some animals, such as the echinoderms and cnidarians, have **radial symmetry**.

Examples of Phyla

The **Porifera** phylum contains sea sponges, which have two layers of cells, pores, and a low degree of cellular specialization. Sponges are usually sessile, meaning they cannot move on their own during most of their life.

Cnidaria is a phylum with species that contain a digestive sac that is sealed at one end (gastrovascular cavity). Two layers of cells are present: the **ectoderm** and the **endoderm**. Cnidarians can have many specialized features, including tentacles, stinging cells, and nerve nets. Examples of cnidarians include hydra, jellyfish, sea anemones, and coral.

The **Platyhelminthes** phylum is characterized by flatworms with ribbon-like, **bilaterally symmetrical** bodies that possess three layers of cells, including a solid mesoderm. They do not have circulatory systems, and their nervous system consist of eyes, an anterior brain ganglion, and a pair of longitudinal nerve cords.

The **Nematoda** phylum contains roundworms that possess long digestive tubes and anuses. A solid mesoderm is present. Nematodes lack circulatory systems but possess nerve cords and an anterior nerve ring. Examples include hookworms, trichina, and free-living soil nematodes.

The phylum **Annelida** contains segmented worms that possess a **coelom** (true body cavity) contained in the mesoderm. Annelids have well-defined systems, including nervous, circulatory, and excretory systems. Examples of annelids include earthworms and leeches.

Members of the phylum **Mollusca** are soft-bodied and possess mantels that often secrete calcareous (calcium carbonate) exoskeletons. They breathe by gills and contain chambered hearts, blood sinuses, and a pair of ventral nerve cords. Examples include clams, snails, and squid.

Arthropoda species have jointed appendages, chitinous exoskeletons, and open circulatory systems (**sinuses**). The three most important classes of arthropods are insects, arachnids, and crustaceans. **Insects** possess spiracles and tracheal tubes designed for breathing outside of an aquatic environment. They also have three pairs of legs. **Arachnids** have four pairs of legs and book lungs. Examples include scorpions and spiders. **Crustaceans** have segmented bodies with a variable number of appendages and also possess gills. Examples include lobsters, crayfish, and shrimp.

Echinodermata members are spiny, radially symmetrical, contain a water-vascular system, and possess the capacity for regeneration of parts. There is evolutionary evidence suggesting a link between echinoderms and chordates. Echinoderms include the starfish and the sea urchin.

Members of the phylum **Chordata** are characterized by a stiff dorsal rod, called the **notochord**, present at some stage of embryologic development. They have paired gill slits and a tail extending beyond the anus at some point during development. The lancelets and tunicates (like amphioxus) are chordates but not **vertebrates.** This means they have notochords but no backbones.

Vertebrata is an important subphylum of Chordata. Vertebrates include **amphibians**, **reptiles**, **birds**, **fish**, and **mammals**. In addition to the chordate characteristics described above, vertebrates also possess bones, called vertebrae, which form the backbone. Bony vertebrae replace the notochord of the embryo and protect the nerve cord. A bony case (the skull) protects the brain. Vertebrates can be divided into fish, amphibians, reptiles, birds, and mammals.

Classes of Vertebrata

Jawless fish make up the superclass **Agnatha**. Jawless fish are eel-like, retain the notochord throughout life, and have a cartilaginous internal skeleton. They have no jaws and possess a sucking mouth. Examples include the lamprey and the hagfish.

Cartilaginous fish possess jaws and teeth and are in the **Chondrichthyes** class. A reduced notochord exists as segments between cartilaginous vertebrae. An example is the shark.

Bony fish are the most prevalent type of fish. They are in the **Osteichthyes** class, have scales, and lack a notochord in the adult form. During development, cartilage is replaced by a bony skeleton. Examples include the sturgeon, trout, and tuna.

Members of the **Amphibia** class have larval stages found in water but adult stages that live on land. Larvae possess gills and a tail with no legs, whereas adults have lungs, two pairs of legs, no tail, a three-chambered heart, and no scales. Amphibians utilize external fertilization; eggs are laid in water with a jellylike secretion and subsequently fertilized. Examples include the frog, salamander, toad, and newt.

Individuals in the class **Reptilia** are **terrestrial** animals since they live on land. They breathe air by means of lungs, lay leathery eggs, and utilize **internal fertilization**. Reptiles are cold-blooded (**poikilothermic**) and have scales and a three-chambered heart. Examples include the turtle, lizard, snake, and crocodile.

Birds, which are in the **Aves** class, possess four-chambered hearts. They are warm-blooded (**homoeothermic**), and their eggs are surrounded by shells. Examples include the hen and the eagle.

Finally, the **Mammalia** class includes animals that are warm-blooded and feed their offspring with milk produced in mammary glands. Members of the **Monotremata** order lay leathery eggs, have horny bills, and produce milk via mammary glands with numerous openings but no nipples. Examples of monotremes include the duck-billed platypus and spiny anteater. Marsupials make up an infraclass of pouched mammals known as **Marsupialia**. The embryo begins development in the uterus and completes development while attached to nipples in the abdominal pouch. Examples include the kangaroo and opossum. Placental mammals of the infraclass **Placentalia** have embryos that develop fully in the uterus. The placenta attaches the embryo to the uterine wall and provides for the exchange of food, oxygen, and waste material. Examples include the bat, whale, mouse, and human.

VIRUSES

Viruses have not been placed in any of the six kingdoms because they do not carry out physiological or biochemical processes outside of a host. Although they are highly advanced parasites, they may be considered **nonliving**. Viruses are capable of taking over their host's cellular machinery and directing the replication of the rival genome and protein coat. Viruses have **lytic** and **lysogenic** life cycles. They contain either **DNA** or **RNA** and some essential enzymes surrounded by a protein coat. Viruses that exclusively infect bacteria are called **bacteriophages**.

BIO

REVIEW PROBLEMS

1. Select the proper progression of the taxonomy classification system.

   A. Kingdom, order, phylum, class, genus, family, species
   B. Kingdom, phylum, class, order, family, genus, species
   C. Kingdom, order, phylum, class, family, genus, species
   D. Kingdom, phylum, order, class, family, genus, species
   E. Kingdom, phylum, order, class, genus, family, species

2. Which of the following is NOT true about viruses?

   A. They may be considered nonliving.
   B. They have lytic and lysogenic life cycles.
   C. They contain only DNA and not RNA.
   D. They are surrounded by protein coats.
   E. They cannot conduct physiological processes outside a host.

3. Which of the following does NOT belong to the kingdom Protista?

   A. Protozoa
   B. Cyanobacteria
   C. Algae
   D. Phytoplankton
   E. Rhizopods

4. Which contains the most number of different species of plants?

   A. Angiospermae
   B. Coniferophyta
   C. Tracheophyta
   D. Bryophyta
   E. Pterophyta

5. Which is NOT a type of worm?

   A. Platyhelminthes
   B. Nematoda
   C. Annelida
   D. Porifera
   E. None of the above

BIO

SOLUTIONS TO REVIEW PROBLEMS

1. **B** See the taxonomic classifications section within this chapter.

2. **C** Viruses can contain either DNA or RNA and also often contain some necessary enzymes within their protein coat.

3. **B** Cyanobacteria are part of the kingdom Monera. All other listed organisms belong to the kingdom Protista.

4. **A** Angiosperms have covered seeds and are the most abundant of all plants. They use flowers as their principal reproductive structures.

5. **D** Porifera are sponges and are not classified as worms. All the other classes of animals listed are types of worms.

Section III

GENERAL CHEMISTRY

SECTION GOALS

General Chemistry is a topic area integral to mastery of the Survey of Natural Sciences portion of the OAT. While it is not the predominant science in the section, general chemistry does account for 30% of the Survey, and is very important to a competitive score. The general chemistry strategies, content, and practice presented within this section are designed to help you to accomplish the following goals:

- Recall key general chemistry concepts, terms, and equations
- Calculate solutions efficiently without a calculator
- Apply previously memorized equations and concepts to new situations presented on the OAT
- Predict answers to OAT General Chemistry questions using the Kaplan methods

CONTENT OVERVIEW

Laboratory Techniques (7%)	Chapter 23: Laboratory Techniques
Atomic & Molecular Structure (10%)	Chapter 24: Atomic and Molecular Structure
Periodic Properties (7%)	Chapter 25: Periodic Properties
Stoichiometry & General Concepts (10%)	Chapter 26: Chemical Bonding Chapter 27: Stoichiometry
Chemical Equilibria (7%)	Chapter 28: Solutions Chapter 33: Chemical Equilibria
Oxidation-Reduction Reactions (7%)	Chapter 29: Reaction Types Chapter 30: Electrochemistry
Chemical Kinetics (7%)	Chapter 31: Chemical Kinetics
Thermodynamics and Thermochemistry (7%)	Chapter 32: Thermochemistry
Liquids and Solids (10%)	Chapter 34: Liquids and Solids
Gases (7%)	Chapter 35: Gases
Acids and Bases (10%)	Chapter 36: Acids and Bases
Nuclear Reactions (3%)	Chapter 37: Nuclear Reactions

KEY STUDY STRATEGIES

In general—especially during early review—study these chapters in order. In later review, skipping around through areas of weakness will be more efficient. The chapters within this section build upon each other to a substantial degree, so if you find a chapter is drawing on background knowledge you do not have, revisit previous chapters. Bolded vocabulary terms are concepts of great importance in the General Chemistry section, but in addition to those terms, there are equations given within the text. These equations will be tested on the OAT, so make sure to memorize them as part of your study. Note that the number of chapters devoted to a topic does not indicate the importance of that topic, but instead reflects the complexity of the topic area. Make sure to complete the associated practice problems. During practice refrain from using a calculator, and be sure to utilize the Kaplan methods. When possible practice with scratch paper set up as it will be on Test Day. For more information on strategy and Test Day refer to Chapters 1–3, and 22.

CHAPTER TWENTY-TWO

General Chemistry Strategies

General chemistry is an important subject for the OAT, not only because it is the main focus for an entire subtest, but also because a strong general chemistry foundation makes learning organic chemistry, which provides the basis for an entire additional subtest of the OAT, much more manageable. General chemistry provides the foundation for many other subjects within the field of chemistry, especially physical chemistry. On the OAT, General Chemistry questions cover stoichiometry; gases, liquids, and solids; solutions; acids and bases; equilibria; thermochemistry; kinetics; redox reactions; atomic and molecular structure; periodic properties; nuclear reactions; and laboratory techniques.

GENERAL CHEMISTRY QUESTION STRATEGY

The General Chemistry subtest of the Survey of Natural Sciences contains questions 41–70 and occurs after the Biology subtest but before the Organic Chemistry subtest. Like the other questions in the Survey of Natural Sciences, General Chemistry questions are susceptible to attack using the Kaplan Stop-Think-Predict-Match question strategy. In particular, the Stop step is extremely important for General Chemistry questions because it helps you decide which questions to attempt right away and which to mark for later, which allows you to better manage your time. In fact, since General Chemistry questions tend to involve many more calculations than the other science questions do, you will likely need to spend an average of 75 seconds per question. Note, however, that this is an average, and you should spend much less time on any fact-based questions so you have more time for the calculation-heavy questions. For more details about how to manage your time in the Survey of Natural Sciences, see Chapter 4, Biology Strategies.

STUDYING GENERAL CHEMISTRY CONTENT

The chemistry you will see on Test Day blends theoretical knowledge with practical application. For the OAT, knowing the reason why intermolecular bonds form is just as important as being able to calculate the energy required to break them. You may be tempted to study these two aspects of chemistry separately, but the best test takers are able to integrate that knowledge to answer even the most difficult chemistry questions. Therefore, when confronted with a new equation, don't focus only on how to perform each mathematical step. Instead, also consider what each variable truly represents, the proportionalities that are implied, and the reasons behind those relationships. Having this conceptual understanding will not only help you answer questions but will also make memorizing equations easier and may even allow you to determine a mathematical relationship on Test Day if you can't recall the correct equation to use.

To facilitate learning the material this way, it's important to intersperse learning content with practicing questions. While reading, take breaks between topics to complete one or two practice questions from the end of the chapter, review relevant material from your online tests, or memorize the important equations from the study sheets at the back of this book. By utilizing a variety of resources, you'll see the material from different perspectives and gain a deeper understanding.

Furthermore, once you've finished a topic or chapter, take some time to reflect on how that knowledge connects to what you've already learned. If you form a narrative describing how an atom is formed, attaches to other atoms with intramolecular bonds to create a molecule, and connects with other molecules via intermolecular forces to determine its phase of matter, then you'll be much more likely to remember the material and apply it on Test Day. Once you've learned the material in the context of General Chemistry alone, you'll be able to apply it to other test sections, allowing you to truly master the OAT.

CHAPTER TWENTY-THREE

Laboratory Techniques

It has been said that a craftsman is only as good as his tools, and the same is true for a scientist working in a laboratory environment. Understanding the different applications of laboratory equipment allows for better technique and thus better results in executing experimental protocols.

SAFETY

One of the foremost considerations in working in a laboratory is maintaining a safe environment, both personally and for the laboratory as a whole. Although it is easy to become complacent when working in a laboratory on an ongoing basis, it is important to remember and follow simple rules, such as no eating or drinking in the lab.

Personal safety involves the consistent use of safety goggles, a laboratory coat or apron, and closed-toed shoes in any laboratory environment. Gloves may be appropriate when handling heated or toxic materials and the choice of glove should match the application (for example, some gloves may not be resistant to certain organic solvents). Volatile or dangerous chemicals should be handled in a hood, and a face mask or respirator may be needed as well.

All laboratories should have an eyewash station and shower station for rapid response to spills that contact the eyes or skin. Also, one or more fire extinguishers should always be present and in working condition. Finally, a laboratory should have more than one exit in the event of an emergency.

Disposal of laboratory waste should be done safely and appropriately, and containers should be set up for different types of waste. These include disposal containers for solvents and excess chemicals, biohazards, and broken glassware.

PRECISION VERSUS ACCURACY

Two important concepts in laboratory experiments are **accuracy** and **precision**. These terms do not mean the same thing and should not be used interchangeably.

Accuracy refers to a measurement giving the actual value for the sample with a limited deviation. For example, correctly determining the weight of a sample to be 1 gram plus or minus 0.001 gram is an accurate measurement.

Precision is the repeatability of a set of measurements on the same sample. For example, measuring the same 1 gram sample three times in a row and finding values of 1.001 g, 1.000 g, and 1.001 g is a precise series of measurements if this is within the limits of experimental error that the scientist wants to achieve.

It is possible to be accurate without being precise, and vice versa. For example, three measurements of the 1 gram sample as 0.9 g, 1.0 g, and 1.1 g give an accurate average value of 1 g for the sample, but are much less precise than the three samples determined to be 1.001 g, 1.000 g, and 1.001 g. Three determinations of the weight of a 1 g sample as 1.100 g, 1.1001 g, and 1.100 g may be precise but are not accurate.

Accuracy and precision are determined by a combination of using the correct laboratory apparatus and using that apparatus properly. In general, calibrated laboratory equipment will provide higher levels of both precision and accuracy than non-calibrated equipment, as long as the user is correctly trained and uses the equipment appropriately. Equipment that is calibrated generally has an acceptable temperature range and is specifically calibrated at one temperature (usually 25°C).

LABORATORY GLASSWARE

Laboratory glassware is a term that applies to a wide variety of vessels, not all of which are actually made of glass. Glass is generally preferred for chemistry applications because of its strength, inertness, transparency, and heat resistance. However, in some instances plastic may be a better choice if using chemicals that can interact with a glass surface. Plasticware also has the benefit of being lightweight and difficult to break.

Solvent compatibility with plastic and rubber labware needs to be considered and may not be obvious. For example, solvent fumes can compromise a pipet bulb, especially if the solvent is allowed to splash up into the bulb. Before using plasticware or rubber, check that no organic solvents will be used because components of the plastic can leach into organic solvents and contaminate the experiment. In some cases plastic labware is made of Teflon to provide chemical inertness.

Non-Calibrated Glassware

A large number of items in the laboratory are uncalibrated because they are simply used for containing, mixing, and reacting without specifically measuring the experimental materials. These include test tubes, beakers, Erlenmeyer flasks, round-bottomed flasks, transfer (or Pasteur) pipets, Petri dishes, watch glasses, bottles, jars and vials, etc. Although these pieces of glassware often have volume markings, they are approximate and should not be used for actual measurements. They are available in a wide range of sizes, as small as a few milliliters to several liters.

Test tubes, beakers, and Erlenmeyer flasks are used for many of the routine mixing and reaction tasks of the lab. **Test tubes** are relatively small and allow a large number of samples to be arrayed in a rack for easy processing. **Beakers** are wide-mouthed cylinders with a lip to allow pouring. **Erlenmeyer flasks** are tapered and therefore minimize accidental spills. The neck of an Erlenmeyer flask also allows it to be clamped in place either on the laboratory bench or above it on a stand. Some Erlenmeyer flasks have a side hose barb to allow connection to a vacuum apparatus. Erlenmeyer flasks can be sealed with rubber, cork, or ground glass stoppers. Both beakers and Erlenmeyer flasks have flat bottoms so they can stand on their own.

Round-bottom flasks are used for reaction, heating, or vacuum applications. The spherical shape and wall thickness of the flask provide extra strength and fit into a heating mantle, and the narrow neck allows the flask to be clamped into place. The top of the neck often has a ground glass joint to allow a stopper or glass tube to be connected to the flask. A **retort** is a round vacuum flask with a long neck that extends to the side. It is used for distillation and must be placed on a ring stand or heating mantle.

An **extraction flask,** also known as a **separatory funnel,** is a teardrop-shaped flask with a ground glass stopper at the top and a stopcock at the bottom. Two different solvents are mixed by shaking the flask and are then allowed to separate; the lower layer is removed by draining through the stopcock. Since the flask cannot stand on its own, it is typically placed in ring stand to keep it vertical.

Liquids are transferred using several different types of non-calibrated glassware. A funnel allows pouring from one vessel to another with minimal spillage. When small amounts are being transferred, a pipet is often used. **Transfer pipets** are often made of plastic and have an integral bulb at the top. **Pasteur pipets** are made of glass with a long tapered tip and require a separate rubber pipet bulb.

Bottles are containers with narrow openings generally used to store reagents or samples. Small bottles are called **vials**. **Jars** are cylindrical containers with wide openings that may be sealed. **Bell jars** are used to contain vacuums. Bottles, jars, and vials can be closed with stoppers or screw top lids. **Watch glasses**, also known as **evaporating dishes**, are shallow glass plates used as evaporating surfaces or to cover beakers. **Petri dishes** are flat dishes with vertical sides used to culture living cells.

Figure 23.1

From left to right, Figure 23.1 shows a test tube, Erlenmeyer flask, retort, and round-bottom flask.

Calibrated Glassware

Calibrated glassware should be used for any laboratory measurement that requires accuracy and precision. It is manufactured to provide exact volumes at a given temperature, which is usually 25°C. Calibrated glassware is available in a broad range of sizes, from a few milliliters or less to several liters.

A **graduated cylinder** is a tall, narrow tube with volume markings increasing from bottom to top and a lip at the top for pouring. A liquid is poured into the graduated cylinder to the approximate desired level and then carefully added to or removed from the cylinder to reach the exact volume required. The fluid is then transferred to another vessel. Graduated cylinders have wide bases and often have protective plastic rings around the top of the cylinder to protect them from spilling and breaking.

Burets and pipets are used to deliver exact volumes of liquids. A **buret** is a long tube that is clamped in place vertically with a stopcock at the bottom. The amount delivered is determined by the difference between the starting volume and the final volume in the buret. Burets are especially useful when liquids are to be dispensed slowly or dropwise. Burets are used to make solutions and to perform titrations.

A **graduated pipet** is hand-held and controlled by a pipet bulb that maintains a slight vacuum at the top of the pipet. Graduated pipets can deliver a variable amount of liquid, as either all of the fluid is dispensed or the stop and start volumes are measured. **Volumetric pipets** have a large bulge in the middle of the tube and deliver a single established volume of liquid with great accuracy and precision. Calibrated pipets are designed to take into account any liquid remaining in the pipet after the desired amount has been dispensed.

A **volumetric flask** is used to make solutions that require a specific volume of liquid, such as molar solutions. The components are added to the flask with less solvent than is required. The contents are mixed, and then a final amount of solvent is added to reach the volume marking on the neck of the flask. Volumetric flasks have flattened bottoms so that they can stand on a laboratory bench and narrow necks so that the volume mark can be easily read.

Figure 23.2

From left to right, Figure 23.2 shows a graduated cylinder, volumetric flask, graduated beaker, pipet, and buret.

pH DETERMINATION

The **pH meter** is an important piece of measurement equipment consisting of a glass probe and an electronic meter. Different pH meters can range from very simple to very complex, but all perform the same essential functions. A pH meter determines the acidity or basicity of a solution by comparing the voltage (electrical potential) produced by the solution compared to the voltage of a known standard solution and uses the difference in voltage (the potential difference) between them to calculate the pH.

The glass probe is first calibrated and then rinsed, dried, and quickly immersed in the solution to be measured. Calibration is done at an appropriate range of pH values to match the samples to be measured; the most commonly used range is pH 4.01 to pH 10.00, often with an initial calibration at pH 7. The sample must be at a known temperature, and the effect of temperature on pH must be compensated for (more complex pH meters can do this automatically).

Litmus paper can also be used to quickly determine pH, although it is less accurate than a pH meter. Traditional litmus paper is red under acidic conditions (below pH 4.5), blue under basic conditions (above 8.3), and purple at neutral pH. Modern litmus paper is available that is calibrated with different colors according to the pH range, typically with a different color at each integer pH value.

WEIGHT DETERMINATION

Laboratory balances are divided into two major categories: standard laboratory balances, and analytical balances. Standard laboratory balances (also called top-loading balances) are used when weights are in the milligram range and require accuracy to within plus or minus 0.5 mg. Analytical balances are used for much more sensitive weighing applications, with accuracy to plus or minus 0.01 mg. Analytical balances have glass sides and sliding doors to protect against slight movements due to drafts and must be used with particular care.

GC

REVIEW PROBLEMS

1. Which of the following is appropriate to use for a procedure that involves simultaneously heating and distilling a reaction mixture?

   A. Erlenmeyer flask

   B. Erlenmeyer flask with a hose barb

   C. Volumetric flask

   D. Round-bottom flask

   E. Either A or B

2. What is the best piece of glassware to use to transfer exactly 50 mL of liquid?

   A. 50 mL beaker

   B. 50 mL Erlenmeyer flask

   C. 50 mL volumetric pipet

   D. 50 mL volumetric flask

   D. 500 mL graduated cylinder

3. What should be used to titrate 50 mL of 0.1 N HCl with 0.2 N NaOH?

   A. 10 mL buret

   B. 30 mL buret

   C. 30 mL graduated pipet

   D. 50 mL volumetric pipet

   E. 50 mL graduated cylinder

4. A scientist is setting up an experiment with 20 samples, each consisting of 0.5 g of a solid. He will pipet 2 mL of liquid into each sample, allow them to stand for 1 hour and then remove 1 mL for analysis. Which of the following is the best glassware to use?

   A. Erlenmeyer flasks

   B. Beakers

   C. Volumetric flasks

   D. Round-bottom flasks

   E. Test tubes

5. Which of the following will provide the most accurate and precise measurement of a sample at approximately pH 5?

   A. pH meter calibrated at pH 5.00

   B. pH meter calibrated at pH 4.01 and pH 10.00

   C. pH meter calibrated at pH 7.00

   D. pH meter calibrated at pH 7.00, pH 4.01, and pH 10.00

   E. Litmus paper

6. A scientist wants to prepare AlCl$_3$ by reacting a large excess of aluminum with exactly 3.0 moles of HCl dissolved in water. How should she measure the solid aluminum?

   A. Weigh 27.0 g of Al (*s*) on a standard laboratory balance.
   B. Weigh 27.00 g of Al (*s*) on an analytical balance.
   C. Weigh 50.0 g of Al (*s*) on a standard laboratory balance.
   D. Weigh 50.00 g of Al (*s*) on an analytical balance.
   E. Add the Al (*s*) by adding double the amount of NaCl by eye.

7. A scientist wants to make 50 mL of a 1.00 molal solution of sodium chloride in water. Which of the following should he use to measure the water to be added?

   A. Graduated cylinder
   B. Volumetric pipet
   C. Volumetric flask
   D. Buret
   E. Balance

8. Which of the following combinations is most suitable for titrating and measuring the pH of a solution with an endpoint of pH 4.4?

   A. Buret, beaker, and litmus paper
   B. Pipet, Erlenmeyer flask, and litmus paper
   C. Buret, volumetric flask, and pH meter
   D. Pipet, volumetric flask, and pH meter
   E. Pipet, Erlenmeyer flask, and pH meter

GC

SOLUTIONS TO REVIEW PROBLEMS

1. **D** A round-bottom flask is best for a heating and distilling application because its round shape gives it extra strength to withstand heat and vacuum.

2. **C** A volumetric pipet is calibrated to deliver one volume with great accuracy. Although a volumetric flask is designed to hold an exact amount, it is not designed to transfer that amount, and some liquid may be left in the flask if it is not drained correctly. A graduated cylinder can be used to transfer liquid, but it will not be as accurate as a volumetric pipet.

3. **B** To solve this problem, the amount of NaOH solution must first be calculated using the formula $N_A V_A = N_B V_B$:

$$VB = \frac{(50\,\text{mL})(0.1\,N)}{(0.2\,N)} = 25\,\text{mL of NaOH solution}$$

Next, the appropriate glassware must be chosen for the titration. The best choice is a buret that allows gradual addition of the NaOH solution as the pH is monitored and that is of the right volume to hold all the solution required without refilling.

4. **E** The best choice is a rack of 20 test tubes, which will allow the scientist to rapidly process the set of samples in order. The test tubes are the correct shape to fit in a rack and allow the liquids to be readily added and removed.

5. **D** A pH meter is much more accurate and precise than litmus paper. For the best accuracy and precision, the three-point calibration is best.

6. **C** First, an appropriate amount of aluminum must be determined. Since the scientist wants to run the reaction with an excess of aluminum, she must have more than 1 mole to react according to the following equation:

$$\text{Al}\,(s) + 3\,\text{HCl}\,(aq) \rightarrow \text{AlCl}_3\,(s) + \frac{3}{2}\,\text{H}_2\,(g)$$

Note that a balanced equation should normally have no fractions, but the above equation is more helpful because it shows the ratios with respect to the three moles of HCl added in this question.

From the periodic table, the atomic mass of aluminum can be found to be 27 g/mol. Thus, weighing 50 g would only provide almost 2 moles, which is an excess. Because exact stoichiometric quantities are not being used, a standard laboratory balance is the correct equipment to use.

7. **E** A molal solution is defined as moles solute/kg of solvent. Since the solvent is measured by weight rather than volume, a balance is the correct measurement device.

8. **A** A buret is the preferred dispensing glassware for a titration since it allows the titrant to be gradually dispensed so the pH can be monitored. Although litmus paper is not as accurate as a pH meter, it will change color almost exactly at the desired pH endpoint, making it a good choice for this application. The use of a beaker as the receiving vessel allows the user to easily check the pH of the solution with the litmus paper.

CHAPTER TWENTY-FOUR

Atomic and Molecular Structure

Chemistry is the study of the nature and behavior of matter. The **atom** is the basic building block of matter, representing the smallest unit of a chemical element. An atom in turn is composed of subatomic particles called **protons, neutrons,** and **electrons**. The protons and neutrons in an atom form the **nucleus**, the core of the atom. The electrons exist outside the nucleus in characteristic regions of space called **orbitals**. All atoms of an **element** show similar chemical properties and cannot be further broken down by chemical means.

SUBATOMIC PARTICLES

In the early 1800s, an English scientist by the name of John Dalton formulated a specific theory of invisible building blocks of matter that are now called atoms. Dalton's atomic theory marks the beginning of the modern era of chemistry. Below is a summary of the key points of his hypothesis:

- All **elements** are composed of very small particles called atoms. All atoms of a given element are identical in size, mass, and chemical properties (although we now know **isotopes**, atoms of the same element with different masses due to different numbers of neutrons, also exist). The atoms of one element are different from atoms of all other elements.
- All **compounds** are composed of atoms of more than one element. For any given compound, the ratio of the numbers of atoms of any two of the elements present is either an integer or a simple fraction.
- A given **chemical reaction** involves only the separation, combination, or rearrangement of atoms; it does NOT result in the creation or destruction of atoms.

Protons

Protons carry a single positive charge and have a mass of approximately one **unified atomic mass unit** (**amu** or **u**), which is equivalent to one **dalton (Da)**. The **atomic number (Z)** of an element is equal to the number of protons found in an atom of that element. All atoms of a given element have the same atomic number. These positively charged particles carry the same quantity of charge as an electron; however, they have a mass that is approximately 1,840 times greater than that of an electron. Although the mass of the nucleus of an atom therefore comprises almost the entire weight of an atom, it occupies only 10^{-13} of the volume of the atom. Putting this in perspective, if the entire atom was the size of a football stadium that seats 100,000 people, the volume of the actual nucleus would be that of a small marble.

Neutrons

Neutrons carry no charge and have a mass only slightly larger than that of protons, so they can still be considered to have a mass of approximately 1 u. Different **isotopes** of one element have different numbers of neutrons but the same number of protons.

Electrons

Electrons carry a charge equal in magnitude but opposite in sign to that of protons. An electron has a very small mass, approximately 1/1,837 the mass of a proton or neutron, which is negligible for the purposes of the exam. The electrons in the electron shell farthest from the nucleus are known as **valence electrons**. The farther the valence electrons are from the nucleus, the weaker the attractive force of the positively charged nucleus and the more likely the valence electrons are to be influenced by other atoms. Generally, the valence electrons and their activity determine the reactivity of an atom. In a neutral atom, the numbers of protons and electrons are equal. Therefore, the atomic number indicates the number of electrons in a neutral atom. A positive or negative charge on an atom is due to a loss or gain of electrons; the result is called an **ion**. Note that a (+) charge indicates a *loss* of negatively-charged electrons, whereas a (−) charges indicates a *gain* of electrons.

Some basic features of the three subatomic particles are shown in the table below:

Subatomic Particle	Symbol	Relative Mass	Charge	Location
Proton	$_{1}^{1}H^{+}$	1	+1	Nucleus
Neutron	$_{0}^{1}n$	1	0	Nucleus
Electron	e^{-}	0	−1	Electron orbitals

Table 24.1

Example: Determine the number of protons, neutrons, and electrons in a nickel-58 atom and in a nickel-60^{2+} cation.

Solution: ^{58}Ni has an atomic number of 28 and a mass number of 58. Therefore, ^{58}Ni has 28 protons, 28 electrons, and (58 – 28), or 30, neutrons.

In the $^{60}Ni^{2+}$ species, the number of protons is the same as in the neutral ^{58}Ni atom (28 protons). However, $^{60}Ni^{2+}$ has a positive charge because it has lost two electrons, so Ni^{2+} has 26 electrons (as opposed to the 28 electrons in ^{58}Ni). Also, the mass number is two units higher than for the ^{58}Ni atom, and this difference in mass must be due to two extra neutrons; thus, it has a total of 32 neutrons (as opposed to 30 neutrons in ^{58}Ni).

MASS NUMBER AND ISOTOPES

Mass Number

The atomic **mass number** (*A*) of an atom is equal to the total number of nucleons (protons and neutrons). The convention $^A_Z X$ is used to show both the atomic number and mass number of an X atom, where *Z* is the atomic number and *A* is the mass number such that:

$$\text{mass number } (A) = \text{number of protons} + \text{number of neutrons}$$

On a larger scale, the **molecular weight** is the weight in grams per one mole (mol) of a given element (g/mol). A **mole** is a unit used to count particles and is represented by **Avogadro's number**, 6.02×10^{23} particles/mol, which is how many atoms of carbon are in 12.0 g of carbon-12. Avogadro's number is the conversion factor between amu and g such that, if one atom of nitrogen has a mass of 14 u, then one mole of nitrogen has a mass of 14 g (see Chapter 27, Stoichiometry).

Isotopes

For a given element, multiple species of atoms with the same number of protons (same atomic number, *Z*) but different numbers of neutrons (different mass numbers, *A*) exist; these are called **isotopes** of the element. Isotopes are referred to either by the convention described above or, more commonly, by the name of the element followed by the mass number. For example, carbon-12 $\left(^{12}_6 C\right)$ is a carbon atom with six protons and six neutrons, while carbon-14 $\left(^{14}_6 C\right)$ is a carbon atom with six protons and eight neutrons. Since isotopes have the same number of protons and electrons, they generally exhibit the same chemical properties.

In nature, almost all elements exist as a collection of two or more isotopes, and these isotopes are usually present in the same proportions in any sample of a naturally occurring element. Therefore, another common convention used to define the mass of an atom is **standard atomic weight**, which is a weighted average of all the isotopes of an element found naturally on Earth. The periodic table lists the atomic weight for the different elements, which accounts for the relative abundance of the various isotopes. The presence of these isotopes accounts for the fact that the accepted atomic weight for most elements is not a whole number. For example, nitrogen has two stable isotopes, ^{14}N and ^{15}N, but ^{14}N is much more common (99.6%), so the weighted average of the two is 14.007.

Example: Element Q consists of three different isotopes, A, B, and C. Isotope A has an atomic mass of 40 u and accounts for 60% of naturally occurring Q. The atomic mass of isotope B is 44 u and accounts for 25% of Q. Finally, isotope C has an atomic mass of 41 u and a natural abundance of 15%. What is the atomic weight of element Q?

Solution: $0.60(40 \text{ u}) + 0.25(44 \text{ u}) + 0.15(41 \text{ u}) = 24 \text{ u} + 11 \text{ u} + 6.15 \text{ u} = 41.15 \text{ u}$

The atomic weight of element Q is 41.15 g/mol.

BOHR'S MODEL OF THE HYDROGEN ATOM

In 1911, Ernest Rutherford provided experimental evidence that an atom has a dense, positively charged nucleus that accounts for only a small portion of the volume of the atom. In 1900, Max Planck developed the first **quantum theory**, proposing that energy emitted as electromagnetic radiation from matter comes in discrete bundles called **quanta**. The energy value of a quantum is given by the equation $E = hf$, where h is a proportionality constant known as **Planck's constant**, equal to 6.626×10^{-34} J·s, and f (sometimes designated ν) is the **frequency** of the radiation.

The Bohr Model

In 1913, Niels Bohr used the work of Rutherford and Planck to develop his model of the electronic structure of the hydrogen atom. Starting from Rutherford's findings, Bohr assumed that the hydrogen atom consisted of a central proton around which an electron traveled in a circular orbit, and that the centripetal force acting on the electron as it revolved around the nucleus was the electrical force between the positively charged proton and the negatively charged electron.

Bohr's model used the quantum theory of Planck in conjunction with concepts from classical physics. In classical mechanics, an object, such as an electron, revolving in a circle may assume an infinite number of values for its radius and velocity. Therefore, the **angular momentum** ($L = mvr$) and **kinetic energy** $\left(KE = \frac{mv^2}{2} \right)$ can take on any value. However, by incorporating Planck's quantum theory into his model, Bohr placed conditions on the value of the angular momentum. Like Planck's energy, the angular momentum (L) of an electron is quantized according to the following equation:

$$L = \frac{nh}{2\pi}$$

where h is Planck's constant and n is the principal quantum number, which can be any positive integer. Since h, 2, and π are constants, the angular momentum changes only in discrete amounts with respect to n.

Bohr then equated the allowed values of the angular momentum to the energy of the electron. He obtained the following equation:

$$E = -\frac{\text{Ry}}{n^2}$$

where Ry is an experimentally determined constant (known as the **Rydberg energy** and representing the product of three different constants: R_H, h, and c) equal to 2.18×10^{-18} J/electron. Therefore, like angular momentum, the energy of the electron changes in discrete amounts with respect to n.

A value of zero energy was assigned to the state in which the proton and electron were separated completely, meaning that there was no attractive force between them. Therefore, the electron in any of its quantized states in the atom would have a negative energy as a result of the attractive forces between the electron and proton. This explains the negative sign in the above equation for energy.

Applications of the Bohr Model

In his model of the structure of hydrogen, Bohr postulated that an electron can exist only in certain fixed-energy states. In terms of quantum theory, the energy of an electron is **quantized**. Using this model, certain generalizations concerning the characteristics of electrons can be made. The energy of the electron is related to its **orbital radius**: the smaller the radius, the lower the energy state of the electron. The smallest orbit (radius) an electron can have corresponds to $n = 1$, which is the ground state of the hydrogen electron. At the **ground state** level, the electron is in its lowest energy state. The Bohr model is also used to explain the atomic emission spectrum and atomic absorption spectrum of hydrogen, and it is helpful in interpretation of the spectra of other atoms.

Atomic emission spectra

At room temperature, the majority of atoms in a sample are in the ground state. However, electrons can be excited to higher energy levels by heat (or other) energy to yield the excited state of the atom. Because the lifetime of the excited state is brief, the electrons will return rapidly to the ground state while emitting energy in the form of photons. The electromagnetic energy of these photons may be determined using the following equation:

$$E = \frac{hc}{\lambda}$$

where h is Planck's constant, c is the velocity of light in a vacuum (3.00×10^8 m/s), and λ is the wavelength of the radiation. This is a derivation of the equation $E = hf$, where $c = \lambda f$.

The different electrons in an atom will be excited to different energy levels. When these electrons return to their ground states, each will emit a photon with a wavelength characteristic of the specific transition it undergoes. The quantized energies of light emitted under these conditions do not produce a continuous spectrum (as expected from classical physics). Rather, the spectrum is composed of light at specific frequencies and is thus known as a **line spectrum**, where each line on the emission spectrum corresponds to a specific electronic transition. Because each element can have its electrons excited to different distinct energy levels, each element possesses a unique **atomic emission spectrum**, which can be used as a fingerprint. One particular application of atomic emissions spectroscopy is in the analysis of stars; although physical samples of the stars cannot be taken, the light from a star can be resolved into its component wavelengths, which are then matched to the known line spectra of the elements.

The Bohr model of the hydrogen atom explained the atomic emission spectrum of hydrogen, which is the simplest emission spectrum among all the elements. The group of hydrogen emission lines corresponding to transitions from upper levels $n > 2$ to $n = 2$ is known as the **Balmer series** (four wavelengths in the visible region), while the group corresponding to transitions between upper levels $n > 1$ to $n = 1$ is known as the **Lyman series** (higher energy transitions in the UV region). Below is a summary of various series in the hydrogen atomic emission spectrum where n_f and n_i are the final and initial states, respectively.

Series	n_f	n_i	Spectrum region
Lyman	1	2, 3, 4 . . .	Ultraviolet
Balmer	2	3, 4, 5 . . .	Visible and Ultraviolet
Paschen	3	4, 5, 6 . . .	Infrared

Table 24.2

When the energy of each frequency of light observed in the emission spectrum of hydrogen was calculated according to Planck's quantum theory, the values obtained closely matched those expected from energy-level transitions in the Bohr model. That is, the energy associated with a change in the quantum number from an initial value n_i to a final value n_f is equal to the energy of Planck's emitted photon. Thus:

$$E = \frac{hc}{\lambda} = -\,\text{Ry}\left(\frac{1}{n_i^2} - \frac{1}{n_f^2}\right)$$

and the energy of the emitted photon corresponds to the precise difference in energy between the higher-energy initial state and the lower-energy final state.

Atomic absorption spectra

When an electron is excited to a higher energy level, it must absorb energy. The energy absorbed as an electron jumps from an orbital of low energy to one of higher energy is characteristic of that transition. This means that the excitation of electrons in a particular element results in energy absorptions at specific wavelengths. Thus, in addition to an emission spectrum, every element possesses a characteristic **absorption spectrum**. Not surprisingly, the wavelengths of absorption correspond directly to the wavelengths of emission since the energy difference between levels remains unchanged. Absorption spectra can thus be used in the identification of elements present in a gas phase sample.

QUANTUM MECHANICAL MODEL OF ATOMS

While the concepts put forth by Bohr offered a reasonable explanation for the structure of the hydrogen atom and ions containing only one electron (such as He^{1+} and Li^{2+}), they did not explain the structures of atoms containing more than one electron. This is because Bohr's model does not take into consideration the repulsion between multiple electrons surrounding one nucleus. Modern quantum mechanics has led to a more rigorous and generalized study of the electronic structure of atoms. The most important difference between the Bohr model and modern quantum mechanical models is that Bohr's assumption that electrons follow a circular orbit at a fixed distance from the nucleus is no longer considered valid. Rather, electrons are described as being in a state of rapid motion within regions of space around the nucleus called **orbitals**. An orbital is a representation of the probability of finding an electron within a given region. In the current quantum mechanical description of electrons, pinpointing both the exact location and momentum of an electron at any given point in time is impossible. This idea is best described by the **Heisenberg uncertainty principle**, which states that it is impossible to simultaneously determine, with perfect accuracy, the momentum (defined as mass times velocity) and the position of an electron. This means that if the momentum of the electron is being measured accurately, its position will not be certain, and vice versa.

Quantum Numbers

Modern atomic theory states that any electron in an atom can be completely described by four **quantum numbers**: n, ℓ, m_ℓ, and m_s. Furthermore, according to the **Pauli exclusion principle**, no two electrons in a given atom can possess the same set of four quantum numbers. The position and energy of an electron described by its quantum numbers is known as its **energy state**. The value of n limits the values of ℓ, which in turn limit the values of m_ℓ. The values of three of the quantum numbers qualitatively give information about the orbitals: n about the size, ℓ about the shape, and m_ℓ about the orientation of the orbital. All four quantum numbers are discussed below.

Principal quantum number

The first quantum number is commonly known as the **principal quantum number** and is denoted by the letter n. This is the quantum number used in Bohr's model that can theoretically take on any positive integer value and represents the **shell** where an electron is present in an atom. The maximum n that can be used to describe the electrons of an element at its ground state corresponds with that element's period (row) in the periodic table. For example, nitrogen is in period 2, so neutral N in its ground state has electrons with n values of 1 and 2. The larger the integer value of n, the higher the energy level and radius of the electron's orbit. The maximum number of electrons in an electron shell n is $2n^2$.

The difference in energy between adjacent shells decreases as the distance from the nucleus increases. For example, the energy difference between the third and fourth shells ($n = 3$ and $n = 4$) is less than that between the second and third shells ($n = 2$ and $n = 3$).

Azimuthal quantum number

The second quantum number is called the **azimuthal (angular momentum) quantum number** and is designated by the letter ℓ. This number tells us the shape of the orbitals and refers to the **subshells** or **sublevels** that occur within each principal energy level. For any given n, the value of ℓ can be any integer in the range of 0 to $n - 1$. The four subshells corresponding to $\ell = 0$, 1, 2, and 3 are known as the sharp, principal, diffuse, and fundamental subshells, or s, p, d, and f subshells, respectively. The maximum number of electrons that can exist within a subshell is given by the equation $4\ell + 2$. The greater the value of ℓ, the greater the energy of the subshell. However, the energies of subshells from different principal energy levels may overlap. For example, the $4s$ subshell will have a lower energy than the 3d subshell because its average distance from the nucleus is smaller.

Magnetic quantum number

The third quantum number is the **magnetic quantum number** and is designated m_ℓ. This number describes the orientation of the **orbital** in space. An orbital is a specific region within a subshell that may contain no more than two electrons. The magnetic quantum number specifies the particular orbital within a subshell where an electron is highly likely to be found at a given point in time. The possible values of m_ℓ are all integers from ℓ to $-\ell$ including 0. Therefore, the s subshell ($\ell = 0$), has only one possible value of m_ℓ (0) and will contain one orbital; in contrast, the p subshell ($\ell = 1$) has three possible m_ℓ values (-1, 0, $+1$) and three orbitals. The d subshell ($\ell = 2$) has five possible m_ℓ values (-2, -1, 0, $+1$, $+2$) and five orbitals; the f subshell ($\ell = 3$) has seven possible m_ℓ values (-3, -2, -1, 0, $+1$, $+2$, $+3$) and contains seven orbitals. The shape and energy of each orbital are dependent upon the subshell in which the orbital is found. For example, a p subshell with its three possible m_ℓ values (-1, 0, $+1$) has three dumbbell-shaped orbitals that are oriented in space around the nucleus along the x, y, and z axes. These three orbitals are often referred to as p_x, p_y, and p_z.

Spin quantum number

The fourth quantum number is also called the **spin quantum number** and is denoted by m_s. The spin of a particle is its intrinsic angular momentum and is a characteristic of a particle. The two spin orientations are designated $+\frac{1}{2}$ and $-\frac{1}{2}$. Whenever two electrons are in the same orbital, they must have opposite spins due to the Pauli exclusion principle. Electrons in different orbitals (different m_ℓ values) with the same m_s values are said to have **parallel** spins. Electrons with opposite spins (different m_s values) in the same orbital (same m_ℓ value) are often referred to as **paired**.

The following table is an example that shows all of the possible quantum numbers for the eight electrons in the second shell ($n = 2$). The numbers in parentheses represent the number of electrons in the region limited by the coresponding quantum number. Thus, all eight electrons in the second shell have $n = 2$, two electrons have $\ell = 0$, six electrons have $\ell = 1$, and so on. Note that the numbers in parentheses for each row must add up to eight, the total number of electrons in the shell.

n	2 (8)						
ℓ	0 (2)	1 (6)					
m_ℓ	0 (2)	−1 (2)		0 (2)		+1 (2)	
m_s	$+\frac{1}{2}(1)$	$-\frac{1}{2}(1)$	$+\frac{1}{2}(1)$	$-\frac{1}{2}(1)$	$+\frac{1}{2}(1)$	$-\frac{1}{2}(1)$	$+\frac{1}{2}(1)$	$-\frac{1}{2}(1)$

Table 24.3

Electron Configuration and Orbital Filling

For a given atom or ion, the pattern by which subshells are filled and the number of electrons within each principal level and subshell are designated by an **electron configuration**. In electron configuration notation, the first number denotes the principal energy level, the letter designates the subshell, and the superscript gives the number of electrons in that subshell. For example, $2p^4$ indicates that there are four electrons in the second subshell (p) of the second principal energy level ($n = 2$). Note that the third and fourth quantum numbers (m_ℓ and m_s) are not indicated in the electron configuration but can be determined for a given electron using the rules from earlier in this chapter if necessary.

When writing the electron configuration of an atom, it is necessary to remember the order in which subshells are filled. According to the **Aufbau principle** subshells are filled from lowest to highest energy, and each subshell will fill completely before electrons begin to enter the next one. The $(n + \ell)$ **rule** is used to rank subshells by increasing energy. This rule states that the lower the sum of the first and second quantum numbers, the lower the energy of the subshell. If two subshells possess the same $(n + \ell)$ value, the subshell with the lower n value has a lower energy and will fill first. The order in which the subshells fill is shown in the following chart:

Figure 24.1

Example: Which will fill first, the 3d subshell or the 4s subshell?

Solution: For 3d, $n = 3$ and $\ell = 2$, so $(n + \ell) = 5$. For 4s, $n = 4$ and $\ell = 0$, so $(n + \ell) = 4$. Therefore, the 4s subshell has a lower energy and will fill first. This can also be determined from examining Figure 24.1.

To determine which subshells are filled, you must know the number of electrons in the atom. In the case of uncharged atoms, the number of electrons equals the atomic number. If the atom is charged, the number of electrons is equal to the atomic number plus the extra electrons if the atom is negative or the atomic number minus the missing electrons if the atom is positive.

In subshells that contain more than one orbital, such as the 2p subshell with its three orbitals, the orbitals will fill according to **Hund's Rule**. Hund's Rule states that, within a given subshell, orbitals are filled such that there are a maximum number of half-filled orbitals with parallel spins. Electrons "prefer" empty orbitals to half-filled ones because a pairing energy must be overcome for two electrons carrying repulsive negative charges to exist in the same orbital.

Example: What are the written electron configurations for nitrogen (N) and iron (Fe) according to Hund's Rule?

Solution: Nitrogen has an atomic number of 7; thus, its electron configuration is $1s^2\ 2s^2\ 2p^3$. According to Hund's Rule, the two s orbitals will fill completely, while the three p orbitals will each contain one electron, all with parallel spins.

$$\underset{1s^2}{\underline{\text{⇅}}} \quad \underset{2s^2}{\underline{\text{⇅}}} \quad \underset{2p^3}{\underline{\text{↑ ↑ ↑}}}$$

Iron has an atomic number of 26, and its 4s subshell fills before the 3d. Using Hund's Rule, the electron configuration will be:

$$\underset{1s^2}{\underline{\text{⇅}}} \quad \underset{2s^2}{\underline{\text{⇅}}} \quad \underset{2p^6}{\underline{\text{⇅ ⇅ ⇅}}} \quad \underset{3s^2}{\underline{\text{⇅}}} \quad \underset{3p^6}{\underline{\text{⇅ ⇅ ⇅}}} \quad \underset{3d^6}{\underline{\text{⇅ ↑ ↑ ↑ ↑}}} \quad \underset{4s^2}{\underline{\text{⇅}}}$$

Iron's electron configuration is written as $1s^2\ 2s^2\ 2p^6\ 3s^2\ 3p^6\ 3d^6\ 4s^2$. Subshells may be listed either in the order in which they fill (e.g., 4s before 3d) or with subshells of the same principal quantum number grouped together, as shown here. Both methods are correct.

The presence of paired or unpaired electrons affects the chemical and magnetic properties of an atom or molecule. If the material has unpaired electrons, a magnetic field will align the spins of these electrons and weakly attract the atom to the field. These materials are said to be **paramagnetic**. Materials that have no unpaired electrons and are slightly repelled by a magnetic field are said to be **diamagnetic**.

Valence Electrons

The valence electrons of an atom are those electrons that exist in its outer energy shell or that are available for chemical bonding. For elements in Groups IA and IIA, only the outermost s electrons are valence electrons. For elements in Groups IIIA through VIIIA, the outermost s and p electrons in the highest energy shell are valence electrons. For transition elements, the valence electrons are those in the outermost s subshell and in the d subshell of the next-to-outermost energy shell. For the inner transition elements (the lanthanide and actinide series), the valence electrons are those in the s subshell of the outermost energy shell, the d subshell of the next-to-outermost energy shell, and the f subshell of the energy shell two levels below the outermost shell.

Group IIIA–VIIA elements beyond Period 2 might, under some circumstances, accept electrons into their empty d subshells, which would give them more than eight valence electrons.

Example: Which are the valence electrons of elemental iron, elemental selenium, and the sulfur atom in a sulfate ion?

Solution: Iron has eight valence electrons: two in its 4s subshell and six in its 3d subshell.

Selenium has six valence electrons: two in its 4s subshell and four in its 4p subshell. Selenium's 3d electrons are not part of its valence shell.

Sulfur in a sulfate ion has 12 valence electrons: its original six plus six more from the oxygen to which it is bonded. Sulfur's 3s and 3p subshells can only contain eight of these electrons; the other four electrons have entered the sulfur atom's 3d subshell, which in elemental sulfur is empty.

REVIEW PROBLEMS

1. The Mg^{2+} ion has how many electrons?

   A. 12
   B. 10
   C. 14
   D. 15
   E. 24

2. It can be shown using mass spectrometry that the ratio of naturally occurring chlorine-35 to its isotope chlorine-37 is 3:1. Assuming no other isotopes exist, what is the standard atomic weight of chlorine?

3. A student represents electrons within the same orbital as having parallel spins. This goes against which of the following principles?

   A. Bohr's model of the hydrogen atom
   B. Pauli exclusion principle
   C. Heisenberg's uncertainty principle
   D. Planck's quantum theory
   E. Aufbau principle

4. What are the four quantum numbers? Discuss how they are related and to what each refers.

5. The maximum number of electrons in a shell with a principal quantum number of 4 is

   A. 2.
   B. 6.
   C. 10.
   D. 16.
   E. 32.

6. In Bohr's model of the hydrogen atom, the energy of an electron is directly dependent on

   A. the spin quantum number (m_s).
   B. Planck's constant (h).
   C. the principal quantum number (n).
   D. the angular momentum quantum number (ℓ).
   E. the magnetic quantum number (m_l).

7. Which of the following describes the excitation exhibited when an electron jumps from its ground state to a higher energy level?

   A. Balmer series
   B. Atomic absorption spectrum
   C. Lyman series
   D. Atomic emission spectrum
   E. Hund's rule

8. The Pauli exclusion principle states that
   A. no two electrons can have the same four quantum numbers.
   B. it is impossible to determine simultaneously the momentum and the position of an electron.
   C. energy is emitted from matter as quantized units.
   D. an electron will enter an empty orbital in a subshell before entering half-filled orbitals.
   E. the standard atomic weight is the most accurate measurement of the mass of atoms.

9. Atoms with the same atomic numbers but with different mass numbers are known as
   A. elements.
   B. isomers.
   C. ions.
   D. isotopes.
   E. compounds.

10. If the principal quantum number of a shell is equal to 2, what type(s) of orbitals will be present?
    A. s
    B. s and p
    C. s, p, and d
    D. s, p, d, and f
    E. s, p, d, f, and g

11. What quantity of energy is emitted when a hydrogen electron relaxes from $n = 3$ to $n = 2$?
    $(Ry = 2.18 \times 10^{-18} \text{ J})$

12. What wavelength (in nm) corresponds to the energy calculated in Question 11?
    $(c = 3 \times 10^8 \text{ m/s})$

13. What is the total number of electrons that could be held in a subshell with an angular momentum number equal to 2?
    A. 2
    B. 6
    C. 8
    D. 10
    E. 12

14. An element with an atomic number of 26 has how many electrons in the 3d subshell?

    A. 0
    B. 2
    C. 6
    D. 8
    E. 10

15. If the energy associated with $n = 1$ is $-1{,}312$ kJ/mol, which principal energy level corresponds with an energy value of -328 kJ/mol?

    A. 1
    B. 2
    C. 3
    D. 4
    E. 5

16. In going from $1s^2\ 2s^2\ 2p^6\ 3s^2\ 3p^6\ 4s^1$ to $1s^2\ 2s^2\ 2p^6\ 3s^2\ 3p^5\ 4s^2$, an electron would

    A. absorb energy.
    B. emit energy.
    C. relax to the ground state.
    D. bind to another atom.
    E. become a proton.

17. The values of the spin quantum number are directly related to

    A. the principal quantum number.
    B. the angular momentum quantum number.
    C. the magnetic quantum number.
    D. none of the above.
    E. the atomic weight.

18. Which of the following orbitals has the lowest energy?

    A. 2p
    B. 3s
    C. 3d
    D. 4s
    E. 4d

19. Which of the following correctly represents the excited state of scandium?

    A. $1s^2\ 2s^2\ 2p^6\ 3s^2\ 3p^6\ 3d^1\ 4s^2$
    B. $1s^2\ 2s^3\ 2p^5\ 3s^2\ 3p^6\ 3d^1\ 4s^2$
    C. $1s^2\ 2s^2\ 2p^6\ 3s^2\ 3p^6\ 3d^2\ 4s^1$
    D. $1s^2\ 2s^2\ 2p^6\ 3s^2\ 3p^6\ 3d^2\ 4s^2$
    E. $1s^2\ 2s^2\ 2p^5\ 3s^2\ 3p^6\ 3d^2\ 4s^1$

20. The photon frequency of red light is 4.51×10^{14} s^{-1}. If Ry $= 2.18 \times 10^{-18}$, what is the energy of the photon? Is this enough energy to cause a hydrogen electron to be excited from $n = 1$ to $n = 3$?

SOLUTIONS TO REVIEW PROBLEMS

1. **B** Magnesium has an atomic number of 12, meaning that it has 12 protons and 12 electrons. However, the Mg^{2+} ion has a positive charge because it has lost 2 electrons. Therefore, the Mg^{2+} ion has 10 electrons.

2. **35.5**

   Mass spectrometry shows that three out of every four chlorine atoms are Cl-35 and one is Cl-37. Thus, 75% of all chlorine atoms are Cl-35, and 25% are Cl-37. Using this information and the atomic weights of the isotopes (Cl-35 = 35 g/mol, Cl-37 = 37 g/mol), the atomic weight of chlorine can be determined as follows:

   $(0.75)(35\ \text{g/mol}) + (0.25)(37\ \text{g/mol})$

   $= (26.25 + 9.25)\ \text{g/mol}$

   $= 35.5\ \text{g/mol}$

3. **B** Discussed in the section on quantum numbers in this chapter.

4. Discussed in the section on quantum numbers in this chapter.

5. **E** The maximum number of electrons within a principal energy level can be calculated using the formula $2n^2$. Therefore, a shell with a principal quantum number equal to 4 will hold a maximum of 32 electrons.

6. **C** In the Bohr model for hydrogen, the energy of the electron is given by the equation

   $E = -\dfrac{\text{Ry}}{n^2}$ where Ry is a constant. Therefore, the energy of the electron is dependent only on n, the principal quantum number.

7. **B** For electrons to jump from ground state to higher energy levels, they must absorb energy. Therefore, the movements from ground state to excited state are characterized by an atomic absorption spectrum.

8. **A** Discussed in the section on quantum numbers in this chapter.

9. **D** Atomic weight equals the number of protons (atomic number) plus the number of neutrons. If two atoms have the same atomic number but different atomic weights, then the number of neutrons must be different. This is the definition of an isotope.

10. **B** When the principal quantum number is equal to 2, then the angular momentum quantum number will have values of $\ell = 0$ and 1. When $\ell = 0$, the subshell is an s subshell, and, when $\ell = 1$, the subshell is a p subshell. Therefore, the second principal energy level contains an s subshell and a p subshell.

11. **3.03×10^{-19} J**

To calculate the energy emitted when a hydrogen electron relaxes from $n = 3$ to $n = 2$, the

equation $E = -\text{Ry}\left(\dfrac{1}{n_i^2} - \dfrac{1}{n_f^2}\right)$ is used, where $\text{Ry} = 2.18 \times 10^{-18}$ J and n_i and n_f are

equal to 3 and 2, respectively. The calculation is performed as follows:

$$E = -2.18 \times 10^{-18}\ \text{J}\left(\frac{1}{3^2} - \frac{1}{2^2}\right)$$

$$E = -2.18 \times 10^{-18}\ \text{J}\left(\frac{1}{9} - \frac{1}{4}\right)$$

$$E = -2.18 \times 10^{-18}\ \text{J}\left(\frac{4}{36} - \frac{9}{36}\right)$$

$$E = -2.18 \times 10^{-18}\ \text{J}\left(-\frac{5}{36}\right)$$

$$E = 3.03 \times 10^{-19}\ \text{J}$$

The value of the energy is positive because energy is released when an electron falls from an excited state back to the ground state.

12. **656 nm**

The wavelength in nm of a photon that carries the 3.03×10^{-19} J of energy found in Question 11 can be determined as follows:

$$E = \frac{hc}{\lambda}, \text{ thus, by rearrangement, } \lambda = \frac{hc}{E}.$$

$$\lambda = \frac{\left(6.626 \times 10^{-34}\ \text{J} \cdot \text{s}\right)\left(3 \times 10^{8}\ \text{m/s}\right)}{3.03 \times 10^{-19}\ \text{J}}$$

$$= 656\ \text{nm}$$

13. **D** The angular momentum number 2 corresponds to the d subshell, and d is capable of holding a maximum of $4(2) + 2 = 10$ electrons.

14. **C** An element with an atomic number of 26 will have six electrons in its 3d subshell. This can be determined by writing the electron configuration for the element: $1s^2\ 2s^2\ 2p^6\ 3s^2\ 3p^6\ 3d^6\ 4s^2$. The number of electrons must equal 26; recall that the 4s subshell must be filled before the 3d because it has the lower energy. Thus, 3d will carry six electrons.

15. **B** You can use the equation $E = \dfrac{\text{Ry}}{n^2}$ to solve for different principle energy levels. However, since you know the value for $n = 1$, you don't need to plug in to the equation and can instead solve by comparing the numbers given. $-1{,}312$ is four times larger in magnitude than -328. Since the n in the denominator of the equation is squared, this means the values of n are only different by a factor of two. Therefore, since the original n was 1, the new n must be $1 \times 2 = 2$.

16. **A** The difference between the first and second electron configurations is that in the second configuration one electron has moved from the 3p subshell to the 4s subshell. Although the 3p and 4s subshells have the same $(n + \ell)$ value, the 3p subshell fills first because it is slightly lower in energy. For an electron to move from the 3p subshell to the 4s subshell, it must absorb energy.

17. **D** The spin quantum number is the intrinsic angular momentum of an electron in an orbital. The spin number can be either $+\frac{1}{2}$ or $-\frac{1}{2}$. These numbers are arbitrary and are not dependent on the other three quantum numbers.

18. **A** To determine which subshell has the lowest energy, the $(n + \ell)$ rule must be used. The values of the first and second quantum numbers are added together, and the subshell with the lowest $(n + \ell)$ value has the lowest energy. The sums of the five choices are $(2 + 1) = 3$, $(3 + 0) = 3$, $(3 + 2) = 5$, $(4 + 0) = 4$, $(3 + 1) = 4$. Choices (A) and (B) have the same $(n + \ell)$ value, so the subshell with the lower principal quantum number has the lower energy. This is the 2p subshell.

19. **C** Scandium has 21 electrons. Its ground-state electron configuration is $1s^2\ 2s^2\ 2p^6\ 3s^2\ 3p^6\ 3d^1\ 4s^2$. When it is in its excited state, one or more of the electrons will be present in a subshell with a higher energy than the one in which it is usually located. The number of electrons and ordering of subshells will not vary from the ground-state electron configuration of scandium. Choice (C) has one of the 4s electrons present in the 3d orbital. This represents an excited state because energy is required to cause an electron to jump from 4s to 3d.

20. **2.988×10^{-19} J; No**

    To determine the energy of a photon with a frequency (ν) of 4.51×10^{14} s^{-1}, the following calculations are performed:

    $E = h\nu$

    $E = (6.626 \times 10^{-34}\ \text{J} \cdot \text{s})\ (4.51 \times 10^{14}\ \text{s}^{-1})$

    $E = 2.988 \times 10^{-19}\ \text{J}$

    The energy from red light will not be sufficient to excite a hydrogen electron from $n = 1$ to $n = 3$. This is because the energy necessary to perform that excitation is:

    $$\Delta E = -\text{Ry} \times \left(\frac{1}{n_i^2} - \frac{1}{n_f^2} \right)$$

    $$\Delta E = -2.18 \times 10^{-18}\ \text{J} \left(\frac{1}{1^2} - \frac{1}{3^2} \right)$$

    $$\Delta E = -2.18 \times 10^{-18}\ \text{J} \left(\frac{8}{9} \right)$$

    $$\Delta E = -1.937 \times 10^{-18}\ \text{J}$$

    The magnitude of this energy is greater than the energy of red light.

CHAPTER TWENTY-FIVE

Periodic Properties

In 1869, the Russian chemist Dmitri Mendeleev published the first version of his periodic table, in which he showed that ordering the elements according to atomic weight produced a pattern where similar properties periodically recurred. This table was later revised, using the work of the physicist Henry Moseley, to organize the elements on the basis of increasing atomic number. Using this revised table, the properties of certain elements that had not yet been discovered were predicted: A number of these predictions were later borne out by experimentation. The substance of this work is summarized in the **periodic law**, which states that the chemical properties of the elements are dependent, in a systematic way, upon their atomic numbers.

In the periodic table used today, the elements are arranged in **periods** (rows) and **groups** (columns). There are seven periods, representing the principal quantum numbers $n = 1$ to $n = 7$, and each period is filled sequentially. Groups represent elements that have the same electronic configuration in their **valence**, or outermost, shell and share similar chemical properties. The electrons in the outermost shell are called **valence electrons**. They are involved in chemical bonding and determine the chemical reactivity and properties of the element. The Roman numeral above each group represents the number of valence electrons. There are two sets of groups, designated A and B. The A elements are the **representative elements**, which have either s or p sublevels as their outermost orbitals. These representative elements are those in Groups IA through VIIA, all of which have incompletely filled s or p subshells of the highest principal number. The B elements are the **nonrepresentative elements**, including the **transition elements**, which have partly filled d sublevels, and the **lanthanide** and **actinide** series, which have partly filled f sublevels. The electron configuration for the valence electrons is indicated by the Roman numeral and letter designations. For example, an element in Group VA has a valence electron configuration of s^2p^3 ($2 + 3 = 5$ valence electrons).

PERIODIC PROPERTIES OF THE ELEMENTS

The properties of the elements exhibit certain trends that can be explained in terms of the position of the element in the periodic table or in terms of the electron configuration of the element. All elements seek to gain or lose valence electrons so as to achieve the stable, fully filled formations possessed by the **inert** or **noble gases** of Group VIIIA. Two other important trends exist within the periodic table. First, from left to right across a period, protons are added one at a time and the electrons of the outermost shell experience an increasing degree of nuclear attraction, becoming closer and more tightly bound to the nucleus. This net positive charge from the nucleus, as felt by an electron, is called the **effective nuclear charge** (Z_{eff}). Second, from top to bottom down a given column, the outermost electrons become less tightly bound to the nucleus. This is because the number of filled principal energy levels (which shield the outermost electrons from attraction by the nucleus) increases downward within each group. Taken together, these trends show that Z_{eff} is at a maximum for elements in the top-right of the table and at a minimum for those in the bottom-left and help explain elemental properties such as atomic radius, ionization potential, electron affinity, and electronegativity.

Atomic Radii

The atomic radius of an element is equal to one-half the distance between the centers of two atoms of that element that are just barely touching each other. For example, the atomic radius of a metal is one-half the distance between the two nuclei in two adjacent atoms. In general, the atomic radius decreases across a period from left to right and increases down a given group; the atoms with the largest atomic radii will be located at the bottom of groups and toward the left of the table (Group IA).

As discussed in Chapter 24, Atomic and Molecular Structure, the electron cloud occupies the majority of the volume of an atom, whereas the nucleus takes up relatively little space. Therefore, something that affects the size of the electron cloud will change the radius of an atom, but altering the size of the nucleus will not directly affect the size of the atom.

From left to right across a period, electrons are added one at a time to the outer energy shell. Electrons within the same shell do not shield one another from the attractive pull of protons. Therefore, since the number of protons is also increasing from left to right across a period, the effective nuclear charge (Z_{eff}) increases as well. The greater the positive charge experienced by the valence electrons (the larger the Z_{eff}), the closer those electrons are pulled toward the nucleus and the smaller the atomic radius.

From top to bottom down a group, the number of electrons and filled electron shells increase. Although the number of valence electrons within a group remains the same, these valence electrons will be found farther from the nucleus as they are in progressively larger energy shells. Z_{eff} will become smaller with distance, so valence electrons in higher energy shells will feel less pull from the nucleus. Also, with more electrons comes increased repulsion from the additional negative ($-$) charges. Thus, the atomic radii will increase.

The **ionic radius** is the radius of a cation or an anion. The ionic radius will affect the physical and chemical properties of an ionic compound. In most situations, cations (positive ions) will be smaller than corresponding neutral atoms since possessing fewer electrons leads to less repulsion among the remaining electrons. Likewise, most anions (negative ions) will be larger than corresponding neutral atoms because having a greater number of electrons causes more repulsion, resulting in a greater distance between electrons and a larger atomic radius.

Ionization Energy

The ionization energy (IE) is the energy required to completely remove an electron from a gaseous atom or ion. Removing an electron from an atom always requires an input of energy and is endothermic. The closer and more tightly bound an electron is to the nucleus, the more difficult it will be to remove and the higher the ionization energy. The **first ionization energy** is the energy required to remove one valence electron from the parent atom, the **second ionization energy** is the energy needed to remove a second valence electron from the univalent ion to form the divalent ion, and so on. Successive ionization energies grow increasingly larger; i.e., the second ionization energy is always greater than the first ionization energy.

For example:

$$Mg(g) \quad \rightarrow \quad Mg^+(g) \quad +e^- \quad \text{First Ionization Energy} \quad = 7.646 \, eV$$

$$Mg^+(g) \quad \rightarrow \quad Mg^{2+}(g) \quad +e^- \quad \text{Second Ionization Energy} = 15.035 \, eV$$

Ionization energy increases from left to right across a period as Z_{eff} increases. Moving down a group, the ionization energy decreases as Z_{eff} decreases. Group IA elements have low ionization energies because the loss of an electron results in the formation of a stable, noble-gas configuration.

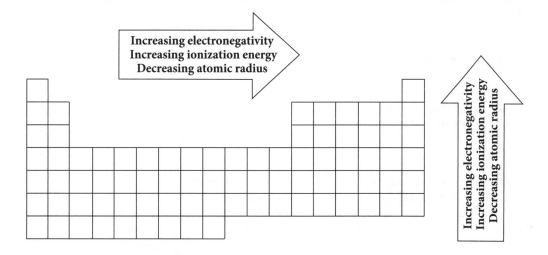

Figure 25.1

Electron Affinity

Electron affinity (EA) is the energy change that occurs when an electron is added to a gaseous atom, and it represents the ease with which the atom can accept an electron. The higher the Z_{eff}, the greater the electron affinity will be. In discussing electron affinities, two sign conventions are used. The more common one states that a positive electron affinity value represents energy release when an electron is added to an atom; the other states that a negative electron affinity represents a release of energy. In this discussion, the first convention will be used.

Electron affinity can be best represented by the following equation, where X is an atom of a given element in the gaseous state (g):

$$X(g) + e^- \rightarrow X^-(g)$$

Generalizations can be made about the electron affinities of particular groups in the periodic table. For example, the Group IIA elements, or **alkaline earth metals**, have low electron affinity values. These elements are relatively stable because their s subshell is filled. Group VIIA elements, or **halogens**, have high electron affinities because the addition of an electron to the atom results in a completely filled shell, which represents a stable electron configuration. Achieving the stable octet involves a release of energy, and the strong attraction of the nucleus for the electron leads to a high change in energy. The Group VIIIA elements (**noble gases**) have electron affinities on the order of zero because they already possess full shells and cannot readily accept electrons. Elements of other groups generally have low values of electron affinity.

Electronegativity

Electronegativity is a measure of the attraction an atom has for electrons in a chemical bond. The greater an atom's electronegativity, the greater its attraction for bonding electrons. Electronegativity values are not determined directly. The most common electronegativity scale is the **Pauling electronegativity scale** where the values range from 0.7 for the most electropositive elements, like cesium, to 4.0 for the most electronegative element, fluorine. Electronegativities are related to effective nuclear charge: Elements with low Z_{eff} will have low electronegativities because their nuclei do not attract electrons strongly, while elements with high Z_{eff} will have high electronegativities because of the strong pull the nucleus has on electrons. Therefore, electronegativity increases from left to right across periods and decreases from top to bottom down a group.

TYPES OF ELEMENTS

The elements of the periodic table may be classified into three categories: **metals**, located on the left side and in the middle of the periodic table; **nonmetals**, located on the right side of the table; and **metalloids** (**semimetals**), found along a diagonal line between the metals and nonmetals.

Metals

Metals are shiny solids (except for mercury) at room temperature and generally have high melting points and densities. Metals have the characteristic ability to be deformed without breaking. The ability of a metal to be hammered into shapes is called **malleability**, and the ability to be drawn into wires is called **ductility**. Many of the characteristic properties of metals, such as large atomic radius, low ionization energy, and low electronegativity, are due to the fact that the few electrons in the valence shell of a metal atom can easily be removed. Because the valence electrons can move freely, metals are good conductors of heat and electricity. Groups IA and IIA represent the most reactive metals and will be discussed below. The transition elements, also discussed later, are metals that have partially filled d orbitals.

Nonmetals

Nonmetals are generally brittle in the solid state and show little or no metallic luster. They have high ionization energies and electronegativities and are usually poor conductors of heat and electricity. Most nonmetals share the ability to gain electrons easily but otherwise display a wide range of chemical behaviors and reactivities. The nonmetals are located on the upper right side of the periodic table and are separated from the metals by a line cutting diagonally through the region of the periodic table containing elements with partially filled p orbitals.

Metalloids

The metalloids or semimetals are found along the line between the metals and nonmetals in the periodic table, and their properties vary considerably. Their densities, boiling points, and melting points fluctuate widely. The electronegativities and ionization energies of metalloids lie between those of metals and nonmetals; therefore, these elements possess characteristics of both those classes. For example, silicon (Si) has a metallic luster, yet it is brittle and is not an efficient conductor. The reactivity of metalloids is dependent upon the element with which they are reacting. For example, boron (B) behaves as a nonmetal when reacting with sodium (Na) and as a metal when reacting with fluorine (F). The elements classified as metalloids are boron (B), silicon (Si), germanium (Ge), arsenic (As), antimony (Sb), and tellurium (Te).

IONS

Ionic solutions are of particular interest to chemists because certain important types of chemical interactions occur in them. For instance, acid-base reactions and oxidation-reduction reactions occur in ionic solutions. Ions and their properties in solution will be introduced here; the chemical reactions mentioned are discussed in detail in Chapter 29, Reaction Types, and Chapter 36, Acids and Bases.

Cations and Anions

Ionic compounds are made up of cations and anions, where a cation is a positive ion and an anion is a negative ion. The nomenclature of ionic compounds is based on the names of the component ions.

- For elements that can form more than one positive ion (usually transition metals), the charge is indicated by a Roman numeral in parentheses following the name of the element.

$$Fe^{2+} \text{ Iron (II)} \qquad\qquad Cu^+ \text{ Copper (I)}$$
$$Fe^{3+} \text{ Iron (III)} \qquad\qquad Cu^{2+} \text{ Copper (II)}$$

- An older, but still commonly used, method is to add the ending *-ous* or *-ic* to the root of the Latin name of the element to represent the ions with lesser or greater charge, respectively.

$$Fe^+ \text{ Ferrous} \qquad\qquad Cu^+ \text{ Cuprous}$$
$$Fe^{3+} \text{ Ferric} \qquad\qquad Cu^{2+} \text{ Cupric}$$

- Monatomic anions are named by dropping the ending of the elemental name and adding *-ide*.

$$H^- \text{ Hydride} \qquad\qquad S^{2-} \text{ Sulfide}$$
$$F^- \text{ Fluoride} \qquad\qquad N^{3-} \text{ Nitride}$$
$$O^{2-} \text{ Oxide} \qquad\qquad P^{3-} \text{ Phosphide}$$

- Many polyatomic anions contain oxygen and are therefore called **oxyanions**. When an element forms two oxyanions, the name of the one with less oxygen ends in *-ite* and the one with more oxygen ends in *-ate*.

$$NO_2^- \text{ Nitrite} \qquad\qquad SO_3^{2-} \text{ Sulfite}$$
$$NO_3^- \text{ Nitrate} \qquad\qquad SO_4^{2-} \text{ Sulfate}$$

- When the series of oxyanions contains four oxyanions, prefixes are also used. **Hypo-** and **per-** are used to indicate less oxygen and more oxygen, respectively.

$$ClO^- \text{ Hypochlorite}$$
$$ClO_2^- \text{ Chlorite}$$
$$ClO_3^- \text{ Chlorate}$$
$$ClO_4^- \text{ Perchlorate}$$

- Polyatomic anions often gain one or more H^+ ions to form anions of lower charge. The resulting ions are named by adding the word hydrogen or dihydrogen to the front of the anion's name. An older method uses the prefix *bi-* to indicate the addition of a single hydrogen ion.

HCO_3^- Hydrogen carbonate or bicarbonate

HSO_4^- Hydrogen sulfate or bisulfate

$H_2PO_4^-$ Dihydrogen phosphate

Ion Charges

Metals, which are found in the left part of the periodic table, generally form positive ions, whereas nonmetals, which are found in the right part of the periodic table, generally form negative ions. Note, however, that anions that contain metallic elements do exist; e.g., MnO_4^- (permanganate) and CrO_4^{2-} (chromate). All elements in a given group tend to form monatomic ions with the same charge. Thus, the alkali metals (Group IA) usually form cations with a single positive charge, the alkaline earth metals (Group IIA) form cations with a double positive charge, and the halogens (Group VIIA) form anions (halides) with a single negative charge. Though other main group elements follow this trend, the intermediate electronegativity of such elements (which makes them less likely to form ionic compounds) and the transition from metallic to nonmetallic character complicates the picture.

THE CHEMISTRY OF GROUPS

Hydrogen

There is no suitable place for hydrogen in the periodic table. Hydrogen does resemble alkali metals because it has a single s valence electron and forms the H^+ ion, which is hydrated in solution. However, it can also form the hydride ion (H^-), which is far too reactive to exist in water. In this respect, hydrogen resembles the halogens in that it only requires one additional electron to reach the next noble gas configuration.

Alkali Metals

The alkali metals are the elements of **Group IA**. They possess most of the physical properties common to metals, yet their densities are lower than those of other metals. The alkali metals have only one loosely bound electron in their outermost shell, giving them the largest atomic radii of all the elements in their respective periods. Their metallic properties and high reactivity are due to their low ionization energies; they easily lose their valence electron to form univalent cations, allowing them to easily form +1 cations. Alkali metals have low electronegativities and react very readily with nonmetals, especially halogens.

Alkaline Earth Metals

The alkaline earth metals are the elements of **Group IIA** and also possess many characteristically metallic properties. Like the alkali metals, these properties are dependent on the ease with which they lose electrons. The alkaline earth metals have two electrons in their outer shell and have smaller atomic radii than the alkali metals. However, the two valence electrons are not held very tightly by the nucleus, so they can be removed to form divalent cations. Therefore, alkaline earth metals commonly form +2 cations. Alkaline earths have low electronegativities and positive electron affinities.

Carbon Group

The family containing carbon, **Group IVA**, exhibits a wide range of characteristics and includes a nonmetal (C), metalloids (Si and Ge), and metals (Sn and Pb). Although these elements do not share many physical properties, they do all have 2 electrons in their outermost p subshells, leading to a configuration that is distant from that of a noble gas. This explains why carbon tends not to form ions (which would need to be +4 or −4 to reach noble gas configuration) but rather participates in electron sharing; it usually is most stable with four covalent bonds (discussed further in Chapter 26, Chemical Bonding).

Pnictogens

Nitrogen and the elements below it in **Group VA** also display a wide variety of properties and include a mixture of nonmetals (N and P), metalloids (As and Sb), and a metal (Bi). Similar to carbon, nitrogen often forms covalent bonds but most commonly forms three per atom instead of carbon's four. Nitrogen also commonly holds a positive charge in organic reactions, making several nitrogen-containing compounds good bases.

Chalcogens

Group VIA, which contains oxygen, is characterized by elements requiring two additional valence electrons to complete their outermost shells. These elements therefore tend to be fairly electronegative and to form −2 anions, but they can also participate in covalent bonds, preferring to have two shared electron pairs and two nonbonded pairs.

Halogens

The halogens, **Group VIIA**, are highly reactive nonmetals with one valence electron less than the closest noble gas. Halogens therefore commonly form −1 anions. Halogens are otherwise highly variable in their physical properties. For instance, the halogens range from gaseous (F_2 and Cl_2) to liquid (Br_2) to solid (I_2) at room temperature. Their chemical properties are more uniform: The electronegativities of halogens are very high, and they are particularly reactive toward alkali metals and alkaline earths, which "want" to donate electrons to the halogens to form stable ionic crystals. Fluorine (F) has the highest electronegativity of all the elements.

Noble Gases

The noble gases, also called the **inert gases**, are found in **Group VIIIA** (also called Group 0). For the purposes of the test, they are completely nonreactive because they each have a complete valence shell, which is an energetically favored arrangement. This gives them no tendency to gain or lose electrons, high ionization energies, and no electronegativities. They possess low boiling points and are gases at room temperature.

Transition Elements

The transition elements, **Groups IB to VIIIB**, are all considered metals; hence, they are also called the **transition metals**. These elements are very hard and have high melting points and boiling points. From left to right across a period, the five d orbitals become progressively more filled. The d electrons are held only loosely by the nucleus and are relatively mobile, contributing to the malleability and high electrical conductivity of these elements. Chemically, transition elements have low ionization energies and may exist in a variety of positively charged forms or **oxidation states**. This is because transition elements are capable of losing various numbers of electrons from the s and d orbitals of their valence shells. Theoretically, the transition metals in Group VIIIB could have eight different oxidation states, from +1 to +8; however, they typically do not exhibit so many. For instance, copper (Cu), in Group IB, can exist in either the +1 or the +2 oxidation state, and manganese (Mn), in Group VIIB, occurs in the +2, +3, +4, +6, or +7 state. Because of this ability to attain positive oxidation states, transition metals form many different ionic and partially ionic compounds. The dissolved ions can form **complex ions** either with molecules of water (**hydration complexes**) or with nonmetals, forming highly colored solutions and compounds (e.g., $CuSO_4 \bullet 5H_2O$, chalcanthite). This complexation may also enhance the relatively low solubility of certain compounds (e.g., AgCl is insoluble in water but quite soluble in aqueous ammonia due to the formation of the complex ion $[Ag(NH_3)_2]^+$). The formation of complexes causes the d orbitals to be split into two energy sublevels. This enables many of the complexes to absorb certain frequencies of light—those containing the precise amount of energy required to raise electrons from the lower to the higher d sublevel. The frequencies not absorbed—known as the **subtraction frequencies**—give the complexes their characteristic colors.

REVIEW PROBLEMS

1. Elements in a given period have the same

    A. atomic weight.
    B. maximum azimuthal quantum number.
    C. maximum principal quantum number.
    D. valence electron structure.
    E. ionic radius.

2. Arrange the following species in terms of increasing atomic (or ionic) radius: Sr, P, Mg, Mg^{2+}.

3. The Ca^{2+} species is electronically similar to the elements in

    A. Group IIA.
    B. Group IA.
    C. Group IVB.
    D. Group 0.
    E. Group IIIB.

4. What is the electron configuration for the outermost electrons of elements found in Group IVB?

    A. $s^2\, p^6\, d^4$
    B. $s^2\, d^2$
    C. $s^2\, d^4$
    D. $s^2\, p^4$
    E. $s^2\, p^2$

5. Which of the following elements has the lowest electronegativity?

    A. Cesium
    B. Strontium
    C. Calcium
    D. Barium
    E. Potassium

6. Arrange the following calcium species in terms of increasing size: Ca, Ca^+, Ca^{2+}, Ca^{3+}, Ca^-, Ca^{2-}.

7. The order of the elements in the periodic table is based on the

    A. number of neutrons.
    B. radius of the atom.
    C. atomic number.
    D. atomic weight.
    E. number of electrons.

8. The elements within each column of the periodic table

    A. have similar valence electron configurations.

    B. have similar atomic radii.

    C. have the same principal quantum number.

    D. will react to form stable elements.

    E. have the same electronegativity.

9. Discuss the properties of nonmetals and give four examples of nonmetallic elements.

10. Arrange the following elements in terms of increasing first ionization energy: Ga, Ba, Ru, F, N.

11. Explain why the Group 0 elements are so unreactive.

12. Arrange the following elements in terms of decreasing electronegativity: Ca, Cl, Fr, P, Zn.

13. Which group contains an element with an electron configuration of $1s^2\ 2s^2\ 2p^6\ 3s^2\ 3p^6\ 4s^2\ 3d^{10}\ 4p^6\ 4d^5\ 5s^2$?

    A. VA

    B. VIIA

    C. VB

    D. VIIB

    E. VIA

14. Discuss the trends in the atomic radii of different elements. How does the atomic number affect the atomic radius of an element?

15. Which element has the greatest electronegativity?

    A. Chlorine

    B. Oxygen

    C. Sulfur

    D. Fluorine

    E. Phosphorus

16. The change in energy that occurs when an electron is added to an atom is known as the

    A. electronegativity.

    B. metallic character.

    C. electron affinity.

    D. ionization energy.

    E. atomic radius.

17. Discuss the properties of metalloids and give three examples of elements exhibiting metalloid behavior.

18. Which of the following elements is most electronegative?

    A. S
    B. Cl
    C. Na
    D. Mg
    E. P

19. Transition metal compounds generally exhibit bright colors because the

    A. electrons in the partially filled d orbitals are easily promoted to excited states.
    B. metals become complexed in water.
    C. metals conduct electricity, producing colored light.
    D. electrons in the d orbitals emit energy as they relax.
    E. compounds are highly reactive and produce colors when they react.

20. Discuss the properties of metals and give four examples of metallic elements.

21. Identify the following elements as metal, nonmetal, or semimetal.

    A. Fr
    B. Pd
    C. I
    D. B
    E. Sc
    F. Si
    G. S

GC

SOLUTIONS TO REVIEW PROBLEMS

1. **C** Discussed in the introduction to this chapter.

2. $Mg^{2+} < P < Mg < Sr$

    The trends in atomic radii are as follows. Going from left to right across a period, the atomic radii decrease because the atomic number increases. The increasing number of protons in the nucleus will have a stronger attraction for the outermost electrons, causing them to be held closer and more tightly to the nucleus. Going down a group, the atomic radius will increase because more filled principal energy levels separate the nucleus and the outermost electrons, shielding the attractive force between them. P has a small radius because it lies far to the right and high in a group. The magnesium species will have smaller radii than the strontium species because they are higher in Group IIA. Finally, positive ions have smaller atomic radii than the corresponding neutral molecules because the loss of electrons leads to a decrease in electron-electron repulsion within the atom, which in turn allows the electrons to move in closer to the nucleus. Therefore, Mg^{2+} will be smaller than Mg. Mg^{2+} has a smaller radius than P because Mg^{2+} has no electrons in orbitals of the third principal energy level.

3. **D** The Ca^{2+} ion is electronically similar to atoms in Group 0 because its outermost valence shell is a complete octet. It is isoelectronic to argon.

4. **B** The electron configuration of the different groups can be written as long as a few basic rules are applied. First, the Roman numeral represents the number of electrons that will lie outside of the noble gas core configuration. Second, the letters A and B tell whether the atom is a representative or a nonrepresentative element. Representative elements will successively fill the s and p orbitals, while the nonrepresentative elements will successively fill the s, d, and maybe f orbitals. Elements in Group IVB are nonrepresentative elements and will have four electrons outside their respective rare gas cores. The correct standard electron configuration for Group IVB elements is thus $s^2 d^2$.

    Using G to represent any noble gas, the full electron configuration of a nonspecified group IVB element can be abbreviated as $[G](n-1)d^2\ ns^2$, where n is the principal quantum number.

5. **A** The least electronegative elements are located at the bottom left of the periodic table. Cesium has the lowest ionization energy, so it is the least electronegative. Note that francium (Fr) would be lower still, but it is not a stable, naturally occurring element.

6. $Ca^{3+}, Ca^{2+}, Ca^+, Ca, Ca^-, Ca^{2-}$

    Positive ions will have smaller radii than the corresponding neutral atoms, and, the greater the positive charge, the smaller the ionic radius. Negative ions will have larger radii than the corresponding neutral atoms, and the greater the negative charge, the larger the ionic radius (see answer to Question 2, above).

7. **C** Discussed in the introduction to this chapter.

8. **A** Discussed in the introduction to this chapter.

9. Nonmetals are brittle, lusterless elements possessing high ionization energies and high electronegativities. They tend to gain electrons to form negative ions. They are poor conductors of heat and electricity. The nonmetals are located on the upper right side of the periodic table.

10. **Ba < Ru < Ga < N < F**

Two common trends should be remembered when ordering atoms according to their ionization energies. First, the ionization energy increases toward the right across a period because the elements are less willing to give up an electron as the attractive pull (Z_{eff}) of the nucleus increases. Second, the ionization energy decreases down a group because the distance separating the valence electrons from the nucleus increases. Therefore, to order the elements according to their first ionization energy, it is necessary to go from the bottom left of the periodic table, where the lowest values are, across to the top right of the periodic table, where the highest values are.

11. Group 0 elements are also known as the noble, rare, or inert gases. They are very unreactive because their outermost shells contain complete, stable formations. There is no reason for these elements to attempt to gain or lose electrons to other atoms because they are electronically stable on their own.

12. **Cl > P > Zn > Ca > Fr**

The two trends to remember with electronegativity are that it increases across a period and decreases down a group. Therefore, chlorine, which is farthest to the top and right, will have the highest value. Francium lies farthest to the left and bottom, so it will have the lowest electronegativity.

13. **D** This element has seven electrons in its outermost shell, so its Roman numeral designation is VII; because the d orbital is being filled, it is a nonrepresentative, or B, element. Thus, it is found in Group VIIB.

14. There are two major trends concerning the atomic radii of elements. The first of these is that the atomic radius decreases across a period. This can be explained by the fact that the atomic number (i.e., the number of protons within the nucleus) increases. Thus, the electrostatic force between the valence electrons and the nucleus increases, and the outermost electrons will be pulled closer to the nucleus, making the atom smaller. The second trend concerning atomic radii is that the atomic radius increases down a group. This can be explained by the fact that with every subsequent element down a group, a filled principal energy level has been added. This increases the distance between the nucleus and the valence electrons because orbital size increases with increasing principal quantum number.

15. **D** The most electronegative elements are located at the top right of the periodic table.

16. **C** Discussed in the section on periodic properties in this chapter.

17. Metalloids are elements that possess characteristics of both metals and nonmetals. Their electronic characteristics, such as ionization energies and electronegativities, lie between those of the metals and nonmetals. When undergoing reactions, the metalloids may act as either

metals or nonmetals depending upon the species with which they are reacting. The elements classified as metalloids are boron, silicon, germanium, arsenic, antimony, and tellurium.

18. **B** Chlorine has the greatest electronegativity because, out of all the choices, it lies farthest to the right and top of the periodic table. Chlorine has a great attraction for electrons in a chemical bond because it needs only one more electron to complete a stable octet formation. Therefore, it has a high electronegativity.

19. **A** The closely spaced d orbitals allow for relatively low energy transitions; these transitions often occur in the visible region of the electromagnetic spectrum, as do other electronic transitions from the transition metal d subshell to other nearby, empty subshells.

20. Metals are shiny, lustrous solids that have high melting points and densities. The ease with which metals lose electrons contributes to their high thermal and electrical conductivities, their malleability and ductility, and the ease with which they form compounds with reactive nonmetals. All of the elements on the left side of the periodic table (except H) and all of the transition elements are metals.

21. **A** Fr: metal

    B Pd: metal

    C I: nonmetal

    D B: semimetal

    E Sc: metal

    F Si: semimetal

    G S: nonmetal

CHAPTER TWENTY-SIX

Chemical Bonding

The atoms of many elements can combine to form **molecules**. The atoms in most molecules are held together by attractive forces called **chemical bonds**. These bonds are formed via the interaction of the valence electrons of the combining atoms. Strong chemical bonds known as **intramolecular bonds** hold atoms together as molecules and include ionic and covalent bonds. The chemical and physical properties of the resulting molecules are often very different from those of their constituent elements. In addition to the very strong forces within a molecule, there are weaker **intermolecular forces** between molecules. Intermolecular forces, although weaker than the intramolecular chemical bonds, are of considerable importance in understanding the physical properties of many substances.

BONDING

Many molecules contain atoms bonded according to the **octet rule**, which states that an atom tends to bond with other atoms until it has eight electrons in its outermost shell, thereby forming a stable electron configuration similar to that of the noble gas neon. Exceptions to this rule are as follows: hydrogen (H) and helium (He), which can have only two valence electrons; lithium (Li) and beryllium (Be), which bond to attain two and four valence electrons, respectively; boron (B), which bonds to attain six; and elements beyond the second row, such as phosphorus (P) and sulfur (S), which can expand their octets to include more than eight electrons by incorporating d orbitals.

When classifying strong chemical bonds, it is helpful to introduce two distinct types: ionic bonds and covalent bonds. In **ionic bonding**, one or more electrons from an atom with a smaller ionization energy are transferred to an atom with a greater electron affinity, and the resulting ions are held together by electrostatic forces. In **covalent bonding**, an electron pair is shared between two atoms. In many cases, the bond is partially covalent and partially ionic; we call such bonds **polar covalent bonds**.

IONIC BONDS

When two atoms with large differences in electronegativity react, there is a complete transfer of electrons from the less electronegative atom to the more electronegative atom. The atom that loses electrons becomes a positively charged ion, or **cation**, and the atom that gains electrons becomes a negatively charged ion, or **anion**. For this transfer to occur, the difference in electronegativity must be greater than 1.7 on the Pauling scale. In general, the elements of Groups IA and IIA (low electronegativities) bond ionically to elements of Group VIIA (high electronegativities). Elements of Groups IA and IIA give up their electrons to achieve a noble gas configuration, while Group VIIA elements gain an electron to achieve a noble gas configuration. For example, $Na + Cl \rightarrow Na^+Cl^-$ (sodium chloride). The electrostatic force of attraction between the charged ions is called an **ionic bond**.

Ionic compounds have characteristic physical properties. They form crystal lattices consisting of arrays of positive and negative ions in which the attractive forces between ions of opposite charge are maximized, while the repulsive forces between ions of like charge are minimized. They therefore have high melting and boiling points due to the strong electrostatic forces between the ions. They also can conduct electricity in the liquid and aqueous states, though not in the solid state.

COVALENT BONDS

When two or more atoms with similar electronegativities interact, the energy required to form ions is greater than the energy that would be released upon the formation of an ionic bond (i.e., the process is not energetically favorable). Since a complete transfer of electrons cannot occur, such atoms achieve a noble gas electron configuration by **sharing** electrons in a covalent bond. The binding force between the two atoms results from the attraction that each electron of the shared pair has for the two positive nuclei.

Covalent compounds generally contain discrete molecular units with weak intermolecular forces. Consequently, they have low melting points and do not conduct electricity in the liquid or aqueous states.

Properties of Covalent Bonds

Atoms can share more than one pair of electrons. Two atoms sharing one, two, or three electron pairs are said to be joined by a **single**, **double**, or **triple covalent bond**, respectively. The number of shared electron pairs between two atoms is called the **bond order**; hence, a single bond has a bond order of one, a double bond has a bond order of two, and a triple bond has a bond order of three.

Two key features characterize covalent bonds: bond length and bond energy.

Bond length

Bond length is the average distance between the two nuclei of the atoms involved in the bond. As the number of shared electron pairs increases, the two atoms are pulled closer together, leading to a decrease in bond length. Thus, for a given pair of atoms, a triple bond is shorter than a double bond, which is shorter than a single bond.

Bond energy

Bond energy is the energy required to separate two bonded atoms. For a given pair of atoms, the strength of a bond (and therefore the bond energy) increases as the number of shared electron pairs increases.

Covalent Bond Notation

The shared valence electrons of a covalent bond are called the **bonding electrons**. The valence electrons not involved in the covalent bond are called **nonbonding electrons**. These unshared electron pairs can also be called **lone electron pairs**. A convenient notation, called a **Lewis structure**, is used to represent the bonding and nonbonding electrons in a molecule, facilitating chemical "bookkeeping." The number of valence electrons attributed to a particular atom in the Lewis structure of a molecule is not necessarily the same as the number would be in the isolated atom, and the difference accounts for what is referred to as the **formal charge** of that atom. Often, more than one Lewis structure can be drawn for a molecule; this phenomenon is called **resonance**. Lewis structures, formal charges, and resonance are discussed in detail below.

Lewis structures

When different atoms interact to form a bond, only their outermost regions come in contact. Hence, only the valence electrons are involved. One of the easiest ways to follow the valence electrons in a chemical reaction is with **Lewis dot symbols**. A Lewis dot symbol contains the symbol of an element and one "dot" for each valence electron in an atom. Magnesium, for example, belongs to Group IIA and has two valence electrons (:Mg). Note: Because the transitional metals, lanthanides, and actinides all have incompletely filled inner shells, Lewis dot symbols are not written for these elements.

·Li	Lithium	$\ddot{N}$	Nitrogen
·Be·	Beryllium	·$\ddot{O}$:	Oxygen
·$\dot{B}$·	Boron	·$\ddot{F}$:	Fluorine
·$\dot{C}$·	Carbon	:$\ddot{N}e$:	Neon

Just as a Lewis symbol is used to represent the distribution of valence electrons in an atom, one can also be used to represent the distribution of valence electrons in a molecule. For example, the Lewis

symbol of an F ion is : $\ddot{F}$:⁻; the Lewis structure of an F_2 molecule is :$\ddot{F}$——$\ddot{F}$:

Certain steps must be followed in assigning a Lewis structure to a molecule. These steps are outlined below, using hydrogen cyanide (HCN) as an example:

1. Count all the valence electrons of the atoms. The number of valence electrons of the molecule is the sum of the valence electrons of all atoms present:

> H has 1 valence electron;
>
> C has 4 valence electrons;
>
> N has 5 valence electrons; therefore,
>
> HCN has a total of 10 valence electrons.

2. Write the skeletal structure of the compound (i.e., the arrangement of atoms). In general, the least electronegative atom is the central atom. Hydrogen (always) and the halogens F, Cl, Br, and I (usually)

occupy the end positions. Draw single bonds between the central atom and the atoms surrounding it, placing an electron pair in each bond (bonding electron pair).

In HCN, H must occupy a terminal position. Of the remaining two atoms, C is the less electronegative and therefore occupies the central position. The skeletal structure is as follows:

$$H:C:N$$

Each bond has 2 electrons, so $10 - 4 = 6$ valence electrons remain.

3. Complete the octets (8 valence electrons) of all atoms bonded to the central atom, using the remaining valence electrons still to be assigned. (Recall that H is an exception to the octet rule since it can have only 2 valence electrons.) In this example H already has 2 valence electrons in its bond with C.

$$H:C:\ddot{\underset{..}{N}}:$$

4. Place any extra electrons on the central atom. If the central atom has less than an octet, try to write double or triple bonds between the central and surrounding atoms using the nonbonding, unshared lone electron pairs. The HCN structure above does not satisfy the octet rule for C because C possesses only 4 valence electrons. Therefore, 2 lone electron pairs from the N atom must be moved to form two more bonds with C, creating a triple bond between C and N.

$$H:C:::N:$$

5. Finally, bonds are drawn as lines rather than pairs of dots.

$$H-C \equiv N$$

Now, the octet rule is satisfied for all three atoms because C and N have 8 valence electrons and H has 2 valence electrons.

Formal charges

The number of electrons officially assigned to an atom in a Lewis structure does not always equal the number of valence electrons of the free atom. The difference between these two numbers is the **formal charge** of the atom. Formal charge can be calculated using the following formula:

$$\text{Formal charge} = V - \frac{1}{2}N_{\text{bonding}} - N_{\text{nonbonding}}$$

where V is the number of valence electrons in the free atom, N_{bonding} is the number of bonding electrons, and $N_{\text{nonbonding}}$ is the number of nonbonding electrons. Using a Lewis dot structure, where 2 bonding electrons are represented by a stick and each nonbonding electron is represented with a dot, the formal charge is also represented by:

$$\text{Formal charge} = V - (\text{\# of sticks} + \text{\# of dots})$$

The formal charge of an ion or molecule is equal to the sum of the formal charges of the individual atoms comprising it.

Example: Calculate the formal charge on the central N atom of $[NH_4]^+$.

Solution: The Lewis structure of $[NH_4]^+$ is

$$
\left[\begin{array}{c} H \\ | \\ H-N-H \\ | \\ H \end{array} \right]^+
$$

Nitrogen is in Group VA; thus, it has 5 valence electrons. In $[NH_4]^+$, N has 4 bonds (i.e., 8 bonding electrons and no nonbonding electrons).

So $V = 5$; $N_{bonding} = 8$; $N_{nonbonding} = 0$

Formal charge $= 5 - \frac{1}{2}(8) - 0 = +1$

Likewise, there are 4 "sticks" and 0 "dots" in the Lewis structure, so formal charge (FC) could be calculated like this too:

$$FC = V - (\text{\# of sticks} + \text{\# of dots})$$
$$FC = 5 - (4 + 0) = 1$$

Thus, the formal charge on the N atom in $[NH_4]^+$ is $+1$.

Resonance

For some molecules, two or more non-identical Lewis structures can be drawn; these arrangements are called **resonance structures**. A resonance structure is one of two or more Lewis structures for a single molecule unable to be described fully with only one Lewis structure. The molecule doesn't actually exist as either one of the resonance structures but is rather a composite, or hybrid, of the two.

For example, SO_2 has three resonance structures, two of which are minor: $O=S-O$ and $O-S=O$. The actual molecule is a hybrid of these three structures (spectral data indicate that the two $S-O$ bonds are identical). This phenomenon is known as resonance, and the actual structure of the molecule is called the **resonance hybrid**. Resonance structures are expressed with a double-headed arrow between them:

$$\ddot{O}=\ddot{S}=\ddot{O} \longleftrightarrow \ddot{O}=\overset{+}{\ddot{S}}-\overset{-}{\ddot{O}}\!: \longleftrightarrow :\overset{-}{\ddot{O}}-\overset{+}{\ddot{S}}=\ddot{O}$$

The last two resonance structures of sulfur dioxide (shown above) have equivalent energy or stability. Often, nonequivalent resonance structures may be written for a molecule. In these cases, the more stable the structure, the more that structure contributes to the character of the resonance hybrid. Conversely, the less stable the resonance structure, the less that structure contributes to the resonance hybrid. The structure on the left of the diagram is the most stable. In this case, the most stable structure has no formal charge on any of the component atoms. Sulfur has more than 8 valence electrons (10 in this case), but that is acceptable because sulfur has a d subshell that can serve to expand the octet. More exceptions to the octet rule are discussed below.

Formal charges are often useful for qualitatively assessing the stability of a particular resonance structure, and the following guidelines should be used:

- A Lewis structure with small or no formal charges is preferred over a Lewis structure with large formal charges.
- A Lewis structure in which negative formal charges are placed on more electronegative atoms is more stable than one in which the formal charges are placed on less electronegative atoms.

Example: Write the resonance structures for the cyanate anion (which contains one nitrogen atom, one oxygen atom, one carbon atom, and an overall charge of negative one).

Solution: First, tally the total number of valence electrons:

N has 5 valence electrons;

C has 4 valence electrons;

O has 6 valence electrons; and the species itself has one negative charge (meaning one additional electron).

Total valence electrons $= 5 + 4 + 6 + 1 = 16$

C is the least electronegative of the three given atoms, N, C, and O. Therefore, the C atom occupies the central position in the skeletal structure of $[NCO]^-$. Draw single bonds between the central C atom and the surrounding atoms, N and O, and place a pair of electrons in each bond.

$$N:C:O$$

Complete the octets of N and O with the remaining $(16 - 4) = 12$ electrons.

$$:\ddot{N}:C:\ddot{O}:$$

The C octet is incomplete. There are three ways in which double and triple bonds can be formed to complete the C octet. Two lone pairs from the O atom can be used to form a triple bond between the C and O atoms:

$$:\ddot{N}-C\equiv O:$$

Or one lone electron pair can be taken from both the O and the N atoms to form two double bonds, one between N and C and the other between O and C:

$$:\ddot{N}=C=\ddot{O}:$$

Or two lone electron pairs can be taken from the N atom to form a triple bond between the C and N atoms:

$$:N\equiv C-\ddot{O}:$$

These three are all resonance structures of $[NCO]^-$.

Assign formal charges to each atom of each resonance structure: In the first structure, the N has a formal charge of -2, and the O has a charge of $+1$. In the second structure, the N has a formal charge of -1, and in the third structure the O has a charge of -1.

The most stable structure is therefore:

$$:N\!\equiv\!C\!-\!\ddot{\underset{..}{O}}:$$

since the negative formal charge is on the most electronegative atom, O.

Exceptions to the octet rule

Atoms found in or beyond the third period can have more than eight valence electrons, since some of the valence electrons may occupy d orbitals. These atoms can be assigned more than four bonds in Lewis structures.

The Lewis structure of the sulfate ion, SO_4^{2-}, for example, can be drawn in six resonance forms by alternating the placement of pi electrons. Giving the sulfur 12 valence electrons permits three of the five atoms to be assigned a formal charge of zero, which is most favorable energetically.

Figure 26.1

Types of Covalent Bonding

The nature of a covalent bond depends on the relative electronegativities of the atoms sharing the electron pairs. Covalent bonds are considered to be polar or nonpolar depending on the difference in electronegativities between the atoms.

Polar covalent bond

Polar covalent bonding occurs between atoms with small differences in electronegativity, generally in the range of 0.4 to 1.7 Pauling units. The bonding electron pair is not shared equally but is pulled more toward the element with the higher electronegativity. As a result, the more electronegative atom acquires a partial negative charge, $\delta-$, and the less electronegative atom acquires a partial positive charge, $\delta+$, giving the molecule a partially ionic character. For instance, the covalent bond in HCl is polar because the two atoms have a small difference in electronegativity (approx. 0.9). Chlorine, the more electronegative atom, attains a partial negative charge, and hydrogen attains a partial positive charge. This difference in charge between the atoms is indicated by an arrow crossed (like a plus sign) at the positive end and pointing to the negative end, as shown below.

Figure 26.2

A molecule that has such a separation of positive and negative charges is called a **polar molecule**. The **dipole moment** itself is a vector quantity μ, measured in **Debye** units (coulomb-meters) and defined as the product of the charge magnitude (q) and the distance between the two partial charges (r):

$$\mu = qr$$

Nonpolar covalent bond

Nonpolar covalent bonding occurs between atoms that have the same electronegativities. The bonding electron pair is shared equally such that there is no separation of charge across the bond. Nonpolar covalent bonds occur in diatomic molecules such as H_2, Cl_2, O_2, and N_2.

Coordinate covalent bond

In a coordinate covalent bond, the shared electron pair comes from the lone pair of one of the atoms in the molecule. Once such a bond forms, it is indistinguishable from any other covalent bond, so identifying such a bond is useful only in keeping track of the valence electrons and formal charges.

Coordinate bonds are typically found in Lewis acid-base compounds (see Chapter 36, Acids and Bases). A **Lewis acid** is a compound that can accept an electron pair to form a covalent bond; a **Lewis base** is a compound that can donate an electron pair to form a covalent bond. For example, in the reaction between boron trifluoride (BF_3) and ammonia (NH_3):

Lewis acid   Lewis base   Lewis acid-base compound

Figure 26.3

NH_3 donates a pair of electrons to form a coordinate covalent bond; thus, it acts as a Lewis base. BF_3 accepts this pair of electrons to form the coordinate covalent bond; thus, it acts as a Lewis acid.

Geometry and Polarity of Covalent Molecules

Molecular geometry

The **valence shell electron-pair repulsion (VSEPR)** theory uses Lewis structures to predict the molecular geometry of covalently bonded molecules. It states that the three-dimensional arrangement of atoms surrounding a central atom is determined by the repulsions between the bonding and the nonbonding electron pairs in the valence shell of the central atom. These electron pairs arrange themselves as far apart as possible, thereby minimizing repulsion.

The following steps are used to predict the geometric structure of a molecule using the VSEPR theory:

1. Draw the Lewis structure of the molecule.
2. Count the total number of bonding and nonbonding electron pairs in the valence shell of the central atom.
3. Arrange the electron pairs around the central atom so that they are as far apart from each other as possible.

4. Determine the bond angle, accounting for the additional repulsion due to nonbonding electrons, which pushes any bonding pairs slightly closer together.

For example, the compound AX_2 has the Lewis structure (X : A : X). A has two bonding electron pairs in its valence shell. To make these electron pairs as far apart as possible, their geometric structure should be linear:

$$X - A - X$$

Valence electron arrangements are summarized in the following table:

Electron Pairs	Nonbonding Pairs	Example	Geometric Arrangement	Shape	Angles
2	0	$BeCl_2$	X —— A —— X	Linear	180°
3	0	BH_3		Trigonal Planar	120°
4	0	CH_4		Tetrahedral	109.5°
4	1	NH_3		Trigonal Pyramidal	107°
4	2	H_2O		Bent	104.5°
5	0	PCl_5		Trigonal Bipyramidal	90°, 120°, 180°
6	0	SF_6		Octahedral	90°, 180°

Table 26.1

Example: Predict the geometry of NH_3.

Solution: The Lewis structure of NH_3 is:

$$H - \underset{\cdot\cdot}{N} - H$$
$$\overset{\displaystyle H}{\overset{|}{}}$$

The central atom, N, has three bonding electron pairs and one nonbonding electron pair for a total of four electron pairs.

The four electron pairs will be farthest apart when they occupy the corners of a tetrahedron. Since one of the four electron pairs is a lone pair, the observed geometry is trigonal pyramidal.

Figure 26.4

In describing the shape of a molecule, only the arrangement of atoms (not electrons) is considered. Even though the electron pairs are arranged in a tetrahedron, the shape of NH_3 is pyramidal. It is not trigonal planar because the lone pair repels the three bonding electron pairs, causing them to move as far away as possible.

Example: Predict the geometry of CO_2.

Solution: The Lewis structure of CO_2 is $:\!O::C::O\!:$.

The double bond behaves just like a single bond for purposes of predicting molecular shape. This compound has two groups of electrons around the carbon. According to the VSEPR theory, the two sets of electrons will orient themselves 180° apart, on opposite sides of the carbon atom, to minimize electron repulsion. Therefore, the molecular structure of CO_2 is linear.

Polarity of molecules

A molecule with a net dipole moment is called polar, as previously mentioned, because it has positive and negative poles. The polarity of a molecule depends on the polarity of the constituent bonds and on the shape of the molecule. A molecule with nonpolar bonds is always nonpolar; a molecule with polar bonds may be polar or nonpolar depending on the orientation of the bond dipoles.

A molecule of two atoms bound by a polar bond must have a net dipole moment and therefore be polar. The two equal and opposite partial charges are localized at the ends of the molecule on the two atoms. A molecule consisting of more than two atoms bound with polar bonds may be either polar or nonpolar since the overall dipole moment of a molecule is the vector sum of the individual bond dipole moments. If the molecule has a particular shape such that the bond dipole moments cancel each other (i.e., if the vector sum is zero), then the result is a nonpolar molecule. For instance, CCl_4 has four polar C–Cl bonds. According to the VSEPR theory, the shape of CCl_4 is tetrahedral. The four bond dipoles point to the vertices of the tetrahedron and cancel each other, resulting in a nonpolar molecule:

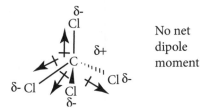

No net dipole moment

Figure 26.5

However, if the orientation of the bond dipoles are such that they do not cancel out, the molecules will have a net dipole moment and therefore be polar. For instance, H_2O has two polar O–H bonds. According to the VSEPR model, its shape is angular. The two dipoles add together to give a net dipole moment to the molecule, making the H_2O molecule polar:

Net dipole moment

Figure 26.6

Atomic and Molecular Orbitals

A description of the quantum numbers has already been given in Chapter 24, Atomic and Molecular Structure. The azimuthal quantum number (ℓ) describes the orbitals of each n shell. The shapes of these orbitals represent the probability of finding an electron at any given instant. $\ell = 0$ represents an s orbital, and s orbitals are spherically symmetric. The 1s orbital ($n = 1$, $\ell = 0$) is plotted below.

s orbital

Figure 26.7

When $\ell = 1$ there are three possible orbitals (since the magnetic quantum number, m_ℓ, may equal -1, 0, or $+1$). These are called p orbitals and have dumbbell shapes. The three p orbitals, designated p_x, p_y, and p_z, are oriented at right angles to each other; the p_x orbital is plotted below.

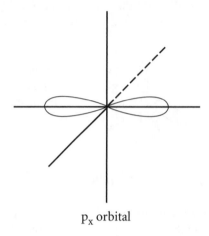

p_x orbital

Figure 26.8

The shapes of the five d orbitals ($\ell = 2$, $m_\ell = -2, -1, 0, 1, 2$) and the seven f orbitals ($\ell = 3$, $m_\ell = -3$, $-2, -1, 0, 1, 2, 3$) are more complex and need not be memorized for the exam.

When two atoms bond to form a molecule, the atomic orbitals interact to form a molecular orbital that describes the probability of finding the bonding electrons. Molecular orbitals are obtained by adding the wave functions of the atomic orbitals. Qualitatively, this is described by the overlap of two atomic orbitals. If the signs of the two atomic orbitals are the same, a **bonding orbital** is formed. If the signs are different, an **antibonding orbital** is formed. When two orbitals of different atoms overlap head-to-head, the resulting bond is called a **sigma (σ) bond**. When parallel p orbitals interact, a **pi (π) bond** is formed.

THE INTERMOLECULAR FORCES

The attractive forces that exist between molecules are collectively known as intermolecular forces. These include **dipole-ion interactions**, **hydrogen bonding**, **dipole-dipole interactions**, and **London dispersion forces (LDF)**. In order of decreasing strength, these are as follows:

dipole-ion > hydrogen bonding > dipole-dipole > LDF

Those forces not due to the interactions of ions or hydrogen bonding (i.e., dipole-dipole and LDF) are also collectively referred to as **van der Waals forces**.

Evaluating intermolecular forces is most important on the exam for determining melting and boiling points. Stronger intermolecular forces hold molecules together more tightly, so more energy (generally represented by higher temperatures) is required to weaken those bonds to allow for phase changes.

Dipole-Dipole Interactions

Polar molecules tend to orient themselves such that the positive region of one molecule is close to the negative region of another molecule. This arrangement is energetically favorable because an attractive dipole force is formed between the two molecules.

Dipole-dipole interactions are present in the solid and liquid phases but become negligible in the gas phase because the molecules are generally much farther apart. Polar species tend to have higher boiling points than nonpolar species of comparable molecular weight.

Hydrogen Bonding

Hydrogen bonding is a specific, particularly strong form of dipole-dipole interaction. When hydrogen is bound to either fluorine, oxygen, or nitrogen, the hydrogen atom carries little of the electron density of the covalent bond. This positively charged hydrogen atom interacts with the partial negative charge located on the electronegative atoms of nearby molecules. This interaction between the δ^+ on the H and the δ^- on the nearby molecule is the hydrogen bond. On the exam, a hydrogen can only hydrogen bond to adjacent molecules if that H is covalently bound to either F, O, or N. Substances that display hydrogen bonding tend to have unusually high boiling points compared with compounds of similar molecular weight that do not hydrogen bond. Hydrogen bonding is particularly important in the behavior of water, alcohols, amines, and carboxylic acids.

Dispersion Forces

The bonding electrons in covalent bonds may appear to be shared equally between two atoms, but, at any particular point in time, they will be located randomly throughout the orbital. This permits unequal sharing of electrons, causing rapid polarization and counterpolarization of the electron cloud and formation of short-lived dipoles. These dipoles interact with the electron clouds of neighboring molecules, inducing the formation of more dipoles. The attractive interactions of these short-lived dipoles are called London dispersion forces (LDF).

Dispersion forces are generally weaker than other intermolecular forces. They do not extend over long distances and are therefore most important when molecules are close together. The strength of these interactions within a given substance depends directly on how easily the electrons in the molecules can move (i.e., be polarized). Large molecules in which the electrons are far from the nucleus are relatively easy to polarize and therefore possess greater dispersion forces. If not for dispersion forces, the noble gases would not liquefy at any temperature since no other intermolecular forces exist between the noble gas atoms. The low temperature at which the noble gases liquefy is to some extent indicative of the magnitude of dispersion forces between the atoms.

Carbon-Carbon Bonding

Carbon-carbon bonds can be categorized based on length and energy level as well as hybridization. In Chapter 39, Nomenclature, we will review the hybridization of carbon-carbon bonds. The table below compares the bond length and energy levels of the different carbon-carbon bonds.

	Bond Length	Bond Energy
C−C	longest	lowest
C=C	middle	middle
C≡C	shortest	highest

Table 26.2

REVIEW PROBLEMS

1. Is Cl^- an anion or a cation?

2. Consider the following reaction:

    $$H_2\ (g) + F_2\ (g) \longrightarrow HF\ (g)$$

    Is the HF bond more or less polar than an H−H bond?

3. Arrange the following compounds in terms of increasing polarity:

    $$HCN,\ NaCl,\ Cl_2$$

4. **(A)** Which has a greater C−C bond distance, C_2H_4 or C_2H_2?

    (B) Which has a greater C−C bond energy?

5. Which of the following compounds would you expect to be weakly drawn into a magnetic field?

    $$H_2,\ NaCl,\ NO,\ NO_2,\ BF_3,\ PCl_5,\ SO_2$$

6. Which represents the proper Lewis structure of:

    A. $CHCl_3$?

    1. H:C̈:C̈l: with :C̈l: above and :C̈l: below

    2. H=C̈−C̈l−C̈l−C̈l:

    3. :C̈l−H−C̈l: with :C̈l: above and :C̈: below

    4. H−C−C̈l: with :C̈l: above and :C̈l: below

    B. N_2?

    1. N≡N

    2. N̈=N̈

    3. :N̈=N̈:

    4. Ṅ≡Ṅ

C. $[ClO_4]^-$?

1.

$$\left[\begin{array}{c} :\overset{..}{O}: \\ \overset{..}{O}=Cl-\overset{..}{O}: \\ :\overset{..}{O}: \end{array} \right]^-$$

2.

$$\left[\begin{array}{c} :\overset{..}{O}: \\ \overset{..}{O}=Cl-\overset{..}{O}: \\ :\overset{..}{O}: \end{array} \right]^-$$

3.

$$\left[\begin{array}{c} :O: \\ \overset{..}{O}=Cl-\overset{..}{O}: \\ :O: \end{array} \right]^-$$

4.

$$\left[\begin{array}{c} :\overset{..}{O}: \\ :\overset{..}{O}-Cl-\overset{..}{O}: \\ :\overset{..}{O}: \end{array} \right]^-$$

7. Which is not a resonance form of:

A. $\left(\begin{array}{c} :\overset{..}{O}: \\ \overset{..}{O}=N-\overset{..}{O}: \end{array} \right)^-$ **?**

1. $\left(\begin{array}{c} :\overset{..}{O}: \\ :\overset{..}{O}-N=\overset{..}{O} \end{array} \right)^-$

2. $\left(:\overset{..}{O}-\overset{..}{O}-N=\overset{..}{O} \right)^-$

3. $\left(\begin{array}{c} :\overset{..}{O}: \\ \| \\ :\overset{..}{O}-N-\overset{..}{O}: \end{array} \right)^{-}$

B. $\left(:\overset{..}{N}\equiv N-\overset{..}{N}: \right)^{-}?$

1. $\left(:\overset{..}{N}-N\equiv \overset{..}{N} \right)^{-}$

2. $\left(:\overset{..}{N}\overset{N}{\underset{}{\diagup}}\overset{\diagdown}{\underset{}{\equiv}} N \right)^{-}$

3. $\left(:\overset{..}{N}=N=\overset{..}{N}: \right)^{-}$

8. Using formal charges, predict which is the most likely resonance structure for N_2O.

A. $:N\equiv N=\overset{..}{O}:$

B. $:\overset{..}{N}=O=\overset{..}{N}:$

C. $:\overset{..}{N}=N=\overset{..}{O}:$

D. $:N\equiv N-\overset{..}{O}:$

E. $:N\equiv O\equiv N:$

9. Draw Lewis structures of the most likely ions of the elements from Na to Ca (atomic numbers 11 to 20).

10. Draw Lewis structures for each of the following:
    A. Nitrate ion ($[NO_3]^-$)
    B. Phosphoric acid (H_3PO_4)
    C. Aluminum chloride ($AlCl_3$)
    D. Sodium phosphate (Na_3PO_4)

11. A hydride is a compound containing the hydride ion, H^-. Predict two elements whose hydrides would contain incomplete octets.

12. Which of the following sets of molecules contains only nonpolar species?
    A. BH_3, NH_3, AlH_3
    B. NO_2, CO_2, ClO_2
    C. HCl, HNO_2, $HClO_3$
    D. BeH_2, BH_3, CH_4
    E. H_2O, SO_3, BCl_3

13. Arrange the following compounds in order of increasing boiling point: C_2H_6, CH_3OH, LiF, HCl.

SOLUTIONS TO REVIEW PROBLEMS

1. Cl^- is an anion. Negative ions are called anions, and positive ions are called cations.

2. The HF bond is more polar than an H–H bond. *Polar* denotes unequal sharing of electrons; H–H must have equal sharing because the two atoms are the same. H and F are different atoms with different electronegativities, and so the electrons are unequally shared.

3. **Cl_2 < HCN < NaCl**

    Cl_2 is the least polar because it contains two identical atoms that must share electrons equally. HCN is a linear molecule with a triple bond between C and N; it has a dipole moment pointing from the relatively electropositive H atom toward the rather electronegative N atom. Still, we should expect HCN to be less polar than NaCl; the bond between Na and Cl, a metal and a nonmetal whose electronegativities differ greatly, is completely ionic.

4. **A** C_2H_4 has greater bond distance because it is a double bond and is therefore held less closely than C_2H_2, which is a triple bond.

    B C_2H_2 has a greater bond energy because it is a triple bond and more energy is needed to break it.

5. NO and NO_2 would be weakly drawn into a magnetic field because they are paramagnetic. All paramagnetic molecules are weakly drawn into a magnetic field, and any compound with an odd number of valence electrons is paramagnetic. Thus:

    H_2: H has 1 valence electron; $1 + 1 = 2$, so H_2 is not paramagnetic.

    NaCl: Na has 1 valence electron, Cl has 7; $1 + 7 = 8$, so NaCl is not paramagnetic.

    NO: N has 5 valence electrons, O has 6; $6 + 5 = 11$, so NO is paramagnetic.

    NO_2: $5 + (2)(6) = 17$, so NO_2 is paramagnetic.

    BF_3: B has 3 valence electrons, F has 7; $3 + 3(7) = 24$, so BF_3 is not paramagnetic.

    PCl_5: P has 5 valence electrons, Cl has 7; $5 + 5(7) = 40$, so PCl_5 is not paramagnetic.

    SO_2: S has 6 valence electrons, O has 6; $6 + 2(6) = 18$, so SO_2 is not paramagnetic.

6. **A 4**

    Choice 4 is correct. Choice 1 is incorrect because covalent bonds are not marked with lines. Choice 2 has an impossible configuration; H can never be double-bonded to anything since the maximum number of electrons it may possess is 2. Choice 3 is also impossible since having four bonds around H would imply 8 electrons are present, which again would mean that H would have more than its maximum of 2 electrons.

    B 2

    Choices 1 and 3 must be incorrect because, although they satisfy the octet rule, they have the wrong total number of electrons; choice 1 has 8 valence electrons, whereas choice 3 has 12. Given two N atoms, there can be only $(2)(5) = 10$ valence electrons, as in correct choice 2. (Choice 1 is also incorrect because quadruple bonding is impossible due to orbital geometries.) Choice 4 is doubly incorrect because, in addition to only having 8 total electrons, the octet rule is not satisfied as each nucleus has 7, not 8, valence electrons.

C 3

Choice 3 is the preferred structure because four of the five atoms have a formal charge of zero. Since Cl is in the third period, its number of valence electrons can exceed 8.

7. **A 2**

In resonance forms, only the electrons change place; atoms are not rearranged. Choices 1 and 3 are both resonance structures. Choice 2 requires rearrangement of the atoms.

B 2

By the same reasoning as above.

8. **D** There is no formal charge on the structure of choice A or E; therefore, either of these structures could be the most likely resonance structure. However, the expanded octects of N and O make both impossible since both are in period 2, and $n = 2$ and does not have d orbitals. Choice C is incorrect because the negative formal charge is on N, which is not the most electronegative atom. Choice B is incorrect because O, which is the most electronegative atom, has a formal charge of $+2$. Choice D is most likely because the negative formal charge is on O, the more electronegative element.

9. **Na^+ Mg^{2+} Al^{3+} Si^{4+} $:\ddot{P}:^{3-}$ $:\ddot{S}:^{2-}$ $:\ddot{Cl}:^-$ (Ar has none)**

K^+ Ca^{2+}

Note that a correct ionic Lewis structure must always show the charge on the ion.

10. **A** $[NO_3]^-$

	has	needs
charge:	1 electron	
N:	5 electrons	8 electrons
3 O:	18 electrons	24 electrons
	24 electrons	32 electrons

$(32 - 24)$ electrons $= 8$ electrons $= 4$ bonds

Place N at the center:

(N and O both have a formal charge.)

$$\left(\begin{array}{c} :\ddot{O} \quad \ddot{O}: \\ \diagdown \quad \diagup \\ N \\ | \\ :\ddot{O}: \end{array} \right)^-$$

They cannot be reduced because the N octet cannot be expanded. However, since resonance will be present, a better version might be:

$$\left(\begin{array}{c} \ddot{O} \diagup \!\!\!\! = \underset{\underset{\displaystyle :\ddot{O}:}{\|}}{N} = \diagdown \!\!\!\! \ddot{O} \end{array} \right)^{-}$$

B H_3PO_4

	has	needs
3 H	3 electrons	$3(2) = 6$ electrons
P	5 electrons	8 electrons (at least)
4 O	24 electrons	32 electrons
	32 electrons	46 electrons

$(46 - 32)$ electrons $= 14$ electrons $= 7$ bonds (at least).

Place the P at the center, the 4 O around it, and H on 3 of the O with single bonds between them; this will use all 7 bonds.

Now check the formal charges:

$$\begin{array}{c} H\!-\!\ddot{O} \qquad \ddot{O}\!-\!H \\ \diagdown \overset{+}{} \diagup \\ P \\ \diagup \diagdown \\ H\!-\!\ddot{O}: \quad \ddot{O}:^{-} \end{array}$$

The P has a formal charge of $+1$, and the O has a formal charge of -1. These can be eliminated by moving a pair of electrons around from the O into a double bond:

$$\begin{array}{c} H\!-\!\ddot{O} \qquad \ddot{O}\!-\!H \\ \diagdown \diagup \\ P \\ \diagup \diagdown\!\!\diagdown \\ H\!-\!\ddot{O}: \quad \ddot{O} \end{array}$$

C Both aluminum chloride and sodium phosphate are ionic.

$AlCl_3$

$$\left(:\ddot{\underset{..}{C}}l: \right)^{-}$$

$$Al^{+3} \qquad \left(:\ddot{\underset{..}{C}}l: \right)^{-}$$

$$\left(:\ddot{\underset{..}{C}}l: \right)^{-}$$

D Na_3PO_4

$$O=P-O^-Na^+$$

with O^-Na^+ above and O^- Na^+ below the phosphorus.

11. Be and B, because they can join to only two or three H, respectively, since they have fewer than 4 valence electrons. The elements Mg and Al may also do this, as could Na, Ca, and the other active metals of Groups IA and IIA.

12. **D**

   A. NH_3 is polar (positive end at base of pyramid, negative end at N).

   B. NO_2 and ClO_2 are both angular molecules; therefore, they are polar.

   C. All three are polar.

   D. H_2O is polar because it is a bent molecule.

13. $C_2H_6 < HCl < CH_3OH < LiF$

   For each compound, the following intermolecular forces are present:

   C_2H_6: London dispersion forces

   HCl: dipole-dipole

   CH_3OH: H-bonding

   LiF: ionic

CHAPTER TWENTY-SEVEN

Stoichiometry

A **compound** is a pure substance composed of two or more elements in a fixed proportion. Compounds can be broken down chemically to produce their constituent elements or other compounds. All elements, except for some of the noble gases, can react with other elements or compounds to form new compounds. These new compounds can react further to form yet different compounds.

MOLECULES AND MOLES

A molecule is a combination of two or more atoms held together by covalent bonds and is the smallest unit of a compound that still displays the properties of that compound. Molecules may contain two atoms of the same element, as in N_2 and O_2, or may be comprised of two or more different atoms, as in CO_2 and $SOCl_2$. Molecules are usually discussed in terms of **molecular mass** and **moles**.

Ionic compounds do not form true molecules. In the solid state, they can be considered to be a nearly infinite, three-dimensional array of the charged particles of which the compound is composed. Because no actual molecule exists, molecular mass becomes meaningless, and the term **formula mass** is used in its place.

Molecular Mass

Like atoms, molecules can be characterized by their mass. The molecular mass (also known as **molecular weight**) is the sum of the atomic masses of the atoms in the molecule. Similarly, the formula mass of an ionic compound is found by adding up the atomic masses of each constituent atom according to the empirical formula of the substance.

Example: What is the molecular mass of $SOCl_2$?

Solution: To find the molecular mass of $SOCl_2$, add together the atomic masses of each of the atoms:

$$1\ S\ =\ 1\times 32\ \text{amu}\ \ =\ 32\ \text{amu}$$
$$1\ O\ =\ 1\times 16\ \text{amu}\ \ =\ 16\ \text{amu}$$
$$2\ Cl\ =\ 2\times 35.5\ \text{amu}\ =\ \underline{71\ \text{amu}}$$
$$\text{molecular mass}\ =\ 119\ \text{amu}$$

Mole

A mole is defined as the amount of a substance that contains the same number of particles found in a 12 g sample of carbon-12. This quantity, **Avogadro's number,** is equal to 6.022×10^{23}. One mole of a compound has a mass in grams equal to the molecular mass of that compound in amu and contains 6.022×10^{23} molecules of the compound. For example, 62 g of H_2CO_3 represents one mole of carbonic acid and contains 6.022×10^{23} H_2CO_3 molecules. The mass of one mole of a compound is called its **molar mass** or **molar weight** and is usually expressed as g/mol. Therefore, the molar mass of H_2CO_3 is 62 g/mol.

The following formula is used to determine the number of moles present in a sample:

$$\text{mol} = \frac{\text{Weight of Sample (g)}}{\text{Molar\ Weight (g/mol)}}$$

Example: How many moles are in 9.52 g of $MgCl_2$?

Solution: First find the molar mass of $MgCl_2$:

$$1(24.31\ \text{g/mol}) + 2(35.45\ \text{g/mol}) = 95.21\ \text{g/mol}$$

Now solve for the number of moles:

$$\frac{9.52\ \text{g}}{95.21\ \text{g/mol}} = 0.10\ \text{mol of } MgCl_2$$

Gram Equivalents

For some substances it is useful to define a measure of reactive capacity. This expresses the fact that some molecules are more potent than others in performing certain reactions. An example of this is the ability of different acids to donate protons (H^+ ions) in solution (see Chapter 36, Acids and Bases). For instance, one mole of HCl can donate one mole of hydrogen ions, while one mole of H_2SO_4 can donate two moles of hydrogen ions. This difference is expressed using the term **equivalent**: one mole of HCl contains one equivalent of hydrogen ions, while one mole of H_2SO_4 contains two equivalents of hydrogen ions. To determine the number of equivalents a compound contains, a new measure of weight, called **gram-equivalent weight (GEW)**, was developed such that:

$$\text{equivalents} = \frac{\text{weight of compound}}{\text{gram equivalent weight}}$$

and

$$\text{gram equivalent weight} = \frac{\text{molar mass}}{n}$$

where n is usually either the number of **hydrogen** ions an Arrhenius or Brønsted-Lowry acid could donate per molecule or the number of **hydroxyl groups** an Arrhenius base could donate (or number of hydrogen ions a Brønsted-Lowry base could accept) in a reaction. Gram equivalent weight is dependent on reaction conditions and is determined experimentally; however, on the exam, gram equivalent weight can be estimated from the molecular structure. By using equivalents, it is possible to say one equivalent of acid will neutralize one equivalent of base, a statement that is not necessarily true when dealing in moles.

REPRESENTATION OF COMPOUNDS

Law of Constant Composition

The law of constant composition states that all samples of a given compound will contain the same elements in identical mass ratios. For instance, every sample of H_2O will contain two atoms of hydrogen for every atom of oxygen and therefore one gram of hydrogen for every eight grams of oxygen.

Empirical and Molecular Formulas

There are two ways to express a formula for a compound. The **empirical formula** gives the simplest whole number ratio of the elements in the compound. The **molecular formula** gives the exact number of atoms of each element in the compound and is a multiple of the empirical formula. For example, the empirical formula for benzene is CH, whereas the molecular formula is C_6H_6. For some compounds the empirical and molecular formulas are the same, as in the case of H_2O. An ionic compound, such as NaCl or $CaCO_3$, will have only an empirical formula.

Note that, given a molecular formula, the empirical formula for that molecule can be calculated by simplifying the ratio of the subscripts next to each component. However, given only an empirical formula, the molecular formula of a specific molecule cannot be determined without more information since several different molecules could share the same empirical formula. For example, the empirical formula CH_2 is shared by ethylene (C_2H_4), butane (C_4H_8), and cyclohexane (C_6H_{12}).

Percent Composition

The percent composition by mass of an element is the mass percent of the element in a specific compound. To determine the percent composition of an element X in a compound, the following formula is used:

$$\% \text{ composition} = \frac{\text{Mass of X in Formula}}{\text{Formula Weight of Compound}} \times \mathbf{100\%}$$

The percent composition of an element may be determined using either the empirical or molecular formula. If the percent compositions are known, the empirical formula can be derived. It is possible to determine the molecular formula if both the percent compositions and molecular mass of the compound are known.

Example: What is the percent composition of chromium in $K_2Cr_2O_7$ (potassium's molecular mass is 39 g/mol, chromium's is 52 g/mol, and oxygen's is 16 g/mol)?

Solution: The formula mass of $K_2Cr_2O_7$ is: $2(39 \text{ g/mol}) + 2(52 \text{ g/mol}) + 7(16 \text{ g/mol}) = 294$ g/mol

$$\% \text{ composition of Cr} = \frac{2(52\text{g/mol})}{294 \text{ g/mol}} \times 100\%$$
$$= 0.354 \times 100\%$$
$$= 35.4\%$$

Example: What are the empirical and molecular formulas of a compound that contains 40.9% carbon, 4.58% hydrogen, and 54.52% oxygen by mass and has a molecular mass of 264 g/mol (carbon's molar mass is 12 g/mol, hydrogen's is 1 g/mol, and oxygen's is 16 g/mol)?

Method One: First, determine the number of moles of each element in the compound by assuming a 100 g sample; this converts the percentage of each element present directly into grams of that element. Then convert grams to moles:

$$\# \text{ mol of C} = \frac{40.9 \text{ g}}{12 \text{ g/mol}} = 3.41 \text{ mol}$$

$$\# \text{ mol of H} = \frac{4.58 \text{ g}}{1 \text{ g/mol}} = 4.58 \text{ mol}$$

$$\# \text{ mol of O} = \frac{54.52 \text{ g}}{16 \text{ g/mol}} = 3.41 \text{ mol}$$

Next, find the simplest whole number ratio of the elements by dividing the number of moles of each element by the smallest number obtained in the previous step:

$$C: \frac{3.41}{3.41} = 1.0 \qquad H: \frac{4.58}{3.41} = 1.3 \qquad O: \frac{3.41}{3.41} = 1.0$$

Finally, the empirical formula is obtained by converting the numbers obtained into whole numbers (multiplying them by an integer value).

$$C_1H_{1.3}O_1 \times 3 = C_3H_4O_3$$

Multiplying all the subscripts by 3 to obtain all whole numbers for the subscripts shows that $C_3H_4O_3$ is the empirical formula.

To determine the molecular formula, divide the molecular mass by the mass represented by the empirical formula. The resulting value is the number of empirical formula units in the molecular formula.

The empirical formula mass of $C_3H_4O_3$ is:

$3(12 \text{ g/mol}) + 4(1 \text{ g/mol}) + 3(16 \text{ g/mol}) = 88 \text{ g/mol}$

$$\frac{264 \text{ g/mol}}{88 \text{ g/mol}} = 3$$

$C_3H_4O_3 \times 3 = C_9H_{12}O_9$ is the molecular formula.

Method Two: When the molecular mass is given, it can be faster to find the molecular formula first. This is accomplished by multiplying the molecular mass by the given percentages to find the grams of each element present in one mole of compound, then dividing by the respective atomic masses to find the mole ratio of the elements:

$$\# \text{ mol of C} = \frac{(0.409)(264 \text{ g})}{12 \text{ g/mol}} = 9 \text{ mol}$$

$$\# \text{ mol of H} = \frac{(0.0458)(264 \text{ g})}{1 \text{ g/mol}} = 12 \text{ mol}$$

$$\# \text{ mol of O} = \frac{(0.5452)(264 \text{ g})}{16 \text{ g/mol}} = 9 \text{ mol}$$

Thus, the molecular formula, $C_9H_{12}O_9$, is the direct result.
The empirical formula can now be found by reducing the subscript ratio to the simplest integral values.

BALANCING EQUATIONS

Chemical equations express how much and what type of reactants must be used to obtain a given quantity of product. From the **law of conservation of mass**, the mass of the reactants in a reaction must be equal to the mass of the products. More specifically, chemical equations must be balanced so that there are the same number of atoms of each element in the products as there are in the reactants. **Stoichiometric coefficients** are used to indicate the number of moles of a given species involved in the reaction. For example, the reaction for the formation of water is:

$$2 \text{ H}_2 \ (g) + \text{O}_2 \ (g) \rightarrow 2 \text{ H}_2\text{O} \ (g)$$

The coefficients indicate that two moles of H_2 gas must be reacted with one mole of O_2 gas to produce two moles of water. In general, stoichiometric coefficients are given as whole numbers.

Example: Balance the following reaction:

$$C_4H_{10} \ (l) + O_2 \ (g) \rightarrow CO_2 \ (g) + H_2O \ (l)$$

Solution: First, balance the carbon in reactants and products.

$$C_4H_{10} + O_2 \rightarrow 4 \ CO_2 + H_2O$$

Second, balance the hydrogen in reactants and products.

$$C_4H_{10} + O_2 \rightarrow 4 \ CO_2 + 5 \ H_2O$$

Third, balance the oxygen in reactants and products.

$$C_4H_{10} + 6.5 \ O_2 \rightarrow 4 \ CO_2 + 5 \ H_2O$$

Stoichiometric coefficients are typically written as integers, so double everything to remove the decimal.

$$2 \ C_4H_{10} + 13 \ O_2 \rightarrow 8 \ CO_2 + 10 \ H_2O$$

Finally, check that all of the elements and the total charge are balanced correctly. If there is a difference in total charge between the reactants and products, then the charge will also have to be balanced. Instructions for balancing charge are found in Chapter 29 in the context of redox reactions.

Applications of Stoichiometry

Once an equation has been balanced, the ratio of moles of reactant to moles of products is known, and that information can be used to solve many types of stoichiometry problems. It is important to use proper units when solving such problems. When performing these calculations, the units should cancel out such that the units obtained in the answer represent those asked for in the problem.

Example: How many grams of calcium chloride are needed to prepare 72 g of silver chloride according to the following equation (calcium's molar mass is 40 g/mol, chlorine's is 35.5 g/mol, and silver's is 108 g/mol)?

$$CaCl_2 \ (aq) + 2 \ AgNO_3 \ (aq) \rightarrow Ca(NO_3)_2 \ (aq) + 2 \ AgCl \ (s)$$

Solution: First, note that the equation is balanced. Then, identify that one mole of $CaCl_2$ yields two moles of AgCl when reacted with two moles of $AgNO_3$. The molar mass of $CaCl_2$ is 110 g/mol, and the molar mass of AgCl is approximately 144 g/mol. Starting with the goal mass of AgCl, convert to moles, find the number of moles of $CaCl_2$ required, and then convert into g of $CaCl_2$ (as grams are the units that the question specifies).

$$72 \text{ g AgCl} \times \frac{1 \text{ mol AgCl}}{144 \text{ g AgCl}} \times \frac{1 \text{ mol CaCl}_2}{2 \text{ mol AgCl}} \times \frac{110 \text{ g CaCl}_2}{1 \text{ mol CaCl}_2} = 27.5 \text{ g of CaCl}_2$$

Thus, 27.5 g of $CaCl_2$ are needed to produce 72 g of AgCl.

Limiting reactant

When reactants are mixed, they are seldom added in the exact stoichiometric proportions as shown in the balanced equation. Therefore, in most reactions, one of the reactants will be consumed first. This reactant is known as the limiting reactant or **limiting reagent** because it limits the amount of product that can be formed in the reaction. The reactant(s) that remains after all of the limiting reactant is used up is called the **excess reactant**.

Example: If 28 g of Fe are reacted with 24 g of S to produce FeS, what is the limiting reactant? How many grams of excess reactant are present in the vessel at the end of the reaction?

The balanced equation is: $Fe + S \xrightarrow{\Delta} FeS$

Solution: First, the number of moles for each reactant must be determined.

$$28 \text{ g Fe} \times \frac{1 \text{ mol Fe}}{56 \text{ g}} = 0.5 \text{ mol Fe}$$

$$24 \text{ g S} \times \frac{1 \text{ mol S}}{32 \text{ g}} = 0.75 \text{ mol S}$$

Since one mole of Fe is needed to react with one mole of S, and there are 0.5 moles of Fe for every 0.75 moles of S, the limiting reagent is Fe. Thus, 0.5 moles of Fe will react with 0.5 moles of S, leaving an excess of 0.25 moles of S in the vessel. The mass of the excess reactant will be:

$$\text{mass of S} = (0.25 \text{ mol S}) \frac{32 \text{ g}}{1 \text{ mol S}} = 8 \text{ g of S}$$

Yields

The yield of a reaction, which is the amount of product predicted or obtained when the reaction is carried out, can be predicted from the balanced equation. There are three distinct ways of reporting yields. The **theoretical yield** is the amount of product that can be predicted from a balanced equation, assuming that all of the limiting reagent has been used, no competing side reactions have occurred, and all of the product has been collected. However, the theoretical yield is seldom obtained in real-world conditions; therefore, chemists speak of the **actual yield,** which is the amount of product isolated from the reaction experimentally. There are a variety of reasons why the actual yield is less than the theoretical yield. For example, many reactions are **reversible** (i.e., do not proceed 100 percent from left to right) or use reactants that interact with one another to produce additional end products.

The term **percent yield** is used to express the relationship between the actual yield and the theoretical yield and is given by the following equation:

$$\text{Percent yield} = \frac{\text{Actual yield}}{\text{Theoretical yield}} \times 100\%$$

Example: What is the percent yield for a reaction in which 27 g of Cu is produced by reacting 32.5 g of Zn in excess $CuSO_4$ solution (copper's molar mass is 63.5 g/mol, zinc's is 65 g/mol, sulfur's is 32 g/mol, and oxygen's is 16 g/mol)?

Solution: The balanced equation is as follows:

$$Zn\ (s) + CuSO_4\ (aq) \rightarrow Cu\ (s) + ZnSO_4\ (aq)$$

Calculate the theoretical yield for Cu.

$$32.5\ g\ Zn \times \frac{1\ mol\ Zn}{65\ g} = 0.5\ mol\ Zn$$

$$0.5\ mol\ Zn \times \frac{1\ mol\ Cu}{1\ mol\ Zn} = 0.5\ mol\ Cu$$

$$0.5\ mol\ Cu \times \frac{64g}{1\ mol\ Cu} = 32\ g\ Cu\ (theoretical\ yield)$$

Finally, determine the percent yield.

$$Percent\ yield = \frac{Actual\ yield}{Theoretical\ yield} \times 100\% = \frac{27\ g}{32\ g} \times 100\% = 84\%$$

REVIEW PROBLEMS

1. What is the sum of the coefficients of the following equation when it is balanced?

$$C_6H_{12}O_6 + O_2 \rightarrow CO_2 + H_2O$$

    A. 19
    B. 20
    C. 21
    D. 38
    E. 40

2. Determine the molecular formula and calculate the percent composition of each element present in nicotine, which has an empirical formula of C_5H_7N and a molecular mass of 162 g/mol.

3. Acetylene, used as a fuel in welding torches, is produced in a reaction between calcium carbide and water:

$$CaC_2 + 2\ H_2O \rightarrow Ca(OH)_2 + C_2H_2$$

How many grams of C_2H_2 are formed from 0.400 moles of CaC_2?

    A. 0.400
    B. 0.800
    C. 4.00
    D. 5.20
    E. 10.4

4. Aspirin ($C_9H_8O_4$) is prepared by reacting salicylic acid ($C_7H_6O_3$) and acetic anhydride ($C_4H_6O_3$).

$$C_7H_6O_3 + C_4H_6O_3 \rightarrow C_9H_8O_4 + C_2H_4O_2$$

How many moles of salicylic acid should be used to prepare six 5-grain aspirin tablets? (1 g = 15.5 grains)

    A. 0.01
    B. 0.10
    C. 1.00
    D. 1.94
    E. 2.01

5. The percent composition of an unknown element X in CH_3X is 32 percent. Which of the following is element X?

    A. H
    B. F
    C. Cl
    D. Li
    E. N

6. Twenty-seven grams of silver were reacted with excess sulfur, according to the following equation:

$$2\,Ag + S \rightarrow Ag_2S$$

Twenty-five grams of silver sulfide were collected. What are the theoretical yield, actual yield, and percent yield?

7. What is the mass in grams of a single chlorine atom? Of a single molecule of O_2?

The following reaction will be used to answer questions 8–10.

$$Ag(NH_3)_2^+ \rightarrow Ag^+ + 2\,NH_3$$

8. How many moles of $Ag(NH_3)_2^+$ are required for the production of 11 moles of ammonia?

9. If 5.80 g of $Ag(NH_3)_2^+$ yields 1.40 g of ammonia, how many moles of silver are produced?
   A. 0.041
   B. 0.054
   C. 2.20
   D. 4.40
   E. 5.80

10. What are the percent compositions of Ag, N, and H in $Ag(NH_3)_2^+$?

11. A hydrocarbon (which by definition contains only C and H atoms) is heated in an excess of oxygen to produce 58.67 g of CO_2 and 27 g of H_2O. What is the empirical formula of the hydrocarbon?

12. Balance the following reaction:

$$NF_3 + H_2O \rightarrow HF + NO + NO_2$$

How many grams of HF are expected to form if 1.5 kg of a 5.2% NF_3 sample is used?

13. Balance the following reactions:
   A. $I_2 + Cl_2 + H_2O \rightarrow HIO_3 + HCl$
   B. $MnO_2 + HCl \rightarrow H_2O + MnCl_2 + Cl_2$
   C. $BCl_3 + P_4 + H_2 \rightarrow BP + HCl$
   D. $C_3H_5(NO_3)_3 \rightarrow CO_2 + H_2O + N_2 + O_2$
   E. $HCl + Ba(OH)_2 \rightarrow BaCl_2 + H_2O$

SOLUTIONS TO REVIEW PROBLEMS

1. **A** To answer this question, the equation must first be balanced. Starting with carbon, it can be seen that there are 6 carbons on the reactant side and only one on the product side, so a coefficient of 6 should be placed in front of the carbon dioxide. For the hydrogen, there are 12 atoms on the left and only 2 on the right; thus, a coefficient of 6 should go in front of water. Now, for oxygen, there are 8 atoms on the left and 18 on the right. To balance the oxygen, 10 more atoms of oxygen must be added to the left side. The best way to do this is to put a coefficient of 6 in front of oxygen, since putting a stoichiometric coefficient in front of the glucose molecule would unbalance the equation in terms of carbon and hydrogen. Therefore, the final balanced equation is:

$$C_6H_{12}O_6 + 6\,O_2 \rightarrow 6\,CO_2 + 6\,H_2O$$

Remember that $C_6H_{12}O_6$ has a coefficient of 1, and this must be added to the total number. So $1 + 6 + 6 + 6 = 19$.

2. $C_{10}H_{14}N_2$; 74.1% C, 8.6% H, 17.3% N

To determine the molecular formula of nicotine, the empirical mass of the compound must be calculated.

$5(C) + 7(H) + 1(N) = $ empirical mass

$5(12 \text{ g/mol}) + 7(1 \text{ g/mol}) + 14 \text{ g/mol} = 81 \text{ g/mol}$

The empirical mass (81 g/mol) is then divided into the molecular mass (162 g/mol) to determine the number by which each subscript in the empirical formula must be multiplied to obtain the molecular formula.

$$\frac{162\text{g/mol}}{81\text{g/mol}} = 2$$

$2(C_5H_7N) = C_{10}H_{14}N_2 = $ molecular formula

To find the percent composition of each element, divide the molar mass of each element by the molecular mass of nicotine:

$$\% \text{ C} = \frac{120}{162} \times 100\% = 74.1\%$$

$$\% \text{ H} = \frac{14}{162} \times 100\% = 8.6\%$$

$$\% \text{ N} = \frac{28}{162} \times 100\% = 17.3\%$$

The same percentages would be obtained if we used the empirical formula for this calculation.

3. **E** According to the balanced equation, one mole of CaC_2 yields one mole of C_2H_2. Therefore, if 0.400 mol of CaC2 were used, 0.400 mol of C_2H_2 would be produced. Now the number of moles must be converted to grams using the following formula:

$$mol = \frac{\text{Weight in g}}{\text{Molecular weight}}$$

The molecular mass of C_2H_2 is
$2(12 \text{ g/mol}) + 2(1 \text{ g/mol}) = 26 \text{ g/mol}$

Substituting into the above equation:

$$0.400 \text{ mol} = \frac{x}{26 \text{g/mol}}$$
$$x = 10.4 \text{ g}$$

4. **A** According to the balanced equation, one mole of salicylic acid will yield one mole of aspirin. Therefore, to solve this question, the number of moles of aspirin in six 5-grain tablets, or 30 grains of aspirin, must be determined using the following relationship.

$$\frac{1 \text{ g}}{15.5 \text{ grains}} = \frac{x}{30 \text{ grains}}$$
$$x \approx 2 \text{ g}$$

Therefore, the mass of the aspirin produced is about 2 grams, which must be converted to moles. The molecular mass of aspirin is:
$9(C) + 8(H) + 4(O) = 9(12 \text{ g/mol}) + 8(1 \text{ g/mol}) + 4(16 \text{ g/mol}) = 180 \text{ g/mol}$
Then, the number of moles in two grams of aspirin is calculated.

$$\frac{2 \text{ g}}{180 \text{g/mol}} = 0.01 \text{ mol}$$

5. **D** The easiest way to solve this problem, short of trying every choice, is to work through the problem with slightly backward logic. Because we know that element X comprises 32% of the compound, CH_3 must comprise 68% (100% – 32%). We must calculate the formula mass of CH_3 (12 + 3 = 15 g). The fact that 15 g = 68% of the total mass can be restated as the equation 15 g = 0.68 × total mass; we can solve this to show that the total molecular mass must be 22 g. The mass of X = total mass – 15 g = 7 g. Choice (D), Li, has an atomic mass of 7 g/mol.

6. **31 g, 25 g, 81%**

According to the balanced equation, two moles of silver react with one mole of sulfur to form one mole of silver sulfide. The theoretical yield is the amount of product that would be collected if all of the limiting reagent reacts. Using a stoichiometric calculation, the theoretical yield of silver sulfide if 27 g of silver is used would be as follows:

$$27 \text{ g Ag} \times \frac{1 \text{ mol Ag}}{108 \text{ g Ag}} \times \frac{1 \text{ mol Ag}_2\text{S}}{2 \text{ mol Ag}} \times \frac{248 \text{ g Ag}_2\text{S}}{1 \text{ mol Ag}_2\text{S}} = 31 \text{ g Ag}_2\text{S}$$

The actual yield is the amount of product that is obtained from the experiment. It is usually less than the theoretical yield since the reagents may not react completely and the product may be difficult to collect. In this experiment, the actual yield is given to be 25 g

GC

of silver sulfide. The percent yield represents the percentage of product actually collected in reference to the theoretical yield. Thus, the percent yield for this experiment would be:

$$\frac{25 \text{ g}}{31 \text{ g}} \times 100\% = 81\%$$

7. **5.81×10^{-23} g/atom Cl; 5.31×10^{-23} g/molecule O_2**

The mass of a single atom is determined by dividing the atomic mass by Avogadro's number. Therefore, the mass of a chlorine atom is

$$\frac{35.5 \text{ g/mol}}{6.022 \times 10^{23} \text{ atoms/mol}} = 5.89 \times 10^{-23} \text{ g/atom}$$

The mass of an oxygen molecule (O_2) is similarly determined by dividing the molecular mass of oxygen by Avogadro's number.

$$\frac{32 \text{ g/mol}}{6.022 \times 10^{23} \text{ molecules/mol}} = 5.31 \times 10^{-23} \text{ g/molecule}$$

8. **5.5 mol**

From the balanced equation, it can be seen that the ratio between $Ag(NH_3)_2^+$ and NH_3 is 1:2. Thus, to form 11 mol of ammonia, the following calculation must be performed.

$$\frac{1 \text{ mol Ag(NH}_3)_2^+}{2 \text{ mol NH}_3} = \frac{x \text{ mol Ag(NH}_3)_2^+}{11 \text{ mol NH}_3}$$

$$x = 5.5 \text{ mol Ag(NH}_3)_2^+$$

9. **A** To answer this question, the law of conservation of mass, which says that the mass of the products must be equal to the mass of the reactants, is used. Therefore, if 5.8 g of $Ag(NH_3)_2^+$ are allowed to dissociate to form 1.4 g of ammonia, 5.8 g − 1.4 g = 4.4 g of silver must be formed. The following calculation is used to determine the number of moles of silver formed.

$$x \text{ mol} = \frac{4.4 \text{ g}}{108 \text{ g/mol}}$$

$$x = 0.041 \text{ mol}$$

10. **76.1% Ag, 19.7% N, 4.2% H**

The percent composition of elements in a compound or formula is determined by dividing the mass of the element by the total formula mass of the compound. Therefore, in the complex ion $Ag(NH_3)_2^+$, which has a formula mass of 142 g/mol, the percent compositions of Ag, N, and H are as follows:

$$\%Ag = \frac{108 \text{ g/mol}}{142 \text{ g/mol}} \times 100\% = 76.1\%$$

$$\%N = \frac{2(14 \text{ g/mol})}{142 \text{ g/mol}} \times 100\% = 19.7\%$$

$$\%H = \frac{6(1 \text{ g/mol})}{142 \text{ g/mol}} \times 100\% = 4.2\%$$

11. **C_4H_9**

To answer this problem, several calculations must be performed. First, the number of moles of carbon and hydrogen present in the hydrocarbon must be determined using the assumption that the number of moles of atoms on the reactant side is equal to the number of moles of atoms on the product side. From this information, the empirical formula can be determined.

First, the moles of carbon and hydrogen are calculated.

$$\frac{58.67 \text{ g CO}_2}{44 \text{ g/mol}} = 1.33 \text{ mol CO}_2$$

Since each mole of CO_2 contains 1 mole of carbon, 1.33 moles of CO_2 contains 1.33 moles of carbon. Therefore, the hydrocarbon contains 1.33 moles of carbon.

$$\frac{27 \text{ g H}_2\text{O}}{18 \text{g/mol H}_2\text{O}} = 1.5 \text{ mol H}_2\text{O}$$

Since one mole of H_2O contains 2 moles of hydrogen atoms, 1.5 moles of H_2O contains 3.0 moles of hydrogen. Therefore, the hydrocarbon contains 3 moles of hydrogen.

Using these calculations, the simplest formula that can be written is $C_{1.33}H_3$. However, molecular formulas are not expressed with decimals or fractions, so these coefficients should be multiplied by 3 to give an empirical formula of C_4H_9.

12. **66 g**

The balanced equation will be:

$$2 \text{ NF}_3 + 3 \text{ H}_2\text{O} \rightarrow 6 \text{ HF} + \text{NO} + \text{NO}_2$$

According to the balanced equation, 2 moles of NF_3 is needed to produce 6 moles of HF. To determine the number of grams of HF that will be formed, the amount of NF_3 used must first be calculated.

$$1,500 \text{ g} \times 0.052 = 78 \text{ g NF}_3 \text{ used}$$

Then a stoichiometric calculation can be set up to see what the theoretical yield of HF would be.

$$78 \text{ g NF}_3 \times \frac{1 \text{ mol NF}_3}{71 \text{ g NF}_3} \times \frac{6 \text{ mol HF}}{2 \text{ mol NF}_3} \times \frac{20 \text{ g HF}}{1 \text{ mol HF}} = 66 \text{ g HF}$$

Thus, 66 g of HF would be produced.

13. The following are the correct balanced equations:

A. $I_2 + 5 \text{ Cl}_2 + 6 \text{ H}_2\text{O} \rightarrow 2 \text{ HIO}_3 + 10 \text{ HCl}$

B. $\text{MnO}_2 + 4 \text{ HCl} \rightarrow 2 \text{ H}_2\text{O} + \text{MnCl}_2 + \text{Cl}_2$

C. $4 \text{ BCl}_3 + \text{P}_4 + 6 \text{ H}_2 \rightarrow 4 \text{ BP} + 12 \text{ HCl}$

D. $4 \text{ C}_3\text{H}_5(\text{NO}_3)_3 \rightarrow 12 \text{ CO}_2 + 10 \text{ H}_2\text{O} + 6 \text{ N}_2 + \text{O}_2$

E. $2 \text{ HCl} + \text{Ba(OH)}_2 \rightarrow \text{BaCl}_2 + 2 \text{ H}_2\text{O}$

CHAPTER TWENTY-EIGHT

Solutions

Solutions are **homogeneous** (uniform in composition) mixtures of substances that combine to form a single phase, generally the liquid phase. Many important chemical reactions, both in the laboratory and in nature, take place in solution.

NATURE OF SOLUTIONS

A solution consists of a solute (e.g., NaCl, NH_3, or $C_{12}H_{22}O_{11}$) dispersed (**dissolved**) in a solvent (e.g., H_2O or benzene). The solvent is the component of the solution whose phase remains the same after mixing. If the two substances are already in the same phase, the solvent is the component present in greater quantity. Solute molecules move about freely in the solvent and can interact with other molecules or ions; consequently, chemical reactions occur easily in solution.

Solvation

The interaction between solute and solvent molecules is known as solvation or **dissolution**; when water is the solvent, it is called **hydration**, and the resulting solution is known as an **aqueous solution**. Solvation is possible when the attractive forces between solute and solvent are stronger than those between the solvent particles. For example, when NaCl dissolves in water, its component ions dissociate from one another and become surrounded by water molecules. Because water is polar, ion-dipole interactions can occur between the Na^+ and Cl^- ions and the water molecules, which are stronger and more favorable than the hydrogen-bonding found between H_2O molecules in pure water. For nonionic solutes, solvation involves van der Waals forces between the solute and solvent molecules. The general rule is that like dissolves like: Ionic and polar solutes are soluble in polar solvents, and nonpolar solutes are soluble in nonpolar solvents.

Solubility

The solubility of a substance is the maximum amount of that substance that can be dissolved in a particular solvent at a particular temperature. When this maximum amount of solute has been added, the solution is saturated; if more solute is added, it will not dissolve. For example, at 18°C, a maximum of 83 g of glucose ($C_6H_{12}O_6$) will dissolve in 100 mL of H_2O. Thus, the solubility of glucose is 83 g/100 mL. If more glucose is added, it will remain in solid form, precipitating to the bottom of the container. A solution in which the proportion of solute to solvent is small is said to be **dilute,** and one in which the proportion is large is said to be **concentrated**.

When a dissolved solute comes out of solution and forms crystals, this process is known as **crystallization.** It is also important to note that some substances can form **supersaturated** solutions, which are solutions that contain more solute than found in a saturated solution. Supersaturated solutions are formed by manipulating temperature or pressure. In a supersaturated solution, the addition of more solute will cause the excess solute in the supersaturated solution to separate, and a saturated solution with a precipitate will subsequently form.

Electrolytes

The electrical conductivity of aqueous solutions is governed by the presence and concentration of ions in solution. Therefore, pure water does not conduct an electrical current well since the concentrations of hydrogen and hydroxide ions are very small. Solutes that make conductive solutions are called electrolytes. A solute is considered a strong electrolyte if it dissociates completely into its constituent ions. Examples of **strong electrolytes** include ionic compounds, such as NaCl and KI, and molecular compounds with highly polar covalent bonds that dissociate into ions when dissolved, such as HCl in water. A **weak electrolyte**, on the other hand, ionizes or hydrolyzes incompletely in aqueous solution, and only some of the solute is present in ionic form. Examples include acetic acid and other weak acids, ammonia and other weak bases, and $HgCl_2$. Many compounds do not ionize at all in aqueous solution, retaining their molecular structure in solution, which usually limits their solubility. These compounds are called **nonelectrolytes** and include many nonpolar gases and organic compounds, such as oxygen and sugar.

CONCENTRATION

Units of Concentration

Concentration denotes the amount of solute dissolved in a solvent. The concentration of a solution is most commonly expressed as **percent composition by mass, mole fraction (X), molarity (M), molality (m),** or **normality (N).**

Percent composition by mass

The percent composition by mass (%) of a solute is the mass of the solute divided by the mass of the solution (solute plus solvent) and multiplied by 100.

Example: What is the percent composition by mass of NaCl of a saltwater solution if 100 g of the solution contains 20 g of NaCl?

Solution: $\dfrac{20\text{ g NaCl}}{100\text{ g}} \times 100\% = 20\%$ NaCl solution

Mole fraction

The mole fraction (X) of a compound is equal to the number of moles of the compound divided by the total number of moles of all species within the system. The sum of all the mole fractions in a system will always equal 1.

The mole fraction can be calculated with the following equation:

$$X_B = \frac{\text{moles of B}}{\text{sum of moles of all components}}$$

where X_B is the mole fraction of component B.

Example: If 92 g of glycerol is mixed with 90 g of water, what will be the mole fractions of the two components (the molecular mass of H_2O = 18 g/mol and the molecular mass of $C_3H_8O_3$ = 92 g/mol)?

Solution:

$$90 \text{ g water} = 90 \text{ g} \times \frac{1 \text{ mol}}{18 \text{ g}} = 5 \text{ mol}$$

$$92 \text{ g glycerol} = 92 \text{ g} \times \frac{1 \text{ mol}}{92 \text{ g}} = 1 \text{ mol}$$

$$\text{Total mol} = 5 + 1 = 6 \text{ mol}$$

$$X_{\text{water}} = \frac{5 \text{ mol}}{6 \text{ mol}} = 0.833$$

$$X_{\text{glycerol}} = \frac{1 \text{ mol}}{6 \text{ mol}} = 0.167$$

As a check, note that the sum of X_{water} and X_{glycerol} is 1:

$$X_{\text{water}} + X_{\text{glycerol}} = 0.833 + 0.167 = 1.000$$

Molarity

The molarity (M) of a solution is the number of moles of solute per liter of solution. Solution concentrations are usually expressed in terms of molarity. Molarity depends on the total volume of the solution, not on the volume of solvent used to prepare the solution.

Example: If enough water is added to 11 g of $CaCl_2$ to make 100 mL of solution, what is the molarity of the solution (the molecular mass of $CaCl_2$ is 110 g/mol)?

Solution:

$$\frac{11 \text{ g CaCl}_2}{110 \text{ g/mol CaCl}_2} = 0.10 \text{ mol CaCl}_2$$

$$100 \text{ mL} \times \frac{1 \text{ L}}{1{,}000 \text{ mL}} = 0.10 \text{ L}$$

$$\text{Molarity} = \frac{\text{mol solute}}{\text{L solution}} = \frac{0.10 \text{ mol CaCl}_2}{0.10 \text{ L solution}} = 1.0 \text{ M CaCl}_2$$

Molality

The molality (m) of a solution is the number of moles of solute per kilogram of solvent. For dilute aqueous solutions at 25°C, the molality is approximately equal to the molarity because the density of water at this temperature is 1 kilogram per liter, but note that this is an approximation and true only for dilute aqueous solutions.

Example: If 10 g of NaOH are dissolved in 500 g of water, what is the molality of the solution (the molecular mass of NaOH is 40 g/mol)?

Solution:

$$\frac{10\text{ g NaOH}}{40\text{ g/mol NaOH}} = 0.25\text{ mol NaOH}$$

$$500\text{ g H}_2\text{O} \times \frac{1\text{ kg}}{1{,}000\text{ g}} = 0.50\text{ kg H}_2\text{O}$$

$$\text{Molality} = \frac{\text{mol solute}}{\text{kg solvent}} = \frac{0.25\text{ mol NaOH}}{0.50\text{ kg H}_2\text{O}} = 0.50\text{ m NaOH}$$

Normality

The normality (N) of a solution is equal to the number of gram equivalent weights of solute per liter of solution. A gram equivalent weight, or **equivalent**, is a measure of the reactive capacity of a molecule (see Chapter 27, Stoichiometry).

To calculate the normality of a solution, we must know for what purpose the solution is being used because it is the concentration of the reactive species with which we are concerned. Normality is unique among concentration units in that it is reaction dependent. For example, each mole of sulfuric acid contributes two equivalents for acid-base reactions (because each mole of sulfuric acid provides two moles of H^+ ions) but contributes only one equivalent for a sulfate precipitation reaction (because each mole of sulfuric acid provides only one mole of sulfate ions). You can calculate normality by multiplying the molarity (M) of a solution by the number of equivalents per mol:

$$N = \text{Molarity} \times \frac{\text{equivalents}}{\text{mol}} = \frac{\text{mol}}{\text{L}} \times \frac{\text{equivalents}}{\text{mol}} = \frac{\text{equivalents}}{\text{L}}$$

Therefore, a 3 M solution of H_2SO_4 would be 6 N in acid-base reactions (3 M × 2 equivalents/mol = 6 N) and 3 N in sulfate precipitation reactions (3 M × 1 equivalents/mol = 3 N).

Dilution

A solution is **diluted** when solvent is added to a solution of higher concentration to produce a solution of lower concentration. The concentration of a solution after dilution can be conveniently determined using the equation below:

$$M_iV_i = M_fV_f$$

where M is molarity, V is volume, and the subscripts i and f refer to initial and final values, respectively.

Example: How many mL of a 5.5 M NaOH solution must be used to prepare 300 mL of a 1.2 M NaOH solution?

Solution:

$$5.5 \text{ M} \times V_i = 1.2 \text{ M} \times 300 \text{ mL}$$
$$V_i = \frac{1.2 \text{ M} \times 300 \text{ mL}}{5.5 \text{ M}}$$
$$V_i = 65 \text{ mL}$$

Factors Affecting Solubility

The solubility of a substance varies depending on the temperature of the solution, the solvent, and, in the case of a gas-phase solute, the pressure. Solubility is also affected by the addition of other substances to the solution.

Aqueous Solutions

The most common solutions you will encounter on Test Day are aqueous solutions (in which the solvent is water). The aqueous state is denoted by the symbol (*aq*). When discussing the chemistry of aqueous solutions and answering questions on the exam, it is useful to know how soluble various salts are in water; this information is given by the solubility rules below:

Soluble salts (with exceptions):

- All salts of alkali metal ions (e.g., Li^+, Na^+, K^+, Rb^+, Cs^+, Fr^+) are water soluble.
- All salts of the ammonium ion (NH_4^+) are water soluble.
- All salts with chloride (Cl^-), bromide (Br^-), and iodide (I^-) ions are water soluble, with the exception of salts containing Ag^+, Pb^{2+}, and Hg_2^{2+}.
- All salts of the sulfate ion (SO_4^{2-}) are water soluble, with the exception of those containing Ca^{2+}, Sr^{2+}, Ba^{2+}, and Pb^{2+}.

Insoluble salts (with exceptions):

- All metal oxides (a metal combined with oxygen) are insoluble, with the exception of alkali metal oxides and CaO, SrO, and BaO, all of which hydrolyze to form solutions of the corresponding metal hydroxides.
- All hydroxides (containing OH^-) are insoluble, with the exception of the alkali metal hydroxides and $Ca(OH)_2$, $Sr(OH)_2$, and $Ba(OH)_2$.
- All salts with carbonates (CO_3^{2-}), phosphates (PO_4^{3-}), sulfides (S^{2-}), and sulfites (SO_3^{2-}) are insoluble, with the exception of those that contain alkali metals or ammonium.

REVIEW PROBLEMS

1. Which of the following choices correctly describes the solubility behavior of potassium chloride (KCl)?

    A. Solubility in CCl_4 > Solubility in CH_3CH_2OH > Solubility in H_2O
    B. Solubility in H_2O > Solubility in CH_3CH_2OH > Solubility in CCl_4
    C. Solubility in CH_3CH_2OH > Solubility in CCl_4 > Solubility in H_2O
    D. Solubility in H_2O > Solubility in CCl_4 > Solubility in CH_3CH_2OH
    E. Solubility in CH_3CH_2OH > Solubility in H_2O > Solubility in CCl_4

2. A simple cake icing can be made by dissolving a large quantity of sugar (sucrose) in boiling water, cooling the solution, and applying it to the cake before it reaches room temperature. The icing appears to harden as it cools in part because the

    A. sugar molecules freeze from liquid to solid.
    B. common ion effect limits the dissolution of sucrose.
    C. K_{sp} of sucrose increases as the solution cools.
    D. sugar concentration increases as water boils off, and the solubility of sugar in water decreases as the solution cools.
    E. sucrose molecules dissociate to form fructose and glucose, which are insoluble in water.

3. How much NaOH must be added to 200 mL of water to make a 1.0 M NaOH solution?

    A. 8.0 g
    B. 16 g
    C. 40 g
    D. 56 g
    E. 80 g

4. To what volume must 10.0 mL of 5.00 M of HCl be diluted to make a 0.500 M HCl solution?

    A. 1.00 mL
    B. 50.0 mL
    C. 100 mL
    D. 250 mL
    E. 500 mL

5. What is the normality of a 2.0 M solution of phosphoric acid, H_3PO_4, for an acid-base titration?

    A. 0.67
    B. 2.0
    C. 3.0
    D. 4.0
    E. 6.0

6. Given that the molecular mass of ethyl alcohol, CH_3CH_2OH, is 46 g/mol and that of water is 18 g/mol, how many grams of ethyl alcohol must be mixed with 100 mL of water for the mole fraction (X) of ethyl alcohol to be 0.2?

7. Name the following ionic compounds:
    A. $NaClO_4$
    B. $NaClO$
    C. $NaNO_3$
    D. KNO_2
    E. Li_2SO_4
    F. $MgSO_3$

8. Which of the following will be the most electrically conductive?
    A. Sugar dissolved in water
    B. Saltwater
    C. Salt dissolved in an organic solvent
    D. An oil and water mixture
    E. Pure water

GC

GC

SOLUTIONS TO REVIEW PROBLEMS

1. **B** KCl is an ionic salt and, therefore, is soluble in polar solvents and insoluble in nonpolar solvents. Water, H_2O, is a highly polar liquid. The carbon atom in carbon tetrachloride, CCl_4, is bonded to four atoms, so the molecule is tetrahedral. This geometry means that the individual dipole moments of the bonds cancel and CCl_4 is nonpolar. Ethanol (CH_3CH_2OH) has two carbon atoms in tetrahedral arrangements; most of the dipole moments associated with the bonds are the same, but the C−C and C−OH bonds are different, so ethanol is somewhat polar. Thus, the polarities of the three solvents decrease in the following sequence: $H_2O > CH_3CH_2OH > CCl_4$, with the solubility of KCl decreasing along that sequence as well.

2. **D** The sugar-water solution hardens because it becomes supersaturated as it cools since the solubility (K_{sp}) of sucrose in water decreases significantly with temperature. Evaporation of water during boiling also contributes to the solution's supersaturated state by reducing the amount of solvent present, which is the opposite of choice (C). Choice (A) is incorrect: in this example the sugar is dissolved, not melted (sucrose melts at 185°C, well above the boiling point of even sucrose-saturated water). Since there are no other sources of sucrose present, choice (B) is not relevant. Choice (E) is also incorrect; although sucrose is made from fructose and glucose, all are soluble in water.

3. **A** To answer this question, first find the formula mass of NaOH from the periodic table. Rounding to whole numbers, the atomic mass of Na is 23 g/mol, the atomic mass of O is 16 g/mol, and the atomic mass of H is 1 g/mol, so the formula mass of NaOH is 40 g/mol. Thus, 40 g of NaOH is 1 mol, and 40 g of NaOH dissolved in 1 L of water is a 1 M solution of NaOH. To determine how much of the solute is needed to make 200 mL of such a solution, set up the following ratio:

$$\frac{x}{200 \text{ mL}} = \frac{40 \text{ g}}{1 \text{ L}} \times \frac{1 \text{ L}}{1,000 \text{ mL}}$$

$$\frac{x}{200 \text{ mL}} = \frac{40 \text{ g}}{1,000 \text{ mL}}$$

$$x = \frac{(40 \text{ g})(200 \text{ mL})}{1,000 \text{ mL}} = 8 \text{ g}$$

4. **C** When a solution is diluted, more solvent is added, yet the number of moles of solute remains the same. To solve a dilution problem, the following equation is used:

$$M_iV_i = M_fV_f$$

where i represents the initial conditions and f represents the final conditions. Therefore, the calculation to solve for the final volume is:

$$(5.0 \text{ M})(10 \text{ mL}) = (0.50 \text{ M})(V_f)$$

$$V_f = 100 \text{ mL}$$

and the correct answer is (C).

5. **E** Each mole of H_3PO_4 contains three moles of hydrogen and (since this is an acid) three mole equivalents. A 2 M solution of this acid is thus:

$$2\,M \times \frac{3\,N}{1\,M} = 6\,N$$

6. **64.4 g**

The number of moles of water is found by estimating the density of water to be 1 g/mL.

$$\text{mol } H_2O = \frac{(100 \text{ mL } H_2O)(1 \text{ g/mL})}{18 \text{ g/mol}} = 5.6 \text{ mol}$$

If the mole fraction of ethyl alcohol is to be 0.2, then the mole fraction of water must be 0.8. If n equals the total number of moles:

$$5.6 \text{ mol} = 0.8n$$
$$n = 7 \text{ mol}$$

Then:

mol ethyl alcohol $= (0.2)(7 \text{ mol}) = 1.4 \text{ mol}$

and:

grams ethyl alcohol $= (1.4 \text{ mol ethyl alcohol})(46 \text{ g/mol}) = 64.4 \text{ g ethyl alcohol.}$

7. (Oxidation numbers—discussed in detail in Chapter 29, Reaction Types—have been placed in parentheses for additional practice.)

    A Sodium perchlorate (Cl: +7)
    B Sodium hypochlorite (C: +11)
    C Sodium nitrate (N: +5)
    D Potassium nitrite (N: +3)
    E Lithium sulfate (S: +6)
    F Magnesium sulfite (S: +4)

8. **B** Only ionic compounds (electrolytes) dissolved in polar solvents will conduct electricity. Sugar is a covalent solid and therefore is not an electrolyte even when dissolved in water. Answers (C) and (D) are incorrect because salt will not dissolve appreciably in an organic solvent and oil and water are immiscible. Answer (E) is incorrect because, while pure water is a polar solvent, no electrolyte is present to conduct electricity. NaCl is an ionic compound, so (B) is correct.

CHAPTER TWENTY-NINE

Reaction Types

TYPES OF CHEMICAL REACTIONS

Elements and compounds can react to form other species in many ways, and memorizing every reaction would be impossible as well as unnecessary. However, nearly every inorganic reaction can be classified into at least one of five general categories.

Combination Reactions

Combination reactions are reactions in which two or more **reactants** form one **product**. This can occur when elements react to form compounds, such as during the formation of sulfur dioxide by burning sulfur:

$$S\ (s) + O_2\ (g) \rightarrow SO_2\ (g)$$

Combination reactions can also occur when two compounds react to form a new compound. For example, in the equation below, gaseous ammonia is reacted with gaseous hydrogen chloride and forms ammonium chloride:

$$NH_3\ (g) + HCl\ (g) \rightarrow NH_4Cl\ (s)$$

Decomposition Reactions

A decomposition reaction is defined as one in which a compound breaks down into two or more substances, usually as a result of heating or electrolysis. For example, when compounds that contain oxygen are heated, most will decompose to form molecular oxygen. **Electrolysis** is a specific process that causes the decomposition of a compound by passing an electric current through the reactant. Another example of a decomposition reaction is the breakdown of mercury (II) oxide (the sign Δ represents the addition of heat):

$$2\ HgO\ (s) \xrightarrow{\ \Delta\ } 2\ Hg\ (l) + O_2\ (g)$$

Single-Displacement Reactions

Single-displacement reactions occur when an atom (or ion) of one compound is replaced by an atom of another element. For example, zinc metal will displace copper ions in a copper sulfate solution to form zinc sulfate:

$$Zn\ (s) + CuSO_4\ (aq) \rightarrow Cu\ (s) + ZnSO_4\ (aq)$$

Single-displacement reactions are often further classified as **redox** reactions, discussed below.

Net ionic equations

Because many reactions, including some displacements, involve ions in solution, their net equations can also be written in ionic form. In the example where zinc is reacted with copper sulfate, the **ionic equation** is:

$$Zn\ (s) + Cu^{2+}\ (aq) + SO_4^{2-}\ (aq) \rightarrow Cu\ (s) + Zn^{2+}\ (aq) + SO_4^{2-}\ (aq)$$

When displacement reactions occur, there are usually **spectator ions** that do not take part in the overall reaction but simply remain in solution throughout. The spectator ion in the equation above is sulfate, which does not undergo any transformation during the reaction. A **net ionic reaction** can be written showing only the species that actually participate in the reaction:

$$Zn\ (s) + Cu^{2+}\ (aq) \rightarrow Cu\ (s) + Zn^{2+}\ (aq)$$

Net ionic equations are important for demonstrating the actual reaction that occurs during a displacement reaction.

Double-Displacement Reactions

In double-displacement reactions, also called **metathesis reactions**, elements from two different compounds displace each other to form two new compounds. This type of reaction occurs when one of the products is removed from the solution as a precipitate or gas, or when two of the original species combine to form a weak electrolyte that remains undissociated in solution. For example, when solutions of calcium chloride and silver nitrate are combined, insoluble silver chloride forms in a solution of calcium nitrate:

$$CaCl_2\ (aq) + 2\ AgNO_3\ (aq) \rightarrow Ca(NO_3)_2\ (aq) + 2\ AgCl\ (s)$$

Neutralization reactions

Neutralization reactions are a specific type of double displacement that occurs when an acid reacts with a base to produce a solution of a salt and water. For example, hydrochloric acid and sodium hydroxide will react to form sodium chloride and water:

$$HCl\ (aq) + NaOH\ (aq) \rightarrow NaCl\ (aq) + H_2O\ (l)$$

This type of reaction will be discussed further in Chapter 36, Acids and Bases.

Oxidation-Reduction Reactions

A reaction that involves the transfer of electrons from one species to another is an oxidation-reduction (redox) reaction. This type of reaction can be divided into two half-reactions, **oxidation** (loss of electrons) and **reduction** (gain of electrons). The law of conservation of charge states that an electrical charge can be neither created nor destroyed. Thus, an isolated loss or gain of electrons cannot occur; oxidation and reduction must occur simultaneously, resulting in an electron transfer called a **redox reaction**. An **oxidizing agent** causes another atom in a redox reaction to undergo oxidation and is itself reduced. A **reducing agent** causes the other atom to be reduced and is itself oxidized.

Assigning oxidation numbers

It is important, of course, to know which atom is oxidized and which is reduced. **Oxidation numbers** are assigned to atoms to keep track of the redistribution of electrons during a chemical reaction. From the oxidation numbers of the reactants and products, it is possible to determine how many electrons are gained or lost by each atom. The oxidation number is the number of charges an atom would have in a molecule if electrons were completely transferred in the direction indicated by the difference in electronegativity. Along the same lines, an element is said to be oxidized (loses electrons) if its oxidation number increases in a given reaction, and an element is said to be reduced (gains electrons) if the oxidation number of the element decreases in a given reaction. The oxidation number of an atom in a compound is assigned according to the following rules:

- The oxidation number of a free element (an element in its elemental state) is zero, irrespective of how complex the molecule is.

- The oxidation number for a monatomic ion is equal to the charge of the ion. For example, the oxidation numbers for Na^+, Cu^{2+}, Fe^{3+}, Cl^-, and N^{3-} are $+1$, $+2$, $+3$, -1, and -3, respectively.

- The oxidation number of each Group IA element in a compound is $+1$. The oxidation number of each Group IIA element in a compound is $+2$.

- The oxidation number of each Group VIIA element in a compound is -1, except when combined with an element of higher electronegativity. For example, in HCl, the oxidation number of Cl is -1; in HOCl, however, the oxidation number of Cl is $+1$ because oxygen is more electronegative and has an oxidation state of -2 (oxygen is discussed further below).

- The oxidation number of hydrogen is generally $+1$. However, the oxidation number can be -1 when H is placed with less electronegative elements (Groups IA and IIA). Examples of hydrogen's oxidation state being -1 occur with NaH and CaH_2. Nevertheless, the most common oxidation number of hydrogen is $+1$.

- In most compounds, the oxidation number of oxygen is -2. This is not the case, however, in molecules such as OF_2. Here, because F is more electronegative and has an oxidation state of -1, the oxidation number of oxygen is $+2$. Also, in peroxides such as BaO_2, the oxidation number of O is -1 instead of -2 because of the structure of the peroxide ion, $[O-O]^{2-}$ (for confirmation, note that Ba, a Group IIA element, cannot be a $+4$ cation).

- The sum of the oxidation numbers of all the atoms present in a neutral compound is zero. The sum of the oxidation numbers of the atoms present in a polyatomic ion is equal to the charge of the ion. Thus, for SO_4^{2-}, the sum of the oxidation numbers must be -2.

- Fluorine has an oxidation number of -1 in all compounds because it has the highest electronegativity of all the elements.

- Metallic elements have only positive oxidation numbers; however, nonmetallic elements may have a positive or negative oxidation number.

Example: Assign oxidation numbers to the atoms in the following reaction to determine the oxidized and reduced species and the oxidizing and reducing agents:

$$SnCl_2 + PbCl_4 \rightarrow SnCl_4 + PbCl_2$$

Solution: All these species are neutral, so the oxidation numbers of each compound must add up to zero. In $SnCl_2$, since there are two chlorines present and chlorine has an oxidation number of -1, Sn must have an oxidation number of $+2$. Similarly, the oxidation number of Sn in $SnCl_4$ is $+4$; the oxidation number of Pb is $+4$ in $PbCl_4$ and $+2$ in $PbCl_2$. Notice that the oxidation number of Sn increases from $+2$ to $+4$; it loses electrons and thus is oxidized, making it the reducing agent. Since the oxidation number of Pb has decreased from $+4$ to $+2$, it has gained electrons and been reduced. Pb is the oxidizing agent. The sum of the charges on both sides of the reaction is equal to zero, so charge has been conserved.

Balancing redox reactions

Balancing any reaction requires not only stoichiometric balance but also charge balance. Because redox reactions involve the transfer of electrons (and therefore of charge) between different elements, balancing redox reactions introduces an additional level of complexity. However, with a straightforward, stepwise method, balancing chemical reactions on the test becomes more manageable.

By assigning oxidation numbers to the reactants and products, one can determine how many moles of each species are required for conservation of charge and mass, which is necessary to balance the equation. To balance a redox reaction, both the net charge and the number of atoms must be equal on both sides of the equation. The most common method for balancing redox equations is the **half-reaction method**, also known as the **ion-electron method**, in which the equation is separated into two half-reactions—the oxidation part and the reduction part. Each half-reaction is balanced separately, and they are then added to give a balanced overall reaction:

Example: Balance the redox reaction between MnO_4 and I in an acidic solution:

$$MnO_4^- + I^- \rightarrow I_2 + Mn^{2+}$$

Solution: Note how the oxidation numbers for I and Mn change (I changes from an oxidation state of -1 to 0, and Mn changes from $+7$ to $+2$) and that the reaction is not balanced. So, use the following five-step method to balance redox reactions:

Step 1: *Separate the two half-reactions.*

$$I^- \rightarrow I_2$$
$$MnO_4^- \rightarrow Mn^{2+}$$

Step 2: *Balance the atoms of each half-reaction.* First, balance all atoms except H and O. Next, add H_2O to balance the O atoms and then add H^+ to balance the H atoms.

To balance the iodine atoms, place a coefficient of two before the I^- ion:

$$2\,I^- \rightarrow I_2$$

For the permanganate half-reaction, Mn is already balanced. Balance the oxygen atoms by adding 4 H_2O to the right side:

$$MnO_4^- \rightarrow Mn^{2+} + 4\,H_2O$$

Finally, add H^+ to the left side to balance the 4 H_2Os. These two half-reactions are now balanced:

$$MnO_4^- + 8\,H^+ \rightarrow Mn^{2+} + 4\,H_2O$$

Step 3: *Balance the electrons of each half-reaction.* Each half-reaction must have the same net charge on the left and right sides, and the only species that can be used to balance charges are electrons, each with a -1 charge. Additionally, the reduction half-reaction must consume the same number of electrons as supplied by the oxidation half.

For the oxidation reaction, the left side has a charge of -2, and the right side has a charge of 0. Add two electrons to the right side of the reaction to balance both sides to be -2:

$$2\,I^- \rightarrow I_2 + 2\,e^-$$

For the reduction reaction, there is a charge of $+7$ on the left and $+2$ on the right. By adding five electrons to the left side, the charges on both sides become $+2$, balancing the half-reaction:

$$MnO_4^- + 8\,H^+ + 5\,e^- \rightarrow Mn^{2+} + 4\,H_2O$$

Next, both half-reactions must have the same number of electrons so that, when the half-reactions are combined, the electrons cancel. Therefore, multiply the oxidation half by five and the reduction half by two.

$$5(2\,I^- \rightarrow I_2 + 2\,e^-)$$
$$2(MnO_4^- + 8\,H^+ + 5\,e^- \rightarrow Mn^{2+} + 4\,H_2O)$$

Step 4: *Combine the half-reactions.*

$$10\,I^- \rightarrow 5\,I_2 + 10\,e^-$$
$$2\,MnO_4^- + 10\,e^- + 16\,H^+ \rightarrow 2\,Mn^{2+} + 8\,H_2O$$

The sum of the two equations is:

$$10\,I^- + 10\,e^- + 16\,H^+ + 2\,MnO_4^- \rightarrow 5\,I_2 + 10\,e^- + 2\,Mn^{2+} + 8\,H_2O$$

To find the final equation, cancel out the electrons and anything that appears on both sides of the equation:

$$10\,I^- + 16\,H^+ + 2\,MnO_4^- \rightarrow 5\,I_2 + 2\,Mn^{2+} + 8\,H_2O$$

Step 5: *Confirm that mass and charge are balanced.* Here, there is a $+4$ net charge on each side of the reaction equation, and the atoms are stoichiometrically balanced.

For redox reactions in a basic (instead of acidic) solution, an additional step is required because H^+ will not be readily available and should not appear as a reactant. Use the same initial steps 1–4, but then add enough hydroxide (OH^-) to both sides to completely combine with the free H^+, forming water. Then, remove any species that appears on both sides and complete step 5 as usual to confirm everything is still balanced.

For example, in order to balance the same redox reaction of MnO_4 and I in a basic solution (instead of acidic), start by completing the same steps 1–3. Recall that during step 4, you combined the half-reactions:

Step 4: *Combine the half-reactions in basic solution.*

$$10\,I^- + 10\,e^- + 16\,H^+ + 2\,MnO_4^- \rightarrow 5\,I_2 + 10\,e^- + 2\,Mn^{2+} + 8\,H_2O$$

Then, add 16 OH$^-$ to both sides to neutralize the H$^+$:

$$10\,I^- + 10\,e^- + 16\,H^+ + 16\,OH^- + 2\,MnO_4^- \rightarrow 5\,I_2 + 10\,e^- + 2\,Mn^{2+} + 8\,H_2O + 16\,OH^-$$

Combine the H$^+$ and OH$^-$ into water:

$$10\,I^- + 10\,e^- + 16\,H_2O + 2\,MnO_4^- \rightarrow 5\,I_2 + 10\,e^- + 2\,Mn^{2+} + 8\,H_2O + 16\,OH^-$$

Cancel out any species (here, e$^-$ and H$_2$O) that appear on both sides to find the balanced redox reaction in a basic solution:

$$10\,I^- + 8\,H_2O + 2\,MnO_4^- \rightarrow 5\,I_2 + 2\,Mn^{2+} + 16\,OH^-$$

Step 5: Finally, confirm that mass and charge are balanced. Here, there is a -12 net charge on each side of the reaction equation, and the atoms are stoichiometrically balanced.

Redox reaction examples

Redox reactions can occur as variations of the major types of reactions above: combination, decomposition, and displacement.

1. **Combination reactions**: These types of reactions occur with two or more substances.

   Example: Equation $N_2\,(g) + 3\,H_2\,(g) \rightarrow 2\,NH_3\,(g)$
                Oxidation #s $\quad 0 \qquad\qquad 0 \qquad\qquad -3\ +1$

2. **Decomposition reactions**: These types of reactions lead to the production of two or more substances.

   Example: Equation $2\,H_2O\,(l) \rightarrow H_2\,(g) + O_2\,(g)$
                Oxidation #s $\quad +1\ -2 \qquad\ 0 \qquad\quad 0$

3. **Displacement reactions**: In this type of reaction, an atom or molecule is displaced from a given compound by a different atom or molecule.

   Example: Equation $2\,Na\,(s) + 2\,H_2O\,(l) \rightarrow 2\,NaOH + H_2\,(g)$
                Oxidation #s $\quad\ 0 \qquad\ +1\ -2 \qquad +1\ -2\ +1\ \ 0$

REVIEW PROBLEMS

1. The reaction below is best classified as which type of reaction?
$$CH_3CO_2Na + HClO_4 \rightarrow CH_3CO_2H + NaClO_4$$
   A. Double-displacement reaction
   B. Combination reaction
   C. Decomposition reaction
   D. Single-displacement and decomposition reaction
   E. Single-displacement reaction

2. Which of the following represents the net ionic equation for the reaction given?
$$AgNO_3\ (aq) + Cu\ (s) \rightarrow CuNO_3\ (aq) + Ag\ (s)$$
   A. $AgNO_3\ (aq) + Cu\ (s) \rightarrow CuNO_3\ (aq) + Ag\ (s)$
   B. $Ag^+\ (aq) + Cu\ (s) \rightarrow Cu^+\ (aq) + Ag\ (s)$
   C. $AgNO_3\ (aq) + Cu\ (s) \rightarrow Cu^+\ (aq) + NO_3^-\ (aq) + Ag\ (s)$
   D. $Ag^+\ (aq) + NO_3^-\ (aq) + Cu\ (s) \rightarrow CuNO_3\ (aq) + Ag\ (s)$
   E. $Ag\ (aq) + NO_3\ (aq) + Cu\ (s) \rightarrow Cu\ (aq) + NO_3\ (aq) + Ag\ (s)$

3. Assign oxidation numbers to each atom of the following reaction equation:
$$2\ Fe\ (s) + O_2\ (g) + 2\ H_2O\ (l) \rightarrow 2\ Fe(OH)_2\ (s)$$

4. Using the ion-electron method, balance the following equation of a reaction taking place in an acidic solution:
$$ClO_3^- + AsO_2^- \rightarrow AsO_4^{3-} + Cl^-$$

SOLUTIONS TO REVIEW PROBLEMS

1. **A** Because the only change is that the Na from CH_3CO_2Na exchanges with the H from $HClO_4$, this is a double-displacement reaction. Alternately, this reaction could be classified as a neutralization, since it is a reaction between an acid and a base.

2. **B** In displacement reactions, there are often ionic species that do not play a role in the overall reaction. Instead, they remain in solution throughout the entire reaction. Thus, displacement reactions can be written in terms of net ionic equations, which express the reactions of the participating species. In the reaction between aqueous silver nitrate and copper metal to form aqueous copper (I) nitrate and metallic silver, the nitrate ion does not participate in the reaction; thus, it is a spectator ion. Therefore, the only species that are involved in the reaction are copper metal and the Ag^+ ion, which react to form the Cu^+ ion and silver metal.

3. **Fe (s): Fe 0;**

    O_2 (g): O 0;

    H_2O (l): H +1, O −2;

    Fe(OH)$_2$ (s): Fe +2, O −2, H +1

    To assign oxidation numbers, use the rules given in the text. Fe (s) and O_2 (g) have oxidation numbers of zero because they are free elements. Hydrogen in H_2O (l) has an oxidation number of +1 because oxygen is more electronegative than hydrogen; likewise, oxygen in H_2O (l) has an oxidation number of −2. Oxygen and hydrogen in Fe(OH)$_2$ (s) have the same oxidation numbers as in H_2O (l). Each OH group contributes a charge of −1 to Fe(OH)$_2$, and since there are 2 OH groups, their overall contribution to the compound is −2. Since Fe(OH)$_2$ (s) is a neutral compound and thus has no overall charge, the sum of all the oxidation numbers of the atoms in this compound is zero. Consequently, the Fe in Fe(OH)$_2$ (s) must possess a charge of +2 to make the overall charge on the compound zero.

4. The balanced equation is:

$$ClO_3^- + 3\,H_2O + 3\,AsO_2^- \rightarrow 3\,AsO_4^{3-} + Cl^- + 6\,H^+$$

CHAPTER THIRTY

Electrochemistry

Electrochemistry is the study of the relationships between chemical reactions and electrical energy. **Electrochemical reactions** include spontaneous reactions that produce electrical energy and nonspontaneous reactions that use electrical energy to produce a chemical change. Both types of reactions always involve a transfer of electrons through the processes of oxidation and reduction, and like other chemical reactions they result in conservation of charge and mass.

ELECTROCHEMICAL CELLS

Electrochemical cells are contained systems in which a redox reaction occurs, either to provide electrical energy or to use electrical energy for a useful purpose. There are two types of electrochemical cells: galvanic cells (also known as voltaic cells) and electrolytic cells. Spontaneous reactions occur in galvanic cells, and nonspontaneous reactions in electrolytic cells. Both types contain electrical conductors known as **electrodes,** where oxidation and reduction occur. For all electrochemical cells, the electrode where oxidation occurs is called the **anode**, and the electrode where reduction occurs is called the **cathode.** A helpful mnemonic for this is "An Ox" and a "Red Cat" (*Ox*idation occurs at the *An*ode, while *Red*uction occurs at the *Cat*hode).

Galvanic Cells

A redox reaction occurring in a **galvanic cell** has a negative ΔG and is therefore a **spontaneous reaction.** Galvanic cell reactions supply energy and are used to do work. This energy is harnessed by placing the oxidation and reduction half-reactions in separate containers called half-cells. The half-cells are then connected by an apparatus that allows the flow of electrons between the half-cells, creating a circuit.

A common example of a galvanic cell is the Daniell cell shown in Figure 30.1.

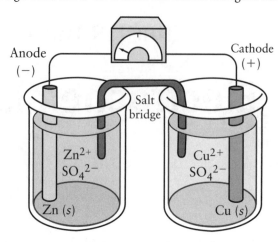

Figure 30.1

In the Daniell cell, a zinc bar is placed in an aqueous $ZnSO_4$ solution, and a copper bar is placed in an aqueous $CuSO_4$ solution. The anode of this cell is the zinc bar, where Zn (*s*) is oxidized to Zn^{2+} (*aq*). The cathode is the copper bar and is the site of the reduction of Cu^{2+} (*aq*) to Cu (*s*). The half-cell reactions are written as follows:

$$Zn\ (s) \rightarrow Zn^{2+}\ (aq) + 2\ e^-\ (anode)$$

$$Cu^{2+}\ (aq) + 2\ e \rightarrow Cu\ (s)\ (cathode)$$

If the two half-cells were not separated, the Cu^{2+} ions would react directly with the zinc bar, and no useful electrical work would be obtained. However, to complete the circuit, the two solutions must be connected somehow; without connection, the electrons from the zinc oxidation half-reaction would not be able to get to the copper ions, and no reaction would occur. Thus, a wire or other conductor is necessary.

Because of the flow of electrons away from the anode and toward the cathode, negative charge can begin to build up in the solution surrounding the cathode, and positive charge can begin to build up in the solution surrounding the anode. If enough charge were to build up, the reaction would become unfavorable and cease. However, this charge gradient can be dissipated by the presence of an additional component that permits the exchange of cations and anions between the two cells, such as a salt bridge or semipermeable membrane. A salt bridge contains an inert electrolyte, usually KCl or NH_4NO_3, whose ions will not react directly with the electrodes or the ions in solution.

In the previous example with a KCl salt bridge, the inert anions (Cl^-) flow from the salt bridge toward the anode to balance the new Zn^{2+} ions being created, and the inert cations (K^+) flow toward the cathode to balance the Cu^{2+} being deposited onto the cathode. This flow depletes the salt bridge and, along with the finite quantity of Cu^{2+} in the solution, accounts for the relatively short lifetime of the cell. Note that the *cat*ions from the salt bridge flow to the *cat*hode, and the *an*ions flow to the *an*ode; this is where the electrodes get their names from!

A cell diagram is a shorthand notation representing the reactions in an electrochemical cell. A cell diagram for the Daniell cell is as follows:

$$\text{Zn } (s) \mid \text{Zn}^{2+}(x \text{ M SO}_4{}^{2-}) \ (aq) \mid\mid \text{Cu}^{2+}(y \text{ M SO}_4{}^{2-}) \ (aq) \mid \text{Cu } (s)$$

The following rules are used in constructing a cell diagram:

1. The reactants and products are always listed from left to right in the form:

anode | anode solution || cathode solution | cathode

2. A single vertical line indicates a phase boundary.

3. A double vertical line indicates the presence of a salt bridge or some other type of barrier.

Electrolytic Cells

A redox reaction occurring in an **electrolytic cell** has a positive ΔG and is therefore **nonspontaneous**. In **electrolysis**, electrical energy is required to induce reaction. Since the reaction is nonspontaneous, the oxidation and reduction half-reactions can be placed in the same container, and no salt bridge is required.

An example of an electrolytic cell, in which molten NaCl is electrolyzed to form Cl_2 (g) and Na (l), is given in Figure 30.2. An electrolytic cell is most easily recognized by the presence of a battery or power source used to drive the nonspontaneous redox reaction.

Figure 30.2

In this cell, Na^+ ions migrate toward the cathode, where they are reduced to Na (l) according to the reaction $\text{Na}^+ + \text{e}^- \rightarrow \text{Na } (l)$. Similarly, Cl^- ions migrate toward the anode, where they are oxidized to Cl_2 (g) by the reaction $2 \text{ Cl}^- \rightarrow \text{Cl}_2$ $(g) + 2 \text{ e}^-$. The electrons liberated at the anode travel through the wire to provide the electrons used at the cathode.

This type of cell is used in industry as the major means of sodium and chlorine production. Sodium is a liquid at the temperature of molten NaCl and is less dense than the molten salt, meaning it is easily removed as it floats to the top of the reaction vessel.

Electrode Charge Designations

The anode of an **electrolytic cell** is considered **positive** because it is attached to the positive pole of the battery. Just like any anode, it attracts anions from the solution. The anode of a **galvanic cell,** on the other hand, is considered **negative** because the spontaneous oxidation reaction that takes place at the galvanic cell's anode is the original source of that cell's negative charge (i.e., is the source of electrons). In spite of this difference in designating charge, oxidation always takes place at the anode in both types of cells, and electrons always flow through the wire from the anode to the cathode.

In a galvanic cell, charge is spontaneously created as electrons are released by the oxidizing species at the anode. Since this is the source of electrons, the anode of a galvanic cell is considered the negative electrode. A mnemonic for this is: "The a*N*ode of a galva*N*ic cell is always *N*egative."

In an electrolytic cell, electrons are forced through the cathode, where they encounter the oxidizing agent. The cathode is providing electrons, and thus the cathode of an electrolytic cell is considered the negative electrode. You can also think of the cathode as the electrode attached to the negative pole of the battery (or other power source) used for the electrolysis. Like in any cell, the cathode attracts cations.

One common topic in which this distinction arises is electrophoresis, a technique often used to separate amino acids based on their isoelectric points, or pIs (see Chapter 51, Separation). The positively charged amino acid cations (i.e., those that are protonated at the pH of the solution) will migrate toward the cathode; negatively charged amino acid anions (i.e., those that are deprotonated at the solution pH) migrate instead toward the anode.

Quantitative Electrochemistry

The number of moles exchanged in an electrochemical cell can be determined from the balanced reaction for that cell. For a half-reaction that involves the transfer of n electrons per atom, one mole of M (s) will be produced if n moles of electrons are supplied.

$$M^{n+} + n\,e^- \rightarrow M$$

One electron carries a charge of 1.6×10^{-19} coulombs (C). The charge carried by one mole of electrons can be calculated by multiplying this number by Avogadro's number:

$$(1.6 \times 10^{-19})(6.022 \times 10^{23}) = 96{,}487 \text{ C/mol e}^-$$

This number is called the **Faraday constant**, and one **farad (F)** is equivalent to the amount of charge contained in one mole of electrons (1 F = 96,487 coulombs, or J/V, but can be rounded to 10^5 coulombs). This can be used to determine the number of moles of electrons transferred by an electrochemical cell according to the equation:

$$i \times t = n \times F$$

where i = current in amperes, t = time in seconds, n = number of moles of electrons, and F = the Faraday constant.

Example: How many moles of solid copper are produced during a redox reaction that generates 4 A of current for three seconds according to the reaction:

$$Zn\ (s) + Cu^{2+}\ (aq) \rightarrow Zn^{2+}\ (aq) + Cu\ (s)$$

Solution: First, determine the number of moles of electrons transferred using:

$$i \times t = n \times F$$

$$n = \frac{it}{F} = (4)(3)/10^5 = 12 \times 10^{-5} = 1.2 \times 10^{-4} \text{ moles of electrons}$$

Next, determine how many moles of electrons are transferred in the reaction. Copper is reduced from Cu^{2+} to $Cu\ (s)$, which requires two electrons:

$$Cu^{2+}\ (aq) + 2\ e^- \rightarrow Cu\ (s)$$

Thus, one mole of Cu will be produced for every two electrons transferred, and you can use this final conversion to calculate the number of moles of solid copper produced:

$$1.2 \times 10^{-4} \text{ mol } e^- \times \frac{1\,\text{mol Cu}}{2\,\text{mol}\,e^-} = 0.6 \times 10^{-4} \text{ mol Cu} = 6 \times 10^{-5} \text{ mol Cu}$$

REDUCTION POTENTIALS AND THE ELECTROMOTIVE FORCE

Reduction Potentials

The species in a redox reaction that will be oxidized or reduced can be determined from the **reduction potential** of each species, defined as the tendency of a species to acquire electrons and be reduced. Each has its own intrinsic reduction potential; the more positive the potential, the greater the tendency to be reduced.

A reduction potential is measured in volts (V) and is defined relative to the **standard hydrogen electrode (SHE)**, which is arbitrarily given a potential of 0.00 volts and is based on the half-reaction $2\ H^+\ (aq) + 2\ e^- \rightarrow H_2\ (g)$. **Standard reduction potential**, ($E°$), is measured under **standard conditions**: 25°C, a 1 M concentration for each ion participating in the reaction, a partial pressure of 1 atm for each gas that is part of the reaction, and metals in their pure state. A higher $E°$ means a greater tendency for reduction to occur, while a lower $E°$ means a greater tendency for oxidation to occur. When two half-reactions are occurring, only one can be a reduction; the half-reaction with the lower reduction potential will occur in reverse as an oxidation.

Example: Given the following half-reactions and $E°$ values, determine which species would be oxidized and which would be reduced.

$$Ag^+\ (aq) + e^- \rightarrow Ag\ (s) \qquad\qquad E° = +0.80 \text{ V}$$

$$Tl^+\ (aq) + e^- \rightarrow Tl\ (s) \qquad\qquad E° = -0.34 \text{ V}$$

Solution: $Ag^+\ (aq)$ would be reduced to $Ag\ (s)$, and $Tl\ (s)$ would be oxidized to $Tl^+\ (aq)$, because $Ag^+\ (aq)$ has the higher $E°$. Therefore, the net redox reaction equation would be:

$$Ag^+\ (aq) + Tl\ (s) \rightarrow Tl^+\ (aq) + Ag\ (s)$$

which is the sum of the two spontaneous half-reactions.

Since reduction and oxidation are opposite processes, the half-reaction and the sign of the reduction potential are both reversed for the oxidation half-reaction. For instance, from the example above, the oxidation half-reaction and oxidation potential of Tl (s) are as follows:

$$\text{Tl } (s) \rightarrow \text{Tl}^+ (aq) + e^- \qquad\qquad E° = +0.34 \text{ V}$$

Electromotive Force

Standard reduction potentials are also used to calculate the **standard electromotive force (emf or $E°_{cell}$)** of a reaction, the difference in potential between two half-cells. Note that electromotive force is NOT a force in the traditional sense but is rather an electrical potential. The $E°_{cell}$ of a reaction is determined by adding the standard reduction potential of the reduced species and the standard oxidation potential of the oxidized species. When adding standard potentials, do *not* multiply by the number of moles oxidized or reduced.

$$E°_{cell} = E°_{red} + E°_{ox}$$

The standard $E°_{cell}$ of a galvanic cell is positive, while the standard $E°_{cell}$ of an electrolytic cell is negative.

Example: Given that the standard reduction potentials for Sm^{3+} and $[RhCl_6]^{3-}$ are -2.41 V and $+0.44$ V, respectively, calculate the $E°_{cell}$ of the following reaction:

$$Sm^{3+} (aq) + \text{Rh } (s) + 6 \text{ Cl}^- (aq) \rightarrow [RhCl_6]^{3-} (aq) + \text{Sm } (s)$$

Solution: First, determine the oxidation and reduction half-reactions. As written, the Rh is oxidized, and the Sm^{3+} is reduced. Thus, the Sm^{3+} reduction potential is used as is, while the reverse reaction for Rh, $[RhCl_6]^{3-} \rightarrow \text{Rh} + 6 \text{ Cl}^-$, applies, and the oxidation potential of $[RhCl_6]^{3-}$ must be used. Then, using $E°_{cell} = E°_{red} + E°_{ox}$, the $E°_{cell}$ can be calculated to be $(-2.41 \text{ V}) + (-0.44 \text{ V}) = -2.85$ V. The cell is thus electrolytic as written because $E°_{cell}$ is negative. This means that the reaction would proceed spontaneously to the left, in which case Sm would be oxidized, while $[RhCl_6]^{3-}$ would be reduced. The $E°_{cell}$ would then be $+2.85$ V.

THERMODYNAMICS OF REDOX REACTIONS

E_{cell} and Gibbs Free Energy

The thermodynamic criterion for determining the spontaneity of a reaction is ΔG, Gibbs free energy, a measure of the maximum amount of useful work produced by a chemical reaction. In an electrochemical cell, the work done is dependent on the number of coulombs and the energy available. Thus, ΔG and E_{cell} are related as follows:

$$\Delta G = -n\text{F}E_{cell}$$

where n is the number of moles of electrons exchanged, and F is the Faraday constant. Keep in mind that if the Faraday constant is expressed in coulombs (J/V), ΔG must be expressed in J, not kJ.

If the reaction takes place under standard conditions (25°C, 1 atm pressure, and all solutions at 1 M concentration), then the ΔG is the standard Gibbs free energy and E_{cell} is the standard cell potential $E°_{cell}$. The above equation then becomes:

$$\Delta G° = -n\mathrm{F}E°_{cell}$$

The relationship demonstrates that the signs of ΔG and $E°_{cell}$ are opposite. A galvanic cell has a negative ΔG and a positive $E°_{cell}$, whereas an electrolytic cell has a positive ΔG and negative $E°_{cell}$.

In addition, as Chapter 32, Thermochemistry, demonstrates:

$$\Delta G° = -RT \ln K_{eq}$$

This relates ΔG to K_{eq}. When $K_{eq} > 1$, products are favored over reactants, the forward reaction is spontaneous, and $\Delta G < 0$. When $K_{eq} < 1$, reactants are favored, the reverse reaction is preferred, and $\Delta G > 0$. Combining the different equations for ΔG gives:

$$n\mathrm{F}E°_{cell} = RT \ln K_{eq}$$

This relationship shows that when $K_{eq} > 1$, $\ln K_{eq} > 0$, and $E°_{cell}$ is positive; thus, the reaction goes forward. When $K_{eq} < 1$, $\ln K_{eq} < 0$, and $E°_{cell}$ is negative; thus, the reaction goes in the reverse direction.

Effect of Concentration

The above equations assume standard conditions, which require 1 M concentrations for all the ionic species present and for all gases to be at a pressure of 1 atm. However, concentration does have an effect on the E_{cell}, which varies with the changing concentrations of the species involved. This can be determined by using the **Nernst equation**:

$$E_{cell} = E°_{cell} - \left(\frac{RT}{n\mathrm{F}}\right)(\ln Q)$$

Q is the reaction quotient for a given reaction and gives the concentrations of reactants and products when the reaction is not at equilibrium. For example, in this reaction:

$$a\mathrm{A} + b\mathrm{B} \rightarrow c\mathrm{C} + d\mathrm{D}$$

the reaction quotient would be:

$$Q = \frac{[\mathrm{C}]^c\,[\mathrm{D}]^d}{[\mathrm{A}]^a\,[\mathrm{B}]^b}$$

This allows the actual E_{cell} to be determined based on the $E°_{cell}$ and reagent concentrations.

Note that the Nernst equation can be rewritten as:

$$E_{cell} = E°_{cell} - \left(\frac{RT}{n\mathrm{F}}\right)(\ln Q) = \left(\frac{RT}{n\mathrm{F}}\right)(\ln K_{eq}) - \left(\frac{RT}{n\mathrm{F}}\right)(\ln Q)$$

If $Q = 1$, as under standard conditions, when all concentrations are 1 M, then $\ln Q = 0$, and the entire last term of the equation disappears. This again confirms the relationship between ΔG, K_{eq}, and E_{cell}.

REVIEW PROBLEMS

1. If one F is equivalent to 96,487 C/mol e^-, what is the charge of an individual electron?

   A. 6.0×10^{-19} C
   B. 1.6×10^{-19} C
   C. 1.6×10^{19} C
   D. 5.8×10^{23} C
   E. 6.0×10^{28} C

2. If one F is equivalent to 96,487 C/mol e^-, how many F are required for the reduction of one mole of Ni^{2+} (aq) to Ni (s)?

   A. 0.5 F
   B. 1 F
   C. 2 F
   D. 96,487 F
   E. 6.022×10^{23} F

3. If the gold-plating process occurs according to the following half-reaction, how many coulombs would be required to plate 0.600 g of Au onto a metal?

   $$Au^{3+} (aq) + 3 e^- \rightarrow Au (s)$$

   A. 299 C
   B. 600 C
   C. 868 C
   D. 2,990 C
   E. 8,680 C

4. When the half-reactions below are combined in a galvanic cell, which species will be reduced, and which will be oxidized?

$F_2 (g) + 2 e^- \rightarrow 2 F^- (aq)$	$E° = +2.87$ V
$Ca^{2+} (aq) + 2 e^- \rightarrow Ca (s)$	$E° = -2.76$ V

   A. F^- (aq) will be oxidized, and Ca^{2+} (aq) will be reduced.
   B. Ca^{2+} (aq) will be oxidized, and F_2 (g) will be reduced.
   C. Ca (s) will be oxidized, and F_2 (g) will be reduced.
   D. F_2 (g) will be oxidized, and Ca (s) will be reduced.
   E. Ca (s) will be oxidized, and F^- (aq) will be reduced.

5. What is the standard EMF if the following half-reactions are combined in a galvanic cell?

$$Co^{3+} (aq) + e^- \rightarrow Co^{2+} (aq) \qquad\qquad E° = +1.82$$

$$Na^+ (aq) + e^- \rightarrow Na (s) \qquad\qquad E° = -2.71$$

   A. −4.53 V
   B. −0.89 V
   C. +0.89 V
   D. +4.53 V
   E. +6.31 V

6. What is the $E°_{cell}$ for a reaction in which $\Delta G° = -553.91$ kJ and two electrons are transferred?
   A. −2.87 V
   B. -2.87×10^{-3} V
   C. 2.87×10^{-3} V
   D. 2.87 V
   E. 2.87×10^3 V

SOLUTIONS TO REVIEW PROBLEMS

1. **B** The Avogadro constant (6×10^{23} mol^{-1}) defines the numbers of particles present in one mole of any substance, including electrons, and the Faraday constant (10^5 $C \cdot (mol\ e^-)^{-1}$) defines the charge per mole of electrons. Therefore:

$$1\ mol\ e^- \times \frac{mol\ e^-}{6 \times 10^{23}\ e^-} \times \frac{10^5\ C}{mol\ e^-} = 1.67 \times 10^{-19}\ C$$

   The only answer choice that is close is (B), which is the correct answer. Note that you may have already memorized this value as e, the elementary charge, in which case you could have quickly selected that answer and moved on to the next question.

2. **C** The reduction of one mole of Ni^{2+} (*aq*) to one mole of Ni (*s*) requires two moles of electrons. The transfer of one mole of electrons is equivalent to the transfer of 1F of charge. Therefore, transferring two moles of electrons requires 2F of charge.

3. **C** In order to solve this problem, first determine the number of moles of Au present in 0.6 g of Au.

$$0.6\ g\ Au \times \frac{mol\ Au}{197.0\ g} = 0.003\ mol\ Au$$

   Next, determine the number of moles of electrons used to reduce Au^{3+} (*aq*) to 0.0030 mol of Au (*s*). From the given reduction half-reaction of Au, you can see that, for every mole of Au^{3+} reacted, three moles of electrons are consumed. Therefore:

$$0.003\ mol\ Au \times \frac{3\ mol\ e^-}{mol\ Au} = 0.009\ mol\ e^-$$

   Finally, convert 0.009 mol e^- to C using 10^5 as an approximation of the Faraday constant:

$$0.009\ mol\ e^- \times \frac{10^5\ C}{mol\ e\ e^-} = 9 \times 10^3\ C$$

   The closest answer choice is (C), which is correct.

4. **C** The half-reaction with the greater reduction potential will proceed forward as written, while the half-reaction with the smaller reduction potential will proceed in the opposite direction. The reaction with F_2 has the greater standard reduction potential, so it will process in the forward direction, and F_2 (*g*) will be reduced. The other reaction will proceed in the opposite direction, meaning that Ca (*s*) will be oxidized.

5. **D** A galvanic cell always has a positive standard electrical potential, which means that (A) and (B) can be eliminated right away. To achieve the maximum, most favorable cell potential with the two provided half-reactions, cobalt will be reduced and sodium will be oxidized. The total EMF of the combined reaction can be calculated by adding together the reduction potential of cobalt and the oxidation potential of sodium (which has the opposite sign of its reduction potential). Therefore:

$$EMF = 1.82\ V + 2.71\ V = 4.53\ V$$

6. D Based on the question stem and your outside knowledge of F, you know that $\Delta G° = -553.91 \approx -6 \times 10^2$ kJ, $n = 2$ mol e$^-$, and F $= 10^5$ C/mol e$^-$, and are asked to calculate the voltage, which is equivalent to J/C. Since the units do not match, you must convert $\Delta G°$ to J such that $\Delta G° \approx -6 \times 10^5$ J. That being done, you can rearrange the relationship $\Delta G° = -nFE°$ to calculate $E°$:

$$E° = -\frac{\Delta G°}{nF}$$

$$E° = -\frac{(-6 \times 10^5)}{(2 \times 10^5)}$$

$$E° = 3 \text{ V}$$

The closest answer choice is (D), which is correct.

CHAPTER THIRTY-ONE

Chemical Kinetics

When studying a chemical reaction, it is important to consider not only the chemical properties of the reactants but also the **conditions** under which the reaction occurs, the **mechanism** by which it takes place, the **rate** at which it occurs, and the **equilibrium** toward which it proceeds.

REACTION MECHANISMS

The **mechanism** of a chemical reaction is the actual series of steps through which it occurs. Knowing the accepted mechanism of a reaction often helps to explain the reaction's rate, position of equilibrium, and thermodynamic characteristics. Consider the reaction below:

$$A_2 + 2\,B \rightarrow 2\,AB$$

This equation seems to imply a mechanism in which two molecules of B collide with one molecule of A_2 to form two molecules of AB. But suppose instead that the reaction actually takes place in two steps.

$$\text{Step 1:} \quad A_2 + B \rightarrow A_2B \qquad \text{(slow)}$$

$$\text{Step 2:} \quad A_2B + B \rightarrow 2\,AB \qquad \text{(fast)}$$

Note that these two steps add up to the overall (net) reaction. A_2B, which does not appear in the overall reaction because it is neither a reactant nor a product, is called an **intermediate**. Reaction intermediates are often difficult to detect, but a proposed mechanism can be supported through experiments.

The slowest step in a proposed mechanism is called the **rate-determining step**, because the overall reaction cannot proceed faster than that step.

REACTION RATES

Chemical kinetics is the study of the rates (or speed) of reactions. The **reaction rate** is the change of concentration of reactant or finished product with respect to time. Any given chemical reaction can be represented by the following equation:

$$\text{Reactants} \rightarrow \text{Products}$$

This equation indicates that reactant molecules are decreasing or being consumed and the product molecules are increasing or being formed. The process of chemical kinetics is concerned with how "fast" the reactants are being transformed into products.

Definition of Rate

Consider a reaction $2A + B \rightarrow C$, in which one mole of C is produced from every two moles of A and one mole of B. The rate of this reaction may be described in terms of either the disappearance of reactants over time or the appearance of products over time.

$$\text{rate} = \frac{\text{decrease in concentration of reactants}}{\text{time}} = \frac{\text{increase in concentration of products}}{\text{time}}$$

Because the concentration of a reactant decreases during the reaction, a minus sign is placed before a rate that is expressed in terms of reactants. For the reaction above, the rate of reaction with respect to A is $-\frac{\Delta[A]}{\Delta t}$, with respect to B is $-\frac{\Delta[B]}{\Delta t}$, and with respect to C is $\frac{\Delta[C]}{\Delta t}$.

Rate is expressed in the units of moles per liter per second ($mol/[L \times s]$) or molarity per second (molarity/s).

Rate Law

For nearly all forward, irreversible reactions, the rate is proportional to the product of the concentrations of the reactants, each raised to some power. For the general reaction:

$$aA + bB \rightarrow cC + dD$$

the rate is proportional to $[A]^x[B]^y$, that is:

$$\text{rate} = k[A]^x[B]^y$$

This expression is the **rate law** for the general reaction above, where k is the **rate constant**. The rate constant is defined as a constant of proportionality between the chemical reaction rate and the concentration of the reactants. Multiplying the units of k by the concentration factors raised to the appropriate powers gives the rate in units of concentration/time. The exponents x and y are called the **orders of reaction**; x is the order with respect to A, and y is the order with respect to B. These exponents may be integers (including zero) or fractions and must be determined experimentally.

It is important to note that the exponents of the rate law are **not** necessarily equal to the stoichiometric coefficients in the overall reaction equation. The exponents **are** equal to the stoichiometric coefficients of the rate-determining step. If one of the reactants or products in the rate-determining step is an intermediate not included in the overall reaction, then calculating the rate law in terms of the original reactants is more complex.

The **overall order of a reaction** (or the **reaction order**) is defined as the sum of the exponents, here equal to $x + y$.

Experimental determination of rate law

The values of k, x, and y in the rate law equation (rate $= k[A]^x[B]^y$) must be determined experimentally for a given reaction at a given temperature. The rate is usually measured as a function of the initial concentrations of the reactants, A and B.

Example: Given the data below, find the rate law for the following reaction at 300 K:

$$A + B \rightarrow C + D$$

Solution: First, look for two trials in which the concentrations of all but one of the substances are held constant.

Trial	$[A]_{initial}$ (M)	$[B]_{initial}$ (M)	$r_{initial}$ (M/s)
1	1.00	1.00	2.0
2	1.00	2.00	8.1
3	2.00	2.00	15.9

a) In trials 1 and 2, the concentration of A is kept constant while the concentration of B is doubled. The rate increases by a factor of 8.1/2.0, or approximately 4. Write down the rate expression for each of the two trials.

Trial 1: $r_1 = k[A]^x[B]^y = k(1.00)^x(1.00)^y$
Trial 2: $r_2 = k[A]^x[B]^y = k(1.00)^x(2.00)^y$

Divide the second equation by the first:

$$\frac{r_2}{r_1} = \frac{8.1}{2.0} = \frac{k(1.00)^x(2.00)^y}{k(1.00)^x(1.00)^y} = (2.00)^y$$

$$4 = (2.00)^y$$

$$y = 2$$

b) In trials 2 and 3, the concentration of B is kept constant while the concentration of A is doubled; the rate is increased by a factor of 15.9/8.1, or approximately 2. The rate expressions of the two trials are:

Trial 2: $r_2 = k(1.00)^x(2.00)^y$
Trial 3: $r_3 = k(2.00)^x(2.00)^y$

Divide the second equation by the first:

$$\frac{r_3}{r_2} = \frac{15.9}{8.1} = \frac{k(2.00)^x(2.00)^y}{k(1.00)^x(2.00)^y} = (2.00)^x$$

$$2 = (2.00)^x$$

$$x = 1$$

So $r = k[A][B]^2$.

The order of the reaction with respect to A is 1 and with respect to B is 2; the overall reaction order is $1 + 2 = 3$.

To calculate k, substitute the values from any one of the above trials into the rate law. For example:

$$2.0 \text{ M/s} = k \times 1.00 \text{ M} \times (1.00 \text{ M})^2$$

$$k = 2.0 \text{ M}^{-2} \cdot \text{s}^{-1}$$

Therefore, the rate law is $r = (2.0 \text{ M}^{-2} \cdot \text{s}^{-1}) [A][B]^2$.

Reaction Orders

Chemical reactions are often classified on the basis of kinetics as zero-order, first-order, second-order, mixed-order, or higher-order reactions. The general reaction $aA + bB \rightarrow cC + dD$ will be used in the following discussion.

Zero-order reactions

A zero-order reaction has a constant rate, which is independent of the reactants' concentrations. Thus, the rate law is:

$$\text{rate} = k, \text{ where } k \text{ has units of M} \cdot \text{s}^{-1}$$

With respect to the administration of a medication, a zero-order reaction is one in which the amount of drug administered/eliminated per unit time remains constant. For example, 25 mg of a drug are administered/eliminated each hour.

Plasma Drug Concentration vs. Time Plot

A_0

Drug A

Slope = $-k$ Graph of drug
eliminated by
Conc.   a zero-order process

Time

The concentration of Drug A can be calculated at any given time with the equation:

$$[A] = [A_0] - (k_0)(t)$$

where: A_0 = initial concentration of Drug A in the body
k_0 = zero-order rate constant
t = time

The zero-order half-life changes with time and is proportional to the initial drug concentration. It is inversely proportional to the zero-order rate constant and can be represented with the following equation:

$$\text{half-life} = \frac{1}{2}\frac{A_0}{k_0}$$

First-order reactions

A first-order reaction (order = 1) has a rate proportional to the concentration of one reactant.

$$\text{rate} = k[A] \text{ or rate} = k[B]$$

First-order rate constants have units of s^{-1}.

The classic example of a first-order reaction is the process of radioactive decay. The concentration of radioactive substance A at any time t can be expressed mathematically as:

$$[A_t] = [A_0]\, e^{-kt}$$

where $[A_0]$ = initial concentration of A
$[A_t]$ = concentration of A at time t
k = rate constant
t = elapsed time

The half-life ($t_{1/2}$) of a reaction is the time needed for the concentration of the radioactive substance to decrease to one-half of its original value. Half-lives can be calculated from the rate law as follows:

$$t_{1/2} = \frac{\ln 2}{k} = \frac{0.693}{k}$$

where k is the first-order rate constant.

With respect to medicine, a first-order reaction is one in which the percentage of drug administered/eliminated per unit time remains constant. In other words, the amount of drug administered/eliminated is proportional to the amount of drug remaining. For example, 25 percent of the drug is eliminated each hour.

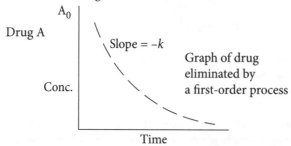

Plasma Drug Concentration vs. Time Plot

Drug A — A_0 — Slope = $-k$ — Conc. — Time

Graph of drug eliminated by a first-order process

The concentration of Drug A can be calculated at any given time with the equation:

$$\ln [A] = \ln [A_0] - k_e(t)$$

Remember: $\ln x = (\log x)(2.3)$

where

$[A_0]$ = initial concentration of Drug A in the body
k_e = first-order elimination rate constant
t = time

Regarding the first-order half-life, the time to reduce the remaining portion of the drug in the body by one-half remains constant irrespective of the drug's concentration in the blood. The first-order half-life = $\frac{0.693}{k}$.

Second-order reactions

A second-order reaction (order = 2) has a rate proportional to the product of the concentration of two reactants or to the square of the concentration of a single reactant. For example, rate = $k[A]^2$, rate = $k[B]^2$, or rate = $k[A][B]$. The units of second-order rate constants are $M^{-1} \cdot s^{-1}$.

Higher-order reactions

A higher-order reaction has an order greater than two. These can be calculated the same way as lower-order reactions, but more possible combinations must be considered.

Mixed-order reactions

A mixed-order reaction has a fractional order; e.g., rate = $k[A]^{1/3}$. These are unlikely to appear on Test Day and describe relationships involving radicals, such as square roots.

Efficiency of Reactions

Collision theory of chemical kinetics

For a reaction to occur, molecules must collide with each other. The collision theory of chemical kinetics states that the rate of a reaction is proportional to the **number of collisions per second** between the reacting molecules. It is important to note that reaction rates almost always increase with increasing temperatures. On the other hand, reaction rates decrease with decreasing temperatures.

GC

Not all collisions, however, result in a chemical reaction. An **effective collision** (one that leads to the formation of products) occurs only if the molecules collide with the correct orientation and sufficient force to break the existing bonds and form new ones. The minimum energy of collision necessary for a reaction to take place is called the **activation energy**, E_a, or the **energy barrier**. Only a fraction of colliding particles have enough kinetic energy to exceed the activation energy. This means that only a fraction of all collisions are effective. The rate of a reaction can therefore be expressed as:

$$rate = fZ$$

where Z is the total number of collisions occurring per second and f is the fraction of collisions that are effective.

Transition state theory

When molecules collide with sufficient energy, they form a **transition state** in which the old bonds are weakened and the new bonds are beginning to form. The transition state then dissociates into products, and the new bonds are fully formed. For a reaction $A_2 + B_2 \rightarrow 2AB$, the change along the **reaction coordinate** (a measure of the extent to which the reaction has progressed from reactants to products; see below) can be represented as follows:

$$A - A \qquad \longrightarrow \qquad A \cdots A \qquad \longrightarrow \qquad A \quad A$$
$$B - B \qquad \qquad \qquad B \cdots B \qquad \qquad \qquad B \quad B$$

Figure 31.1

The **transition state**, also called the **activated complex**, has greater energy than either the reactants or the products and is denoted by the symbol ‡. The activation energy is required to bring the reactants to this particular energy level. Once an activated complex is formed, it can either dissociate into the products or revert to reactants without any additional energy input. Transition states are distinguished from intermediates in that, existing as they do at energy maxima, transition states do not have a finite lifetime.

A **potential energy diagram** illustrates the relationship between the activation energy, the heats of reaction, and the potential energy of the system before and after the reaction. The most important factors in such diagrams are the **relative** energies of the products and reactants. The **enthalpy change** of the reaction (ΔH) is the difference between the potential energy of the products and the potential energy of the reactants. A negative enthalpy change indicates an **exothermic reaction** (where heat is given off), and a positive enthalpy change indicates an **endothermic reaction** (where heat is absorbed).

The activated complex exists at the top of the energy barrier. The difference in potential energies between the activated complex and the reactants is the activation energy of the forward reaction; the difference in potential energies between the activated complex and the products is the activation energy of the reverse reaction.

For example, consider the formation of HCl from H_2 and Cl_2:

$$H_2 + Cl_2 \rightleftharpoons 2\,HCl$$

The following figure gives the energy profile of the reaction. It shows that the reaction is exothermic. The potential energy of the products is less than the potential energy of the reactants; heat is evolved, and the heat of reaction is negative.

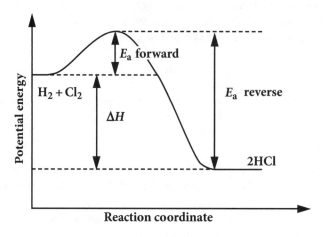

Figure 31.2

Factors Affecting Reaction Rate

The rate of a chemical reaction depends on the individual species undergoing reaction and on the reaction environment. The rate of reaction will increase if there is an increase in the number of effective collisions or a stabilization of the activated complex compared to the reactants.

Reactant concentrations

The greater the concentrations of the reactants (the more particles per unit volume), the greater the number of effective collisions per unit time, so the reaction rate will increase as reactant concentrations increase for all but zero-order reactions. For reactions occurring in the gaseous state, the partial pressures of the reactants can serve as measures of concentration.

Temperature

For nearly all reactions, the reaction rate will increase as the temperature of the system increases. Since the temperature of a substance is a measure of the particles' average kinetic energy, increasing the temperature increases the average kinetic energy of the molecules. Consequently, the proportion of molecules having energies greater than E_a (and thus capable of undergoing reaction) increases with higher temperature.

Medium

The rate of a reaction may also be affected by the medium in which it takes place. Due to differences in intermolecular forces and other stabilizing factors, certain reactions proceed more rapidly in aqueous solution, whereas other reactions proceed more rapidly in nonpolar solvents. The state of the medium (liquid, solid, or gas) can also have a significant effect.

Catalysts

Catalysts are substances that increase reaction rate without themselves being consumed; they do this by lowering the activation energy. Catalysts are important in biological systems and in industrial chemistry; **enzymes** are biological catalysts. Catalysts may increase the frequency of collision between the reactants, change the relative orientation of the reactants to make a higher percentage of collisions effective, donate electron density to the reactants, or reduce intramolecular bonding within reactant molecules. The following figure compares the energy profiles of catalyzed and uncatalyzed reactions.

Figure 31.3

The energy barrier for the catalyzed reaction is much lower than the energy barrier for the uncatalyzed reaction. Note that the rates of both the forward and the reverse reactions are increased by the catalyst, since E_a of the forward and reverse reactions are lowered by the same amount. Therefore, the presence of a catalyst causes the reaction to proceed more quickly toward equilibrium.

REVIEW PROBLEMS

1. All of the following are true statements concerning reaction orders EXCEPT

    A. The rate of a zero-order reaction is constant.
    B. After three half-lives, a sample will have one-ninth of its original activity.
    C. The units for the rate constant for first-order reactions are s^{-1}.
    D. Higher-order reactions are those with an order greater than two.
    E. The decrease in concentration of reactants equals the increase in concentration of the products as a function of time.

2. Consider the following hypothetical reaction and experimental data:

    $$A + B \rightarrow C + D \qquad\qquad T = 273\ K$$

	$[A]_0\ (mol\cdot L^{-1})$	$[B]_0\ (mol\cdot L^{-1})$	rate $(mol\cdot L^{-1}\cdot s^{-1})$
Exp 1	0.10	1	0.035
Exp 2	0.10	4	0.070
Exp 3	0.20	1	0.140
Exp 4	0.10	16	0.140

    A. What is the order with respect to A?
    B. What is the order with respect to B?
    C. What is the rate equation?
    D. What is the overall order of the reaction?
    E. Calculate the rate constant.

3. Consider the following chemical reaction and experimental data:

    $$A\ (aq) \rightarrow B\ (aq) + C\ (g)$$

Trial 1		**Trial 2**	
[A] (mol/L)	rate (M/s)	[A] (mol/L)	rate (M/s)
0.10	0.6	0.10	0.9
0.20	0.6	0.20	0.9
0.30	0.6	0.30	0.9
0.40	0.6	0.40	0.9

    A. What is the rate expression for trial 1?
    B. What is the rate constant for trial 1?
    C. What is the most likely reason for the increased rate in trial 2?

4. Consider the following reaction and experimental data:

    $$SO_3 + H_2O \rightarrow H_2SO_4$$

	$[SO_3]\ (mol\cdot L^{-1})$	$[H_2O]\ (mol\cdot L^{-1})$	rate $(mol\cdot L^{-1}\cdot s^{-1})$
Trial 1	0.1	0.01	0.013
Trial 2	0.2	0.01	0.052
Trial 3	X	0.02	0.234
Trial 4	0.1	0.03	0.039

A. What is the value of *X*?

    B. What is the order of the reaction?

    C. What is the rate constant?

    D. What would be the rate if $[SO_3]$ in trial 4 were raised to 0.2 mol/L?

5. In the following diagram, which labeled arrow represents the activation energy for the reverse reaction?

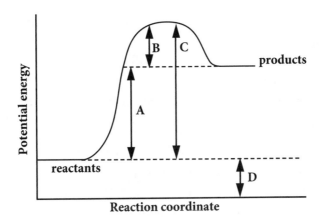

    A. A

    B. B

    C. C

    D. D

    E. The sum of B and D

6. The activation energy for a reaction in the forward direction is 78 kJ. The activation energy for the same reaction in reverse is 300 kJ. If the energy of the products is 25 kJ, then:

    A. What is the energy of the reactants?

    B. Is the forward reaction endothermic or exothermic?

    C. Is the reverse reaction endothermic or exothermic?

    D. What is the enthalpy change for the forward reaction?

7. According to chemical kinetic theory, a reaction can occur

    A. if the reactants collide with the proper orientation.

    B. if the reactants possess sufficient energy of collision.

    C. if the reactants are able to form a correct transition state.

    D. for all of the above.

    E. for none of the above.

8. The number of undecayed nuclei in a sample of bromine-87 decreased by a factor of four over a period of 112 s. What is the decay constant for bromine-87?

    A. $6.19 \times 10^{-3}\,s^{-1}$

    B. $1.24 \times 10^{-2}\,s^{-1}$

    C. $6.93 \times 10^{-1}\,s^{-1}$

    D. $28\,s^{-1}$

    E. $56\,s^{-1}$

9. Which of the following is most likely to increase the rate of a reaction?

    A. Decreasing the temperature

    B. Increasing the volume of the reaction vessel

    C. Reducing the activation energy

    D. Decreasing the concentration of the reactant in the reaction vessel

    E. Decreasing the pressure in the reaction vessel

10. All of the following are true statements concerning catalysts EXCEPT

    A. a catalyst will speed the rate-determining step.

    B. a catalyst will be used up in a reaction.

    C. a catalyst may induce steric strain in a molecule.

    D. a catalyst will lower the activation energy of a reaction.

    E. a catalyst will speed up the rates of both the forward and the reverse reactions.

SOLUTIONS TO REVIEW PROBLEMS

1. **B** Discussed in the section on reaction orders in this chapter.

2. First, the general rate equation must be written out. It is:

   rate $= k[A]^x[B]^y$

   where:

   $k =$ the rate constant

   $x =$ the order with respect to reactant A

   $y =$ the order with respect to reactant B

   A $x = 2$

   To solve for x, it is necessary to find two trials in which B is held constant; here, experiments 1 and 3. The data shows that if the concentration of A is doubled, the rate increases by a factor of 4. Thus, the rate varies as the square of the concentration of A. The order with respect to A, x, is therefore equal to 2.

   B $y = 0.5$

   To solve for y, follow the steps as in x. In experiments 1 and 2 (and 2 and 4) A is held constant, the concentration of B quadruples, and the rate doubles. The rate, therefore, varies as the square root of the concentration of B. The order, y, is therefore equal to 0.5.

   C **rate $= k[A]^2[B]^{0.5}$**

   D **order $= 2.5$**

   The overall order is equal to $x + y = 2.5$.

   E **3.5**

   Given the rate expression, the rate constant can easily be calculated by substituting the rate and concentrations for any of the four trials into the rate expression; the rate constant will work out to 3.5 in each case.

   Trial 1: $0.035 = k[0.10]^2[1]^{0.5}$; $k = 3.5$ M$^{-1.5}$·s^{-1}

   Trial 2: $0.070 = k[0.10]^2[4]^{0.5}$; $k = 3.5$ M$^{-1.5}$·s^{-1}

   Trial 3: $0.140 = k[0.20]^2[1]^{0.5}$; $k = 3.5$ M$^{-1.5}$·s^{-1}

   Trial 4: $0.140 = k[0.10]^2[16]^{0.5}$; $k = 3.5$ M$^{-1.5}$·s^{-1}

3. **A** **rate $= k[A]^0 = k$**

   This reaction has only one reactant. It is evident from the data that the rate of the reaction is not affected by reactant concentration. This is a zero-order reaction, and the rate is equal to its rate constant, k.

   B **$k = 0.6$**

   C The most likely reason for the increased rate in trial 2 is a change in temperature. We know that in a zero-order reaction, changing the concentration of the reactant will not cause a change in rate; the factor most likely to affect the rate is temperature.

4. **A** $X = 0.3$

To calculate X, first write the rate expression for this reaction. From the data, the rate expression is calculated as:

$$\text{rate} = k[SO_3]^2[H_2O]$$

The order with respect to SO_3 is 2, since the rate quadruples when the concentration of SO_3 doubles (with the concentration of H_2O remaining constant) between trials 1 and 2. The order with respect to H_2O is 1, as the rate triples as the concentration of H_2O triples (with the concentration of SO_3 remaining constant) between trials 1 and 4.

X can be calculated by plugging the values from trial 3 into the rate expression. First, however, calculate the rate constant, k, by plugging in the known values from trial 1, 2, or 4. For instance:

Trial 4: $0.039 = k[0.1]^2[0.03]$; $k = 130$ $M^{-2} \cdot s^{-1}$

To calculate X, plug in the values of rate and $[H_2O]$ for trial 3, using $k = 130$ $M^{-2} \cdot s^{-1}$.

$0.234 = 130[X]^2[0.02]$

$X = 0.3$ M

B 3

The order of the reaction is the sum of the exponents in the rate expression: in this case, $(2 + 1) = 3$.

C 130 $M^{-2} \cdot s^{-1}$

For calculations see solution to part A.

D **0.156 units**

Substitute 0.2 M instead of 0.1 M for $[SO_3]$:

$\text{rate} = (130)(0.2)^2(0.03) = 0.156$ M/s

5. **B** The activation energy is the minimum amount of energy needed for a reaction to proceed. The activation energy for the reverse reaction is the change in potential energy between the products and the transition state indicated by arrow B.

6. **A** **247 kJ**

The best way to visualize the solution to this set of problems is to draw a diagram.

$\Delta H = \text{Activation Energy}_{\text{forward}} - \text{Activation Energy}_{\text{reverse}}$
$= 78\,\text{kJ} - 300\,\text{kJ} = -222\,\text{kJ}$

And because $\Delta H = \text{Energy}_{\text{products}} - \text{Energy}_{\text{reactants}}$:
$-222\,\text{kJ} = 25\,\text{kJ} - X$
$X = 247\,\text{kJ} = \text{energy of reactants}$

B The forward reaction is exothermic because ΔH is negative.

C The reverse reaction is endothermic.

D The enthalpy change, ΔH, of the reaction is $-222\,\text{kJ}$.

7. **D** Discussed in the section on the efficiency of reactions in this chapter.

8. **B** If the number of nuclei decaying in a sample has decreased by a factor of 4, the sample has been through two half-lives, and the half-life will be

$\dfrac{112\,\text{s}}{2} = 56\,\text{s} = t_{1/2}$

The equation to determine the decay constant for the first-order reaction is

$t_{1/2} = \dfrac{0.693}{k}$

Thus, given that the half-life is 56 s, the decay constant will be

$56\,\text{s} = \dfrac{0.693}{k}$
$k = 0.0124\,\text{s}^{-1}$

9. **C** Various conditions can affect the rate of reaction: increased temperature, increased concentration of reactants, decreased volume or increased pressure (if any reactants are gases), or addition of a suitable catalyst. The effect of a catalyst is to decrease the activation energy; therefore, choice (C) is correct.

10. **B** Discussed in the section on factors affecting reaction rate in this chapter.

CHAPTER THIRTY-TWO

Thermochemistry

All chemical reactions are accompanied by energy changes. Thermal, chemical, potential, and kinetic energies are all interconvertible, as they must obey the **law of conservation of energy.** Energy changes determine whether reactions can occur and how easily they will do so. **Thermodynamics** helps determine whether a chemical reaction is **spontaneous,** meaning whether or not it will go forward without assistance. The application of thermodynamics to chemical reactions is called **thermochemistry.**

A thermodynamic **system** is the particular part of the universe being studied; everything outside the system is considered the **surroundings** or **environment.** A system may be:

Isolated: It cannot exchange energy or matter with the surroundings, as with an insulated bomb reactor.

Closed: It can exchange energy but not matter with the surroundings, as with a steam radiator.

Open: It can exchange both matter and energy with the surroundings, as with a pot of boiling water.

A system undergoes a **process** when one or more of its properties changes, such as volume, temperature, or pressure.

Some processes are limited such that only certain variables change while others are held constant. Isothermal processes occur when systems do not change temperature ($\Delta T = 0$), while adiabatic processes occur when there is no heat exchanged between systems and their surroundings ($\Delta q = 0$), a concept discussed below. Similarly, isobaric processes occur in systems at constant pressure ($\Delta P = 0$), while isochoric processes occur at constant volume ($\Delta V = 0$).

HEAT

Definition

Heat (q) is a form of energy that can easily transfer to or from a system due to a temperature difference between the system and its surroundings; this transfer will occur spontaneously from a warmer system to a cooler system. According to convention, heat absorbed by a system (from its surroundings) is considered positive, while heat lost by a system (to its surroundings) is considered negative. Heat is measured in **calories (cal)** or **joules (J)** and is often expressed in kcal or kJ (1 cal = 4.184 J).

Heat change is the most common energy change in chemical processes. Reactions that absorb heat energy are said to be **endothermic**, while those that release heat energy are said to be **exothermic**. The heat absorbed or released in a given process is calculated from this equation:

$$q = mc\Delta T$$

where m is the mass, c is the **specific heat capacity**, and ΔT is the change in temperature. Specific heat is a property of a material that describes how much energy it takes to raise its temperature.

STATES AND STATE FUNCTIONS

The state of a system is described by the properties of the system, such as temperature (T), pressure (P), and volume (V). When the state of a system changes, the values of the properties also change. Properties whose magnitude depends only on the initial and final states of the system and not on the path of the change are known as **state functions**. Pressure, temperature, and volume are important state functions. Other examples are **enthalpy (H)**, **entropy (S)**, **free energy (G)**, and **internal energy (E or U)**. Although independent of path, state functions are not necessarily independent of one another.

A set of **standard conditions** (298 K, 1 atm, and 1 M concentrations) is normally used for measuring the enthalpy, entropy, and free energy of a reaction. A substance in its most stable form under standard conditions is said to be in its **standard state**. Examples of substances in their standard states include hydrogen as H_2 (g), water as H_2O (l), and salt as $NaCl$ (s). The changes in enthalpy, entropy, and free energy that occur when a reaction takes place under standard conditions are called the **standard enthalpy**, **standard entropy**, and **standard free energy** changes, respectively, and are symbolized by $\Delta H°$, $\Delta S°$, and $\Delta G°$. Note that standard conditions are not the same as the conditions for standard temperature and pressure (STP), which are 273 K and 1 atm and is used for gas law calculations.

ENTHALPY

The change in **enthalpy (ΔH)** of a process is equal to the heat absorbed or given off by the system at constant pressure. The enthalpy of a process depends only on the enthalpies of the initial and final states, *not* on the path. Thus, to find the enthalpy change of a reaction, ΔH_{rxn}, subtract the enthalpy of the reactants from the enthalpy of the products:

$$\Delta H_{rxn} = H_{products} - H_{reactants}$$

A positive ΔH corresponds to an endothermic process in which enthalpy is added to the system, and a negative ΔH corresponds to an exothermic process in which the system gives off enthalpy. Figure 32.1 shows the reaction coordinate diagrams for an exothermic reaction with $\Delta H_{rxn} < 0$ and an endothermic reaction with $\Delta H_{rxn} > 0$. Note that the transition state for each reaction gives an indirect path from starting to final state, but the overall enthalpy change is determined only by the beginning and ending enthalpy values.

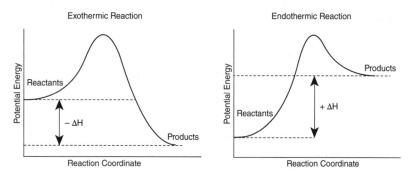

Figure 32.1

Several different enthalpy calculations can be done for reactions depending on the type of information provided: standard heats of formation, standard heats of reaction, or bond dissociation enthalpies.

STANDARD HEAT OF FORMATION

The enthalpy of formation of a compound, $\Delta H°_f$, is the enthalpy change that occurs if one mole of a compound is formed directly from its elements in their standard states. Note that the $\Delta H°_f$ of an element in its standard state is defined as zero, so the heat of formation of a compound gives its increase or decrease in enthalpy from zero.

For example, the $\Delta H°_f$ for water is the change in enthalpy when H_2 gas and O_2 gas are combined to form one mole of water vapor:

$$H_2\ (g) + \frac{1}{2}\ O_2\ (g) \rightarrow H_2O\ (g) \qquad \Delta H°_f = -241.8 \text{ kJ/mol}$$

Note that the equation must be balanced for one mole of the product because $\Delta H°_f$ is defined for one mole of a substance.

STANDARD HEAT OF REACTION

The standard heat of a reaction, $\Delta H°_{rxn}$, is the enthalpy change that occurs when the reaction is carried out under standard conditions (298 K, 1 atm, and 1 M concentrations). The equation for standard heat of reaction demonstrates the same concept as the reaction coordinate diagrams in Figure 32.1:

$\Delta H°_{rxn} = $ (sum of $\Delta H°_f$ of products) $-$ (sum of $\Delta H°_f$ of reactants)

Example: What is the $\Delta H°_{rxn}$ of CO_2 and H_2O combining to form glucose according to the following reaction ($\Delta H°_f$ for liquid water is -285.8 kJ/mole, $\Delta H°_f$ for CO_2 (g) is -393.5 kJ/mole, and the $\Delta H°_f$ for glucose is -1271 kJ/mole)?

$$6\ CO_2\ (g) + 6\ H_2O\ (l) \rightarrow C_6H_{12}O_6\ (s) + 6\ O_2\ (g)$$

Solution: The $\Delta H°_f$ for each compound in the reaction must be multiplied by its stoichiometric coefficient and then combined according to the equation:

$$\Delta H°_{rxn} = (\text{sum of } \Delta H°_f \text{ of products}) - (\text{sum of } \Delta H°_f \text{ of reactants})$$

$$\Delta H°_{rxn} = [(6 \ \Delta H°_f \text{ for CO}_2) + (6 \ \Delta H°_f \text{ for H}_2\text{O})] - [(\Delta H°_f \text{ for glucose}) + (6 \ \Delta H°_f \text{ for O}_2)]$$

$$\Delta H°_{rxn} = [6(-393.5) + 6(-285.8)] - (-1271 + 0)$$

$$\Delta H°_{rxn} = -2361 + -1714 + 1271 = -2{,}804 \text{ kJ/mole}$$

HESS'S LAW

Since enthalpy is a state function, the enthalpy of a reaction does not depend on the path taken but only on the initial and final states. Hess's Law states that enthalpies of reactions are additive; if a reaction is broken down into individual steps, the overall enthalpy of the reaction is the sum of enthalpies for each step.

Example: Given the following thermochemical equations, calculate ΔH_d:

a) $C_3H_8 \ (g) + 5 \ O_2 \ (g) \rightarrow 3 \ CO_2 \ (g) + 4 \ H_2O \ (l)$ $\Delta H_a = -2{,}220.1 \text{ kJ}$

b) $C \ (graphite) + O_2 \ (g) \rightarrow CO_2 \ (g)$ $\Delta H_b = -393.5 \text{ kJ}$

c) $H_2 \ (g) + \dfrac{1}{2} O_2 \ (g) \rightarrow H_2O \ (l)$ $\Delta H_c = -285.8 \text{ kJ}$

d) $3 \ C \ (graphite) + 4 \ H_2 \ (g) \rightarrow C_3H_8 \ (g)$ $\Delta H_d = \ ?$

Solution: Equations (a), (b), and (c) must be combined to obtain equation (d), similar to the combination of several algebraic equations. Since equation (d) contains only C, H_2, and C_3H_8, we must eliminate O_2, CO_2, and H_2O from the first three equations. Equation (a) is reversed to move C_3H_8 to the product side in order to match the net equation, giving equation (e). Because the direction of the equation is reversed, the sign of the ΔH for the reaction must also be reversed:

e) $3 \ CO_2 \ (g) + 4 \ H_2O \ (l) \rightarrow C_3H_8 \ (g) + 5 \ O_2 \ (g)$ $\Delta H_e = 2{,}220.1 \text{ kJ}$

Next, the other two equations must be multiplied by the appropriate integer to match the stoichiometric coefficients in the net equation. Equation (b) is multiplied by three, giving equation (f), and equation (c) is multiplied by four, giving equation (g). The ΔH values for each equation must also be multiplied by the same integer values. Finally, the three equations are added, terms on either side are cancelled to reach the net reaction, and the ΔH values are added to calculate the net ΔH_{rxn}.

f) $3 \ CO_2 \ (g) + 4 \ H_2O \ (l) \rightarrow C_3H_8 \ (g) + 5 \ O_2 \ (g)$ $\Delta H_e = 2{,}220.1 \text{ kJ}$

g) $3 \times [C \ (graphite) + O_2 \ (g) \rightarrow CO_2 \ (g)]$ $\Delta H_f = 3 \times -393.5 \text{ kJ}$

h) $4 \times [H_2 \ (g) + \dfrac{1}{2} O_2 \ (g) \rightarrow H_2O \ (l)]$ $\Delta H_g = 4 \times -285.8 \text{ kJ}$

$3 \ C \ (graphite) + 4 \ H_2 \ (g) \rightarrow C_3H_8 \ (g)$ $\Delta H_d = -103.6 \text{ kJ}$

where $\Delta H_d = \Delta H_e + \Delta H_f + \Delta H_g$.

BOND DISSOCIATION ENERGY

Heats of reaction can also be determined by the energy required for the breakdown and formation of chemical bonds. **Bond dissociation energy** is the energy required to break a specific chemical bond in one mole of gaseous molecules. Since it takes energy to pull two atoms apart, bond breaking is always endothermic and bond formation is always exothermic.

For example, the reaction below shows that a molecule of H_2 gas is cleaved to produce two gaseous, unassociated hydrogen atoms. For each mole of H_2 gas cleaved, 436 kJ of energy is required, and the reaction is therefore endothermic.

$$H_2 \ (g) \rightarrow 2 \ H \ (g) \qquad\qquad \Delta H = 436 \text{ kJ}$$

Bond energies can be used to calculate enthalpies of reactions. Using the convention that bond dissociation enthalpies are always positive, whether for bond breaking or bond formation, the enthalpy change of a reaction is given by:

$$\Delta H_{rxn} = (\Delta H \text{ of bonds broken}) - (\Delta H \text{ of bonds formed})$$
$$= \text{total energy input} - \text{total energy released}$$

Example: Calculate the enthalpy change for the following reaction:

$$C \ (graphite) + 2 \ H_2 \ (g) \rightarrow CH_4 \ (g) \qquad \Delta H = ?$$

The bond dissociation energies of H–H and C–H bonds are 436 kJ/mol and 415 kJ/mol, respectively. $\Delta H°_f$ of C $(g) = 715$ kJ/mol.

Solution: CH_4 is formed from free elements in their standard states (C as solid graphite and H_2 as a gas). The C–C bonds of C $(graphite)$ must be broken and thus form C (g), the H–H bonds of two molecules of H_2 (g) must be broken, and four C–H bonds must be formed to create CH_4 (g). Because all of the enthalpies are provided as bond dissociation energies, they are all positive; thus, bonds that are broken are added, and bonds that are formed are subtracted:

$$\Delta H_{rxn} = (\Delta H \text{ of bonds broken}) - (\Delta H \text{ of bonds formed})$$
$$\Delta H_{rxn} = [(\Delta H_{bond} \text{ for C–C}) + 2(\Delta H_{bond} \text{ for H–H})] - [4(\Delta H_{bond} \text{ for C–H})]$$
$$\Delta H_{rxn} = [715 + 2(436)] - [4(415)] = -73 \text{ kJ/mol}$$

HEATS OF COMBUSTION

One specific type of enthalpy of reaction is the standard heat of combustion, $\Delta H°_{comb}$. Combustion of hydrocarbons follows the general unbalanced reaction:

$$\text{Hydrocarbon} + O_2 \rightarrow CO_2 + H_2O$$

The reactions used in enthalpy calculations for C_3H_8 (g) are combustion reactions, and the corresponding values ΔH_a, ΔH_b, and ΔH_c are thus heats of combustion.

ENTROPY

Entropy (S) is a measure of the disorder, or randomness, of a system. The units of entropy are energy/temperature, commonly J/K or cal/K. The greater the order in a system, the lower the entropy; the greater the disorder or randomness, the higher the entropy.

At any given temperature, a solid will have lower entropy than a liquid, and a liquid will have lower entropy than a gas. Individual molecules in the gaseous state are moving randomly, whereas molecules in a liquid are less able to move freely, and molecules in a solid are constrained in place. Relative entropy changes accompanying phase changes can be estimated.

For example, freezing is accompanied by a decrease in entropy, as the relatively disordered liquid becomes a well-ordered solid. Meanwhile, boiling is accompanied by a large increase in entropy, as the liquid becomes a much more highly disordered gas. For any substance, sublimation will be the phase transition with the greatest entropy change.

Entropy is a state function, so a change in entropy depends only on the initial and final states:

$$\Delta S = S_{final} - S_{initial}$$

A standard entropy change for a reaction, ΔS°_{rxn}, is calculated using the standard entropies of reactants and products:

$$\Delta S^{\circ}_{rxn} = (\text{sum of } S^{\circ}_{products}) - (\text{sum of } S^{\circ}_{reactants})$$

The second law of thermodynamics states that all spontaneous processes proceed such that the entropy of the system plus its surroundings (i.e., the entropy of the universe) increases:

$$\Delta S_{universe} = \Delta S_{system} + \Delta S_{surroundings} > 0$$

However, it is possible for entropy to decrease in a localized part of the system, as long as there is an accompanying increase in entropy elsewhere in the system. For example, water can turn to ice inside a freezer, thus lowering the entropy of the water. However, the entropy of the air surrounding the freezer will increase as the heat pumped out the back of the freezer coils increases the randomness of movement of air molecules.

A system reaches its maximum entropy at **equilibrium**, a state in which no observable change takes place as time goes on. For a reversible process, $\Delta S_{universe}$ is zero:

$$\Delta S_{universe} = \Delta S_{system} + \Delta S_{surroundings} = 0$$

A system will spontaneously tend toward an equilibrium state if left alone.

GIBBS FREE ENERGY

Spontaneity of Reaction

The thermodynamic state function G, known as **Gibbs free energy,** combines the two factors that affect the spontaneity of a reaction: changes in enthalpy, ΔH; and changes in entropy, ΔS. The change in the free energy of a system, ΔG, represents the maximum amount of energy released (i.e., work done) by a process occurring at constant temperature and pressure. ΔG is defined by the equation:

$$\Delta G = \Delta H - T\Delta S$$

where T is the absolute temperature in kelvin.

In the equilibrium state, free energy is at a minimum. A process can occur spontaneously if the Gibbs function decreases (i.e., $\Delta G < 0$).

1. If ΔG is negative, the reaction is spontaneous and proceeds forward.

2. If ΔG is positive, the reaction is not spontaneous, and the reverse reaction occurs.

3. If ΔG is zero, the system is in a state of equilibrium; thus, $\Delta G = 0$ and $\Delta H = T\Delta S$.

It is important to note that the **rate** of a reaction depends on the **activation energy,** not on ΔG. Spontaneity indicates whether or not a reaction will occur but not the rate of the reaction. For example, conversion of C (*diamond*) to C (*graphite*) is spontaneous under standard conditions. However, its rate is so slow that the reaction is never practically observed.

Gibbs free energy provides information on how both enthalpy and entropy changes affect a reaction. Enthalpy and entropy may act together to drive a reaction forward or backward, or they may oppose each other. In the latter case, the temperature will determine whether entropy or enthalpy has a greater effect on the spontaneity of a reaction, and the reaction is considered to be **temperature-dependent**. The effects of the signs of ΔH and ΔS and the effect of temperature on spontaneity can be summarized as follows, keeping in mind that temperature is always positive because it is on the kelvin scale:

ΔH	ΔS	Outcome
$-$	$+$	spontaneous at all temperatures (temperature-independent)
$+$	$-$	nonspontaneous at all temperatures (temperature-independent)
$+$	$+$	spontaneous only at high temperatures (temperature-dependent)
$-$	$-$	spontaneous only at low temperatures (temperature-dependent)

STANDARD FREE ENERGY

Standard free energy, $\Delta G°$, is defined as the ΔG of a process occurring with reactants in their standard states at standard conditions: 25°C (298 K) and 1 atm pressure. Standard free energies are similar to standard enthalpies and are calculated by similar formulas. The standard free energy of formation of a compound, $\Delta G°_f$, is the free energy change that occurs when 1 mol of a compound in its standard state is formed from its elements in their standard states under standard conditions. The standard free energy of formation of any element in its most stable, standard state is defined as zero. The standard free energy of a reaction, $\Delta G°_{rxn}$, is the free energy change that occurs when that reaction is carried out under standard state conditions.

$$\Delta G°_{rxn} = (\text{sum of } \Delta G°_f \text{ of products}) - (\text{sum of } \Delta G°_f \text{ of reactants})$$

REACTION QUOTIENT

ΔG°_{rxn} can also be derived from the equilibrium constant using the equation:

$$\Delta G^{\circ} = -RT \ln K_{eq}$$

where K_{eq} is the equilibrium constant, R is the gas constant, and T is the temperature in kelvin. This equation demonstrates the relationship between the equilibrium constant and Gibbs free energy. If $K_{eq} > 1$, then $\ln K_{eq} > 0$ and $\Delta G^{\circ} < 0$; thus the reaction will proceed forward. If $K_{eq} < 1$, then $\ln K_{eq} < 0$ and $\Delta G^{\circ} > 0$; thus the reaction will proceed in reverse.

Once a reaction commences, however, the standard state conditions no longer hold. K_{eq} must be replaced by another parameter, the **reaction quotient** (Q). For the reaction $a\text{A} + b\text{B} \rightleftarrows c\text{C} + d\text{D}$,

$$Q = \frac{[\text{C}]^{c}\,[\text{D}]^{d}}{[\text{A}]^{a}\,[\text{B}]^{b}}$$

Likewise, ΔG must be used in place of ΔG°. The relationship between the two is as follows:

$$\Delta G = \Delta G^{\circ} + RT \ln Q$$

where R is the gas constant and T is the temperature in K. Keep in mind that since $\Delta G^{\circ} = -RT \ln K_{eq}$ it is opposite in sign to $RT \ln Q$ in this equation. If $Q < K_{eq}$, then $RT \ln Q$ is smaller in magnitude than ΔG° and ΔG is a negative quantity; thus, the reaction will proceed forward until $Q = K_{eq}$ and equilibrium is reached. If $Q > K_{eq}$, then $RT \ln Q$ is greater in magnitude than ΔG° and ΔG is a positive quantity; thus, the reaction will proceed in reverse until $Q = K_{eq}$ and equilibrium is reached.

EXAMPLES

Vaporization of water at one atmosphere pressure

$$\text{H}_2\text{O}\ (l) + \text{heat} \rightarrow \text{H}_2\text{O}\ (g)$$

When water boils, hydrogen bonds are broken (see Chapter 26, Chemical Bonding). Energy is absorbed, so the reaction is endothermic, and ΔH is positive. Entropy increases as the closely packed molecules of the liquid become the more randomly moving molecules of a gas; thus, $T\Delta S$ is also positive. Since ΔH and $T\Delta S$ are each positive, the reaction will proceed spontaneously only if $T\Delta S > \Delta H$ such that $\Delta G < 0$. This is true only at temperatures above 373 K (100°C). Below 373 K, ΔG is positive, and the water remains a liquid. At 373 K, $\Delta H = T\Delta S$ and $\Delta G = 0$, so an equilibrium is established between water and water vapor. The opposite is true when water vapor condenses. H-bonds are formed, and energy is released; the reaction is exothermic, so ΔH is negative. Entropy decreases, since a liquid is forming from a gas and $T\Delta S$ is negative. Condensation will be spontaneous only if $\Delta H < T\Delta S$. This is the case at temperatures below 373 K. Above 373 K, $T\Delta S$ is more negative than ΔH, ΔG is positive, and condensation is not spontaneous.

The combustion of C_6H_6 (benzene)

$$2\ \text{C}_6\text{H}_6\ (l) + 15\ \text{O}_2\ (g) \rightarrow 12\ \text{CO}_2\ (g) + 6\ \text{H}_2\text{O}\ (g) + \text{heat}$$

In this reaction, heat is released, and thus ΔH is negative as the benzene combusts. The entropy is increased ($T\Delta S$ is positive) because two gases (18 moles total) have greater entropy than a gas and a liquid (15 moles gas and 2 liquid). Overall, ΔG is negative, and the reaction is spontaneous.

REVIEW PROBLEMS

1. A process involving no heat exchange is known as

    A.   isothermal.
    B.   isobaric.
    C.   adiabatic.
    D.   isometric.
    E.   isochoric.

2. What is the heat capacity of a 10.0 g sample that has absorbed 100 calories over a temperature change of 30.0°C?

    A.   0.333 cal/(g·°C)
    B.   0.667 cal/(g·°C)
    C.   3.00 cal/(g·°C)
    D.   67 cal/(g·°C)
    E.   300 cal/(g·°C)

3. What is the enthalpy of formation of N (g) in the following reaction?

    $$N_2\ (g) \rightarrow 2\ N\ (g) \qquad\qquad \Delta H_{rxn} = 945.2\ kJ$$

    A.   −945.2 kJ/mol
    B.   −472.6 kJ/mol
    C.   0.0 kJ/mol
    D.   472.6 kJ/mol
    E.   945.2 kJ/mol

4. A 50 g sample of metal was heated to 100°C and then dropped into a beaker containing 50 g of water at 25°C. If the specific heat capacity of the metal is 0.25 cal/(g·°C), what is the final temperature of the water?

    A.   27°C
    B.   40°C
    C.   50°C
    D.   60°C
    E.   86°C

5. What is the maximum amount of work than can be done by the following reaction at 30°C if $\Delta H = -125$ kJ and $\Delta S = -200$ J/K?

    A.   64.4 kJ
    B.   119 kJ
    C.   2,250 kJ
    D.   5,880 kJ
    E.   60,500 kJ

SOLUTIONS TO REVIEW PROBLEMS

1. **C** Discussed at the beginning of this chapter.

2. **A** In calorimetry, the amount of heat absorbed in a given process is calculated using the equation $q = mc\Delta T$. Knowing that the heat absorbed is 100 cal, the mass is 10 g, and the temperature change is 30°C, you can calculate the specific heat capacity as follows:

$$q = mc\Delta T$$
$$100 \text{ cal} = 10(c)(30)$$
$$c = 0.333 \text{ cal/(g°·C)}$$

3. **D** This problem requires the equation:

$$\Delta H_{rxn} = \Delta H_{products} - \Delta H_{reactants}$$

The equation for the enthalpy of formation of N is:

$$945.2 \text{ kJ} = 2(\Delta H_N) - (\Delta H_{N_2})$$

The ΔH of N_2 is 0 kJ because the heat of formation of any element in its elemental state is zero. Use that to solve for the enthalpy of formation of N:

$$\Delta H_N = \frac{945.2 \text{ kJ}}{2 \text{ mol}} = 472.6 \text{ kJ/mol}$$

4. **B** This problem uses the concept of conservation of energy. When the metal is put in the water, the metal will lose heat, which is transferred to the water. The amount of heat released by the metal is the same as the amount of heat absorbed by the water. The equation for heat transfer, $q = mc\Delta T$, can be used to show that the expressions for the heat released and absorbed by the metal and water, respectively, are:

$$q_m = 50(0.25)(x - 100)$$
$$q_w = 50(1.0)(x - 25)$$

Since heat is lost by the metal, it has a negative value $(-q_m)$; therefore, we can set $-q_m = q_w$, and these equations can be combined to solve for x:

$$-50(0.25)(x - 100) = 50(1.0)(x - 25)$$
$$-(0.25)(x - 100) = (1.0)(x - 25)$$
$$25 - 0.25x = x - 25$$
$$1.25x = 50$$
$$x = 40°C$$

5. **A** The maximum amount of work that can be done by a spontaneous reaction is the absolute value of its Gibbs free energy change, which can be calculated according to $\Delta G = \Delta H - T\Delta S$. Substituting the values from the question (being sure to use units consistently) gives:

$$\Delta G = -125 - (30 + 273)(-0.2)$$
$$\Delta G = -125 - (303)(-0.2)$$
$$\Delta G = -125 + 60.6 = -64.4 \text{ kJ}$$

CHAPTER THIRTY-THREE

Chemical Equilibria

Often, reactions are discussed under the assumption that they are **irreversible** (i.e., only proceed in one direction) and that they proceed to completion. However, a **reversible** reaction often does not proceed to completion because (by definition) the products can react to reform the reactants. This is particularly true of reactions occurring in closed systems, where products are not allowed to escape. When there is no **net** change in the concentrations of the products and reactants during a reversible chemical reaction, equilibrium exists. This is not to say that a reaction in equilibrium is static; change continues to occur in both the forward and reverse directions. Equilibrium can be thought of as a balance between the two reaction directions.

Consider the following reaction:

$$A \rightleftharpoons B$$

At equilibrium, the concentrations of A and B are constant, yet the reactions $A \rightarrow B$ and $B \rightarrow A$ continue to occur at equal rates.

LAW OF MASS ACTION

Consider the following **one-step** reaction:

$$2A \rightleftharpoons B + C$$

Since the reaction occurs in one step, the rates of the forward (rate$_f$) and reverse (rate$_r$) reactions are given by:

$$\text{rate}_f = k_f[A]^2 \text{ and rate}_r = k_r[B][C]$$

When rate$_f$ = rate$_r$, equilibrium is achieved. Since the rates are equal, it can be stated that

$$k_f[A]^2 = k_r[B][C] \text{ or } \frac{k_f}{k_r} = \frac{[B][C]}{[A]^2}$$

Since k_f and k_r are both constants, this equation may be rewritten as:

$$K_c = \frac{[B][C]}{[A]^2}$$

where K_c is called the **equilibrium constant**, and the subscript c indicates that it is in terms of concentration. When dealing with gases the equilibrium constant is referred to as K_p, and the subscript p indicates that it is in terms of partial pressure. For dilute solutions, K_c and K_{eq} are used interchangeably; the symbol K is also often used, though it is not completely correct to do so.

While the forward and reverse reaction rates are equal at equilibrium, the **molar concentrations** of the reactants and products usually are not equal. This means that the forward and reverse rate constants, k_f and k_r, respectively, are also usually unequal. For the one-step reaction described above:

$$k_f [A]^2 = k_r [B][C]$$

$$k_f = k_r \left(\frac{[B][C]}{[A]^2} \right)$$

In a reaction of more than one step, the equilibrium constant for the overall reaction is found by multiplying together the equilibrium constants for each step of the reaction. When this is done, the equilibrium constant for the overall reaction is equal to the concentrations of products divided by reactants in the overall reaction, each raised to its stoichiometric coefficient. The forward and reverse rate constants for any step n are designated k_n and k_{-n} respectively. For example, if the reaction

$$aA + bB \rightleftharpoons cC + dD$$

occurs in three steps, then

$$K_{eq} = \frac{k_1 k_2 k_3}{k_{-1} k_{-2} k_{-3}} \text{ will equal } \frac{[C]^c [D]^d}{[A]^a [B]^b}$$

This expression is known as the **law of mass action**.

Example: What is the expression for the equilibrium constant for the following reaction?

$$3 H_2 (g) + N_2 (g) \rightleftharpoons 2 NH_3 (g)$$

Solution:

$$K_{eq} = \frac{[NH_3]^2}{[H_2]^3 [N_2]}$$

PROPERTIES OF THE EQUILIBRIUM CONSTANT

The equilibrium constant, K_{eq}, has the following characteristics:

- Pure solids and liquids do not appear in the equilibrium constant expression.
- K_{eq} is characteristic of a given system at a given temperature.
- If the value of K_{eq} is much larger than 1, an equilibrium mixture of reactants and products will contain very little of the reactants compared to the products.
- If the value of K_{eq} is much smaller than 1 (i.e., less than 0.1), an equilibrium mixture of reactants and products will contain very little of the products compared to the reactants.
- If the value of K_{eq} is close to 1, an equilibrium mixture of products and reactants will contain approximately equal amounts of reactants and products.

LE CHÂTELIER'S PRINCIPLE

The French chemist Henry Louis Le Châtelier indicated that, if an external stress is applied to a system currently at equilibrium, the system will attempt to adjust itself to partially offset the stress. This rule, known as Le Châtelier's principle, is used to determine the direction in which a reaction at equilibrium will proceed when subjected to a stress, such as a change in concentration, pressure, temperature, or volume.

Changes in Concentration

Increasing the concentration of a species will tend to shift the equilibrium in the direction that will reestablish the equilibrium concentration of the species that is added, and decreasing its concentration will shift the equilibrium in the opposite direction. For example, in the reaction:

$$A + B \rightleftharpoons C + D$$

if the concentration of A and/or B is increased, the equilibrium will shift toward (or favor production of) C and D. Conversely, if the concentration of C and/or D is increased, the equilibrium will shift away from the production of C and D, favoring production of A and B. Similarly, decreasing the concentration of a species will tend to shift the equilibrium toward the production of that species. For example, if A and/or B is removed from the above reaction, the equilibrium will shift so as to favor increasing the concentrations of A and B.

This effect is often used in industry to increase the yield of a useful product or drive a reaction to completion. If D were constantly removed from the above reaction, the net reaction would produce more D and concurrently more C. Likewise, using an excess of the least expensive reactant helps to drive the reaction forward.

Change in Pressure or Volume

In a system at constant temperature, a change in pressure causes a change in volume, and vice versa. Since liquids and solids are practically incompressible, a change in the pressure or volume of systems involving only these phases has little or no effect on their equilibrium. Reactions involving gases, however, may be greatly affected by changes in pressure or volume; since gases are highly compressible, changing the volume of a container effectively changes the concentration of the gases it contains.

Pressure and volume are inversely related. An increase in the pressure of a system will shift the equilibrium so as to decrease the number of moles of gas present. This reduces the volume of the system and relieves the stress of the increased pressure. Consider the following reaction:

$$N_2\,(g) + 3\,H_2\,(g) \rightleftharpoons 2\,NH_3\,(g)$$

The left side of the reaction has four moles of gaseous molecules, whereas the right side has only two moles. When the pressure of this system is increased, the equilibrium will shift so that the side of the reaction producing fewer moles is favored. Since there are fewer moles on the right, the equilibrium will shift toward the right. Conversely, if the volume of the same system is increased, its pressure immediately decreases, which, according to Le Châtelier's principle, leads to a shift in the equilibrium to the left.

Change in Temperature

Changes in temperature also affect equilibrium. To predict this effect, heat may be considered as a product in an exothermic ($\Delta H < 0$) reaction and as a reactant in an endothermic reaction ($\Delta H > 0$). Consider the following exothermic reaction:

$$A \rightleftharpoons B + heat$$

If this system were placed in an ice bath, its temperature would decrease, driving the reaction to the right to replace the heat lost. Conversely, if the system were placed in a boiling-water bath, the reaction equilibrium would shift to the left due to the increased "concentration" of heat.

Not only does a temperature change alter the position of the equilibrium, it also alters the numerical value of the equilibrium constant. In contrast, changes in the concentration of a species in the reaction, in the pressure, or in the volume alter the position of the reaction quotient without changing the numerical value of the equilibrium constant itself.

SOLUTION EQUILIBRIA

The process of solvation, like other reversible chemical and physical changes, tends toward equilibrium. Immediately after a solute has been introduced into a solvent, most of the change taking place is dissociation because no dissolved solute is initially present. However, according to Le Châtelier's principle, as solute dissociates, the reverse reaction (precipitation of the solute) also begins to occur. Eventually, equilibrium is reached and the rate of solute dissociation is equal to the rate of precipitation. At equilibrium, the net concentration of the dissociated solute remains unchanged regardless of the amount of solute added.

An ionic solid introduced into a polar solvent dissociates into its component ions. The dissociation of such a solute in solution may be represented by:

$$A_m B_n\,(s) \rightleftharpoons mA\,(aq) + nB\,(aq)$$

For example: $$CaCl_2\,(s) \rightleftharpoons Ca^{2+}\,(aq) + 2\,Cl^-\,(aq)$$

The Solubility Product Constant

A slightly soluble ionic solid exists in equilibrium with its saturated solution. In the case of AgCl, for example, the solution equilibrium is as follows:

$$AgCl \ (s) \rightleftarrows Ag^+ \ (aq) + Cl^- \ (aq)$$

The **ion product (Q_{sp})** of a compound in solution is defined as follows:

$$Q_{sp} = [A]^m[B]^n$$

The same expression for a saturated solution at equilibrium defines the **solubility product constant (K_{sp}).**

$$K_{sp} = [A]^m[B]^n \text{ in a saturated solution}$$

However, Q_{sp} is defined with respect to initial concentrations and does not necessarily represent either an equilibrium or a saturated solution, while K_{sp} does.

Each salt has its own distinct K_{sp} at a given temperature. If at a given temperature a salt's Q_{sp} is equal to its K_{sp}, the solution is saturated, and the rate at which the salt dissolves equals the rate at which it precipitates out of solution. If a salt's Q_{sp} exceeds its K_{sp}, the solution is supersaturated (holding more salt than it should be able to at a given temperature) and unstable. If the supersaturated solution is disturbed by adding more salt, other solid particles, or jarring the solution by a sudden decrease in temperature, the solid salt will precipitate until Q_{sp} equals the K_{sp}. If Q_{sp} is less than K_{sp}, the solution is unsaturated and no precipitate will form.

Example: The solubility of $Fe(OH)_3$ in an aqueous solution was determined to be 4.5×10^{-10} mol/L. What is the value of the K_{sp} for $Fe(OH)_3$?

Solution: The molar solubility (the solubility of the compound in mol/L) is given as 4.5×10^{-10} M. The equilibrium concentration of each ion can be determined from the molar solubility and the balanced dissociation reaction of $Fe(OH)_3$. The dissociation reaction is:

$$Fe(OH)_3 \ (s) \rightleftarrows Fe^{3+} \ (aq) + 3 \ OH^- \ (aq)$$

Thus, for every mole of $Fe(OH)_3$ that dissociates, one mole of Fe^{3+} and three moles of OH^- are produced. Since the solubility is 4.5×10^{-10} M, the K_{sp} can be determined as follows:

$$K_{sp} = [Fe^{3+}][OH^-]^3$$

$$[OH^-] = 3[Fe^{3+}]; \quad [Fe^{3+}] = 4.5 \times 10^{-10} \, M$$

$$K_{sp} = [Fe^{3+}](3[Fe^{3+}])^3 = 27[Fe^{3+}]^4$$

$$K_{sp} = 27(4.5 \times 10^{-10})^4 = 27(410 \times 10^{-40}) = 11{,}070 \times 10^{-40}$$

$$K_{sp} = 1.1 \times 10^{-36}$$

Example: What are the concentrations of each of the ions in a saturated solution of $PbBr_2$, given that the K_{sp} of $PbBr_2$ is 2.1×10^{-6}? If 5 g of $PbBr_2$ are dissolved in water to make 1 L of solution at 25°C, would the solution be saturated, unsaturated, or supersaturated?

Solution: The first step is to write out the dissociation reaction:

$$PbBr_2 \ (s) \rightleftarrows Pb^{2+} \ (aq) + 2 \ Br^- \ (aq)$$

$$K_{sp} = [Pb^{2+}][Br^-]^2$$

If x equals the concentration of Pb^{2+}, then $2x$ equals the concentration of Br^- in the saturated solution at equilibrium (since $[Br^-]$ is twice as large as $[Pb^{2+}]$).

$$K_{sp} = [x][2x]^2 = 4x^3$$

$$2.1 \times 10^{-6} = 4x^3$$

Solving for x, the concentration of Pb^{2+} in a saturated solution is 8.07×10^{-3} M, and the concentration of Br^- ($2x$) is 1.61×10^{-2} M.

To solve the second part of the question, convert 5 g of $PbBr_2$ into moles:

$$5 \ g \times \frac{1 \ mol \ PbBr_2}{367 \ g} = 1.36 \times 10^{-2} \ mol$$

1.36×10^{-2} mol of $PbBr_2$ is dissolved in 1 L of solution, so the concentration of the solution is 1.36×10^{-2} M. Since this is higher than the concentration of a saturated solution of $PbBr_2$ (8.07×10^{-3} M), this solution would be supersaturated.

Factors Affecting Solubility

The quantity of a salt that can be dissolved is considerably reduced when it is dissolved in a solution that already contains one of its ions rather than in a pure solvent. This reduction in solubility, called the **common ion effect,** is another example of Le Châtelier's principle. The common ion effect will not change K_{sp}, but it will change the molar solubility (the concentrations of the individual ions, or x, in the solution).

Example: The K_{sp} of AgI in aqueous solution is 1×10^{-16} mol/L. If a 1×10^{-5} M solution of $AgNO_3$ is saturated with AgI, what will be the final concentration of the iodide ion?

Solution: The concentration of Ag^+ in the original $AgNO_3$ solution will be 1×10^{-5} mol/L. After AgI is added to saturation, the iodide concentration can be found with the K_{sp} equation:

$$AgI \ (s) \rightleftarrows Ag^+ \ (aq) + I^- \ (aq)$$

$$K_{sp} = [Ag^+][I^-]$$

$$1 \times 10^{-16} = [Ag^+][I^-]$$

$$1 \times 10^{-16} = [1 \times 10^{-5}][I^-]$$

$$[I^-] = 1 \times 10^{-11} \ mol/L$$

If the AgI had been dissolved in pure water, the concentration of both Ag^+ and I^- would have been 1×10^{-8} mol/L. The presence of the common ion, Ag^+, at a concentration 1,000 times higher than what it would be in a solution of just water and silver iodide has reduced the iodide concentration to one-thousandth of what it would have been otherwise. An additional 1×10^{-11} mol/L of silver will dissolve in solution along with the iodide ion, but this will not significantly affect the final silver concentration, which is one million times greater.

REVIEW PROBLEMS

1. The equilibrium constant, K_{eq}, of a certain single-reactant reaction is 0.16. Suppose an appropriate catalyst is added in twice the concentration of the reactant.

   A. What will be the equilibrium constant?
   B. Will the activation energy increase or decrease?

2. At equilibrium

   A. the forward reaction will continue.
   B. a change in reaction conditions will shift the equilibrium.
   C. the reverse reaction will not continue.
   D. the forward reaction will not continue.
   E. both A and B will occur.

3. What is the general equation for K_{eq} for the following reaction?

$$2\ NO_2\ (g) + 2\ H_2\ (g) \rightleftharpoons N_2\ (g) + 2\ H_2O\ (g)$$

4. If $K_{eq} > 1$,

   A. the equilibrium mixture will contain more product than reactant.
   B. the equilibrium mixture will contain more reactant than product.
   C. the equilibrium amounts of reactants and products are equal.
   D. the reaction is irreversible.
   E. the reaction will not occur spontaneously.

5. Answer the following questions using the reaction given below.

$$CH_3OH\ (l) + H_2\ (g) \rightleftharpoons CH_4\ (g) + H_2O\ (l) \qquad \Delta H = -30\ \text{kcal}$$

   A. In which direction would the reaction be shifted if the temperature were increased?
   B. In which direction would the reaction be shifted if the volume were doubled?
   C. In which direction would the reaction be shifted if methane (CH_4) were removed from the reaction vessel?

6. What is the concentration of the Ag^+ ion in a saturated solution of AgCl? (K_{sp} for AgCl = 1.7×10^{-10})

$$AgCl\ (s) \rightleftharpoons Ag^+\ (aq) + Cl^-\ (aq)$$

   A. $1.7 \times 10^{-10}\,M$
   B. $3.4 \times 10^{-10}\,M$
   C. $1.3 \times 10^{-5}\,M$
   D. $2.6 \times 10^{-5}\,M$
   E. $5.8 \times 10^{-4}\,M$

7. Explain the common ion effect in terms of K_{sp}.

SOLUTIONS TO REVIEW PROBLEMS

1. **A** K_{eq} remains constant at 0.16. Catalysts do not affect equilibrium position.

    B Addition of a catalyst decreases the activation energy.

2. **E** At equilibrium, both the forward and reverse reactions are proceeding. Any change in the equilibrium conditions will shift the equilibrium to alleviate the stress on the reaction.

3. $$K_{eq} = \frac{[N_2][H_2O]^2}{[NO_2]^2[H_2]^2}$$

    K_{eq} can also be written in terms of partial pressures as:

    $$K_{eq} = \frac{\left(P_{N_2} \times P_{H_2O}^2\right)}{\left(P_{NO_2}^2 \times P_{H_2}^2\right)}$$

4. **A** Discussed in the section on the equilibrium constant in this chapter.

5. **A** The reaction shifts to the left. This is an exothermic reaction, as seen by the negative ΔH, and any increase in temperature will favor the reverse reaction.

    B The reaction will remain unchanged. Changing the volume constraints on a reaction that involves gases will affect the equilibrium only when one side of the reaction has a greater number of moles of gas than the other.

    C The reaction would shift to the right. By removing methane gas from the reaction vessel, the reactant concentrations are effectively increased relative to the product concentrations, and the reaction will go to the right to correct for this.

6. **C** $K_{sp} = [Ag^+][Cl^-]$

    Let $x = [Ag^+]$

    Since $[Ag^+] = [Cl^-]$: $1.7 \times 10^{-10} = x^2$

    $x = 1.3 \times 10^{-5}$ M

7. Consider as an example a dilute solution of AgCl. The K_{sp} of AgCl at 25°C is 1.7×10^{-10}. If the original concentration of AgCl is 1×10^{-6} M, then $Q_{sp} = (1 \times 10^{-6})^2 = 1 \times 10^{-12}$, which is less than the K_{sp}; thus, all the salt is dissolved.

    Now suppose NaCl is added to this solution until the NaCl concentration is 1×10^{-2}. $[Cl^-]$ will now be the sum of $[Cl^-]$ due to AgCl and $[Cl^-]$ due to NaCl; $[Cl^-] = 1 \times 10^{-2} + 1 \times 10^{-6} = 1.0001 \times 10^{-2}$, or approximately 1×10^{-2}.

    Thus, the Q_{sp} for AgCl is $(1 \times 10^{-6})(1 \times 10^{-2}) = 1 \times 10^{-8}$, which is greater than the K_{sp}. AgCl will therefore precipitate until Q_{sp} is reduced to the K_{sp}. Because of the high concentration of Cl^-, the final concentration of Ag^+ will be lower than it would have been otherwise.

CHAPTER THIRTY-FOUR

Liquids and Solids

Matter can exist in three different physical forms called **phases** or **states**: gas, liquid, and solid. The primary difference between the three phases is how tightly the constituent pieces are held together. When the attractive forces between gaseous molecules overcome the kinetic energy that keeps them apart, the molecules move closer together such that they can no longer move about freely, entering the **liquid** or **solid** phase. Because of their smaller volume relative to gases, liquids and solids are also referred to as **condensed phases**.

The table below contrasts the general properties of each phase.

Phase	Volume and Shape	Motion Principles	Density	Ability to be Compressed
Gas	Conforms to the volume and shape of the container it is in	Continual motion	Low	Easily compressed to smaller volume
Liquid	Conforms to the shape of the container; however, has definite volume	Sliding motion of particles past one another	Moderate	Small ability to be compressed (considered incompressible on the exam)
Solid	Defined volume and shape	Particles in a fixed position	High	Difficult to compress (considered incompressible on the exam)

Table 34.1

GASES

Gases display similar behavior and follow similar laws regardless of their identity. The atoms or molecules in a gaseous sample move rapidly and are far apart from each other. In addition, only very weak intermolecular forces exist between gas particles; this results in certain characteristic physical properties, such as the ability to expand to fill any volume, to take on the shape of a container, and to flow as fluids. Furthermore, gases are easily, though not infinitely, compressible. This chapter will mainly focus on principles of liquids and solids, but gases will be discussed more in Chapter 35, Gases.

LIQUIDS

In a liquid, atoms or molecules are held close together with little space between them. As a result, liquids have definite volumes and cannot easily be expanded or compressed. However, the molecules can still move around and are in a state of relative disorder. Consequently, the liquid can change shape to fit its container, and its molecules are able to **diffuse** and **evaporate**.

One of the most important properties of liquids is their ability to mix, both with each other and with other phases, to form **solutions** (see Chapter 28, Solutions). The degree to which two liquids can mix is called their **miscibility**. Oil and water are almost completely **immiscible**; that is, their molecules tend to repel each other due to their polarity difference. Oil and water normally form separate layers when mixed, with oil on top because it is less dense. Under extreme conditions, such as violent shaking, two immiscible liquids can form a fairly homogeneous mixture called an **emulsion**. Although they look like solutions, emulsions are actually mixtures of discrete particles too small to be seen distinctly.

SOLIDS

In a solid, the attractive forces between atoms, ions, or molecules are strong enough to hold them rigidly together. Thus, the particles' only motion is vibration about fixed positions, and the kinetic energy of solids is predominantly **vibrational energy**. As a result, solids have definite shapes and volumes.

A solid may be **crystalline** or **amorphous**. A crystalline solid, such as NaCl, possesses an ordered structure; its atoms exist in a specific, three-dimensional geometric arrangement with repeating patterns of atoms, ions, or molecules. An amorphous solid, such as glass, has no ordered three-dimensional arrangement, although the molecules are also fixed in place.

Most solids are crystalline in structure. The two most common forms of crystals are **metallic** and **ionic** crystals.

Ionic solids are aggregates of positively and negatively charged ions; there are no discrete molecules. The physical properties of ionic solids include high melting points, high boiling points, and poor electrical conductivity in the solid phase. These properties are due to the compounds' strong electrostatic interactions, which also cause the ions to be relatively immobile. Ionic structures are given by empirical formulas that describe the ratio of atoms in the lowest possible whole numbers. For example, the empirical formula $BaCl_2$ gives the ratio of barium to chloride within the crystal.

Metallic solids consist of metal atoms packed together as closely as possible. Metallic solids have high melting and boiling points as a result of their strong covalent attractions. Pure metallic structures (consisting of a single element) are usually described as layers of spheres of roughly similar radii.

Crystals (both ionic and metallic) are defined by their **unit cells**, which represent the smallest repeating units that compose the larger crystalline structure. Although there are many types of unit cells, the cubic unit cells are the most important: **simple cubic**, **body-centered cubic**, and **face-centered cubic**.

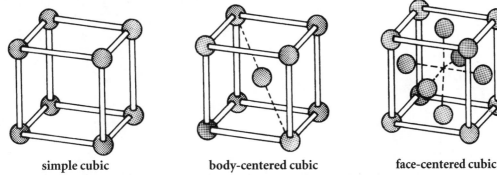

| simple cubic | body-centered cubic | face-centered cubic |

Figure 34.1

Each point in a unit cell diagram represents the exact same atom or ion. Additional atoms or ions of other elements may also be present, but these are not included in the unit cell diagram. For example, the ions of cesium chloride (CsCl) arrange in simple cubic units such that each of the eight corners of the cube are occupied by Cl^- ions. The center of the cube is occupied by one Cs^+ ion (creating a final structure similar to the body-centered cubic diagram), but the Cs^+ ion is not represented in the simple cubic diagram since Cs^+ is not the same ion as the corners, which are Cl^-.

ENERGY OF PHASE CHANGES

Phase changes between solids, liquids, and gases involve the exchange of heat. First, the substance's temperature must reach the correct temperature for the phase change to occur. Then, heat must be transferred to or from the material in order for it to go through a phase change. Units of heat are either the calorie (cal) or the joule (J); one calorie is equal to 4.184 J.

Specific Heat

The heat Q gained or lost by a substance when the temperature of that substance is changed by T is given by:

$$Q = mc\Delta T = mc(T_f - T_i)$$

where m is the mass of the object and c is a constant called the specific heat. The specific heat is defined as the amount of heat required to raise a unit mass of a substance 1 K or 1°C and depends solely on the material of the object. For water, specific heat is often given as $c = 1 \text{ cal·g}^{-1}\text{·K}^{-1} = 1 \text{ cal·g}^{-1}\text{·}°\text{C}^{-1} = 4.184 \text{ J·g}^{-1}\text{·K}^{-1}$. Figure 34.3 shows the heating curve for water; the formula $Q = mc\Delta T$ applies to the angled portions of the curve.

Figure 34.2

Heat of Transformation

The $Q = mc\Delta T$ applies only when there is no conversion between gas, liquid or solid phases. During a phase change the temperature of the substance remains constant and the heat gained or lost is related to the amount of material that changes phase. The amount of heat needed to change the phase of 1 kg of a substance is the latent heat of transformation H_L. The total amount of heat gained or lost by a substance during a phase change is given by:

$$Q = mH_L$$

where Q is the heat gained or lost, m is the mass of the substance, and H_L is the latent heat of transformation of the substance.

The phase change from liquid to solid, or solid to liquid, occurs at the melting-point temperature. The corresponding heat of transformation is often referred to as the heat of fusion and is written as ΔH_f. On the other hand, the phase change from liquid to gas, or gas to liquid, occurs at the boiling-point temperature. Here the heat of transformation is often referred to as the heat of vaporization and is written as ΔH_v. In Figure 34.3 the flat portions of the curve represent the phase changes, with no change in temperature occurring as water changes from either solid to liquid or liquid to gas.

Example: How much heat must be added to bring 20 g of ice at 0°C to water vapor at 100°C? (The heat of fusion of ice is 80 cal/g. The heat of vaporization of water is 540 cal/g.)

Solution: The different parts of the heating curve must be calculated separately. Start with melting the ice at 0°C:

$$Q_{melting} = mH_f = 20g \times 80 \text{ cal/g} = 1{,}600 \text{ cal}$$

Next, calculate the heat needed to raise the water temperature from 0°C to 100°C:

$Q = mc\Delta T = 20 \text{ g} \times 1 \text{ cal·g}^{-1}\cdot{}^{\circ}\text{C}^{-1} \times (100 - 0{}^{\circ}\text{C}) = 2{,}000 \text{ cal}$

Now calculate the heat needed to turn the water from liquid to vapor:

$Q_{vaporization} = mH_v = 20 \text{ g} \times 540 \text{ cal/g} = 10{,}800 \text{ cal}$

Finally, add together the three quantities from the three sections of the heating curve:

$Q_{total} = 1{,}600 + 2{,}000 + 10{,}800 = 14{,}400 \text{ cal}$

PHASE EQUILIBRIA

In an isolated system, phase changes (solid to liquid to gas) are reversible, and an equilibrium exists between phases. For example, at 1 atm and 0°C in an isolated system, an ice cube floating in water is in equilibrium. Some of the ice may absorb heat and melt, but an equal amount of water will release heat and freeze. Thus, the relative amounts of ice and water remain constant.

Gas-Liquid Equilibrium

The temperature of a liquid is related to the average kinetic energy of the liquid molecules; however, the kinetic energy of the molecules will vary. A few molecules near the surface of the liquid may have enough energy to leave the liquid phase and escape into the gaseous phase. This process is known as **evaporation** or **vaporization**. Each time the liquid loses a high-energy particle, the temperature of the remaining liquid decreases; thus, evaporation is a cooling process. Nevertheless, given enough kinetic energy, the liquid will completely evaporate.

If a cover is placed on a beaker of liquid, the escaping molecules are trapped above the solution. These molecules exert a countering pressure, which forces some of the gas back into the liquid phase; this process is called **condensation**. Atmospheric pressure acts on a liquid in a similar fashion as a solid lid. As evaporation and condensation proceed, an equilibrium is reached in which the rates of the two processes become equal. Once this equilibrium is reached, the pressure that the gas exerts over the liquid is called the **vapor pressure** of the liquid. Vapor pressure increases as temperature increases, since more molecules have sufficient kinetic energy to escape into the gas phase. The temperature at which the vapor pressure of the liquid equals the external pressure is called the **boiling point**.

Liquid-Solid Equilibrium

The liquid and solid phases can also coexist in equilibrium (e.g., the ice water mixture discussed above). Even though the atoms or molecules of a solid are confined to definite locations, each atom or molecule can undergo motions about some equilibrium position. These motions (vibrations) increase when heat is applied. If atoms or molecules in the solid phase absorb enough energy in this fashion, the solid's three-dimensional structure breaks down, and the liquid phase begins. The transition from solid to liquid is called **fusion** or **melting**. The reverse process, from liquid to solid, is called **solidification**, **crystallization**, or **freezing**. The temperature at which these processes occur is called the **melting point** or **freezing point**, depending on the direction of the transition. Whereas pure crystals have distinct melting points, amorphous solids, such as glass, tend to melt over a larger range of temperatures due to their less-ordered molecular distribution.

Gas-Solid Equilibrium

A third type of phase equilibrium is that between a gas and a solid. When a solid goes directly into the gas phase, the process is called **sublimation**. Dry ice (solid CO_2) sublimes at room temperature, becoming CO_2 (g); the absence of the liquid phase makes it a convenient refrigerant. The reverse transition, from the gaseous to the solid phase, is called **deposition**.

The Gibbs Function

The thermodynamic criterion for each of the above equilibria is that the change in Gibbs free energy must equal zero, meaning no net energy is required for or released from the forward or reverse reaction. For an equilibrium between a gas and a solid:

$$\Delta G = G\,(g) - G\,(s)$$

$$\text{so } G\,(g) = G\,(s) \text{ at equilibrium}$$

The same is true of the Gibbs functions for the other two equilibria.

PHASE DIAGRAMS

Single Component

A standard **phase diagram** depicts the phases and phase equilibria of a substance at defined temperatures and pressures. In general, the gas phase is found at high temperature and low pressure; the solid phase is found at low temperature and high pressure; and the liquid phase is found at high temperature and high pressure. A typical phase diagram is shown below:

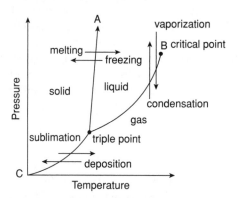

Figure 34.3

The three phases are demarcated by lines indicating the temperatures and pressures at which two phases are in equilibrium. Line A represents freezing/melting, line B vaporization/condensation, and line C sublimation/deposition. The intersection of the three lines is called the **triple point**. At this temperature and pressure, unique for a given substance, all three phases are in equilibrium. The point at B is known as the **critical point**, the temperature and pressure above which the liquid and gas phases are not possible and supercritical fluids exist instead.

Multiple Components

The phase diagram for a mixture of two or more components is complicated by the requirement that the composition of the mixture, as well as the temperature and pressure, must be specified. Consider a solution of two liquids, A and B. The vapor above the solution is a mixture of the vapors of A and B. The pressures exerted by vapor A and vapor B on the solution are the vapor pressures that each exerts above its individual liquid phase. **Raoult's law** (described below) enables one to determine the relationship between the vapor pressure of vapor A and the concentration of liquid A in the solution.

COLLIGATIVE PROPERTIES

Colligative properties are physical properties derived solely from the number of particles present, not the nature of those particles. These properties are usually associated with dilute solutions.

Freezing-Point Depression

Pure water (H_2O) freezes at 0°C; however, for every mole of solute particles dissolved in 1 L of water, the freezing point is lowered by 1.86°C. This is because the solute particles interfere with the process of crystal formation that occurs during freezing; the solute particles lower the temperature at which the molecules can align themselves into a crystalline structure.

The formula for calculating this freezing-point depression is:

$$\Delta T_f = iK_f m$$

where ΔT_f is the freezing-point depression, K_f is a proportionality constant characteristic of a particular solvent, m is the molality of the solution (mol solute/kg solvent), and i is the van't Hoff factor, which accounts for the number of particles that dissociate from the original molecule. For example, NaCl dissociates into two ions in water, Na^+ and Cl^-, so its $i = 2$ to represent that 1 mol NaCl becomes 2 mol solute particles.

One of the best examples of this principle is when salt is sprinkled on roads to make ice melt. This thawing occurs because the salt depresses the freezing point of the water.

Boiling-Point Elevation

A liquid boils when its vapor pressure equals the atmospheric pressure. If the vapor pressure of a solution is lower than that of the pure solvent, more energy (and consequently a higher temperature) will be required before its vapor pressure equals atmospheric pressure. The extent to which the boiling point of a solution is raised relative to that of the pure solvent is given by the following formula:

$$\Delta T_b = iK_b m$$

where ΔT_b is the boiling-point elevation, K_b is a proportionality constant characteristic of a particular solvent, m is the molality of the solution, and i is the van't Hoff factor.

One commonly misunderstood example of this principle is the addition of salt (NaCl) to a boiling pot of water on the stove, such as before cooking pasta, supposedly to speed cooking by raising the temperature of the water. Although adding Na^+ and Cl^- ions does increase the boiling point, the molality of salt normally added only results in an increase in boiling point of approximately 0.1°C (in fact, the main values of adding salt are to decrease sticking and add flavor).

Osmotic Pressure

Consider a container separated into two compartments by a semipermeable membrane (which, by definition, selectively permits the passage of only certain molecules). One compartment contains pure water, while the other contains water with dissolved solute. The membrane allows water but not solute to pass through. Because substances tend to flow, or **diffuse**, from higher to lower concentrations (which increases entropy), water will diffuse from the compartment containing pure water to the compartment containing the water-solute mixture. This net flow will cause the water level in the compartment containing the solution to rise above the level in the compartment containing pure water.

However, the pressure exerted by the water level in the solute-containing compartment due to gravity will eventually oppose the influx of water due to diffusion, and the water will stop flowing once this point is reached. This pressure is defined as the **osmotic pressure** (Π) of the solution and is given by the formula:

$$\Pi = iMRT$$

where M is the molarity of the solution, R is the ideal gas constant, T is the temperature on the kelvin scale, and i is the van't Hoff factor. This equation shows that molarity and osmotic pressure are directly proportional (i.e., as the concentration of the solution increases, the osmotic pressure also increases). Thus, the osmotic pressure depends only on the amount of solute, not its identity.

Vapor-Pressure Lowering (Raoult's Law)

When solute B is added to pure solvent A, the vapor pressure of A above the solvent decreases. If the vapor pressure of A above pure solvent A is designated by P°_A and the vapor pressure of A above the solution containing B is P_A, the vapor pressure decreases as follows:

$$\Delta P = P^\circ_A - P_A$$

In the late 1800s, the French chemist François Marie Raoult determined that this vapor pressure decrease is also equivalent to:

$$\Delta P = X_B P^\circ_A$$

where X_B is the mole fraction of the solute B in solvent A (mol B/total moles). Because $X_B = 1 - X_A$ and $\Delta P = P^\circ_A - P_A$, substitution into the above equation leads to the common form of Raoult's law:

$$P_A = X_A P^\circ_A$$

Similarly, the expression for the vapor pressure of the solute in solution (assuming it is volatile) is given by:

$$P_B = X_B P^\circ_B$$

Raoult's law holds only when the attraction between molecules of the different components of the mixture is equal to the attraction between the molecules of any one component in its pure state. When this condition does not hold, the relationship between mole fraction and vapor pressure will deviate from Raoult's law. Solutions that obey Raoult's law are called **ideal solutions**.

REVIEW PROBLEMS

1. Which of the following indicates the relative randomness of molecules in the three states of matter?

   A. solid > liquid > gas
   B. liquid < solid < gas
   C. liquid > gas > solid
   D. gas > liquid > solid
   E. gas < solid < liquid

2. What factor determines whether or not two liquids are miscible?

   A. Molecular size
   B. Molecular polarity
   C. Density
   D. Both B and C
   E. Both A and C

3. Discuss the physical properties of ionic crystals.

4. Alloys are mixtures of pure metals in either the liquid or solid phase. Which of the following is usually true of alloys?

   A. The melting/freezing point of an alloy will be lower than that of either of the component metals because the new bonds are stronger.
   B. The melting/freezing point of an alloy will be lower than that of either of the component metals because the new bonds are weaker.
   C. The melting/freezing point of an alloy will be greater than that of either of the component metals because the new bonds are weaker.
   D. The melting/freezing point of an alloy will be greater than that of either of the component metals because the new bonds are stronger.
   E. None of the above.

Refer to the phase diagram below for questions 5–8.

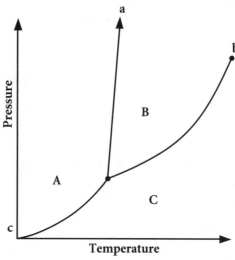

5. What is the typical form of a substance in state B?

    A. Pure crystalline solid

    B. Amorphous solid

    C. Gas

    D. Liquid

    E. Supercooled liquid

6. What is the typical form of a substance in state C?

    A. Pure crystalline solid

    B. Amorphous solid

    C. Gas

    D. Liquid

    E. Supercooled liquid

7. If line a was instead a band covering a range of temperatures, what would state A be?

    A. Pure crystalline solid

    B. Amorphous solid

    C. Gas

    D. Liquid

    E. Supercooled liquid

8. What is the triple point?

9. A semipermeable membrane separates a container of fresh water from one of salt water. If the volume of fresh water decreases significantly, what must be true of the semipermeable membrane? Assume that evaporation is negligible.

10. Once equilibrium is reached, if the temperature in Question 9 is suddenly increased, the osmotic pressure

    A. will decrease.
    B. will increase.
    C. will remain the same.
    D. will decrease and then increase.
    E. cannot be determined.

11. What is the freezing point of a solution containing 0.5 mol of glucose dissolved in 200 g of H_2O? (The K_f for water is 1.86°C·m^{-1}.)

12. The osmotic pressure at STP of a solution in which 1 L of solution contains 117 g of NaCl is

    A. 44.8 atm.
    B. 48.9 atm.
    C. 89.54 atm.
    D. 97.7 atm.
    E. 117 atm.

13. At 18°C and 1 atm, the vapor pressure of pure water is 0.02 atm, and the vapor pressure of pure ethyl alcohol (MW = 46 g/mol) is 0.50 atm. For a water-alcohol mixture with the alcohol present in a mole fraction of 0.2, find the vapor pressure due to the alcohol and the vapor pressure due to the water.

SOLUTIONS TO REVIEW PROBLEMS

1. **D** Because gas molecules have the greatest freedom to move around, gases have the greatest disorder. Liquids are denser than gases, and therefore the molecules are less free to move around. The arrangement of molecules in solids is the least random. Thus, melting and boiling are accompanied by an increase in entropy (i.e., $\Delta S > 0$).

2. **B** The miscibility of two liquids strongly depends on their polarities. In general, polar and nonpolar liquids are not miscible, while a polar liquid can usually be mixed with another polar liquid and a nonpolar liquid with another nonpolar liquid. Choice (A), molecular size, and choice (C), the density of a liquid, do not directly affect the miscibility. However, (C) should remind you that two immiscible liquids will form separate layers, with the denser liquid on the bottom. Thus, (B) is the only correct choice.

3. Ionic crystals contain repeating units of cations and anions. Because of the strong electrostatic attraction between the ions, these crystals have high melting points. Since the charges in these crystals are tightly fixed in the lattice, ionic solids are poor conductors of electricity. In the liquid or solution phase, the charged particles can move around, and thus liquid ionic compounds will conduct electricity, as will solutions of such salts.

4. **B** The bonds between different metal atoms in an alloy are much weaker than those between the atoms in pure metals. Therefore, breaking these bonds requires less energy than breaking the bonds in pure metals. Since melting and freezing points are inversely proportional to the stability of bonds, they tend to be lower for alloys than for pure metals. Alternately, an alloy can be looked at as a solid solution; adding impurities is similar to adding solutes in that it results in melting point depression.

5. **D** Discussed in the section on phase diagrams in this chapter.

6. **C** Discussed in the section on phase diagrams in this chapter.

7. **B** Discussed in the section on phase diagrams in this chapter.

8. The unique combination of temperature and pressure at which the solid, liquid, and gas phases coexist at equilibrium.

9. The membrane must be permeable to water but not to salt. If it were permeable to salt, the salt would diffuse across the membrane into the fresh water container (down its concentration gradient) until the molarities of the two containers were the same. However, the volume of the salt water container increased, indicating that fresh water diffused across the membrane from a region of low solute concentration to one of high solute concentration. The water level rose until it exerted enough pressure to counterbalance the tendency to diffuse; this pressure is known as the osmotic pressure.

10. **B** Using the formula $\Pi = iMRT$, we see that osmotic pressure and temperature are directly proportional (i.e., if temperature increases, osmotic pressure will also increase). Thus, (B) is the correct answer.

11.   **−4.65°C**

This question applies the concept of freezing-point depression. If 0.5 mol of a nonelectrolyte solute such as glucose is dissolved in 200 g of H_2O, then the molality of the solution is:

$$\frac{0.5\,\text{mol}}{0.200\,\text{kg}\,H_2O} = 2.5 \text{ mol solute/kg } H_2O = 2.5 \text{ m}$$

Using the equation $\Delta T_f = iK_f m$, the freezing point depression is $1 \times 2.5 \text{ m} \times 1.86°\text{C}\cdot\text{m}^{-1} = 4.65°\text{C}$ ($i = 1$ for glucose because it does not dissociate in solution). The new freezing point is $0°\text{C} - 4.65°\text{C} = -4.65°\text{C}$. Note that ΔT_f is the change in freezing point and not the freezing point itself.

12. **C**   The osmotic pressure (Π) of a solution is given by $\Pi = iMRT$. At STP, $T = 273$ K; R, the ideal gas constant, equals 8.2×10^{-2} L·atm/(K·mol). To determine the molarity, find the formula weight of NaCl from the periodic table; FW = 58.5 g/mol. The number of moles in the solution described is:

$$\frac{117\,\text{g/L}}{58.5\,\text{g/mol}} = 2 \text{ mol undissociated} = \text{NaCl/L}$$

But since NaCl is a strong electrolyte, it dissociates in aqueous solution into two particles, so i is 2, and there are actually four moles of particles per liter of solution (two moles of Na^+ and two moles of Cl^-). Thus:

$$\Pi = (2)(2 \text{ mol/L})(8.2 \times 10^{-2} \text{ L·atm/(K·mol)})(273 \text{ K})$$
$$= 89.54 \text{ atm}$$

Remember that colligative properties depend on the number of particles, not their identity.

13.   Use Raoult's law to answer this question, with $A = H_2O$ and $B = $ ethyl alcohol.

$$P_A = X_A P°_A$$
$$P_B = X_B P°_B$$

Because we are given that $X_B = 0.2$, then $X_A = 1 - X_B = 1 - 0.2 = 0.8$.

$$P°_A = 0.02 \text{ atm}$$
$$P°_B = 0.50 \text{ atm}$$
$$P_A = (0.8)(0.02 \text{ atm}) = 0.016 \text{ atm}$$
$$P_B = (0.2)(0.50 \text{ atm}) = 0.10 \text{ atm}$$

Thus, the vapor pressure due to water is 0.016 atm, and the vapor pressure due to alcohol is 0.10 atm.

CHAPTER THIRTY-FIVE

Gases

Gases, as defined in Chapter 34, Liquids and Solids, are unique in that their molecules have very weak intermolecular forces, allowing gases both to flow and to change volume to fill and take the shape of their containers. The state of a gaseous sample is generally defined by four variables: **pressure (P), volume (V), temperature (T)**, and **number of moles (n)**. Pressure describes force per area, such as the force per area an enclosed gas exerts on the walls of its container. The SI unit of pressure is the pascal (Pa), but pressure is also often expressed in units of atmospheres (atm) or millimeters of mercury (mm Hg or torr), which are related as follows:

$$1 \text{ atm} = 10^5 \text{ Pa} = 760 \text{ mm Hg} = 760 \text{ Torr}$$

Volume is generally expressed in liters (L) or milliliters (mL). The temperature of a gas is usually given in Kelvin (K, not °K). Gases are also often discussed in terms of **standard temperature and pressure (STP)**, which refers to conditions of 273.15 K (0°C) and 1 atm. It is important not to confuse STP with **standard conditions**—the two standards involve different temperatures and are used for different purposes. STP (0°C or 273 K) is generally used for gas law calculations; standard conditions (25°C or 298 K) are used when measuring standard enthalpy, entropy, Gibbs free energy, or voltage.

IDEAL GASES

When examining the behavior of gases under varying conditions of temperature and pressure, scientists speak of ideal gases. An ideal gas represents a hypothetical gas whose molecules have no intermolecular forces and occupy no volume. Although gases actually deviate from this idealized behavior, under conditions of relatively low pressure (i.e., atmospheric pressure) and high temperature, many gases behave in a nearly ideal fashion. Therefore, the assumptions used for ideal gases can be applied to real gases with reasonable accuracy.

Boyle's Law

Experimental studies performed by Robert Boyle in 1660 led to the formulation of Boyle's law. His work showed that, for a given gaseous sample held at a constant temperature (isothermal conditions), the product of pressure and volume is constant: $PV = k$. Another way to think about this mathematical relationship is that pressure and volume are inversely proportional.

It is important to note that the individual values of pressure and volume can vary greatly for a given sample of gas. However, as long as the temperature remains constant and the amount of gas does not change, the product of both P and V will equal the same constant (k). Subsequently, for a given sample of gas under two sets of conditions, the following equation can be derived:

$$P_1V_1 = k_1 = P_2V_2 \quad \text{or simply} \quad P_1V_1 = P_2V_2$$

where k is a proportionality constant and the subscripts 1 and 2 represent two different sets of conditions. A plot of pressure versus volume for a gas is shown below.

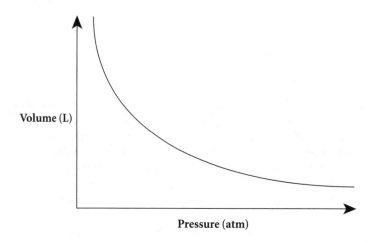

Figure 35.1

Example: Under isothermal conditions, what would be the volume of a 1 L sample of helium after its pressure is changed from 12 atm to 4 atm?

Solution:

$$P_1 = 12 \text{ atm} \qquad P_2 = 4 \text{ atm}$$
$$V_1 = 1 \text{ L} \qquad V_2 = \text{?}$$

$$P_1V_1 = P_2V_2$$

$$12 \text{ atm} (1 \text{ L}) = 4 \text{ atm}(V_2)$$

$$\frac{12 \text{ atm}}{4 \text{ atm}} \times 1 \text{ L} = V_2$$

$$V_2 = 3 \text{ L}$$

Charles's Law

The law of volumes, also known as Charles's law, was developed at the turn of the 19th century. The law states that, at constant pressure, the quotient of the volume and temperature of gas is constant. Or, put another way, the volume of a gas is directly proportional to its absolute temperature

$$\frac{V}{T} = k \quad \text{or} \quad \frac{V_1}{T_1} = \frac{V_2}{T_2}$$

where k is a constant and the subscripts 1 and 2 represent two different sets of conditions. The absolute temperature (T) is the temperature expressed in kelvins, which can be calculated from the expression $T_K = T_{°C} + 273.15$. It is important to note that the temperature $-273.15°C$ is the theoretical lowest attainable temperature, known as **absolute zero**. Below is a summary to help understand this principle:

absolute zero	0 K	−273.15°C
water freezes	273.15 K	0°C
water boils	373.15 K	100°C

A plot of temperature versus volume is shown below.

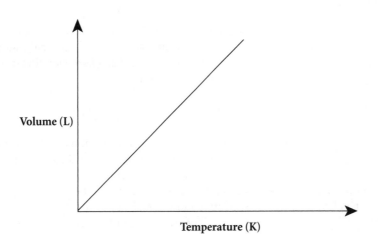

Figure 35.2

Example: If the absolute temperature of 2 L of gas at constant pressure is changed from 283.15 K to 566.30 K, what would be the final volume?

Solution:

$$T_1 = 283.15 \text{ K} \qquad V_1 = 2 \text{ L}$$
$$T_2 = 566.30 \text{ K} \qquad V_2 = ?$$

$$\frac{V_1}{T_1} = \frac{V_2}{T_2}$$

$$\frac{2 \text{ L}}{283.15 \text{ K}} = \frac{V_2}{566.30 \text{ K}}$$

$$V_2 = \frac{2 \text{ L} (566.30 \text{ K})}{283.15 \text{ K}}$$

$$V_2 = 4 \text{ L}$$

Avogadro's Principle

In 1811, Amedeo Avogadro proposed that, for all gases at a constant temperature and pressure, the volume of the gas will be directly proportional to the number of moles of gas present; therefore, all gases have the same number of moles in the same volume.

$$\frac{n}{V} = k \quad \text{or} \quad \frac{n_1}{V_1} = \frac{n_2}{V_2}$$

The subscripts 1 and 2 once again apply to two different sets of conditions with the same temperature and pressure.

Ideal Gas Law

A theoretical gas whose volume-pressure-temperature behavior can be completely understood by the ideal gas equation is known as an "ideal gas." The ideal gas law combines the relationships outlined in Boyle's law, Charles's law, and Avogadro's principle to yield an expression that can be used to predict the behavior of a gas and is represented by the equation

$$PV = nRT$$

The constant R is known as the **gas constant**. Under STP conditions (273.15 K and 1 atmosphere), one mole of ideal gas has a volume of 22.4 L. Substituting these values into the ideal gas equation gives $R = 8.21 \times 10^{-2}$ L·atm/(mol·K). The gas constant may also be expressed in many other units; another common value is 8.314 J/(K·mol), which is derived when the SI units of pascals (for pressure) and cubic meters (for volume) are substituted into the ideal gas law. When carrying out calculations based on the ideal gas law, it is important to choose a value of R that matches the units of the variables.

Example: What volume would 12 g of helium occupy at 20°C and a pressure of 380 mm Hg?

Solution: The ideal gas law can be used, but first all the variables must be converted to yield units that correspond to the expression of the gas constant as 0.0821 L·atm/(mol·K):

$$P = 380 \, \text{mm Hg} \times \frac{1 \, \text{atm}}{760 \, \text{mm Hg}} = 0.5 \, \text{atm}$$

$$T = 20°C + 273.15 = 293.15 \, \text{K}$$

$$n = 12 \, \text{g He} \times \frac{1 \, \text{mol He}}{4.0 \, \text{g}} = 3 \, \text{mol He}$$

Substituting into the ideal gas equation:

$$PV = nRT$$

$$(0.5 \, \text{atm})(V) = (3 \, \text{mol})(0.0821 \, \text{L} \cdot \text{atm/(mol} \cdot \text{K})) (293.15 \, \text{K})$$

$$V = 144.4 \, \text{L}$$

Sometimes, it is advantageous to compare gases under different conditions. To do this quickly, divide the ideal gas law from one condition by another condition:

$$\frac{P_1 V_1}{P_2 V_2} = \frac{n_1 R T_1}{n_2 R T_2}$$

One great advantage of this approach is that the ideal gas constant (R) cancels out, leaving:

$$\frac{P_1 V_1}{P_2 V_2} = \frac{n_1 T_1}{n_2 T_2}$$

And from this point, some straightforward algebra can find pressure, volume, moles, or temperature under either condition. Removing R from the equation can certainly help with mental math, but not all ideal gas questions compare gases under two separate conditions. However, by remembering that 1 mole of gas at STP (1 atm and 273.15K) occupies 22.4 L, one can use the comparative ideal gas equation and still remove the ideal gas constant from the solution (as long as all the units align!):

$$\frac{PV}{P_{STP}V_{STP}} = \frac{nT}{n_{STP}T_{STP}}$$

Using the above simplification as a guide, let's go through the previous example again:

Example: What volume would 12 g of helium occupy at 20°C and a pressure of 380 mm Hg?

Solution: Convert the given information on mass, temperature, and pressure to units that match the STP information (mol, atm, K, and L):

12 g of He is 3 mol

20°C is 293.15 K

380 mm Hg is 0.5 atm

Then, rearrange the simplification to solve for V and plug in the values given:

$$\frac{PV}{P_{STP}V_{STP}} = \frac{nT}{n_{STP}T_{STP}}$$

$$V = \frac{V_{STP}P_{STP}nT}{Pn_{STP}T_{STP}} = (22.4\ \text{L})\left(\frac{1\ \text{atm}}{0.5\ \text{atm}}\right)\left(\frac{3\ \text{mol}}{1\ \text{mol}}\right)\left(\frac{293.15\ \text{K}}{273.15\ \text{K}}\right)$$

$$= (22.4\ \text{L})\left(\frac{3}{0.5}\right)\left(\frac{293.15\ \text{K}}{273.15\ \text{K}}\right) \approx (22\ \text{L})(6)(1.1)$$

$$V = 145\ \text{L (actual volume} = 144.4\ \text{L)}$$

Density

In addition to standard calculations to determine the pressure, volume, or temperature of a gas, the ideal gas law may also be used to determine the **density** and **molar mass** of a gas. Density is defined as the mass per unit volume (m/V) of a substance and, for gases, is usually expressed in units of g/L. By rearrangement, the ideal gas equation can be used to calculate the density of a gas:

$$PV = nRT$$

where:

$$n = \frac{m}{MM} \frac{\text{(mass in g)}}{\text{(molar mass)}}$$

therefore:

$$PV = \frac{m}{MM} RT$$

and:

$$\frac{P(MM)}{RT} = \frac{m}{V} = d$$

Another way to find the density of a gas is to start with the volume of a mole of gas at STP, 22.4 L, calculate the effect of pressure and temperature on the volume, and finally calculate the density by dividing the mass by the new volume.

Example: What is the density of HCl gas at 2 atm and 45°C? (The molar mass of H is 1 g/mol and Cl is 35.5 g/mol).

Solution: At STP, a mole of gas occupies 22.4 liters. Since the increase in pressure to 2 atm decreases volume, 22.4 L must be multiplied by $\left(\frac{1\,\text{atm}}{2\,\text{atm}}\right)$. Since the increase in temperature increases volume, the temperature factor will be $\left(\frac{318\,\text{K}}{273\,\text{K}}\right)$. Given the molar mass information in the question, the mass of 1 mol of HCl is 36.5 g. Plugging that into the ideal gas law comparing different conditions gives the following:

$$V = \frac{V_{STP} P_{STP} nT}{Pn_{STP} T_{STP}} = (22.4\,\text{L})\left(\frac{1\,\text{atm}}{2\,\text{atm}}\right)\left(\frac{1\,\text{mol}}{1\,\text{mol}}\right)\left(\frac{318\,\text{K}}{273\,\text{K}}\right) = (22\,\text{L})\left(\frac{1}{2}\right)(1.2) = 13\,\text{L}$$

$$d = \left(\frac{36.5\,\text{g}}{13\,\text{L}}\right) = 2.8\,\text{g/L} \quad \text{(actual value is 2.77 g/L)}$$

Molar mass

Sometimes the identity of a gas is unknown, and the molar mass must be determined to identify it. Using the concept of density, the molar mass of a gas can be determined experimentally using the ideal gas law.

Example: What is the molar mass of an 8 g sample of gas that occupies 2 L at a temperature of 15°C and a pressure of 1.5 atm?

Solution: The mass of the gas (8 g) and therefore the moles of gas are constant regardless of the volume, temperature, or pressure. To find the molar mass (g/mol), calculate how many moles (mol) of gas are present in the 2 L sample at 15°C and 1.5 atm:

$$\frac{PV}{P_{STP}V_{STP}} = \frac{nT}{n_{STP}T_{STP}}$$

$$n = n_{STP}\frac{PVT_{STP}}{P_{STP}V_{STP}T} = (1\ \text{mol})\left(\frac{1.5\ \text{atm}}{1\ \text{atm}}\right)\left(\frac{2\ \text{L}}{22.4\ \text{L}}\right)\left(\frac{273.15\ \text{K}}{288.15\ \text{K}}\right)$$

$$= \left(\frac{3}{22.4}\right)\left(\frac{273.15\ \text{K}}{288.15\ \text{K}}\right) \approx \left(\frac{6}{45}\right)(0.95)$$

$$n = \frac{6}{45} = \frac{2}{15}\ \text{mol}$$

Therefore, the molar mass of the unknown substance is:

$$MM = \left(\frac{m}{n}\right) = \left(\frac{8}{2/15}\right) = \frac{8 \times 15}{2} = 4 \times 15$$

$$MM = 60\ \text{g/mol (actual value} = 63.1\ \text{g/mol)}$$

REAL GASES

In general, the ideal gas law is a good approximation of the behavior of real gases, but all real gases deviate from ideal gas behavior to some extent, particularly when the gas atoms or molecules are forced into close proximity under high pressure and at low temperature so that molecular volume and intermolecular attractions become significant.

Deviations Due to Pressure

As the pressure of a gas increases, the particles are pushed closer and closer together. As the condensation pressure for a given temperature is approached, intermolecular attraction forces become more and more significant until the gas condenses into the liquid state (see Gas-Liquid Equilibrium in Chapter 34).

At moderately high pressure (a few hundred atm) the volume of a gas is less than would be predicted by the ideal gas law; this is due to intermolecular attraction. At extremely high pressure the size of the particles becomes relatively large compared to the distance between them, and this causes the gas to take up a larger volume than would be predicted by the ideal gas law.

Deviations Due to Temperature

As the temperature of a gas is decreased, the average velocity of the gas molecules decreases and the attractive intermolecular forces become increasingly significant. As the condensation temperature (which is the same as the boiling point) is approached for a given pressure, intermolecular attractions eventually cause the gas to condense to a liquid state, and the increasing intermolecular attractions cause the gas to have a smaller volume than would be predicted by the ideal gas law. The closer the temperature of a gas is to its boiling point, the less ideal is its behavior.

DALTON'S LAW OF PARTIAL PRESSURES

When two or more gases are found in one vessel without chemical interaction, each gas will behave independently of the other(s). Therefore, the pressure exerted by each gas in the mixture will be equal to the pressure that gas would exert if it were the only one in the container. The pressure exerted by each individual gas is called the **partial pressure** of that gas. In 1801, John Dalton derived an expression, now known as Dalton's law of partial pressures, which states that the total pressure of a gaseous mixture is equal to the sum of the partial pressures of the individual components. The equation is:

$$P_T = P_A + P_B + P_C + \cdots$$

The partial pressure of a gas is related to its mole fraction and can be determined using the following equations:

$$P_A = P_T X_A$$

$$X_A = \frac{n_A \text{ (moles of A)}}{n_T \text{ (total moles)}}$$

Example: A vessel contains 0.75 mol of nitrogen, 0.20 mol of hydrogen, and 0.05 mol of fluorine at a total pressure of 2.5 atm. What is the partial pressure of each gas?

Solution: First, calculate the mole fraction of each gas.

$$X_{N_2} = \frac{0.75 \text{ mol}}{1.0 \text{ mol}} = 0.75 \qquad X_{H_2} = \frac{0.20 \text{ mol}}{1.0 \text{ mol}} = 0.20 \qquad X_{F_2} = \frac{0.05 \text{ mol}}{1.0 \text{ mol}} = 0.05$$

Then, calculate the partial pressures.

$$P_A = X_A P_T$$

$$P_{N_2} = (0.75)(2.5 \text{ atm}) \qquad P_{H_2} = (0.20)(2.5 \text{ atm}) \qquad P_{F_2} = (0.05)(2.5 \text{ atm})$$
$$= 1.875 \text{ atm} \qquad\qquad = 0.5 \text{ atm} \qquad\qquad = 0.125 \text{ atm}$$

KINETIC MOLECULAR THEORY OF GASES

As indicated by the gas laws, all gases show similar physical characteristics and behavior. A theoretical model to explain the behavior of gases was developed during the second half of the 19th century. The combined efforts of Boltzmann, Maxwell, and others led to a simple explanation of gaseous molecular behavior based on the motion of individual molecules. This model is called the kinetic molecular theory of gases. Like the gas laws, this theory was developed in reference to ideal gases, but it can be applied with reasonable accuracy to real gases as well.

Assumptions of the Kinetic Molecular Theory

- Gases are made up of particles whose volumes are negligible compared to the container volume.
- Gas atoms or molecules are inert and exhibit no intermolecular attractions or repulsions.

- Gas particles are in continuous, random motion, undergoing collisions with other particles and the container walls.
- Collisions between any two gas particles are elastic, meaning that there is no overall gain or loss of energy.
- The average kinetic energy of gas particles is proportional to the absolute temperature of the gas and is the same for all gases at a given temperature.

Applications of the Kinetic Molecular Theory of Gases

Average molecular speeds

According to the kinetic molecular theory of gases, the average kinetic energy (and therefore average velocity) of a gas particle is proportional to the absolute temperature of the gas:

$$K = \frac{1}{2}mv^2 = \frac{3}{2}kT$$

where k is the Boltzmann constant. However, because of the large number of rapidly and randomly moving gas particles, the speed of an individual gas molecule is nearly impossible to define. Instead, it is the average speed of all the gas particles that can be related exactly to the temperature. Some particles will be moving at higher speeds and some at lower speeds.

A **Maxwell-Boltzmann distribution curve** shows the distribution of speeds of gas particles at a given temperature. The curve below shows a distribution curve of molecular speeds at two temperatures, T_1 and T_2, where $T_2 > T_1$. Notice that the bell-shaped curve flattens and shifts to the right as the temperature increases, indicating that, at higher temperatures, more molecules are moving at high speeds.

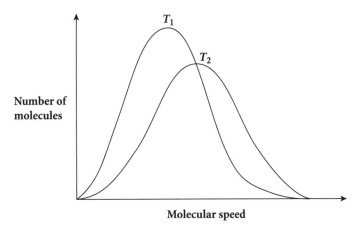

Figure 35.3

Graham's law of diffusion and effusion

Diffusion of gases can provide a demonstration of random motion when the molecules of these gases mix with one another by virtue of their individual kinetic properties. Diffusion occurs when gas molecules move through a mixture. Diffusion accounts for the fact that an open bottle of perfume can quickly be smelled across a room. The kinetic molecular theory of gases predicts that heavier gas molecules diffuse more slowly than lighter ones because of their differing average speeds. In 1832,

Thomas Graham showed mathematically that, under isothermal and isobaric conditions, the rates at which two gases diffuse are inversely proportional to the square root of their molar masses. Thus:

$$\frac{r_1}{r_2} = \left(\frac{MM_2}{MM_1}\right)^{\frac{1}{2}} = \sqrt{\frac{MM_2}{MM_1}}$$

where r_1 and MM_1 represent the diffusion rate and molar mass of gas 1, respectively, and r_2 and MM_2 represent the diffusion rate and molar mass of gas 2.

Effusion is the flow of gas particles under pressure from one compartment to another through a small opening. Graham used the kinetic molecular theory of gases to show that for two gases at the same temperature, the rates of effusion are proportional to the average speeds. He then expressed the rates of effusion in terms of molar mass and found that the relationship is the same as that for diffusion.

REVIEW PROBLEMS

1. Boyle's law can be used for which of the following?

    A. Predicting the expected volumes of two party balloons
    B. Predicting the relative pressures inside a hot air balloon
    C. Predicting the change in volume of an inflatable toy from summer to winter
    D. Predicting the change in volume of a party balloon inside a bell jar as a vacuum is being drawn
    E. Predicting the change in pressure inside a hot air balloon as it rises into cooler air

2. The word *kinetic* appears in the kinetic molecular theory of gases because

    A. the properties of a gas are dependent primarily on the motion of its component particles.
    B. gases only possess kinetic energy in closed systems.
    C. gases possess more kinetic than potential energy.
    D. collisions in real gases do not dissipate kinetic energy.
    E. potential energy depends upon kinetic energy.

3. A sample of argon occupies 50 L at standard temperature. Assuming constant pressure, what volume will the gas occupy if the temperature is doubled?

    A. 25 L
    B. 50 L
    C. 100 L
    D. 200 L
    E. 250 mL

4. What is the molecular weight of an unknown gas if 2.5 g of it occupies 2 L at 630 torr and a temperature of 600 K?

5. Explain the conditions under which real gases follow ideal gas behavior.

6. If a 360 mL sample of helium contains 0.25 mol of the gas, how many molecules of chlorine gas would occupy the same volume at the same temperature and pressure?

    A. 1.51×10^{23}
    B. 3.01×10^{23}
    C. 6.022×10^{23}
    D. 1.2×10^{24}
    E. 2.4×10^{24}

7. In the kinetic molecular theory of gases, the speed of molecules is most often discussed in terms of the average speed. Which of the following statements concerning average speeds is true?

    A. Most of the molecules are moving faster than the average speed, but a few outliers skew the average.

    B. The average speed is independent of pressure and volume in a closed system.

    C. When the temperature increases, more of the molecules will move at the new average speed.

    D. When the temperature increases, fewer molecules will move at the new average speed.

    E. The average speed is independent of temperature in a closed system.

8. What is the density of a gas at 76.0 torr and 37.0°C (MM = 25.0 g/mol)?

    A. 0.098 g/L

    B. 0.800 g/L

    C. 22.4 g/L

    D. 75.0 g/L

    E. 107 g/L

9. The following reaction represents the production of hydrogen chloride gas:

$$H_2 + Cl_2 \rightarrow 2\,HCl$$

How many grams of chlorine gas are needed to produce 3 L of HCl gas at a pressure of 2 atm and a temperature of 19°C?

10. Dalton's law of partial pressures says that the total pressure of all the gases in a system

    A. is less than the sum of the partial pressures of the gases.

    B. is more than the sum of the partial pressures of the gases.

    C. is equal to the sum of the partial pressures of the gases.

    D. is not related to the partial pressures of the gases.

    E. is equal to the product of the partial pressures of the gases.

11. A student performing an experiment has a bulb containing 14 g of N_2, 64 g of O_2, 8 g of He, and 35 g of Cl_2 at a total pressure of 380 torr. What are the partial pressures of each gas?

12. A 1.74 g sample of gas is found to occupy 1 L at 10°C and 2 atm. What is the molar mass of the gas?

13. All of the following assumptions underlie the kinetic molecular theory of gases EXCEPT that:

    A. gas molecules have no intermolecular forces.

    B. gas particles are in random motion.

    C. the collisions between gas particles are elastic.

    D. the average kinetic energy is directly proportional to the number of moles present of a gas.

    E. gas particles have a volume negligible compared to that of their container.

14. What will be the final pressure of a gas that expands from 1 L at 10°C to 10 L at 100°C if the original pressure was 3 atm?

15. In the reaction $N_2 + 2\,O_2 \rightarrow 2\,NO_2$, what volume of NO_2 is produced from 7 g of nitrogen gas at 27°C and 0.9 atm?

SOLUTIONS TO REVIEW PROBLEMS

1. **D** Boyle's law states that, when a gas is held at constant temperature, its pressure and volume are inversely proportional. This means that, as the pressure increases, the volume decreases, and vice versa. Of the answer choices, the only one that involves both pressure and volume—in addition to a controlled variation of one of the variables—is (D). When a balloon is placed in a bell jar, the volume of the balloon will increase as a vacuum is being drawn in the jar. Boyle's law can be used to predict this behavior.

2. **A** In developing the kinetic molecular theory of gases, it was found that the properties of a gas sample, such as pressure, volume, and temperature, can be explained in terms of the motion of the individual gas molecules. Because *kinetic* is defined as "relating to motion," this theory of gases was called the kinetic molecular theory.

3. **C** This question is an application of Charles's law, which states that, at constant pressure, the volume and temperature of a gas will vary in direct proportion to each other. If a 50 L volume of gas is heated from standard temperature, which is 273 K, to two times standard temperature, 546 K, the volume will double as well. Therefore, the volume of the gas will increase from 50 L to 100 L. The answer can also be calculated using proportions.

$$\frac{V_1}{V_2} = \frac{T_1}{T_2}$$

$$\frac{50 \text{ L}}{x} = \frac{273 \text{ K}}{546 \text{ K}}$$

$$x = (2)(50 \text{ L})$$

$$x = 100 \text{ L}$$

4. **74.1 g/mol**
   The molecular weight of a gas is the number of grams that occupy 22.4 L at STP. At 630 torr and 600 K, the density of this gas is 2.5 g per 2 L. First, find the volume at STP:

$$V = (2 \text{ L}) \left(\frac{630 \text{ torr}}{760 \text{ torr}} \right) \left(\frac{273 \text{K}}{600 \text{K}} \right) = 0.754 \text{ L}$$

   Next, find the density at STP:

$$d = \frac{2.5 \text{ g}}{0.754 \text{ L}} = \frac{3.31 \text{ g}}{\text{L}}$$

   Finally, find the gram molecular weight of 22.4 L of gas at STP:

$$MM = d(V \text{ for 1 mol gas at STP}) = (3.31 \text{ g/L})(22.4 \text{ L/mol}) = 74.1 \text{ g/mol}$$

5. The conditions that define an ideal gas are low pressure and high temperature. Under these conditions, the gas molecules are assumed to have no intermolecular forces and to occupy no volume. Therefore, it is possible to predict their behavior.

6. **A** This question is an application of Avogadro's principle, which states that, at a constant temperature and pressure, all gases will have the same number of moles in the same volume. This is true regardless of the identity of the gas. Thus, to answer the question, the number of particles in 0.25 mol of helium must be calculated; that value will represent the number of molecules of chlorine gas in the same volume. The number of helium atoms is $(0.25 \text{ mol})(6.022 \times 10^{23} \text{ atoms/mol}) = 1.51 \times 10^{23}$ atoms.

7. **D** The average speed of a gas is defined as the mathematical average of all the speeds of the gas particles in a sample. To answer this question, you must understand the Maxwell-Boltzmann distribution curve, which shows the distribution of speeds of all the gas particles in a sample at a given temperature. The distribution curve is a bell-shaped curve that flattens and shifts to the right as the temperature increases. The flattening of the curve means that gas particles within the sample are traveling at a greater range of speeds. As a result, a smaller proportion of the molecules will move at exactly the new average speed.

8. **A** A gas weighing 25 g/mol will have a density of 25 g per 22.4 L at STP. The density at 76 torr and 37°C is found by calculating the change in volume of a mole of gas under these conditions:

$$\frac{P_1 V_1}{T_1} = \frac{P_2 V_2}{T_2}$$

$$V_2 = \frac{P_1 V_1 T_2}{T_1 P_2}$$

$$V_2 = \frac{(760 \text{ torr})(22.4 \text{ L})(310 \text{ K})}{(273 \text{ K})(76 \text{ torr})} = 254 \text{ L/mol}$$

$$d = \frac{25 \text{ g/mol}}{254 \text{ L/mol}} = 0.098 \text{ g/L}$$

9. **8.88 g**

   First, let's find out how many moles of HCl would occupy 3 L at the pressure and temperature given.

$$n = \frac{(2 \text{ atm})(3 \text{ L})}{(0.0821 \text{ Latm/molK})(293 \text{ K})} = 0.25 \text{ mol}$$

   Because 2 mol of HCl are produced from each mol of Cl_2, 0.25 mol HCl would be produced from 0.125 mol of Cl_2. The molecular weight of Cl_2 is 71 g/mol, so the answer is $(71 \text{ g } Cl_2/\text{mol}) (0.125 \text{ mol}) = 8.88 \text{ g } Cl_2$.

10. **C** Discussed in the section on Dalton's law of partial pressures in this chapter.

11. **N_2: 38 torr, O_2: 152 torr, He: 152 torr, Cl_2: 38 torr**

   According to Dalton's law of partial pressures, the sum of the partial pressures of the gases in a mixture is equal to the total pressure of the mixture. Therefore, the partial pressures of nitrogen, oxygen, helium, and chlorine will add up to 380 torr. The partial pressure of a gas is calculated as follows:

$$P_p = X P_T$$

where X is the mole fraction of the gas. Thus, the mole fractions of each of the gases must be determined.

$$X = \frac{n}{n_T}$$

$$X_{N_2} = \frac{0.5 \text{ mol}}{5 \text{ mol}} = 0.1$$

$$X_{O_2} = \frac{2 \text{ mol}}{5 \text{ mol}} = 0.4$$

$$X_{He} = \frac{2 \text{ mol}}{5 \text{ mol}} = 0.4$$

$$X_{Cl_2} = \frac{0.5 \text{ mol}}{5 \text{ mol}} = 0.1$$

Now the partial pressures may be calculated.

$P_{N_2} = (380 \text{ torr})(0.1) = 38 \text{ torr}$
$P_{O_2} = (380 \text{ torr})(0.4) = 152 \text{ torr}$
$P_{He} = (380 \text{ torr})(0.4) = 152 \text{ torr}$
$P_{Cl_2} = (380 \text{ torr})(0.1) = 38 \text{ torr}$

12. **20.2 g/mol**

Convert the density given to the density at STP.

$$(1 \text{ L})\left(\frac{273 \text{ K}}{283 \text{ K}}\right)\left(\frac{2 \text{ atm}}{1 \text{ atm}}\right) = 1.93 \text{ L at STP}$$

$$\frac{1.74 \text{ g}}{1.93 \text{ L}} = 0.902 \text{ g/L at STP}$$

Now find the molar mass by multiplying by 22.4.

$MM = (0.902 \text{ g/L})(22.4 \text{ L/mol}) = 20.2 \text{ g/mol}$

13. **D** Kinetic energy is proportional to temperature, not number of moles. In an isolated system, increasing the number of moles of a gas while maintaining constant temperature and pressure will cause a decrease in temperature and therefore kinetic energy, indicating an inverse relationship.

14. **0.4 atm**

This question is different from the previous ones in that the new volume is given and you are looking for the final pressure. Rearranging the equation

$$\frac{P_1 V_1}{T_1} = \frac{P_2 V_2}{T_2}$$

gives

$$P_2 = \frac{P_1 V_1 T_2}{T_1 V_2}$$

$$P_2 = \frac{(3 \text{ atm})(1 \text{ L})(373 \text{ K})}{(283 \text{ K})(10 \text{ L})}$$

$$P_2 = 0.4 \text{ atm}$$

15.   **13.7 L**

$$\frac{7 \text{ g N}_2}{28 \text{ g N}_2/\text{mol}} = 0.25 \text{ mol N}_2$$

From the balanced reaction equation, 2 mol of NO_2 are produced from each mol of N_2, so 0.50 mol of NO_2 will be produced from 0.25 mol of N_2. Therefore, the volume at STP will be (0.5 mol NO_2) (22.4 L/mol at STP) = 11.2 L NO_2.

Now find the volume under the conditions given.

$$V = (11.2 \text{ L}) \left(\frac{1 \text{ atm}}{0.9 \text{ atm}} \right) \left(\frac{300 \text{ K}}{273 \text{ K}} \right) = 13.7 \text{ L}$$

CHAPTER THIRTY-SIX

Acids and Bases

Many important reactions in chemical and biological systems involve **acids** and **bases** (defined below). Acids and bases cause color changes in certain compounds called **indicators**, which may be in solution or on paper. A particularly common indicator is **litmus paper**, which turns red in acidic solutions and blue in basic solutions. A more extensive discussion of the chemical properties of acids and bases is outlined below.

Acids	Bases
• Have a sour taste.	• Have a bitter taste.
• Aqueous solutions can conduct electricity.	• Aqueous solutions can conduct electricity.
• React with bases to form water and a salt.	• React with acids to form water and a salt.
• Nonoxidizing acids react with metals to produce hydrogen gas.	• Feel slippery to the touch.
• Cause color changes in plant dyes— turn litmus paper red.	• Cause color changes in plant dyes—turn litmus paper blue

Table 36.1

DEFINITIONS

Arrhenius Definition

The first definitions of acids and bases were formulated by Svante Arrhenius toward the end of the 19th century. Arrhenius defined an acid as a species that produces H^+ (a proton) in an aqueous solution and a base as a species that produces OH^- (a hydroxide ion) in an aqueous solution. These definitions, though useful, fail to describe acidic and basic behavior in nonaqueous media.

An example of an Arrhenius acid (HCl), base (NaOH), and acid-base reaction, respectively, are as follows:

$$HCl\ (aq) \rightarrow H^+\ (aq) + Cl^-\ (aq)$$

$$NaOH\ (aq) \rightarrow Na^+\ (aq) + OH^-\ (aq)$$

$$HCl\ (aq) + NaOH\ (aq) \rightarrow NaCl\ (aq) + H_2O\ (l)$$

Brønsted-Lowry Definition

A more general definition of acids and bases was proposed independently by Johannes Brønsted and Thomas Lowry in 1923. A Brønsted-Lowry acid is a species that donates protons, while a Brønsted-Lowry base is a species that accepts protons. For example, $NH_3\ (g)$ is a Brønsted-Lowry base because it can accept a proton. However, it cannot be called an Arrhenius base since it is not in an aqueous solution.

Brønsted-Lowry acids and bases always occur in pairs, called **conjugate acid-base pairs**. The two members of a conjugate pair are related by the transfer of a proton. For example, H_3O^+ is the conjugate acid of the base H_2O, and NO_2^- is the conjugate base of HNO_2:

$$H_3O^+\ (aq) \rightarrow H_2O\ (aq) + H^+\ (aq)$$
$$HNO_2\ (aq) \rightarrow NO_2^-\ (aq) + H^+\ (aq)$$

Lewis Definition

At approximately the same time as Brønsted and Lowry, Gilbert Lewis also proposed definitions of acids and bases. Lewis defined an acid as an electron-pair acceptor and a base as an electron-pair donor. Lewis's are the most inclusive definitions. Just as every Arrhenius acid is a Brønsted-Lowry acid, every Brønsted-Lowry acid is also a Lewis acid (and likewise for bases). However, the Lewis definition encompasses some species not included within the Brønsted-Lowry definition. For example, BCl_3 and $AlCl_3$ can each accept an electron pair and are therefore Lewis acids, despite their inability to donate protons.

NOMENCLATURE OF ARRHENIUS ACIDS

The name of an acid is related to the name of the parent anion (the anion that combines with H^+ to form the acid). Acids formed from anions whose names end in -**ide** have the prefix **hydro-** and the ending -**ic**.

F^-	Fluoride	HF	Hydrofluoric acid
Br^-	Bromide	HBr	Hydrobromic acid

Acids formed from oxyanions are called **oxyacids**. If the anion ends in -**ite** (less oxygen), then the acid will end with -**ous acid**. If the anion ends in -**ate** (more oxygen), then the acid will end with -**ic acid**. Prefixes in the names of the anions are retained. Some examples:

ClO^-	Hypochlorite	HClO	Hypochlorous acid
ClO_2^-	Chlorite	$HClO_2$	Chlorous acid
ClO_3^-	Chlorate	$HClO_3$	Chloric acid
ClO_4^-	Perchlorate	$HClO_4$	Perchloric acid
NO_2^-	Nitrite	HNO_2	Nitrous acid
NO_3^-	Nitrate	HNO_3	Nitric acid

PROPERTIES OF ACIDS AND BASES

Hydrogen Ion Equilibria (pH and pOH)

Hydrogen ion concentration, $[H^+]$, is generally measured as **pH**, where:

$$pH = -\log[H^+]$$

Likewise, hydroxide ion concentration, $[OH^-]$, is measured as **pOH** where:

$$pOH = -\log[OH^-]$$

In any aqueous solution, the H_2O solvent dissociates slightly in a process called autoionization:

$$H_2O\ (l) \leftrightharpoons H^+\ (aq) + OH^-\ (aq)$$

This dissociation is an equilibrium reaction and is therefore described by a constant, K_w, the water dissociation constant:

$$K_w = [H^+][OH^-] = 10^{-14}$$

Rewriting this equation in logarithmic form gives:

$$pH + pOH = 14$$

In pure H_2O, $[H^+]$ is equal to $[OH^-]$ because, for every mole of H_2O that dissociates, one mole of H^+ and one mole of OH^- are formed. At STP, a solution with equal concentrations of H^+ and OH^- is neutral and has a pH of 7 ($-\log(10^{-7}) = 7$). A pH below 7 indicates a relative excess of H^+ ions and, therefore, an acidic solution; a pH above 7 indicates a relative excess of OH^- ions and, therefore, a basic solution.

Math note: estimating p-scale values

A useful skill for various problems involving acids and bases, as well as their corresponding buffer solutions, is the ability to quickly convert pH, pOH, pK_a, and pK_b into nonlogarithmic form and vice versa (pK_a and pK_b are acid and base dissociation constants, discussed below).

When the original value is a power of 10, the operation is relatively simple; changing the sign on the exponent gives the corresponding p-scale value directly. For example:

If $[H^+] = 0.001$, or 10^{-3}, then pH $= 3$.
If $K_b = 1.0 \times 10^{-7}$, then $pK_b = 7$.

More difficulty arises when the original value is not an exact power of 10; exact calculation would be onerous without a calculator, but a simple method of approximation exists. If the nonlogarithmic value is written in proper scientific notation, it will look like $n \times 10^{-m}$, where n is a number between 1 and 10. The log of this product can be written as $\log(n \times 10^{-m}) = -m + \log n$, and the negative log is thus $m - \log n$. Now, since n is a number between 1 and 10, its logarithm is a fraction between 0 and 1; thus, $m - \log n$ is between $m - 1$ and m. Furthermore, the larger the n, the larger the $\log n$, and therefore the closer the answer is to $m - 1$.

Example: If $K_a = 1.8 \times 10^{-5}$, then $pK_a = 5 - \log 1.8$. Because 1.8 is small, its log will be small, and the answer will be closer to 5 than to 4. (The actual answer is 4.74.)

Relative Strengths of Acids and Bases

The strength of an acid or base will depend largely upon its ability to ionize. The strength of an acid, for example, can be measured by the fraction of the molecules of that acid undergoing ionization. Subsequently, the acid strength can be expressed by the following equation:

$$\text{Percent ionization} = \frac{\text{ionized acid concentration at equilibrium}}{\text{inital concentration of acid}} \times 100\%$$

When an acid or base is strong (has more complete dissociation), its conjugate base or acid will be weak. The stronger the acid, the weaker the conjugate base. For incredibly strong acids (near complete dissociation), the conjugate base is so weak that it is practically inert. Within a series of weak acids, the stronger the acid, the weaker its conjugate base for all acids and bases included. For example, HF is a stronger acid than HCN; therefore, F^- is a weaker base than CN^-.

Strong Acids and Bases

Strong acids and bases are those that completely dissociate into their component ions in aqueous solution. For example, when NaOH is added to water, it dissociates completely:

$$\text{NaOH } (s) + \text{ excess H}_2\text{O } (l) \rightarrow \text{Na}^+ (aq) + \text{OH}^- (aq)$$

Hence, in a 1 M solution of NaOH, complete dissociation gives one mole of OH^- ions per liter of solution.

$$\text{pH} = 14 - (-\log[\text{OH}^-]) = 14 + \log[1] = 14$$

Because NaOH is a strong base, virtually no undissociated NaOH remains. Note that the $[OH^-]$ contributed by the autoionization of H_2O is considered to be negligible in this case. In fact, the contribution of OH^- and H^+ ions from the dissociation of H_2O can always be neglected if the concentration of the acid or base is significantly greater than 10^{-7} M.

As a counterexample, consider the pH of a 1×10^{-8} M HCl solution. HCl is a strong acid and will dissociate completely, so the $[H^+] = 1 \times 10^{-8}$ M. At first glance, the pH of the solution might appear to be 8 because $-\log (1 \times 10^{-8}) = 8$. However, a pH of 8 is in the basic pH range, and an HCl solution should be acidic (pH < 7), not basic. This discrepancy arises from the fact that, at low HCl concentrations, H^+ from the dissociation of water contributes significantly to the total $[H^+]$.

The total concentration of H^+ can be calculated from:
$$K_w = [\text{H}^+][\text{OH}^-]$$
$$1.0 \times 10^{-14} = [x + 1 \times 10^{-8}][x]$$

(note the H^+ from water and HCl are added together due to the common ion effect).

Solving for x gives $x = 9.5 \times 10^{-8}$ M, so $[\text{H}^+]_{\text{total}} = [\text{H}^+ \text{ from HCl} + \text{H}^+ \text{ from water}] = (9.5 \times 10^{-8} + 1 \times 10^{-8})$ M $= 1.05 \times 10^{-7}$ M, and pH $= -\log (1.05 \times 10^{-7}) = 6.98$. The pH is slightly less than 7, as should be expected for a very dilute yet acidic solution.

Strong acids and bases commonly encountered on the exam include the following:

Acids	Bases
$HClO_4$ (perchloric acid)	NaOH (sodium hydroxide)
HNO_3 (nitric acid)	KOH (potassium hydroxide)
H_2SO_4 (sulfuric acid)	$Ca(OH)_2$ (calcium hydroxide)
HCl (hydrochloric acid)	other soluble hydroxides of Group IA and IIA metals

Table 36.2

Calculation of the pH and pOH of strong acids and bases assumes complete dissociation of the acid or base in solution: $[H^+]$ = normality of strong acid, and $[OH^-]$ = normality of strong base.

Weak Acids and Bases

Weak acids and bases are those that only partially dissociate in aqueous solution. A weak, monoprotic acid (HA) in aqueous solution will achieve the following equilibrium after dissociation (H_3O^+ is equivalent to H^+ in aqueous solution):

$$HA\ (aq) + H_2O\ (l) \leftrightharpoons H_3O^+\ (aq) + A^-\ (aq)$$

The **acid dissociation constant, K_a,** is a specific type of K_{eq} (see Chapter 33, Chemical Equilibria) that measures the degree to which an acid dissociates by showing the ratio of concentrations of the products (the conjugate base and the H^+ donated) to that of the reactant (the original acid).

$$K_a = \frac{[H_3O^+][A^-]}{[HA]}$$

The weaker the acid, the smaller the K_a. Note that K_a does not contain an expression for the pure liquid, water, since pure liquids (and pure solids) are not included in any K_{eq} calculations.

A weak monovalent base (BOH) undergoes dissociation to give B^+ and OH^-. The **base dissociation constant, K_b,** is a measure of the degree to which a base dissociates. The weaker the base, the smaller its K_b. For a monovalent base, K_b is defined as follows:

$$K_b = \frac{[B^+][OH^-]}{[BOH]}$$

A **conjugate acid** is defined as the acid formed when a base gains a proton. Similarly, a **conjugate base** is formed when an acid loses a proton. For example, in the HCO_3^-/CO_3^{2-} conjugate acid/base pair, CO_3^{2-} is the conjugate base, and HCO_3^- is the conjugate acid:

$$HCO_3^-\ (aq) \leftrightharpoons H^+\ (aq) + CO_3^{2-}\ (aq)$$

To find the K_a of the conjugate acid HCO_3^-, the reaction with water must be considered:

$$HCO_3^- \ (aq) + H_2O \ (l) \rightleftharpoons H_3O^+ \ (aq) + CO_3^{2-} \ (aq)$$

Likewise, for the K_b of CO_3^{2-}:

$$CO_3^{2-} \ (aq) + H_2O \ (l) \rightleftharpoons HCO_3^- \ (aq) + OH^- \ (aq)$$

The equilibrium constants for these reactions are as follows:

$$K_a = \frac{[H^+][CO_3^{2-}]}{[HCO_3^-]} \quad \text{and} \quad K_b = \frac{[HCO_3^-][OH^-]}{[CO_3^{2-}]}$$

Adding the two reactions shows that the net reaction is simply the dissociation of water:

$$HCO_3^- \ (aq) + H_2O \ (l) \rightleftharpoons H_3O^+ \ (aq) + CO_3^{2-} \ (aq)$$
$$+ \quad \underline{CO_3^{2-} \ (aq) + H_2O \ (l) \rightleftharpoons HCO_3^- \ (aq) + OH^- \ (aq)}$$
$$2\,H_2O \ (l) \rightleftharpoons H_3O^+ \ (aq) + OH^- \ (aq)$$

The equilibrium constant for this net reaction is $K_w = [H^+][OH^-]$, which is the product of K_a and K_b. Thus, if the **dissociation constant** either for an acid or for its conjugate base is known, then the dissociation constant for the other can be determined using the equation:

$$K_a \times K_b = K_w = 1 \times 10^{-14}$$

Thus, K_a and K_b are inversely related. In other words, the larger the K_a (the stronger the acid), the smaller the conjugate's K_b (the weaker the base), and vice versa. For strong acids and bases, the K_a and K_b are significantly larger than 1. For example, the K_a of HCl is 1.3×10^6. Because the K_a is large, the K_b is expected to be small. Keeping in mind that $K_a \times K_b = 1 \times 10^{-14}$, $K_b = 8.3 \times 10^{-21}$. As expected, the conjugate base (Cl^-) is weak; in fact, 8.3×10^{-21} is such a very small number that Cl^- can, practically speaking, be considered inert.

Applications of K_a and K_b

To calculate the concentration of H^+ in a 2.0 M aqueous solution of acetic acid, CH_3COOH ($K_a = 1.8 \times 10^{-5}$), first write the equilibrium reaction:

$$CH_3COOH \ (aq) \rightleftharpoons H^+ \ (aq) + CH_3COO^- \ (aq)$$

Next, write the expression for the acid dissociation constant:

$$K_a = \frac{[H^+][CH_3COOO^-]}{[CH_3COOH]} = 1.8 \times 10^{-5}$$

Because acetic acid is a weak acid, the concentration of CH_3COOH at equilibrium is equal to its initial concentration, 2.0 M, less the amount dissociated, x. Likewise $[H^+] = [CH_3COO^-] = x$, since each molecule of CH_3COOH dissociates into one H^+ ion and one CH_3COO^- ion. Thus, the equation can be rewritten as follows:

$$K_a = \frac{[x][x]}{[2.0 - x]} = 1.8 \times 10^{-5}$$

We can approximate that $2.0 - x \approx 2.0$ since acetic acid is a weak acid that only slightly dissociates in water, and x will be small. Multiplying or dividing by small numbers can have large effects, but adding or subtracting small numbers is not statistically significant. On the exam, the math can be made much simpler be ignoring x values that are added or subtracted from (comparably) large numbers:

$$K_a = \frac{[x][x]}{[2.0]}$$
$$1.8 \times 10^{-5} = \frac{x^2}{2}$$
$$3.6 \times 10^{-5} = x^2$$
$$x = 6 \times 10^{-3}\,\text{M}$$

The fact that x is so much less than the initial concentration of acetic acid (2.0 M) validates the approximation; otherwise, it would have been necessary to solve for x using the quadratic formula. (A rule of thumb is that the approximation is valid as long as x is less than 5 percent of the initial concentration.)

SALT FORMATION

Acids and bases may react with one another, forming a salt and (often, but not always) water in what is termed a **neutralization reaction**. For example:

$$HA + BOH \rightarrow BA + H_2O$$

The salt may precipitate out or remain ionized in solution depending on its solubility and the amount produced. Neutralization reactions generally go to completion. The reverse reaction, in which the salt ions react with water to give back the acid or base, is known as **hydrolysis**.

Four combinations of strong and weak acids and bases are possible:

1. strong acid + strong base: e.g., $HCl + NaOH \rightarrow NaCl + H_2O$
2. strong acid + weak base: e.g., $HCl + NH_3 \rightarrow NH_4Cl$
3. weak acid + strong base: e.g., $HClO + NaOH \rightarrow NaClO + H_2O$
4. weak acid + weak base: e.g., $HClO + NH_3 \leftrightarrows NH_4ClO$

The products of a reaction between equal concentrations of a strong acid and a strong base are a salt and water. The conjugate acids and bases (Na^+ and Cl^- from combination 1, above) are so very weak that they are practically inert and will not contribute to the pH of the solution. The only other remaining product is water, meaning the resulting solution is neutral (pH = 7).

The product of a reaction between a strong acid and a weak base is also a salt, but usually no water is formed since weak bases are usually not hydroxides. In this case, the cation of the salt is the conjugate acid of a weak base, which will not be inert and will contribute to the pH. Instead of a neutral salt and water (as in the strong acid and strong base reaction), an inert anion and a weak acid cation (Cl⁻ and NH4⁺ from combination 2 above, respectively) are formed, meaning the solution will be slightly acidic (pH < 7).

Another way to consider this reaction is that the weak-acid cation will react with the water solvent, reforming the weak base. This reaction constitutes hydrolysis. Revisiting combination 2:

$$HCl\,(aq) + NH_3\,(aq) \leftrightharpoons NH_4^+\,(aq) + Cl^-\,(aq) \qquad \text{Reaction I}$$
$$NH_4^+\,(aq) + H_2O\,(aq) \leftrightharpoons NH_3\,(aq) + H_3O^+\,(aq) \qquad \text{Reaction II}$$

By increasing the amount of H_3O^+, the pH of the strong acid/weak base reaction product will be slightly acidic (pH < 7).

On the other hand, when a weak acid reacts with a strong base, the opposite occurs. The cation product is practically inert, and the anion product is a weak base (Na^+ and ClO^- from combination 3 above, respectively). The presence of the weak base anion will cause the water solvent to become slightly alkaline (pH > 7); the weak base anion (ClO^- in our example) will react with the H_2O solvent, which leaves OH^- to raise the pH.

The pH of a solution containing a weak acid and a weak base depends on the relative strengths of the reactants. For example, the acid HClO has a $K_a = 3.2 \times 10^{-8}$, and the base NH_3 has a $K_b = 1.8 \times 10^{-5}$. Thus, an aqueous solution of HClO and NH_3 is basic, since the K_a for HClO is smaller than the K_b for NH_3, and therefore NH_3 is the stronger reactant.

POLYVALENCE AND NORMALITY

The relative acidity or basicity of an aqueous solution is determined by the relative concentrations of **acid** and **base equivalents**. An acid equivalent is equal to one mole of H^+ (or H_3O^+) ions; a base equivalent is equal to one mole of OH^- ions. Some acids and bases are polyvalent, that is, each mole of the acid or base liberates more than one acid or base equivalent. For example, the diprotic acid H_2SO_4 undergoes the following dissociation in water:

$$H_2SO_4\,(aq) \rightarrow H^+\,(aq) + HSO_4^-\,(aq)$$
$$HSO_4^-\,(aq) \leftrightharpoons H^+\,(aq) + SO_4^{2-}\,(aq)$$

One mole of H_2SO_4 can thus produce two acid equivalents (two moles of H^+). The acidity or basicity of a solution depends upon the concentration of acidic or basic equivalents that can be liberated. The quantity of acidic or basic capacity is directly indicated by the solution's normality (N) where

$N = \text{Molarity} \times \dfrac{\text{equivalents}}{\text{mol}}$ (see Chapter 28, Solutions). Because each mole of H_3PO_4 can liberate three moles (equivalents) of H^+, a 2 M H_3PO_4 solution would be 6 N (6 normal).

Another useful measurement is **equivalent weight**. The equivalent weight is calculated by taking the molecular weight and dividing by the number of equivalents per mole. For example, the gram molecular weight of H_2SO_4 is 98 g/mol. Because each mole liberates two acid equivalents, the gram equivalent weight of H_2SO_4 would be $\frac{98}{2} = 49$ g; that is, the dissociation of 49 g of H_2SO_4 would release one acid equivalent. Common polyvalent acids include H_2SO_4, H_3PO_4, and H_2CO_3.

AMPHOTERIC SPECIES

An amphoteric, or **amphiprotic,** species is one that can act either as an acid or a base, depending on its chemical environment. In the Brønsted–Lowry sense, an amphoteric species can either gain or lose a proton. Water is the most common example. When water reacts with a base, it behaves as an acid:

$$H_2O + B^- \rightleftharpoons HB + OH^-$$

When water reacts with an acid, it behaves as a base:

$$HA + H_2O \rightleftharpoons H_3O^+ + A^-$$

The partially dissociated conjugate base of a polyprotic acid is usually amphoteric (e.g., HSO_4^- can either gain an H^+ to form H_2SO_4 or lose an H^+ to form SO_4^{2-}). The hydroxides of certain metals (e.g., Al, Zn, Pb, and Cr) are also amphoteric. Furthermore, species that can act as either oxidizing or reducing agents (see Chapter 29, Reaction Types) are considered to be amphoteric as well, since by accepting or donating electron pairs, they act as Lewis acids or bases, respectively.

TITRATION AND BUFFERS

Titration is a procedure used to determine the molarity of an acid or base. This is accomplished by reacting a known volume of a solution of unknown concentration with a known volume of a solution of known concentration. When the number of acid equivalents equals the number of base equivalents added, or vice versa, the **equivalence point** is reached. It is important to emphasize that, while a strong acid/strong base titration will have an equivalence point at pH 7, the equivalence point need *not* always occur at pH 7. Also, when titrating polyprotic acids or bases, there are several equivalence points, as each acidic or basic species is titrated separately (see Polyprotic Acids and Bases later in this chapter).

The equivalence point in a titration is estimated in two common ways: either by plotting the pH (measured with a **pH meter**) of the solution as a function of added titrant on a graph or by watching for a color change of an added **indicator**. Indicators are weak organic acids or bases that have different colors in their undissociated and dissociated states. Indicators are used in low concentrations and therefore do not significantly alter the equivalence point. The point at which the indicator actually changes color is not the equivalence point but is called the **end point**; this point is not significant mathematically but rather is a practical way to ensure the reaction has gone to completion. If the titration is performed well, the volume difference (and therefore the error) between the end point and the equivalence point is small and may be corrected for or ignored.

Strong Acid and Strong Base

Consider the titration of 10 mL of a 0.1 N solution of HCl with a 0.1 N solution of NaOH. Plotting the pH of the reaction solution versus the quantity of NaOH added gives the curve shown in Figure 36.1. Because HCl is a strong acid and NaOH is a strong base, the equivalence point of the titration will be at pH 7, and the solution will be neutral.

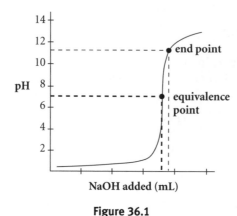

Figure 36.1

In the early part of the curve (when little base has been added), the acidic species predominates, so the addition of small amounts of base will not appreciably change either the $[OH^-]$ or the pH. Similarly, in the last part of the titration curve (when an excess of base has been added), the addition of small amounts of base will not change the $[OH^-]$ significantly, and the pH remains relatively constant. The addition of base most alters the concentrations of H^+ and OH^- near the equivalence point, and thus the pH changes most drastically in that region.

Weak Acid and Strong Base

Titration of a weak acid, HA, with a strong base produces the titration curve shown in Figure 36.2.

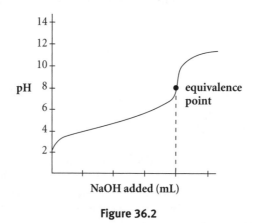

Figure 36.2

Comparing Figure 36.2 with Figure 36.1 shows that the initial pH of the weak acid solution is greater than the initial pH of the strong acid solution. The pH changes most significantly early on in the titration, and the equivalence point is in the basic range. Although the original weak acid and strong base are completely neutralized at the equivalence point (forming water with pH = 7), the side product of weak conjugate base from the original weak acid will be able to react with water in solution, consuming H⁺, thereby lowering [H⁺] and raising pH.

Buffers

A **buffer solution** consists of a mixture of a weak acid and its salt (which consists of its conjugate base and a cation) or a mixture of a weak base and its salt (which consists of its conjugate acid and an anion). Two examples of buffers are a solution of acetic acid (CH_3COOH) and its salt, sodium acetate (CH_3COONa), and a solution of ammonia (NH_3) and its salt, ammonium chloride (NH_4Cl). Buffer solutions have the useful property of resisting changes in pH when small amounts of acid or base are added.

Consider a buffer solution of acetic acid and sodium acetate:

$$CH_3COOH \leftrightharpoons H^+ + CH_3COO^-$$

$$CH_3COONa \leftrightharpoons Na^+ + CH_3COO^-$$

When a small amount of NaOH is added to the buffer, the OH⁻ ions from the NaOH react with the acetic acid in the buffer solution such that:

$$CH_3COOH + NaOH \leftrightharpoons H_2O + CH_3COO^- + Na^+$$

Subsequently, the solution contains less acetic acid and more acetate ion. Instead of a strong base (OH⁻) in solution, there is now a weak base (CH_3COO^-). Though the strong base may have considerably changed the pH, the substitution by a weak base does not appreciably change pH. Likewise, when a small amount of HCl is added to the buffer, the acid will react with the acetate ion (CH_3COO^-):

$$CH_3COONa + HCl \leftrightharpoons NaCl + CH_3COOH$$

Instead of the addition of a strong acid (HCl), there is now a weak acid present (CH_3COOH). Just as with the strong base, the pH shift will be quite small.

The **Henderson-Hasselbalch equation** is used to estimate the pH of a solution in the buffer region where the concentrations of the species and its conjugate are present in approximately equal concentrations. For a weak acid buffer solution:

$$pH = pK_a + \log\frac{[\text{conjugate base}]}{[\text{weak acid}]}$$

Note that when [conjugate base] = [weak acid] (in a titration, halfway to the equivalent point), the pH = pK_a because log 1 = 0. Likewise, for a weak base buffer solution:

$$pOH = pK_b + \log\frac{[\text{conjugate acid}]}{[\text{weak base}]}$$

$pOH = pK_b$ when [conjugate acid] = [weak base].

Polyprotic Acids and Bases

The titration curve for a polyprotic acid or base looks different from that for a monoprotic acid or base. Figure 36.3 shows the titration of Na_2CO_3 with HCl in which the polyprotic acid H_2CO_3 is the ultimate product.

Figure 36.3

In the region between I and II, little acid has been added, and the predominant species is CO_3^{2-}. Point II represents the half-equivalence point where $[CO_3^{2-}]$ and $[HCO_3^-]$ are equal. Around this point the pH remains relatively constant at pH = 10.3; this is the first buffer region, and the pH corresponds to the pK_a of HCO_3^-.

In the region between II and III, HCO_3^- begins to predominate until point III, the first equivalence point, where all of the original CO_3^- has been consumed, leaving only HCO_3^-.

The same pattern occurs again as HCO_3^- reacts to form H_2CO_3. Point IV represents the second half-equivalence point (with a pH of 6.4 to correspond with the pK_a of H_2CO_3), and point V represents the second equivalence point where no original HCO_3^- remains, leaving only H_2CO_3.

REVIEW PROBLEMS

1. A certain aqueous solution has $[OH^-] = 6.2 \times 10^{-5}$ M.
   A. Calculate $[H^+]$.
   B. Calculate the pH of the solution.
   C. Is the solution acidic or basic?

2. What is the ratio of $[H^+]$ of a solution of pH $= 4$ to the $[H^+]$ of a solution of pH $= 7$?

3. Write equations expressing what happens to each of the following bases in aqueous solutions:
   A. LiOH
   B. $Ba(OH)_2$
   C. NH_3
   D. NO_2^-

4. What volume of a 3 M solution of NaOH is required to titrate 0.05 L of a 4 M solution of HCl to the equivalence point?

5. If 10 mL of 1 M NaOH is titrated with 1 M of HCl to a pH of 2, what volume of HCl was added?

6. Identify the conjugate acids and bases in the following equation:

$$NH_3 + H_2O \leftrightarrows NH_4^+ + OH^-$$

7. Identify each of the following as an Arrhenius acid or base, Brønsted-Lowry acid or base, or Lewis acid or base.
   A. NaOH, in $NaOH \rightarrow Na^+ + OH^-$
   B. HCl, in $HCl \rightarrow H^+ + Cl^-$
   C. NH_3, in $NH_3 + H^+ \rightarrow NH_4^+$
   D. NH_4^+, in $NH_4^+ \rightarrow NH_3 + H^+$
   E. $(CH_3)_3N{:}$, in $(CH_3)_3N{:} + BF_3 \rightarrow (CH_3)_3N{:}BF_3$
   F. BF_3 in the above equation

8. At equilibrium, a certain acid, HA, in solution yields $[HA] = 0.94$ M and $[A^-] = 0.060$ M.
   A. Calculate K_a.
   B. Is this acid stronger or weaker than sulfurous acid ($K_a = 1.7 \times 10^{-2}$)?
   C. Calculate K_b.
   D. Calculate pH.
   E. Calculate the pK_a.

9. For each of the following pairs, choose which one describes the weaker acid:
   A. $K_a = x$, $K_a = 3x$
   B. $[H^+] = x$, $[H^+] = 3x$
   C. $pK_a = x$, $pK_a = 3x$
   D. $pH = x$, $pH = 3x$

10. For a certain acid HA, $K_b(A^-) = 2.22 \times 10^{-11}$. Calculate the pH of a 0.5 M solution of HA.

11. Which of the following sets of materials would make the best buffer solution?
    A. H_2O, 1 M NaOH, 1 M H_2SO_4
    B. H_2O, 1 M $HC_2H_3O_2$, 1 M $NaC_2H_3O_2$
    C. H_2O, 1 M $HC_2H_3O_2$, 6 M $NaC_2H_3O_2$
    D. H_2O, 1 M $HC_2H_3O_2$, 1 M NaOH
    E. H_2O, 1 M NaOH, 1 M HCl

12. A certain buffer solution is 3 M in HF and 2 M in NaF. Calculate the pH of this buffer given that the K_a of HF $= 7.0 \times 10^{-4}$.

13. Which of the following combinations would produce a buffer solution of pH $= 4$?
    (K_a $HNO_2 = 4.5 \times 10^{-4}$)
    A.   0.30 M HNO_2, 0.22 M $NaNO_2$
    B.   0.22 M HNO_2, 0.30 M $NaNO_2$
    C.   0.11 M HNO_2, 0.50 M $NaNO_2$
    D.   0.50 M HNO_2, 0.11 M $NaNO_2$
    E.   0.22 M HNO_2, 0.80 M $NaNO_2$

14. Write chemical equations describing the buffer activity that prevents drastic pH changes when (A) a strong acid and (B) a strong base is added.

SOLUTIONS TO REVIEW PROBLEMS

1. **A** 1.6×10^{-10} **M**

    Water is composed of hydronium and hydroxide ions, and the dissociation constant of water, K_w, is defined as $[H^+][OH^-] = 1.0 \times 10^{-14}$ M. If $[OH^-] = 6.2 \times 10^{-5}$, then:

    $$[H^+] = \frac{K_w}{[OH^-]} = \frac{1.0 \times 10^{-14}}{6.2 \times 10^{-5}} = 1.6 \times 10^{-10} \text{ M.}$$

    B **9.79**

    The pH of a solution is a logarithmic measurement of $[H^+]$, which expresses the degree of acidity.

    pH is defined as $-\log[H^+]$. In this case, pH $= -\log(1.6 \times 10^{-10}) = 9.79$.

    C **Basic**

    A pH of 9.79 indicates a basic solution, as does any $[OH^-] > 1.0 \times 10^{-7}$ M.

2. **1,000:1**

    This problem can be solved by calculating the $[H^+]$ of the pH $= 4$ solution and the $[H^+]$ of the pH $= 7$ solution. Then divide the former by the latter: because pH $= -\log[H^+]$, $[H^+] = $ antilog $(-pH)$. For pH $= 4$, antilog $(-4) = 1.0 \times 10^{-4}$. For pH $= 7$, antilog $(-7) = 1.0 \times 10^{-7}$. $1 \times 10^{-4} : 1 \times 10^{-7} = 1,000:1$. Alternately, we could subtract the pHs first, and then find the antilog: $7 - 4 = 3$ implies 10^3, or $1,000:1$.

3. **A** $LiOH \rightarrow Li^+ + OH^-$

    B $Ba(OH)_2 \rightarrow Ba^{2+} + 2\,OH^-$

    C $NH_3 + H_2O \rightarrow NH_4^+ + OH^-$

    D $NO_2^- + H_2O \rightarrow HNO_2 + OH^-$

4. **0.067 L**

    At the equivalence point,

    $(Normality)_{acid}(Volume)_{acid} = (Normality)_{base}(Volume)_{base}$

    4 M HCl $=$ 4 N HCl

    3 M NaOH $=$ 3 N NaOH

    Plugging into the formula,

    $(4)(0.05) = (3)(V_B)$

    $V_B = 0.067$ L

5. **10.2 mL**

    First, add enough HCl to neutralize the solution. Because both the acid and the base are 1 M, 10 mL of HCl will neutralize 10 mL of NaOH, from $N_A V_A = N_B V_B$. This produces 20 mL of 0.5 M NaCl solution.

    Next calculate how much more HCl must be added to produce a $[H^+]$ of 1×10^{-2}. Let x be the amount of HCl to be added. The total volume of the solution will be $(20 + x)$ mL. Since this is now a dilution problem, the amount of HCl to be added can be found by using the formula:

$$M_1V_1 = M_2V_2$$
$$(1 \text{ M})(x \text{ mL}) = (0.01 \text{ M})[(20 + x) \text{ mL}]$$

When this equation is solved, x is found to have an approximate value of 0.2 mL, so a total of 10.2 mL of HCl was added to the original NaOH solution.

6. NH_4^+ is the conjugate acid of the weak base, NH_3; OH^- is the conjugate base of the weak acid, H_2O.

   The reaction in question is:

   $$NH_3 + H_2O \leftrightarrows NH_4^+ + OH^-$$

   According to the Brønsted-Lowry theory of acids and bases, an acid releases a proton, whereas a base accepts a proton. In the case of weak acids and bases, an equilibrium is established whereby a weak acid, in this case H_2O, dissociates partially, donating a proton to a weak base, which is NH_3. The weak acid, H_2O, loses a proton and becomes a relatively stronger conjugate base, OH^-. This is one conjugate acid-base pair (H_2O, OH^-). Meanwhile, the weak base, NH_3, picks up a proton to become a relatively stronger conjugate acid, NH_4^+. This is the second conjugate acid-base pair (NH_4^+, NH_3).

7. **A** NaOH is an Arrhenius base.

   B HCl is an Arrhenius acid and a Brønsted-Lowry acid.

   C NH_3 is a Brønsted-Lowry base and a Lewis base.

   D NH_4^+ is an Arrhenius acid and a Brønsted-Lowry acid.

   E $(CH_3)_3N$: acts only as a Lewis base.

   F BF_3 acts only as a Lewis acid.

8. **A** 3.8×10^{-3}

   K_a is the equilibrium constant for an acid, also called the dissociation constant for the particular equilibrium state that is achieved by the dissociation of an acid. We are told that at equilibrium [HA] is 0.94 M, whereas [A$^-$] is 0.060 M. The dissociation of HA can be written as follows:

   $$HA \rightarrow H^+ + A^-$$

   The molar ratio of A$^-$ to H$^+$ is 1:1, so [H$^+$] must also be 0.060 M at equilibrium. It follows, then, that:

   $$K_a = \frac{[A^-][H^+]}{[HA]} = \frac{(0.060)(0.060)}{0.94} = 3.8 \times 10^{-3}$$

   B **Weaker**

   K_a is a measure of the strength of an acid. An acid with a high K_a is a strong acid because its equilibrium position lies farther to the right (more product increases the numerator of the equilibrium expression and makes K_a larger), meaning that dissociation is more complete. Greater dissociation means a stronger acid. The K_a of sulfurous acid is 1.7×10^{-2} and the K_a of HA is 3.8×10^{-3}. The K_a of HA is less than that of sulfurous acid; therefore, HA is a weaker acid.

   C 2.6×10^{-12}

   Just as K_a is the dissociation constant for an acid, K_b is the dissociation constant of a base. Whereas K_a measures the degree to which H$^+$ is liberated, K_b measures the degree to which

OH⁻ is liberated. Because H^+ and OH^- are related by $K_w = 1.0 \times 10^{-14}$, K_b can be easily calculated. In this case,

$$K_b = \frac{1.0 \times 10^{-14}}{3.8 \times 10^{-3}} = 2.6 \times 10^{-12}$$

D **1.22**

$pH = -\log [H^+] = -\log (0.060) = 1.22$

E **2.42**

$pK_a = -\log K_a = -\log (3.8 \times 10^{-3}) = 2.42$

9. **A** $K_a = x$

K_a is a measure of the dissociation of an acid and, therefore, the strength of an acid. A higher K_a indicates a stronger acid; a lower K_a indicates a weaker acid. x is one-third the value of $3x$ and, therefore, a weaker acid.

B $[H^+] = x$

$[H^+]$ is a direct measure of the strength of an acid. The greater the concentration of H^+ in solution, the stronger the acid. An acid that liberates x moles of H^+ per liter is weaker, therefore, than an acid that liberates $3x$ moles of H^+ per liter.

C $pK_a = 3x$

$pK_a = -\log K_a$; therefore, a pK_a of $3x$ corresponds to a K_a lower in value than that of a pK_a of x. A lower K_a means a weaker acid, and a lower pK_a means a stronger acid. $3x$ is greater than x, so the acid whose pK_a is $3x$ is weaker than the acid whose pK_a is x.

D $pH = 3x$

The acid with a pH of $3x$ is the weaker acid, using the same reasoning as for part (C).

10. **1.82**

If $K_b = 2.22 \times 10^{-11}$, then

$$K_a = \frac{K_w}{K_b} = \frac{1.0 \times 10^{-14}}{2.22 \times 10^{-11}}$$

$$K_a = 4.5 \times 10^{-4}$$

If HA dissociates according to the following expression,

$HA \leftrightarrows H^+ + A^-$,

then the equilibrium expression for this dissociation is:

$$K_a = \frac{[H^+][A^-]}{[HA]}$$

We can let $[H^+] = x$ at equilibrium and, since $[H^+]:[A^-] = 1:1$, $[A^-] = x$.

If the original $[HA]$ was 0.5 M, and x mol/L are dissociated, then at equilibrium, $[HA] = 0.5 - x$.

Thus the equilibrium expression becomes:

$$4.5 \times 10^{-4} = \frac{[x][x]}{(0.5 - x)}$$

We can approximate that $0.5 - x \approx 0.5$ since HA has a small K_a, which indicates it is a weak acid.

$$4.5 \times 10^{-4} \approx \frac{x^2}{0.5}$$

$$x^2 = 2.25 \times 10^{-4}$$

$$x = 0.015 = [H^+]$$

$$pH = -\log [H^+] = -\log [0.015] = 1.82$$

11. **B** A buffer solution is prepared from a weak acid and its conjugate base, preferably in near-equal quantities. Choices (A), (D), and (E) are incorrect because they do not show conjugate acid/base pairs. (C) is incorrect because it shows a weak acid and its conjugate base, where the concentrations of the acid and the base are quite different. Thus, the best buffer solution would be that prepared from (B), which shows a conjugate acid/base pair, both present in 1 M concentrations.

12. **2.98**

$$K_a = \frac{[H^+][F^-]}{[HF]}$$

$$7 \times 10^{-4} = \frac{[H^+](2)}{3}$$

$$[H^+] = 1.05 \times 10^{-3}$$

$$pH = -\log[H^+] = 2.98$$

Another way to solve this problem is by using the Henderson-Hasselbalch equation:

$$pH = pK_a + \log\frac{[\text{conjugate base}]}{[\text{weak acid}]}$$

Using the Henderson-Hasselbalch equation for this problem:

$$pH = -\log K_a + \log\frac{[F^-]}{[HF]}$$

$$pH = -\log(7.0 \times 10^{-4}) + \log\left(\frac{2}{3}\right)$$

$$pH = 3.155 - 0.176 = 2.98$$

13. C The Henderson-Hasselbalch equation may again be used here:

$$pH = pK_a + \log\frac{[A^-]}{[HA]}$$

$$4 = 3.35 + \log\frac{[A^-]}{[HA]}$$

$$0.65 = \log\frac{[A^-]}{[HA]}$$

$$\frac{[A^-]}{[HA]} = 4.5$$

Only choice (C) fulfills this criterion, as $\frac{0.50}{0.11} = 4.5$.

14. A Strong acid:

Salt in buffer dissociates completely:

$$NaX \leftrightarrows Na^+ + X^-$$

Added strong acid dissociates completely:

$$HCl \leftrightarrows H^+ + Cl^-$$

Protons from the acid are absorbed by the strong conjugate base of the salt:

$$H^+ + X^- \leftrightarrows HX$$

B Strong base:

Weak acid in buffer hardly dissociates:

$$HX \leftrightarrows HX$$

Added strong base dissociates completely:

$$NaOH \leftrightarrows Na^+ + OH^-$$

OH^- is a strong base, which attracts protons from the weak acid:

$$OH^- + HX \leftrightarrows H_2O + X^-$$

GC

CHAPTER THIRTY-SEVEN

Nuclear Reactions

Nuclear phenomena describe interactions with and changes to nuclei, which is distinctly different from many other topics in general chemistry focused on the behavior of electrons outside the nucleus. Therefore, to begin, it is important to understand the standard terminology used in nuclear chemistry and physics. Briefly, an amount of energy, called the **binding energy**, is required to break up a given nucleus into its constituent protons and neutrons. That energy is converted to mass via Einstein's $E = mc^2$ equation, resulting in a larger mass for the constituent protons and neutrons than that of the original nucleus; this difference is called the **mass defect**. The remainder of the chapter is concerned with a brief discussion of nuclear reactions (**fission** and **fusion**) and an extended treatment of radioactive decay, which itself is presented in two distinct parts. The first deals with the four different types of **radioactive decay** and a discussion of the reaction equations that describe them. The second covers the general problem of determining the number of nuclei that have not decayed as a function of time along with the associated concept of the half-life of a decay process.

NUCLEI

At the center of an atom lies its nucleus, consisting of one or more **nucleons** (protons or neutrons) held together with considerably more energy than the energy needed to hold electrons in orbit around the nucleus. The radius of the nucleus is about 100,000 times smaller than the radius of the atom. As described in Chapter 24, Atomic and Molecular Structure, the atomic number (Z) of an element describes the number of protons, whereas the mass number (A) describes the number of protons + neutrons. Z is used as a presubscript and A is used as a presuperscript to the chemical symbol in **isotopic notation**. The number of protons determines the identity (name) of an element, and varying numbers of neutrons determine different isotopes of that same element. The term **radionucleotide** is another generic name used to refer to any radioactive isotope, especially those used in nuclear medicine.

Nuclear versus Chemical Reactions

All nuclei of atoms, with the exception of hydrogen, contain protons and neutrons. When the nucleus of an atom is unstable, it may spontaneously emit particles or electromagnetic radiation (otherwise known as **radioactivity**). Nuclei may also change composition when nuclear transmutation occurs. This process involves the bombardment of the nucleus by electrons, neutrons, or other nuclei. These are all specific types of nuclear reactions, which involve changes to nuclei rather than solely electrons. Below is a summary of the major differences between nuclear and chemical reactions.

Nuclear reactions	Chemical reactions
• Elements or isotopes are changed from one to another.	• Atoms can be rearranged by the formation or breaking of chemical bonds.
• Reactions result in the release or absorption of large amounts of energy.	• Reactions generally result in the release or absorption of small amounts of energy.
• Reaction rates are generally not affected by catalysts, temperature, or pressure.	• Reaction rates are generally affected by catalysts, temperature, or pressure.
• Protons, neutrons, or electrons can be involved.	• Only electrons in the affected orbital of the atom are involved in the formation and breaking of bonds.

Table 37.1

Nuclear Binding Energy and Mass Defect

Every nucleus (other than $_1^1H$) has a smaller mass than the combined mass of its constituent protons and neutrons. This difference is called the **mass defect**. Scientists had difficulty explaining why this mass defect occurred until Einstein discovered the equivalence of matter and energy, embodied by the equation $E = mc^2$. The mass defect is a result of matter that has been converted to energy. This energy, called **binding energy**, holds the nucleons together in the nucleus.

Note: The binding energy per nucleon peaks at iron, which implies that iron is the most stable atom. In general, intermediate-sized nuclei are more stable than large and small nuclei.

The mass defect and binding energy of ^4He are calculated in the following example.

Example: Measurements of the atomic mass of a neutron and a proton yield these results:

proton $= 1.00728$ amu

neutron $= 1.00867$ amu

A measurement of the atomic mass of a ^4He nucleus yields:

$^4He = 4.00260$ amu

^4He consists of two protons and two neutrons, which should theoretically give a ^4He mass of:

$Z(m_p) + N(m_n) = 2(1.00728) + 2(1.00867)$

$= 4.03190$ amu

What is the mass defect and binding energy of this nucleus?

Solution: The difference $4.03190 - 4.00260 = 0.02930$ amu is the mass defect for ^4He and is interpreted as the conversion of mass into the binding energy of the nucleus. The rest energy (the energy equivalent of a given mass times the speed of light squared) of

1 amu is 932 MeV, so using $E = mc^2$, we find that $c^2 = 932$ MeV/amu. Therefore, the binding energy (BE) of ^{4}He is:

$$\mathrm{BE} = \Delta mc^2$$
$$= (0.02930 \text{ amu})(932 \text{ MeV/amu})$$
$$= 27.3 \text{ MeV}$$

NUCLEAR REACTIONS AND DECAY

Nuclear reactions such as fusion, fission, and radioactive decay involve either combining or splitting the nuclei of atoms. Since the binding energy per nucleon is greatest for intermediate-sized atoms, when small atoms combine or large atoms split, a great amount of energy is released.

Fusion

Fusion occurs when small nuclei combine into a larger nucleus. As an example, many stars, including the sun, power themselves by fusing four hydrogen nuclei to make one helium nucleus. By this method, the sun produces 4×10^{26} J every second. Here on Earth, researchers are trying to find ways to use fusion as an alternative energy source. Because these fusion reactions can only take place at extremely high temperatures, they are generally referred to as **thermonuclear reactions**.

Fission

Fission is a process in which a large, heavy (mass number >200) atom splits to form smaller, more stable nuclei (especially noble gases) and one or more neutrons. It is important to note that, because the original large nucleus is more unstable than its products, there is the release of a large amount of energy. Spontaneous fission rarely occurs. However, by the absorption of a low-energy neutron, fission can be induced in certain nuclei. Of special interest are those fission reactions that release more neutrons since those other neutrons will cause other atoms to undergo fission. This in turn releases more neutrons, creating a **chain reaction**. By bombarding large, unstable nuclei with neutrons, scientists can use fission reactions to power commercial nuclear electric-generating plants.

Example: A fission reaction occurs when uranium-235 (U-235) absorbs a low-energy neutron, briefly forming an excited state of U-236, which then splits into xenon-140, strontium-94, and x more neutrons. In isotopic notation form the reactions are:

$$^{235}_{92}\mathrm{U} + {}^{1}_{0}\mathrm{n} \rightarrow {}^{236}_{92}\mathrm{U} \rightarrow {}^{140}_{54}\mathrm{Xe} + {}^{94}_{38}\mathrm{Sr} + x{}^{1}_{0}\mathrm{n}$$

How many neutrons are produced in the last reaction?

Solution: The question is asking "What is x?" By treating each arrow as an equal sign, the problem is simply asking you to balance the last "equation." The mass numbers (A) on either side of each arrow must be equal. This is an application of **nucleon** or **baryon number conservation,** which says that the total number of neutrons plus protons remains the same, even if neutrons are converted to protons and vice versa, as they are in some decays. Because $235 + 1 = 236$, the first arrow is indeed balanced. To find the number of neutrons, solve for x in the last equation (arrow):

$$236 = 140 + 94 + x$$
$$x = 236 - 140 - 94$$
$$x = 2$$

So two neutrons are produced in this reaction. These neutrons are free to go on and be absorbed by more ^{235}U and cause more fission, and the process continues in a chain reaction. Note that it really was not necessary to know that the intermediate state $^{236}_{92}U$ was formed.

Some radioactive nuclei may be induced to fission via more than one **decay channel** or **decay mode**. For example, a different fission reaction may occur when uranium-235 absorbs a slow neutron and then immediately splits into barium-139, krypton-94, and three more neutrons with no intermediate state:

$$^{235}_{92}U + ^{1}_{0}n \rightarrow ^{139}_{56}Ba + ^{94}_{36}Kr + 3^{1}_{0}n$$

Radioactive Decay

Radioactive decay is a naturally occurring spontaneous decay of certain nuclei accompanied by the emission of specific particles. It could be classified as a certain type of fission. Radioactive decay problems are of three general types:

1. The integer arithmetic of particle and isotope species
2. Radioactive half-life problems
3. The use of exponential decay curves and decay constants

Isotope decay arithmetic and nucleon conservation

Let the letters X and Y represent nuclear isotopes such that the **parent isotope** $^{A}_{Z}X$ decays into a **daughter isotope** $^{A'}_{Z'}Y$ as in:

$$^{A}_{Z}X \rightarrow ^{A'}_{Z'}Y + \text{emitted decay particle}$$

Alpha decay

Alpha decay is the emission of an α-particle, which is a $^{4}_{2}He$ nucleus that consists of two protons and two neutrons. The alpha particle is very massive (compared to a beta particle) and doubly charged (since it contains two protons and has a +2 charge). Alpha particles interact with matter very easily; hence, they do not penetrate shielding (such as lead sheets) very far.

The emission of an α-particle means that the daughter's atomic number (Z') will be two less than the parent's atomic number, and the daughter's mass number (A') will be four less than the parent's mass number. This can be expressed in two equations:

$$Z_{daughter} = Z_{parent} - 2$$
$$A_{daughter} = A_{parent} - 4$$

The generic alpha decay reaction is then:

$$^{A}_{Z}X \rightarrow ^{A-4}_{Z-2}Y + ^{4}_{2}\alpha$$

Note that alpha decay and fission are the only radioactive processes on the exam during which the mass number (A') changes.

Example: Suppose a parent X alpha decays into a daughter Y such that:

$$^{238}_{92}X \rightarrow {}^{A'}_{Z'}Y + \alpha$$

What are the mass number (A') and atomic number (Z') of the daughter isotope Y?

Solution: Since $\alpha = {}^4_2He$, balancing the mass numbers and atomic numbers is all that needs to be done:

$238 = A' + 4$

$A' = 234$

$92 = Z' + 2$

$Z' = 90$

So $A' = 234$ and $Z' = 90$. Note that it was not necessary to know the chemical species of the isotopes to do this problem. However, the periodic table does show that $Z = 92$ means X is uranium-238 $\left({}^{238}_{92}U\right)$ and that $Z = 90$ means Y is thorium-234 $\left({}^{234}_{90}Th\right)$.

Beta decay

Beta decay is the emission of a β-particle, which could be either β^- (electron) or β^+ (positron), from the nucleus. A **positron** (e^+) is similar to an electron (so has minimal mass) but has a positive charge. Electrons and positrons do not normally reside in the nucleus but are emitted when a proton or neutron in the nucleus decays. This is because protons and neutrons are composed of elementary particles called quarks, which can recombine to form different particles. Specifically, in β^- decay, a neutron decays into a proton and a β^- particle (and an antineutrino), whereas in β^+ decay, a proton decays into a neutron and a β^+ particle (and a neutrino). Note that neither of these reactions is concerned with electrons in orbitals outside the nucleus, which are generally ignored during radioactive decay.

β^- decay means that a neutron is consumed and a proton takes its place. Hence, the parent's mass number is unchanged, and the parent's atomic number is increased by one. In other words, the daughter's A is the same as the parent's, and the daughter's Z is one more than the parent's.

$$Z_{daughter} = Z_{parent} + 1$$
$$A_{daughter} = A_{parent}$$

In β^+ decay, a proton is consumed and a neutron takes its place. Therefore, β^+ decay means that the parent's mass number is unchanged, and the parent's atomic number is decreased by one. In other words, the daughter's A is the same as the parent's, and the daughter's Z is one less than the parent's.

$$Z_{daughter} = Z_{parent} - 1$$
$$A_{daughter} = A_{parent}$$

The generic negative beta-minus decay reaction is:

$$^A_ZX \rightarrow {}^A_{Z+1}Y + \beta^-$$

Note that β^- decay is the only radioactive decay on the test where the atomic number (Z') increases. The generic beta-plus decay reaction is:

$$_Z^A X \rightarrow \,_{Z-1}^{A}Y + \beta^+$$

Since β particles are singly charged and about 1,836 times lighter than protons, the beta radiation from radioactive decay is more penetrating than alpha radiation.

Example: Suppose a cobalt-60 nucleus undergoes beta-minus decay such that:

$$_{27}^{60}\text{Co} \rightarrow \,_{Z+1}^{A}Y + \beta^-$$

What are the A' and Z' of the daughter isotope?

Solution: Balance mass numbers:

$60 = A' + 0$

$A' = 60$

Now balance the atomic numbers, taking into account that cobalt has 27 protons (the Z value, or presubscript, given in the question) and that there is one more proton on the right-hand side:

$Z' = Z + 1$

$Z' = 27 + 1$

$Z' = 28$

The answer is an element with 28 protons and 60 nucleons. Although the question does not ask for the identity of the daughter, the periodic table shows that it is:

$Y = \,_{28}^{60}\text{Ni}$

Gamma decay

Gamma decay is the emission of γ-particles, which are high-energy photons. Gamma decay usually follows another type of nuclear decay and is a way for the nucleus to shed excess energy (similar to how an electron in an excited state emits a photon to shed energy). Gamma particles carry no charge and simply lower the energy of the emitting (parent) nucleus without changing the mass number or the atomic number. In other words, the daughter's A is the same as the parent's, and the daughter's Z is the same as the parent's.

$$Z_{\text{parent}} = Z_{\text{daughter}}$$
$$A_{\text{parent}} = A_{\text{daughter}}$$

The generic gamma decay reaction is thus:

$$_Z^A X^* \rightarrow \,_Z^A X + \gamma$$

Example: Suppose a parent isotope $_Z^A X$ emits a β^+ and turns into an excited state of the isotope $_{Z'}^{A'} Y^*$, which then γ-decays to $_{Z''}^{A''} Y$, which in turn α-decays to $_{Z'''}^{A'''} W$. If W is ^{60}Fe (Z = 26), what is $_Z^A X$?

Solution: Since the final daughter in this chain of decay is given, it will be necessary to work backward through the reactions. First, work backward from the α-decay, then use that answer to work backward from the β^+-decay. Note that the γ-decay simply releases energy from the nucleus but does not alter the atomic number or the mass number of the parent and so can be disregarded for these calculations.

First, the α-decay:

$$_{Z''}^{A''} Y \rightarrow _{26}^{60} Fe + _2^4 He^{2+}$$

By balancing the atomic numbers you find:

$Z'' = 26 + 2 = 28$

A balancing of the mass numbers implies:

$A'' = 60 + 4 = 64$

So the γ-decay was:

$$_{28}^{64} Y^* \rightarrow _{28}^{64} Y + \gamma$$

The first reaction was a β^+-decay that must have looked like:

$$_Z^A X \rightarrow _{28}^{64} Y^* + \beta^+$$

Again, balance the atomic numbers:

$Z = 28 + 1 = 29$

Since A remains unchanged during β^+-decay, $A' = A = 64$.

While the question did not ask for it, it is possible again to look at the periodic table to find that the total chain of decays can be written as:

$$_{29}^{64} Cu \rightarrow _{28}^{64} Ni^* + \beta^+$$
$$_{28}^{64} Ni^* \rightarrow _{28}^{64} Ni + \gamma$$
$$_{28}^{64} Ni \rightarrow _{26}^{60} Fe + \alpha$$

Electron capture

Certain unstable radionuclides are capable of capturing an inner electron that combines with a proton to form a neutron. The atomic number is now one less than the original, but the mass number remains the same. Electron capture is a rare process best thought of as an inverse β^- decay, following the exact same process as beta-minus decay but in reverse.

$$_Z^A X + e^- \rightarrow _{Z-1}^A Y$$

Radioactive decay half-life

In a collection of a great many identical radioactive isotopes, the **half-life** $(t_{1/2})$ of the sample is the time it takes for half of the sample to decay by any of the above processes. After n half-lives, $\left(\frac{1}{2}\right)^n$ of the original sample will remain, whereas $1 - \left(\frac{1}{2}\right)^n$ will have decayed.

Example: If the half-life of a certain isotope is 4 years, what fraction of a sample of that isotope will remain after 12 years?

Solution: If 4 years is one half-life, then 12 years is three half-lives and $n = 3$. During the first half-life—the first 4 years—half of the sample will have decayed. During the second half-life (years 4 to 8), half of the remaining half will decay, leaving one-fourth of the original. During the third and final period (years 8 to 12), half of the remaining fourth will decay, leaving one-eighth of the original sample. Thus the fraction remaining after 3 half-lives is $\left(\frac{1}{2}\right)^3$ or $\frac{1}{8}$.

Exponential decay

Let N be the number of radioactive nuclei that have not yet decayed in a sample. It turns out that the **rate** at which the nuclei decay $\left(\frac{\Delta N}{\Delta t}\right)$ is proportional to the number that remain (N). This suggests the equation:

$$\frac{\Delta N}{\Delta t} = -\lambda N$$

where λ is known as the **decay constant.** The solution of this equation tells us how the number of radioactive nuclei changes with time, which is known as **exponential decay:**

$$N = N_0 e^{-\lambda t}$$

where N_0 is the number of undecayed nuclei at time $t = 0$. (The decay constant is related to the half-life by $\lambda = \frac{\ln(2)}{t_{1/2}} = \frac{0.693}{t_{1/2}}$.)

Example: If at time $t = 0$ there is a two-mole sample of radioactive isotopes of decay constant $2\ (hour)^{-1}$, how many nuclei remain after 45 minutes?

Solution: Because 45 minutes is three-fourths of an hour, the exponent $(-\lambda t)$ is

$$-\lambda t = -2\left(\frac{3}{4}\right) = -\frac{6}{4} = -\frac{3}{2}$$

The exponential factor will be a number smaller than 1:

$$e^{-\lambda t} = e^{-3/2} = 0.22$$

So only 0.22 or 22% of the original two-mole sample will remain. To find N_0, multiply the number of moles by the number of particles per mole (Avogadro's number):

$$N_0 = 2(6.02 \times 10^{23}) = 1.2 \times 10^{24}$$

From the equation that describes exponential decay, you can calculate the number of nuclei that remain after 45 minutes:

$$\begin{aligned} N &= N_0 e^{-\lambda t} \\ &= (1.2 \times 10^{24})(0.22) \\ &= 2.6 \times 10^{23} \text{ particles} \end{aligned}$$

REVIEW PROBLEMS

1. Element $^{102}_{20}\varsigma$ is formed as a result of 3 α and 2 β^- decays. Which of the following is the parent element?

    A. $^{90}_{16}\Gamma$

    B. $^{114}_{24}\Phi$

    C. $^{114}_{28}\Theta$

    D. $^{12}_{8}\Delta + ^{90}_{12}\vartheta$

    E. $^{114}_{25}\Lambda$

2. Element X is radioactive and decays via α-decay with a half-life of four days. If 12.5% of an original sample of element X remains after t days, then determine t.

3. A patient undergoing treatment for thyroid cancer receives a dose of radioactive iodine (^{131}I), which has a half-life of 8.05 days. If the original dose contained 12 mg of ^{131}I, what mass of ^{131}I remains after 16.1 days?

4. In an exponential decay, if the natural logarithm of the ratio of intact nuclei (N) at time t to the intact nuclei at time $t = 0$ (N_0) is plotted against time, what does the slope of the graph correspond to?

5. The half-life of radioactive sodium is 15 hours. How many hours would it take for a 64 g sample to decay to one-eighth of its original activity?

    A. 3
    B. 15
    C. 30
    D. 45
    E. 60

SOLUTIONS TO REVIEW PROBLEMS

1. **B** Emission of three alpha particles by the (as yet unknown) parent results in the following changes:

   Mass number: decreases by 3×4 or 12 units

   Atomic number: decreases by 3×2 or 6 units

   Emission of two negative betas results in the following changes:

   Mass number: no change

   Atomic number: increases by 2×1 or 2 units

   So the net change is: mass number decreases by 12 units; atomic number decreases by 4 units. Therefore, the mass number of the parent is 12 greater than 102, or 114; the atomic number of the parent is 4 greater than 20, or 24. The only choice given with these numbers is (B).

2. **$t = 12$ days**

   Because the half-life of element X is 4 days, 50% of an original sample remains after 4 days, 25% of an original sample remains after 8 days, and 12.5% of an original sample remains after 12 days. Thus, $t = 12$ days. A different approach is to set $\left(\frac{1}{2}\right)^n = 0.125,$ where n is the number of half-lives that have elapsed. Solving for n gives $n = 3$. Thus, 3 half-lives have elapsed, and given the half-life is 4 days, $t = 12$ days.

3. **3 mg**

   Given that the half-life of ^{131}I is 8.05 days, we know that two half-lives have elapsed after 16.1 days, which means that 25% of the original amount of ^{131}I is still present. Thus, only 25% of the original number of ^{131}I nuclei remain, which also means that only 25% of the original mass of ^{131}I remain. Because the original dose contained 12 mg of ^{131}I, only 3 mg remain after 16.1 days.

4. **$-\lambda$**

   The expression $N = N_0 e^{-\lambda t}$ is equivalent to $\frac{N}{N_0} = e^{-\lambda t}$. Taking the natural logarithm of both sides of the latter expression you find:

   $$\ln\left(\frac{N}{N_0}\right) = -\lambda t$$

   From this expression it is clear that plotting $\ln\left(\frac{N}{N_0}\right)$ versus t will give a straight line of slope $-\lambda$.

5. **D** For a 64 g sample to decay to one-eighth of its original activity, or 8 g, the sample would have to go through three half-lives. Therefore, the amount of time needed for the decay is 3 half-lives × 15 hours per half-life = 45 hours.

Section IV

ORGANIC CHEMISTRY

SECTION GOALS

Organic Chemistry is the final section in the Survey of Natural Sciences section of the OAT. The organic chemistry strategies, terminology, reaction mechanisms, and practice presented within this section are designed to help you to accomplish the following goals:

- Recall functional group structure, nomenclature, and reactivity trends
- Predict reaction mechanisms of novel compounds
- Distinguish key differences in compounds with similar structures
- Apply known reagents to new reaction schema
- Predict answers to OAT Organic Chemistry questions efficiently

CONTENT OVERVIEW

Nomenclature (7%)**	Chapter 39: Nomenclature
Stereochemistry (10%)	Chapter 40: Isomers
Aromatics and Bonding (10%)	Chapter 41: Bonding Chapter 44: Aromatic Compounds
Reactions (30%), Reaction Mechanisms (17%)	Chapter 42: Alkanes Chapter 43: Alkenes and Alkynes Chapter 45: Alcohols and Ethers Chapter 46: Aldehydes and Ketones Chapter 47: Carboxylic Acids* Chapter 48: Carboxylic Acid Derivatives* Chapter 49: Amines
Acid-Base Chemistry (10%)	Chapter 47: Carboxylic Acids* Chapter 48: Carboxylic Acid Derivatives*
Chemical and Physical Properties of Molecules (17%)**	Chapter 50: Spectroscopy Chapter 51: Separation

*Chapters 47 and 48 are required for Reactions, Reaction Mechanisms, and Acid-Base Chemistry
**These test areas require both the listed chapters, and understanding of Chapters 42–49.

KEY STUDY STRATEGIES

The organic chemistry in this section is best studied in order. After an initial review, the content should be used for spot checks on content and reactions. As noted in the table above, there is extensive overlap of the topics within this section. Each chapter is designed to build on knowledge from prior chapters, so if a particular chapter is giving you trouble refer back to previous readings. Later chapters should be used after thoroughly working through the previous chapters and their practice questions. Within each chapter, extra focus should be placed on the boldface terms, as well as the recurring reaction schema. The same simple steps within reaction mechanisms will be repeated throughout the Organic Chemistry section, making comfort with this content a key OAT skill. When solving the practice problems at the end of each chapter, attempt to do so without referring back to the associated chapter in order to demonstrate mastery of the content.

CHAPTER THIRTY-EIGHT

Organic Chemistry Strategies

The final subtest of the Survey of Natural Sciences is Organic Chemistry. Questions 71–100 will assess your knowledge of reaction mechanisms, properties of molecules, stereochemistry, nomenclature, reactions, acids and bases, and aromatics.

ORGANIC CHEMISTRY QUESTION STRATEGY

Organic Chemistry questions should always be approached using Kaplan's Stop-Think-Predict-Match question strategy. In particular, making good use of the *Think* and *Predict* steps will allow you to quickly eliminate impossible answer choices, such as those that don't use correct Lewis structures or don't reflect the key change caused by a reaction. In this way, a general, well-thought-out prediction may be sufficient for narrowing down the choices to the correct answer without requiring you to ever draw out an entire reaction or complex molecule. This does vary, though: Some questions will be fact-based or require only a simple mental assessment, but others will necessitate writing out complex reactions or drawing molecules based on their IUPAC names. On average, expect each question to take you 60 seconds, but plan for this to fluctuate from question to question. Note that if you did not follow the Kaplan timing guidelines for the first two subtests of the Survey of Natural Sciences, you may have less time per Organic Chemistry question. This isn't an ideal situation and might mean that your time will elapse before you are able to attempt every question. Complete enough timed practice to ensure you stay on time throughout this and every other section on Test Day. For more details about how to apply the question and timing strategies to any question in the Survey of Natural Sciences, see Chapter 4, Biology Strategies.

STUDYING ORGANIC CHEMISTRY CONTENT

Initially, the Organic Chemistry content on the OAT may appear quite dissimilar to what you studied in your previous courses. The OAT is a multiple-choice test, so you can't be asked to draw out complicated molecules, deduce elaborate reaction mechanisms, or synthesize specific products based on memory alone. If the test makers ask you to determine the reactant required for a certain reaction or the identity of an unknown molecule based on its IR absorption spectrum, the answer must be one of five choices in front of you. The nature of the test dictates that the focus be more on generalizations, patterns, and critical thinking rather than straight memorization, which may seem more difficult at first but is actually easier for most students to learn in the long term!

To that end, study concepts rather than memorizing a long list of specific reactions. Although it won't hurt you to know the mechanisms for the Wittig reaction, the Newman-Kwart rearrangement, and the Takai olefination, a basic understanding of the properties of a carbonyl and the kinds of reactions it can take part in (the carbonyl carbon is partially positive and will react with nucleophiles, and the carbonyl oxygen is partially negative and will act as a base; see Chapter 46, Aldehydes and Ketones) will be much more beneficial for Test Day.

The chapters in this section are arranged by functional group to help you pay attention to these kinds of general properties. While reading, don't attempt to memorize every reaction initially but instead focus on the general types of reactions each functional group can undergo. Only 30 percent (nine questions) of the Organic Chemistry subtest is about individual reactions, and the named reactions make up only a small fraction of those questions. Much more of the subtest is devoted to broader topics, such as nomenclature, physical properties, stability, and stereochemistry. Even questions that do require analyzing reactions can often be answered correctly using critical thinking based on a strong fundamental understanding of why reactions take place and a solid knowledge of General Chemistry. Learn the basics first by reading the following chapters and analyzing the reactions from the study sheets at the end of this book. Only focus on memorizing specific reactions once you feel comfortable with the concepts, which yield more points on Test Day and make memorizing the specifics easier, too.

Finally, with that understanding, don't panic if you see a reaction or molecule that you don't recognize on Test Day. Instead, examine the reactants and products for components you do recognize. If you see that xylitol (pentane-1,2,3,4,5-pentol) is a reactant for a reaction-based question, you might not initially know its structure or how it behaves. However, you can identify that it's an alcohol right away based on its name alone, which means you know it's likely to be a water-soluble weak acid that can undergo deprotonation. If only one of the five answer choices shows the transfer of a hydrogen, then you have a very good chance of getting that question right; no further knowledge is required. Once you have the concepts down and put them into practice using the Kaplan strategies, you'll be ready to think like this on Test Day and correctly answer even the questions that seem difficult to you now.

CHAPTER THIRTY-NINE

Nomenclature

Nomenclature, the set of accepted conventions for naming compounds, is crucial to a discussion of organic chemistry. Nomenclature represents the basic language of organic chemistry; if you don't know it, you may feel like you're taking a test in a foreign language! Note that the rules of nomenclature presented in this chapter are for general cases only. More specific examples will be discussed in the chapters dealing with particular types of compounds.

ALKANES

Alkanes are the simplest organic molecules, consisting only of carbon and hydrogen atoms held together by single bonds.

Straight-Chain Alkanes

The names of the four simplest alkanes are:

$$CH_4 \qquad CH_3CH_3 \qquad CH_3CH_2CH_3 \qquad CH_3CH_2CH_2CH_3$$
methane   **eth**ane   **prop**ane   **but**ane

The names of the longer-chain alkanes consist of prefixes derived from the Greek root for the number of carbon atoms with the ending **-ane.**

$C_5H_{12} =$ **pent**ane $C_9H_{20} =$ **non**ane

$C_6H_{14} =$ **hex**ane $C_{10}H_{22} =$ **dec**ane

$C_7H_{16} =$ **hept**ane $C_{11}H_{24} =$ **undec**ane

$C_8H_{18} =$ **oct**ane $C_{12}H_{26} =$ **dodec**ane

These prefixes are applicable to more complex organic molecules, too, and should be memorized.

Branched-Chain Alkanes

The International Union of Pure and Applied Chemistry (IUPAC) proposed a set of simple rules for naming complex molecules. This basic system can be used to name all classes of organic compounds. Throughout these notes, the IUPAC names will be listed as the primary name, and common names will appear in parentheses.

1. Find the longest chain in the compound.

The longest continuous carbon chain within the compound is taken as the backbone. If two or more chains are of equal length, the most highly substituted chain (the one with the greatest number of other groups attached) takes precedence. The longest chain may not be as obvious from the structural formula as when it is drawn. For example, the backbone shown below is an octane (it contains eight carbon atoms).

Figure 39.1

2. Number the chain.

Number the chain from one end in such a way that the lowest set of numbers is obtained for the substituents (which in alkanes are carbon groups not part of the main carbon chain).

Figure 39.2

3. Name the substituents.

Substituents are named according to their appropriate prefix with the ending **-yl.** For example:

CH_3-	CH_3CH_2-	$CH_3CH_2CH_2-$
methyl	ethyl	*n*-propyl

The prefix *n*- in the above example indicates an unbranched ("normal") compound. There are special names for some common branched alkanes (see Figure 39.3), and these are usually used in the naming of substituents.

$$CH_3 - \underset{\underset{CH_3}{|}}{\overset{\overset{CH_3}{|}}{C}} -$$

tert —butyl

$$CH_3 - \underset{\underset{CH_3}{|}}{\overset{\overset{CH_3}{|}}{C}} - CH_2 -$$

neopentyl

$$\underset{\underset{CH_3}{/}}{\overset{\overset{CH_3}{\backslash}}{HC}} -$$

isopropyl

$$CH_3 - CH_2 - \underset{}{\overset{\overset{CH_3}{|}}{CH}} -$$

sec —butyl

$$CH_3 - \underset{}{\overset{\overset{CH_3}{|}}{CH}} - CH_2 -$$

isobutyl

Figure 39.3

If two or more equivalent groups are present, the prefixes **di-, tri-, tetra-,** etc. are used.

4. Assign a number to each substituent.

Each substituent is assigned a number to identify its point of attachment to the principal chain. If the prefixes **di-, tri-, tetra-,** etc., are used, a number is still necessary for each individual group.

5. Complete the name.

List the substituents in alphabetical order with their corresponding numbers. Prefixes such as di-, tri-, etc., as well as the hyphenated prefixes (*tert-* [or *t-*], *sec-, n-*), are ignored in alphabetizing. In contrast, **cyclo-, iso-,** and **neo-** are considered part of the group name and are alphabetized. Commas should be placed between numbers, and hyphens should be placed between numbers and words. For example:

4-ethyl-5-isopropyl-3,3-dimethyl octane

Figure 39.4

You may also need to indicate the isomer you are describing—e.g., *cis* or *trans, R* or *S*, etc. Isomers are discussed in detail in Chapter 40.

Cycloalkanes

Alkanes can also form rings rather than straight chains. These are named according to the number of carbon atoms in the ring with the prefix **cyclo-**.

cyclopropane   cyclobutane   cyclooctane

Figure 39.5

Substituted cycloalkanes are named as derivatives of the parent cycloalkane. The substituents are named, and the carbon atoms are numbered around the ring *starting from the point of greatest substitution*. Again, the goal is to provide the lowest series of numbers, as in rule number 2 for naming complex molecules.

methylcyclobutane   3-isopropyl-1,1-dimethylcyclohexane

Figure 39.6

MULTIPLE BONDS

Organic molecules more complicated than simple alkanes can also be named using the 5-step process but with a few additional considerations.

Alkenes

Alkenes (or **olefins**) are compounds containing carbon-carbon double bonds. The nomenclature rules are essentially the same as for alkanes except that the ending **-ene** is used rather than **-ane**. Note the exceptions of the common names *ethylene* and *propylene,* which are used preferentially over the IUPAC names *ethene* and *propene.*

When identifying the carbon backbone, select the longest chain that contains the double bond (or the greatest number of double bonds if more than one is present).

Figure 39.7

Number the backbone so the double bond receives the lowest number possible. Remember that multiple double bonds must be named using the prefixes di-, tri-, etc. and that each must receive a number. Also, you may need to name the configurational isomer (*cis/trans*, *Z/E*). This topic will be discussed further in Chapter 40.

Substituents are named as they are for alkanes, and their positions are specified by the number of the backbone carbon atom to which they are attached.

Frequently, an alkene group must be named as a substituent. In these cases, the systematic names may be used, but common names are more popular. **Vinyl-** derivatives are monosubstituted ethylenes (**ethenyl-**), and **allyl-** derivatives are propylenes substituted at the C–3 position (**2-propenyl-**). **Methylene** refers to the –CH_2 group.

chloroethene
(vinyl chloride)

3-bromo-1-propene
(allyl bromide)

methylene cyclohexane

Figure 39.8

Cycloalkenes

Cycloalkenes are named like cycloalkanes but with the suffix -**ene** rather than -**ane**. If the molecule has only one double bond and no other substituents, a number is not necessary.

cyclohexene

Figure 39.9

Alkynes

Alkynes are compounds that possess carbon-carbon triple bonds. The suffix **-yne** replaces -*ane* in the parent alkane. The position of the triple bond is indicated by a number when necessary. The common name for ethyne is **acetylene,** and this name is used almost exclusively.

$$HC \equiv CH$$
ethyne
(acetylene)

4-methyl-2-hexyne

cyclohexyne

Figure 39.10

SUBSTITUTED ALKANES

Haloalkanes

Compounds containing a halogen substituent are named following similar rules as those above while including the halogen as a substituent. If the halogen is the highest priority substituent, ensure it has the lower number when deciding from which end of the carbon chain to start counting. For example:

2-chloro-3-iodopentane

1-chloro-2-methylcyclohexane

Figure 39.11

Alternatively, the haloalkane may be named as an **alkyl halide.** In this system, chloroethane is called **ethyl chloride**. Other examples are:

2-bromo-2-methylpropane
(*t*-butyl bromide)

2-iodopropane
(isopropyl iodide)

Figure 39.12

Alcohols

In the IUPAC system, **alcohols** are named by replacing the *-e* of the corresponding alkane with **-ol**. The chain is numbered such that the carbon attached to the hydroxyl group (–OH) receives the lowest number possible.

In compounds that possess a multiple bond and a hydroxyl group, numerical priority is given to the carbon attached to the –OH.

ethanol

5-methyl-2-heptanol

hept-6-en-1-ol

Figure 39.13

A common system of nomenclature exists for alcohols in which the name of the alkyl group is combined with the word *alcohol*. These common names are used for simple alcohols. For example, methanol may be named "methyl alcohol," while 2-propanol may also be named "isopropyl alcohol."

Molecules with two hydroxyl groups are called **diols** (or **glycols**) and are named with the suffix **-diol**. Two numbers are necessary to locate the two functional groups. Diols with hydroxyl groups on adjacent carbons are referred to as **vicinal**, and diols with hydroxyl groups on the same carbon are **geminal**. These terms apply for any two functional groups. Geminal diols (also called **carbonyl hydrates**) are not commonly observed because they spontaneously lose water (**dehydrate**) to produce carbonyl compounds (containing C=O; see Chapter 44, Aromatic Compounds).

Ethers

In the IUPAC system, **ethers** are named as derivatives of alkanes, and the larger alkyl group is chosen as the backbone. The ether functionality is specified as an **alkoxy-** prefix, indicating the presence of an ether (*oxy-*), and the corresponding smaller alkyl group (*alk-*). The chain is numbered to give the ether the lowest position. Common names for ethers are frequently used. They are derived by naming the two alkyl groups in alphabetical order and adding the word *ether*. The generic term "ether" refers to diethyl ether, a commonly used solvent.

For **cyclic ethers**, numbering of the ring begins at the oxygen and proceeds to provide the lowest numbers for the substituents. Three-membered rings are termed **oxiranes** by IUPAC. The simplest of these are commonly called **epoxides**.

methoxyethane
(ethyl methyl ether)

1-isopropoxyhexane
(*n*-hexyl isopropyl ether)

oxirane
(ethylene oxide)

2-methyloxirane
(propylene oxide)

tetrahydrofuran
(THF)

Figure 39.14

Aldehydes and Ketones

Aldehydes are named according to the longest chain containing the aldehyde functional group. The suffix **-al** replaces the *-e* of the corresponding alkane. The carbonyl carbon receives the lowest number, although numbers are not always necessary since by definition an aldehyde is terminal and receives the number (1).

n-butanal

5,5-dimethylhexanal

Figure 39.15

The common names *formaldehyde*, *acetaldehyde*, and *propionaldehyde* are used almost exclusively instead of the IUPAC names *methanal*, *ethanal*, and *propanal*, respectively.

methanal
(formaldehyde)

ethanal
(acetaldehyde)

propanal
(propionaldehyde)

Figure 39.16

Ketones are named analogously with aldehydes but with **-one** as a suffix. If highest priority, the carbonyl group must be assigned the lowest possible number. In complex molecules, the carbonyl group can be named as a prefix with the term **oxo-**. Alternatively, the individual alkyl groups may be listed in alphabetical order and followed by the word **ketone**.

2-pentanone

3-(5-oxohexyl)cyclohexanone

2-propanone
(dimethyl ketone)
(acetone)

3-butene-2-one
(methyl vinyl ketone)

Figure 39.17

A commonly used alternative to the numerical designation of substituents is to term the carbon atom adjacent to the carbonyl carbon as α and the carbon atoms successively along the chain as β, γ, δ, etc. This system is encountered with dicarbonyl compounds and halocarbonyl compounds.

Carboxylic Acids

Carboxylic acids are named with the ending **-oic acid** replacing the *-e* ending of the corresponding alkane. Carboxylic acids are terminal functional groups and, like aldehydes, are numbered one (1).

The common names *formic acid* (methanoic acid), *acetic acid* (ethanoic acid), and *propionic acid* (propanoic acid) are used almost exclusively.

| methanoic acid | ethanoic acid | propanoic acid |
| (formic acid) | (acetic acid) | (propionic acid) |

Figure 39.18

Amines

The longest chain attached to the nitrogen atom is taken as the backbone. For simple compounds, name the alkane and replace the final -*e* with **-amine**. More complex molecules are often named using the prefix **amino-**.

ethanamine   4-aminohept-2-en-1-ol

Figure 39.19

The prefix N- is used to specify the location of an additional alkyl group attached to the nitrogen:

N-ethylpentanamine
(ethylpentylamine)

Figure 39.20

SUMMARY OF FUNCTIONAL GROUPS

Table 39.1 lists the major functional groups you need to know.

Functional Group	Structure	IUPAC Prefix	IUPAC Suffix
Carboxylic acid	R–C(=O)OH	carboxy-	-oic acid
Ester	R–C(=O)OR	alkoxycarbonyl-	-oate
Acyl halide	R–C(=O)X	halocarbonyl-	-oyl halide
Amide	R–C(=O)NH₂	amido-	-amide
Nitrile	$RC\equiv N$	cyano-	-nitrile
Aldehyde	R–C(=O)H	oxo-	-al
Ketone	R–C(=O)–R	oxo-	-one
Alcohol	ROH	hydroxy-	-ol
Thiol	RSH	sulfhydryl-	-thiol
Amine	RNH_2	amino-	-amine
Imine	$R_2C{=}NR'$	imino-	-imine
Ether	ROR	alkoxy-	-ether
Sulfide	R_2S	alkylthio-	
Halide	-I, -Br, -Cl, -F	halo-	
Nitro	RNO_2	nitro-	
Azide	RN_3	azido-	
Diazo	RN_2^+	diazo-	

Table 39.1

REVIEW PROBLEMS

1. What is the IUPAC name of the following compound?

    A. 2,5-dimethylheptane
    B. 2-ethyl-5-methylhexane
    C. 3,6-dimethylheptane
    D. 5-ethyl-2-methylhexane
    E. 3,5-dimethylhexane

2. What is the structure of 5-ethyl-2,2-dimethyloctane?

3. What is the name of the following compound?

    A. 1-ethyl-3,4-dimethylcycloheptane
    B. 2-ethyl-4,5-dimethylcyclohexane
    C. 1-ethyl-3,4-dimethylcyclohexane
    D. 4-ethyl-1,2-dimethylcyclohexane
    E. 4-ethyl-1,3-dimethylcyclohexane

4. What is the name of the following compound?

    A. 2-bromo-5-butyl-4,4-dichloro-3-iodo-3-methyloctane
    B. 7-bromo-4-butyl-5,5-dichloro-6-iodo-6-methyloctane
    C. 2-bromo-4,4-dichloro-3-iodo-3-methyl-5-propylnonane
    D. 2-bromo-5-butyl-4,4-dichloro-3-iodo-3-methylnonane
    E. 7-bromo-4-butyl-5,5-dichloro-4-iodo-3-methylnonane

5. What is the name of the following compound?

A. *trans*-3-ethyl-4-hexen-2-ol
B. *trans*-4-ethyl-2-hexen-5-ol
C. *trans*-3-ethanol-2-hexene
D. *trans*-4-ethanol-2-hexene
E. *trans*-2-ethyl-3-hexen-4-ol

6. Indicate the α, β, γ, and δ carbons in the following compound.

7. An alkane can be synthesized from its corresponding alkene by a reaction with hydrogen in the presence of a platinum catalyst. If 5-methenyl-3-methyloctane (shown below) were treated with hydrogen in the presence of a platinum catalyst, what would be the name and structure of the alkane that would be produced?

8. What is the correct structure for *cis*-1-ethoxy-2-methoxycyclopentane?

A.

B.

C.

D.

E. None of the above

9. Do the following structures show the same compound or different compounds? Give a name for each structure.

A. B.

10. Match each name with the correct structure below.

A. *t*-butyl
B. diene
C. β-keto acid
D. cyclohexanol
E. *sec*-butyl

1. R⌒⌒⌒R

2. ⬡—OH

3. CH₃—CH—
     |
     C₂H₅

$$CH_3-CH-$$
$$C_2H_5$$

4. (CH₃)₃C—

$$(CH_3)_3C-$$

5. R ⟍⟋⟍ OH (β-keto acid structure)

11. Which of the following are always considered terminal functional groups?

A. Aldehydes
B. Ketones
C. Carboxylic acids
D. Alkenes
E. Both A and C

SOLUTIONS TO REVIEW PROBLEMS

1. **A** The first task in naming alkanes is identifying the longest chain. In this case, the longest chain has seven carbons, so the parent alkane is heptane. Choices (B) and (D) can be eliminated. The next step is to identify the substituents on the alkane chain. This compound has two methyl groups at carbons 2 and 5, so the correct IUPAC name is 2,5-dimethylheptane. Choice (C) is incorrect because the position numbers of the substituents are not minimized.

2. The structure of 5-ethyl-2,2-dimethyloctane is shown below.

3. **D** Substituted cycloalkanes are named as derivatives of their parent cycloalkane, which in this case is cyclohexane. Thus, choice (A) can be ruled out immediately. Then, the substituents are listed in alphabetical order, and the carbons are numbered so as to give the lowest sum of substituent numbers. This cyclohexane has an ethyl and two methyl substituents; it is therefore an ethyl dimethyl cyclohexane. All the remaining answer choices recognize this; they only differ in the numbers assigned. In order to give the lowest sum of substituent numbers, the two methyl substituents must be numbered 1 and 2, and the ethyl substituent must be numbered 4. The correct name for this compound is thus 4-ethyl-1,2-dimethylcyclohexane.

4. **C** This question requires the application of the same set of rules laid out in Question 1. The longest backbone has nine carbons, so the compound is a nonane. Thus, choices (A) and (B) can be ruled out immediately. The substituent groups are, in alphabetical order: bromo, chloro, iodo, methyl, and propyl; these substituents must be given the lowest possible number on the hydrocarbon backbone. The resulting name is 2-bromo-4,4-dichloro-3-iodo-3-methyl-5-propylnonane.

5. **A** The first step is to locate the longest carbon chain containing the functional groups (C=C and OH). The backbone has six carbons (hex-). Since the alcohol group has higher priority than the double bond, it dictates the ending (-ol) and is given the lower position (2). The alkene is named according to the position of the double bond followed by -ene (4-hexene). Thus, the chain is called 4-hexene-2-ol. The substituents on the backbone are an ethyl group and an alkene group on C–3 and C–4, respectively. Since these constituents lie on opposite sides of the double bond, the molecule is *trans*. Therefore, this compound is called *trans*-3-ethyl-4-hexen-2-ol.

6. Numbering the carbons on the backbone from left to right, C–2 and C–4 are α carbons, C–1 and C–5 are β carbons, C–6 is a γ carbon, and C–7 is a δ carbon. This nomenclature is used to specify how far a given carbon in the backbone is from a reactive center, usually a carbonyl carbon.

7. Treating this alkene with hydrogen in the presence of a platinum catalyst will cause hydrogen atoms to be added across the double bond. The product will be 3,5-dimethyloctane, shown below.

8. **B** A cyclopentane is a cyclic alkane with five carbons. A *cis* cyclic compound has both of its substituents on the same side of the ring. Only choices (B) and (C) have two substituents, so (A) and (D) can be ruled out. In fact, choice (C) is a *trans* compound, so the correct answer must be (B). Ethoxy and methoxy represent ether substituents, and they must be on adjacent carbons on the same side of the molecule. Thus, the structure of *cis*-1-ethoxy-2-methoxycyclopentane is given in choice (B).

9. These structures both represent the same compound, 5-ethyl-3,5-dimethylnonane. The best way to see this is to name each one; this forces you to determine both the backbone and the substituents.

10. A. 4

    B. 1

    C. 5

    D. 2

    E. 3

11. **E** Both aldehyde and carboxylic acid functional groups are located on the terminal ends of carbon backbones. As a result, the carbon to which they are attached is named C–1, and choice (D) is correct. Ketones are always internal to the carbon chain, and alkenes can be internal or terminal so are not *always* terminal.

CHAPTER FORTY

Isomers

Isomers are chemical compounds that have the same molecular formula but differ in structure—that is, in their atomic connectivity or the spatial orientation of their atoms. Isomers may be similar, sharing most or all of their physical and chemical properties, or they may be very different.

Stereoisomers

Most
Different

Most
Similar

Structural
Isomers

Diastereomers
and
Geometric Isomers

Enantiomers

Conformational
Isomers

Figure 40.1

STRUCTURAL ISOMERISM

Structural isomers, also known as constitutional isomers, are compounds that share only a molecular formula. Structural isomers differ in where and how atoms are connected to each other and thus often have very different chemical and physical properties (such as melting point, boiling point, and solubility). For example, five different structures exist for compounds with the formula C_6H_{14}.

n-hexane   2-methylpentane

3-methylpentane   2,3-dimethylbutane   2,2-dimethylbutane

Figure 40.2

All have the same formula, but they differ in their carbon framework and in the number and type of atoms bonded to one another.

STEREOISOMERISM

Stereoisomers are compounds that have the same connectivity between their atoms and differ from each other only in the way that their atoms are oriented in space. *Cis-trans* isomers, enantiomers, diastereomers, *meso* compounds, and conformational isomers are all types of stereoisomers.

Cis-Trans Isomers

Cis-trans isomers, formerly known as **geometric isomers**, are compounds that differ in the position of substituents attached to the two carbons that form a double bond. Because a double bond cannot rotate, the substituents are fixed relative to one another and to the bond. If the substituents on the carbons are both above the double bond, they are on the same side, and the double bond is called *cis*. If one is above and one below, they are on opposite sides, and it is called a *trans* double bond.

For compounds with more than one substituent on either carbon of the double bond, an alternative method of naming applies. The highest priority substituent attached to each double bonded carbon has to be determined:

1. From the carbon of interest, determine the atomic weight of the first *atom* encountered along each bond. The group with the highest atomic weight atom has the highest priority.

2. If two atoms are the same, look at the next atom attached to each; the group that has the second atom with higher molecular weight is higher priority.

3. If two atoms are the same, a double bond takes priority over a single bond. This is a tie-breaker only; higher atomic weight will always take priory over a double bond.

The alkene is called (*Z*) (from German *zusammen*, meaning together) if the two highest priority substituents on each carbon are both above or both below the double bond or (*E*) (from German *entgegen*, meaning opposite) if they are on opposite sides. A simple mnemonic is that (*Z*) isomers are on "ze zame zide" of the double bond, while (*E*) isomers are "epposite."

(*Z*)-2-chloro-2-pentene   (*E*)-2-bromo-3-*t*-butyl-2-heptene

Figure 40.3

Enantiomers and Chirality

A molecule that is not superimposable upon its mirror image is called **chiral**. Your right and left hands are illustrations of chirality. Although essentially identical, your hands differ in their ability to fit into a right-handed glove. They are mirror images of each other yet cannot be superimposed. **Achiral** molecules are mirror images that can be superimposed; for example, the letter A is identical to its mirror image and therefore is achiral.

Figure 40.4

Carbon atoms are chiral only if they have four different substituents. Such a carbon atom is called **asymmetric** because it lacks a plane or point of symmetry. For example, the C−1 carbon atom in 1-bromo-1-chloroethane has four different substituents. The molecule is chiral because it is not superimposable on its mirror image. Pairs of chiral molecules that are nonsuperimposable mirror images are called **enantiomers** and are a specific type of stereoisomer discussed later in this chapter.

Figure 40.5

A carbon atom with only three different substituents, such as 1,1-dibromoethane, has a plane of symmetry and is therefore achiral. A simple 180° rotation along the *y*-axis allows the compound to be superimposed upon its mirror image.

Figure 40.6

Fischer projections

A three-dimensional molecule can be conveniently represented in two dimensions in a **Fischer projection**. In this system, horizontal lines indicate bonds that project out from the plane of the page, while vertical lines indicate bonds behind the plane of the page. The point of intersection of the lines represents a carbon atom. The Fischer projection of a molecule can be manipulated by interchanging any two pairs of substituents or by rotating the projection in the plane of the page by 180°, and it will keep the same absolute configuration. If only one pair of substituents is interchanged or if the molecule is rotated by 90°, the mirror image and thus the opposite enantiomer of the original compound is obtained.

Figure 40.7

Fischer projections allow straightforward determination of the configuration at a chiral center, discussed next.

Relative and absolute configuration

A **configuration** describes the spatial arrangement of the atoms or functional groups of a stereoisomer. The **relative configuration** of a chiral molecule is its configuration in relation to another chiral molecule.

The **absolute configuration** of a chiral molecule describes the spatial arrangement of these atoms or groups within the molecule relative to each other. Absolute configuration is determined using the *R/S* naming convention, and relative configuration is compared between the *R* and the *S* enantiomers.

Figure 40.8

The set sequence to determine the absolute configuration of a molecule at a single chiral center is as follows:

Step 1:

Assign priority to the four substituents using the same rules as for *E/Z* isomers:

1. From the carbon of interest, determine the atomic weight of the first *atom* encountered along each bond. The group with the highest atomic weight atom has the highest priority.
2. If two atoms are the same, look at the next atom attached to each; the group that has the second atom with higher molecular weight is higher priority.
3. If two atoms are the same, a double bond takes priority over a single bond. This is a tie-breaker only; higher atomic weight will always take priority over a double bond.

For example:

$$^2 CH_2CH_3$$
$$^4 H\text{''''} \overset{}{\underset{^3CH_3}{\diagup}} Cl ^1$$

Figure 40.9

Step 2:

Proceeding from highest priority (1st) to second lowest (3rd), determine the order of substituents around the wheel as either clockwise or counterclockwise by drawing a loop that connects 1st to 2nd to 3rd priority, ignoring the 4th group. If the order is clockwise, the chiral center temporarily is called

R (from Latin *rectus,* meaning right). If it is counterclockwise, it is temporarily called ***S*** (from Latin *sinister,* meaning left).

Step 3:

Finally, look at the lowest (4th) priority group. If group 4 is on the vertical line in a Fischer projection or otherwise is going into the page, the molecule is oriented correctly, and the designation remains the same. If group 4 is on the horizontal line or otherwise coming out of the page, the molecule is in the opposite orientation that it should be, so the temporary designation is swapped to the opposite designation (i.e., if the designation obtained in Step 2 was *R* but the 4th priority group is coming out of the page, the actual absolute configuration is *S*).

To provide a full name for a stereoisomer with a chiral center, the terms *R* and *S* are put in parentheses and separated from the rest of the name by a dash. If more than one asymmetric carbon is present, the location is specified by a number preceding the *R* or *S* within the parentheses and without a dash.

Note that in the traditional approach to determining chirality, the molecule initially must be rotated to place the lowest priority group pointing toward the back. However, this can be problematic as it is easy to lose track of the relative positions of the substituents during this step. The simpler Kaplan strategy, as described above, recognizes that if the lowest priority group is coming out of the page, it will appear the opposite of its true configuration, which avoids the difficult work of mentally rearranging the molecule.

Optical activity

Pairs of enantiomers (with opposite *R* and *S* designations) have identical chemical and physical properties with one exception: **optical activity**. A compound is optically active if it has the ability to rotate plane-polarized light. Ordinary light is unpolarized. It consists of waves vibrating in all possible planes perpendicular to its direction of motion. A polarizing filter allows light waves oscillating only in a particular direction to pass, producing plane-polarized light.

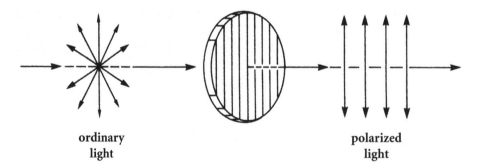

ordinary   polarized
light   light

Figure 40.10

If plane-polarized light is passed through a solution of an optically active compound, the molecule rotates the orientation of the polarized light by an angle α. The enantiomer of this compound will rotate light by the same amount, but in the opposite direction. A compound that rotates the plane-polarized light to the right, or clockwise (from the point of view of an observer seeing the light approach), is **dextrorotatory** and is indicated by (+). A compound that rotates light toward the left, or counterclockwise, is **levorotatory** and is labeled (−). The direction of rotation cannot be determined from the structure of a molecule and is not related to its *R* or *S* designation. Instead, it must be determined experimentally.

The amount of rotation depends on the number of molecules that a light wave encounters. This depends on two factors: the concentration of the optically active compound and the length of the tube through which the light passes. Chemists have set standard conditions of 1 g/mL for concentration and 1 dm for length in order to compare the optical activities of different compounds. Rotations measured at different concentrations and tube lengths can be converted to a standardized **specific rotation** (α) using the following equation:

$$\frac{\text{observed rotation}(\alpha)}{\text{concentration}(\text{g/ml}) \times \text{length}(\text{dm})}$$

A racemic mixture, or racemate, is a mixture of equal concentrations of both the (+) and (−) enantiomers. The rotations cancel each other, and no optical activity is observed.

Diastereomers

Many compounds have more than one chiral center, and thus multiple forms of stereoisomers exist for them. For any molecule with *n* chiral centers, there are 2^n possible stereoisomers. Thus, if a compound has two chiral carbon atoms, it has four possible stereoisomers (see Figure 40.11).

Figure 40.11

Compounds I and II are mirror images of each other and are therefore enantiomers. Similarly, compounds III and IV are enantiomers. However, compounds I and III are not. They are stereoisomers that are not mirror images, and so they are called diastereomers. Notice that other combinations of non–mirror image stereoisomers are also possible, and form diastereomer pairs. Hence compounds I and IV, compounds II and III, compounds I and III, and compounds II and IV are all pairs of diastereomers.

Diastereomers that differ at only one carbon make up special pairs called epimers, which are particularly important in the chemistry of carbohydrates.

Meso Compounds

Meso compounds are molecules with multiple chiral centers that also have an internal plane of symmetry. One half of the molecule has an *S* enantiomer, and the other half has its matching *R* enantiomer. If such a plane of symmetry exists, the molecule is not optically active, because the rotation of light by one chiral center is matched by the opposite rotation by the other chiral center. For example:

L-tartaric acid   *Meso*-tartaric acid   D-tartaric acid

Figure 40.12

D- and L-tartaric acid are both optically active, but *meso*-tartaric acid has a plane of symmetry and is not optically active. Although *meso*-tartaric acid has two chiral carbon atoms, the lack of optical activity is a function of the molecule as a whole.

Conformational Isomers

Conformational isomers are compounds that differ only by rotation about one or more single bonds. These isomers represent the same compound in a slightly different position—analogous to a person who may be either standing up or sitting down. These different conformations can be seen when the molecule is depicted in a **Newman projection**, in which the line of sight extends along a carbon-carbon bond axis. Because the view of the second carbon atom is blocked by the first, the second carbon is depicted as a large circle at the back, and the first carbon is depicted as the intersection of its three other bonds in front. The different conformations are encountered as the molecule is rotated about the axis between the two carbons. The classic example for demonstrating conformational isomerism in a straight chain molecule is *n*-butane. In a Newman projection, the line of sight extends through the C−2-C−3 bond axis.

Figure 40.13

Straight-chain conformations

The most stable conformation of *n*-butane is found when the two methyl groups (C–1 and C–4) are oriented 180° from each other. There is no overlap of atoms along the line of sight (besides C–2 and C–3), so the molecule is said to be in a **staggered** conformation. Specifically, it is called the *anti* conformation, because the two methyl groups are antiperiplanar to each other. This particular orientation is very stable and thus represents an energy minimum because all atoms are far apart, minimizing repulsive steric interactions.

The other type of staggered conformation, called *gauche*, occurs when the two methyl groups are 60° apart. In order to convert from the *anti* to the *gauche* conformation, the molecule must pass through an eclipsed conformation, in which the two methyl groups are 120° apart and overlap with the H atoms on the adjacent carbon. When the two methyl groups overlap with each other, the molecule is said to be totally eclipsed and is in its highest energy state.

Figure 40.14

A plot of potential energy versus the degree of rotation about the C–2–C–3 bond shows the relative minima and maxima the molecule encounters throughout its various conformations.

Figure 40.15

It is important to note that these barriers are rather small (3–4 kcal/mol) and are easily overcome at room temperature, when the molecule is rotating freely. Very low temperatures will slow conformational interconversion. If the molecules do not possess sufficient energy to cross the energy barrier, they may not rotate at all.

Cyclic conformations

In cycloalkanes, ring strain arises from three factors: angle strain, torsional strain, and nonbonded strain. Angle strain results when bond angles deviate from their ideal values (109.5° for sp³ hybridized carbons); torsional strain results when cyclic molecules must assume conformations that have eclipsed interactions; and nonbonded strain (van der Waals repulsion) results when atoms or groups compete for the same space. In order to alleviate these three types of strain, cycloalkanes attempt to adopt nonplanar conformations. Cyclobutane puckers into a slight V shape, cyclopentane adopts what is called the **envelope** conformation, and cyclohexane exists mainly in three conformations called the **chair,** the **boat,** and the **twist** or **skew-boat.**

| puckered cyclobutane | envelope cyclopentane | chair cyclohexane | boat cyclohexane | twist boat cyclohexane |

Figure 40.16

Cyclohexane

Unsubstituted

The most stable conformation of cyclohexane is the chair conformation. In this conformation, all three types of strain are eliminated. The hydrogen atoms that are perpendicular to the plane of the ring are called axial, and those parallel to the plane of the ring are called equatorial. The axial-equatorial orientations alternate around the ring.

The chair conformation has two forms that can be thought of as "left facing" and "right facing." The boat conformation is adopted when the chair "flips" and converts to the other chair conformation. When this happens, hydrogen atoms that were equatorial become axial, and vice versa, in the new chair.

In the boat conformation, all of the atoms are eclipsed, creating a high-energy state. To avoid this strain, the boat can twist into a slightly more stable form called the twist or skew-boat conformation. In the chair form, the atoms are in the staggered gauche conformation, thus contributing to the greater stability compared to the boat form.

Monosubstituted

The interconversion between the two chairs can be slowed or even prevented if a sterically bulky group is attached to the ring. The equatorial position is favored over the axial position because of steric repulsion with other axial substituents. Hence, a large group such as *t*-butyl can lock the molecule in one conformation.

Bulky groups prefer equatorial positions

Figure 40.17

Disubstituted

Different isomers can exist for disubstituted cycloalkanes. If both substituents are located on the same side of the ring, the molecule is called *cis*; if the two groups are on opposite sides of the ring, it is called *trans*.

cis-1,2-dimethylcyclohexane   *trans*-1,2-dimethylcyclohexane

Figure 40.18

Note that the chair form shows that equatorial constituents can be either above or below the plane of the ring, shown by the "slant" of the bond connecting them to their ring carbons. For example, in *trans*-1,4-dimethylcyclohexane, both of the methyl groups are equatorial in one chair conformation and axial in the other, but in either case they point in opposite directions relative to the plane of the ring.

trans-1,4-dimethylcyclohexane

Figure 40.19

REVIEW PROBLEMS

1. Categorize the following pairs as enantiomers, diastereomers, structural isomers, molecules of the same compound, or different compounds.

    A. dimethyl ether and ethanol

    B. and

    C. and **D.** and

2. Which of the following does NOT show optical activity?

    A. (*R*)-2-butanol

    B. (*S*)-2-butanol

    C. A solution containing 1 M (*R*)-2-butanol and 2 M (*S*)-2-butanol

    D. A solution containing 2 M (*R*)-2-butanol and 2 M (*S*)-2-butanol

    E. A solution containing 3 M (R)-2-butanol and 3 M (S)-2-methanol

3. How many stereoisomers exist for the following aldehyde?

    A. 2

    B. 4

    C. 8

    D. 16

    E. 32

4. Which of the following compounds is optically inactive?

A.
$$CH_3$$
H——Cl
Cl——H
$$CH_3$$

B.
$$CH_3$$
Cl——H
H——Cl
$$CH_3$$

C.
$$CH_3$$
H——Cl
H——Cl
$$CH_3$$

D.
$$CH_2Cl$$
H——Cl
H——H
$$CH_3$$

E. None of the above

5. Which isomer of 2-pentene is more stable, the *cis* isomer or the *trans* isomer?

6. Assign (R) and (S) designations to the following compounds:

A.
$$Cl$$
H——Cl
$$CH_3$$——H
$$Br$$

B.
$$O$$
$$\|$$
$$C—H$$
H——OH
$$CH_2OH$$

7. Cholesterol, shown below, contains how many chiral centers?

A. 5
B. 7
C. 8
D. 9
E. 10

8. Which isomer of the following compound is the most stable?

A.

B.

C.

D. They are all equally stable.

E. A and B are equally stable and more stable than C.

9. Designate the following compounds as (R) or (S):

A. CH_3—$\overset{CH_3}{\underset{OH}{C}}$—H   Cl—C—H with OH

B. HO_2C—$\overset{H}{\underset{CH_3}{C}}$—$CH_2CH_3$

C. HO—$\overset{Br}{\underset{F}{C}}$—Cl

D. H—$\overset{HC=CH_2}{\underset{C(CH_3)_3}{C}}$—$CH_2CH_3$

E. H—$\overset{C\equiv CH}{\underset{Br}{C}}$—$CH_3$

F. H—$\overset{CH_3}{\underset{CH_2CH_3}{C}}$—$CH_2OH$

G. H—$\overset{CH_3}{\underset{CH_2CH_3}{C}}$—$CH_2Cl$

H. Br—$\overset{F}{\underset{I}{C}}$—Cl

I. H_3C—$\overset{NH_2}{\underset{OH}{C}}$—Br

10. The following reaction results in:

A. retention of relative configuration and a change in the absolute configuration.
B. a change in the relative and absolute configurations.
C. retention of the relative and absolute configurations.
D. retent0ion of the absolute configuration and a change in the relative configuration.
E. retention of the relative configuration and a change in the absolute configuration.

11. The following structures are:

I   II

    A. enantiomers.
    B. diastereomers.
    C. *meso* compounds.
    D. structural isomers.
    E. *cis-trans* isomers.

12. MSG ([*S*]-monosodium glutamate) is a compound widely used as a flavor enhancer. MSG has the following structure:

(S)-MSG

This enantiomer of MSG has a specific rotation of +24°. In a racemic mixture of MSG, what would be the specific rotation? What is the specific rotation of (*R*)-monosodium glutamate?

SOLUTIONS TO REVIEW PROBLEMS

1. **A. Structural isomers and different compounds**

   The two compounds, CH_3CH_2OH and CH_3OCH_3, have the same molecular formula, C_2H_6O, but differ in how the atoms are connected to each other. For instance, the oxygen atom of ethanol is bonded to a carbon atom on one side and to a hydrogen atom on the other, whereas the oxygen atom of dimethyl ether is bonded to carbon atoms on both sides.

   B. Molecules of the same compound

   The two structures are achiral. Rotating one gives the other.

   Also note that, in order for a compound to be chiral, at least one of its carbons must be bonded to four different substituents. In both of these compounds, all the carbons are attached to two identical groups, so the compounds are achiral.

   C. Enantiomers

   These two compounds look alike, but the Cl and the Br have been interchanged. You may remember that one exchange of two substituents produces the mirror image of the original compound. Thus, these two molecules are enantiomers.

   Another way to solve this problem is to remember that, according to the rules governing Fischer projections, interchanging two pairs of substituents in a compound will give the original compound. Interchanging two pairs of substituents in the compound on the right in pair (C), as shown below, allows you to see that the two compounds of pair (C) are mirror images of each other; hence, they are enantiomers.

D. Diastereomers

Rotate the second compound in the plane of the paper by 180°. The two compounds now are:

Assign (R) and (S) designations to the compounds:

The above figure shows that one compound is an S, R stereoisomer and the other is an R, R stereoisomer; hence, they are diastereomers.

2. **D** A racemic mixture of 2-butanol consists of equimolar amounts of (R)-2-butanol and (S)-2-butanol. The (R)-2-butanol molecule rotates the plane of polarized light in one direction, and the (S)-2-butanol molecule rotates it by the same angle but in the opposite direction. If for every one (R)-2-butanol molecule there is one (S)-2 butanol molecule, exact cancellation of all rotation occurs, and no net rotation of polarized light is observed. Hence, the correct answer is (D).

Choice (A) is incorrect because all the molecules of the (R)-2-butanol solution rotate the plane of light in the same direction, so rotations do not cancel, and optical activity is observed. In the same way, the (S)-2-butanol solution also shows optical activity. Thus, choices (A) and (B) are incorrect. Choice (C) has more (S)-2-butanol molecules than (R)-2-butanol molecules. All the rotation produced by the (R)-2-butanol molecules is canceled by half of the (S)-2-butanol molecules; the rotation produced by the other half of (S)-2-molecules contributes to the optical activity observed in this solution. Thus, choice (C) is incorrect. Finally, choice (D) shows two different molecules; although one is (R) and the other (S), the two won't perfectly cancel one another out, and (D) is incorrect.

3. **C** The maximum number of stereoisomers of a compound equals 2^n, where n is the number of chiral carbons in the compound. Here, there are three chiral carbon atoms ($n = 3$) marked by asterisks in the following figure:

$$
\begin{array}{c}
\text{O} \\
\parallel \\
\text{C—H} \\
| \\
\text{HO—C*—H} \\
| \\
\text{HO—C*—H} \\
| \\
\text{HO—C*—H} \\
| \\
\text{HO—C—H} \\
| \\
\text{H}
\end{array}
$$

So the number of stereoisomers it can form is $2^n = 2^3 = 8$. Hence, the correct choice is (C).

4. **C** The correct answer choice is an example of a *meso* compound: a compound that contains chiral centers but is superimposable on its mirror image. A *meso* compound can also be recognized by the fact that one half of the compound is the mirror image of the other half:

$$
\begin{array}{c}
\text{CH}_3 \\
| \\
\text{H——Cl} \\
\text{- - - - - - - -} \quad \text{plane of} \\
\text{H——Cl} \quad \text{symmetry} \\
| \\
\text{CH}_3
\end{array}
$$

As a result of this internal plane of symmetry, the molecule is achiral and hence optically inactive. Choices (A) and (B) are enantiomers of each other and will certainly show optical activity on their own. Choice (D), since it contains a chiral carbon, is optically active as well.

5. The *trans* isomer of 2-pentene is the most stable. When you draw out this isomer, you can see that one side of the double bond has a methyl group and a hydrogen, and the other side has an ethyl group and a hydrogen. In this configuration, the van der Waals repulsion (nonbonding interaction) between the methyl and the ethyl groups is minimized. If these groups were oriented *cis* to each other (on the same side of the double bond), the van der Waals repulsion would be maximized.

trans   *cis*

6. A **(R)-2-bromo-1,1-dichloropropane**

In the above compound, C–1 is not chiral because it has two C-1 atoms bound to it. Only C–2 is chiral, so the molecule is designated as (*R*) or (*S*) with respect to only C–2. Assign priority numbers to the atoms connected directly to C–2. The atom with the highest atomic number is given priority 1, followed by the atom with next highest atomic number, which is given the priority number 2, and so on. In this compound, Br has the highest atomic number and so is assigned priority 1. Next come two carbon atoms connected to the chiral carbon. Since these have the same atomic number, you must consider their substituents. C–1 has two Cl atoms and one hydrogen, whereas C–3 has three hydrogen. Since chlorine has a higher atomic number than hydrogen, C–1 is the higher priority. Thus, C–1 is 2 and C–3 is 3. The hydrogen is the lowest priority, 4.

Draw a curved arrow from 1 → 2 → 3. The direction of the arrow is counterclockwise, so the molecule is temporarily designated (*S*). Finally, check the orientation of group 4, which in this case is coming out of the page, which is the opposite way it should be; thus the (*S*) should be swapped to the (*R*) designation.

B **(*R*)-2,3-dihydroxypropanal**

For the purposes of prioritization, double- or triple-bonded atoms are considered to be linked by multiple single bonds. For instance, in −C=O, C would be considered to have two single bonds with O, and O would be considered to have two single bonds with carbon. In this question, −OH is assigned the highest priority, 1; −C=O (here considered to be two −C−O) is assigned the next priority, 2; −CH$_2$OH is assigned priority 3; and hydrogen, with the lowest atomic number, is assigned the lowest priority, 4. The direction of the curved arrow from 1 → 2 → 3 is clockwise, and the molecule is designated (*R*).

7. **C** To be a chiral center, a carbon must have four different substituents. There are eight stereocenters in this molecule, marked below with asterisks.

The other carbons are not chiral, for various reasons. Many are bonded to two hydrogen; others participate in double bonds, which count as two bonds to the same thing (another C atom).

8. **B** This is a chair conformation in which the two equatorial methyl groups are *trans* to each other. Since the methyl hydrogens do not compete for the same space as the (unshown) hydrogens attached to the ring, this conformation ensures the least amount of steric strain. Choice (A) would be more unstable than choice (B) since the diaxial methyl group hydrogens are closer to the hydrogens on the ring, causing greater steric strain. Choice (C) is incorrect because it is in the more unstable boat conformation. Choices (D) and (E) are incorrect because these are all different structures with different stabilities.

9.

10. **C** The relative configuration is retained because the bonds between the chiral carbon and its substituents are not broken. The bond that is cleaved is one between a substituent of the chiral carbon (the O atom) and another atom attached to the substituent (the H attached to the O). The absolute configuration is also retained because the (R)/(S) designation is the same for the reactant and the product.

11. **A** Compared side by side, the two structures are mirror images of each other. Rotating one of the structures by 180° (structure III) shows that structures I and III are nonsuperimposable.

Choice (B) is incorrect because diastereomers are stereoisomers that are not mirror images of each other. Choice (C) is incorrect because, in order for a compound to be designated as a *meso* compound, it must have a plane of symmetry, which neither of these structures contains. Choice (D) is incorrect because structural isomers are compounds with the same molecular formula but different connectivity. These compounds do have the same connectivity. The only difference is that they do not have the same spatial arrangement of atoms. As a result, they are stereoisomers, not structural isomers.

12. The specific rotation of a racemic mixture of MSG, or any other racemic mixture, is zero. A racemic mixture by definition is a mixture that contains equal amounts of the (+) and (−) enantiomers, which cancel each other's optical rotations. The specific rotation of (*R*)-monosodium glutamate is −24°. An enantiomer of a chiral compound rotates plane-polarized light by the same amount but in the opposite direction.

CHAPTER FORTY-ONE

Bonding

As discussed in general chemistry, there are two types of chemical bonds: **ionic**, in which an electron is transferred from one atom to another, and **covalent**, in which pairs of electrons are shared between two atoms. In organic chemistry, it is important to understand the details of covalent bonding, as these play a crucial role in determining the properties and reactions of organic compounds.

ATOMIC ORBITALS

The first three quantum numbers, n, l, and m, describe the size, shape, and number of the atomic orbitals an element possesses. The quantum number n corresponds to the energy levels in an atom and is essentially a measure of size. Within each electron shell, there can be several types of orbitals (s, p, d, and f, corresponding to the quantum numbers $l = 0$, 1, 2, 3, and 4). Each type of atomic orbital has a specific shape. An s orbital is spherical and symmetrical, centered around the nucleus. A p orbital is composed of two lobes located symmetrically about the nucleus and contains a **node** (an area where the probability of finding an electron is zero). A d orbital is composed of four symmetrical lobes and contains two nodes. Both d and f orbitals are complex in shape and are rarely encountered in organic chemistry.

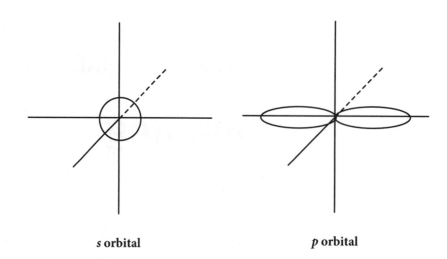

s orbital   p orbital

Figure 41.1

MOLECULAR ORBITALS

Single Bonds

Two atomic orbitals can be combined to form a **molecular orbital**. Molecular orbitals are obtained mathematically by adding the wave functions of the atomic orbitals. If the signs of the wave functions are the same, a lower-energy **bonding orbital** is produced. If the signs are different, a higher-energy **antibonding orbital** is produced. Figure 41.2 below shows examples of combining two s orbitals in both bonding and antibonding orbitals as well as the bonding orbitals formed from an s orbital and p orbital and from two p orbitals.

Figure 41.2

When a molecular orbital is formed by head-to-head overlap, the resulting bond is called a **sigma (σ) bond**. All single bonds are sigma bonds and contain two electrons. Shorter single bonds are stronger than longer single bonds.

Double and Triple Bonds

When two p orbitals overlap in a parallel fashion, a bonding MO is formed, called a **pi (π) bond**. When both a sigma and a pi bond exist between two atoms, a **double bond** is formed. When a sigma bond and two pi bonds exist, a **triple bond** is formed. As can be seen in Figure 41.3, the overlap of the p orbitals involved in a pi bond prevents rotation about double and triple bonds. Pi bonds contain two electrons each.

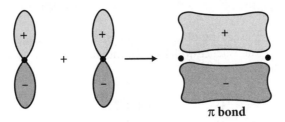

π bond

Figure 41.3

A pi bond cannot exist independently of a sigma bond. The formation of the sigma bond between two atoms orients their p orbitals to overlap from side to side, allowing the pi bond to form. In general, pi bonds are weaker than sigma bonds. It is possible to break the pi bond of a double bond but leave the sigma bond intact; however, the sigma bond cannot be broken unless the pi bond is broken first.

HYBRIDIZATION

Carbon has the electronic configuration $1s^2\, 2s^2\, 2p^2$ with 4 valence electrons; it therefore needs four additional electrons to complete its octet. A typical carbon-containing molecule is methane, CH_4. Experimentation shows that the four sigma bonds in methane are equal. This is inconsistent with the asymmetrical distribution of valence electrons: two electrons in the 2s orbital, one in the p_x orbital, one in the p_y orbital, and none in the p_z orbital. The theory of **orbital hybridization** was developed to account for this discrepancy.

sp^3

Hybrid orbitals are formed by mixing different types of atomic orbitals. If one s orbital and three p orbitals are mathematically combined, the result is four identical sp^3 hybrid orbitals that have a new shape.

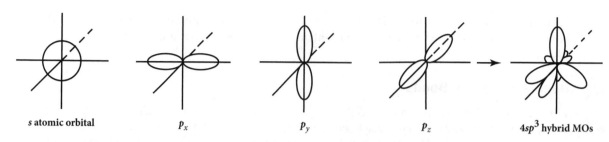

Figure 41.4

These four orbitals will point toward the vertices of a tetrahedron, minimizing repulsion. This explains the preferred tetrahedral geometry adopted by carbon when it has four single bonds to other atoms.

The hybridization is accomplished by promoting one of the 2s electrons into the $2p_z$ orbital (see Figure 41.5). This produces four valence orbitals, each with one electron, which can be mathematically mixed to create the hybrids.

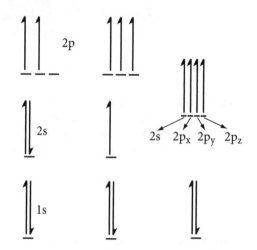

Figure 41.5

sp²

Although carbon is often found bonded to four other atoms with sp³ hybridization, there are other possibilities. If one s orbital and two p orbitals are mixed, three identical sp² hybrid orbitals are obtained.

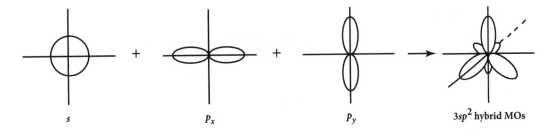

Figure 41.6

For example, this occurs in ethylene. The third p orbital of each carbon atom is left unhybridized and participates in the pi bond. The three sp² orbitals are 120° apart, allowing maximum separation. These orbitals participate in the formation of the C=C and C−H sigma bonds.

sp

If two p orbitals are used to form the pi bonds of a triple bond and the remaining p orbital is mixed with an s orbital, two identical sp hybrid orbitals are obtained. The remaining two p orbitals of each carbon atom are left unhybridized and participate in creating two pi bonds, resulting in a triple bond. The two sp hybrid orbitals are oriented 180° apart, explaining the linear structure of molecules such as acetylene.

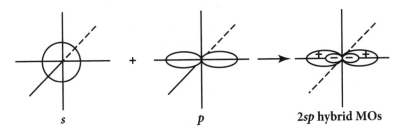

Figure 41.7

BONDING SUMMARY

The following table summarizes the major features of bonding orbitals in organic molecules.

Bond Order	Component Bonds	Hybridization	Angles	Examples
single	sigma	sp³	109.5°	C−C; C−H
double	sigma pi	sp²	120°	C=C; C=O
triple	sigma pi pi	sp	180°	C≡C; C≡N

Table 41.1

REVIEW PROBLEMS

1. Within one principal quantum level of a many-electron atom, which orbital has the minimum energy?

    A. s
    B. p
    C. d
    D. f
    E. g

2. Which of the following compounds possesses at least one σ bond?

    A. CH_4
    B. C_2H_2
    C. C_2H_4
    D. CH_2O
    E. All of the above

3. In a double-bonded carbon atom

    A. hybridization between the s orbital and one p orbital occurs.
    B. hybridization between the s orbital and two p orbitals occurs.
    C. hybridization between the s orbital and three p orbitals occurs.
    D. hybridization between the two s orbitals and one p orbital occurs.
    D. no hybridization between s and p orbitals occurs.

4. The hybridizations of the carbon atom and the nitrogen atom in the ion CN^- are

    A. sp^3 and sp^3, respectively.
    B. sp^3 and sp, respectively.
    C. sp and sp^3, respectively.
    D. sp and sp, respectively.
    E. sp^2 and sp^2, respectively.

5. Which of the following hybridizations does the Be atom in BeH_2 assume?

    A. sp
    B. sp^2
    C. sp^3
    D. sp^4
    E. No hybridization occurs.

6. Two atomic orbitals combine to form:

    I. a bonding molecular orbital.
    II. an antibonding molecular orbital.
    III. new atomic orbitals.

    A. I
    B. I, II, and III
    C. III
    D. I and II
    E. II and III

7. Molecular orbitals can contain a maximum of

    A.   1 electron.

    B.   2 electrons.

    C.   4 electrons.

    D.   6 electrons.

    E. $2n^2$ electrons, where n is the principal quantum number.

8. π bonds are formed by which of the following orbitals?

    A.   Two s orbitals

    B.   Two p orbitals

    C.   One s and one p orbital

    D.   One s and one f orbital

    E.   One p and one f orbital

9. How many σ bonds and π bonds are present in the following compound?

    A.   6 σ bonds and 1 π bond

    B.   6 σ bonds and 2 π bonds

    C.   7 σ bonds and 1 π bond

    D.   7 σ bonds and 2 π bonds

    E.   7 σ bonds and no π bonds

10. The four C−H bonds of CH_4 point toward the vertices of a tetrahedron. This indicates that the hybridization of a carbon atom is

    A.   sp.

    B. sp^2.

    C. sp^3.

    D. sp^4

    E.   none of the above.

SOLUTIONS TO REVIEW PROBLEMS

1. **A** In a many-electron atom, the energy of the orbitals within the principal quantum numbers is as follows: 2s < 2p; 3s < 3p < 3d; 4s < 4p < 4d < 4f. For any given principal quantum level, the s orbital is always the lowest in energy; thus, the correct choice is (A).

2. **E** σ bonds are formed when orbitals overlap end-to-end. All single bonds are σ bonds; double and triple bonds contain one σ bond each. The compounds CH_4, C_2H_2, C_2H_4, and CH_2O all contain at least one single bond, so the correct choice is (E).

3. **B** In a double-bonded carbon, sp^2 hybridization occurs, i.e., one s orbital hybridizes with two p orbitals to form three sp^2 hybrid orbitals. Therefore, the correct choice is (B). Note that the sp^2 orbitals take part in σ bond formation, making choice (D) incorrect. The third p orbital of the carbon atom remains unhybridized and takes part in the formation of the pi bond of the double bond.

4. **D** The carbon atom and the nitrogen atoms are connected by a triple bond in CN^-.

$$:N \equiv C:^-$$

   A triple-bonded atom is sp hybridized; one s orbital hybridizes with one p orbital to form two sp hybridized orbitals. The two remaining unhybridized p orbitals take part in the formation of two π bonds. The correct choice, therefore, is (D).

5. **A** BeH_2 is a linear molecule, which means that the angle between the two Be−H bonds is 180°. Since the sp orbitals are oriented at an angle of 180°, the Be atom is sp hybridized. Therefore, the correct choice is (A). Note that sp^2 orbitals are oriented at an angle of 120°, and sp^3 orbitals are oriented at an angle of 109.5°.

6. **D** When atomic orbitals combine to form molecular orbitals, the number of molecular orbitals obtained equals the number of atomic orbitals that take part in the process. Half of the molecular orbitals formed are bonding molecular orbitals, and the other half are antibonding molecular orbitals. In this case, therefore, two atomic orbitals combine to form one low-energy bonding molecular orbital and one high-energy antibonding molecular orbital. New atomic orbitals do not form, but the bonding molecular orbital will have a corresponding antibonding molecular orbital. The correct choice is (D).

7. **B** Each molecular orbital, like an atomic orbital, can contain a maximum of two electrons with opposite spins.

8. **B** Pi bonds are formed by the parallel overlap of unhybridized p orbitals. The electron density is concentrated above and below the bonding axis. A sigma bond can be formed by the head-to-head overlap of two s orbitals, two p orbitals, or one s and one p orbital. In a σ bond, the density of the electrons is concentrated between the two nuclei of the bonding atoms.

9. **A** Each single bond has 1 σ bond, and each double bond has one σ and one π bond. In this question, there are five single bonds (5 σ bonds) and one double bond (one σ bond and one π bond), which gives a total of six σ bonds and one π bond. Thus, the correct choice is (A).

10. **C** The four bonds point to the vertices of a tetrahedron, which means that the angle between two bonds is 109.5°. sp^3 orbitals have an angle of 109.5° between them. Hence, the carbon atom of CH_4 is sp^3 hybridized. The correct choice, therefore, is (C).

CHAPTER FORTY-TWO

Alkanes

Alkanes are hydrocarbons that have the maximum possible number of hydrogen atoms attached to each carbon, and thus are said to be saturated. These compounds consist only of hydrogen and carbon atoms joined by single bonds and their general formula is C_nH_{2n+2}. However, alkanes can be modified with additional functional groups as well, such as alcohols, halogens, or amines.

A brief overview of nomenclature and properties of alkanes will be followed by a discussion of substitution reactions and then additional types of reactions.

NOMENCLATURE

Alkanes are named for their longest, straight carbon chain. The names of the four simplest alkanes are:

CH_4 CH_3CH_3 $CH_3CH_2CH_3$ $CH_3CH_2CH_2CH_3$

methane   **eth**ane   **prop**ane   **but**ane

The names of the longer-chain alkanes consist of prefixes derived from the Greek root for the number of carbon atoms with the ending -**ane**.

$C_5H_{12} =$	**pent**ane	$C_9H_{20} =$	**non**ane
$C_6H_{14} =$	**hex**ane	$C_{10}H_{22} =$	**dec**ane
$C_7H_{16} =$	**hept**ane	$C_{11}H_{24} =$	**undec**ane
$C_8H_{18} =$	**oct**ane	$C_{12}H_{26} =$	**dodec**ane

For detailed information on naming branched chain alkanes and alkanes with substituent groups, refer to Chapter 39.

Carbon atoms can be characterized by the number of other carbon atoms to which they are directly bonded. A **primary** carbon atom (written as **1°**) is bonded to only one other carbon atom. A **secondary (2°)** carbon is bonded to two; a **tertiary (3°)** to three, and a **quaternary (4°)** to four other carbon atoms. In addition, hydrogen atoms or other functional groups attached to 1°, 2°, or 3° carbon atoms are referred to as 1°, 2°, or 3°, respectively.

$1° \longrightarrow CH_3$

$3°$

$2° \longrightarrow$

Figure 42.1

PHYSICAL PROPERTIES

Most of the physical properties of alkanes vary in a predictable manner. In general, as the molecular weight of a straight chain alkane increases, the melting point, boiling point, and density also increase. At room temperature, the straight-chain compounds C_1H_4 through C_4H_{10} are gases, C_5H_{12} through $C_{16}H_{34}$ are liquids, and the longer-chain compounds are waxes and harder solids.

Branched molecules have slightly lower boiling and melting points than their straight-chain isomers. Greater branching reduces the surface area of a molecule, decreasing the weak intermolecular attractive forces (London dispersion forces). The molecules are held together less tightly, thus lowering the boiling point. In addition, branched molecules are more difficult to pack into a tight, three-dimensional structure, which is reflected in the lower melting points of branched alkanes.

SUBSTITUTION REACTIONS OF ALKANES

Alkyl halides and other substituted carbon molecules can take part in reactions known as *nucleophilic substitutions*. Substitution reactions involve removing an atom or a functional group from a molecule and replacing it with another. Substitution reactions can occur in many different types of molecules; however, this chapter will specifically discuss substitution reactions of alkanes. In all substitution reactions, identifying the nucleophile and the leaving group are critical to an understanding of the mechanism.

Nucleophiles

Nucleophiles are molecules that are attracted to positive charge, as seen by their name: nucleophile means "nucleus lover." Nucleophiles are electron-rich species that are often but not always negatively charged. Nucleophiles are attracted to atoms with partial or full positive charges.

Basicity

If a group of nucleophiles are based on the same atom (for example, oxygen) then nucleophilicity is roughly correlated to basicity. In other words, the stronger the base, the stronger the nucleophile. This is because bases act as electron donors, and stronger nucleophiles are also better electron donors. For example, nucleophilic strength decreases in the order:

$$RO^- > HO^- > RCO_2^- > ROH > H_2O$$

Size and polarizability

If a series of nucleophiles is based on different atoms, nucleophilic ability doesn't necessarily correlate to basicity. In a protic solvent (a solvent that is able to form hydrogen bonds), large atoms or ions tend to be better nucleophiles. Larger ions more easily shed their solvent molecules and are more polarizable. Hence, nucleophilic strength decreases in the order:

$$CN^- > I^- > RO^- > HO^- > Br^- > Cl^- > F^- > H_2O$$

In contrast, in an aprotic solvent (a solvent that cannot form hydrogen bonds) the nucleophiles are "naked"; they are not solvated. In this case, nucleophilic strength is directly related to basicity. For example, in DMSO (an aprotic solvent), the order of nucleophilic strength is the same as base strength:

$$F^- > Cl^- > Br^- > I^-$$

Leaving Groups

The ease with which nucleophilic substitution takes place is dependent on the nature of the leaving group. The best leaving groups are those that are weak bases, as these can accept a negative charge and dissociate to form a stable ion in solution. In the case of the halogens, therefore, this is the opposite of base strength:

$$I^- > Br^- > Cl^- > F^-$$

Other leaving groups besides halogens can be used for substitution reactions. For example, an $-OH$ group that is a poor leaving group can be protonated to form $-H_2O^+$, which leaves as a water molecule.

S_N1 Reactions

S_N1 designates a **unimolecular nucleophilic substitution** reaction. It is unimolecular because the rate of the reaction is dependent upon only one molecule in the reaction; in other words, the rate expression is first order. The rate-determining step of an S_N1 reaction is the dissociation of the substrate (the starting molecule) to form a stable, positively charged ion called a **carbocation.** The formation and stabilization of the carbocation determine all other aspects of S_N1 reactions.

Mechanism

S_N1 reactions involve two steps: the dissociation of a substrate molecule into a carbocation and a leaving group, followed by the combination of the carbocation with a nucleophile to form the substituted product.

Figure 42.2

In the first step, a carbocation intermediate is formed. Carbocations are stabilized by polar solvents that have lone electron pairs available to donate (e.g., water or ethyl alcohol). Carbocations are also stabilized by charge delocalization throughout the molecule. More highly substituted carbocations are more stable, because hydrocarbon substituent groups donate electron density toward the positive charge. The order of stability for carbocations is:

$$\text{tertiary} > \text{secondary} > \text{primary} > \text{methyl}$$

To drive the reaction forward, the original leaving group should be a weaker nucleophile than the replacement nucleophile. The second step, in which the nucleophile combines with the carbocation, occurs very rapidly compared to the first step, and is essentially irreversible.

Rate

The rate at which a reaction occurs can never be greater than the rate of its slowest step. Such a step is termed the **rate-limiting** or **rate-determining step** of the reaction (see Chapter 31, Chemical Kinetics, for a more detailed discussion of rate expressions). In an S_N1 reaction, the slowest step is the dissociation of the molecule to form a carbocation intermediate, a step that is energetically unfavorable. The formation of a carbocation is therefore the rate-limiting step of an S_N1 reaction. The only reactant in this step is the original substrate molecule, and so the rate of the entire reaction depends only on the concentration of the substrate (a so-called *first-order reaction*): rate = k[substrate]. The rate is *not* dependent on the concentration or the nature of the nucleophile, because it plays no part in the rate-limiting step.

The rate of an S_N1 reaction can be increased by anything that promotes the formation and stability of the carbocation. The most important factors are as follows:

a. Structural factors: Highly substituted alkanes allow for distribution of the positive charge over a greater number of carbon and hydrogen atoms, and thus form the most stable carbocations. The order of reactivity of substrates for S_N1 reactions is tertiary > secondary > primary > methyl; in general, primary and methyl substrates do not react by the S_N1 mechanism.

b. Solvent effects: Highly polar solvents are better at surrounding and isolating ions than are less polar solvents. Polar protic solvents such as water or alcohols work best for two reasons. Protic solvents can form hydrogen bonds with the leaving group, solvating it and preventing it from returning to the carbocation. Also, lone electron pairs on oxygen or nitrogen atoms in the solvent molecule can stabilize the carbocation intermediate.

c. Nature of the leaving group: Weak bases dissociate more easily from the alkyl chain and thus make better leaving groups, increasing the rate of carbocation formation.

d. Nature of the nucleophile: S_N1 reactions do not require a strong nucleophile. S_N1 reactions run equally well with either strong (fully charged) or weak (electron-rich but uncharged) nucleophiles.

Stereochemistry

S_N1 reactions involve carbocation intermediates, which are sp² hybridized and have trigonal planar geometry. The attacking nucleophile can approach the carbocation from either above or below with equal probability, and thus create either the (*R*) or (*S*) enantiomer with equal probability.

Figure 42.3

If the original compound is optically active because of the presence of a chiral center, then a racemic mixture will be produced. In some cases, the nucleophile may react so rapidly that it approaches the carbocation from the opposite side of the leaving group with greater frequency; in this case, the product will be characterized as a partial racemate.

S_N2 Reactions

S_N2 designates a **bimolecular nucleophilic substitution** reaction. S_N2 reactions involve a nucleophile pushing its way into a compound while simultaneously displacing the leaving group. Its rate-determining and only step involves two molecules: the substrate and the nucleophile.

Figure 42.4

Mechanism

S_N2 reactions are **concerted** reactions, meaning that the entire mechanism occurs in single coordinated process. The nucleophile attacks the reactant from the backside of the leaving group, forming a trigonal bipyramidal **transition state**. As the reaction progresses, the bond to the nucleophile strengthens while the bond to the leaving group weakens. The leaving group is displaced as the bond to the nucleophile becomes complete.

Rate

The single step of an S_N2 reaction involves *two* reacting species: the substrate and the nucleophile. The concentrations of both therefore play a role in determining the rate of an S_N2 reaction; the two species must "meet" in solution, and raising the concentration of either will make such a meeting more likely. Since the rate of the S_N2 reaction depends on the concentration of two reactants, it follows **second-order kinetics**. The rate expression for an S_N2 reaction is: rate $= k$[substrate][nucleophile].

Other factors that can affect the rate of S_N2 reactions include:

- Structural factors: The nucleophile must have unhindered access to the central carbon of the substrate. Therefore S_N2 reactions occur most readily with substrates with little branching in order to minimize steric hindrance. The order of reactivity of substrates for S_N2 is methyl > primary > secondary > tertiary; in general, tertiary substrates do not react by the S_N2 mechanism.

- Solvent effects: S_N2 reactions occur most readily in polar aprotic solvents, meaning solvents that are unable to form hydrogen bonds. Typical polar aprotic solvents include acetone and DMSO (dimethylsulfoxide). Because these solvents cannot form hydrogen bonds, they do not create a solvation shell around the nucleophile and thus do not interfere with its attack on the substrate.

- Nature of the leaving group: Weak bases dissociate more easily from the alkyl chain and thus make better leaving groups, increasing the ease of displacement by the nucleophile.

- Nature of the nucleophile: Because the nucleophile must attack a neutral molecule and displace the leaving group, it must be strongly nucleophilic. This typically means that the nucleophile is a negatively charged ionic species, and can be either a strong or weak base.

Stereochemistry

The single step of an S_N2 reaction involves a chiral transition state. Since the nucleophile attacks from one side of the central carbon and the leaving group departs from the opposite side, the reaction "flips" the bonds attached to the carbon.

Figure 42.5

If the reactant is chiral, optical activity will be retained, but will invert between (R) and (S) as long as the nucleophile and leaving group have the same priority relative to the other groups in the substrate.

If the nucleophile and leaving group have different priorities compared to the rest of the molecule, however, the absolute configuration must be determined for the substituted product.

S$_N$1 versus S$_N$2

Certain reaction conditions favor one substitution mechanism over the other, and provide distinctive "fingerprints" that allow the determination of whether S$_N$1 or S$_N$2 will proceed. Sterics, nucleophilic strength, leaving group ability, reaction conditions, and solvent effects are all important in determining which reaction will occur.

	S$_N$1	S$_N$2
Substrate reactivity	$3° > 2° > 1° > CH_3$	$CH_3 > 1° > 2° > 3°$
Leaving group	Cl^-, Br^-, I^-, weak bases $-OH$ if protonated to form OH_2^+	Cl^-, Br^-, I^-, weak bases
Nucleophile	Any nucleophile	Strong (charged) nucleophile
Solvent	Polar protic	Polar aprotic
Reaction mechanism	2-step: carbocation, then nucleophilic attack	Concerted 1-step
Rate law	1st order: rate = k[substrate]	2nd order: rate = k[substrate][nucleophile]
Stereochemistry	Chiral → racemic mix	Inversion of R/S

Table 42.1

Free Radical Substitution Reactions

Alkanes can react by a **free radical substitution mechanism** in which one or more hydrogen atoms are replaced by Cl, Br, or I atoms. These reactions involve three steps:

1. **Initiation:** Diatomic halogens are cleaved by either UV light (shown as UV or hv) or peroxide (H-O-O-H or R-O-O-H), resulting in the formation of free radicals (heat can also be used, but is not specific for radical formation). Free radicals are uncharged species with unpaired electrons (such as Cl• or R$_3$C•). They are extremely reactive and readily attack alkanes.

$$\text{Initiation: } X_2 \xrightarrow{\text{hv}} 2X\bullet$$

2. **Propagation**—A propagation step is one in which a radical produces another radical that can continue the reaction. A free radical reacts with an alkane, removing a hydrogen atom to form HX, and creating an alkyl radical. The alkyl radical can then react with X$_2$ to form an alkyl halide (the substiuted product) and generate another X•, thus propagating the radical.

$$\text{Propagation: } \quad X\bullet + RH \longrightarrow HX + R\bullet$$
$$R\bullet + X_2 \longrightarrow RX + X\bullet$$

3. **Termination**—Two free radicals combine with one another to form a stable molecule.

$$\text{Termination: } X\bullet + X\bullet \longrightarrow X_2$$
$$X\bullet + R\bullet \longrightarrow RX$$
$$R\bullet + R\bullet \longrightarrow R_2$$

A single free radical can initiate many reactions before the reaction chain is terminated.

Larger alkanes have many hydrogens that the free radical can attack. Bromine radicals react fairly slowly, and primarily attack the hydrogens on the carbon atom that can form the most stable free radical, i.e., the most substituted carbon atom.

$$\bullet CR_3 > \bullet CR_2H > \bullet CRH_2 > \bullet CH_3$$
$$3° > 2° > 1° > \text{methyl}$$

Thus, a tertiary radical is the most likely to be formed in a free-radical bromination reaction. As a result, the substitution product will have the bromine on the most highly substituted carbon. Note the same pattern of stability and the same resulting product compared to a carbocation-based mechanism.

Figure 42.6

Free-radical chlorination is a more rapid process and depends on both the stability of the intermediate and on the number of hydrogens present. Free-radical chlorination reactions are likely to replace primary hydrogens that are found abundantly in most molecules, despite the relative instability of primary radicals. Unfortunately, free-radical chlorination reactions produce mixtures of products, and are useful only when a single type of hydrogen is present.

ADDITIONAL REACTIONS OF ALKANES

Combustion

The reaction of alkanes with molecular oxygen to form carbon dioxide, water, and heat is a process of great practical importance. It is an unusual reaction because heat, not a chemical species, is generally the desired product. The reaction mechanism is very complex and is believed to proceed through a radical process. The equation for the complete **combustion** of propane is:

$$C_3H_8 + 5\,O_2 \longrightarrow 3\,CO_2 + 4\,H_2O + \text{heat}$$

All combustion reactions take this basic form, with different hydrocarbons used as the starting molecule, and each reaction must be balanced appropriately for the number of carbons, hydrogens, and oxygens present. Combustion is often incomplete, producing significant quantities of carbon monoxide instead of carbon dioxide. This frequently occurs, for example, in the burning of gasoline in an internal combustion engine.

Pyrolysis

Pyrolysis occurs when a molecule is broken down by heat in the absence of oxygen. Pyrolysis, also called **cracking,** is most commonly used to reduce the average molecular weight of heavy oils and to increase the production of more desirable volatile compounds. In the pyrolysis of alkanes, the C—C bonds are cleaved, producing smaller-chain alkyl radicals. These radicals can recombine to form a variety of alkanes:

$$CH_3CH_2CH_3 \xrightarrow{\Delta} CH_3\bullet + \bullet CH_2CH_3$$

$$2\,CH_3\bullet \longrightarrow CH_3CH_3$$

$$2\,\bullet CH_2CH_3 \longrightarrow CH_3CH_2CH_2CH_3$$

Figure 42.7

Alternatively, in a process called **disproportionation,** a radical transfers a hydrogen atom to another radical, producing an alkane and an alkene:

$$\bullet CH_3 + \bullet CH_2CH_3 \longrightarrow CH_4 + H_2C{=}CH_2$$

Figure 42.8

REVIEW PROBLEMS

1. Under the following conditions,

    Br‿‿‿Y $\xrightarrow{\text{CN}^-}$ CN‿‿‿Y $+ \text{ Br}^-$

    1-bromo-4-methylpentane will most probably react via

    A. S_N1.
    B. S_N2.
    C. both S_N1 and S_N2.
    D. E1.
    E. both E1 and E2.

2. The following molecule can be classified as having

    $CH_2C(CH_3)_3$

    CH_2CH_3

    A. 4 primary, 2 secondary, 4 tertiary, and 3 quaternary carbon atoms.
    B. 3 methyl groups, 2 ethyl groups, and 4 secondary carbon atoms.
    C. 4 primary, 6 secondary, 2 tertiary, and 1 quaternary carbon atoms.
    D. 3 primary, 3 secondary, 4 tertiary, and 3 quaternary carbon atoms.
    E. 3 primary, 2 secondary, 5 tertiary, and 1 quaternary carbon atoms.

3. The following reactions are part of a free-radical halogenation sequence:

		ΔH (kcal/mol)
A.	$Cl_2 \longrightarrow 2\ Cl\bullet$	$+58$
B.	$Cl\bullet + CH_4 \longrightarrow \bullet CH_3 + HCl$	$+1$
C.	$\bullet CH_3 + Cl_2 \longrightarrow CH_3Cl + Cl\bullet$	-26
D.	$\bullet CH_3 + Cl\bullet \longrightarrow CH_3Cl$	-84

    Identify the initiation, propagation, and termination steps.

4. S_N1 reactions show first-order kinetics because

    A. the rate-limiting step is the first step to occur in the reaction.
    B. the rate-limiting step involves only one molecule.
    C. there is only one rate-limiting step.
    D. the reaction involves only one molecule.
    E. the reaction only involves one step.

5. The following reaction sequence is typical of S_N1 reactions. Which is the rate-limiting step(s)?

Step 1 $(CH_3)_3C—Cl \longrightarrow (CH_3)_3C^+ + Cl^-$

Step 2 $(CH_3)_3C^+ \xrightarrow{CH_3CH_2OH} (CH_3)_3C—\overset{+}{\underset{H}{O}}—CH_2CH_3$

Step 3 $(CH_3)_3C—\overset{+}{\underset{H}{O}}—CH_2CH_3 \longrightarrow (CH_3)_3C—O—CH_2CH_3 + H^+$

A. Step 1
B. Step 2
C. Step 3
D. Steps 1 and 2
E. Steps 1 and 3

6. Which of the following would be the best solvent for an S_N2 reaction?

A. H_2O
B. CH_3CH_2OH
C. CH_3SOCH_3
D. $CH_3CH_2CH_2CH_2CH_2CH_3$
E. NH_3

7. What choices for X and Y would most favor the following reaction?

$$R_3C–X \xrightarrow{-X^-} R_3C^+ \xrightarrow{+Y^-} R_3C–Y$$

A. $X = I^-, Y = Cl^-$
B. $X = EtO^-, Y = $ tosylate $(CH_3C_6H_4SO_2)$
C. $X = $ tosylate, $Y = CN^-$
D. $X = OH^-, Y = H_2O$
E. $X = EtO^-, Y = CN^-$

8. What would be the major product of the following reaction?

$$CH_3CH_2CH_3 + Br_2 \xrightarrow{h\nu}$$

A. $CH_3CH_2CH_2Br$
B. $CH_3CH_2CH_2CH_2CH_2CH_3$
C. $H_3CCHBrCH_3$
D. CH_3CH_2Br
E. CH_2CHBr

9. Treatment of (S)-2-bromobutane with sodium hydroxide results in the production of a compound with an (R) configuration. The reaction has most likely taken place through

   A. an S_N1 mechanism.
   B. an S_N2 mechanism.
   C. both an S_N1 and S_N2 reaction.
   D. an elimination reaction.
   E. an addition reaction.

10. What is the correct decreasing order of the boiling points of the following compounds?

    I. *n*-hexane
    II. 2-methylpentane
    III. 2,2-dimethylbutane
    IV. *n*-heptane

    A. I > IV > II > III
    B. IV > III > II > I
    C. IV > I > II > III
    D. I > II > III > IV
    E. I > II > IV > III

11. The reaction of isobutane with an unknown halogen is catalyzed by light. The two major products obtained are:

    What is the unknown halogen?
    A. Cl_2
    B. Br_2
    C. I_2
    D. F_2
    E. At

12. Place the following species in order of increasing stability.

    A. (i) $CH_3CH_2CH_2^{\bullet}$ (ii) $(CH_3)_2\overset{\displaystyle |}{\underset{\displaystyle H}{C}}{}^{\bullet}$ (iii) $CH_3^{\bullet}$ (iv) $(CH_3)_3C^{\bullet}$

    B. (i) $R_2\overset{\displaystyle |}{\underset{\displaystyle H}{C}}{}^+$ (ii) R_3C^+ (iii) H_3C^+ (iv) $H_2\overset{\displaystyle |}{\underset{\displaystyle R}{C}}{}^+$

SOLUTIONS TO REVIEW PROBLEMS

1. **B** In this question, a primary alkyl halide is treated with cyanide, which is a good nucleophile. Primary alkyl halides are not sterically hindered and are readily displaced in S_N2 reactions. Cyanide will displace the bromide to produce 5-methylheptanenitrile in good yield. The correct answer is therefore choice (B). An S_N1 reaction will probably not occur because formation of a primary carbocation, which would result from the loss of bromide, is highly unfavorable. Elimination reactions would form a product with a double bond instead.

2. **C** The molecule shown in question 2 is 2-ethyl-1-neopentylcyclohexane. A primary carbon atom is one that is bonded to only one other carbon atom, a secondary carbon atom is bonded to two, a tertiary to three, and a quaternary to four. Thus, this molecule has four primary, six secondary, two tertiary, and one quaternary carbon atoms, so choice (C) is correct.

3. Step (A) is an initiation step because a nonradical species forms two radicals. Both steps (B) and (C) are propagation steps in which one radical species reacts to form another radical species. Step (D) is a termination step in which two radicals form a nonradical species.

4. **B** An S_N1 reaction is a first-order nucleophilic substitution reaction. It is called first-order because the rate-limiting step involves only one molecule; thus the correct answer is choice (B). Choice (A) is incorrect because the rate-limiting step is not necessarily the first step to occur in a reaction. It is simply the slowest step. Choice (C) is a true statement, but is incorrect because it is irrelevant to the term "first-order." Choice (D) is incorrect because it is the rate-limiting step, not the reaction, that involves only one molecule. Finally, (E) is false: S_N1 reactions involve two steps.

5. **A** The formation of a carbocation is the rate-limiting step. This step is the slowest to occur and its rate determines the rate of the reaction. Step 2 is a nucleophilic attack on the carbocation by ethanol. In step 3 a proton is lost from the protonated ether. Both steps 2 and 3 occur very rapidly in solution and are not rate-limiting steps. Choices (D) and (E) are incorrect because there can be only one rate-limiting step.

6. **C** The correct answer is choice (C), dimethyl sulfoxide. S_N2 reactions give the best results if a polar aprotic solvent is used. S_N2 reactions occur via a one-step mechanism in which a nucleophile attacks a substrate. Polar aprotic solvents accelerate this reaction by allowing the nucleophile to be "naked," i.e., not surrounded by hydrogen-bonded solvation spheres. The nucleophile therefore has easy access to the substrate. In addition, the solvent should be polar to dissolve the reactants. Choice (A), water; choice (B), ethanol; and choice (E), ammonia, are incorrect because, although these are polar, they are also protic and would diminish the power of the nucleophile. Choice (D) is hexane and is incorrect because it is a nonpolar solvent.

7. **C** This reaction is S_N1 and therefore must have a good leaving group and a strong incoming nucleophile. In choice (C), X is a tosylate ion, an excellent leaving group, and Y is a cyanide ion, an excellent nucleophile. Therefore, choice (C) is the correct answer. Choice (A) is incorrect; even though iodide is a good leaving group (favoring the forward reaction), it is also a good nucleophile (favoring the reverse reaction) because the solvent will be polar protic and it is an S_N1 reaction. Choices (B) and (E) are incorrect because ethoxide is a

poor leaving group (and tosylate is a weak nucleophile). Finally, choice (D) is incorrect because hydroxide is a poor leaving group and water is a poor nucleophile.

8. **C** This question concerns the free-radical bromination of an alkane. The bromination reaction occurs in such a way as to produce the most stable alkyl radical. This is because bromine radicals are very selective, as opposed to chlorine radicals, which react indiscriminately. In this question, the most stable radical is a secondary radical, which further reacts to form 2-bromopropane, choice (C), the correct answer. Choice (A) is incorrect because 1-bromopropane results from reaction of a primary radical, and although this may occur to an extent, the major product will be 2-bromopropane. Choice (B) would result from the combination of two primary radicals and is expected to be a very minor product. Choice (D) is incorrect because a carbon atom is lost in the reaction, and this does not occur in free-radical bromination. Finally, choice (E) is incorrect because it is an alkene, and bromination is a substitution or addition reaction, not an elimination.

9. **B** Inversion of configuration is a trademark of the S_N2 reaction, whereas racemization is typical of S_N1 reactions. When (S)-2-bromobutane is treated with hydroxide, a compound with an *R* configuration is obtained. The most likely occurrence is a substitution reaction, and the fact that the absolute configuration has changed suggests an S_N2 reaction. If the reaction proceeded by S_N1, the products would have both *R* and *S* configurations because the hydroxide ion could attack the planar carbocation from either side and would form a racemic mix. There is only one configuration in this case, and therefore the correct answer is S_N2.

10. **C** The correct answer is choice (C), IV > I > II > III, corresponding to: *n*-heptane > *n*-hexane > 2-methylpentane > 2,2-dimethylbutane. As the chain length of a straight-chain alkane is increased, the boiling point also increases, approximately $25-30°C$ for each additional carbon atom. Therefore, *n*-heptane is expected to boil at a higher temperature than *n*-hexane. Isomeric alkanes follow a typical trend: as branching increases, boiling point decreases. Compounds I, II, and III are isomeric hexanes, listed in increasing order of branching. Therefore, *n*-hexane boils at a higher temperature than 2-methylpentane, which boils at a higher temperature than 2,2-dimethylbutane.

11. **A** Free-radical halogenation reactions are practical only for bromine and chlorine; iodine, fluorine, and astatine do not react efficiently, and can therefore be eliminated. Bromine radicals react slowly in comparison to chlorine radicals, and are therefore more likely to react in a manner that forms the most stable alkyl radical, i.e., the most substituted radical. This leads to the production of one major bromination product. Chlorine radicals, on the other hand, react so quickly that they become rather indiscriminate, and generally produce several different products. In this particular reaction, two different products are isolated in comparable yields.

12. **A** III < I < II < IV

The order of stability of free radicals follows this sequence: $CH_3 < 1° < 2° < 3°$. Stability is enhanced by an increase in the number of alkyl substituents bonded directly to the radical carbon atom. These substituents allow the extra electron density to be spread out or delocalized throughout the molecule.

B III < IV < I < II

The stability of carbocations is increased when the positive charge can be distributed over more than one carbon atom. This means that tertiary carbocations are more stable than secondary, and so on.

CHAPTER FORTY-THREE

Alkenes and Alkynes

Alkenes and alkynes are hydrocarbons that contain double and triple bonds between carbons. They are called unsaturated, because they contain fewer than the maximum possible number of hydrogens. Double and triple bonds are considered functional groups, and alkenes and alkynes are more reactive than the corresponding alkanes. The double and triple bonds of alkenes and alkynes are made from first forming a single sigma bond, and then by forming one or two additional pi bonds (for a review of bonding, please see Chapter 41, Bonding).

For both alkenes and alkynes, a brief overview of nomenclature and properties will be followed by a discussion of their synthesis and then of their reactions.

ALKENES

Alkenes are hydrocarbons that contain carbon-carbon double bonds. The general formula for a straight-chain alkene with one double bond is C_nH_{2n}. The degree of unsaturation (the number N of double bonds or rings) of a compound of molecular formula C_nH_m can be determined according to the equation:

$$N = \frac{1}{2}(2n + 2 - m)$$

The carbons at either end of a double bond are sp² hybridized and both form planar bonds with bond angles of 120°. Alkenes are not able to rotate around their double bond and thus are constrained to unique configurations.

NOMENCLATURE OF ALKENES

Alkenes, also called olefins, may be described by the terms *cis, trans, E,* and *Z* to distinguish the configuration of functional groups around the double bond. The common names *ethylene, propylene,* and *isobutylene* are often used over the IUPAC names ethene, propene, and 2-methyl-1-propene, respectively. For a review of *cis-trans* isomers, see Chapter 40, Isomers; to review nomenclature, see Chapter 39.

$$CH_2{=}CH_2 \qquad\qquad CH_3CH{=}CH_2$$

ethene
(ethylene)

propene
(propylene)

2-methyl-1-propene
(isobutylene)

trans-2-butene

(Z)-3-methyl-3-heptene

Figure 43.1

PHYSICAL PROPERTIES OF ALKENES

The physical properties of alkenes are similar to those of alkanes. For example, their melting and boiling points increase with increasing molecular weight and are similar in value to those of the corresponding alkanes. Terminal alkenes (or 1-alkenes) usually boil at a lower temperature than internal alkenes. *Trans*-alkenes generally have higher melting points than *cis*-alkenes because their higher symmetry allows better packing in the solid state. They also tend to have lower boiling points than *cis*-alkenes because they are less polar.

Polarity is a property that results from the asymmetrical distribution of electrons in a particular molecule. In alkenes, this distribution creates dipole moments that are oriented from the electropositive alkyl groups toward the electronegative alkene. In *trans*-2-butene, the two dipole moments are oriented in opposite directions and cancel each other. The compound possesses no net dipole moment and is not polar. On the other hand, *cis*-2-butene has a net dipole moment, resulting from addition of the two smaller dipoles. The compound is polar, and the additional intermolecular forces raise the boiling point.

(nonpolar)

(polar)

Figure 43.2

SYNTHESIS OF ALKENES

Alkenes can be synthesized in a number of different ways. The most common method involves elimination reactions of either alcohols or alkyl halides. In these reactions the molecule loses either HX (where X is a halide) or a molecule of water from two adjacent carbons to form a double bond:

Figure 43.3

Elimination occurs by two distinct mechanisms, unimolecular and bimolecular, which are referred to as E1 and E2, respectively.

Unimolecular Elimination

Unimolecular elimination, abbreviated **E1**, is a two-step process proceeding through a carbocation intermediate. The rate of reaction is dependent on the concentration of only the substrate. The elimination of a leaving group and a proton results in the production of a double bond. In the first step, the leaving group departs, producing a carbocation. In the second step, a proton is removed by a base and the double bond forms.

Because both involve the formation of a carbocation intermediate, E1 is favored by the same factors that favor S_N1: protic solvents, highly branched carbon chains, good leaving groups, and weak nucleophiles in low concentration. After the identical first step, the reaction can proceed by either the E1 or S_N1 pathway. E1 and S_N1 are therefore competitive, and occur simultaneously under the same conditions. In fact, E1 and S_N1 have exactly the same rate law, given by rate $= k$[substrate], including having the same value of k. Directing a reaction toward either E1 or S_N1 alone is difficult, although high temperatures tend to favor E1; this means that a mixture of both E1 and S_N1 products will always be present.

Bimolecular Elimination

Bimolecular elimination, termed **E2**, occurs in one step. Its rate is dependent on the concentration of two species, the substrate and the base. A strong base such as the ethoxide ion ($C_2H_5O^-$) removes a proton, while simultaneously a halide ion *anti* to the proton leaves, resulting in the formation of a double bond.

Figure 43.4

Often there are two possible hydrogens that can be removed from carbons on either side of the leaving group, resulting in two different products. In such cases, the more substituted double bond is formed preferentially; this is known as Zaitsev's rule.

Controlling E2 vs. S_N2 is easier than controlling E1 vs. S_N1:

1. Steric hindrance does not greatly affect E2 reactions. Therefore, highly substituted carbon chains, which form the most stable alkenes, undergo E2 easily and S_N2 rarely.
2. A strong, bulky base such as *t*-butoxide favors E2 over S_N2. S_N2 is favored over E2 by strong nucleophiles that are weak bases, such as CN^- or I^-.

In general, heat and basic conditions will result in an E2 mechanism; heat and acidic conditions will result in E1 combined with S_N1.

REACTIONS OF ALKENES

Alkenes undergo several types of reactions, including:

- reduction by hydrogen
- addition by electrophiles and free radicals
- hydroboration
- a variety of oxidations
- polymerization

Reduction

Catalytic hydrogenation is the reductive process of adding molecular hydrogen (H_2) to a double bond with the aid of a metal catalyst. Typical catalysts are platinum, palladium, and nickel (usually Raney nickel, a special powdered form), but on rare occasions rhodium, iridium, or ruthenium are used.

The reaction takes place on the surface of the metal. One face of the double bond is coordinated to the metal surface, and thus the two hydrogen atoms are added to the same face of the double bond. This type of addition is called *syn* addition and results in a *meso* compound if the starting molecule was symmetrical (see Chapter 40, Isomers, for a review of *meso* compounds).

Figure 43.5

Electrophilic Additions

The π bond is somewhat weaker than the σ bond, and can therefore be broken without breaking the σ bond. As a result, compounds can *add* to double bonds while leaving the carbon skeleton intact. Although many different addition reactions exist, most operate via the same essential mechanism.

The electrons of the π bond are particularly exposed and are thus easily attacked by molecules that seek to accept an electron pair (Lewis acids). Because these groups are electron-seeking, they are known as electrophiles (literally, "lovers of electrons").

Addition of HX

The electrons of the double bond act as a Lewis base and react with electrophilic HX (hydrogen halide) molecules. The first step yields a carbocation intermediate after the double bond reacts with a proton. In the second step, the halide ion combines with the carbocation to give an alkyl halide. In cases where the alkene is asymmetrical, the initial protonation creates the *most stable carbocation*. The proton will add to the less substituted carbon atom (the carbon atom with the most hydrogens), and the positive charge of the carbocation will reside on the more substituted carbon. The halogen will then add to the carbocation, and thus create the product with the halide on the most substituted carbon. This phenomenon is called Markovnikov's rule. An example is:

Figure 43.6

Addition of X₂

The addition of halogens to a double bond is a rapid process. The addition of bromine and resulting change in color of the solution is frequently used as a diagnostic tool to test for the presence of double bonds. In the example shown, the double bond acts as a nucleophile and attacks a Br_2 molecule, displacing Br^-. The Br^+ attaches to the double bond and a cyclic bronomium ion is formed. This is attacked by Br^-, giving the dibromo compound. Note that this addition is *anti* because the Br^- attacks the cyclic bronomium ion in a standard S_N2 displacement from the opposite side.

Anti-addition

Figure 43.7

If the reaction is carried out in a nucleophilic solvent, the solvent molecules can compete in the displacement step, producing, for example, a bromo alcohol rather than the dibromo compound.

Addition of H₂O

Water can be added to alkenes under acidic conditions. The double bond is protonated according to Markovnikov's rule, forming the most stable carbocation. This carbocation reacts with water, forming a protonated alcohol, which then loses a proton to yield the alcohol. The reaction is performed at low temperature because the reverse reaction is an acid-catalyzed dehydration favored by high temperatures.

Figure 43.8

Direct addition of water is generally not useful in the laboratory because yields vary greatly with reaction conditions; therefore, this reaction is generally carried out indirectly using mercuric acetate, $Hg(CH_3COO)_2$.

Free Radical Additions

An alternate mechanism exists for the addition of HX (hydrogen halide) to alkenes, which proceeds through free-radical intermediates, and occurs when peroxides, oxygen, or other impurities are present. Free-radical additions are called anti-Markovnikov because X• adds first to the double bond, producing the most stable free radical on the most substituted carbon. The hydrogen then adds to the free radical, resulting in the less substituted product. The reaction is useful for HBr but is not practical for HCl or HI because the energies are unfavorable.

most stable
radical

Figure 43.9

Hydroboration

Diborane (B_2H_6) adds readily to double bonds. The boron atom is a Lewis acid and attaches to the less sterically hindered carbon atom. The second step is an oxidation-hydrolysis with peroxide and aqueous base, producing the alcohol with overall anti-Markovnikov, *syn* orientation.

R =

Figure 43.10

Oxidation

Potassium permanganate

Alkenes can be oxidized with $KMnO_4$ to provide different types of products, depending upon the reaction conditions. Cold, dilute, aqueous $KMnO_4$ reacts to produce 1,2 diols (vicinal diols), which are also called glycols, with *syn* orientation:

Figure 43.11

Under acidic conditions, manganate ions (MnO_4^{2-}) are reduced to manganese ions (Mn^{2+}), and this reaction can be coupled to the complete cleavage of a double bond. If a hot, basic solution of potassium permanganate is added to the alkene and then acidified, the product will be determined by the nature of the alkene substrate. Nonterminal alkenes are cleaved to form two molar equivalents of carboxylic acid, and terminal alkenes are cleaved to form a carboxylic acid and carbon dioxide. If the nonterminal double bonded carbon is disubstituted, however, a ketone will be formed:

Figure 43.12

Ozonolysis

Treatment of alkenes with ozone followed by reduction with zinc and water is a milder reaction. This treatment results in cleavage of the double bond to produce two aldehyde molecules as shown (or ketones if the double bond is substituted with alkyl groups):

Figure 43.13

If the reaction mixture is reduced with sodium borohydride, $NaBH_4$, the corresponding alcohols are produced:

Figure 43.14

Peroxycarboxylic acids

Alkenes can be oxidized with peroxycarboxylic acids. Peroxyacetic acid (CH_3CO_3H) and *m*-chloroperoxybenzoic acid (mCPBA) are commonly used. The products formed are oxiranes (also called epoxides) and are highly reactive. This makes them ideal for further nucleophilic reactions such as substitutions and the formation of alcohols, glycols, and amines:

Figure 43.15

Polymerization

Polymerization is the creation of long, high molecular weight chains (polymers), composed of repeating subunits (called monomers). Polymerization usually occurs through a radical mechanism, although anionic and even cationic polymerizations are commonly observed. A typical example is the formation of polyethylene from ethylene (ethene) that requires high temperatures and pressures:

$$CH_2\!=\!CH_2 \xrightarrow[\text{high pressure}]{R\cdot,\ \text{heat}} RCH_2CH_2(CH_2CH_2)_nCH_2CH_2R$$

Figure 43.16

ALKYNES

Alkynes are hydrocarbon compounds that possess one or more carbon-carbon triple bonds. The general formula for a straight-chain alkyne with one triple bond is C_nH_{2n-2}. Triple bonds are sp hybridized and are therefore linear, imparting unique characteristics to molecules that contain them.

NOMENCLATURE OF ALKYNES

The suffix **-yne** is used to designate an alkyne, and the position of the triple bond is specified when necessary. A common exception to the IUPAC rules is ethyne, which is called *acetylene*. Frequently, compounds are named as derivatives of acetylene.

$$CH_3CH_2CH_2\underset{\underset{\text{Cl}}{|}}{CH}C\!\equiv\!CCH_3 \qquad CH\!\equiv\!CH \qquad CH_3C\!\equiv\!CH$$

4-chloro-2-heptyne   ethyne   propyne

(acetylene)   (methylacetylene)

Figure 43.17

PHYSICAL PROPERTIES OF ALKYNES

The physical properties of the alkynes are similar to those of their analogous alkenes and alkanes. In general, the shorter-chain compounds are gases, boiling at somewhat higher temperatures than the corresponding alkenes. Internal alkynes, like alkenes, boil at higher temperatures than terminal alkynes.

Asymmetrical distribution of electron density causes alkynes to have dipole moments that are larger than those of alkenes, but still small in magnitude. Thus, solutions of alkynes can be slightly polar.

Terminal alkynes are relatively acidic, having pK_a values of approximately 25. This property is exploited in some of the reactions of alkynes, which will be discussed later.

SYNTHESIS OF ALKYNES

Triple bonds can be made by the elimination of two molecules of HX from a geminal or vicinal dihalide:

Figure 43.18

This reaction is not always practical and requires high temperatures and a strong base. A more useful method adds an already existing triple bond onto a particular carbon skeleton. A terminal triple bond is converted to a nucleophile by removing the acidic proton with strong base, producing an acetylide ion. This ion will perform nucleophilic displacements on alkyl halides at room temperature using an S_N2 mechanism:

$$CH\equiv CH \xrightarrow{\text{n-BuLi}} CH\equiv C^-Li \quad + \quad CH_3Cl \xrightarrow{} CH\equiv CCH_3$$

Figure 43.19

REACTIONS OF ALKYNES

Alkynes undergo several types of reactions, most of which are closely related to the reactions of alkenes:

- a variety of reduction mechanisms by hydrogen and catalysts
- addition by electrophiles and free radicals
- hydroboration
- oxidation

Reduction

Alkynes, just like alkenes, can be hydrogenated with a metal catalyst to produce alkanes in a reaction that goes to completion:

$$CH_3\text{-}C\equiv C\text{-}CH_3 \rightarrow CH_3CH_2CH_2CH_3 \text{ in the presence of Pt, Pd, or Ni}$$

A more useful reaction stops the reduction after addition of just one equivalent of H_2, producing alkenes. This partial hydrogenation can take place in two different ways. The first uses Lindlar's catalyst, which is palladium on barium sulfate ($BaSO_4$) with quinoline, a poison that stops the reaction at the alkene stage. Because the reaction occurs on a metal surface, the product alkene is the *cis* isomer. The other method uses sodium in liquid ammonia below $-33°C$ (the boiling point of ammonia), and produces the *trans* isomer of the alkene via a free radical mechanism:

$$CH_3C \equiv CCH_3 \xrightarrow[\substack{\text{Quinoline} \\ \text{(Lindlar's catalyst)}}]{H_2, \text{Pd/BaSO}_4} \text{cis-2-butene}$$

2-butyne   cis-2-butene

$$CH_3C \equiv CCH_3 \xrightarrow{Na, NH_3(l)} \text{trans-2-butene}$$

2-butyne   trans-2-butene

Figure 43.20

Addition

Electrophilic

Electrophilic addition to alkynes occurs in the same manner as it does to alkenes, with the reaction following Markovnikov's rule. The addition can generally be stopped at the intermediate alkene stage, or carried further:

$$CH_3C \equiv CH \xrightarrow{HBr}$$

$$CH_3C \equiv CH \xrightarrow{Br_2}$$

$$CH_3C \equiv CH \xrightarrow{2Br_2} CH_3CBr_2CBr_2H$$

Figure 43.21

Free radical

Radicals add to triple bonds as they do to double bonds—with anti-Markovnikov placement of the halogen. The reaction product is usually the *trans* isomer, because the intermediate vinyl radical can isomerize to its more stable form as shown:

$$CH_3CH_2C \equiv CH + X \cdot \longrightarrow$$

Figure 43.22

Hydroboration

Addition of boron to triple bonds occurs by the same method as addition of boron to double bonds. Addition is *syn*, and the boron atom adds first. The boron atom can be replaced with a proton from acetic acid, to produce a *cis* alkene:

$$3 \; H_3CC \equiv CCH_3 + \frac{1}{2} B_2H_6 \longrightarrow$$

Figure 43.23

With terminal alkynes, a disubstituted borane is used to prevent further boration of the vinylic intermediate to an alkane. The vinylic borane intermediate can be oxidatively cleaved with hydrogen peroxide (H_2O_2), creating an intermediate vinyl alcohol, which rearranges to the more stable carbonyl compound via keto-enol tautomerism (discussed in Chapter 46, Aldehydes and Ketones).

$$CH_3C \equiv CH \xrightarrow[\;H_2O_2, \; OH^-\;]{R_2BH}$$

Figure 43.24

Oxidation

Alkynes can be oxidatively cleaved with either basic potassium permanganate (followed by acidification) or ozone. In both instances shown, carboxylic acids are produced, but treatment of a terminal alkyne with basic permanganate will produce carbon dioxide.

Figure 43.25

Figure 43.26

REVIEW PROBLEMS

1. The major product of the reaction below is

   A. 3-methyl-1-butene.
   B. 2-methyl-3-butene.
   C. 3-methyl-2-butene.
   D. 2-methyl-2-butene.
   E. 3-methyl-3-butene.

2. The below reaction takes place mostly by which of the following mechanisms?

   A. S_N1
   B. S_N2
   C. E1
   D. E2
   E. None of the above

3. Which of the following products will be formed if 2-methyl-2-butene is reacted with hot basic $KMnO_4$?
   A. 1 mole of acetic acid and 1 mole of propanoic acid
   B. 2 moles of pentanoic acid
   C. 1 mole of acetic acid and 1 mole of acetone
   D. 2 moles of acetic acid and 1 mole of CO_2
   E. 1 mole of pentanoic acid

4. Which of the following is true about E2 reactions?
   A. They are greatly affected by steric hindrance.
   B. They need a strong base to abstract the proton.
   C. They are favored over S_N2 by weak Lewis bases.
   D. They are favored over S_N1 and E1 by polar solvents.
   E. They don't need a strong leaving group.

5. What is the product of the following reaction?

A. (isopropanol-OH) + (formaldehyde H–CO–H) **B.** (acetone) + CH_3OH

C. (acetone) + CO_2 **D.** (formaldehyde H–CO–H) + (acetone)

E. None of the above

6. What is the product of the following reaction?

$$CH_3-C\equiv C-\underset{\underset{CH_3}{|}}{\overset{\overset{CH_3}{|}}{CH}} \xrightarrow[\text{2) H}^+]{\text{1) hot KMnO}_4, \text{OH}^-} \; ?$$

A. (acetaldehyde) + (isobutyraldehyde) **B.** (acetaldehyde) + (HO–isobutyryl)

C. (acetic acid) + (HO–isobutyric acid) **D.** (enediol structure with OH, OH)

E. None of the above

7. What is the product of the following reaction?

(propene) $\xrightarrow[\text{peroxides}]{\text{HBr}}$?

A. (1-bromopropane with Br) **B.** (propene skeleton)

C. (2-bromopropane, Br) **D.** (2-bromopropene, Br)

E. None of the above

SOLUTIONS TO REVIEW PROBLEMS

1. **D** Heating an alcohol generally leads to loss of a water molecule and the formation of a double bond. Two products can be obtained depending on which H atom is used by the OH group to form water; either

OR

The most stable alkene, which is the most substituted one, is formed. Of the two alkenes, 2-methyl-2-butene is more stable, and the correct choice is (D).

2. **D** Since tertiary butyl chloride has been converted to an alkene, this is an elimination reaction. This particular compound, formally named 2-chloro-2-methylpropane, can react through either E1 or E2 depending on the conditions: reaction with strong bases leads to E2, and reaction with weak bases leads to E1. Since methoxide is a strong base, elimination occurs by the E2 mechanism. Choice (D) is the correct response.

3. **C** The double bond of 2-methyl-2-butene is cleaved by hot, basic potassium permanganate to form acetone and acetic acid. If the double-bonded carbon is a monosubstituted carbon as seen on the right side of the molecule, a carboxylic acid is obtained; if it is a disubstituted carbon as seen on the left side, a ketone is obtained. Thus, the correct choice is (C).

acetone   acetic acid

4. **B** Answer choice (A) is incorrect; E2 reactions are not affected by steric hindrance. Answer choice (C) is also incorrect, as S_N2 reactions are favored over E2 by weak Lewis bases. Answer choice (D) is a distortion, as all four substitution and elimination mechanisms require polar solvents to keep the polar reactants and products in solution. The correct answer choice is (B), as E2 requires a strong base to remove a proton at the same time that the leaving group departs on the opposite side of the molecule.

5. **D** Ozonolysis of an alkene and subsequent treatment with zinc and water produces carbonyl compounds. The double bond is broken and a disubstituted double-bonded carbon is converted to a ketone, whereas a monosubstituted double-bonded carbon is converted to an aldehyde. In this reaction, C−1 is a monosubstituted carbon and C−2 is a disubstituted carbon, and thus the products obtained are a ketone and an aldehyde.

6. **C** Treating alkynes with hot basic $KMnO_4$ leads to the cleavage of the triple bond and the formation of carboxylic acids.

7. **A** In the presence of peroxides, the addition of HBr to the double bond takes place in an anti-Markovnikov manner in a series of free-radical reactions initiated by peroxides.

1. ROOR → 2RO•

2. HBr + RO• → ROH + Br•

3. $CH_3CH=CH_2$ + Br• → CH_3-CH_2Br

4. CH_3-CH_2Br + HBr → $CH_3-CH_2-CH_2Br$ + Br •

In step 3, CH_3-CH_2Br is formed instead of CH_3-CHBr^-, since the more substituted free-radical is more stable than the less substituted one. Thus, the correct choice is (A). Note that in the absence of peroxides, HBr adds to the double bond in a Markovnikov manner.

O C

K 537

CHAPTER FORTY-FOUR

Aromatic Compounds

The terms **aromatic** and **aliphatic,** meaning "fragrant" and "fatty," respectively, were used originally to distinguish types of organic compounds. The terms are still used by organic chemists but with new definitions. "Aromatic" now describes an unusually stable ring system with several unique characteristics. Aromatic compounds are cyclic, conjugated molecules that possess $4n + 2$ pi electrons and adopt planar conformations to allow maximum overlap of the conjugated pi orbitals. Aliphatic describes all compounds that are not aromatic.

All aromatic compounds are conjugated, but not all conjugated molecules are aromatic. A conjugated system consists of alternating single and double bonds, creating a delocalized pi electron network. This allows one or more resonance structures to exist; resonance indicates stability, which is a key characteristic of aromatics. Because every other bond is a double bond, every carbon in the conjugated system is sp^2 hybridized, and thus is trigonal planar in shape. When confined to a ring system, all of the sp^2 hybridized carbons must lie flat relative to each other, giving another characteristic of aromatics: they are cyclic and planar.

The criterion of possessing $4n + 2$ pi electrons is known as **Hückel's rule,** and is an important indicator of aromaticity. If a cyclic conjugated molecule follows Hückel's rule, then it is an aromatic compound. The integer n can be any nonnegative whole number, including 0, and thus $4n + 2$ can be 2, 6, 10, 14, 18, etc. It is often easier to remember and recognize these allowable values for Hückel's rule than to calculate them. To determine the number of pi electrons, determine the number of pi bonds and multiply by two. Unbonded p orbitals that contain lone pairs of electrons sometimes take part in the conjugation of an aromatic compound. Resonance forms are possible that include these electrons and usually have formal charges; when this is possible, the lone pairs are counted toward Hückel's rule.

Neutral compounds, anions, and cations may all be aromatic, and many compounds must be in their ionic form in order to be aromatic. Some typical aromatic compounds and ions are:

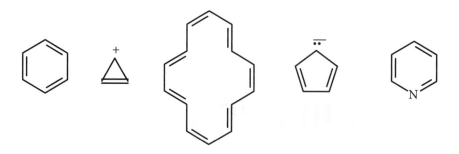

Figure 44.1

A cyclic, conjugated molecule that possesses $4n$ pi electrons is said to be **anti-aromatic** (a cyclic, conjugated molecule that is unstable and highly reactive). Some typical anti-aromatic compounds are:

Figure 44.2

NOMENCLATURE

Aromatic compounds are referred to as **aryl** compounds, or **arenes**, and are represented by the symbol **Ar**. Aliphatic compounds are called **alkyl** and are represented by the symbol **R**. Common names exist for many mono- and disubstituted aromatic compounds.

Toluene   Phenol   Aniline   Anisole

Figure 44.3

The benzene group is called a **phenyl** group (**Ph**) when named as a substituent. The term **benzyl** refers to a toluene molecule substituted at the methyl position.

methyl phenyl ketone   benzyl chloride

Figure 44.4

Substituted benzene rings are named as alkyl benzenes, with the substituents numbered to produce the lowest sequence. A 1,2-disubstituted compound is called *ortho-* or *o-*; a 1,3-disubstituted compound is called *meta-* or *m-*; and a 1,4-disubstituted compound is called *para-* or *p-*.

2,4,6-trinitrotoluene   *o*-nitrotoluene   *m*-dichlorobenzene
(TNT)

p-methylbenzoic acid

Figure 44.5

There are many polycyclic and heterocyclic aromatic compounds, many of which have common names:

Naphthalene   Anthracene   Pyridine   Pyrrole

Figure 44.6

PROPERTIES

The physical properties of aromatic compounds are generally similar to those of other hydrocarbons. In contrast, chemical properties are significantly affected by aromaticity. The characteristic planar shape of benzene permits the ring's six pi orbitals to overlap, delocalizing the electron density. All six carbon atoms are sp^2 hybridized, and each of the six orbitals overlaps equally with its two neighbors. As a result, the delocalized electrons form two pi electron clouds, one above and one below the plane of the ring. This delocalization stabilizes the molecule, making it fairly unreactive: in particular, benzene does not undergo addition reactions as alkenes do. The same stability holds true for other aromatic compounds, since the definition of an aromatic compound includes the presence of a delocalized pi electron system.

REACTIONS

Electrophilic Aromatic Substitution

The most important reaction of aromatic compounds is electrophilic aromatic substitution. In this reaction an electrophile replaces a proton on an aromatic ring, producing a substituted aromatic compound. Because benzene is nonreactive, a form of acidic catalyst is required for the substitution reaction to proceed. The most common examples of substitution reactions are halogenation, sulfonation, nitration, and acylation.

Halogenation

Aromatic rings react with bromine or chlorine in the presence of a Lewis acid, such as $FeCl_3$, $FeBr_3$, or $AlCl_3$, to produce monosubstituted products in good yield. Reaction of fluorine and iodine with aromatic rings is less useful, as fluorine tends to produce multisubstituted products, and iodine's lack of reactivity requires special conditions for the reaction to proceed.

Figure 44.7

Sulfonation

Aromatic rings react with fuming sulfuric acid (a mixture of sulfuric acid and sulfur trioxide) to form sulfonic acids.

Figure 44.8

Nitration

The nitration of aromatic rings is another synthetically useful reaction. A mixture of nitric and sulfuric acids is used to create the nitronium ion, NO_2^+, a strong electrophile. This reacts with aromatic rings to produce nitro compounds.

Figure 44.9

Acylation (Friedel-Crafts reactions)

In a Friedel-Crafts acylation reaction, a carbocation electrophile, usually an acyl group, is incorporated into the aromatic ring. These reactions are usually catalyzed by Lewis acids such as $AlCl_3$. This reaction can also be used to add alkyl groups, but the reaction is difficult to control and can lead to multiple products.

Figure 44.10

Substituent effects

The first substituent on an aromatic ring strongly influences the susceptibility of the ring to further electrophilic aromatic substitution, and also strongly affects what position on the ring another electrophile is most likely to attack. Substituents can be grouped into three different classes according to whether they are activating or deactivating, and where on the ring the next reaction is likely to take place. Activators cause the next reaction to occur more quickly and more easily; deactivators cause the next reaction to occur more slowly and with greater difficulty. These effects depend on whether the group tends to donate or withdraw electron density.

The three classes of substituents, each in decreasing strength of effect, are:

a. Activating, *ortho/para*-directing substituents (electron-donating): $NH_2 > NR_2 > OH > NHCOR > OR > OCOR > R$

b. Deactivating, *ortho/para*-directing substituents (weakly electron-withdrawing): $F > Cl > Br > I$

c. Deactivating, *meta*-directing substituents (electron-withdrawing): $NO_2 > SO_3H >$ carbonyl compounds, including COOH, COOR, COR, and CHO

Example: When toluene undergoes electrophilic aromatic substitution, the methyl group directs substitution to occur primarily at the *ortho* and *para* positions:

Figure 44.11

Reduction

Catalytic Reduction

Benzene rings can be reduced by catalytic hydrogenation under vigorous conditions (elevated temperature and pressure) to yield cyclohexane. Ruthenium or rhodium on carbon are the most common catalysts; platinum or palladium may also be used.

Figure 44.12

REVIEW PROBLEMS

1. Predict aromatic, anti-aromatic, or nonaromatic behavior for each of the following compounds.

A.

B.

C.

D.

E.

2. Which of the following represents the correct structure for *para*-nitrotoluene?

A. CH_2NH_2

B. NO_2 CH_3

C. NO_2 H_3C

D. NH_2 H_3C

E. None of the above

3. What would be the major product of the following reaction?

    + C_2H_5COCl $\xrightarrow{AlCl_3}$?

A.

B.

C.

D.

E. None of the above

4. Nitration of benzene at 30°C leads to a 95 percent yield of nitrobenzene. When the temperature is increased to 100°C, dinitrobenzene is produced. Which of the following is the predominant product?

A.

B.

C.

D.

E. None of the above

5. What is the major product of the nitration reaction below?

$$\xrightarrow[\text{HNO}_3]{\text{H}_2\text{SO}_4}$$?

A.

C.

B.

D.

E. None of the above

6. Which represents the predominant product(s) of the reaction below?

$$\xrightarrow[\text{FeBr}_3]{\text{Br}_2}$$?

A.

B.

C.

D.

E. None of the above

7. Which sequence of reaction conditions should be used to produce the compound below from benzene?

A. $AlCl_3/Cl_2$; H_2/Pt
B. Cl_2/UV light; H_2/Pt
C. H_2/Pt; $AlCl_3/Cl_2$
D. HCl; H_2/Pt
E. Cl_2/UV light; $AlCl_3/Cl_2$

SOLUTIONS TO REVIEW PROBLEMS

1. **A** Nonaromatic. This compound has $4n + 2 = 6$ pi electrons ($n = 1$), and is a conjugated system; however, it is not cyclic.

   B Nonaromatic. This compound has $4n + 2 = 6$ pi electrons ($n = 1$) and is cyclic. However, there is no conjugation of the double bonds.

   C Aromatic. This compound (naphthalene) is cyclic, has $4n + 2 = 8$ pi electrons ($n = 2$), and has a conjugated system of double bonds.

   D Anti-aromatic. This compound is cyclic and conjugated. However, it has only $4n = 4$ pi electrons ($n = 1$).

   E Aromatic. This class of compounds (alkyl anilinium ions) has $4n + 2 = 6$ pi electrons ($n = 1$), is cyclic, and has conjugated double bond systems.

2. **C** Toluene is the common name for methylbenzene: a methyl group attached to a benzene ring. In *para*-nitrotoluene, the nitro group (NO_2) is attached to the ring directly across from the methyl group. Choice (C) is the correct response. Choice (B) is incorrect because the nitro group is *meta*, not *para* substituted. Choices (A) and (D) can be eliminated since nitro groups are not present in these compounds.

3. **B** The reaction shown, a Friedel-Crafts acylation of toluene, will yield a product containing a $-CH_3$ substituent and a $-C=O$ substituent. Chlorination of the ring also uses $AlCl_3$ as a reagent, but the second reagent would have to be Cl_2, not C_2H_5COCl; thus, choices (C) and (D) (both chlorotoluenes) can be eliminated. Since CH_3 is an activating, *ortho/para*-directing group, the *meta* isomer, choice (A), would be a minor product at best. Choice (B), the *para* isomer, would be favored by the substituent effect of the methyl group, and along with the *ortho* isomer (which is not among these choices) would be the major product.

4. **C** *meta*-dinitrobenzene is the predominant product since $-NO_2$ is a *meta*-directing group.

5. **A** All three substituents of 2-bromo-1,3-dinitrobenzene direct reaction to C−5, which is *meta* to both nitro groups and *para* to the bromine atom, so choice (A) will be the major product. Since all three groups are deactivating, the reaction will be slow and require elevated temperatures to proceed.

6. **B** This reaction shows the bromination of nitrobenzene. Choices (A) and (D) are actually different views of the same compound. Since aromatic rings are planar, rings that are mirror images are identical (although alkyl substituents of benzene rings may still have chiral centers, and molecules containing such groups may be chiral). Choice (B) shows *meta*-bromonitrobenzene, which is the favored product of this reaction since the nitro substituent is *meta*-directing. Choices (A) and (D) show the *para* isomer, while (C) shows the *ortho* isomer, both of which are less favored in this reaction.

7. **A** In order to produce chlorocyclohexane, two different procedures must be carried out: the benzene ring must be chlorinated and then hydrogenated. A suitable way to chlorinate the ring is to use Cl_2 and the Lewis acid $AlCl_3$, which is choice (A). Using chlorine in the

presence of UV light will not be effective, so choices (B) and (E) are incorrect. Choice (D) is incorrect because HCl will not chlorinate the ring. Now for the second step: hydrogenation. Hydrogenation of the benzene ring can be accomplished by using hydrogen in the presence of a platinum catalyst, so choice (A) is the correct answer. If the procedure were carried out according to choice (C), reduction would occur, forming cyclohexane, but chlorination would not, since cyclohexane is unreactive towards chlorine and the Lewis acid catalyst.

CHAPTER FORTY-FIVE

Alcohols and Ethers

Alcohols are compounds with the general formula **ROH**. The functional group –**OH** is called the **hydroxyl** group. An alcohol can be thought of as a substituted water molecule, with an alkyl group R replacing one **H** atom.

An ether is a compound with two alkyl or aryl groups bonded to a single oxygen atom. The general formula for an ether is R-O-R, and ethers can be thought of as disubstituted water molecules.

The nomenclature, properties, synthesis, and reactions of alcohols will be discussed in the following sections; subsequently the same topics will be reviewed for ethers.

NOMENCLATURE OF ALCOHOLS

Alcohols are named in the IUPAC system by replacing the -**e** ending of the root alkane with the ending -**ol**. The —OH group has high priority for naming; the carbon atom attached to the hydroxyl group usually must be included in the longest chain and receive the lowest possible number. Some examples are:

2-propanol   4,5-dimethyl-2-hexanol

Figure 45.1

The common names for alcohols are given by naming the alkyl group as a derivative, followed by the word *alcohol*.

ethyl alcohol   isobutyl alcohol

Figure 45.2

Compounds of the general formula ArOH, with a hydroxyl group attached to an aromatic ring, are called **phenols**.

phenol   *p*-nitrophenol   *m*-cresol   *o*-bromophenol
(*m*-methylphenol)

Figure 45.3

PHYSICAL PROPERTIES OF ALCOHOLS

Alcohols have a hydrogen attached directly to an oxygen, and thus are able to form **hydrogen bonds**. As a result of these strong intermolecular attractions, the boiling points of alcohols are significantly higher than those of their analogous hydrocarbons.

Figure 45.4

Molecules with more than one hydroxyl group show greater degrees of hydrogen bonding, as shown by the following boiling points:

Boiling
Point (°C)   − 42.1   97.4   189.0   290.0

Figure 45.5

The hydrogen atom of the hydroxyl group is weakly acidic, and alcohols can dissociate into protons and alkoxy ions just as water dissociates into protons and hydroxide ions. pK_a values of several compounds are listed below. The presence of electron withdrawing groups such as fluorine stabilize the negatively charged conjugate base of the alcohol, thus decreasing the pK_a. Conversely, alkyl groups destabilize the anionic form because of their electron donating properties, thereby increasing the pK_a. Note that as pK_a decreases, acidity increases; acids and pK_a values are discussed in Chapter 36, Acids and Bases.

	Dissociation	pK_a
H_2O	$\rightleftharpoons$ $HO^- + H^+$	15.7
CH_3OH	$\rightleftharpoons$ $CH_3O^- + H^+$	15.5
C_2H_5OH	$\rightleftharpoons$ $C_2H_5O^- + H^+$	15.9
i-PrOH	$\rightleftharpoons$ i-PrO$^- + H^+$	17.1
t-BuOH	$\rightleftharpoons$ t-BuO$^- + H^+$	18.0
CF_3CH_2OH	$\rightleftharpoons$ $CF_3CH_2O^- + H^+$	12.4
PhOH	$\rightleftharpoons$ $PhO^- + H+$	≈ 10.0

Table 45.1

Phenols are more acidic than aliphatic alcohols, due to resonance structures that distribute the negative charge of the conjugate base throughout the ring, thus stabilizing the anion. This acidity allows phenols to readily form salts with inorganic bases such as NaOH. Phenols readily form intermolecular hydrogen bonds and have relatively high melting and boiling points. However, phenol and many of its derivatives are only slightly soluble in water due to the conflicting effects of the hydrophobicity of the phenyl ring and the ability of the −OH group to hydrogen bond. The presence of other substituents on the ring has significant effects on the acidity, boiling point, and melting point of phenols. As with other aromatic compounds, electron-withdrawing substituents increase acidity by stabilizing the negatively charged conjugate base, and electron-donating groups decrease acidity.

OVERVIEW OF ALCOHOLS

Key Reaction Mechanisms for Alcohols

Several basic reaction mechanisms occur over and over in the chemistry of alcohols (and ethers in many cases as well). These reactions provide a framework for understanding and learning how the alcohols behave, and specific examples will be shown in the sections on both synthesis and reactions of alcohols that follow.

1. S_N1 and S_N2 nucleophilic substitution to create alcohols. Conversely, protonation of an alcohol allows it act as a leaving group in these reactions. See Chapter 42, Alkanes, for a review of S_N1 and S_N2 reaction mechanisms.

2. Electrophilic addition of water to a double bond to create an alcohol. Conversely, elimination reactions (E1, E2) remove hydroxyls to create a double bond. Addition and elimination reactions are discussed in Chapter 43.

3. Nucleophilic addition to a carbonyl to create an alcohol. This reaction type is discussed further in Chapters 44−46.

4. Oxidation and reduction: Alcohols are at the most reduced end of the oxidation-reduction continuum (shown in Table 45.2 below), as they have only single bonds to oxygen. Carbonyl-containing compounds are more oxidized, as demonstrated by the larger number of bonds to oxygen from a single carbon. Additional discussion of alcohols relative to aldehydes, ketones, and carboxylic acids is found in chapters 46 and 47.

Oxidation ⟶

1° alcohols ⟷ aldehydes ⟷ carboxylic acids

2° alcohols ⟷ ketones

⟵ *Reduction*

Table 45.2

SYNTHESIS OF ALCOHOLS

Alcohols can be prepared from a variety of different types of compounds. Methanol, also called wood alcohol, is obtained from the destructive distillation of wood. It is toxic and can cause blindness if ingested. Ethanol, or grain alcohol, is produced from the fermentation of sugars and can be metabolized by the body; however, in large enough quantities, it too is toxic.

Addition Reactions

Alcohols can be prepared via several reactions that involve addition of water to double bonds (discussed in Chapter 41).

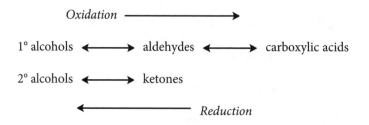

Figure 45.6

Alcohols can also be prepared from the addition of organometallic compounds (Grignard reagents) to carbonyl groups (discussed in Chapter 46).

Figure 45.7

Substitution Reactions

Both S_N1 and S_N2 reactions can be used to produce alcohols under the appropriate reaction conditions (discussed in Chapter 42). For example:

$$CH_3Br + OH^- \rightarrow CH_3OH + Br^-$$

Reduction Reactions

Alcohols can be prepared from the reduction of aldehydes, ketones, carboxylic acids, or esters. Lithium aluminum hydride ($LiAlH_4$, or LAH) and sodium borohydride ($NaBH_4$) are the two most frequently used reducing reagents. LAH is stronger and less specific, whereas $NaBH_4$ is milder and more selective. For example, LAH will reduce carboxylic acids and esters to alcohols, while $NaBH_4$ will not. Both LAH and $NaBH_4$, however, will reduce aldehydes and ketones to alcohols.

Figure 45.8

Phenol Synthesis

Phenols may be synthesized from arylsulfonic acids with heat and NaOH. However, this reaction is useful only for phenol or its alkylated derivatives, as most functional groups are destroyed by the harsh reaction conditions.

A more versatile method of synthesizing phenols proceeds using hydrolysis of diazonium salts.

Figure 45.9

REACTIONS OF ALCOHOLS

Elimination Reactions

Alcohols can be **dehydrated** in strongly acidic solution (usually H_2SO_4) to produce alkenes. The mechanism of this dehydration reaction is E1, and proceeds by first protonating the alcohol and then removing a water molecule to form the double bond.

Figure 45.10

Notice that two products are obtained, with the more stable alkene being the major product. This occurs via movement of a proton to produce the more stable 2° carbocation. This type of rearrangement is commonly encountered with carbocations.

Substitution Reactions

The direct displacement of hydroxyl groups in substitution reactions is rare because the hydroxide ion is a poor leaving group. However, the hydroxyl group can be converted to a good leaving group using two different approaches. Protonating the alcohol makes water the leaving group, which works well for S_N1 reactions. Alternatively, the alcohol can be converted into a tosylate (p-toluenesulfonate) group, which is an excellent leaving group for S_N2 reactions (see Figures 45.11a and 45.11b).

Figure 45.11a

Figure 45.11b

Another substitution reaction that serves as a common method of converting alcohols into alkyl halides is through the formation of inorganic esters, which then readily undergo S_N2 reactions. Alcohols react with thionyl chloride to produce a chlorosulfite intermediate and HCl. The chloride ion of HCl then displaces SO_2 and regenerates Cl^-, forming the desired alkyl chloride.

$$CH_3OH + SOCl_2 \longrightarrow CH_3OSOCl + HCl$$

$$Cl^- \quad CH_3-O-\overset{\overset{O}{\|}}{S}-Cl \longrightarrow ClCH_3 + SO_2 + Cl^-$$

Figure 45.12

An analogous reaction in which the alcohol is treated with PBr_3 instead of thionyl chloride produces alkyl bromides.

Phenols readily undergo electrophilic aromatic substitution reactions. Because the $-OH$ group of phenol has lone pairs that can be donated to the ring, the $-OH$ is a strongly activating, *ortho/ para*-directing ring substituent (see Chapter 44, Aromatic Compounds).

Oxidation Reactions

The oxidation of alcohols generally involves a metal oxidizing agent such as chromium or manganese. For example, some form of chromium (VI) is reduced to chromium (III) during the reaction. PCC (pyridinium chlorochromate, $C_5H_6NCrO_3Cl$) is commonly used as a mild oxidant. It converts primary alcohols to aldehydes but does not continue the oxidation to the carboxylic acid. PCC can also be used to convert a secondary alcohol to a ketone.

Figure 45.13

Potassium permanganate ($KMnO_4$) is a very strong oxidizing agent that will react with a primary alcohol to create a carboxylic acid or with a secondary alcohol to create a ketone. Another reagent used to oxidize primary or secondary alcohols is alkali (either sodium or potassium) dichromate salt.

Figure 45.14

A stronger oxidant is chromium trioxide, CrO_3. This is often dissolved with dilute sulfuric acid in acetone; the mixture is called Jones reagent. It oxidizes primary alcohols to carboxylic acids and secondary alcohols to ketones.

Figure 45.15

Tertiary alcohols cannot be oxidized as the carbon-carbon bonds are resistant to oxidizing agents, and therefore no second bond to the oxygen can be created.

Treatment of phenols with oxidizing reagents produces compounds called quinones (2,5-cyclohexadiene-1, 4-diones).

1,4-Benzenediol   p-Benzoquinone

Figure 45.16

ETHERS

An ether is a compound with two alkyl (or aryl) groups bonded to an oxygen atom. The general formula for an ether is **ROR**. Ethers can be thought of as disubstituted water molecules. The most familiar ether is diethyl ether, once used as a medical anesthetic. The following sections describe the nomenclature, properties, synthesis, and reactions of ethers.

NOMENCLATURE OF ETHERS

Ethers are named according to IUPAC rules as **alkoxyalkanes,** with the smaller chain as the prefix and the larger chain as the suffix. There is a common system of nomenclature in which ethers are named as alkyl alkyl ethers. In this system, methoxyethane would be named ethyl methyl ether. The alkyl substituents are alphabetized.

methoxyethane

(ethyl methyl ether)

ethoxybenzene

(ethyl phenyl ether)

Figure 45.17

Exceptions to these rules occur for cyclic ethers, also known as oxiranes, for which many common names also exist.

oxirane

(epoxide)

oxyethane

oxacyclopentane

(tetrahydrofuran)

Figure 45.18

PHYSICAL PROPERTIES

Ethers do not undergo hydrogen bonding because they have no hydrogen atoms bonded to the ether oxygen atoms. Ethers therefore boil at relatively low temperatures compared to alcohols; in fact, they boil at approximately the same temperatures as alkanes of comparable molecular weight.

Ethers are only slightly polar and therefore only slightly soluble in water. They are relatively inert to most organic reagents and are frequently used as solvents. However, ethers can form highly reactive peroxides (see Reactions of Ethers), requiring careful storage and handling.

SYNTHESIS OF ETHERS

Ethers are readily synthesized by the condensation of two molecules of an alcohol in the presence of acid, producing a symmetrical ether and water in a substitution reaction:

Figure 45.19

The Williamson ether synthesis produces asymmetrical ethers from the reaction of metal alkoxide ions with primary alkyl halides or tosylates. The alkoxides behave as nucleophiles and displace the halide or tosylate in an S_N2 reaction, producing an ether.

Figure 45.20

Because this is an S_N2 mechanism, alkoxides will attack only nonhindered halides. Thus, to synthesize a methyl ether, an alkoxide must attack a methyl halide; the reaction cannot be accomplished with the methoxide ion attacking a highly substituted alkyl halide substrate.

The Williamson ether synthesis can also be applied to phenols. Relatively mild reaction conditions are sufficient, due to the acidity of phenols.

Figure 45.21

Cyclic ethers, also known as oxiranes, are prepared in a number of ways. Oxiranes can be synthesized by means of an internal S_N2 displacement. Since the nucleophile and substrate are part of the same molecule, they are in close proximity, facilitating the reaction.

Figure 45.22

Oxidation of an alkene with a **peroxy acid** (general formula RCOOOH) such as mCPBA (*m*-chloroperoxybenzoic acid) will also produce an oxirane.

Figure 45.23

REACTIONS

Peroxide Formation

Ethers react with the oxygen in air to form highly explosive compounds called **peroxides** (general formula ROOR). For this reason, ethers are typically stored at low temperature and away from light.

Cleavage

Cleavage of straight-chain ethers will take place only under vigorous conditions: usually at high temperatures in the presence of HBr or HI. Cleavage is initiated by protonation of the ether oxygen. The reaction then proceeds by an S_N1 or S_N2 mechanism, depending on the conditions and the structure of the ether (note the difference in substitution of the substrates in Figure 45.24). Although not shown below, the alcohol products usually react with a second molecule of hydrogen halide to produce a second alkyl halide.

Figure 45.24

The same basic principles and reaction mechanisms of substitution reactions apply to epoxides. Since epoxides are highly strained cyclic ethers, they are susceptible to S_N2 reactions. Unlike straight-chain ethers, these reactions can be catalyzed by acids or bases. In symmetrical epoxides, either carbon can be attacked by a nucleophile; however, in asymmetrical epoxides, the most substituted carbon is attacked by the nucleophile in the presence of acid, and the least substituted carbon is attacked in the presence of base:

Figure 45.25

Reactions of epoxides provide additional insight into S_N1 and S_N2 reaction mechanisms. Base-catalyzed cleavage of epoxides has the most S_N2 character, so it occurs at the least hindered (least substituted) carbon. The basic environment provides the strong nucleophile required for S_N2 reactions.

In contrast, acid-catalyzed cleavage is thought to have some S_N1 character as well as some S_N2 character. The epoxide oxygen can be protonated, making it a better leaving group. This gives the carbons partial positive charges. Since substitution stabilizes this charge (3° carbons provide the most stable carbocations), the more substituted C becomes a good target for nucleophilic attack.

REVIEW PROBLEMS

1. Provide IUPAC names for the following alcohols and classify them as primary, secondary, or tertiary.

   A. [structure: HO on a branched chain]

   B. [structure with —OH]

   C. [structure with —OH]

   D. [cyclohexanol structure with OH]

   E. [cyclopentane with OH and CH₃]

   F. [structure with HO on a branched chain]

2. Alcohols have higher boiling points than their analogous ethers and hydrocarbons because

   A. the oxygen atoms in alcohols have shorter bond lengths.
   B. hydrogen bonding is present in alcohols.
   C. alcohols are more acidic than their analogous ethers or hydrocarbons.
   D. alcohols are lighter than their analogous ethers or hydrocarbons.
   E. ether and hydrocarbons are more electronegative than alcohols.

3. Why are alcohols of lower molecular weight more soluble in water than those of higher molecular weight?

4. Tertiary alcohols are oxidized with difficulty because

   A. there is no hydrogen attached to the carbon with the hydroxyl group.
   B. there is no hydrogen attached to the α-carbon.
   C. they contain hydroxyl groups with no polarization.
   D. they are relatively inert.
   E. they don't contain any oxygen atoms.

5. Which of the following reagents should be used to convert $CH_3(CH_2)_3CH_2OH$ into $CH_3(CH_2)_3CHO$?

   A. $KMnO_4$
   B. Jones reagent
   C. PCC
   D. $LiAlH_4$
   E. H_2/Pd

6. The reaction of 1 mole of diethyl ether with excess hydrobromic acid results in the production of

    A. 2 moles of ethyl bromide.
    B. 2 moles of ethanol.
    C. 1 mole of ethylbromide and 1 mole of ethanol.
    D. 1 mole of methylbromide and 1 mole of propanol.
    E. 1 mole of methylbromide only.

7. Which of the following reagents should be used to oxidize the steroid hormone testosterone to 4-androsterone-3,17-dione?

testosterone   4-androsterone-3,17-dione

    A. Dilute $KMnO_4$
    B. O_3/CH_2Cl_2; Zn/H_2O
    C. PCC
    D. $LiAlH_4$
    E. H_2/Pd

SOLUTIONS TO REVIEW PROBLEMS

1. A **3-methyl-1-heptanol**

    A primary alcohol

    B **2-methyl-2-propanol,** commonly called *t*-butyl alcohol or *t*-butanol

    A tertiary alcohol

    C **2-methyl-1-propanol,** commonly called isobutyl alcohol

    A primary alcohol

    D **cyclohexanol**

    A secondary alcohol

    E *cis*-**2-methylcyclopentanol**

    A secondary alcohol

    F **5-methyl-3-propyl-1-hexanol**

    A primary alcohol

2. B Alcohols have higher boiling points than their analogous ethers and hydrocarbons because alcohols have a polarized O−H bond in which the oxygen is partially negative and the hydrogen is partially positive. This enables the oxygen atoms of other alcohol molecules to be attracted to the hydrogen to form a hydrogen bond. These hydrogen bonds make it difficult for the alcohol to vaporize, thereby increasing the boiling point. The analogous hydrocarbons and ethers do not form hydrogen bonds and therefore vaporize at lower temperatures. Choice (A) is a nonsense choice. The bond length of the oxygen is not a factor in determining the boiling point of a substance. Choice (C) is incorrect because, although alcohols are more acidic than their analogous ethers or hydrocarbons, this property does not affect the boiling point of a substance. Choices (D) and (E) are not always true and even if so would promote lower boiling points rather than higher since either would result in the alcohols having relatively weaker intermolecular forces.

3. Alcohols of lower molecular weight are more soluble in water than larger alcohols because the hydrophilic hydroxyl group can form hydrogen bonds with water. The nonpolar hydrocarbon chain is not solvated by the water because the alkyl group is hydrophobic. As the molecular weight of an alcohol increases, so does the length of the hydrocarbon chain, making the alcohol more hydrophobic. As the molecule becomes more hydrophobic, the alcohol becomes less soluble in water.

4. A Tertiary alcohols can be oxidized only under extreme conditions because they do not have a hydrogen attached to the carbon with the hydroxyl group. Alcohol oxidation involves the removal of such a hydrogen; if none is present, a carbon-carbon bond must be cleaved instead. This requires a great deal of energy and will therefore occur only under extreme conditions. Choice (B) is incorrect because the number of hydrogens attached to the α-carbon is irrelevant to the mechanism of alcohol oxidation. Choices (C), (D), and (E) are false statements.

5. C The best way to prepare aldehydes from primary alcohols is to use PCC (pyridinium chlorochromate, $C_5H_6NCrO_3Cl$), which is choice (C). $KMnO_4$, choice (A), is a strong oxidizing agent and converts a primary alcohol to a carboxylic acid. Jones reagent, choice (B), also converts a primary alcohol into a carboxylic acid. $LiAlH_4$, choice (D), and H_2/Pd, choice (E), are a reducing agents so would not add more bonds to oxygen.

6. **A** When 1 mole of an ether reacts with excess HBr, the initial products are 1 mole alcohol and 1 mole alkyl bromide, choice (C). However, under these acidic conditions, Br displaces H_2O, resulting ultimately in 1 mole each of two alkyl bromides. In this case, since the ether is symmetric, the product is 2 moles ethyl bromide, choice (A). Choice (B) is incorrect because under these conditions, the alcohol is protonated, and H_2O (a good leaving group) is replaced by Br to form ethyl bromide. Choice (D) is incorrect because the ether molecule is split at the oxygen atom; it does not rearrange, as would be required to produce a 3-carbon and a 1-carbon fragment. Choice (E) is incorrect because it does not account for all of the carbons of the original reactants.

7. **C** The best way to oxidize this 2° alcohol to a ketone is with PCC, choice (C). $KMnO_4$, choice (A), would oxidize the double bond to a diol, while $LiAlH_4$, choice (D), and H_2/Pd, choice (E), are reducing agents, not oxidizing agents. Choice (B) is incorrect because ozone would cleave the double bond in testosterone.

CHAPTER FORTY-SIX

Aldehydes and Ketones

Aldehydes and **ketones** are compounds that contain the **carbonyl group, C=O**, a double bond between a carbon atom and an oxygen atom. A ketone has two alkyl or aryl groups bonded to the carbonyl, placing the carbon-oxygen group in the middle of the molecule. An aldehyde has one alkyl group and one hydrogen (or, in the case of formaldehyde, two hydrogens) bonded to the carbonyl; thus, an aldehyde is always a terminal group found at the end of a molecule.

The carbonyl group is one of the most important functional groups in organic chemistry and should always be visualized with a dipole moment: The carbon carries a partial positive charge, and the oxygen carries a partial negative charge. In addition to its presence in aldehydes and ketones, it is also found in carboxylic acids, esters, amides, and more complicated compounds. These additional carbonyl compounds are discussed in Chapters 47 and 48.

NOMENCLATURE

Because of their high degree of oxidation, aldehydes and ketones are usually the priority group in naming compounds. Note that the shorthand for an aldehyde group is always written –CHO; this should not be confused with the shorthand for an alcohol, which is C–OH.

In the IUPAC system, **aldehydes** are named with the suffix **-al**. The position of the aldehyde group does not need to be specified: it must occupy the terminal (C–1) position and usually is the highest priority group in the molecule. Common names exist for the first five aldehydes: formaldehyde, acetaldehyde, propionaldehyde, butyraldehyde, and valeraldehyde.

methanal
(formaldehyde)

ethanal
(acetaldehyde)

propanal
(propionaldehyde)

butanal
(butyraldehyde)

pentanal
(valeraldehyde)

Figure 46.1

In more complicated molecules, the suffix **-carbaldehyde** can be used. In addition, the aldehyde can be named as a functional group with the prefix **formyl-** when combined in a molecule with an even higher priority carboxylic acid group.

cyclopentanecarbaldehyde

m-formylbenzoic acid

Figure 46.2

Ketones are named with the suffix **-one**. The location of the carbonyl group must be specified with a number, except in cyclic ketones, where it is assumed to occupy the number 1 position. The common system of naming ketones lists the two alkyl groups followed by the word *ketone*. When it is necessary to name the carbonyl as a substituent, the prefix **oxo-** is used.

2-propanone
(dimethyl ketone)
(acetone)

2-butanone
(ethyl methyl ketone)

3-oxobutanoic acid

cyclopentanone

Figure 46.3

PHYSICAL PROPERTIES

The physical properties of aldehydes and ketones are governed by the presence of the carbonyl group and its strong dipole moment. Due to differences in electronegativity, the carbon carries a strong partial positive charge, and the oxygen carries a strong partial negative charge. The dipole moments associated with the polar carbonyl groups of nearby molecules align, causing an elevation in boiling point of aldehydes and ketones relative to similar alkanes. However, aldehydes and ketones show lower boiling points than comparable alcohols because –OH groups can form hydrogen bonds, but carbonyls cannot.

Figure 46.4

OVERVIEW OF ALDEHYDES AND KETONES

Aldehydes and ketones are midway along the oxidation-reduction continuum (shown below). The carbonyl carbon has two bonds to oxygen, placing it between the single C–O bond of alcohols and the three carbon-oxygen bonds of the carboxyl group.

Table 46.1

There are numerous methods of preparing aldehydes and ketones, but three are of particular interest: oxidation of alcohols, oxidative cleavage of alkenes, and Friedel-Crafts acylation of benzenes. These three mechanisms are important to study both as synthetic pathways of aldehydes and ketones and also as reaction pathways for other compounds.

The reactions of aldehydes and ketones are likewise interrelated with those of other compounds and are often driven by the dipole moment of the carbon-oxygen double bond. Aldehydes and ketones can be oxidized or reduced to form carboxylic acids or alcohols, respectively. They can act as either the nucleophile or substrate in S_N1 and S_N2-type reactions. They can serve as the substrate for nucleophilic attack on the carbonyl to produce alcohols, ethers, amides, and related compounds. They can condense to form larger molecules and to create double bonds.

Although the variety of aldehyde and ketone reaction pathways can appear overwhelming, studying them in the context of other organic molecules allows a greater understanding of the overall mechanisms involved.

SYNTHESIS OF ALDEHYDES AND KETONES

Oxidation of Alcohols

An aldehyde can be obtained from the oxidation of a primary alcohol; a ketone can be obtained from a secondary alcohol. These reactions are usually performed with PCC (one of the only options to create an aldehyde), potassium permanganate, sodium or potassium dichromate, or chromium trioxide (Jones reagent). These reactions are discussed in Chapter 45, Alcohols and Ethers.

Figure 46.5

Figure 46.6

Oxidative Cleavage of Alkenes

Double bonds can be oxidatively cleaved with ozone to yield aldehydes and/or ketones (see Chapter 43, Alkenes and Alkynes).

Figure 46.7

Ketones can also be synthesized by the cleavage of disubstituted alkenes with potassium permanganate:

$$\text{1) KMnO}_4\text{, OH}^-\text{, heat} \quad\quad \text{2) H}^+$$

Figure 46.8

Friedel-Crafts Acylation

This reaction, discussed in Chapter 44, produces ketones of the form R–CO–Ar from benzene and an acyl halide in the presence of a Lewis acid such as $AlCl_3$.

Figure 46.9

REACTIONS OF ALDEHYDES AND KETONES

Oxidation and Reduction

Aldehydes and ketones occupy the middle of the oxidation-reduction continuum. They are more oxidized than alcohols but less oxidized than carboxylic acids.

Aldehydes can be oxidized with a number of different reagents, such as $KMnO_4$, $K_2Cr_2O_7$, CrO_3, Ag_2O (Tollen's reagent), or H_2O_2. The product of oxidation of an aldehyde is a carboxylic acid. Ketones cannot undergo further oxidation unless extraordinarily harsh conditions are used to break C–C bonds.

Figure 46.10

A number of different reagents will reduce aldehydes and ketones to alcohols. The two most common are lithium aluminum hydride (LAH), which is a stronger reducing agent, and sodium borohydride ($NaBH_4$), which is milder; both, however, are effective on aldehydes and ketones.

Figure 46.11

Aldehydes and ketones can be completely reduced to alkanes by two common methods. In the **Wolff-Kishner** reduction, the carbonyl is first converted to a hydrazone, which then releases molecular nitrogen (N_2) when heated and forms an alkane. The Wolff-Kishner reaction is performed in basic solution and therefore is only useful when the product is stable under basic conditions.

Figure 46.12

An alternative reduction to the alkane is the **Clemmensen reduction**, where an aldehyde or ketone is heated with amalgamated zinc in hydrochloric acid.

Figure 46.13

Enolization and Reactions of Enols

Aldehydes and ketones can act as nucleophiles when they undergo rearrangement to a slightly different form. Protons alpha to carbonyl groups (one carbon away) are relatively acidic ($pK_a \approx$ 20), due to resonance stabilization of the conjugate base. A hydrogen atom that detaches itself from the alpha carbon has a finite probability of reattaching itself to the oxygen instead of the carbon. Therefore, aldehydes and ketones exist in solution as a mixture of two structural isomers, the familiar **keto** form and the **enol** form, representing the unsaturated alcohol (**ene** = the double bond, **ol** = the alcohol, so **ene** + **ol** = **enol**). The two isomers, which differ only in the placement of a proton, are called **tautomers**. The equilibrium between the tautomers lies far to the keto side. The process of interconverting from the keto to the enol tautomer is called **enolization**.

Figure 46.14

Enols are the necessary intermediates in many reactions in which aldehydes and ketones act as nucleophiles. The enolate carbanion can be created with a strong base such as lithium diisopropyl amide (LDA) or potassium hydride, KH, either of which remove the proton from the –OH group. The resulting nucleophilic carbanion will react via an S_N2 mechanism with an α,β-unsaturated carbonyl compound in a reaction called a **Michael addition**.

Figure 46.15

Addition Reactions

General reaction mechanism: nucleophilic addition to a carbonyl

A key property of aldehydes and ketones is the dipole created by the partially positive carbonyl carbon and the partially negative oxygen. The partial positive charge on the carbon creates a site for attack by a wide variety of electron-rich nucleophiles. Nucleophilic attack creates a tetrahedral intermediate in which the carbon-oxygen bond is reduced to a single bond and the oxygen carries a full negative charge. Because there is no good leaving group present in an aldehyde or a ketone, the carbonyl cannot re-form and an alcohol will be the end product after protonation. This general mechanism is the basis for many reactions of aldehydes and ketones that appear to be different but actually follow the same principles.

Figure 46.16

Hydration

In the presence of water, aldehydes and ketones react to form **geminal diols** (1,1-diols or *gem* diols). In this case, water acts as the nucleophile attacking at the carbonyl carbon. This hydration reaction proceeds slowly; the rate may be increased by the addition of a small amount of acid or base.

a gem diol

Figure 46.17

Acetal and ketal formation

A reaction similar to hydration occurs when aldehydes and ketones are treated with alcohols. When one equivalent of alcohol (the nucleophile in this reaction) is added to an aldehyde or ketone, the product is a **hemiacetal** or a **hemiketal,** respectively. When two equivalents of alcohol are added, the product is an **acetal** or a **ketal,** respectively. The reaction mechanism is the same as for hydration and is catalyzed by anhydrous acid. Acetals and ketals, which are comparatively inert, are frequently used as protecting groups for carbonyl functionalities. They can easily be converted back to the carbonyl with aqueous acid.

aldehyde   hemiacetal

Figure 46.18

Figure 46.19

Reaction with hydrogen cyanide

Aldehydes and ketones react with HCN (hydrogen cyanide) to produce stable compounds called **cyanohydrins.** HCN dissociates and the strongly nucleophilic cyanide anion attacks the carbonyl carbon atom. Protonation of the oxygen produces the cyanohydrin. The cyanohydrin gains its stability from the newly formed C–C bond (in contrast, when a carbonyl reacts with HCl, a weak C–Cl bond is formed, and the resulting chlorohydrin is unstable).

Figure 46.20

Condensations with ammonia derivatives

Ammonia and some of its derivatives are nucleophiles and can add to carbonyl compounds, but a different final product is created than in other nucleophilic attacks. In the net reaction, the C=O bond is replaced by a C=N bond. In the simplest case, ammonia adds to the carbon atom and the –OH group is protonated and lost as a molecule of water. This reaction produces an **imine,** a compound with a nitrogen atom double-bonded to a carbon atom. (A reaction in which water is lost between two molecules is called a **condensation reaction.**)

Figure 46.21

Some common ammonia derivatives that react with aldehydes and ketones are hydroxylamine (H_2NOH), hydrazine (H_2NNH_2), and semicarbazide ($H_2NNHCONH_2$); these form oximes, hydrazones, and semicarbazones, respectively.

Figure 46.22

The Aldol Condensation

The aldol condensation is an important reaction that follows the same mechanism of nucleophilic addition to a carbonyl. In this case, an aldehyde acts both as nucleophile (enol form) and target (keto form). When acetaldehyde is treated with base, an enolate ion is produced. The nucleophilic enolate ion will attack the carbonyl group of another acetaldehyde molecule. The product is 3-hydroxybutanal, which contains both an alcohol and an aldehyde group. This type of compound is called an **aldol,** from **ald**ehyde and alcoh**ol.**

3-hydroxybutanal
(an aldol)

Figure 46.23a

When heated, this molecule can undergo elimination and lose H_2O to form a double bond, producing an α,β-unsaturated aldehyde. This type of condensation reaction is known as the **aldol condensation**.

Figure 46.23b

The aldol condensation is most useful when only one type of aldehyde or ketone is present, since mixed condensations usually result in a mixture of products.

The Wittig Reaction

The **Wittig reaction** is a method of forming carbon-carbon double bonds by converting aldehydes and ketones into alkenes; in other words, the C=O bond ultimately becomes a C=C bond. The first step involves the formation of the necessary reactant: a phosphonium salt from the S_N2 reaction of an alkyl halide with the nucleophile triphenylphosphine, $(C_6H_5)_3P$. The phosphonium salt is then deprotonated (losing the proton α to the phosphorus) with a strong base, yielding a neutral compound called an **ylide** (pronounced "ill-ide") or **phosphorane**.

$$(C_6H_5)_3P \ + \ CH_3Br \ \longrightarrow \ (C_6H_5)_3\overset{+}{P}CH_3 + \ Br^-$$

$$(C_6H_5)_3\overset{+}{P}{-}CH_3 \ \xrightarrow{\text{Base}} \ (C_6H_5)_3P{=}CH_2 \ \longleftrightarrow \ (C_6H_5)_3\overset{+}{P}{-}\overset{-}{C}H_2$$

phosphonium
salt

ylide

Figure 46.24

Notice that an ylide is a type of carbanion and has nucleophilic properties. When combined with an aldehyde or ketone, an ylide attacks the carbonyl carbon, giving an intermediate called a *betaine*, which forms a four-membered ring intermediate called an oxaphosphetane. This decomposes to yield an alkene and triphenylphosphine oxide.

Figure 46.25

The decomposition reaction is driven by the strength of the phosphorus-oxygen bond that is formed. Although the overall mechanism has many complex steps, the net reaction is simply the substitution of a C=C bond for the original C=O bond of the cyclic ketone.

REVIEW PROBLEMS

1. The product of the reaction below is

O=CH—CH₃ + HO⟍⟍ ⟶ ?

A.

B.

C.

D.

E. None of the above

2. The major product of the reaction below is

O=C(H₃C)(C₂H₅) + ⟍⟍OH ⟶ ?

A. H₃C—C(OCH₃)(OC₂H₅)—CH₃

B. CH₃CH(OCH₃)—OH

C. H₃C—C(OH)(OC₂H₅)—C₂H₅

D. O=C(CH₃)—C₂H₅

E. None of the above

3. The product of the reaction below is

O
‖
(acetone) + (with NH₂) → ether → ?

A. (imine structure) ═N─

B. OH / N─ (with OH)

C. (structure with O─N)

D. O‖ / N─ (amide structure)

E. None of the above

4. All of the following properties are responsible for the reactivity of the carbonyl bond in propanone EXCEPT the fact that

A. the carbonyl carbon is electrophilic.
B. the carbonyl oxygen is electron-withdrawing.
C. a resonance structure of the compound places a positive charge on the carbonyl carbon.
D. the π electrons are mobile and pulled toward the carbonyl carbon.
E. the molecule is polar.

5. The reaction below is an example of

keto ⇌ HO enol

A. esterification.
B. tautomerization.
C. elimination.
D. dehydration.
E. neutralization.

6. Which of the following reactions produces the compound below?

   A. $CH_3CHO + CH_3CH_2CH_2CHO$
   B. $CH_3COCH_3 + CH_3CH_2CH_2CHO$
   C. $CH_3CH_2COCH_3 + CH_3CHO$
   D. $CH_3CH_2CHO + CH_3CH_2CHO$
   E. $CH_3COCH_3 + CH_3CHO$

7. The product of the reaction below is

$$\diagup\!\!\diagdown\!\!\diagup^O \xrightarrow{\text{KMnO}_4} \quad ?$$

   A. C_3H_7OH
   B. C_2H_5COOH
   C. C_3H_7CHO
   D. CH_3COOH
   E. C_5H_7COH

8. Heating an aldehyde with Zn in HCl produces
   A. a ketone.
   B. an alkane.
   C. an alcohol.
   D. a carboxylic acid.
   E. an ester.

9. Which hydrogen atom in the compound below is the most acidic?

   A. a
   B. b
   C. c
   D. d
   E. All exhibit the same acidity.

10. The product obtained in the reaction below is

LiAlH₄ → ?

A. [structure] + [structure with OH]

B. [structure with OH]

C. [structure]

D. [structure with OH, OH]

E. None of the above

11. Draw the following compounds.
  - **A.** 3-Methyl-2-pentanone
  - **B.** 3-Hydroxypentanal
  - **C.** Benzyl phenyl ketone
  - **D.** Cyclohexane carboaldehyde

12. The product of the reaction between benzaldehyde and an excess of ethanol (C_2H_5OH) in the presence of anhydrous HCl is

A. [structure with OC₂H₅, OH]

B. [structure with OC₂H₅, OC₂H₅]

C. [structure with OC₂H₅, OH, H]

D. [structure with OC₂H₅, OC₂H₅, H]

E. None of the above

SOLUTIONS TO REVIEW PROBLEMS

1. **D** One mole of aldehyde reacts with one mole of alcohol via a nucleophilic addition reaction to form a product called a *hemiacetal*. In a hemiacetal, an –OH group, an –OR group, a H atom, and a –R group are attached to the same carbon atom.

2. **C** The reaction between one molecule of a ketone and one molecule of an alcohol produces a compound analogous to a hemiacetal called a *hemiketal*. This has an –OH group, an –OR group, and two –R groups attached to the same carbon atom. Of the given choices, only choice (C) represents a hemiketal. Choice (A) has two –OR groups and two –R groups attached to the same carbon atom; this compound is called a *ketal*. Choice (B) is a hemiacetal since it has an –OH group, an –OR group, a H atom, and a –R group attached to the same carbon atom. Choice (D) is a ketone. The correct choice, therefore, is (C). Note that a hemiketal is a very unstable compound; it reacts rapidly with a second molecule of alcohol to form a ketal.

3. **A** Aldehydes and ketones react with ammonia and primary amines to form imines (also called *Schiff bases*), compounds with a double bond between a carbon atom and a nitrogen atom.

$$(CH_3)_2C{=}O + H_2N - C_2H_5 \rightarrow (CH_3)_2C{=}NCH_2CH_3 + H_2O$$

4. **D** The reactivity of the carbonyl bond in propanone, and in aldehydes and ketones in general, is due to the difference in electronegativity between the carbon and oxygen atoms. The oxygen atom has higher electronegativity and is therefore electron-withdrawing. Thus, the carbonyl carbon is electrophilic and the carbonyl oxygen is nucleophilic. The π electrons of the carbonyl bond are pulled toward the more electronegative element, which is oxygen, not carbon; thus, choice (D) is a false statement and the correct answer choice. That means the other choices are all true.

5. **B**

keto ⇌ enol

Esterification, choice (A), is the formation of esters from carboxylic acids and alcohols. Tautomerization, choice (B), is the interconversion of keto and enol forms of a compound. An elimination reaction, choice (C), is a reaction in which a substituent is lost and a double bond is introduced. A dehydration reaction, choice (D), is one in which a molecule of water is eliminated. A neutralization reaction, choice (E), involves an acid and a base. The reaction in the question stem involves an interconversion of keto and enol forms of ethanal. The correct choice is therefore (B). Note that equilibrium lies to the left in the reaction since the keto form is more stable.

6. **D**

The above reaction is an example of aldol condensation. In the presence of a base, the alpha H is removed from an aldehyde, forming an enolate ion, CH_3CH^-CHO. The enolate ion then attacks the carbonyl group of another aldehyde molecule, CH_3CH_2CHO, forming the above aldol.

7. **B** Aldehydes are easily oxidized to the corresponding carboxylic acids by $KMnO_4$. The –CHO group is converted to –COOH. In this reaction, therefore, C_2H_5CHO is oxidized to C_2H_5COOH, which is choice (B). In choices (A) and (E) the aldehyde has been reduced to an alcohol. In choice (C), a $-CH_2$ group has been added. In choice (D), the –CHO group has been oxidized to –COOH, but a $-CH_2$ group has been deleted.

8. **B** Heating an aldehyde or a ketone with amalgamated Zn/HCl converts it to the corresponding alkane; this reaction is called the Clemmensen reduction. Note that aldehydes and ketones can also be converted to alkanes under basic conditions by reaction with hydrazine (the Wolff-Kishner reduction).

9. **B** The hydrogen alpha to the carbonyl group is the most acidic, since its resultant carbanion is resonance-stabilized:

10. **B** $LiAlH_4$ reduces carboxylic acids, esters, and aldehydes to primary alcohols, and ketones to secondary alcohols. In this reaction, therefore, the ketone is converted to a secondary alcohol. Thus, the correct answer is choice (B), $C_6H_5CH(CH_3)CHOHCH_2CH_3$, a secondary alcohol.

11.

A.

B.

C.

D.

12. **D** This product of this reaction is an acetal: two ethoxy groups bonded to the same carbon, represented by choice (D). This question states that an excess of ethanol is present, so benzaldehyde will first be converted to a hemiacetal, having an ethoxy and a hydroxy group bonded to the same carbon. Then the hemiacetal will be converted to the acetal by another equivalent of ethanol. Choices (A) and (B) are incorrect because they show the presence of two benzene rings in the final product. Choice (C) is incorrect since this is the hemiacetal that is formed initially, which then goes on to react with excess ethanol to produce the acetal.

CHAPTER FORTY-SEVEN

Carboxylic Acids

Carboxylic acids contain a hydroxyl group (–OH) attached to a carbonyl carbon (C=O), represented by the formula –COOH. This functionality is known as a **carboxyl group,** which is always a terminal group on a molecule. Carboxylic acids are the most highly oxidized organic compounds (other than carbon dioxide). The carbonyl carbon of a carboxylic acid has three bonds to oxygen, two within the carbonyl C=O and the other to the –OH group from the same carbon.

Table 47.1

The hydrogen atoms of the –OH group are highly acidic with pK_a values in the general range of 3 to 6. As with other carbonyl compounds, the C=O group is polarized with a partial positive charge on the carbon and a partial negative charge on the oxygen. Carboxylic acids occur widely in nature and are synthesized by many living organisms.

There are numerous methods of preparing carboxylic acids, but three are of particular interest: oxidation of alcohols and alkenes, carbonation with Grignard reagents, and hydrolysis of nitriles. These three mechanisms are important to study both as synthetic pathways of carboxylic acids and also as reaction pathways of other compounds.

The reactions of carboxylic acids are likewise interrelated with those of other compounds and are often driven by the dipole moment of the carbon-oxygen double bond. Carboxylic acids can be reduced to form alcohols. They can serve as the substrate for nucleophilic attack and substitution to form acyl halides, anhydrides, esters, and amides. They can decarboxylate to produce CO_2, and long-chain carboxylic acids can form soaps and micelles.

NOMENCLATURE

In the IUPAC system of nomenclature, carboxylic acids are named by adding the suffix **-oic acid** to the alkyl root. Since carboxylic acids are highly oxidized, they have very high priority in naming, and the chain is numbered so that the carboxyl group receives the lowest possible number.

2-methylpentanoic acid

4-isopropyl-5-oxohexanoic acid

Figure 47.1

Carboxylic acids were among the first organic compounds discovered. Their original names continue today in the common system of nomenclature. For example, formic acid (from Latin *formica*, meaning ant) was found in ants and butyric acid (from Latin *butyrum*, meaning butter) in rancid butter. The common and IUPAC names of the first three carboxylic acids are listed in Figure 47.2.

methanoic acid
(formic acid)

ethanoic acid
(acetic acid)

propanoic acid
(propionic acid)

Figure 47.2

Cyclic carboxylic acids are usually named as cycloalkane carboxylic acids. The carbon atom to which the carboxyl group is attached is numbered 1 because of the group's high priority. When a carboxylic acid is deprotonated, its name is changed to end in the suffix **-ate**. Thus, acetic acid becomes acetate when ionized and is called sodium acetate when in its sodium salt form. Typical examples are:

1-chloro-2-methylcyclo-
pentane carboxylic acid

sodium hexanoate

Figure 47.3

Dicarboxylic acids—compounds with two carboxyl groups—are common in biological systems. The first six straight-chain terminal dicarboxylic acids are oxalic, malonic, succinic, glutaric, adipic, and pimelic acids. Their IUPAC names are ethanedioic acid, propanedioic acid, butanedioic acid, pentanedioic acid, hexanedioic acid, and heptanedioic acid.

PHYSICAL PROPERTIES

Hydrogen Bonding

Carboxylic acids are polar and form hydrogen bonds between the –OH group of one molecule and the lone pairs of electrons on the oxygen of another molecule. As a result, carboxylic acids can form dimers: pairs of molecules connected by hydrogen bonds. The boiling points of carboxylic acids are therefore even higher than those of the corresponding alcohols. The boiling points follow the usual trend of increasing with molecular weight.

Acidity

The acidity of carboxylic acids is due to the resonance stabilization of the carboxylate anion (the conjugate base). When the hydroxyl proton dissociates from the acid, the negative charge left on the carboxylate group is delocalized and shared by both oxygen atoms.

Figure 47.4

Substituents on carbon atoms adjacent to a carboxyl group can influence acidity. Electron-withdrawing groups such as –Cl or –NO_2 further delocalize the negative charge and increase acidity. Electron-donating groups such as –NH_2 or –OCH_3 destabilize the negative charge, making the compound less acidic.

In dicarboxylic acids, one –COOH group (which is electron-withdrawing) influences the other, making the first carboxyl group more acidic than the analogous monocarboxylic acid. The second carboxyl group is then influenced by the carboxylate anion. Ionization of the second group will create a doubly charged species, in which the two negative charges repel each other. Since this is unfavorable, the second proton is less acidic than that of a monocarboxylic acid.

β-dicarboxylic acids are notable for the high acidity of the α-hydrogens located between the two carboxyl groups ($pK_a \sim 10$). Loss of this acidic hydrogen atom produces a carbanion that is stabilized by the electron-withdrawing effect of the two carboxyl groups.

Figure 47.5

The same effect is also seen in β-ketoacids, $RC{=}OCH_2{-}COOH$. The resonance structures of the representative β-ketoacid below demonstrate the additional stability due to delocalization of the electrons from the carbonyl groups:

β-ketoacid

$-H^+$

Figure 47.6

SYNTHESIS

Oxidation Reactions

Carboxylic acids can be prepared via oxidation of aldehydes, primary alcohols, and certain alkylbenzenes. Any strong oxidizing agent, including $KMnO_4$, $K_2Cr_2O_7$, and CrO_3, will create a carboxylic acid, as in Figure 47.7. A primary alcohol can also be oxidized first with PCC to create an aldehyde and then further oxidized with Tollen's reagent to create the carboxylic acid.

$KMnO_4$

Figure 47.7

Carboxylic acids can also be prepared by the oxidative cleavage of alkenes:

$$\text{(alkene)} \xrightarrow[\text{2) H}^+]{\text{1) KMnO}_4,\ \text{OH}^-,\ \text{heat}} \text{(carboxylic acid)} + \text{(carboxylic acid)}$$

Figure 47.8

Carbonation of Organometallic Reagents

Organometallic reagents, such as Grignard reagents, react with carbon dioxide (CO_2) to form carboxylic acids. This reaction is useful for the conversion of tertiary alkyl halides into carboxylic acids, which cannot be accomplished through other methods. Note that this reaction adds one carbon atom to the chain.

$$\text{Br} \xrightarrow[\text{ether}]{\text{Mg}} \text{MgBr} \xrightarrow[\text{2) H}^+,\ \text{H}_2\text{O}]{\text{1) CO}_2\ \text{gas}} \text{COOH}$$

Figure 47.9

Hydrolysis of Nitriles

Nitriles, also called cyanides, are compounds containing the functional group $-C\equiv N$. The cyanide anion CN^- is a strong nucleophile and will displace primary and secondary halides in typical S_N2 fashion.

Nitriles can be hydrolyzed under either acidic or basic conditions. The products are carboxylic acids and ammonia (or ammonium salts).

$$\text{CH}_3\text{Cl} \longrightarrow \text{CH}_3\text{CN} \longrightarrow \text{CH}_3\overset{\overset{\text{O}}{\|}}{\text{C}}\text{OH} + \text{NH}_4^+$$

Figure 47.10

This allows the conversion of alkyl halides into carboxylic acids. As in the carbonation reaction, an additional carbon atom is introduced to the carbon chain. For instance, if the desired product is acetic acid, a possible starting material would be methyl iodide.

REACTIONS

Nucleophilic Substitution

Many of the reactions of carboxylic acids can be explained by a single mechanism: nucleophilic substitution. This mechanism is very similar to nucleophilic addition to a carbonyl, discussed in Chapter 46, Aldehydes and Ketones. The key difference between the two is that nucleophilic substitution concludes with re-formation of the C=O double bond and elimination of a leaving group.

Figure 47.11

Reduction

Carboxylic acids occupy the most oxidized position of the oxidation-reduction continuum. Carboxylic acids can be reduced with lithium aluminum hydride (LAH) to their corresponding primary alcohols. Note that this reaction will not occur when the milder reducing agent $NaBH_4$ is used. Aldehyde intermediates that may be formed in the course of the reaction with LAH are also reduced to the primary alcohol. The reaction occurs by nucleophilic addition of hydride (the H^- ion) to the carbonyl group and elimination of water as a leaving group.

Figure 47.12

Ester formation

Carboxylic acids react with alcohols under acidic conditions to form esters and water. In acidic solution, the oxygen on the carbonyl group can become protonated. This increases the polarity of the carbon-oxygen bond, putting even more positive charge on the carbon and making it even more susceptible to nucleophilic attack. Again, water is eliminated as a leaving group, and the carbonyl re-forms. This condensation reaction occurs most rapidly with primary alcohols. Esters are discussed in more detail in Chapter 48, Carboxylic Acid Derivatives.

Figure 47.13

Acyl halide formation

Acyl halides, also called acid halides, are compounds with carbonyl groups bonded to halides. Several different reagents can accomplish this transformation; thionyl chloride, $SOCl_2$, is the most common.

Figure 47.14

Acid chlorides are very reactive, as the greater electron-withdrawing power of the Cl^- makes the carbonyl carbon more susceptible to nucleophilic attack than the carbonyl carbon of a carboxylic acid. Also, chlorine is an excellent leaving group, making acid chlorides highly reactive. They are frequently used as intermediates in the conversion of carboxylic acids to esters and amides. Acyl halides, esters, and amides are discussed further in Chapter 48, Carboxylic Acid Derivatives.

Decarboxylation

Carboxylic acids can undergo decarboxylation reactions, resulting in the loss of carbon dioxide and thus loss of the entire carboxyl group.

1,3-dicarboxylic acids and other β-keto acids may spontaneously decarboxylate when heated. The carboxyl group is lost and replaced with a hydrogen. The reaction proceeds through a six-membered ring transition state. The enol initially formed tautomerizes to the more stable keto form as the final product.

Figure 47.15

Soap Formation

When long-chain hydrocarbon carboxylic acids react with sodium or potassium hydroxide, they form salts. These salts, called soaps, are able to solubilize nonpolar organic compounds in aqueous solutions because they possess both a nonpolar "tail" and a polar carboxylate "head."

Figure 47.16

When placed in aqueous solution, soap molecules arrange themselves into spherical structures called **micelles**. The polar heads face outward, where they can be solvated by water molecules, and the nonpolar hydrocarbon chains are inside the sphere, protected from the solvent. Nonpolar molecules such as grease can dissolve in the hydrocarbon interior of the spherical micelle, while the micelle as a whole is soluble in water because of its polar shell.

Figure 47.17

REVIEW PROBLEMS

1. Which compound in each of the following pairs is more acidic?

   A. CH_3COOH or $CH_2ClCOOH$

   B. $HOOCCH_2COOH$ or $HOOCCH_2COO^-$

   C. NH_2CH_2COOH or NO_2CH_2COOH

2. Which of the following molecules could be classified as a soap?

   A. $CH_3(CH_2)_{17}CH_2COOH$

   B. CH_3COOH

   C. $CH_3(CH_2)_{19}CH_2COO^-Na^+$

   D. $CH_3COO^-Na^+$

   E. CH_3CH_2OH

3. Which of the following compounds would be expected to decarboxylate when heated?

   A.

   B.

   C.

   D.

   E. None of the above.

4. Oxidation of which of the following compounds is most likely to yield a carboxylic acid?

   A. Acetone

   B. Cyclohexanone

   C. 2-Propanol

   D. Methanol

   E. 2-Methyl-2-propanol

5. Give the IUPAC name for each of the following carboxylic acids:

A.

B.

C.

D. Br⎯⟨ ⟩⎯COOH

E. None of the above.

6. Draw the structures of the following carboxylic acids:

A. 2,3-Dimethylpentanoic acid
B. 3-Butenoic acid
C. *p*-Hydroxybenzoic acid
D. 4-Bromohexanoic acid

7. Carboxylic acids have higher boiling points than the corresponding alcohols because

A. the molecular weight of a carboyxlic acid is less than that of its corresponding alcohol.
B. the pH of a carboxlyic acid is lower than that of its corresponding alcohol.
C. acid salts are soluble in water.
D. hydrogen bonding is much stronger among carboxylic acids than among alcohols.
E. the average kinetic energy of a carboxylic acid is much lower than that of its corresponding alcohol at the same temperature.

8. Which of the following carboxylic acids will be the most acidic?

A. $CH_3CHClCH_2COOH$
B. $CH_3CH_2CCl_2COOH$
C. $CH_3CH_2CHClCOOH$
D. $CH_3CH_2CH_2COOH$
E. CH_3CH_2COOH

9. Which of the following substituted benzoic acid compounds will be the least acidic?

A.

B.

C.

D.

E. All of the above compounds are equally acidic.

10. Rank the following compounds in order of increasing acidity.

A.

I   II   III

B.

I   II   III

11. Predict the final product of the following reaction:

$$CH_3(CH_2)_4CH_2OH \xrightarrow[\text{acetone}]{CrO_3,\ H_2SO_4}$$

A. $CH_3(CH_2)_4CHO$
B. $CH_3(CH_2)_4COOH$
C. $CH_3(CH_2)_4CH_3$
D. $HOOC(CH_2)_4COOH$
E. $CH_3(CH_2)_4CH_2Cr$

12. The reduction of a carboxylic acid by lithium aluminum hydride will yield what final product?
A. An aldehyde
B. An ester
C. A ketone
D. An alcohol
E. A sulfide

SOLUTIONS TO REVIEW PROBLEMS

1. **A** $CH_2ClCOOH$

   Acetic acid is a fairly acidic compound and has a pK_a of 4.8. However, chloroacetic acid is more acidic because the chlorine atom is electron-withdrawing. This withdrawing effect stabilizes the carboxylate anion by delocalizing the charge more than the carboxyl group alone and thus facilitating the acid's dissociation.

   B $HOOCCH_2COOH$

   The maleate anion is less acidic than maleic acid because formation of a second negative charge is hindered by the presence of the first negative charge.

   C NO_2CH_2COOH

   Nitroacetic acid is more acidic than aminoacetic acid because the nitro group is electron-withdrawing while the amino group is electron-donating. The withdrawing effect delocalizes the negative charge on the anion, making it more stable. In contrast, the donating effect of the amino group concentrates the negative charge on the carboxylate group, creating a higher-energy state and destabilizing the anion.

2. **C** A soap is a long-chain hydrocarbon with a highly polar end. Generally, this polar end or head is a salt of a carboxylic acid. Choice (C) fits these criteria and is the correct answer. The remaining choices all fail one or both of the criteria and are therefore wrong. Choices (A), (B), and (E) are not salts. Choice (D) is sodium acetate, which is a salt but does not have a long hydrocarbon chain.

3. **D** Choice (D) is a β-keto acid: a keto group β-bonded to a carboxyl group. Decarboxylation occurs with β-keto acids and 1,3-diacids because they can form a cyclic transition state that permits simultaneous transfer of a hydrogen and loss of carbon dioxide. Choice (B) is a diketone, and this will definitely not decarboxylate. Choices (A) and (C) are 1,4- and 1,5-diacids, respectively, and will decarboxylate but with more difficulty. The correct answer is choice (D).

4. **D** Oxidation of methanol, choice (D), will yield first formaldehyde and then formic acid; this is the correct answer. Acetone, choice (A), cannot be oxidized further unless extremely harsh conditions are used. This is because the carbonyl carbon is bonded to two alkyl groups, and further oxidation would necessitate cleavage of a carbon-carbon bond. Choice (B), cyclohexanone, is likewise limited in its options for further oxidation. Choice (C), 2-propanol, can be oxidized to acetone but no further without harsh conditions. Choice (E), also known as *tert*-butyl alcohol, is similar but is even more resistant to oxidation because it is a tertiary alcohol and would also require cleavage of a carbon-carbon bond to undergo oxidation.

5. **A** **Hexanoic acid**

   B **3-Methylpentanoic acid**

   C **5-Ethyl-2-propylhexanedioic acid**

   D **4-Bromocyclohexanecarboxylic acid**

6.

A.

B.

C.

D.

7. **D** The boiling points of compounds depend on the strength of the attractive forces between molecules. In both alcohols and carboxylic acids, the major form of intermolecular attraction is hydrogen bonding; however, the hydrogen bonds of carboxylic acids are much stronger than those of alcohols since the acids are much more polar than the alcohols. This makes the boiling points of carboxylic acids higher than those of the corresponding alcohols, so choice (D) is correct. Boiling points are also dependent on molecular weight, choice (A), but in this case the influence of the small difference in molecular weight is negligible compared with the effect of hydrogen bonding, and in fact carboxylic acids are generally heavier than alcohols. Therefore, choice (A) is incorrect. Choice (B) describes the behavior of acids in solution; although this is also dependent on intermolecular forces, it is not otherwise related to the behavior of the pure acid, so choice (B) is incorrect. Choice (C) discusses the behavior of an acid's salt in solution, which is incorrect for the same reason. Finally, choice (E) is a false statement since having the same temperature means having the same average kinetic energy.

8. **B** The acidity of carboxylic acids is significantly increased by the substitution of highly electronegative halogens onto the carbon chain. Their electron-withdrawing effect upon the carboxyl group increases the stability of the carboxylate anion, favoring the dissociation of the proton. This effect is especially strong for α-halogenated carboxylic acids. Choices (D) and (E) are unsubstituted and therefore must have the lowest acidity. Choice (A) is β-halogenated, while choices (B) and (C) are α-halogenated, so (A) may be rejected. Finally, choice (B) contains 2 α-halogens and choice (C) includes only 1, so the electron-withdrawing effect in choice (B) is stronger; thus, (B) is the correct answer.

9. **C** The effects of different substituents on the acidity of benzoic acid compounds is correlated with their effects on the reactivity of the benzene ring (see Chapter 44). Activating substituents donate electron density into the benzene ring, and the ring in turn donates electron density to the carboxyl group, destabilizing the benzoate ion formed and therefore decreasing a compound's acidity. Deactivating substituents have the opposite effect: they withdraw electrons from the ring, which in turn withdraws negative charge from the carboxyl group, thus stabilizing the carboxylate anion and increasing the compound's acidity. Choice (A) contains a nitro group attached to the ring, and choice (B) has a chloride; both of these substituents have deactivating effects, so these choices may be rejected.

Choice (D) is an unsubstituted benzoic acid, while choice (C) has a strongly activating hydroxyl substituent. Thus, choice (C) will be the least acidic and is the correct answer.

10. **A** $II < I < III$

An ethyl substituent has an activating and therefore electron-donating effect on the benzene ring; thus, the acidity of compound II is very low. The bromine substituent, on the other hand, has a deactivating and electron-withdrawing effect on the benzene ring, which makes compound III highly acidic. The acidity of unsubstituted benzoic acid (compound I) is somewhere in the middle. Therefore the order of increasing acidity is II, I, III.

B $III < II < I$

In this case, compound I is the strongest acid because the nitro group is a powerful deactivating and therefore electron-withdrawing substituent. On the other hand, II is a stronger acid than III because the methyl group in compound III donates electron density to the carboxyl group, decreasing the acidity of III. Here the order of increasing acidity is III, II, I.

11. **B** Jones reagent (chromium trioxide in aqueous sulfuric acid) oxidizes primary alcohols directly to monocarboxylic acids, so choice (B) is correct. This oxidizer is too strong to give an aldehyde as the final product (aldehyde will be formed but will immediately be oxidized further), so choice (A) is incorrect. Choice (D), a dicarboxylic acid, cannot form because there is no functional group "handle" on the other end of the molecule for the reagent to attack, and it cannot attack the inert alkane. Nor will it produce an alkane such as choice (C), so this is also incorrect. Finally, (E) represents a substitution reaction with the chromium, but the chromium from Jones reagent will enter solution as as a relatively stable Cr^{3+} ion rather than reacting.

12. **D** Lithium aluminum hydride is a very strong reducing agent. Its reaction with carboxylic acids yields alcohols, choice (D). Aldehydes are intermediate products of this reaction and will be further reduced to alcohols; therefore, choice (A) is incorrect. Esters are formed from carboxylic acids by reaction with alcohols, so choice (B) is incorrect. Ketones are formed by the Friedel-Crafts acylation of the acyl chloride derivatives of acids, so choice (C) is incorrect. Sulfides (E) are S^{2-} ions and are not directly related to carboxylic acids.

CHAPTER FORTY-EIGHT

Carboxylic Acid Derivatives

Carboxylic acids can be converted into several types of derivatives: **acyl halides**, **anhydrides**, **amides**, and **esters**. These are compounds in which the –OH of the carboxyl group has been replaced with **–X, –OCOR, –NH$_2$**, or **–OR**, respectively:

- Acyl halide: R-CO-X
- Anhydride: R-CO-O-CO-R
- Ester: R-CO-OR′
- Amide: R-CO-NH$_2$ or R-CO-NR$_2$

Carboxylic acid derivatives all have the highly polarized C=O group in which the carbon carries a partial positive charge and the oxygen has a partial negative charge. As a result, these compounds readily undergo nucleophilic substitution reactions, including hydrolysis (with H$_2$O as the nucleophile). They also undergo other additions and substitutions, including various interconversions between different acid derivatives. In general, the acyl halides are the most reactive of the carboxylic acid derivatives, followed by the anhydrides, the esters, and the amides.

Each of these types of carboxylic acid derivatives will be discussed in turn. Although the variety of reaction pathways can appear overwhelming, they are all closely interwoven and should be studied in relation to each other. To aid your studies, a summary of the different reactions of carboxylic acid derivatives is included at the end of this chapter.

ACYL HALIDES

Nomenclature of Acyl Halides

Acyl halides are also called **acid** or **alkanoyl halides**. The acyl group is written RCO–, and with the halide attached it is written as RCOX. Acyl halides are the most reactive of the carboxylic acid derivatives. They are named in the IUPAC system by changing the *-ic acid* ending of the carboxylic acid to **-yl halide**. Some typical examples are ethanoyl chloride (also called acetyl chloride), benzoyl chloride, and *n*-butanoyl bromide.

| ethanoyl chloride | benzoyl chloride | *n*-butanoyl bromide |

(acetyl chloride)

Figure 48.1

Properties of Acyl Halides

Because the –OH of the carboxyl group has been replaced by a halogen, an acyl halide is not able to form hydrogen bonds. Acyl halides are therefore less polar than comparable carboxylic acids, and demonstrate significantly lower melting and boiling points. For example, acetyl chloride boils at 51°C, compared to acetic acid which boils at 118°C.

Synthesis of Acyl Halides

The most common acyl halides are the acid chlorides, although acid bromides and iodides are occasionally encountered. Acyl chlorides are prepared by reaction of a carboxylic acid with thionyl chloride, $SOCl_2$, producing SO_2 and HCl as side products. Alternatively, PCl_3 or PCl_5 (or PBr_3, to make an acid bromide) can be used for this synthesis.

Figure 48.2

Reactions of Acyl Halides

Nucleophilic acyl substitution

Acyl halides are very reactive, as the greater electron-withdrawing power of the halogen makes the carbonyl carbon more susceptible to nucleophilic attack than the carbonyl carbon of a carboxylic acid. Because halides are excellent leaving groups, nucleophilic attack will always be followed by re-formation of the carbonyl. As a result, acyl halides readily undergo nucleophilic substitution reactions, including hydrolysis (with H_2O as the nucleophile), which produces the original carboxylic acid. Acyl halides are also frequently used as intermediates in the conversion of carboxylic acids to anhydrides, esters, and amides.

Hydrolysis

The simplest reaction of acid halides is their conversion back to carboxylic acids by classic nucleophilic attack. Acyl halides react very rapidly with water to form the corresponding acid, along with HCl, which is responsible for their irritating odor.

Figure 48.3

Conversion into anhydrides

Reaction of an acyl chloride with a carboxylate salt will produce an anhydride through nucleophilic attack and re-formation of the carbonyl:

Figure 48.4

Conversion into esters

Acyl halides can be converted into esters by reaction with alcohols. The same type of nucleophilic attack found in hydrolysis leads to the formation of a tetrahedral intermediate, with the hydroxyl oxygen of the alcohol acting as the nucleophile. Chloride is displaced as the carbonyl re-forms, and HCl is released as a side-product.

Figure 48.5

Conversion into amides

Acyl halides can be converted into amides (compounds of the general formula $RCONR_2$) by nucleophilic substitution with amines. An amine, such as ammonia, attacks the carbonyl group, displacing chloride. The side product is ammonium chloride, formed from excess ammonia and HCl. Primary and secondary amines can also be used as the nucleophile to create N-substituted amides.

Figure 48.6

Other Reactions of Acyl Halides

Friedel-Crafts acylation

Aromatic rings can be acylated in a Friedel-Crafts reaction, as discussed in Chapter 44, Aromatic Compounds. The mechanism is electrophilic aromatic substitution, and the attacking reagent is an acylium ion, formed by reaction of an acid chloride with $AlCl_3$ or another Lewis acid. The product is an alkyl aryl ketone.

Figure 48.7

Reduction

Acid halides can be reduced to alcohols with a strong reducing agent such as LAH. They can also be selectively reduced to the intermediate aldehydes by catalytic hydrogenation in the presence of a "poison" such as quinoline, also called Lindlar's catalyst. These reaction conditions are also discussed in Chapter 43, Alkenes and Alkynes.

Figure 48.8

ANHYDRIDES

Nomenclature of Anhydrides

Anhydrides, also called **acid anhydrides**, are the condensation dimers of carboxylic acids, with the general formula RCOOCOR. They are named by substituting the word **anhydride** for the word *acid* in a carboxylic acid. Most anhydrides are symmetrical, although asymmetrical anhydrides exist and can be important in biological systems. The most common and important anhydride is acetic anhydride, the dimer of acetic acid. Other common anhydrides, such as succinic, maleic, and phthalic anhydrides, are **cyclic anhydrides** arising from intramolecular condensation or dehydration of diacids (Figure 48.9).

acetic anhydride

(ethanoic anhydride)

phthalic anhydride

succinic anhydride

Figure 48.9

Properties of Anhydrides

Since acid anhydrides no longer have an –OH group, they do not have the ability to form hydrogen bonds. Anhydrides therefore are less polar and demonstrate lower melting and boiling points than comparable carboxylic acids of the same molecular weight (MW). For example, ethanoic anhydride and pentanoic acid are approximately the same MW, but the anhydride boils at 140°C and the carboxylic acid at 186°C.

However, because anhydrides are often formed from the condensation of two other molecules, the product will have a higher melting or boiling point due to its larger size compared to the starting materials. For example, acetic anhydride ($CH_3CO-O-COCH_3$) boils at 140°C, compared to acetic acid (CH_3COOH) which boils at 118°C. In this case, the much larger MW of the anhydride is more influential than the effect of hydrogen bonding for the carboxylic acid.

Although anhydrides are polar, they are not considered to be soluble in water because they immediately decompose in aqueous conditions to form carboxylic acids.

Synthesis of Anhydrides

The synthesis pathways of anhydrides all involve some form of nucleophilic attack on a carboxylic acid, followed by the release of a leaving group and re-formation of the carbonyl.

Acyl chloride reaction

Anhydrides can be readily synthesized by reaction of an acyl chloride with a carboxylate salt. This is the most efficient and most commonly used method of anhydride synthesis.

Figure 48.10

Cyclic anhydride self-condensation

Certain cyclic anhydrides can be formed simply by heating carboxylic acids. The reaction is driven by the increased stability of the newly formed ring; hence, only five- and six-membered ring anhydrides are easily made. In this case, the hydroxyl of one –COOH group acts as a nucleophile, attacking the carbonyl on the other –COOH group and releasing water.

o-phthalic acid   phthalic anhydride

Figure 48.11

Condensation of two carboxylic acids

Two carboxylic acid molecules can condense to form an anhydride in a reaction releasing water; however, this reaction requires anhydrous conditions. Therefore a dehydrating reagent that will remove the water produced in the reaction is needed to prevent immediate conversion back to the carboxylic acids. Reagents such as acetic anhydride, trifluoroacetic anhydride, phosphorus pentachloride, or dicyclohexylcarbodiimide (DCC) can be used for this purpose.

Figure 48.12

Reactions of Anhydrides

Anhydrides react under the same conditions as acid chlorides, but since anhydrides are somewhat more stable, they are less reactive. Nucleophilic attack on an anhydride is slower and produces a carboxylic acid as the side product instead of HCl. Cyclic anhydrides are also subject to these reactions, which cause ring opening at the anhydride group along with formation of the new functional groups.

Hydrolysis

Anhydrides are converted into carboxylic acids when exposed to water. Note that in this reaction, the leaving group is actually a carboxylic acid; because the anhydride is symmetrical, it produces two molecules of the same carboxylic acid.

Figure 48.13

Conversion into amides

Anhydrides are cleaved by ammonia, producing an amide and a carboxylic acid. The carboxylic acid then further reacts with ammonia to form an ammonium carboxylate.

Then:

Figure 48.14

Conversion into esters and carboxylic acids

Anhydrides react with alcohols to form esters; a single anhydride molecule will produce one ester and also one molecule of carboxylic acid.

Figure 48.15

Acylation

Friedel-Crafts acylation occurs readily with anhydrides in the presence of $AlCl_3$ or other Lewis acid catalysts. This reaction produces an aryl ketone and a carboxylic acid.

Figure 48.16

ESTERS

Nomenclature of Esters

Esters are the dehydration products of carboxylic acids and alcohols. They are commonly found in many fruits and perfumes. They are named in the IUPAC system as **alkyl** or **aryl alkanoates**. The alkyl chain attached to the non-carbonyl oxygen is named as a functional group; the carboxylic acid suffix *-oic acid* is replaced by **-oate** while retaining the carbon chain from the acid. For example, propyl acetate, derived from the condensation of acetic acid and propanol, has the structure $CH_3COO-CH_2CH_2CH_3$ and is called propyl ethanoate according to IUPAC nomenclature.

ethyl
ethanoate

isopropyl
butanoate

Figure 48.17

Properties of Esters

Since esters do not have an –OH group, they do not have the same ability to form hydrogen bonds. Esters, therefore, are less polar and demonstrate lower melting and boiling points than comparable carboxylic acids of the same size. For example, ethyl acetate ($CH_3COOCH_2CH_3$) and butanoic acid ($CH_3CH_2CH_2COOH$) are approximately the same molecular weight, but the ester boils at 77°C and the carboxylic acid boils at 164°C.

The water solubility of esters depends on the length of the hydrocarbon chain on the ester oxygen. Smaller esters have good water solubility, but as the chain becomes longer, water solubility decreases. This becomes important for very long chain esters that make up fats and oils.

Synthesis of Esters

Conversion of acyl chlorides into esters

Esters can be readily obtained from the reaction of acid chlorides with alcohols under anhydrous conditions. Phenolic (aromatic) esters are produced in the same way, although the aromatic acid chlorides are less reactive than aliphatic acid chlorides, requiring base to be added as a catalyst.

Figure 48.18

Conversion of anhydrides into esters and carboxylic acids

Anhydrides react with alcohols to form esters; a single anhydride molecule will produce one ester and also one molecule of carboxylic acid.

Figure 48.19

Condensation of carboxylic acids and alcohols

Mixtures of carboxylic acids and alcohols will condense into esters under anhydrous conditions, liberating water. Use of sulfuric acid as a catalyst and dehydrating reagent will drive the reaction forward:

Figure 48.20

Reactions of Esters

Esters react with nucleophiles at the carbonyl carbon, although they are less reactive than acyl halides or anhydrides. Almost all reactions of esters can be recognized as nucleophilic substitutions (in which the carbonyl is retained) or nucleophilic additions (in which the carbonyl is lost).

Hydrolysis

Esters, like the other derivatives of carboxylic acids, can be hydrolyzed, yielding carboxylic acids and alcohols. Hydrolysis can take place under either acidic or basic conditions. Under acidic conditions, the first step is protonation of the carbonyl oxygen, followed by water attacking the carbonyl carbon:

Figure 48.21

Under basic conditions, the nucleophile is OH⁻, which directly attacks the carbonyl carbon. **Triacylglycerols,** also called fats or triglycerides, are esters of long-chain carboxylic acids, often called fatty acids, and glycerol (1,2,3-propanetriol). **Saponification** is the process whereby fats are hydrolyzed under basic conditions to produce soaps.

Triacylglycerol   Soap   Glycerol

Figure 48.22

Conversion into amides

Nitrogen bases, such as ammonia, act as a nucleophile and attack the electrophilic carbonyl carbon atom, displacing the ester functional group to yield an amide and an alcohol side-product:

Figure 48.23

Transesterification

Alcohols can act as nucleophiles and displace the alkoxy groups on esters. This process, which transforms one ester into another, is called **transesterification**.

Figure 48.24

Grignard addition

Grignard reagents add to the carbonyl groups of esters to form ketones; however, these ketones are more reactive than the initial esters and are readily attacked by more Grignard reagent. Two equivalents of Grignard reagent can thus be used to produce tertiary alcohols with good yield. The intermediate ketone can be isolated only if the alkyl groups are sufficiently bulky to prevent further attack. This reaction proceeds via nucleophilic substitution followed by nucleophilic addition.

3-methyl-3-pentanol

Figure 48.25

Condensation Reactions

An important reaction of esters is the **Claisen condensation**. In the simplest case, two moles of ethyl acetate react under basic conditions to produce a β-keto ester, ethyl 3-oxobutanoate, which is also known by its common name, acetoacetic ester. (The Claisen condensation is also called the **acetoacetic ester condensation**.) The reaction proceeds by addition of an enolate anion to the carbonyl group of another ester, followed by displacement of ethoxide ion (the formation of enolate ions is discussed in Chapter 46, Aldehydes and Ketones). This mechanism is analogous to that of the aldol condensation (also covered in Chapter 46).

Figure 48.26

Reduction

Esters may be reduced to primary alcohols with LAH, but not with $NaBH_4$. This allows for selective reduction in molecules with multiple functional groups. Note that different alcohols are produced from the ester alkoxy functional group and the carbonyl-containing carbon chain.

Figure 48.27

Phosphate Esters

While phosphoric acid derivatives are not carboxylic acid derivatives, they form esters with many similar properties and reactivities.

where R = H or hydrocarbon

phosphoric acid   phosphoric ester

Figure 48.28

Phosphoric acid and the mono- and diesters are acidic (more so than carboxylic acids) and usually exist as anions. Like carboxylic acid esters, under acidic conditions they can be cleaved into the parent acid (here, H_3PO_4) and alcohols.

Phosphate esters are found in living systems in the form of **phospholipids** (phosphoglycerides), in which glycerol is attached to two carboxylic acids and one phosphoric acid.

phosphatidic acid
diacylglycerol phosphate
(a phosphoglyceride)

Figure 48.29

Phospholipids are the main component of cell membranes, and phosphate/carbohydrate polymers form the backbone of nucleic acids, the hereditary material of life. The nucleic acid derivative **adenosine triphosphate (ATP)** can give up and regain one or more phosphate groups. ATP facilitates many biological reactions by releasing phosphate groups to other compounds, thereby increasing their reactivities.

AMIDES

Nomenclature of Amides

Amides are compounds with the general formula $RCONR_2$, in which the R group can be either a hydrocarbon, a hydrogen, or one of each. Amides are particularly important in biological systems, as the peptide bonds that link amino acids into proteins are actually amide bonds. Amides are named by replacing the -**oic** acid ending with -**amide**. Alkyl substituents on the nitrogen atom are listed as prefixes, and their location is specified with the letter N. For example, N-methylpropanamide has a methyl and a hydrogen as the substituents on the nitrogen and a 3-carbon chain, including the carbonyl:

N-methylpropanamide

Figure 48.30

Properties of Amides

Although amides do not have an –OH group, those that have hydrogens as substituents on the amide nitrogen have the ability to form hydrogen bonds. In fact, when two hydrogens are present on the amide nitrogen, it has the ability to form twice as many hydrogen bonds as the corresponding carboxylic acid. As a result, amides have very high melting and boiling points, and good water solubility (with the exception of tertiary amides that have two alkyl groups on the amide nitrogen). For example, acetamide (CH_3CONH_2) boils at 221°C, while acetic acid boils at 118°C.

Synthesis of Amides

Amides are generally synthesized by the reaction of acid chlorides with amines or by the reaction of acid anhydrides with ammonia.

Conversion of acyl halides to amides

Acyl halides can be readily converted into amides by nucleophilic substitution with amines. An amine such as ammonia attacks the carbonyl group, displacing chloride. The side product is ammonium chloride, formed from excess ammonia and HCl. Primary and secondary amines can also be used as the nucleophile to create substituted amides; tertiary amines are not able to lose a hydrogen and thus cannot participate in this reaction.

Figure 48.31

Conversion of anhydrides into amides

Anhydrides are cleaved by ammonia, producing an amide and a carboxylic acid. The carboxylic acid then further reacts with ammonia to form ammonium carboxylate.

Then:

Figure 48.32

Conversion of esters into amides

Nitrogen bases such as ammonia act as nucleophiles and will attack the electrophilic carbonyl carbon atom, displacing the ester functional group to yield an amide and an alcohol side-product.

Figure 48.33

Reactions

Amides are the least reactive of the carboxylic acid derivatives but are still susceptible to nucleophilic attack as well as rearrangements and reductions.

Hydrolysis

Amides can be hydrolyzed under acidic conditions, via nucleophilic substitution, to produce carboxylic acids. Under basic conditions amides react to form carboxylates.

Figure 48.34

Hofmann rearrangement

The **Hofmann rearrangement** converts amides to primary amines with the loss of the carbonyl carbon as a molecule of CO_2. The mechanism involves the formation of a **nitrene**, the nitrogen analog of a carbene. The nitrene is attached to the carbonyl group and rearranges to form an **isocyanate**, which under aqueous reaction conditions is hydrolyzed to the amine.

nitrene   isocyanate

Figure 48.35

Reduction

Amides can be reduced with LAH to the corresponding amine. Notice that this differs from the product of the Hofmann rearrangement in that no carbon atom is lost. Note that, unlike with a carboxylic acid reduction with LAH, the oxygen atom is completely removed:

Figure 48.36

SUMMARY OF REACTIONS

- The most important derivatives of carboxylic acids are acyl halides, anhydrides, esters, and amides. These are listed in order from most reactive (least stable) to least reactive (most stable).

ACYL HALIDES:

- can be formed by adding $RCOOH + SOCl_2$, PCl_3 or PCl_5, or PBr_3
- undergo many different nucleophilic substitutions; H_2O yields carboxylic acid, while ROH yields an ester and NH_3 yields an amide
- can participate in Friedel-Crafts acylation to form an alkyl aryl ketone
- can be reduced to alcohols or, selectively, to aldehydes

ANHYDRIDES:

- can be formed by $RCOO^- + RCOCl$ (substitution) or by $RCOOH + RCOOH$ (condensation)
- undergo many nucleophilic substitution reactions, forming products that include carboxylic acids, amides, and esters
- can participate in Friedel-Crafts acylation

ESTERS:

- formed by acid chlorides or anhydrides + ROH or by $RCOOH + ROH$
- hydrolyze to yield acids + alcohols; adding ammonia yields an amide
- undergo transesterification with alcohol to exchange alkoxy functional group
- react with Grignard reagent (2 moles) to produce a tertiary alcohol
- can be formed by the Claisen condensation, analogous to the aldol condensation, which combines two molecules of ester acting both as nucleophile and target
- are very important in biological processes, particularly phosphate esters, which can be found in membranes, nucleic acids, and metabolic reactions

AMIDES:

- can be formed by acid chlorides + amines, acid anhydrides + ammonia, or ester + ammonia
- can hydrolyze, yielding carboxylic acids or carboxylate anions
- can be transformed to primary amines via Hofmann rearrangement or reduction
- are very important in formation of proteins because all amino acids are linked by amide bonds known as peptide bonds

OC

REVIEW PROBLEMS

1. Name each of the following compounds according to the IUPAC system.

A.   B.

C.   D.

E.

2. What would be the product of the following reaction?

A.   B.

C.   D.

E.

3. During the hydrolysis of an acid chloride, pyridine (a base) is usually added to the reaction vessel. This is done because

   A. the reaction leads to the production of hydroxide ions.
   B. the acyl chloride is unreactive.
   C. the hydrolysis reaction leads to the formation of HCl.
   D. the pyridine reacts in a side-reaction with the carboxylic acid product.
   E. the oxidation leads to the formation of an ester.

4. What would be the primary product of the following reaction?

OH

+

O ‖ Cl

⟶

?

A.

B.

OH

C.

OH

D.

O

E. None of the above

5. In order to produce a primary amide, an acid chloride should be treated with

    A.   ammonia.

    B.   an alcohol.

    C.   a primary amine.

    D.   a tertiary amine.

    E.   a sulfide.

OC

6. Which of the following would be the best method of producing methyl propanoate?
   A. Reacting propanoic acid with methanol in the presence of a mineral acid
   B. Reacting propanyl chloride with ethanol in the presence of a base
   C. Reacting propanoyl chloride alone with an aqueous base
   D. Reacting propanoic acid with ethanol in the presence of a mineral acid
   E. Reacting propanoic acid with methanol in the presence of a base

7. What would be the product(s) of the following reaction?

A.   B. 2

C.   D.

E. None of the above

8. Which of the following correctly shows the intermediates and products of the reaction below?

E. None of the above

9. Prepare the following compounds from pentanoic acid. Give all reactants and reaction conditions.

   A. 1-Pentanol
   B. Pentanoyl bromide
   C. *N*-Methylpentanamide
   D. Ethyl pentanoate
   E. Pentanoic anhydride

10. What is saponification?

SOLUTIONS TO REVIEW PROBLEMS

1. **A** N-methyl-3-butenamide
   B Propanoyl bromide
   C Pentanamide
   D Propyl propanoate
   E Ethanoic anhydride (common name: acetic anhydride)

2. **D** Treating a carboxylic acid with thionyl chloride results in the production of an acyl chloride. In this reaction, butanoic acid is converted to butanoyl chloride, which is choice (D). Since none of the other choices are acyl chlorides, they can be eliminated.

3. **C** Hydrolysis of an acid chloride results in the formation of a carboxylic acid and HCl. Since pyridine can act as a base, it serves to neutralize the HCl that is formed. The reaction does not result in the formation of hydroxide ions, so choice (A) is incorrect. Pyridine does not react with the carboxylic acid product, it reacts with the HCl, so choice (D) is incorrect. Finally, choice (B) is incorrect because the acyl chloride is very reactive. The correct answer is choice (C).

4. **B** In this question, an acid chloride is treated with an alcohol, and the product will be an ester. However, the esterification process is affected by the presence of bulky side-chains on either reactant. It is easier to esterify an unhindered alcohol than a hindered one. In this reaction, the primary hydroxyl group is less hindered and will react with benzoyl chloride more rapidly, so choice (B) is correct. Choice (A) is incorrect because the hydroxyl group is a hindered secondary hydroxyl, and the reaction rate will be slower. Choice (C) is incorrect because it is not an ester. Choice (D) is incorrect because steric hindrance would prevent this product from being formed.

5. **A** Acid chlorides react with ammonia or other amines to form amides. Since the amine is replacing the hydroxyl group of the carbonyl, there must be at least one hydrogen on the amine. Therefore, only ammonia and primary or secondary amines can undergo this reaction. In order to obtain a primary amide, ammonia, choice (A), must be used. The reaction of an alcohol with an acid chloride produces an ester, so choice (B) is incorrect. A primary amine reacting with an acid chloride would give an N-substituted amide; thus, choice (C) is incorrect. Choice (D) is incorrect because tertiary amines will not react with acid chlorides.

6. **A** Methyl propanoate is an ester, which can be synthesized by reacting a carboxylic acid with an alcohol in the presence of acid: choice (A). Choice (E) is close, but adding both acid and base at the same time will cause a neutralization reaction and severely diminish yields. Reacting ethanol with propanoyl chloride, choice (B), will also result in the formation of an ester, but because ethanol is used, ethyl propanoate will be formed, not methyl propanoate. This is also the case for choice (D), since ethanol is used here as well. Therefore, choices (B) and (D) are incorrect. Choice (C) is incorrect because propanoyl chloride will not form an ester in the presence of base alone. Therefore, choice (A) is the correct response.

7. **D** This question asks for the products when ammonia reacts with acetic anhydride. Recall from the text that an amide and an ammonium carboxylate will be formed. The only choice showing such a pair is (D), acetamide and ammonium acetate.

8. C This question gives a reaction scheme for the interconversion of propanoic acid to various derivatives, and asks what intermediate products are formed. The first reaction involves the formation of an acid chloride using thionyl chloride. Acid chlorides are made by replacing the hydroxyl group with chlorine. Thus, choices (A) and (B), which depict intact hydroxyl groups, can be eliminated. The second reaction is nucleophilic attack by ammonia on propanoyl chloride. The product should be propanamide, since ammonia will replace the chloride on the carbonyl carbon, which is correctly shown in both answer choices (C) and (D). The final reaction involves amide hydrolysis in the presence of base; therefore, the resulting carboxylic acid will exist in solution as a carboxylate salt. Thus, choice (C) is the correct answer, since it has sodium propanoate as the product of the third reaction.

9. This question asks about preparation of pentanoic acid derivatives. Where there is more than one way to make the products, the most efficient method will be given.

A 1-Pentanol

Carboxylic acids are easily reduced by LAH to produce the corresponding primary alcohol.

B Pentanoyl bromide

To form pentanoyl bromide, pentanoic acid is reacted with PBr_3. The bromide replaces the hydroxyl on the carbonyl carbon.

C *N*-Methylpentanamide

N-Methylpentanamide can be prepared by first producing the acid chloride using thionyl chloride, and then reacting it with methylamine to yield the amide.

D Ethyl pentanoate

The ethyl ester of pentanoic acid can be formed by reacting it directly with ethanol in the presence of hydrochloric acid.

E Pentanoic anhydride

The most common method of preparing anhydrides is the reaction between an acid chloride and a carboxylate anion. To form pentanoic anhydride, one mole of pentanoic acid must be treated with thionyl chloride to yield pentanoyl chloride. This reacts with one mole of sodium pentanoate to form pentanoic anhydride.

10. Saponification is the process whereby fats are hydrolyzed under basic conditions to produce soaps.

CHAPTER FORTY-NINE

Amines

Amines are nitrogen-containing compounds of the general formula NR_3, with R representing either hydrogens, alkyl groups, or a combination of both. One of the most important features of amines is the lone pair of electrons on the nitrogen, which determines many of the chemical and physical properties of these compounds. Other nitrogen-containing compounds are similar to amines, including those with double or triple bonds between a carbon and a nitrogen (imines and nitriles), compounds with two or three nitrogens (diazides and azides), and compounds with both nitrogen and oxygen (amides, isocyanates, and nitrates).

Amines have a great deal of biological significance since they are part of amino acids, nucleic acids, and many other biomolecules. They are also are important in medicine. Many nitrogen-containing compounds act as relaxants, including nitroglycerin and nitrous oxide. Nitroglycerin is given either sublingually or transdermally to relieve coronary artery spasms and angina (chest pain). Nitrous oxide is also known as laughing gas and is used as a dental anesthetic. Nitroglycerin and trinitrotoluene also have nonmedical significance as explosives due to their high reactivities.

NOMENCLATURE OF AMINES

Amines are classified according to the number of alkyl (or aryl) groups to which the nitrogen is bound. A **primary (1°)** amine is attached to one alkyl group and can be written as RNH_2; a **secondary (2°)** amine is bound to two alkyl groups and can be written as R_2NH; and a **tertiary (3°)** amine is bound to three alkyl groups and is written as R_3N. A nitrogen atom attached to four alkyl groups is called a **quaternary ammonium compound** and is written as R_4N^+; the nitrogen carries a positive charge, and these compounds generally exist as salts.

In the common naming system, amines are generally named as alkylamines. The groups are designated individually or by using the prefixes di- or tri- if they are the same. In the IUPAC system, amines are named by substituting the suffix **-amine** for the final -*e* of the name of the alkane to which the nitrogen is attached. *N* is used to label substituents attached to the nitrogen in secondary or tertiary amines. The prefix **amino-** is used for naming compounds containing a higher priority OH or a CO_2H group. Aromatic amines are named as derivatives of aniline ($C_6H_5NH_2$), the IUPAC name for which is benzenamine. Table 49.1 gives three examples of compounds named by both the common and IUPAC system:

Formula:	$CH_3CH_2NH_2$	$CH_3CH_2N(CH_3)_2$	$H_2NCH_2CH_2OH$
IUPAC Name:	Ethanamine	*N,N*-Dimethylethanamine	2-Aminoethanol
Common Name:	Ethylamine	Dimethylethylamine	2-Aminoethanol

Table 49.1

Many other nitrogen-containing organic compounds are listed in Table 49.2 with their key characteristics, and Figure 49.1 gives several example structures.

Class of compound	Characteristics
Amides	$RCONR_2$ Discussed in Chapter 48, Carboxylic Acid Derivatives
Carbamates (urethanes)	$RNHC(O)OR'$ Form polymers called **polyurethanes** Derived from isocyanates + alcohol
Isocyanates	RNCO Combine with alcohols to create carbamates
Enamines	$C=CH-NR_2$ Analogous to enols
Imines	$C=NR$
Nitriles (Cyanides)	$C\equiv N$ Named as either cyano- or -nitrile
Nitro compounds	$-NO_2$
Diazo compounds	$-N_2$ Lose N_2 to form carbenes $R-(C:)-R'$ or $R=C:$
Azides	$-N_3$ Readily lose N_2 to form nitrenes
Nitrenes	R-N: Nitrogen analog of carbenes Formed from azides upon loss of N_2 Highly unstable; usually a reaction intermediate

Table 49.2

Figure 49.1

PROPERTIES OF AMINES

The boiling points of amines are between those of alkanes and alcohols. For example, methylamine (CH_3NH_2, MW = 31 g/mol) boils at $-6°C$, whereas ethane (CH_3CH_3, MW = 30 g/mol) boils at $-89°C$ and methanol (CH_3OH, MW = 32 g/mol) boils at $64.5°C$. Ammonia and primary and secondary amines can form hydrogen bonds, while tertiary amines cannot; therefore, tertiary amines have lower boiling points. Since nitrogen is not as electronegative as oxygen, the hydrogen bonds of amines are not as strong as those of alcohols.

The nitrogen atom in an amine is approximately sp^3 hybridized. Nitrogen bonds to only three substituents in order to complete its octet; a lone pair occupies the last sp^3 orbital. This lone pair is very important to the chemistry of amines; it is associated with their basic and nucleophilic properties.

Nitrogen atoms bonded to three different substituents are chiral because of the geometry of the orbitals. However, these enantiomers cannot be isolated, because they interconvert rapidly in a process called **nitrogen inversion**: an inversion of the sp^3 orbital occupied by the lone pair. The activation energy for this process is only 6 kcal/mol, and only at very low temperatures is it significantly slowed or stopped.

Figure 49.2

Amines are Brønsted-Lowry bases and readily accept protons to form ammonium ions; they are also classified as Lewis bases because of their ability to donate electrons (for a review of acids and bases, see Chapter 36). The pK_b values of alkyl amines are around 4, making them slightly more basic than ammonia ($pK_b = 4.76$). Aromatic amines such as aniline ($pK_b = 9.42$) are far less basic than aliphatic amines, because the electron-withdrawing effect of the ring reduces the electron-donating ability of the amino group. The presence of other substituents on the ring alters the basicity of anilines: electron-donating groups (such as $-OH$, $-CH_3$, and $-NH_2$) increase basicity, while electron-withdrawing groups (such as $-NO_2$) reduce basicity.

Amines also function as very weak acids. The pK_a values of amines are around 35, and a very strong base is required for deprotonation. For example, the proton of diisopropylamine may be removed with butyllithium, forming the sterically hindered base lithium diisopropylamide, LDA.

Figure 49.3

SYNTHESIS OF AMINES

Alkylation of Ammonia

Direct alkylation

Alkyl halides react with ammonia to produce alkylammonium halide salts. Ammonia functions as a nucleophile and displaces the halide atom. When the salt is treated with base, the alkylamine product is formed.

$$CH_3Br + NH_3 \longrightarrow CH_3\overset{+}{N}H_3Br^- \xrightarrow{NaOH} CH_3NH_2 + NaBr + H_2O$$

Figure 49.4

This reaction often leads to side products, because the alkylamine formed is more nucleophilic than ammonia. The alkylamine product therefore reacts with the alkyl halide faster than ammonia, leading to increasingly complex products. The final result will be a mixture of primary, secondary, tertiary and sometimes quaternary amines:

$$NH_3 + R-X \longrightarrow RNH_2 \quad (1°)$$

$$RNH_2 + R-X \longrightarrow R_2NH \quad (2°)$$

$$R_2NH + R-X \longrightarrow R_3N \quad (3°)$$

$$R_3N + R-X \longrightarrow R_4N^+ \quad (4°)$$

Gabriel synthesis

The preferred method for synthesizing amines is the **Gabriel synthesis.** This pathway converts a primary alkyl halide to a primary amine without the uncontrolled additional reactions seen in the direct alkylation of amines. The first step is the creation of phthalimide, a nitrogen source based on ammonia, but with more controlled reactivity:

Figure 49.5

Phthalimide, the condensation product of phthalic acid and ammonia, acts as a good nucleophile when deprotonated. It displaces halide ions, forming N-alkylphthalimides, which do not further react with other alkyl halides. When the reaction is complete, the N-alkylphthalimide can be hydrolyzed with aqueous base to produce the alkylamine.

Figure 49.6

Reduction

Amines can be obtained from other nitrogen-containing functionalities through reduction reactions using typical reducing agents.

From nitro compounds

Nitro compounds are easily reduced to primary amines. The most common reducing agent is iron or zinc and dilute hydrochloric acid, although many other reagents can be used. This reaction is especially useful for aromatic compounds, because aromatic rings are readily nitrated and thus provide an efficient route for amine synthesis.

Figure 49.7

From nitriles

Nitriles can be reduced with hydrogen and a catalyst, or with lithium aluminum hydride (LAH), to produce primary amines.

$$CH_3CH_2C{\equiv}N \xrightarrow{\text{LAH}} CH_3CH_2CH_2NH_2$$

Figure 49.8

From imines

Amines can be synthesized by **reductive amination**: a process in which an aldehyde or ketone is reacted with ammonia, a primary amine, or a secondary amine to form a primary, secondary, or tertiary amine, respectively. When the amine reacts with the aldehyde or the ketone, an imine intermediate is produced. Similar to a carbonyl, the imine can then undergo hydride reduction. When the imine is reduced with hydrogen in the presence of a catalyst, an amine is produced.

acetone   imine   amine
isopropylimine   isopropylamine
(aminoisopropane)

Figure 49.9

From amides

Amides can be reduced with LAH to form amines (see Chapter 48, Carboxylic Acid Derivatives, to review amides).

Figure 49.10

REACTIONS OF AMINES

Exhaustive Methylation

Exhaustive methylation is also known as **Hofmann elimination**. In this process, an amine is converted to a quaternary ammonium iodide salt by reacting with excess methyl iodide. Treatment with silver oxide and water converts this to the ammonium hydroxide, which, when heated, undergoes elimination to form an alkene and an amine. The predominant alkene formed is the least substituted, in contrast with normal elimination reactions, where the predominant alkene product is the most substituted.

Figure 49.11

REVIEW PROBLEMS

1. A compound with the general formula $R_4N^+X^-$ is classified as a
   A. secondary amine.
   B. quaternary ammonium salt.
   C. tertiary amine.
   D. primary amine.
   E. tertiary ammonium salt.

2. A compound with the structural formula $C_6H_5N^-N^+{\equiv}N$ is called
   A. a urethane.
   B. a diazo compound.
   C. an azide.
   D. a nitrile.
   E. an amide.

3. Amines have lower boiling points than the corresponding alcohols because
   A. amines have higher molecular masses.
   B. amines form much stronger hydrogen bonds.
   C. amines form weaker hydrogen bonds.
   D. amines are less dense.
   E. amines contain fewer total atoms per molecule.

4. Which of the following would be formed if methyl bromide was reacted with phthalimide and then hydrolyzed with aqueous base?
   A. $C_2H_5NH_2$
   B. CH_3NH_2
   C. $(C_2H_5)_3N$
   D. $(CH_3)_4N^+Br^-$
   E. CH_4

5. The reaction of benzamide with $LiAlH_4$ yields which of the following compounds?
   A. Benzoic acid
   B. Benzonitrile
   C. Benzylamine
   D. Ammonium benzoate
   E. Benzopyrene

6. Suggest a method of converting RCOOH to RNH_2.

7. Which of the following amines has the highest boiling point?
   A. CH_3NH_2
   B. $CH_3(CH_2)_6NH_2$
   C. $CH_3(CH_2)_3NH_2$
   D. $(CH_3)_3CNH_2$
   E. $CH_3CH_2NH_2$

8. If 2-amino-3-methylbutane were treated with excess methyl iodide, silver oxide, and water, what would be the major reaction products?

    A. Ammonia and 2-methyl-2-butene

    B. Trimethylamine and 3-methyl-1-butene

    C. Trimethylamine and 2-methyl-2-butene

    D. Ammonia and 3-methyl-1-butene

    E. Ammonia alone

9. Nylon, a polyamide, is produced from hexanediamine and a substance X. This substance X is most probably

    A. an amine.

    B. a carboxylic acid.

    C. a nitrile.

    D. an alcohol.

    E. a sulfide.

10. A researcher wants to prepare a primary amine (RNH_2). He uses an alkyl halide (RX) and ammonia to produce an alkyl ammonium halide salt ($RNH_3^+X^-$), which he then treats with sodium hydroxide to produce the primary amine. He finds that the product is always contaminated with a secondary amine (R_2NH) and a tertiary amine (R_3N). What has he done wrong and how can he produce only the primary amine he desires?

OC

SOLUTIONS TO REVIEW PROBLEMS

1. **B** A quaternary ammonium salt has four substituents attached to the nitrogen, resulting in a positive charge on this atom. As a result, this compound forms a salt, where X^- is usually a halide. Primary amines have the general formula RNH_2, secondary amines have the general formula R_2NH, and tertiary amines have the general formula R_3N.

2. **C** This is an azide, which is unstable and readily loses nitrogen to yield a nitrene. A urethane, choice (A), has the formula RNHCOOR'. A diazo compound, choice (B), has the formula $R-N\equiv N$. A nitrile, choice (D), also called a *cyanide*, has the formula $R-C\equiv N$. An amide does contain nitrogen but also has a carbonyl.

3. **C** Amines form weaker hydrogen bonds than alcohols, since nitrogen has a lower electronegativity than oxygen. The molecules are not held together as tightly and are therefore more volatile. Density and number of atoms may indicate other properties but do not affect intermolecular forces or boiling point directly.

4. **B** The reaction between methyl bromide and phthalimide results in the formation of methyl phthalimide. Subsequent hydrolysis then yields methylamine, so answer choice (B) is the correct response. The overall reaction is the conversion of a primary alkyl halide into a primary amine. Choice (A) is incorrect because this contains an ethyl group, not a methyl group. In order to form this compound, the initial reactant would need to be ethyl bromide. Choices (C) and (D) are incorrect as these are tertiary and quaternary nitrogen compounds, respectively, and the reaction only converts primary alkyl halides into primary amines. Choice (E) is methane, which does not take into account the nitrogen from phthalimide.

5. **C** Lithium aluminum hydride is a good reducing agent and is used to reduce amides to amines. Reduction of benzamide will result in the formation of benzylamine, choice (C). Hydrolysis of benzamide would result in the formation of benzoic acid, so choice (A) is incorrect. Benzonitrile would be formed by the dehydration of amides, so choice (B) is also incorrect. To form ammonium benzoate, choice (D), benzamide would first have to be hydrolyzed and then reacted with ammonia, so this answer choice is also incorrect. Choice (E), benzopyrene, is a structure composed of five different rings and has the formula $C_{20}H_{12}$. This structure has a complex synthesis that could not be achieved with the given reactants alone, especially not in a 1:1 ratio as implied.

6. One method is transformation of the carboxylic acid to an acid chloride, followed by reaction with ammonia and then reduction with LAH (see Chapter 48, Carboxylic Acid Derivatives).

Another approach is the Curtius rearrangement:

1. $\underset{R}{\overset{O}{C}}{-}OH \xrightarrow{SOCl_2} \underset{R}{\overset{O}{C}}{-}Cl$

2. $\underset{R}{\overset{O}{C}}{-}Cl \xrightarrow{NaN_3} \underset{R}{\overset{O}{C}}{-}N{-}\overset{+}{N}{\equiv}N \xrightarrow{-N_2} O{=}C{=}N{-}R$

Curtius rearrangement

3. $O{=}C{=}N{-}R \xrightarrow[-CO_2]{H_2O} \overset{H}{\underset{H}{N}}{-}R$

7. **B** As the molecular masses of comparable amines having the same degree of substitution increase, so do their boiling points. Of the choices given, choice (B), heptylamine, has the highest molecular mass (115 g/mol) and therefore the highest boiling point, 142−144°C. Choice (A), methylamine, has a mass of 31 g/mol and a boiling point of −6.3°C. Butylamine, choice (C), has a boiling point of 77.5°C, and *t*-butylamine, choice (D), has a boiling point of 44.4°C. Butylamine and *t*-butylamine have the same mass (73 g/mol), demonstrating the effect branching has on decreasing the boiling point. Finally, choice (E), ethylamine, has a mass of 45 g/mol and a boiling point of 16.6°C.

8. **B** Treatment of an amine with excess methyl iodide, silver oxide, and water is called exhaustive methylation or Hofmann elimination. The products formed are a trisubstituted amine and an alkene. Since 2-amino-3-methylbutane is a primary amine, it will take up three methyl groups; the trisubstituted amine produced will be trimethylamine. The predominant alkene product will be the least substituted alkene, because removal of a secondary hydrogen is sterically hindered. Therefore, this reaction will produce 3-methyl-1-butene, plus trimethylamine, choice (B). Choices (A) and (D) are incorrect; ammonia cannot be a product of this reaction since the mechanism involves the addition of methyl groups. Choice (C) is incorrect because 2-methyl-2-butene, the more substituted alkene, would not be the predominant product.

9. **B** An amide is formed from an amine and a carboxyl group or its acyl derivatives. In this question, an amine is already given; the compound to be identified must be an acyl compound. The only acyl compound among the choices given is a carboxylic acid, choice (B).

10. The researcher gets a contaminated product because he is using a direct alkylation process, which does not stop cleanly after the first alkylation. The primary amine produced by

direct alkylation is an excellent nucleophile and will react with other alkyl halides to produce secondary and tertiary amines.

$$NH_3 + R-X \longrightarrow RNH_2 \quad (1°)$$
$$RNH_2 + R-X \longrightarrow R_2NH \quad (2°)$$
$$R_2NH + R-X \longrightarrow R_3N \quad (3°)$$

Instead he should use the Gabriel synthesis, which converts an alkyl halide to a primary amine without unwanted side products. In this reaction, an imide, not ammonia, is used as the nucleophile. The product is an N-alkylimide, which cannot react further with alkyl halides. After the reaction is complete, the N-alkylimide is hydrolyzed with base to produce the primary alkylamine.

CHAPTER FIFTY

Spectroscopy

When an organic compound has been synthesized or separated from a mixture, it often must be characterized and identified. **Spectroscopy** is the process of measuring the frequencies of electromagnetic radiation (light) absorbed by a molecule. The frequencies of light that are absorbed are related to the energy levels of the molecule and different types of motion, including rotation, vibration of bonds, and electron movement. Different types of spectroscopy measure these different types of motion, allowing identification of specific functional groups and how they are connected within a molecule.

INFRARED SPECTROSCOPY

Basic Theory

Infrared (IR) spectroscopy measures molecular vibrations. The infrared spectrum of a sample is determined by passing light through the sample and recording the frequencies at which light is absorbed. These absorption frequencies correspond to the vibrations of the molecule, including **stretching, bending,** and **rotation.** The useful absorptions of infrared light occur in the frequency range from $400-4,000$ cm^{-1} (called **wavenumbers**). The wavenumber of the absorption is related to specific functional groups in a molecule, and can be used to identify these functional groups.

Bond stretching is observed in the region of $1,500-4,000$ cm^{-1}. Bending vibrations are observed in the region of $400-1,500$ cm^{-1}. Four different types of vibration that can occur are shown in Figure 50.1.

symmetric
bend

asymmetric
bend

symmetric
stretch

asymmetric
stretch

Figure 50.1

In addition to bending and stretching vibrations, more complex vibrations may occur. These can be combinations of bending, stretching, rotation, or motion of the whole molecule. Absorptions of these types are seen in the region of $400-1{,}500$ cm^{-1}, known as the **fingerprint region**, which is unique to a molecule.

In order for IR light to be absorbed, the vibration of the molecule must result in a change in a bond dipole moment. Symmetrical molecules do not have a dipole moment and therefore do not absorb IR light. For example, O_2 and Br_2 do not absorb IR light, but HCl and CO do. The more complicated a molecule, the more peaks observed in its IR spectrum.

Characteristic IR Absorptions

Specific functional groups absorb at well-defined frequencies. For example, carbon-carbon single bonds absorb at around $1{,}200$ cm^{-1}, double bonds around $1{,}600$ cm^{-1}, and triple bonds around $2{,}200$ cm^{-1}. Table 50.1 lists the specific absorptions of key functional groups and the vibrations that occur at those frequencies.

Functional Group	Frequency (cm^{-1})	Vibration
Alkanes	2800–3000	C—H
	1200	C—C
Alkenes	3080–3140	=C—H
	1645	C=C
Alkynes	2200	C≡C
	3300	≡C—H
Aromatic	2900–3100	C—H
	1475–1625	C—C
Alcohols	3100–3500	O—H (broad)
Ethers	1050–1150	C—O
Aldehydes	2700–2900	(O)C—H
	1725–1750	C=O
Ketones	1700–1750	C=O
Acids	1700–1750	C=O
	2900–3300	O—H (broad)
Amines	3100–3500	N—H (sharp)

Table 50.1

Some of the most useful information in an IR spectrum can often be quickly and easily determined by reviewing two key areas of absorption—from 1,700–1,750 and 3,100–3,500 cm^{-1}—to determine the presence of oxygen and nitrogen functional groups:

Functional Group	1,700–1,750 cm^{-1}	3,100–3,500 cm^{-1}
Alcohol	No	Broad peak
Aldehyde or Ketone	Yes	No
Carboxylic Acid	Yes	Broad peak
Amine	No	Sharp peak

Table 50.2

Application

A great deal of information can be obtained from an IR spectrum. Percent transmission, the inverse of absorbance, is plotted versus frequency; this gives areas of absorption the appearance of valleys on the spectrum.

Figure 50.2 shows the IR spectrum of an aliphatic alcohol. The broad peak at 3,300 cm^{-1} is due to the hydroxyl group, while the peak at 3,000 cm^{-1} is created by the large number of C−H bonds in the molecule.

Figure 50.2

Summary of IR Spectroscopy

1. IR spectroscopy is based on the vibrations of molecules, including bending and stretching.
2. IR absorption is measured in the frequency range of 400−4,000 cm^{-1}, and is plotted as transmittance vs. wave number, with absorption appearing as "valleys" in the spectrum.
3. Different functional groups show IR absorption at different wave numbers. Some of the most useful absorption ranges to note are at 1,700 cm^{-1} (C=O bond) and at 3,100–3,500 cm^{-1} (O−H if broad, N−H if narrow). However, other absorption frequencies can also be important.

NUCLEAR MAGNETIC RESONANCE

Basic Theory

Nuclear magnetic resonance (**NMR**) spectroscopy is one of the most widely used spectroscopic tools in organic chemistry. Certain nuclei have magnetic moments that are normally oriented at random. When such nuclei are placed in a magnetic field, their magnetic moments tend to align either with or against the direction of the field. Nuclei whose magnetic moments are aligned with the field are said to be in the **α-state** (lower energy), while those whose moments are aligned against the field are said to be in the **β-state** (higher energy).

If the nuclei are then exposed to electromagnetic radiation, some in the lower energy α-state will be excited into the β-state; this transition is known as **resonating.** The absorption corresponding to this excitation occurs at different frequencies depending on the atom's environment. Other nearby atoms in the same molecule (or sometimes in the solvent) can shift the frequency at which an atom transitions between the α- and β-states. A compound may contain many nuclei that resonate at different frequencies, producing a very complex spectrum.

Since different NMR spectrometers operate at different magnetic field strengths, a standardized method of plotting the NMR spectrum has been adopted. A variable called **chemical shift**, represented by the symbol δ and with units of **parts per million** (**ppm**), is plotted on the *x*-axis. Chemical shift is compared to the standard organic molecule tetramethylsilane (TMS). TMS is always shown by a peak at 0 ppm, and the peaks of interest always appear to the left of TMS. A peak further to the left is said to be **shifted downfield**.

NMR is most commonly used to study ^1H nuclei (protons) and ^{13}C nuclei, although any atom possessing a nuclear spin (any nucleus with an odd atomic number or odd mass number) can be studied, such as ^{19}F, ^{17}O, ^{14}N, ^{15}N, or ^{31}P.

^1H NMR (Proton NMR)

Peak location

Most ^1H nuclei come into resonance between 0 and 10 δ downfield from TMS. Each distinct set of nuclei gives rise to a separate peak. The compound dichloromethyl methyl ether ($Cl_2HC–O–CH_3$) has two distinct sets of ^1H nuclei. The single proton attached to the dichloromethyl group is in a different magnetic environment compared to the three protons on the methyl group, and the two types of protons resonate at different frequencies. The three protons on the methyl group are magnetically equivalent, due to rotation about the oxygen-carbon single bond, and resonate at the same frequency. Thus, two separate peaks are seen, as shown in Figure 50.3.

Figure 50.3

The peak at 6 ppm corresponds to the single dichloromethyl proton and the peak at 3 ppm to the three methyl protons. The size of the peaks is also significant; if the areas under the peaks are integrated, the ratio between them is 3:1, corresponding to the number of protons producing each peak. This can be roughly approximated as the relative heights of the peaks when quickly evaluating an NMR spectrum.

The single proton comes into resonance downfield from (to the left of) the methyl protons. This shift downfield is due to the electron-withdrawing effect of the chlorine atoms. The electron cloud that surrounds the ${}^1H$ nucleus ordinarily screens the nucleus from the magnetic field. The chlorine atoms pull the electron cloud away and **deshield** the nucleus, moving its resonance to the left. Conversely, electron-donating atoms **shield** the ${}^1H$ nuclei, causing them to appear further to the right. Different bonds also have different affinities for electrons. As a result, different functional groups can deshield protons in predictable ways, as shown in Table 50.3:

Type of Proton	Approximate Shift δ (ppm)
RCH_3	0.9
R_2CH_2	1.25
R_3CH	1.5
$-CH=CH$	4.6−6.0
$-C\equiv CH$	2.0−3.0
$Ar-H$	6.0−8.5
$-CHX$	2.0−4.5
$-CHOH / -CHOR$	3.4−4.0
$RCHO$	9.0−10.0
$RCHCO-$	2.0−2.5
$-CHCOOH / -CHCOOR$	2.0−2.6
$-CHOH / -CH_2OH$	1.0−5.5
$ArOH$	4.0−12
$-COOH$	10.5−12.0
$-NH_2$	1.0−5.0

Table 50.3

Peak splitting

If two magnetically different protons are within three bonds of each other, a phenomenon known as **coupling** or **splitting** occurs. Consider two protons, H_a and H_b, on the molecule 1,1-dibromo-2,2-dichloroethane (Figure 50.4).

<figure>

    Cl Br

H—C—C—H
 a   b

    Cl Br

</figure>

Figure 50.4

At any given time, H_a can experience two different magnetic environments, since H_b can be in either the α or the β state. These different states of H_b influence nucleus H_a, causing slight upfield and downfield shifts. Since there is a 50 percent chance that H_b will be in either state, this results in a **doublet**, two peaks of equal intensity equally spaced around the true chemical shift of H_a. H_b experiences the two different states of H_a and is likewise split into a doublet. In 1,1-dibromo-2-chloroethane (Figure 50.5), the H_a nucleus is affected by two nearby H_b nuclei, which, taken together, can be in four different states: αα, αβ, βα, or ββ.

$$
\begin{array}{c}
\overset{\displaystyle Cl}{|}\ \ \overset{\displaystyle Br}{|}\\
H_b-C-C-H_a\\
\underset{\displaystyle H_b}{|}\ \ \underset{\displaystyle Br}{|}
\end{array}
$$

Figure 50.5

The $\alpha\beta$ and $\beta\alpha$ states have the same net effect on the H_a nucleus, and the resonances occur at the same frequency. The $\alpha\alpha$ and $\beta\beta$ states resonate at frequencies different from each other and from the $\alpha\beta$ / $\beta\alpha$ frequency. The result is three peaks centered around the true chemical shift, with an area ratio of 1:2:1. The number of peaks that will appear when splitting occurs can be determined as follows: n hydrogen atoms couple to give $n + 1$ peaks, whose area ratios are given by Pascal's triangle, shown in Table 50.4.

Number of Adjacent Hydrogens	Total Number of Peaks	Area Ratios
0	1	1
1	2	1:1
2	3	1:2:1
3	4	1:3:3:1
4	5	1:4:6:4:1
5	6	1:5:10:10:5:1
6	7	1:6:15:20:15:6:1
7	8	1:7:21:35:35:21:7:1

Table 50.4

Summary of ¹H NMR Spectroscopy

1. NMR spectroscopy is based on the magnetic moment of nuclei, which resonate between two states.

2. Each peak in an NMR spectrum represents a single proton or a group of equivalent protons. The size of each peak represents the number of equivalent protons in a group.

3. The position of the peak (distance downfield, or to the left) is determined by the shielding or deshielding effects of other functional groups nearby.

4. The splitting of a peak is determined by the number of adjacent protons n, and the number of peaks is given by $n + 1$.

¹³C NMR (Carbon NMR)

¹³C NMR is very similar to ¹H NMR. Most ¹³C NMR signals, however, occur $0-200\ \delta$ downfield from the carbon peak of TMS, so a spectrum for ¹³C NMR is easily recognized by the larger scale of the x-axis. Another significant difference is that only 1.1 percent of carbon atoms are ¹³C atoms. This has two effects: First, a much larger sample is needed to run a ¹³C spectrum (about 50 mg compared with 1 mg for ¹H NMR), and second, coupling between carbon atoms is generally not observed.

Coupling *is* observed, however, between carbon atoms and the protons directly attached to them. For example, if a carbon atom is attached to two protons, it can experience four different states of those protons (αα, αβ, βα, and ββ), and the carbon signal is split into a triplet with the area ratio 1:2:1.

An additional feature of ^{13}C NMR is the ability to record a spectrum *without* the coupling of adjacent protons. This is called **spin decoupling**, and produces a spectrum of **singlets**, each corresponding to a separate magnetically equivalent carbon atom. For example, compare the following two spectra, both of 1,1,2-trichloropropane. One (Figure 50.6) is a typical **spin-decoupled spectrum**, and the other (Figure 50.7) is spin-coupled.

Figure 50.6

Figure 50.7

Summary of ¹H and ¹³C NMR Spectroscopy

In general, NMR spectroscopy provides information about the carbon and hydrogen skeleton of a molecule along with some suggestion of its functional groups. Specifically, NMR can provide the following types of information:

1. The number of nonequivalent nuclei, determined from the number of peaks.

2. The magnetic environment of a nucleus, determined by the chemical shift.

3. The relative numbers of nuclei, determined by integrating the peak areas.

4. The number of neighboring nuclei, determined by the splitting pattern observed (except for ¹³C in the spin-decoupled mode).

ULTRAVIOLET-VISIBLE SPECTROSCOPY

Basic Theory

Ultraviolet-visible (UV-vis) spectra are obtained by passing ultraviolet or visible light through a chemical sample (usually dissolved in an inert, nonabsorbing solvent) and plotting absorbance versus wavelength. The higher the concentration of the compound in solution, the greater the absorbance. The wavelength of absorption depends on functional groups of the molecule; in particular, conjugation leads to greater UV-vis absorption.

UV-vis spectra are often used to simply identify the presence or absence of a compound by measuring the absorbance at a characteristic wavelength for that molecule. For example, to follow the progress of an oxidation reaction using $K_2Cr_2O_7$, the absorbance of the solution at 350 nm is monitored. When large amounts of $K_2Cr_2O_7$ are present, high absorbance is recorded; when the reaction has gone to completion and the $K_2Cr_2O_7$ is no longer present, the absorption peak disappears.

Atomic absorption and emission spectra related to the energy levels of electrons are measured in the UV-vis range, and provide information on the quantum states of atoms. Atomic spectra are discussed in more detail in Chapter 24, Atomic and Molecular Structure.

MASS SPECTROMETRY

Basic Theory

Mass spectrometry is a means of determining the molecular weight and structure of a molecule based on how it ionizes and decomposes under specific conditions. Mass spectrometry differs from other spectroscopic methods in two ways: No absorption of electromagnetic radiation is involved, and it is a destructive technique that does not allow the sample to be recovered and reused.

Mass spectrometers ionize the sample in a high-speed beam of electrons. The ionized sample then enters a magnetic field that deflects the ionic fragments into a detector. The net charge and mass of each particle is determined, along with the number of each type of particle (known as the **abundance**). The first ion formed is the $+1$ cation (M^+) resulting from the removal of a single electron. This unstable ion usually decomposes rapidly into more cationic fragments. A typical mass spectrum is composed of many lines, each corresponding to a fragment with a specific **mass to charge ratio** (*m/e*, also written as *m/z*). The spectrum itself plots mass/charge on the horizontal axis and relative abundance of the various cationic fragments on the vertical axis (see Fig. 50.8).

Characteristics

The tallest peak, belonging to the most common ion, is called the **base peak**, and is assigned the relative abundance value of 100 percent; thus the amount of any other ion is a percent of the base peak. The peak with the highest *m/e* ratio (see Figure 50.8) is almost always the **molecular ion peak** (**parent ion peak**), M^+, from which the molecular weight, M, can be obtained. The charge value is usually 1; hence the *m/e* ratio can usually be read as the mass of the fragment.

Application

Fragmentation patterns often provide information that helps identify the compound's structure. For example, while IR spectroscopy would be of little use in distinguishing between propionaldehyde and butyraldehyde, a mass spectrum would assist in identification.

Figure 50.8 shows the mass spectrum of butyraldehyde. The peak at *m/e* $= 72$ corresponds to the molecular cation-radical, M^+. Additional peaks represent a variety of fragments derived from the loss of groups of carbons and hydrogens.

Figure 50.8

Summary of Mass Spectrometry

1. Mass spectrometry is based on the mass to charge (m/e) ratio of fragments of the molecule of interest.

2. Each peak in a mass spectrum corresponds to one fragment, and its height gives the relative abundance (amount) of that fragment.

3. The original molecule can be identified as the highest mass/charge ratio peak in the spectrum, as it is the +1 cation of the original compound.

4. The fragmentation pattern can give additional information about the structure of the compound.

REVIEW PROBLEMS

1. IR spectroscopy is most useful for distinguishing
    A. double and triple bonds.
    B. C$-$H bonds.
    C. chirality of molecules.
    D. composition of racemic mixtures.
    E. electronegativity.

2. Oxygen (O_2) does not exhibit an IR spectrum because
    A. it has no molecular motions.
    B. it is not possible to record IR spectra of a gaseous molecule.
    C. molecular vibrations do not result in a change in the dipole moment of the molecules.
    D. it has a molar mass less than 20 g/mol.
    E. it reacts too quickly to be measured.

3. If IR spectroscopy were employed to monitor the oxidation of benzyl alcohol to benzaldehyde, which of the following would provide the best evidence that the reaction was proceeding as planned?
    A. Comparing the fingerprint region of the spectra of starting material and product.
    B. Noting the change in intensity of the peaks corresponding to the phenyl ring.
    C. Noting the appearance of a broad absorption peak in the region of 3,100–3,500 cm^{-1}.
    D. Noting the appearance of a strong absorption peak in the region of 1,700 cm^{-1}.
    E. Noting the appearance of a sharp absorption peak in the region of 675–870 cm^{-1}.

4. Which of the following chemical shifts would correspond to an aldehyde proton signal in a ^{1}H NMR spectrum?
    A. 1.2 ppm
    B. 2.6 ppm
    C. 4.8 ppm
    D. 7.0 ppm
    E. 9.5 ppm

5. The isotope ^{12}C is not useful for NMR because
    A. it is not abundant in nature.
    B. its resonances are not sensitive to the presence of neighboring atoms.
    C. it has no magnetic moment.
    D. the signal-to-noise ratio in the spectrum is too low.
    E. its density is too high to be affected by magnetic fields.

6. The NMR spectra of ethanol in the presence and absence of water are shown below.

NMR spectrum of ethanol

δ(ppm)

NMR spectrum of anhydrous ethanol

δ(ppm)

Which of the following explains the differences between the two spectra?

A. Water also resonates, doubling the number of peaks.

B. Carbon atoms do not couple in the presence of water.

C. The hydroxyl proton of ethanol exchanges with protons from water, preventing it from coupling.

D. Anhydrous ethanol forms dimers, causing the signal to split.

E. The solvent is not as effective at dissolving anhydrous ethanol, so more must be added.

7. In ^{13}C NMR, splitting of spectral lines is due to

   A. coupling between a carbon atom and protons attached to that carbon atom.

   B. coupling between a carbon atom and protons attached to adjacent carbon atoms.

   C. coupling between adjacent carbon atoms.

   D. coupling between two adjacent protons.

   E. coupling between a carbon atom, a proton directly attached, and an adjacent proton.

8. In the ^{13}C NMR spectrum of methyl phenyl ketone, which carbon atom will appear the farthest downfield?

   A. The methyl carbon

   B. The carbon at the first position of the phenyl ring

   C. The carbon at the *para* position of the phenyl ring

   D. The carbonyl carbon

   E. The carbon at the *meta* position of the phenyl ring

9. UV spectroscopy is most useful for detecting

   A. aldehydes and ketones.

   B. unconjugated alkenes.

   C. conjugated alkenes.

   D. aliphatic acids and amines.

   E. alkanes.

10. Mass spectroscopy results in the separation of fragments according to

    A. atomic mass.

    B. mass-to-charge ratio.

    C. viscosity.

    D. absorption wavelength.

    E. principal quantum number.

SOLUTIONS TO REVIEW PROBLEMS

1. **A** IR is most useful for distinguishing between different functional groups. Almost all organic compounds have C—H bonds (B), so that except for "fingerprinting" a compound, these absorptions are not useful. Very little information about the optical properties of a compound, such as choices (C) and (D), can be obtained by IR spectroscopy. Electronegativity (E) can be determined from the periodic table and does not require spectroscopy.

2. **C** Since molecular oxygen is a diatomic molecule with no initial net dipole, there is no net change in its dipole moment during vibration or rotation. Diatomic nitrogen and chlorine exhibit similar behavior. IR spectroscopy is based on the principle that when the molecule vibrates or rotates, there is a change in dipole moment; therefore, choice (C) is the correct answer. Choice (A) is incorrect because oxygen does have molecular motions. Choice (B) is incorrect because it is possible to record the IR of a gaseous molecule as long as it shows a change in its dipole moment when it vibrates. Choices (D) and (E) are false statements.

3. **D** In this reaction, the functional group is changing from a hydroxyl to an aldehyde. This means that a sharp peak will appear at around 1700 cm^{-1}, which corresponds to the carbonyl functionality. Therefore, choice (D) is the correct response. Choice (C) is incorrect because the reaction will be characterized by the disappearance of a peak at $3,100–3,500 \text{ cm}^{-1}$, not the appearance of one (this peak corresponds to the hydroxyl functionality). Choice (A) is possible, but the complexity of the information makes it a poor choice compared to (D). Choices (B) and (E) are the least useful, as the IR absorbance of the phenyl ring, which is in the $675–870 \text{ cm}^{-1}$ band, will not change in this reaction.

4. **E** The peak at 9.5 ppm corresponds to an aldehyde proton. This signal lies relatively far downfield because the carbonyl oxygen is strongly electron-withdrawing and deshields the proton. The other peaks are too upfield and represent more shielded molecules.

5. **C** This isotope has no magnetic moment and will therefore not exhibit resonance. Nuclei that possess a magnetic moment are those with odd-numbered masses (^{1}H, ^{11}B, ^{13}C, ^{15}N, ^{19}F, etc.) or those with an even mass but an odd atomic number (^{2}H, ^{10}B).

6. **C** The normal spectrum of CH_3CH_2OH has a CH_3 group split into a triplet by the CH_2 group protons, a CH_2 group split into a quartet by the CH_3 group protons, and a hydroxyl proton singlet. This proton exchanges rapidly with the protons of water and is not able to participate in splitting. Under anhydrous conditions, this proton can couple, and it splits the neighboring quartet into a doublet such that an octet is observed. The —OH signal itself appears as a triplet due to splitting by the protons of the neighboring CH_2 group. Answer choice (A) is incorrect because it is opposite of what is true: The peaks are split in the absence of water, not its presence. Choice (B) is incorrect because the spectra are for ^{1}H NMR, not ^{13}C NMR. Answer choice (D) is incorrect because ethanol does not form dimers in solution. Choice (E) is a false statement since the presence or absence of water doesn't affect solubility.

7. **A** Coupling between adjacent carbon atoms, choice (C), is rarely seen due to the low abundance of ^{13}C. Coupling between carbon and protons on the adjacent carbon, choices (B) and (E), is never observed. Since proton coupling is only relevant to ^{1}H NMR, choice (D) is incorrect.

8. **D** The carbonyl carbon atom will be furthest downfield because of the electron-withdrawing ability of the oxygen atom. ^{13}C NMR follows the same rules of chemical shift as ^{1}H NMR. Choices (A), (B), and (E) are farther from the oxygen than the carbonyl carbon and thus will not be shifted as far downfield. Choice (C), the carbon at the *para* position of the phenyl ring, is the furthest from the oxygen and will therefore be shifted downfield the least. Choice (D), the carbonyl carbon, is closest to the oxygen and therefore will experience the greatest shift and is the correct answer.

9. **C** Most conjugated alkenes, choice (C), give an intense UV absorption and are therefore most readily detected by UV spectroscopy. Aldehydes, ketones, acids, and amines, choices (A) and (D), all absorb in the UV, but other forms of spectroscopy (mainly IR and NMR) are more useful for their precise identification. Isolated alkanes and alkenes, choices (B) and (E), can rarely be identified by UV.

10. **B** In mass spectrometry, a molecule is broken down into smaller charged fragments. These fragments are passed through a magnetic field and are identified according to their mass-to-charge ratios; therefore, choice (B) is the correct answer. Choice (D) is the basis for IR and NMR, not mass spectrometry, so this is incorrect. Viscosity, choice (C), doesn't form the basis for any of the spectroscopic techniques discussed, so it is also incorrect. Choice (A) is incorrect because the separation of fragments does not depend solely on mass but on charge as well, and the fragments are mostly polyatomic. Choice (E), principal quantum number, indicates the distance electrons are from the nucleus and isn't directly indicated by mass spectroscopy.

OC

CHAPTER FIFTY-ONE

Separation

Much of organic chemistry is concerned with the isolation and purification of the desired reaction product. A reaction itself may be completed in a matter of minutes, but separating the product from the reaction mixture is often a difficult and time-consuming process. Many techniques have been developed to accomplish the objective of obtaining a pure compound separated from solvents, reagents, and other products.

BASIC TECHNIQUES

Extraction

One way of separating out a desired product is through extraction, the transfer of a dissolved compound from one solvent into another in which the product is more soluble. Most impurities will be left behind in the first solvent. The two solvents should be immiscible (form two layers that do not permanently mix because of mutual insolubility). The two layers are temporarily mixed together so the solute can pass from one to the other.

For example, isobutyric acid in solution with diethyl ether can be extracted with water; isobutyric acid is more soluble in water than in ether, so isobutyric acid transfers to the water phase when the two solvents are placed together. The water (**aqueous**) and ether (**organic**) phases are separated in a specialized piece of glassware called a separatory funnel (see Figure 51.1). Once separated, the isobutyric acid can be isolated from the aqueous phase in pure form. Some isobutyric acid will remain dissolved in the ether phase, so the extraction should be repeated several times with fresh solvent (water). More product can be obtained with successive extractions (e.g., it is more effective to perform three successive extractions of 10 mL each than to perform one extraction of 30 mL). Once the compound has been isolated in its purified form in a solvent, it can then be obtained by evaporation of the solvent.

Extraction depends on the basic rule of solubility: "like dissolves like." This rule can be observed by comparing the types of intermolecular forces the solute forms, such as in the following examples:

1. Hydrogen bonding: Compounds that can do this, such as alcohols or acids, will move most easily into the aqueous layer, which also can form hydrogen bonds.

2. Dipole–dipole interactions: Compounds with these interactions are less likely to move into the aqueous layer because doing so requires breaking the hydrogen bonds of the solvent and replacing them with weaker dipole–dipole bonds.

3. London dispersion forces: Compounds with only these interactions are least likely to move into the aqueous layer because breaking the hydrogen bonds of the solvent without replacing them with any significant bonds takes large amounts of energy.

The properties of acids and bases also can be used to advantage in extraction:

$$HA + \text{base} \rightarrow A^- + \text{Base: } H^+$$

When the acid dissociates, the anion formed will be more soluble in the aqueous layer than the original form. This is because the charged anions will form ion–dipole bonds with the solvent, which are even stronger than the hydrogen bonds they are displacing. Thus, adding a *base* will help extract an acid into an aqueous layer.

Figure 51.1

An extraction carried out to remove unwanted impurities rather than to isolate a pure product is called a **wash**.

Filtration

Filtration is used to isolate a suspended solid from a liquid. In this technique, a liquid/solid mixture is poured onto a paper filter that allows only the solvent to pass through. The result of this process is the separation of the solid (the **residue**) from the liquid (the **filtrate**). The two basic types of filtration are gravity filtration and vacuum filtration.

In **gravity filtration**, the solvent's own weight pulls it through the filter. Frequently, however, the pores of the filter become clogged with solid, slowing the rate of filtration. For this reason, in gravity filtration it is generally desirable for the substance of interest to be in solution (dissolved in the solvent), while impurities remain undissolved and can be filtered out. This allows the desired product to flow more easily and rapidly through the apparatus. To ensure the product remains dissolved, gravity filtration is usually carried out with hot solvent, since increasing heat generally increases K_{sp}.

In **vacuum filtration** (see Figure 51.2), the solvent is forced through the filter by a vacuum on the other side. Vacuum filtration is used to isolate relatively large quantities of solid, usually when the solid is the desired product.

residue
filter paper

to vacuum trap

clean filter flask

filtrate

Figure 51.2

Recrystallization

Recrystallization is a process in which impure crystals are dissolved in a minimum amount of hot solvent. As the solvent is cooled, the crystals re-form, leaving the impurities in solution. For recrystallization to be effective, the solvent must be chosen carefully. It must dissolve the solid while hot but not while cold. In addition, it must dissolve the impurities at both temperatures so they remain in solution even after being cooled.

Solvent choice is usually a matter of trial and error, although some generalizations can be made. Ideally, the desired product should have solubility that depends on temperature—it should be more soluble at high temperature and less so at low. In contrast, impurities should be equally soluble at various temperatures. An estimate of polarity is useful since polar solvents dissolve polar compounds, whereas nonpolar solvents dissolve nonpolar compounds. A solvent with intermediate polarity is generally desirable in recrystallization. In addition, the solvent should have a low enough freezing point that the solution may be sufficiently cooled without turning to a solid.

In some instances, a mixed solvent system may be used. Here, the crude compound is dissolved in a solvent in which it is highly soluble. Another solvent in which the compound is less soluble is then added in drops until the solid just begins to precipitate. The solution is heated a bit more to redissolve the precipitate and then slowly cooled to induce crystal formation.

Sublimation

Sublimation occurs when a heated solid turns directly into a gas without an intervening liquid stage. It is used as a method of purification because the impurities found in most reaction mixtures will not sublime easily. The vapors are made to condense on a **cold finger**, a piece of glassware packed with dry ice or with cold water running through it (see Figure 51.4). Most sublimations are performed under vacuum because at higher pressures more compounds will pass through a liquid phase rather than subliming. Low pressure also reduces the temperature required for sublimation and thus the danger that the compound will decompose. The optimal conditions depend on the compound to be purified since each compound has a different phase diagram.

Figure 51.3

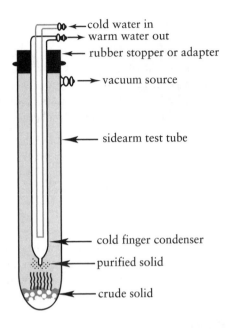

- cold water in
- warm water out
- rubber stopper or adapter
- vacuum source
- sidearm test tube
- cold finger condenser
- purified solid
- crude solid

Figure 51.4

Centrifugation

Particles in a solution settle, or **sediment**, at different rates depending upon their mass, density, and shape. Sedimentation can be accelerated by **centrifuging** the solution. A centrifuge is an apparatus in which test tubes containing the solution are spun at high speed. This subjects them to centrifugal force (see Figure 51.5). Compounds of greater mass and density settle toward the bottom of the test tube, while lighter compounds remain near the top. This method of separation is effective for many different types of compounds and is frequently used in biochemistry to separate cells, organelles, and biological macromolecules.

A handy mnemonic for centrifugation is "*Se*Dimentation depends on *Si*ze (mass) and *D*ensity."

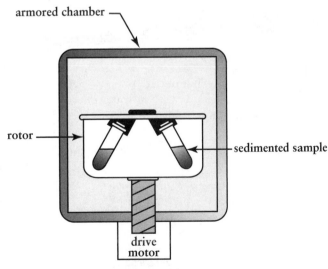

armored chamber

rotor

sedimented sample

drive motor

Figure 51.5

DISTILLATION

Distillation is the separation of one liquid from another through vaporization and condensation. A mixture of two or more miscible liquids is slowly heated. The compound with the lowest boiling point is preferentially vaporized, condensed on a water-cooled distillation column, and separated from the other, higher-boiling-point compound(s). Note that immiscible liquids can be separated in a separatory funnel and thus do not require distillation.

Boiling point is strongly affected by intermolecular forces, with stronger intermolecular forces requiring more energy (higher temperature) to break. This is why H_2O (with hydrogen bonds) has such a high boiling point and why longer molecules (with more London dispersion forces) tend to have higher boiling points than shorter ones.

Simple distillation

Simple distillation is used to separate liquids that have boiling points that are *below* 150°C and that are at least 25°C apart from one another. The apparatus consists of a distilling flask containing the two liquids, a distillation column consisting of a thermometer and a condenser, and a receiving flask to collect the distillate.

Vacuum distillation

Vacuum distillation is used to separate liquids that have boiling points *above* 150°C and that are at least 25°C apart (see Figure 51.6). The entire system is operated under reduced pressure, lowering the boiling points of the liquids and preventing their decomposition due to excessive temperature.

Figure 51.6

Fractional distillation

Fractional distillation is used to separate liquids that have boiling points that are less than 25°C apart (see Figure 51.7). A fractionating column is used to connect the distilling flask to the distillation column. It is filled with inert objects, such as glass beads, that have a large surface area. The vapors condense on these surfaces, re-evaporate, and then condense further up the column. Each time the liquid evaporates, the vapors contain a greater proportion of the lower-boiling-point component. Eventually, the vapor near the top of the fractionating column is composed solely of one component, which condenses on the distillation column and collects in the receiving flask.

Figure 51.7

CHROMATOGRAPHY

Chromatography is a technique that allows the separation and identification of individual compounds from a complex mixture based on their differing chemical properties. Chromatography separates compounds based on how strongly they adhere to a stationary phase versus a mobile phase.

First, the sample is loaded onto the stationary phase, which is a solid medium also called the **adsorbent**. Then, the **mobile phase**, which is a fluid, is run through the stationary phase to displace (or **elute**) adhered substances. Different compounds will adhere to the stationary phase with different strengths and therefore migrate with different speeds. This causes separation of the compounds within the stationary phase, allowing each compound to be isolated.

How quickly a compound travels through the stationary phase depends on a variety of factors. Several forms of media are used as the stationary phase in order to separate compounds based on different chemical properties. Chromatography is often done with silica gel as the adsorbent because it is very polar and hydrophilic. The mobile phase, usually an organic solvent of weak to moderate polarity, is then used to run the sample through the gel. In this situation, nonpolar compounds move very quickly because they dissolve well in the nonpolar mobile phase, whereas polar molecules stick tightly to the polar stationary phase.

Reverse-phase chromatography is just the opposite. In this process, the stationary phase is very nonpolar, so polar molecules run very quickly, while nonpolar molecules stick more tightly.

Size or charge may also play a role, as in column chromatography. Newer techniques, such as affinity chromatography, take advantage of unique properties of a substance, such as its ability to bind to a specific antibody, receptor, or ligand, in order to bind it to the stationary phase.

Compounds can be distinguished from each other because they travel across the stationary phase (adsorbent) at different rates. In practice, a substance can be identified based on how far it travels in a given amount of time (as in thin-layer chromatography) or how rapidly it travels a given distance (e.g., how quickly it elutes off the column in gas or column chromatography).

The four most commonly used types of chromatography are thin-layer chromatography, column chromatography, gas chromatography, and high-performance liquid chromatography.

Thin-Layer Chromatography

The adsorbent, or plate, in **thin-layer chromatography** (TLC) is either a piece of paper or a thin layer of silica gel or alumina on a plastic or glass sheet (see Figure 51.8). The mixture to be separated is placed on the adsorbent; this is called **spotting** because a small, well-defined spot is desirable. The TLC plate is then **developed**—placed upright in a developing chamber (usually a wide-mouthed jar or a beaker with a lid) containing **eluent** (solvent) approximately one-fourth of an inch deep (this value depends on the size of the plate). It is imperative that the initial spots on the plate be above the level of the solvent, or else they will simply elute off the plate into the solvent rather than moving up the plate itself. The solvent creeps up the plate by capillary action, with different compounds moving at different rates depending on their affinity for the plate versus the solvent. When the **solvent front** nears the top of the plate, the plate is removed from the chamber and allowed to dry.

The spots of individual compounds are not usually visible on the white TLC plate. They are instead **visualized** by placing the TLC plate under UV light, which shows any compounds that are UV-sensitive, or by allowing iodine to stain the spots. Other chemical staining agents include phosphomolybdic acid and vanillin. Note that these compounds destroy the product, and it cannot be recovered for further study.

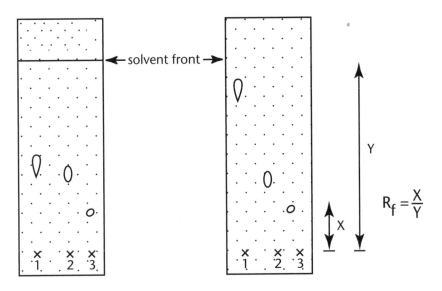

Figure 51.8

The distance a compound travels divided by the distance the solvent travels is called the **Rf value**. This value is relatively constant for each unique compound in a particular solvent and can therefore be used for identification.

TLC is most frequently used for qualitative identification (i.e., determining the identity of a compound) rather than separation. Nevertheless, it can also be used on a larger scale as a means of purification. **Preparative** or **prep TLC** uses a large TLC plate upon which a sizeable streak of a mixture is placed. As the plate develops, the streak splits into bands of individual compounds, which can then be scraped off. Rinsing with a polar solvent will recover the pure compounds from the silica.

Column Chromatography

The principle behind **column chromatography** is the same as for TLC. Column chromatography, however, uses silica gel or alumina as an adsorbent (not paper), and this adsorbent is in the form of a poured or packed column, which allows much more separation (see Figure 51.9). In TLC, the solvent and compounds move up the plate due to capillary action, whereas in column chromatography they move down the column due to the force of gravity. Sometimes the solvent is forced through the column with nitrogen gas; this is called **flash column chromatography**.

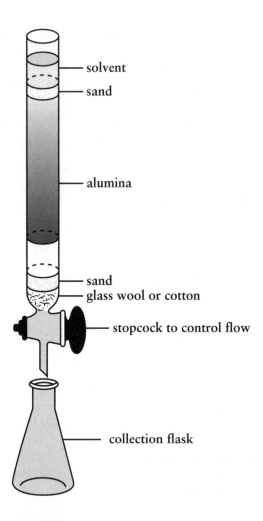

Figure 51.9

The solvent drips out of the end of the column, and fractions are collected in flasks or test tubes. These fractions contain bands corresponding to the different compounds. When the solvents are evaporated, the compounds can be isolated. In column chromatography, the silica/alumina packing is highly polar. Hence, the nonpolar fraction will be collected in the collection flasks.

Column chromatography is particularly useful in biochemistry because it can be used to separate macromolecules, such as proteins or nucleic acids.

Several specialized techniques exist:

1. In *ion exchange chromatography*, the beads in the column are coated with charged substances so they will attract or bind compounds with an opposing charge. For instance, a positively charged column will attract and hold negative substances while letting those with positive charge pass through.

2. In *size-exclusion chromatography*, the column contains beads with many tiny pores. Very small molecules can enter the beads, which slows down their progress, while large molecules move around the beads and thus travel through the column faster.

3. In *affinity chromatography*, columns can be customized to bind a substance of interest. For example, to purify substance A, a scientist might use a column of beads coated with something that binds A very tightly, such as a receptor for A, A's biological target, or even a specific antibody. This will cause substance A to bind to the column very tightly. Substance A can later be eluted by washing with free receptor (or target or antibody), which will compete with the bead-bound receptor and ultimately free substance A from the column.

Gas Chromatography

Gas chromatography (GC) is another method of qualitative separation. In gas chromatography, also called **vapor-phase chromatography** (VPC), the eluent that passes through the adsorbent is a gas, usually helium or nitrogen. The adsorbent is inside a 30-foot column that is coiled and kept inside an oven to control its temperature (see Figure 51.10). The mixture to be separated is injected into the column and vaporized. The gaseous compounds travel through the column at different rates because they adhere to the adsorbent to different degrees and will separate by the time they reach the end of the column. At this point, they are registered by a detector, which records the presence of a compound as a peak. To identify a compound or distinguish between two different compounds, the **retention times** (how long it took for each to travel through the column) are compared.

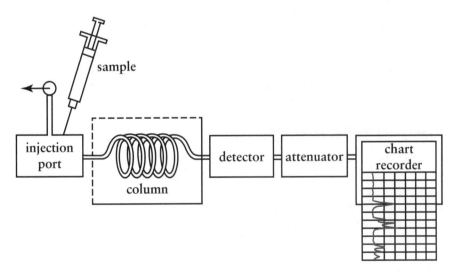

Figure 51.10

GC can be used on a larger scale for quantitative separation; it is then called preparative, or prep, GC. However, this is very tedious and difficult to perform and is rarely done.

HPLC

HPLC stands for either **high-pressure** or **high-performance liquid chromatography**. The eluent is a liquid that travels through a column similar to a GC column, but it is under pressure. In the past, very high pressures were used. Now much lower pressures can be used, hence the change from high *pressure* to high *performance*.

In HPLC, a sample is injected into the column, and separation occurs as it is pumped through. The compounds pass through a detector and are collected as the solvent flows out of the end of the apparatus. The eluent may vary, as in thin-layer or column chromatography.

The additional pressure allows for the separation of even very small samples and an increased resolving power, making HPLC a good choice when fine detail is needed, as in medical applications.

ELECTROPHORESIS

When a molecule is placed in an electric field, it will move toward either the cathode or the anode, depending on its size and charge. **Electrophoresis** employs this phenomenon to separate macromolecules, such as proteins or DNA. The migration velocity, v, of a molecule is directly proportional to the electric field strength, E, and to the net charge on the molecule, z, and is inversely proportional to a frictional coefficient, f, which depends on the mass and shape of the migrating molecules. Therefore, in a constant electric field, highly charged, small molecules will move most rapidly. Note that, in most forms of electrophoresis, the size of a macromolecule is the most important factor—small molecules move faster, whereas large ones move more slowly and may in fact take hours to leave the well.

Agarose Gel Electrophoresis

Agarose gel electrophoresis is used by molecular biologists to separate pieces of **nucleic acid** (usually **deoxyribonucleic acid**, but sometimes **ribonucleic acid** as well). Agarose is an organic gel derived from seaweed that is nontoxic and easy to manipulate. Since every piece of nucleic acid is highly negatively charged, nucleic acids can be separated effectively on the basis of size without any additional treatment to create or manage charge.

Agarose gels are stained with a compound called ethidium bromide, which binds to nucleic acids and is visualized by its fluorescence under ultraviolet light. Agarose gel electrophoresis can also be used preparatively by cutting the desired band out of the gel and eluting out the nucleic acid.

SDS-Polyacrylamide Gel Electrophoresis

SDS-polyacrylamide gel electrophoresis separates proteins on the basis of mass, not charge. Polyacrylamide gel (PAGE) is the standard medium for electrophoresis. SDS is sodium dodecyl sulfate, which disrupts noncovalent interactions. SDS binds to proteins and creates large negative net charges, overriding the protein's original net charge. Therefore, as proteins move through the gel, the only variable affecting their velocity is f, the frictional coefficient, which is dependent on mass. After separation, the gel is stained so the protein bands can be visualized.

Isoelectric Focusing

A protein may be characterized by its **isoelectric point,** pI, which is the pH at which the sum of the charges on all of its component amino acids (its net charge) is zero. Since amino acids and proteins are organic molecules, the fundamental principles of acid-base chemistry apply to them as well.

At a low pH, [H^+] is relatively high. Thus, at a pH < pI, proteins will tend to be protonated and, as a result, positively charged. At a relatively high (basic) pH, [H^+] is fairly low and proteins will tend to be deprotonated, thus carrying a negative charge.

If a mixture of proteins is placed in an electric field in a gel with a pH gradient, the proteins will move until they reach the point at which the pH is equal to their pI. At this location, the protein will be uncharged and will no longer move in the field. Molecules differing by as little as one charge can be separated in this manner, which is called **isoelectric focusing**.

SUMMARY OF PURIFICATION METHODS

Method	Use
Extraction	Separates dissolved substances based on differential solubility in aqueous versus organic solvents.
Filtration	Separates solids from liquids.
Recrystallization	Separates solids based on differential solubility; temperature is important here.
Sublimation	Separates solids based on their ability to sublime.
Centrifugation	Separates large things (like cells, organelles, and macromolecules) based on mass and density.
Distillation	Separates liquids based on boiling point, which in turn depends on intermolecular forces.
Chromatography	Uses a stationary phase and a mobile phase to separate compounds based on how tightly they adhere (generally due to polarity but sometimes size as well).
Electrophoresis	Used to separate biological macromolecules (such as proteins or nucleic acids) based on size and sometimes charge.

REVIEW PROBLEMS

1. Fractional distillation would be best used to separate which of the following compounds?
   A. Methylene chloride (b.p. 41°C) and water (b.p. 100°C)
   B. Ethyl acetate (b.p. 77°C) and ethanol (b.p. 80°C)
   C. Aniline (b.p. 184°C) and benzyl alcohol (b.p. 22°C)
   D. Aniline (b.p. 184°C) and water (b.p. 100°C)
   E. Ethyl acetate (b.p. 77°C) and aniline (b.p. 184°C)

2. Which of the following compounds would be the most effective in extracting benzoic acid from a diethyl ether solution?
   A. Tetrahydrofuran
   B. Aqueous hydrochloric acid
   C. Aqueous sodium hydroxide
   D. Aqueous acetic acid
   E. Water

3. Which of the following techniques should be used to separate red blood cells from blood plasma?
   A. Gel electrophoresis
   B. Fractional distillation
   C. Isoelectric focusing
   D. HPLC
   E. Centrifugation

Questions 4 and 5 refer to the following table.

	pI	Molecular Weight
Protein A	4.5	25,000
Protein B	6.0	10,000
Protein C	9.5	12,000

4. At which pH can the above proteins be separated by isoelectric focusing?
   A. 4.5
   B. 6.0
   C. 7.0
   D. 8.0
   E. 9.5

5. The above proteins were treated with SDS and separated by gel electrophoresis. Predict the order of migration toward the anode.

SOLUTIONS TO REVIEW PROBLEMS

1. **B** Fractional distillation is the most effective procedure for separating two liquids having boiling points that are less than 25 degrees Celsius from each another. Ethyl acetate and ethanol boil within three degrees of each other and would be good candidates for fractional distillation. In the other answer choices, the compounds have widely separated boiling points; fractional distillation could be used but is not needed since simple or vacuum distillation, which are easier to perform, would be effective.

2. **C** Benzoic acid is not soluble in cold water or acidic solutions because of its large, nonpolar ring. However, sodium hydroxide (a base) will react with benzoic acid (an acid) to produce a soluble salt, sodium benzoate. Sodium benzoate, unlike its acid counterpart, will dissolve in an aqueous solution because of the charge created by deprotonating the benzoic acid. Diethyl is a non-polar solvent that will still remain in the organic layer, which allows for the two to be separated when a basic solvent is added.

3. **E** With centrifugation, the dense blood cells would be forced to the bottom of the tube, and the less dense plasma would stay at the top, allowing for separation. Distillation (B) and high-performance liquid chromatography likely would not work; distillation would degrade the cells and proteins found in solution, whereas HPLC, which is designed for small quantities, would not be able to handle the size of the sample. Electrophoresis, (A) and (C), could separate the cells if set up correctly but is not necessary if centrifugation, which is a much simpler technique, is available.

4. **B** The three proteins may be separated when the isoelectric point of one protein is equal to the pH of the solution. Protein B has the intermediate pI at 6.0, so a good pH to choose is 6.0. At that pH, B will be neutral and will remain stationary, even in the presence of a potential difference. Since protein A is neutral at pH = 4.5, it becomes basic (negatively charged) at the relatively more basic pH of 6. Thus, at this pH, protein A migrates to the anode. On the other hand, protein C is neutral at pH = 9.6; therefore, it becomes acidic (positively charged) at the relatively more acidic pH of 6.0 and migrates to the cathode. Thus, the three proteins become separated.

5. **B > C > A**

    The order of migration in SDS-polyacrylamide gel electrophoresis is inversely proportional to the molecular weight. B, which is lightest, will move most quickly, whereas C, which is heaviest, will move most slowly.

Section V

READING COMPREHENSION

SECTION GOALS

The Reading Comprehension (RC) section of the OAT is designed to test your critical thinking skills. The higher-order components of this skill set are relatively undeveloped in most test takers, and generally require substantial practice for mastery. After completing this section of the book, you will be able to accomplish the following goals:

- Identify different question types common to OAT Reading Comprehension
- Determine the location of relevant information within the passage using a passage map
- Recognize important keywords within the text, question stem and answer choices
- Distinguish the key characteristics of the wrong answer types common to RC questions
- Analyze arguments presented within passages and questions in the RC section

CONTENT OVERVIEW

Section Specific Strategy	Chapter 52: Reading Critically
	Chapter 53: Question Types
Practice Problems	Chapter 54: Reading Comprehension Practice

KEY STUDY STRATEGIES

The Reading Comprehension section of the OAT does not require any previous knowledge of the topics presented in the passages. In fact, in this section, the reader is expected to ignore any outside knowledge of the topic and rely solely on passage information. As such, the following section of this book focuses on the critical thinking and strategy skills required to perform well on RC questions. Read Chapters 52 and 53 before completing any RC practice. After these chapters have been read and understood, use Chapter 54 to practice the strategies and skills. Following completion of the practice in Chapter 54, review the questions thoroughly, ensuring that your approach was consistent with the strategies outlined in Chapters 52 and 53. If your approach differed, develop short reminders such as "Don't rely on memory for detail questions" or "Stay in scope." Build a list of these reminders and review the list before your next practice session. For best results, complete the practice in Chapter 54 prior to any additional practice in RC. Return to the strategy chapters whenever struggling with specific question or wrong answer types.

CHAPTER FIFTY-TWO

Reading Critically

To do well on Reading Comprehension on Test Day, you need to read critically and understand why the author presents certain information. Preparing for this section, therefore, is an interesting task. You won't see any lengthy calculations, and you don't need to memorize complex science concepts. Instead, the best ways to study involve learning strategies, applying them to the reading you do from now until Test Day, and completing practice passages.

THE READING COMPREHENSION PASSAGE

The Reading Comprehension portion of the exam contains three passages consisting of approximately 14 paragraphs each. Each passage will pertain to a scientific topic. The intent of the author may be to inform, persuade, or speculate, but usually the author's tone remains roughly neutral due to the nature of the content. Subtle clues may indicate an author is for or against certain ideas, but these opinions will rarely be extreme.

Outside knowledge of each field is not required to answer questions correctly in this section, and the passages are meant to cover material you do not already know. Nevertheless, rough familiarity with the general vocabulary and writing style used in each field can build your confidence and speed you up on Test Day. Reading through recent editions of journals, such as the *Journal of the American Dental Association* and *Science*, and magazines, such as *National Geographic* and *Scientific American,* will increase your familiarity with this type of material.

Each of the three passages will be accompanied by 16–17 questions for a total of 50 questions per section. Because you will have 60 minutes total to complete this section, allot 20 minutes per passage: up to 8 minutes for reading the passage and at least 12 minutes for answering the questions. This will give you approximately 40–45 seconds per question. Neither every passage nor every question should take the same amount of time due to varying difficulty and length, so use these numbers as guidelines rather than hard rules.

OAT READING

Reading Comprehension questions are *always* about the corresponding passage. You are not necessarily looking for the answer choices that are the most factual but rather those that correspond best with the author and the passage. If you do have prior knowledge in a field, you must be careful not to apply that to the questions and instead only answer based on the information in the passage. Therefore, before you can tackle a Reading Comprehension question, you must read at least some of the corresponding passage.

There are four things you really need to know about Reading Comprehension:

First, you're not reading to learn anything. This is not information you need to carry with you for years, months, weeks, or even hours. You just need to use it in the next few minutes, and you will even be able to refer back to the passage when you need it.

Second, you're not reading to remember anything. If you try to remember what you read, you'll rely on memory—which is notoriously faulty—and your mind will be taken up with what you're trying to remember. That's not helpful. Your mind needs to be open and focused on the really important parts of the OAT: the questions. Anything you think is important enough to remember will go on your map, which is discussed later in this chapter.

Third, you don't need any outside knowledge or your own leaps of logic to read the passage well. All the correct answers are supported in the passage. As stated previously, if you use what you already know, you'll be tempted to answer questions based on your own knowledge and not on the passage. That's a classic way to choose wrong answers.

Finally, keep in mind that you're not reading to understand everything. After all, if there's no question on the part you didn't understand, it doesn't matter anyway. So you're not going to read and reread; you're just going to keep moving ahead and let the questions determine what you need to reread.

Considering all these points together shows that reading on the OAT is quite different from reading almost anything else. Therefore, how you approach the passages in the Reading Comprehension section should be different from how you read anything else. Don't fall into the easy trap of approaching the passages as you would a novel or even a textbook; instead, read critically to set yourself up for success when you get to the questions. After all, answering those questions correctly is your primary goal on Test Day, so everything you do should directly serve that goal, including how you read.

Reading Critically

Ordinarily, people read for one or both of two reasons: to learn something or to pass the time pleasantly. Neither of these reasons has anything to do with the OAT. So what do you really need to get from reading a OAT passage that's different from everyday reading? Broadly stated, there are two primary goals in reading a passage: reading for purpose—the *why* of the text and *what* the author wants you to learn from the passage—and reading for structure—the *how* of the text and the way in which the author presents the ideas. Every Reading Comprehension question type fundamentally hinges on your ability to step back from the text and analyze *what* the author is stating, *why* the author is writing in the first place, and *how* the author puts the text together.

Notice the theme here: it's all about the author. You'll get questions about the author's ideas, her purpose, what can be inferred from what she writes in the passage, and how she puts it all together. If you understand little more than the author's intent, you'll still have enough to get started with the questions, so your focus as you read must always be on the author. Therefore, pay attention not only to what details are present and where they are but also why they are there. Details are the *what* of a passage, and they never exist in a vacuum; they always support an idea.

Since the majority of the Reading Comprehension question types requires only these big-picture ideas, don't get caught up in the details themselves as you read. Instead, skim over details quickly, then reread them more closely only when a question demands it. In fact, if you follow this strategy, you won't ever need to read or understand most of the details in a passage. If you spent a significant portion of your time poring over the passage to learn and memorize all the information contained within it, you would have wasted the majority of your time. Rather than spend your time on a task not directly earning you points, quickly read through the passage for main ideas and only return to specific details when necessary.

Nevertheless, although reading all the content carefully is a waste of time, don't take that too far. There's no payoff in getting through a passage with zero comprehension. Instead, know what is important in a passage and what is not. The author's ideas are important; the details can always be researched if there are questions regarding them (all it takes to find a detail in that case is for you to shift your eyes over to view the passage, which will always be on the screen next to each of its questions). Remember that the OAT is a timed test; use your time wisely and focus on the author when reading the first time through, saving the details for a second, targeted look if a question demands it.

Using Keywords

To help you read quickly without missing important information, pay special attention to keywords, the specific words or phrases that provide structure to text. By training your eye to notice these essential words, you will be able to skim through much of each passage, slowing down to read more thoroughly only when you know an important idea is coming next. As you review the following types of keywords, add your own words to watch out for on Test Day.

Continuation keywords announce that more of the same is about to come up. Some of the most common Continuation words and phrases include:

also	*furthermore*	*in addition*	*as well as*
moreover	*plus*	*at the same time*	*equally*

Also (there's a keyword for you), the colon often does the same job: It tells you that what follows expands upon what came before, as do commas, semicolons, and dashes. When you see a Continuation keyword of any type, you can generally keep skimming if you understood what came before it since no new ideas are likely to follow.

Sequence keywords tell you there's an order to the author's ideas. Some examples are:

second (and third, fourth, etc.)	*next*
finally	*recently*

Similar to Continuation keywords, Sequence keywords show you more of the same is coming, so keep skimming.

Illustration keywords signal that an example is about to arrive. *For example* and *for instance* are very common. But think about these:

in the words of Hannah Arendt	*according to* these experts
as Maya Angelou *says*	*for* historians
to Proust	Toynbee *claims* that

In each case, what's about to follow is an example of that person's thinking. Illustration keywords also indicate you can keep skimming, but you may want to take note of any vocabulary terms or other important words that follow so you know where to return should you be required to answer a question about that detail.

Evidence keywords tell you that the author is about to provide support for a point. Here are the four most common evidence keywords:

because	*for*	*since*	*the reason is*

Although evidence keywords do show you the same point is continued, they also indicate that the author's underlying logic is coming next. If you don't have a strong grasp of the *why* behind an argument yet, you may need to pay more attention here. Otherwise, keep moving.

Contrast keywords signal an opposition or shift. There are lots of these words:

but	*however*	*although*	*not*
nevertheless	*despite*	*alternatively*	*unless*
though	*by contrast*	*yet*	*still*
otherwise	*while*	*notwithstanding*	

Contrast keywords are among the most significant in Reading Comprehension because so many passages are based on contrast or opposition. Almost certainly, something important is happening when a Contrast keyword shows up, so slow down here to ensure you follow where the argument is going next. If you are an advanced reader, you may be able to anticipate what's coming next, saving you the time of slowing down, but verify that you anticipated correctly before continuing.

Emphasis keywords may be the most welcome. Since you are reading for the author's point of view, there are no better sections to pay attention to than those where the author announces that he finds something to be important. Note these well:

above all	*most of all*	*primarily*	*in large measure*
essentially	*especially*	*particularly*	*indeed*

These words serve as great hints that the information will show up on a question, so definitely read what follows.

Conclusion keywords signal the author is about to sum up or announce the thesis. The most common is *therefore*, together with the following:

thus	*consequently*	*hence*	*in conclusion*
it can be seen	*so*	*we conclude*	*in summary*

Because these keywords have to do with the author's logic, they are especially crucial for Reading Comprehension, especially when determining the overall purpose of the passage. Slow down and read these.

THE PASSAGE MAP

To make the most of your limited reading time, take quick notes on your noteboard as you finish reading each paragraph. These notes will make up your roadmap, a literal map of the passage that shows you where to look when you need to go back and find a specific detail. Forming a roadmap also helps guide your thought processes during your first pass. You can feel confident reading quickly and focusing on the big picture ideas while ignoring most of the details because you will know exactly where to look should the need for one of those details arise.

Every passage map has four major components:

Topic: the author's basic, broad subject matter, such as *antibiotics* or *volcanoes*. The passages on the OAT will be titled according to their Topics, so you should be able to ascertain this within the first five seconds of reading.

Scope: the specific aspect of the topic that is the focus of an individual paragraph. The scope shifts throughout the passage but always relates back to the topic. For example, if the topic of a passage is *antibiotics*, an individual paragraph might have a scope of *penicillins and cephalosporins, mechanisms,* or *side effects.*

Tone: the author's attitude toward the material at hand. Since the passages are related to science topics, most authors attempt to maintain relatively neutral stances, but subtle clues can indicate if an author is *positive, negative,* or truly *neutral* toward the subject matter.

Purpose: the reason why the author wrote the passage or how he is trying to change your mind. The purpose is always a verb, such as to *explain, evaluate, argue,* or *compare.*

Figure 52.1

Each passage map component can convey extensive meanings, but your actual notes only need to contain enough information to help you remember the broader ideas. Make use of your own shorthand to ensure your notes for each item average approximately two to three words each. When you've finished your passage map, you should have written one overall topic, purpose, and tone for the entire passage and one scope for each individual paragraph, such as in Figure 52.1, above.

DISSECTING AN ARGUMENT

Some Reading Comprehension questions ask about the structure of a passage and the function of specific words, sentences, or paragraphs. Being able to characterize each component of the passage into categories—such as supporting evidence or refutation, analogy or example, detail or inference, and fact or opinion—means you not only will be able to answer questions that ask for exactly that, but you will also have a deeper understanding of the passage as a whole, which is helpful for any question.

Parts of an Argument

An **argument**, in literary terms, is a set of reasons an author uses to convince you of some point. Sometimes an author is attempting to persuade you into supporting (or dismissing) a theory; other times, he is simply teaching you new information. Either way, the author wants you to believe his main idea or **conclusion**. The evidence, examples, and logic the author uses to support that conclusion and prove he is correct are the **evidence**.

When the author directly states these ideas in the passage, they can be called **explicit**. However, sometimes the author doesn't include either the conclusion or all the evidence plainly in his writing and instead requires you to determine some of them on your own because the ideas are only **implied**.

If the author sets up all the evidence but forces you to realize his conclusion yourself, then you are making an **inference**. This can be a strong literary technique; if you come to a conclusion on your own rather than being told, you often are more likely to believe it. However, this does require some (minimal) work on your part, so the test makers use Inferences as one of their question types.

Assumptions, or implied evidence, are tested much less often. Not all possible types of evidence qualify as assumptions; instead, only the pieces of evidence required for the argument to make sense logically are classified as assumptions.

Consider the example of this statement: *Doberman Pinschers have bitten children, so no one should own any dogs.* The conclusion the speaker wants you to believe is that *no one should own any dogs;* the evidence is that *Doberman Pinschers have bitten children.* Since the conclusion is stated explicitly, you don't need to make an inference. However, several assumptions that the speaker believes to be obvious must be true for the logic to make sense: Doberman Pinschers must be representative of all dogs; otherwise, the evidence does not connect to the conclusion of *any* dog. Additionally, children being bitten must be unfavorable; if the listener actually wants children to be bitten, then the conclusion once again does not align with the evidence.

Facts and Opinions

The evidence of an argument can be further classified as fact or opinion. A **fact** is an unbiased observation or something that is irrefutable. An **opinion** interjects the author's feelings on or evaluation of a subject. To identify each, watch for the specific phrasing the author uses. Words like *should* and *seems* and phrases like *in my opinion* and *I believe* are good clues that the author is describing an opinion, but sometimes the clues are more subtle. When you need to differentiate between fact and opinion, such as in the following exercise, consider whether everyone would agree given the same data (fact) or if there could be multiple interpretations (opinion).

Practice exercise

Directions: Determine whether each statement is a fact or the author's opinion.

1. To assert that the ideal of democratic rule began with the Magna Carta is to misunderstand that the document was actually the product of a power struggle between two factions—the throne and the nobility—that were completely unconcerned about the rights of the common man.

2. Frank Lloyd Wright's designs are still held in very high regard by both the architectural community and the general public.

3. The federal government has claimed for years that reforms to make the income tax system more progressive will soon be enacted, but this seems very unlikely in light of the government's disinterest in easing the burden on low- and middle-income wage earners.

4. Some scientists believe that a layer of iridium in the Earth's crust proves a comet struck the planet, wiping out the dinosaurs; others argue that this layer was formed as the result of volcanic activity.

5. Astronomers long ago established that nebulae—clouds of interstellar gas and dust—are regions of space that give birth to new stars.

6. Literary critics have rightly concluded that the interest in "ethnic inheritance" displayed by George Eliot in her novels was sparked by her inability to feel comfortable in her own surroundings.

Solutions to practice exercise

1. **Opinion:** the statement refutes a *misunderstanding* of the Magna Carta held by others.

2. **Fact:** the statement repeats a generally acknowledged truth about Frank Lloyd Wright.

3. **Opinion:** the statement takes issue with the government's claim about taxes that *seems* unlikely.

4. **Fact:** the statement describes two different views about the origins of the iridium layer.

5. **Fact:** the statement repeats a scientific observation about the birth of stars.

6. **Opinion:** the statement describes a generally accepted interpretation of George Eliot's work as *right*.

CHAPTER FIFTY-THREE

Question Types

The test makers use the same types of questions in every Reading Comprehension section. You'll see some **comprehension** questions that test about basic facts from the passage, but you also can expect other questions that test a deeper understanding of the ideas through **analysis** and **evaluation**, so it's important to be prepared for various levels of critical thinking. Although you won't earn any points directly by identifying what type each question is on Test Day, identifying question types will help you make efficient predictions and avoid wrong answers.

QUESTION TYPES

Global

Global questions test how well you understand the passage as a whole and ask for the main idea, conclusion, or thesis of a passage or paragraph. If you follow Kaplan's passage mapping strategy (see Chapter 52, Reading Critically), then you will already have determined the overall topic and purpose of the passage as well as the scope of each paragraph before reading any of the questions. When you do reach a Global question, all you need to do is predict the answer based on your written passage map. You can identify Global questions by their use of phrases such as *main purpose, title,* or *overall point.* Although each passage generally does not have more than one Global question, these can be quick points on Test Day.

Detail

Detail questions are by far the most common question type and ask about statements found explicitly in the passage. These questions are often preceded by the phrase *according to the passage.* Detail questions are *not* asking about your own logic but merely about a statement directly from the passage. The best strategy for these questions is to use your notes as a literal map to show you where in the passage you should go to research the answer. You should be able to find phrasing in the passage that exactly or nearly exactly matches the correct answer choice. If you find yourself frequently missing Detail questions, ensure you are spending enough time researching; one hint is to not let yourself select the correct answer until you can point to the place in the passage that directly supports the answer choice you believe is correct.

Detail EXCEPT

Many questions ask you to choose the one answer that is true based on the passage. Detail EXCEPT questions reverse this and ask you to choose the one answer that is FALSE. These questions have phrasing similar to *the author mentions all of these items EXCEPT*. Four of the answer choices will appear in the passage, and one won't, so using the process of elimination is useful for these questions. Note, however, that finding four separate facts from a passage can be a slow process, so consider making quick educated guesses and saving thorough evaluation of these questions for last if you are running out of time in a section.

Tone

The author's tone or bias is rarely stated directly in a passage but is often heavily implied. Although the author of a passage may not say "I love penguins" verbatim, he may use words to describe them that indicate his opinion, such as *fascinating, remarkable, interesting,* and *superior,* to make his bias clear. Looking for these types of Opinion keywords while initially reading makes answering Tone questions straightforward, and a good prediction is one based on the overall tone of positive, negative, or neutral from your passage map. Tone questions tend to include clear indicators of their type, such as the words *tone, bias,* or *feels.*

Function

Function questions require you to evaluate the way the author constructed his argument. A limited knowledge of rhetorical strategies is helpful in answering these kinds of questions. Authors might use rhetorical questions, analogies, counterexamples, or other techniques that can be asked about in Function questions. There are two subtypes of Function questions: Structure and Evaluation. As with other question types, you will want to refer back to the passage and to your map to identify the correct answers.

Structure

Structure questions are types of Function questions that ask about how the author organized the passage or a part of the passage. For example, a Structure question might ask about the flow of the passage, requiring you to identify where the author's conclusion is within the passage and how other paragraphs relate to the author's main point. Your roadmap will be especially helpful in these kinds of questions because you'll already have an idea of how the passage was put together and can use that as your prediction. Other questions might be about specific sentences and require you to determine if the author is stating a fact or offering an opinion. When answering questions about fact versus opinion, refer back to the passage to check the context of the clause referred to in the question stem. These questions rely heavily on your ability to recognize keywords in the passage, which will frequently be sufficient to clue you in to the answer.

Evaluation

An Evaluation question takes the task in the Structure subtype one step further. Not only do you need to recognize how the author constructed the argument using rhetorical techniques, but you need to be able to consider *why* the author did something in the passage. Evaluation questions will ask you something like *Why did the author include X phrase?* or *What function does X serve in the passage?* To answer this kind of question, start by determining in which paragraph the detail occurred, then evaluate how that sentence or clause relates to the paragraph's scope, which should already be in your roadmap. If the relationship is unclear, you can find more clues by going back to the passage and looking at the surrounding sentences to identify more of the context. Consider what effect the phrase has on the rest of the paragraph or overall argument. Often these questions can be answered by identifying whether a statement is the author's conclusion or supporting evidence.

Some Evaluation questions might ask about the purpose of one paragraph and how it fits in with the rest of the passage. The question stems are usually very straightforward in these instances, asking things like *What was the purpose of paragraph X?* For this style of question, check how the paragraph's scope relates to the entire passage's purpose, both of which should already be in your roadmap. You'll likely find that these questions are fairly quick to answer.

Inference

Inference questions test your ability to use the information in the passage to draw conclusions. They may be worded in a variety of ways, such as *it can be inferred from the passage* or *the phrase X implies.* Inference questions ask you to read between the lines and find the relationships between ideas. The correct answer will be a small step from what is said directly in the passage—but only a small step. Most Inference questions have strong clues in the passage, such as a specific detail, word choice, or tone, that will help you determine just what the author is trying to convey. Although the correct answer may not be stated explicitly in the passage, you can still determine it by restating something that was said or by combining ideas from two different sentences in the passage. Stick to the evidence in the text and avoid any answer choices that seem far-fetched.

Strengthen/Weaken

The final question type tends to be the least common and pertains to how new information affects an existing argument from the passage. These questions may ask you to find the statement among the answer choices that most strengthens or weakens an argument, such as *Which of the following best supports the author's contention that X?* Other Strengthen/Weaken questions may give you new information in the question stem and ask you to determine whether it strengthens, weakens, or has no effect on a position from the passage. In either format, your task is to determine how the new information fits with what the author has already written. As when attempting the other question types, beware of applying too much of your own reasoning or outside knowledge. Instead, treat these as matching exercises. For each piece of new information, you generally will be able to find a statement in the passage that almost exactly matches (meaning the new information strengthens that argument) or that is almost exactly the opposite (meaning the new information weakens that argument). If you can't find a match, that usually means a statement has no relevant effect on what's in the passage. Sticking with the mindset that you need to find a match will allow you to quickly answer these questions and avoid the trap statements that sound good but really don't directly affect what the author is actually saying.

TRIAGING

Another benefit of identifying question types is that some types are answered in less time than others. The order of the question types listed above is an approximate order of difficulty. Typically, Global and Tone questions can be answered fairly quickly by referring to your map. Most Detail questions direct you to a specific place in the passage and require that you simply recognize or comprehend the detail in question. However, remember that Detail EXCEPT questions may be more time-consuming since they can require the process of elimination, which is slower than prediction. Function, Inference, and Strengthen/Weaken questions all require higher level skills so may be more challenging and slightly more time-consuming. Answer the lower-level questions first and then tackle the higher-level questions when working on a passage. Often, a lower-level question will help you answer a more challenging question, saving you time and earning you even more points on Test Day.

WRONG ANSWER PATHOLOGIES

Although identifying question types can help with making clear predictions of the correct answer choices, it can sometimes be just as important to know what makes an answer choice wrong as what makes one right. Wrong answer choices fall into predictable categories, and analyzing those categories allows you to get inside the mind of the test writers, which is key to maximizing your score. By identifying the common traps the test makers use, you can quickly avoid them and more easily match your predictions.

Note that many wrong answer choices correspond with multiple wrong answer pathologies. It's not important to definitively identify what makes an answer choice most wrong. Instead, as soon as you realize an answer choice is incorrect for any reason, eliminate it and keep moving. Likewise, if you have found the correct answer, don't spend time evaluating why each wrong answer choice is incorrect; in fact, evaluating all of the choices is one of the most common reasons for running out of time during a section. Instead, only use the wrong answer pathologies to aid in quickly making matches and when using the process of elimination due to being unsure of the correct answer.

Although recognizing these wrong answer pathologies is most useful in the Reading Comprehension section, the test makers use the same patterns in the other sections as well, so feel free to apply these ideas throughout the entire test!

Faulty Use of Detail

A Faulty Use of Detail is when an answer choice comes directly from the passage but does not answer the question being asked. These incorrect choices can come from a different paragraph than the one being asked about or describe ideas that are too narrow or too broad to answer the given question.

For example, Faulty Uses of Detail often are used with Global questions asking for the main idea of an entire passage. Such questions are looking for the overall topic and purpose, so any answer choices that describe only one specific scope or focus too much on only one example are incorrect. Although these specific Faulty Uses of Detail may accurately describe what is in the passage, they don't accurately reflect the main idea so are incorrect. To avoid these kinds of traps, always paraphrase and think about every question stem before tackling it to ensure you don't miss what's being asked.

Opposite

Opposite choices tend to be entirely correct except for one word, such as *not, false*, or *except*, that completely changes their meanings. Although Opposite choices are completely false as written, it can be easy to overlook that one important word in the question stem or answer choice. To avoid Opposite choices, slow down to ensure you carefully read the entire question stem and the answer you have chosen.

Distortion

Some answer choices contain parts that are correct alongside parts that are not. These often come in the form of Distortions, in which information is taken from the passage but then slightly changed to be incorrect. Similar to Opposite choices, Distortions can be wrong because of just one word, but for Distortions that word often ascribes an opinion that wasn't expressed in the passage, such as *more, better, worse*, or *preferred*.

One very common form of Distortion is the **Extreme** answer choice, which takes those ideas even further. An Extreme choice uses an idea from the passage but then adds an absolute word, such as *always, must, all, cannot*, or *never*. This tends to make a reasonable statement, such as "Most mammals bear live young," into an incorrect statement, such as "All mammals bear live young" (which is incorrect because monotremes, such as the playtpus and echidna, are mammals that lay eggs).

To avoid Distortions, ensure you have read every word of the answer choice you have chosen as correct, paraphrasing that choice to ensure it is completely right.

Out of Scope

Sometimes, an answer choice for a Reading Comprehension question describes a true statement, but that statement is not supported by information from the passage. Other times, an answer choice will seem perfectly logical but, again, is not mentioned in the passage. These are examples of Out of Scope answer choices. In the Reading Comprehension section, every correct answer must be directly supported by the passage, so using outside knowledge or even excessive reasoning can lead to choosing an incorrect answer choice. Since Out of Scope answer choices make logical sense, the best way to avoid falling into this trap is to make a strong prediction based on the passage before reading the answer choices, allowing you to bypass most choices completely since they will not match with that kind of clear prediction.

CHAPTER FIFTY-FOUR

Reading Comprehension Practice

60 minutes—50 questions

DIRECTIONS: The following test consists of several reading passages and questions that test your comprehension of the passages. Read each passage carefully, and when you believe you have sufficient comprehension of the passage, go on to the questions. You may look back at a passage as often as you wish. Each question item consists of a question or an unfinished sentence followed by possible answers or completions. After reading a question, decide which choice is best and mark your answer. For an even more realistic experience, take your online full-length practice tests.

Growth of Mammalian Teeth

The growth and development of mammalian teeth is the result of a complex series of tissue interactions that occurs during the embryonic and post-natal periods. The permanent tooth and its associated structures are composed of a wide variety of tissue types, including bone, epithelium, connective tissue, nerves, and blood vessels. Its anatomic structure is based upon a central pulp cavity containing the neural and vascular supply. This is surrounded by a layer of dentin, a yellowish material that is somewhat harder than bone. Finally, the dentin is covered by a layer of mineralized enamel, the hardest substance in the body. The dentin and enamel are each produced by highly specialized cells known as odontoblasts and ameloblasts, respectively.

The nerves responsible for pain sensation in the teeth are the superior and inferior alveolar nerves, which are derived from the fifth cranial (trigeminal) nerve. These are the sole sensory nerves for the teeth. The autonomic nervous system also innervates the teeth through the parasympathetic vasodilator fibers of the otic ganglion of the ninth cranial (glossopharyngeal) nerve and the fibers of the cervical sympathetic chain.

The blood supply to the upper jaw is provided by the superior alveolar arteries, which arise from the infraorbital and maxillary arteries. Blood to the lower jaw is carried by the inferior alveolar artery, another branch of the maxillary artery. These arteries are controlled by the vasoconstrictor fibers of the cervical sympathetic system, which stimulates contraction of the arterial smooth muscle fibers. All of the blood to the teeth comes originally from the right and left common carotid arteries, which supply the entire head and face.

The rate of tooth eruption in mammals has been studied for over 150 years. Early observations in 1823 led Oudet to conclude that rat incisors were capable of persistent growth, even in mature animals. Although it was long suspected that innervation might be responsible for control of this growth, it was not until 1919 that Moral and Hosemann were the first to measure tooth growth after cutting the inferior alveolar nerve. In 1927, Leist reported increased growth of guinea pig incisors after cutting the inferior alveolar nerve and the cervical sympathetic chain. However, he believed that the observed increase may have been due to secondary hyperemia of the pulp following the cervical sympathectomy.

This belief shifted attention, at least temporarily, away from the nervous system and toward the circulatory system. Despite the wide range of possible explanations for the control of tooth growth, the most commonly accepted theory was that first proposed by Leist—that blood supply was the important regulatory influence. it was not until the work of Butcher and Taylor in 1951 that any significant change in thought evolved.

The two investigators, working at New York University, studied five factors—blood supply, innervation, the shape of the tooth, physical stress, and the consistency of the diet—and their influence upon tooth growth rates. They explained that rat incisors were capable of two processes, eruption and attrition. The former refers to extrusion of a tooth into the oral cavity, while the latter results in a shortening of the tooth due to breakage or grinding, usually the result of normal feeding activity. Changes in tooth length were measured by initially cutting a notch in the tooth at the gingival crest. Eruption was quantified by measuring the distance between the notch and the gingival crest after a period of a few days, during which the tooth was allowed to grow. Attrition was measured as the decrease in distance from the notch to the incisal edge after breaking or grinding had occurred.

Studying the blood supply, Butcher and Taylor found that unilateral ligation of the common carotid artery decreased blood supply to teeth on the corresponding side but also produced bilateral fluctuation in eruption rate, although there was no clear decrease in tooth growth. Further, they showed that ligation of the inferior alveolar artery, while decreasing blood flow considerably, had no effect on rate of eruption. However, when all blood flow to a tooth was stopped by applying retroactive tension to the tooth, eruption ceased. Thus, the demonstration that only complete ischemia, or total lack of blood, would drastically reduce tooth growth led Butcher and Taylor to conclude that circulation was not the most important regulatory factor.

Considering innervation, they discovered that cutting the inferior alveolar nerve resulted in an average increase in growth rate of 26 to 30 percent. Teeth so denervated appeared microscopically normal, except for a decrease in nerve fibers in the periodontal tissue and pulp cavity. Sympathetic denervation in the rats had no effect on tooth growth, despite contrary results observed in guinea pigs. Likewise, removal of the rat's otic ganglion had no effect upon the rate of growth. Thus, Butcher and Taylor surmised that the role of the inferior alveolar nerve was due to its sensory fibers, since the autonomic system had no apparent influence. They hypothesized that the phenomenon was due to sensory impulses conducted from the tooth by the inferior alveolar nerve whenever the tooth met its antagonist in occlusion. This suggested the presence of a feedback system where lack of sensory impulse served as a stimulus to additional growth and presence of sensory impulse served to inhibit additional growth. A loss of the sensory nerve, then, would render the animal unable to detect normal occlusion of the tooth or injury to the tooth.

This hypothesis was tested by artificially altering the physical stress upon a tooth by adjusting its shape. When all occlusal stress was relieved by repeated fracture of the incisor, eruption rate was accelerated. Extrusion rate was increased in every case of relieved functional pressure, and the increase reached a maximum of 200 percent above normal with prolonged repeated fracture. This was considered to be the maximum growth potential of the tooth. When the tooth was allowed to resume normal contact with its antagonist, there was an immediate return of growth rate to the normal levels. Rapidly erupting teeth were found to be abnormal in cross-sectional appearance, with decreased content of dentin and enamel and a widely dilated pulp cavity. Individual odontoblasts and ameloblasts, however, were found to be normal.

Finally, the consistency of the diet and its relation to functional stress were considered, and the results further supported the sensory feedback hypothesis. The standard consistency diet of all experiments was Purina Dog Chow. To prevent fracture and grinding, a soft consistency diet of cornmeal was used; to promote fracture and grinding, a hard consistency diet of whole kernel corn was used. When animals were placed on the soft consistency diet, eruption rate decreased 20 percent from the normal value of 0.5 mm/day. The rate gradually returned to normal when the animals were returned to the dog chow.

Similarly, eruption rate increased when the rats were fed whole kernel corn, a food that caused increased fracture and grinding. The overall difference in eruption rate from the hard to soft consistency diets was 35 percent.

Thus, the work of Butcher and Taylor shifted the focus of attention from the circulatory system to the nervous system and was largely responsible for the direction and emphasis of future research. To date, no major evidence in opposition to the theory of Butcher and Taylor has been found.

1. Vasodilator nerve fibers that innervate teeth in mammals are found in

   A. the trigeminal nerve.
   B. the otic ganglion.
   C. the cervical sympathetic chain.
   D. the inferior alveolar nerve.
   E. the superior alveolar nerves.

2. Since the work of Butcher and Taylor, the accepted theory for control of tooth eruption rate has been based upon

   A. sensory nerve feedback.
   B. blood supply.
   C. the role of odontoblasts.
   D. the role of ameloblasts.
   E. None of the above

3. In the experiment described in the passage, when a rat on a soft diet was returned to the standard consistency diet, its tooth growth rate

   A. remained depressed.
   B. immediately returned to normal.
   C. gradually returned to normal.
   D. remained elevated.
   E. decreased even further.

4. Which of the following statements correctly summarizes the sensory feedback hypothesis of Butcher and Taylor?

   A. Lack of sensory impulse causes increased blood flow to the tooth.
   B. Lack of sensory impulse causes decreased tooth growth rate.
   C. Lack of sensory impulse causes gradual pulp ischemia.
   D. Lack of sensory impulse causes increased tooth growth rate.
   E. The absence of a feedback system allows for an increased tooth growth rate.

5. Teeth that are denervated by cutting the inferior alveolar nerve show

   A. an average decrease in growth rate of 30 percent.
   B. no change in normal growth rate.
   C. an average increase in growth rate of 45 percent.
   D. no change in microscopic appearance except for a proliferation of capillaries.
   E. no change in microscopic appearance except for a decrease in nerve fibers.

6. Removal of the otic ganglion in rats

   A. caused an immediate increase in growth rate.
   B. caused an immediate decrease in growth rate.
   C. caused a delayed decrease in growth rate.
   D. caused a delayed increase in growth rate.
   E. had no effect on growth rate.

7. Before 1951, tooth growth was commonly thought to be regulated by

   A. diet.
   B. physical stress.
   C. blood supply.
   D. innervation.
   E. both (C) and (D).

8. Which of the following would be most likely to cause the greatest increase in blood supply to the teeth in mammals?

   A. A cervical sympathectomy
   B. Ligation of the common carotid artery
   C. Cutting the inferior alveolar nerve
   D. Removal of the otic ganglion
   E. Ligation of the inferior alveolar nerve

9. Based on information in the passage, which of the following statements best defines the term *antagonistic teeth*?

   A. Two adjacent teeth on the upper jaw

   B. Two adjacent teeth on the lower jaw

   C. Two teeth with opposite functional properties

   D. One tooth on the upper jaw, one on the lower

   E. Upper and lower teeth that meet in normal biting

10. According to the author, odontoblasts are responsible for the production of

    A. enamel.

    B. dentin.

    C. pulp.

    D. gingival tissue.

    E. dentin and enamel.

11. In the experiments on normal adult rats, significant incisor growth could be measured within

    A. 24 hours.

    B. 48 hours.

    C. 72 hours.

    D. 1 week.

    E. 2 weeks.

12. The greatest increase in eruption rate was achieved by

    A. altering the consistency of the diet.

    B. relieving the tooth of all functional stress.

    C. ligating the common carotid artery.

    D. removing the otic ganglion.

    E. returning the tooth to normal contact with its antagonist.

13. The central structure of the adult tooth is composed of

    A. epithelium.

    B. mineralized enamel.

    C. cementum.

    D. nerves and blood vessels.

    E. bone.

14. To destroy pain sensation in the teeth, which of the following nerves must be cut?

    A. The ninth cranial nerve

    B. The cervical sympathetic fibers

    C. The otic ganglion

    D. The glossopharyngeal nerve

    E. The inferior alveolar nerve

15. What observation was made about rat teeth that were permitted to grow at their maximum potential rate?

    A. They were more prone to fracture.

    B. They were lacking in nerve fibers.

    C. They had decreased amounts of dentin and enamel.

    D. They had unusually small pulp cavities.

    E. They appeared normal at the microscopic level.

16. Which of the following may be concluded from the observation of Butcher and Taylor?

    A. Teeth are more likely to fracture in older mammals.

    B. Occlusal stress may account for suppression of the maximum tooth growth rate.

    C. Mammals fed a "soft" diet will exhibit an increased number of ameloblasts.

    D. Occlusion involves only antagonistic teeth.

    E. Circulation plays a critical role in the regulation of tooth growth.

17. Butcher and Taylor's findings on the effects of dietary consistency upon tooth growth rate

    A. are inconsistent with the hypothesis of a sensory feedback system.

    B. show that consistency of the diet has little effect on rate of tooth eruption in rats, even if the diet consists solely of Purina Dog Chow.

    C. suggest that a mechanism other than sensory feedback affects tooth growth rate.

    D. are irrelevant, since rats would never duplicate the experimental diet under normal circumstances.

    E. indicate that tooth growth rate is affected by more than one factor.

RC

Population Estimates

Since estimates of future population growth are based on projections regarding complex and changeable social factors, it is not surprising to find that the estimates are often markedly inaccurate. For several decades following World War II, unprecedented population growth in the United States exceeded all projections. A 1947 Census Bureau prediction of the U.S. population in 1970, for example, underestimated the actual 1970 population by 65 million, falling far short of the count of 205 million that year. Today, predicting population growth is still an inexact science, but discrepancies often stem from overestimation rather than underestimation. Only a few years ago, demographers projected that our national population would reach the 300 million mark in the year 2000, but even after the turn of the century, the nation's population has not reached that mark. Such discrepancies stem from the fact that population predictions involve a certain amount of guesswork. The complexity and variability of social and economic factors involved in predicting population make the enterprise one of educated speculation.

Population predictions are based primarily upon studies of the "total fertility rate" of a country, defined as the average number of births a woman is expected to have over the course of her reproductive life. This rate is related to the "replacement level," a constant that describes the fertility rate at which a population neither grows nor declines. Today, the U.S. fertility rate is 1.7, considerably less than the replacement level of 2.1, so our population is expected to decrease. While demographers differ on exactly why and to what extent this diminution will occur, many agree that the decline in fertility is related to changes in the status and expectations of women.

Radical and rapid changes in attitudes toward marriage and family partly explain recent unanticipated declines in the rate of U.S. population growth. In the past few decades, there has been a considerable decline in the number of women who marry young. In 1960, only 29 percent of women under 24 had never married; by 1978, that percentage had jumped to 48 percent. This seems related to the tendency for unmarried couples to postpone marriage and live together, an arrangement that has become increasingly popular in recent years. Whether cohabitation is a likely prelude to marriage or an indication of a basic change in attitudes toward that institution, it is clear that cohabitation results in lower fertility than does marriage. Growing instability of marital relationships also affects fertility rates: As marriage rates have declined, divorce rates have increased, with half of all American marriages ending in divorce.

The shifting economic role that women play in society also effects childbearing. The relationship between fertility and the growing participation of women in the workplace is complex. A few demographers actually suggest that there is a positive correlation between women's working and fertility; this school of thought speculates that because increased prosperity positively affects fertility, women's economic gains will result in boosted fertility rates. But most demographers agree that work and fertility are negatively correlated in women. Some believe that women will have fewer children in order to facilitate their ability to join the workforce and gain financial stability. Others claim that, at the same time as increasingly effective methods of contraception have given women greater control over their own childbearing, the growing financial independence of women has weakened the economic rationale for marriage. This theory suggests that marriage offers women financial security in return for their childbearing and housekeeping services. Thus, if women no longer need to "barter" for economic support, childbearing becomes less of an automatic and expected social response.

In addition to the changing attitudes and status of women, even larger, more sweeping processes are at work in declining birthrates. Broad societal trends, including increasing urbanization and decreasing religiosity, are playing a significant role in lowering fertility rates. Migration to urban areas, for instance, has stripped away a powerful economic incentive for childbearing. In agrarian economies, there is a need for large families, as children play an important role in agricultural production. But in industrial economies, children are—in an economic sense—burdens, as they consume limited resources without producing much in return.

Similarly, declining subscription to traditional religious values weakens the emphasis formerly placed upon, and reduces attachment to, family and childbearing. Some demographers have argued that the spread of evangelical religious movements, with their strong emphasis on traditional values, may eventually reverse this trend, but this seems doubtful. While these movements are certainly attracting an increasing number of followers, they appeal mainly to rural elements of the population. Put differently, evangelical movements tend to attract people who are already very religious, so it is unlikely that their ultimate impact on demographic trends will be significant.

Hence, most demographers now agree that a declining birthrate is a long-term feature of U.S. society, especially since there does not appear to be any sense of urgency about altering the status quo. Indeed, the general belief about desirable population levels in this country was best summed up by the Commission on Population Growth and the American Future, which concluded that declining fertility was a positive development, since it may—in sheer terms of numbers—help to alleviate many of our most pressing social and economic problems.

Consequently, the United States has expressed no interest in pronatalist policies. In contrast, many nations in both Eastern and Western Europe have instituted a wide variety of pronatalist measures. In most instances, national security was cited as the reason for their introduction—demographic projections for many of these nations predicted rapid falls in population by the 21st century. Whatever the case, pronatalist polices led to an almost immediate rise in European birthrates. In former East Germany, for example, the birthrate went from 10.6 per 1,000 inhabitants in 1975 to 13.3 in 1977. Most of these countries have thus far restricted themselves mainly to liberal economic measures, such as family cash allowances, generous tax relief, subsidized child care services, and improved housing.

Should the U.S. government ever decide that the declining birthrate has become a threat to the nation's well-being, it may very well take steps to encourage population growth similar to those adopted by European countries. If that were to occur, once again demographers would have to drastically revise today's population predictions.

18. According to the passage, in 1947 the Census Bureau estimated that the 1970 U.S. population would be

    A. 205 million.
    B. 65 million.
    C. 283 million.
    D. 140 million.
    E. 270 million.

19. Which of the following statements best expresses the author's opinion about the relationship between marriage and the economic status of women?

    A. Lower economic status generally results in reduced fertility.
    B. Working women give birth to fewer children than do nonworking women.
    C. The effect of women's economic position on fertility has not yet been determined.
    D. Women who receive economic support tend to exhibit lower fertility rates.
    E. Urban women of lower economic status have higher birth rates than do rural women of lower economic status.

20. The "replacement level" is defined as

    A. the number of births the average woman has over her lifetime.
    B. the difference between a nation's birth and death rates.
    C. the birthrate necessary to ensure population growth.
    D. the number of deaths that must occur in order to keep the population from increasing.
    E. the birthrate at which a nation's population will remain stable.

21. Which of the following "total fertility rates" would most probably signal an increase in U.S. population?

    A. 2.0
    B. 1.7
    C. 1.8
    D. 2.1
    E. 2.4

22. The author mentions the increasingly popular trend of cohabitation in order to

    A. make a generalization about shifting moral values.
    B. support the claim that marriage is losing its economic rationale.
    C. provide an example of a social factor that contributes to lower fertility rates.
    D. underscore the relationship between cohabitation and increased divorce rates.
    E. recommend it as a guarantor of increased fertility.

23. Which of the following would most demographers probably NOT consider a factor in decreasing fertility rates?

    A. Increasingly effective methods of birth control
    B. Greater societal acceptance of childless marriages
    C. Growing demand for women in the workplace
    D. Liberalized attitudes toward unwed motherhood
    E. An increasing divorce rate

24. It can be inferred from the author's discussion of the economic rationale for marriage that

    A. the institution of marriage has generally lost its romantic veneer.
    B. women seek financial security when choosing husbands.
    C. romantic illusions often mask exploitive financial relationships.
    D. marriage is an idyllic state of shared responsibility.
    E. some demographers consider marriage primarily an economic relationship.

25. Which of the following is the most appropriate alternative title for the passage?

    A. Decline in Birthrate Illustrates New Social Realities

    B. Growth Rate Falls as Women's Economic Status Improves

    C. Demographers Admit Futility of Population Prediction

    D. Shifting Social Values Lessen Nation's Social and Economic Ills

    E. New Women's Attitudes and National Birthrate Trends

26. According to the passage, the Commission on Population Growth and the American Future concluded that declining fertility will

    A. harm our national security.

    B. improve our quality of life.

    C. make our political problems more severe.

    D. convince our government to adopt pronatalist policies.

    E. escalate the divorce rate.

27. Which of the following is NOT mentioned in the passage as a pronatalist measure?

    A. Tax relief

    B. Cash allowances

    C. Subsidized child care

    D. Land grants

    E. Improved housing

28. According to most demographers, the U.S. birthrate will

    A. decline for a few more years but then increase.

    B. decline steadily for the indefinite future.

    C. increase over the next decade but then decline.

    D. increase drastically over the next couple of centuries.

    E. remain stable, without decline or increase.

29. The primary purpose of the first paragraph is to

    A. suggest that demographers are poor statisticians.

    B. argue that predicting population is difficult.

    C. prove that Census Bureau figures are highly accurate.

    D. discuss the social and economic factors that affect population estimates.

    E. analyze the Census Bureau's prediction of the U.S. population in 1970.

30. Many European nations have adopted pronatalist measures because

    A. their immigrant populations are expanding at alarming rates.

    B. they want to encourage long-term economic growth.

    C. they wish to reflect American pronatalist policies.

    D. their populations are heavily influenced by traditional religious values.

    E. they believe that population levels affect national security.

31. Rural families tend to be larger than their urban counterparts. The passage implies that this is because

    A. children are important as productive members of agrarian economies.

    B. rural couples are more likely to be traditional and religious.

    C. women are less likely to pursue careers in an agrarian environment.

    D. rural couples experience less difficulty conceiving than urban couples.

    E. urban couples are better educated about the use of contraception.

32. The author believes that the growth of evangelical religious movements will

    A. eventually lead to an upswing in the U.S. birthrate.

    B. cause an immediate drop in the U.S. birthrate.

    C. have no real impact on the U.S. birthrate.

    D. cause an upswing in the U.S. birthrate initially but a drop in the long run.

    E. cause an eventual decline in the U.S. birthrate.

33. The passage suggests that, in the future, young women will become

    A. more interested in marrying at a young age.

    B. less likely to give birth out of wedlock.

    C. more interested in pursuing a career.

    D. less interested in being financially independent.

    E. uninterested in maintaining a long-term career.

34. The author suggests that current population predictions

    A. are extremely accurate.

    B. overestimate the actual population.

    C. underestimate the actual population.

    D. ignore the growth of illegal immigrant populations.

    E. are anomalous in their inaccuracy.

RC

Nutrition

Adequate nutrition is essential to the development, growth, and sustenance of the human organism. A good diet must supply the body with sufficient energy to power all life support activities. Amino acids play an important role in this dietary process.

The amino acid molecule is composed of an amino group (-NH$_2$), a carboxyl group (-COOH), a hydrogen atom (-H), and a unique R group (or side chain), all bonded to a central alpha carbon atom (C). Although amino acids occur in two stereoisomeric forms, *D*- (dextrorotary) and *L*- (levorotary), only the *L*-form is nutritionally active in the human body. There are twenty *L*-amino acids in total, each identifiable by its side chains, which differ in terms of size, shape, charge, hydrogen-bonding capacity, and chemical reactivity.

The primary role of *L*-amino acids is to provide the biologically active building blocks for proteins. Proteins are formed when groups of amino acids become linked in polypeptide chains. Peptide bonds are formed between the alpha-carboxyl group of one amino acid and the alpha-amino group of the next. These polypeptide chains link in turn to become proteins—in certain cells, they become the precursors of neurotransmitters, skin pigments, or hormones. All twenty amino acids must be present for the complete range of body proteins to be synthesized. The human body is capable of synthesizing several amino acids, such as alanine, glutamate, and proline, and these are classified as nonessential in dietary terms. Others, however, designated essential amino acids, must be supplied in the diet. The absence of any single amino acid disrupts protein synthesis and can result in a negative nitrogen balance within the body. When this occurs, protein degradation exceeds protein synthesis, and the body excretes a greater quantity of nitrogen than it ingests to replace it.

The body obtains essential amino acids by extracting them from food proteins in the digestive process, which begins in the stomach. Firstly, the oxyntic (parietal) cells of the fundic gastric glands lower the pH level of the stomach by secreting 0.15 M HCl into the stomach. Zymogenic (chief) cells secrete quantities of pepsin, the first proteolytic enzyme to break down the ingested proteins, as well as rennin, an enzyme that curdles milk. The pepsin is secreted in an inactive form (pepsinogen) and is converted to the active enzymatic form by the acid. In this state, it catalyzes the hydrolysis of the peptide bonds between amino acids within the proteins.

The majority of protein degradation and absorption occurs in the small intestine. The two primary proteolytic enzymes of the small intestine are trypsin and chymotrypsin. Trypsin breaks polypeptide chains on the carboxyl side of arginine and lysine residues. Chymotrypsin, on the other hand, cleaves preferentially on the carboxyl side of aromatic and other bulky, nonpolar amino acids.

The major end products of digestion are *L*-amino acids, which are absorbed by the intestinal mucosa cells through a complex transport mechanism. First, a basolateral membrane Na$^+$-K$^+$-ATPase pump (powered by cellular ATP) sets up a favorable concentration gradient, where the concentration of sodium ions is greater outside the cell than inside. Then, as sodium ions diffuse into the cell, *L*-amino acids are transported simultaneously with sodium ions across the cell membrane.

The intestinal mucosal cells are also capable of absorbing dipeptides and tripeptides; their microvillus membranes contain enzymes that specifically split off dipeptides from the amino terminal end of protein polypeptide chains prior to absorption. All of the amino acids absorbed from the lumen of the intestine are then transported by the mucosal cells into the blood, where they proceed to the liver via the hepatic portal system. Any excess of absorbed amino acids, above that required for protein synthesis, is not stored in the body and is much too valuable to be excreted. Instead, surplus amino acids are degraded in the liver and utilized as metabolic fuel.

Amino acid degradation primarily involves conversion of the alpha-amino group to urea. This group is transferred to the molecule alpha-ketoglutarate to form glutamate, which is subsequently oxidatively deaminated to the ammonium ion (NH_4^+) by the enzyme glutamate dehydrogenase, then converted via the enzymes of the urea cycle into the excretion product.

A special class of enzymes called transaminases catalyzes the transfer of the amino group from an alpha-amino acid to an alpha-keto acid, such as alpha-ketoglutarate. These transaminases require a prosthetic group (or coenzyme) called pyridoxal phosphate, which is derived from pyridoxine (vitamin B6) to become active. The transaminase enzyme has a terminal lysine residue at its active site that combines with the aldehyde group of pyridoxal phosphate in a covalent Schiff-base linkage prior to the binding of the amino acid substrate. The transaminases form a new covalent Schiff-base intermediate with the alpha-amino group of the amino acid, which displaces an epsilon-amino group of the enzyme's active site lysine. As a result of this reaction, the pyridoxal phosphate is converted to pyridoxamine phosphate, and the alpha-amino becomes an alpha-keto acid. The pyridoxamine phosphate-enzyme complex subsequently combines with alpha-ketoglutarate to yield glutamates and a regenerated pyridoxal phosphate enzyme. Other pyridoxal phosphate enzymes can catalyze decarboxylations, deaminations, racemizations, and aldol cleavages of amino acid substrates.

The main benefits of the transamination process are that it enables the glutamate formed to be oxidatively deaminated by glutamate dehydrogenase to regenerate alpha-ketoglutarate and thus form ammonium ions for the urea cycle. In this particular process, either NAD^+ or $NADP^+$ are energized with electrons to form NADH or NADPH respectively, and both can be used as electron carriers. NADH is an active electron carrier in oxidative phosphorylation, which generates cellular ATP, whereas NADPH is more active in reductive biosynthesis.

The process of energy production is controlled by the enzyme glutamate dehydrogenase and pre-existing cellular energy levels. It is an allosterically regulated enzyme (i.e., it is only active when low-energy precursors are present, such as ADP and GDP). Conversely, it is inhibited when high-energy molecules are in abundance, such as ATP and GTP. Thus, under low-energy states, surplus amino acids can generate high-energy molecules and raise the caloric content in the body. In contrast, amino acid carbon skeletons are transformed into acetyl-CoA, pyruvate, or one of the intermediates of the citric acid cycle. The citric acid cycle is the final common route of oxidation of fuel molecules such as carbohydrates, fatty acids, and amino acids. The reactions of this cycle occur within the cells' mitochondria, and most fuel molecules enter as acetyl-CoA. However, some amino acids enter the cycle in the form of intermediates. Phenylalanine (derived from phenylpyruvate) is degraded to tyrosine by phenylalanine hydroxylase, and tyrosine is further transaminated back to p-hydroxyphenylpyruvate (the precursor of tyrosine), which is in turn oxidized to homogentisate. Homogentisate oxidase then converts homogentisate to 4-maleylacetoacetate, which is subsequently isomerized and hydrolyzed to become acetoacetate and fumarate, a cycle intermediate.

Those amino acids that are degraded to acetyl-CoA or acetoacetyl-CoA are called ketogenic and ultimately may also give rise to the ketone bodies acetone, D-3-hydroxybutyrate, and acetoacetate, which is a preferred fuel of heart muscle and renal cortex cells. Other amino acids are called glucogenic because they are degraded to pyruvate and fumarate or oxaloacetate. Of all the twenty acids, only leucine is purely ketogenic, while isoleucine, lysine, phenylalanine, tryptophan, and tyrosine are both ketogenic and glucogenic. The remaining fourteen amino acids are purely glucogenic.

35. Negative nitrogen balance is a state in the body in which

    A. essential amino acids are absent.

    B. protein synthesis exceeds protein degradation.

    C. protein degradation exceeds protein synthesis.

    D. the body ingests too much nitrogen.

    E. both (A) and (C) are correct.

36. When the alpha-carboxyl group of one amino acid is bonded to the alpha-amino group of the subsequent amino acid, this is called

    A. a hydrogen bond.

    B. a polar covalent.

    C. a nonpolar covalent bond.

    D. a peptide bond.

    E. an ionic bond.

37. The low pH of the stomach is provided by the

    A. secretion of 0.25 M HCl by chief cells.

    B. secretion of 0.15 M HCl by parietal cells.

    C. secretion of 0.15 M phosphoric acid by oxyntic cells.

    D. secretion of 10 M HCl by oxyntic cells.

    E. secretion of 0.15 M HCl by zymogenic cells.

38. In the process of absorption, an L-amino acid is cotransported with

    A. a K^+ ion.

    B. a Cl^- ion.

    C. a Na^+ ion.

    D. a Na^+ and a Cl^- ion simultaneously.

    E. a glucose molecule.

39. Transamination is the enzymatic process

    A. of transferring the alpha-amino group of an alpha-amino acid to an alpha-keto acid.

    B. of transferring the alpha-amino group of an alpha-keto acid to an alpha-amino acid.

    C. of transferring the carboxyl group of an alpha-amino acid to a lysine residue.

    D. used to split and transfer a carboxyl group from an alpha-amino acid to an alpha-keto acid.

    E. used to create pyridoxine.

40. Which of the following amino acids is purely ketogenic?

    A. Tyrosine

    B. Phenylalanine

    C. Leucine

    D. Isoleucine

    E. Tryptophan

41. Ketone bodies are

    A. D-3-hydroxybutyrate molecules.

    B. acetone molecules.

    C. used by renal and heart cells as fuel.

    D. products of degradation.

    E. All of the above

42. Pyridoxal phosphate enzymes

    A. can only catalyze transaminations.

    B. catalyze aldol cleavages of amino acids.

    C. catalyze carboxylations of amino acids.

    D. All of the above

    E. None of the above

43. The bond formed by a transaminase and its coenzyme

    A. is a covalent Schiff-base reaction.

    B. is a noncovalent Schiff-base reaction.

    C. occurs between a lysine residue of the enzyme and an aldehyde group of the coenzyme.

    D. occurs between a tyrosine residue of the enzyme and a carboxyl group of the coenzyme.

    E. both (A) and (C) are correct.

44. The main benefit of transamination is the

    A. conversion of coenzyme to NH_4^+.

    B. decrease in the caloric content of the body.

    C. generation of GDP and ADP.

    D. generation of NADH to participate in oxidative phosphorylation.

    E. catabolism of ammonium ions.

45. The main site of amino acid degradation in the body is
    A. the pancreas.
    B. the stomach.
    C. the small intestine.
    D. the liver.
    E. the gall bladder.

46. Side chains of amino acids differ in regard to which of the following?
    A. Size
    B. Hydrogen-binding capacity
    C. Shape
    D. Charge
    E. All of the above

47. The enzyme glutamate dehydrogenase is allosterically regulated, such that
    A. an increase in GTP and ATP levels activates the enzyme.
    B. an increase in UTP and GTP levels activates the enzyme.
    C. an increase in GDP and ADP levels activates the enzyme.
    D. only an increase in UTP activates the enzyme.
    E. only a decrease in UTP activates the enzyme.

48. Trypsin and chymotrypsin cleave protein polypeptide chains at or between
    A. the same site.
    B. different sites.
    C. arginine and lysine residues for trypsin and aromatic residues for chymotrypsin.
    D. (A), (B), and (C) are correct.
    E. both (B) and (C) are correct.

49. Amino acid degradation involves
    A. transamination.
    B. change of amino acids to acetyl-CoA and acetoacetyl-CoA.
    C. change of amino acids to pyruvate and fumarate.
    D. conversion of the alpha-amino group to urea.
    E. All of the above

50. Which of the following compounds can act as electron carriers in oxidative phosphorylation?
    A. $NADP^+$
    B. NAD^+
    C. Both NADPH and NADH
    D. ATP
    E. None of the above

Answers and explanations begin on the next page ▶ ▶ ▶

ANSWERS AND EXPLANATIONS

Answer Key

1.	B	26.	B
2.	A	27.	D
3.	C	28.	B
4.	D	29.	B
5.	E	30.	E
6.	E	31.	A
7.	C	32.	C
8.	A	33.	C
9.	E	34.	B
10.	B	35.	E
11.	C	36.	D
12.	B	37.	B
13.	D	38.	C
14.	E	39.	A
15.	C	40.	C
16.	B	41.	E
17.	E	42.	B
18.	D	43.	E
19.	B	44.	D
20.	E	45.	D
21.	E	46.	E
22.	C	47.	C
23.	D	48.	E
24.	E	49.	E
25.	A	50.	C

EXPLANATIONS

1. B

The passage states that the vasodilator nerve fibers are parasympathetic fibers found in the otic ganglion of the glossopharyngeal nerve, making choice (B) correct. They are not found in the inferior alveolar nerve, the superior alveolar nerve, a branch of the trigeminal nerve, or the cervical sympathetic chain. Thus, answer choices (A), (C), (D), and (E) are all incorrect.

2. A

Each of the five factors (blood supply, innervation, shape of the tooth, physical stress, and the consistency of the diet) that Butcher and Taylor examined pointed to sensory nerve feedback, choice (A), as the predominant controller of the rate of tooth growth. While the blood supply was thought at one point in time to be important in tooth eruption, Taylor and Butcher concluded that it was not the most important regulatory factor. In addition, the accepted theory for control of tooth eruption rate since Butcher and Taylor has not been based in the roles of odontoblasts or of ameloblasts.

3. C

Although animals which were placed on a soft consistency diet experienced decreases of tooth eruption rate of up to 20 percent from the normal value of 0.5 mm/day, the passage states that the animals' eruption rates gradually returned to normal when the animals returned to the dog chow (the standard consistency diet).

4. D

The passage states that Butcher and Taylor surmised that the sensory fibers of the inferior alveolar nerve would provide a feedback system where a lack of sensory impulse would serve as a stimulus for a tooth to grow—choice (D)—and, conversely, the presence of a sensory impulse would serve to inhibit a tooth's growth. The sensory feedback hypothesis did not address the lack of sensory impulses and their relation to blood flow or ischemia.

5. E

After cutting the inferior alveolar nerve, Butcher and Taylor discovered that teeth demonstrated an average increase in growth rate of 26–30 percent, not 45 percent as in choice (C). When examined microscopically, these teeth were normal except for a decrease in nerve fibers. Therefore, choice (D) is incorrect.

6. E

In contrast to the question above, denervation of the otic ganglion had no effect on growth rate. Butcher and Taylor surmised that this was due to the presence of sensory fibers in the inferior alveolar nerve that were not present in the autonomic nerves.

7. C

The passage states that prior to 1951 and subsequent to 1927, the most commonly accepted theory of tooth growth was the one proposed by Leist—that blood supply was the important regulatory influence. Although innervation was considered at one time, it is not the optimal answer because in the years pursuant to 1951, blood supply was more highly considered. Physical stress and diet were never thought to be extremely important regulators of tooth growth.

8. A

The passage states that following cervical sympathectomy, a secondary hyperemia (increase in blood flow to the site of innervation) occurs. Therefore, choice (A) would be most correct. Ligation of the common carotid artery would decrease the amount of blood flow to teeth, and the denervation of the inferior alveolar nerve would have little to do with blood supply. Finally, the removal of the otic ganglion may actually decrease the amount of blood to the teeth due to the presence of parasympathetic autonomic nerve fibers in the otic ganglion.

9. E

The use of the word *antagonist* in the passage refers to a tooth that makes normal contact with another. Therefore, answer choice (E) is most correct. While the word *antagonists* might conjure up images of teeth with opposite functional properties—choice (C), it was not used in this context in the passage. Clearly, answer choices (A) and (B) are incorrect; they are not mentioned as valid choices in the passage. Finally, answer choice (D) is too vague—choice (E) is far more accurate.

10. B

The author states that odontoblasts are responsible for the production of dentin and that ameloblasts are responsible for the production of enamel. The pulp is littered with neural and vascular supply, and the author does not mention the origin of gingival tissue.

11. C

The passage states that eruption (the extrusion of a tooth into the oral cavity) was measured by examining the distance between the notch (cut initially at the gingival crest) and the gingival crest after a period of a few days (during which time the tooth was allowed to grow). Three days, or 72 hours, is the best choice.

12. B

The passage states that ligating the common carotid artery or removing the otic ganglion did nothing to affect the eruption rate. Altering the consistency of the diet, while affecting the eruption rate slightly, could not compare to relieving the tooth of all functional stress (which was shown to increase eruption by 200 percent). Finally, returning the tooth to normal contact with its antagonist reinstituted normal growth rates.

13. D

The passage specifically states that the central pulp cavity of a tooth contains the neural and vascular supply. The mineralized enamel is a layer that covers the dentin, which in turn surrounds the central pulp cavity. No mention is made of cementum or bone in the composition of the central structure of the adult tooth.

14. E

The inferior alveolar nerve carries sensory nerve fibers that the cervical sympathetic fibers and the otic ganglion do not. While the glossopharyngeal nerve does have sensory fibers, this nerve does not innervate the teeth. Therefore, the inferior alveolar nerve is the most correct answer.

15. C

The passage states that Butcher and Taylor found that rapidly erupting teeth were abnormal in cross-sectional appearance (thus, answer choice (E) is not correct). They possessed decreased contents of dentin and enamel—choice (C)—and a widely dilated pulp cavity (therefore, choice (D) is not correct). No mention was made of their propensity for fracture or their abundance of nerve fibers; therefore, these answers—choices (A) and (B)—are incorrect.

16. B

According to the sensory feedback hypothesis proposed by Butcher and Taylor, it is the absence of sensory influences that causes an increase in the growth rate of teeth. No mention is made of tooth fracture and older mammals or of the occlusive ability of nonantagonistic teeth. Mammals fed on a "soft" diet exhibit a decrease in the eruption rate, indicating—if anything—a decrease in the number of ameloblasts.

17. E

Butcher and Taylor's experiments revealed that both occlusal stress and diet consistency affected tooth eruption. This corresponds to many other findings in science, namely that they are multifactorial. The fact that dietary consistency affected tooth growth rate does not obviate the hypothesis of a sensory feedback system, nor does it suggest that a sole mechanism other than sensory feedback affects tooth growth rate. These diet consistency experiment results are relevant and should be examined from a multifactorial perspective.

18. D

The passage states the census count for the year 1970 was 205 million people and that the 1947 Census Bureau prediction was 65 million short of that. Therefore, 140 million was the predicted number.

19. B

Although the author concedes that some demographers believe that there is a positive correlation between women's working and fertility, he argues that most demographers agree that work and fertility are negatively correlated in women. He also believes that higher economic status of women generally results in reduced fertility and that women who receive economic support (i.e., are dependent upon it) tend to exhibit higher fertility rates. Finally, although the author states that higher economic status is associated with lower fertility, he never compares the fertility rates of women of lower economic status in rural and urban areas. One factor that immediately undermines this supposition is the indication that urbanization provides fewer incentives for childbearing and has thus played a role in lowering fertility rates.

20. E

The passage defines "replacement level" as a birthrate at which a nation's population will remain stable (will neither decline nor grow). Note that the question stem refers to "replacement," which implies a need for production to fill a void (or births to fill the population void caused by deaths). Thus, one could automatically eliminate choice (D), which only focuses on deaths, and choice (C), which refers to actual growth, not just replacement. Choice (A) is incorrect, as well, as it refers to "total fertility rate" as defined in the passage, and choice (B) is incorrect as it refers to a measurement of a status quo, not of a determined "level."

21. E

The total fertility rate of a country is defined as the average number of births a woman is expected to have over the course of her reproductive life. This rate is related to the replacement level (the fertility rate at which population remains stable), which is defined as 2.1 in the passage. As the total fertility rate must exceed the replacement rate for population growth to occur, the answer choice must be greater than 2.1. Choice (E) satisfies this requirement.

22. C

The author cites cohabitation as an example of a social factor that contributes to lower fertility rates. She makes little judgment about shifting moral values; she does not support the claim that marriage is losing its economic rationale. In addition, the author never correlates cohabitation with increased divorce rates. Finally, cohabitation is anything but a guarantor of fertility, as the author indicates that it is more clearly associated with lower fertility rates than is marriage.

23. D

The author cites several factors that demographers believe to be important in decreasing fertility rates. They include contraception, more women working, increased societal acceptance of childless marriages, and increased divorce rates. However, the author does not address the role of liberalized attitudes toward unwed motherhood, implying that it is not a factor.

24. E

The passage discusses the rationale behind marriage in strictly economic terms and indicates that many demographers regard marriage in this way. While it might be argued that choice (B) is also correct, it is not, since it makes an assumption about all women's reasons for marriage—an inference that is too drastic. Note that choice (E) makes a less inclusive conclusion by referring to "some demographers." Finally, answers (A), (C), and (D) are poor choices because they are not addressed in the passage.

25. A

Whether the author talks about urbanization, contraception, or cohabitation, it is clear that she is referring to the relationship of new social realities and decline in birthrate. While answer choice (B) is factually correct, it is a limited title because it does not include other causes of declining birthrates. The author does not deem population prediction futile; she only admits that it is an "enterprise of educated speculation." In addition, the author never correlates shifting social values with a lessening of the nation's social and economic ills. Finally, national birthrate trends are related not just to women's new attitudes but to other issues such as divorce, cohabitation, and contraception (all of which might involve men's attitudes, as well).

26. B

The passage states that the Commission on Population Growth and the American Future concluded that declining fertility was a positive development because it may help to alleviate many of our most pressing social and economic problems.

27. D

The passage mentions that European pronatalist policies included family cash allowances, generous tax relief, subsidized child-care services, and improved housing. There is no mention in the passage of land grants, choice (D).

28. B

The passage states that most demographers now agree that the present declining birthrate is a long-term feature of U.S. society, especially since there does not appear to be any sense of urgency about altering the status quo.

29. B

The purpose of the first paragraph can be identified in its last sentence, which states, "The complexity and variability of social and economic factors involved in predicting population make the enterprise one of educated speculation." In other words, it is difficult. The paragraph never states that demographers are poor statisticians. Rather, it says population growth prediction is an inexact science. And, on the contrary, it reveals the inaccuracy of Census Bureau figures. Finally, while the paragraph mentions social and economic factors, as well as the Census Bureau's prediction of the 1970 U.S. population, it does not focus on any of these points as its central purpose.

30. E

The passage states that in most instances, European pronatalist policies have been introduced for reasons of national security. Thus, choice (E) is the most directly applicable choice.

31. A

The author states that rural families have higher fertility rates than urban families. This is, she argues, because in agrarian (i.e., more rural) economies, children play an important role in agricultural production and are thus necessities of life. While it may be that rural couples are more likely to be traditional and religious, this cannot be argued from the passage. Further, the passage provides no indication that women are less likely to pursue careers in rural areas, that rural couples experience less difficulty conceiving than urban couples, or that urban couples are better educated about contraception.

32. C

The author does correlate a decline in subscription to religious values with a reduced attachment to childbearing, which would imply that an extension of religious values through evangelism would potentially increase birthrates. However, the author specifically indicates that "evangelical movements tend to attract people who are already very religious," or who already embrace values of family and childbearing. Thus, evangelism, according to the passage, causes neither an increase nor decline in the birthrate.

33. C

The author claims that there is a growing financial independence of women owing to an increased number of women in the workplace. Therefore, it follows that women will be less interested in marrying at a young age, more likely to give birth out of wedlock, more interested in remaining financially independent, and more interested in maintaining a long-term career. These are opposite to the responses seen in choice (A), (B), (D), and (E), respectively.

34. B

The first paragraph of the passage states that discrepancies in current population predictions for the year 2000 reflect an overestimation rather than an underestimation. Thus, choices (A) and (C) are automatically eliminated as possibilities. In terms of choice (D), the author never indicates that current population predictions fail to account for the growth of illegal immigrant populations. Finally, the author's description of the 1947 underestimation of the population for 1970 indicates that present inaccuracies in prediction are not anomalous.

35. E

The passage defines negative nitrogen balance as a process in which protein degradation exceeds protein synthesis, so the body excretes a greater quantity of nitrogen than it ingests to replace it. In this state, essential amino acids are absent, making choice (E) the most correct one.

36. D

The passage states that peptide bonds are formed between the alpha-carboxyl group of one amino acid and the alpha-amino group of another. Therefore, choice (D) is most correct.

37. B

The passage states that the first process in gastric digestion of food is the secretion of 0.15 M HCl from the oxyntic, or parietal, cells of the fundus of the stomach. Therefore, choice (B) is most correct.

38. C

The passage states that end products of digestion—*L*-amino acids—are absorbed by the intestinal mucosal cells via a complex transport mechanism that involves cotransport of sodium ion. It makes no mention of the simultaneous transport of chloride ions, making choice (C) optimal.

39. A

Transamination, mediated by enzymes called transaminases, catalyzes the transfer of amino groups from alpha amino acids to alpha-keto acids (e.g., alpha-ketoglutarate).

40. C

The last few sentences of the passage categorize amino acids, which are either gluconeogenic, ketogenic, or both. Leucine is the only ketogenic amino acid; therefore, choice (C) is the correct answer.

41. E

All of the answer choices work. Amino acids that are degraded to acetyl-CoA or acetoacetyl-CoA are considered ketogenic. They may give rise to *D*-3-hydroxybutyrate, acetone molecules, and acetoacetate. They are the preferred fuel of cardiac muscle and renal cortical cells; thus, choice (E) is correct.

42. B

Pyridoxal phosphate enzymes may cause transamination, decarboxylation deamination, racemization, and aldol cleavage of amino acids. Therefore, choice (B) is correct.

43. E

The bond between pyridoxal phosphate and a transaminase occurs at a terminal lysine residue. The bond is a Schiff-base linkage, which is covalent in property. Therefore, choice (E) correct.

44. D

According to the passage, the main benefit of the transamination process is that it enables the glutamate formed to be oxidatively deaminated (by glutamate dehydrogenase) to regenerate alpha-ketoglutarate. This results in the formation of ammonium ions (from the glutamate, not the coenzyme pyridoxal phosphate) for the urea cycle and the regeneration of NADH and NADPH (involved in oxidative phosphorylation and reductive biosynthesis, respectively). Therefore, answer choice (D) is correct.

45.   D

The passage states that the main degradation site of amino acids is in the liver, although the main absorption site is the small intestine. Therefore, choice (D) is correct.

46.   E

The passage states the differences in amino acids are in their side chains, which themselves differ in size, shape, charge, hydrogen bonding capacity, and chemical reactivity. The passage does not indicate that side chains differ in carbon-binding capacity or number. Therefore, choice (E) is correct.

47.   C

The passage states that glutamate dehydrogenase is an allosterically regulated enzyme that is active only when low-energy precursors are present, such as ADP and GDP. In contrast, the activity of glutamate dehydrogenase is low when ATP and GTP are present. Therefore, choice (C) is correct.

48.   E

The passage states that trypsin breaks polypeptide chains on the carboxyl side of arginine and lysine residues, while chymotrypsin cleaves preferentially on the carboxyl side of aromatic and other bulky, nonpolar amino acids. Therefore, choice (E) is correct.

49.   E

The passage states that amino acid degradation involves primarily the conversion of an alpha-amino group to urea. The alpha-amino group is initially transferred to the molecule alpha-ketoglutarate to form glutamate, which is oxidatively deaminated to form NH4+. The ammonium ion is then converted to an excretion product and launched into the urea cycle. Amino acid skeletons may be converted to acetyl-CoA, pyruvate, or one of the intermediates of the citric acid cycle (e.g., fumarate). Alternatively, for ketogenic amino acids, degradation may involve the formation of acetyl-CoA or acetoacetyl-Coa and may give rise to ketone bodies, such as acetone, D-3-hydroxybutyrate, and acetoacetate. Therefore, choice (E) is correct.

50.   C

The passage states that while NADH is an active electron carrier in the oxidative phosphorylation that generates cellular ATP, NADPH is more active in reductive biosynthesis. However, this implies that NADPH has some activity in oxidative phosphorylation. Therefore, choice (C) is correct.

Section VI

QUANTITATIVE REASONING

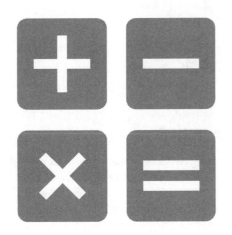

SECTION GOALS

The Quantitative Reasoning section of the OAT requires considerable outside knowledge, proficient test-taking skills, and strategic use of the calculator. The following section provides the content and guidance necessary for Test Day success. The section is designed to help you achieve the following goals:

- Recall key mathematical concepts likely to show up on Test Day
- Utilize non-traditional strategies effectively
- Identify when and how to use the on-screen calculator
- Predict answers to Quantitative Reasoning questions accurately and quickly, using the Kaplan methods

CONTENT OVERVIEW

Applied Mathematics (25%)**	Chapter 55: Quantitative Strategies
Numerical Calculations (15%)	Chapter 56: Numerical Calculations and Conversions*
Conversions (7.5%)	Chapter 56: Numerical Calculations and Conversions*
Algebra (22.5%)	Chapter 57: Algebra
Probability and Statistics (10%)	Chapter 58: Probability and Statistics
Geometry (10%)	Chapter 59: Plane Geometry Chapter 60: Solid Geometry Chapter 61: Coordinate Geometry
Trigonometry (10%)	Chapter 62: Trigonometry

*Chapter 56 contains materials relevant to Numerical Calculations and to Conversions
**Applied Mathematics problems are heavily dependent on strategy, but can contain math from any chapter.

KEY STUDY STRATEGIES

The Quantitative Reasoning section is the only section of the OAT which allows the use of a calculator. However, the calculator tends to be fairly time consuming. As such, its value tends to be overestimated. To avoid this trap, start your review with Chapter 55, which discusses strategies relevant to all Quantitative Reasoning questions as well as specific tips for certain question types. Following review of Chapter 55, prioritize the chapters that cover the test materials you have the most trouble with. Consider making flashcards for any rules or equations you have trouble with, as these are important materials to recall when solving OAT Quantitative Reasoning problems. Note that the number of chapters devoted to a topic is not correlated to the importance of that topic on the OAT. As you work through the associated practice problems, practice with the calculator on your computer, but make sure to use only the functionalities available on the actual OAT calculator. Try to complete the practice problems at the end of the chapter without referring back to the chapter, as you will not have access to a formula sheet on Test Day.

CHAPTER FIFTY-FIVE

Quantitative Strategies

The Quantitative Reasoning section of the OAT is designed to test the math skills required in dental school. The section contains 40 multiple-choice questions, and you will have 45 minutes to complete it. A basic on-screen calculator similar to the one below will be available only in this section. It can be opened by clicking the "Calculator" button at the bottom of the screen. The calculator can add, subtract, multiply, and divide as well as take square roots, percentages, and reciprocals.

Note that the calculator *cannot* perform the complex functions of a scientific or graphing calculator. You also cannot input to the calculator by typing and instead will need to click every number and operation you want to perform, which can be quite time consuming and lead to making mistakes. For these reasons, avoid using the calculator as much as possible and instead use mental math and quick scratch-work calculations, saving the calculator for the rare questions with difficult multiplication or long division. Developing your ability to complete calculations without a calculator will also be helpful for the Survey of Natural Sciences since you won't have access to a calculator during any of that section.

Scored items in the Quantitative Reasoning section directly test your abilities with Numerical Calculations (15%), Conversions (7.5%), Algebra (22.5%), Probability and Statistics (10%), Geometry (10%), and Trigonometry (10%). The remaining 25% of the questions are word problems that require applying one or more of those topics to a story problem. These topics are discussed in detail in Chapters 56–62.

This chapter will introduce you to the most common Kaplan strategies that you will use for calculations on the OAT. Although these strategies are most useful for the Quantitative Reasoning section, you may find them helpful throughout the test, especially in the Chemistry section. Additionally, remember that you can skip questions within a section and come back to them if you have time. Use this ability to your advantage by tackling questions you know you can answer with relative ease and skipping questions you know will take longer to answer.

PICKING NUMBERS

Picking Numbers is a powerful alternative to solving problems by brute force. Rather than working with unknown variables, you can pick concrete values for those variables or unknowns. In essence, you're transforming algebra or abstract math rules into basic arithmetic, giving yourself a much simpler task.

To successfully use Picking Numbers, follow these rules:

- Pick **permissible** numbers. Some problems have explicit rules such as "x is odd." Other problems have implicit rules. For example, if a word problem says, "Betty is five years older than Tim," don't pick $b = -2$ and $t = -7$; these numbers wouldn't work in the problem.
- Pick **manageable** numbers. Some numbers are simply easier to work with than others. $d = 2$ will probably be a more successful choice than $d = 492\sqrt{\pi}$, for example. The problems themselves will tell you what's manageable. For instance, $d = 2$ wouldn't be a great pick if an answer choice were $\frac{d}{12}$. (The number 12, 24, or even 120 would be much better in that case, since each is divisible by 12.)
- Once you've picked numbers to substitute for unknowns, approach the problem as basic arithmetic instead of algebra or number properties.
- Test every answer choice—sometimes certain numbers will yield a "false positive" in which a wrong answer looks right. If you get more than one "right answer," just pick a new set of numbers. The truly correct answer must work for all permissible numbers.

There are four signals that Picking Numbers will be a possible approach to the problem:

1. Variables in the answer choices
2. Percents in the answer choices
3. Answers that are fractions of an unknown value
4. Number property questions

These aren't in any particular order. You'll see many instances of each case on Test Day, so become familiar with all of them to ensure you recognize all your options on Test Day.

Picking Numbers with Variables in the Answer Choices

Whenever the answer choices contain variables, you should consider Picking Numbers. The correct answer choice is the one that yields the result that you got when you plugged the same number(s) into the question stem. Make sure that you test each answer choice, just in case more than one answer choice produces the desired result. In such a case, you will need to pick a new set of numbers and repeat the process only for the answer choices that worked out the first time.

Example: If $a > 1$, which of the following is equal to $\dfrac{2a + 6}{a^2 + 2a - 3}$?

    A. a

    B. $a + 3$

    C. $\dfrac{2}{a - 1}$

    D. $\dfrac{2a}{a - 3}$

    E. $a - 6$

Solution: The question says that $a > 1$, so the most manageable permissible number is 2.

Then $\dfrac{2(2) + 6}{2^2 + 2(2) - 3} = \dfrac{4 + 6}{4 + 4 - 3} = \dfrac{10}{5} = 2$.

Now substitute 2 for a in each answer choice, looking for choices that equal 2 (the answer you just solved for) when $a = 2$. Eliminate choices that do not equal 2 when $a = 2$.

    A. $a = 2$. Choice (A) is possibly correct.

    B. $a + 3 = 2 + 3 = 5$. This is not 2. Discard.

    C. $\dfrac{2}{a - 1} = \dfrac{2}{2 - 1} = \dfrac{2}{1} = 2$. Possibly correct.

    D. $\dfrac{2a}{a - 3} = \dfrac{2(2)}{2 - 3} = \dfrac{4}{-1} = -4$. This is not 2. Discard.

    E. $a - 6 = 2 - 6 = -4$. This is not 2. Discard.

You're down to (A) and (C). When more than one answer choice remains, you must pick another number. Try $a = 3$. Then $\dfrac{2(3) + 6}{3^2 + 2(3) - 3} = \dfrac{6 + 6}{9 + 6 - 3} = \dfrac{12}{12} = 1$.

Now work with the remaining answer choices.

Choice (A): $a = 3$. This is not 1. Discard.

Now that all four incorrect answer choices have been eliminated, you know that (C) must be correct. On Test Day, you should select (C) and move on, but just to verify right now, check to see whether (C) equals 1 when $a = 3$:

$\dfrac{2}{a - 1} = \dfrac{2}{3 - 1} = \dfrac{2}{2} = 1$. Choice (C) does equal 1 when $a = 3$.

This approach to Picking Numbers also applies to many confusing word problems. Picking Numbers can resolve a lot of that confusion. The key to Picking Numbers in word problems is to reread the question stem after you've picked numbers, substituting the numbers in place of the variables.

Example: A car rental company charges for mileage as follows: x dollars per mile for the first n miles and $x + 1$ dollars per mile for each mile over n miles. How much will the mileage charge be, in dollars, for a journey of d miles, where $d > n$?

A. $d(x + 1) - n$
B. $xn + d$
C. $xn + d(x + 1)$
D. $x(n + d) - d$
E. $xd + n$

Solution: Suppose you pick $x = 4$, $n = 3$, and $d = 5$. Now the problem would read like this:

A car rental company charges for mileage as follows: $4 per mile for each of the first 3 miles and $5 per mile for each mile over 3 miles. How much will the mileage charge be, in dollars, for a journey of 5 miles?

All of a sudden, the problem has become much more straightforward. The first 3 miles are charged at $4/mile. So that's $4 + $4 + $4, or $12. There are 2 miles remaining, and each one costs $5. So that's $5 + $5, for a total of $10. If the first 3 miles cost $12 and the next 2 cost $10, then the total charge is $12 + $10, which is $22.

Plugging $x = 4$, $n = 3$, and $d = 5$ into the answer choices, you get:

A. $d(x + 1) - n = 5(4 + 1) - 3 = 22$
B. $xn + d = 4 \times 3 + 5 = 17$
C. $xn + d(x + 1) = 4 \times 3 + 5(4 + 1) = 37$
D. $x(n + d) - d = 4(3 + 5) - 5 = 27$
E. $xd + n = 4 \times 5 + 3 = 23$

Only (A) yields the same number you calculated when you plugged these numbers into the question stem, so (A) is the answer. There's no need for complex algebra at all.

Picking Numbers with Percents in the Answer Choices

Picking Numbers also works well on Problem Solving questions for which the answer choices are given in percents. When the answers are in percents, 100 will almost always be the most manageable number to pick. Using 100 not only makes your calculations easier, but it also simplifies the task of expressing the final value as a percent of the original.

Example: The manufacturer of Sleep-EZ mattresses is offering a 10% discount on the price of its king-size mattress. Some retailers are offering additional discounts. If a retailer offers an additional 20% discount, then what is the total discount available at that retailer?

A. 10%
B. 25%
C. 28%
D. 30%
E. 32%

Solution: Since the answers are in percents, pick $100 as the original price of the mattress. (Remember, realism is irrelevant—only permissibility and manageability matter.) The manufacturer offers a 10% discount: 10% of $100 is $10. So now the mattress costs $90.

Then the retailer offers an additional 20% discount. Since the price has fallen to $90, that 20% is taken off the $90 price. A 20% discount is now a reduction of $18. The final price of the mattress is $90 − $18, or $72.

The mattress has been reduced to $72 from an original price of $100. That's a $28 reduction. Since you started with $100, you can easily calculate that $28 is 28% of the original price. Choice (C) is correct.

Notice that choice (D) commits the error of simply adding the two percents given in the question stem. An answer choice like (D) will never be correct on a question that gives you information about multiple percent changes.

Picking Numbers with Answers That Are Fractions of an Unknown

Similar to when a question asks for a percent, when a question asks about any fraction of an unknown, pick numbers to represent the unknown(s) in the question stem and walk through the arithmetic of the problem using those. Look in the question stem and the answer choices for clues about what the most manageable numbers might be.

Example: Carol spends $\frac{1}{4}$ of her savings on a stereo, and then she spends $\frac{1}{3}$ less than she spent on the stereo for a television. What fraction of her savings did she spend on the stereo and television together?

    A. $\frac{1}{4}$

    B. $\frac{2}{7}$

    C. $\frac{5}{12}$

    D. $\frac{7}{12}$

    E. $\frac{3}{4}$

Solution: Lowest common denominators of fractions in the question stem are good choices for numbers to pick. So are numbers that appear frequently as denominators in the answer choices. In this case, the common denominator of the fractions in the stem is 12, so let the number 12 represent Carol's total savings (12 dollars).

That means she spends $\frac{1}{4} \times 12$ dollars, or 3 dollars, on her stereo, and $\frac{2}{3} \times 3$ dollars, or 2 dollars, on her television. That comes out to be $3 + 2 = 5$ dollars; that's how much she spent on the stereo and television combined. You're asked what *fraction* of her savings she spent. Because her total savings was 12 dollars, she spent $\frac{5}{12}$ of her savings; (C) is correct. Notice how picking a common denominator for the variable (Carol's savings) made it easy to convert each of the fractions $\left(\frac{1}{4} \text{ and } \frac{2}{3} \times \frac{1}{4} \text{ of her savings}\right)$ to a simple integer.

A tricky part of this question is understanding how to determine the price of the television. The television does not cost $\frac{1}{3}$ of her savings. It costs $\frac{1}{3}$ *less* than the stereo; that is, it costs $\frac{2}{3}$ as much as the stereo.

By the way, some of these answers could have been eliminated quickly using basic logic. Choice (A) is too small; the stereo alone costs $\frac{1}{4}$ of her savings. Choices (D) and (E) are too large; the television costs *less* than the stereo, so the two together must cost less than $2 \times \frac{1}{4}$, or half, of Carol's savings. Although you may not be used to approaching questions using this type of broad, logical approach, you can save significant time during any section of the test by looking for these kinds of patterns!

Picking Numbers with Number Property Questions

Number properties questions deal with categorizing numbers and explaining the expected behavior of numbers based on certain rules. The most common topics you will encounter include integers/non-integers, odds/evens, positives/negatives, factors/multiples, remainders, and primes. When you see a question that asks about any of these topics and that includes any unknown values, you should immediately consider the Picking Numbers strategy. As always, remember to select permissible and manageable numbers for yourself when you pick numbers to make the math as easy as possible.

Example: If 2 is the remainder when m is divided by 5, what is the remainder when $3m$ is divided by 5?

     A. 0

     B. 1

     C. 2

     D. 3

     E. 4

Solution: This question tests your ability to think critically about the characteristics of remainders in division. You are told that some number, m, has a remainder of 2 when divided by 5. Pick simple, permissible numbers and apply them to the problem in the question stem.

Since m has a remainder of 2 when divided by 5, m could be any number that is 2 greater than a multiple of 5. The simplest number to substitute for m is 7. You know that 5 goes into 7 one time with a remainder of 2. Now, apply 7 to the rest of the question stem: $3m$ divided by 5. Multiplying 3 and 7 gives you 21, and 21 divided by 5 leaves a remainder of 1. Thus, answer choice (B) is correct; no more work is required!

BACKSOLVING

Backsolving is just like Picking Numbers except, instead of coming up with the number yourself, you use the numbers in the answer choices. You'll literally work backward through the problem, looking for the answer choice that agrees with the information in the question stem. This is a good approach whenever the task of plugging a choice into the question would allow you to confirm its details in a straightforward way.

You want to Backsolve systematically, not randomly. Start with either choice (B) or (D), depending on whether you anticipate the correct answer being closer to one or the other. If the choice you pick isn't correct, you'll often be able to figure out whether you need to try a number that's larger or one that's smaller. Since numerical answer choices will always be in ascending or descending order, you'll be able to use that information to eliminate several choices at once.

For example, you might choose to start with (B). If (B) works, then choose it as the correct answer and move to the next question. If (B) is too large, then (A) must be the correct answer since it is the only choice that is smaller. If (B) is too small, then eliminate both (A) and (B) and try (D) next. (D) will either be correct, too large, in which case (C) is the correct answer; or too small, in which case (E) is the correct answer.

Using this strategy, you'll only need to check two answer choices at most, which makes Backsolving a quick and efficient method to use for many questions. It is also an exceptional choice when you don't know how to begin a question using traditional math.

Example: Ron begins reading a book at 4:30 p.m. and reads at a steady pace of 30 pages per hour. Michelle begins reading a copy of the same book at 6:00 p.m. If Michelle started 5 pages behind the page that Ron started on and reads at an average pace of 50 pages per hour, at what time would Ron and Michelle be reading the same page?

    A.   7:00 p.m.
    B.   7:30 p.m.
    C.   8:00 p.m.
    D.   8:30 p.m.
    E.   9:00 p.m.

Solution: You could perhaps set up a complex system of equations to solve this problem, but even if you knew exactly what those equations would be and how to solve them, that's not a very efficient use of your time. Backsolving would work better here. Pick an answer choice and see whether Michelle and Ron are on the same page at that time. There's no compelling reason to prefer one choice to another, so just quickly choose (B) or (D).

Let's say you choose (B). On what page is Ron at 7:30 p.m.? He started reading at 4:30 p.m., so he has been reading for 3 hours. His pace is 30 pages per hour. So he has read 30×3, or 90 pages. Since Michelle started 5 pages behind Ron, she would need to read 95 pages to be at the same place. She has been reading since 6:00 p.m., so she has read for 1.5 hours. At 50 pages per hour, she has read 75 pages. That's 20 short of what she needs. So (B) is not the right answer.

Since Michelle is reading faster than Ron, she'll catch up to him with more time. Therefore, they will be on the same page sometime later than 7:30 p.m., so eliminate (A) as well and try (D).

At 8:30 p.m. Ron has read for 4 hours. At a pace of 30 pages per hour he's read $30 \times 4 = 120$ pages. Since Michelle started 5 pages behind, she'd need to read 125 pages to be at the same place. She's been reading for 2.5 hours at this point; at 50 pages per hour, she's read 125 pages. That's exactly what you're looking for—choice (D) must be correct.

As happened with this question, sometimes you may have to test more than one choice. But as you saw above, you should never have to test more than two answer choices. Stick to (B) or (D), and you'll save valuable time.

STRATEGIC GUESSING AND ESTIMATION

A well-placed guess can sometimes be the best tool you can use for a problem. Because of the severe time constraints, you need to stay on a steady pace. If you fall behind, it's a good idea to guess on the hardest problems and mark them for later rather than completing the full calculations right away. That way you'll get back lost time instead of falling further behind. And while you shouldn't be afraid to guess, you should be afraid to rush! The test makers write problems in complicated ways, and rushing almost always leads to misperception of questions (not to mention errors in arithmetic). This is a problem because the test makers base many wrong answers on the most common misperceptions. Rushing through a problem almost always guarantees a wrong answer. It's far better to guess as needed, skipping some questions and taking the time you need on others, than to rush through an entire section.

Even if you are ahead of schedule during a section, sometimes you simply will have no idea how to approach a problem. Instead of throwing away three or four minutes becoming frustrated, make a guess. If you don't know how to approach a problem, you aren't likely to choose the right answer anyway, and you can use the time you save to solve other problems that you stand a better chance of answering correctly.

Estimation can also be useful when answering questions as it can save you time and help you avoid mistakes when working through lengthy arithmetic calculations. You should consider estimation on questions that involve difficult or lengthy calculations and have answer choices that are spread fairly far apart. Once you decide to estimate, you'll want to follow a couple of general rules.

First, use scientific notation and fractions to simplify calculations. Although mastering both may take practice, you'll find the arithmetic required for either to be much simpler than leaving the number as a regular decimal. Review the rules in Chapter 56, Numerical Calculations and Conversions, if you don't feel comfortable with manipulating fractions yet; you'll need to know them to do well on certain questions anyway, so becoming adept at them now will allow you to master content and strategies at the same time.

Second, feel free to round numbers or only use powers of 10 when the answer choices vary widely. When you add or multiply numbers, round one number up and the other number down. When you subtract or divide numbers, round both numbers in the same direction. By doing so, you'll minimize the effect of rounding and arrive at a closer answer than you would if rounding randomly.

REVIEW PROBLEMS

1. Each writer for the local newspaper is paid as follows: a dollars for each of the first n stories each month and $a + b$ dollars for each story thereafter, where $a > b$. How many more dollars will a writer who submits $n + a$ stories in a month earn than a writer who submits $n + b$ stories?

    A. $(a - b)(a + b + n)$
    B. $a - b$
    C. $a^2 - b^2$
    D. $n(a - b)$
    E. $n(a + b)$

2. A crate of apples contains 1 bruised apple for every 30 apples in the crate. Three out of every four bruised apples are considered not fit to sell, and every apple that is not fit to sell is bruised. If there are 12 apples not fit to sell in the crate, then how many total apples are there in the crate?

    A. 270
    B. 360
    C. 480
    D. 600
    E. 720

3. Company Z spent $\frac{1}{4}$ of its revenues last year on marketing and $\frac{1}{7}$ of the remainder on maintenance of its facilities. What fraction of last year's original revenues did company Z have left after its marketing and maintenance expenditures?

    A. $\frac{5}{14}$
    B. $\frac{1}{2}$
    C. $\frac{17}{28}$
    D. $\frac{9}{14}$
    E. $\frac{41}{56}$

4. The positive difference between Sam and Lucy's ages is a, and the sum of their ages is z. If Lucy is older than Sam, then which of the following represents Lucy's age?

    A. $\frac{z - a}{2}$
    B. $\frac{z + a}{2}$
    C. $a - \frac{z}{2}$
    D. $\frac{a - z}{2}$
    E. $\frac{a + 2z}{2}$

5. If a bicyclist in motion increases his speed by 30 percent and then increases this speed by 10 percent, what percent of the original speed is the total increase in speed?

   A. 40%

   B. 43%

   C. 64%

   D. 140%

   E. 180%

6. If p, q, and r are positive integers such that q is a factor of r and r is a multiple of p, which of the following must be an integer?

   A. $\dfrac{p+q}{r}$

   B. $\dfrac{p}{q}$

   C. $\dfrac{r(p+q)}{pq}$

   D. $\dfrac{r+p}{q}$

   E. $\dfrac{rp+q}{p}$

SOLUTIONS TO THE REVIEW PROBLEMS

1. **C** You are given information about the number of dollars reporters are paid to write newspaper stories. They are paid at one rate for each of a certain number of stories and another rate for each remaining story after that. You are also given information about two specific writers and the number of stories that they write. Although it is possible to complete this question using traditional math, the set up would be quite difficult. Since there are variables in the question stem and the answer choices, this is a good question to use Picking Numbers instead.

   The only permissibility rule given in the question is that $a > b$, so you could pick $a = 3$ and $b = 2$. The remaining variable is n; there are no constraints on this number, so pick a number that is easy to work with, such as 10.

   Once you have chosen your numbers, reread the question stem but mentally substitute your new numbers for the variables as this can help the problem make more sense. You want to know how much more a writer who writes $n + a = 10 + 3 = 13$ stories will make than will a writer who writes $n + b = 10 + 2 = 12$ stories.

   Start with the writer who writes 13 stories. She makes $3 for each of the first 10 stories or $30 total for the first ten stories. Then, she makes $a + b = 3 + 2 = \$5$ for each story after that. She wrote 3 more stories, so she earned $15 more for the additional stories. In total, the writer earned $45.

   Next, look at the writer who wrote 12 stories. He too will make $3 for each of the first 10 stories or $30 total. Then he will make $5 for each of the remaining 2 stories, another $10. In total, the second writer earns $40. Therefore, the difference between the two writers' earnings is $5. Now, plug your variables into the answer choices to find one that equals $5:

   A. $(3 - 2)(3 + 2 + 10) = (1)(15) = 15$. Eliminate.

   B. $3 - 2 = 1$. Eliminate.

   C. $3^2 - 2^2 = 9 - 4 = 5$. This could be the correct answer, but keep checking to ensure no other answer choices also calculate to 5.

   D. $10(3 - 2) = 10(1) = 10$. Eliminate.

   E. $10(3 + 2) = 10(5) = 50$. Eliminate.

   Since only one answer choice yields the number 5, pick choice (C) and move on.

2. **C** This is another difficult-sounding question. Since the answer choices are all numbers, Backsolving is a great approach to use instead of traditional math. Start with choice (B). Suppose that there are 360 apples in the crate. Then $\frac{360}{30}$ apples, or 12 apples, are bruised. Then, $\frac{3}{4}$ of those 12 apples, or 9 apples, are unsellable. This is too few unsellable apples, so (B) is too small. The answer must be larger than 360, so eliminate choices (A) and (B). Try choice (D) next. Suppose that there are 600 apples in the crate. Then $\frac{600}{30}$ apples, or 20 apples, are bruised. Of those 20, $\frac{3}{4}$ or 15, are unsalable. That's too many, so choice (C) must be correct.

3. **D** Company Z spends portions of its revenues on two things. It is important to note that the answer choices are fractions and represent the fraction of last year's revenues that company Z had left after the expenses. Notice that you are given absolutely no way to know how much revenue company Z received last year, so you can use Picking Numbers to determine the total revenue. Since you must take $\frac{1}{4}$ and $\frac{1}{7}$ of the revenue, a number divisible by both 4 and 7 will be most manageable. Make the calculations as easy as possible by picking the lowest common multiple of 4 and 7: 28.

Now, "Company Z spent $\frac{1}{4}$ of its revenues last year on marketing," becomes "Company Z spent \$7 last year on marketing." The next sentence mentions "the remainder," so you need to know what that is. Since \$28 − \$7 = \$21, "Company Z spent $\frac{1}{7}$ of the remainder on maintenance," means "Company Z spent \$3 on maintenance."

What's left from \$28 after company Z spent \$7 and then \$3 is \$18. So the answer is $\frac{18}{28}$. A common factor of 2 can be canceled from both the numerator and the denominator, leaving $\frac{9}{14}$. Choice (D) is correct.

4. **B** There are two people—Sam and Lucy—whose ages are related in some way. While you could set up an algebraic equation here, notice that the answer choices all contain variables and thus allow for Picking Numbers. You are solving for Lucy's age, so be careful not to answer with Sam's age because that's likely to be one of the wrong answers.

It's easy enough to pick two numbers for a and z. But then you would still have to backtrack from those to calculate the two ages. If this happens, consider reevaluating your approach. Are there other variables you could pick first that would make things easier?

If you pick numbers for Lucy's and Sam's ages, then all you need to do to figure out the values of a and z is basic arithmetic. You might pick that Lucy is 5 years old and Sam is 3 years old. That makes a, their difference, equal to 2. And z, their sum, is equal to 8.

Plug in $a = 2$ and $z = 8$ to see which choices yield Lucy's age of 5.

A. is $\frac{8-2}{2} = \frac{6}{2} = 3$. Eliminate.

B. is $\frac{8+2}{2} = \frac{10}{2} = 5$. Possibly right.

C. is $2 - \frac{8}{2} = 2 - 4 = -2$. Eliminate.

D. is $\frac{2-8}{2} = \frac{-6}{2} = -3$. Eliminate.

E. is $\frac{2+8(2)}{2} = \frac{18}{2} = 9$. Eliminate.

Since it is the only choice that matches, (B) is correct.

5. **B** The question gives you information about two increases to the speed of a bicyclist and asks for the total percent increase in the cyclist's speed. When you encounter a percentage problem with an unknown value in the question and percentages in the answer choices, you should use the strategy of Picking Numbers and pick 100.

If the bicyclist initially rides at 100 (the units aren't mentioned in this problem, and in any case, the numbers don't need to be realistic, just permissible and manageable) and then increases his speed by 30%, he now rides at 130. He then increases this speed by 10%, so find 10% of 130, which is 13, and add it to 130. That makes his final speed 143. That is an increase of 43 over his original speed of 100. Recalling that 100 was the number you initially picked shows that 43 is 43% (or $\frac{43}{100}$) of the original speed. Answer choice (B) is correct.

6. **C** This question gives information about three variables and how they relate to each other. Since q is a factor of r, r is a multiple of q. The question stem also says r is a multiple of p. Thus, r is a multiple of both p and q. This question is very abstract and relies on your knowledge of number properties, so picking numbers that are permissible will help you make quick work of the answer choices.

Pick numbers for p, q, and r and apply them to the answer choices. Since you know r is a multiple of both p and q, start with p and q. You might pick that $p = 2$ and $q = 3$. From there, you can pick a value for r; such as $r = 6$. Now plug these values into the answer choices and eliminate any choice that does not yield an integer.

A. is $\frac{2+3}{6} = \frac{5}{6}$. Eliminate.

B. is $\frac{2}{3}$. Eliminate.

C. is $\frac{6(2+3)}{2(3)} = \frac{6(5)}{6} = 5$. Possibly correct.

D. is $\frac{6+2}{3} = \frac{8}{3}$. Eliminate.

E. is $(6 \times 2) + 3 = 15$. Eliminate.

As the only choice that fit, (C) is correct.

CHAPTER FIFTY-SIX

Numerical Calculations and Conversions

The test makers describe the arithmetic covered in this chapter as basic math, but that doesn't mean it's all easy to calculate, especially when you do not have access to a calculator and are under the time constraints of Test Day. Even if you once had a strong, working knowledge of number properties and how to manipulate fractions, decimals, ratios, logarithms, and means, you may find that your knowledge has deteriorated through disuse, especially if you haven't taken a math class in several years. Even if this content seems straightforward at first glance, spend some time with the practice problems and worked examples to ensure your knowledge is fresh and you won't need to waste time on Test Day recalling basic rules or formulas.

NUMBER OPERATIONS

Important terms and concepts to be familiar with for Test Day:

- **Real number:** All numbers on the number line.
- **Integers**: All numbers with no fractional or decimal parts, including negative whole numbers and zero; multiples of 1. See the number line below.
- **Operation**: A process that is performed on one or more numbers. The four basic arithmetic operations are addition, subtraction, multiplication, and division.
- **Sum**: The result of addition.
- **Difference**: The result of subtraction.
- **Product**: The result of multiplication.
- **Reciprocal**: The result of switching the numerator and denominator of a fraction. The reciprocal of $\frac{3}{5}$ is $\frac{5}{3}$. The reciprocal of 2 is $\frac{1}{2}$ because 2 can be considered to be the fraction $\frac{2}{1}$. Multiplying any number by its reciprocal will result in 1.

Numbers and the Number Line

A number line is a straight line, extending infinitely in either direction, on which real numbers are represented as points. Decimals and fractions can also be depicted on a number line, as can numbers such as $\sqrt{2}$.

The values of numbers get larger as you move to the right along the number line. Numbers to the right of zero are **positive**; numbers to the left of zero are **negative**. **Zero** is neither positive nor negative, but it is an even integer. Any positive number is larger than any negative number. For example, 4 is larger than -300.

Laws of Operations

Commutative laws of addition and multiplication

Addition and multiplication are both **commutative**; switching the order of any two numbers being added or multiplied together does not affect the result. For example, $5 + 12 = 12 + 5$; both sums equal 17. Similarly $2 \times 6 = 6 \times 2$; both products equal 12.

$$a + b = b + a$$
$$a \times b = b \times a$$

Subtraction and division are *not* commutative; switching the order of the numbers changes the result. For instance, $3 - 2 \neq 2 - 3$; the left side yields a result of 1, whereas the right side yields a result of -1.

Similarly, $6 \div 2 \neq 2 \div 6$; the left side gives 3, whereas the right side gives $\frac{1}{3}$.

Associative laws of addition and multiplication

$$(a + b) + c = a + (b + c)$$
$$(a \times b) \times c = a \times (b \times c)$$

Addition and multiplication are both **associative**. This means that the terms can be regrouped without changing the result.

Example: $(3 + 5) + 8 = 3 + (5 + 8)$
$8 + 8 = 3 + 13$
$16 = 16$

Example: $(4 \times 5) \times 6 = 4 \times (5 \times 6)$
$20 \times 6 = 4 \times 30$
$120 = 120$

Because addition and multiplication are both commutative and associative, numbers can be added or multiplied in any order. Subtraction and division are *not* associative.

Example: $(7 - 10) - 4 = -3 - 4 = -7$, whereas $7 - (10 - 4) = 7 - 6 = 1$.
So $(7 - 10) - 4 \neq 7 - (10 - 4)$.

Example: $(24 \div 12) \div 3 = 2 \div 3 = \frac{2}{3}$, whereas $24 \div (12 \div 3) = 24 \div 4 = 6$.

So $(24 \div 12) \div 3 \neq 24 \div (12 \div 3)$.

Distributive law

The distributive law of multiplication allows you to "distribute" a factor among the terms being added or subtracted by multiplying that factor by each number in the group.

$$a(b + c) = ab + ac.$$

Example: $4(3 + 7) = (4 \times 3) + (4 \times 7)$

$\qquad 4 \times 10 = 12 + 28$

$\qquad\qquad 40 = 40$

Division can be distributed in a similar way, because dividing by a number is equivalent to multiplying by that number's reciprocal.

Example: $\frac{3+5}{2} = \frac{1}{2}(3 + 5) = \frac{1}{2}(3) + \frac{1}{2}(5)$

$\qquad \frac{8}{2} = \frac{3}{2} + \frac{5}{2}$

$\qquad \frac{8}{2} = \frac{3+5}{2}$

$\qquad \frac{8}{2} = \frac{8}{2}$

Don't get carried away, though. When the sum or difference is in the denominator—that is, when you're dividing by a sum or difference—no distribution is possible. $\frac{9}{4+5}$ is NOT equal to $\frac{9}{4} + \frac{9}{5}$; $\frac{9}{4+5} = \frac{9}{9} = 1$. But $\frac{9}{4}$ and $\frac{9}{5}$ are both greater than 1, so their sum can't equal 1.

Operations with signed numbers

Numbers can be treated as though they have two parts: a positive or negative sign and a number part. For example, the sign of the number -3 is negative, and the number part is 3. Numbers without any sign are understood to be positive. To add two numbers that have the same sign, add the number parts and keep the sign.

Example: What is the sum of -6 and -3?

Solution: To find $(-6) + (-3)$, add 6 and 3, and then attach the negative sign from the original numbers to the sum:

$$(-6) + (-3) = -9.$$

To add two numbers that have different signs, find the difference between the number parts and keep the sign of the number whose number part is larger.

Example: What is the sum of -7 and $+4$?

Solution: To find $(-7) + (+4)$, subtract 4 from 7 to get 3. $7 > 4$; that is, the number part of -7 is greater than the number part of $+4$, so the final sum will be negative. $(-7) + (+4) = -3$.

Subtraction is the opposite of addition. You can rephrase any subtraction problem as an addition problem by changing the operation sign from a minus to a plus and switching the sign on the second number. For instance, $8 - 5 = 8 + (-5)$. There's no real advantage to rephrasing if you are subtracting a smaller positive number from a larger positive number. But the concept comes in very handy when you are subtracting a negative number from any other number, a positive number from a negative number, or a larger positive number from a smaller positive number.

To subtract a negative number, rephrase as an addition problem and follow the rules for addition of signed numbers.

For instance, $9 - (-10) = 9 + 10 = 19$.

Here's another example: $(-5) - (-2) = (-5) + 2$. The difference between 5 and 2 is 3, and the number with the larger number part is -5, so the answer is -3.

To subtract a positive number from a negative number or from a smaller positive number, change the sign of the number that you are subtracting from positive to negative and follow the rules for addition of signed numbers.

For example, $(-4) - 1 = (-4) + (-1) = -5$.

Example: Subtract 8 from 2.

Solution: $2 - 8 = 2 + (-8)$. The difference between the number parts is 6, and the -8 has the larger number part, so the answer is -6.

Multiplying or dividing two numbers with the same sign gives a positive result.

$$(-4) \times (-7) = +28$$
$$(-50) \div (-5) = +10$$

Multiplying or dividing two numbers with different signs gives a negative result.

$$(-2) \times (+3) = -6$$
$$8 \div (-4) = -2$$

Properties of 0, 1, and -1

Properties of 0

Adding zero to or subtracting zero from a number does not change the number.

$$x + 0 = x$$
$$0 + x = x$$
$$x - 0 = x$$

Example: $5 + 0 = 5$
$0 + (-3) = -3$
$4 - 0 = 4$

Notice, however, that subtracting a number from zero switches the number's sign. It's easier to see why if you rephrase the problem as an addition problem.

Example: Subtract 5 from 0.

Solution: $0 - 5 = -5$. That's because $0 - 5 = 0 + (-5)$, and according to the properties of zero, $0 + (-5) = -5$.

The product of zero and any number is zero.

$$0 \times z = 0$$
$$z \times 0 = 0$$

Example: $0 \times 12 = 0$

Division by zero is undefined. For practical purposes, that translates as "it can't be done." Because fractions are essentially division (that is, $\frac{1}{4}$ means $1 \div 4$), any fraction with zero in the denominator is also undefined.

Properties of 1 and −1

Multiplying or dividing a number by 1 does not change the number.

$$a \times 1 = a$$
$$1 \times a = a$$
$$a \div 1 = a$$

Example: $4 \times 1 = 4$
$1 \times (-5) = -5$
$(-7) \div 1 = -7$

Multiplying or dividing a nonzero number by −1 changes the sign of the number.

$$a \times (-1) = -a$$
$$(-1) \times a = -a$$
$$a \div (-1) = -a$$

Example: $6 \times (-1) = -6$
$(-3) \times (-1) = 3$
$(-8) \div (-1) = 8$

QR

Order of Operations

Whenever you have a string of operations, be careful to perform them in the proper order. Otherwise, you will probably get the wrong answer.

The acronym PEMDAS stands for the correct order of operations:

> Parentheses
>
> Exponents
>
> Multiplication
>
> Division
>
> Addition
>
> Subtraction

Multiplication and division should be performed together in order from left to right, and then addition and subtraction should be performed together in order from left to right. If you have trouble remembering PEMDAS, you can think of the mnemonic phrase Please Excuse My Dear Aunt Sally.

Example: $66 \times (3 - 2) \div 11 = ?$

Solution: If you were to perform all the operations sequentially from left to right, without regard to the rules for the order of operations, you would arrive at the answer $\frac{196}{11}$. To do this correctly, however, perform the operation inside the parentheses first: $3 - 2 = 1$. Now you have:

$$66 \times 1 \div 11 = 66 \div 11 = 6$$

Example: $30 - 5 \times 4 + (7 - 3)^2 \div 8 = ?$

Solution: First perform any operations within parentheses. (If the expression has parentheses within parentheses, work from the innermost set out.)

$30 - 5 \times 4 + 4^2 \div 8$

Next, do the exponent.

$30 - 5 \times 4 + 16 \div 8$

Then, do all multiplication and division in order from left to right.

$30 - 20 + 2$

Last, do all addition and subtraction in order from left to right.

$10 + 2$

The answer is 12.

FRACTIONS

Basic Arithmetic with Fractions

$\frac{7}{8}$ → Numerator
→ Denominator

Multiplying fractions: Multiply numerators by each other and denominators by each other.

$$\frac{3}{4} \times \frac{9}{7} = \frac{3 \times 9}{4 \times 7} = \frac{27}{28}$$

Dividing fractions: Flip the numerator and denominator of the fraction you're dividing by, then multiply.

$$\frac{1}{5} \div \frac{4}{11} = \frac{1}{5} \times \frac{11}{4} = \frac{1 \times 11}{5 \times 4} = \frac{11}{20}$$

Adding fractions: You can add fractions only when they have the same denominator. When you add, add only the numerators, NOT the denominators.

$$\frac{2}{3} + \frac{5}{3} = \frac{2 + 5}{3} = \frac{7}{3}$$

If you don't have a common denominator, you have to find one. The fastest way to get a common denominator is to multiply each fraction by a fraction whose numerator and denominator are the same as the denominator of the other fraction. (You can do this because any fraction with the same numerator and denominator is equal to 1, and multiplying any number by 1 doesn't change the value of the number.)

$$\frac{1}{3} + \frac{2}{5} = \left(\frac{1}{3} \times \frac{5}{5}\right) + \left(\frac{2}{5} \times \frac{3}{3}\right) = \frac{5}{15} + \frac{6}{15} = \frac{11}{15}$$

Subtracting fractions: This works the same way as adding fractions, except you subtract the numerators instead of adding them.

$$\frac{6}{7} - \frac{1}{2} = \left(\frac{6}{7}\right)\left(\frac{2}{2}\right) - \left(\frac{1}{2}\right)\left(\frac{7}{7}\right) = \frac{12}{14} - \frac{7}{14} = \frac{5}{14}$$

Remember, parentheses can be used to indicate multiplication instead of the "×" sign.

Reducing fractions: Whenever there is a common factor in the numerator and denominator, you can reduce the fraction by removing the factor from both parts of the fraction. You can do this because dividing the numerator and denominator by the same number doesn't change the value of the fraction as a whole. This will often make working with the fraction much easier because you'll be using smaller numbers.

$$\frac{4}{12} = \frac{1 \times 4}{3 \times 4} = \frac{1}{3} \times 1 = \frac{1}{3}$$

On Test Day, you don't actually have to write out all this math. For example, you might work like this:

$$\frac{4}{12} = \frac{1 \times 4}{3 \times 4} = \frac{1}{3}.$$

Or, even more simply, you might keep track of the multiplication operations mentally, only writing down the results. For example, if attempting to reduce $\frac{42}{28}$, you might write your work by cancelling like this:

$$\frac{{}^{6}\cancel{42}}{{}_{4}\cancel{28}} = \frac{{}^{3}\cancel{6}}{{}_{2}\cancel{4}} = \frac{3}{2}.$$

Because both 42 and 28 are divisible by 7, you can divide both the numerator (42) and the denominator (28) by 7. Thus, $\frac{42}{28}$ reduces to $\frac{6}{4}$. Because both 6 and 4 are divisible by 2, you can divide both the numerator (6) and the denominator (4) by 2. Thus, $\frac{6}{4}$ reduces to $\frac{3}{2}$.

Canceling: Whenever you have to multiply two or more fractions, you should cancel common factors before you multiply. This is a lot like reducing and has the same advantages. $\frac{1}{7} \times \frac{7}{3}$ can be canceled like this:

$$\frac{1}{\cancel{7}} \times \frac{\cancel{7}^{1}}{3} = \frac{1}{1} \times \frac{1}{3} = \frac{1}{3}$$

$\frac{4}{5} \times \frac{15}{12}$ can be canceled like this:

$$\frac{\cancel{4}^{1}}{\cancel{5}} \times \frac{\cancel{15}^{3}}{\cancel{12}} = \frac{1}{1} \times \frac{3}{3} = 1$$

Notice that both the 5 in the denominator of the first fraction and the 15 in the numerator of the second fraction are divisible by 5. Similarly, the 4 in the numerator of the first fraction and the 12 in the denominator of the second fraction are both divisible by 4. Simplifying fractions requires identifying these types of relationships and dividing accordingly.

Comparing Fractions

One way to compare fractions is to re-express them with a **common denominator**. $\frac{3}{4} = \frac{21}{28}$ and $\frac{5}{7} = \frac{20}{28}$. $\frac{21}{28}$ is greater than $\frac{20}{28}$ so $\frac{3}{4}$ is greater than $\frac{5}{7}$. Another way to compare fractions is to convert them both to decimals. $\frac{3}{4}$ converts to 0.75, and $\frac{5}{7}$ converts to approximately 0.714.

Mixed Numbers and Fractions

A mixed number consists of an integer and a fraction. For example, $3\frac{1}{4}$, $12\frac{2}{5}$, and $5\frac{7}{8}$ are all mixed numbers.

To convert an improper fraction (a fraction whose numerator is greater than its denominator) to a mixed number, divide the numerator by the denominator. The number of "whole" times that the denominator goes into the numerator will be the integer portion of the mixed number; the remainder will be the numerator of the fractional portion.

Example: Convert $\frac{23}{4}$ to a mixed number.

Solution: Dividing 23 by 4 gives you 5 with a remainder of 3, so $\frac{23}{4} = 5\frac{3}{4}$.

To change a mixed number to a fraction, keep the denominator of the fraction. To figure out the numerator, multiply the integer portion of the mixed number by the number in the denominator. Then add this result to the numerator of the mixed number.

Example: Convert $2\frac{3}{7}$ to a fraction.

Solution: $2\frac{3}{7} = \frac{(2 \times 7) + 3}{7} = \frac{17}{7}$

Example: Convert $5\frac{8}{9}$ to a fraction.

Solution: $5\frac{8}{9} = \frac{(5 \times 9) + 8}{9} = \frac{53}{9}$

Adding and Subtracting Mixed Numbers

Adding or subtracting mixed numbers whose fractional parts have the same denominator will probably be on the test.

Example: $3\frac{12}{17} + 4\frac{10}{17} = ?$

Solution: First, add the integer parts: $3 + 4 = 7$.

Next, add the fractional parts: $\frac{12}{17} + \frac{10}{17} = \frac{22}{17}$.

Now, $\frac{22}{17} = 1\frac{5}{17}$.

Therefore, $3\frac{12}{17} + 4\frac{10}{17} = 7 + 1\frac{5}{17} = 8\frac{5}{17}$.

Example: $4\frac{5}{8} - 2\frac{7}{8} = ?$

Solution: The wrinkle here is that the fractional part of the first number is smaller than the fractional part of the second number (i.e., $\frac{5}{8}$ is smaller then $\frac{7}{8}$). What you need to do, therefore, is borrow from the integer part of the first number to make the fractional part of the first number bigger. Borrow 1 from the integer part and add it to the fractional part (remembering that 1 can be rewritten as $\frac{8}{8}$).

So $4\frac{5}{8} = 3 + \frac{8}{8} + \frac{5}{8} = 3\frac{13}{8}$. So the problem of finding $4\frac{5}{8} - 2\frac{7}{8}$ has been replaced with the problem of finding $3\frac{13}{8} - 2\frac{7}{8}$, which is easier because the fractional part of the first number is greater than the fractional part of the second number.

Notice that all you need to do is replace $4\frac{5}{8}$ with $3\frac{13}{8}$, which is equal to $4\frac{5}{8}$. To find $3\frac{13}{8} - 2\frac{7}{8}$, first subtract the integer parts: $3 - 2 = 1$. Next subtract the fractional parts: $\frac{13}{8} - \frac{7}{8} = \frac{13-7}{8} = \frac{6}{8} = \frac{3}{4}$. So $4\frac{5}{8} - 2\frac{7}{8} = 1\frac{3}{4}$.

QR

Example: $5\frac{1}{4} - 1\frac{3}{4} = ?$

Solution: $5\frac{1}{4} - 1\frac{3}{4} = 5 + \frac{1}{4} - 1\frac{3}{4} = \left(4 + \frac{4}{4}\right) + \frac{1}{4} - 1\frac{3}{4} = 4 + \left(\frac{4}{4} + \frac{1}{4}\right) - 1\frac{3}{4}$

$$= 4\frac{5}{4} - 1\frac{3}{4} = 3\frac{2}{4} = 3\frac{1}{2}$$

When you gain experience with this, you'll be able to skip some of the steps and do this type of problem more quickly.

Example: $8\frac{3}{25} - 4\frac{12}{25} = ?$

Solution: $8\frac{3}{25} - 4\frac{12}{25} = 7 + \frac{25}{25} + \frac{3}{25} - 4\frac{12}{25} = 7\frac{28}{25} - 4\frac{12}{25} = 3\frac{16}{25}$

RATIOS

Setting Up a Ratio

To find a ratio, put the number associated with the word *of* on top and the quantity associated with the word *to* on the bottom and reduce. The ratio of 20 oranges to 12 apples is $\frac{20}{12}$, which reduces to $\frac{5}{3}$.

Part-to-Part Ratios and Part-to-Whole Ratios

If the parts add up to the whole, a part-to-part ratio can be turned into two part-to-whole ratios by putting each number in the original ratio over the sum of the numbers. If the ratio of males to females is 1 to 2, then the males-to-people ratio is $\frac{1}{1+2} = \frac{1}{3}$ and the females-to-people ratio is $\frac{2}{1+2} = \frac{2}{3}$. In other words, $\frac{2}{3}$ of all the people are female.

Solving a Proportion

To solve a proportion, **cross-multiply**:

$$\frac{x}{5} = \frac{3}{4}$$

$$4x = 5 \times 3$$

$$x = \frac{15}{4} = 3.75$$

An Important Point About Ratios

Notice that if you are given a ratio, you can't determine how many there are of each item just from the ratio. For example, if you are told that the ratio of the number of pencils to the number of pens in a drawer is 5 to 4, you don't know that there are 5 pencils and 4 pens in the drawer. All you know is that for every 5 pencils, there are 4 pens. There might be 50 pencils and 40 pens, or there might be 10 pencils and 8 pens in the drawer.

Example: The ratio of dogs to cats in an apartment building is 3 to 2. If there are a total of 50 animals in the apartment building and all of the animals in the building are dogs or cats, how many dogs are in the building?

Solution: The fraction of animals that are dogs is $\frac{3}{3+2}$, or $\frac{3}{5}$. So the number of dogs in the building is $\frac{3}{5} \times 50$, or 30.

DECIMALS

There are two different ways to express numbers that are not integers: as fractions and as decimals. You've already seen fractions; now it's time to talk about decimals.

When a number is expressed in decimal form, it has two parts: the whole number part and the decimal fraction part. The two parts are separated by the decimal point (.). The whole number part is to the left of the decimal point; the decimal fraction part is the decimal point and the numbers to the right of the decimal point. For example, in 4.56, the whole number is 4, and the decimal fraction is 0.56.

You are certainly familiar with decimals from dealing with money: $12.45 is an example of a decimal. The part to the left of the decimal point is the whole number part: 12 in this case. The decimal fraction part is 0.45 in this case.

You can see how decimals work by looking at dollars and cents. What fraction of a dollar is 1 cent? That's 0.01 dollars. Well, there are 100 cents in a dollar, so 1 cent must represent $\frac{1}{100}$ of a dollar. So you know that the fraction $\frac{1}{100}$ is equivalent to the decimal 0.01.

Now, what fraction of a dollar is 10 cents, or 0.10 dollars? That's equal to a dime, and there are 10 dimes in a dollar, so 10 cents must be $\frac{1}{10}$ of a dollar. So you also know that $\frac{1}{10}$ is equivalent to the decimal 0.10.

Now notice this: the fraction $\frac{1}{10}$ is ten times as much as the fraction $\frac{1}{100}$. Similarly, the decimal 0.10 is ten times as much as the decimal 0.01. This should reassure you that you aren't changing the values of the fractions, only the way they're expressed.

You also can tell how each digit in a positive integer will lead to the value of that integer by the place value of that digit. For instance, in the number 27,465, the number 6 is in the tens place, so there will be $6 \times 10 = 60$ going towards the value of the integer 27,465. Each place is worth 10 times as much as the place to its right:

$$
\begin{aligned}
27{,}465 = 2 \times \ & 10{,}000 \\
+\ 7 \times \ & 1{,}000 \\
+\ 4 \times \ & 100 \\
+\ 6 \times \ & 10 \\
+\ 5 \times \ & 1
\end{aligned}
$$

Decimals work the same way. You can tell each digit in a decimal will lead to the value of that decimal by the place of that digit relative to the decimal point. The first place to the right of the decimal point is worth $\frac{1}{10}$ (thus it is called the tenths place). The second place is worth $\frac{1}{100}$ (thus it is the hundredths place). The third place is worth $\frac{1}{1,000}$ (thus it is the thousandths place). The fourth place is worth $\frac{1}{10,000}$ (thus it is the ten-thousandths place), and so on.

As before, each place is worth 10 times as much as the place to its immediate right. That's why 0.10 means $\frac{1}{10}$, and 0.01 means $\frac{1}{100}$. By the way, the decimal point is small and has a habit of getting lost (is that a decimal or a bug?); for this reason, it's best to put the 0 before the decimal. That doesn't change the value; 0.01 is the same as .01. Also, zeros to the right of the last digit of a decimal don't change its value: 0.10 is the same as 0.1; they're both $\frac{1}{10}$. Similarly, 7.59 and 7.59000 have the same value; they're both $7\frac{59}{100}$.

Changing Fractions to Decimals

To change a fraction into a decimal, divide the denominator of the fraction into the numerator.

Example: Change $\frac{415}{3,220}$ into a decimal.

Solution: First write the fraction as long division.

$$3,220\overline{)415}$$

3,220 is much bigger than 415, so add zeros to 415 to make the division work out. The only way you can do this without changing the value of 415 is by adding a decimal point after the 5. Then, change 415 to 415.00 (those zeros don't change the value of anything). Divide normally but put a decimal point in the quotient (the answer) directly above the decimal point in 415.

$$
\begin{array}{r}
.12 \\
3220\overline{)415.00} \\
\underline{3220} \\
9300 \\
\underline{6440} \\
28600
\end{array}
$$

How far you should go depends on how much accuracy you need; here, you can stop at this hundredths place because you can see the answer is going to be close to 0.13.

Changing Decimals to Fractions

How do you express 0.5 as a fraction? 0.1 represents $\frac{1}{10}$, and 0.5 is five times as much as 0.1, so 0.5 must represent 5 times $\frac{1}{10}$ or $\frac{5}{10}$.

How do you express 0.55 as a fraction? Think of it in terms of dollars and cents. $0.01 is one cent, and that's $\frac{1}{100}$ of a dollar. $0.55 is 55 cents, and that's 55 times as much, so $0.55 must be $\frac{55}{100}$ of a dollar. You can reduce this by dividing the top and bottom by 5, giving $\frac{11}{20}$. That's the fractional equivalent of 0.55.

Hopefully by this point you recognize a pattern:

$$0.1 = 1 \times \frac{1}{10} \text{ or } \frac{1}{10}$$

$$0.11 = 11 \times \frac{1}{100} \text{ or } \frac{11}{100}$$

$$0.111 = 111 \times \frac{1}{1,000} \text{ or } \frac{111}{1,000}$$

$$0.1111 = 1,111 \times \frac{1}{10,000} \text{ or } \frac{1,111}{10,000}$$

and so on.

To change decimals that are between 0 and 1 to fractions, put the digits to the right of the decimal point in the numerator. To figure out the denominator, put a 1 in the denominator and follow it with as many zeros as digits to the right of the decimal point.

Example: Change 0.564 to a fraction.

Solution: There are three digits to the right of the decimal point, so the denominator of the fraction will be 1,000 (a 1 followed by three zeros). The numerator of the fraction is 564.

$$0.564 = \frac{564}{1,000}$$

But notice that $\frac{564}{1,000}$ can be reduced. Because both 564 and 1,000 are divisible by 4, divide both the numerator and the denominator by 4; therefore, $\frac{564}{1,000} = \frac{564 \div 4}{1,000 \div 4} = \frac{141}{250}$.

Addition and Subtraction of Decimals

Add and subtract decimals the same way you add and subtract whole numbers, but make sure the decimal points are lined up before adding. In the answer, put the decimal point directly below the other decimal points.

$$0.456 + 1.234 = \begin{array}{r} 0.456 \\ + 1.234 \\ \hline 1.690 \end{array}$$

QR

K 741

If one of the terms you are adding or subtracting is longer than another (has more digits to the right of the decimal point), add zeros to the shorter number before adding or subtracting.

$$6.97 - 3.567 = 6.970$$
$$\underline{- 3.567}$$
$$3.403$$

Multiplication of Decimals

As with addition and subtraction, you multiply decimals as if they were whole numbers and worry about the decimal points later. You don't need to add zeros to make the numbers the same length when you multiply, however.

$$4.5 \times 3.2 = 4.5$$
$$\underline{\times\ 3.2}$$
$$90$$
$$\underline{+\ 1350}$$
$$1440$$

To place the decimal point in the answer, count the number of digits to the right of the decimal point in each number. Here you have 1 decimal place in 4.5, and 1 in 3.2, for a total of $1 + 1$ or 2 places. Put the decimal point 2 places from the right in the answer: 14.40.

It's a good idea when you get the answer to see whether it makes sense and to check that you put the decimal point in the right place. Here the answer should be a little bigger than 4×3 or 12. So 14.40 should be about right. If you placed the decimal point incorrectly and ended up with 144, you would know that was wrong.

Division of Decimals

It's easiest to discuss division of decimals if you express the division in fractional form.

Example: $4.15 \div 32.2 = \dfrac{4.15}{32.2}$

Solution: Make both the numerator and the denominator of the fraction whole numbers; to do this, multiply both top and bottom by a sufficient power of 10. In this example, multiply by 100; this will make the denominator 3,220 and the numerator 415, leaving:

$$\frac{4.15}{32.2} = \frac{415}{3,220}$$

Now divide 3,220 into 415. You should get approximately 0.129.

Rounding Decimals to the Nearest Place

To round a decimal to the nearest place, look at the digit immediately to the right of that place. If that digit is 5, 6, 7, 8, or 9, then round up. If the digit immediately to the right of the place you are rounding to is 0, 1, 2, 3, or 4, then don't change the digit at the place you are rounding. In either case, in the rounded-off number, there will be no digits to the right of the place you are rounding.

Example: Round 0.12763 to the nearest thousandth.

Solution: The digit in the thousandths place is 7. The digit immediately to the right of the 7 is a 6. Because 6 is among the digits that are 5 or more, round up the thousandths digit from 7 to 8. So 0.12763 rounded to the nearest thousandth is 0.128.

Example: Round 0.5827 to the nearest hundredth.

Solution: The digit in the hundredths place is 8. Immediately to the right of the 8 is a 2. Because 2 is among the digits 0 through 4, keep the digit in the hundredths place the same. So 0.5827 rounded to the nearest hundredth is 0.58.

Scientific Notation

Scientific notation is a convention for expressing numbers that simplifies computation and standardizes results. To write a nonzero number in scientific notation, write the number in the form $a \times 10^n$, where n is an integer and $1 \leq a < 10$ or $-10 < a \leq -1$.

Example: $123 = 1.23 \times 10^2$

1.23 is the **coefficient**, and 2 is the **exponent**.

Example: $0.042 = 4.2 \times 10^{-2}$

You can obtain products and quotients of numbers expressed in scientific notation. When multiplying, one simply multiplies the coefficients and adds the exponents to find the new coefficient and exponent of the answer. Some additional conversion may be necessary so that the new coefficient a is such that $1 \leq a < 10$ or $-10 < a \leq -1$, as in the example below.

Example: $(1.1 \times 10^6)(5.0 \times 10^{17}) = ?$

Solution: Multiply the coefficients 1.1 and 5.0 and add the exponents 6 and 17. The answer is 5.5×10^{23}.

The quotient of two numbers expressed in scientific notation is obtained by dividing the coefficient in the numerator by the coefficient in the denominator and subtracting the exponent in the denominator from the exponent in the numerator.

Example: $\dfrac{6.2 \times 10^5}{2.0 \times 10^{-7}} = ?$

Solution: Divide 6.2 by 2.0 and subtract -7 from 5 (note that $5 - (-7) = 5 + 7 = 12$). The answer is 3.1×10^{12}.

When a number expressed in scientific notation is raised to an exponent, the coefficient is raised to that exponent, and the original exponent is multiplied by that exponent.

Example: $(6.0 \times 10^4)^2$

Solution: Square the 6.0 and multiply the exponent by 2:

$(6.0)^2 \times 10^{4 \times 2} = 36.0 \times 10^8 = 3.6 \times 10^9$

Note that when you move the decimal point one place to the left you must increase the exponent of the 10 by one, from 8 to 9.

QR

When adding or subtracting numbers expressed in scientific notation, they must have the same exponent; when they do not, the appropriate conversion must be made first.

Example: $3.7 \times 10^4 + 1.5 \times 10^3 = ?$

Solution: First, convert 1.5×10^3 to 0.15×10^4 so both numbers have the same exponent:

$3.7 \times 10^4 + 0.15 \times 10^4 = 3.85 \times 10^4$, which can be rounded to 3.9×10^4.

PERCENTS

Percents are a special kind of ratio. Any percent can be expressed as a fraction with a denominator of 100 (*cent* means "one hundred," so *percent* means "per one hundred"). When you see the symbol %, think of it as the factor $\frac{1}{100}$. Thus, $70\% = 70\left(\frac{1}{100}\right)$.

To convert a percent to a fraction or decimal, divide the percent by 100%. Because $100\% = 1$, you are dividing the percent by 1 and are not changing the value of the percent. In the case where the percent is in the form of a decimal number followed by the percent symbol %, the shortcut is to drop the percent symbol and move the decimal point in the number two places to the left.

Percent to fraction: $78\% = \frac{78\%}{100\%} = \frac{78}{100}$

Note that in going from $\frac{78\%}{100\%}$ to $\frac{78}{100}$, the percent symbol %, which represents the factor $\frac{1}{100}$, was cancelled from the numerator and denominator.

Percent to decimal: $78\% = 0.78$

$$78\% = \frac{78\%}{100\%} = \frac{78}{100} = 0.78$$

To convert any fraction or decimal to a percent, just multiply by 100%. For decimals, just move the decimal point two places to the right and add a percent sign. For fractions, remember to reduce if you can before you multiply.

Decimal to percent: $0.29 = 0.29 \times 100\% = 29\%$

$0.3 = 0.30 \times 100\% = 30\%$

$1.45 = 1.45 \times 100\% = 145\%$

Fraction to percent: $\frac{3}{5} = \frac{3}{5} \times 100\% = \frac{3(100)}{5}\% = 3(20)\% = 60\%$

Know these common conversions. They come up frequently on the test, and you can avoid errors and save time by memorizing them instead of having to calculate them on the test.

In general, a digit with a bar over it means that the digit repeats indefinitely. In the table below, $0.3\overline{3}$ means that the 3 with the bar over it repeats indefinitely. Thus, $0.3\overline{3} = 0.3333\ldots$

Fraction	Decimal	Percent
$\frac{1}{1}$	1.0	100%
$\frac{3}{4}$	0.75	75%
$\frac{2}{3}$	$0.6\overline{6}$	$66\frac{2}{3}\%$
$\frac{1}{2}$	0.5	50%
$\frac{1}{3}$	$0.3\overline{3}$	$33\frac{1}{3}\%$
$\frac{1}{4}$	0.25	25%
$\frac{1}{5}$	0.2	20%
$\frac{1}{8}$	0.125	$12\frac{1}{2}\%$
$\frac{1}{10}$	0.1	10%
$\frac{1}{20}$	0.05	5%

The Percent Formula

The percent formula is commonly expressed in two different ways that are mathematically identical. Memorize and use whichever version of the formula you prefer. Notice how easy it is to get from one formula to the other—just multiply or divide both sides of the equation by the Whole.

$$\text{Percent} = \frac{\text{Part}}{\text{Whole}}$$

$$\text{Percent} \times \text{Whole} = \text{Part}$$

If the Part is 3 and the Whole is 4, then the Percent $= \frac{3}{4} = 0.75 = 75\%$.

If the Percent is 20% and the Whole is 8, then the Part $= 20\%(8) = (0.2)(8) = 1.6$.

If the Percent is 60% and the Part is 12, then $60\% \times (\text{Whole}) = 12$. So:

$$\text{Whole} = \frac{12}{60\%} = \frac{12}{\left(\frac{6}{10}\right)} = 12\left(\frac{10}{6}\right) = 20.$$

Translating

Translating percent word problems into math is relatively easy. Whenever you see the phrase "what percent *of* . . . *is* . . . ?," whatever follows the word *of* is the Whole and whatever follows the verb (often *is* or *are*) is the Part.

Example: 25% of 48 is 12.

$$\frac{\text{(part)}\,12}{\text{(whole)}\,48} = 25\%$$

Example: What percent of the songbirds are cardinals?

You don't really have to know what the question is talking about to know that the Whole is the number of songbirds and the Part is the number of cardinals.

Percent Increase/Decrease

Once you understand percents, percent increase and decrease are not as difficult as they may seem.

$$\% \text{ increase} = \frac{\text{Amount of increase}}{\text{Original whole}} \times 100\%$$

$$\% \text{ decrease} = \frac{\text{Amount of decrease}}{\text{Original whole}} \times 100\%$$

$$\text{New whole} = \text{Original whole} \pm \text{Amount of change}$$

Look at the first equation above. To find a percent increase, divide the amount of increase by the original whole. Then multiply this fraction by 100%.

Example: If a number increases from 50 to 70, what is the percent increase?

Solution: The amount of increase is $70 - 50$, or 20. The original whole is 50. So the percent increase is

$$\frac{20}{50} \times 100\% = \frac{2}{5} \times 100\%.$$

What you learned about reducing fractions can help here:

$$\frac{2}{5} \times 100\% = 2 \times 20\% = 40\%$$

If the new price of an item is 130% of its previous price, then it has increased in price by 30%. If an item goes on sale at 60% of its previous price, then it has decreased in price by 40%.

The percent increase or decrease is just the difference in percent from the whole (which is always equal to 100%).

The following table shows which formula to use—percent increase or percent decrease—when you come across different phrases in word problems:

Percent increase	Percent decrease
percent higher than	percent lower than
percent greater than	percent less than
percent gain	percent loss
percent more than	percent less than

Table 56.1

If X is $n\%$ greater than Y, then X is $(100 + n)\%$ of Y. For example, if X is 10% greater than Y, then X is 110% of Y.

If X is $n\%$ less than Y, then X is $(100 - n)\%$ of Y. For example, If X is 70% less than Y, then X is 30% of Y.

Example: If the value of a certain piece of property now is 350% of its original value when Kim purchased it, by what percent has the value of the property increased since Kim purchased it?

Solution: The percent increase is the difference from 100%. So there was a $350\% - 100\% = 250\%$ increase.

AVERAGES

Formula for Computing Averages (**Mean**)

The average formula is $\text{Average} = \dfrac{\text{Sum of the terms}}{\text{Number of terms}}$

To find the mean of a set of numbers, add them up (the sum of the terms) and divide by the number of numbers (the number of terms).

Example: To find the average of the five numbers 12, 15, 23, 40, and 40, first add them: $12 + 15 + 23 + 40 + 40 = 130$. Then divide the sum by 5: $130 \div 5 = 26$.

Using the Average to Find the Sum

$\text{Sum} = (\text{Average}) \times (\text{Number of terms})$

Example: If the average of 10 numbers is 50, then they add up to 50×10, or 500.

Finding the Missing Number

To find a missing number when you're given the average, use the sum.

Example: If the average of four numbers is 7, then the sum of those four numbers is 4×7, or 28. Suppose that three of the numbers are 3, 5, and 8. These three numbers add up to 16 of that 28, which leaves $28 - 16 = 12$ for the fourth number.

CONVERSIONS

Occasionally you will be asked to convert a quantity in a question. The quantity will be a number of units of something. Examples of quantities are 450 miles and 12 pounds. Converting a quantity means expressing the quantity in a different unit.

Example: If the distance between the city of New York and the city of London is approximately 3,500 miles, how many inches apart are these cities?

Solution: To convert from miles to inches, first convert miles to feet and then convert feet to inches:

3,500 miles (5,280 feet/1 mile)

$= 18,480,000$ feet (12 inches/1 foot)

$= 221,760,000$ feet.

Now 221,760,000 rounded to the nearest million is 222,000,000, which in scientific notation is 2.2×10^8.

Example: The moon revolves around the Earth at a speed of approximately 1.02 kilometers per second. How many kilometers per hour is this approximate speed?

Solution: Since the question asks for kilometers per hour, begin by converting seconds to minutes and then converting minutes to hours.

(1.02 kilometers/1 second) (60 seconds/1minute)

$= (61.2$ kilometers/1 minute) (60 minutes/1 hour)

$= 3,672$ kilometers/hour.

LOGARITHMS

The properties of logarithms are dependent on the laws of exponents; therefore, a review of exponents is necessary before the introduction of logarithms.

In the equation: $b^c = x$

 b is the base

 c is the exponent

 x is b raised to the exponent c , where b is positive and not equal to 1.

In the equation above, the exponent c may be an integer, a fraction, or an irrational number. The value of c may be positive, negative, or 0.

In the equation $b^c = x$, the exponent c is the exponent to which b must be raised to obtain the number x . This relationship is described by the statement "The logarithm of x to the base b ," which means if $b^c = x$, then the logarithm to the base b of x is c . In other words:

The logarithm to the base b of a positive number x is equal to the exponent to which b must be raised to obtain x :

$$\text{If: } \log_b (x) = c, \text{ then: } b^c = x$$

Examples: $\log_4 (16) = 2$, since $4^2 = 16$

$\log_{10} (10{,}000) = 4$, since $10^4 = 10{,}000$

$\log_{25} (5) = \frac{1}{2}$, since $25^{\frac{1}{2}} = 5$

Example: If $\log_5 (x) = 3$, then $x = ?$

Solution: The expression $\log_5 (x) = 3$ means that $5^3 = x$; therefore, $x = 125$.

Example: If $\log_b (36) = 2$, then $b = ?$

Solution: The expression $\log_b (36) = 2$ means that $b^2 = 36$; therefore, $b = 6$. If $b^2 = 36$, then $b = 6$ or $b = -6$. However, since you are working with a logarithm to the base b , b must be positive and not equal to 1. Thus, you cannot have $b = -6$. In this example, the only possible value of b is 6.

Example: If $\log_{10} (100) = c$, then $c = ?$

Solution: The expression $\log_{10} (100) = c$ means that $10^c = 100$. Now $100 = 10^2$. Thus, $10^c = 10^2$. Therefore, $c = 2$.

Properties of Logs

The logarithm of the product of two numbers equals the sum of the individual logarithms:

$$\log_b (s \times t) = \log_b (s) + \log_b (t)$$

The logarithm of a quotient of two numbers is the logarithm of the numerator minus the logarithm of the denominator:

$$\log_b \left(\frac{s}{t}\right) = \log_b(s) - \log_b(t)$$

The logarithm of a power with a positive base is equal to the exponent of the power multiplied by the logarithm of the base of that power:

$$\log_b (s^p) = p \times \log_b (s)$$

Log Base 10

Most commonly, logs are expressed in base 10. This means that an increase of one logarithmic unit (in base 10) corresponds to a multiplication of 10 of the actual total.

$$\log_{10}(0.1) = -1, \text{ since } 10^{-1} = 0.1$$
$$\log_{10}(1) = 0, \text{ since } 10^{0} = 1$$
$$\log_{10}(10) = 1, \text{ since } 10^{1} = 10$$
$$\log_{10}(100) = 2, \text{ since } 10^{2} = 100$$
$$\log_{10}(1,000) = 3, \text{ since } 10^{3} = 1,000$$

When working with logarithms to the base of 10, $\log_{10}(x)$ is often written $\log(x)$. For example, $\log(5.3)$ means $\log_{10}(5.3)$. When working with logarithms to the base 10, the integer of the logarithm of a number is called the **characteristic** and the decimal fraction of the logarithm of the number is called the **mantissa**. For example, consider $\log(7,435)$ (note that $\log(7,435)$ means $\log_{10}(7,435)$.) You have that $\log(7,435) = 3.87128$. In this case, for $\log(7,435)$, the characteristic is 3 and the mantissa is 0.87128. Shifting the decimal point to the right or left in a number increases or decreases the characteristic of the logarithm of that number as seen below:

Example: $\log(4.26) = \log(1 \times 4.26) = \log(10^{0}) + \log(4.26) = 0 + 0.62941 = 0.62941 + 0$

$\log(0.426) = \log(0.1 \times 4.26) = \log(10^{-1}) + \log(4.26) = -1 + 0.62941 = 0.62941 - 1$

$\log(0.0426) = \log(0.01 \times 4.26) = \log(10^{-2}) + \log(4.26) = -2 + 0.62941 = 0.62941 - 2$

$\log(42.6) = \log(10 \times 4.26) = \log(10^{1}) + \log(4.26) = 1 + 0.62941 = 0.62941 + 1$

$\log(426) = \log(10^{2} \times 4.26) = \log(10^{2}) + \log(4.26) = 2 + 0.62941 = 0.62941 + 2$

REVIEW PROBLEMS

1. The average of 3, 15, 18, and 8 is

   A. 5
   B. 9
   C. 11
   D. 15
   E. 18

2. Which of the following fractions is largest?

   A. $\frac{2}{5}$

   B. $\frac{1}{2}$

   C. $\frac{2}{7}$

   D. $\frac{2}{10}$

   E. $\frac{3}{9}$

3. $\frac{2}{7} + \frac{1}{4} =$

   A. $\frac{1}{11}$

   B. $\frac{3}{28}$

   C. $\frac{15}{28}$

   D. $\frac{7}{8}$

   E. $\frac{13}{11}$

4. $6\frac{1}{7} - 3\frac{4}{7} =$

   A. $2\frac{3}{7}$

   B. $2\frac{4}{7}$

   C. $3\frac{3}{7}$

   D. $3\frac{4}{7}$

   E. $3\frac{6}{7}$

5. Which of the following numbers is smallest?

   A. 0.1
   B. 0.01
   C. 0.0407
   D. 0.03995
   E. 0.043999

6. What is the value of $5\frac{1}{4} \div 7$?

   A. $\dfrac{7}{20}$

   B. $\dfrac{5}{7}$

   C. $\dfrac{3}{4}$

   D. $\dfrac{6}{7}$

   E. 3

7. $16 + 0.267 + 36.78 =$

   A. 5.347
   B. 8.26
   C. 50.036
   D. 52.047
   E. 53.047

8. What is the cost of a blouse that is priced at $50.00 with a tax of 7%?

   A. $35.00
   B. $50.35
   C. $53.50
   D. $62.75
   E. $85.00

9. If a pencil costs $0.26, what is the cost of 96 pencils?

   A. $2.49
   B. $12.00
   C. $24.00
   D. $22.96
   E. $24.96

10. What is the value of $2,886 \div 37$?

   A. 78
   B. 708
   C. 780
   D. 7,008
   E. 7.800

SOLUTIONS TO REVIEW PROBLEMS

1. **C** Average $= \dfrac{\text{Sum of the terms}}{\text{Number of terms}}$

   Here, the average is $\dfrac{3+15+18+8}{4} = \dfrac{44}{4} = 11$.

2. **B** Begin by comparing choice (A), $\dfrac{2}{5}$, and choice (B), $\dfrac{1}{2}$. $\dfrac{2}{5}$ has a numerator that is less than half of its denominator, so choice (A) is less than $\dfrac{1}{2}$. Choice (A) can be eliminated. Choices (C),(D) and (E) both have numerators that are less than half of their denominators, so these choices are also less than $\dfrac{1}{2}$ and can therefore also be eliminated. This means that choice (B), $\dfrac{1}{2}$, is the largest.

3. **C** $\dfrac{2}{7} + \dfrac{1}{4} = \left(\dfrac{2}{7} \times \dfrac{4}{4}\right) + \left(\dfrac{1}{4} \times \dfrac{7}{7}\right) = \dfrac{8}{28} + \dfrac{7}{28} = \dfrac{15}{28}$

4. **B** $6\dfrac{1}{7} - 3\dfrac{4}{7} = \left(6 + \dfrac{1}{7}\right) - 3\dfrac{4}{7} = \left(5 + \dfrac{7}{7} + \dfrac{1}{7}\right) - 3\dfrac{4}{7} = 5\dfrac{8}{7} - 3\dfrac{4}{7} = 2\dfrac{4}{7}$

5. **B** Choice (A) has a tenths digit of 1, while choices (B), (C), (D), and (E) each have a tenths digit of 0. So choice (A) can be eliminated. Next, look at the hundredths digit: choice (B) has the smallest value at 1, so (B) is the smallest number.

6. **C** When you divide one fraction by another, you invert the second fraction and multiply.

   Think of the integer 7 as the fraction $\dfrac{7}{1}$, so that you can invert it to get the fraction $\dfrac{1}{7}$. Rewrite $5\dfrac{1}{4}$ as an improper fraction. $5\dfrac{1}{4} = \dfrac{5 \times 4 + 1}{4} = \dfrac{20 + 1}{4} = \dfrac{21}{4}$.

   Then $5\dfrac{1}{4} \div 7 = \dfrac{21}{4} \div \dfrac{7}{1} = \dfrac{21}{4} \times \dfrac{1}{7} = \dfrac{21 \times 1}{4 \times 7} = \dfrac{21}{28} = \dfrac{3}{4}$.

7. **E** Write the numbers in a column, making sure to align the decimal points. Write 16 as 16.000 and write 36.78 as 36.780.

$$16.000$$
$$0.267$$
$$\underline{+36.780}$$
$$53.047$$

8. **C** Add 7% of 50 to 50. 7% of 50 is $\dfrac{7}{100} \times 50 = \dfrac{7}{2} \times 1 = \dfrac{7}{2} = 3\dfrac{1}{2} = 3.5$. So the cost of the blouse is $50 + \$3.50$, or $\$53.50$.

9. **E** Multiply the cost of one pencil by the number of pencils. The cost of all the pencils is $0.26 \times 96 = \$24.96$.

10. **A**

$$
\begin{array}{r}
78 \\
37\overline{)2886} \\
\underline{259} \\
296 \\
\underline{296} \\
0
\end{array}
$$

CHAPTER FIFTY-SEVEN

Algebra

Algebra uses the concepts of arithmetic and number properties but adds a twist: variables. **Variables** represent unknown quantities, and many algebraic questions task you with determining what numerical values variables actually represent. Variables are often defined by the rules of **equations** and **inequalities**, statements that show the relationship between two or more expressions as equal (equations) or greater than or less than each other (inequalities).

WORD PROBLEMS

Often the most challenging aspect of algebra problems is the odd way in which information is presented. Don't get frustrated; just break down the information into small pieces and take things one step at a time. Word problems can usually be translated from left to right, but this is not always the case. Say you see this sentence: "The number of stamps in George's stamp collection is twice the number that is 5 less than the number of stamps in Bill's stamp collection." Instead of trying to translate it into math all in one step, approach it piece by piece.

Whenever possible, choose letters for the variables that make sense in the context of the problem. For example, start by calling the number of stamps in George's stamp collection G and the number of stamps in Bill's stamp collection B. Now, think about the relationship between the two amounts: G is not compared to B but to 5 less than B, or $(B - 5)$. So G is twice as large as $(B - 5)$. To set them *equal* to each other, multiply $(B - 5)$ by two. The equation is $G = 2(B - 5)$.

The hardest part of word problems is the process of taking the English sentences and extracting the math from them. The actual math in word problems tends to be the easiest part. The following translation table will help you start dealing with English-to-math translation:

Word Problems Translation Table	
English	**Math**
equals, is, was, will be, has, costs, adds up to, the same as, as much as	$=$
times, of, multiplied by, product of, twice, double, by	$\times$
divided by, per, out of, each, ratio	$\div$
plus, added to, and, sum, combined	$+$
minus, subtracted from, smaller than, less than, fewer, decreased by, difference between	$-$
a number, how much, how many, what	x, n, etc.

Table 57.1

Example: w is x less than y.

Solution: $w = y - x$

Example: Giuseppa's weight is 75 pounds more than twice Jovanna's weight.

Solution: $G = 2J + 75$

Example: In 5 years, Sandy will be 4 years younger than twice Tina's age.

Solution: $(S + 5) = 2(T + 5) - 4$

Notice here that the statement discusses the ages of Sandy and Tina *in five years*, so you must represent their ages as $(S + 5)$ and $(T + 5)$, respectively. One common mistake is to translate the right side of the equation as $2T + 5 - 4$, but that is not equivalent to $2(T + 5) - 4$.

Example: The sum of Richard's age and Cindy's age in years is 17 more than the amount by which Tim's age is greater than Kathy's age.

Solution: $R + C = (T - K) + 17$

EXPONENTS

You can't be adept at algebra unless you're completely at ease with exponents. Here's what you need to know:

Multiplying powers with the same base: To multiply powers with the same base, keep the base and add the exponents:

$$x^3 \times x^4 = x^{3+4} = x^7$$

Dividing powers with the same base: To divide powers with the same base, keep the base and subtract the exponents:

$$y^{13} \div y^8 = y^{13-8} = y^5$$

Raising a power to an exponent: To raise a power to an exponent, keep the base and multiply the exponents:

$$(x^3)^4 = x^{3 \times 4} = x^{12}$$

Multiplying powers with the same exponent: To multiply powers with the same exponent, multiply the bases and keep the exponent:

$$(3^x)(4^x) = (3 \times 4)^x = 12^x$$

Dividing powers with the same exponent: To divide powers with the same exponent, divide the bases and keep the exponent:

$$\frac{6^x}{2^x} = \left(\frac{6}{2}\right)^x = 3^x$$

Example: For all $xyz \neq 0$, $\dfrac{6x^2 y^{12} z^6}{(2x^2 yz)^3} = ?$

Solution: The first step is to eliminate the parentheses. Everything inside gets cubed:

$$\frac{6x^2 y^{12} z^6}{(2x^2 yz)^3} = \frac{6x^2 y^{12} z^6}{8x^6 y^3 z^3}$$

The next step is to look for factors common to the numerator and denominator. The 6 on the top and the 8 on the bottom reduce to 3 over 4. The x^2 on the top cancels with the x^6 on the bottom, leaving x^4 on the bottom.

You're actually subtracting the exponents: $2 - 6 = -4$. The x^{-4} on the top is the same as $\dfrac{1}{x^4}$. The y^{12} on the top cancels with the y^3 on the bottom, leaving y^9 on the top. And the z^6 on the top cancels with the z^3 on the bottom, leaving z^3 on the top:

$$\frac{6x^2 y^{12} z^6}{8x^6 y^3 z^3} = \frac{3y^9 z^3}{4x^4}$$

ADDING, SUBTRACTING, AND MULTIPLYING POLYNOMIALS

Algebra is the basic language of mathematics, and you will want to be fluent in that language. You might not get a whole lot of questions that ask explicitly about such basic algebra procedures as combining like terms, multiplying binomials, or factoring algebraic expressions, but you will do all of those things in the course of working out the answers to more advanced questions. So it's essential that you be at ease with the mechanics of algebraic manipulations.

Combining like terms: To combine like terms, keep the variable part unchanged while adding or subtracting the coefficients:

$$2a + 3a = (2 + 3)a = 5a$$

Adding or subtracting polynomials: To add or subtract polynomials, combine like terms:

$$(3x^2 + 5x - 7) - (x^2 + 12)$$
$$= 3x^2 + 5x - 7 - x^2 - 12$$
$$= (3x^2 - x^2) + 5x + (-7 - 12)$$
$$= 2x^2 + 5x - 19$$

Multiplying monomials: To multiply monomials, multiply the coefficients and the variables separately:

$$2x \times 3x = (2 \times 3)(x \times x) = 6x^2$$

Multiplying binomials: To multiply binomials, use FOIL. To multiply $(x + 3)$ by $(x + 4)$, first multiply the First terms: $x \times x = x^2$; next the Outer terms: $x \times 4 = 4x$; then the Inner terms: $3 \times x = 3x$; and finally the Last terms: $3 \times 4 = 12$. Then add and combine like terms:

$$x^2 + 4x + 3x + 12 = x^2 + 7x + 12$$

Multiplying polynomials: To multiply polynomials with more than two terms, make sure you multiply each term in the first polynomial by each term in the second. (FOIL works only when you want to multiply two binomials.)

$$(x^2 + 3x + 4)(x + 5) = x^2(x + 5) + 3x(x + 5) + 4(x + 5)$$
$$= x^3 + 5x^2 + 3x^2 + 15x + 4x + 20$$
$$= x^3 + 8x^2 + 19x + 20$$

After multiplying two polynomials together, the number of terms in your expression before simplifying should equal the number of terms in one polynomial multiplied by the number of terms in the second. In the example above, you should have $3 \times 2 = 6$ terms in the product before you simplify like terms.

DIVIDING POLYNOMIALS

To divide polynomials, you can use long division. For example, to divide $2x^3 + 13x^2 + 11x - 16$ by $x + 5$:

$$x + 5 \overline{)2x^3 + 13x^2 + 11x - 16}$$

The first term of the quotient is $2x^2$, because that's what will give you a $2x^3$ as a first term when you multiply it by $x + 5$:

$$
\begin{array}{r}
2x^2 \\
x + 5 \overline{)2x^3 + 13x^2 + 11x - 16} \\
2x^3 + 10x^2
\end{array}
$$

Subtract and continue in the same way as when dividing numbers:

$$\begin{array}{r} 2x^2 + 3x - 4 \\ x+5\overline{)2x^3+13x^2+11x-16} \\ \underline{2x^3+10x^2} \\ 3x^2+11x \\ \underline{3x^2+15x} \\ -4x-16 \\ \underline{-4x-20} \\ 4 \end{array}$$

The result is $2x^2 + 3x - 4$ with a remainder of 4.

Example: When $2x^3 + 3x^2 - 4x + k$ is divided by $x + 2$, the remainder is 3. What is the value of k?

Solution: To answer this question, start by cranking out the long division:

$$\begin{array}{r} 2x^2 - x - 2 \\ x+2\overline{)2x^3+3x^2-4x+k} \\ \underline{2x^3+4x^2} \\ -x^2-4x \\ \underline{-x^2-2x} \\ -2x+k \\ \underline{-2x-4} \\ k+4 \end{array}$$

The question says that the remainder is 3, so whatever k is, when you add 4, you get 3:

$k + 4 = 3$

$k = -1$

FACTORING

Performing operations on polynomials is largely a matter of cranking it out. Once you know the rules, adding, subtracting, multiplying, and even dividing is automatic. Factoring algebraic expressions is a different matter. To factor successfully, you have to do more thinking and less cranking. You have to try to figure out what expressions multiplied will give you the polynomial you're looking at. Sometimes that means having a good eye for the test makers' favorite factorables:

- Factor common to all terms

- Difference of squares

- Square of a binomial

Factor common to all terms: A factor common to all the terms of a polynomial can be factored out. This is essentially the distributive property in reverse. For example, all three terms in the polynomial $3x^3 + 12x^2 - 6x$ contain a factor of $3x$. Pulling out the common factor yields $3x(x^2 + 4x - 2)$.

Difference of squares: You will want to be especially keen at spotting polynomials in the form of the difference of squares. Whenever you have two identifiable squares with a minus sign between them, you can factor the expression like this:

$$a^2 - b^2 = (a + b)(a - b)$$

$4x^2 - 9$, for example, factors to $(2x + 3)(2x - 3)$.

Squares of binomials: Learn to recognize polynomials that are squares of binomials:

$$a^2 + 2ab + b^2 = (a + b)^2$$
$$a^2 - 2ab + b^2 = (a - b)^2$$

Polynomials such as those seen above can be expressed as a product of two or more polynomials of lower positive degree. Each of these polynomials is referred to as a factor of the given polynomial. Unless stated in the question otherwise, one can assume only integer coefficients for the factors of a polynomial with integer coefficients.

For example, $4x^2 + 12x + 9$ factors to $(2x + 3)^2$, and $a^2 - 10a + 25$ factors to $(a - 5)^2$.

Sometimes you'll want to factor a polynomial that's not in any of these classic factorable forms. When that happens, factoring becomes a kind of logic exercise with some trial and error thrown in. To factor a quadratic expression, think about what binomials you could use FOIL on to get that quadratic expression. For example, to factor $x^2 - 5x + 6$, think about what First terms will produce x^2, what Last terms will produce $+6$, and what Outer and Inner terms will produce $-5x$. Some common sense—and a little trial and error—will lead you to $(x - 2)(x - 3)$.

Example: For all $x \neq \pm 3$, $\dfrac{3x^2 - 11x + 6}{9 - x^2} =$

    A. $\dfrac{2x - 3}{x + 3}$

    B. $\dfrac{2 - 3x}{x + 3}$

    C. $\dfrac{2x + 3}{x + 3}$

    D. $\dfrac{3x - 2}{x - 3}$

    E. $\dfrac{x - 3}{2x + 3}$

Solution: To reduce a fraction, you eliminate factors common to the top and the bottom. So the first step in reducing an algebraic fraction is to *factor the numerator and denominator*. Here, the denominator is the difference of squares: $9 - x^2 = (3 - x)(3 + x)$. The numerator takes some thought and some trial and error. For the first term to be $3x^2$, the first terms of the factors must be $3x$ and x. For the last term of the polynomial in the numerator to be $+6$, the last terms of the binomials must be either $+2$ and $+3$, -2 and -3, $+1$ and $+6$, or -1 and -6. After a few tries, you should come up with: $3x^2 - 11x + 6 = (3x - 2)(x - 3)$. Now the fraction looks like this:

$$\frac{3x^2 - 11x + 6}{9 - x^2} = \frac{(3x - 2)(x - 3)}{(3 - x)(3 + x)}$$

In this form there are no precisely common factors, but there is a factor in the numerator that's the opposite (negative) of a factor in the denominator: $x - 3$ and $3 - x$ are opposites. Factor -1 out of the numerator and get:

$$\frac{(3x - 2)(x - 3)}{(3 - x)(3 + x)} = \frac{(-1)(3x - 2)(3 - x)}{(3 - x)(3 + x)}$$

Now $(3 - x)$ can be eliminated from both the top and the bottom:

$$\frac{(-1)(3x - 2)(3 - x)}{(3 - x)(3 + x)} = \frac{-(3x - 2)}{3 + x} = \frac{-3x + 2}{3 + x}$$

That's the same as choice (B):

$$\frac{-3x + 2}{3 + x} = \frac{2 - 3x}{x + 3}$$

Alternative: Here's another way to answer this question. Pick a number for x, and see what happens. At least one of the answer choices, the correct answer choice, will give you the same value as the original fraction, no matter what you plug in for x. However, some of the incorrect answer choices might give you the same value as the original fraction for the value that you plug in. Pick a number that's easy to work with—like 0.

When you plug $x = 0$ into the original expression, any term with an x drops out, and you end up with $\frac{6}{9}$, or $\frac{2}{3}$. Now plug $x = 0$ into each answer choice to see which ones equal $\frac{2}{3}$. Eliminate any answer choices that do not equal $\frac{2}{3}$ when $x = 0$.

When you get to (B), it works, but you can't stop there. Sometimes one or more incorrect answer choices will work for the particular value that you choose. When you pick numbers, *look at every answer choice*. All the incorrect answer choices must be eliminated when using the method of picking numbers. Choice (D) also works for $x = 0$. At least you know one of those is the correct answer, and you can decide between them by picking another value for x.

This is not a sophisticated approach, but who cares? You don't get points for elegance. You get points for right answers.

Example: Factor the following polynomial: $8xy + 18y^2$.

Solution: You can see that $2y$ is greatest common factor of each term in the polynomial. Therefore, by the distributive law, you can factor:

$8xy + 18y^2 = 2y(4x + 9y)$

In this example, $2y$ is referred to as the greatest monomial factor of the given polynomial because it is the monomial with the greatest numerical coefficient that is a factor of each term in the polynomial and each variable of the monomial is raised to the greatest exponent that is a factor of each term of the polynomial. The other factor, $4x + 9y$, cannot be reduced to a product of factors of lower positive degree and therefore is irreducible. Moreover, the greatest monomial factor of $4x + 9y$ is 1. A polynomial is said to be completely factored when it is expressed as a product of a monomial, which may or may not be a constant, and one or more irreducible polynomials, each of which has 1 as its greatest monomial factor.

THE GOLDEN RULE OF EQUATIONS

You probably remember the basic procedure for solving algebraic equations: *do the same thing to both sides.* You can do almost anything you want to one side of an equation as long as you preserve the equality by doing the same thing the other side. Your aim in whatever you do to both sides is to get the variable (or expression) you're solving for all by itself on one side.

Example: If $\sqrt[3]{8x+6} = -3$, what is the value of x ?

Solution: To solve this equation for x, do whatever you must to both sides of the equation to isolate x on one side. Layer by layer you want to peel away all those extra symbols and numbers around the x. First you want to get rid of that cube-root symbol. The way to undo a cube root is to cube both sides:

$$\sqrt[3]{8x+6} = -3$$
$$\left(\sqrt[3]{8x+6}\right)^3 = (-3)^3$$
$$8x + 6 = -27$$

Next, subtract 6 from both sides and divide both sides by 8:

$$8x + 6 = -27$$
$$8x = -27 - 6$$
$$8x = -33$$
$$x = -\frac{33}{8} = -4.125$$

The test makers have a few favorite equation types that you should be prepared to solve. Solving linear equations is usually straightforward. Generally it's obvious what to do to isolate the unknown. But when the unknown is in a denominator or an exponent, how to proceed might not be so obvious.

UNKNOWN IN A DENOMINATOR

The basic procedure for solving an equation is the same even when the unknown is in a denominator: do the same thing to both sides. In this case, you multiply to undo division.

If you wanted to solve $1 + \dfrac{1}{x} = 2 - \dfrac{1}{x}$, you would multiply both sides by x:

$$1 + \frac{1}{x} = 2 - \frac{1}{x}$$
$$x\left(1 + \frac{1}{x}\right) = x\left(2 - \frac{1}{x}\right)$$
$$x + 1 = 2x - 1$$

Now you have an equation with no denominators, which is easy to solve:

$$x + 1 = 2x - 1$$
$$x - 2x = -1 - 1$$
$$-x = -2$$
$$x = 2$$

Another good way to solve an equation with the unknown in the denominator is to *cross multiply*. That's the best way to do the following example.

Example: If $\dfrac{5}{x+3} = \dfrac{1}{x} + \dfrac{1}{2x}$, what is the value of x?

Solution: Before you can cross multiply, you need to re-express the right side of the equation as a single fraction. That means giving the two fractions a common denominator and adding them. The common denominator to use is $2x$:

$$\frac{5}{x+3} = \frac{1}{x} + \frac{1}{2x}$$
$$\frac{5}{x+3} = \frac{2}{2x} + \frac{1}{2x}$$
$$\frac{5}{x+3} = \frac{3}{2x}$$

Now cross multiply:

$$\frac{5}{x+3} = \frac{3}{2x}$$
$$(5)(2x) = (x+3)(3)$$
$$10x = 3x + 9$$
$$10x - 3x = 9$$
$$7x = 9$$
$$x = \frac{9}{7}$$

UNKNOWN IN AN EXPONENT

The procedure for solving an equation when the unknown is in an exponent is a little different. What you want to do in this situation is to re-express one or both sides of the equation so that the two sides have the same base.

Example: If $8^x = 16^{x-1}$, then $x =$

A. $\dfrac{1}{8}$

B. $\dfrac{1}{2}$

C. 2

D. 4

E. 8

Solution: In this case, the base on the left is 8 and the base on the right is 16. They're both powers with bases of 2 and integer exponents, so you can re-express both sides as powers with bases of 2:

$$(2^3)^x = (2^4)^{(x-1)}$$

$$2^{3x} = 2^{4(x-1)}$$

$$2^{3x} = 2^{(4x-4)}$$

Thus, $2^{3x} = 2^{(4x-4)}$. When two powers have the same base, they must have equal exponents. Here, you can simply set the exponent expressions equal and solve for x:

$$3x = 4x - 4$$

$$3x - 4x = -4$$

$$-x = -4$$

$$x = 4$$

Choice (D) is correct.

Alternative: Here's another way to answer this question: Use Backsolving. Here, if you start with choice (C) and $x = 2$, you get $8^x = 8^2 = 64$ on the left side of the equation and $16^{(x-1)} = 16^{(2-1)} = 16^1 = 16$ on the right side. It's not clear whether (C) was too small or too large, so you should probably try (D) next—it's easier to work with than (B), which is a fraction (and that's also why you didn't want to start with it first). If $x = 4$, then $8^x = 8^4 = 4,096$ on the left side, and $16^{(x-1)} = 16^{(4-1)} = 16^3 = 4,096$ on the right side. No need to do any more. Choice (D) works, so it's the answer.

QUADRATIC EQUATIONS

To solve a quadratic equation, put it in the $ax^2 + bx + c = 0$ form, factor the left side (if you can), and set each factor equal to 0 separately to get the two solutions. To solve $x^2 + 12 = 7x$, first rewrite it as $x^2 - 7x + 12 = 0$. Then factor the left side:

$$x^2 - 7x + 12 = 0$$
$$(x - 3)(x - 4) = 0$$
$$x - 3 = 0 \text{ or } x - 4 = 0$$
$$x = 3 \text{ or } x = 4$$

Sometimes the left side may not be obviously factorable. You can always use the *quadratic formula*. Just plug the coefficients a, b, and c from $ax^2 + bx + c = 0$ into the formula:

$$x = \frac{-b \pm \sqrt{b^2 - 4ac}}{2a}$$

To solve $x^2 + 4x + 2 = 0$, plug $a = 1$, $b = 4$, and $c = 2$ into the formula:

$$x = \frac{-4 \pm \sqrt{4^2 - 4 \cdot 1 \cdot 2}}{2 \cdot 1}$$

$$= \frac{-4 \pm \sqrt{8}}{2} = \frac{-4 \pm 2\sqrt{2}}{2} = -2 \pm \sqrt{2}$$

For all real numbers b and c, and all nonzero real numbers a, the quadratic equation $ax^2 + bx + c = 0$ has:

- Two different real roots if $b^2 - 4ac > 0$

- One double real root if $b^2 - 4ac = 0$

- Two complex conjugate roots if $b^2 - 4ac < 0$

"In Terms Of"

So far in this chapter, solving an equation has meant finding a numerical value for the unknown. When there's more than one variable in one equation, it's generally impossible to get numerical solutions. Instead, what you do is solve for the unknown *in terms of* the other variables.

To solve an equation for one variable in terms of another means to isolate the one variable on one side of the equation, leaving an expression containing the other variable on the other side of the equation.

For example, to solve the equation $3x - 10y = -5x + 6y$ for x in terms of y, isolate x:

$$3x - 10y = -5x + 6y$$
$$3x + 5x = 6y + 10y$$
$$8x = 16y$$
$$x = 2y$$

Example: If $a = \dfrac{b + x}{c + x}$, what is the value of x in terms of a, b, and c?

Solution: You want to get x on one side by itself. The first thing to do is eliminate the denominator by multiplying both sides by $c + x$:

$$a = \frac{b + x}{c + x}$$
$$a(c + x) = \frac{b + x}{c + x}(c + x)$$
$$ac + ax = b + x$$

Next, move all terms with x to one side and all terms without x to the other:

$$ac + ax = b + x$$
$$ax - x = b - ac$$

Now factor x out of the left side and divide both sides by the other factor to isolate x:

$$ax - x = b - ac$$

$$x(a - 1) = b - ac$$
$$x = \frac{b - ac}{a - 1}$$

SIMULTANEOUS EQUATIONS

You can get numerical solutions for more than one unknown if you are given more than one equation. Simultaneous Equations questions take a little thought to answer. Solving simultaneous equations almost always involves combining equations, but you have to figure out the best way to combine each unique set of equations.

You can solve for two variables only if you have two distinct equations. Two forms of the same equation will not be adequate. Combine the equations in such a way that one of the variables cancels out. For example, to solve the two equations $4x + 3y = 8$ and $x + y = 3$, multiply both sides of the second equation by -3 to get $-3x - 3y = -9$. Now add the two equations; the $3y$ and the $-3y$ cancel out, leaving $x = -1$. Plug that back into either one of the original equations and you'll find that $y = 4$.

Example: If $2x - 9y = 11$ and $x + 12y = -8$, what is the value of $x + y$?

Solution: If you just plow ahead without thinking, you might try to answer this question by solving for one variable at a time. That would work, but it would take a lot more time than this question needs. As usual, the key to this Simultaneous Equations question is to combine the equations, but combining the equations doesn't necessarily mean losing a variable. Look what happens here if you just add the equations as presented:

$$2x - 9y = 11$$
$$+ \underline{(x + 12y = -8)}$$
$$3x + 3y = 3$$

Suddenly you're almost there! Just divide both sides by 3 and you get $x + y = 1$.

ABSOLUTE VALUE AND INEQUALITIES

To solve an equation that includes absolute value signs, think about the two different cases. For example, to solve the equation $|x - 12| = 3$, think of it as two equations:

$$x - 12 = 3 \text{ or } x - 12 = -3$$
$$x = 15 \text{ or } 9$$

To solve an inequality, do whatever is necessary to both sides to isolate the variable. Just remember that when you multiply or divide both sides by a negative number, you must reverse the inequality sign. To solve $-5x + 7 < -3$, subtract 7 from both sides to get $-5x < -10$. Now divide both sides by -5, remembering to reverse the inequality sign: $x > 2$.

Example: What is the solution set of $|2x - 3| < 7$?

      A. $\{-5 < x < 2\}$

      B. $\{-5 < x < 5\}$

      C. $\{-2 < x < 5\}$

      D. $\{x < -5 \text{ or } x > 2\}$

      E. $\{x < -5 \text{ or } x < 2\}$

Solution: What does it mean if $|2x - 3| < 7$? It means that if the expression between the absolute value bars is positive, it's less than $+7$, or if the expression between the bars is negative, it's greater than -7. If the expression between the absolute value bars is 0, its absolute value is less than 7. In other words, $2x - 3$ is between -7 and $+7$:

$$-7 < 2x - 3 < 7$$
$$-4 < 2x < 10$$
$$-2 < x < 5$$

Choice (C) is correct.

In fact, there's a general rule that applies here: to solve an inequality in the form $|\text{whatever}| < p$, where $p > 0$; just put that "whatever" inside the range $-p$ to p:

      $|\text{anything}| < p$ means: $-p < \text{anything} < p$

      For example, $|x - 5| < 14$ becomes $-14 < x - 5 < 14$.

And here's another general rule: to solve an inequality in the form $|\text{whatever}| > p$, where $p > 0$; just put that "whatever" outside the range $-p$ to p:

      $|\text{anything}| > p$ means: $\text{anything} < -p$ OR $\text{anything} > p$

      For example, $\left|\dfrac{3x + 9}{2}\right| > 7$ becomes $\dfrac{3x + 9}{2} < -7$ or $\dfrac{3x + 9}{2} > 7$.

GRAPHING EQUATIONS

When graphing an equation, it's best to identify a few key parameters initially to get an overall sense of the function. Doing these in order provides a repeatable way to tackle almost any equation:

1. **Determine what type of function is presented.**

    Equations can be linear, absolute value, quadratic, polynomial, radical, and piecewise. Knowing what general category the equation or function falls under gives you an idea as to what the graph should look like.

    - **Linear:** These come in one of two general forms:
        - The graph of the equation $y = mx + b$ is a straight line where $m = $ slope and $b = y$-intercept.
        - The graph of the equation $x = $ constant is a vertical line. This is not a function.
    - **Absolute Value:** The graph of the equation $y = |ax + b|$, where a and b are constants and $a \neq 0$, has a V-shape.
    - **Quadratic:** The graph of the equation $y = ax^2 + bx + c$, where $a \neq 0$, is a parabola.
    - **Polynomial:** The graph of the equation $y = p(x)$, where $p(x)$ is a polynomial, can take on any squiggly-line shape. When $p(x) = ax^2 + bx + c$, where $a \neq 0$, $p(x)$ is a quadratic polynomial.
    - **Radical:** The radical function cannot take a negative value under the radical.
    - **Piecewise:** These have no general form because they can be continuous or discontinuous functions that may take on the characteristic shapes of other general functions over certain ranges.

2. **Identify the y-intercepts and the x-intercepts.**

    Obvious points on the graph of an equation are points where the graph in question crosses the x- and y-axes. A y-intercept is the y-coordinate of a point where the graph crosses the y-axis. An x-intercept is the x-coordinate of a point where the graph crosses the x-axis. At a y-intercept, $x = 0$. At an x-intercept, $y = 0$. You find the y-intercept or y-intercepts by letting $x = 0$ and find the x-intercept or x-intercepts by letting $y = 0$.

3. **Identify the zeros of functions.**

    Find the zeros of the function f by finding the x-intercepts of the graph of the equation $y = f(x)$.

4. **Find the domain.**

    The domain of a function defines all the values that x can have for the function.

5. **Determine the range.**

    The range of a function defines all the values that y can have for the function.

The following examples illustrate these five steps.

Example: Graph $y = 3x + 2$.

Solution: 1. This is a nonvertical straight line.

2. The y-intercept (where $x = 0$) is $y = 2$. The x-intercept (where $y = 0$) is $x = -\dfrac{2}{3}$

3. If the function is f, where $f(x) = 3x + 2$, then there are no other zeros for this function.

4. The domain is all real numbers because x can be any real number.

5. The range is all real numbers because y can be any real number.

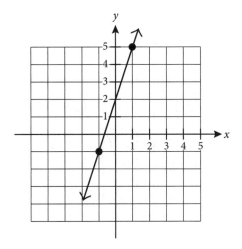

Example: Graph $y = |x + 1|$.

Solution: 1. This is an absolute value and fits in the general form of the equation $y = |ax + b|$, so it should have a V-shape.

2. The y-intercept is $y = 1$. The x-intercept is $x = -1$.

3. There are no other zeros for the function $|x + 1|$.

4. The domain is all real numbers.

5. The range is $[0, \infty)$. This means y can be any value from 0 to ∞, including 0.

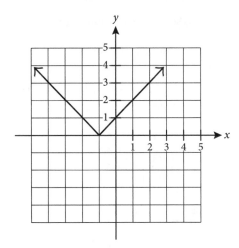

Example: Graph $y = \sqrt{2x - 5}$.

Solution: 1. This is a radical. The graph of this particular equation is part of a parabola.

2. When $x = 0$, $y = \sqrt{-5}$. That means the graph never crosses the y-axis. The x-intercept is $x = \frac{5}{2}$.

3. There are no other zeros for the function $f(x) = \sqrt{2x - 5}$.

4. The domain for this function is $\frac{5}{2}, \infty$).

5. The range for this function is $[0, \infty)$.

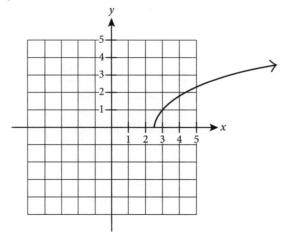

Example: Graph $y = \dfrac{2x - 6}{x^2 - 9}$ $x \leq 0, x \neq -3$

$$= x^2 - 6x + 5, x > 0$$

Solution: 1. This fits the piecewise general form, so look at the general form of each piece.

$$\frac{2x - 6}{x^2 - 9} = \frac{2(x - 3)}{(x + 3)(x - 3)} = \frac{2}{x + 3}.$$

The first piece is $y = \dfrac{2}{x + 3}$, $x \leq 0, x \neq -3$.

The second piece takes on a quadratic general form and will be part of a parabola.

2. The only y-intercept is $y = \dfrac{2}{3}$. The x-intercepts are $x = 1$ and $x = 5$.

3. The vertical asymptote has the equation $x = -3$, and the horizontal asymptote has the equation $y = 0$.

4. The domain is $(-\infty, -3) \cup (-3, \infty)$. This means x can be any number but -3.

5. The range is all real numbers.

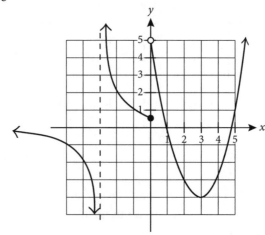

REVIEW PROBLEMS

1. If $x = 3 - y^2$ and $y = -2$, what is the value of x ?

    A. -2

    B. -1

    C.   1

    D.   2

    E.   3

2. For all x, $2^x + 2^x + 2^x + 2^x =$

    A. $2^{(x+2)}$

    B. $2^{(x+4)}$

    C. 2^{3x}

    D. 2^{4x}

    E. 8^x

3. For all $x \neq \pm\frac{1}{2}, \dfrac{6x^2 - x - 2}{4x^2 - 1} =$

    A. $\dfrac{2-3x}{2x+1}$

    B. $\dfrac{3x+2}{2x+1}$

    C. $\dfrac{3x+2}{2x-1}$

    D. $\dfrac{3x-2}{2x-1}$

    E. $\dfrac{2-3x}{2x-1}$

4. When $3x^3 - 7x + 7$ is divided by $x + 2$, the remainder is:

    A. -5

    B. -3

    C.   1

    D.   3

    E.   5

5. If $\sqrt[4]{\dfrac{x+1}{2}} = \dfrac{1}{2}$, then $x =$

    A. -0.969

    B. -0.875

    C.   0

    D.   0.875

    E.   0.985

6. If $\dfrac{19}{5x + 17} = \dfrac{19}{31}$, then $x =$

    A. 0.4
    B. 1.4
    C. 2.8
    D. 3.4
    E. 4.8

7. If $(3^{x^2})(9^x)(3) = 27$ and $x > 0$, what is the value of x?

    A. 0.27
    B. 0.41
    C. 0.73
    D. 1.41
    E. 1.92

8. If $y \neq 4a$ and $x = \dfrac{y + a^2}{y - 4a}$, what is the value of y in terms of a and x?

    A. $\dfrac{4a - 4a^2 x}{x + 1}$

    B. $\dfrac{a^2 - 4ax}{x + 1}$

    C. $\dfrac{a^2 + 4ax}{x + 1}$

    D. $\dfrac{a^2 + 4ax}{x - 1}$

    E. $\dfrac{4a - 4a^2 x}{x - 1}$

9. If $4x + ky = 15$ and $x - ky = -25$, which of the following could be the values of x and y?

    A. $x = -3$ and $y = -5$
    B. $x = -2$ and $y = 3$
    C. $x = 0$ and $y = -2$
    D. $x = 2$ and $y = 3$
    E. $x = 3$ and $y = 2$

10. How many integers are in the solution set of $|4x + 3| < 8$?

    A. None
    B. Two
    C. Three
    D. Four
    E. Five

SOLUTIONS TO REVIEW PROBLEMS

1. **B** Substitute -2 for y into the equation $x = 3 - y^2$:

$$x = 3 - y^2 = 3 - (-2)^2 = 3 - 4 = -1$$

2. **A** The sum of 4 identical quantities is 4 times one of those quantities, so the sum of the four terms 2^x is 4 times 2^x:

$$2^x + 2^x + 2^x + 2^x = 4(2^x) = 2^2(2^x) = 2^{x+2}$$

3. **D** Factor the top and the bottom and cancel the factors they have in common:

$$\frac{6x^2 - x - 2}{4x^2 - 1} = \frac{(2x+1)(3x-2)}{(2x+1)(2x-1)}$$
$$= \frac{3x-2}{2x-1}$$

4. **B** Use long division. Watch out: The expression that goes under the division sign needs a place-holding $0x^2$ term:

$$
\begin{array}{r}
3x^2 - 6x + 5 \\
x+2\overline{)3x^3 + 0x^2 - 7x + 7} \\
\underline{3x^3 + 6x^2} \\
-6x^2 - 7x \\
\underline{-6x^2 - 12x} \\
5x + 7 \\
\underline{5x + 10} \\
-3
\end{array}
$$

The remainder is -3.

5. **B** To undo the fourth-root symbol, raise both sides to the exponent 4:

$$\sqrt[4]{\frac{x+1}{2}} = \frac{1}{2}$$
$$\left(\sqrt[4]{\frac{x+1}{2}}\right)^4 = \left(\frac{1}{2}\right)^4$$
$$\frac{x+1}{2} = \frac{1}{16}$$

Now cross multiply:

$$(x+1)(16) = (2)(1)$$
$$16x + 16 = 2$$
$$16x = -14$$
$$x = -\frac{14}{16} = -\frac{7}{8} = -0.875$$

6.   **C**   This might look at first glance like a candidate for cross multiplication, but that would just make things more complicated. Notice that the fractions on both sides have the same numerator, 19. If the two fractions are equal and they have the same numerator, then they must have the same denominator, so just write an equation that says that one denominator is equal to the other denominator:

$$\frac{19}{5x+17} = \frac{19}{31}$$

$$5x + 17 = 31$$
$$5x = 31 - 17$$
$$5x = 14$$
$$x = \frac{14}{5} = 2.8$$

7.   **C**   Watch what happens when you express everything as powers with a base of 3:

$$(3^{x^2})(9^x)(3) = 27$$

$$(3^{x^2})(3^2)^x(3^1) = 3^3$$

When you raise a power to an exponent, multiply the exponents, and keep the same base. So $(3^2)^x = 3^{2x}$:

$$(3^{x^2})(3^2)^x(3^1) = 3^3$$

$$(3^{x^2})(3^{2x})(3^1) = 3^3$$

The left side of the equation is the product of powers with the same base, so just add the exponents:

$$(3^{x^2})(3^{2x})(3^1) = 3^3$$

$$3^{x^2+2x+1} = 3^3$$

Now the two sides of the equation are powers with the same base, so you can just set the exponents equal:

$$x^2 + 2x + 1 = 3$$
$$(x + 1)^2 = 3$$
$$x + 1 = \pm\sqrt{3}$$
$$x = -1 \pm \sqrt{3}$$

The positive value is $-1 + \sqrt{3}$, which is approximately 0.732.

8. **D** First multiply both sides by $y - 4a$ to clear the denominator:

$$x = \frac{y + a^2}{y - 4a}$$

$$x(y - 4a) = y + a^2$$

$$xy - 4ax = y + a^2$$

Now move all terms with y to the left and all terms without y to the right:

$$xy - 4ax = y + a^2$$
$$xy - y = a^2 + 4ax$$

Now factor the left side and divide to isolate y:

$$xy - y = a^2 + 4ax$$
$$y(x - 1) = a^2 + 4ax$$

$$y = \frac{a^2 + 4ax}{x - 1}$$

9. **B** With only two equations, you won't be able to get numerical solutions for three unknowns. But apparently you can get far enough to rule out three of the four answer choices. How? Look for a way to combine the equations that leads somewhere useful. Notice that the first equation contains $+ky$ and the second equation contains $-ky$, so if you add the equations as they are, you'll lose those terms:

$$4x + ky = 15$$
$$\underline{x - ky = -25}$$
$$5x = -10$$
$$x = -2$$

There's not enough information to get numerical solutions for k or y, but you do know that $x = -2$, so the correct answer is the only choice that has an x-value of -2.

QR

K 775

10.   D   If the absolute value of something is less than 8, then that something is between -8 and 8:

$$|4x + 3| < 8$$

$$-8 < 4x + 3 < 8$$

$$-11 < 4x < 5$$

$$-\frac{11}{4} < x < \frac{5}{4}$$

$$-2\frac{3}{4} < x < 1\frac{1}{4}$$

There are four integers in that range: $-2, -1, 0,$ and 1.

CHAPTER FIFTY-EIGHT

Probability and Statistics

Questions involving probability and statistics tend to be some of the most dreaded by test takers. This isn't without good reason: The equations can appear confusing, and the questions can be time-consuming. Nevertheless, these question types can be broken down into predictable formulations that appear time and again. With good understanding of the terminology and experience with the calculations, you will find these questions to be much more manageable and possibly even a source of quick points on Test Day.

PROBABILITY

Probability is the branch of mathematics concerned with calculating the likelihood that an event will occur. This likelihood is assigned a numerical value. If p is the probability that an event will occur, then you always have that $0 \leq p \leq 1$. Thus, the probability of an event is always greater than or equal to 0 and less than or equal to 1. A probability of 0 means there is *no* chance an event will occur; while a probability of 1 means the event will *definitely* occur.

Basic Terms

While you do not need to memorize the following terms verbatim, understanding what each means is important for understanding test questions. As you read through each, consider the example of a fair die with sides numbered 1, 2, 3, 4, 5, and 6 being rolled.

Experiment: When some process is conducted, it is called an experiment. An experiment could be the process of rolling the die one time.

Outcome: One of the possible results of the experiment. An example of an outcome is the rolling of a 3.

Sample space: The set of all possible outcomes. The set of possible outcomes can be considered to be the rolling of a 1, the rolling of a 2, the rolling of a 3, the rolling of a 4, the rolling of a 5, and the rolling of a 6. Thus, the sample space in this case is {1, 2, 3, 4, 5, 6}. The probability of the sample space is always 1. Therefore, if the sample space is S, then $P(S) = 1$.

Empty set: The unique set having no elements. The empty set is often represented by ϕ, so $P(\phi) = 0$.

Event: One particular set of possible outcomes. An example of an event is the rolling of a 3 or a 5. Thus, one event, which you can call event A, is $\{3, 5\}$. So $A = \{3, 5\}$.

Elementary event: An event that is a set consisting of only one outcome, such as rolling a 4. If B is the event of rolling a 4, then $B = \{4\}$. 4 is an outcome, whereas $\{4\}$ is an event. This is consistent with the definition since an event is a set of possible outcomes. Note that, as is the case with the event of rolling a 4, it is possible that the set contains just one outcome.

The sample space of an experiment can be defined in different ways, which can affect how you will need to consider outcomes and events. For example, suppose the experiment is the rolling of the die once. You can define the outcomes to be these:

One outcome is the rolling of a 1 or a 2. Define this outcome as s_1.
One outcome is the rolling of a 3. Define this outcome as s_2.
One outcome is the rolling of a 4, a 5, or a 6. Define this outcome as s_3.

In this experiment, because of how you have defined it, the only possible outcomes are s_1, s_2, and s_3. The sample space in this case is $\{s_1, s_2, s_3\}$. Under these conditions, an event could be the set consisting of s_1 and s_2. Thus, if B is the event consisting of the outcomes s_1 and s_2, then $B = \{s_1, s_2\}$.

Notation

In mathematics, the probability that event A occurs is written $P(A)$.

Describing Probability

Probability can be expressed as a percent (for example, there's a 50% chance of getting heads in a fair coin toss), as a fraction (for example, the probability of getting heads is $\frac{1}{2}$), or as a decimal (for example, there's a 0.5 chance of getting heads). What does this value mean? It's a statement of what's *likely* to happen and not a guarantee of what *will* actually happen. It's certainly possible, for example, to flip a coin 10 times and get 10 tails.

What's behind probability?

Now, how do you know that, when a fair coin is tossed, there's a 50% chance of getting heads? You figure out how many different outcomes there are for the coin toss (two: heads or tails) and then figure out how many of those outcomes give a result of heads (just 1). So one out of the two possible outcomes (or 50% of them) result in heads. That's the basic formula for probability when all the outcomes are equally likely:

$$\text{Probability} = \frac{\text{Number of desired outcomes}}{\text{Number of possible outcomes}}$$

You can see now that probability is a fraction with the number of desired outcomes on the top and the number of possible outcomes on the bottom. In other words, probability is just a way of predicting the likelihood of a specific event by figuring out what fraction of all possible outcomes have the characteristic you're looking for. Stated yet another way, probability is the fraction of all the possible outcomes that are members of the set of outcomes that is a specified event. In every probability question, your goal is to find the total number of possible outcomes and the number of desired outcomes. Keep in mind that "desired" means only that these are the outcomes that have the characteristic you're interested in, not that you necessarily want these outcomes to happen.

Example: A bag contains 10 identical balls numbered 1 through 10 inclusive. If a ball is drawn from the bag at random, what is the probability (as a percent) that it bears a number less than 4?

Solution: If there are 10 balls in the bag, and you're picking only one ball, then there are 10 possible outcomes. So you now have the bottom of our probability fraction. What you still need to do is determine the number of desired outcomes. You're interested in numbers less than 4, and the only balls that have this characteristic are 1, 2, and 3, so 3 out of the 10 balls would give us a number less than 4. That's $\frac{3}{10}$ or 30%.

So to find a probability for a single event:

1. Figure out how many outcomes are possible overall.
2. Figure out how many of the possible outcomes have the characteristic you're looking for.
3. Plug these numbers into the probability formula.

As you can see, every probability problem starts with two basic things:

1. Total possible outcomes
2. Desired outcomes

Example: A fair six-sided die with sides numbered 1, 2, 3, 4, 5, and 6 is thrown. What is the probability it lands with an even number facing up?

Solution: Desired outcomes = 3
Total possible outcomes = 6

The regular six-sided die has six numbers (1, 2, 3, 4, 5, and 6) on its faces. That gives us a total of six possible outcomes. You're interested only in the even numbers, of which there are three (2, 4, and 6). So the number of desired outcomes is three. This gives us a probability of $\frac{3}{6}$, or $\frac{1}{2}$.

Example: Of the 1,000 employees of a company, 5 employees have the job title of accountant. If one of these employees is selected at random, what is the probability this employee has the job title of accountant?

Solution: Desired outcomes = 5
Total possible outcomes = 1,000

There are 1,000 employees that could be selected. So the total number of possible outcomes is 1,000. There are 5 employees with the job title of accountant. So the number of desired outcomes here is 5. That gives a probability of $\frac{5}{1,000}$, or $\frac{1}{200}$.

Example: A certain pet store has 13 mice in a single tank. Five of the mice are white, and 8 of the mice are brown. If the store clerk reaches into the mice's tank to select a mouse at random, what is the probability that the mouse is white?

Solution: Desired outcomes $= 5$
Total possible outcomes $= 13$

If there are 13 mice total, then the number of possible outcomes is 13. Only 5 of the mice are white, so the number of desired outcomes is 5. This gives us a probability of $\frac{5}{13}$.

Probability an Event Does Not Occur

Now that you've seen how to find the probability of a single event, consider what happens when you're interested in more than one event. Let A be an event and $\overline{A}$ be the event that event A does not occur. Added together, these two events represent the entire sample set (with a probability of 1). Therefore, the probability event A does not occur is equal to 1 minus the probability that event A does occur: $P(\overline{A}) = 1 - P(A)$.

For example, suppose a fair sided die with sides numbered 1 through 6 is tossed. The probability that a 4 is rolled is $\frac{1}{6}$. Therefore, the probability that a 4 is not rolled is $1 - \frac{1}{6} = \frac{5}{6}$.

The event that a 4 is not rolled is the event that a 1, 2, 3, 5, or 6 is rolled. There are 5 desired outcomes and 6 possible outcomes. So the probability that a 4 is not rolled is $\frac{\text{Number of desired outcomes}}{\text{Number of possible outcomes}} = \frac{5}{6}$.

Multiple-Event Probability

When all the outcomes are equally likely, the probability for a single event is just $\frac{\text{Number of desired outcomes}}{\text{Number of possible outcomes}}$. But what if you're interested in the probability that *at least* one of two different events occurs? Or in the probability that two different events *both* occur? Or in the probability that one of two different events occurs and the other does *not*? In those cases, it's not enough just to determine the probabilities of the individual events; you must combine the probabilities somehow.

Probability at least one of two events will occur when both events cannot occur

Some probability questions test your ability to determine the probability of what are known technically as **mutually exclusive events**. Mutually exclusive events are those events for which the occurrence of one event eliminates the possibility of the occurrence of the other event (in other words, where the two events *exclude* each other). To find the probability that one *or* another of two mutually exclusive events will occur, you add the probabilities of the two events.

For example, what is the probability that a certain machine randomly fills a box with all pennies *or* with all dimes? If the box contains all pennies, then it can't contain all dimes. If it contains all dimes, it can't contain all pennies. So these two events are mutually exclusive in that the occurrence of one means the other can't happen at the same time. If you wanted to figure out the probability that a box contains either all pennies or all dimes, the first thing you'd need is the probabilities of the two events separately.

Say that the probability that the machine fills the box with all pennies is $\frac{1}{2}$ and the probability that the machine fills the box with all dimes is $\frac{1}{3}$. To calculate the probability that one or the other of these two events occurs, add their respective probabilities:

$$\frac{1}{2} + \frac{1}{3} = \frac{3}{6} + \frac{2}{6} = \frac{5}{6}$$

So the probability that the box contains all pennies *or* all dimes is $\frac{5}{6}$.

Remember, if two events A and B cannot both occur, then to calculate the probability that either event A *or* event B occurs (but not both), find the probabilities of A and B separately and then *add* them together.

Why do you need to add in such cases? Because with many repetitions, close to $\frac{1}{2}$ of the boxes can be expected to be filled with pennies, and close to $\frac{1}{3}$ of the boxes can be expected to be filled with dimes. Close to $\frac{1}{2} + \frac{1}{3}$ or $\frac{5}{6}$ of all the boxes will be filled with pennies or dimes, which is the same as saying that the probability that any given box contains all pennies or all dimes is $\frac{5}{6}$. Remember that a probability tells you how likely it is that something will occur.

Example: A bag contains 20 identical plastic tiles. Eleven of the tiles are marked with the numbers 1 through 11 inclusive. The remaining 9 tiles are marked with the letters A through I inclusive. If a single tile is drawn at random from the bag, what is the probability that it bears either an even number or a vowel?

Solution: To find the probability of getting either an even number *or* a vowel, you need to find the probability of each of these occurrences separately and then add them together. Start off with the even numbers. There are 20 tiles in the bag, so you know the number of total possible outcomes is 20. The even numbers in the bag are 2, 4, 6, 8, and 10, so there are five desired outcomes. The probability of withdrawing an even number is $\frac{5}{20}$ (don't reduce the fraction yet; you'll see why). Now for the vowels: The number of possible outcomes is still 20. There are three vowels in the bag (A, E, and I), so there are three desired outcomes. The probability of withdrawing a vowel is $\frac{3}{20}$. Therefore, the probability of withdrawing an even number *or* a vowel is $\frac{5}{20} + \frac{3}{20}$ (this is why you didn't want to reduce before), which sums to $\frac{8}{20}$, or $\frac{2}{5}$.

Probability Two Events Occur

So far, you have looked at the probability of one or another of two events happening, but what about the case in which *both* happen? In general, the probability that events A *and* B both occur is equal to the probability that event A occurs multiplied by the conditional probability that event B occurs given that event A occurs. You can also say that the probability that events A *and* B both occur is equal to the probability that event B occurs *multiplied* by the conditional probability that event A occurs, given that event B occurs.

Example: There are 4 blue disks and 12 green disks in a container. Two disks are to be removed from the container, one after the other. What is the probability that the first disk selected is blue and the second disk selected is green?

Solution: There are 4 blue disks and a total of $4 + 12 = 16$ disks in the container. The probability that the first disk selected is blue is $\frac{4}{16} = \frac{1}{4}$. Once a blue disk is removed from the container, there remain 3 blue disks and 12 green disks. So there are 12 green disks and $3 + 12 = 15$ disks in the container. The probability that the second disk selected is green given that the first disk selected is blue is $\frac{12}{15} = \frac{4}{5}$. Then the probability that the first disk selected is blue and the second disk selected is green is $\frac{1}{4} \times \frac{4}{5} = \frac{1}{5}$.

Independent events

Two events are said to be independent if one of these events has absolutely no effect on the probability of the other event occurring. For example, suppose a fair coin with heads and tails is tossed once and then a fair die with sides number 1, 2, 3, 4, 5, and 6 is rolled once. For the coin toss, you are interested in the event that a head is tossed (say that's event A), and for the die roll you are concerned with the event that a 1 or a 4 is rolled (say that's event B). The tossing of the coin has absolutely no effect on the rolling of the die. Thus, the event that a head results when a fair coin is tossed is independent of the event that a 1 or a 4 is tossed when a fair die is rolled.

In the case of independent events A and B, the probability that events A and B both occur is equal to the probability that event A occurs multiplied by the probability that event B occurs. Returning to the above situation, you can use that relationship to find the probability that both events A and B occur.

There are 2 possible outcomes when the coin is tossed, heads or tails. So the number of possible outcomes is 2. For the event that a head is tossed, you have one desirable outcome, heads. So the probability that, when a fair coin is tossed, the result is heads is $\frac{1}{2}$.

When the fair die is rolled, all the possible outcomes are 1, 2, 3, 4, 5, and 6. The number of possible outcomes is 6. For the event that a 1 or a 4 is rolled, there are 2 desired outcomes, which are 1 and 4. So the probability that, when the fair die is rolled, a 1 or 4 results is $\frac{2}{6} = \frac{1}{3}$.

Finally, the probability that both events A and B occur is $\frac{1}{2} \times \frac{1}{3} = \frac{1}{6}$.

Example: If the probability of finding a pearl in any given oyster is $\frac{1}{3}$ and the probability of any given pearl being black is $\frac{2}{5}$, what's the probability that if you crack open a randomly chosen oyster, you'll find a black pearl?

Solution: In $\frac{1}{3}$ of the cases when you crack open an oyster, you'll find a pearl. And in $\frac{2}{5}$ of the cases when you find a pearl, that pearl will be black. Therefore, you should find a black pearl in $\frac{2}{5}$ of $\frac{1}{3}$ of the times you open an oyster, which is $\frac{2}{5} \times \frac{1}{3}$ or $\frac{2}{15}$ of all the times you open an oyster. Therefore, the probability of finding a pearl *and* having the pearl be black is $\frac{2}{15}$.

Example: A bag contains ten identically shaped plastic tiles. Six of the tiles are red, three are blue, and one is black. If two tiles are drawn at random from the bag, without replacement, what is the probability that the first tile drawn is red and the second tile drawn is black?

Solution: First find the individual probabilities of drawing a red tile and then drawing the black tile. For the first tile drawn, there are 10 tiles in the bag, and 6 of them are red, so the probability of drawing a red tile first is $\frac{6}{10}$ or $\frac{3}{5}$. For the second tile, there are only 9 tiles left in the bag, and 1 of them is black, so the probability of getting a black tile on the second draw is $\frac{1}{9}$. Now you need to find the probability of getting a red tile on the first draw *AND* a black tile on the second draw. To do so, you multiply the individual probabilities: $\frac{3}{5} \times \frac{1}{9} = \frac{3}{45} = \frac{1}{15}$.

Probability at Least One of Two Events Occurs

Suppose you have two events A and B. You want to find the probability that at least one of the events A or B occurs. A picture of the events A and B would look like this:

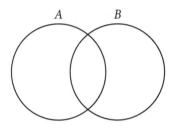

If you just add the probability that event A occurs and the probability that B occurs, the sum will include the probability of *both* events A and B occurring (the overlapping area on the Venn diagram) twice, which is included in both the probability that A occurs and the probability that B occurs. So you must subtract the probability that both events A and B occur from that sum. Remember that $P(E)$ means the probability that event E occurs. You can say that $P(A$ or $B) = P(A) + P(B) - P(A$ and $B)$.

Notice that the rule for finding the probability that at least one of events A or B occurs, $P(A$ or $B) = P(A) + P(B) - P(A$ and $B)$, also accounts for cases in which the events are mutually exclusive. If the events A and B are mutually exclusive, $P(A$ and $B) = 0$. So, if the events A and B are mutually exclusive, $P(A$ or $B) = P(A) + P(B) - P(A$ and $B) = P(A) + P(B) - 0 = P(A) + P(B)$.

Example: Suppose a fair coin is tossed and a fair die with sides numbered 1, 2, 3, 4, 5, and 6 is rolled. Let A be the event that the coin toss results in a head. Let B be the event that the roll of the die results in a 5. What is the probability that at least one of the events A or B occurs?

Solution: For the coin toss, $P(A) = \frac{1}{2}$. For the roll of the die, $P(B) = \frac{1}{6}$. The toss of the coin and the roll of the die are independent, so $P(A$ and $B) = P(A)P(B) = \frac{1}{2} \times \frac{1}{6} = \frac{1}{12}$. Then $P(A$ or $B) = \frac{1}{2} + \frac{1}{6} - \frac{1}{12} = \frac{6}{12} + \frac{2}{12} - \frac{1}{12} = \frac{6+2-1}{12} = \frac{7}{12}$.

Summary Comparison: And/Or

You've seen two different ways to calculate probabilities for situations involving more than one event. It's essential you understand which method to use in any given probability question. To recap:

- To find the probability of event *A or* event *B* when the events *A* and *B* are mutually exclusive, find the probability of *A* and the probability of *B* and then *add* these two probabilities. Thus, if the events *A* and *B* are mutually exclusive, $P(A \text{ or } B) = P(A) + P(B)$. (The same rule applies if you're trying to figure out the probability that *A or B or C* occurs where the events *A*, *B*, and *C* are mutually exclusive, etc.)

- For any two events *A* and *B*, to find the probability that *at least one of* event *A or* event *B* occurs, find the probability of event *A* and the probability of event *B*, *add* these two probabilities, then *subtract* from this sum the probability that both events *A* and *B* occur. Thus, for any events *A* and *B*, $P(A \text{ or } B) = P(A) + P(B) - P(A \text{ and } B)$.

- To find the probability of event *A and* event *B*, find the probability that event *A* occurs and the conditional probability that *B* occurs given that event *A* occurs, then *multiply* the probability that event *A* occurs by the conditional probability that event *B* occurs given that event *A* occurs. (The same rule applies if you're trying to figure out *A and B and C*, etc.)

MEDIAN, MODE, RANGE, AND STANDARD DEVIATION

Probability is just one way to look at statistical patterns. Using other techniques, such as determining median, mode, range, and standard deviation, also can provide equally useful information.

Median

If a group containing an odd number of terms is arranged in numerical order, the median is the middle value.

If a group containing an even number of terms is arranged in numerical order, the median is the average, or arithmetic mean, of the two middle numbers.

Example: What is the median of 4, 5, 100, 1, and 6?

Solution: First, arrange the numbers in numerical order: 1, 4, 5, 6, and 100. The middle number (the median) is 5.

Example: What is the median value of 2, 7, 8, 16, 12, and 37?

Solution: If a set has an even number of terms, then the median is the average (arithmetic mean) of the two middle terms after the terms are arranged in numerical order. Arrange the values in numerical order: 2, 7, 8, 12, 16, 37. The two middle numbers are 8 and 12. The median is the average of 8 and 12, that is, 10.

The median can be quite different from the mean (average). For instance, in the first set of numbers above, {1, 4, 5, 6, 100}, the median is 5, but the average is $\frac{1+4+5+6+100}{5} = \frac{116}{5} = 23.2$.

Mode

The mode is the number that appears most frequently in a set. For example, in the set {1, 2, 2, 2, 3, 4, 4, 5, 6}, the mode is 2.

It is possible for a set to have more than one mode. For example, in the set {35, 42, 35, 57, 57, 19}, the two modes are 35 and 57. When more than one mode exists, do not calculate the mean of these numbers but rather report each as a separate value. It may also be worthy to note that not all sets have a mode.

Range

The range is the positive difference between the largest term in the set and the smallest term. For example, in the set {2, 4, 10, 20, 26}, the range is $26 - 2 = 24$.

Standard Deviation

Standard deviation measures the dispersion of a set of numbers around the mean. If you let σ be the standard deviation of the N values $x_1, x_2, \ldots x_N$ and let μ be the average, or arithmetic mean, of the N values $x_1, x_2, \ldots x_N$, that is, $\mu = \dfrac{x_1 + x_2 + \ldots + x_N}{N}$,

then the formula looks like this:

$$\sigma = \sqrt{\frac{1}{N}\left[\left(x_1 - \mu\right)^2 + \left(x_2 - \mu\right)^2 + \cdots + \left(x_N - \mu\right)^2\right]}$$

It can be intimidating, so it helps to break up the process into the following steps:

1. Find the arithmetic mean of the set.
2. Subtract the mean of the set from each term in that set.
3. Square each result.
4. Take the mean of those squares.
5. Calculate the positive square root of that average.

Fortunately, you will only very rarely be required to apply this formula and only on the most difficult questions. When standard deviation is tested, all you will generally need to understand is the basic concept: Standard deviation represents how close or far the terms in a set or list are from the average. Thus, standard deviation is a measure of how widely dispersed the terms of a list are, or how widely dispersed the members of a set are.

Thus, {1, 2, 3} and {101, 102, 103} have the same standard deviation since they both have one term on the mean and two terms exactly one unit away from the mean. Quickly sketching number lines can confirm this:

The set {1, 3, 5} will have a smaller standard deviation than {0, 3, 6}. Both sets have a mean of 3, but the first has terms 2, 0, and 2 units from the average, while the second has terms 3, 0, and 3 units from the average. Again, you can confirm this by quickly sketching number lines:

You could also calculate the standard deviation for the sets {1, 3, 5} and {0, 3, 6} to confirm:

{1, 3, 5}

mean $= 3$

$$\sigma = \sqrt{\frac{1}{3}\left[(1-3)^2 + (3-3)^2 + (5-3)^2\right]}$$

$$= \sqrt{\frac{1}{3}\left[(-2)^2 + 0^2 + 2^2\right]}$$

$$= \sqrt{\frac{1}{3}(8)}$$

$$= \sqrt{\frac{8}{3}}$$

{0, 3, 6}

mean $= 3$

$$\sigma = \sqrt{\frac{1}{3}\left[(0-3)^2 + (3-3)^2 + (6-3)^2\right]}$$

$$= \sqrt{\frac{1}{3}\left[(-3)^2 + 0^2 + 3^2\right]}$$

$$= \sqrt{\frac{1}{3}(9+0+9)}$$

$$= \sqrt{\frac{1}{3}(18)}$$

$$= \sqrt{6}$$

Since 6 is larger than $\frac{8}{3}$, the standard deviation of the second, more widely spaced set of numbers is larger than that of the first set.

Below are the key concepts to remember about median, mode, range, and standard deviation.

- When the numbers in a list with an odd number of numbers is arranged in ascending or descending order, the median is the middle number.
- When the numbers in a list with an even number of numbers is arranged in ascending or descending order, the median is the average of the two middle numbers.
- The mode of a list of terms is the term that appears most frequently. Having more than one mode, or no mode at all, is possible.
- The range is the positive difference between the largest term in the list and the smallest term.
- Standard deviation measures the dispersion of a set of numbers around the mean. You will rarely be required to apply the formula for standard deviation. Instead, use critical thinking and quick sketches of number lines to determine how close the terms in a list are from the mean.

COMBINATIONS AND PERMUTATIONS

Some questions ask you to count the number of possible ways to select a small subgroup from a larger group. If the selection is **unordered**, then it's a combination question. But if the selection is **ordered**, it is a permutation question.

For example, if a question asks you to count the possible number of different slates of officers who could be elected to positions in class government, then order matters—President Joseph and Vice President Rose is a different slate than President Rose and Vice President Joseph. You would use the permutations formula in this scenario. But if you had to count the number of possible pairs of flavors of jelly beans, you are solving a combinations question; cherry and lemon is the same pair as lemon and cherry, so order does not matter (that is, you wouldn't count those as two different pairs).

The very first thing you need to do is use critical thinking to figure out whether a given question calls for an ordered or an unordered selection; otherwise, you won't know which formula to use.

Combinations

The combinations formula is used when solving for the number of k unordered selections one can make from a group of n items where $k \leq n$. This is usually referred to as $_nC_k$, which is said as "n choose k." It is often helpful to say it this way to yourself because that's what making combinations is: an act of choosing small groups from a larger group.

Here's the formula, in which $n!$, or n-factorial, is the product of n and every positive integer smaller than n (for example, $5! = 5 \times 4 \times 3 \times 2 \times 1$), where n is a positive integer:

$$_nC_k = \frac{n!}{k!(n-k)!}$$

Example: A company is selecting 4 members of its board of directors to sit on an ethics subcommittee. If the board has 9 members, any of whom may serve on the subcommittee, how many different selections of members could the company make?

Solution: Since the order in which you select the members doesn't change the composition of the committee in any way, this is a combinations question. The size of the group from which you choose is n, and the size of the selected group is k. So $n = 9$ and $k = 4$.

$$_9C_4 = \frac{9!}{4!(9-4)!}$$
$$= \frac{9!}{4!5!}$$
$$= \frac{9\times8\times7\times6\times5\times4\times3\times2\times1}{4\times3\times2\times1\times5\times4\times3\times2\times1}$$

Save yourself some work. There's rarely a need to multiply out factorials since many of the factors can quickly be canceled.

$$_9C_4 = \frac{9\times8^2\times7\times6\times5\times4\times3\times2\times1}{4\times3\times2\times1\times5\times4\times3\times2\times1}$$
$$= 9\times2\times7 = 126$$

Sometimes the problems will be more complicated and will require multiple iterations of the formula.

Example: County X holds an annual math competition to which each county high school sends a team of 4 students. If school A has 6 boys and 7 girls whose math grades qualify them to be on their school's team, and competition rules stipulate that the team must consist of 2 boys and 2 girls, how many different teams might school A send to the competition?

Solution: The order of selection doesn't matter here, so you can use the combinations formula. But be careful … if you lump all the students together in a group of 13 and calculate $_{13}C_4$, you'd wind up including some all-boy teams and all-girl teams. The question explicitly says you can only select 2 boys and 2 girls. So you aren't really choosing 4 students from 13 but rather choosing 2 boys from 6 and 2 girls from 7. Multiply the two combinations together to get the answer.

$$_6C_2 \quad \text{and} \quad _7C_2$$

$$\frac{6!}{2!4!} \times \frac{7!}{2!5!} =$$

$$\frac{6\times5\times4\times3\times2\times1}{2\times1\times4\times3\times2\times1} \times \frac{7\times6\times5\times4\times3\times2\times1}{2\times1\times5\times4\times3\times2\times1} =$$

$$\frac{6^3\times5\times4\times3\times2\times1}{2\times1\times4\times3\times2\times1!} \times \frac{7\times6^3\times5\times4\times3\times2\times1}{2\times1\times5\times4\times3\times2\times1} =$$

$3 \times 5 \times 7 \times 3 = 315$ possible teams consisting of 2 boys and 2 girls.

Permutations

If the order of selection matters, use the permutation formulas instead:

Number of permutations (arrangements) of n items $= n!$

Number of permutations of k items selected from n items $= {}_nP_k = \dfrac{n!}{(n-k)!}$

Example: How many ways are there to arrange the letters in the word ASCENT?

Solution: Order matters here since ASCENT is different from TNECSA. There are 6 letters in the word, so you must calculate the permutations of 6 items:

$$6! = 6 \times 5 \times 4 \times 3 \times 2 \times 1 = 720$$

Another way to solve this question is to draw a quick sketch of the problem with blanks for the arranged items, then write in the number of possibilities for each blank in order. Finally, multiply the numbers together. Many high-difficulty permutation questions resist formulaic treatment but are easier to complete with the *draw blanks* or *slot filling* approach.

Here's how you would use this technique to solve the ASCENT problem:

ASCENT has 6 letters, so you need 6 blanks:

$$\_\_\times\_\_\times\_\_\times\_\_\times\_\_\times\_\_$$

There are 6 letters you might place in the first blank (A, S, C, E, N, or T):

$$\underline{6}\times\_\_\times\_\_\times\_\_\times\_\_\times\_\_$$

No matter which letter you placed there, there will be 5 possibilities for the next blank:

$$\underline{6} \times \underline{5} \times \underline{} \times \underline{} \times \underline{} \times \underline{}$$

There will be 4 for the next, 3 thereafter, 2 after that, and just 1 letter left for the last:

$$\underline{6} \times \underline{5} \times \underline{4} \times \underline{3} \times \underline{2} \times \underline{1} = 720$$

Notice that you wind up reproducing the arrangements formula, $n!$. It's quite possible to solve most permutation problems without knowing the right formulas ahead of time, although knowing the formulas can save you time on Test Day.

Example: There are 6 children at a family reunion, 3 boys and 3 girls. They will be lined up single-file for a photo, alternating genders. How many arrangements of the children are possible for this photo?

Solution: You may not be sure how to approach this with a formula, so draw a picture. You know you'll have 6 blanks, but you don't know whether to begin with a boy or with a girl. It could be either one. So try both:

bgbgbg or *gbgbgb*

$$\underline{} \times \underline{} \times \underline{} \times \underline{} \times \underline{} \times \underline{} + \underline{} \times \underline{} \times \underline{} \times \underline{} \times \underline{} \times \underline{}$$

Any of the three boys could go in the first spot, and any of the three girls in the second:

$$\underline{3} \times \underline{3} \times \underline{} \times \underline{} \times \underline{} \times \underline{} + \underline{} \times \underline{} \times \underline{} \times \underline{} \times \underline{} \times \underline{}$$

The next spot can be filled with either of the remaining two boys; the one after by either of the two remaining girls. Then the last boy and the last girl take their places:

$$\underline{3} \times \underline{3} \times \underline{2} \times \underline{2} \times \underline{1} \times \underline{1} + \underline{} \times \underline{} \times \underline{} \times \underline{} \times \underline{} \times \underline{}$$

That's the boy-first possibility. The same numbers of boys and girls apply to the girl-first possibility, and so you get:

$$\underline{3} \times \underline{3} \times \underline{2} \times \underline{2} \times \underline{1} \times \underline{1} + \underline{3} \times \underline{3} \times \underline{2} \times \underline{2} \times \underline{1} \times \underline{1}$$

$$9 \times 4 \times 1 + 9 \times 4 \times 1$$

There are $36 + 36 = 72$ possible arrangements of 3 boys and 3 girls, with alternating genders.

Hybrids of Combinations and Permutations

Some questions involve elements of both ordered and unordered selection.

Example: How many ways are there to arrange the letters in the word ASSETS?

Solution: Earlier you saw that the rearrangement of ASCENT was a permutation. But what about ASSETS? The order of the E, the A, the T, and the Ss matter, but the order of the three Ss themselves does not.

Think about it this way: Put a tag on the Ss ... $AS_1S_2ETS_3$. If you just calculated 6! again, you'd be counting $AS_1S_2ETS_3$ and $AS_3S_1ETS_2$ as different words, even though with the tags gone, you can see they aren't (ASSETS is the same as ASSETS). So you'll need to eliminate all the redundant arrangements from the 6! total.

For each specification of the positions of the different letters A, E, and T, there are 3! ways to permute 3 distinguishable Ss, like S_1, S_2, and S_3. For each specification of the positions of the different letters A, E, and T, there is just one way to permute 3 indistinguishable Ss. So the total number of permutations, for 6 distinguishable letters, which is 6!, must be divided by 3! because of the 3 indistinguishable Ss.

So instead of 6! arrangements, as there were for ASCENT, the word ASSETS has $\frac{6!}{3!}$ arrangements.

$$\frac{6!}{3!} = \frac{6 \times 5 \times 4 \times 3 \times 2 \times 1}{3 \times 2 \times 1} = 6 \times 5 \times 4 = 120$$

The same logic would apply to the arrangements of ASSESS ... $\frac{6!}{4!}$.

And if two letters repeat, you need two corrections to eliminate the counting of redundant arrangements. For instance, the number of arrangements of the letters in the word REASSESS is $\frac{8!}{4!2!}$.

Some difficult problems boil down to the same logic as this rearranging letters problem.

Example: A restaurant is hanging 7 large tiles on its wall in a single row. How many arrangements of tiles are possible if there are 3 white tiles and 4 blue tiles?

Solution: This problem essentially asks for the arrangements of *WWWBBBB*. Although there are 7 total tiles to arrange, all the white tiles are indistinguishable from one another, as are the blue tiles. Therefore, you will need to divide out the number of redundant arrangements from the 7! total arrangements:

$$\frac{7!}{3!4!} = \frac{7 \times 6 \times 5 \times 4 \times 3 \times 2 \times 1}{3 \times 2 \times 1 \times 4 \times 3 \times 2 \times 1} = 7 \times 5 = 35$$

Did you notice that $\frac{7!}{3!4!}$ is the same as $_7C_3$? This is also the same as $_7C_4$, $\frac{7!}{4!3!}$.

Whether you consider "rearrange *WWWBBBB*" to mean "choose 3 of the 7 tiles to be white (the rest will be blue)," or consider "rearrange *WWWBBBB*" to mean "choose 4 of the 7 tiles to be blue (the rest will be white)," the result is the same. As you'll soon see, many probability questions involve just this kind of calculation.

REVIEW PROBLEMS

1. A certain school has 50 students assigned to five distinct classes so that the numbers of students in the classes are consecutive and each student is assigned to only one class. What is the probability that a student selected at random from the 50 students is in one of the two largest classes?

   A. 38%

   B. 42%

   C. 46%

   D. 48%

   E. 56%

2. A certain machine produces toy cars in a repeating cycle of blue, red, green, yellow, and black. If a string of six consecutively produced cars is selected at random from all the possible strings of six consecutively produced cars, what is the probability that, in the string selected, two of the cars are red?

   A. $\frac{1}{6}$

   B. $\frac{1}{5}$

   C. $\frac{1}{3}$

   D. $\frac{2}{5}$

   E. $\frac{1}{2}$

3. A certain circular stopwatch has exactly 60 second marks and a single hand. If the hand of the watch is randomly set to one of the marks and allowed to count exactly 10 seconds, what is the probability that the hand will stop less than 10 marks on either side of the 53-second mark?

   A. $\frac{1}{6}$

   B. $\frac{19}{60}$

   C. $\frac{1}{3}$

   D. $\frac{29}{60}$

   E. $\frac{41}{60}$

4. A certain board game is played by rolling a pair of fair six-sided dice and then moving one's piece forward the number of spaces indicated by the sum showing on the dice. A player is "frozen" if her opponent's piece comes to rest in the space already occupied by her piece. If player A is about to roll and is currently six spaces behind player B, what is the probability that player B will be frozen after player A rolls?

A. $\frac{1}{36}$

B. $\frac{5}{36}$

C. $\frac{1}{6}$

D. $\frac{1}{3}$

E. $\frac{1}{2}$

5. A machine is made up of two components, A and B. Each component either works or fails. The failure or nonfailure of one component is independent of the failure or nonfailure of the other component. The machine works if at least one of the components works. If the probability that each component works is $\frac{2}{3}$, what is the probability that the machine works?

A. $\frac{1}{9}$

B. $\frac{4}{9}$

C. $\frac{1}{2}$

D. $\frac{2}{3}$

E. $\frac{8}{9}$

6. In the list 3, 4, 5, 5, 5, 5, 7, 11, 21, what fraction of the data is less than the mode?

A. $\frac{2}{9}$

B. $\frac{1}{3}$

C. $\frac{2}{3}$

D. $\frac{7}{9}$

E. $\frac{8}{9}$

7. Amanda goes to the toy store to buy 1 ball and 3 different board games. If the toy store is stocked with 3 types of balls and 6 types of board games, how many different selections of the 4 items can Amanda make?

A. 20

B. 23

C. 40

D. 60

D. 80

8. A code is to be made by arranging 7 letters. Three of the letters used will be the letter A, two of the letters used will be the letter B, one of the letters used will be the letter C, and one of the letters used will be the letter D. If there is only one way to present each letter, how many different codes are possible?

   A. 42
   B. 210
   C. 420
   D. 5,040
   E. 6,025

SOLUTIONS TO THE REVIEW PROBLEMS

1. **C** The correct answer is 46%. To find the probability, you need possible outcomes and desired outcomes. The possible outcomes here are just the total number of students you have to choose from. The desired outcomes are the number of students in the two largest classes. How can you find that, though? The key to this problem is the fact that the numbers of students in the classes are consecutive. Whenever you see *consecutive* in a math problem, it's there for a specific reason. It tells you that each number in the series is separated from the next by a fixed amount. Consecutive integers are separated by 1, consecutive even integers by 2, etc. So here you know that if you add up the numbers of students in all the classes, you'll get 50. You also know that the numbers of students in the classes are separated by 1. So let's call the number of students in the smallest class x. The next largest class would have $x + 1$ students, then $x + 2$ students, $x + 3$ students, and $x + 4$ students. If you add these up, you get $5x + 10 = 50$. Now you can solve for x: subtract 10 from both sides to get $5x = 40$, then divide both sides by 5 to get $x = 8$. So the smallest class has 8 students, and the two largest classes then will have $8 + 3$ and $8 + 4$ students respectively, which gives a total of 23 students in the two largest classes. So the probability is $\frac{23}{50} = \frac{23}{50} \times \frac{2}{2} = \frac{46}{100} = 46\%$.

2. **B** The correct answer is $\frac{1}{5}$. You need to find the number of possible and the number of desired outcomes. You're going to be randomly selecting a possible string of six consecutively produced cars, and you want to know what the probability is that the string will contain two red cars. How many different possible strings of six consecutive cars are there? You have five colors, so any one of them could be the first in the string of six that you choose. That gives five different strings of six, so 5 is the number of possible outcomes here. What about desired outcomes? You need to know how many of those five strings have two red cars. What does getting two red cars depend on? It depends on the color of the first car of the string of six. For example, if blue is the first car of the string, then you'd get blue, red, green, yellow, black, and then blue again. So, the only way to get two red cars is if the first car of the string is red because then you'd have red, green, yellow, black, blue, and then red again as the sixth car. So one out of the five strings will contain two red cars, and that's a probability of $\frac{1}{5}$.

3. **B** The correct answer is $\frac{19}{60}$. There's a watch with a single hand and 60 second marks. Say you randomly spin the hand so it points to one of those marks and then you let the watch count 10 seconds. What are the chances that the hand will end up pointing to a mark that's less than 10 marks from the 53-second mark? What would it depend on? It would depend on the mark the hand began counting from. How many marks are less than 10 marks from 53 seconds? This is a good question for scrap paper. If you jot down 53 and then count 9 in either direction (remember, you need less than 10, so you don't want to count 10), you start with 44 seconds and count all the way past 53 seconds to the mark that is 2 seconds after the minute mark, with the minute mark also being the 0-second mark. This gives 19 marks that are less than 10 marks from 53 seconds. To end up less than 10 marks from 53 seconds, you need to end on one of those 19 marks. Each one of those 19 marks corresponds to another mark that's exactly 10 seconds earlier than it, which would be marks 34–52. If the hand begins counting from any of the 19 marks that go from 34 to 52, it will end up on a mark between 44 and 02. So there are 19 marks that have the characteristic you're looking for. That's 19 out of 60, or $\frac{19}{60}$.

4. B The correct answer is $\frac{5}{36}$. In this game, a player is "frozen" whenever another player lands on the spot where the first player already has her piece. The question asks for the probability that player *B* will be frozen by player *A*, who's six spaces behind. What does it depend on? It depends on whether player *A* gets a roll of exactly 6 on the dice. So what's the probability of getting 6 on the dice? First, figure out the total possible outcomes for the roll. Since there are six numbers on each die, the total number of possible rolls is 6 × 6, or 36. So there are 36 possible rolls. How many of them would allow player *A* to move exactly six spots? Any roll that adds up to 6 will. So you could have (1, 5), (2, 4), and (3, 3). But since there are two dice, there are two ways to get (1, 5) and (2, 4) because either die could get the 1 or the 5, etc. So there's (1, 5), (5, 1), (2, 4), (4, 2), and (3, 3). That's five possible rolls that add up to exactly 6. So 5 out of the 36 possible rolls would allow player *A* to freeze player *B*, which gives a probability of $\frac{5}{36}$.

5. E The fastest way to do this is to find the probability that neither component works and subtract that from 1. Since the probability of a component working is $\frac{2}{3}$, the probability of a component not working is $1 - \frac{2}{3} = \frac{1}{3}$. Therefore, the probability that neither component works is $\frac{1}{3} \times \frac{1}{3} = \frac{1}{9}$, and the probability that the machine works is $1 - \frac{1}{9} = \frac{8}{9}$.

6. A This question can be answered by using the definitions of mode and fraction. Determine the mode, the total number of items in the list, and the number of items in the list less than the mode. The mode of any list of numbers is the number that appears most frequently in the list. In this case, the mode is 5. The total number of items in the list is 9. Finally, the number of items in the list less than the mode, or 5, is 2. So the final fraction is $\frac{2}{9}$.

7. D Amanda is buying 1 ball and 3 different board games from a selection of 3 balls and 6 types of board games. You need to find the number of different selections of 4 items that Amanda can make. Amanda is choosing 3 board games from a total of 6, so you can use the combination formula (since a different arrangement of the same board games is not considered a different selection) to find the number of combinations of board games:

$$_nC_k = \frac{n!}{k!(n-k)!}$$

$$_6C_3 = \frac{6!}{3!(6-3)!}$$

$$_6C_3 = \frac{6 \times 5 \times 4 \times 3!}{3! \times 3!}$$

$$_6C_3 = 20$$

Amanda has 20 ways to choose 3 board games from a total of 6. For each of those 20 ways, Amanda can choose 1 of 3 balls, so there are 20 × 3 = 60 different ways for Amanda to choose 1 ball and 3 games from 3 balls and 6 games.

8. **C** You need to make a seven-letter code, but some of the letters are repeated. You have three *A*s, two *B*s, one *C*, and one *D*. Calculate the number of different permutations, remembering to take the repeated letters into account. To calculate the number of permutations where some of the elements are indistinguishable, divide the total number of permutations (here, 7!) by the factorial of the number of indistinguishable elements. So you have $\frac{7!}{3!2!} = \frac{(7 \times 6 \times 5 \times 4 \times 3 \times 2 \times 1)}{(3 \times 2 \times 1)(2 \times 1)} = 420$.

CHAPTER FIFTY-NINE

Plane Geometry

Geometry is a wide and varied subject. The next three chapters, Plane Geometry, Solid Geometry, and Coordinate Geometry, cover the concepts and equations you will need to succeed on these challenging questions. However, it's important to note that, of the 40 questions in the Quantitative Reasoning section, only four questions, or 10 percent of the section, will be related to geometry (although you may see additional word problems that rely on geometry concepts). Another four questions in the section will be specifically about trigonometry. Plan your studying accordingly to ensure you spend the right amount of time reviewing these topics in relation to the other subjects you'll see on Test Day.

LINE SEGMENTS

One of the most fundamental skills in geometry is the ability to manipulate **line segments**, which make up the sides of **polygons**, such as triangles and rectangles. In general, the lengths of line segments can be added or subtracted just like any other numbers, but this may still require algebraic skills when one or more of the sides are unknown.

Example:

In the figure above, the length of segment PS is $2x + 12$, and the length of segment PQ is $6x - 10$. If R is the midpoint of segment QS, what is the length of segment PR?

Solution: Usually the best way to start on a plane geometry question is to draw a figure. Put as much of the information into the figure as you can. That's a good way to organize your thoughts, and that way you don't have to go back and forth between the figure and the question.

Now you can plan your attack. First, subtract *PQ* from the whole length *PS* to get *QS*:

$$QS = PS - PQ = (2x + 12) - (6x - 10) = 2x + 12 - 6x + 10 = -4x + 22$$

Then, because *R* is the midpoint of *QS*, you can divide *QS* by 2 to get *QR* and *RS*:

$$QR = RS = \frac{QS}{2} = \frac{-4x+22}{2} = -2x+11$$

What you're looking for is *PR*, so you have to add:

$$PR = PQ + QR = (6x - 10) + (-2x + 11) = 4x + 1$$

TRIANGLES

Most plane geometry questions are about **closed figures**: polygons and circles. The test makers' favorite closed figure is the three-sided polygon; that is, the **triangle**. All three-sided polygons are interesting because they share so many characteristics, and certain unique three-sided polygons—equilateral, isosceles, and right triangles—are interesting because of their special characteristics.

First, let's look at the traits all triangles share:

Sum of the interior angles: The three interior angles of any triangle add up to 180°.

In the figure above, $x + 50 + 100 = 180$, so $x = 30$.

Measure of an exterior angle: The measure of an exterior angle of a triangle is equal to the sum of the measures of the remote interior angles.

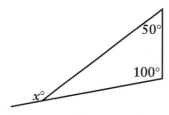

In the figure above, the measure of the exterior angle labeled $x°$ is equal to the sum of the measures of the remote interior angles: $x = 50 + 100 = 150$.

Sum of the exterior angles: The measures of the three exterior angles of any triangle add up to 360°.

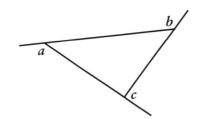

In the previous figure, $a + b + c = 360°$. In fact, the measures of the exterior angles of any polygon add up to 360°.

Area formula: The general formula for the area of a triangle is always the same:

$$\text{Area of Triangle} = \frac{1}{2}(\text{base})(\text{height})$$

The height is the perpendicular distance between the side that's chosen as the base and the opposite vertex. In the triangle shown below, 4 is the height when the 7 side is chosen as the base.

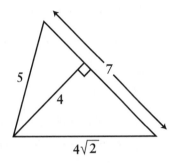

$$\text{Area of Triangle} = \frac{1}{2}(\text{base})(\text{height})$$
$$= \frac{1}{2}(7)(4) = 14$$

Triangle inequality theorem: The length of any one side of a triangle must be greater than the positive difference and less than the sum of the lengths of the other two sides. For example, if it is given that the length of one side is 3 and the length of another side is 7, then the length of the third side must be greater than $7 - 3 = 4$ and less than $7 + 3 = 10$.

Triangles Summary:

1. Interior angles add up to 180°
2. Exterior angle equals sum of remote interior angles
3. Exterior angles add up to 360°
4. Area of a triangle = ½ (base)(height)
5. Each side is greater than the difference and less than the sum of the other two sides

SIMILAR TRIANGLES

Similar triangles are triangles that have the same shape: Corresponding angles are equal, and corresponding sides are proportional.

Example:

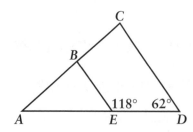

In the figure above, $AB = BC$. If the area of $\triangle ABE$ is x, what is the area of $\triangle ACD$?

Solution: You might wonder here how you're supposed to find the area of $\triangle ACD$ when you're given no lengths you can use for a base or an altitude. The only numbers you have are the angle measures. They must be there for some reason—the test makers rarely provide superfluous information. In fact, because the two angle measures provided add up to 180°, they tell you that BE and CD are parallel. That, in turn, tells you that $\triangle ABE$ is similar to $\triangle ACD$—because they have the same three angles.

In this case, it's given that $AB = BC$, so you know that AC is twice AB and that corresponding sides are in a ratio of 2:1. Each side of the larger triangle is twice the length of the corresponding side of the smaller triangle. That doesn't mean, however, that the ratio of the areas is also 2:1. In fact, the area ratio is the square of the side ratio, and the larger triangle has four times the area of the smaller triangle, so the answer is $4x$.

TYPES OF TRIANGLES

Three unique triangle types deserve extra attention: isosceles triangles, equilateral triangles, and right triangles. Be sure you know not just the definitions of these triangle types but, more importantly, their special characteristics: side relationships, angle relationships, and area formulas.

Isosceles triangle: An isosceles triangle is a triangle that has two equal sides. Not only are two sides equal, but the angles opposite the equal sides, called *base angles*, are also equal.

Equilateral triangle: An equilateral triangle is a triangle that has three equal sides. Since all the sides are equal, all the angles are also equal. All three angles in an equilateral triangle measure 60 degrees, regardless of the lengths of the sides. You can find the area of an equilateral triangle by dividing it into two 30°-60°-90° triangles, or you can use this formula in terms of the length of one side s:

$$\text{Area of Equilateral Triangle} = \frac{s^2\sqrt{3}}{4}$$

Right triangle: A right triangle is a triangle with one right angle. The two sides that form the right angle are called **legs**, and you can use them as the base and height to find the area of a right triangle. The side opposite the right angle is called the **hypotenuse** and is always the longest of the three sides.

$$\text{Area of Right Triangle} = \frac{1}{2}(\text{leg}_1)(\text{leg}_2)$$

Pythagorean theorem: If you know any two sides of a right triangle, you can find the third side by using the Pythagorean theorem:

$$(\text{leg}_1)^2 + (\text{leg}_2)^2 = (\text{hypotenuse})^2$$

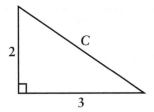

For example, if one leg is 2, and the other leg is 3, then

$$2^2 + 3^2 = c^2$$
$$c^2 = 4 + 9$$
$$c = \sqrt{13}$$

Pythagorean triplet: A Pythagorean triplet is a set of integers that fits the Pythagorean theorem. The simplest Pythagorean triplet is (3, 4, 5). In fact, any integers in a 3:4:5 ratio make up a Pythagorean triplet, including (6, 8, 10) and (9, 12, 15). There are many other Pythagorean triplets as well: (5, 12, 13); (7, 24, 25); (8, 15, 17); (9, 40, 41); all their multiples; and infinitely many more.

3-4-5 triangle: If a right triangle's leg-to-leg ratio is 3:4, or if the leg-to-hypotenuse ratio is 3:5 or 4:5, then it's a 3-4-5 triangle, and you don't need to use the Pythagorean theorem to find the third side. Just figure out what multiple of 3-4-5 it is.

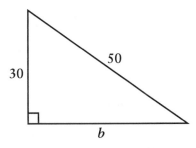

In the right triangle shown, one leg is 30 and the hypotenuse is 50. This is 10 times 3-4-5. The other leg b is 40.

5-12-13 triangles: If a right triangle's leg-to-leg ratio is 5:12, or if the leg-to-hypotenuse ratio is 5:13 or 12:13, then it's a 5-12-13 triangle, and you don't need to use the Pythagorean theorem to find the third side. Just figure out what multiple of 5-12-13 it is.

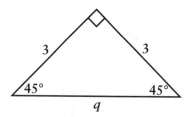

Here one leg is 36 and the hypotenuse is 39. This is 3 times 5-12-13. The other leg a is 3×5 or 15.

45°-45°-90° triangles: The sides of a 45°-45°-90° triangle are in a ratio of $1:1:\sqrt{2}$

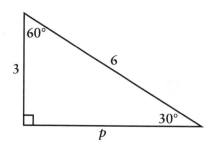

If one leg is 3, then the other leg is also 3, and the hypotenuse q is equal to a leg times $\sqrt{2}$ or $3\sqrt{2}$.

30°-60°-90° triangles: The sides of a 30°-60°-90° triangle are in a ratio of $1:\sqrt{3}:2$. You don't need to use the Pythagorean theorem.

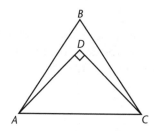

If the hypotenuse is 6, then the shorter leg is half that, or 3, and then the longer leg p is equal to the short leg times $\sqrt{3}$, or $3\sqrt{3}$.

Example: In the figure below, $\triangle ABC$ is equilateral and $\triangle ADC$ is isosceles. If $AC = 1$, what is the distance from B to D?

Solution: To get the answer to this question, you need to know about equilateral, 45°-45°-90°, and 30°-60°-90° triangles. If you drop an altitude from B through D, you will divide the equilateral triangle into two 30°-60°-90° triangles, and you will divide the right isosceles (or 45°-45°-90°) triangle into two smaller right isosceles triangles:

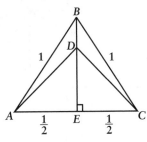

Using the side ratios for 30°-60°-90° and 45°-45°-90° triangles, you know that $BE = \frac{\sqrt{3}}{2}$ and that $DE = \frac{1}{2}$.

Therefore, $BD = BE - DE = \frac{\sqrt{3}}{2} - \frac{1}{2} = \frac{\sqrt{3}-1}{2}$.

HIDDEN SPECIAL TRIANGLES

Often, the key to solving a geometry problem is to add a line segment or two to the figure, which can result in forming one or more special triangles.

Example: In the figure below, the perimeter of isosceles trapezoid $ABCD$ is 50. If $BC = 9$ and $AD = 21$, what is the length of diagonal AC?

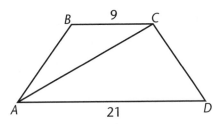

Solution: As you read the stem, you might wonder what an *isosceles trapezoid* is. If you've never heard the term before, you still might be able to extrapolate its meaning from what you know of isosceles triangles. *Isosceles* means "having two equal sides." When applied to a trapezoid, it tells you that the two nonparallel sides—the legs—are equal. In this case, that's AB and CD. If the total perimeter is 50, and the two marked sides add up to 21 + 9 = 30, then the two unmarked sides split the difference of 50 – 30 = 20. In other words, $AB = CD = 10$.

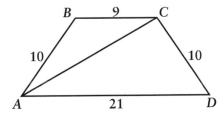

There aren't any special triangles yet. As so often happens, though, you can get some by constructing altitudes. Drop perpendiculars from points B and C, and you make two right triangles. The length 21 of side AD then gets split into 6, 9, and 6.

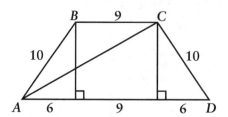

Now you can see that those right triangles are (3, 4, 5) triangles (times 2) and that the height of the trapezoid is 8. Next, look at the right triangle of which AC is the hypotenuse.

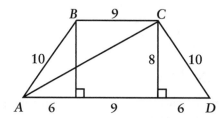

One leg is $6 + 9 = 15$, and the other leg is 8; therefore, the hypotenuse AC is as follows:

$$\text{hypotenuse} = \sqrt{(\text{leg}_1)^2 + (\text{leg}_2)^2}$$
$$= \sqrt{15^2 + 8^2}$$
$$= \sqrt{225 + 64} = \sqrt{289} = 17$$

QUADRILATERALS

The trapezoid is just one of five special quadrilaterals you need to be familiar with. As with triangles, there is some overlap among these categories, and some figures fit into none of these categories. Just as a 45°-45°-90° triangle is both right and isosceles, a quadrilateral with four equal sides and four right angles is not only a square but also a rhombus, a rectangle, and a parallelogram. It is wise to have a solid grasp of the definitions and special characteristics of these five quadrilateral types.

TRAPEZOID

A trapezoid is a four-sided figure with one pair of parallel sides and one pair of nonparallel sides.

$$\text{Area of Trapezoid} = \left(\frac{\text{base}_1 + \text{base}_2}{2} \right) \times \text{height}$$

Think of this formula as the average of the bases (the two parallel sides) times the height (the length of the perpendicular altitude).

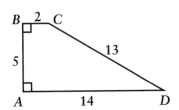

In the trapezoid *ABCD* above, you can use side *AB* for the height. The average of the bases is $\frac{2+14}{2} = 8$, so the area is 8×5, or 40.

PARALLELOGRAM

A parallelogram is a four-sided figure with two pairs of parallel sides. Opposite sides are equal. Opposite angles are equal. Consecutive angles add up to 180°.

Area of Parallelograms = base × height

In parallelogram *KLMN* above, 4 is the height when *LM* or *KN* is used as the base. Base × height = $6 \times 4 = 24$.

To find the area of a parallelogram, you need the height, which is the perpendicular distance from the base to the opposite side. You can use a side of a parallelogram for the height only when the side is perpendicular to the base, in which case you have a rectangle.

RECTANGLE

A rectangle is a four-sided figure with four right angles. Opposite sides are equal. Diagonals are equal. The perimeter of a rectangle is equal to the sum of the lengths of the four sides, which is equal to 2(length + width).

Area of Rectangle = length × width

The area of a 7-by-3 rectangle is $7 \times 3 = 21$.

RHOMBUS

A rhombus is a four-sided figure with four equal sides.

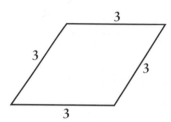

All four sides of the quadrilateral above have the same length, so it's a rhombus. A rhombus is also a parallelogram, so to find the area of a rhombus, you need its height to plug into the equation area = base × height. The more a rhombus "leans over," the smaller the height and, therefore, the smaller the area.

SQUARE

A square is a four-sided figure with four right angles and four equal sides. A square is also a rectangle, a parallelogram, and a rhombus. The perimeter of a square is equal to 4 times the length of one side.

$$\text{Area of Square} = (\text{side})^2$$

The square above, with sides of length 5, has an area of $5^2 = 25$.

PERIMETER AND AREA

The test makers like to write problems that combine the concepts of perimeter and area. What you need to remember is that perimeter and area are not directly related. In the following example, for instance, you have two figures with the same perimeter, but that doesn't mean they have the same area.

Example: A square and a regular hexagon have the same perimeter. If the area of the square is 2.25, what is the area of the hexagon?

Solution: The way to get started is to sketch what's described in the question. A square of area 2.25 has sides each of length $\sqrt{2.25} = 1.5$. So the perimeter of the square is $4(1.5) = 6$. Since that's also the perimeter of the regular hexagon, and a regular hexagon has six equal sides, the length of each side of the hexagon is 1.

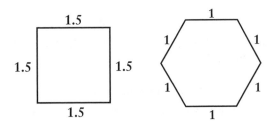

Now the problem is one of finding the area of a regular hexagon of side length 1. The fastest way to do that would be to use the formula. If the length of one side is s,

$$\text{Area of Hexagon} = \frac{3s^2\sqrt{3}}{2}$$

This formula is not one the test makers expect you to know—there's always a way around it—but if you like formulas and you're good at memorizing them, it can only help. Let's proceed, however, as if we didn't know the formula.

Another way to go about finding this area is to add a line segment or two to the figure and divide it up into more familiar shapes. You could, for example, draw in three diagonals and turn the hexagon into six equilateral triangles of side 1:

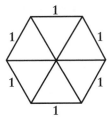

Each of those six triangles has base 1 and height $\frac{\sqrt{3}}{2}$, and therefore,

$$\text{Area of one triangle} = \frac{1}{2}(\text{base})(\text{height}) = \frac{1}{2}(1)\left(\frac{\sqrt{3}}{2}\right) = \frac{\sqrt{3}}{4}$$

The area of the hexagon is 6 times that.

$$\text{Area of Hexagon} = 6\left(\frac{\sqrt{3}}{4}\right) = \frac{3\sqrt{3}}{2} \approx 2.598 \,.$$

CIRCLES

After the triangle, the test makers' favorite plane geometry figure is the circle. Circles don't come in as many varieties as triangles do. In fact, all circles are similar—they're all the same shape. The only difference among them is size. So you don't have to learn to recognize types or remember names. All you have to know about circles is how to find four things: circumference, length of an arc, area, and area of a sector. You could think of the task as one of memorizing four formulas, but you'll be better off in the end if you have some idea of where the arc and sector formulas come from and how they are related to the circumference and area formulas.

CIRCUMFERENCE

Circumference is a measurement of length. You could think of it as the perimeter: It's the total distance around the circle. If the radius of the circle is r,

$$\text{Circumference} = 2\pi r$$

Since the diameter is twice the radius, you can easily express the formula in terms of the diameter d:

$$\text{Circumference} = \pi d$$

In the circle above, the radius is 3, so the circumference is $2\pi(3) = 6\pi$.

LENGTH OF AN ARC

An arc is a piece of the circumference. If n is the degree measure of the arc's central angle, then the formula is

$$\text{Length of an Arc} = \left(\frac{n}{360}\right)(2\pi r)$$

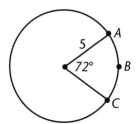

In the figure above, the radius is 5 and the measure of the central angle is 72°. The arc length is $\frac{72}{360}$ or $\frac{1}{5}$ of the circumference:

$$\left(\frac{72}{360}\right)(2\pi)(5) = \left(\frac{1}{5}\right)(10\pi) = 2\pi$$

QR

AREA

The area of a circle is found using this formula in terms of the radius r:

$$\text{Area of a Circle} = \pi r^2$$

The area of the circle above is $\pi(4)^2 = 16\pi$.

AREA OF A SECTOR

A sector is a piece of the area of a circle. If n is the degree measure of the sector's central angle, then the area formula is

$$\text{Area of a Sector} = \left(\frac{n}{360}\right)(\pi r^2)$$

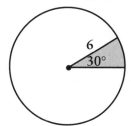

In the figure above, the radius is 6 and the measure of the sector's central angle is 30°. The sector has $\frac{30}{360}$ or $\frac{1}{12}$ of the area of the circle:

$$\left(\frac{30}{360}\right)(\pi)(6^2) = \left(\frac{1}{12}\right)(36\pi) = 3\pi$$

CIRCLES SUMMARY

1. Circumference $= 2\pi r = \pi d$

2. Length of an arc $= \left(\frac{n}{360}\right)(2\pi r)$

3. Area of a circle $= \pi r^2$

4. Area of a sector $= \left(\frac{n}{360}\right)(\pi r^2)$

COMPLEX FIGURES

Some of the most challenging plane geometry questions are those that combine circles with other figures.

Example: In the figure below, rectangle *ABCD* is inscribed in a circle. If the radius of the circle is 1 and $AB = 1$, what is the area of the shaded region?

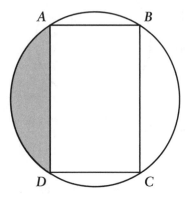

Solution: Once again, the key here is to add to the figure. And in this case, as is so often the case when there's a circle, what you should add is radii. The equilateral triangles tell you that the central angles are 60° and 120°.

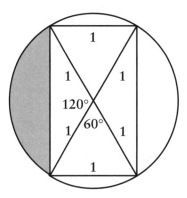

The shaded region is what's left of the 120° sector after you subtract the area of the triangle with the 120° vertex angle.

To find the area of the shaded region, you want to find the areas of the sector and triangle, then subtract. The sector is exactly one-third of the circle (because 120° is one-third of 360°), so

$$\text{Area of sector} = \frac{1}{3}\pi r^2 = \frac{1}{3}\pi(1)^2 = \frac{\pi}{3}$$

You can divide the triangle into two $30°-60°-90°$ triangles:

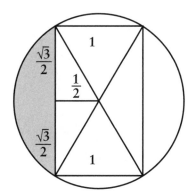

The area of each $30°-60°-90°$ triangle is $\frac{1}{2}\left(\frac{1}{2}\right)\left(\frac{\sqrt{3}}{2}\right)=\frac{\sqrt{3}}{8}$, so the area of the triangle with the $120°$ vertex is twice that, or $\frac{\sqrt{3}}{4}$.

The area of the shaded region is, therefore:

$$\frac{\pi}{3}-\frac{\sqrt{3}}{4}$$

CHAPTER SIXTY

Solid Geometry

Solids are three-dimensional objects with length, width, and height. **Solid geometry** takes concepts from two-dimensional plane geometry and adds another dimension such that area becomes volume. With a strong understanding of the planar shapes, however, you'll find that the rules for solid geometry follow the same format and are only slightly more complicated.

UNIFORM SOLIDS

A **uniform solid** is what you get when you take a plane and move it, without tilting it, through space. Here are some uniform solids.

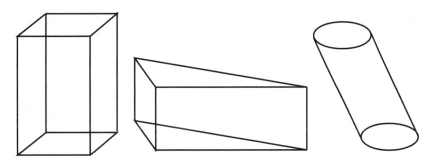

The way these solids are drawn, the top and bottom faces are parallel and congruent. These faces are called the **bases**. You can think of each of these solids as the result of sliding the base through space. The perpendicular distance through which the base slides is called the **height**.

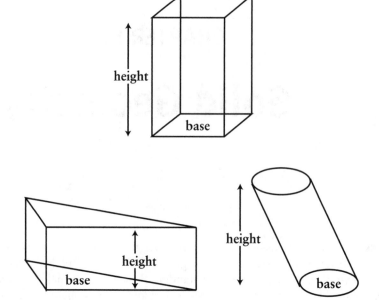

In every one of the above cases—indeed, in the case of any uniform solid—the volume is equal to the area of the base times the height. So you can say that for any uniform solid, given the area of the base B and the height h:

$$\text{Volume of a Uniform Solid} = Bh$$

Surface area can be much more time-consuming to calculate and involves adding together the areas of all the faces of a three-dimensional object, which can be calculated using the equations from Chapter 59, Plane Geometry.

Example: In the figure below, the bases of the right uniform solid are triangles with sides of lengths 3, 4, and 5. If the volume of the solid is 30, what is the total surface area?

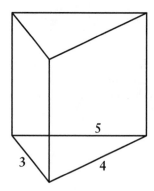

Solution: The surface area is the sum of the areas of the faces. To find the areas of the faces, you need to figure out what kinds of polygons they are so that you'll know what formulas to use. Start with the bases, which are triangles with sides of lengths 3, 4, and 5. This is a 3-4-5 triangle, which means that it's a right triangle, and you can use the legs as the base and height to find the area:

$$\text{Area of Right Triangle} = \frac{1}{2}(\text{leg}_1)(\text{leg}_2) = \frac{1}{2}(3)(4) = 6$$

That's the area of each of the bases. The other three faces are rectangles. To find their areas, you need first to determine the height of the solid. If the area of the base is 6 and the volume is 30, then

$$\text{Volume} = Bh$$
$$30 = 6h$$
$$h = 5$$

So the areas of the three rectangular faces are $3 \times 5 = 15$, $4 \times 5 = 20$, and $5 \times 5 = 25$. The total surface area, then, is $6 + 6 + 15 + 20 + 25 = 72$.

Rectangular Solids

A rectangular solid is a uniform solid whose base is a rectangle and whose height is perpendicular to its base. Rectangular solids have six rectangular faces and 12 edges that meet at right angles at eight vertices.

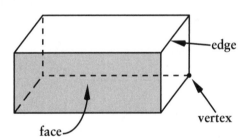

Given the length l, width w, and height h, the area of the base is lw, so the volume formula is:

Volume of a Rectangular Solid = ℓwh

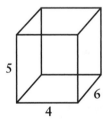

The volume of a 4-by-5-by-6 box is

$$4 \times 5 \times 6 = 120$$

The surface area of a rectangular solid is the sum of the areas of the faces, according to the formula **Surface Area = $2lw + 2wh + 2lh$**. If the length is l, the width is w, and the height is h, then two rectangular faces have area lw, two have area wh, and two have area lh. The total surface area is the sum of those three pairs of areas.

You may also be asked to find the distance between opposite vertices of a rectangular solid.

Example: In the rectangular solid in the figure below, what is the distance from vertex A to vertex B?

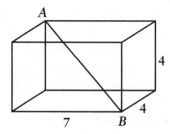

Solution: One way to find this distance is to apply the Pythagorean theorem twice. First plug the dimensions of the base into the Pythagorean theorem to find the diagonal of the base:

$$\text{Diagonal of base} = \sqrt{(4^2 + 7^2)} = \sqrt{(16 + 49)} = \sqrt{65}$$

Notice that the base diagonal combines with an edge and with the segment AB you're looking for to form a right triangle:

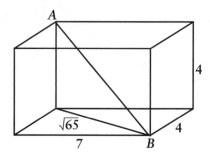

So you can plug the base diagonal and the height into the Pythagorean theorem to find AB:

$$AB = \sqrt{(\sqrt{65})^2 + 4^2} = \sqrt{65 + 16} = \sqrt{81} = 9$$

Another way to find this distance is to take the Pythagorean theorem to another dimension. If the length is l, the width is w, and the height is h, the formula is:

$$\text{Distance} = \sqrt{l^2 + w^2 + h^2}$$

Volume of a Cube

A cube is a rectangular solid with length, width, and height all equal. If e is the length of an edge of a cube, the volume formula is:

$$\text{Volume of a Cube} = e^3$$

The volume of this cube is $2^3 = 8$.

Volume of a Cylinder

A cylinder is a uniform solid whose base is a circle. Given base radius r and height h, the area of the base is πr^2, so the volume formula is:

$$\text{Volume of a Cylinder} = \pi r^2 h$$

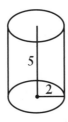

In the cylinder above, $r = 2$ and $h = 5$, so:

$$\text{Volume} = \pi(2^2)(5) = 20\pi$$

CONES

In common terms, a **cone** is formed from a round base connected to a point called a **vertex**.

Lateral Area of a Cone

Given base circumference c and slant height l,

$$\text{Lateral Area of Cone} = \frac{1}{2}cl$$

The **lateral area** of a cone is the area of the part that extends from the vertex to the base. It does not include the base.

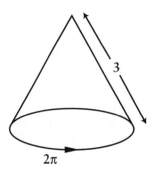

For example, in the figure above, $c = 2\pi$ and $l = 3$, so

$$\text{Lateral Area} = \frac{1}{2}(2\pi)(3) = 3\pi$$

Volume of a Cone

Given base radius r and height h:

$$\text{Volume of Cone} = \frac{1}{3}\pi r^2 h$$

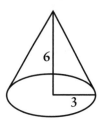

For example, in the figure, $r = 3$ and $h = 6$, so:

$$\text{Volume} = \frac{1}{3}\pi(3^2)(6) = 18\pi$$

PYRAMIDS

A **pyramid** is also formed from a base connected to a point, but the base is polygonal rather than circular The most common pyramids have bases that are triangular or rectangular.

Volume of a Pyramid

Given base area B and height h:

$$\text{Volume of Pyramid} = \frac{1}{3}Bh$$

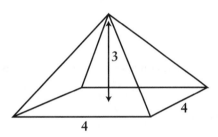

For example, in the figure above, $h = 3$, and the base is a square, $B = 16$. Thus:

$$\text{Volume} = \frac{1}{3}(16)(3) = 16$$

Example: A right circular cone and a sphere have equal volumes. If the radius of the base of the cone is $2x$ and the radius of the sphere is $3x$, what is the height of the cone in terms of x?

Solution: As you can see, this question is hard enough even with the formulas provided. This is no mere matter of plugging values into a formula and cranking out the answer. This question is more algebraic than that and takes a little thought. It's really a word problem. It describes in words a mathematical situation (in this case, geometric) that can be translated into algebra. The pivot in this situation is that the cone and sphere have equal volumes. You're looking for the height h in terms of x, and fortunately you can express both volumes in terms of those two variables. Be careful. Both formulas include r, but they're not the same r. In the case of the cone, $r = 2x$, but in the case of the sphere, $r = 3x$:

$$\text{Volume of cone} = \frac{1}{3}\pi r^2 h = \frac{1}{3}\pi(2x)^2 h = \frac{4}{3}\pi x^2 h$$

$$\text{Volume of sphere} = \frac{4}{3}\pi r^3 = \frac{4}{3}\pi(3x)^3 = 36\pi x^3$$

QR

Now write an equation that says that the expressions for the two volumes are equal to each other and therefore: solve for h:

$$\frac{4}{3}\pi x^2 h = 36\pi x^3$$

$$\pi x^2 h = \frac{3}{4}(36\pi x^3)$$

$$\pi x^2 h = 27\pi x^3$$

$$h = \frac{27\pi x^3}{x^3 \pi}$$

$$h = 27x$$

SPHERES

A **sphere** is a three-dimensional circle that makes a perfectly round ball.

Surface Area of a Sphere

Given radius r:

$$\text{Surface Area of Sphere} = 4\pi r^2$$

For example, if the radius of a sphere is 2, then

$$\text{Surface Area} = 4\pi(2^2) = 16\pi$$

Volume of a Sphere

Given radius r:

$$\text{Volume} = \frac{4}{3}\pi r^3$$

For example, if the radius of a sphere is 2, then

$$\text{Volume} = \frac{4}{3}\pi(2)^3 = \frac{32\pi}{3}$$

CHAPTER SIXTY-ONE

Coordinate Geometry

MIDPOINTS AND DISTANCES

Some of the more basic coordinate geometry questions are concerned with the layout of grids, the location of points and the distances between them, midpoints, and similar concepts.

Example:

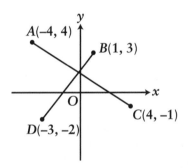

In the above figure, what is the distance from the midpoint of segment AC to the midpoint of segment BD?

Solution: To find the **midpoint** of a segment, average the x-coordinates and average the y-coordinates of the endpoints:

$$\text{midpoint of } AC = \left(\frac{-4+4}{2}, \frac{4-1}{2}\right) = (0, 1.5)$$

$$\text{midpoint of } BD = \left(\frac{-3+1}{2}, \frac{-2+3}{2}\right) = (-1, 0.5)$$

To find the distance between two points, use the distance formula:

$$\text{Distance} = \sqrt{(x_1 - x_2)^2 + (y_1 - y_2)^2}$$

The distance from (0, 1.5) to (–1, 0.5) is calculated as follows:

$$\text{Distance} = \sqrt{(-1-0)^2 + (0.5-1.5)^2}$$
$$= \sqrt{1+1}$$
$$= \sqrt{2}$$

SLOPE-INTERCEPT FORM

Slopes and **intercepts** are descriptions of lines and points on the grid, but the processes of finding and using slopes or intercepts are generally algebraic processes.

Example: Which of the following lines has no point of intersection with the line $y = 4x + 5$?

A. $y = \dfrac{1}{4}x - 5$

B. $y = -\dfrac{1}{4}x - 5$

C. $y = 4x + \dfrac{1}{5}$

D. $y = -4x + \dfrac{1}{5}$

E. $y = -4x - \dfrac{1}{5}$

Solution: What does "has no intersection with" mean? It means that the lines are parallel, which in turn means that the lines have the same slope. If you know the slope-intercept form, you're able to spot the correct answer instantly.

When an equation is in the form $y = mx + b$, the letter m represents the slope, and the letter b represents the y-intercept. The equation in the stem is $y = 4x + 5$. That's in slope-intercept form, so the coefficient of x is the slope.

$$y = ④x + 5$$
$$\text{slope} = 4$$

Now look for the answer choice with the same slope. Conveniently, all the answer choices are presented in slope-intercept form, so spotting the one with $m = 4$ is straightforward; it's (C):

$$y = ④x + \dfrac{1}{5}$$
$$\text{slope} = 4$$

Test takers who are good at memorizing methods and formulas are not necessarily the ones who get the best scores; instead, it's the people who have a deeper understanding of mathematics. If you really want to ace coordinate geometry questions, it's not enough to memorize the midpoint formula, the distance formula, the slope definition, the slope-intercept equation form, and so on. What you want is to have a real grasp of what slope is and what perpendicular, parallel, positive, negative, zero, and undefined slopes tell you.

Slope is a description of the "steepness" of a line. Lines that go uphill (from left to right) have positive slopes, and the steeper the uphill grade, the greater the slope.

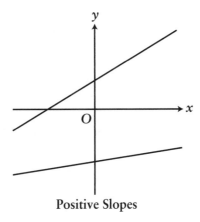

Positive Slopes

Lines that go downhill have negative slopes. The steeper the downhill grade, the less the slope:

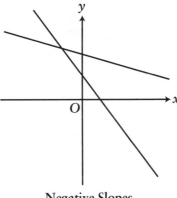

Negative Slopes

Lines parallel to the x-axis have slope $= 0$, and lines parallel to the y-axis have *undefined slopes*.

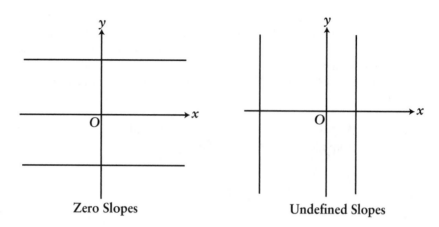

Zero Slopes   Undefined Slopes

Lines that are parallel to each other have the same slope, and lines that are perpendicular to each other have negative-reciprocal slopes.

In the figure below, the two parallel lines both have slope $= 2$, and the line that's perpendicular to them has slope $= -\dfrac{1}{2}$:

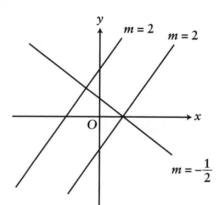

Parallel and Perpendicular Lines

ABSOLUTE VALUE AND INEQUALITIES

Example: Which of the following shaded regions shows the graph of the inequality $y \leq |x + 2|$?

A.

B.

C.

D.

E.
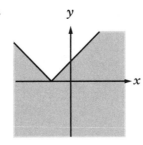

Solution: The way to handle an inequality is to think of it as an equation first, plot the line, and then figure out which side of the line to shade. This inequality is more complicated because of the absolute value. When you graph an equation with an absolute value, you generally get a line with a bend, as in all of the answer choices above. To find the graph of an absolute value equation, figure out where the bend is. In this case, $|x + 2|$ has a turning-point value of 0, which happens when $x = -2$. So the bend is at the point $(-2, 0)$. That narrows the choices down to (A) and (E).

Next, figure out which side gets shaded. Pick a convenient point on either side and see if that point's coordinates fit the given inequality. The point $(0, 0)$ is an easy one to work with. Do those coordinates satisfy the inequality?

$$y \leq x + 2$$
$$0 \overset{?}{\leq} 0 + 2$$
$$0 \overset{?}{\leq} 2 \quad \text{Yes.}$$

The point $(0, 0)$ must be on the shaded side of the bent line. The answer is (E).

CHAPTER SIXTY-TWO

Trigonometry

RIGHT TRIANGLES

Trigonometry is really all about right triangles—and you're concerned not with the right angle, per se, but with one of the other angles of the triangle. The **sine** of angle θ is the length of the side opposite the angle divided by the length of the hypotenuse (the **hypotenuse** is the side opposite the right angle). The mathematical abbreviation for sine is sin, and the sine of the angle θ is written $\sin \theta$.

The **cosine** is the length of the side adjacent to angle θ (actually, there will be two sides adjacent to the angle, but one of those sides will be the hypotenuse, so by adjacent, we really mean the side adjacent to angle that is not the hypotenuse) divided by the length of the hypotenuse. The mathematical abbreviation for cosine is cos, and the cosine of the angle θ is written $\cos \theta$.

Finally, the **tangent** of an angle is the length of the opposite side over the length of the adjacent side. The mathematical abbreviation for tangent is tan, and the tangent of the angle is written $\tan \theta$.

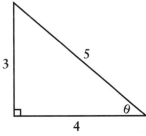

So for instance, in the figure above, the sine of angle θ, $\sin \theta$, is the length of the side opposite angle θ (3) divided by the length of the hypotenuse (5). So the sine is $\frac{3}{5} = 0.60$. That is, $\sin \theta = 0.60$.

The cosine of angle θ is the length of the side adjacent to angle θ (4) divided by the length of the hypotenuse (5). So the cosine of angle θ is $\frac{4}{5} = 0.80$, or $\cos \theta = 0.80$.

Finally, the tangent is the length of the side opposite angle θ (3) divided by the length of the side adjacent to angle θ (4). So the tangent of angle θ is $\frac{3}{4} = 0.75$, or $\tan \theta = 0.75$. To help you remember the definitions of sine, cosine, and tangent as they apply to right triangles, use the mnemonic **SOHCAHTOA** (the first letters of each of the words below).

$$\text{Sine} = \frac{\text{Opposite}}{\text{Hypotenuse}} \qquad \text{Cosine} = \frac{\text{Adjacent}}{\text{Hypotenuse}} \qquad \text{Tangent} = \frac{\text{Opposite}}{\text{Adjacent}}$$

We can also use this information to help us figure out the lengths of sides of triangles.

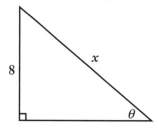

Example: In the right triangle above, if the sine of angle $\theta = 0.5$, what is the value of x?

Solution: The angle is opposite the given side, and the side you're looking for is the hypotenuse, so you can use the sine formula to find x:

$$\sin \theta = \frac{\text{Opposite}}{\text{Hypotenuse}}$$

$$0.5 = \frac{8}{x}$$

$$x = \frac{8}{0.5}$$

$$x = 16$$

There are three other trig functions you should be aware of—and each is the *reciprocal* of one of the trig functions introduced above. They are called **cotangent**, **secant**, and **cosecant**.

$$\text{Cotangent} = \frac{\text{Adjacent}}{\text{Opposite}} \qquad \text{Secant} = \frac{\text{Hypotenuse}}{\text{Adjacent}} \qquad \text{Cosecant} = \frac{\text{Hypotenuse}}{\text{Opposite}}$$

These are also equal to:

$$\text{Cotangent} = \frac{1}{\text{Tangent}} \qquad \text{Secant} = \frac{1}{\text{Cosine}} \qquad \text{Cosecant} = \frac{1}{\text{Sine}}$$

The mathematical abbreviation for cotangent is cot, and the cotangent of the angle θ is written cot θ. The mathematical abbreviation for secant is sec, and the secant of the angle θ is written sec θ. The mathematical abbreviation for cosecant is csc, and the cosecant of the angle θ is written csc θ.

There are also three identities that you should be aware of:

$$\sin^2 x + \cos^2 x = 1$$
$$\tan^2 x + 1 = \sec^2 x$$
$$1 + \cot^2 x = \csc^2 x$$

So for any angle x, you could take the sine and cosine, square them both, and the squares will add up to 1. These relationships are really just restatements of the Pythagorean theorem. To make it easier for you to remember them, the proof of the first identity is presented below, but you certainly don't need to know the proof for Test Day.

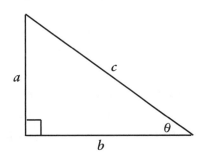

PYTHAGOREAN THEOREM

The Pythagorean theorem says that in a right triangle, the square of the hypotenuse is equal to the sum of the squares of the legs. In the right triangle in the figure above, $c^2 = a^2 + b^2$. Write this as $a^2 + b^2 = c^2$. Now divide both sides of this equation by c^2. Then $\dfrac{a^2 + b^2}{c^2} = \dfrac{c^2}{c^2}, \dfrac{a^2}{c^2} + \dfrac{b^2}{c^2} = 1$, and $\left(\dfrac{a}{c}\right)^2 + \left(\dfrac{b}{c}\right)^2 = 1$. Now $\dfrac{a}{c} = \sin\theta$ and $\dfrac{b}{c} = \cos\theta$. So $\sin^2\theta + \cos^2\theta = 1$.

The identity $\tan^2 x + 1 = \sec^2 x$ is proved by dividing both sides of the equation $a^2 + b^2 = c^2$ by b^2, and the identity $1 + \cot^2 x = \csc^2 x$ is proved by dividing both sides of the equation $a^2 + b^2 = c^2$ by a^2.

Example: Simplify $5 \sin^2 x + 5 \cos^2 x$.

Solution: When you spot a trigonometric expression where quantities are being squared, as in $5 \sin^2 x + 5 \cos^2 x$, you should think immediately about how to extract $\sin^2 x + \cos^2 x$ from it. You do that by factoring out a 5:

$$5 \sin^2 x + 5 \cos^2 x = 5(\sin^2 x + \cos x)$$
$$= 5(1)$$
$$= 5$$

DEGREES AND RADIANS

By definition, if you go all the way around a circle, you have traveled 360 degrees. The **degree** is a unit of measure for describing angles. An angle that is 1 degree is $\frac{1}{360}$ of a complete circle.

The **radian** is another measure used to describe an angle and is often used in trigonometry.

The word *radian* is related to the word *radius*. Remember that, in a circle, a **central angle** is the angle formed by two radii of the circle. This leads to the definition of a radian. If a central angle of a circle intercepts an arc of a circle with length ℓ, then the number of radians in the central angle that contains this arc is $\frac{\ell}{r}$.

If a central angle in a circle intercepts an arc equal in length to 1 radius of a circle, that central angle has a radian measure of 1. So an angle can be described by its degree measure or by its radian measure. The circumference C of a circle is related to its radius r by the formula $C = 2\pi r$. The number of radians in the circumference of any circle is 2π because there are precisely 2π radii in the length of the circumference of any circle. However, there are also 360 degrees in any full circle, so 2π radians is equal to 360 degrees. Therefore, 1 radian is equal to $\frac{360}{2\pi} = \frac{180}{\pi}$ degrees, $\frac{180}{\pi}$ is approximately 57.3.

You are best off if you remember that 2π radians is equal to 360 degrees. Then, you can work with this to convert from some other given number of degrees to the corresponding number of radians, or you can convert from the number of radians to the corresponding number of degrees. You may also remember that π radians is equal to 180 degrees and do your converting based on this, if you are more comfortable doing so.

Example: How many degrees are in $\frac{5\pi}{6}$ radians?

Solution: Let x be the number of degrees. Then:

$$\frac{x}{\left(\frac{5\pi}{6}\right)} = \frac{360}{2\pi}$$

$$x = \frac{5\pi}{6} \times \frac{360}{2\pi} = \frac{5}{6} \times \frac{360}{2} = \frac{5}{1} \times \frac{60}{2} = 5 \times 30 = 150.$$

So there are 150 degrees in $\frac{5\pi}{6}$ radians.

Example: How many radians are there in 270 degrees?

Solution: Let y be the number of radians. Then $\frac{y}{270} = \frac{2\pi}{360}$. So:

$$y = 270 \times \left(\frac{2\pi}{360}\right) = \left(\frac{270}{360}\right) \times \pi = \left(\frac{27}{36}\right) \times \pi = \frac{3\pi}{2}.$$

There are $\frac{3\pi}{2}$ radians in 270 degrees.

Notice that in the first example, we had the number of degrees in the numerator and the number of radians in the denominator, while in the second example, our equation had the number of radians in the numerator and the number of degrees in the denominator. This is just a matter of setting up an equation so it will be easier to work with, since it's generally easier to begin with the unknown in the numerator. Both are correct.

TRIGONOMETRIC FUNCTIONS OF OTHER ANGLES

To find a trigonometric function of an angle greater than or equal to 90°, sketch a circle of radius r and centered at the origin of the coordinate grid (known as the **unit circle**). Start from the point $(r, 0)$ and rotate the appropriate number of degrees θ counterclockwise.

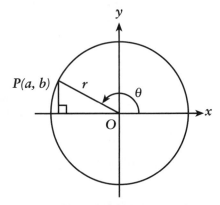

In this circle setup, the basic trigonometric functions are defined in terms of the coordinates a and b:

$$\sin \theta = \frac{b}{r}$$

$$\cos \theta = \frac{a}{r}$$

$$\tan \theta = \frac{b}{a}$$

$$\cot \theta = \frac{a}{b}$$

$$\sec \theta = \frac{r}{a}$$

$$\csc \theta = \frac{r}{b}$$

Notice that tan and sec are undefined if $a = 0$ and cot and csc are undefined if $b = 0$. Notice also that you are working with a right triangle whose hypotenuse is a radius of the circle. One of the legs of this right triangle is on the part of the x-axis that is closest to the hypotenuse (which is the rotated radius).

Example: What is sin 210°?

Solution: Sketch a 210° angle in the coordinate plane:

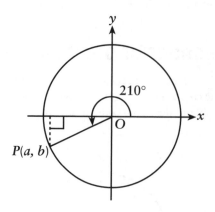

Because the triangle shown in the figure above is a 30°−60°−90° right triangle whose side lengths are in the ratio of $1:\sqrt{3}:2$, it is convenient to use a radius of 2. The coordinates of point P are $(-\sqrt{3}, -1)$.

Therefore $b = -1$, $r = 2$, and $\sin 210° = \dfrac{b}{r} = \dfrac{-1}{2} = -\dfrac{1}{2}$.

GRAPHS OF TRIGONOMETRIC FUNCTIONS

The graph of $y = \sin x$ repeats itself every interval of length 360 degrees (or 2π radians), and the values of $y = \sin x$ can be read off the unit circle and plotted against angle as shown below. When $0 \leq x \leq 90°$, sin x increases from 0 (when $x = 0°$) to 1 (when $x = 90°$). When $90 \leq x \leq 180°$, sin x decreases from 1 (when $x = 90°$) to 0 (when $x = 180°$). When $180 \leq x \leq 270°$, sin x decreases from 0 (when $x = 180°$) to -1 (when $x = 270°$). When $270 \leq x \leq 360°$, sin x increases from -1 (when $x = 270°$) to 0 (when $x = 360°$).

Right after 360°, sin x begins another cycle. Sin x increases from 0 to 1 (in the interval $360° \leq x \leq 450°$), then decreases from 1 to 0 (in the interval $450° \leq x \leq 540°$), then continues to decrease from 0 to -1 (interval $540° \leq x \leq 630°$), and then increases from -1 to 0 (in the interval $630° \leq x \leq 720°$). This graph also repeats its cycle for values of x less than 0°.

This is the graph of $y = \sin x$.

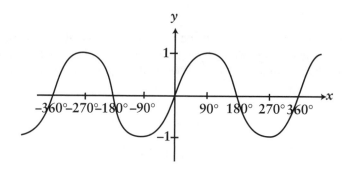

The graph of $y = \cos x$ also repeats itself every 360 degrees or 2π radians; values can be read from the unit circle and plotted against angle as shown below. It begins at 1 when $x = 0°$, and in the interval $0 \leq x \leq 90°$, it decreases from 1 to 0. When $90° \leq x \leq 180°$, $\cos x$ continues its decrease from 0 when $x = 90°$ to -1 when $x = 180°$. When $180 \leq x \leq 270°$, $\cos x$ increases from -1 when $x = 180°$ to 0 when $x = 270°$. When $270 \leq x \leq 360°$, $\cos x$ increases from 0 when $x = 270°$ to 1 when $x = 360°$. Then, for $360° \leq x \leq 720°$, the graph repeats itself again with one more complete cycle in the interval $360° \leq x \leq 720°$.

This is the graph of y = cos x:

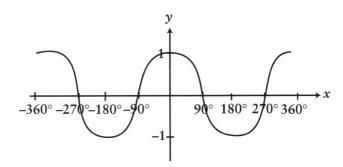

The graph of $y = \tan x$ repeats itself every 180°, which is unlike the graphs of $y = \sin x$ and $y = \cos x$, which repeat themselves every 360°. This is because $\tan x$ is positive for $0° < x < 90°$, $\tan x$ is negative for $90° < x < 180°$, $\tan x$ is positive again for $180° < x < 270°$, and $\tan x$ is negative again for $270° < x < 360°$.

Notice that $\tan x$ is undefined for every odd multiple of 90° or $\frac{\pi}{2}$. Thus, $\tan x$ is undefined when x is any of..., $-630°$, $-450°$, $-270°$, $-90°$, 90°, 270°, 450°, 630°, ..., or in terms of radians, $\tan x$ is undefined when x is any of...,

$$-\frac{7\pi}{2}, -\frac{5\pi}{2}, -\frac{3\pi}{2}, -\frac{\pi}{2}, \frac{\pi}{2}, \frac{3\pi}{2}, \frac{5\pi}{2}, \frac{7\pi}{2}, ...$$

When $-90° < x < 0°$, $\tan x$ is negative, and $\tan x$ increases from negative numbers with very large absolute values when x is near, but greater than $-90°$ to negative values with small absolute values when x is near but less than 0°. So in the interval $-90° < x < 0°$, $\tan x$ is increasing. When $x = 0°$, $\tan x = 0$. When $0 < x < 90°$, $\tan x$ continues to increase from positive values that are small for values of x that are near but greater than 0° to positive values are large for values of x that are close to but less than 90°. The graph of $y = \tan x$ in the interval $-90° < x < 90°$ is repeated in the interval $90° < x < 270°$.

In trigonometry, scales are often given in terms of radians. The x-axis of the graph of $y = \tan x$ will be labeled with radians, unlike the graphs of $y = \sin x$ and $y = \cos x$, which had their x-axes labeled with degrees.

This is the graph of $y = \tan x$:

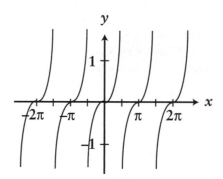

It can be seen from the graph that when x approaches $\frac{\pi}{2}$ through values of x that are greater than $\frac{\pi}{2}$, $y = \tan x$ approaches negative infinity. When x approaches $\frac{\pi}{2}$ through values of x that are less than $\frac{\pi}{2}$, $y = \tan x$ approaches positive infinity.

PERIODIC FUNCTIONS

A **function** f is a set of instructions that associates each number of a set A (which is called the **domain**) with a number in a set B (which is called the **range**). Often the domain and/or the range are not specified. What is important is that you just follow the instructions: For each given number, use the function to find the number associated with it. While f is the most common symbol, other letters, such as g, h, and r, may also be used to denote functions.

If x is a point of the domain, then $f(x)$ is the number associated with x by the function f. Notice the difference between f and $f(x)$ while f refers to the entire process of using the instructions to associate numbers with other numbers, $f(x)$ means the exact number that the function f associates with the number x. So $f(x)$ is a number for any specified x.

The trigonometric function $f(x) = \sin x$ repeats itself every 360°. For example, $\sin 30°$ equals $\sin 390°$; both of these equal $\frac{1}{2}$.

Let R be a positive constant. If f is a function such that $f(x) = f(x + R)$ for all x, and R is the smallest positive number for which this is true, then the function is said to be periodic with period R. Notice that for the function f defined by $f(x) = \sin x$, $\sin (x + 2\pi) = \sin x$ for all x. Because 2π is the smallest possible positive value for R for which $\sin (x + R) = \sin x$ for all x, 2π is the period of $\sin x$. While it is also true that $\sin (x + 4\pi) = \sin x$ for all x, 4π is not the smallest possible positive value for R such that $\sin (x + R) = \sin x$ for all x. So even though for any x, $\sin x$ does have the same value at $x + 4\pi$ that is has at x, we would not say that the period of $f(x) = \sin x$ is 4π. Again, the period of $\sin x$ is 2π.

INVERSE FUNCTIONS

The inverse sine function of x, which is denoted by arcsin x, or $\sin^{-1} x$, determines the angle y such that $\sin y = x$ and $-90° \le y \le 90°$. Because $-1 \le \sin y \le 1$, the inverse sine function cannot be defined for values of x such that $x < -1$ or $x > 1$. Therefore, the inverse sine function of x is defined only for x such that $-1 \le x \le 1$.

For example, $\arcsin\left(\frac{1}{2}\right) = \sin^{-1}\left(\frac{1}{2}\right) = 30°$ because $\sin 30° = \frac{1}{2}$ and 30° is in the interval $-90° \le y \le 90°$.

The reason why, for a given x, the value of $\sin^{-1} x$ is defined to be in the interval $-90° \leq y \leq 90°$ is that there are infinitely many y such that $\sin y = x$, and a function must associate exactly one number with each number in the domain.

For example, look at $\sin^{-1}\left(\frac{1}{2}\right)$ again. It is true that $\sin(-570°) = \frac{1}{2}$, $\sin(-330°) = \frac{1}{2}$, $\sin(-210°) = \frac{1}{2}$, $\sin 30° = \frac{1}{2}$, $\sin 150° = \frac{1}{2}$, $\sin 30° = \frac{1}{2}$, $\sin 510° = \frac{1}{2}$, $\sin 750° = \frac{1}{2}$, and so on. To be able to assign a unique value to $\sin^{-1}\left(\frac{1}{2}\right)$, the requirement that the angle be in the interval $-90° \leq y \leq 90°$ is included.

The inverse tangent function of x, which is denoted by arctan x, or $\tan^{-1} x$, determines the angle y such that $-90° < y < 90°$ and $\tan y = x$. The inverse tangent function is defined for all real x. For example, $\arctan(-1) = \tan^{-1}(-1) = -45°$ because $-45°$ is in the interval $-90° < y < 90°$ and $\tan(-45°) = -1$.

The reason why, for any given real number x, the value of $\tan^{-1} x$ is defined to be in the interval $-90° < y < 90°$ is that there are infinitely many values of y such that $\tan y = x$, and a function must associate exactly one number with each number in the domain.

For example, look at $\tan^{-1}(-1)$ again. It is true that $\tan(-765°) = -1$, $\tan(-585°) = -1$, $\tan(-405°) = -1$, $\tan(-225°) = -1$, $\tan(-45°) = -1$, $\tan(135°) = -1$, $\tan 315° = -1$, $\tan 495° = -1$, $\tan 675° = -1$, and so on. To be able to assign a unique value to $\tan^{-1}(-1)$, the requirement that the angle be in the interval $-90° < y < 90°$ is included.

Notice that the possible values of the inverse sine function are in the interval $-90° \leq y \leq 90°$, while the possible values of the inverse tangent function are in the interval $-90° < y < 90°$. The values of $-90°$ and $90°$ are not possible values of the inverse tangent function because $\tan 90°$ and $\tan(-90°)$ are both undefined.

Example: Which of the following is equal to $\tan\left(\sin^{-1}\left(\frac{7}{\sqrt{74}}\right)\right)$?

A. $\dfrac{\sqrt{74}}{7}$

B. $\dfrac{5}{\sqrt{74}}$

C. $\dfrac{5}{7}$

D. $\dfrac{7}{\sqrt{74}}$

E. $\dfrac{7}{5}$

Solution: You want to find the tangent of a certain angle. That angle is $\sin^{-1}\left(\frac{7}{\sqrt{74}}\right)$. Call $\sin^{-1}\left(\frac{7}{\sqrt{74}}\right)$ the angle y. Then $y = \frac{7}{\sqrt{74}}$. In a right triangle, the sine of an angle is equal to the length of the leg opposite that angle divided by the length of the hypotenuse. So draw a picture of a right triangle with an angle y whose sine is $\frac{7}{\sqrt{74}}$:

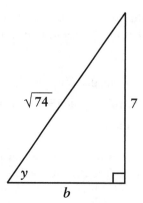

If you can find the length of b, you can find $\tan\left[\sin^{-1}\left(\dfrac{7}{\sqrt{74}}\right)\right] = \tan y$ by remembering that, in a right triangle, the tangent of an angle is equal to the length of the leg opposite that angle divided by the length of the leg adjacent to that angle. The length b of the other leg can be found by using the Pythagorean theorem, which says that the square of the hypotenuse is equal to the sum of the squares of the legs. Here,

$$7^2 + b^2 = (\sqrt{74})^2$$
$$49 + b^2 = 74$$
$$b^2 = 25$$
$$b = 5$$

Note that $b = -5$ is also a solution of the equation $b^2 = 25$, but you're concerned with lengths, and you can't have a negative length; therefore, $b = -5$ does not apply here.

So $b = 5$, and $\tan y = \tan\left(\sin^{-1}\left(\dfrac{7}{\sqrt{74}}\right)\right) = \dfrac{7}{5}$. Choice (E) is correct.

REVIEW PROBLEMS

1. In the figure below, what is the value of $\cos \theta$?

Figure 1

   A.   0.25
   B.   0.66
   C.   0.75
   D.   0.80
   E.   1.25

2. Which of the following equals $\dfrac{\cos^4 \theta - \sin^4 \theta}{\cos^2 \theta - \sin^2 \theta}$ where defined?

   A.   1
   B.   2
   C. $\cos \theta + \sin \theta$
   D. $\cos \theta - \sin \theta$
   E. $\cos^2 \theta + \sin^2 \theta$

3. If $\sin \theta = \dfrac{1}{2} \cos \theta$, and $0 < \theta < \dfrac{\pi}{2}$, the value of $\dfrac{1}{2} \sin \theta$ is

   A.   0.22
   B.   0.25
   C.   0.45
   D.   0.50
   E.   0.75

4. If θ is an acute angle for which $\tan^2 \theta = 6 \tan \theta - 9$, what is the approximate measure of θ?

   A.   30°
   B.   45°
   C.   75°
   D.   90°
   E.   105°

5. What is the y-coordinate of the point at which the graph of $y = 2 \sin x - \cos 2x$ intersects the y-axis?

   A. -2
   B. -1
   C.   0
   D.   1
   E.   2

SOLUTIONS TO REVIEW PROBLEMS

1. **B** The cosine is the ratio of the adjacent side to the hypotenuse. Use the Pythagorean theorem $a^2 + b^2 = c^2$ to find the adjacent leg, then approximate cosine based on that value and the given value of hypotenuse, which is 4:

$$\text{leg} = \sqrt{4^2 - 3^2}$$
$$= \sqrt{16 - 9}$$
$$= \sqrt{7}$$

$$\cos\theta = \frac{\text{adjacent}}{\text{hypotenuse}} = \frac{\sqrt{7}}{4} = 0.66$$

On Test Day, you could use your calculator to take the square root of seven, or you could estimate that it would be smaller than the square root of nine, meaning the final fraction would be smaller than three-fourths, and answer choice (B) is the best fit without being too small.

2. **A** The numerator is the difference of squares and so can be factored:

$$\frac{\cos^4\theta - \sin^4\theta}{\cos^2\theta - \sin^2\theta} = \frac{\left(\cos^2\theta + \sin^2\theta\right)\left(\cos^2\theta - \sin^2\theta\right)}{\cos^2\theta - \sin^2\theta}$$
$$= \cos^2\theta + \sin^2\theta$$

This is a trigonometric identity and equals one.

3. **A** Rewrite the given equation in terms of only sine by using the identity $\sin^2\theta + \cos^2\theta = 1$ to determine that $\cos^2\theta = (1 - \sin^2\theta)$, then solve for θ and divide by two:

$$\sin\theta = \frac{1}{2}\cos\theta$$
$$\sin^2\theta = \frac{1}{4}\cos^2\theta$$
$$\sin^2\theta = \frac{1}{4}(1 - \sin^2\theta)$$
$$4\sin^2\theta = 1 - \sin^2\theta$$
$$5\sin^2\theta = 1$$
$$\sin^2\theta = \frac{1}{5}$$

Since one-fifth is less than one-fourth, and the square root of one-fourth is one-half:

$$\sin\theta < \frac{1}{2}$$
$$\frac{1}{2}\sin\theta < \frac{1}{4}$$

Only (A) is less than (and not equal to) 0.25.

4.   **C**   This is a quadratic equation for which the unknown is tan θ:

$$\tan^2 \theta = 6 \tan \theta - 9$$
$$\tan^2 \theta - 6 \tan \theta + 9 = 0$$
$$(\tan \theta - 3)^2 = 0$$
$$\tan \theta = 3$$
$$\theta = \arctan (3) < 75°$$

Note that the answer choices are widely separated, so you only need a rough approximation of tangent. Remembering that tangent is the ratio of sine to cosine, you can recall that tan $45° = 1$ because that is where sine equals cosine. A tangent larger than one occurs when sine is larger (the angle is larger than 45° and smaller than 90°), and a tangent small than one occurs when cosine is larger (the angle is smaller than 45° and larger than 0°). Only answer choice (C) lies in the correct range. Note that the tangent of 90° (D) is undefined since it's a fraction with a denominator of 0, and the tangent of 105° (E) would be negative since it's past 90° and in a different quadrant.

5.   **B**   The graph intersects the y-axis at the point where $x = 0$:

$$y = 2 \sin x - \cos x$$
$$= 2 \sin (0) - \cos (0)$$
$$= 2 (0) - 1$$
$$= -1$$

Section VII

PHYSICS

SECTION GOALS

The Physics section of the OAT requires strong knowledge of testable concepts and equations, as well as strategic testing skills. This section of the book will focus on supplying the content required for the Physics section of the OAT. This section is designed to help you achieve the following goals:

- Associate key physics terms with relevant equations and related concepts
- Recall concepts and equations necessary for success on the Physics section
- Connect new information and examples to existing content knowledge
- Troubleshoot time-consuming calculations with time-saving strategies
- Predict answers to OAT Physics questions accurately and quickly, using the Kaplan methods

CONTENT OVERVIEW

Units and Vectors, Linear Kinematics, Rotational Motion, and Force Statistics and Dynamics (40%)	Chapter 63: Units, Vectors, and Kinematics Chapter 64: Newtonian Mechanics
Energy and Momentum (10%)	Chapter 65: Energy and Momentum
Thermal Chemistry and Thermodynamics (7.5%)	Chapter 66: Thermodynamics
Fluid Statics (5%)	Chapter 67: Fluid Statics
Electrostatics, DC Circuits, and Magnetism (15%)	Chapter 68: Electrostatics Chapter 69: Magnetism Chapter 70: Circuits
Simple Harmonic Motion and Waves (10%)	Chapter 71: Simple Harmonic Motion and Waves
Optics (10%)	Chapter 72: Light and Optics
Modern Physics (2.5%)	Chapter 73: Modern Physics

KEY STUDY STRATEGIES

The physics section of this book is devoted entirely to content relevant to this section of the OAT exam. For strategies relevant to this section, refer back to the strategies for the Survey of Natural Sciences in Chapters 2–3, especially those you found most useful in your General Chemistry review. Start your review of this section with Chapter 63 for basic information needed in calculations. From there, jump to the chapters most relevant to your areas of concern within the Physics section. Place extra focus in studying the bolded vocabulary terms and equations, as you will need to be able to recall those materials on Test Day. After reviewing a chapter, answer the associated practice questions. These should be completed from memory only, to simulate testing conditions.

CHAPTER SIXTY-THREE

Units, Vectors, and Kinematics

This first physics chapter will review some of the basic mathematics necessary for the study of OAT physics, such as scientific notation, basic trigonometric functions, and vectors. In addition, the topic of units is presented, with emphasis on the three systems of units found on the test: meter-kilogram-second (MKS), centimeter-gram-second (CGS), and foot-pound-second (FPS). Finally, the topic of kinematics, which is the study of motion, is discussed, starting with a review of the basic quantities of displacement, speed, velocity, and acceleration. These basic quantities are then applied to the study of motion with constant acceleration in both one dimension and two dimensions with examples of free fall and projectile motion.

UNITS

Fundamental Measurements and Dimensions

Physics is the most basic of all the sciences. Everything in the world around us is subject to the laws of physics. In order to describe nature, physicists use the language of mathematics in the form of equations to make their quantitative descriptions.

These descriptions, however, mean nothing if they are not expressed in some kind of units. While explaining how you were pulled over on the highway "doing seventy" might mean something among a group of friends, a scientist would ask whether your speed was 70 miles per hour, 70 kilometers per hour, or some other speed. Scientists have developed systems of units that give meaning to all the numbers in the formulas. The "British" **foot-pound-second** (**FPS**) system is commonly used in America but virtually nowhere else in the world (not even in Britain). Basic units for length, weight, and time are the foot (ft), pound (lb), and second (s), respectively, which is the source of the system's name. The most common system of units is the **metric** system, in which the basic units include length, mass (instead of weight like in FPS), and time. The metric system comes in two main variations. One metric system uses meter (m), kilogram (kg), and second (s) as its base and is referred to as **MKS** or **SI** (SI being the initials of the French abbreviation for the International System of Units). The other metric system uses centimeter (cm), gram (g), and second (s) and is referred to as **CGS**. The SI system is usually considered standard, and the majority of physics concepts are presented in this system. Be aware, though, that the test may give you different units.

The following chart lists some important units in the three different systems:

Quantity	CGS	SI	FPS
Length	centimeter (cm)	meter (m)	foot (ft)
Mass	gram (g)	kilogram (kg)	slug (sl)
Force	dyne (dyn)	newton (N)	pound (lb)
Time	second (s)	second (s)	second (s)
Work & Energy	erg	joule (J)	foot-pound (ft·lb)
Power	erg/second	watt (W)	foot-pound/sec

Due to the extremely small scale of the interactions in atomic-sized systems, some different scales are used that make the numbers a little easier to handle. Useful length units on the atomic scale include the angstrom (Å, where 1 Å $= 10^{-10}$ m) and the nanometer (nm, where 1 nm $= 10^{-9}$ m). The unit of energy called the electron volt (eV) is also important at this level and represents the energy acquired by an electron accelerating through a potential difference of 1 volt. Compared to the SI unit of energy, the joule, the electron volt is very small (1 eV $= 1.6 \times 10^{-19}$ J).

Metric system prefixes are often added to units to make numbers easier to handle. The chart below lists prefixes sometimes encountered. These are worth memorizing for Test Day, as are the most common prefix abbreviations: m $= 10^{-3}$, k $= 10^3$, μ $= 10^{-6}$, M $= 10^6$, and n $= 10^{-9}$.

Multiples

Factor	Prefix	Prefix abbreviation
10^9	giga	G (or B)
10^6	mega	M
10^3	kilo	k

Submultiples

Factor	Prefix	Prefix abbreviation
10^{-2}	centi	c
10^{-3}	milli	m
10^{-6}	micro	μ
10^{-9}	nano	n
10^{-12}	pico	p

Scientific Notation

Scientific notation is a convention for expressing numbers that simplifies computation and standardizes results. To express a number in scientific notation, convert it into a number between 1 and 10, then multiply it by 10 raised to the appropriate power.

Example: $123 = 1.23 \times 10^2$

1.23 is the **mantissa,** and 2 is the **exponent** (power of ten).

Example: $0.042 = 4.2 \times 10^{-2}$.

Products and quotients of numbers expressed in scientific notation are readily calculated. When multiplying, multiply the mantissas and add the exponents to find the mantissa and exponent of the answer.

Some additional conversion may be necessary so that the new mantissa is again between 1 and 10, as in the third example below.

Example: $(1.1 \times 10^6)(5.0 \times 10^{17}) = ?$

Solution: Multiply the mantissas 1.1 and 5.0 and add the exponents 6 and 17.

The answer is 5.5×10^{23}.

The quotient of two numbers expressed in scientific notation is obtained by dividing the mantissa in the numerator by the mantissa in the denominator and then subtracting the power of 10 in the denominator from the power of 10 in the numerator.

Example: $\dfrac{6.2 \times 10^5}{2.0 \times 10^{-7}}$

Solution: Divide 6.2 by 2.0 and subtract -7 from 5 (note that $5 - (-7) = 5 + 7 = 12$).

The answer is 3.1×10^{12}.

When a number expressed in scientific notation is raised to a power, the mantissa is raised to that power, and the exponent is multiplied by that number. Think of this as distributing the power to both the mantissa and the exponent.

When the decimal point is moved one place to the left, the power of ten must be increased by one. In other words, if the mantissa becomes smaller, the exponent becomes larger; if the mantissa becomes larger, the exponent becomes smaller.

Example: $(6.0 \times 10^4)^2$

Solution: Square the 6.0 and multiply the exponent by 2.

$(6.0)^2 \times 10^{4 \times 2} = 36.0 \times 10^8 = 3.6 \times 10^9$

When adding or subtracting numbers expressed in scientific notation, they must have the same power of 10; when they do not, the appropriate conversion must be made first.

Example: $3.7 \times 10^4 + 1.5 \times 10^3 = ?$

Solution: First convert 1.5×10^3 to 0.15×10^4 so that both numbers have the same exponent. Then $3.7 \times 10^4 + 0.15 \times 10^4 = 3.85 \times 10^4$, rounded to 3.9×10^4.

TRIGONOMETRIC RELATIONS

For the right triangle, the trigonometric functions for angle θ can be remembered by using the mnemonic SOHCAHTOA:

$$\sin\theta = \frac{y}{h} = \frac{\text{opposite side}}{\text{hypotenuse}}$$

$$\cos\theta = \frac{x}{h} = \frac{\text{adjacent side}}{\text{hypotenuse}}$$

$$\tan\theta = \frac{y}{x} = \frac{\text{opposite side}}{\text{adjacent side}}$$

Some important values of the trigonometric functions are as follows:

θ	$\sin\theta$	$\cos\theta$
0°	0	1
30°	$\frac{1}{2}$	$\frac{\sqrt{3}}{2}$
45°	$\frac{\sqrt{2}}{2}$	$\frac{\sqrt{2}}{2}$
60°	$\frac{\sqrt{3}}{2}$	$\frac{1}{2}$
90°	1	0
180°	0	−1

VECTORS AND SCALARS

Scalars are those numerical quantities that have **magnitude** but no direction, such as distance, speed, and mass. **Vector** quantities have both **magnitude** and **direction.** Some vector quantities are displacement, velocity, and force.

Vector Representation

Common notations for a vector quantity are either an arrow or **boldface.** If an arrow is used, its direction and length may or may not correspond to the direction and magnitude of the vector. For example, the vector A can be written as $\vec{A}$ or **A**, and the magnitude of vector **A** can be represented as $|\vec{A}|$, $|\mathbf{A}|$, or simply A (no arrow or boldface).

Vector Addition

The **sum** of two or more vectors is called the **resultant** of the vectors. The terms vector sum and resultant are interchangeable.

One method of finding the resultant **A** + **B** of the two vectors **A** and **B** is to place the tail of **B** at the tip of **A** without changing the length or direction of either arrow. In this method of vector addition, the lengths of the arrows must be proportional to the magnitudes of the vector. The vector sum

A + **B** is the vector joining the tail of **A** to the tip of **B** and pointing toward the tip of **B**. For three or more vectors, proceed similarly (see Figure 63.1).

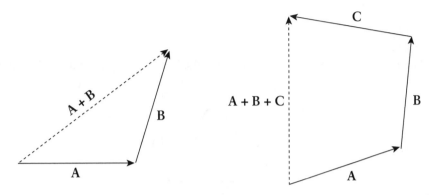

Figure 63.1

A method more commonly used for finding the resultant of several vectors involves breaking each vector into perpendicular (**X** and **Y**) components and combining the components of the different vectors. These components are often, but not always, horizontal and vertical.

Given any vector **V**, the $\mathbf{V_X}$ and $\mathbf{V_Y}$ components are found by drawing a right triangle with **V** as the hypotenuse (see Figure 63.2). If θ is the angle between **V** and the x direction, then $\cos \theta = \mathbf{V_X}/\mathbf{V}$ and $\sin \theta = \mathbf{V_Y}/\mathbf{V}$. Rearranging these gives:

$$\mathbf{V_X} = \mathbf{V} \cos \theta$$

$$\mathbf{V_Y} = \mathbf{V} \sin \theta$$

Example: If **V** = 10 m/s and $\theta = 30°$, then what are $\mathbf{V_X}$ and $\mathbf{V_y}$?

Solution: $\mathbf{V_X} = 10 \cos 30° = \dfrac{10\sqrt{3}}{2} = 5\sqrt{3}$ m/s

$\mathbf{V_Y} = 10 \sin 30° = \dfrac{10}{2} = 5$ m/s

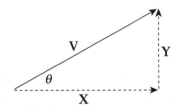

Figure 63.2

Conversely, if $\mathbf{V_X}$ and $\mathbf{V_Y}$ are known, **V** is found by using the Pythagorean theorem: $\mathbf{V_X}^2 + \mathbf{V_Y}^2 = \mathbf{V}^2$.

Example: $V_X = 3$ m/s

$V_Y = 4$ m/s

$V = \sqrt{3^2 + 4^2} = \sqrt{25}$

$= 5$ m/s

Also note that θ can be determined from $\tan \theta = V_Y/V_X$. In this example $\tan \theta = 4/3$, so $\theta = 53°$.

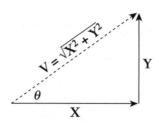

Figure 63.3

The X component of the resultant vector is the sum of the X components of the vectors being added. Similarly, the Y component of the resultant vector is the sum of the Y components of the vectors being added.

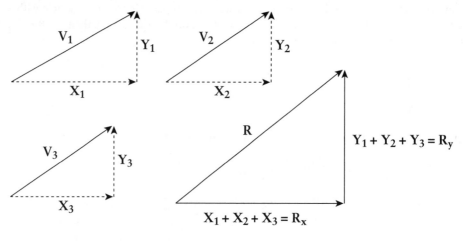

Figure 63.4

To find the resultant (**R**) using the components method:

1. Resolve the vectors to be summed into their X and Y components.

2. Add the X components to get the X component of the resultant ($\mathbf{R_x}$). In the same way, add the Y components to get the Y component of the resultant ($\mathbf{R_y}$).

3. Find the magnitude of the resultant by using the Pythagorean theorem. If $\mathbf{R_x}$ and $\mathbf{R_y}$ are the components of the resultant, then:

$$R = \sqrt{R_x^2 + R_y^2}$$

4. Find the direction (θ) of the resultant by using the relation $\tan \theta = \dfrac{R_y}{R_x}$. From the value of $\tan \theta$ you can find θ, which is the angle **R** makes with the x axis.

Example: Find the horizontal and vertical components of **V**.

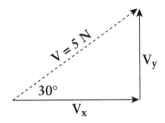

Figure 63.5

Solution: Let X be the horizontal direction and Y be the vertical direction, then:

$$\mathbf{V_x} = V \cos \theta = 5 \cos 30° = \frac{5\sqrt{3}}{2} = 2.5\sqrt{3}\,N \approx 4.3\ N$$

$$\mathbf{V_y} = V \sin \theta = 5 \sin 30° = \frac{5}{2} = 2.5\ N$$

Example: Find the resultant of **A, B, C,** and **D.**

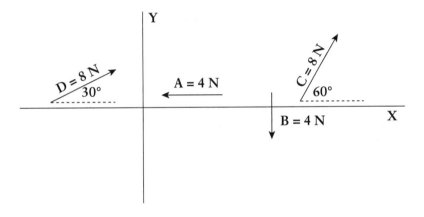

Figure 63.6

Solution: Resolve the vectors into their horizontal (X) and vertical (Y) components. Note that X components go both left and right, and Y components go both up and down. In each case choose one direction as the positive direction. The other direction is then automatically the negative direction.

In this example going to the right is the positive X direction, so to the left is negative. Likewise, up is the positive Y direction, so down is negative.

a. $\mathbf{A_x} = -4\ N$

$\mathbf{B_x} = 0$

$\mathbf{C_x} = 8 \cos 60° = \dfrac{8}{2} = 4\ N$

$\mathbf{D_x} = 8 \cos 30° = \dfrac{8\sqrt{3}}{2} = 4\sqrt{3}\ N$

b. $\mathbf{A}_y = 0$

$\mathbf{B}_y = -4 \text{ N}$

$\mathbf{C}_y = 8 \sin 60° = \dfrac{8\sqrt{3}}{2} = 4\sqrt{3} \text{ N}$

$\mathbf{D}_y = 8 \sin 30° = \dfrac{8}{2} = 4 \text{ N}$

Add the components of **A, B, C,** and **D** to get the components of the resultant, **R:**

a. $\mathbf{R}_x = (-4) + 0 + 4 + 4\sqrt{3} = 4\sqrt{3} \text{ N}$

b. $\mathbf{R}_y = 0 + (-4) + 4\sqrt{3} + 4 = 4\sqrt{3} \text{ N}$

Find the magnitude of the resultant:

$$R = \sqrt{R_x^2 + R_y^2}$$

$$R = \sqrt{(4\sqrt{3})^2 + (4\sqrt{3})^2} = \sqrt{96} = 4\sqrt{6} \text{ N}$$

Find the angle the resultant makes with the horizontal:

$$\tan \theta = \dfrac{4\sqrt{3}}{4\sqrt{3}} = 1; \ \theta = 45°$$

Thus, we have found that **R** is a vector with a magnitude of $4\sqrt{6}$ N, making an angle of 45° with the horizontal. In general, $\tan \theta = |R_y/R_x|$ where θ is the smallest angle with the x-axis.

Vector Subtraction

Subtracting two vectors is exactly the same as adding the negative of the vector being subtracted. When expressed in a mathematical formula, the idea looks like this:

$$\mathbf{A} - \mathbf{B} = \mathbf{A} + (-\mathbf{B})$$

In this case $-\mathbf{B}$ is a vector with the same magnitude as **B** but pointing in the opposite direction.

Example: What is the resultant of $\mathbf{A} - \mathbf{B}$ as pictured below?

Figure 63.7

Solution: The first step is to make the vector $-\mathbf{B}$. This is done by erasing the arrowhead at the tip of **B** and redrawing it where the tail used to be (see Figure 1.8(a)). Now, add this to

A. To do this, move the tip of **A** to the tail of −**B**, then join the tail of **A** to the tip of −**B** (see Figure 63.8(b)).

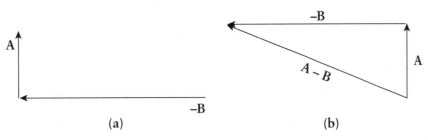

(a)   (b)

Figure 63.8

To find −**B** by breaking the vectors into their horizontal and vertical components, first multiply each vector component by −1 before adding.

Example: If **A** has components $A_x = 3$ and $A_y = 4$ and **B** has components $B_x = 2$ and $B_y = 1$, then what is **A** − **B**?

Solution: First, remember **A** − **B** = **A** + (−**B**). Since **B** has components B_x and B_y, −**B** has components $−B_x$ and $−B_y$.

$$R_x = A_x − B_x = 3 − 2 = 1$$
$$R_y = A_y − B_y = 4 − 1 = 3$$

To get the magnitude of the final resultant vector **R**:

$$R = \sqrt{(1^2 + 3^2)}$$
$$= \sqrt{(1+9)} = \sqrt{10}$$

To get the direction:

$$\tan \theta = \frac{R_y}{R_x} = 3$$
$$\theta = 72°$$

Multiplying a Vector by a Scalar

Now consider the case where a vector is multiplied by a scalar, **B** = n**A**. To find the magnitude of **B**, multiply the magnitude of **A** by the absolute value of n, **B** = $|n|$**A**. If n is a positive number, then **B** and **A** are in the same direction. However, if n is a negative number, then **B** and **A** are in opposite directions. For example, if vector **A** is multiplied by +3, the resultant vector **B** will be three times as long as **A** and point in the same direction. However, if **A** is multiplied by −3, then **B** would again be three times as long as **A** but would point in the opposite direction.

KINEMATICS

Kinematics is the branch of mechanics dealing with the description of motion. In physics, the **position** of an object or particle is defined on a three-dimensional coordinate axis. However, most questions you will have to deal with concerning motion on Test Day will involve only one or two dimensions.

Displacement

The **displacement** (Δx) of an object is a vector quantity that describes the change in position of the object. Displacement goes in a straight line from the initial position to the final position without regard to the actual path taken. Since this is a vector quantity, displacement has both direction and magnitude.

Example: A man walks 2 km east, 2 km north, 2 km west, and 2 km south. Find his total distance traveled and his net displacement.

Solution: His actual total distance traveled is 8 km, since distance is a scalar, but his displacement is a vector quantity that is the change in position. In this case his displacement is zero since the man ends up in the same place he started (see Figure 63.9).

Figure 63.9

Velocity

Average velocity

The **average velocity** of a particle is the ratio of the displacement vector over the change in time. It is a vector quantity such that:

$$\mathbf{v} = \Delta x\,/\,\Delta t$$

v has the same direction as $\Delta \mathbf{x}$.

Instantaneous velocity

The **instantaneous velocity** or simply **velocity** refers to a single instant of time. It is the average velocity as Δt approaches 0. This can be represented as:

$$v = \lim_{\Delta t \to 0} \frac{\Delta x}{\Delta t}$$

The most important concept to understand for the OAT is the graph of instantaneous velocity. Instantaneous velocity is defined as the slope of the graph of the object's position with respect to time at the particular time, *t*.

Speed

The **average speed** is given by:

$$s = d / \Delta t$$

where d is the actual distance traveled. It is a scalar. Since actual distance traveled is not always the same as the magnitude of the displacement vector, average speed is not always the same as the magnitude of the average velocity.

The **instantaneous speed** is the magnitude of the instantaneous velocity vector. It is also a scalar.

Example: A car starts from rest and travels a distance of 120 miles in two hours. What are the average speed and average velocity? Is the instantaneous speed ever less than the average speed?

Solution: The average speed is a scalar that represents distance per time, so $\frac{120}{2} = 60$ mph. However, the average velocity is a vector that is unknown because the path of the car is unknown. Finally, the instantaneous speed must be less than the average speed at some point because the car has an initial speed of zero and must accelerate through slower speeds to reach its average speed, which is not zero.

Acceleration

Average acceleration

Acceleration is the rate of change of an object's velocity. It is a vector quantity. **Average acceleration** is the change in instantaneous velocity over the time period Δt:

$$\mathbf{a} = \Delta v / \Delta t$$

Instantaneous acceleration

Instantaneous acceleration—the acceleration at one point of a particle's path—is defined the same way as instantaneous velocity, i.e., it is the average acceleration as Δt approaches 0.

$$a = \lim_{\Delta t \to 0} \frac{\Delta v}{\Delta t}$$

Instantaneous acceleration is the slope of the line giving the object's velocity with respect to time at a particular time, t. The direction of the acceleration vector is not always in the same direction as the direction of the velocity vector; for an object that is slowing down, the acceleration vector is in the opposite direction of the velocity vector. Consider a ball thrown straight up into the air. The velocity vector is directed up, but the acceleration of the ball due to gravity is directed down, causing the ball to slow down and eventually stop and come back to Earth.

Motion with Constant Acceleration

The acceleration of a body is proportional to the net force (see Chapter 64, Newtonian Mechanics) applied to that body. When a body is under the influence of a constant force, the acceleration is also constant. The OAT will only ask questions based on constant acceleration.

PHYSICS

Linear motion

In linear motion the acceleration and velocity vectors are along the line of motion. Note that the linear motion need not be in the horizontal direction. One-dimensional motion of this kind can be fully described by the following equations:

Notes:

$$v = v0 + at$$

1. v_0, x_0 are defined as v and x at $t = 0$.

$$x - x_0 = v_0 t + \frac{at^2}{2}$$

2. When the motion is vertical, use y instead of x.

$$v^2 = v0^2 + 2a(x - x0)$$

$$\mathbf{v} = \frac{(v_0 + v)}{2}$$

$$x - x_0 = \mathbf{v}t = \frac{(v_0 + v)}{2}t$$

3. Always remember that velocity and acceleration are vector quantities.

The first example involves free-falling bodies. Free fall means that the only force acting on a body is its own weight (gravity) and neglects other forces, such as air resistance. All objects in free fall have the same acceleration, which is called the acceleration due to gravity (g) and is 9.8 m/s². The following example demonstrates the use of the above equations in the analysis of free-falling bodies.

Example: A ball is thrown vertically up into the air with an initial velocity of 10 m/s.

    a. Find the position and velocity of the ball after 2 seconds.

    b. Find the distance and time at which the ball reaches its maximum height.

Solution: a. Velocity and acceleration are vector quantities. Taking the initial position of the ball $y_0 = 0$ and defining "up" as positive, the initial velocity is $\mathbf{v_0} = +10$ m/s, and the acceleration is $\mathbf{g} = -9.8$ m/s². Notice $\mathbf{g}$ is negative because its direction is down, whereas we are taking "up" to be the positive direction.

Velocity after two seconds can be found using the equation:

$$v = v_0 + at$$
$$= (+10) + (-9.8)(2) \qquad \text{(The minus sign for } \mathbf{v} \text{ means the ball is coming down.)}$$
$$= -9.6 \text{ m/s}$$

After two seconds, the position of the ball is found using the equation:

$$y = v_0 t + \frac{at^2}{2}$$
$$= 10(2) + \frac{(-9.8)(2)^2}{2}$$
$$= 20 - 19.6$$
$$= +0.4m$$

b. When the ball is at its maximum height, the velocity, **v**, which has been decreasing on the way up, is zero. The maximum height the ball reaches above the ground is found by using the following equation and plugging in values:

$$v^2 = v_0^2 + 2ay$$
$$0 = (10)^2 + 2(-9.8)y$$
$$y = 5.1m$$

The time at which the ball reaches its maximum height can be found from the equation:

$$v = v_0 + at$$
$$0 = 10 + (-9.8)t$$
$$t = 1.0s$$

Projectile motion

The example above uses only linear motion because the ball only traveled in the y direction. In the case of **projectile motion,** however, the object has velocity and position components in both the vertical and horizontal directions. The two components of the velocity vector, v_x and v_y, are independent, so the change in the vertical velocity v_y due to gravity does not affect and is not affected by the constant horizontal velocity, v_x. The following example demonstrates how projectile motion is analyzed.

Example: A projectile is fired from ground level with an initial velocity of 50 m/s and an initial angle of elevation of 37°. Assuming g = 10 m/s², find:

a. the projectile's total time in flight.

b. the maximum height attained.

c. the total horizontal distance traveled.

d. the final horizontal and vertical velocities just before it hits the ground.

(sin 37° = 0.6; cos 37° = 0.8)

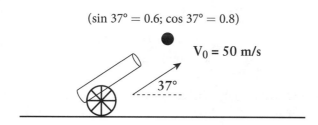

Figure 63.10

Solution: a. Let y equal the vertical height, and let "up" be the positive direction. Acceleration will be defined as **g** for any projectile motion problem, but it will be negative if up is defined as positive.

$$a = -10\text{m/s}^2$$

$$y = v_{0_y}t + \frac{1}{2}at^2$$

$$v_{0_y} = v_0 \sin 37°$$

$$v_{0_y} = 50(0.6) = 30 \text{ m/s}$$

$$y = 30t - 5t^2$$

$y = 0$ both when the projectile is first fired and when it hits the ground later. Its time of flight will be the time from the launch ($y_0 = 0$) until landing ($y = 0$). Note that in any projectile motion problem there is no acceleration in the x direction, so the particle moves with constant horizontal speed.

$$30t - 5t^2 = 0$$

$$5t(6 - t) = 0$$

$$t = 0 \text{ (first fired)}, \ t = 6 \text{ (hits the ground)}$$

Time in flight $= 6 - 0 = 6 \ s$

b. To find the maximum height attained (using y instead of x):

$$v_y^2 = v_{0y}^2 + 2a(y - y_0)$$

$$0 = 30^2 + 2(-10)(y - 0)$$

$$y = \frac{900}{20}$$

$$y = 45 \text{ m}$$

c. To find the horizontal distance traveled:

$$x = v_x t \ (a_x = 0)$$

$$v_x = 50 \cos 37° = 40 \text{ m/s}$$

$$x = 40(6) = 240 \text{ m}$$

d. The horizontal velocity remains constant, so $v_x = 40$ m/s. To find the vertical velocity at impact:

$$v_y = v_{0y} + at$$

$$v_y = 30 - 10(6)$$

$$v_y = 30 - 60$$

$$v_y = -30 \text{ m/s}$$

Since up was chosen as positive, the minus sign means the vertical component of the velocity is directed down.

REVIEW PROBLEMS

1. A man walks three blocks (30 m) east and then another five blocks (50 m) north to the drug store (point A).

   a. What distance did he walk?

   b. What is his final displacement from his original location (point X)?

   c. Instead of the motion described, imagine that the man simply walks three blocks (30 m) in one direction and five blocks (50 m) in another (possibly the same) direction; what's the minimum displacement from his original location?

   d. How does his average speed compare with the magnitude of his average velocity?

2. A submarine sends out a sonar signal (sound wave) in a direction directly downward. It takes 2.3 s for the sound wave to travel from the submarine to the ocean bottom and back to the submarine. How high up from the ocean floor is the submarine? (The speed of sound in water is 1,490 m/s.)

3. A car is traveling at 40 km/hr, and the driver applies the brakes to bring the car to rest in a time of six seconds. What's the magnitude of the average acceleration of the car in units of km/hr^2?

4. If an object is released 19.6 m above the ground, how long does it take the object to reach the ground?

5. At a place where g is 9.8 m/s^2, an object is thrown vertically downward with a speed of 10 m/s. Meanwhile, a different object is thrown vertically upward with a speed of 20 m/s. Which object undergoes a greater change in speed in a time of two seconds?

6. A firefighter jumps horizontally from a burning building with an initial speed of 1.5 m/s. At what time is the angle between his velocity and acceleration the greatest?

7. A circus clown is catapulted straight up in the air from a catapult opening 1.5 m above ground level. If his velocity as he leaves the catapult is 4 m/s:

   a. How high does he get as measured from the ground?

   b. How does his velocity when he lands compare to his initial velocity?

SOLUTIONS TO REVIEW PROBLEMS

1. a. **80 m**

   The total distance the man walked to point A is 30m + 50m = 80 m. Since distance is a scalar quantity, direction is irrelevant.

   b. **58 m from where he started in a direction 59.0° north of east**

   His displacement from point X is the vector sum of 30 m east and 50 m north or D m in the direction of $\theta°$ north of east. Remember, to completely describe a vector, both magnitude and direction must be stated.

   From the Pythagorean theorem:

   $$D^2 = (30)^2 + (50)^2$$
   $$= 900 + 2,500$$
   $$= 3,400$$

   Therefore:

   $$D = 10\sqrt{34}\, m = 58\ m$$

   θ is given by:

   $$\theta = \arctan\left(\frac{50}{30}\right)$$
   $$= \arctan(1.666...)$$
   $$= 59°$$

   c. **20 m (two blocks)**

   The minimum displacement is obtained when the five-block section is in the direction opposite to the three-block section. In that case, the net displacement is two blocks or 20 m.

   d. **His average speed is greater than the magnitude of his average velocity.**

   Average speed is distance traveled divided by time taken, whereas the magnitude of the average velocity is the magnitude of the displacement vector divided by the time taken. The displacement vector is along the hypotenuse of a right triangle, so its magnitude is smaller than the distance traveled (the sum of the two legs of the right triangle). So we conclude that the magnitude of the average velocity is less than the average speed.

2. **1,713.5 m**

   The distance travelled by an object is given by:

   $$d = vt$$
   $$= (1,490)(2.3)$$
   $$= 3,427\, m$$

   However, this distance represents the distance from the submarine to the ocean floor and back to the submarine, or in other words, twice the distance from the submarine to the ocean floor. It follows, therefore, that the submarine is 3,427/2, or 1,713.5 m from the bottom of the ocean.

3. **24,000 km/hr²**

The magnitude of the average acceleration is the change in speed divided by the time taken. The speed changes by 40 km/hr, since the car comes to rest. The time taken, in hours, is $(6 \text{ s}) \times (1 \text{ hr})/(3{,}600 \text{ s}) = (\frac{1}{600})$ hr. Average acceleration is then: $(40 \text{ km/hr})/(\frac{1}{600} \text{ hr}) = 24{,}000$ km/hr².

4. **2 s**

We solve for t taking "down" as positive:

$$d = v_0 t + \frac{1}{2} a t^2$$

Since $\mathbf{v}_0 = 0$ we can say:

$$d = \frac{1}{2} a t^2$$

Solving for t:

$$t^2 = \frac{2d}{a}$$
$$= \frac{2(19.6)}{9.8}$$
$$t = \sqrt{4}$$
$$= 2 \text{ s}$$

In all problems dealing with falling objects or projectiles, if air resistance is neglected, the acceleration is constant (9.8 m/s² or 32 ft/s²) and acts in a downward direction. Unless otherwise stated, there is no acceleration in the horizontal direction and the initial velocity is zero. Aside from these rules, these problems are the same as all other problems dealing with constant acceleration.

5. **Each object undergoes the same change in speed.**

Each object experiences an acceleration of 9.8 m/s², which means that each object's speed changes by 9.8 m/s each second. Both objects thus experience the same change in speed over the two-second period, i.e., 19.6 m/s.

6. **The angle is the greatest the instant he jumps.**

The firefighter's acceleration is always directed downward, whereas his velocity starts out horizontal and gradually rotates downward as his downward velocity increases. As time progresses, the angle between his velocity and acceleration decreases, which means the maximum angle occurs at the instant he jumps.

7. a. **2.3 m**

At the instant the clown reaches his maximum height, his vertical velocity is zero. Taking "up" as positive:

$$v^2 = v_0^2 + 2a(y - y_0)$$
$$v^2 = v_0^2 + 2(-g)(h)$$
$$v^2 = v_0^2 - 2gh$$

Since $v = 0$, we can solve for h:

$$h = \frac{v_0^2}{2g}$$

$$= \frac{4^2}{2(9.8)}$$

$$= \frac{16}{19.6}$$

$$= 0.8\,\mathrm{m}$$

Since the catapult opening is 1.5 m above the ground, the maximum height is $1.5 + 0.8 = 2.3$ m.

b. **The landing velocity is opposite in direction and greater in magnitude than the initial velocity.**

On his way down, the clown will have a speed of 4 m/s at a height of 1.5 m off the ground, since that was his speed at that height on the way up. The clown will then gain speed in falling the additional 1.5 m to the ground.

CHAPTER SIXTY-FOUR

Newtonian Mechanics

This chapter covers an important area of OAT physics: Newton's laws of motion. Basic concepts for the study of Newton's laws are force and mass, which are discussed in this chapter along with the distinction between mass and weight and a detailed example of obtaining the resultant of two or more forces. The classic example of a block sliding down a frictionless incline is also presented as an exercise for applying Newton's second law to a situation in which there are forces in two directions. Translational and rotational equilibrium are discussed as examples of cases where the net force or net torque vanishes. The real-world problem of motion in the presence of friction is briefly discussed qualitatively, followed by a detailed numerical example. Lastly, the topic of circular motion is discussed along with the associated concepts of tangential and centripetal acceleration and centripetal force.

NEWTON'S THREE LAWS

Force

Force is a vector quantity. Forces are observed as the push or pull on an object. Forces can be exerted either between bodies in contact (such as the force a person exerts to push a box across the floor) or between bodies not in contact (such as the force of gravity holding the Earth in its orbit around the sun). The unit for force in SI units is the **newton (N)** and is equivalent to kilogram $\cdot$ meter/second^2. Note that newtons can be broken down into fundamental units using $\mathbf{F} = m\mathbf{a}$.

Mass and Weight

The mass of an object should not be mistaken for the weight of an object. **Mass (m)** is a scalar quantity that measures a body's inertia, while **weight (W)** is a force vector that measures a body's gravitational attraction to the Earth. The two are related by the equation:

$$\mathbf{W} = m\mathbf{g}$$

where $\mathbf{g}$ is the acceleration due to gravity. The unit for weight is the same as for any other force, the newton (N).

When one of the forces acting on a body is its own weight, the entire force due to gravity can be thought of as applied at a single point, called the center of gravity. For a homogeneous body, the center of gravity is at its geometric center.

Newton's Laws of Motion

Mechanics is the study of bodies in motion and at rest. Newtonian mechanics is a way of describing the effect forces have on macroscopic bodies. In order to carry out such a description, it is first necessary to have an understanding of Newton's three laws of motion and how to apply them to various situations.

Newton's three laws are:

1. A body either at rest or in motion with constant velocity will remain that way unless a net force acts upon it.

2. A net force applied to a body of mass m will result in that body undergoing acceleration in the same direction as the net force. The magnitude of the body's acceleration is directly proportional to the magnitude of the net force and inversely proportional to the body's mass. This can be expressed in general terms as:

$$\mathbf{F}_{net} = \Sigma\mathbf{F} = m\mathbf{a}$$

   or in components as:

$$\Sigma\mathbf{F}_x = m\mathbf{a}_x$$
$$\Sigma\mathbf{F}_y = m\mathbf{a}_y$$

   Note that the acceleration in the x direction depends only on the forces (or components of forces) in the x direction (and the same is true for the y direction). Also, when $\mathbf{F}_{net} = 0$, then $\mathbf{a} = 0$; forces may be present, but if no *net* force is present, no acceleration will occur.

3. If body A exerts a force $\mathbf{F}$ on body B, then B exerts a force $-\mathbf{F}$ back on A that is equal in magnitude and opposite in direction. In Newton's words, "to every action there is always an opposed but equal reaction." Note that action and reaction forces always act on separate objects.

$$\mathbf{F}_{BA} = -\mathbf{F}_{AB}$$

Example: Why are collapsible guard rails on a highway actually safer than more rigid ones?

Solution: What's dangerous in a collision is the average impact force, which equals the mass of the colliding vehicle times the average acceleration experienced ($\mathbf{F} = m\mathbf{a}$). The average acceleration equals the change in speed experienced by the vehicle divided by the time over which the change occurs or the collision time ($\mathbf{a} = \Delta\mathbf{v}/\Delta t$). Given equal changes in speed, a collapsible guard rail results in a longer collision time and thus a smaller average impact force.

Free-Body Diagram

Another concept useful in force problems is the **free-body diagram**, which helps to visually show what forces are applied and what their directions are. The examples below demonstrate the use of this technique.

Example: Three people are pulling on ropes tied to a tire with forces of 100 N, 150 N, and 200 N, as shown in Figure 64.1. Find the magnitude and direction of the resultant force.

Solution: First draw a free-body diagram that shows the forces acting on the tire. Its purpose is to identify and better visualize the acting forces.

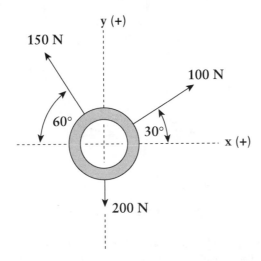

The resultant force is the sum of the x and y components of the forces. To find the resultant force vector, first sum each of the force components:

$$\mathbf{R}_x = \Sigma\mathbf{F}_x = 100 \cos 30° - 150 \cos 60°$$
$$= 86.6 - 75$$
$$= 11.6 \text{ N (positive } x \text{ direction, to the right)}$$

$$\mathbf{R}_y = \Sigma \mathbf{F}_y = 100 \sin 30° + 150 \sin 60° - 200$$
$$= 50 + 129.9 - 200$$
$$= -20.1 \text{ N (negative } y \text{ direction, down)}$$

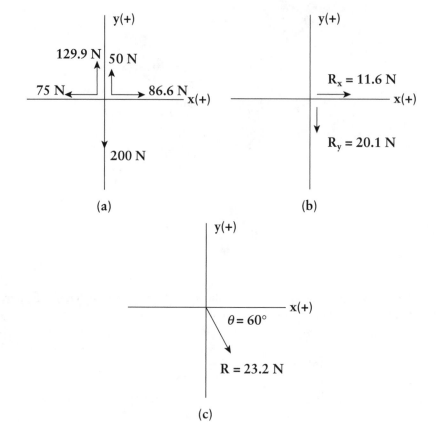

(a)

(b)

(c)

$$\mathbf{R} = \sqrt{(11.6)^2 + (-20.1)^2}$$
$$= 23.3 \text{N}$$

$$\tan \theta = \frac{-20.1}{11.6}$$

$$\theta \cong -60° \ (\mathbf{R} \text{ is in the 4th quadrant})$$

Example: Starting from rest, a 5 kg block takes 4 s to slide down a frictionless incline. Find the normal force, the acceleration of the block, and the vertical height h where the block started if the plane is at an angle of 30°.

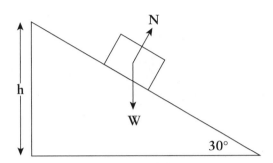

Solution: Choose the x- and y- axes such that one of the axes is parallel to the surface. The force that the surface exerts on the block is broken up into two components, one perpendicular to the surface, called the **normal force (N)**, and the other parallel to the surface, called the **friction force (f)**. In this problem the incline is frictionless (i.e., $\mathbf{f} = 0$), so of the two it experiences only the normal force, **N**. The block's weight **W** is vertically down. To solve, first find the components of **W** that are parallel and perpendicular to the inclined surface (i.e., the components of **W** in the x and y directions, $\mathbf{W}_x$ and $\mathbf{W}_y$).

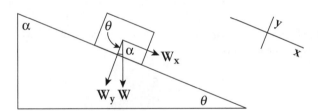

Note that in Figure 64.5 the angle **W** makes with the x-axis is α, and we would normally use this angle in expressing the components of **W** such that $\mathbf{W}_x = \mathbf{W}\cos\alpha$ and $\mathbf{W}_y = \mathbf{W}\sin\alpha$. However, it is more useful to express the components of **W** in terms of the angle θ, which the inclined surface makes with the horizontal. In other words, resolve the weight ($m\mathbf{g}$) into its components parallel to and perpendicular to the incline. In terms of θ the components of **W** are:

$$\mathbf{W}_x = \mathbf{W}\sin\theta = m\mathbf{g}\sin\theta$$
$$\mathbf{W}_y = \mathbf{W}\cos\theta = m\mathbf{g}\cos\theta$$

So let the x-axis be parallel to the inclined surface, and let the y-axis be perpendicular to it. The motion is along the inclined surface so is along the x-axis. Therefore, any acceleration is only in the x direction, and a_y is automatically zero.

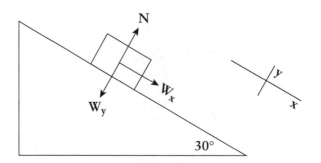

Only the forces in the x direction affect the motion of the block. Since there is no acceleration in the y direction, the sum of those forces equals zero.

$$\Sigma \mathbf{F}_x = \mathbf{W}_x = (5)(9.8) \sin 30° = 24.5 \text{ N} = m\mathbf{a}_x$$
$$\Sigma \mathbf{F}_y = m\mathbf{a}_y = \mathbf{N} - \mathbf{W}_y = 0$$

From the second equation, solve the first part of the problem, which asks for **N**:

$$\mathbf{N} = (5)(9.8) \cos 30° = 42.4 \text{ N}$$

From the first equation solve the second part of the problem which asks for $\mathbf{a}_x$: (Note that $\mathbf{a}_x = \mathbf{a}$ since $\mathbf{a}_y = 0$.)

$$\mathbf{a} = \frac{\mathbf{F}}{m}$$
$$= \frac{24.5}{5}$$
$$= 4.9 \text{ m/s}^2$$

For the third part of the problem, start by finding the length d of the incline from where the block started:

$$d = \frac{at^2}{2} \qquad (V_0 = 0)$$
$$= \frac{(4.9)(4)^2}{2}$$
$$= 39.2 \text{ m}$$

From trigonometry, the vertical height h is can be calculated:

$$\sin 30° = \frac{h}{d}$$
$$h = 39.2 \sin 30°$$
$$= 19.6 \text{ m}$$

Gravity

Gravity is an attractive force that is felt by all forms of matter. The **gravitational force (F_g)** is given as:

$$F = \frac{Gm_1m_2}{r^2}$$

where G is the **gravitational constant** (6.67×10^{-11} N $\cdot$ m^2/kg^2), m_1 and m_2 are the masses of the two objects, and r is the distance between their centers. The force due to gravity is the reaction force of m_1 on m_2 and of m_2 on m_1. Gravity increases directly as the masses of the objects increase and decreases as the square of the distance between them increases.

Example: Find the gravitational attraction between an electron and a proton at a distance of 10^{-11}m. (Proton mass $= 10^{-27}$ kg; electron mass $= 10^{-30}$ kg)

Solution: Using Newton's law of gravitation:

$$
\begin{aligned}
F &= \frac{Gm_1m_2}{r^2} \\
&= \frac{(6.67 \times 10^{-11})(10^{-27})(10^{-30})}{(10^{-11})^2} \\
&= 6.67 \times 10^{-46} \text{ N}
\end{aligned}
$$

EQUILIBRIUM

If several forces act on an object simultaneously, their vector sum may cancel, leaving the motion of the body unchanged. This balancing phenomenon is called **equilibrium,** and $F_{net} = 0.$

Translational Equilibrium

An unbalanced force acting on an object accelerates the object in the direction of the force because $F = ma$. For an object to be in **translational equilibrium,** the sum of the forces pushing the object through space in one direction must be counterbalanced by the sum of the forces acting in the opposite direction. This is called the first condition of equilibrium and can be written as:

$$\Sigma F = 0 \text{ (vector sum)}$$

or, if the vectors are resolved into their x and y components:

$$\Sigma F_x = 0 \text{ and } \Sigma F_y = 0$$

Example: A block of mass 20 kg is supported as shown in the diagram. Find the tensions T_1 and T_2.

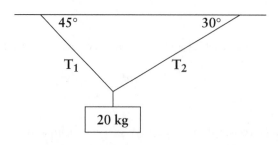

Solution: A free-body diagram at the point of intersection of the three cords will help solve this problem. Cords, strings, and the like can only exert pulling forces, and these are in the direction of each cord. Note also that the tension in the vertical cord is equal to the weight of the 20 kg mass, as shown in the other free-body diagram on the right of Figure 64.8.

The force components are:

$$\Sigma F_x = 0 = T_2 \cos 30° - T_1 \cos 45°$$
$$\Sigma F_y = 0 = T_1 \sin 45° + T_2 \sin 30° - 20(9.8)$$

Solve the second equation for T_1:

$$T_1 = \frac{20(9.8) - T_2 \sin 30°}{\sin 45°}$$

$$= \frac{20(9.8) - T_2/2}{\sqrt{2}/2}$$

$$= \frac{196 - T_2}{\sqrt{2}}$$

Solve the first equation for $\mathbf{T}_2$:

$$\frac{\mathbf{T}_2\sqrt{3}}{2} - \frac{\sqrt{2}}{2}\left(\frac{196 - \mathbf{T}_2}{\sqrt{2}}\right) = 0$$

$$\mathbf{T}_2(\sqrt{3} + 1) = 196$$

$$\mathbf{T}_2 = \frac{196}{\sqrt{3} + 1}$$

$$= 71.8 \text{ N}$$

Substitute the value of $\mathbf{T}_2$ in to the equation for $\mathbf{T}_1$ and solve:

$$\mathbf{T}_1 = \frac{196 - 71.8}{\sqrt{2}}$$

$$= 87.8 \text{ N}$$

Rotational Equilibrium

Unlike translational motion, rotational motion depends not only on the magnitude and direction of the force but also on the distance from the force to the axis of rotation. The greater the distance, the greater the change in rotational motion that will be produced by a given force. As an example, try closing a door first by pushing on it a few inches from the hinge and then by pushing far from the hinge. You'll find it's much easier to close the door when you push farther from the hinge because the distance between the axis and the force is greater. The quantity that causes rotation is called the **moment of the force** or the **torque** τ, and is given by:

$$\tau = rF \sin \theta$$

where F is the magnitude of the force, r is the distance between the axis and the force (also called the lever arm), and θ is the angle between F and r. The $\sin \theta$ term indicates that maximum torque occurs when $\theta = 90°$ ($\tau_{max} = rF$), and minimum torque occurs when $\theta = 0°$ ($\tau_{min} = 0$). Torque can act in two directions about a pivot point: clockwise and counterclockwise. Counterclockwise is the positive direction, and clockwise the negative direction. For **rotational equilibrium** to occur, the sum of the torques in both these directions must be equal. Since torques causing a rotation in the clockwise direction are negative and torques causing counterclockwise rotations are positive, we can also say that the sum of all the torques must be zero:

$$\Sigma\tau = 0$$

This is called the second condition of equilibrium.

Example: A seesaw with a mass of 5 kg has one block of mass 10 kg located 2 meters to the left of the fulcrum and another block located 0.5 m to the right of the fulcrum. If the seesaw is in equilibrium:

a. find the mass of the second block.

b. find the force exerted by the fulcrum.

Solution: a. To find t, take the point of the fulcrum as the pivot point. This way the weight of the seesaw will be eliminated from the equation because $r = 0$ for the center of the seesaw, and the weight of it to the right cancels the weight of it to the left. Call the 10 kg mass object 1 and the block whose mass is unknown object 2.

$$\Sigma \tau = 0 = m_1 g r_1 - m_2 g r_2$$

$$m_2 = \frac{m_1 r_1}{r_2}$$

$$= \frac{10(2)}{0.5}$$

$$= 40 \text{ kg}$$

b. To find the normal force, $\mathbf{N}$, exerted by the fulcrum, combine all vertical forces such that $\Sigma \mathbf{F}_y = 0$. There is the upward force exerted by the fulcrum and the downward weights of the seesaw and the two masses. Don't forget that $\mathbf{W} = m\mathbf{g}$. Taking "up" as positive:

$$\mathbf{N} - (m_{\text{seesaw}}\mathbf{g} + m_1\mathbf{g} + m_2\mathbf{g}) = 0$$

$$\mathbf{N} - 5(9.8) - 10(9.8) - 40(9.8) = 0$$

$$\mathbf{N} = 49 + 98 + 392 = 539 \text{ N}$$

MOTION

Translational Motion

Translational motion is defined as motion in which there is no rotation. An example of translational motion is a block sliding on an inclined plane. With Newton's three laws and enough information about initial conditions, you can solve any translational motion problem.

Friction

Whenever two objects are in contact, their surfaces rub together creating a friction force. **Static friction, $\mathbf{f}_s$,** is the force which must be overcome to set an object in motion. Its equation is:

$$0 \leq \mathbf{f}_s \leq \mu_s \mathbf{N}$$

where μ_s is the **coefficient of static friction** and $\mathbf{N}$ is the normal force. Note that static friction can have any value up to some maximum $\mu_s\mathbf{N}$. For example, to send a book that is at rest sliding across a table, a force greater than the maximum static friction force is required. Any force less than or equal to $\mu_s\mathbf{N}$ will result in the book not moving. Once the book starts to slide, though, the friction force is not quite as strong. This new friction force is called **kinetic friction, f_k,** and its equation is:

$$\mathbf{f_k} = \mu_k \mathbf{N}$$

where μ_k is the **coefficient of kinetic friction** and $\mathbf{N}$ is the normal force. Remember that friction always acts to oppose motion.

Example: Two blocks are in static equilibrium as shown in Figure 64.10.

    a. If block A has a mass of 15 kg and the coefficient of static friction μ_s equals 0.20, then find the maximum mass of block B.

    b. If an extra 5 kg are added to B, find the acceleration of A and the tension in the rope (μ_k equals 0.14).

Solution: a.

For block B:

Since block B is in static equilibrium, the tension in the rope must equal the weight of the block:

$$\Sigma F_y = 0 = T - W_B$$
$$T = W_B = m_B g$$

For block A: Note that asking for the maximum mass of block B means that the coefficient of static friction holding block A must be at its maximum, $\mathbf{f_s} = \mu_s \mathbf{N}$.

$$\Sigma F_y = 0 = N - W_A$$

$$N = W_A = m_A g$$
$$\Sigma F_x = 0 = T - \mu_s N$$
$$T = \mu_s m_A g$$
$$T = (0.2)(15)(9.8)$$
$$T = 29.4 \text{ N}$$

As determined above, the tension in the rope must equal the weight of block B, giving:

$$m_B g = 29.4$$
$$m_B = 3 \text{ kg}$$

b.

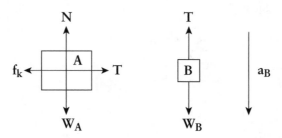

In the first part of the solution to this problem, we determined the maximum mass of block B for the system to be in static equilibrium. Adding an extra 5 kg to B means that the system is now in motion.

For block B: Motion means that net force and net acceleration are given by:

$$\Sigma F_y = m_B g - T = m_B a_B$$

For block A: Motion means that net force and net acceleration are given by:

$$\Sigma F_x = T - \mu_k N$$
$$= T - \mu_k m_A g$$
$$= m_A a_A$$

Since the blocks are connected by the string, the magnitude of the acceleration for both of them is the same:

$$\mathbf{a}_A = \mathbf{a}_B = \mathbf{a}$$

and

$$m_B g - T = m_B a$$
$$T - \mu_k m_A g = m_A a$$

Adding the two equations gives:

$$m_B g - T + T - \mu_k m_A g = (m_A + m_B) a$$

Solving for **a**:

$$a = \frac{(m_B - \mu_k m_A)g}{(m_A + m_B)}$$

$$= \frac{[8 - (0.14)(15)]9.8}{(15 + 8)}$$

$$= 2.5 \text{ m/s}^2$$

Substituting this value into the equation $m_A\mathbf{a} = \mathbf{T} - \mu_k m_A\mathbf{g}$ and solving for the tension gives:

$$\mathbf{T} = m_A(\mu_k\,\mathbf{g} + \mathbf{a})$$

$$= 15(0.14(9.8) + 2.5)$$

$$= 58.1 \text{ N}$$

CIRCULAR MOTION

In circular motion, the velocity vector is always tangent to the circular path. In other words, if the force holding the object in a circular path were suddenly to disappear, the object would fly off in a straight line at a right angle to the radius of the circular path.

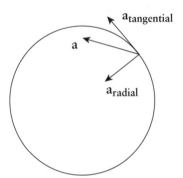

Figure 64.1

In uniform circular motion, the speed of the object remains constant. The acceleration is always directed toward the center of the circle and is called **centripetal acceleration.** Centripetal acceleration changes only the direction of the velocity so the object travels in a circle and does not change the speed of the object. The magnitude of centripetal acceleration is given by:

$$a = \frac{v^2}{r}$$

The centripetal acceleration toward the center of the circle must be the result of some force also directed toward the center. Whatever that particular force happens to be caused by, it is called the **centripetal force.** Using the relationship $a = \mathbf{v}^2/r$ for the centripetal acceleration, the magnitude of the centripetal force on a particle in circular motion is given by:

$$F = ma = \frac{mv^2}{r}$$

Consider a mass tied to a string, moving with circular motion. To keep the mass moving in a circular path, the string must constantly pull the object toward the center. In this particular case, the force exerted by the string is the centripetal force. If at some point the string breaks, the inward force no longer acts and the mass flies off along a path tangential to the circle.

There is always some force that causes circular motion. As another example, consider a planet in orbit around the sun. In this case, the centripetal force is the force of gravity, and the formula for F_g can be set equal to the centripetal force F_c:

$$F = \frac{Gm_1 m_2}{r^2} = m_1 v^2/r$$

REVIEW PROBLEMS

1. A 1,000 kg rocket ship, traveling at 100 m/s, is acted on by an average force of 20 kN applied in the direction of its motion for 8 s. What is the change in velocity of the rocket?

2. An elevator is designed to carry a maximum weight of 9,800 N (including its own weight) and to move upward at a speed of 5 m/s after an initial period of acceleration. What is the relationship between the maximum tension in the elevator cable and the maximum weight of 9,800 N when:

   a) the elevator is accelerating upward and

   b) the elevator reaches its constant speed of 5 m/s.

3. A 10 kg wagon rests on a frictionless inclined plane. The plane makes an angle of 30° with the horizontal. What is the force required to keep the wagon from sliding down the plane?

4. A 20 kg wagon is released from rest from the top of a 15 m long plane which is angled at 30° with the horizontal. Assuming there is friction between the ramp and the wagon, how is the frictional force affected if the angle of the incline is increased?

5. An astronaut weighs 700 N on Earth. What will her weight be on a planet with a radius that is two times that of Earth and a mass three times that of Earth?

6. A 30-kg girl sits on a seesaw at a distance of 2 m from the fulcrum. Where must her father sit to balance the seesaw if he has a mass of 90 kg?

7. An object is moving uniformly in a circle whose diameter is 200 m. If the centripetal acceleration of the object is 4 m/s^2, what is the time for one revolution of the circle?

8. A distant solar system is made up of one small planet of mass 1.48×10^{24} kg revolving in a circular orbit about a large, stationary star of mass 7.30×10^{30} kg. The distance between their centers is 5.00×10^{11} m. What happens to the speed of the planet if the distance between the star and the planet increases, assuming the new orbit is also circular?

SOLUTIONS TO REVIEW PROBLEMS

1.   **160 m/s**

The average force on the rocket equals its mass times the average acceleration, and the average acceleration equals the change in velocity divided by the time over which the change occurs. So the change in velocity equals the average force (20,000 N) multiplied by the time (8 s) and divided by the mass (1,000 kg), which equals 160 m/s.

2. a. **The tension is greater than 9,800 N.**

    b. **The tension equals 9,800 N.**

The forces on the elevator are the tension upward and the weight downward, so the net force on the elevator is the difference between the two. While the elevator is accelerating upward, the tension in the cable must be greater than the maximum weight so that the difference produces a nonzero acceleration. While the elevator is moving at a constant speed, its acceleration is zero, so the net force on the elevator is also zero This means that the tension and the weight are equal.

3.   **49 N**

The weight of the wagon ($\mathbf{W} = m\mathbf{g}$) acts in a direction straight down. This force can be broken up into x- and y- components, with the x-axis parallel to and the y-axis perpendicular to the plane of the incline.

$$\mathbf{W}_x = \mathbf{W} \sin 30°$$
$$\mathbf{W}_y = \mathbf{W} \cos 30°$$

In order to keep the wagon from moving (i.e., to keep it in equilibrium), the sum of the forces must be zero. In terms of components:

$$\Sigma\mathbf{F}_x = 0 \qquad \Sigma\mathbf{F}_y = 0 \; (x, y \text{ coordinates})$$

From a free-body diagram, it can be seen that the y-component of the weight is counteracted by an equal and opposite force from the surface of the plane (the normal force, $\mathbf{N}$). Similarly, the x-component of the weight, which tends to cause the wagon to roll down the plane, must be counteracted by an equal and opposite force parallel to the plane (the unknown force, $\mathbf{F}$).

Here, we'll let up the plane be the positive x-direction. We could also have taken down the plane to be the positive x-direction as long as we use the correct signs when we take components. The choice of positive direction is arbitrary.

The magnitude of the required force can be determined by recognizing that the sum of the forces in the x-direction must be zero:

$$\Sigma\mathbf{F}_x = \mathbf{F} - \mathbf{W}\sin 30° = 0$$
$$\mathbf{F} = \mathbf{W}\sin 30°$$
$$= mg \sin 30°$$
$$= 10(9.8)(0.5)$$
$$= 49\,\text{N}$$

4.   **The frictional force decreases.**

The force of friction on an object sliding down an incline equals the coefficient of friction times the normal force. The normal force, which is given by $mg \cos \theta$, decreases as the angle of the incline, q, increases. Thus, the frictional force decreases as the angle of the incline increases.

5.   **525 N**

The weight of an object on a planet can be found using Newton's law of gravitation with one minor simplification. Since the planet is much larger than the person (or object), **r**, which is the distance between the centers of the two objects (planet and person), can be taken simply as the radius of the planet, and the additional few meters to the center of the astronaut can be ignored. Since the astronaut's weight equals:

$$\mathbf{F} = \frac{GmM_e}{r_e^2} = 700 \text{ N on Earth},$$

then on a planet that is three times as massive as Earth ($M_p = 3M_e$) and that has twice the radius of Earth ($r_p = 2r_e$):

$$\begin{aligned}
\mathbf{F} &= \frac{GmM_p}{r_p^2} \\
&= \frac{Gm(3M_e)}{(2r_e)^2} \\
&= \frac{3GmM_e}{4r_e^2} \\
&= \frac{3}{4}\left(\frac{GmM_e}{r_e^2}\right) \\
&= \frac{3}{4}\text{(the astronaut's weight on Earth)} \\
&= \frac{3}{4}(700) \\
&= 525 \text{ N}
\end{aligned}$$

6.   **67 cm from the fulcrum**

In order for the seesaw to be balanced, the moment (torque) due to the girl must be exactly counteracted by the moment due to her father. More generally stated, the sum of the moments about any point must equal zero.

Taking moments about the fulcrum, with the subscript f denoting the father and the subscript g denoting the girl, gives:

$$\sum \tau_{fulcrum} = m_f \, \mathbf{g}x - m_g \mathbf{g}x_g = 0$$

$$m_f \, \mathbf{g}x = m_g \mathbf{g}x_g$$

$$x = \frac{m_g x_g}{m_f}$$

$$= \frac{30 \times 2}{90}$$

$$= \frac{2}{3} \, m$$

$$= 67 \text{ cm from the fulcrum}$$

The problem can actually be solved by taking moments about any point, not just the fulcrum. However, doing so is usually more complicated because the force of the fulcrum on the seesaw first has to be determined.

7. **10π s**

Start with centripetal acceleration: $\mathbf{a} = \mathbf{v}^2/\mathbf{r}$. Given $\mathbf{r} = 100$ m and $\mathbf{a} = 4$ m/s^2, we have $\mathbf{v} = 20$ m/s. Velocity, $\mathbf{v}$, and time of revolution, $\mathbf{T}$, are related by $\mathbf{v} = 2\pi\mathbf{r}/\mathbf{T}$; i.e., in a time equal to one revolution, the distance covered is the circumference. Thus, $\mathbf{T} = 2\pi(100)/20$ s $= 10\pi$ s.

8. **The speed of the planet decreases.**

The force on the planet due to the star is: $\mathbf{F} = \dfrac{Gm_{star}m_{planet}}{r^2}$. Since this force provides the

centripetal force, it's also true that $\mathbf{F} = m_{planet}\mathbf{v}^2/r$. Equating the two expressions for $\mathbf{F}$ gives $\mathbf{v}^2 = Gm_{star}/r$. Increasing the distance between the planet and the star then means the speed of the planet, $\mathbf{v}$, decreases.

CHAPTER SIXTY-FIVE

Energy and Momentum

This chapter reviews the fundamental concepts of energy and momentum and the associated concepts of work and impulse. Essentially, work is responsible for changing the energy of an object, and impulse is responsible for changing the momentum of an object. Regarding energy and momentum, the laws of conservation of energy and conservation of momentum are discussed along with concrete examples of problems that make use of these laws for their solution. The topic of collisions is discussed in detail as the most common example on the OAT of the application of conservation of momentum. The concept of work is applied to the problem of pulley systems, resulting in the definition of the efficiency of a simple machine. The chapter closes with a review of the equivalent concepts of center of mass and center of gravity.

WORK

Work Defined

As shown in Chapter 64, Newtonian Mechanics, solving mechanics problems using Newtonian methods involves analyzing the forces acting on a system. In this chapter, energy and momentum considerations, rather than forces, will be used to solve problems. To understand the different forms and applications of energy, it is important to first talk about one specific type of energy: work. **Work (W)** is a measure of mechanical energy that is transferred. For a constant force F acting on an object which moves through a distance d, the work is:

$$W = Fd \cos \theta$$

where θ is the angle between F and d. Units for work (and other forms of energy) are the joule (J) in SI (1 joule = 1 newton · meter) and the foot · pound in FPS. Only the component of the force parallel to the path, $F \cos \theta$, is relevant. For a force perpendicular to the motion, $W = 0$ (since $\theta = 90°$ and $\cos 90° = 0$). Note that for a force opposite to the motion ($\theta > 90°$), the work will be negative ($\cos \theta < 0$).

Example: A block weighing 100 N is pushed up a frictionless incline over a distance of 20 m to a height of 10 m. Find:

  a. the minimum force required to push the block;

  b. the work done by the force;

  c. the force required and the work done by the force if the block were simply lifted vertically 10 m.

Solution:

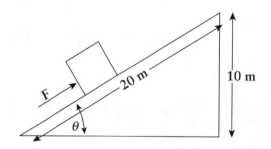

a. A free-body diagram of the forces acting on the block:

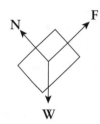

The minimum force needed is a force that is parallel to the inclined plane and that will push the block with no acceleration. Since $a = 0$, $\Sigma F = 0$:

$$\Sigma F = 0 = F - mg \sin \theta$$
$$F = mg \sin \theta$$
$$mg = 100 \text{ N}; \sin \theta = \frac{10}{20}. \text{ Therefore:}$$
$$F = 100\frac{10}{20}$$
$$= 50 \text{ N}$$

b. The work done by F is:

$$W = Fd \cos \theta$$

In this case θ is the angle between the force vector and the displacement vector. Since they are parallel, $\theta = 0$, and therefore $\cos \theta = 1$. Substituting the numbers into the equation:

$$W = 50(20)(1)$$
$$= 1{,}000 \text{ J}$$

c. To raise the block vertically, the force should also be vertical and equal to the object's weight.

$$F = mg$$
$$= 100 \text{ N}$$

The work done by the lifting force is:

$$W = Fd \cos \theta$$
$$= 100(10)(1)$$
$$= 1{,}000 \text{ J}$$

The same amount of work is required in both cases, but twice the force is needed to raise the block vertically compared to pushing it up the incline. Note, however, that pushing the block up the incline doubles the distance compared to lifting straight up, thus resulting in the same amount of work being done.

Power

Often, the amount of work required to perform an operation is less important than the amount of time required to do the work. The rate at which work is done is called **power** (P) and is given as:

$$P = \frac{W}{t}$$

Units of power are the watt (W) in SI (1 watt = 1 joule/sec) and foot $\cdot$ pound/sec in FPS.

Example: Find the power required to raise the block (of the previous example) in four seconds in each case.

Solution: When lifting up the incline, power is:

$$P = \frac{W}{t}$$
$$= \frac{1{,}000}{4}$$
$$= 250 \text{ W}$$

When lifting straight up, power equals:
$$P = \frac{1{,}000}{4}$$
$$= 250 \text{ W}$$

ENERGY

Kinetic Energy

A body in motion possesses energy. This energy of motion is called kinetic energy and is defined for a body of mass m and velocity v as:

$$K = \frac{mv^2}{2}$$

Units for kinetic energy are joules (J) in SI.

Example: A 15 kg block, initially at rest, slides down a frictionless incline and comes to the bottom with a velocity of 7 m/s. What is the kinetic energy at the top and at the bottom?

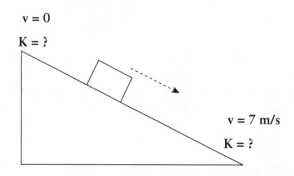

v = 0

K = ?

v = 7 m/s

K = ?

Solution: At the top $v = 0$, so kinetic energy is:

$$K = \frac{mv^2}{2}$$
$$= \frac{15(0)}{2}$$
$$= 0$$

At the bottom:

$$K = \frac{15(7)^2}{2}$$
$$= 367.5\,\text{J}$$

Potential Energy

Another form of energy a body can possess is **potential energy.** Unlike kinetic energy, which depends upon a body's motion, potential energy depends upon a body's **position.** One example of potential energy is the gravitational potential energy an object has when it is raised to a height h. Objects on the Earth possess greater potential energy the higher they are from the surface. **Gravitational potential energy (U)** is given as:

$$U = mgh$$

where m is the mass of the body, g is the acceleration due to gravity, and h is the height of the body. Just as for work and kinetic energy, potential energy's units are joules (J).

Example: An 80 kg diver leaps from a 10 m cliff into the sea. Find the diver's potential energy at the top of the cliff and just as he hits the water (set height equal to zero at sea level).

cliff

10 m

sea

Solution: At the top of the cliff:

$$U = mgh$$
$$= 80(9.8)(10)$$
$$= 7,840 \text{ J}$$

At the water's surface:

$$U = 80(9.8)(0)$$
$$= 0 \text{ J}$$

Total Mechanical Energy

Kinetic and potential energy are both forms of **mechanical energy**. The total mechanical energy (E) is defined as the sum of the kinetic and potential energies such that $E = K + U$ when K is the kinetic energy of a system and U is the potential energy. Mechanical energy is conserved when the sum of the potential and kinetic energies remains constant.

Mechanical energy is not always conserved, though. For example, when friction is present, mechanical energy is drained away in the form of heat (which is another form of energy). Note that in the example of friction and heat, *total* energy is still conserved even though *mechanical* energy is not conserved.

CONSERVATION OF ENERGY

Work–Energy Theorem

The work–energy theorem relates the work performed by all the forces acting on a body in a certain time interval to the change in kinetic energy during that time. In equation form, the theorem is:

$$W = \Delta K = K_f - K_i$$

Example: A baseball of mass 0.25 kg is thrown straight up in the air with an initial velocity of 30 m/s. Assuming no air resistance, find the work done by the force of gravity when the ball is at its maximum height.

Solution: Neglecting air resistance, the only force acting on the ball is gravity. Since the ball's speed is 0 at its maximum height, using the work–energy theorem:

$$W = \Delta K$$
$$= 0 - \frac{mv^2}{2}$$
$$= \frac{-(0.25)(30)^2}{2}$$
$$= -112.5 \text{ J}$$

Conservative and Nonconservative Forces

Conservative forces have associated potential energies (e.g., gravity). There are two equivalent tests that are used to determine whether a force is conservative or not:

1. If the work done to move a particle in any round-trip path is zero, the force is conservative.

2. If the work needed to move a particle between two points is the same regardless of the path taken, then the force is conservative.

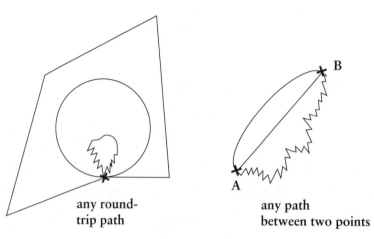

any round-
trip path

any path
between two points

Figure 65.1

Use the following rule of thumb: A force that has an associated potential energy (e.g., gravity) is conservative. Since an object's weight is just another name for the gravitational force on the object, an object's weight is a conservative force. Other examples of conservative forces include spring, electrostatic, and magnetic forces. Nonconservative forces cause energy to be transferred to another form such as heat. Friction, air resistance, and viscosity are examples of nonconservative forces.

Conservation of Energy

When the work done by the nonconservative forces is 0 or when there are no nonconservative forces, such as when an object is falling without air resistance, the total mechanical energy remains constant, and we have **conservation of energy:**

$$E = K + U = \text{constant}$$

or equivalently:

$$\Delta E = \Delta K + \Delta U = 0$$

However, when nonconservative forces such as friction or air resistance are present, mechanical energy is *not* conserved. The equation for a nonconservative system is:

$$W' = \Delta E = \Delta K + \Delta U$$

where W' is the work done by the nonconservative forces only. Note that if the work done by the nonconservative forces is zero (which is automatically true if there aren't any such forces), $W' = 0 = \Delta E = \Delta K + \Delta U$, and we have conservation of energy.

Example: A baseball of mass 0.25 kg is thrown in the air with an initial speed of 30 m/s, but because of air resistance the ball returns to the ground with a speed of 27 m/s. Find the work done by air resistance.

Solution: Air resistance is a nonconservative force. To solve this problem, the energy equation for a nonconservative system is needed. The work done by air resistance is W'.

$$W' = \Delta E = \Delta K + \Delta U$$

Since $\Delta U = 0$ (since final height = initial height):

$$W' = \Delta K$$
$$= \frac{mv_f^2}{2} - \frac{mv_i^2}{2}$$
$$= \frac{1}{2}(0.25)[(27)^2 - (30)^2]$$
$$= -21.4\,\text{J}$$

Pulleys

Pulley systems allow heavy weights to be lifted using a much smaller force than used for directly lifting the weight. The same amount of work is done with or without a pulley, but pulleys allow for smaller forces to be applied over longer distances to obtain the same product as applying greater forces over shorter distances. The weight of the object being lifted (mg) is the **load,** and the distance it rises is the **load distance.** The force exerted on the rope when lifting the load is known as the **effort,** and the distance through which the effort is exerted is the **effort distance.**

Consider the heavy block in Figure 65.2 suspended from two ropes. The force that the block exerts downward is equaled by the sum of the tensions in the two ropes. For a symmetrical system, the tensions in the two ropes are the same, and each is equal to half the weight of the block.

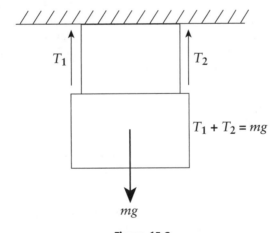

Figure 65.2

Now consider the pulley setup in Figure 65.3 with the block being held stationary. The tension in both vertical ropes will be equal; if they were different, the pulleys would turn until the tensions on both sides were equal. Since the tensions are equal, each rope supports half the total weight of the block. If the rope is pulled at the far right, the block will move upward a certain distance, but the rope will shorten by that distance in two places: between the two pulleys and between the lower pulley and the hook. This means that only half the force is now required to lift the block because the length of rope that must be pulled through on the far right is twice the distance the block moves upward.

For example, think about raising the block five meters. For this to happen, both sides of the supporting rope have to shorten by five meters, and the only way to accomplish this is by pulling through ten meters of rope. Work = force × distance, so the work done with or without the pulley is the same, but since the total distance the rope is pulled is doubled with the pulley, the force is cut in half.

Figure 65.3

In a frictionless pulley system where the pulleys themselves have no mass, the work expended pulling the rope and the potential energy gained by the mass are equal. However, no pulley system has these properties since pulleys do have mass and are not frictionless. This implies that no real pulley system is 100 percent efficient. **Efficiency** gives a measure of the amount of work a person puts into a machine that comes out as useful work as a ratio:

$$\text{Efficiency} = \frac{W_{\text{out}}}{W_{\text{in}}}$$
$$= \frac{\text{Load} \times \text{Load distance}}{\text{Effort} \times \text{Effort distance}}$$

Work input is the product of the effort and the effort distance, and work output is the product of the load and the distance the load moves through.

Consider the pulley system in Figure 65.4. By increasing the number of pulleys, it is possible to reduce the effort still further. Treating this as an ideal case, the load has been divided among six strands of the rope, so the effort required is now only one-sixth the load, and the effort distance is six times the load distance. However, note that, generally speaking, as the number of pulleys increases, the efficiency decreases in nonideal situations. This decrease in efficiency is caused by the added weight of each pulley as well as the increase in frictional forces.

Figure 65.4

Example: The pulley system of Figure 65.4 has an efficiency of 80%, and a person is required to lift 200 kg. Find:

a. the distance through which the effort must move to raise the load a distance of 4 m.

b. the effort required to lift the load.

c. the work done by the person lifting the load through a height of 4 m.

Solution: a. For the load to move through a vertical distance of 4 m, all six of the supporting ropes must shorten 4 m also. This may only be accomplished by pulling $6 \times 4 = 24$ m of rope through. So the effort must move through a distance of 24 m.

b To calculate the effort required, the equation for efficiency must be used. The load is the weight of the object being lifted and is equal to the mass times the acceleration due to gravity g. Since g is approximately 10 m/s^2 and all the other parameters except the effort are known, it is possible to substitute into this equation to calculate the effort:

$$\text{Efficiency} = \frac{\text{Load} \times \text{Load distance}}{\text{Effort} \times \text{Effort distance}}$$

$$0.80 = \frac{(200)(10)(4)}{(\text{Effort})(24)}$$

$$\text{Effort} = \frac{(2{,}000)(4)}{(0.80)(24)}$$

$$= 417 \text{ N}$$

c. The work done is given by:

$$\text{Work done} = \text{Effort} \times \text{Effort distance}$$
$$= 417 \times 24$$
$$= 10{,}000 \text{ J}$$

MOMENTUM

Momentum Defined

In nonrelativistic physics, **momentum (p)** is the product of mass and velocity and can be thought of as the tendency of an object to keep moving. Momentum, like velocity, is a vector quantity. In equation form it is given as:

$$\mathbf{p} = m\mathbf{v}$$

For two or more objects, the total momentum is the vector sum of the individual momentums.

Impulse

Applying a force to an object over time will cause that object's momentum to change. The product of the force applied **F** and the time it was applied t is a vector quantity and is given the name **impulse (J)**. For constant forces, impulse and momentum are related by the equation:

$$\mathbf{J} = \mathbf{F}t = m\mathbf{v} - m\mathbf{v}_0 = \Delta\mathbf{p}$$

In one-dimensional problems, the forces and velocities are either in the positive or negative direction, and the equation becomes a single scalar equation:

$$J = Ft = mv - mv_0$$

In this equation, J, F, v, and v_0 are positive or negative depending on whether the corresponding vectors are in the positive or negative direction.

Example: A 7 kg bowling ball initially at rest is acted on by a 110 N force for 3.5 s. Find the final speed of the ball.

Solution: From the equation for impulse:

$$Ft = mv - mv_0$$
$$v = v_0 + \frac{Ft}{m}$$
$$= 0 + \frac{110(3.5)}{7}$$
$$= 55 \text{ m/s}$$

Example: Many cars are now equipped with airbags as a safety feature. From the viewpoint of basic physics, why do airbags make cars safer?

Solution: The answer has to do with the concept of impact force, which is the average force exerted on a passenger during a collision (F_{avg}). The definition of impulse says that the average force exerted on an object multiplied by the time over which the force is applied equals the change in momentum of the object: $J = F_{avg} \times t$. The impact force then equals the change in momentum divided by the time over which the force is applied: $F_{avg} = J/t$.

The change in momentum of a passenger in a collision is fixed by the mass of the passenger and the initial speed of the vehicle. Airbags, however, can increase the time over which the passenger's momentum changes, thereby reducing the impact force. Since impact force is what's dangerous, airbags are useful as safety devices.

Conservation of Momentum

Those forces that one part of a system exerts on another part are called **internal forces.** Those forces that are exerted on any part of a system from outside the system are called **external forces.** The principle of **conservation of momentum** states that, when the net impulse of the external forces acting on a system is zero, the total momentum of the system remains constant. This condition is automatically satisfied when there are no external forces or when their vector sum is zero. Thus, for internal forces only, conservation of momentum means $\mathbf{p}_{initial} = \mathbf{p}_{final}$ for the entire system.

Collisions

One of the most common applications of conservation of momentum occurs when two objects collide in an idealized collision, one that occurs instantaneously at a specific location. Because there are no external forces, conservation of momentum applies. Conservation of momentum means that the total momentum before the collision equals the total momentum after the collision.

For a collision between two objects, a and b, this is given by:

$$\mathbf{p}_{ai} + \mathbf{p}_{bi} = \mathbf{p}_{af} + \mathbf{p}_{bf}$$

where $\mathbf{p}_{ai}$, $\mathbf{p}_{bi}$ are the momenta before the collision, and $\mathbf{p}_{af}$, $\mathbf{p}_{bf}$ are the momenta after the collision. Since momentum has been defined previously as $\mathbf{p} = m\mathbf{v}$, the conservation of momentum equation may be written as:

$$m_a\mathbf{v}_{ai} + m_b\mathbf{v}_{bi} = m_a\mathbf{v}_{af} + m_b\mathbf{v}_{bf}$$

where $\mathbf{v}_{ai}$ and $\mathbf{v}_{bi}$ are the velocity vectors before the collision, and $\mathbf{v}_{af}$ and $\mathbf{v}_{bf}$ are the velocity vectors after the collision.

In one-dimensional problems, velocities are either in the positive direction or in the negative direction, and the conservation of momentum equation becomes a simpler scalar equation:

$$m_a v_{ai} + m_b v_{bi} = m_a v_{af} + m_b v_{bf}$$

v_{ai}, v_{bi}, v_{af}, and v_{bf} are the magnitudes of the respective velocity vectors. They have positive signs if the velocities are in the positive direction and negative signs if the velocities are in the negative direction. The positive direction is chosen arbitrarily.

Example: The image below shows two bodies moving toward each other on a frictionless air track. Body A has a mass of 2 kg and a speed of 4 m/s; body B has a mass of 3 kg and has a speed of 1 m/s. After the bodies collide, body A moves away with a velocity of 2 m/s to the left. What is the final velocity of body B?

4 m/s   1 m/s

A   B

$m_a = 2$ kg $m_b = 3$ kg

Solution: This problem may be solved by equating the total momentum before the collision with the total momentum after the collision. Let the final velocity of body B be v_{Bf}. Taking the right as positive (and therefore the left as negative):

$$m_A v_{Ai} + m_B v_{Bi} = m_A v_{Af} + m_B v_{Bf}$$
$$2(4) + 3(-1) = 2(-2) + 3(v_{bf})$$
$$3v_{Bf} = 8 - 3 + 4 = 9$$
$$v_{Bf} = 3 \text{ m/s}$$

The fact that the solution is positive means that body B is moving to the right after the collision.

In many typical one-dimensional problems, the velocities before the collision are known and the velocities after the collision are unknown. The most common types of such problems involve completely inelastic collisions or completely elastic collisions.

Completely inelastic collisions

A **completely inelastic collision** is one in which the colliding bodies stick together after the collision with a combined mass of $m_a + m_b$. Since there is only one final object, the only velocity that exists after the collision is for that single object: $v_{af} = v_{bf} = v_f$

Thus, there is only one unknown final velocity. This can be combined with the principle of the conservation of momentum to give:

$$m_a v_{ai} + m_b v_{bi} = (m_a + m_b)v_f$$

Example: Two rail freight cars are being hitched together. The first car has a mass of 15,750 kg and is moving at a speed of 4 m/s toward the second car, which is stationary and has a mass of 19,250 kg. Calculate the final velocity of the two cars after they collide and are hitched together.

Solution: Using the modified equation above for the conservation of momentum:

$$m_a v_{ai} + m_b v_{bi} = (m_a + m_b)v_f$$

$$v_f = \frac{m_a v_{ai} + m_b v_{bi}}{m_a + m_b}$$

Taking the direction of the initial velocity of the car as the positive direction gives:

$$v_f = \frac{15,750(4) + 19,250(0)}{(15,750 + 19,250)}$$

$$v_f = 1.8 \text{ m/s}$$

The fact that v_f is positive means that, after the collision, the two cars together are moving in the same direction that the first car was moving initially.

Completely elastic collisions

A **completely elastic collision** is one in which both momentum and kinetic energy are conserved. The final velocities are not necessarily equal. If neither final velocity is given, then there are two unknowns in the momentum equation. However, since the kinetic energy is conserved, this provides the needed second equation.

Conservation of momentum:

$$m_a v_{ai} + m_b v_{bi} = m_a v_{af} + m_b v_{bf}$$

Conservation of kinetic energy:

$$\frac{1}{2} m_a v_{ai}^2 + \frac{1}{2} m_b v_{bi}^2 = \frac{1}{2} m_a v_{af}^2 + \frac{1}{2} m_b v_{bf}^2$$

Example: Using the results obtained from the example above, establish whether the collision was completely elastic.

Solution: For the collision to be completely elastic, both the kinetic energy and the momentum must be conserved. The second condition has already been satisfied. Next, the kinetic energy before the collision and the kinetic energy after the collision must be calculated, and only if these values are equal can it be said that the collision was completely elastic.

The kinetic energy before the collision is:

$$\frac{1}{2} m_a v_{ai}^2 + \frac{1}{2} m_b v_{bi}^2$$
$$= \frac{1}{2}(2)(4)^2 + \frac{1}{2}(3)(-1)^2$$
$$= 17.5 \text{ J}$$

The kinetic energy after the collision is:

$$\frac{1}{2} m_a v_{af}^2 + \frac{1}{2} m_b v_{bf}^2$$
$$= \frac{1}{2}(2)(-2)^2 + \frac{1}{2}(3)(3)^2$$
$$= 17.5 \text{ J}$$

Since the kinetic energy is not changed by the collision, it can be said that the collision was completely elastic.

CENTER OF MASS

Every object has a special point known as the **center of mass.** The center of mass can be considered to be the single point where an object would be steady if it were balanced on top of a pole or fulcrum or hung from a string. For two or more objects that are connected, the center of mass is analogous to a weighted average of the masses. For a system of two masses m_1 and m_2 lying along the x-axis at points x_1 and x_2, respectively, the center of mass is:

$$X = \frac{m_1 x_1 + m_2 x_2}{m_1 + m_2}$$

For a system with several masses strung out along the x-axis, the center of mass is given by:

$$X = \frac{m_1 x_1 + m_2 x_2 + m_3 x_3 + \cdots}{m_1 + m_2 + m_3 + \cdots}$$

For a system in which the particles are distributed in all three dimensions, the center of mass is defined by the three coordinates:

$$X = \frac{m_1 x_1 + m_2 x_2 + m_3 x_3 + \cdots}{m_1 + m_2 + m_3 + \cdots}$$

$$Y = \frac{m_1 y_1 + m_2 y_2 + m_3 y_3 + \cdots}{m_1 + m_2 + m_3 + \cdots}$$

$$Z = \frac{m_1 z_1 + m_2 z_2 + m_3 z_3 + \cdots}{m_1 + m_2 + m_3 + \cdots}$$

The **center of gravity** is the point at which the entire force due to gravity can be thought of as acting. It takes into account weight rather than mass and is found from similar formulas:

$$X = \frac{W_1 x_1 + W_2 x_2 + W_3 x_3 + \cdots}{W_1 + W_2 + W_3 + \cdots}$$

$$Y = \frac{W_1 y_1 + W_2 y_2 + W_3 y_3 + \cdots}{W_1 + W_2 + W_3 + \cdots}$$

$$Z = \frac{W_1 z_1 + W_2 z_2 + W_3 z_3 + \cdots}{W_1 + W_2 + W_3 + \cdots}$$

Since $W = mg$, the center of gravity and the center of mass will be the same point as long as g is constant.

Example: Find the center of mass with respect to the x- and y-axes of two uniform metal cubes that are attached to each other as shown. One cube has a mass of 2 kg and is 0.4 m on each side; the other has a mass of 0.5 kg and is 0.2 m on each side.

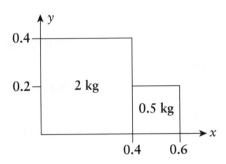

Solution: The fact that the cubes are uniform implies that the center of mass for each cube is located at the center of that cube. Therefore, the problem becomes one of finding the center of mass of two point masses; one is a 2 kg mass located at 0.2 m along the x-axis and 0.2 m along the y-axis, and the other is a 0.5 kg mass located at 0.5 m along the x-axis and 0.1 m along the y-axis.

Consider the x-coordinate first. The x component of the center of mass can be determined by the following formula:

$$X = \frac{m_1 x_1 + m_2 x_2 + m_3 x_3 + \cdots}{m_1 + m_2 + m_3 + \cdots}$$

Taking m_1 as 2 kg, x_1 as 0.2 m, m_2 as 0.5 kg, and x_2 as 0.5 m gives:

$$X = \frac{m_1 x_1 + m_2 x_2}{m_1 + m_2}$$
$$= \frac{2(0.2) + 0.5(0.5)}{2 + .05}$$
$$= \frac{0.65}{2.5}$$
$$= 0.26\,\text{m}$$

The y component of the center of mass can be determined by the following formula:

$$Y = \frac{m_1 y_1 + m_2 y_2 + m_3 y_3 + \cdots}{m_1 + m_2 + m_3 + \cdots}$$

Taking m_1 as 2 kg, y_1 as 0.2 m, m_2 as 0.5 kg, and y_2 as 0.1 m:

$$Y = \frac{m_1 y_1 + m_2 y_2}{m_1 + m_2}$$
$$= \frac{2(0.2) + 0.5(0.1)}{2 + 0.5}$$
$$= \frac{0.45}{2.5}$$
$$= 0.18\,\text{m}$$

PHYSICS

REVIEW PROBLEMS

1. A weightlifter lifts a 275 kg barbell from the ground to a height of 2.4 m.

    a How much work has he done?

    b. How much work is required to hold the weight at that height?

2. A tractor pulls a log that has a mass of 500 kg along the ground for 100 m. The rope (between the tractor and the log) makes an angle of 30° with the ground, and is acted on by a tensile force of 5,000 N.

    a. How much work does the tractor do?

    b. Does the work done by the tractor change if, keeping everything else the same, the angle between the rope and the ground increases?

3. A 2,000 kg experimental car can accelerate from zero to 30 m/s in 6.3 s. What is the average power of the engine needed to achieve this acceleration?

4. A 40 kg block is resting at a height of 5 m off the ground.

    a. What is its potential energy?

    b. What is its kinetic energy?

    c. If the block is released and falls to the ground, what is its total energy at a height of 2m?

5. A 2,000 kg rollercoaster car is brought to the top of a 150 m long section of track that is inclined at 30° with the horizontal. The speed of the car is 3 m/s at the top.

    a. In the absence of friction, what is the change in kinetic energy when going from the top to the bottom of the track?

    b. If the friction force between the car and the track is 2,000 N, how much energy is lost to heat as the car traverses the length of the track (neglect air resistance)?

6. A 25 g bullet is fired horizontally into a 2 kg block of wood that is suspended by a massless rope. The bullet is fired with a speed of 100 m/s. After impact the bullet remains embedded in the wood, and the two swing upward together.

    a. What is the relationship between the momentum of the bullet before impact and the momentum of the bullet once it is embedded in the wood?

    b. What is the relationship between the kinetic energy of the bullet before impact and the potential energy of the bullet plus block at the highest point of their swing?

7. Two billiard balls, one moving at 0.5 m/s and the other at rest, undergo a perfectly elastic collision.

    a. If the masses of the billiard balls are equal and the speed of the stationary one after the collision is 0.5 m/s, then what is the speed of the other ball after the collision?

    b. If the stationary ball is more massive than the moving ball, the moving ball will rebound after the collision. Relative to the direction and speed of the incoming ball, discuss the direction and speed of the stationary ball after the collision.

8. A 2,500 kg car traveling at 20 m/s crashes into a 6,000 kg truck that is originally at rest. Assuming no friction, what is the speed of the truck after the collision if the car comes to rest at the point of impact?

SOLUTIONS TO REVIEW PROBLEMS

1. a. **6,468 J**

    Since the weight of the barbell (force acting downward) is 275 kg × 9.8 m/s² = 2,695 N, it follows that the weightlifter must exert an equal and opposite force of 2,695 N on the barbell. The work done in lifting the barbell is defined as:

    $$W = Fd$$
    $$= 2,695(2.4)$$
    $$= 6,468 \text{ J}$$

    b. **Zero work**

    By the same equation as above, the work done to hold the barbell in place is:

    $$W = Fd$$
    $$= 2,695(0)$$
    $$= \text{zero work}$$

2. a. **433 kJ**

    The total force on the rope is 5,000 N. However, the force in the direction of motion (the horizontal direction) is only (5,000 N)(cos 30°) = 4,330 N. Therefore the work done by the tractor is:

    $$W = Fd \cos \theta$$
    $$= 5,000(100) \cos 30°$$
    $$= 433,000 \text{ J}$$
    $$= 433 \text{ kJ}$$

    b. **Yes, the work done decreases.**

    Increasing the angle between the rope and the ground means that the cos θ factor in the expression for work decreases, so the work done also decreases. The work done if the angle = 0° is:

    $$W = Fd \cos \theta$$
    $$= Fd \cos (0)$$
    $$= 5,000(100)(0)$$
    $$= 0 \text{ J}$$

3. **143 kW**

   The work done by the engine is equal to the change in kinetic energy of the car:

   $$W = \Delta K = \frac{1}{2}mv_2^2 - \frac{1}{2}mv_1^2$$

   $$v_2 = 30 \text{ m/s}$$

   $$v_1 = 0$$

   $$W = \Delta K = \frac{1}{2}mv_2^2$$

   $$= \frac{1}{2}(2{,}000)(30)^2$$

   $$= 900{,}000 \text{ J}$$

   The average power supplied is therefore equal to:

   $$P = \frac{W}{t}$$

   $$= 900{,}000 / 6.3$$

   $$= 143{,}000 \text{ W}$$

   $$= 143 \text{ kW}$$

4. a. **1,960 J**

   The potential energy of an object is defined as:

   $$U = mgh$$

   $$= 40(9.8)(5)$$

   $$= 1{,}960 \text{ J}$$

   b. **Zero**

   The kinetic energy of an object is equal to one half its mass times the square of its speed, and since the block is stationary, it consequently has zero kinetic energy.

   c. **1,960 J**

   Conservation of energy says that the total mechanical energy of the block is constant as it falls (neglecting air resistance). Since the total initial energy is 1,960 J, the total energy at any other time during its fall is also 1,960 J.

5. a. **1.47×10^6 J**

   Using conservation of energy:

   $$K_{initial} + U_{initial} = K_{final}, \text{ so } \Delta K = U_{initial}$$

   $$U_{initial} = mgh = (2000)(9.8)(150 \sin 30°) = 1.46 \times 106 \text{ J} = \Delta K$$

   b. **3×10^5 J**

   The amount of energy lost to heat is simply the work done by friction:

   $$W = Fd = (2{,}000)(150) = 3 \times 10^5 \text{ J}$$

6. a. **The momentum after the bullet is embedded is less than the momentum before it was embedded.**

    Although total momentum is conserved in this inelastic collision, the momentum of the bullet alone is not. Some of the momentum of the bullet is transferred into the momentum of the wood block in the collision, so the bullet itself loses momentum in the collision process.

    b. **The initial kinetic energy of the bullet is greater than the maximum potential energy of the bullet and block together.**

    Because the collision is inelastic, the bullet loses some of its initial energy to heat. Thus the total energy of the bullet and block at the bottom of their swing (equal to the maximum potential energy at the top of the swing) is less than the initial kinetic energy of the bullet.

7. a. **0 m/s**

    Either conservation of momentum or conservation of kinetic energy can be applied here. The momentum and kinetic energy of the stationary ball after the collision equal the momentum and kinetic energy of the moving ball before the collision, respectively, so there is no more momentum or kinetic energy to give to the other ball, meaning it's at rest after the collision.

    b. **The stationary ball moves with a speed less than and in the same direction as the incoming ball.**

    In order for momentum to be conserved, the stationary ball must be moving in the same direction after the collision as the incoming ball was before the collision. This is because the incoming ball has negative momentum after the collision relative to its initial momentum. The stationary ball must make up for the lost initial positive momentum by itself acquiring positive momentum. Conservation of kinetic energy requires that the speed of the stationary ball after the collision be less than the speed of the incoming ball because it is more massive. In other words, if the stationary ball moved as fast or faster than the incoming ball, it would have more kinetic energy than the incoming ball, and this would violate conservation of kinetic energy.

8.   **8.33 m/s**

    In all collision problems, it is important to remember that the vector sum of the momentum before the collision is equal to the vector sum of the momentum after:

    $$mv_{(car)i} + mv_{(truck)i} = mv_{(car)f} + mv_{(truck)f}$$
    $$2,500(20) + 0 = 0 + 6,000\,v$$
    $$v = 50,000\,/\,6,000$$
    $$= 8.33\,\text{m/s}$$

CHAPTER SIXTY-SIX

Thermodynamics

Thermodynamics is the study of heat and its effects. Primary to this study are the concepts of temperature, heat, pressure, volume, work, internal energy, and entropy. These ideas will be applied to thermal expansion, heat transfer processes, specific heat, heat of transformation (latent heat), and pressure vs. volume diagrams, including the relationship between work, pressure, and volume. The first law of thermodynamics involving conservation of energy in the presence of heat transfer will be reviewed along with the second law of thermodynamics and the associated concept of entropy.

TEMPERATURE

Temperature

All bodies possess a property called **temperature.** In common usage, temperature is the relative measure of how hot or cold something is. In the study of thermodynamics, however, temperature is a measure of the internal energy of the object and must be identified quantitatively on a defined scale. There are three scales used to make these measurements of temperature on a thermometer: the **Fahrenheit** (°F), the **Celsius** (°C), and the **kelvin** (K) scales. Absolute zero and the boiling and freezing points of water for the three scales are listed in the table below.

Situation	K	°C	°F
Absolute zero	0	−273	−460
Freezing point of water	273	0	32
Boiling point of water	373	100	212

Table 66.1

The kelvin scale is most commonly used for scientific measurements and is a base unit in SI. The Celsius scale is convenient for everyday usage because it sets the phase change points for water to be 0°C and 100°C. A kelvin and a degree Celsius are the same size, which means a change of 1 K equals a change of 1°C. The following formulas are used to convert from one scale to another:

$$T_C = T_K - 273$$

$$T_F = \frac{9}{5} T_C + 32$$

where T_C stands for temperature in degrees Celsius, T_K stands for temperature in kelvins, and T_F stands for temperature in degrees Fahrenheit.

Example: If a meteorologist says that the temperature will reach a high of 303 K today, what will be the temperature in °C and in °F?

Solution: To convert from kelvin to Celsius, use:

$$T_C = T_K - 273$$
$$= 303 - 273$$
$$= 30°C$$

To convert from Celsius to Fahrenheit, use:

$$T_F = \frac{9}{5} T_C + 32$$
$$= \frac{9}{5} (32) + 32$$
$$= 86° \text{ F}$$

Thermal Expansion

Rising temperatures cause most solids to increase in size. The amount of expansion, known as **thermal expansion**, is proportional to the length of the solid and the increase in temperature:

$$\Delta L = \alpha L_0 \Delta T$$

where ΔL is the change in length, L_0 is the original length, and ΔT is the change in temperature. The **coefficient of linear expansion** (α) is a constant that characterizes how a specific material's length changes as the temperature changes. This usually has units of K^{-1} but may sometimes be quoted as $°C^{-1}$ since a change of 1 K is the same as a change of 1°C.

Example: A metal rod of length 2 m and with a coefficient of expansion of 11×10^{-6} K^{-1} is heated from 30°C to 1,080°C. By what length does the rod expand?

Solution: By using the information given in the problem, we can substitute directly into the thermal expansion formula. The value of α can be changed directly from K^{-1} to $°C^{-1}$ to match the units of the temperature change:

$$\Delta L = \alpha L_0 \Delta T$$
$$= (11 \times 10^{-6} \, °C^{-1})(2m)(1,080 - 30°C)$$
$$= 0.023 \text{ m}$$

Liquids also expand when heated, but in their case the only meaningful parameter of expansion is **volume expansion.** The formula that governs this expansion for both solids and liquids is:

$$\Delta V = \beta V_0 \Delta T$$

where ΔV is the change in volume, V_0 is the original volume, and the coefficient $\beta = 3\alpha$.

Example: Assume that a thermometer with 1 mL of mercury is taken from a freezer with a temperature of –25°C and placed near an oven at 225°C. If the coefficient of volume expansion of mercury is 1.8×10^{-4} K^{-1}, by how much will the liquid expand?

Solution: Using the information given, and changing the value of β directly from K^{-1} to $°C^{-1}$ to match the units of the temperature change:

$$\Delta V = \beta V_0 \Delta T$$
$$= (1.8 \times 10^{-4}\,°C)(1\text{ mL})[225°C - (-25°C)]$$
$$= 0.045\text{ mL}$$

HEAT

All macroscopic objects have a property called temperature. What exactly does a body's temperature say about that body? The answer is that a body's temperature is related to the internal energy of that body. At constant volume, an increase in temperature indicates an increase in internal energy, and a decrease in temperature indicates a decrease in internal energy.

When two objects at different temperatures are brought into contact, the object with a higher temperature will give off **heat** energy to the cooler body until both objects have the same temperature. Heat can be defined as the energy transferred between two objects as a result of a difference in temperature. Note that heat can never be transferred from a cooler body to a warmer body without doing work on the system.

Units of heat are either the **calorie** (cal) for SI or the **British thermal unit** (Btu) for English units. Note that the calorie defined here (lowercase c) and the term **Calorie** used in nutrition (uppercase C) are not the same; one food Calorie is equal to one thousand calories or one kilocalorie. Since heat is a form of energy transfer, the **joule** is also used as a unit of heat.

The conversion factors among the heat units are as follows:

$$1\text{ Cal} = 10^3\text{ cal} = 3.97\text{ Btu} = 4,184\text{ J}$$

Heat Transfer

Heat energy can be transferred by conduction, convection, or radiation (or any combination of these processes).

Conduction is the direct transfer of energy from molecule to molecule through molecular collisions. Metals are the best heat conductors, since mobile electrons play a role in the transfer of heat from one molecule to the next. Gases tend to be the poorest heat conductors. An example of heat transfer through conduction is the heat that is rapidly conducted to your finger when you touch a hot stove.

Convection is the transfer of heat by the physical motion of the heated material. Since convection involves a flow of material, it can take place only in fluids (liquids and gases). During convection, heated portions of fluid rise from the source of heat, while colder portions sink. An example of convection is a pot of water boiling on the stove; hot water from the bottom of the pot rises to the top, carrying heat with it. At the same time, cooler water from the top of the pot moves down to the heat source at the bottom, creating a "rolling boil" effect. This process is due to the differences of densities between the hot and cold segments; the cold water is more dense and therefore feels a greater force due to gravity, causing it to sink past the less-dense hot water.

Radiation is the transfer of energy by electromagnetic waves and is the only method that allows transfer of heat through a vacuum. An example of this form of heat transfer is the warming effect the sun has on the Earth and objects on its surface, such as a person sitting on the beach. A beach umbrella can block the sun's radiation and provide an immediate cooling effect.

Specific Heat

The heat (Q) gained or lost by an object and the change in temperature of that object (T) are related by the equation:

$$Q = mc\Delta T = mc(T_f - T_i)$$

where m is the mass of the object and c is a proportionality constant called the **specific heat.** The specific heat can be defined as the amount of heat required to raise a unit mass of a substance 1 K or 1°C, and depends solely on the material of the object. This formula applies to any substance that does not undergo a phase change. For water, specific heat is often given as:

$$c = 1 \text{ cal/g·K} = 1 \text{ cal/g·°C} = 4.184 \text{ J/g·K}$$

Figure 66.1 shows a heating curve for water in which the formula $Q = mc\Delta T$ applies to the angled portions of the curve.

Figure 66.1

Heat of Transformation

The formula discussed in the preceding section, $Q = mc\Delta T$, applies only when there is no change of phase, or in other words, no conversion between the gas, liquid, or solid phases. During a phase change, the temperature remains constant, and the heat gained or lost is related to the amount of material that changes phase. The amount of heat needed to change the phase of 1 kg of a substance is the **heat of transformation** (L). The total amount of heat gained or lost by a substance during a phase change is given by:

$$Q = mL$$

where Q is the heat gained or lost, m is the mass of the substance, and L is the heat of transformation of the substance.

The phase change from liquid to solid or solid to liquid occurs at the melting point temperature. The corresponding heat of transformation is often referred to as the **heat of fusion** and is written as ΔH_f. On the other hand, the phase change from liquid to gas or gas to liquid occurs at the boiling point temperature. Here, the heat of transformation is often referred to as the **heat of vaporization** and is written as ΔH_v. In Figure 66.1 the flat portions of the curve represent the phase changes, showing that no change in temperature occurs as water moves from either solid to liquid or liquid to gas.

Example: Silver has a melting point of roughly 1,000°C and a heat of fusion of 105 kJ/kg. The specific heat of silver is roughly 250 J/kg·°C. Approximately how much heat is required to completely melt a 1 kg silver chain with an initial temperature of 20°C?

Solution: Before melting the chain, first determine the temperature change in order for the chain to reach the melting point. To calculate how much heat is required use the formula:

$$Q = mc\Delta T = mc(T_f - T_i)$$
$$= 1\ \text{kg}(250\ \text{J/kg·°C})(1{,}000°\text{C} - 20°\text{C})$$
$$= 245{,}000\ \text{J}$$
$$= 245\ \text{kJ}$$

At this point, the chain is still in the solid phase but has reached the melting point. To melt it (change its phase to liquid), continue to add heat in accordance with the formula:

$$Q = mL$$
$$= 1\ \text{kg}(105\ \text{kJ/kg})$$
$$= 105\ \text{kJ}$$

The total heat needed to heat and melt the solid silver chain from the starting temperature is 245 kJ + 105 kJ = 350 kJ.

FIRST LAW OF THERMODYNAMICS

Thermodynamics is governed by several fundamental laws that describe thermodynamic systems. However, for Test Day, you will only need to know the first and second laws. The first law of thermodynamics describes the internal energy of systems and how that energy can change due to an exchange of heat or work. Heat was discussed earlier in this chapter, but it's also necessary to have an understanding of what pressure and work are before exploring the first law in more detail.

Pressure

Consider a gas contained in a box: The gas particles move in random directions, and some of them hit the walls of the box. As the gas particles hit the walls of the box, they impart a force to the walls. If many particles hit a wall, the net force on the wall increases. The force per unit area is the **pressure** of the gas:

$$P = \frac{F}{A}$$

The SI unit of pressure is the pascal (Pa). The pascal is equivalent to a newton/meter². Since this unit is relatively small, often you will see the pressure quoted in kilopascals (kPa); $1 \text{ kPa} = 10^3$ Pa. The pressure at sea level can also be used as a unit. This is called an atmosphere (atm), and one atm is equal to 1.013×10^5 Pa.

Work

When dealing with the various problems of thermodynamics, the concept of a system is used. To describe a physical process, there are two things to take into account: the system whose behavior is being observed and everything else (the environment).

A good example of a system is a gas contained in a cylinder with a piston that is able to move up when the gas expands and down when the gas is compressed. When the piston moves up, it is because a force is exerted by the gas inside the cylinder to physically expand the system. Since the volume of the system has increased because of a pressure applied by the gas within the system, work is said to have been done *by* the system. When the piston is compressed, causing the system's volume to decrease, work is done *on* the system by the environment. This implies that work, in thermodynamics problems, depends on pressure and volume.

During any thermodynamic process, a system goes from some initial state with an initial pressure and volume to some other state with a different final pressure or volume. These thermodynamic processes are often represented in graphical form with volume on the x-axis and pressure on the y-axis (see Figure 66.2). There are an infinite number of paths between an initial and final state. Different paths require different amounts of work. The work done on or by a system is calculated by finding the area under the pressure–volume curve. If volume doesn't change, then there can be no work done, because there is no area to calculate. On the other hand, if pressure remains constant, the area under the curve is a rectangle of length P and width $(V_f - V_i)$ or ΔV. Thus, for processes in which the pressure remains constant, $W = P\Delta V$.

Figure 66.2

Figure 66.2(a) shows that the system undergoes a decrease in pressure from P_1 to P_2. The work done in this process is zero because volume is constant, and therefore there is no area under the curve.

In Figure 66.2(b) the system expands from V_1 to V_2 at constant pressure. When the pressure remains constant, the process is called **isobaric.** Here the work done is found using the formula:

$$W = P\Delta V = P(V_f - V_i)$$

The work in this case is positive.

Figure 66.2(c) shows a case in which neither pressure nor volume is held constant. The total area under the graph (regions I and II) gives the work done. Region I is a triangle with base V and height P, so the area is:

$$A_I = \frac{1}{2}\Delta V \Delta P$$

Region II is a rectangle with base V and height P_2 such that its area is:

$$A_{II} = P_2 V$$

Work now is the sum of Regions I and II:

$$W = A_I + A_{II}$$

Figure 66.2(d) shows a closed cycle in which, after certain interchanges of work and heat, the system returns to its initial state. Here, the work done is the area enclosed by the curve.

First Law

Internal energy (U or E) is the measure of all the energy, potential and kinetic, possessed by molecules in a system. The internal energy of a system can be increased by doing work on it or by adding heat to it. This change in internal energy ΔU is calculated from the **first law of thermodynamics:**

$$\Delta U = Q - W$$

where Q is the heat energy transferred to the system and W is the work done *by* the system. Note the **sign convention:** Work done *by* the system is positive, but work done *on* the system is negative. This is because work done by the system reduces the system's energy by "giving away" energy in the form of work done, whereas work done on the system increases the internal energy because it is energy "brought in." Similarly, heat flow into the system is positive, but heat flow out of the system is negative. This is because heat flowing into the system increases the internal energy, whereas heat flowing out "gives away" that internal energy. The table below gives some special cases of the first law:

Process	First Law Becomes
Adiabatic ($Q = 0$)	$\Delta U = -W$
Constant Volume ($W = 0$)	$\Delta U = Q$
Closed Cycle ($U = 0$)	$Q = W$

Table 66.2

Example: A gas in a cylinder was kept at a constant pressure of 3.5×10^5 Pa while 300 kJ of heat was added to it, causing the gas to expand from 0.9 m^3 to 1.5 m^3. Find:

a. the work done by the gas.

b. the change in internal energy of the gas.

Solution: a. The pressure is held constant through the entire process, so the work can be found using the equation:

$$W = PV$$
$$= (3.5 \times 10^5 \text{ Pa})(1.5\text{m}^3 - 0.9\text{m}^3)$$
$$= 2.1 \times 10^5 \text{ J}$$

b. The change in internal energy can be found from the first law of thermodynamics:

$$U = Q - W$$
$$= 3 \times 10^5 \text{ J} - 2.1 \times 10^5 \text{ J}$$
$$= 0.9 \times 10^5 \text{ J}$$
$$= 9 \times 10^4 \text{ J}$$

THE SECOND LAW OF THERMODYNAMICS

Before investigating the second law of thermodynamics, it's important to know the definition of entropy, which it describes. **Entropy** can be defined as the measure of disorder of a system. One way to picture entropy is to imagine a pool divided in two by an impermeable barrier that has one side filled with water and the other with ink. This system is highly ordered because the ink molecules and water molecules are physically separated. The position of a particular ink molecule is limited to one half of the pool; therefore, there is some degree of certainty as to where a given ink molecule can be found. If someone were to remove the barrier, however, the water and ink would mix until there was no discernible difference between them. The position of a particular ink molecule would be less certain now because it would have access to the entire pool, as opposed to half of it. Therefore, the order of the system would be decreased, and its entropy would be increased.

Second Law

The **second law of thermodynamics** states that, in any thermodynamic process that moves from one equilibrium state to another, the entropy of the system and environment together will either increase or remain unchanged. The entropy of the system and environment together will not change during a totally reversible process, but the entropy will increase in an irreversible process. Reexamination of the pool described above shows that it is essentially impossible to get the ink back to one side of the pool and the water to the other after they have been mixed. This is because the entropy of an isolated system (the pool) increases for all real (irreversible) processes. However, the entropy of a system that is not isolated can decrease as long as the entropy of its surroundings increases by at least as much. Consider a freezer that turns water to ice; the ice has lower entropy than the starting water, but the entropy of the air around the freezer increases from the heat output of the refrigeration mechanism. Freezing the ice is reversible because it can be melted to form liquid water again.

Isothermal processes are processes in which the temperature remains constant throughout. For reversible isothermal processes, the change in entropy of the system or of the environment can be found from:

$$\Delta S = \frac{Q}{T}$$

where T is the constant temperature of the system or environment in Kelvins.

Example: If, in a reversible process, 6.66×10^4 J of heat is used to change a 200 g block of ice to water at a temperature of 273 K, what is the change in the entropy of the system?

Solution: We know that during a change of phase the temperature is constant, which in this case is 273 K. From the information given,

$$\Delta S = \frac{Q}{T}$$
$$= \frac{6.66 \times 10^4}{273}$$
$$= 244$$

REVIEW PROBLEMS

Specific Heats of Different Substances

Substance	Specific Heat	
	cal/g·°C	J/kg·°C
Lead	0.0305	128
Tungsten	0.0321	134
Mercury	0.033	140
Silver	0.0564	236
Brass	0.092	380
Copper	0.0923	386
Glass	0.200	840
Aluminum	0.215	900
Water	1.00	4,190

1. Is there any difference between the temperature of an object and the total random kinetic energy of the molecules of the object?

2. Name the method of heat transfer responsible for:
   a) heat transferred from the sun to the Earth,
   b) a metal spoon heating up when placed in a pot of hot soup,
   c) a rising plume of smoke from a fire.

3. A 20 m steel rod at 10°C is dangling from the edge of a building and is just 2.5 cm from the ground. If the rod is now heated to 90°C, what is its increase in length? Does it touch the ground? ($\alpha = 11 \times 10^{-6}$ K^{-1})

4. What is the final temperature of a 5 kg silver pendant with an initial temperature of 20°C that was left for ten minutes in front of an electric heater that imparts heat energy at a rate of 100 W?

5. Materials that store heat are very important for energy-saving techniques. For such materials, it is optimal to store the greatest amount of heat for a given mass of material with the smallest rise in temperature. Which of the materials in the preceding chart of specific heats is the most suitable for storing heat, and why?

6. From the cycle below, determine the work done by the gas along path A, path B, and path C. What is the total work done by the gas in the cycle?

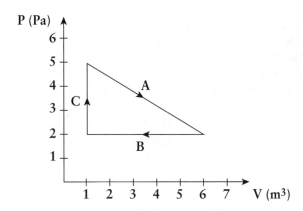

7. When a volume of hot air rises rapidly, it undergoes essentially an adiabatic expansion. What happens to the temperature of the gas in this process?

8. Thermal equilibrium exists when

   A. the specific heat of two objects is the same.

   B. the change in volume of one object is equal to the change in volume of another.

   C. the amount of heat released by one object exactly equals the amount absorbed by another.

   D. there is no net heat flow between two bodies that are in thermal contact.

   E. two objects have the same total kinetic energy.

SOLUTIONS TO REVIEW PROBLEMS

1. **Yes**

    The temperature measures the average random kinetic energy of each of the molecules of the substance but tells nothing about the total random kinetic energy of an object, which depends on the total number of particles in the object. Thus, it's possible to have an object (say a dilute gas) with a high temperature and low thermal energy content. However, if the number of gas particles is known, the total kinetic energy of the gas can then be calculated.

2. **a) radiation, b) conduction, c) convection**

    Since there is essentially only empty space between the sun and the Earth, the only means of heat transfer is by radiation, e.g., electromagnetic waves that propagate from the sun to the Earth.

    When a metal spoon is placed in a pot of hot soup, the molecules in the soup collide with those on the surface of the spoon, thereby transferring heat by conduction.

    Fires warm the air above them; the warmed air is less dense than the surrounding air, so it rises. A rising column of warm air means that heat is being transported in the air mass, which is the process of convection. The smoke particles ride along with the upward moving air mass and create a plume of smoke.

3. $\Delta L = 1.8$ **cm; The rod will not touch the ground.**

    First find the change in length due to thermal expansion:

    $$\begin{aligned}
    \Delta L &= \alpha L \Delta T \\
    &= (11 \times 10^{-6})(20)(80) \\
    &= 0.0176 \, \text{m} \\
    &= 1.8 \, \text{cm}
    \end{aligned}$$

    Since the rod is originally 2.5 cm above the ground and the increase in length is less than that, the rod will not touch the ground.

4. $T_f = 71°C$

    Watts are joules (energy) per second, so in ten minutes (600 seconds) the pendant absorbs the following amount of energy (Q):

    $$\text{Energy} = \text{Power} \times \text{Time}$$
    $$Q = 100 \times 600 = 60,000 \, \text{J}$$

    Now that you know the heat added, find the final temperature from the equation:

    $$Q = mc\Delta T = mc(T_f - T_i)$$
    $$60,000 = 5(236)(T_f - 20)$$
    $$T_f = 71°C$$

5. **Water, because it has the highest specific heat**

    When a material has a high specific heat, it means that you can add a lot of heat to it with only a small increase in temperature. This is seen from the equation $Q = mc\Delta T$, which can be rearranged to show that $\Delta T = Q/(mc)$.

6. $W_A = 17.5 \text{ J}; W_B = -10 \text{ J}; W_c = 0; W_{tot} = 7.5 \text{ J}$

    The total work done by the cycle is the sum of the work of paths A, B, and C.

    W_A is the area under the curve and can be broken down into a triangle on top of a rectangle:

    $$\begin{aligned} W_A &= \frac{1}{2}(5)(3) + 2(5) \\ &= 17.5 \text{J} \\ W_B &= P_2 \Delta V \\ &= 2(-5) \\ &= 10 \text{J} \\ W_C &= 0 (\text{constant volume}) \\ W_{tot} &= W_A + W_B + W_C \\ &= 17.5 - 10 + 0 \\ &= 7.5 \text{J} \end{aligned}$$

7. **The temperature drops.**

    An adiabatic expansion means that no heat enters or leaves the rising volume of gas. However, the gas does expand, which means that it does work on its surroundings. Using the first law of thermodynamics, $\Delta U = Q - W$, where $Q = 0$ and $W > 0$, we see that $\Delta U < 0$. Therefore, the gas loses internal energy, and the temperature drops.

8. **D** Equilibrium in general implies no net flow, movement, force, change, etc., in a system. Thermal equilibrium specifically implies that there is no net heat flow between two or more objects in thermal contact.

CHAPTER SIXTY-SEVEN

Fluid Statics

This chapter reviews the physics of both fluids and solids, with the greatest emphasis on fluid statics. The basic concepts of density and pressure are covered, as well as the applied concept of pressure as a function of depth in a fluid. Hydrostatics, the study of fluids at rest, is presented from the point of view of the two dominant concepts of the field: Pascal's principle and Archimedes' principle. Hydrodynamics, the study of fluids in motion, includes a brief discussion of the continuity equation and Bernoulli's equation, as well as viscosity and behavior of real fluids. Finally, the elastic properties of solids are briefly discussed, along with the associated concepts of stress, strain, Young's modulus, shear modulus, and the bulk modulus.

FLUIDS AND SOLIDS

Both liquids and gases are classified as fluids; solids are not. Fluids are characterized by their ability to flow and to conform to the boundaries of any container they are put in. Solids, however, are characterized by their rigidity. While both fluids and solids can exert forces perpendicular to their surfaces, only solids can withstand shear (tangential) forces.

DENSITY AND PRESSURE

Density (ρ) is a scalar quantity that is defined as mass (m) per unit volume (V). In equation form:

$$\rho = \frac{m}{V}$$

The units of density are kg/m^3. From the definition of density, the weight of an object can be expressed as the product of its density, volume, and the acceleration due to gravity:

$$W = mg$$
$$m = \rho V$$
$$W = \rho V g$$

The density of water is 10^3 kg/m^3 (1 gm/cm^3). The ratio of the density of a substance to the density of water is called **specific gravity.** Since it is a ratio, specific gravity has no units.

Example: Find the specific gravity of benzene (density $= 879$ kg/m^3).

Solution: The ratio of the density of benzene to the density of water is the specific gravity.

$$\text{specific gravity} = \frac{\rho_{benzene}}{\rho_{water}}$$
$$= \frac{879}{1,000}$$
$$= 0.879$$

Pressure P is also a scalar quantity. It is defined as the magnitude of the normal force F per unit area A. As an equation it reads:

$$P = \frac{F}{A}$$

The SI unit of pressure is the newton per square meter, also called the pascal (1 Pa $= 1$ N/m^2). Another commonly used unit of pressure is the atmosphere (atm), which is the average atmospheric pressure at sea level. It is related to the SI unit of pressure by:

$$1 \text{ atm} = 1.013 \times 10^5 \text{ Pa}$$

Example: The window of a skyscraper measures 2.0 m by 3.5 m. If a storm passes by and lowers the pressure outside the window to 0.997 atm while the pressure inside the building remains at 1 atm, what net force is pushing the window out?

Solution: The forces acting inside and outside the building are needed. However, before the forces may be calculated, the values of the pressure both inside and outside the building must be converted from atmospheres to pascals:

$$1 \text{ atm} = 1.013 \times 10^5 \text{ Pa}$$
$$0.997 \text{ atm} = (0.997)(1.013 \times 10^5)$$
$$= 1.010 \times 10^5 \text{ Pa}$$

Using the equation for pressure, the force inside pushing out is:

$$F_i = P_i A$$
$$F_i = (1.013 \times 10^5)(7.0)$$
$$= 7.091 \times 10^5 \text{ N}$$

and the force outside pushing in is:

$$F_o = P_o A$$
$$F_o = (1.010 \times 10^5)(7.0)$$
$$= 7.070 \times 10^5 \text{ N}$$

The net force is the difference of these two:

$$F_{net} = 7.091 \times 10^5 - 7.070 \times 10^5$$
$$= 2,100 \text{ N}$$

To find the **absolute pressure (P)** in a fluid due to gravity on an object somewhere below the surface, use the equation for hydrostatic pressure:

$$P = P_0 + \rho g h$$

where P_0 is the pressure at the surface, ρ is the density of the fluid, g is the acceleration due to gravity, and h is the depth below the surface.

Pressure increases linearly with depth below the surface of a liquid and depends on the density of the liquid but not on the density of the object in the liquid. The pressure is created by the weight of the fluid above the submerged object pressing down on that object. In many applications the pressure at the surface is atmospheric pressure such that $P_0 = P_{atm} = 1.013 \times 10^5$ Pa.

More common in everyday usage than absolute pressure is **gauge pressure (P_g).** For example, automobile tire pressure is reported as gauge pressure. Gauge pressure is the difference between the absolute and atmospheric pressure. The equation for gauge pressure is:

$$P_g = P - P_{atm}$$

Note from the equation for hydrostatic pressure that, if $P_0 = P_{atm}$, then $P_g = \rho g h$ at a depth h below the surface.

Example: A diver in the ocean is 20 m below the surface of sea water with a density of 1,025 kg/m^3.

a. What is the absolute pressure he experiences?

b. What is the gauge pressure?

Solution: a. Using the equation for absolute pressure in a liquid:

$$P = P_{atm} + \rho g h$$
$$= 1.013 \times 10^5 + (1,025)(9.8)(20)$$
$$= 3.02 \times 10^5 \text{ Pa}$$

b. Using the equation for gauge pressure:

$$P_g = P - P_{atm}$$
$$= (3.02 - 1.013) \times 10^5$$
$$= 2.01 \times 10^5 \text{ Pa}$$

HYDROSTATICS

Pascal's Principle

Pascal's principle deals with the pressure of a fluid that is completely enclosed and is related to pressure being a scalar rather than vector quantity. The principle states that a change in the pressure applied to an enclosed fluid is transmitted undiminished to every portion of the fluid and to the walls of the containing vessel. For example, a fluid in a tube exerts pressure on an object at any depth below the surface of the fluid. When the pressure on the fluid is increased, pressure will be increased throughout the fluid and on any submerged object in the fluid.

Pascal's principle is the basis of the hydraulic lever (see Figure 67.1). Consider the case when an external force of magnitude F_1 is applied to the left-hand piston of area A_1. To keep the system in equilibrium, a force of magnitude F_2 must be applied to the right-hand piston of area A_2.

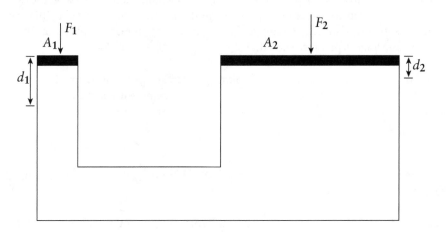

Figure 67.1

Since the system remains in equilibrium as the pressure changes, the change in pressure in both pistons must be equal and is given by:

$$\Delta P = \frac{F_1}{A_1} = \frac{F_2}{A_2}$$

$$F_2 = F_1 \frac{A_2}{A_1}$$

This equation shows that F_2 can be made larger if $A_2 > A_1$.

When piston 1 is moved down a distance d_1, piston 2 moves up a distance d_2. If the fluid is incompressible, then the volume in the system must remain constant. This implies that:

$$V = A_1 d_1 = A_2 d_2$$

$$d_2 = d_1 \frac{A_1}{A_2}$$

By combining both equations, the expression below is obtained:

$$F_1 d_1 = F_2 d_2 = W$$

where work, W, is the product of force and distance. This shows that the same amount of work is being done by both pistons; a greater force is moving through a smaller distance, and a smaller force is moving through a larger distance, but the products are the same. This is another example of the conservation of energy.

Example: A hydraulic press has two pistons. One piston of radius 5 cm pushes down on an enclosed fluid and has a 45 kg weight resting on it. The other, larger piston has a radius of 20 cm. What force is needed on the larger piston to keep the press in equilibrium?

Solution: Using Pascal's principle:

$$\frac{F_2}{A_2} = \frac{F_1}{A_1}$$

$$F_2 = \frac{F_1 A_2}{A_1}$$

Since $F_1 = mg$ and $A = \pi r^2$, it is possible to solve for F_2 by plugging in the known values, including that $g = 10$ m/s^2:

$$F_2 = \frac{45(10)\pi(0.2)^2}{\pi(0.05)^2}$$
$$= 7,200 \text{ N}$$

Archimedes' Principle

Archimedes' principle deals with the buoyancy of objects when placed in a fluid. It explains why ships float and why objects seem lighter when underwater. The principle states that a body wholly or partially immersed in a fluid will be buoyed up by a force equal to the weight of the fluid that it displaces. This buoyant force is given by:

$$F_B = \rho_{\text{fluid}} \, g \, V_{\text{submerged}}$$

where F_B is the buoyant force, ρ_{fluid} is the density of the fluid, g is acceleration due to gravity, and $V_{submerged}$ is the volume of the submerged object. Note that this is the same as the weight of the fluid displaced when the object was submerged.

The weight of the displaced fluid equals the magnitude of the upward buoyant force the fluid exerts on the object; the fluid is trying to "push" its way back into the volume that the object now occupies. If the average density of the object is less than or equal to that of the surrounding fluid, then the object will float. However, if the average density of the object is greater than that of the surrounding fluid, then the object will sink.

Example: A wooden block floats in the ocean with half its volume submerged. Find the density of the wood ρ_b if the density of seawater is 1,024 kg/m^3.

Solution: The weight of the block of total volume V_b is:

$$W_b = m_b g = \rho_b V_b g$$

The weight of the displaced seawater is the buoyant force and is given by:

$$W_w = F_B = m_w g = \rho_w V_w g$$

where ρ_w is the density of seawater (1,024 kg/m^3) and V_w is the volume of displaced water, which is also the volume of that part of the block that is submerged. Since the block is floating, the buoyant force equals the block's weight:

$$W_b = F_B$$

$$\rho_b V_b g = \rho_w V_w g$$

We are given that half the block is submerged, so

$$V_w = \frac{V_b}{2}$$

$$\rho_b V_b g = \frac{1}{2}\rho_w V_b g$$

$$\rho_b = \frac{1}{2}\rho_w$$

$$\rho_b = \frac{1}{2}(1,024)$$

$$= 512 \text{ kg/m}^3$$

Surface Tension

There are two types of forces that the molecules of a liquid experience. The first type is **adhesion,** which is the attractive force that a molecule of the liquid feels toward the molecules of some other substance. For example, the adhesive force causes water droplets to stick to the windshield of a car even though gravity is pulling them downward.

The second type of force experienced by the molecules in a liquid is **cohesion.** Cohesion is the attractive force that a molecule of the liquid feels toward the other molecules of the liquid. Below the surface of the liquid, the cohesive forces cancel out since any one molecule is surrounded on all sides by the other molecules of the liquid. However, on the surface, the molecules feel an unbalanced force pulling them back toward the liquid. This causes the surface to behave like a skin and results in what is known as the **surface tension.** An example of the force of the surface tension can be seen with an insect walking on water; even though its density is greater than that of water, the surface tension of the water is enough to oppose the weight of the insect.

HYDRODYNAMICS

Hydrodynamics refers to the physics of fluids that are in motion. Although it is rarely tested, an understanding of hydrodynamics can be useful. Two major concepts encompass much of hydrodynamics: conservation of mass and conservation of energy.

Figure 67.2

Figure 67.2 shows a tube with a fluid flowing from cross-sectional area A_1 to A_2. The mass of fluid flowing per second through cross-sectional area A is given by $Av\rho$, where v is the velocity and ρ is the density. Since matter is conserved, the mass flow rate of fluid must remain constant from one cross section to another. Assuming that the fluid is incompressible and therefore that the densities are equal cancels the density terms from each side, leaving:

$$v_1 A_1 = v_2 A_2 = \text{constant}$$

This is known as the **continuity equation** and shows that the flow is faster in narrow passages than in wider passages. For example, a river flowing through a wide valley flows slowly and peacefully, but the same river in a narrow canyon will travel at a very high velocity.

Bernoulli's Equation

The continuity equation results from the conservation of mass of the fluid, but energy is also conserved as the fluid flows. Bernoulli formulated this fact into the following equation that bears his name:

$$P_1 + \frac{\rho v_1^2}{2} + \rho g y_1 = P_2 + \frac{\rho v_2^2}{2} + \rho g y_2 = \text{a constant}$$

where P is the absolute pressure of the fluid, ρ is the density of the fluid, v is the velocity of the fluid, g is the acceleration due to gravity, and y is the height of the fluid relative to some reference height. Bernoulli's equation says that, when height is constant ($y_1 = y_2$), increased velocity means decreased pressure and decreased velocity means increased pressure.

Viscosity

Viscosity is a measure of the internal friction of a fluid. Because of viscosity, a force must be exerted to cause one layer of fluid to slide past another. Both liquids and gases have viscosity, but the viscosity of gases tends to be much lower than that of liquids since gases generally have much lower densities. Consider a person moving a hand through air. Little effort is required to move the air out of the way; hence, the viscosity of air is very low. However, it would be much more difficult for the same person to move the same hand through a tub of water; this is because water has a much higher viscosity than air, and so a greater force is required to move the water out of the way.

The SI unit of viscosity is the newton · second/meter^2 (N · s/m^2). The CGS unit is the dyne · second/centimeter^2 (dyn · s/cm^2), also called the poise. 1 N · s/m^2 = 10 poise.

ELASTIC PROPERTIES OF SOLIDS

Young's Modulus

The elasticity of a solid is characterized by a factor called a **modulus.** When subjected to a force F, a material will change its length by ΔL. The force is applied to a cross-sectional area A, and the quantity F/A is defined as **stress.** The change in length normalized to the starting length of the material is known as **strain,** which is $\Delta L/L$. **Young's modulus (Y)** is defined as stress over strain and is given by:

$$Y = \frac{(F/A)}{(\Delta L/L)} = \frac{\text{stress}}{\text{strain}}$$

A large Young's modulus means a large stress produces only a small strain, which indicates a strong material.

Figure 67.3

Yield strength is the point beyond which a material will not return to its original dimensions once the force is removed. If more stress is applied, eventually the ultimate strength is reached. Beyond that point, rupture occurs.

Shear Modulus

Another type of deforming stress is **shearing,** which is also force per area, F/A. However, in this case the force vector lies parallel to the area, as in Figure 67.4. The corresponding strain is x, the movement in the direction of the force, divided by h, the height. The **shear modulus (S)** is defined as the ratio of the stress to the strain and is given by:

$$S = \frac{(F/A)}{(x/h)}$$

Figure 67.4

Bulk Modulus

The **bulk modulus (B)** relates the change in pressure acting on the surfaces of a solid or fluid to the change in volume that is produced. The stress is the change in pressure (ΔP), and the strain is $\Delta V/V$, where V is the original volume and ΔV is the decrease in volume. This leads to the following equation for the bulk modulus:

$$B = \frac{\Delta P}{\Delta V/V}$$

PHYSICS

REVIEW PROBLEMS

1. An aluminum cube is suspended by a cable in a tank of water such that it is completely submerged but remains at a fixed depth. Is there a net vertical force on the cube due only to the water pressure? (Ignore the cube's weight and the tension in the cable.)

2. An anchor made of iron weighs 833 N on the deck of a ship. If the anchor is now suspended in seawater by a massless chain, what is the tension in the chain? The density of iron is 7,800 kg/m^3, and the density of seawater is 1,024 kg/m^3.

3. Two wooden balls of equal volume but different density are held beneath the surface of a container of water. Ball A has a density of 0.5 gm/cm^3, and ball B has a density of 0.7 gm/cm^3. When the balls are released, they will accelerate upward to the surface. What is the relationship between the acceleration of ball A and that of B? ($\rho_{water} = 1$ gm/cm^3)

4. Water flows from a pipe of diameter 0.15 m into one of diameter 0.20 m. If the speed in the 0.15 m pipe is 4.88 m/s, what is the speed in the 0.20 m pipe?

5. A cup in the shape of a cylinder is filled with soda. If a hole is cut in the side of the cup so the soda shoots out, what is the direction of the soda flow the instant it leaves the cup?

6. The figure below represents a section through a horizontal pipe of varying diameters into which open four vertical pipes. If water is allowed to flow through the pipe in the direction indicated, in which of the vertical pipes will the water level be lowest?

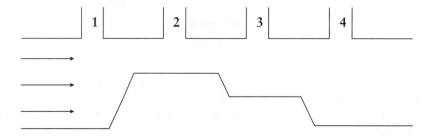

7. Assume water in a tank and pipe are at rest as pictured.

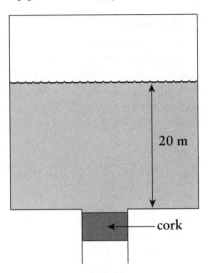

The cork is removed, allowing the water to flow out. Assume the downward velocity of the water at the top of the tank is negligible. Does the velocity of the water as it leaves the pipe depend on the air pressure at the surface of the water, and if so, how?

8. Approximately how much pressure must be exerted on a given volume of water in order to compress it to 99.8% of its volume? (The bulk modulus for water is approximately 2.2×10^9 newtons/meter^2.)

SOLUTIONS TO REVIEW PROBLEMS

1. **Yes, there is a net vertical force upward.**

   The water pressure exerts forces perpendicular to all of the faces of the cube. The top face of the cube experiences a downward force, and the bottom face of the cube experiences an upward force. Remembering that the water pressure increases with depth, we see that the pressure on the bottom surface is greater than the pressure on the top surface. Since both surfaces have the same area, the upward force on the bottom surface is greater than the downward force on the top surface. Thus, there is a net vertical force upward.

2. **724 N**

   The tension in the chain is the difference between the anchor's weight and the buoyant force:

   $$T = W - F_B$$

   where T is the tension, W is the anchor's weight, and F_B is the buoyant force on the anchor. The object's weight is 833 N, and the buoyant force may now be found from Archimedes' principle. The buoyant force is equal to the weight of the seawater that the anchor displaces:

   $$F_B = \rho_w V_w g$$

   Since the anchor is submerged entirely, $V_w = V_A$. To find the volume of the anchor, use:

   $$
   \begin{aligned}
   V_A &= \frac{m_A}{\rho_A} \\
   &= \frac{W_A}{g\rho_A} (W = mg) \\
   &= \frac{833}{(9.8)(7,800)} \\
   &= 1.09 \times 10^{-2}\,\text{m}^3
   \end{aligned}
   $$

   This can be used to find the buoyant force:

   $$
   \begin{aligned}
   F_B &= \rho_w V_A g \\
   &= 1,024(1.09 \times 10^2)(9.8) \\
   &= 109\,\text{N}
   \end{aligned}
   $$

   Now the tension may be found as follows:

   $$
   \begin{aligned}
   T &= W - F_B \\
   &= 833 - 109 \\
   &= 724\,\text{N}
   \end{aligned}
   $$

3. **Ball A has the greater acceleration.**

   Using Newton's second law, $F_{net} = ma$, you have: $F_B - mg = ma$, so $a = F_B/m - g$. Both balls experience the same buoyant force since they both have the same volume. Thus, the ball with the smaller mass experiences the greater acceleration. Again, since both balls have the same volume, the ball with the smaller density has the smaller mass, which is ball A.

4. **2.7 m/s**

   Water flows faster through a narrower pipe; its speed is inversely proportional to the cross-sectional area of the pipe since the same volume of water must pass by each point at each time interval. Let A be the 0.15 m pipe and B the 0.20 m pipe. Then:

   $$V_A A_A = V_B A_B$$

   Since v is inversely proportional to the cross-sectional area and area is proportional to the square of the diameter $A = \pi r^2 = \pi d^2/4$:

   $$V_B = V_A \frac{\pi d_A^2 / 4}{\pi d_B^2 / 4}$$

   $$V_B = V_A \frac{d_A^2}{d_B^2}$$

   $$= (4.88)\frac{(0.15)^2}{(0.20)^2}$$

   $$= (4.88)\frac{0.0225}{0.04}$$

   $$= 2.7 \text{ m/s}$$

5. **Horizontal**

   The pressure of a liquid is always perpendicular to the walls of its container. This means that the soda is pushing outward or in the horizontal direction on the sides of the cup. If a hole is cut and the soda flows out, its initial velocity will be in the same direction as the pressure at the hole. So, the initial velocity is in the horizontal direction.

6. **Pipe 2**

   It is not necessary to do any calculation to answer this question. Since the fluid at the top of the four open pipes is at atmospheric pressure, the pipe with the lowest level will be above the fluid with the lowest pressure. Looking at Bernoulli's equation, the height at which the open pipes meet the horizontal pipe is the same for each one; thus, the third term ρgh is the same for each segment of pipe. If the pressure is lower for one, then the velocity must be larger; all you need to do is determine which segment of horizontal pipe has the highest velocity. From the continuity equation, you know that this will be at the point at which the horizontal pipe has the smallest cross-sectional area. This is under open pipe 2.

7. **Yes: the greater the pressure, the greater the velocity**

   The intuitive explanation is that the velocity at the bottom depends on the force that pushes the water out, and that force consists of the weight of the water above the opening and the force of air pressure at the surface. Thus, increased air pressure means increased velocity.

   This problem can also be solved by a qualitative application of Bernoulli's equation. Denoting the surface of the water as point t and the point at which it leaves as point b, recall that Bernoulli's equation says:

   $$p_t + \frac{1}{2}\rho vt^2 + \rho gy_t = p + \frac{1}{2}\rho v_b^2 + \rho gy_b$$

You're told that $v_t = 0$ and can choose $y_b = 0$, so $P_t + \rho g y_t = P_b + \frac{1}{2}\rho v_b^2$ where v_b is the velocity of the water leaving the pipe. From this expression, you can see that the greater P_t (air pressure at the surface of the water), the greater the velocity.

8. **4.4×10^6 N/m^2**

The new volume is 99.8% of the original volume, so the change in volume is $100\% - 99.8\% = 0.2\%$. This can be represented as $\Delta V/V = 0.2\% = 0.002$. Using the equation for bulk modulus:

$$B = \frac{P}{\Delta V/V}$$
$$P = B(\Delta V/V)$$
$$= (2.2\times10^9)(0.002)$$
$$= 4.4\times10^6 \text{ N/m}^2$$

CHAPTER SIXTY-EIGHT

Electrostatics

Electrostatics is the study of stationary charges and the forces between them. This chapter reviews Coulomb's law, which gives the electrostatic force between two charges, and then discusses the concept of the electric field, which gives the electrostatic force per unit charge. The topic of electric potential energy is discussed along with the related topic of the electric potential, which is defined as electric potential energy per unit charge. One can think of the electric potential being related to the electric potential energy in the same way as the electric field is related to the electric force. Associated with the electric field and electric potential are the concepts of field lines and equipotential lines, which are reviewed separately.

CHARGES

Charge may be either positive or negative. A positive charge and a negative charge attract one another; positive repels positive; and negative repels negative. To summarize: **unlike charges attract, and like charges repel.** The force that exists between stationary charges is known as the **electrostatic** force.

Materials are usually electrically neutral, but can sometimes be charged by stripping off loose surface charges simply by friction. If a glass rod is rubbed on a piece of silk, electrons, which are negatively charged, flow from the glass rod to the silk cloth. This results in the glass rod being positively charged and the silk cloth being negatively charged. The rod and cloth then attract each other; this is known as static cling.

In calculations, a charged particle is represented by the variable q. The SI unit of charge is the **coulomb (C)**, and the **fundamental unit of charge (e)** is:

$$e = 1.60 \times 10^{-19} \, C$$

Both protons and electrons have this amount of charge, though protons are positively charged ($q = +e$), and electrons are negatively charged ($q = -e$).

COULOMB'S LAW

Coulomb's law gives the magnitude of the electrostatic force F between two charges, q_1 and q_2, whose centers are separated by a distance r:

$$F = k\frac{q_1 q_2}{r^2}$$

where k is **Coulomb's constant,** also known as the **electrostatic constant,** and is a number that depends on the units used in the equation. In SI units, $k = \dfrac{1}{4\pi\varepsilon_0} = 8.99 \times 10^9$ N·m²·C⁻². ε_0 is the **permittivity of free space** and equals 8.85×10^{-12} C²·N⁻¹·m⁻².

Coulomb's law in SI units is therefore:

$$F = k\frac{q_1 q_2}{r^2} = \frac{1}{4\pi\varepsilon_0}\frac{q_1 q_2}{r^2} = 8.99 \times 10^9 \frac{q_1 q_2}{r^2}$$

where the electrostatic force F is in newtons, the charges q_1 and q_2 are in coulombs, and the distance r is in meters. Since force is a vector, the direction of the force is determined using the signs of the charges. Unlike charges have opposite signs, giving a negative force between them that causes them to attract. Like charges have the same sign, giving a positive force that causes the charges to repel. The force always points along the line connecting the centers of the two charges.

Example: A positive charge is attracted to a negative charge a certain distance away. The charges are then moved so that they are separated by twice the distance. How has the force of attraction changed between them?

Solution: Coulomb's law states that the force between two charges varies with the inverse of the square of the distance between them. Therefore, if the distance is doubled, the square of the distance is quadrupled, and the force is reduced to one-fourth of what it was originally. Note that it was not necessary to know the distance or the units being used but only the fact that the distance was doubled and that the relation was an inverse square law.

Example: Negatively-charged electrons are electrostatically attracted to positively-charged protons (together they form hydrogen atoms). Because electrons and protons have mass, they will be gravitationally attracted to each other as well. Compare the two forces using Coulomb's law and Newton's law of gravitation.
(Use the equations $m_p = 1.67 \times 10^{-27}$ kg and $m_e = 9.11 \times 10^{-31}$ kg and a Bohr radius separation between the electron and proton such that $r = 5.29 \times 10^{-11}$ m.)

Solution: Both Coulomb's law and Newton's law state that the attractive forces between the electron and proton vary with the inverse of the square of the distance between them. As calculated in Chapter 64, the gravitational attractive force is:

$$F_{\mathrm{N}} = \frac{Gm_{\mathrm{p}}m_{\mathrm{e}}}{r^2}$$

$$= \frac{(6.67 \times 10^{-11})(1.67 \times 10^{-27})(9.11 \times 10^{-31})}{(5.29 \times 10^{-11})^2}$$

$$= 3.63 \times 10^{-47} \ \mathrm{N} \approx 10^{-47} \ \mathrm{N}$$

On the other hand, the magnitude of the electrostatic attractive force is:

$$F_{\mathrm{c}} = \frac{1}{4\pi\varepsilon_0} \frac{q_{\mathrm{p}}q_{\mathrm{e}}}{r^2}$$

$$= \frac{(8.99 \times 10^9)(1.60 \times 10^{-19})(1.60 \times 10^{-19})}{(5.29 \times 10^{-11})^2}$$

$$= 8.22 \times 10^{-8} \ \mathrm{N} \approx 10^{-7} \ \mathrm{N}$$

Note that the electrostatic attraction between the electron and proton is stronger than the gravitational attraction by a factor of approximately 10^{40}.

ELECTRIC FIELD

Every electric charge sets up a surrounding **electric field.** The electric field can be detected by the force it exerts on other electric charges. Electric field is defined as the force a charge exerts on another stationary positive test charge q_0 divided by the test charge. It is therefore a vector quantity given by:

$$\mathbf{E} = \frac{\mathbf{F}}{q_0}$$

The electric field $\mathbf{E}$ points in the same direction as the force $\mathbf{F}$ exerted on the positive test charge q_0. In SI units, $\mathbf{E}$ is measured in newtons/coulomb, which equals volts/meter.

Given an electric field $\mathbf{E}$ in some region of space, any charge q placed in the field experiences a force $\mathbf{F}$ given by:

$$\mathbf{F} = q\mathbf{E}$$

This vector equation uses the sign of the charge, whether positive or negative, so that the force $\mathbf{F}$ is in the direction of $q\mathbf{E}$. Thus, a positive test charge in an electric field feels a force in the direction of the field, and a negative test charge in an electric field feels a force in the direction opposite the field.

As defined above, the force on a positive test charge q_0 placed a distance r from a charge q is given by Coulomb's Law:

$$\mathbf{F} = k\frac{q\,q_0}{r^2}$$

Using this equation combined with the equation for an electric field $\mathbf{E} = \mathbf{F}/q_0$, the electric field at any distance r from a charge q is determined to be:

$$\mathbf{E} = k\frac{q}{r^2}$$

Just as Coulomb's law states that the force between two charges varies with the inverse of the square of the distance between them, the electric field $\mathbf{E}$ also varies with the inverse of the square of the distance from the source charge.

The **direction** of the electric field vector is determined by the sign of the source charge. The electric field of a positive charge points radially outward from the charge. The electric field of a negative charge points radially inward toward the charge.

In order to visualize the direction and magnitude of the electric field vector over a wide number of points, it is helpful to think in terms of field lines. **Field lines**, also sometimes called **lines of force**, are imaginary lines that represent how a positive test charge would be accelerated in the electric field. For example, the field lines for a negatively-charged source particle, such as an electron, would point radially toward the charge because the positive test charge would be attracted toward a negative charge. Similarly, the field lines point radially away from a positive source charge, such as a proton, because the positive test charge would be repelled away from another positive charge. Figure 68.1 shows the field lines for a positive source charge on the left and for a negative source charge on the right.

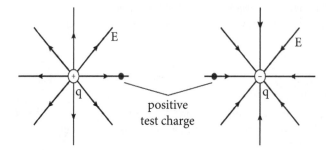

Figure 68.1

Field lines also indicate the relative strength of the electric field. Where the field lines are closer together, the electric field is stronger; where the field lines are farther apart, the electric field is weaker.

For a collection of charges, the total electric field at a point in space is the **vector sum** of the electric field due to each charge:

$$\mathbf{E}_{total} = \mathbf{E}_{q1} + \mathbf{E}_{q2} + \mathbf{E}_{q3} + \ldots \text{(vector sum)}$$

Figure 68.2 shows the vector sum of the individual electric fields for a positive source charge on the left and negative source charge on the right.

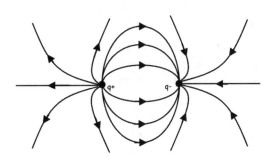

Figure 68.2

The vector sum must be carried out using the rules of vector addition, as shown in the following example:

Example: A positive charge of $+1 \times 10^{-5}$ C is located one meter away from another positive charge of $+2 \times 10^{-5}$ C. At what point along the line between the two charges is the electric field equal to zero?

Solution: In order for the sum of two vectors to be zero, they must be equal in magnitude and opposite in direction. Because both of the charges are positive, the electric field vector of each charge points away from that charge. Along the line between the two charges, the two electric field vectors point in opposite directions. If the charges were equal in magnitude, the point at which the two fields have the same magnitude (and therefore where the resultant field is zero) would be exactly halfway between them. However, the charges are not equal since one charge is one-half the magnitude of the other. Let x be the distance from the $+1 \times 10^{-5}$ C charge. The distance from the other charge is the total distance of one meter minus x.

Setting the magnitudes of the two fields equal to each other to find the distance x that will make them equal, the equation is:

$$k\frac{(1\times10^{-5})}{x^2}=k\frac{(2\times10^{-5})}{(1-x)^2}$$

$$\frac{1}{x^2}=\frac{2}{(1-x)^2}$$

$$2x^2=(1-x)^2$$

$$\sqrt{2}x=1-x$$

$$x(1+\sqrt{2})=1$$

$$x=\frac{1}{\sqrt{2}+1}$$

$$x=0.41\,\text{m}$$

As might be expected, this point is closer to the smaller charge since the field of the larger charge is stronger.

ELECTRIC POTENTIAL

Just as work is required to lift an object against the Earth's gravitational field, work must be done to move an electric charge in an electric field. The **electric potential** at a point is defined as the amount of work needed to move a positive test charge q_0 from infinity to that point, divided by the quantity of charge q_0:

$$V = \frac{W}{q_0}$$

In SI units electric potential is measured in **volts** (V) where 1 volt = 1 joule/coulomb. The electric potential at a distance r from a point charge q is:

$$V = k\frac{q}{r}$$

V is a scalar quantity, and its sign is determined by the sign of the charge q. For a positive charge, V is positive, but for a negative charge, V is negative. For a collection of charges, the total electric potential at a point in space is the **scalar sum** of the electric potential due to each charge:

$$V_{total} = V_{q1} + V_{q2} + V_{q3} + \ldots \text{(scalar sum)}$$

Potential difference (voltage) is the difference in potential between two points and is the same as the term voltage used in circuits (see Chapter 70, Circuits). If V_a and V_b are the electric potentials at points a and b, then the potential difference between a and b is $V_b - V_a$. From the definition of electric potential, it follows that the potential difference between a and b can be expressed as:

$$V_b - V_a = \frac{W_{ab}}{q_0}$$

where W_{ab} is the work needed to move a test charge q_0 through an electric field from a to b. The work depends only on the potentials at the two points a and b and is independent of the path. This means that, like the gravitational force described in Chapter 64, Newtonian Mechanics, the electrostatic force is a conservative force.

EQUIPOTENTIAL LINES

An **equipotential line** is one for which the potential at every point is the same; in other words, the potential difference between any two points on an equipotential line is zero. From the equation above for potential difference, it follows that no work is done when moving a test charge q_0 from one point to another on an equipotential line. Work will be done in going from one line to another, but the work depends only on the potential difference of the two lines and not on the path.

Example: In Figure 68.3 an electron goes from point a to point b in the vicinity of a very large positive charge. The electron could be made to follow any of the paths shown. Which path requires the least work to get the electron charge from a to b?

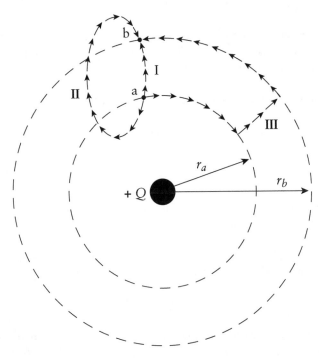

Figure 68.3

Solution: Work depends only on the potential difference and not on the path, so any of the paths shown would require the same amount of work in moving the electron from a to b, namely:

$$W_{ab} = q_e(V_b - V_a)$$
$$= q_e(k\frac{Q}{r_b} - k\frac{Q}{r_a})$$

So paths I, II, and III all require the same amount of work to move the electron. Note that W_{ab} is positive in this example because $r_a < r_b$ and $q_e = -e$. This makes sense intuitively because a negative charge is being moved away from a positive charge.

ELECTRIC POTENTIAL ENERGY

Electric potential at a point in space is defined as the amount of work W required to move a positive test charge q_0 from infinity to that point, divided by q_0. Next, a different quantity needs to be defined: electric potential energy. Despite the similarity in names, it is important to distinguish between **electric potential (V)** and **electric potential energy (U)**. The electric potential energy of a test charge q_0 at a point in space is defined as the amount of work needed to move the charge from infinity to that point through an electric field created by a separate source charge. Using the definition of the electric potential as a starting point and rearranging gives:

$$U = W = qV$$

where V is the electric potential due to the source charge. Note that the sign of U depends on the signs of q and V. Since $U = qV$, it may be said that $V = U/q$, so electric potential can also be thought of as electric potential energy per unit charge.

When V is due to just one other charge Q, V is given by kQ/r, and U may be rewritten as:

$$U = k\frac{qQ}{r}$$

$$= \left(\frac{1}{4\pi\varepsilon_0}\right)\frac{qQ}{r}$$

If the charges are both positive or both negative (like charges), U will be positive, but if one charge is positive and the other negative (unlike charges), U will be negative.

Example: If a charge of $+2e$ and a charge of $-3e$ are separated by a distance of 3 nm, what is the potential energy of the system? (e is the fundamental unit of charge equal to 1.6×10^{-19} C.)

Solution: $$U = k\frac{qQ}{r}$$

From the question stem you know that $r = 3$ nm $= 3 \times 10^{-9}$ m, $q = +2e$, and $Q = -3e$. Substituting in these values and approximating k as 9.0×10^9 gives:

$$U = (9 \times 10^9)\frac{(2)(1.6 \times 10^{-19})(-3)(1.6 \times 10^{-19})}{3 \times 10^{-9}}$$

$$= -4.6 \times 10^{-19} \text{ J}$$

THE ELECTRIC DIPOLE

Two equal and opposite charges a small distance (d) away from each other form an **electric dipole.** Suppose there is a dipole with charges $+q$ and $-q$, as shown in Figure 68.4.

Figure 68.4

The product of qd is defined as the **dipole moment (p)** with SI units of C·m. This is a vector quantity. Its magnitude is equal to the product qd, and its direction lies along the line connecting the charges (dipole axis) and points from the negative charge toward the positive charge.

The electric field produced by the dipole at any point is the vector sum of each of the individual fields due to each of the two charges. Along the perpendicular bisector of the dipole (a plane that lies halfway between $+q$ and $-q$), the magnitude of the electric field can be approximated as:

$$E = \left(\frac{1}{4\pi\varepsilon_0}\right)\frac{p}{r^3} = \frac{kp}{r^3}$$

The field will point in the opposite direction to **p**.

Example: The H_2O molecule has a dipole moment of 1.85 D, where D = debye unit = 3.34×10^{-30} C·m. Calculate the electric field due to an H_2O molecule at a point 89 nm away along the axis of the dipole if k = 9×10^9 N·m²/C².

Solution: Substituting the values into the equation for the field due to a dipole gives:

$$E = \frac{kp}{r^3} = \frac{(9\times10^9)[1.85(3.34\times10^{-30})]}{(89\times10^{-9})^3} \approx 49 \text{ N/C}$$

Next, consider the case when an electric dipole is placed in a uniform external electric field, as shown in Figure 68.5. If there is no field present, the dipole moment will assume any random orientation. With a uniform external electric field present, however, each of the equal but opposite charges that make up the dipole will feel a force exerted on it by the external electric field. The net force will be zero, since the force on each charge is equal in magnitude but opposite in direction. Therefore, the dipole feels no translational force. However, there will be a nonzero torque about the center. This torque will cause the dipole to reorient itself by rotating so that its dipole moment, **p**, aligns with the electric field **E**, and $\theta = 0°$ relative to the external electric field.

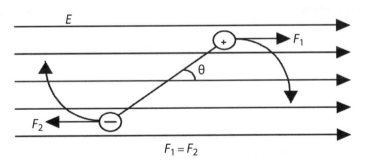

Figure 68.5

PHYSICS

REVIEW PROBLEMS

Base your answers to questions 1–3 on the information below.

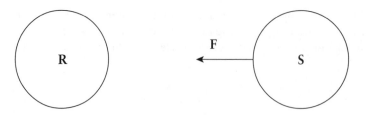

A metal sphere, R, has a charge of $-q$ coulombs. An identical metal sphere, S, has a charge of $+2q$ coulombs. The magnitude of the electrical force on S due to R is F newtons.

1. The magnitude of the electric force on R due to S is

   A. $F/2$.
   B. F.
   C. $2F$.
   D. $3F$.
   E. $4F$.

2. If the distance between the centers of the spheres is halved, the magnitude of the force on S due to R will be

   A. $F/4$.
   B. $F/2$.
   C. $2F$.
   D. $3F$.
   E. $4F$.

3. If an electron were placed midway between R and S, the resultant electric force on the electron would be

   A. toward R.
   B. toward S.
   C. up.
   D. down.
   E. zero.

4. Which of the following is a unit of energy?

   A. eV
   B. V·m
   C. V/m
   D. W
   E. N

Base your answers to questions 5 and 6 on the figure below.

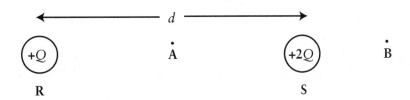

A positive charge of $+Q$ is fixed at point R a distance d away from another positive charge of $+2Q$ fixed at point S. Point A is located midway between the charges, and point B is a distance $d/2$ from the $+2Q$ charge.

5. Is the total electric field stronger at A or B?

6. In which direction will a positive charge move if placed at point A?

7. Two parallel conducting plates, one carrying a charge of $+Q$ and the other a charge of $-Q$, are separated by a distance d. The voltage between the plates is 12 V.

    a. What is the change in potential energy of a charge of $+2 \ \mu C$ as it is moved from the negative plate to the positive plate, and is the work done in this process positive or negative?

    b. If the $+2 \ \mu C$ charge is released from rest at the positive plate, how much kinetic energy does it have when it reaches the negative plate?

8. The $-1 \ \mu C$ negative charge in the figure below goes from $y = -5$ to $y = +5$ and is made to follow the dashed line in the vicinity of two equal $+5$ C positive charges. What is the work required to move the negative charge along the dashed line?

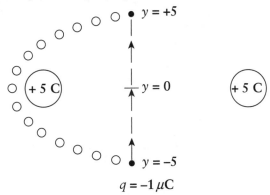

9. If the negative charge in question 8 were made instead to follow the path shown by the dotted line, what would be the net work done in moving the charge?

10. Given an electric dipole, the electric potential is zero

    A.   only at the midpoint of the dipole axis.

    B.   anywhere on any perpendicular bisector of the dipole axis and at infinity.

    C.   anywhere on the dipole axis.

    D.   only for points at infinity.

    E.   only when a second dipole is introduced to the system.

SOLUTIONS TO REVIEW PROBLEMS

1. **B** According to Newton's third law, if R exerts a force on S, then S exerts an equal but oppositely directed force back on R. Therefore, the magnitude of the force on R due to S is also F.

2. **E** The force is inversely proportional to r^2. Thus:

$$F \propto \frac{1}{r^2}$$

If r_2 equals $\frac{r_1}{2}$, then,

$$F_{old} \propto \frac{1}{r_1^2}$$

and:

$$F_{new} \propto \frac{1}{r_2^2}$$

$$\propto 1 / \left(\frac{r_1}{2}\right)^2$$

$$\propto 1 / \left(\frac{r_1^2}{4}\right)$$

$$\propto \frac{4}{r_1^2}$$

$$= 4 \, F_{old}$$

So the new force is 4 times greater.

3. **B** If an electron with its negative charge ($-e$) were to be placed midway between R and S, the electron would be attracted by S (unlike charges attract) and repelled by R (like charges repel). Thus, the resultant force would be toward S and away from R.

4. **A** The eV is a unit of energy: $1 \text{ eV} = 1.6 \times 10^{-19}$ J. Even if you weren't sure of this, the other answers can be eliminated because none of them has a unit of energy:

   B. V·m = potential × length = (energy/charge) × length

   C. V/m = units used to measure electric fields = energy/(charge × length)

   D. W = watts = unit of power = energy/time

   E. N = newton = unit of force = (mass × length)/(time^2) = energy/length

5. **B** The total electric field due to the two charges is the vector sum of the electric field due to each. The magnitude of the electric field of a given charge is proportional to the magnitude of the charge and inversely proportional to the square of the distance from the charge.

   Compare the strength of the field at A versus that at B. Both are the same distance from the $+2Q$ charge (so the contribution from $+2Q$ is the same at A and B), but when the field from the $+Q$ charge is added in, it will increase the total field at B (since the fields from $+Q$ and $+2Q$ are in the same direction at B) and decrease the total field at A (since the fields from $+Q$ and $+2Q$ are in opposite directions at A). Thus, the field at B is larger than at A.

6.   **Toward the $+Q$ charge.**

A positive charge placed at A will experience two forces: a force to the left due to $+2Q$ and a force to the right due to $+Q$. Since point A is the same distance from $+Q$ and $+2Q$, the force due to $+2Q$ will be larger than that due to $+Q$. Therefore, there will be a net force to the left toward $+Q$.

7.   a. **2.4×10^{-5} J, positive work**

    b. **2.4×10^{-5} J**

Recall that change in potential energy, ΔU, and change in potential, ΔV, are related by $\Delta U = q\Delta V$. So $\Delta U = (2 \times 10^{-6})(12)$ J $= 2.4 \times 10^{-5}$ J. In order to move a positive charge away from negative charges and toward positive charges, you must exert a force to counteract the attractive force of the negative charges on the negative plate and the repulsive force of the positive charges on the positive plate. Thus, positive work must be done.

Conservation of energy applies to charges as it does to masses, so the loss in electric potential energy as the charge moves from the positive plate to the negative plate must equal the gain in the kinetic energy of the charge. The loss in potential energy is just the amount of potential energy it gained in originally going from the negative to the positive plate, 2.4×10^{-5} J. So the gain in kinetic energy is also 2.4×10^{-5} J.

8.   **No net work is done.**

There will be work done in moving the negative charge from its initial position to the origin. However, in moving the negative charge from the origin to the final position, the same amount of work is done but with the opposite sign. This is because the force changes direction as the electron crosses $y = 0$. Therefore, both quantities of work cancel each other out. Note that this argument depends on the symmetry of initial and final positions.

9.   **Zero**

The electrostatic force is conservative, and the work done is independent of the path. The work done along the dashed line path was shown to be zero. Since the endpoints of the dotted line path are the same as the endpoints of the dashed line path, it may be concluded that the net work done along the dotted line path is zero as well.

10.   **B**   Potential is a scalar quantity. The total potential is the sum of the potentials of the positive and negative charges. $V_+ = kq_+/r_+$ and $V_- = kq_-/r_-$. In a dipole $q_- = -q_+$ and the total potential equals zero wherever $r_+ = r_-$. This will be at any point along any perpendicular bisector of the dipole axis. The potential is also zero for all points at infinity, since $kq/\infty = 0$, but choice (D) says *only* points at infinity, which is too extreme.

CHAPTER SIXTY-NINE

Magnetism

This chapter reviews the subject of magnetism. Unlike electrostatics, in which electric charges create electric fields that exert forces on other electric charges, magnetism has no fundamental magnetic charge. Instead, magnetic fields are created by moving charges, currents in wires, and permanent magnets. These magnetic fields, in turn, exert magnetic forces on the same types of things that create them, i.e., moving charges, currents in wires, and permanent magnets.

The first half of the chapter is concerned with the determination of the magnetic force due to a given magnetic field. Since force is a vector, both the magnitude and direction of the magnetic force are considered. The second half of the chapter then examines sources of magnetic fields, including a brief review of magnetic materials and a discussion of the two most common current configurations, the straight wire and the loop of wire.

THE MAGNETIC FIELD

In discussing the magnetic force exerted on moving charges and on current-carrying wires, assume the presence of a fixed and uniform magnetic field **B**. This field must be produced by some external source, such as a magnet or arrangement of current-carrying wires, but only the strength and direction of this field need to be considered.

Like most physical quantities, magnetic fields have units. The SI unit of the magnetic field is the **tesla (T)** where $1\,T = 1\dfrac{N \cdot s}{m \cdot C}$. Small magnetic fields are sometimes measured in **gauss**, where 1 tesla = 10^4 gauss.

Force on a Moving Charge

When a charge moves in a magnetic field, a magnetic force is exerted on it. This force, like all forces, is a vector, and its magnitude is given by:

$$F = qvB \sin \theta$$

In using this formula, θ is the angle between the vectors $q\mathbf{v}$ and **B**, q is the charge of the moving particle, v is the particle's speed, and B is the magnitude of the magnetic field vector. Note that if q or v is zero, then the magnetic force will be zero; a neutral particle or a charge that is not moving will not experience a force.

Right-Hand Rule for the Direction of the Magnetic Force on a Moving Charge

The **direction** of the magnetic force on the moving charge depends on the velocity vector **v** and the sign of the charge q. If q is positive, then qv points in the same direction as **v**. If q is negative, then qv points in the opposite direction from **v.**

The direction of the magnetic force will be **perpendicular** to the plane defined by qv and **B,** but this could be either of two directions. To find the correct direction for a positive charge, use your *right hand* to visualize the scenario (for a negative charge, reverse the direction of the velocity by 180°). Let your *thumb* of the right hand point in the direction of the vector qv, aligned with where the positive charge is moving. Let the remaining *fingers* of your right hand point in the direction of **B**, the existing magnetic field. Your *palm* will now point in the direction of **F,** the magnetic force on q, which shows the direction toward which the charge will begin to accelerate. This **right-hand rule** is illustrated in Figure 69.1. Note that slightly different versions of the right-hand rule are sometimes used that represent these same three factors differently; if you have an alternative rule that works for you, feel free to continue using that. However, if you aren't confident with your rule, then learn the rule above, which will always work.

When dealing with the direction of magnetic fields, there are six possibilities: up or down relative to the page, right or left across the page, and into or out of the page. Because of the three-dimensional nature of problems involving magnetic fields, scientists have chosen the following conventions to denote magnetic fields going into the page, or coming out of the page. The symbol "x" represents a field going into the page. The x represents the tail end (fletching) of an arrow traveling into the page. The symbol "•" represents a field coming out of the page. The • represents the tip of an arrowhead coming out of the page. Figure 69.4 at the end of this chapter shows both symbols being used to designate the direction of a magnetic field.

Example: Suppose a proton with charge of $+1.6 \times 10^{-19}$ C is moving with a speed of 15 m/s in a direction parallel to a uniform magnetic field of 3.0 T. What are the magnitude and direction of the magnetic force on the proton?

Solution: Because the proton is positively charged, the vector qv is in the same direction as **v,** which is the same direction as **B** as stated in the problem. Since qv and **B** are pointing in the same direction, the angle between the vectors is zero. Because sin 0° = 0, and $F = qvB \sin \theta$, the magnetic force on the proton is zero.

Note that if the charge had been negative (an electron, for example), the angle between qv and **B** would have been 180°. Since sin 180° = 0, the magnetic force on a negative charge moving parallel to a uniform magnetic field would be zero as well. Thus, the magnetic force on a moving charge will be zero if the charge is moving parallel or antiparallel to the magnetic field.

Example: Suppose a proton with charge equal to $+1.6 \times 10^{-19}$ C is moving with a speed of 15 m/s toward the top of the page and through a uniform magnetic field of 3.0 T directed into the page (see Figure 69.1(a)). What are the magnitude and direction of the magnetic force on the proton?

Figure 69.1

Solution: Because the proton is positively charged, the vector $q\mathbf{v}$ is in the same direction as $\mathbf{v}$, which is perpendicular to $\mathbf{B}$ as stated in the problem. Because $q\mathbf{v}$ and $\mathbf{B}$ are perpendicular, the angle between the vectors, θ, is 90°. Since $\sin 90° = 1$, the magnetic force on the proton will be the largest possible value and is given by:

$$F = qvB \; sin\theta$$
$$= qvB$$
$$= (1.6 \times 10^{-19})(15)(3.0)$$
$$= 7.2 \times 10^{-18} \text{ N}$$

By holding the thumb of your right hand so it is directed toward the top of the page and then holding the remaining fingers of your right hand so that they point toward (into) the page, your right hand palm will point to the left (see Figure 69.1(b)). Hence, the force vector points to the left, and the proton is deflected to the left on its upward journey.

Note that if the charge had been negative (an electron, for example), the angle between $q\mathbf{v}$ and $\mathbf{B}$ still would have been 90°, but the direction of the force would be reversed by 180°. Hence, an electron would be deflected to the right on its upward journey.

Current

When two points at different electric potentials are connected with a conductor (such as a metal wire), positive charge flows between the two points. The flow of positive charge is called an **electric current (I)**. The magnitude of the current is the amount of charge (Δq) passing through the conductor per unit time (Δt). In the form of an equation, that is:

$$I = \frac{\Delta q}{\Delta t}$$

The SI unit of current is the **ampere** (1 A = 1 C/s). Electric current will be covered in more detail in Chapter 70, Circuits.

Charge is transmitted by a flow of electrons in a conductor. Since electrons are negatively charged, they go from lower potentials to higher potentials. By convention, the direction of current is the direction in which positive charge would flow, which is from high to low potential. Thus, the direction of current is opposite to the direction of electron flow.

Force on a Current-Carrying Wire

Since moving charge is subject to magnetic forces and electric current is a flow of charge, magnetic forces also act on a current-carrying wire. For a straight wire of length L carrying a current I in a direction that makes an angle θ with a uniform magnetic field **B**, the magnitude of the magnetic force on the current-carrying wire is:

$$F = ILB \sin \theta$$

The direction of the force is given by the same right-hand rule given for moving charges, with the thumb of the right hand pointing in the direction of the flow of conventional current since this is the same as the positive charge vector.

Example: Suppose a wire of length 2.0 m is conducting a current of 5.0 A toward the top of the page and through a 30 gauss uniform magnetic field directed into the page (see Figure 69.2(a)). What are the magnitude and direction of the magnetic force on the wire?

(a)   (b)

Figure 69.2

Solution: Since 1 T $= 10^4$ gauss, 1 gauss $= 10^{-4}$ T, 30 gauss $= 30 \times 10^{-4}$ T $= 3 \times 10^{-3}$ T. The wire is conducting current toward the top of the page, and the magnetic field points into the page. Therefore, the current is perpendicular to **B**. The angle between them is 90°, and since sin 90° = 1, the magnetic force on the wire is the maximum possible force given by:

$$F = ILB\sin\theta = ILB$$
$$= 5.0(2.0)(3.0\times 10^{-3})$$
$$= 3.0\times 10^{-2}\ \text{N} = 0.03\ \text{N}$$

By holding the thumb of your right hand so it is directed toward the top of the page and then holding the remaining fingers toward (into) the page, the palm of your right hand will point to the left. Hence, the force on the wire is to the left.

SOURCES OF MAGNETIC FIELDS

The previous section dealt with the magnetic force on a moving charge and a current-carrying wire, but did not discuss how the field was generated. Any moving charge creates a magnetic field. Magnetic fields may be set up by the flow of charge in permanent magnets, by electric currents, or by individual moving charges (e.g., an electron moving through space). This section deals only with permanent magnets and current-carrying wires, but it is important to realize that each of these sources of magnetic fields has, in one sense or another, a flow of charge or a current—it is the movement of charge that gives rise to a magnetic field.

As with electric fields, magnetic **field lines** can be used to visualize the magnetic field.

Magnetic Materials

Materials are classified as diamagnetic, paramagnetic, and ferromagnetic.

Diamagnetic materials are very slightly repelled from the pole of a strong bar magnet but are not permanent magnets. All materials exhibit some diamagnetism, but this is generally a very weak effect not easily observable in everyday life, and it can be overcome in those materials also displaying paramagnetism or ferromagnetism. Most materials with only diamagnetism are referred to as nonmagnetic in colloquial terms. Examples include wood, plastic, and water.

Paramagnetic materials are slightly attracted toward the pole of a strong bar magnet but are also not permanent magnets because they do not retain magnetism when the magnetic field (such as the bar magnet) is removed. Paramagnets do, however, have permanent dipoles due to uneven distributions of electrons caused by having unpaired valence electrons. These dipoles align in the presence of a magnetic field, but their orientations become random again when the field is removed. Examples include aluminum, platinum, and some solutions.

Ferromagnetic materials are strongly magnetic and include iron, nickel, cobalt, and many of their alloys. Similar to paramagnets, these materials have permanent dipoles, but their dipoles can be permanently oriented in the same direction, such as when exposed to a magnetic field while at the correct temperature. Examples of ferromagnets include bar magnets and the magnets commonly used on refrigerators.

All permanent magnets have **north** and **south** poles. The north pole is the place where the magnetic field lines emerge; the south pole is where they enter. If two magnets are placed in close proximity, the opposite poles will attract each other, and the like poles will repel one another.

When a paper with iron filings is placed on top of a permanent bar magnet, the iron filings form lines connecting the top of the magnet to the bottom of the magnet. The iron filings show the magnetic field lines.

Current-Carrying Wires

A current-carrying wire will produce a magnetic field surrounding it. The magnetic field of a current-carrying wire is the vector sum of the magnetic fields due to the individual moving charges of the current. The two most important examples are a long straight wire and the center of a circular loop of wire.

At a perpendicular distance r from an infinitely long and *straight* current-carrying wire, the magnitude of the magnetic field produced by the current I in the wire is given by:

$$B = \frac{\mu_0 I}{2\pi r}$$

where μ_0 is the **permeability of free space** and equals $4\pi \times 10^{-7}\,\text{T}\cdot\text{m/A} = 1.26 \times 10^{-6}\,\text{T}\cdot\text{m/A}$. This shows that, for a long straight wire, the field strength drops off with distance from the wire.

Magnetic field lines around wires form concentric, perpendicular circles and can be thought of as a rotating cylinder surrounding the wire. For example, for a wire in the plane of the page, the field lines will go into the page on one side of the wire and come out of the page on the other side of the wire.

You can use the right-hand rule to find the direction of the magnetic field produced by a straight wire. This rule is the same as previously described but with curled fingers, since the field is circular: The **right thumb** points in the direction of the current (the movement of positive charges), and the remaining **right fingers** follow the magnetic field lines by curling around the wire. The fingers now show the direction of the magnetic field lines and the direction of **B** itself at any point.

Example: A straight wire carries a current of 5 A toward the top of the page (see Figure 69.3(a)). What are the magnitude and direction of the magnetic field at point P, which is 10 cm to the left of the wire? What are the magnitude and direction of the magnetic field at point Q, which is 2 cm to the right of the wire?

Figure 69.3

Solution: To find the magnitude of the magnetic field at point P:

$$B = \frac{\mu_0 I}{2\pi r}$$
$$= \frac{(4\pi \times 10^{-7})(5)}{2\pi(0.1)}$$
$$= 10^{-5} \text{ T} = 0.1 \text{ G}$$

To find the magnitude of the magnetic field at point Q:

$$B = \frac{(4\pi \times 10^{-7})(5)}{2\pi(0.02)}$$
$$= 5 \times 10^{-5} \text{ T} = 0.5 \text{ G}$$

To get the direction of the field for each of these points, use the right-hand rule. Hold the right thumb toward the top of the page. Now curl the fingers around the wire. At Q the fingers should point into the page. Keep curling around and notice that at point P the fingers come out of the page. (See Figure 69.3 (b).) This gives $\mathbf{B}_P = 0.1$ gauss pointing out of the page and $\mathbf{B}_Q = 0.5$ gauss pointing into the page. Note that, as the points move farther from the wire, the magnitude of magnetic field decreases.

The magnitude of the magnetic field at the center of a *circular* loop of current-carrying wire of radius r is:

$$B = \frac{\mu_0 I}{2r}$$

Notice that this is similar to the equation for a straight wire, in which r refers to the perpendicular distance from the wire and gives B for any point at that distance from the wire. However, in the case of the circular loop, r is the radius of the loop, and the expression gives the magnetic field at the loop's center point only. The same right-hand rule is used to find the direction of the magnetic field. Since the magnetic field forms a circle around the current, the field will always go opposite directions inside the loop compared to outside the loop.

Example: Suppose a wire is formed into a loop that carries current clockwise, as in Figure 69.4(a). Find the direction of the magnetic field produced by this loop:

a. within the loop.

b. outside of the loop.

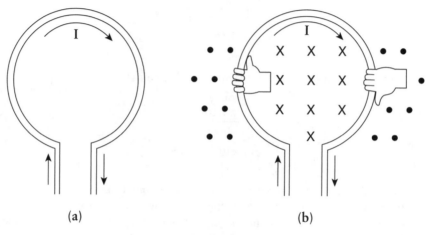

(a)   (b)

Figure 69.4

Solution: Figure 69.4(b) shows the orientation of the right hand and of the magnetic field. By holding the right thumb anywhere around the loop in the direction of current flow (clockwise) and encircling the wire with the remaining fingers of the right hand, the right-hand fingers point into the page inside of the loop. Thus, the magnetic field within the loop points into the page. The right-hand fingers point out of the page outside of the loop. Thus the magnetic field outside the loop points out of the page.

REVIEW PROBLEMS

1. A negative charge placed in an external magnetic field circulates counterclockwise in the plane of the paper as shown below. In which direction is the magnetic field pointing?

    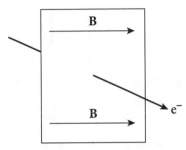

2. If, as in the accompanying figure, an electron is traveling straight out of the page crossing a magnetic field that is directed from left to right, in which direction will the electron be deflected?

3. A long, straight wire carrying current **I** is placed between the poles of a horseshoe magnet as shown in the figure below. Does the force on the wire depend on the width of the pole faces, and why or why not? Assume that the strength of the field is independent of the width of the pole faces.

    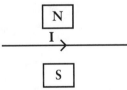

4. A long, straight wire carries a current from right to left as in the figure below.
    a. In what direction is the magnetic field pointing at A?
    b. In what direction is the magnetic field pointing at B?

    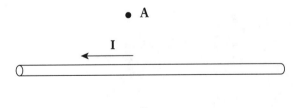

5. A long, straight wire carries a current of 5×10^{-4} A as shown in the figure below. A charged particle moving parallel to the wire experiences a force of 1×10^{-6} N at point P. Assuming the same charge and same velocity, what is the magnetic force on the charge at point R and at point S?

6. A positively charged particle enters a region with a uniform electric field, as shown, and is initially moving perpendicular to the field. In what direction must a uniform magnetic field be oriented so the net force on the particle is zero (assuming that the strength of the magnetic field can be appropriately adjusted)?

7. A circular loop of wire of radius 20 cm carries a current of 5.0 A. A positively charged particle with velocity perpendicular to the plane of the loop passes directly through the center of the loop. What is the force on the charged particle the instant it passes through the center?

8. A certain urban hospital wants to expand its radio-oncology department and will need a source of short-lived radioisotopes. A 6.5 MeV proton cyclotron is to be built but must fit into an existing 10×10 m room in the basement of the hospital. Assuming that the maximum magnetic field attainable is 1 T, can the hospital go ahead with its plans? (The mass of a proton is 1.67×10^{-27} kg, and the charge of a proton is $+1.6 \times 10^{-19}$ C.)

SOLUTIONS TO REVIEW PROBLEMS

1. **Out of the page**

   This problem is an application of the right-hand rule. The velocity vector **v** is always tangent to the circle. Since the question describes a negative charge, q**v** is also tangent to the circle but going clockwise the other way. The magnetic force is the centripetal force and points toward the center of the circle.

   Apply the directions of q**v** and **F** to the right-hand rule to find the direction of **B**. Pick a convenient point along the circular path. Using your right hand, put your thumb in the clockwise direction. **F** points toward the center of the circle, so orient your open palm toward the center. With your thumb pointing in the direction of q**v** and palm facing the center of the circle, find your remaining fingers pointing out of the page. Therefore, the direction of the magnetic field is out of the page.

2. **Downward**

   The problem asks only for the direction of deflection, so it will only be necessary to apply the right-hand rule to find the direction of the force. An electron travels straight out of the page, so **v** is out of the page, and q**v** is into the page (the electron has negative charge). Holding the thumb of your right hand into the page and your remaining fingers pointing toward the right, your palm, and therefore the force, points down.

3. **Yes, because the width of the pole faces determines the length of the wire in the magnetic field.**

   Recall that the force on a wire in a magnetic field is $F = ILB \sin \theta$, where L is the length of the wire in the magnetic field. The wider the pole faces, the larger is the region of space where the magnetic field exerts an appreciable force on the wire and thus the larger the value of L.

4. a. **Into the page**
   b. **Out of the page**

   Apply the right-hand rule for the direction of the magnetic field produced by a current-carrying wire. Let the thumb of the right hand point in the direction of the current—that is, from right to left. Now let the remaining fingers of the right hand curl around the wire. The fingers show the direction of the magnetic field lines. The direction of the magnetic field is tangent to the field line in the same direction. Hence, if your fingers point into the page or out of the page, the magnetic field is along the tangent line in the same direction. Therefore, the direction of the field is into the page at point A and out of the page at point B.

5. **1×10^{-6} N at point R and 0.5×10^{-6} N at point S**

    The magnetic force on a charge moving in the vicinity of the given wire is $F = qvB \sin \theta$, where B is given by the magnetic field of a straight wire and $B = \mu_o I/2\pi r$. Thus, F is inversely proportional to the distance between the charge and the wire. Since point R is the same distance from the wire as point P, the force at R is the same as at P. Point S is given to be twice as far from the wire as point P, so the magnetic force at S will be one-half the force at P.

6. **Out of the page**

    The positively charged particle will experience a force in the direction of the electric field pushing it toward the top of the page. Using the right-hand rule for magnetic forces on charged particles, you can see that a magnetic field coming out of the page will give a force toward the bottom of the page. Assuming that the strength of the magnetic field is appropriately set as stated in the question, the net force on the charged particle due to both the electric and magnetic fields will be zero.

7. **Zero**

    The magnetic field at the center of the loop is directed perpendicular to the plane of the loop. Thus, the particle's velocity is parallel to the magnetic field, which means that the field doesn't exert any force on the particle.

8. **Yes**

    This problem is asking whether the proposed cyclotron will fit in the room with the given dimensions. Assume that the protons in the cyclotron will orbit such that they are just contained by the room and then calculate the necessary field and see if it is feasible.

    For circular motion, the centripetal acceleration $a = v^2/r$. The centripetal force is the magnetic force $F = qvB \sin \theta$ where $\theta = 90°$; thus, $F = qvb$. From $F = ma$:

    $$qvB = \frac{mv^2}{r}$$

    Now solve for B:

    $$B = \frac{mv}{qr}$$

    To determine velocity, start with the energy of the proton:

    $$E = 6.5 \text{ MeV} = 6.5 \times 10^6 \text{ eV} = (6.5 \times 10^6 \text{ eV})(1.6 \times 10^{-19} \text{ J/eV}) = 1.04 \times 10^{-12} \text{ J.}$$

    Find v by using the definition of kinetic energy:

    $$\frac{1}{2}mv^2 = E$$
    $$v^2 = \frac{2E}{m}$$
    $$v = \sqrt{2E/m}$$

    The orbit diameter must fit into the 10×10 m room, so the orbit radius must be less than or equal to 5 m.

Combining the above expressions yields an upper limit to the required field:

$$B = \frac{mv}{qr}$$

$$= \frac{m}{qr}\sqrt{2E/m}$$

$$= \frac{\sqrt{2mE}}{qr}$$

$$= \frac{\sqrt{2(1.67 \times 10^{-27})(1.04 \times 10^{-12})}}{(1.6 \times 10^{-19})(5.0)}$$

$$= 0.074\ T$$

Since the maximum field needed is only 0.074 T, and the maximum field that can be generated is 1 T, it will be possible to go ahead with the project.

CHAPTER SEVENTY

Circuits

Electric circuits pervade our everyday world, powering the various necessities of modern-day living such as cell phones, TVs, and light fixtures. This chapter reviews the essentials of DC circuits, touching only briefly and qualitatively on the subject of AC circuits. Topics include emf, resistance, power dissipated by resistors, Kirchhoff's laws, resistors, capacitors, and dielectrics.

CIRCUIT COMPONENTS

An understanding of circuits begins with a short review of conductors and insulators, the essential materials of the wires of any circuit.

Some materials allow electric charge to move freely within the material. These materials are called electrical **conductors.** Metal atoms can easily lose one or more of their outer electrons, which are then free to move around in the metal. This makes most metals good electrical conductors. In most conductors the positive ions remain fixed, and the liberated electrons are free to move. In other materials electric charge is bound to the atoms and is not free to move. These materials severely retard the flow of electricity and are called **insulators.** Most nonmetals are good insulators.

For example, the wires connecting to most electrical devices have a core made of a conductor, such as copper, with an insulating sheath of plastic. The copper wire conducts the electricity to the device from the wall socket. The insulating sheath protects anyone from touching the wire and getting an electric shock.

DIRECT CURRENT

Current and Circuit Voltage

The flow of charge is called an **electric current.** The magnitude of the current, I (also sometimes written as i), is the amount of charge, Δq, passing a given point per unit time, Δt, and is given by:

$$I = \frac{\Delta q}{\Delta t}$$

The SI unit of current is the **ampere** (1 A = 1 coulomb/second). The two basic types of current flow are **direct current** (DC), in which the charge flows in one direction only, and **alternating current** (AC), in which the flow changes direction periodically. The OAT focuses on DC current, so AC current will be only briefly discussed at the end of this chapter for comparison.

When two points at different electric potentials are connected by a conductor such as a metal wire, charge flows between the two points. In a conductor, only negatively charged electrons are free to move. These act as the charge carriers and move from low to high potentials. By convention, however, the direction of the current is taken as the direction in which *positive* charge would flow, which is from high to low potential. Thus, the direction of current is opposite the direction of electron flow. Current flows from higher potential (the positive terminal of a battery) to lower potential (the negative terminal of a battery) in the same way that a mass will fall from higher to lower heights in a gravitational field.

A voltage (potential difference) can be produced by an electric generator, a voltaic cell, or a group of cells wired into a battery. **Electromotive force (emf or ε)** is the voltage across the terminals of a cell when no current is flowing. Despite its name, electromotive force is not actually a force and should not be confused with forces or electric fields; it is instead a potential difference and is measured in volts.

When a cell is supplying current it is **discharging**, and the current flows out of the positive terminal and into the negative terminal. When a cell is being **recharged**, current from another source is sent into the positive terminal. Ideally, a cell has no internal resistance, and all of the potential is available as ε. However, in the real world, a cell has an internal resistance, R_{int}, and the available voltage is decreased such that $V - IR_{int} = \varepsilon$. Thus, a real-world cell provides less voltage than an ideal cell.

Resistance

Resistance and Ohm's law

Resistance (R) can be thought of as the opposition to the flow of an electric current that occurs within a conductor. This opposition takes the form of an energy loss or drop in potential. **Ohm's law** states that the voltage drop across a resistor is proportional to the current it carries, with R being the proportionality constant known as resistance:

$$V = IR$$

This equation applies to a single resistor within a circuit, to any part of a circuit, or to an entire circuit. Note that the current is unchanged as it passes through the resistor since no charge is lost inside the resistor. The SI derived unit of electrical resistance is the **ohm (Ω)**.

Resistance of a conductor

The resistance of an object depends on its size, the type of material from which it is made, and its temperature. Resistance of a wire depends on three factors: length, cross-sectional area, and resistivity. These three factors give the following equation for resistance of a conductor:

$$R = \rho \frac{L}{A}$$

where R is resistance in ohms, L is the length in meters, A is the cross-sectional area in m^2, and ρ is the resistivity of the material. Temperature is also a factor in determining resistance.

Length (L)

Resistance is directly proportional to length of a wire. A longer conductor means greater resistance because there is a longer path that current-carrying electrons must travel. For example, consider two wires that are identical in every respect except that one is twice as long as the other. The longer wire will have twice the resistance of the shorter wire because the electrons need to travel twice as far.

Cross-sectional area (A)

The resistance of a conductor is inversely proportional to its cross-sectional area. An increase in cross-sectional area causes a decrease in resistance because there is an increase in the number of conduction paths electrons can follow. For example, consider two wires that are identical in every respect except that one has twice the cross-sectional area of the other. The thinner wire will have twice the resistance of the thicker wire.

Major home appliances such as ovens, washers, and dryers require large currents for their operation and so have very thick wires. Thicker wire means a larger cross-sectional area and a smaller resistance and thus a larger current for a given voltage.

Resistivity (ρ)

Some materials are intrinsically better conductors of electricity than others. For example, copper conducts electricity much better than glass does. The value that characterizes the intrinsic resistance to current flow in a material is called its **resistivity** (ρ), and the SI unit of resistivity is the ohm · meter. For example, consider two wires that are identical in every respect except that one has resistivity ρ that is twice the value compared to the other wire. The wire with the higher value of ρ will have twice the resistance of the wire with the smaller value of ρ. Thus, good conductors have low resistivities, whereas poor conductors are good insulators and have high resistivity values.

Temperature

Most conductors have greater resistance at higher temperatures. This is due to increased thermal oscillations of atoms in the conductor, which produce a greater resistance to electron flow. The resistivity is therefore a function of temperature. However, a few materials, such as glass, pure silicon, and most semiconductors are exceptions to this general rule.

Power dissipated by a resistor

Electric potential is defined in Chapter 68, Electrostatics, as electric potential energy per unit of positive charge. Since current is a flow of charge, a current-carrying resistor also has a **flow of energy.** In a resistor, this electric energy is converted into heat, light, or electrical work. Since power is defined as change in energy over change in time, the **rate** at which the energy conversion occurs is equal to the power dissipated by the resistor and is given by:

$$P = IV$$

where I is the current flowing through the resistor and V is the drop in electric potential across the resistor. Using Ohm's law this expression can be rewritten as:

$$P = I^2 R = \frac{V^2}{R}$$

PHYSICS

Circuit Laws

An electric circuit is a conducting path that usually has one or more voltage sources (such as a cell) connected to one or more **passive circuit elements** (such as resistors). A discussion of DC circuits deals primarily with voltages, resistances, and currents. Kirchhoff's laws provide an understanding of how these three factors are related to DC circuits.

Kirchhoff's laws

Kirchhoff's current (1st) law states that at any junction in a circuit the sum of currents directed into that point equals the sum of currents directed away from that point. This is a consequence of the conservation of electric charge.

Example: Three wires (a, b, and c) meet at a junction point P as in Figure 70.1. A current of 5 A flows into P along wire a, and a current of 3 A flows away from P along wire b. What is the magnitude and direction of the current along wire c?

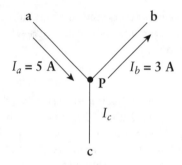

Figure 70.1

Solution: The sum of the currents entering P must equal the sum of the currents leaving P.

$$I_a = I_b + I_c$$
$$I_c = 5 - 3$$
$$I_c = 2 \text{ A}$$

Thus a current of 2 A flows **out** of P along wire c. Note that the total current into and out of P is then zero.

Kirchhoff's voltage (2nd) law states that the sum of voltage sources is equal to the sum of voltage (potential) drops around a closed circuit loop. This is a consequence of the conservation of energy, since voltage is energy per unit charge. All the electrical energy supplied by a source is fully used up by the resistors of the circuit. No excess energy appears or disappears. Energy is conserved in one complete loop of a circuit. Energy lost in the resistors is gained back in the battery.

Resistors in series

Kirchhoff's two laws provide the framework for understanding resistors in series. When resistors are wired in series, there is only one pathway for current to follow; thus, all resistors see the same current. Because the voltage must decrease from the positive terminal to the negative terminal, the voltage drop across each resistor must add up to the total voltage drop for the circuit. Therefore, resistances add in series:

$$R_s = R_1 + R_2 + R_3 + \dots + R_n$$

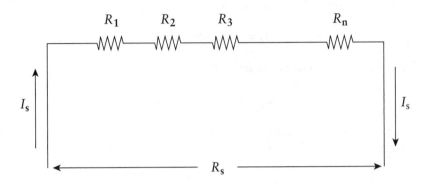

Figure 70.2

Example: The circuit below is wired with a battery supplying 5 V together with three resistors of 3 Ω, 5 Ω, and 7 Ω wired in series. What is the resulting voltage across, and current through, each resistor of this circuit, as well as for the entire circuit?

Solution: The total resistance of the resistors in series is:

$$R_s = R_1 + R_2 + R_3$$
$$= 3 + 5 + 7$$
$$= 15\ \Omega$$

Now use Ohm's law ($V = IR$) to find the current through the entire circuit. Since everything is in series, this is also the current through each resistor:

$$I_s = \frac{V_s}{R_s} = \frac{5}{15} = \frac{1}{3}\text{A}$$

Now use Ohm's law to determine the voltage drop for each of the resistors in turn. From a to b the voltage drop across R_1 is:

$$IR_1 = (1/3)(3) = 1.0 \text{ V}$$

From b to c the voltage drop across R_2 is:

$$IR_2 = (1/3)(5) = 1.67 \text{ V}$$

From c to d the voltage drop across R_3 is:

$$IR_3 = (1/3)(7) = 2.33 \text{ V}$$

Note that the three voltage drops across the three resistors adds to the total voltage of the battery:

$$1.0 + 1.67 + 2.33 = 5 \text{ V}$$

Resistors in parallel

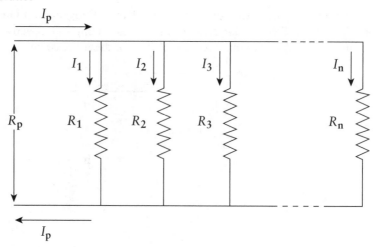

Figure 70.3

When resistors are wired in parallel, they are all wired with a common high-potential terminal and a common low-potential terminal (see Figure 70.3). The effect of **adding resistors in parallel** is the same as that of increasing the cross-sectional area of a conductor. This increases the paths by which current can flow and thereby **decreases resistance.**. Note that the voltage across each of the parallel resistors is equal, and that for equal resistances the current flowing through each of the resistors is also equal. For different resistors, the current must be calculated using Ohm's law, as shown below. The rule for combining resistances in parallel states that the reciprocal of the equivalent resistance equals the sum of the reciprocals of the individual parallel resistances:

$$\frac{1}{R_p} = \frac{1}{R_1} + \frac{1}{R_2} + \frac{1}{R_3} + \ldots + \frac{1}{R_n}$$

When resistors are in parallel, the voltage drop across each is the same and is equal to the voltage drop across the entire combination:

$$V_p = V_1 = V_2 = V_3 = \ldots = V_n$$

Example: Consider two identical resistors wired in parallel. What is the equivalent resistance of the two combined?

Solution: The equation for summing resistors in parallel is:

$$\frac{1}{R_p} = \frac{1}{R_1} + \frac{1}{R_2}$$

Find the common denominator of the right-hand side and take the inverse to find:

$$R_p = \frac{R_1 R_2}{(R_1 + R_2)}$$

Since $R_1 = R_2$ in this special case, let $R = R_1 = R_2$:

$$R_p = \frac{R^2}{2R} = \frac{R}{2}$$

In this example, the total resistance is halved by wiring two identical resistors in parallel.

More generally, when n identical resistors are wired in parallel, the total resistance is given by R/n. Equivalent resistance can also be calculated by substituting the values of each resistor and then combining the fractions; however, care must be taken to take the reciprocal of the result to determine the final equivalent resistance.

Example: Consider two resistors wired in parallel with $R_1 = 5\ \Omega$ and $R_2 = 10\ \Omega$. If the voltage across them is 10 V, what is the current through each of the two resistors?

Solution: First, the combined resistance must be determined:

$$\frac{1}{R_p} = \frac{1}{R_1} + \frac{1}{R_2} \qquad \text{OR} \qquad R_p = \frac{R_1 R_2}{(R_1 + R_2)}$$

$$= \frac{1}{10} + \frac{1}{5} \qquad\qquad\qquad R_p = \frac{(5)(10)}{(5+10)}$$

$$= \frac{3}{10} \qquad\qquad\qquad\qquad R_p = \frac{50}{15}\Omega = \frac{10}{3}\Omega$$

$$R_p = \frac{10}{3}\Omega$$

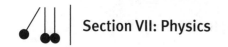

Using Ohm's law to calculate the current flowing through the circuit gives:

$$I_p = \frac{V_p}{R_p}$$

$$= \frac{10}{(10/3)}$$

$$= 3\,A$$

Three amps flow through the combination R_1 and R_2. Since the resistors are in parallel, $V_p = V_1 = V_2 = 10$ V. Apply Ohm's law to each resistor individually:

$$I_1 = \frac{V_p}{R_1} = \frac{10}{5} = 2A$$

$$I_2 = \frac{V_p}{R_2} = \frac{10}{10} = 1A$$

As a check, note that $I_p = 3$ A $= I_1 + I_2 = 2 + 1 = 3$ A. More current flows through the smaller resistance. In particular note that R_1, with half the resistance of R_2, has twice the current. Once I_p was found to be 3 A, the problem could have been solved by noting that because R_1 is half of R_2, $I_1 = 2I_2$, and $I_1 + I_2 = 3$ A. In general, $V_p = I_1 R_1 = I_2 R_2$, which demonstrates that there is a reciprocal relationship between current and resistance; as resistance increases, current decreases, and as resistance decreases, current increases.

Capacitors and Dielectrics

Capacitors and dielectrics are means of storing charge in a circuit based on a voltage difference between two parallel plates. Dielectrics are insulating materials that increase the ability of a capacitor to store charge.

Capacitors and capacitance

When two electrically neutral plates of metal are connected to a voltage source, positive charge builds up on the plate connected to the positive terminal and an equal amount of negative charge builds up on the plate connected to the negative terminal. The two-plate system stores charge and is called a **capacitor**. It is important to remember that charge collects on a capacitor any time there is a potential difference between the plates. The **capacitance (C)** of a capacitor is defined as the ratio of charge stored to the total potential difference across the capacitor. If a voltage difference V is applied across the plates of the capacitor and a charge Q collects on it (with $+Q$ on the positive plate and $-Q$ on the negative plate), then the capacitance is given by:

$$C = \frac{Q}{V}$$

The SI unit of capacitance is the **farad** (where 1 F = 1 C/V). Because one coulomb is such a large amount of charge, one farad is a very large capacitance. Capacitances are therefore quoted in submultiples of the farad such as microfarads (1 μF $= 10^{-6}$ F), nanofarads (1 nF $= 10^{-9}$ F), or picofarads (1 pF $= 10^{-12}$ F). Note also that the farad should not be confused with the faraday, the unit of charge equal to one mole of elementary charges (1 faraday $= 9.65 \times 10^4$ C).

The capacitance of a capacitor is dependent on the geometry of the two conducting surfaces. For the simple case of the parallel plate capacitor, the capacitance is given by:

$$C = \varepsilon_0 \frac{A}{d}$$

where ε_0 is the **permittivity of free space** ($\varepsilon_0 = 8.85 \times 10^{-12}$ F/m), A is the area of overlap of the two plates, and d is the separation of the two plates. The separation of charges sets up an electric field between the plates of the capacitor. The electric field between the plates of a parallel plate capacitor is a uniform field whose magnitude at any point is given by:

$$E = \frac{V}{d}$$

This equation can often be more easily remembered in the form $V = Ed$. The direction of the electric field at any point between the plates is toward the negative plate and away from the positive plate.

Dielectric materials

When an insulating material (such as glass, plastic, or certain metal oxides) is placed between the plates of a charged-up capacitor that is disconnected from its source of charge, the voltage across the capacitor decreases. Such insulating materials are called **dielectrics.** By lowering the voltage across the charged-up capacitor the dielectric has "made room for" even more charge; hence, the capacitance of the capacitor is increased. Dielectric materials are characterized by a dimensionless number called the **dielectric constant k,** which tells by what factor the capacitance of a capacitor is increased:

$$C' = kC$$

where C' is the new capacitance with the dielectric, and C is the original capacitance.

Example: The voltage across the terminals of an isolated 3 μF capacitor is 4 V. If a piece of ceramic having dielectric constant $k = 2$ is placed between the plates, find:

    a. the new charge on the capacitor.

    b. the new capacitance of the capacitor.

    c. the new voltage across the capacitor.

Solution: a. The introduction of a dielectric by itself has no effect on the charge stored on the isolated capacitor, as the capacitor has been disconnected from any source of additional charge. The charge stored is therefore given by:

$$\begin{aligned}
Q' &= Q \\
&= CV \\
&= (3 \times 10^{-6})(4) \\
&= 12 \times 10^{-6} \text{ C} \\
&= 12 \ \mu\text{C}
\end{aligned}$$

b. By introducing a dielectric with a value of 2, the capacitance of the capacitor is doubled ($C' = kC$). Hence the new capacitance is $C' = 2(3) = 6\ \mu\text{F}$.

c. Using the relationship $V' = Q'/C'$, the new voltage across the capacitor may be determined. Putting numbers into the equation gives:

$$V' = \frac{12 \times 10^{-6}}{6 \times 10^{-6}}$$
$$= 2\ \text{V}$$

Example: The voltage across the terminals of a 3 μF capacitor is 4 V. Now suppose a piece of ceramic having dielectric constant $k = 2$ is placed between the plates and the voltage is held constant (e.g., by keeping the capacitor connected to a battery). What is the new charge on the capacitor?

Solution: By introducing the dielectric ceramic, the capacitance of the capacitor has been altered. But because the voltage was held constant, the charge on the capacitor plates must have been altered. From the definition of dielectric constant the new capacitance is:

$$C' = kC$$
$$= 6\ \mu\text{F}$$

However, the new voltage is still 4 V, so the new charge must be:

$$Q' = C'V'$$
$$= (6 \times 10^{-6})(4)$$
$$= 24 \times 10^{-6}\ \text{C}$$
$$= 24\ \mu\text{C}$$

Since the original charge was $Q = CV = (3 \times 10^{-6})(4) = 12\ \mu$C, by keeping the voltage constant the battery had to supply an additional $+12\ \mu$C of charge to the positive plate and $-12\ \mu$C to the negative plate.

Capacitors in parallel

When wired in parallel, capacitors can be added directly. Capacitors wired in parallel can be thought of as combining to form a single larger capacitor with increased overlapping area and increased capacitance. Since the wire from one capacitor to the next is a conductor and an equipotential surface, the potential of all the plates on one side are the same (see Figure 70.4).

$$C_\text{p} = C_1 + C_2 + C_3 + \ldots + C_\text{n}$$

The voltage across each parallel capacitor is the same, and is equal to the voltage across the entire combination:

$$V_\text{p} = V_1 = V_2 = V_3 = \ldots = V_\text{n}$$

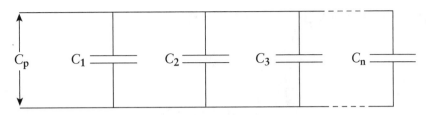

Figure 70.4

Capacitors in series

When wired in series, the total voltage drop across a series of capacitors must add up to the total voltage drop for the circuit. Each additional capacitor added in series decreases the total capacitance of the circuits. Just as for resistors in parallel, the reciprocal of the total capacitance in series is equal to the sum of the reciprocals of the individual capacitances (see Figure 70.5).

$$\frac{1}{C_s} = \frac{1}{C_1} + \frac{1}{C_2} + \frac{1}{C_3} + \ldots + \frac{1}{C_n}$$

For capacitors in series, the total voltage is the sum of the individual voltages:

$$V_s = V_1 + V_2 + V_3 + \ldots + V_n$$

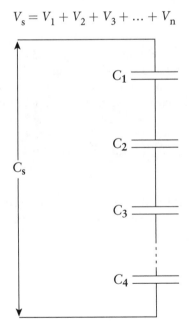

Figure 70.5

A SUMMARY OF CIRCUIT ELEMENT ADDITION

Series

$$R_s = R_1 + R_2 + R_3 + ... + R_n$$

$$\frac{1}{C_s} = \frac{1}{C_1} + \frac{1}{C_2} + \frac{1}{C_3} + ... + \frac{1}{C_n}$$

Parallel

$$\frac{1}{R_p} = \frac{1}{R_1} + \frac{1}{R_2} + \frac{1}{R_3} + ... + \frac{1}{R_n}$$

$$C_p = C_1 + C_2 + C_3 + ... + C_n$$

ALTERNATING CURRENT

Although alternating current is rarely tested on the OAT, the brief review below gives insight into the most important elements of this topic.

Alternating Current

Alternating current (AC) changes its direction of flow periodically. The most common form of AC current oscillates in a sinusoidal wave, as shown in Figure 70.7. Note that for half of the cycle the current flows in one direction, and for the other half of the cycle the current flows in the opposite direction; therefore the sign of the current alternates between positive and negative. Such a current can be described by the equation

$$i = I_{max} \sin (2\pi f t)$$
$$= I_{max} \sin \omega t$$

where i is the instantaneous current at the time t, I_{max} is the maximum current, f is the frequency, and $\omega = 2\pi f$ is the angular frequency. The most common sinusoidal current is the ordinary AC house current that oscillates with a frequency of 60 Hz in the U.S and Canada.

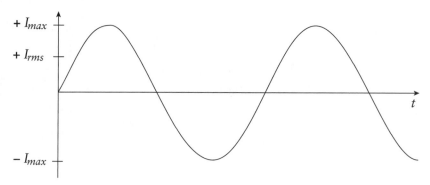

Figure 70.6

RMS Current

In AC circuits the magnitude of the current varies from a maximum positive value to a minimum negative value. A problem arises when calculating the average current for AC circuits: For one cycle, the sum of the positive current flowing in one direction is exactly canceled by the sum of the negative current that flows in the other direction. Yet the AC current exists; it delivers power. Consider the power dissipated in a resistor R that carries an AC current I. It is given by the equation $P = I^2 R$; the square of the current is a positive number. This makes it possible to find the average power dissipated over one cycle. This can then be used to determine I_{rms}^2 where I_{rms} is the root-mean-square (rms) current given by:

$$I_{rms} = \frac{I_{max}}{\sqrt{2}}$$

Example: What is the rms current of an AC circuit that will produce a maximum current of 1.00 A?

Solution:

$$I_{rms} = \frac{I_{max}}{\sqrt{2}}$$
$$= \frac{1.00}{\sqrt{2}}$$
$$= \frac{1.00}{1.41}$$
$$= 0.71 \text{ A}$$

RMS Voltage

Voltage in AC circuits, like current, is sinusoidal and changes sign back and forth over time. Just as for current, it is possible to calculate **rms voltage:**

$$V_{rms} = \frac{V_{max}}{\sqrt{2}}$$

Example: The AC current used in a home is frequently called "120 V AC." Assuming that this refers to the rms voltage, what is the maximum voltage?

Solution: Using the above equation gives the following:

$$V_{max} = \sqrt{2} V_{rms}$$
$$= \sqrt{2}(120)$$
$$= 170 \text{ V}$$

REVIEW PROBLEMS

1. If a current of 1.0 A flows through a circuit for 5.0 s, how much charge has flowed?

2. A charge of 2 μC flows from the positive terminal of a 6 V battery, through a 100 Ω resistor, and back through the battery to the positive terminal. What is the total voltage drop experienced by the charge?

3. If the resistance of two conductors of equal cross-sectional area and equal lengths are compared, it is found that they are in the ratio 1:2. The resistivities of the materials from which they are constructed must therefore be in what ratio?

4. A DC battery is connected to a circuit containing a number of resistors in series. The connecting wire has a nonnegligible resistance and can thus be treated as another resistor in the series. How is the current through the circuit affected if the original connecting wire is replaced with wire that is thicker but made from the same material?

5. A transformer is a device that takes an input voltage and produces an output voltage that can be either larger or smaller than the input voltage depending on the transformer design. Although the voltage is changed by the transformer, energy is not, so the input power equals the output power. A particular transformer produces an output voltage that is 300% of the input voltage. What is the ratio of the output current to the input current?

6. Given three identical resistors, find:
   a. the ratio of total resistance for the three resistors connected in series compared to the resistance of an individual resistor.
   b. the ratio of the total resistance for the three resistors connected in parallel compared to the resistance of an individual resistor.

7. For the circuit shown below, how is the total current through the circuit affected if a third resistor is added in parallel with the 2 Ω and 2/3 Ω resistors?

8. A parallel plate capacitor is fully charged and then disconnected from the charging source. Assuming that the charge on the plates remains fixed, is work required to increase the separation between the plates?

9. Given three identical capacitors, find:

    a. the ratio of total capacitance for the three capacitors connected in series compared to the capacitance of an individual capacitor.

    b. the ratio when the three are connected in parallel.

10. The circuit shown below consists of an AC voltage source in series with a $1/2\ \Omega$ resistor. The current through the resistor is also shown in the graph below. At time $t = 0$, the current flows clockwise around the circuit. In which direction, clockwise or counterclockwise, does the current flow at $t = 1/120\,\text{s}$?

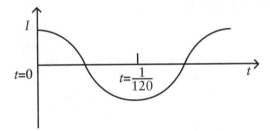

11. The energy stored in a fully charged capacitor is given by $E = (1/2)CV^2$. In a typical cardiac defibrillator, a capacitor charged to 7,500 V has a stored energy of 400 W·s. If the charge Q and voltage V on a capacitor are related by $Q = CV$, what is the charge on the capacitor in the cardiac defibrillator?

12. A 10.0 Ω resistor carries a current that varies as a function of time as shown below. What energy has been dissipated by the resistor after 5 s?

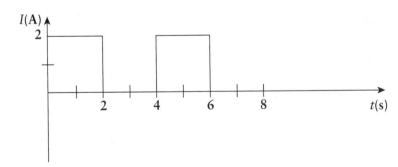

SOLUTIONS TO REVIEW PROBLEMS

1. **5.0 C**

$$\Delta q = I\Delta t$$
$$= 1.0\,(5.0)$$
$$= 5.0\,\text{C}$$

2. **Zero**

Kirchhoff's second law states that the total voltage drop around a complete circuit loop is zero. Another way of saying this is that the voltage lost through the resistors is gained in going through the battery so the net change in voltage is zero. Since voltage is electric potential energy per unit charge, this is also equivalent to saying that the amount of potential energy lost by the charge in going through the resistor is gained back when the charge goes through the battery.

3. **1:2**

The resistance of a resistive material is given by:

$$R = \frac{\rho L}{A}$$

For two different materials:

$$R_1 = \frac{\rho_1 L_1}{A_1}$$

$$R_2 = \frac{\rho_2 L_2}{A_2}$$

From the information given in the problem, $A_1 = A_2$, $L_1 = L_2$, and $R_1:R_2 = 1:2$; therefore, $\rho_1:\rho_2 = 1:2$. (Resistance is directly proportional to resistivity.)

4. **The current increases.**

The current in a series circuit is proportional to the emf of the battery and inversely proportional to the total resistance of the circuit. From the equation $R = \rho L/A$ we see that thicker wire will mean larger cross-sectional area A, which will in turn mean that the resistance of the wire will decrease. Since the wire is in series with the other resistors, the total resistance of the circuit will decrease, resulting in a larger current.

5. $\dfrac{1}{3}$

We are told that transformers conserve energy so that the output power equals the input power. Thus $P_{out} = P_{in}$, where $P_{out} = I_{out}V_{out}$, and $P_{in} = I_{in}V_{in}$. So $I_{out}V_{out} = I_{in}V_{in}$, which means that $\dfrac{I_{out}}{I_{in}} = \dfrac{V_{in}}{V_{out}}$. Given that $\dfrac{V_{in}}{V_{out}} = \dfrac{1}{3}$ we find that $\dfrac{I_{out}}{I_{in}} = \dfrac{1}{3}$.

6. a. **3:1**

    The total resistance for three resistors in series is given by:

    $$R_{tot} = R_1 + R_2 + R_3$$
    $$= R + R + R$$
    $$= 3R$$

    Therefore:

    $$\mathbf{R_{tot}} = 3R$$

    The ratio of total resistance to the resistance of an individual resistor is 3:1.

    b. **1:3**

    Using the equation for three resistors in parallel:

    $$\frac{1}{R_{tot}} = \frac{1}{R_1} + \frac{1}{R_2} + \frac{1}{R_3}$$
    $$= \frac{3}{R}$$
    $$R_{tot} = \frac{R}{3}$$

    Therefore the ratio of the total resistance to the resistance of an individual resistor is 1:3.

7. **The total current increases.**

    The total current in the circuit is inversely proportional to the total resistance of the circuit. If a third resistor is added in parallel with the 2 Ω and 2/3 Ω resistors, the effective resistance of the parallel resistors will decrease. The reason is that $1/R_{eff} = 1/R_1 + 1/R_2 + \ldots$ so that adding another resistor means that $1/R_{eff}$ will increase, which means that R_{eff} will decrease. The total resistance in the circuit shown is $1/2\ \Omega + R_{eff}$, so a decrease in R_{eff} means a decrease in the total resistance. A decrease in the total resistance then means an increase in the total current.

8. **Yes**

    A fully charged parallel plate capacitor has a charge $+Q$ on one plate and a charge $-Q$ on the other. The positive and negative plates thus attract each other because of the electrostatic force. In order to increase the plate separation, work must be done against this attractive force.

9. a. **1:3**

    Using the equation for three capacitors arranged in series:

    $$\frac{1}{C_{tot}} = \frac{1}{C_1} + \frac{1}{C_2} + \frac{1}{C_3}$$
    $$= \frac{1}{C} + \frac{1}{C} + \frac{1}{C}$$
    $$= \frac{3}{C}$$

PHYSICS

Therefore:

$$C_{tot} = \frac{C}{3}$$

The ratio of the total capacitance to the capacitance of an individual capacitor is 1:3.

b. **3:1**

The total capacitance for three identical capacitors in parallel is given by:

$$C_{tot} = C_1 + C_2 + C_3 = 3C$$

The ratio of the total capacitance to the capacitance of an individual capacitor is 3:1.

10. **Counterclockwise**

In an AC circuit the current alternates between positive and negative values. A negative current simply means that the charges flow in the direction opposite to the positive current direction. Thus if the current flows clockwise at $t = 0$, it will flow counterclockwise at $t = 1/120$ s. The reason for the switch in current direction is that the voltage also alternates between positive and negative values. Essentially, a negative voltage means that the positive and negative poles of the voltage source have interchanged places, causing the current to flow in the opposite direction.

11. **0.11 C**

$$Q = CV$$
$$E = \frac{CV^2}{2}$$
$$\frac{Q}{E} = \frac{2}{V}$$
$$Q = \frac{2E}{V}$$
$$= \frac{2 \times 400}{7,500}$$
$$= 0.11 \, C$$

12. **120 J**

Power is energy dissipated per unit time, therefore energy dissipated is:

$$E = Pt$$

The power dissipated in a resistor R carrying a current I is:

$$P = I^2 R$$

Therefore, the energy dissipated in the first 2 s is:

$$E = I^2 Rt$$
$$= (2)^2(10)(2)$$
$$= 80 \, J$$

The energy dissipated in the next 2 s is zero, since there is no current, and therefore no power is dissipated. The energy dissipated during the one-second interval from $t = 4$ s to $t = 5$ s is:

$$E = I^2Rt$$
$$= (2)^2(10)(1)$$
$$= 40 \text{ J}$$

The total energy dissipated is therefore:

$$80 + 40 = 120 \text{ J}$$

CHAPTER SEVENTY-ONE

Simple Harmonic Motion and Waves

Harmonic motion shows repetitive movement of some kind. There are many different examples of harmonic motion in the natural world, from the waves of water in the ocean to the waves of light that allow us to see to the waves of sound that bring music to our ears. This chapter will first lay the foundation for understanding wave phenomena by reviewing the subject of simple harmonic motion. General properties of waves are then introduced, including the concepts of amplitude, wavelength, frequency, wave speed, and resonance. The superposition of two waves is discussed along with the related concepts of constructive versus destructive interference and the production of standing waves. Finally, the subject of sound is briefly reviewed as it relates to harmonic motion.

SIMPLE HARMONIC MOTION

Uniform Circular Motion

Consider a particle moving around a circular path at constant speed. The time it takes for the particle to complete one revolution is the **period** (T) in seconds. The number of cycles the particle makes in a given time period is the **frequency** (f) in cycles/second, which is often shown as s^{-1} or Hz. The frequency is converted to **angular frequency** (ω) by multiplying it by 2π, the number of radians in a circle. Angular frequency is the change in angle per time described by the particle's path as it moves around the circle. These variables are all related as follows:

$$\omega = 2\pi f = 2\pi/T$$

If the particle's path is projected onto a line adjacent to the circle (Figure 71.1), the particle's position oscillates between $+X$ and $-X$. This is the basis for most types of simple harmonic motion.

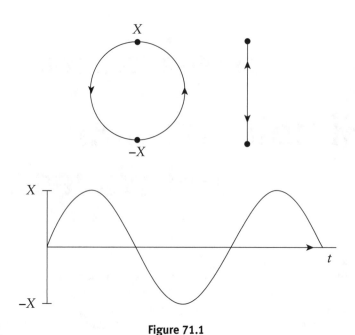

Figure 71.1

Simple Harmonic Motion

In **simple harmonic motion (SHM)**, an object oscillates back and forth from an equilibrium point with an angular frequency ω and is subject to a linear restoring force. A linear restoring force has two characteristics: It is always directed back toward the equilibrium position, and its magnitude is directly proportional to the displacement from the equilibrium position. By Newton's second law, the particle's acceleration **a** is also proportional to the displacement from equilibrium:

$$\mathbf{F} = -k\mathbf{x}$$
$$\mathbf{a} = -\omega^2\mathbf{x}$$

where the angular frequency ω is given by:

$$\omega = \sqrt{k/m} = 2\pi f$$

The negative signs in these equations demonstrate that the force and the acceleration are opposite to the direction of the particle's displacement from equilibrium. Maximum acceleration occurs at maximum force, and maximum force occurs at maximum displacement.

Two examples of simple harmonic motion are a mass attached to a spring and a simple pendulum. A stretched or compressed spring exerts a linear restoring force, where the constant k is called the **spring constant** (or force constant), and the equation $\mathbf{F} = -k\mathbf{x}$ is called **Hooke's Law.** The spring constant k is a measure of the stiffness of the spring; a larger value of k means a stronger spring, and a smaller value of k means a less-resistant spring. Figure 71.2(a) shows a spring–mass system with the mass at the equilibrium position. Figure 71.2(b) shows the same system when the mass has a displacement of $\mathbf{x}_1$.

Similarly, in the case of a simple pendulum, $k = mg/L$ where m is the mass and L is the length of the pendulum. Combining this with the formula for angular frequency gives:

$$\omega = \sqrt{\frac{k}{m}} = \sqrt{\frac{\frac{mg}{L}}{m}} = \sqrt{\frac{g}{L}} = 2\pi f$$

For pendulums, the angular frequency is related to acceleration due to gravity g and the length of the pendulum L. Note that neither the mass of the pendulum nor the angle of displacement from the vertical affects the angular frequency.

Figure 71.2(c) shows a simple pendulum displaced at an angle θ from the vertical.

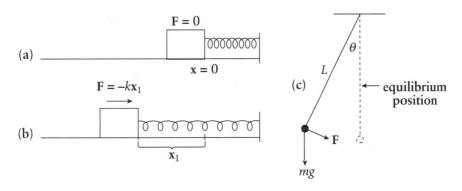

Figure 71.2

For either a spring or a pendulum, position can be plotted against time on a graph. Let A be the particle's amplitude, defined as the maximum distance x from the equilibrium position. Starting so the particle is at $\mathbf{x} = 0$ at $t = 0$, the equation that describes the particle's displacement $\mathbf{x}$ is:

$$\mathbf{x} = A \sin (\omega t)$$

where t is the time and ω is the angular frequency. This results in the sinusoidal wave shown in Figure 71.1, which shows the plot of position versus time. Note that the amplitude is independent of angular frequency and thus also independent of frequency and period.

Another consideration in SHM is energy. In an ideal system, the forces are conservative and the system is frictionless. Thus, the conservation of energy gives:

$$E = K + U = \text{constant}$$

where K is the kinetic energy and U is the potential energy. Kinetic energy for both the mass attached to the spring and the pendulum mass is given by:

$$K = \frac{1}{2}mv^2$$

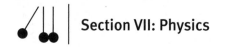

For the pendulum, the potential energy is the gravitational potential energy (mgh) as it swings up. For the spring, the potential energy is given by:

$$U = \frac{1}{2}kx^2$$

When the mass is at the equilibrium position, the potential energy is zero, and the kinetic energy is a maximum given by $E = K_{max}$. However, when the oscillation reaches its maximum displacement, the mass has zero speed. At this point the kinetic energy is zero, and the potential energy is a maximum given by $E = U_{max} = \frac{1}{2}kA^2$ where A is the amplitude.

The chart below summarizes the mass–spring system and the simple pendulum and shows the similarities between them.

	Mass–spring	Simple pendulum
force constant k	spring constant k	mg/L
period T	$2\pi\sqrt{\dfrac{m}{k}}$	$2\pi\sqrt{\dfrac{L}{g}}$
ang. freq. ω	$\sqrt{\dfrac{k}{m}}$	$\sqrt{\dfrac{g}{L}}$
frequency f	$\dfrac{1}{T}$ or $\dfrac{\omega}{2\pi}$	$\dfrac{1}{T}$ or $\dfrac{\omega}{2\pi}$
kinetic energy K	$\frac{1}{2}mv^2$	$\frac{1}{2}mv^2$
K_{max} occurs at	$x = 0$	$\theta = 0$ (vertical position)
potential energy U	$\frac{1}{2}kx^2$	mgh
U_{max} occurs at	$x = \pm A$	max value of θ
max acceleration at	$x = \pm A$	max value of θ

Example: What is the length of a pendulum that has a period of 1 second?

Solution: Use the equation for the period of a simple pendulum to find the length:

$$T = 2\pi\sqrt{\frac{L}{g}}$$

Squaring both sides and rearranging gives:

$$L = \frac{T^2 g}{4\pi^2}$$
$$= \frac{g}{4\pi^2}$$
$$= 0.25 \text{ m}$$

GENERAL WAVE CHARACTERISTICS

Transverse and Longitudinal Waves

Waves can be divided into two basic groups based on their geometry. **In transverse waves** the particles oscillate perpendicular to the direction of the wave motion, as shown in Figure 71.3(a). The oscillating string elements are moving at right angles to the direction of travel of the wave. In **longitudinal waves** the particles oscillate along the direction of the wave motion, as illustrated in Figure 71.3(b). The longitudinal wave created by the person moving the piston back and forth consists of oscillating air molecules that move parallel to the direction of motion of the wave.

(a)

(b)

Figure 71.3

Describing Waves

The displacement **y** of a particle may be plotted at each point x along the direction of the wave's motion. It is given mathematically by:

$$\mathbf{y} = A \sin (k\mathbf{x} - \omega t)$$

where A is the amplitude (maximum displacement), k is the wave number (not to be mistaken with the k of Hooke's law), ω is the angular frequency, and t is the time. Plotting this function gives the familiar sine wave associated with waves and harmonic motion.

The distance from one maximum (crest) of the wave to the next is the wavelength, λ. The frequency f is the number of wavelengths passing a fixed point per second measured in cycles per second (cps), s^{-1}, or hertz (Hz). The speed of the wave v is related to the frequency and wavelength by a small but important equation:

$$v = f\lambda$$

The wave number k is related to ω:

$$k = \frac{2\pi}{\lambda}$$

$$\omega = 2\pi f = \frac{2\pi}{T}$$

where the period T is the time for the wave to move one wavelength ($f = 1/T$). Combining these formulas into the equation for velocity gives:

$$\upsilon = f\lambda = \frac{\omega}{k} = \frac{\lambda}{T}$$

Example: If a wave on a string were described by the equation $y = (0.01) \sin (2x - 10t)$, find the frequency, wavelength, and speed of the wave. (Assume units of meters and seconds.)

Solution: Work from the wave equation $y = A \sin (kx - \omega t) = (0.01) \sin(2x - 10t)$. This gives A = amplitude = 0.01 m, k = wave number = 2, and ω = angular frequency = 10. Since angular frequency $\omega = 2\pi f$:

$$f = \frac{\omega}{2\pi}$$

$$= \frac{5}{\pi}$$

$$= 1.59 \text{ Hz}$$

The wavelength is given by:

$$k = \frac{2\pi}{\lambda}$$

$$\lambda = \frac{2\pi}{k}$$

$$= 2\pi/2$$

$$= \pi$$

$$= 3.14 \text{ m}$$

and the speed by:

$$v = f\lambda$$

$$= \left(\frac{5}{\pi}\right)\pi$$

$$= 5 \text{ m/s}$$

Phase

Two similar waves often show a **phase difference.** This phase difference describes how aligned two waves are with each other. Consider two separate waves that have the same frequency, amplitude, and wavelength. If the waves are perfectly in phase, the maxima and minima of each wave coincide. In this case the phase difference is zero. However, if the two waves are out of phase, then one wave is shifted with respect to the other by some fraction of a cycle. This phase difference is usually expressed as an angle. In Figure 71.4(a), waves y_1 and y_2 are nearly in phase; their phase difference is approximately $0°$. In Figure 71.4(b), wave y_2 is shifted nearly one-half wavelength with respect to y_1. The phase difference in this case is almost $180°$.

Principle of Superposition

The principle of superposition states that when waves interact with each other the result is a sum of the waves. When the waves are in phase, the amplitudes add together (**constructive interference**), but when waves are $180°$ out of phase, the resultant amplitude is the difference between interacting amplitudes (**destructive interference**). Figures 71.4(a) and (b) show the interference between two waves when they are nearly in phase and when they are nearly $180°$ out of phase.

Figure71.4(a)

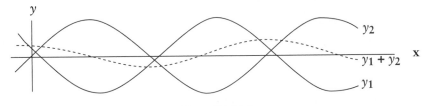

Figure 71.4(b)

Traveling and Standing Waves

If a string fixed at one end is moved from side to side, a wave propagates down the string. Such a wave is known as a **traveling wave.** When the wave reaches the fixed boundary, it is reflected and inverted (see Figure 71.5). If the free end of the string is continuously moved from side to side, then there will then be two waves: the original wave moving down the string and the reflected wave moving the other way. These waves will then interfere with each other.

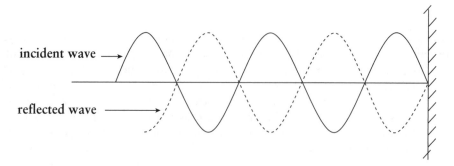

incident wave →

reflected wave →

Figure 71.5

Consider now a situation in which both ends of the string are fixed and traveling waves are excited in the string. Certain wave frequencies can result in a waveform remaining in a stationary position while the amplitude fluctuates. These waves are known as **standing waves.** Points in the wave that remain at rest are known as **nodes,** and points that are midway between these nodes are known as **antinodes.** Antinodes are points that fluctuate with maximum amplitude. It is also possible to set up standing waves in pipes in much the same way as in a string.

For strings, pipes that are closed at both ends, and pipes that are open at both ends, standing waves are described by the equations:

$$\lambda = \frac{2L}{n} \qquad (n = 1, 2, 3, \ldots)$$

$$f = \frac{nv}{2L} \qquad (n = 1, 2, 3, \ldots)$$

For pipes that are closed at one end and open at the other, the equations are:

$$\lambda = \frac{4L}{n} \qquad (n = 1, 3, 5, \ldots \text{odd integers only})$$

$$f = \frac{nv}{4L} \qquad (n = 1, 3, 5, \ldots \text{odd integers only})$$

In these equations, n is the *harmonic* and is related to the wavelength and number of nodes.

Resonance

In any oscillatory system there will be one or more **natural frequencies** (normal modes) of vibration; the system will oscillate at one of these natural frequencies if there are no external forces involved. However, if a periodically varying force is applied to the system, the system will then be driven at a frequency equal to the frequency of the force. This is known as a **forced oscillation.** The amplitude of this motion will generally be small. However, if the frequency of the applied force is close to that of the natural frequency of the system, then the amplitude will be much larger. In fact, if the frequency of the periodically varying force is equal to a natural frequency of the system, then the system is said to be **resonating,** and the amplitude of the oscillation is a maximum. This type of oscillation has been known to destroy suspension bridges when the wind exerts enough force at the right frequency on a bridge to cause resonance, amplifying the force and potentially leading to destruction.

SOUND

Sound is a longitudinal wave that can be transmitted through solids, liquids, and gases but not through a vacuum. Sound travels faster in a solid than in a liquid and faster in a liquid than in a gas.

For humans, detectable sound waves are called **audible waves** and have frequencies ranging from 20 Hz to 20,000 Hz. Waves with frequencies below 20 Hz are called **infrasonic waves,** and those with frequencies above 20,000 Hz are called **ultrasonic waves.** In air at 0°C, the speed of sound is 331 m/s.

Characteristics of Sound

Intensity is defined as the power transported per unit area by a sound wave. In SI it has units of W/m^2. The amplitude of the sound wave is a measure of its energy. The total power P carried across a surface area (such as an eardrum) is:

$$P = IA$$

where I is the intensity of the wave and A is the surface area.

The intensity of sound is often expressed as a ratio known as the **decibel**, which is defined as:

$$\beta = 10 \log \frac{I}{I_0}$$

where I_0 is a reference intensity of 10^{-12} W/m^2, corresponding to the faintest sound that can be heard by humans. Another characteristic of sound is **pitch.** This is a change in the frequency of a sound wave that enables the hearer to recognize a change in a musical note.

Production of Sound

For sound to be produced, there must be a longitudinal oscillation of the medium the sound is traveling through, such as air molecules. This oscillation can be produced by the vibration of a solid object that sets adjacent air molecules into motion or by means of an acoustic vibration in an enclosed space. Sound can also be transmitted through a solid such as the Earth or a liquid such as the ocean, as in the case of an earthquake. In general, sound travels fastest through solids, slower in liquids, and slowest in gases. Within the same medium, the speed of sound is proportional to the stiffness, pressure, and temperature of a material but inversely proportional to its density. All of these factors can be summarized as the elasticity of a material; substances that are able to easily distort to absorb sound waves cause the sound waves to move more slowly, whereas substances that are rigid transmit the sound wave more quickly because they cannot easily absorb the sound and instead quickly transmit it.

REVIEW PROBLEMS

1. Two blocks of equal mass hang respectively from two different springs. The weight of the blocks causes spring 1 to stretch by 5 cm and spring 2 to stretch by 10 cm. Which spring has the greater spring constant?

2. Masses M_a and M_b hang respectively from two identical springs A and B. What is the ratio of M_a to M_b if the period of oscillation of spring A is twice that of spring B?

3. A mass is attached to a horizontal spring and allowed to move horizontally on a frictionless surface. The mass is displaced from equilibrium and released.

    a. At what point does the mass experience the minimum force from the spring?
    b. At what point does the mass experience its maximum acceleration?

4. A pendulum has a period of 1 s on the surface of the Earth. How is this period affected if the same pendulum is operated on the surface of the moon, where the acceleration due to gravity is less?

5. A traveling sinusoidal wave is described by $y = (0.006) \sin(67.7x - 1.71t)$. Assume units of meters and seconds. Find the:

    a. amplitude.
    b. wavelength.
    c. period.
    d. frequency.
    e. speed.

6. A water wave with a period of 4 s is traveling toward shore. A point of zero amplitude passes a stationary swimmer at time $t = 0$. How long does the swimmer have to wait for the next point of zero amplitude, assuming that the swimmer remains stationary?

7. A battery-powered motor drives a pendulum at its natural frequency in order to ensure that the pendulum swings at a constant rate. If the same motor is to be used on a longer pendulum, should the frequency of the motor be increased or decreased?

8. A certain sound level is increased by 20 dB. By how much does its intensity increase?

9. Standing waves are set up in a string that is fixed at both ends so the ends are nodal points. Higher harmonics in the string have progressively smaller wavelengths. Do the frequencies of higher harmonics get progressively smaller or larger? Assume the wave velocity is constant.

SOLUTIONS TO REVIEW PROBLEMS

1. **Spring 1**

   Recall from Hooke's law that the spring constant, k, is related to the magnitude of the displacement, x, and the applied force, F, by: $k = \frac{F}{x}$. Since both springs experience the same applied force (the blocks have equal mass), the spring with the smaller displacement has the larger spring constant.

2. **4:1**

   The period of oscillation of a mass–spring system is inversely proportional to the frequency of oscillation. The frequency of oscillation is proportional to the square root of the ratio of the mass to the spring constant. So $T \propto \sqrt{m/k}$. We're given $T_a/T_b = 2$, so $\sqrt{M_a/k} / \sqrt{M_b/k} = 2$, which tells us that $M_a/M_b = 4$.

3. a. **The equilibrium point**

   Hooke's law gives the force, F, of the spring on the mass as $F = kx$. The minimum force is zero and occurs where $x = 0$. By definition, $x = 0$ is the equilibrium point, i.e., the position of the mass at which the spring is neither stretched nor compressed.

   b. **At the point of maximum compression or maximum expansion of the spring**

   Newton's second law states that $a = F/m$, so the point of maximum acceleration of the mass is the point at which the mass experiences the greatest force. From Hooke's law, the greatest force occurs at the point of the largest displacement from equilibrium. Since the displacement at maximum expansion equals the displacement at maximum compression, the largest force and hence the largest acceleration occurs at either maximum expansion or maximum compression.

4. **Increases**

   The frequency of a pendulum is proportional to $\sqrt{g/L}$, where g is the acceleration due to gravity and L is the length of the pendulum. Given that $T = 1/f$, $T \propto \sqrt{L/g}$. Thus, decreasing the acceleration of gravity results in a larger period.

5. **The general wave equation is:**

   $$y = A \sin(kx - \omega t)$$

   This may be compared with the equation given in the question:

   $$y = (0.006) \sin(67.7x - 1.71t).$$

   a. **0.006 m**

   b. **0.0928 m**

   Wavelength is given by:

   $$\lambda = \frac{2\pi}{k}$$
   $$= \frac{2\pi}{67.7}$$
   $$= 0.0928 \text{ m}$$

c. **3.67 s**

Period is given by:

$$T = \frac{2\pi}{\omega}$$

$$= \frac{2\pi}{1.71}$$

$$= 3.67 \text{ s}$$

d. **0.272 Hz**

The frequency is given by:

$$f = \frac{1}{T}$$

$$= 0.272 \text{ Hz}$$

e. **0.0253 m/s**

The wave's velocity is given by:

$$v = \frac{\omega}{k}$$

$$= \frac{1.71}{67.7}$$

$$= 0.0253 \text{ m/s}$$

6. **2 s**

Points of zero amplitude of a wave are separated by half a wavelength. Since half a wavelength of a wave passes by any given point in half a period, the next point of zero amplitude occurs at 2 s, given a wave period of 4 s.

7. **Decreased**

The natural or resonant frequency of a pendulum is proportional to $\sqrt{g/L}$ where g is the acceleration due to gravity and L is the length of the pendulum. Since the motor is set to this frequency, increasing the length necessitates decreasing the frequency of the motor.

8. **The intensity is increased by a factor of 100.**

If I_a is the intensity before the increase and I_b is the intensity after the increase, then:

$$\Delta\beta = 10 \log \frac{I_b}{I_a}$$

$$\log \frac{I_b}{I_a} = \frac{20}{10}$$

$$\frac{I_b}{I_a} = 10^2$$

$$= 100$$

$$I_b = 100 \ I_a$$

9. **Larger**

Standing waves on a string are produced by the interference of two or more traveling waves on the string. The traveling waves obey the usual relationship $v = \lambda f$, and the question states that v is constant. Thus, as the wavelength decreases, the frequency must increase to keep the velocity constant.

CHAPTER SEVENTY-TWO

Light and Optics

This chapter reviews the basics of light and optics, which is the study of the reflection and transmission of light through material media and through constrictions such as apertures and slits. Geometrical optics pertains to the study of mirrors and lenses along with the concepts of reflection and refraction. The wave nature of light demonstrates that light does not travel in straight-line paths when it is passed through apertures and slits. The concepts of superposition and interference are explained in order to understand this behavior. A brief review is also provided of the physical nature of light itself as a wave.

ELECTROMAGNETIC SPECTRUM

Electromagnetic Waves

A changing magnetic field can cause a change in the electric field, and a changing electric field can cause a change in the magnetic field. Since changing electric fields affect changing magnetic fields that affect changing electric fields (and so on, and so on), the end result is an **electromagnetic wave.** One field affects the other, totally independent of matter, and electromagnetic waves can travel through a vacuum.

Electromagnetic waves are transverse waves because the oscillating electric and magnetic field vectors are perpendicular to the direction of propagation. Furthermore, the electric field and the magnetic field are perpendicular to each other, as shown in Figure 72.1.

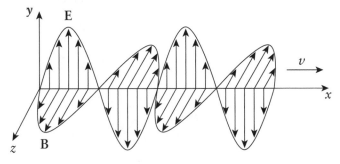

Figure 72.1

The **electromagnetic spectrum** is a term used to describe the full range of electromagnetic waves. The following prefixes are often used when describing wavelength: 1 mm = 10^{-3} m, 1 μm = 10^{-6} m, 1 nm = 10^{-9} m, and 1 Å = 10^{-10} m. The full spectrum is broken up into many regions which, in descending order of wavelength, include radio (10^9 m to 1 mm), infrared (1 mm to 700 nm), visible light (700 nm to 400 nm), ultraviolet (400 nm to 50 nm), X-ray (50 nm to 10^{-2} nm), and gamma ray (smaller than 10^{-2} nm).

Electromagnetic waves can vary in frequency and wavelength, but in a vacuum all electromagnetic waves travel at the same speed, commonly called the **speed of light.** This constant is represented by the letter c and is equal to 3.00×10^8 m/s.

The relationship between speed, frequency, and wavelength is given by:

$$c = f\lambda$$

for all electromagnetic waves in a vacuum. Note that frequency and wavelength are inversely related; higher frequencies have shorter wavelengths, and lower frequencies have longer wavelengths.

Color and the Visible Spectrum

The visible part of the electromagnetic spectrum is the only part that is perceived as light by the human eye. Within this region different wavelengths induce sensations of different colors, with violet at one end of the visible spectrum (400 nm) and red at the other end of the visible spectrum (700 nm).

Light that contains all of the colors in equal intensity is seen as white. The color of an object that does not emit its own light is dependent on the color of light that it reflects. So, an object that appears red is one that absorbs all light except red. This implies that a red object receiving green light will appear black since it absorbs the green light and has no light to reflect.

GEOMETRICAL OPTICS

When light travels through a single medium, it travels in a straight line. The behavior of light at the boundary of a medium or interface between two media is described by the theory of geometrical optics.

Reflection

Reflection is the rebounding of incident light waves at the boundary of a medium.

Figure 72.2

The law of reflection states that the angle of incidence equals the angle of reflection:

$$\theta_1 = \theta_2$$

In optics, angles are always measured from a line drawn perpendicular to the boundary of a medium, also referred to as the **normal line.**

Refraction

Snell's law

Refraction is the bending of light due to changing speed when passing from one medium to another. When light is traveling in any other medium than a vacuum, its speed is less than c, although when light is in air, $v \cong c$. For a given medium:

$$n = \frac{c}{v}$$

where c is the speed of light in a vacuum, v is the speed of light in the medium, and n is a dimensionless quantity called the **index of refraction** of the medium. Because $v < c$, $n > 1$ for any medium; however air can be approximated to have $v = c$ and $n = 1$.

Refracted rays of light obey **Snell's law** as they pass from one medium to another:

$$n_1 \sin \theta_1 = n_2 \sin \theta_2$$

where n_1 and θ_1 represent the medium the light is coming from, and n_2 and θ_2 are for the medium the light is going into. Note that θ is always measured with respect to the normal that is perpendicular to the boundary, as shown in Figure 72.3

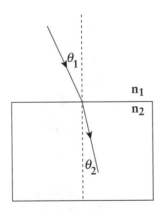

Figure 72.3

When light enters a medium with a higher index of refraction ($n_2 > n_1$), it slows down and bends toward the normal so that $\theta_2 < \theta_1$. Conversely, if the light travels into a medium with an index of refraction that is smaller ($n_2 < n_1$), the light will speed up and bend away from the normal so that $\theta_2 > \theta_1$.

PHYSICS

Example: A penny sits at the bottom of a pool of water ($n = 1.33$) at a depth of 3.0 m. If an observer 1.8 m tall stands 30 cm away from the ledge, how close to the side of the pool can the penny be and still be visible?

Solution: First, draw a picture of the situation, as in Figure 72.4. Note that the light is coming from the penny in the water ($n_1 = 1.33$) and going into the air ($n_2 = 1$), so the light is bent away from the normal ($\theta_2 > \theta_1$).

Figure 72.4

To find the angles the light rays make with the normal to the water's surface, use the trigonometric relationships for the right triangle based on the person and θ_2:

$$\tan \theta_2 = \frac{0.3}{1.8}$$
$$\theta_2 = 9.51°$$

Next, use Snell's law to solve for θ_1:

$$\sin \theta_1 = \frac{n_2}{n_1} \sin \theta_2$$
$$= \frac{0.165}{1.33}$$
$$\theta_1 = 7.1°$$

Finally, find x using the trigonometric relationships for the right triangle based on the penny's depth and θ_2:

$$x = 3 \tan \theta_1$$
$$= 0.37 \text{ m}$$
$$= 37 \text{ cm}$$

Total internal reflection

When light travels from a medium with a higher index of refraction to a medium with a lower index of refraction, the refracted angle is larger than the angle of incidence ($\theta_2 > \theta_1$). As the angle of incidence is increased, a special angle is reached, called the **critical angle** (θ_c). When $\theta_1 = \theta_c$ the refracted angle θ_2 equals 90°. The critical angle can be found from Snell's law:

$$n_1 \sin \theta_1 = n_2 \sin \theta_2$$
$$n_1 \sin \theta_c = n_2 \sin 90° = n_2$$
$$\sin \theta_c = \frac{n_2}{n_1}$$

Since $\theta_2 = 90°$, all light in the second medium is bent along the surface boundary; in essence, it has not escaped the first medium and is instead reflected back into it. Total **internal reflection,** a condition that occurs when all the light incident on a boundary is reflected back into the original material, results for any angle of incidence greater than θ_c. Total internal reflection is illustrated in Figure 72.5.

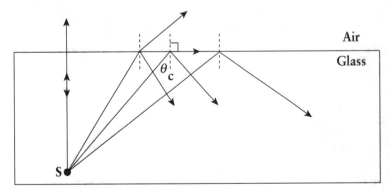

Figure 72.5

Example: From the previous example, suppose another penny is ten times farther out than the first one. Will a light ray going from this penny to the top edge of the pool emerge from the water?

Solution: First, find the critical angle:

$$\sin \theta_c = \frac{n_2}{n_1}$$

$$= \frac{1}{1.33}$$

$$\theta_c = 48.8°$$

The angle made by the second penny's light ray is:

$$\tan \theta_1 = \frac{0.37 \times 10}{3} = 1.23$$

$$\theta_1 = 51°$$

$\theta_1 > \theta_c$, therefore the light ray will be totally internally reflected and will not emerge.

Plane mirrors

Parallel incident rays remain parallel after reflection from a plane mirror. In general, images created by a mirror can be either real or virtual. An image is said to be **real** if the light actually converges at the position of the image. An image is **virtual** if the light only *appears* to be coming from the position of the image but does not converge there. If a screen (or the retina of an eye) is placed where the virtual image seems to be, no actual image will appear at that point in space.

Plane mirrors always create virtual images. In a plane mirror, the image appears to be the same distance behind the mirror as the object's distance in front of it, as shown in Figure 72.6. Because the reflected light remains in front of the mirror but the image is behind the mirror, the image is virtual.

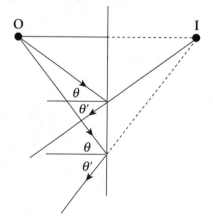

Figure 72.6

Spherical mirrors

Spherical mirrors can be either **concave** or **convex.** The word *spherical* implies that the surface of the mirror has the shape of part of a sphere. In other words, if you had a sphere made out of a mirror-like material, a spherical mirror would be a small portion cut out of that sphere. Therefore, spherical mirrors have a **center of curvature (C)** and a **radius of curvature (r)** associated with them.

If you were to look from the inside of a sphere to its surface, you would see a concave surface. However, if you were to look from outside the sphere you would see a convex surface. The **focal length (f)** is the distance between the focal point and the mirror, and the focal point is the point where all light reflected from the mirror will converge. For all spherical mirrors $f = r/2$. For a concave surface the center of curvature and focal point are in front of the mirror and are defined as positive. For a convex surface the center of curvature and the focal point are behind the mirror and are defined as negative. Concave mirrors are called **converging mirrors,** and convex mirrors are called **diverging mirrors.**

There are several important distances associated with mirrors. To summarize, the focal length f is the distance between the focal point F and the mirror; the radius of curvature r is the distance between the mirror and the center of the sphere it is based on. Additionally, the distance of the object from the mirror is o or d_o; the distance of the image from the mirror is i or d_i. Possible placements for these variables are illustrated for a concave mirror in Figure 72.7.

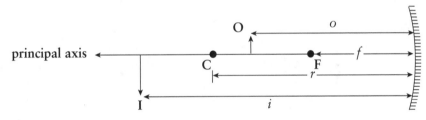

Figure 72.7

These distances are combined in the thin lens equation:

$$\frac{1}{o} + \frac{1}{i} = \frac{1}{f} = \frac{2}{r}$$

The thin lens equation is most frequently used to calculate the image distance of an object placed in front of a mirror or lens. If the image has a positive distance, it is a real image, which implies that the image is in front of the mirror. If the image has a negative distance, it is virtual and thus located behind the mirror. For a plane mirror, $r = f = \infty$, and the equation becomes $1/o + 1/i = 0$, and thus $i = -o$ (virtual image).

Magnification (m) is a dimensionless value that is the ratio of the image's height to the object's height and is calculated as:

$$m = -\frac{i}{o}$$

The sign of the magnification gives the orientation of the image compared with the object. A negative magnification signifies an inverted image, whereas a positive value means the image is upright.

The magnitude of magnification provides the relative size of the image to the object. If $|m| < 1$, the image is reduced; if $|m| > 1$, the image is enlarged; and if $|m| = 1$, the image is the same size as the object.

Figure 72.8 shows **ray diagrams** for a concave spherical mirror with the object at three different points. A ray diagram is useful for approximating where the image appears. In general, there are three important rays to draw. For a concave mirror, a ray that strikes the mirror parallel to the horizontal is reflected back through the focal point. A ray that passes through the focal point before reaching the mirror is reflected back parallel to the horizontal. A ray that strikes the mirror right where the normal intersects it is reflected back at the same angle measured from the normal. The point where these three rays intersect, whether in real or virtual space, identifies where the image appears.

The image formed by a single converging mirror depends on the position of the object, as shown in Figure 72.8. When the object is farther away from the mirror than the focal point, the image is real and inverted. By moving the object to the focal point, the image disappears because the light rays reflect off the mirror parallel to each other and never converge. Moving the object closer to the mirror than the focal length makes an image that is virtual and erect. A single diverging mirror (not shown) forms only a virtual erect image, regardless of the position of the object.

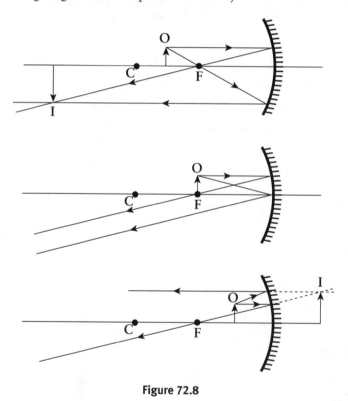

Figure 72.8

Sign convention

The following chart gives the proper signs for various instances when dealing with single mirrors. Note that R side is used to denote Real side, which for mirrors is in front of the mirror. Similarly, V side stands for Virtual side, which is behind the mirror.

Symbol	Positive	Negative
o	object is in front of mirror (real)	object is behind mirror (virtual)
i	image is in front of mirror (real)	image is behind mirror (virtual)
r	concave mirrors	convex mirrors
f	concave mirrors	convex mirrors
m	image is upright (erect)	image is inverted

Table 72.1

Note that in almost all problems the object will be in front of the mirror, and thus the object distance o will be positive. Negative objects are typically found only in multi-lens systems in which the image from one lens becomes the object for the next.

Example: An object is placed 7 cm in front of a concave mirror that has a 10 cm radius of curvature. Determine the image distance, the magnification, whether the image is real or virtual, and whether it is inverted or upright.

Solution: Using the thin lens equation:

$$\frac{1}{i} + \frac{1}{o} = \frac{2}{r}$$

$$\frac{1}{i} = \frac{2}{r} - \frac{1}{o}$$

$$\frac{1}{i} = \frac{2}{10} - \frac{1}{7}$$

$$i = +17.5 \,\text{cm}$$

The magnification is:

$$m = -\frac{i}{o}$$

$$= -\frac{17.5}{7}$$

$$= -2.5$$

The image is in front of the mirror (i is positive) and therefore real. The image is also inverted (m is negative) and 2.5 times larger ($|m| = 2.5$).

Thin spherical lenses

One important difference between lenses and mirrors is that lenses refract light, whereas mirrors reflect it (although in the real world lenses will also reflect some incident light). Also, when working with lenses, there are *two* boundary surfaces that affect the light path. For example, a person wearing glasses sees light that travels from an object through the air into the glass lens (the first boundary surface). Then, the light travels through the glass until it reaches the other side, where again it travels out of the glass into the air (the second boundary surface).

PHYSICS

A thin lens is a lens with thickness that can be neglected. Since light can be coming from either side of a lens, a lens has two focal points, one on each side of the lens (see Figure 72.9). However, for thin spherical lenses, the focal lengths are equal, and the lenses can be treated as having only one focal length.

Figure 72.9(a) illustrates that a **converging lens** is always thicker at the center, and Figure 72.9(b) illustrates that a **diverging lens** is always thinner at the center.

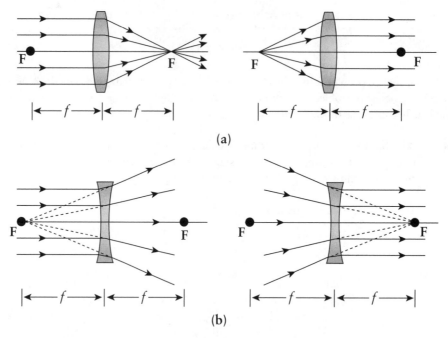

(a)

(b)

Figure 72.9

The same formulas for finding image distance and magnification for spherical mirrors also apply to lenses. The object distance o, image distance i, focal length f, and magnification m are related by the same equations.

$$\frac{1}{o} + \frac{1}{i} = \frac{1}{f}$$

$$m = -\frac{i}{o}$$

For lenses in which the curvature of the two boundary surfaces is different, the focal length is related to the curvature of the lens surfaces and the index of refraction of the lens by the **lensmaker's equation:**

$$\frac{1}{f} = (n-1)\left(\frac{1}{r_1} - \frac{1}{r_2}\right)$$

where r_1 is the radius of curvature of the first lens surface and r_2 is the radius of curvature of the second lens surface.

Note that sign conventions change slightly for lenses. For both lenses and mirrors, positive magnification means upright images, and negative magnification means inverted images, and a positive image distance means that the image is real, whereas a negative image distance means that the image is virtual.

However, where to place the real side and virtual side is different for mirrors and lenses. The real side is where the light actually goes after interacting with the mirror or lens. For mirrors, light is reflected and therefore stays in front of the mirror. The image may either appear in front of or behind the mirror, but the light rays always remain in front of the mirror. Since the real side is in front of the mirror, the virtual side is behind the mirror.

Lenses are different because light travels through the lens and comes out on the other side, and therefore the real side is on the opposite side of the lens from the light source. Thus, the virtual side must be the side of the lens that the light came from.

Although the object of a single lens is on the virtual image side, this does not make the object virtual. Objects are always real and have a positive object distance unless they are in certain multiple-lens systems. In summary, real images are always on the side that the light actually goes to; this is the same side as the object for mirrors and the opposite side from the object for lenses.

Focal lengths have a much simpler sign convention. For both mirrors and lenses, converging lenses and mirrors have positive focal lengths, and diverging mirrors and lenses have negative focal lengths.

Sign Chart for Single Lenses

Symbol	Positive	Negative
o	object on side of lens light is coming from	object on side of lens light is going to
i	image on side of lens light is going to (real)	image on side of lens light is coming from (virtual)
f	converging lens	diverging lens
m	image erect	image inverted
r	when on real side (convex surface as seen from side the light is coming from)	when on virtual side (concave surface as seen from side the light is coming from)

Table 72.2

Optometrists often describe a lens in terms of its **power** (P). This is measured in **diopters** when f is in meters and is given by the equation:

$$P = \frac{1}{f}$$

P has the same sign as f and is therefore positive for a converging lens and negative for a diverging lens.

Example: An object is 15 cm to the left of a thin diverging lens with a 45 cm focal length, as shown in Figure 72.10. Find:

a. where the image is formed, if it is upright or inverted, and if it is real or virtual.

b. the radii of curvature, assuming the lens is symmetrical and made of glass ($n = 1.50$).

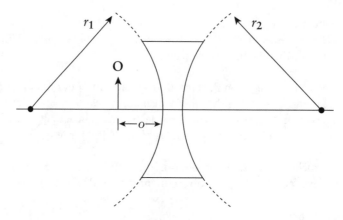

Figure 72.10

Solution: a. The image distance (i) is found using the equation:

$$\frac{1}{i} + \frac{1}{o} = \frac{1}{f}$$

$$\frac{1}{i} = \frac{1}{f} - \frac{1}{o}$$

Since the lens is diverging, the focal length has a negative sign, and $f = -45$ cm. The object has a positive sign such that $o = 15$ cm. Solving for i:

$$\frac{1}{i} = \frac{-1}{45} - \frac{1}{15}$$

$$= \frac{-1}{45} - \frac{3}{45}$$

$$= \frac{-4}{45}$$

$$i = -11.25 \text{ cm}$$

The negative sign indicates that the image is on the left side of the lens and therefore virtual (the light went through the lens and is on the right side as shown in the left-hand drawing in Figure 72.9(b)). To find out whether the image is upright or inverted, calculate the magnification:

$$m = -\frac{i}{o}$$

$$= -\frac{(-11.25)}{15}$$

$$= \frac{11.25}{15}$$

$$= 0.75$$

Since the magnification is positive, the image is upright. Furthermore, since $|m| < 1$, the image is smaller than the object.

b. Since the lens is symmetrical, the radii are equal but opposite in sign. They can be found from the lensmaker's equation:

$$\frac{1}{f} = (n-1)\left(\frac{1}{r_1} - \frac{1}{r_2}\right)$$

As the light progresses from left to right, the first surface of the lens is concave (r_1 negative), and the second surface of the lens is convex (r positive). So:

$$\frac{1}{f} = (n-1)\left(\frac{1}{-r} - \frac{1}{r}\right)$$

$$= (n-1)\left(-\frac{2}{r}\right)$$

Substituting $f = -45$ cm for a diverging lens and $n = 1.5$ from the question stem gives:

$$-\frac{1}{45} = (1.5-1)\left(-\frac{2}{r}\right)$$

$$= \frac{-1}{r}$$

$$r = 45\,\text{cm}$$

Multiple-lens systems

Lenses in contact or with negligible distances between them behave as a single lens with the equivalent focal length given by:

$$\frac{1}{f} = \frac{1}{f_1} + \frac{1}{f_2} + \dots$$
$$(P = P_1 + P_2 + \dots)$$

For lenses *not* in contact that have significant distances between them, the image of the first lens is used as the object of the second lens and so on. The image from the last lens is the final image of the system. The magnification for the system is $M = m_1 \times m_2 \times m_3 \times \dots$. Microscopes and telescopes are good examples of multiple-lens systems with significant distances between the eyepieces and objectives.

Dispersion

The speed of light for all wavelengths in a vacuum is the same. However, when light travels through a medium other than a vacuum, different wavelengths travel at different velocities. This fact also implies that the index of refraction of a medium is a function of the wavelength of the light traveling through it, since the index of refraction is related to the velocity of the wave by $n = c/v$. When the speed of a wave passing through it varies with wavelength, a material exhibits **dispersion.** The most common example of dispersion is the splitting of white light into its component colors using a prism.

If a source of white light is incident on one of the faces of a prism, the light emerging from the prism is spread out into a fan-shaped beam, as shown in Figure 72.11, in which the light has been dispersed into a spectrum. This occurs because violet light experiences a greater index of refraction than red does and so is bent to a greater extent. All wavelengths in between are bent at angles in between those of red and violet.

Figure 72.11

DIFFRACTION

In geometrical optics, light travels in straight lines, but there are other situations in which this is not strictly true. For example, when light passes through a narrow opening (an opening with a size close to one wavelength), the light waves seem to spread out, as is seen in Figure 72.12. As the slit narrows, the light is spread out more. This spreading out of light as it passes through a narrow opening is called **diffraction.** Diffraction is caused by the interference of an infinite number of waves when each point along the slit acts as a wave source.

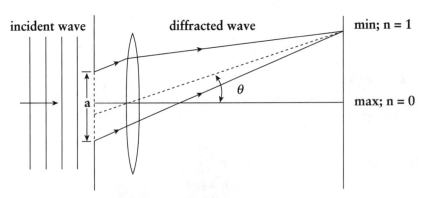

Figure 72.12

INTERFERENCE

By the superposition principle, when waves interact with each other, the amplitudes of the waves add together in a process called **interference** (see Chapter 71, Simple Harmonic Motion and Waves). Young's famous double-slit experiment showed that two light waves can interfere with one another, and this contributed to the wave theory of light. Figure 72.13 shows the results of Young's experiment: When light illuminates the slits, an interference pattern is observed on a screen placed behind the slits. Regions of constructive interference between the two light waves appear as regions of maximum light intensity on the screen. Conversely, in regions where the light waves interfere destructively, the light is at a minimum intensity and the screen is dark.

Figure 72.13

POLARIZATION

Plane-polarized light is light in which the electric fields of all the waves are oriented in the same direction, i.e., their electric field vectors are parallel. It is true that their magnetic field vectors are also parallel, but convention dictates that the plane of the electric field identifies the plane of polarization. Plane-polarized light is used to determine the presence of enantiomers in chiral chemistry.

Unpolarized light corresponds to a random orientation of the electric field vectors. Unfiltered sunlight is a prime example because its waves travel in all directions. However, there are filters called polarizers that are often used in cameras and sunglasses and allow only light waves with their electric fields pointing in a particular direction to pass. By holding one polarizer in sunlight or another unpolarized light source, it will let through only the portion of the light that has a given vector orientation. If a second polarizer is placed in front of the first and slowly turned, the light transmitted through the two polarizers will vary from total darkness to the level of the original polarizer alone; when both the first and second polarizer are polarizing in the same direction, all the light that passed through the first also passes through the second, but when the second polarizer is turned so that it polarizes in a direction perpendicular to the first, no light passes through at all.

REVIEW PROBLEMS

1. An electromagnetic wave has electric field vectors and magnetic field vectors that oscillate in the plane of the page. What is the propagation direction of the wave?

2. What is the focal length of a plane mirror?

3. An object is placed at the center of curvature of a concave mirror. The image it creates must be
    A. real and inverted.
    B. virtual and inverted.
    C. virtual and upright.
    D. real and upright.
    E. nonexistent.

4. When monochromatic light is refracted as it passes from air to glass, which of the following does not remain the same? (Assume that the wave is fully transmitted.)
    A. Wavelength
    B. Frequency
    C. Amplitude
    D. Period
    E. Energy

5. Light rays from a very distant object are reflected by a concave mirror. What is the size of the image produced by the mirror?

6. Why can you see an image of yourself in a window pane at night but usually not during the day?

7. Which phenomenon would cause monochromatic light entering the prism along path AB to leave along path CD?

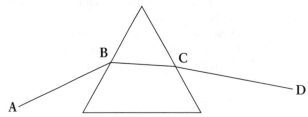

    A. Reflection
    B. Refraction
    C. Diffraction
    D. Polarization
    E. Diffusion

8. A simple film projector consists of a converging lens and an object (the film) located somewhere between one and two focal lengths from the lens. The image produced by this object is located on the other side of the lens. Is the image upright or inverted?

9. A magnifying glass simply consists of a converging lens. An object is placed between the focal point of the lens and the lens itself. What type of image, real or virtual, is produced?

10. A camera is a device that can take a large object and reduce it to a much smaller image which fits on the film. Assume that the camera uses a single lens to produce a real image of an object, such that the object distance is much greater than the image distance. What type of lens, converging or diverging, should be used?

11. The maxima of a two-slit interference experiment are located at angles θ that satisfy the equation $d \sin\theta = m\lambda$ where d is the distance between the slits, λ is the wavelength of the light, and m is an integer that takes on the values $m = 0,1,2,\ldots$ What happens to the angle of the $m = 2$ maximum if the light frequency is increased?

SOLUTIONS TO REVIEW PROBLEMS

1.   **Into or out of the page**

The electric and magnetic field vectors of an electromagnetic wave are perpendicular to the direction of motion of the wave. For field vectors in the plane of the page, the wave must propagate either into the page or out of the page.

2.   **Infinity**

Recall that a plane mirror always produces a virtual image, the same distance from the mirror as the object distance, thus $i = -o$. Using $1/f = 1/i + 1/o$, we have $1/f = (-1/o) + 1/o = 0$, which says that $f = $ infinity.

3.   **A**   First draw a diagram:

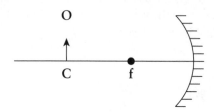

You know $o = r$, and since $1/f = 2/r$, you can substitute into the thin lens equation:

$$\frac{1}{i} = \frac{1}{f} - \frac{1}{o}$$

$$\frac{1}{i} = \frac{2}{r} - \frac{1}{r}$$

$$= \frac{1}{r}$$

$$i = r$$

Because i is positive, the image is real, eliminating **choices (B), (C),** and **(E)**. The magnification will then tell you the image's orientation:

$$m = -\frac{i}{o}$$

$$= -\frac{r}{r}$$

$$= -1$$

The negative sign tells you the image is inverted.

4.   **A**   If you don't know right away that **(A)** is the correct answer, you can still solve by process of elimination. Frequency is related to period ($f = 1/T$), so if either quantity changes, the other would have to change as well. Since they cannot both be correct, **choices (B)** and **(D)** can both be eliminated. Furthermore, because the wave is fully transmitted, there is no absorption or reflection, and the amplitude and energy should not change. Therefore, answer **choices (C)** and **(E)** are eliminated.

Looking at the equation c = fλ, you might be tempted to eliminate wavelength, too. However, when light is refracted, its speed changes. So, although the frequency cannot change, the wavelength will.

5. **The image is a point that is essentially of zero size.**

Light rays from a distant object only reach the mirror if they're essentially parallel rays. Parallel rays, in turn, produce an image at the focal point. Using the magnification factor $m = -i/o$ with $i = f$ and $o = $ infinity, you have $m = 0$, which says that the image is a point and has essentially no size.

6. **The reflected image is too weak during the day.**

Light reflected from your body hits the window pane, and some of it is reflected back to you, allowing you to see your image in the window pane. This is true during the day and at night. During the day, however, the much greater intensity of light coming through the window pane usually overpowers the weak reflected light. At night, with little incoming light, the reflected image is easily seen.

7. **B** Even though the light is traveling through a prism, the change in the light's direction is caused by refraction and not dispersion. Dispersion involves the breaking up of multi-wavelength light into its component wavelengths because of the index of refraction's dependence on wavelength. If the incident light is monochromatic, or in other words, of only one wavelength, the light will not be dispersed.

8. **Inverted**

Whether an image is upright or inverted can be determined from the magnification $m = -i/o$. When $m > 0$ the image is upright, and when $m < 0$ the image is inverted. Since the image is on the other side of the lens from the object, the image is real, and thus $i > 0$, which says that $m < 0$ and that the image is inverted.

9. **Virtual**

The type of image, real or virtual, is determined by the sign of the image distance. Positive image distances mean real images, and negative image distances mean virtual images. The sign of the image distance is determined from the thin lens equation: $1/i + 1/o = 1/f$. Since the lens is converging, $f > 0$. Since the question stem states that $o < f$, $1/o > 1/f$. The thin lens equation can only be satisfied if $1/i < 0$, which means that $i < 0$, meaning the image must be virtual.

10. **Converging**

To evaluate whether the lens is converging or diverging, determine the sign of the focal length. Positive focal lengths mean converging lenses, and negative focal lengths mean diverging lenses. Given that both i and o are positive, you have that $1/f = 1/o + 1/i$ is positive, which says that f is positive. Thus, the lens is converging.

11. **The angle decreases**

Recall that the frequency and wavelength of the incident light are related by c = λf where c is the speed of light in a vacuum. Increasing the frequency means decreasing the wavelength. Given the equation $\sin \theta = m\lambda/d$, we see that, for all m, decreasing the wavelength means decreasing the angle.

CHAPTER SEVENTY-THREE

Modern Physics

Toward the end of the 19th century and through today, research has shown that different laws of physics take effect at short distances due to the wave nature of the discrete bits of matter. The theory that was developed to explain such phenomena is known as quantum mechanics. This chapter will cover particular applications of quantum mechanical ideas to atomic phenomena but will not cover the formal theory of quantum mechanics. The first two topics covered here, blackbody radiation and the photoelectric effect, address the particle nature of light. The quantum theory was later applied to the structure of the hydrogen atom, leading to Bohr's theory. This is reviewed along with a discussion of the interaction of photons with atoms. However, the application of quantum mechanics to nuclear phenomena is discussed in Chapter 37, Nuclear Reactions.

THERMAL BLACKBODY RADIATION

At any temperature above absolute zero, matter emits electromagnetic radiation. The amount of radiant energy emitted at a given wavelength depends on the temperature of the emitter. Blackbody radiation is based on an ideal radiator known as a **blackbody** because any ideal radiator is also an ideal absorber and would appear totally black if it were at a lower temperature than its surroundings. Physicist Max Planck developed the theoretical derivation of the blackbody spectrum. His radiant spectrum for two blackbodies at different temperatures is shown in Figure 73.1. The graph shows that the energy radiated varies with the wavelength that is given off. In the derivation, Planck had to use a number called **Planck's constant (h)** whose value is given by:

$$h = 6.63 \times 10^{-34}\,\text{J}\cdot\text{s} = 4.14 \times 10^{-15}\,\text{eV}\cdot\text{s}$$

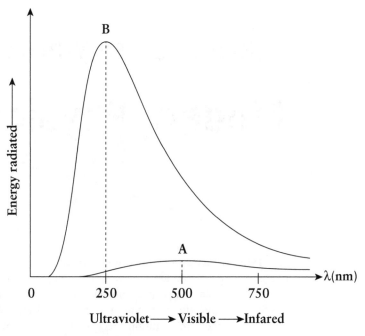

Figure 73.1

For any given blackbody there is one wavelength at which the maximum amount of energy is emitted (λ_{peak}). **Wien's displacement law** relates the peak wavelength to temperature:

$$\lambda_{peak}T = 2.90 \times 10^{-3} \text{ m} \cdot \text{K}$$

Note that λ_{peak} is the wavelength at which more energy is emitted than any other wavelength. λ_{peak} does *not* refer to the maximum wavelength emitted.

The **Stefan–Boltzmann law** relates the total energy being emitted (E_T = energy per unit area per unit time) to temperature:

$$E_T = \sigma T^4$$

where σ is the Stefan–Boltzmann constant ($5.67 \times 10^{-8} \text{ J/s} \cdot \text{m}^2 \cdot \text{K}^4$).

Example: In Figure 73.1 the radiant spectrum for two blackbodies is plotted. The first body is at temperature T_a, and the second body is at temperature T_b.

a. How do the temperatures of the two blackbodies compare?

b. How much greater is the energy per unit area per second of the second body compared to the first?

Solution: a. The plots in Figure 73.1 show that $\lambda_{peak-a} = 500$ nm, and $\lambda_{peak-b} = 250$ nm; thus:

$$\lambda_{peak-a} = 2\lambda_{peak-b}$$

Wien's law says: $\lambda_{\text{peak}}T = $ constant. Combining information gives:

$$\lambda_{\text{peak-a}}T_a = \lambda_{\text{peak-b}}T_b$$
$$2\lambda_{\text{peak-b}}T_a = \lambda_{\text{peak-b}}T_b$$
$$T_b = 2T_a$$

b. The Stefan–Boltzmann law states: $E_T = \sigma T^4$. Combining the result from part (a) gives:

$$E_{Ta} = \sigma T_a{}^4$$
$$E_{Tb} = \sigma T_b{}^4 \text{ and } T_b = 2T_a$$
$$E_{Tb} = \sigma(2T_a)^4 = 16\sigma T_a{}^4 = 16E_{Ta}$$

Thus, the E_T of blackbody b is $2^4 = 16$ times greater than that of blackbody a.

PHOTOELECTRIC EFFECT

When light of a sufficiently high frequency (typically blue or ultraviolet light) strikes a metal in a vacuum, the metal emits electrons. This phenomenon is called the **photoelectric effect.** The minimum frequency of light able to eject electrons is known as the **threshold frequency (f_T)** and depends on the type of metal. The photoelectric effect demonstrates that a light beam consists of particles called photons with the energy of each photon proportional to the frequency f of the light:

$$E = hf$$

where h is **Planck's constant**, 6.63×10^{-34} J·s $= 4.14 \times 10^{-15}$ eV·s. Wavelength and frequency of light in a vacuum are related to speed of light by $c = \lambda f$, just as wavelength, frequency, and velocity of any wave are related by $v = \lambda f$. The wavelength of light that is able to eject electrons is given by:

$$\lambda = \frac{c}{f}$$

where c is the speed of light (3.00×10^8 m/s). Combining equations gives $E = hf = hc/\lambda$, which says that a shorter wavelength means higher frequency and therefore higher-energy photons (toward the blue and ultraviolet end of the spectrum). A longer wavelength means lower frequency and therefore lower-energy photons (toward the red and infrared end of the spectrum). Common units used for wavelength include nanometers (1 nm $= 10^{-9}$ m) and angstroms (1 Å $= 10^{-10}$ m).

If the frequency of a photon striking a metal is at the threshold frequency, the electron barely escapes from the metal. However, if the frequency of an incident photon is above the threshold frequency of the metal, there will be excess energy that is converted to kinetic energy of the ejected electron. The maximum kinetic energy can be calculated from the formula:

$$K = hf - W$$

where W is the **work function**, the minimum energy required to eject an electron. A photon can liberate an electron from a metal surface only if the energy of the photon, $E = hf$, is greater than or equal to the work function of the metal. The work function is related to the threshold frequency of that metal by:

$$W = hf_T$$

When $f > f_T$ the photon will eject electrons, and the excess energy appears as kinetic energy (K). When $f < f_T$ the photon does not carry enough energy to eject an electron from the metal, and no effect is observed.

The electrons released from the metal by the photoelectric effect produce a net charge flow per unit time, which is the same as a current. The higher the intensity of the beam, the greater the number of photons per unit time that fall on the metal and the greater the number of electrons per unit time. When the light's frequency is above threshold frequency, the current is directly proportional to the intensity of the light beam.

Example: If the work function of a metal is 2.00 eV and blue light of frequency 6.00×10^{14} Hz is incident on the metal, will there be photo-ejection of electrons? If so, how much kinetic energy will an electron carry away?

Solution: If the photons have a frequency of 6.00×10^{14} Hz, each photon has an energy given by:

$$E = hf$$
$$= (4.14 \times 10^{-15})(6.00 \times 10^{14})$$
$$= 2.48 \text{ eV}$$

Thus a photon has more than enough energy to get an electron in the metal to overcome the 2.00 eV threshold barrier. The kinetic energy carried away by the electron is:

$$K = hf - W$$
$$= 2.48 - 2.00$$
$$= 0.48 \text{ eV}$$

THE BOHR MODEL OF THE HYDROGEN ATOM

Energy Levels

The hydrogen atom consists of an electron in orbit about a single, more massive proton. Niels Bohr postulated that there were specific stable, or allowed, orbits of quantized (discrete) energy in which electrons maintained stable orbits and did not radiate energy. This led him to deduce an **energy level formula.**

The Bohr energy corresponding to the closest orbit to the nucleus is called the **ground state** ($n = 1$) and has an energy of −13.6 eV. The energies corresponding to orbits farther away from the nucleus ($n = 2,3,4,...$) are higher because they are less negative in value. If the electron is given so much energy that it reaches an energy of zero or higher, it pulls free from the nucleus. The electron can now have any positive energy level, and the atom is **ionized.**

An electron occupying a higher-energy orbit but still bound to the proton is said to be in an **excited state.** The energy of the electron is greater than -13.6 eV but still less than zero. The quantum energy levels in the Bohr model of the hydrogen atom can be arranged from lowest ($n = 1$) to highest ($n = \infty$), where n is the **principal quantum number**. The energy levels for different orbits for hydrogen are given by the formula:

$$E_n = \frac{-13.6}{n^2}$$

The following table gives the calculated values for the energy levels for the hydrogen atom for principal quantum numbers 1 through 4. Note that, as n increases, the energy levels become larger (less negative). At $n = \infty$, the energy reaches zero, and the hydrogen atom loses the electron and becomes ionized.

The table below shows the electron energy levels in hydrogen.

Principal quantum number	Energy level
n	E_n
1	$\frac{-13.6}{1}\,\text{eV} = -13.6\ \text{eV}$
2	$\frac{-13.6}{4}\,\text{eV} = -3.40\ \text{eV}$
3	$\frac{-13.6}{9}\,\text{eV} = -1.51\ \text{eV}$
4	$\frac{-13.6}{16}\,\text{eV} = -0.85\ \text{eV}$
∞	$\frac{-13.6}{\infty}\,\text{eV} = 0\ \text{eV}$

Table 73.1

Emission and Absorption of Light

Hydrogen atoms radiate light only at particular frequencies and follow a set of rules set forth by Bohr:

1. Energy levels of the electron correspond to specific orbits.
2. An electron emits or absorbs radiation only when making a transition from one energy level (orbit) to another.
3. To jump from a lower energy (inner orbit) to a higher energy (outer orbit), an electron must **absorb** a photon of precisely the right frequency such that the photon's energy ($E = hf$) exactly equals the energy difference between the two orbits.

4. When jumping from a higher energy (outer orbit) to a lower energy (inner orbit), an electron must **emit** a photon of a frequency such that the photon's energy ($E = hf$) is exactly the energy difference between the two orbits.

An electron in the lowest allowed energy level ($n = 1$) cannot emit any more energy; it can only absorb radiation and jump up to a higher energy level. An electron occupying an **excited state** can either emit radiation and jump down to a lower energy level or absorb radiation and jump up to a higher energy level.

The frequency of radiation emitted or absorbed by an electron in going from energy level E_i to energy level E_f is $\Delta E = E_f - E_i$. If ΔE is negative, then the electron has jumped from a higher energy state (less tightly bound state) to a lower energy state (more tightly bound state). There is then an **emission** of a photon of frequency f where:

$$\Delta E < 0$$
$$hf = -\Delta E \text{ (emission)}$$

The negative sign is necessary to give the photon a positive energy even though the energy change of the electron is negative.

On the other hand, if ΔE is positive, then the electron has **absorbed** a photon and jumped from a lower energy state to a higher energy state. The absorbed photon has a frequency f where:

$$\Delta E > 0$$
$$hf = \Delta E \text{ (absorption)}$$

A single equation can be used to ensure that photon energies are always positive, whether the photon is emitted or absorbed:

$$hf = |\Delta E|$$

Example: What wavelength of light is emitted by a hydrogen electron going from the $n = 5$ to the $n = 2$ energy level?

Solution: For hydrogen, the energy for a given principal quantum number n is given by

$$E = \frac{-13.6}{n^2}$$

Since the electron goes from $n = 5$ to $n = 2$, the initial energy level is:

$$E_i = E_5 = \frac{-13.6}{25} = -0.544 \text{ eV}$$

The final energy is:

$$E_f = E_2 = \frac{-13.6}{4} = -3.40 \text{ eV}$$

Therefore:

$$\Delta E = E_f = E_i$$
$$= -3.40 + 0.544$$
$$= -2.856 \text{ eV}$$

The negative value of ΔE confirms that the light is emitted. The frequency is found by:

$$f = \frac{|\Delta E|}{h}$$
$$= \frac{2.856}{4.14 \times 10^{-15}}$$
$$= 6.90 \times 10^{14} \text{ Hz}$$

To find the wavelength of the emitted photon:

$$\lambda = \frac{c}{f}$$
$$= \frac{3.00 \times 10^8}{6.90 \times 10^{14}}$$
$$= 4.35 \times 10^{-7} \text{ m}$$
$$= 435 \text{ nm}$$
$$= 4350 \text{ Å}$$

Example: What wavelength of light is needed to free an electron from the ground state of hydrogen?

Solution: The electron in the ground state ($n = 1$) of hydrogen has an energy of -13.6 eV. Negative energies mean a bound state; positive energies mean a free state. It would take a photon of at least $+13.6$ eV for the electron to jump to $E = 0$ and escape. To find the frequency:

$$f = \frac{E}{h}$$
$$= \frac{13.6}{4.14 \times 10^{-15}}$$
$$= 3.29 \times 10^{15} \text{ Hz}$$

Now the wavelength is given by:

$$\lambda = \frac{c}{f}$$
$$= \frac{3.00 \times 10^8}{3.29 \times 10^{15}}$$
$$= 9.12 \times 10^{-8} \text{ m}$$
$$= 91.2 \text{ nm}$$

Fluorescence

Fluorescence is a process by which certain substances emit visible light when excited by radiation of another wavelength, usually ultraviolet radiation. Photons corresponding to ultraviolet radiation have relatively high frequencies, short wavelengths, and high energies. After being excited to a higher energy state by the ultraviolet radiation, the electron returns to its original state in two or more steps. By returning in two or more steps, each step involves a smaller energy drop. In each step a lower-frequency, longer-wavelength, and lower-energy photon is emitted whose wavelength may fall in the visible portion of the spectrum. This is the principle of fluorescent light.

REVIEW PROBLEMS

1. If the work function of a certain metal is 4.14 eV, and light of frequency 2.42×10^{14} Hz is incident on this metal, will there be ejection of electrons? (Use $h = 4.14 \times 10^{-15}$ eV·s.)

2. What is the threshold frequency of the metal in Question 1?

3. When light of frequency 7×10^{14} Hz is directed onto a particular metal surface, no electrons are ejected. How should the wavelength of the light be changed so that electrons may be ejected from the metal surface?

4. All of the following are characteristic of the photoelectric effect EXCEPT that

   A. the intensity of the light beam does not affect the photocurrent.

   B. the kinetic energies of the emitted electrons do not depend on the light intensity.

   C. a weak beam of light of frequency greater than the threshold frequency yields more current than an intense beam of light of frequency lower than the threshold.

   D. for light of a given frequency, the kinetic energy of emitted electrons increases as the value of the work function decreases.

   E. it shows that light can behave as a particle.

5. In the hydrogen atom, how many electron states fall in the energy range -10.2 eV to -1.4 eV?

6. For a large n, the difference in energy between the $(n + 1)$ state and the n state is given by $E_{n+1} - E_n = 27.2/n^3$ eV. As n increases, what happens to the frequency of light emitted in the transition from $(n + 1)$ to n?

7. What is the difference in ionization energy for a hydrogen atom with its electron in the ground state and a hydrogen atom with its electron in the $n = 4$ state?

8. When a hydrogen atom electron falls to the ground state from the $n = 2$ state, 10.2 eV of energy is emitted. What is the wavelength of this radiation? (Use 1 eV $= 1.60 \times 10^{-19}$ J, $h = 6.63 \times 10^{-34}$ J·s.)

SOLUTIONS TO REVIEW PROBLEMS

1. **No**

    Each photon has an energy given by:

    $$E = hf$$
    $$= (4.14 \times 10^{-15})(2.42 \times 10^{14})$$
    $$= 1.00 \text{ eV}$$

    Thus, the photons do not have enough energy to allow an electron in the metal to overcome the 4.14 eV barrier, and there will be no ejection of electrons.

2. **1.00×10^{15} Hz**

    From the relation between the work function and the threshold frequency of a metal, $W = hf_T$, you can solve for the threshold frequency:

    $$f_T = \frac{W}{h}$$
    $$= \frac{4.14}{4.14 \times 10^{-15}}$$
    $$= 1.00 \times 10^{15} \text{ Hz}$$

3. **The wavelength must be decreased.**

    An electron is ejected from the surface of a metal when the energy of the incident light is greater than or equal to the work function (the minimum energy needed to eject an electron). Since no electrons are ejected with light frequency 7×10^{14} Hz, higher-energy light must be needed. Since the energy of light is proportional to its frequency ($E = hf$), a greater frequency than 7×10^{14} Hz is required. Given that frequency, wavelength, and speed are related by $c = \lambda f$ and that c is a constant, the requirement for a greater frequency means a decreased wavelength is needed.

4. **A** The greater the intensity, the greater the number of incident photons, and therefore the greater the number of photoelectrons that will be ejected from the metal surface (assuming that the frequency of the light is above the threshold). This means a larger current. Choice (A) is not a characteristic of the photoelectric effect and is therefore the answer to the question. All the other choices are characteristics of the photoelectric effect.

5. **2**

    The energy states of an electron in hydrogen are given by the equation $E_n = -13.6 \text{ eV}/n^2$ where $n = 1,2,3...$. For $n = 1$, $E_1 = -13.6$ eV. For $n = 2$, $E_2 = -(13.6/4) = -3.4$ eV. For $n = 3$, $E_3 = -13.6/9 = -1.5$ eV. For $n = 4$, $E_4 = -13.6/16 = -0.85$. Thus, there are two energy states in the range -10.2 eV to -1.4 eV, the states $n = 2$ and $n = 3$.

6. **The frequency decreases.**

    The frequency of light emitted in a transition from $(n + 1)$ to n is given by $f = (E_{n+1} - E_n)/h$ where E_{n+1} and E_n are the energies of the $(n + 1)$ and n states, respectively. Given the equation stated in the question, $f = (27.2/n^3)/h$. Thus, as n increases, the frequency of light decreases.

7. **12.75 eV**

The energy required to ionize an atom is the energy needed to bring the electron energy up to 0 eV. For a hydrogen atom with its electron in the ground state ($E_1 = -13.6$ eV), the ionization energy is 13.6 eV. For a hydrogen atom with its electron in the $n = 4$ state ($E_4 = -0.85$ eV), the ionization energy is 0.85 eV. The difference in ionization energies is $(13.6 - 0.85)$ eV $= 12.75$ eV.

8. **1.22×10^{-7} m**

First, you need consistent units. Convert $\Delta E = 10.2$ eV to joules:

$$\Delta E = (10.2 \text{ eV}) \times (1.6 \times 10^{-19} \text{ J/eV}) = 1.63 \times 10^{-18} \text{ J}$$

To find the frequency, use the formula:

$$f = \frac{\Delta E}{h}$$
$$= \frac{1.63 \times 10^{-18}}{6.63 \times 10^{-34}}$$
$$= 2.46 \times 10^{15} \text{ Hz}$$

From the wave equation, $c = \lambda f$, so:

$$\lambda = \frac{c}{f}$$
$$= \frac{3.00 \times 10^8}{2.46 \times 10^{15}}$$
$$= 1.22 \times 10^{-7} \text{ m}$$

Index

A

Abdominal cavity, 167, 195
ABO blood groups, 87, 156
Absolute configuration, 479–480
Absolute refractory period, 144
Absolute value and inequalities, 767, 826
Absolute zero, 409
Absorption, definition, 65
Acceleration
average acceleration, 853
free-falling bodies, motion and
acceleration, 855
instantaneous acceleration, 853
motion with constant acceleration, 856
Acetals, 574–575
Acetoacetic ester condensation, 615
Acetylcholine, 131
Acetylene (ethyne), 464, 529
Achiral molecules, definition, 477
Acid-base disorders, 178
Acid-base indicators, 423
Acid chlorides, from carboxylic acids, 593
Acid halides. *See* Acyl halides
Acidosis, 178
Acids
acid-base indicators, 423
acid dissociation constant (K_a), 427, 427–429
acid equivalents, 430–431
amphoteric species, 431
Arrhenius definition, 423–424
Brønsted-Lowry definition, 424
buffer solutions, 433
conjugate acid/base pairs, 424, 427–428,
429–430, 433
equivalence points, 431–432, 434
equivalent weight, 431
Henderson-Hasselbalch equation, 433
Lewis definition, 298, 424
neutralization reactions, 338, 429
nomenclature, 424
normality (N), 430–431
pH, 425–426
pH meters, 431
polyprotic acids, 434
polyvalence, 430–431
properties, 423, 425–429
salt formation, 429–430
strong acids and bases, 426–427
titration, 431–434
water dissociation constant (K_w), 425, 428
weak acids and bases, 427–428. *See also* Bases;
Titration
Acquired characteristics, 99
Acquired immunodeficiency syndrome (AIDS),
117
Acquired or specific immunity, 119
Acromegaly, 183
Acrosomal process, 197
Acrosome, 195
ACTH-releasing factor (ACTH-RF), 185

Actin, 38, 143, 145
Actinides, 277
Action potentials, 123, 124–125
Activated complexes, 363
activation energy, 379
Activation energy (E_a), 363
Active immunity, 118
Actual yield, 319–320
Acyl halides (acid halides, alkanoyl halides)
conversion into amides, 606, 617–618
conversion into anhydrides, 605
conversion into esters, 605
formation, 593
Friedel-Crafts acylation, 571, 606, 620
hydrolysis, 605
nomenclature, 603–604
nucleophilic acyl substitution, 604
properties, 604
reactions, 604–606, 620
reduction, 606
synthesis, 604
Adaptive immunity, 119
Adaptive radiation, 102
Adenine, 54, 57
Adenosine triphosphate (ATP)
and muscle contraction, 144, 146
from glucose catabolism, 65, 66–70
gain and loss of phosphate groups, 617
Adhesion, 918
Adiabatic processes, 905
Adrenal cortex, 182, 183, 187
Adrenal glands, 182
Adrenal medulla, 154, 182, 204
Adrenocortical steroids, 182
Adrenocorticotropic hormone (ACTH), 182,
183
Adsorbents, 664
Aerobic respiration
development of, 107
waste products, 173
Afferent neurons, 128
Affinity chromatography, 667
Agarose gel electrophoresis, 668
Agnatha, 245
Agonistic displays, 217
Airways, 158
Alcohol fermentation, 68
Alcohols
common names, 465, 551–552
dehydration reactions, 556
diols (or glycols), 465, 527, 574
elimination reactions, 556
geminal diols (carbonyl hydrates), 465, 574
hydrogen bonds, 552–553
hydroxyl group, 551, 552–553
nomenclature, 465, 551–552
oxidation reactions, 557–558, 570
phenols, 552, 553, 555, 557, 558, 560
physical properties, 552–553
reaction mechanisms, 553–554

substitution reactions, 556–557
synthesis by addition reactions, 554
synthesis by reduction reactions, 555
synthesis by substitution reactions, 555
vicinal diols, 465, 527
Aldehydes
acetal formation, 574–575
addition reactions, 573–576
aldol condensation, 576–577
Clemmensen reduction, 572
common names, 467, 567–568
condensation with ammonium derivatives,
575–576
cyanohydrin formation, 575
enol form, 572–573
enolization, 572–573
hemiacetal formation, 574–575
hydration to form geminal diols, 574
keto form, 572–573
Michael addition, 573
nomenclature, 465–466, 567–568
nucleophilic addition to carbonyl, 573
overview, 569–570
oxidation reactions, 571
physical properties, 569
reduction reactions, 571–572
synthesis, 570–571
Wittig reaction, 578
Wolff-Kishner reduction, 572
Aldol condensation, 576–577
Aldosterone, 177, 182, 187, 188
Algae, 241
Algebra
absolute value and inequalities, 767
differences of squares, 760
equations, definition, 755, 777
exponents, operations, 756–757
factor common to all terms, 760
factoring, 759–761
FOIL for multiplying binomials, 758
golden rule of equations, 762
inequalities, definition, 755, 778
polynomials, adding, subtracting, or
multiplying, 757–758
polynomials, dividing, 758–759
quadratic equations, 764–766
quadratic formula, 765
simultaneous equations, 766
squares of binomials, 760
unknown in a denominator, 762–763
unknown in an exponent, 763–764
word problems, 745–746, 755–756, 778–779
Aliphatic compounds (alkyl compounds), 540
Alkali metals (Group IA), 282
Alkaline earth metals (Group IIA), 279, 282
Alkanes
branched-chain alkanes, 460–462
common names, 462
nomenclature, 459–462
prefixes for number of carbon atoms, 459

Index

Index

Index

Index

Index

Index

Ion exchange chromatography, 666
Ionic bonds, 291–292, 497
Ionic equations, 338
Ionic radii, 278
Ionic solids, 394
Ionization energy (IE), 278–279
Ion product (Q_{sp}) of a compound in solution, 387
Ions, 261, 281–282
Irreversible reactions, 358, 383
Irritability, definition, 65
Islets of Langerhans, 186
Isobaric processes, 905
Isocyanates, 619
Isoelectric focusing, 668
Isoelectric point, 668
Isolated systems, 373
Isomers
  absolute configuration, 479–480
  achiral molecules, definition, 477
  anti conformation, 483
  asymmetric (chiral) carbon atoms, 477
  boat conformation, 484
  chair conformation, 484
  chirality, 477–482
  chiral molecules, definition, 477
  cis-trans isomers, 476, 521
  configuration, definition, 478
  conformational isomers, 482–485
  cyclic conformations, 484–485
  dextrorotatory compounds, 480
  diastereomers, 481–482
  eclipsed conformation, 483
  (*E*) isomers, 476
  enantiomers, definition, 477
  envelope conformation, 484
  Fischer projections, 478
  gauche conformation, 483, 484
  geometric isomers, 476
  levorotatory compounds, 480–481
  meso compounds, 482
  Newman projections, 482–483
  optical activity, 480–481
  plane of symmetry, 482
  relative configuration, 478–479
  R/S naming convention, 479–480
  specific rotation, 481
  staggered conformation, 483
  stereoisomers, definition, 476
  structural isomers (constitutional isomers), 475–476
  twist boat conformation, 484
  (*Z*) isomers, 476
Isometric contraction, 144
Isosceles triangles, 800
Isotonic contraction, 143
Isotonic solutions, 39–40
Isotopes, 261, 262, 263
Isotopic notation, 443

J

Jejunum, 167
Joints, 140–141
Joule, 879, 901

K

Karyokinesis (nuclear division), 42
Kelvin temperature (K), 407, 900
Ketals, 574–575
Keto-enol tautomerism, 532
Ketones
  addition reactions, 573–576
  Clemmensen reduction, 572
  common names, 567–568

condensation with ammonium derivatives, 575–576
  cyanohydrin formation, 575
  enol form, 572–573
  enolization, 572–573
  hemiketal formation, 574–575
  hydration to form geminal diols, 574
  ketal formation, 574–575
  keto form, 572–573
  Michael addition, 573
  nomenclature, 567–568
  nucleophilic addition to carbonyl, 573
  overview, 569–570
  oxidation reactions, 571
  physical properties, 569
  reduction reactions, 571–572
  synthesis, 570–571
  Wittig reaction, 578
  Wolff-Kishner reduction, 572
Keywords
  Conclusion keywords, 678–679
  Continuation keywords, 677
  Contrast keywords, 678
  Emphasis keywords, 678
  Evidence keywords, 678
  Illustration keywords, 678
  Sequence keywords, 677–678
  using keywords in reading, 677–679
Kidneys
  aldosterone, 177, 182, 187, 188
  and urethra, 174
  and urinary bladder, 174
  antidiuretic hormone (ADH; vasopressin), 177, 184
  aquaporins (water channels), 177
  Bowman's capsule, 174, 175
  collecting duct, 174, 176–177
  concentrated urine formation, 176–177
  cortex, 174, 177
  counter-current-multiplier system, 177
  distal convoluted tubule, 174, 176–177
  effect of diuretics, 177
  erythropoietin (EPO), 156, 187
  filtrate, 175
  filtration, 175
  glomerulus, 174, 175
  hyperosmolar spaces, 177
  loop of Henle, 174, 176–177
  medulla, 174, 177
  nephron function, 175–178
  nephron structure, 174–176
  osmolarity gradient, 176, 177
  osmosis, 177
  passive and active transport, 175
  pH maintenance, 177–178
  proximal convoluted tubule, 174, 176
  reabsorption of water and nutrients, 177, 182
  renal pelvis, 174
  renin, 187
  secretion of waste, 176
  selective permeability of nephrons, 176, 177
  structure, 174–176
  urine formation, 175–176
Kinematics
  average acceleration, 853
  average velocity, 852
  definition, 843, 852
  displacement, 852
  equations of linear motion, 854
  free-falling bodies, motion and acceleration, 855
  instantaneous acceleration, 853
  instantaneous velocity, 853
  linear motion, 855

  motion with constant acceleration, 856
  position of an object, 852
  projectile motion, 856
  speed, 853
Kinetic energy, 264, 882
Kinetic molecular theory of gases, 414–416
Kinetochore, 43, 47
Kingdoms of life, 36
Kingdoms (taxonomy), 239
Kirchoff's voltage (second) law, 958
Krebs cycle (citric acid cycle), 69

L

Labor and childbirth, 206
Laboratory techniques
  calibrated laboratory glassware, 256
  laboratory glassware, overview, 254
  non-calibrated laboratory glassware, 255
  pH determination, 257
  precision and accuracy, 254
  safety, 253
  See also Separation of mixtures.
  weight determination, 257
Lactase, 77, 168
Lacteals, 155
Lactic acid fermentation, 68
Lactose intolerance, 168
Lamarckian evolution, 99
Lamellae, 139
Lanthanides, 277
Large intestine, 166, 169
Lateral meristem or cambium, 207
Law of conservation of energy, 373
Law of conservation of mass, 317
Law of constant composition, 315
Law of Independent Assortment (Mendel's second law), 84–86
Law of mass action, 383–384
Law of Segregation (Mendel's first law), 81–84
Le Châtelier's principle, 385–386
Lenses
  converging lenses, 996
  diverging lenses, 996
  focal length, 997, 998
  lensmaker's equation, 996, 999
  magnification, 999
  multiple-lens systems, 1000
  real side and virtual side, 997
  See also Optics.
  signs for single lenses, 997, 998
  thin lens equation, 993, 995
  thin spherical lenses, 999
Lensmaker's equation, 996, 999
Leukocytes (white blood cells), 115–117, 155
Levorotatory compounds, 480–481
Lewis acids as electron acceptors, 298, 424, 525
Lewis bases as electron donors, 298, 424, 525
Lewis dot symbols, 293
Lewis structures, 293–297
Ligaments, 141
Light
  color, 988
  diffraction, 1001
  dispersion, 1000
  emission and absorption, 1014
  energy of photons, 1009, 1013
  interference, 1001
  photoelectric effect, 1010
  plane-polarized light, 1001
  polarization, 1001
  ray diagrams, 994
  reflection, 989
  refraction, 991
  See also Electromagnetic waves; Optics.

Index

cardiac muscle, 145, 146
concentric contraction, 144
Cori cycle, 145
creatine phosphate, 146
dynamic contraction, 143–144
eccentric contraction, 144
energy reserves of muscles, 146
H zone, 143
isometric contraction, 144
isotonic contraction, 143
M line, 143
muscle contraction, 143–144
myofibrils, 142
myoglobin, 146
neuromuscular junction, 143
rigor mortis, 143
sarcolemma, 142
sarcomeres, 142, 143
sarcoplasmic reticulum, 142
simple twitch, 144
skeletal muscle, 142–145, 146
smooth muscle, 145, 146
stimulus and muscle response, 144–145
striated muscle, 142
temporal summation, 144
tetanus, 144
tonus, 145
T system (transverse tubules in muscle fibers), 142
Z lines, 143
Muscular System, 141–146
Musculoskeletal system
    A band, 143
    absolute refractory period, 144
    appendicular skeleton, 140
    ATP and muscle contraction, 143, 145, 146
    axial skeleton, 140
    bone, 139–140
    bone formation, 140
    cardiac muscle, 145, 146
    cartilage, 139
    chrondrocytes, 139
    compact bone, 139
    concentric contraction, 144
    Cori cycle, 145
    creatine phosphate, 146
    dynamic contraction, 143–144
    eccentric contraction, 144
    endochondral ossification, 140
    energy reserves of muscles, 146
    extension (joints), 141
    extrapyramidal system, 141
    flexion (joints), 141
    Haversian canals, 139
    H zone, 143
    insertion (muscles), 141
    intramembranous ossification, 140
    isometric contraction, 144
    isotonic contraction, 143
    joints, 140–141
    lamellae, 139
    ligaments, 141
    M line, 143
    muscle contraction, 143–144
    muscular system, 141–146
    myofibrils, 142
    myoglobin, 146
    neuromuscular junction, 143
    origin (muscles), 141
    osteoblasts, 140
    osteoclasts, 140
    osteocytes, 140
    osteons (Haversian systems), 139
    pyramidal system (motor cortex), 141

red marrow, 140
rigor mortis, 143
sarcolemma, 142
sarcomeres, 142, 143
sarcoplasmic reticulum, 142
simple twitch, 144
skeletal muscle, 142–145, 146
skeletal system, 139–141
smooth muscle, 145, 146
spicules (trabeculae), 140
spongy bone, 140
stimulus and muscle response, 144–145
striated muscle, 142
sutures (immovable joints), 140
temporal summation, 144
tendons, 141
tetanus, 144
tonus, 145
T system (transverse tubules in muscle fibers), 142
yellow marrow, 140
Z lines, 143
Mutation
    added, deleted, or substituted bases in, 89
    and evolution, 53, 105
    DNA, 53
    frameshift mutation, 89
    in phenylketonuria (PKU), 90
    in sickle-cell anemia, 90
    missense mutation, 89
    nonsense mutation, 89
    point mutation, 89
    silent mutation, 89
mutations, 104
Mutualism, 225
Myelin, 123, 126
Myofibrils, 142
Myoglobin, 146

N

Nails (fingers and toes), 114
Nanometer (nm), 844
Natural frequencies of vibration, 982
Natural killer T (NKT) cells, 116
Natural selection, 99–100, 104
Negative numbers, 730
Negative reinforcement, 215
Nekton, 235
Nematoda, 245
Nernst equation, 351
Nervous system
    acetylcholine as neurotransmitter, 131
    autonomic nervous system (ANS), 131–132, 154
    brain, 129–130
    brainstem, 130
    brainstem, 212
    central nervous system (CNS), 123, 129–131
    cerebellum, 130
    cerebral cortex, 129
    cerebrum, 212
    diencephalon, 129
    dorsal horn, 130
    dorsal root ganglia, 130
    electrochemical signals, 123
    epinephrine as neurotransmitter, 182
    extrapyramidal system, 141
    "flight or fight" responses, 131
    forebrain (prosencephalon), 129
    hindbrain (rhombencephalon), 130
    hypothalamus, 129
    medulla oblongata, 160
    midbrain (mesencephalon), 130
    neuroglia, 123

norepinephrine as neurotransmitter, 131, 182
olfactory bulb, 129
organization of, 129–132
parasympathetic nervous system, 131–132
peripheral nervous system (PNS), 123, 131–132
pons, 130
pyramidal system (motor cortex), 141
reflexes, 130
reflexes, 212
"rest and digest" responses, 131
reticular activating system, 212
somatic nervous system (SNS), 131
spinal cord, 130–131
stimuli and responses, 123
sympathetic nervous system, 131, 132
telencephalon, 129
thalamus, 129
types of cells, 124–125
vagus nerve, 154
ventral horn, 130. See also Neurons
Net ionic equations, 338
Neural crest cells, 204
Neural tube, 204
Neuroglia, 123
Neuromuscular junction, 143
Neurons
    action potentials, 123, 124–125
    afferent neurons, 128
    axons, 123
    cell body (soma), 123
    dendrites, 123
    depolarized cells, 125
    effect of drugs, 128
    effector cells, 127
    efferent neurons, 128
    electrochemical signals and, 123
    function, 124–128
    ganglia, 129
    hyperpolarization, 126
    impulse propagation and speed, 126–127
    motor neurons, 128
    myelin, 123, 126
    neurotransmitters and, 41, 123–124, 125, 127–128, 143
    nodes of Ranvier, 123
    nuclei (central nervous system), 129
    oligodendrocytes, 123
    plexus, 129
    polarization, 125
    presynaptic neuron, 127
    refractory period, 126
    repolarization, 126
    resting potential, 124–125
    Schwann cells, 123, 204
    sensory neurons, 128
    structure, 123–124
    synapses (synaptic clefts), 123, 126–127
    synaptic terminals (boutons or knobs), 123
    synaptic vesicles, 125
    threshold potential, 125
    types of, 128–129
    voltage-gated ion channels, 125. See also Nervous system
Neurosecretory cells (hypothalamus), 183, 184, 185
Neurotransmitters
    acetylcholine, 131
    and neurons, 41, 123–124, 126, 127–128, 143
    endorphins, 183
    epinephrine, 182
    norepinephrine, 131, 182
Neurulation, 204
Neutralization reactions, 338, 429

Index

Index

Index

STUDY SHEETS

TEAR-OUT, QUICK REFERENCE STUDY SHEETS FOR BIOLOGY, GENERAL CHEMISTRY, ORGANIC CHEMISTRY, AND PHYSICS

The following OAT Study Sheets are your one-stop resource for the key diagrams, charts, equations, and formulas that you are sure to see on the exam. This color-coded guide is separated into four OAT subtopics: Biology, General Chemistry, Organic Chemistry, and Physics. Each topic features the most important highlights you will want to review in between study sessions and before your Test Day. Carefully tear out the pages to create a light and portable on-the-go resource that you can use to study anytime, anywhere.

Periodic Table of the Elements

1 IA	2 IIA	3 IIIB	4 IVB	5 VB	6 VIB	7 VIIB	8	9 VIIIB	10	11 IB	12 IIB	13 IIIA	14 IVA	15 VA	16 VIA	17 VIIA	18 VIIIA
1 H 1.01																	2 He 4.00
3 Li 6.94	4 Be 9.01											5 B 10.81	6 C 12.01	7 N 14.01	8 O 16.00	9 F 19.00	10 Ne 20.18
11 Na 22.99	12 Mg 24.31											13 Al 26.98	14 Si 28.09	15 P 30.97	16 S 32.07	17 Cl 35.45	18 Ar 39.95
19 K 39.10	20 Ca 40.08	21 Sc 44.96	22 Ti 47.88	23 V 50.94	24 Cr 52.00	25 Mn 54.94	26 Fe 55.85	27 Co 58.93	28 Ni 58.69	29 Cu 63.55	30 Zn 65.39	31 Ga 69.72	32 Ge 72.61	33 As 74.92	34 Se 78.96	35 Br 79.90	36 Kr 83.80
37 Rb 85.47	38 Sr 87.62	39 Y 88.91	40 Zr 91.22	41 Nb 92.91	42 Mo 95.94	43 Tc (98)	44 Ru 101.07	45 Rh 102.91	46 Pd 106.42	47 Ag 107.87	48 Cd 112.41	49 In 114.82	50 Sn 118.71	51 Sb 121.75	52 Te 127.60	53 I 126.90	54 Xe 131.29
55 Cs 132.91	56 Ba 137.33	57 La * 138.91	72 Hf 178.49	73 Ta 180.95	74 W 183.85	75 Re 186.21	76 Os 190.20	77 Ir 192.22	78 Pt 195.08	79 Au 196.97	80 Hg 200.59	81 Tl 204.38	82 Pb 207.20	83 Bi 208.98	84 Po (209)	85 At (210)	86 Rn (222)
87 Fr (223)	88 Ra 226.03	89 Ac † (227)	104 Rf (261)	105 Db (262)	106 Sg (263)	107 Bh (262)	108 Hs (265)	109 Mt (266)	110 Ds (264)	111 Rg (272)	112 Cn (277)	113 Uut (286)	114 Fl (289)	115 Uup (288)	116 Lv (289)	117 Uus (291)	118 Uuo (294)

*	58 Ce 140.12	59 Pr 140.91	60 Nd 144.24	61 Pm 145.00	62 Sm 150.36	63 Eu 151.97	64 Gd 157.25	65 Tb 158.93	66 Dy 162.50	67 Ho 164.93	68 Er 167.26	69 Tm 168.93	70 Yb 173.04	71 Lu 174.97
†	90 Th 232.04	91 Pa 231.04	92 U 238.03	93 Np 237.05	94 Pu (244)	95 Am (243)	96 Cm (247)	97 Bk (247)	98 Cf (254)	99 Es (252)	100 Fm (257)	101 Md (258)	102 No (259)	103 Lr (262)

OAT STUDY SHEET – BIOLOGY

THE CELL

FLUID MOSAIC MODEL AND MEMBRANE TRAFFIC

- Phospholipid bilayer with cholesterol and embedded proteins
- Exterior: hydrophilic, phosphoric-acid region
- Interior: hydrophobic, fatty-acid region

carbohydrate
phospholipid head (hydrophilic)
outside cell
fatty acid tails (hydrophobic)
inside cell
carrier proteins

HOMEOSTASIS

HORMONAL REGULATION

Aldosterone
- Stimulates Na^+ reabsorption and K^+ secretion, increasing water reabsorption, blood volume, and blood pressure
- Secreted from adrenal cortex
- Regulated by renin-angiotensin system

ADH
- Increases collecting duct's permeability to water to increase water reabsorption
- Secreted from posterior pituitary with high [solute] in the blood

THE LIVER'S ROLES IN HOMEOSTASIS

1. Gluconeogenesis
2. Processing of nitrogenous wastes (urea)
3. Detoxification of wastes/chemicals/drugs
4. Storage of iron and vitamin B_{12}
5. Synthesis of bile and blood proteins
6. Beta-oxidation of fatty acids to ketones
7. Interconversion of carbs, fat, and amino acids

ENZYMES

REGULATION

- **Allosteric**: Binding of an effector molecule at allosteric site.
- **Feedback inhibition**: End product inhibits initial enzyme pathway.
- **Reversible inhibition**: Competitive inhibitors bind to active site; noncompetitive inhibitors bind to allosteric site.

GLUCOSE CATABOLISM

Glycolysis occurs in the cytoplasm: $C_6H_{12}O_6 + 2\ ADP + 2\ P_i + 2\ NAD^+ \rightarrow$ 2 Pyruvate + 2 ATP + 2 NADH + 2 H^+ + 2 H_2O.

Fermentation occurs in anaerobic conditions. Pyruvate is converted into lactic acid (in muscle) or ethanol (in yeast).

Respiration occurs in aerobic conditions.

- **Pyruvate decarboxylation**: Pyruvate converted to acetyl CoA in the mitochondrial matrix.
- **Citric acid cycle**: Acetyl CoA enters; coenzymes exit.
- **Electron transport chain**: Coenzymes are oxidized; energy is released as electrons are transferred from carrier to carrier.
- **Oxidative phosphorylation**: Electrochemical gradient caused by NADH and $FADH_2$ oxidation provides energy for ATP synthase to phosphorylate ADP into ATP.

MUSCULOSKELETAL SYSTEM

Sarcomere
- Contractile unit of the fibers in skeletal muscle.
- Contains thin actin and thick myosin filaments.

sarcomere
Z line   M line   Z line
H zone
I band   A band

CONTRACTION

Initiation
- Depolarization of a neuron leads to action potential.

BONE FORMATION AND REMODELING

- **Osteoblast:** Builds bone.
- **Osteoclast:** Breaks down bone.
- **Reformation:** Inorganic ions are absorbed from the blood for use in bone.
- **Resorption:** Inorganic ions are released into the blood.

ENDOCRINE SYSTEM

Direct hormones directly stimulate organs. **Tropic** hormones stimulate other glands.
Mechanisms of hormone action: **Peptides** act via secondary messengers. **Steroids** act via a hormone/receptor binding to DNA. **Monoamines** may do either.

Hormone	Source	Action
Follicle-stimulating (FSH)	Anterior pituitary	Stimulates follicle maturation, spermatogenesis
Luteinizing (LH)		Stimulates ovulation, testosterone synthesis
Adrenocorticotropic (ACTH)		Stimulates adrenal cortex to make and secrete corticosteroids
Thyroid-stimulating (TSH)		Stimulates thyroid to produce thyroid hormones
Prolactin		Stimulates milk production and secretion
Endorphins		Inhibit the perception of pain in the brain
Growth hormone		Stimulates bone and muscle growth, lipolysis
Oxytocin	Hypothalamus; stored in posterior pituitary	Stimulates uterine contractions during labor, milk secretion during lactation
Vasopressin (ADH)		Stimulates water reabsorption in kidneys
Thyroid hormones (T_4, T_3)	Thyroid	Stimulate metabolic activity
Calcitonin		Decreases (tones down) blood calcium level
Parathyroid hormone	Parathyroid	Increases blood calcium level
Glucocorticoids	Adrenal cortex	Increase blood glucose level, decrease protein synthesis
Mineralocorticoids		Increase water reabsorption in kidneys
Epinephrine, Norepinephrine	Adrenal medulla	Increases blood glucose level, heart rate
Glucagon	Pancreas	Stimulates conversion of glycogen to glucose in the liver, increases blood glucose
Insulin		Lowers blood glucose, increases glycogen stores
Somatostatin		Suppresses secretion of glucagon and insulin
Testosterone	Testes	Maintains male secondary sexual characteristics
Estrogen	Ovary/Placenta	Maintains female secondary sexual characteristics
Progesterone		Promotes growth/maintenance of endometrium
Melatonin	Pineal	Maintains circadian rhythms
Atrial natriuretic peptide	Heart	Involved in osmoregulation and vasodilation
Thymosin	Thymus	Stimulates T lymphocyte development

REPRODUCTION

CELL DIVISION

- **G_1:** Cell doubles its organelles and cytoplasm
- **S:** DNA replication
- **G_2:** Same as G_1
- **M:** Cell divides in two
- Mitosis = PMAT
- Meiosis = PMAT × 2

Mitosis

centrosome — centriole
nuclear membrane — chromatin
interphase 2N
spindle mitosis
aster
2 chromosomes — prophase
metaphase plate
2 chromosomes — metaphase
4 chromosomes — anaphase
4 chromosomes — telophase
daughter cell
2N 2N
2 chromosomes 2 chromosomes

Meiosis

centrosome — centriole
nuclear membrane — chromatin
interphase 2N
meiosis
prophase I — 2 chromosomes
metaphase I — 2 chromosomes
disjunction
anaphase I — 2 chromosomes
telophase I — 2 chromosomes
1 chromosome metaphase II — 1 chromosome daughter cells
2 chromosomes anaphase II — 2 chromosomes
telophase II
1 chromosome in each daughter cell
N N N N
gametes

SEXUAL REPRODUCTION

Meiosis I

- Two pairs of sister chromatids form tetrads during prophase I.
- Crossing over leads to genetic recombination in prophase I.

Meiosis II

- Identical to mitosis but without replication.
- Meiosis occurs in **spermatogenesis** (sperm formation) and **oogenesis** (egg formation).

FOUR STAGES OF EARLY DEVELOPMENT

Cleavage: Mitotic divisions
Implantation: Embryo implants during blastulation
Gastrulation: Ectoderm, endoderm, and mesoderm form
Neurulation: Germ layers develop a nervous system

morula   blastula   blastocoel   ectoderm
archenteron
blastopore
endoderm

Ectoderm "Attract-o-derm"	Nervous system, epidermis, lens of eye, inner ear	**Endoderm** "Endernal" organs	Lining of digestive tract, lungs, liver, pancreas	**Mesoderm** "Means-o-derm"	Muscles, skeleton, circulatory system, gonads, kidney

DIGESTION

CARBOHYDRATE DIGESTION

Enzyme	Site of Production	Site of Function	Hydrolysis Reaction
Salivary amylase (ptyalin)	Salivary glands	Mouth	Starch → maltose
Pancreatic amylase	Pancreas	Small Intestine	Starch → maltose
Maltase	Intestinal glands	Small Intestine	Maltose → 2 glucoses
Sucrase	Intestinal glands	Small Intestine	Sucrose → glucose, fructose
Lactase	Intestinal glands	Small Intestine	Lactose → glucose, galactose

PROTEIN DIGESTION

Enzyme	Production Site	Function Site	Function
Pepsin	Gastric glands (chief cells)	Stomach	Hydrolyzes specific peptide bonds
Trypsin	Pancreas	Small Intestine	Hydrolyzes specific peptide bonds. Converts chymotrypsinogen to chymotrypsin
Chymotrypsin	Pancreas	Small Intestine	Hydrolyzes specific peptide bonds
Carboxypeptidase	Pancreas	Small Intestine	Hydrolyzes terminal peptide bond at carboxyl
Aminopeptidase	Intestinal glands	Small Intestine	Hydrolyzes terminal peptide bond at amino
Dipeptidases	Intestinal glands	Small Intestine	Hydrolyzes pairs of amino acids
Enterokinase	Intestinal glands	Small Intestine	Converts trypsinogen to trypsin

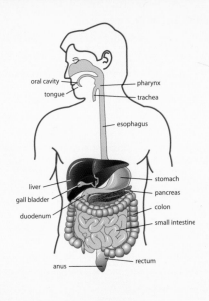

oral cavity, tongue, pharynx, trachea, esophagus, liver, gall bladder, duodenum, stomach, pancreas, colon, small intestine, anus, rectum

IMMUNE SYSTEM

- The body distinguishes between "self" and "nonself" (antigens).

HUMORAL IMMUNITY (specific defense)

B lymphocytes

Memory cells
remember antigen, speed up secondary response

Plasma cells
make and release antibodies (**IgG, IgA, IgM, IgD, IgE**), which induce antigen phagocytosis

- **Active immunity**: Antibodies are produced during an immune response.

- **Passive immunity**: Antibodies produced by one organism are transferred to another organism.

CELL-MEDIATED IMMUNITY

T lymphocytes

Cytotoxic T cells
destroy cells directly

Suppressor cells
regulate B and T cells to decrease anti-antigen activity

Helper T cells
activate B and T cells and macrophages by secreting lymphokines

Memory cells

NONSPECIFIC IMMUNE RESPONSE

Includes skin, passages lined with cilia, macrophages, inflammatory response, and interferons (proteins that help prevent the spread of a virus).

LYMPHATIC SYSTEM

- Lymph vessels meet at the thoracic duct in the upper chest and neck, draining into the veins of the cardiovascular system.

- Vessels carry **lymph** (excess interstitial fluid), and capillaries (**lacteals**) collect fats by absorbing chylomicrons in the small intestine.

- **Lymph nodes** are swellings along the vessels with phagocytic cells (leukocytes) that remove foreign particles from lymph.

CIRCULATION

BLOOD TYPING

Antigens are located on the surface of red blood cells.

Blood type	RBC antigen	Antibodies	Donates to:	Receives From:
A	A	Anti-B	A, AB	A, O
B	B	Anti-A	B, AB	B, O
AB	A, B	None	AB only	All
O	None	Anti-A, B	All	O

Blood cells with Rh factor are Rh+ and produce no antibody. Rh− lack antigen and produce an antibody.

MOLECULAR GENETICS

NUCLEIC ACID

- Basic unit: nucleotide (sugar, nitrogenous base, phosphate)
- DNA's sugar: deoxyribose. RNA's sugar: ribose.
- 2 types of bases: double-ringed **purines** (adenine, guanine) and single-ringed **pyrimidines** (cytosine, thymine, uracil).
- **DNA double helix:** antiparallel strands joined by base pairs (AT, GC).
- RNA is usually single-stranded: A pairs with U, not T.

TRANSCRIPTION REGULATION, PROKARYOTES

Regulated by the **operon**

- **Structural genes:** have DNA that codes for protein
- **Operator gene:** repressor binding site
- **Promoter gene:** RNA polyermase's 1st binding site
- **Inducible systems:** need an inducer for transcription to occur
- **Repressible systems:** need a corepressor to inhibit transcription

MUTATIONS

- **Point:** One nucleotide is substituted by another; they are silent if the sequence doesn't change.
- **Frameshift:** Insertions or deletions shift reading frame. Protein doesn't form or is nonfunctional.

VIRUSES

- Acellular structures of double- or single-stranded DNA or RNA in a protein coat.
- **Lytic cycle:** Virus kills the host.
- **Lysogenic cycle:** Virus enters host genome.

DNA REPLICATION

- **Semiconservative:** each new helix has an intact strand from the parent helix and a newly synthesized strand.

EUKARYOTIC PROTEIN SYNTHESIS

- **Transcription:** RNA polymerase synthesizes hnRNA using a DNA, "antisense strand" as a template.
- **Post-transcriptional processing:** Introns cut out of hnRNA, exons spliced to form mRNA.
- **Translation:** Occurs on ribosomes in the cytoplasm.

- **Post-translational modifications:** (e.g., disulfide bonds) made before the polypeptide becomes a functional protein.

EVOLUTION

- When frequencies are stable, the population is in Hardy-Weinberg equilibrium: no mutations, large population, random mating, no net migration, and equal reproductive success.

$$p + q = 1; p^2 + 2pq + q^2 = 1$$

p = freq. of dom. allele q = freq. of rec. allele

p^2 = freq. of dom homozygotes

$2pq$ = freq. of heterozygotes

q^2 = freq. of recessive homozygotes

CLASSICAL GENETICS

- If both parents are Rr, the alleles separate to give a genotypic ratio of 1:2:1 and a phenotypic ratio of 3:1.

Law of independent assortment: Alleles of unlinked genes assort independently in meiosis.

- For two traits: AaBb parents will produce AB, Ab, aB, and ab gametes.
- The phenotypic ratio for this cross is 9:3:3:1.

STATISTICAL CALCULATIONS

- The probability of producing a genotype that requires multiple events to occur equals the *product* of the probability of each event.
- The probability of producing a genotype that can be the result of multiple events equals the *sum* of each probability.

GENETIC MAPPING

- Crossing over during meiosis I can unlink genes during prophase I.
- Genes are most likely unlinked when far apart.
- One map unit is 1% recombinant frequency.

Given recombination frequencies

X and Y: 8%

X and Z: 12%

Y and Z: 4%

INHERITED DISORDERS in PEDIGREES

- **Autosomal recessive:** Skips generations
- **Autosomal dominant:** Appears in every generation
- **X-linked (sex-linked):** No male-to-male transmission, more males are affected.

OAT STUDY SHEET – GENERAL CHEMISTRY

ATOMIC STRUCTURE

Atomic weight: The weight in grams of one mole (mol) of a given element and is expressed in terms of g/mol.

A **mole** is a unit used to count particles and is represented by **Avogadro's number**, 6×10^{23} particles.

$$\text{Moles} = \frac{\text{grams}}{\text{atomic or molecular weight}}$$

Isotopes: For a given element, multiple species of atoms with the same number of protons (same atomic number) but different numbers of neutrons (different mass numbers).

Planck's quantum theory: Energy emitted as electromagnetic radiation from matter exists in discrete bundles called quanta.

Bohr's Model of the Hydrogen Atom

Angular momentum: $\dfrac{nh}{2\eta}$

Energy of electron: $E = \dfrac{-RH}{n^2}$

Electromagnetic energy of photons: $E = \dfrac{hc}{\lambda}$

The group of hydrogen emission lines corresponding to transitions from upper levels $n > 2$ to $n = 2$ is known as the **Balmer series**. The group corresponding to transitions between upper levels $n > 1$ to $n = 1$ is known as the **Lyman series.**

Absorption spectrum: Characteristic energy bands where electrons absorb energy.

Quantum Mechanical Model of Atoms

Heisenberg uncertainty principle: It is impossible to determine with perfect accuracy the momentum and the position of an electron simultaneously.

Quantum Numbers:

#	Character	Symbol	Value
1st	Shell	n	n
2nd	Subshell	l	From zero to $n - 1$
3rd	Orbital	m_ℓ	Between l and $-l$
4th	Spin	m_s	½ or −½

Principal Quantum Number (n): The larger the integer value of n, the higher the energy level and radius of the electron's orbit. The maximum number of electrons in energy level n is $2n^2$.

Azimuthal Quantum Number (l): Refers to subshells, or sublevels. The four subshells corresponding to $l = 0, 1, 2,$ and 3 are known as s, p, d and f, respectively. The maximum number of electrons that can exist within a subshell is given by the formula $4l+2$.

Magnetic Quantum Number (m_ℓ): This specifies the particular orbital within a subshell where an electron is highly likely to be found at a given point in time.

Spin Quantum Number (m_s): The spin of a particle is its intrinsic angular momentum and is a characteristic of a particle.

Electron Configuration

Hund's rule: Within a given subshell, orbitals are filled such that there are a maximum number of half-filled orbitals with parallel spins.

Valence electrons: Electrons of an atom that are in its outer energy shell or that are available for bonding.

KINETICS AND EQUILIBRIUM

Experimental Determination of Rate Law: The values of k, x, and y in the rate law equation (rate $= k[A]^x[B]^y$) must be determined experimentally for a given reaction at a given temperature. The rate is usually measured as a function of the initial concentrations of the reactants, A and B.

Efficiency of Reactions

Factors affecting reaction rates: Reactant Concentrations, Temperature, Medium, Catalysts

Catalysts are unique substances that increase reaction rate without being consumed; they do this by lowering the activation energy.

Law of Mass Action

$$aA + bB \rightleftharpoons cC + dD$$

$$K_c = \frac{[C]^c[D]^d}{[A]^a[B]^b}$$

K_c is the equilibrium constant. (c stands for concentration.)

Properties of The Equilibrium Constant

Pure solids/liquids don't appear in expression.

- K_{eq} is characteristic of a given system at a given temperature.
- If $K_{eq} > 1$, an equilibrium mixture of reactants and products will contain very little of the reactants compared to the products.
- If $K_{eq} < 1$, an equilibrium mixture of reactants and products will contain very little of the products compared to the reactants.
- If K_{eq} is close to 1, an equilibrium mixture of products and reactants will contain approximately equal amounts of the two.

$A + B \rightleftharpoons C +$ **heat**	
Will shift to **RIGHT:**	Will shift to **LEFT:**
1. if more A or B added	1. if more C added
2. if C taken away	2. if A or B taken away
3. if pressure applied or volume reduced (assuming A, B, and C are gases)	3 if pressure reduced or volume increased (assuming A, B, and C are gases)
4. if temperature reduced	4. if temperature increased

BONDING AND CHEMICAL INTERACTIONS

Formal Charges

Formal charge $=$ Valence electrons $- \frac{1}{2} N_{bonding} - N_{nonbonding}$

Intermolecular Forces

1. **Hydrogen Bonding:** The partial positive charge of the hydrogen atom interacts with the partial negative charge located on the electronegative atoms (F, O, N) of nearby molecules.

2. **Dipole-Dipole Interactions:** Polar molecules orient themselves such that the positive region of one molecule is close to the negative region of another molecule.

3. **Dispersion Forces:** The bonding electrons in covalent bonds may appear to be equally shared between two atoms, but at any particular point in time they will be located randomly throughout the orbital. This permits unequal sharing of electrons, causing rapid polarization and counter-polarization of the electron clouds of neighboring molecules, inducing the formation of more dipoles.

COMPOUNDS AND STOICHIOMETRY

A **compound** is a pure substance composed of two or more elements in a fixed proportion.

A **mole** is the amount of a substance that contains the same number of particles found in a 12.0 g sample of carbon-12.

Combination Reactions: two or more reactants form one product.

$$S\ (s) + O_2\ (g) \rightarrow SO_2\ (g)$$

Decomposition Reactions: A compound breaks down into two or more substances, usually as a result of heating or electrolysis.

$$2\ HgO\ (s) \rightarrow 2\ Hg\ (l) + O_2\ (g)$$

Single-Displacement Reactions: An atom (or ion) of one compound is replaced by an atom of another element.

$$Zn\ (s) + CuSO_4\ (aq) \rightarrow Cu\ (s) + ZnSO_4\ (aq)$$

Double-Displacement Reactions: Also called metathesis reactions, elements from two different compounds displace each other to form two new compounds.

$$CaCl_2\ (aq) + 2\ AgNO_3\ (aq) \rightarrow Ca(NO_3)_2\ (aq) + 2\ AgCl\ (s)$$

Net Ionic Equations: These types of equations are written showing only the species that actually participate in the reaction. So in the following equation,

$$Zn\ (s) + Cu^{2+}\ (aq) + SO_4^{2-}\ (aq) \rightarrow Cu\ (s) + Zn^{2+}\ (aq) + SO_4^{2-}\ (aq)$$

the spectator ion (SO_4^{2-}) does not take part in the overall reaction, but simply remains in solution throughout. The net ionic equation would be:

$$Zn\ (s) + Cu^{2+}\ (aq) \rightarrow Cu\ (s) + Zn^{2+}\ (aq)$$

Neutralization Reactions: These are a specific type of double displacements that occur when an acid reacts with a base to produce a solution of a salt and water:

$$HCl\ (aq) + NaOH\ (aq) \rightarrow NaCl\ (aq) + H_2O\ (l)$$

ACIDS AND BASES

Arrhenius: An acid is a species that produces H+ (a proton) in an aqueous solution, and a base is a species that produces OH^- (a hydroxide ion).

Brønsted-Lowry: An acid is a species that donates protons, while a base is a species that accepts protons.

Lewis: An acid is an electron-pair acceptor, and a base is an electron-pair donor.

Properties of Acids and Bases

$$pH = -\log[H^+] = \log\left(\frac{1}{[H^+]}\right)$$

$$pOH = -\log[OH^-] = \log\left(\frac{1}{[OH^-]}\right)$$

$$H_2O(l) \rightleftharpoons H^+ (aq) + OH^- (aq)$$

$$K_w = [H^+][OH^-] = 10^{-14}$$

$$pH + pOH = 14$$

Weak Acids and Bases

$$HA\ (aq) + H_2O\ (l) \rightleftharpoons H_3O^+ (aq) + A^- (aq)$$

$$K_a = \frac{[H_3O^+][A^-]}{[HA]}$$

$$K_b = \frac{[B^+][OH^-]}{[BOH]}$$

Salt Formation: Acids and bases may react with each other, forming a salt and (often, but not always) water in a neutralization reaction.

$$HA + BOH \rightarrow BA + H_2O$$

Titration and Buffers

Strong Acid and Strong Base

Weak Acid and Strong Base

Titration is a procedure used to determine the molarity of an acid or base by reacting a known volume of a solution of unknown concentration with a known volume of a solution of known concentration.

ACIDS AND BASES *(cont.)*

Henderson-Hasselbalch equation is used to estimate the pH of a solution in the buffer region where the concentrations of the species and its conjugate are present in approximately equal concentrations.

$$pH = pK_a + \log \frac{[\text{conjugate base}]}{[\text{weak acid}]}$$

$$pOH = pK_b + \log \frac{[\text{conjugate acid}]}{[\text{weak base}]}$$

THE GAS PHASE

1 atm = 760 mm Hg = 760 torr

Do not confuse STP with standard conditions—the two standards involve different temperatures and are used for different purposes. STP (0°C or 273 K) is generally used for gas law calculations; standard conditions (25°C or 298 K) is used when measuring standard enthalpy, entropy, Gibbs free energy, and voltage.

Boyle's Law

$$PV = k \text{ or } P_1V_1 = P_2V_2$$

Charles's Law

$$\frac{V}{T} = k \text{ or } \frac{V_1}{T_1} = \frac{V_2}{T_2}$$

Avagadro's Principle

$$\frac{n}{T} = k \text{ or } \frac{n_1}{T_1} = \frac{n_2}{T_2}$$

Ideal Gas Law

$$PV = nRT$$

Deviations due to Pressure: As the pressure of a gas increases, the particles are pushed closer and closer together. At moderately high pressure a gas's volume is less than would be predicted by the ideal gas law, due to intermolecular attraction.

Deviations due to Temperature: As the temperature of a gas decreases, the average velocity of the gas molecules decreases, and the attractive intermolecular forces become increasingly significant. As the temperature of a gas is reduced, intermolecular attraction causes the gas to have a smaller volume than would be predicted.

SOLUTIONS

Units of Concentration

Percent Composition by Mass: $= \dfrac{\text{Mass of solute}}{\text{Mass of solution}} \times 100\ (\%)$

Mole Fraction: $\dfrac{\text{\# of mol of compound}}{\text{total \# of moles in system}}$

Molarity: $\dfrac{\text{\# of mol of solute}}{\text{liter of solution}}$

Molality: $\dfrac{\text{\# of mol of solute}}{\text{kg of solvent}}$

Normality: $\dfrac{\text{\# of gram equivalent weights of solute}}{\text{liter of solution}}$

PHASES AND PHASE CHANGES

simple cubic   body-centered cubic   face-centered cubic

Colligative Properties: Physical properties derived solely from the number of particles present, not the nature of those particles, usually associated with dilute solutions.

Freezing Point Depression

$$\Delta T_f = K_f m$$

Boiling Point Elevation

$$\Delta T_b = K_b m$$

Osmotic Pressure

$$\Pi = MRT$$

Vapor-pressure Lowering (Raoult's Law)

$$P_A = X_A P^\circ_A;\ P_B = X_B P^\circ_B$$

Solutions that obey Raoult's Law are called ideal solutions.

Graham's Law of Diffusion and Effusion

Diffusion: occurs when gas molecules diffuse through a mixture.

Effusion: is the flow of gas particles under pressure from one compartment to another through a small opening.

Effusion

Both diffusion and effusion have the same formula:

$$\frac{r_1}{r_2} = \left(\frac{MM_2}{MM_1}\right)^{\frac{1}{2}}$$

REDOX REACTIONS AND ELECTROCHEMISTRY

Oxidation: Loss of electrons

Reduction: Gain of electrons

Oxidizing agent: Causes another atom to undergo oxidation, and is itself reduced

Reducing agent: Causes another atom to be reduced, and is itself oxidized

THERMOCHEMISTRY

Constant-volume and constant-pressure calorimetry: used to indicate conditions under which the heat changes are measured.

$Q = mc\Delta T$, where Q is the heat absorbed or released in a given process, m is the mass, c is the specific heat, and ΔT is the change in temperature.

States and State Functions: are described by the macroscopic properties of the system. These are properties whose magnitude depends only on the initial and final states of the system, and not on the path of the change.

Enthalpy (H): is used to express heat changes at constant pressure.

Standard Heat of Formation (ΔH°_f): the enthalpy change that would occur if one mole of a compound were formed directly from its elements in their standard states.

Standard Heat of Reaction (ΔH°_{rxn}): the hypothetical enthalpy change that would occur if the reaction were carried out under standard conditions.

$$\Delta H^\circ_{rxn} = (\text{sum of } \Delta H^\circ_{rxn} \text{ of products}) - (\text{sum of } \Delta H^\circ_{rxn} \text{ of reactants})$$

Hess's Law: Enthalpies of reactions are additive.

The reverse of any reaction has an enthalpy of the same magnitude as that of the forward reaction, but its sign is opposite.

Bond Dissociation Energy: Average of the energy required to break a particular type of bond in one mole of gaseous molecules:

Entropy (S): Measure of the disorder, or randomness, of a system.

$$\Delta S_{universe} = \Delta S_{system} + \Delta S_{surroundings}$$

Gibbs Free Energy (G): combines the two factors that affect the spontaneity of a reaction—changes in enthalpy, ΔH, and changes in entropy, ΔS.

$$\Delta G = \Delta H - T\Delta S$$

if ΔG is negative, the rxn is spontaneous

if ΔG is positive, the rxn is not spontaneous

if ΔG is zero, the system is in a state of equilibrium; thus, $\Delta G = 0$ and $\Delta H = T\Delta S$

ΔH	ΔS	Outcome
−	+	Spontaneous at all temps.
+	−	Nonspontaneous at all temps.
+	+	Spontaneous only at high temps.
−	−	Spontaneous only at low temps.

Reaction Quotient (Q): Once a reaction commences, the standard state conditions no longer hold. For the reaction,

$$aA + bB \rightleftharpoons cC + dD$$

$$Q = \frac{[C]^c[D]^d}{[A]^a[B]^b}$$

OAT STUDY SHEET – ORGANIC CHEMISTRY

NOMENCLATURE

1. Find the longest carbon chain containing the principle functional group (highest priority groups are generally more oxidized).
2. Number the carbon chain so the principle functional group gets lowest number (1).
3. Proceed to number the chain so the lowest set of numbers is obtained for the substituents.
4. Name the substituents and assign each a number.
5. Complete the name by listing substituents in alphabetical order; place commas between numbers and dashes between numbers and words.

t-butyl   neopentyl   isopropyl

sec-butyl   isobutyl

Functional Group	Suffix	Functional Group	Suffix
Carboxylic Acid	-oic acid	Ketone	-one
Ester	-oate	Thiol	-thiol
Acyl halide	-oyl halide	Alcohol	-ol
Amide	-amide	Amine	-amine
Nitrile/Cyanide	-nitrile	Imine	-imine
Aldehyde	-al	Ether	-ether

ISOMERS

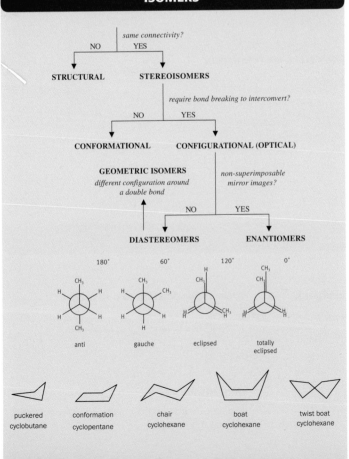

anti   gauche   eclipsed   totally eclipsed

puckered cyclobutane

conformation cyclopentane

chair cyclohexane

boat cyclohexane

twist boat cyclohexane

BONDING

	single	double	triple
Bond order	single	double	triple
Bond type	sigma	sigma	sigma
		pi	2 pi
Hybridization	sp^3	sp^2	sp
Angles	109.5°	120°	180°
Example	C–C	C=C	C≡C

ALKANES

CH_3

Free radical halogenation
- Initiation
- Propagation
- Termination

Combustion

$$C_3H_8 + 5\,O_2 \rightarrow 3\,CO_2 + 4\,H_2O + heat$$

Nucleophilicity and basicity

$$RO^- > HO^- > RCO_2^- > ROH > H_2O$$

Nucleophilicity, size, and polarity

$$CN^- > I^- > RO^- > HO^- > Br > Cl^- > F^- > H_2O$$

Leaving groups (weak bases best)

$$I^- > Br^- > Cl^- > F^-$$

S_N1	S_N2
2 steps	1 step
Favored in polar protic solvents	Favored in polar aprotic solvents
3° > 2° > 1° > Methyl	Methyl > 1° > 2° > 3°
Rate = k[RX]	Rate = k[Nu][RX]
Racemic products	Optically active and inverted products
Strong nucleophile not required	Favored with strong nucleophile

AMINO ACIDS, PEPTIDES, AND PROTEINS

Amino acids have four substituents: amine group, carboxyl group, hydrogen, and R group. Amino acids are **amphoteric**—they can act as either acids or bases and often take the form of **zwitterions** (dipolar ions).

amino acid   →   zwitterion

neutral solution

Structure

Primary: Sequence of amino acids

Secondary: α-helix, β-pleated sheet

Tertiary: Disulfide bridges, hydrophobic/hydrophilic interactions

Quaternary: Arrangement of polypeptides

Henderson–Hasselbalch Equation

$$pH = pK_a + \log \frac{[\text{conj. base}]}{[\text{conj. acid}]}$$

ALKYNES

Alkynes have a terminal hydrogen that is appreciably more acidic than hydrogens on alkanes and alkenes.

Synthesis via double elimination of geminal or vicinal dihalide

Oxidation with KMnO₄, O₃

Reduction with Lindlar's catalyst or liquid ammonia

Free radical addition

Electrophilic addition (anti orientation)

Hydroboration (cis alkene formed)

ALKENES

Catalytic Reduction

Electrophilic Addition of HX

Electrophilic Addition of X₂

anti-addition

Electrophilic Addition of H₂O

Free Radical Addition (anti-Markovnikov)

most stable radical

Hydroboration (anti-Markovnikov, syn orientation)

Oxidation with KMnO₄

Oxidation with O₃

ALDEHYDES

The dipole moment of aldehydes causes an elevation of boiling point, but not as high as alcohols since there is no hydrogen bonding.

Synthesis

- Oxidation of primary alcohols
- Ozonolysis of alkenes
- Friedel-Crafts acylation

Reactions

Reactions of Enols (Michael additions)

Nucleophilic Addition to a Carbonyl

Aldol condensation

An aldehyde acts both as nucleophile (enol form) and target (keto form).

CARBOXYLIC ACIDS

Carboxylic acids have pK_as of around 4.5 due to resonance stabilization of the conjugate base. Electronegative atoms increase acidity with inductive effects. Boiling point is higher than alcohols because of the ability to form two hydrogen bonds.

Synthesis

Oxidation of Primary Alcohols with KMnO₄

Organometallic Reagents with CO₂ (Grignard)

Hydrolysis of Nitriles

Reactions

Formation of soap by reacting carboxylic acids with NaOH; arrange in micelles.

nonpolar tail   polar head

Nucleophilic Acyl Substitution

Ester formation

Acyl halide formation

Reduction to alcohols

carboxylic acid

aldehyde

alcohol

ALCOHOLS

- Higher boiling points than alkanes
- Weakly acidic hydroxyl hydrogen

Synthesis

- Addition of water to double bonds
- S_N1 and S_N2 reactions
- Reduction of carboxylic acids, aldehydes, ketones, and esters
  - Aldehydes and ketones with $NaBH_4$
  - Esters and carboxylic acids with $LiAlH_4$

Reactions

E1 dehydration reactions in strongly acidic solutions

minor — Hoffman product

major — Zaitsev product

Substitution reactions after protonation or leaving group conversion

tosyl chloride

Oxidation

- PCC takes a primary alcohol to an aldehyde.

- Jones's reagent, $KMnO_4$, and alkali dichromate salts will convert secondary alcohols to ketones and primary alcohols to carboxylic acids.

- Tertiary alcohols cannot be oxidized without breaking a carbon-to-carbon bond.

Oxidation and Reduction

Wittig Reaction

$$(C_6H_5)_3P + CH_3Br \longrightarrow (C_6H_5)_3\overset{+}{P}CH_3 + Br^-$$

phosphonium salt

ylide

CARBOXLIC ACID DERIVATIVES

Acyl halides

Nucleophilic acyl substitution

Friedel–Crafts acylation

Reduction

Anhydrides

Synthesis via reaction of carboxylic acid with an acid chloride

Addition of ammonia to form amides

Friedel–Crafts acylation

Amines and Nitrogen-Containing Compounds

Amide   Carbamate   Imine   Enamine

Azide   Nitrile   Isocyanate

Direct alkylation of ammonia

$$CH_3Br + NH_3 \longrightarrow CH_3\overset{+}{N}H_3Br^- \xrightarrow{NaOH} CH_3NH_2 + NaBr + H_2O$$

Reduction from nitro compounds, nitriles, imines, and amides

$$CH_3CH_2C\equiv N \xrightarrow{LAH} CH_3CH_2CH_2NH_2$$

Exhaustive methylation (Hoffman elimination)

Gabriel Synthesis

Amides

Hoffman rearrangement converts amides to primary amines

Reduction with LAH

Esters

Synthesis via condensation of carboxylic acids and alcohols

Conversion to amides

Claisen condensation

KINEMATICS

Displacement (Δx): The change in position that goes in a straight-line path from the initial position to the final; it is independent of the path taken (SI unit: m).

Average velocity: $v = \frac{\Delta x}{\Delta t}$ (SI units: m/s).

Acceleration: the rate of change of an object's velocity; it is a vector quantity: $\mathbf{a} = \frac{\Delta \mathbf{v}}{\Delta t}$ (SI units: m/s²).

Linear Motion

$v = v_0 + at$

$\Delta x = v_0 t + \frac{1}{2} at^2$

$v^2 = v_0^2 + 2a\Delta x$

$v_{avg} = \left(\frac{v_0 + v}{2}\right)$

$\Delta x = v_{avg}t = \left(\frac{v_0 + v}{2}\right)t$

- When solving for time, there will be two values for t: when the projectile is initially launched, and when it impacts the ground.
- To find max height, remember that the vertical velocity of the projectile is 0 at the highest point of the path.

Projectile Motion

- Vertical component of velocity = $v \sin \theta$.
- Horizontal component of velocity = $v \cos \theta$.

Frictional Forces

Static friction (f_s): The force that must be overcome to set an object in motion. It has the formula $0 \le f_s \le \mu_s N$.

Kinetic friction (f_k): Opposes the motion of objects moving relative to each other. It has the formula $f_k = \mu_k N$.

WORK, ENERGY, AND MOMENTUM

Work: For a constant force F acting on an object that moves distance d, the work is $W = Fd\cos\theta$. For a force perpendicular to the displacement, $W = 0$ [SI unit: joule = N·m].

Power: The rate at which work is performed, given by

$$P = \frac{W}{t} \text{ (SI unit: watt = J/s)}$$

Mechanical Energy

Energy is a scalar quantity (SI unit: joule).

Kinetic energy: The energy associated with moving objects, given by

$$K = \frac{1}{2}mv^2$$

Potential energy: The energy associated with a body's position. Gravitational potential energy of an object is due to the force of gravity acting on it, expressed as $U = mgh$.

Total Mechanic Energy

$$E = U + K$$

Mechanical energy is conserved when the sum of kinetic and potential energies remains constant.

Work–Energy Theorem

Relates the work performed by all forces acting on a body in a particular time interval to the change in kinetic energy at that time. The expression is

$$W = \Delta K$$

Conservation of Energy

When there are no nonconservative forces (e.g., friction) acting on a system, the total mechanical energy remains constant: $\Delta E = \Delta K + \Delta U = 0$

Conservation of Momentum

Momentum: A vector quantity, given by

$$\boldsymbol{p} = m\boldsymbol{v}$$

Momentum is always conserved in an isolated system.

NEWTON'S LAWS

Newton's First Law (Law of Inertia): A body in a state of motion or at rest will remain in that state unless acted upon by a net force.

Newton's Second Law: When a net force is applied to a body of mass m, the body will be accelerated in the same direction as the force applied to the mass. This is expressed by the formula $\mathbf{F} = m\mathbf{a}$ (SI unit: newton (N) = kg·m/s²).

- $F_{gravity} > F_{parachute}$: person accelerates downward.
- $F_g = F_{parachute}$: terminal velocity is reached (person travels at constant velocity).

Newton's Third Law: If body A exerts a force on body B, then B will exert a force back onto A that is equal in magnitude but opposite in direction. This can be expressed as $F_B = -F_A$.

Newton's Law of Gravitation: All forms of matter experience an attractive force to other forms of matter in the universe.

The magnitude of the force is represented by $F = \frac{Gm_1 m_2}{r^2}$.

- **Mass (m):** A scalar quantity that measures a body's inertia
- **Weight (W):** A vector quantity that measures a body's gravitational attraction to the Earth ($\mathbf{W} = m\mathbf{g}$)

Uniform Circular Motion:

$\mathbf{a}_c = \frac{\mathbf{v}^2}{r}$

$\mathbf{F}_c = \frac{m\mathbf{v}^2}{r}$

center of the circle

THERMODYNAMICS

Specific Heat

$Q = mc\Delta T$

- Can only be used to find Q when object does not change phase.
- $Q > 0$ means heat is gained; $Q < 0$ means heat is lost [SI units: joules or calories].

Heat of transformation: The quantity of heat required to change the phase of 1 kg of a substance.

$Q = mL$ (phase changes are isothermal processes).

System Work

- When the piston expands, work is done by the system ($W > 0$).
- When the piston compresses the gas, work is done on the system ($W < 0$).
- The area under a P vs. V curve is the amount of work done in a system.

First Law of Thermodynamics: $\Delta U = Q - W$.

Process	First Law Becomes
Adiabatic ($Q = 0$)	$\Delta U = -W$
Constant Volume ($W = 0$)	$\Delta U = Q$
Closed Cycle ($\Delta U = 0$)	$Q = W$

Second Law of Thermodynamics: In any thermodynamic process that moves from one state of equilibrium to another, the entropy of the system and environment together will either increase or remain unchanged.

FLUIDS & SOLIDS

Density $(\rho) = \frac{m}{V}$ [SI units: kg/m³].

Specific gravity $= \frac{\rho_{substance}}{\rho_{water}}$ [no units].

$$\rho_{water} = 10^3 \text{ kg/m}^3$$

Weight (W) $= \rho g V$

Pressure: A scalar quantity defined as force per unit area:

$P = \frac{F}{A}$ [SI units: Pascal = N/m²].

- For static fluids of uniform density in a sealed vessel, $P = \rho g h$.
- **Absolute pressure** in a fluid due to gravity somewhere below the surface is given by the equation $P = P_o + \rho g h$.
- **Gauge pressure:** $P_g = P_{abs} - P_{environment}$.

Continuity equation: $v_1 A_1 = v_2 A_2$.

Bernoulli's equation: $P + \frac{1}{2}\rho v^2 + \rho g h = $ constant.

Pascal's Principle

- A change in the pressure applied to an enclosed fluid is transmitted undiminished to every portion of the fluid and to the walls of the containing vessel.

$\Delta P = \frac{F_1}{A_1} = \frac{F_2}{A_2}$ and $W = F_1 d_1 = F_2 d_2$

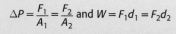

PERIODIC MOTION AND WAVES

Wave Formulas

$f = \frac{1}{T}$

$v = f\lambda$

	mass-spring	simple pendulum
force constant (k)	spring constant (k)	mg/L
ang. freq. ω	$\frac{k}{m}$	$\frac{g}{L}$
frequency f	$\frac{1}{T}$ or $\frac{\omega}{2\pi}$	$\frac{1}{T}$ or $\frac{\omega}{2\pi}$
Kinetic energy K	$\frac{1}{2}mv^2$	$\frac{1}{2}mv^2$
K_{max} occurs at	$x = 0$	$\theta = 0$ (vertical position)
potential energy U	$\frac{1}{2}kx^2$	mgh
U_{max} occurs at	$x = \pm x_{max}$	Max value of θ
max acceleration	$x = \pm x_{max}$	Max value of θ

OPTICS

Spherical Mirrors

Mirror Equation: $\frac{1}{i} + \frac{1}{o} = \frac{1}{f} = \frac{2}{r}$.

- Any of units of distance may be used, but all units used must be the same.

Concave Mirrors

- If an object is placed inside the focal length of a concave mirror, the image formed is behind the mirror, enlarged and virtual.

Convex Mirrors

- Regardless of the position of the object, a convex mirror forms only a virtual erect image.

Thin Spherical Lenses

Lens Equation: $\frac{1}{f} = \frac{1}{o} + \frac{1}{i}$.

Converging (Convex) Lenses

- For an object beyond the focal point, the image formed is real and inverted.
- For an object inside the focal length, the image formed is virtual, erect, and enlarged.
- No image at focal point.

Diverging (Concave) Lenses

Magnification $(m) = \frac{-i}{o}$

- $|m| < 1$ image reduced; $|m| > 1$ image enlarged; $|m| = 1$ image same size.
- Inverted image has a negative m; erect image has a positive m.

MAGNETISM

The Magnetic Field (B)

Magnetic fields are created by permanent magnets and moving charges.

Magnetic field lines depict the direction a compass needle would point if placed in the field from the North Pole to the South Pole [SI Units = tesla(T) = N·s/m·C].

Force on a Moving Charge

A charge moving in a magnetic field experiences a force exerted on it.

The magnetic force is zero when charges move parallel or antiparallel to the magnetic field.

Right-Hand Rule for Force on a Moving Charge

$F = qvB\sin\theta$

Note that the right-hand rule gives the direction of magnetic force exerted on a proton. The direction of force on an electron is simply in the opposite direction of the force on a proton.

Right-Hand Rule for Force on a Current-Carrying Wire

$F = ILB\sin\theta$

X $\rightarrow$ represents B fields pointing into the page; • $\rightarrow$ represents B fields pointed out of the page.

Special Cases

Center of Wire Loop
$$B = \frac{\mu_0 I}{2r}$$

Around a Straight Wire
$$B = \frac{\mu_0 I}{2\pi r}$$

Right-Hand Rule for Direction of B Field Produced by Current-Carrying Wires

- Right thumb points in the direction of current flow.
- Wrap your fingers around the wire as if you were grabbing it with your palm.
- The direction that the fingers curl is the direction of the magnetic field.

Wave Superposition

Constructive

Waves can also be shifted with respect to one another by other fractions of a cycle, such as $\frac{1}{4}\lambda$, or 90° out of phase.

Destructive

SOUND

Sound propagates through a deformable medium by the oscillation of particles along the direction of the wave's motion.

Intensity $(I) = \frac{P}{A}$ [SI units: W/m²].

Sound level $(\beta) = 10 \log (I/I_o)$ $(I_o = 10^{-12}$ W/m²) [unit = decibel = dB]

(Note that an increase in intensity by a factor of 100, for instance 40 W/m² to 4,000 W/m², corresponds to an increase of 20 dB.)

Beats occur when two waves that have slightly different frequencies are superimposed:

$f_{\text{beat}} = |f_1 - f_2|$.

Refraction

$n = \frac{c}{v}$ (speed of light = 3×10^8 m/s).

Snell's Law: $n_1 \sin \theta_1 = n_2 \sin \theta_2$. When $n_2 > n_1$, light bends toward normal; when $n_2 < n_1$, light bends away from normal.

Doppler effect: When a source and a detector move relative to one another, the perceived frequency of the sound received differs from the actual frequency emitted, even though the source velocity and frequency is unchanged.

$$f' = f\frac{(v \pm v_D)}{(v \pm v_S)}$$

ATOMIC AND NUCLEAR PHENOMENA

Blackbody Radiation

A **blackbody** is an object that absorbs all incident electromagnetic radiation upon it and emits energy that is characteristic to the system itself.

Wien's Displacement Law: $\lambda_{\text{peak}}T = $ constant.

Stefan-Boltzmann Law: $E_{\text{total}} = \sigma T^4$.

Photoelectric Effect

$E = hf = \frac{hc}{\lambda}$

$K = hf - W$

K is the maximum kinetic energy of the ejected electron; W is the minimum energy required to eject an electron.

Nuclear Binding Energy

Mass defect: The difference between the sum of the masses of nucleons in the nucleus and the mass of the nucleus. The mass defect results from the conversion of matter to energy, embodied by $E = mc^2$. This energy is the **binding energy** that holds nucleons within the nucleus.

Exponential Decay

Half-Life
$n = n_0 e^{-\lambda t}$

Beta Minus Decay
$^{137}_{55}\text{Cs} \rightarrow {}^{137}_{56}\text{Ba} + {}^{0}_{-1}e^- + \overline{v}_e$

Alpha Decay
$^{238}_{92}\text{U} \rightarrow {}^{234}_{90}\text{Th} + {}^{4}_{2}\text{He}$

Beta Plus Decay
$^{22}_{11}\text{Cs} \rightarrow {}^{22}_{10}\text{Ne} + {}^{0}_{+1}e^+ + v_e$

Direct Current

Current: The flow of electric charge. Current is given by

$I = \frac{\Delta q}{\Delta t}$ [SI units: Amp (A) = C/s].

(The direction of current is the direction positive charge would flow, or from high to low potential.)

Ohm's Law and Resistance

$V = IR$ (can be applied to entire circuit or individual resistors).

Resistance: Opposition to the flow of charge. $R = \frac{\rho L}{A}$ (resistance increases with increasing temperatures with most conductors) [SI units: ohm (Ω)].

Circuit Laws

Kirchoff's Laws:

1. At any junction within a circuit, the sum of current flowing into that point must equal the current leaving.
2. The sum of voltage sources equals the sum of voltage drops around a closed circuit loop.

Alternating Current

$V_{rms} = \frac{V_{max}}{\sqrt{2}}$

$I_{rms} = \frac{I_{max}}{\sqrt{2}}$

Series Circuits

$R_{eff} = R_1 + R_2 + R_3...$
$V_{eff} = V_1 + V_2 + V_3...$
$I_{eff} = I_1 = I_2 = I_3...$

Parallel Circuits

$\frac{1}{R_{eff}} = \frac{1}{R_1} + \frac{1}{R_2} + \frac{1}{R_3} ...$

$V_{eff} = V_1 = V_2 = V_3 = ...$

$I_{eff} = I_1 + I_2 + I_3 + ...$

Power Dissipated by Resistors

$P = IV = \frac{V^2}{R} = I^2 R$

Capacitors

Capacitance: The ability to store charge per unit voltage. It is given by $C = \frac{Q}{V}$.

$C = \kappa \frac{\varepsilon_0 A}{d}$ for parallel plates.

Capacitors in parallel add
$C_{eff} = C_1 + C_2 + C_3$

Energy Stored by Capacitors:

$U = \frac{1}{2}QV = \frac{1}{2}CV^2 = \frac{1}{2}\frac{Q^2}{C}$

Capacitors in series add as reciprocals

$\frac{1}{C_{eff}} = \frac{1}{C_1} + \frac{1}{C_2} + \frac{1}{C_3} ...$

Coulomb's Law

$F = \frac{kq_1 q_2}{r^2}$ [SI units: Newtons]

Electric field

$E = \frac{F}{q} = \frac{kq}{r^2}$ [SI units: N/C or V/m]

- A positive point charge will move in the same direction as the electric field vector; a negative charge will move in the opposite direction.

Electric potential energy (U): The electric potential energy of a charge q at a point in space is the amount of work required to move it from infinity to the point.

$U = q\Delta V = qEd = \frac{kq_1 Q}{r}$ [SI units: V or J/C]

Electric Dipoles

- p is the dipole moment ($p = qd$).
- The dipole feels no translational force but experiences a torque about the center causing it to rotate so that the dipole moment aligns with the electric field.

Electric Potential

The amount of work required to move a positive test charge q_0 from infinity to a particular point divided by the test charge:

$V = \frac{W}{q_0}$ [SI units: volt = J/C].

Potential Difference (Voltage)

Voltage $(V) = \frac{w}{q} = \frac{kq}{r}$ [SI units: volt = J/C].

- When two oppositely charged parallel plates are separated by a distance d, an electric field is created, and a potential difference exists between the plates, given by $V = Ed$.